The Oliver Wendell Holmes Devise
HISTORY OF THE SUPREME COURT
OF THE UNITED STATES

General Editors: PAUL A. FREUND and STANLEY N. KATZ

THE
Oliver Wendell Holmes
DEVISE

HISTORY OF
THE SUPREME COURT
OF THE UNITED STATES

VOLUME IX

THE OLIVER WENDELL HOLMES DEVISE

History of the

SUPREME COURT

of the United States

VOLUME IX

The Judiciary and Responsible Government

1910–21

PART ONE

by Alexander M. Bickel

MEMBER OF THE MASSACHUSETTS BAR, LATE STERLING
PROFESSOR OF LAW, YALE UNIVERSITY

PART TWO

by Benno C. Schmidt, Jr.

MEMBER OF THE DISTRICT OF COLUMBIA BAR,
HARLAN FISKE STONE PROFESSOR OF CONSTITUTIONAL
LAW, COLUMBIA UNIVERSITY SCHOOL OF LAW

MACMILLAN PUBLISHING COMPANY
NEW YORK
COLLIER MACMILLAN PUBLISHERS
LONDON

Macmillan Publishing Company
866 Third Avenue, New York, N.Y. 10022
Collier Macmillan Canada, Inc.

Library of Congress Cataloging in Publication Data
(Revised for Volume 9)
Main entry under title:

History of the Supreme Court of the United States.

At head of title: The Oliver Wendell Holmes Devise.
Includes bibliographical footnotes.
CONTENTS: v. 1. Antecedents and beginnings to 1801,
by J. Goebel, Jr.—v. 2. Foundations of power, John
Marshall, 1801–15, by G. L. Haskins and H. A. Johnson.—
v. 9. The Judiciary and responsible government, 1910–21,
pt. 1, by Alexander M. Bickel, pt. 2, by Benno C.
Schmidt, Jr.
1. United States. Supreme Court—History.
I. Oliver Wendell Holmes Devise.
KF8742.A45H55   347.73'26   78–30454
ISBN 0–02–541420–8   347.30735

10 9 8 7 6 5 4 3 2 1

Printed in the United States of America

Contents

PART TWO

Illustrations

Foreword

T HE *History of the Supreme Court of the United States* is being prepared under the auspices of the Permanent Committee for the
Oliver Wendell Holmes Devise with the aid of the estate left by Mr.
Justice Oliver Wendell Holmes, Jr. Mr. Justice Holmes died in 1935
and the Permanent Committee for the Devise was created by Act of
Congress in 1955. Members of the Committee are appointed by the
President of the United States, with the Librarian of Congress, an *ex
officio* member, as Chairman. The present volume is the fifth in the
series. The Committee hopes to complete the history expeditiously while
maintaining the high quality of the scholarship. The volumes in the
Holmes Devise *History of the Supreme Court of the United States* bring
to this subject some of the best legal scholarship of the decades since
Mr. Justice Holmes' death. They will also have such advantages (not
anticipated at the time of the Justice's death) as can be secured from
a more than ample measure of judicious deliberation. We hope that,
when completed, the series will widen and deepen our understanding
of the Supreme Court and bring honor to the memory of one of
its great Justices.

Daniel J. Boorstin
LIBRARIAN OF CONGRESS

Editor's Foreword

THE PERIOD COVERED by this volume (1910–1921) marks a single Chief Justiceship, that of Edward Douglass White, the Confederate soldier from Louisiana turned nationalist statesman. He was the third of President Taft's six Supreme Court appointments in one term—a record unmatched since George Washington's time—and when he left the Court he was succeeded by Taft himself. Whether Taft had greater impact on the Court as anointer or anointed is a fair question the answer to which must await the completion of the succeeding volume, dealing with the period of the Taft Chief Justiceship.

The two volumes were originally planned as one, under the deliberately ambiguous title "The Court and Responsible Government," and authorship was entrusted to the gifted and expert hands of Professor Alexander Bickel of the Yale Law School. He soon determined that the richness of the two decades would require two volumes to present adequately both the inner workings of the Court and its relation to the life of the nation.

The grievously untimely and deeply lamented death of Professor Bickel forced a reassignment of responsibilities. At his death he left seven full-scale completed chapters of the first projected volume, covering the politics of appointments, the inner workings of the Court and judicial review of social and economic measures, federal and state, the most distinctive aspect of the Court's business in those years. Confronted with the legislative fruits of the Progressive movement, the Court was vacillating, frequently divided, unprepared (apart from Holmes) philosophically, and yet, if not hospitable, at least tolerant to a perhaps surprising degree toward measures of industrial and financial change. Helping the Court to this position in cases of federal power was a spirit of nationalism, and in cases of state power, a revulsion against the efforts of the bar to trivialize the Fourteenth Amendment guarantees of liberty and equality by seeking to convert political defeats into constitutional grievances. The era of judicial vetoes, emerging toward the end of the period, would not reach its zenith until the next decade.

These chapters display Bickel's combination of analytical acuity, human sensitivity, and pungent exposition. To enliven and enlighten the narrative he has drawn fully on the personal papers of the Justices and on unpublished notes taken by Professor (as he then was) Felix Frankfurter of unbuttoned conversations with Justice Brandeis in the relaxing summer atmosphere of the latter's cottage on Cape Cod. He has also drawn, for insights into the decision-making process, on Brandeis' working papers, which he had combed in preparing his remarkable early volume *The Unpublished Opinions of Mr. Justice Brandeis* (1957).

The remaining chapters are the work of Professor Benno Schmidt, Jr., of the Columbia Law School, a former student of Professor Bickel at Yale, who there is good reason to believe would have been Bickel's choice to complete the volume. His account of the race-relations cases, tentative forerunners of the civil-rights movement decades later, is vivid social no less than legal history, and a contribution to both. Written with controlled passion and ranging widely in the sources, the story exposes the grim actualities beneath the decorous locutions of the law.

Consistent with the original design, themes that were emerging but reached more mature development in the next decade (notably freedom of speech and press) will be incorporated in the succeeding volume, under the authorship of Professor Robert Cover.

Paul A. Freund

PART ONE

By Alexander M. Bickel

CHAPTER I

Mr. Taft Rehabilitates the Court

MR. JUSTICE DAVID JOSIAH BREWER died in March 1910, after twenty years of service. On May 31, 1910, in accordance with a custom almost uniformly observed, there were proceedings in his memory in open court. It was the last day of the October Term 1909. Chief Justice Melville W. Fuller, who had preceded Brewer on the Bench by no more than a year and a half, opened his response to a eulogy by Attorney General George W. Wickersham as follows:

> During the years of my occupancy of a seat upon this Bench it has been my sad duty to accept for the Court tributes of the Bar in memory of many members of this tribunal who have passed to their reward. As our brother Brewer joins the great procession, there pass before me the forms of Matthews and Miller, of Field and Bradley and Lamar and Blatchford, of Jackson and Gray and of Peckham, whose works follow them now that they rest from their labors.

All excellent, illustrious men, though quite different from each other, Fuller continued. Very briefly he dwelt on Brewer, "one of the most lovable of them all," on death and the hereafter, on Brewer's eloquence, and on his humor, which, like Mr. Lincoln's, served to lighten the load.[1]

And so Fuller ended. It was the last time he sat, and these were virtually his last words spoken from the Bench, for he had no substantial opinion to deliver that day. Before the beginning of the next term, Fuller died, aged seventy-seven, in Sorrento, in his native Maine, on Independence Day, 1910. Less than a year earlier, Rufus W. Peckham had gone. William H. Moody, quite ill for the past term, retired shortly

---

[1] 218 U.S. vii, xv (1910).

thereafter and soon also died. John Marshall Harlan, in his thirty-third year of service, had but one more to go. By 1912, five men were on the Court who had not been there in 1909. A new majority under a new Chief Justice.

It is tempting to hold that Fuller's emotional evocation of the men he had served with marks the end of an era. The temptation is the stronger as one can marshal other indicia of change. Fuller was fourth in succession to John Marshall: a total of five Chief Justices from 1801 to 1910. Of these Marshall served thirty-four years; Roger B. Taney twenty-eight; Fuller himself over twenty-one. Fuller's predecessor, Morrison Waite, sat for only fourteen years, and before him there was the brief, troubled interlude of Salmon P. Chase. Yet it signifies in the history of the Court, and it affected the character of the institution, that only five men headed it in over a century, and that for eighty-four years of that period just three men sat as Chief Justice. The era that opened in 1910 was to be quite different. Fuller's successor, Edward Douglass White, though a side judge for sixteen years, was Chief Justice for a mere ten and a half. He was followed by William Howard Taft for eight, Charles Evans Hughes eleven, Harlan Fiske Stone less than five, Fred M. Vinson seven. The next substantial tenure after Fuller's was that of Earl Warren, from 1953 to 1969. Again, White's was the first appointment of a Chief Justice from within the Court. Stone's appointment in 1941 was to provide the only like instance.

The year 1910 was also something of a turning point in the political history of the country. It was a year of Republican insurgency in Congress. It marked the first time in eight elections that a Democratic House of Representatives was sent to Washington. It saw Theodore Roosevelt's decisive turn to progressive agitation. It was a time, in short, of "one of those significant divides in American history which signalize a reversal in political trends before a complete transfer of power occurs."[2]

And yet there was no significant divide in the history of the Supreme Court. The single appointment of Louis D. Brandeis in 1916 more nearly qualifies for such a description, as do the appointments made by President Harding in 1921 and 1922. Brandeis was a new man, of an entirely different cast from that of the colleagues he joined, different in experience and outlook, the first of many new men who were to constitute the Court a generation thence, and perhaps the single most powerful judicial influence on them. Harding's appointment of George Sutherland and Pierce Butler, both rigidly committed conservatives, created an almost unvarying majority, which set the institution firmly

---

[2] G. E. Mowry, *The Era of Theodore Roosevelt* (1958), 272.

on one of the several courses it had been pursuing. And this was the course that led, in essential attitudes if not in all niceties of doctrine, to the struggle of 1937, and to the veritable revolution that followed.

The five new appointments made by President Taft in the three years from 1909 to 1912 had no such effect. Neither attitude nor doctrine was to harden for another decade. Both remained more or les ambivalent under White. If there was a movement away from such unpopular decisions as *Lochner* v. *New York*[3] and the *First Employers' Liability Cases*,[4] the movement was as far from being radical as it was from being permanent, it did not involve a firm settlement of doctrine, and it proceeded from other precedents that had grown up more quietly alongside these highly notorious cases; it was, indeed, a movement not away, but alongside.[5]

The William Howard Taft who in 1922, as Chief Justice, heartily welcomed the appointment of Sutherland and actively sought the appointment of Butler was in some measure a different man and, what is more important, a man acting in different political circumstances and from different motives from those of the President of 1910. The Taft of 1922 viewed conservative Republican principles as being at once happily ascendant in the White House and dangerously menaced within the Court. This was the Court, after all, on which sat a Brandeis, boring from within, as Taft sometimes was wont to say, and an Oliver Wendell Holmes, whom Taft, in common with the rest of the country, perceived rather differently now from the way he had a decade earlier. Taft was, therefore, quite clear in 1921–22 and to the end of his life that only men whom he could trust as sound, men of definite, ascertainable conservative principles should be appointed. Each appointment had to be utterly safe. Even a Henry L. Stimson, a Benjamin Cardozo, or a Learned Hand seemed to Taft at this time a dubious risk.[6] But Taft the President of 1910 gave scarcely a thought to the danger that the Court's conservative soundness might be impaired from within. If anything, he shared the general regret about some conservative excesses of the past, and he was not yet entirely free of the dominating influence of Theodore Roosevelt. It was the election of 1912, says his biographer, that heightened in Taft "the conservatism he had shaken off under the influence of Roosevelt."[7]

Soundness, in 1910, therefore, meant men of balance; conserva-

---

[3] 198 U.S. 45 (1905).

[4] 207 U.S. 463 (1908).

[5] See C. Warren, "The Progressiveness of the United States Supreme Court," *Colum. L. Rev.,* 13:294, 296–309, 1913.

[6] W. H. Taft to W. G. Harding, Dec. 4, 1922; Taft to Elihu Root, Dec. 21, 1922; Taft to C. D. Hilles, Dec. 31, 1922, W. H. Taft Papers, Library of Congress (hereinafter cited as Taft Papers).

[7] H. Pringle, *The Life and Times of William Howard Taft* (1939), II, 841.

tives, to be sure, but moderate ones. So long as a candidate was a substantial and successful lawyer and politician, and certainly if he was a sitting federal judge, there was little need to inquire with precision and in detail into the principles he held, for there was no danger within the Court, and hence no requirement of strict conformity. It might actually strengthen the Court and shore up public confidence in it if the President were to appoint one or two Justices who, while sound, substantial, and well established in the profession, were of relatively progressive reputation; and it was certainly a good thing to have an occasional Democrat, provided he qualified as a lawyer of standing, which would automatically ensure that he was respectable and free of any taint of Populism. As late as the summer of 1912, when selecting a district judge, Taft remarked that

> the times are out of joint and it is exceedingly important that . . . we should not only have men who can administer justice and who know the law, but that we should also have men of sufficient knowledge of affairs not to involve the Court in unnecessary controversy and to retain among the people as great a respect and friendship for it as possible, consistent with its administering proper justice.[8]

Some years later, in July 1923, Brandeis reported a conversation—one of the warmest, he said, in fact, the only near-heated one—he had had with Chief Justice Taft the previous fall. Taft asked Brandeis to suggest possible Democrats for appointment to the Court. Brandeis replied that he didn't believe in appointing men as Democrats or Republicans. Those were not, he said, the lines of cleavage on the Court, and it was wrong to encourage a belief on the part of the public that the Court divided along such lines. The actual differences of opinion among the Justices turned on "progressiveness, so-called—views as to property." Taft replied that he disagreed altogether. "We can't go around looking for men with certain creeds on property." And he brought up his appointments of Democrats in 1909–10. "Don't you think I did a good thing?" Brandeis lowered the temperature by answering that times were different then, and thus apparently ended the conversation. But he believed that Taft was, in fact, hunting for men "with certain creeds on property." And in appointing Democrats when he was President, Taft had not done a particularly good thing, Brandeis believed, and the men he had appointed *did* have certain views on property: White, Lamar, Lurton."[9]

[8] W. H. Taft to O. W. Holmes et al., Aug. 3, 1912, Taft Papers.

[9] Brandeis-Frankfurter Conversations, Brandeis Papers, Harvard Law School Library.

6

I: *Mr. Taft Rehabilitates the Court*

The truth is that Taft was being disingenuous with Brandeis in the fall of 1922, when he surely was looking hard for safe and sound property men. But Brandeis was unjustly identifying the Taft he knew, who had after all undergone the shock of Brandeis' own appointment, with the President of more than a decade before. Times *were* different then, they were differently "out of joint." It can be said of President Taft that he made no effort at all to look for the sort of judges Theodore Roosevelt had insisted on finding. "You know how anxious I am," Roosevelt wrote in 1907 to Justice William H. Moody, his former Attorney General, "to get a man who shall not only be an honest man and a good lawyer, but a liberal-minded man, a man with sympathy for the position of labor . . . a man who is not to be scared by technicalities from exercising the proper control over corporations. . . ."[10] Roosevelt was then looking for a circuit judge, but this is how he had also tried to pick his Supreme Court nominees, notably Holmes.[11] This was not how President Taft picked. He had no mission to reform the judiciary. An "honest man and a good lawyer," professional competence and standing, vigor and effectiveness, and conventional political considerations such as geographic distribution and party representation—these were President Taft's decisive criteria. The rest, including "certain creeds on property," would take care of itself.

Moreover, it was, perhaps, Taft's overriding concern, not excluded in 1922 either, but felt more keenly in 1910, to equip the Court with active men of middle years who could carry the load. For the Court was in a bad way, and needed to be reconstituted. As early as May 1909, Taft wrote to Horace H. Lurton, his good friend, then still a circuit judge:

> The condition of the Supreme Court is pitiable, and yet those old fools hold on with a tenacity that is most discouraging. Really the Chief Justice is almost senile; Harlan does no work; Brewer is so deaf that he cannot hear and has got beyond the point of the commonest accuracy in writing his opinions; Brewer and Harlan sleep almost through all the arguments. I don't know what can be done. It is most discouraging to the active men on the Bench.[12]

Meanwhile Justice Moody was succumbing to a disabling illness, and on September 2, 1909, before the opening of the term, at which Moody would not sit, Taft complained further to Senator Henry Cabot Lodge:

---

[10] T. Roosevelt to W. H. Moody, June 5, 1907, letter in possession of the author.

[11] See D. McHargue, "Appointments to the Supreme Court of the United States" (Ph.D. diss., University of California at Los Angeles, 1949), 344–50; W. Harbaugh, *Power and Responsibility* (1961), 163.

[12] Quoted in Pringle, *Taft,* I, 529–30.

It is an outrage that the four men on the Bench who are over seventy should continue there and thus throw the work and responsibility on the other five. This is the occasion of Moody's illness. It is with difficulty that I can restrain myself from making such a statement in my annual message.[13]

As the October Term 1909 opened, Justice Rufus W. Peckham also was absent. He was ill, and it was not clear how gravely. Attorney General Wickersham reported to the President that Justice White had urged him not to bring any important case before the Court while it was in its present state.[14]

Within the month, the situation cleared somewhat. On October 24, 1909, Peckham died, and Taft had his first chance to make an appointment. His choice was his old friend and colleague on the bench of the Circuit Court for the Sixth Circuit, Horace H. Lurton. There was no doubt of that. "It is just the simple truth to tell you," Taft wrote Lurton after making the appointment, "that the chief pleasure of my administration, as I have contemplated it in the past, has been to commission you a Justice of the Supreme Court; and I never had any other purpose. . . ."[15]

Taft had supported Lurton's candidacy in 1906 for the vacancy which Moody eventually filled. This candidacy had foundered on the partisan rock of Senator Henry Cabot Lodge. "My objection," wrote Lodge to President Roosevelt, "is fundamental. I do not think that you ought to appoint a Democrat to the Supreme Court."[16] Now, in 1909, there was some opposition in different quarters. Samuel Gompers, the labor leader, had misgivings. Taft dismissed them, not as he might have done in 1922, on the ground that they served to confirm the soundness of the appointment, but rather because ideological objections did not seem very relevant. Taft knew Lurton to be a just man, and as liberal minded, he said, as anyone.[17] The difficulty, and there was a difficulty, highlighted Taft's chief concern—to put vigorous, effective men on a Court that sadly lacked them. Lurton was sixty-five. "For this reason," as Taft wrote Lurton after he appointed him, "I took back my determination to appoint you, wiped it off the slate, and gave two or three days to

---

[13] Quoted *ibid.*

[14] G. W. Wickersham to W. H. Taft, Oct. 13, 1909 (two letters), Taft Papers.

[15] W. H. Taft to H. H. Lurton, December 1909, H. H. Lurton Papers, Library of Congress (hereinafter cited as Lurton Papers).

[16] H. C. Lodge to T. Roosevelt, Sept. 1, 1906, T. Roosevelt Papers, Library of Congress (hereinafter cited as Roosevelt Papers); see E. Morison and J. Blum, eds., *Letters of Theodore Roosevelt* (1951), V, 396; *cf.* W. H. Taft to Roosevelt, Sept. 8, 1906, Roosevelt Papers.

[17] S. Gompers to W. H. Taft, December 1909, Taft Papers; see Pringle, *Taft*, I, 531.

the introspective process to know whether I was yielding to personal preference and affection at the expense of the public. I became convinced that I was not . . . that I have the right to gratify my personal predilection by doing what I have done, because the motive in doing it included a desire to strengthen that Court as much as I could strengthen it."[18]

So it was that President Taft, much less ideologically committed than he was later to become, seeking still to occupy the middle ground in politics and not free of reelection worries, cherishing the institution as his predecessor had not, and seeing that it suffered more from old age and incompetence than from ideological division within, anxious to make it effective and enhance its professional prestige—a President thus relatively little intent on a candidate's precise ideological orientation, although in three short years he appointed a whole new majority—left the Court pretty much unchanged. For this ambiguous achievement, he received an ambiguous reward when, at a dinner in his honor in January 1911, Joseph H. Choate, the most accomplished toastmaster and one of the most famous advocates at the American Bar, told him: "Mr. Taft has rehabilitated the Supreme Court of the United States. We will now be able to know what the law means and what the law is."[19] And there was lasting inner satisfaction. On going out of office, Taft told newspapermen that the achievement in which he took greatest pride was the reconstitution of the Court. He had said to his appointees, Taft remarked: "Damn you, if any of you die, I'll disown you."[20]

The Nation and the Court, 1909–12

In 1910, the United States had a population of 91,972,266, which had increased rapidly and continued to grow fast. It was growing westward, although 70 percent of it still lived east of the Mississippi, and it was becoming more and more urban, nearly half so in 1910, if one counts the small towns as well as the big cities. Immigration was steady and large. It came to over 14,500,000 between 1900 and 1915, and in 1910, 13,515,886 people, or 14.7 percent of the total population, were foreign-born. The economy was expanding and the country was prosperous, on the farm as well as in the city. Employment was full, or nearly so. The standard of living was rising, although not very perceptibly for the urban worker; and altogether not very evenly: 1 percent of the population owned about 47 percent of the national wealth and got about 15 percent of the income. As one historian has remarked, "Although the poor were not becoming poorer, the rich were gaining

---

[18] W. H. Taft to H. H. Lurton, December 1909, Lurton Papers.

[19] Quoted in M. Keller, *In Defense of Yesterday* (1958), 89.
[20] See Pringle, *Taft,* II, 853–54.

faster than the lower and middle classes."[21] Moreover, in the persons of a handful of investment bankers and allied or subservient railroad and industrial empire-builders, the very rich, who managed, in Brandeis' phrase, other people's money as well as their own, were gaining also enormous social and economic power that was as yet unmatched and hardly controlled by the federal government. The regulation of railroads was substantially advanced by the Hepburn Act of 1906 and the Mann-Elkins Act of 1910. Also in 1906, a federal pure food law was enacted, and there were other regulatory statutes, state and federal. But the rash of regulatory and remedial legislation placed on the books by the first Wilson Administration is one measure of what had not yet been accomplished in 1910.

A very small portion of the nonagricultural work force put in a forty-eight-hour week or less. The vast majority worked between fifty-four and sixty hours, and a good number worked as many as seventy-two hours and over. Child labor, shockingly widespread at the turn of the century, had been attacked in the states, but far from eradicated. The country stood barely at the threshold of enacting humane and rational systems of employers' liability and workmen's compensation. Labor unions, organized nationally in the American Federation of Labor, were an established fact, although total membership was in a state of temporary decline at this time. But such a prime industry as steel was unorganized, a strike having collapsed in August 1910. And the struggles of labor were still marked by much violence and intransigence on both sides. There were over 9,500,000 blacks in the United States, mostly in the South, and while their economic condition was improving slightly and their educational condition considerably, they were often forced into involuntary servitude, disfranchised, segregated, freely lynched, generally oppressed and despised where they lived, and largely abandoned to their fate by the rest of the country.[22] But in May 1910, following some preparatory work started nearly two years before, there was "organized a permanent body to be known as the National Association for the Advancement of Colored People."[23]

The condition of blacks in 1910 and the launching in the same year of the NAACP—two rather specialized facts unfortunately outside the mainstream of contemporary life—may be taken to symbolize,

---

[21] A. S. Link, *American Epoch* (1955), 23.

[22] This and the preceding paragraph are based on H. U. Faulkner, *The Quest for Social Justice* (1931), 7–13, 21–25, 75–80, and Link, *American*

Epoch, 17–74; also Mowry, *The Era of Theodore Roosevelt*, 1–15.

[23] See M. W. Ovington, *How the National Association for the Advancement of Colored People Began* (1914).

on the one hand, much that was primitive or in need of repair in American society, and, on the other, the spirit of the country and the direction in which events were tending. There were problems and inequities that other civilized governments had long since begun to deal with, and much discontent and even despair. At the same time, however, the Progressive movement, which had been afoot for some years, was scoring solid and permanent achievements, although still suffering many defeats, and was on the point of coming to full power in the federal government. This movement and the pervasive effects of the First World War were to change the nature and shape of American society, fulfilling —albeit not for blacks—a measure of what Herbert Croly in 1909 called "The Promise of American Life."[24]

The Progressives, as historians generally agree, were chiefly a middle-class army,[25] and their objectives, William Allen White said in December 1910, were "political and economic: first, to get the gun, and second, to hit something with it."[26] Intellectually they were in reaction against the Social Darwinism that had been dominant in American political thought. The gun had for some time been in the hands of those who believed, in the words of Richard Hofstadter, that "attempts to reform social processes were efforts to remedy the irremediable, that they interfered with the wisdom of nature, that they could lead only to degeneration."[27] This was the preachment, of course, of Herbert Spencer, whose *Social Statics*, Holmes felt it necessary to say in 1905, was not enacted into the Fourteenth Amendment.[28] However that might be, most of the men who directed private and public affairs were thoroughly committed to the general outlines of the Spencerian philosophy till well after the turn of the century. Holmes himself wrote to Lady Pollock in 1895 that Spencer, though dull, uncharming, and "a lower middle-class British Philistine," was insufficiently appreciated in England, and had done more than "any writer of English except Darwin . . . to affect our whole way of thinking about the universe."[29] It is to be doubted that Holmes had substantially changed his mind ten years

---

[24] H. Croly, *The Promise of American Life* (1909).

[25] But see J. J. Huthmacher, "Urban Liberalism and the Age of Reform," *Miss. Valley Hist. Rev.*, 46: 231, 1962.

[26] Quoted in K. W. Hechler, *Insurgency—Personalities and Politics of the Taft Era* (1940), 220.

[27] R. Hofstadter, *Social Darwinism in American Thought* (rev. ed. 1955), 6-7.

[28] Lochner v. New York, 198 U.S. 45, 75 (1905) (Holmes, J., dissenting).

[29] M. DeW. Howe, ed., *Holmes-Pollock Letters* (1946), I, 55-58 (hereinafter cited as *Holmes-Pollock Letters*).

later, when he was resisting the introduction of Spencer into the Fourteenth Amendment, or, indeed, that he held any different notions to the end of his life. Holmes' view of the judicial function was one thing; his affinity to Spencer was another. And the latter was more widely shared.

Spencer was the apostle of the negative state. He was against state aid to the poor, state-supported education, sanitary and housing regulations, tariffs, state banking, and government postal systems. Few perhaps followed him to such specific extremes, but large numbers of educated men shared the "stark and candid pessimism" that the very influential scholar and publicist, William Graham Sumner of Yale, derived from his philosophy. "At bottom," Sumner wrote, "there are two chief things with which government has to deal. They are the property of men and the honor of women. These it has to defend against crime." "Let it be understood that we cannot go outside of this alternative: liberty, inequality, survival of the fittest; not liberty, equality, survival of the unfittest. The former carries society forward and favors all its best members; the latter carries society downwards and favors all its worst members."[30] Spencer's influence in the United States reached its peak before the turn of the century, but men formed under it wielded power well after 1900. "Those who were brought up in America in the second half of the nineteenth century were young victims of a vast literature of social apologetics."[31]

The Progressives were led, for the most part, by hard-nosed, realistic politicians. But they were optimistic reformers who had somehow escaped being victimized by their education. They were movers and doers. As George E. Mowry has written, they fastened "Jeffersonian idealism on a Hamiltonian structure in a partial realization of social democracy."[32] In the beginnings of its national effectiveness, the movement dates to Theodore Roosevelt's first term. The enactment (if, in a phrase of later currency, with all deliberate speed) of federal remedial and regulatory legislation and the prosecutions under the Sherman Antitrust Act proceeded without a break, indeed in increasingly greater volume, from the Roosevelt through the Taft administrations.[33] But the style of President Taft was not that of his predecessor, and neither temperamentally nor in fundamental outlook was Taft really a Progressive. And so the movement hurtled past, leaving him by the wayside. Congress and ex-President Roosevelt, who returned from a tour of the

---

[30] See Hofstadter, *Social Darwinism in American Thought*, 31–50, 51, 57, 62.

[31] M. G. White, *Social Thought in America* (1949), 64.

[32] G. E. Mowry, *Theodore Roosevelt and the Progressive Movement* (1949), 11.

[33] See A. M. Schlesinger, Sr., *Political and Social Growth of the American People* (1941), 326–27; and see *infra*, p. 96, n.27.

world late in the spring of 1910, nearly simultaneously with the arrival of Halley's Comet,[34] provided the drama and the leadership.

In the spring and summer of 1909, the country's attention had been caught by a stirring revolt staged in the Senate by insurgent Republican Progressives against the Payne-Aldrich tariff, and against the leadership of Nelson W. Aldrich of Rhode Island and his small oligarchy, which had made of the Senate the redoubt of conservatism. Early the following spring, in March 1910, Democrats and Insurgents in the outgoing Republican House, led by George W. Norris of Nebraska in an even more dramatic twenty-nine-hour continuous fight, toppled the authority of the arch-conservative Speaker, Uncle Joe Cannon. On August 31, 1910, in perhaps the most radical speech of his career, at Osawatomie, Kansas, Theodore Roosevelt proclaimed the New Nationalism, combining "Hamiltonian means with Jeffersonian ends,"[35] and calling for, among other reforms, physical valuation of railroad properties, graduated income and inheritance taxes, workmen's compensation legislation, and national regulation of women's and children's labor.[36] The Colonel's candidacy of 1912 was germinating, and that year's triumph of Progressivism in national politics was being ensured.

The state and federal judiciaries, and particularly the Supreme Court of the United States, both specifically and as symbol, figured heavily in the exciting and productive political agitation of the time. No doubt the Supreme Court is seldom far removed from the political consciousness of the nation. Yet this was for the Court one of those recurring periods of the most intense involvement in political agitation. Progressivism was, among other things, a revolt against established orthodoxy and authority, of which the Supreme Court could hardly escape being deemed a symbol. Moreover, many of the specific issues that were being agitated touched unavoidably on the work of the Court. Theodore Roosevelt, for one, was always on the verge of a collision with the judges. In a fiery message on January 31, 1908, he had attacked the labor injunction,[37] and on his Western tour in 1910, addressing the Colorado legislature, he deplored the *Lochner* case, as well as the general tendency of the Supreme Court to develop a "neutral" area between the power of state and the power of federal government.[38] At Osawatomie, a few days later, he declared that the judiciary should be subsidiary to the executive. And it should be more interested in human welfare than in property, he said. By February 1912, in a famous speech at Columbus, Ohio, when he was already more or less

---

[34] See Mowry, *Roosevelt and the Progressive Movement*, 116–17, n.12.

[35] *Ibid.,* 145.

[36] See Harbaugh, *Power and Re-* sponsibility, 392.

[37] *Ibid.,* 343–44.

[38] See Mowry, *Roosevelt and the Progressive Movement*, 142.

13

an active candidate, Roosevelt toned down some of the radicalisms uttered at Osawatomie a year and a half before, but, curiously enough, he chose to cause a sensation and to scandalize conservative opinion by coming out in favor of the popular recall of judicial decisions, albeit decisions of state courts only. Judges were wont to obstruct, Roosevelt had always felt. He was highly exercised over the *Ives* case, of June 1911, in which the New York Court of Appeals had struck down a workmen's compensation statute.[39] Like Franklin K. Lane, Roosevelt felt "that the country would have to satisfy the common man's sense of justice, or worse things than the recall of judges would come to pass."[40] The courts simply had to be curbed. Roosevelt carried this theme into the campaign of 1912, saying, in October of that year: "We stand for the Constitution, but we will not consent to make the Constitution a fetish for the protection of fossilized wrong. We recognize in neither court, nor Congress, nor President, any divine right to override the will of the people."[41]

Others took up the theme, and had indeed sounded it before. But not everyone was as full-throated as TR, and there were differences of substance as well as emphasis among the Progressives on the subject of the Court. Although the recall of judges was adopted, but never successfully used, in seven states, and Colorado briefly had the recall of judicial opinions,[42] and although these and other specific proposals for curbing the judiciary as an institution were bruited about for some little time,[43] they cannot be said ever to have gathered widespread responsible support, even among Progressives, or to have come anywhere near to general adoption by the states, let alone in the federal system.

Aside from specifics, the Progressives do not all appear to have shared even the Rooseveltian premise of distrust and suspicion of the judiciary. Toward the Supreme Court, at least, if not toward state courts, some of the Progressives harbored kindlier feelings. Thus William Allen White, a certified Progressive even though he bore Taft no ill will, wrote

---

[39] Ives v. South Buffalo Ry., 201 N.Y. 271 (1911). The state constitution was subsequently amended, and a new statute was upheld both by the New York court and by the Supreme Court of the United States some years later. See *infra*, pp. 205–213.

[40] See Mowry, *Roosevelt and the Progressive Movement*, 214.

[41] *Ibid.*, 278.

[42] See Link, *American Epoch*, 90. One of these states, Arizona, had adopted the recall of judges in its proposed constitution, which had been vetoed by Taft, however, so that Arizona could readopt the recall of judges only after having become a state. See Mowry, *Era of Theodore Roosevelt*, 264–65.

[43] See M. R. Senior, *The Supreme Court: Its Power of Judicial Review with Respect to Congressional Legislation* (1937), 57–58, and, e.g., S. 3222 (Senator Bourne of Oregon), 47 *Cong. Rec.* 3877, 61st Cong., 1st Sess. (1911).

to the President in 1911: "I am one of the few bomb-throwing radicals who believe that our most progressive institution is the United States Supreme Court. It seems to me today to be the most radical branch of our government."[44] The following year, Dean William Draper Lewis, of the University of Pennsylvania Law School, another Progressive in good standing, but not so vivid a writer, said much the same thing in print.[45] Nevertheless, a degree of hostility toward the judiciary, distrust of it or outright fear, a measure of anxiety that this institution was a threat to all reforms and that it was one gun which could not be readily got, and which could perhaps never be aimed so as to hit what the reformers wanted to hit—such an attitude was decidedly an ingredient of Progressivism. And to the left of the Progressives, among those who could with more justification than William Allen White, although still with some humor, call themselves "bomb-throwing radicals," feelings were quite bitter about the Supreme Court and the Constitution with which it was identified. *Our Dishonest Constitution* ran the title of a Socialist tract published in 1914.[46] And Gustavus Myers' *History of the Supreme Court of the United States*, issued in 1912, while it refrained from bringing charges of venality against the Justices, found them guilty of "class corruption," and labored to establish prior connections between such Justices as Lurton, Hughes, Willis Van Devanter, and Joseph R. Lamar and predatory interests involved in fraudulent ventures.[47]

Quite aside from any decisions, actual or feared, that frustrated Progressive purposes, the attitude of the Progressives is sufficiently explained as a reaction to what was virtually a conservative deification of the judges and of the Constitution of which they were the supposed impersonal voices. "For many years we have been taught the slavish doctrine," Justice Moody wrote President Roosevelt in December 1908, "that the courts are infallible, and the protest against this doctrine has been, in the main, inarticulate until you gave it voice."[48] A year earlier, Moody had written the President: "You know how the Constitution is cherished by many good people who haven't a speaking acquaintance with it, and by many bad people who regard it as a benign gift from

---

[44] W. A. White to W. H. Taft, July 4, 1911, Taft Papers.

[45] See "A New Method of Constitutional Amendment by Popular Vote," Annals, 43:311, 1912; see also F. Frankfurter, *Law & Politics*, A. MacLeish and E. F. Pritchard, eds. (Capricorn ed., 1962), 3, 5–6; and *cf.* C. Warren, "The Progressiveness of the United States Supreme Court," *Colum. L. Rev.* 13:294, 1913.

[46] A. L. Benson, *Our Dishonest Constitution* (1914).

[47] G. Myers, *History of the Supreme Court of the United States* (1912), 8, 718–78.

[48] W. H. Moody to T. Roosevelt, Dec. 3, 1908, letter in possession of the author.

the fathers, designed to protect those of sufficient wealth from the consequences of their misdoing."[49] Moody was counseling Roosevelt against too violent an attack on the judiciary which, he feared, might furnish an argument for the latter class (the "bad people") to use with the former (the "good people" who haven't a speaking acquaintance with the Constitution). But the Progressives were under an ineluctable necessity to counter with the "good people" the arguments about the Supreme Court and the Constitution that the "bad people" were already using.

The symbols of Court and Constitution were instruments of political warfare in conservative hands. Rights and privileges of property identified with these symbols might seem legitimate—because supposedly proceeding from constitutional morality rather than mere interest and expediency—even to those who, if they felt free to follow their own interests and inclinations, would regard the privileges of property as unconscionable. It is one thing to propose reforms, but quite another to subvert sacred documents and institutions. Votes and access to power were, therefore, in play. The Progressives had to contend that their proposals were not subverting the Constitution, and they were well advised, as Moody said, not to let themselves be maneuvered into trampling on the sacred symbols. On the other hand, to be on the safe side, the Progressives had also to contend that the Constitution was, after all, a secular document, and the Court a secular body.

Conservative opinion in these years certainly went beyond mere satisfaction with decisions that appeared to it to safeguard the interests of property. There was such satisfaction, and it was heartfelt, to be sure. Thus, Edward A. Moseley, the Secretary of the Interstate Commerce Commission, regretfully reported to Willis Van Devanter, then a circuit judge, what he had heard a leading army officer remark about *Adair* v. *United States*:[50] "I am delighted to see the Supreme Court put a stop to these miserable labor organizations."[51] In public, more elevated ground was taken, though with full awareness of the uses of the Constitution as an anti-Progressive political weapon. And the Constitution and the Court were one. Writing in 1912, Nicholas Murray Butler, president of Columbia University and a leading Republican, declared his belief

that the independent judiciary, throwing the protection of fundamental law about the humblest individual and holding both legislatures and

---

[49] W. H. Moody to T. Roosevelt, Sept. 26, 1907, letter in possession of the author.

[50] 208 U.S. 161 (1908).

[51] E. A. Moseley to W. Van Devanter, Jan. 28, 1908, Van Devanter Papers, Library of Congress (hereinafter cited as Van Devanter Papers).

administrative officers to the strict observance of their constitutional limitations, is the chief glory of our American system of government and its most original contribution to political science.[52]

In a widely circulated Senate speech, George Sutherland of Utah, the future Justice, said in July 1911:

The judge represents no constituents, speaks for no policy save the public policy of the law. If he be not utterly forsworn, he must at all hazards put the rights of a single individual above the wishes of *all* the people. He has no master but the compelling forces of his own conscience.[53]

And the following, a much-quoted Te Deum, as Ralph H. Gabriel calls it, by Henry R. Estabrook of the New York Bar, was sung in 1913:

Our great and sacred Constitution, serene and inviolable, stretches its beneficent powers over our land . . . like the outstretched arm of God himself. . . . [T]he people of the United States . . . ordained and established one Supreme Court—the most rational, considerate, discerning, veracious, impersonal power—the most candid, unaffected, conscientious, incorruptible power. . . . O Marvelous Constitution! Magic Parchment! Transforming Word! Maker, Monitor, Guardian of Mankind![54]

When they took care not to concede Court and Constitution to the other side, the Progressives demanded, as did Albert J. Beveridge in the keynote speech of the Progressive Convention of 1912, that the judges make of the Constitution "a living thing, growing with the people's growth . . . aiding the people in their struggles for life, liberty and the pursuit of happiness."[55] Many believed that the Constitution was itself a neutral, rather than necessarily, in current political terms, a conservative document, and that what was needed to make it hospitable to Progressive objectives was merely the appointment of Justices "who not only understand the great industrial and political problems now before us, but who are likewise in sympathy with the big movements which have

---

[52] N. M. Butler, *Why Should We Change Our Form of Government?* (1912), xiii.

[53] J. F. Paschal, *Mr. Justice Sutherland—A Man Against the State* (1951), 79. Sutherland was opposing the provision for judicial recall in the Arizona constitution that Taft eventually vetoed, see *supra* n.42.

[54] Quoted in R. H. Gabriel, *The Course of American Democratic Thought* (1940), 402.

[55] Quoted in C. Bowers, *Beveridge and the Progressive Era* (1932), 426–29.

for their aim the promotion of the public welfare. . . ."[56] This was the view that the young Felix Frankfurter, an ardent Progressive, expressed on the great occasion of the twenty-fifth anniversary dinner of the *Harvard Law Review* in 1912, and this is what he came to teach at the Harvard Law School two years later.[57] This was the view taken also in a body of scholarly and professional writings—most of them academic products, but some the work of practicing lawyers—which connected with the older tradition of James Bradley Thayer, John Chipman Gray, and Oliver Wendell Holmes.[58] Thayer had counseled a restricted and restrained role for the Court under what he regarded as a broadly permissive Constitution. The legal realism of Gray's *The Nature and Sources of the Law* and of Holmes' *The Common Law* was altogether incompatible with the deification of the judges and the consecration of the text of the Constitution. Some of the writers of this school went so far—but no further—as to urge one or another structural reform of the state, if not the federal, judiciary (for it was widely agreed that abuses had been more frequent in the former), and even occasionally to try to render Theodore Roosevelt's Columbus speech on the recall of judicial decisions professionally respectable.[59]

But the provocation, by way of politically very useful Te Deums, under which the Progressives labored was great, as we have seen, and hence a more fundamental attack on both Court and Constitution, an effort to secularize them and cut them down to size, was inevitable. In this endeavor also, the Progressives were aided by a considerable scholarly literature. In 1907, Professor J. Allen Smith of the University

---

[56] J. R. Garfield to C. E. Hughes, Apr. 27, 1910, Hughes Papers, Library of Congress (hereinafter cited as Hughes Papers).

[57] See A. M. Bickel, "Applied Politics and the Science of Law: Writings of the Harvard Period," in W. Mendelson, ed., *Felix Frankfurter: A Tribute* (1964), 164–66.

[58] See, e.g., P. Bordwell, "The Function of the Judiciary," *Colum. L. Rev.,* 7:337, 520, 1907; W. F. Dodd, "The Growth of Judicial Power," *Political Science Quarterly,* 24:193, 1909; F. J. Goodnow, *Social Reform and the Constitution* (1911); C. G. Haines, "Judicial Criticism of Legislation by Courts," *Mich. L. Rev.,* 11:26, 1912; M. R. Cohen, "The Process of Judicial Legislation," *Am. L. Rev.,* 48:161, 1914; W. M. Meigs, "Some Recent Attacks on the American Doctrine of Judicial Power," *Am. L. Rev.,* 40: 640, 1906.

[59] See, e.g., H. W. Ballantine, "Labor Legislation and the Recall of the 'Judicial Veto,' " *Case & Comm.,* 19:225, 1912; J. G. Palfrey, "The Constitution and the Courts," *Harv. L. Rev.,* 26:507, 1913; F. A. Maynard, "Five to Four Decisions of the Supreme Court of the United States," *Cent. L. J.,* 89:206, 1919; and see W. L. Ransom, *Majority Rule and the Judiciary* (1912); W. D. Lewis, "A New Method of Constitutional Amendment by Popular Vote," *Annals,* 43:311, 1912.

of Washington published a volume entitled *The Spirit of American Government,* in which he took a rather earthy approach to the Constitution as the product of "the wealthy and conservative classes." The solicitude shown by the members of the Constitutional Convention "for the interests of the well-to-do" was reflected in decisions of the Supreme Court "almost uniformly advantageous to the capital-owning class." This was an influential book. Robert M. La Follette bought hundreds of copies of it for distribution in Wisconsin.[60]

Meanwhile, other writers were resuming a debate over the question of the legitimacy of the Court's power of judicial review. This debate was nearly as old as the Court itself, but it had been quiescent in recent years. It proceeded now from substantial new researches, and continued well into the later years of the decade, having reached something of a climax around 1912. Some writers regarded judicial review as legitimate, but as an implied, judge-created power rather than an expressly granted one. In a series of incisive papers, which he began to publish as early as 1906, and which culminated in his book *The Doctrine of Judicial Review,* issued in 1914, Edward S. Corwin argued that the evidence of the framers' intent was ambivalent; that the doctrine of judicial review was in the air at the time of the framing and was approved by at least some of the authors of the Constitution, although it was impossible to determine with precision just how they visualized the actual exercise of the power; that as applied to test state enactments against the federal Constitution, judicial review was an inescapable concomitant of a federal system; that in general it rested not on textual authority, for the text of the Constitution was ambiguous on the point, or on historical evidence of intent, but on a Lockeian theory of limited government and individual rights; and that as such it had been essentially accepted by the legislature, from the earliest Congress onward. In the exercise of judicial review, Corwin was quite clear, as in the assumption of the power, judges made law rather than distilling it from the constitutional text.[61] Others raised an unqualified cry of usurpation, holding that *Marbury* v.

---

[60] J. A. Smith, *The Spirit of American Government* (1907), 32, 39, 111. See E. F. Goldman, *Rendezvous with Destiny* (1952), 148–49.

[61] E. S. Corwin, "The Supreme Court and Unconstitutional Acts of Congress," *Mich. L. Rev.,* 4:616, 1906; "The Establishment of Judicial Review," *Mich. L. Rev.,* 9:102, 283, 1910, 1911; "*Marbury v. Madison* and the Doctrine of Judicial Review," *Mich. L. Rev.,* 12:538, 1914; and see F. N. Judson, *The Judiciary and the People* (1913); H. Pope, "The Fundamental Law and the Power of Courts," *Harv. L. Rev.,* 27:45, 1913; F. E. Melvin, "The Judicial Bulwark of the Constitution," *American Political Science Review,* 8:167, 1914.

Madison was an invention of John Marshall pure and simple, with no support in the intention of the framers.[62]

In 1912, Charles A. Beard published a little book which, if he said so himself—and he did, in an introduction to a new edition in 1938—"settled" this particular controversy and "became a permanent part of our constitutional literature."[63] Beard's volume, entitled *The Supreme Court and the Constitution*, showed that a majority of active members of the Constitutional Convention favored some form of judicial control over legislation. Quite aside from the considerable ambiguity in what Beard set out to prove, and from ambiguities that some critics have found in his evidence, the book offered more comfort to the Progressives than to conservative defenders of the divine right of the Court. For Beard's argument was joined to a thesis that he elaborated the following year in another book, *An Economic Interpretation of the Constitution*. This work purported to show, through an analysis of the backgrounds and interests of the framers, that the Constitution was written by and for the monied classes, the groups of personalty interests holding money or public securities, or engaged in manufacturing, trade, or shipping. No wonder the framers wanted to lodge a power of judicial review in the Court! Even Holmes, a realist about law and the judicial function and no worshipper of deities, was distressed by Beard's book. It was, he wrote Sir Frederick Pollock some years later, a

---

[62] See, e.g., W. Trickett, "The Great Usurpation," *Am. L. Rev.,* 40:356, 1906; W. Clark (Chief Justice of North Carolina), "Is the Supreme Court Constitutional?" *Independent,* 63:723, 1907; L. B. Boudin, "Government by Judiciary," *Political Science Quarterly,* 26:238, 1911; and see H. A. Davis, "Annulment of Legislation by the Supreme Court," *American Political Science Review,* 7:541, 1913. Judge Clark returned to the attack in later years; see "Back to the Constitution," *Am. L. Rev.,* 50:1, 1916, and "Where Does the Governing Power Reside?" *Am. L. Rev.,* 52:687, 1918. Professional voices were, of course, promptly raised, defending in absolute terms the legitimacy of the Court's function. See, e.g., J. Woodward, "The Courts and the People," *Colum. L. Rev.,* 7:559, 1907; W. G. Hastings, "Is It Usurpation to Hold as Void Unconstitutional Laws?" *Green Bag,* 20:453, 1908; C. H. Burr, "Unconstitutional Laws and the Federal Judicial Power," *U. Pa. L. Rev.,* 60:624, 1912; H. L. Carson, "The Historic Relation of Judicial Power to Unconstitutional Legislation," *U. Pa. L. Rev.,* 60:687, 1912; E. Countryman, *The Supreme Court of the United States* (1913); F. Green, "The Judicial Censorship of Legislation," *Am. L. Rev.,* 47:90, 1913; J. R. Long, "Unconstitutional Acts of Congress," *Va. L. Rev.,* 1:417, 1914; W. A. Sutherland, "Politics and the Supreme Court," *Am. L. Rev.,* 48:390, 1914; G. W. Williams, "The Power of Courts to Declare a Statute Void," *Am. L. Rev.,* 52:497, 1918.

[63] Beard's book was reissued in 1962, in an edition prepared, with an introduction and bibliography, by Professor Alan F. Westin. The bibliography is extremely valuable, and I have made extensive use of that portion of it which appears at pp. 136–39.

rather ignoble though most painstaking investigation of the investments of the leaders, with an innuendo even if disclaimed. I shall believe until compelled to think otherwise that they wanted to make a nation and invested (bet) on the belief that they would make one, not that they wanted a powerful government because they had invested. Belittling arguments always have a force of their own, but you and I believe that highmindedness is not impossible to man.[64]

Later revisionist scholarship lends some support to Holmes' belief.[65] Nevertheless, in its day, Beard's book powerfully bolstered one aspect of the Progressive argument about judicial review.[66]

The two aspects of the Progressive argument were not rigorously consistent, and this may have been another reason for Holmes' dissatisfaction with Beard. If the Constitution was what Beard said it was, then the judges probably were construing it correctly, and even properly applied by humane and enlightened judges, it could not be rendered hospitable to Progressive reforms. The only remedy then would be a radical one, which most Progressives did not favor. They wished only to neutralize the Court, and in the end perhaps bring it over to their side. But if intellectually the Progressives did not walk an altogether straight path, then neither did the conservatives, who, while insisting that the Constitution was not only a divine but also a self-enforcing document, and that the judges made no law, and certainly made none merely because it accorded with their own presuppositions, also kept a wary eye out for the appointment of judges whose social and economic views were safe and sound.

We have seen something of the uses and abuses of the Court and the Constitution as strategic weapons in the contest for power, and of the Progressive defenses and counterattacks. But the federal judiciary as a whole, and the Supreme Court in particular, was also deeply involved in the tactical political struggle for specific objectives. To recur once more to William Allen White's figure of speech, the Progressives' grand design for getting the gun encountered the Court. But so did many of their specific efforts to hit something. This was signally true, for one example, of the battle staged by the Senate Insurgents of 1909 against the Payne-Aldrich tariff. Through the hot summer months, the Insurgents fought against the high, and in many cases increased, pro-

---

[64] *Holmes-Pollock Letters, II,* 222–23; see also *ibid.,* I, 237.

[65] See F. McDonald, *We the People* (1958); R. E. Brown, *Charles Beard and the Constitution* (1956). And see F. McDonald, *E. Pluribus Unum* (1965). For a reaction to the reac-tion to Beard, see L. Benson, *Turner and Beard* (1960).

[66] See R. Hofstadter, "Beard and the Constitution," *American Quarterly,* 2:195, 1950; White, *Social Thought in America,* 64–66.

tective rates which Senator Aldrich had dictatorially written into the bill, in violation of what was, at the least, an implied pledge in the Republican platform of 1908 to lower rates. In coalition with Democrats, the Progressives proposed also to write into the bill an income tax amendment intended bluntly to overrule *Pollock* v. *Farmers' Loan & Trust Co.*,[67] which had held a federal income tax unconstitutional, or, in any event, to invite the Court to overrule itself. The amendment was sponsored by Joseph W. Bailey, the Texas Democrat, and Albert B. Cummins, former Progressive governor of Iowa, who, with Jonathan P. Dolliver, Albert J. Beveridge, Moses E. Clapp, and Robert M. La Follette, was one of the prime figures in the summer's struggle.[68]

The *Pollock* decision had long been unpopular. It had itself gone against earlier precedent, and had been made by a Court divided 5–4. Many conservatives, including, for example, Elihu Root, were at least mildly in favor of an income tax, and Theodore Roosevelt had advocated precisely what the Bailey-Cummins amendment now proposed. Taft had also in the past favored an attempt to revise the *Pollock* decision by statute.[69] But Aldrich was firmly opposed, because even aside from its other undesirable features, an income tax would bring in so much revenue as to render the protective tariff superfluous from a fiscal point of view. The debate in the Senate, which was long and intensive, did not turn on the merits of the income tax. It turned rather on the propriety of the *Pollock* decision, and of an attempt by Congress to invite the Court to overrule itself. The proponents of the amendment were thoroughly candid about their purposes. They wanted, as Cummins said, to force the Court to reexamine the issue, and thus put pressure on it to overrule itself, as it had done in the past more than once.[70] They thought, as Bailey and William E. Borah of Idaho and others argued at length, that the *Pollock* case had been wrongly decided.[71] There was also much argument about the nature of the separation of powers, and the obligation of the other departments of government to make their own constitutional decisions when they considered that the Supreme Court had rendered one that was wrong.[72] At the farther reaches of Democratic Populism, Hernando D. Money of Mississippi went so far as to remark:

---

[67] 157 U.S. 429 (1895).

[68] In the House, on the first day of the first session of the 61st Congress, Cordell Hull of Tennessee had introduced a similar proposal. 44 *Cong. Rec.* 533, 61st Cong., 1st Sess. (1909).

[69] See Mowry, *Roosevelt and the Progressive Movement,* 59–60.

[70] See 44 *Cong. Rec.* 1421–22, 3970–85, 61st Cong., 1st Sess. (1909).

[71] *Ibid.,* 1361–66, 1684, 1693–1701, 1820.

[72] See Hughes of Colorado, *ibid.,* 3444–45.

I: *Mr. Taft Rehabilitates the Court*

I am not one of those who regard the judgment of the Supreme Court as an African regards his deity. I respect such a decision just exactly to the extent that it is founded in common sense and argued out on reasonable logic, but when it violates the law and common sense, then I cease to so regard it, except that as a citizen I am bound by it. . . . As a legislator, I have no more regard for it than I have for the decision of a magistrate in one of the counties of the State of Mississippi. . . .[73]

Elihu Root, then in the Senate, upheld the honor of the Court, as did George Sutherland of Utah and others. It was proposed, he said, to compel the Supreme Court to yield to the force of public opinion. If the Court did, it would lose the respect of the people. If it did not, it would be involved in an open breach with the other branches of the government, and the popular acclaim would be behind the popular branches,

. . . all setting against the independence, the dignity, the respect, the sacredness of that great tribunal whose function in our system of government has made us unlike any republic that ever existed in the world, whose part in our government is the greatest contribution that America has made to political science.[74]

This was, no doubt, the most effective argument made against an income tax statute. Nevertheless, the proponents seemed on the verge of carrying the Senate. Taft thereupon worked out a compromise with Aldrich to drop the income tax and enact instead a corporation tax, which would collide much less, if at all, with the authority of the *Pollock* case. And so Taft sent up a message saying that after "mature consideration," he had come to the conclusion that income taxation should await a constitutional amendment, so that popular confidence in the Court might not be eroded. And he proposed the corporation tax,[75] which was enacted, and later upheld by the Supreme Court.[76] But the Senate insisted on also submitting the Sixteenth Amendment at the same time, and the House concurred.[77] The larger aspect of the debate did not go unnoticed. Calling it memorable, a writer in the *Political*

---

[73] *Ibid.*, 4115. See A. T. Mason, *The Supreme Court from Taft to Warren* (1958), 19; and see A. M. Bickel, *The Least Dangerous Branch* (1962), 254–72.

[74] 44 *Cong. Rec.* 4022, 61st Cong., 1st Sess. (1909); see *ibid.*, 4023, 4067, and (for Sutherland of Utah) 3446.

[75] *Ibid.*, 3344–45, 3985–4067; see *infra*, pp. 242–51.

[76] Flint v. Stone Tracy Co., *infra*, p. 246, n.142.

[77] Despite Hull's continued belief that a statute would have been sufficient. See 44 *Cong. Rec.*, 4400–4404, 61st Cong., 1st Sess. (1909).

Science Quarterly the following year hoped that it would be widely studied. For

> if we come to believe that the Supreme Court in its construction of the Constitution is not infallible, and that, when convinced that this Court has mistakenly voided a desirable law, the legislature should secure that law's reconsideration, we may find ourselves with a more responsive form of government.[78]

Such is the story of the Court's impact on the vivid politics of the day. What impact did the political drama have on the Court? This was a period not merely of agitation, but of gathering momentum, a period leading, as people could doubtless sense, and as happens cyclically, to a new national consensus and a shift of power. The cycle was to close more or less with the death of Roosevelt in 1919, when, as George E. Mowry has written, "the cold grey shadow of Calvin Coolidge fell across America."[79] But this was the middle period of the cycle, the mood of the country was evident, and the shape of events immediately in prospect fairly clear. In such a time, can the Court have remained unaffected?

Writing many years later, Felix Frankfurter thought that Theodore Roosevelt had been right when he remarked: "I may not know much about law, but I do know one can put the fear of God into judges."[80] In 1916, Frankfurter believed that the era of "luxuriant individualism" characterized by the *Lochner* decision was over, that the Court, in other words, had had the fear of God effectively put into it.[81] And on the specific issue of the *Lochner* case, that was, indeed, for a time true. Moreover, as noted earlier, there was a perceptible, if slight, more general movement in Supreme Court adjudication. But it dated back farther than the campaign of 1912 and Roosevelt's sabre rattling, it was not a sharp movement in any event, and no surmises as to the impact of Progressive agitation can safely be based on it. What one can say is that the political configuration of 1910 must have had its subtle effect on the appointments made by President Taft. The power of the Progressive movement played its role in Taft's inclination to welcome, rather than be put off by, the relatively liberal stance of such a candidate for judicial office as Charles Evans Hughes. And it may be that the national mood and the politics of the day had their subtle part also in the formation of the men whom Taft appointed. Van Devanter, Hughes

---

[78] H. M. Bowman, "Congress and the Supreme Court," *Political Science Quarterly*, 25:20, 34, 1910.

[79] Mowry, *Roosevelt and the Pro-gressive Movement*, 377.

[80] See Frankfurter, *Law and Politics*, 3, 15.

[81] *Ibid.*, 109.

reminisced many years later, was not, when appointed, the inflexible conservative he became in the twenties.[82] Perhaps he and Lamar and Mahlon Pitney, and perhaps even Hughes himself, might have been different men had they been appointed at the same respective ages by President Harding in 1923. This is as far as speculation can take one, however, and even this may be too far.

The Appointments of 1910

When Brewer died on March 28, 1910, President Taft did not suffer much doubt about a replacement. He seems almost to have had his choice prepared in advance, and within a month he made the appointment. The week before Brewer's death, Taft had been to Albany, where he had a long talk with Governor Charles Evans Hughes of New York and spent the night at the Executive Mansion.[83] Hughes, born in Glens Falls, New York, on April 11, 1862, was, at forty-eight, a nationally known, successful, if embattled, reform governor. The son of an immigrant Welsh Baptist minister, Hughes attended Colgate University, then Brown University, where he received a bachelor's degree, then Columbia Law School for an LL.B. He practiced law in New York and married Antoinette Carter, daughter of his senior partner. Later he taught law briefly at Cornell. He entered public life early in 1905 as counsel to a committee of the New York legislature investigating the gas and electric utilities. In the fall of the same year, he conducted an even more celebrated investigation of the life insurance business, which propelled him into the governorship in the election of 1906. In 1908, he was a serious, although undeclared, possibility for the Republican Presidential nomination, which Theodore Roosevelt awarded to Taft. Hughes declined the Vice-Presidential nomination.[84]

When Taft visited him in Albany in 1910, Hughes was in the last year of his second term as governor. He was, at this time of life, under considerable inner tension, and easily subject to nervous strain. But impeccably attired, his beard well brushed, if, perhaps, a little longer than it would later be remembered, he cut a vigorous, resolute, altogether imposing public figure. He had already acquired the reputation for stiffness—undeserved, his biographer thinks, and belied by his private personality[85]—which was to remain with him for the rest of his days, and he enjoyed also a reputation for formidable rectitude.

The question of a third two-year term as governor faced Hughes in

---

[82] See C. E. Hughes, *Biographical Notes*, 220–21, Hughes Papers.
[83] See M. Pusey, *Charles Evans*

Hughes (1951), I, 267.
[84] See *ibid.*
[85] *See ibid.*, e.g., 174–75, 339.

March of 1910, and he made it clear to Taft that he had no wish to continue in the office. "I do not dare to run the chance of breaking down mentally," Taft's aide, Captain Archie Butt, who accompanied the President, reports Hughes as saying. He had had warnings from his doctor, Hughes continued, and he felt that he must go out and make his family safe "while I am able." After leaving the governor, Butt reports, Taft remarked: "I don't know the man I admire more than Hughes. If ever I have the chance, I shall offer him the Chief Justiceship."[86]

Taft had not always been so enthusiastic about Hughes. Less than three years earlier, he had declared himself to his brother Charles as sharing President Roosevelt's dislike for Hughes, who was "a man without magnetism," and without sufficient regard for his obligation to the Republican Party.[87] But in 1907, Taft's views were strongly colored by those of Roosevelt; they were indeed a rather simplified reflection of Roosevelt's complex distrust for Hughes. By 1910, Taft was forming a more independent judgment. He was, moreover, in political trouble in quarters in which Hughes might not have been loved, but was certainly respected and accepted. Hughes was also the logical rival if there was to be a contest over Taft's renomination in 1912. To put Hughes on the Supreme Court was, therefore, to gain some credit where Taft needed it—from the center and even slightly right-of-center all the way to the left within the Republican Party—and it would substantially remove Hughes from contention for the Presidency. There is absolutely no evidence that calculations looking to the Presidential contest in 1912 played a primary role in Taft's decision to appoint Hughes. But the evidence is clear that the bearing of the appointment on the prospects for 1912 was in Taft's mind.

Brewer was from Kansas, and there might have been reason to think that Taft would go to the central or western states, the Seventh or Eighth Circuit, for a replacement. But when Peckham had died the year before, Taft had replaced him with Lurton of Tennessee, and had thus left New York, and its Second Circuit, the busiest and most important, unrepresented. And so New York was now a logical place to look for a candidate.

Taft no doubt flirted, however briefly, with one alternative, his Solicitor General, Lloyd W. Bowers of Minnesota. A few days after Brewer's death, Taft told Francis E. Warren of Wyoming, a pillar of the Republican establishment in the Senate, who had come to explore the possibilities in behalf of his friend Judge Willis Van Devanter of the Eighth Circuit Court of Appeals, that he greatly admired Bowers, but

---

[86] See *ibid.*, 267–68; A. Butt, *Taft and Roosevelt: The Intimate Letters* of *Archie Butt* (1924), I, 223.
[87] See Pringle, *Taft*, 331.

would hesitate seriously about appointing him to the Supreme Court now, when Bowers was doing so superb a job as Solicitor General and had so many important causes pending. Warren nevertheless walked away believing that "today Bowers has the inside track." And if Bowers was not appointed now, he would nevertheless land on the Supreme Court, Warren thought, during the remaining three years of Taft's Presidential term.[88] This conviction of Warren's was well grounded. Many years later, Taft recalled that he had "certainly intended to put Lloyd Bowers on the Supreme bench and would have done so had he lived. I clinched the matter by sending word to him . . . that I intended to do so. Bowers was one of the best men I ever knew and was admirably adapted to succeed on the bench."[89]

It seems clear that Van Devanter, Lamar, or Pitney would in the next two years have lost out to Bowers, but he died prematurely, on September 9, 1910. At the time of the Brewer vacancy, Taft was holding him in reserve. The only active candidacies that can be ascertained definitely for this vacancy were those of Van Devanter and of his senior colleague on the Eighth Circuit, Walter H. Sanborn,[90] a perennial, now past the peak of whatever chances were ever his. The Van Devanter candidacy, which was also not being advanced for the very first time, was quite an active one. But it made no great headway.[91] The President's mind was set, and Hughes' name went to the Senate on April 25, 1910.

The tender of the Associate Justiceship came to Hughes in a longhand letter from Taft, dated April 22, 1910. He knew very well, Taft wrote, that there were considerations which might cause Hughes to reject the offer: "I believe as strongly as possible that you are likely to be nominated and elected President some time in the future unless you go upon the Bench or make such associations at the Bar as to prevent." Moreover, in practice, Hughes could in a very short time earn enough to make his family secure for life. But perhaps Hughes preferred a judicial to a political life, and in that event he "might as well take the step now." There was no need for him to resign his governorship until October, when the Court's new term began, and he would thus be de-

---

[88] F. E. Warren to W. Van Devanter, Apr. 2, 1910, Van Devanter Papers.

[89] W. H. Taft to S. Philbrick, Nov. 25, 1927, Taft Papers.

[90] Walter Henry Sanborn (1845–1928) was born in New Hampshire and held an A.B. and an A.M. from Dartmouth. After three years of teaching school, Sanborn moved to St. Paul, Minnesota, where he entered the law office of an uncle. In March 1892, following some twenty years of practice, he was appointed U.S. circuit judge by President Benjamin Harrison. Sanborn served until his death.

[91] See C. D. Clark to W. Van Devanter, Apr. 30, 1910, Van Devanter Papers.

faulting on no more than two and one-half months of the term for which he was elected. The salary of a Justice, then $12,500, would soon be raised, Taft hoped, to $17,500.[92] Finally:

> The Chief Justiceship is soon likely to be vacant and I should never regard the practice of never promoting Associate Justices as one to be followed. Though, of course, this suggestion is only that by accepting the present position you do not bar yourself from the other, should it fall vacant in my term.
>
> Let me hear from you. I make this offer first because I know you will strengthen the Bench as a lawyer and a jurist with a great power of application and second because you will strengthen the Bench in the confidence of the people.

And then a postscript:

> Don't misunderstand me as to the Chief Justiceship. I mean that if that office were now open, I should offer it to you and it is probable that if it were to become vacant during my term, I should promote you to it; but, of course, conditions change, so that it would not be right for me to say by way of promise what I would do in the future. Nor, on the other hand, would I have you think that your declination now would prevent my offering you the higher place, should conditions remain as they are.[93]

Hughes accepted promptly, within two days. His reply was typewritten, but it had been copied from a draft in Hughes' hand which bears the mark of ease in composition, flowing along from beginning to end with only a very occasional correction. It is lengthy, solemn, and not without a tinge of self-righteousness.

> My dear Mr. President,
>
> A careful consideration of the questions raised by your offer to nominate me for the Supreme Court, to succeed Mr. Justice Brewer, has convinced me that I should accept it. The honor of the appointment, great as it would be in any case, is especially enhanced in my estimation because it comes from you,—in view of your distinguished judicial career and intimate knowledge of the requirements of the office. So far as my personal inclinations are concerned, they lie in the direction of judicial work. My training and professional interests have been such that I should undertake this work with a personal satisfac-

---

[92] Taft so proposed to Congress in December. 46 *Cong. Rec.*, 25, 61st Cong., 3d Sess. (1910). It was actually raised only to $14,500. See *infra*, p. 83, n.324.

[93] See Pringle, *Taft*, 532; Pusey, *Hughes*, 271–72.

tion which no other line of effort could command in the same degree. No one could have a more profound sense of the vast responsibilities of the Supreme Court than I have and while this makes me realize the more keenly my shortcomings, it also disposes me to welcome the opportunity to devote my life to such important service. Against such a life-work, to meet the conditions of which an adjustment could be made, I should not for a moment set any prospect of money-making at the bar.

I trust that I should be able, however, to withstand any personal inclination, and not permit it to control my decision, if it were opposed to the obligations of public duty. This is the only question which has occasioned any difficulty. But reflection has re-assured me upon this point. There is no definite sphere of public usefulness, other than the place you offer, which would be open to me at the close of this year and my circumstances would permit me to accept. The opportunities of the future are conjectural. The alternative of your proposal is private practice. Undoubtedly this would permit public service in many ways, but there would also be the exacting demands of active work at the bar. Against this division of effort, and its doubtful fruition, I should have on the bench a definite field of usefulness in the discharge of a function of national government of the gravest consequences to our people and to the future of our institutions.

The question seems to me to be really,—What right have I to refuse this opportunity of public service, which is now presented by you, and upon what grounds could I justify myself in turning aside from such a plain path of usefulness?

I confess that I know of none unless it be found in my present obligations as Governor of this State. But you point out that I need not qualify as Justice of the Supreme Court or resign as Governor until the second week of October. Until that time I can perform my full duty here. This would leave only a few weeks of my time and most of these could follow the election of another Governor to whom inevitably must then be confided the policy of the administration after January 1, next. My retirement in October to accept a call to national service of such importance could not justly be regarded as a violation of any superior obligations here. On the contrary, I should regard a refusal to take up, at your request, the life-work solely because I should have to leave my office here in October instead of remaining until the close of December, as based on a ground too trivial to be just to you or worthy of myself.

After a review, therefore, of the entire situation in its personal and public aspects, I accept your offer. In announcing this, I should be glad to have you state, in order to avoid any misunderstanding, on the part of the public, that I shall be able to serve as Governor until the second week in October.

Your expressions regarding the Chief Justiceship are understood and most warmly appreciated. You properly reserve entire freedom with respect to this and I accept the offer you now make without wishing you to feel committed in the slightest degree. Should the vacancy occur during your term, I, in common with all our citizens, would desire you to act freely and without embarrassment in accordance with your best judgment at that time.

Assuring you of my esteem and warm personal regard, and expressing again my deep sense of the confidence you repose and the responsibility it involves, I am

Very sincerely yours,

Charles E. Hughes[94]

Writing to a friend a few weeks later, Hughes indicated that he had no real taste for private practice, and that the Presidency was a bird in a distant bush. "A refusal on the ground that sometime or other I might be a candidate for the Presidency, particularly in view of the record of the disappointed ambitions of so many historic worthies, would have been absurd."[95]

The Hughes nomination had a glowing reception, although not unanimous. William Jennings Bryan dissented. It would be, he knew, a popular appointment with many good people who thought of Hughes as a reformer. But the reforming reputation rested, in Bryan's judgment, "upon a few official acts which showed him opposed to grafting and to the individual vices." Actually, Hughes was a personal friend of Rockefeller, and indebted to the bankers and to other interests, which he was all too willing to serve. In sum:

Governor Hughes exemplifies the individual virtues, and naturally demands honesty in the public service; but he is a shining illustration of that peculiar type of citizen developed in this country during the present generation—the citizen who personally opposes vice, and is a punisher of small crimes, but shows no indignation at the larger forms of legalized robbery.[96]

Other Democrats, Insurgents, and Progressives, however, were pleased with the nomination.[97] The *Chicago Tribune*, which gave evidence that it had been taught its standards for judicial appointments by Theodore Roosevelt, hailed Hughes as being "in sympathy with the broad general tendencies of the American people."[98] Judge Charles F. Amidon, an admirer of Theodore Roosevelt, wrote Taft that Hughes'

---

[94] C. E. Hughes to W. H. Taft, Apr. 24, 1910, Hughes Papers. See Pusey, *Hughes*, 272–73.

[95] C. E. Hughes to E. J. Ridgway, May 14, 1910, Hughes Papers.

[96] See *Washington Post*, Apr. 26, 1910, p. 2, col. 4.

[97] See, e.g., *ibid.*, p. 1, col. 2.

[98] *Chicago Tribune*, Apr. 26, 1910, p. 6, col. 1.

public experience will have "emancipated" him "from the purely analytical methods of the lawyer," as Marshall, Field, Bradley, and Miller had been emancipated. Amidon hoped that Hughes might eventually succeed to the Chief Justiceship. "I know of no one else in the country so well fitted to guide the Court and unify its decisions."[99] And there was no dissent from the conservatives. William D. Guthrie, who wanted no part of emancipated judges, was also gratified. He offered Hughes "the thanks of your brethren at the New York bar that you have accepted the appointment. . . . We are all confident that you will render the very greatest public service. . . ."[100] In short, as Myron T. Herrick wrote the President, "I congratulate you most heartily upon . . . being able to please everybody,—I mean by that everybody worth while."[101] The only note of regret running through the general expressions of satisfaction—a note of regret sounded, for example, both by James R. Garfield and Maxwell Evarts—was that Hughes could now presumably never be President.[102]

Hughes was confirmed, promptly and painlessly, on May 2, 1910.[103] But on July 4, well before Hughes was ready to resign his governorship, while he was turning from a special session of the legislature to hundreds of applications for pardon pending before him in Albany,[104] Chief Justice Fuller died. Meanwhile a second vacancy also became certain, as the tragedy of Moody was drawing to a close. Rumors were going around that Moody was mentally incapacitated. Actually, as Taft remembered subsequently, Moody was crippled with arthritis.[105] Letters written by Moody in the summer of 1910 give sufficient proof of his lucidity. He had been, however, as he wrote Justice Harlan, fourteen months on his back, and the best he could expect was "to get up a crippled man and perhaps with shattered health which would not enable me to do a full man's work. . . ."[106] On June 23, 1910, at the President's instance, Congress passed a statute enabling Moody to retire with the same benefits that would have been available to a Justice who had served ten years or attained seventy years of age, neither of which was true in his case.[107] On October 3, Moody informed the President, "with inexpressible regret," that he would avail himself of the statute. There were some private reasons, however, "not in any way adversely

[99] C. F. Amidon to W. H. Taft, Apr. 27, 1910, Taft Papers.

[100] W. D. Guthrie to C. E. Hughes, Apr. 26, 1916, Hughes Papers.

[101] M. T. Herrick to W. H. Taft, Apr. 28, 1916, Taft Papers.

[102] J. R. Garfield, Apr. 27, 1910, M. Evarts, Apr. 28, 1910, to C. E. Hughes, Hughes Papers.

[103] See Pusey, *Hughes,* 273.

[104] C. E. Hughes, *Biographical Notes,* 206, Hughes Papers.

[105] W. H. Taft to W. I. Smith, Dec. 1, 1921, Taft Papers.

[106] See J. M. Harlan to H. H. Lurton, July 8, 1910, Lurton Papers.

[107] 36 Stat. 1861 (1910).

affecting the public interest, why I should like to postpone the taking effect of my resignation for a few weeks. I therefore hereby resign my position as Associate Justice of the Supreme Court of the United States to take effect on the 20th of November next." Taft replied warmly the very next day: "[M]y heart goes out to you, my dear friend and old-time associate, in the pain that the relinquishment of such an office and such duties and such opportunity to help your fellow man gives you. . . . I would not appoint your successor until the meeting of the Senate on the first Monday in December. There is not the slightest reason, therefore, why your resignation should take effect until then."[108]

Quite plainly, and in the light of both earlier and later experience of the Court, quite wisely, Taft was resolved not to make recess appointments. And so, when Hughes took his seat on October 10, at the beginning of the Court's new term, it was a seven-member Court, and was to remain so for the rest of the calendar year 1910. The occasion was, as always, solemn and impressive. Hughes took the judicial oath in open court: ". . . I will administer justice without respect to persons, and do equal right to the poor and to the rich. . . ." Harlan, presiding as Senior Justice, extended a cordial welcome.[109] There were no opinions delivered or arguments heard that day, and adjournment followed in respect for Fuller's memory.

Although the Court by no means suspended business for the rest of the year, attention centered on the new appointments that were in the offing, and speculation, both in public and privately among the Justices, was rife. Thus Justice Joseph McKenna, writing to his colleague William R. Day on September 5, 1910, noted that the vacation was running out and work and responsibility were casting their shadows before. Then:

> I repeat your question, who will share them with us? Quien sabe? I have assumed Hughes for C.J. because speculation some time ago assigned it to him and there is no contrary prediction. But the other two? A newspaper the other day ventured a guess (it was said to have been discussed at a judicial luncheon at which the President, Holmes, and other judges were present) that [Solicitor General] Bowers would be one and that the other would go to the Eighth [Circuit]. But n'importe. They will be men of ability, no doubt, and the old duty will be on us "to stop and think." . . .[110]

---

[108] W. H. Moody to W. H. Taft, Oct. 3, 1910, Taft to Moody, Oct. 4, 1910, Taft Papers.

[109] See Pusey, *Hughes*, 274; see also J. M. Harlan to W. R. Day, Oct. 9, 1910, Day Papers, Library of Congress (hereinafter cited as Day Papers).

[110] J. McKenna to W. R. Day, Sept. 5, 1910, Day Papers.

And Lurton, from Hot Springs, Virginia, also to Day, on September 7, 1910:

> I suppose Hughes will sit in the middle, though I only know what the press reports. Moody's successor is not indicated. . . . Can't help but think that Roosevelt has not been loyal to Taft. . . .[111]

The newspapers were indeed full of Hughes.[112] And both Lurton and Day voiced their expectation to Hughes himself.[113] But in writing to Justice White, Lurton must have expressed a preference for White over Hughes. For on July 12, White, from Port Hope in Ontario, Canada, was replying to Lurton:

> My thoughts have been recurring to your kind expression as to the succession to the Chief. No aspiration on the subject has taken possession of me. On the contrary, the very gravest doubt exists in my mind as to whether I am the man for the place and whether the new responsibility, if it were tendered, would be beneficial either to the country or the Court. I say this with perfect candor and absolute directness. I know the necessity of unity and cohesion in the Court and believe we are going to be in a much better position in that respect than we have been. No one knows the needs of the situation better than does the President and I have no doubt that he will deal with the situation for the best and no consideration personal to myself can possibly cause me for a moment to think otherwise. My term of service before retirement is not now so long—and I shall be happy if it be given to me to reach it doing the work which I have been trying to do for the past sixteen years.[114]

White was in a remarkably optimistic mood that summer. By fall, as Hughes recalled, "he was plainly out of sorts," presumably owing to impatience, since, as Hughes thought, he felt himself entitled to the place. He was silent and offish.[115] But during the summer it was otherwise with White. Returning from the funeral services for Fuller in Chicago, White wrote Day:

> To me the services were simple and appropriate and I could not resist the thought how wise was the disposition which called the Chief! The brethren all looked to me so much better than when we parted in

---

[111] H. H. Lurton to W. R. Day, Sept. 7, 1910, Day Papers.

[112] See Pusey, *Hughes,* 279.

[113] See C. E. Hughes, *Biographical Notes,* 216–17, Hughes Papers.

[114] E. D. White to H. H. Lurton, July 12, 1910, Lurton Papers.

[115] C. E. Hughes, *Biographical Notes,* 216–17.

Washington that it was very consoling. Somehow I cannot but think that with the new appointments which are to be made we have good reason to look forward with more of hopeful equanimity to the work of the Court. . . . Have written a few lines to Harlan about our doings at Chicago as I presume he must have been annoyed at not being asked to go.[116]

On August 29, White wrote, again to Day:

I do not think I have been so well for nearly two years. . . . Yes, I share your anxiety . . . as to the two vacancies which are to be filled. If only you or Lurton could take the place of Chief what a blessing it would be for the country. I know nothing as to the intentions of the President. He sent for me to come to Beverly [Massachusetts, where Taft summered] which I was very reluctant to do but found no way to avoid. He did not in the slightest degree indicate his intention as to the vacancies! . . . Somehow I do not feel so anxious as to the future of the Court as I have been in the past. Maybe I am less nervous and thus will give you less trouble in trying to keep me straight than you have had in the past.[117]

Simply and unsentimentally, White was relieved at the death of the aged Chief, who had been failing. But all this well-being and "hopeful equanimity," this sanguine serenity from a notorious and congenital worrier! Was it the mood of a man who sensed the coming fulfillment of ambition? In any case, it was a mood conveyed with winning ingenuousness.

Other ambitions stirred the Court that summer—some more, some less muted, some pretty well abandoned, but not without rue. In Holmes, rue predominated. On September 24, he wrote to his intimate English friend, Sir Frederick Pollock:

The vacation has been interrupted and saddened by these recurring deaths and I am content to make a new start from Washington. The President said he meant to send for me and talk about the new appointments. I know of no one whom I so want to see on our Bench as much as I did the late Solicitor General [Bowers]. As to the Chief Justiceship I am rather at a loss. I should bet he will appoint Hughes who has given up a chance of being Republican nominee for the Presidency, but I know nothing. I think White who is next in Seniority to Harlan (too old, etc.) the ablest man likely to be thought of. I don't know whether his being a Catholic would interfere. I always have assumed absolutely that I should not be regarded as possible—they don't appoint

---

[116] E. D. White to W. R. Day, July 11, 1910, Day Papers.

[117] E. D. White to W. R. Day, Aug. 29, 1910, Day Papers.

side Judges as a rule, it would be embarrassing to skip my Seniors, and I am too old. [But these were considerations militating in considerable degree also against White.] I think I should be a better administrator than White, but he would be more politic. Also the President's inclination so far as I can judge seems to me toward a type for which I have but a limited admiration. I am afraid White has about as little chance as I. I really don't care much who is appointed, if only he is a man who can dispose of the little daily questions with promptitude and decision. Apart from that and the honor of being figurehead, the C.J. like the rest of us must depend on his intellectual power. I know of no first rate man except White.[118]

Justice John Marshall Harlan, apparently, was not satisfied to think of himself, between parentheses, as "too old, etc." It was clear to Hughes "that Justice Harlan desired the appointment as the crown of his judicial service; he thought that he could be appointed with the idea that it would not be long before the post could be given to a younger man."[119] It would not be a costly affair, in other words, to bestow this final honor on him. Attorney General Wickersham recalled later that word of Harlan's ambition, and of the suggestion that it could be inexpensively gratified, reached the White House. Harlan, Wickersham said, using a figure of speech virtually identical to the one embedded in Hughes' memory, wanted "the elevation as the final ornament of his judicial career."[120] And Harlan's good friend, the Court's Reporter of Decisions, Charles Henry Butler, remembered Harlan's deep disappointment when White was finally given the place.[121] Harlan himself, however, wrote to Lurton that he was in the dark about the appointment and knew only what appeared in the newspapers: "The mention of my name in connection with the place has been without my knowledge or procurement. I do not suppose that I will be thought of."[122] Whatever hopes he may or may not have harbored for himself, it is evident that Harlan did not favor the appointment of White, nor even that of Hughes, though he was satisfied of the latter's "eminent fitness for the bench."[123] On July 11, 1910, Harlan wrote to the President:

Although the question as to the vacancy caused by the death of the late Chief Justice is one of great importance to every citizen of the United States, especially to the present members of the Supreme Court,

---

[118] *Holmes-Pollock Letters,* I, 170.
[119] C. E. Hughes, *Biographical Notes,* 216–17, Hughes Papers.
[120] See Pringle, *Taft,* 534–35.
[121] See C. Butler, *A Century at the Bar of the Supreme Court of the United States* (1942), 173–75. See also

J. B. Foraker, *Notes from a Busy Life* (1916), 405.
[122] J. M. Harlan to H. H. Lurton, Sept. 12, 1910, Lurton Papers.
[123] J. M. Harlan to H. H. Lurton, July 3, 1910, Lurton Papers.

I would not volunteer any expression of opinion as to a successor, if a former vacancy had not been heretofore the subject of some conversation between us. [Taft had consulted Harlan about the appointment of Lurton, which Harlan favored, and for which, at the President's request, he had lobbied among some Senators.] I beg to make a few suggestions touching this matter.

Up to this time, there has been, I believe, only one instance of the Chief Justiceship being offered to an Associate Justice of the Court. That occurred in the case of Mr. Justice Cushing who, it was supposed, declined on the ground of infirm health. The usage referred to has, I think, no sound reason in its support. Indeed I have always thought that an Associate Justice ought, as a general rule, succeed a Chief Justice, who had died or resigned, unless, in the judgment of the President, he was disqualified for the position by advanced years, or by ill health; *provided, always,* he was, in character, soundness of judgment, sagacity and legal attainments *equal* to the place.

I beg to say that there is on the Supreme Court an Associate Justice who is equal to the Chief Justiceship, and whose appointment would, I am confident, meet with general approval by the Bench and the Bar, as well as by the people at large. He was born in 1849 and is by no means too old for the place, especially when that fact is considered in connection with his experience in active, judicial life. His appearance at first might impress one with the idea that he was not very strong, physically. But President McKinley once told me that Justice Day was "as hard as a knot" and would likely reach an advanced age. You will know whether he was often absent from his post as a Circuit Judge on account of sickness. Since coming to the Supreme Bench he has not, that I can recall, missed but a few days, if any, on account of sickness. I have found him to be as represented by President McKinley. He has exhibited, on our Bench, an unusual capacity and fondness for judicial work. He has been indefatigable in his judicial labors. Indeed, since he has been with us no member of the Court has held to his work more persistently or steadily nor done a greater amount of work than Justice Day. His opinions in my judgment will always be highly regarded. They show unusual care in preparation. They are not overrun with *dicta* nor with immaterial suggestions. I regard him as a first class lawyer—sagacious, cautious, as firm as a rock, and eminently wise in consultation. And what has become a necessary qualification in a Chief Justice (however great his legal attainments or mental power may be), he has fine executive power and is a "man of affairs." His experience as a judge would enable him to take up the work of the Court where the late Chief Justice left it, and go right ahead without any delay or any friction whatever. He would not be under the necessity of becoming trained in details, upon the "handling" of which with ease and promptness so much depends. He is already fully informed as to the manner in which the business of the Court is transacted. My conviction is strong that, all things considered, the best interests of the country, and the efficient administration of the law, will be promoted by his selection as Chief Justice.

I have the honor to be,

Your Obedient Servant,

John M. Harlan[124]

The President acknowledged this remarkable communication, evidently in longhand, for there is a notation to that effect on Harlan's letter as preserved in Taft's files. There is no evidence, however, that Day was seriously considered, or that he did anything to further his candidacy. But Harlan's recommendation remained a treasured memory in the Day family,[125] and Day either knew it was being made, or learned of it very shortly afterward.[126] And so of the seven sitting Justices who convened in Washington in October 1910, only two—Lurton and McKenna—or possibly three, if one wishes to include Holmes, neither thought of themselves nor were thought of by others as being in contention for the open Chief Justiceship.[127]

The President, who devoted more loving care to the choice of judges than perhaps any of his predecessors or successors, had the matter much in mind. He rejected the notion of crowning Harlan's career, evidently with some heat. "I'll do no such damned thing," his Attorney General later reported him as having exclaimed at a conference of the lawyers in his Cabinet. "I won't make the position of Chief Justice a blue ribbon for the final years of any member of the Court. I want someone who will coordinate the activities of the Court and who has a reasonable expectation of serving ten or twenty years on the bench."[128] He considered Elihu Root, and declared that he would appoint him if he were five years younger, although Root was the same age as the eventual appointee, White.[129] He considered also, but perhaps less seriously, his Secretary of State, Philander C. Knox, who had been

---

[124] J. M. Harlan to W. H. Taft, July 11, 1910, Taft Papers.

[125] Interview with Luther Day, Apr. 26, 1960.

[126] On Jan. 9, 1911, almost exactly a month after White's nomination, Day's son Stephen was writing him: "I received a copy of Justice Harlan's letter and shall cherish and preserve it always." In what may be construed as a mood of resentment that his father was passed over, Stephen Day added: "Some things are beyond human comprehension and the action of our present executive must be thus char-

acterized. He will be the nominee in 1912 and will be defeated simply because he does not excite any enthusiasm, cannot get things warmed up." S. A. Day to W. R. Day, Day Papers, Library of Congress.

[127] Holmes remembered telling McKenna that the two of them were the only ones "who didn't have booms going for us." *Holmes-Laski Letters*, M. DeW. Howe, ed. (1953), I, 846; see also *ibid.*, I, 339, II, 1227.

[128] See Pringle, *Taft*, 534–35.

[129] *Ibid.*

Attorney General under Roosevelt, and to whom Taft the following year tendered the place that ultimately went to Pitney.[130]

Edward Douglass White,[131] Taft's eventual choice, was born on November 3, 1845, in the village of Thibodeaux, Lafourche Parish, Louisiana, the youngest of four children. His father, who died two years after the birth of Edward Douglass, was a lawyer and sugar planter, and had been governor of the state and, for several terms, a member of the United States House of Representatives. His mother was Catherine Sidney Lee Ringgold, of an old Maryland and Virginia family. White was educated in Jesuit schools in Louisiana and at Georgetown College, Maryland, now District of Columbia. The Civil War ended his formal education, as White returned home and despite his youth joined a company of Louisiana volunteers. He saw active service, then read law under a senior member of the bar. He was admitted in 1868, practiced law in New Orleans, and served two terms in the state Senate and a year as an Associate Justice of the state Supreme Court.

On March 4, 1891, White took office as a United States Senator, and early in 1894 he was President Cleveland's fourth choice for a vacancy created by the death of Justice Samuel Blatchford. Cleveland's own mismanagement resulted in the narrow defeat in the Senate of his first nominee, William D. Hornblower of New York. Cleveland then tried again with another New Yorker, Wheeler H. Peckham, brother of the Rufus who was himself appointed two years later. This nomination also failed in the Senate, and an offer by Cleveland to Frederic Coudert of New York was refused. Finally Cleveland sent in the name of Senator White, and the Senate confirmed without question on the same day.[132] In sixteen years as an Associate Justice, White made his mark most distinctly. He dissented ably in *Pollock v. Farmers' Loan & Trust Co.*,[133] and in the *Trans-Missouri Freight* and *Northern Securities* antitrust cases,[134] and won recognition also for his important concurrence in the *Insular Cases*,[135] and for his "pioneer work," as Taft later called it, in administrative law.[136] This was Holmes' opinion of him in 1910:

[130] W. H. Taft to P. C. Knox, Nov. 29, 1911, P. C. Knox Papers, Library of Congress.

[131] Douglass is the spelling in his will, on the oaths he signed as Associate and Chief Justice, and the spelling followed by every volume of the U.S. Reports. His biographer prefers, and offers some evidence that White himself might have preferred, the simpler spelling, but the evidence the other way is overwhelming. See M. C. Klinkhamer, *Edward Douglas White,*

Chief Justice of the United States (1943), I, n.I.

[132] See A. Nevins, *Grover Cleveland* (1932), 569–72.

[133] 157 U.S. 429 (1895).

[134] 166 U.S. 290 (1897); 193 U.S. 197 (1904).

[135] Downes v. Bidwell, 182 U.S. 244 (1901).

[136] 257 U.S. xxvi (1922); see Texas & Pacific Ry. Co. v. Abilene Cotton Oil Co., 204 U.S. 426 (1907).

His writing leaves much to be desired, but his thinking is profound, especially in the legislative direction which we don't recognize as a judicial requirement but which is so, especially in our Court, nevertheless.[137]

White was a large, ponderous man, "with a small face in the center of a great head."[138] He had, certainly in his later years, extremely heavy jowls. As he sat on the Bench, one observer reported in 1911, he shaded his eyes with his hand to keep out the light, "and his bulky presence broods over the whole courtroom." At home he looked like a "jovial monk." "Put a brown cowl on him and you could well fancy him at the porter's wicket of a monastery, offering hospitality with the most genial grace. His welcome is a benediction."[139] Felix Frankfurter recalled many years later visiting White at home on business, and feeling enveloped by the presence of the Chief Justice, as though in a confessional.[140] It was a kindly but elaborate presence. Mrs. Joseph R. Lamar remembered him as "quite early Victorian in his courtesies."[141] Brandeis placed him in an even earlier period. He "had the grand manner," Brandeis said, "and was of the eighteenth century."[142] White was long a bachelor. He married Mrs. Virginia Leita Montgomery Kent, a widow, in 1894, shortly after coming to the Court.[143]

When White's nomination as Chief Justice went to the Senate on December 12, 1910, it was accompanied by two other names. Willis Van Devanter of Wyoming and Joseph Rucker Lamar of Georgia were nominated as Associate Justices. Van Devanter succeeded White, and filled the Western place that had been vacant since the death of Brewer. Lamar succeeded Moody and made the fourth Southerner on the Bench, if one counts also the Kentuckian Harlan. Massachusetts and New England, which lost Moody, remained represented, of course, by Holmes. The search that produced Van Devanter and Lamar was conducted while the President deliberated on the Chief Justiceship, and what little is known of the considerations that moved him with regard

---

[137] See *Holmes-Pollock Letters,* I, 170.

[138] D. Acheson, "Justice Is a Method," *Record of N.Y.C.B.A.,* 12: 143, 145, 1957.

[139] See I. Marcosson, "The New Supreme Court," *Munsey's Magazine* 44:No. 6, March 1911.

[140] H. Phillips, ed., *Felix Frank-* *furter Reminisces* (1960), 94–104.

[141] C. P. Lamar, *The Life of Joseph Rucker Lamar* (1926), 179–80.

[142] Brandeis-Frankfurter Conversations, Brandeis Papers, Harvard Law School Library.

[143] See M. C. Klinkhamer, *Edward Douglas White, Chief Justice of the United States* (1943), 40.

to that appointment can be understood only in the full context of the three nominations that went up together.

Among those to whom Taft gave consideration for appointment as Associate Justice were William C. Hook of Kansas, judge of the Court of Appeals for the Eighth Circuit;[144] William D. McHugh of Nebraska, a practicing lawyer in Omaha; Frederick W. Lehmann of Missouri, whom Taft, on December 19, made Solicitor General in succession to Bowers; Charles Nagel of Missouri, Taft's Secretary of Commerce and Labor, and widowed brother-in-law of Louis D. Brandeis; Senator George Sutherland of Utah; Chief Justice John B. Winslow of Wisconsin; Judge John C. Pollock of the U.S. district court in Kansas; and Francis E. Baker of Indiana, judge of the U.S. Circuit Court of Appeals for the Seventh Circuit.[145] There was even a small movement, but no evidence that it ever got very far, for Dean John H. Wigmore, of Northwestern University Law School, one of the great names in American legal scholarship of this century.

The President's mind did not come to rest till shortly before his nominations actually went up. Judge Hook, as will appear, was in serious contention to the end. And as late as November 28, 1910, the President received a favorable reply from Justice White to an inquiry he had made about McHugh. McHugh was a conservative Democrat, whom Cleveland had tried to put on the U.S. district court, but for whom he had been unable to obtain Senate confirmation. White reported himself and several of his brethren, including Lurton, as having "a very distinct and strong impression as to his ability. . . ."[146] Considered geographically, virtually all of these candidates were in competition with Van Devanter, and none with Lamar. The President would seem to have had it in mind ever since he named Hughes to the Eighth Circuit vacancy created by Brewer's death that a Western appointment was called for in any event. Fuller had been appointed from Illinois, and so the second vacancy in an Associate Justiceship, however the President was going to create it, by the elevation of either White or Hughes, also pointed westward. Yet in the end one appointment went to the South.

Very little is discoverable about the origins of the Lamar nomination. Joseph Rucker Lamar, cousin some few times removed of Lucius

---

[144] William Cather Hook (1857–1921) was born in Waynesburg, Pennsylvania. After receiving an LL.B. from St. Louis Law School in 1878, he practiced law in Kansas until 1899, when he was appointed U.S. district judge there. He was promoted to the Court of Appeals in 1903, and served until his death. See *A.B.A.J.*, 7:552, 1921.

[145] See *Washington Post*, Nov. 29, 1910, p. 2, col. 5.

[146] E. D. White to W. H. Taft, Nov. 28, 1910, Taft Papers.

I: *Mr. Taft Rehabilitates the Court*

Quintus Cincinnatus Lamar of Mississippi, who preceded him on the Supreme Court, was of the Southern gentry. He was born in Ruckersville, Elbert County, Georgia, on October 14, 1857. His father, trained for the bar, had become a minister of the Church of the Disciples of Christ. His mother, a Rucker of Ruckersville, was the daughter of a planter. During Lamar's boyhood, his father was pastor of the First Christian Church in Augusta, where young Joseph attended a school for some years with Thomas Woodrow Wilson, son of a Presbyterian minister. The Wilsons left Augusta in 1870, and the two schoolboys were not to resume relations until they met again in Washington in 1913. Lamar attended the University of Georgia for two years, and then Bethany College in West Virginia, which was the college of the Church of the Disciples. From Bethany he took a degree in 1877, and a wife, in the person of Clarinda Pendleton, the president's daughter. Lamar briefly read law at Washington and Lee University, and then in an office in Augusta, where he was admitted to the bar in 1878. Soon he was engaged in a successful practice in Augusta, chiefly corporate in character, with substantial concentration on railroads. He served two brief terms in the legislature, and between 1893 and 1895 played a leading role in compiling the Civil Code of the state. In January 1903, Lamar was appointed an Associate Justice of the Supreme Court of Georgia, and in 1904, he was elected to a term lasting through January 1907. In March 1905, however, Lamar resigned and returned to law practice in Augusta. The confining nature of the work, his widow recalled later, had begun to tell on his health, and he was homesick for Augusta. He might also have felt a financial strain.[147]

The record Lamar made on the Supreme Court of Georgia is not very revealing.[148] There was not much scope in the cases. And yet there were some opinions at this stage of Lamar's career—as there were not to be in his few years as a Justice—that are barely identifiable as mildly progressive in tone and direction. He invoked the doctrine of *res ipsa loquitur* in favor of an injured employee of a brick company, reversing a directed verdict for the company;[149] he took a dim view of stock dealings by corporate directors seeking to turn their inside knowledge to profit;[150] he held a labor union not liable in damages for urging a boycott against a merchant who resisted its demands;[151] he recoiled from the

---

[147] See Lamar, *Lamar,* 133–34.

[148] Lamar's opinions will be found in Volumes 117–22 (1903–1905) of the *Reports of the Supreme Court of Georgia.*

[149] Chenall v. Palmer Brick Co., 117 Ga. 106 (1903).

[150] Oliver v. Oliver, 118 Ga. 362 (1903).

[151] Watters & Son v. Retail Clerks Union #479, 120 Ga. 424 (1904).

horror of holding children under fourteen guilty of contributory negligence in a factory accident, or foreclosed from recovering because of the fellow-servant rule;[152] and affirming the conviction of a white man on the testimony of a black man, he held: "It was not error to charge that the law is no respecter of persons, and that whether one of the parties interested is white and the other colored should have no weight with the jury. The caution was not improper. It had no tendency to prejudice their minds against the defendant. . . ."[153] His opinions were generally concise, sometimes quite brief, but the style sacrifices nothing of ease, or even of languor. The opinions have a measure of grace, if no flash.

Lamar was a convivial man, with a well-developed gift for friendship. He was tall and handsome and carried himself with the dignity of a civic leader. One decorous lock of his silver-gray hair had a tendency to fall over his broad forehead. The *New York Times*, in 1914, thought that he looked at once the scholar and the judge.[154] In 1910, his reputation was entirely local. He seems to have come to some slight national notice only once, when a speech he delivered in Athens, Georgia, on Memorial Day, 1902, was heard by Albert Shaw, editor of the *Review of Reviews*, and then published with an introduction by Shaw in New York in 1902 as a pamphlet under the title *The Private Soldier of the Confederacy*. Lamar addressed himself in this speech to the question of Race, as he called it. That question, he said, had merely been modified, not solved, by the Civil War, and what it had lost in intensity it had gained in complexity. In the short period since the Emancipation Proclamation, "how impossible to expect the hereditary tendencies and influences of centuries to be reversed. . . ." Then Lamar touched, as Shaw thought, "the very root of remedial policy," by recommending an agrarian paternalism. Southern whites had a responsibility to train the black man in more effective and efficient agriculture, thus making him ready for the benefits of literacy and the ultimate duties of citizenship.

President-elect Taft had spent the late fall and early winter of 1908 in Augusta. He stayed with friends who were friends also of the Lamars, as was his aide, Captain Butt, a native Augustan. The President-elect met and liked the Lamars. In the fall of 1909, it became known that the President was planning to return to Augusta, and Mrs. Lamar wrote Captain Butt inviting the President to stay with the Lamars. Butt replied that the President intended to call, but that he was staying with his friend

---

[152] Canton Cotton Mills v. Edwards, 120 Ga. 447 (1904); Evans v. Josephine Mills, 119 Ga. 448 (1904).

[153] Summerford v. The State, 121 Ga. 390, 391 (1904).
[154] *New York Times*, May 24, 1914, p. 2, col. 1.

Major Joseph V. Cumming, a close friend also of the Lamars, who had been a senior associate of Lamar's in law practice. The President came in November, and the Lamars dined with him at Major Cumming's and also received a morning call from him. Rumors that Lamar was headed for the Supreme Court were by then current locally. In July 1910, Taft offered Lamar appointment to a commission that was to go to Mexico to attend the centenary of Mexican independence. Lamar was unable to go, but replied with much praise for the President's achievements.[155]

Many years later, when Chief Justice, Taft recalled: "I only succeeded in securing a man such as I wanted in the South by going down South and staying there for several vacations. This enabled me to know him. I mean Lamar."[156] But it is doubtful that Taft decided till quite late in 1910 that he did indeed want a man from the South. In the fall of 1910, he seemed to be considering Lamar for a post on the new Commerce Court, which he was staffing at the same time. Or so he wrote, in reply to a letter from retired Justice Henry Billings Brown recommending Lamar. Taft had reached no definite conclusion: "I shall keep his name, however, among the eligible."[157] By early December, Taft, while consulting Congressman William M. Howard of Georgia about Lamar's suitability for the Commerce Court, asked also whether Lamar measured up to the Supreme Court. The Georgia Congressional delegation, led by Senator A. O. Bacon, was assiduously recommending Lamar, although it may have taken them a while to raise their sights from the Commerce Court to the Supreme Court.

Lamar himself was kept informed, and was interested, but discreetly aloof. By December 6—but not before then—Major Cumming in Augusta received a confidential wire: "The President requests that you will telegraph him your opinion of Lamar's qualification as lawyer for Supreme Court Justice. He knows his character and other qualifications. Please emphasize the lawyer in the man. There is favorable chance." Cumming was asked to wire care of Senator Bacon. His reply was measured, and hence, no doubt, the more effective:

> If I were called on to construct a model for a judge, I would take Lamar as he is, only chipping off somewhat of his too painstaking search for finality of truth, which sometimes keeps him reaching out beyond the sea mark where other excellent judges would be willing

---

[155] See Lamar, *Lamar*, 161–68; A. Butt to C. P. Lamar, September 1910; J. R. Lamar to W. H. Taft, July 29, 1910, Lamar Papers, University of Georgia Library (hereinafter cited as Lamar Papers).

[156] W. H. Taft to W. G. Harding, Nov. 2, 1922, Taft Papers.

[157] W. H. Taft to H. B. Brown, Oct. 12, 1910, Taft Papers.

to drop anchor. This characteristic, however, increases the burden but lessens not the excellence of his work.[158]

Even at this late date the President was far from having made up his mind about the names he was to send to the Senate less than a week hence. Conceivably Lamar had been decided upon. But there is good indication that the Chief Justiceship was still in doubt, and that no definite settlement had yet been reached on the place that finally went to Willis Van Devanter.[159]

Van Devanter, destined to sit on the Supreme Court for nearly twenty-seven years, was one of the most enduring achievements of the Taft Administration, and very possibly its greatest. He "was of the stuff of which pioneers are made."[160] Born in Marion, Indiana, on April 17, 1859, Van Devanter attended what is now DePauw University, and in 1881 received an LL.B. from the Cincinnati Law School, of which Taft was also an alumnus. He then joined his father's law practice in Marion for three years. But in July 1884, shortly after having married Dollie Burhans of Ionia, Michigan, he moved to Cheyenne, Wyoming Territory, where his brother-in-law and later partner, John W. Lacey, had been appointed territorial Chief Justice.

Cheyenne, during Van Devanter's first year there, was in his own words "a lively, busy and substantial city with a population something in excess of 8,000. This spring's assessment shows a property valuation in the city of 7 millions."[161] By the spring of 1888, Van Devanter could report to a friend on his rapid rise, on his widening professional experience, and on the flavor of the community that was shaping him:

> In our office we have all the business we can attend to and it yields us a fair return for the labor expended.
>   The experience acquired in some of the positions I have held here has been of benefit to me. I have been the City Attorney of Cheyenne at a salary of $750, and was a member of the Commission which prepared the revised statutes of the Territory (compensation $1,000) and I was a member of the last legislative assembly, which but recently adjourned. . . . As a rule, lawyers work much harder here, and get

---

[158] See C. D. Norton to W. C. Adamson, Dec. 7, 1910; A. V. Lawton to J. V. Cumming, Dec. 6, 1910; Cumming to W. H. Taft, Dec. 7, 1910, Lamar Papers.

[159] On Dec. 8, 1910, one newspaper guessed Hughes, Hook, and Lamar.

Washington Post, Dec. 8, 1910, p. 4, col. 5.

[160] 316 U.S. xxix (1942) (Attorney General Biddle).

[161] W. Van Devanter to L. A. Von Behren, May 2, 1885, Van Devanter Papers.

better fees accordingly. There are no really old practitioners in Wyoming, but what is lacking in experience is more than made up by constant study and application. . . .

Our lawyers usually have good libraries. I have all the Reports of Ohio, New York, Michigan and Wisconsin, and the American and English railroad cases, and also a large and well selected list of text books. My partner has about the same number . . . making in all a fair library.

Having no established decisions by our own Supreme Court, and having but few local precedents and established rules of decision, it is very common in important cases to cite authorities from the entire range of American Reports. . . .

Money is often so invested here as to give quick and good returns, but the risk taken generally corresponds with the profits received.

The current rates of interest are from 1 to 1¼ per cent per month. At points distant from the railroad, the rates are higher.

People are generally active and one must keep moving to keep up with the procession. . . .

Litigation at Cheyenne often involves very large amounts, which makes the fees here good. . . .[162]

On August 31, 1889, the youthful Van Devanter was appointed Justice of the territorial Supreme Court by President Harrison. When Wyoming became a state in 1890, Van Devanter was elected the state's first Chief Justice. But he promptly resigned, in October 1890, to resume private practice, which prospered and was varied, including some substantial railroad clients. He resumed also an active, if managerial rather than elective, political career. His politics were Republican, as were those of his father and of his father's family, evolving out of a more distant Whig past.

The Chief Justiceship of Wyoming had evidently not been satisfying. But judicial office became henceforth a fixed ambition. Thus within a few months after his resignation as Chief Justice, Van Devanter unsuccessfully tried for appointment to the newly-created federal Circuit Court of Appeals, and in the alternative, to virtually any other available federal court.[163] He never sought a nonprofessional office, and never failed to consider the bearing of any office on his chances for a judicial

---

[162] W. Van Devanter to A. A. Frazier, Apr. 9, 1888, Van Devanter Papers.

[163] See W. Van Devanter to F. E.

Warren, Feb. 28, 1891; Warren to Van Devanter, Mar. 1, 1891, Van Devanter Papers.

career. Van Devanter's man in Washington was Francis E. Warren,[164] Civil War veteran, rancher, Senator from Wyoming, a shrewd, energetic, and durable Republican regular. Senator Warren's man in Wyoming, his confidant, counsel, and political manager, was Van Devanter.

"It is time," Van Devanter noted in the spring of 1892, at the end of one of his long periodic reports to the Senator on Wyoming affairs, "to quietly consider the selection of a chairman of the State Republican Central Committee. . . ."[165] The sentence characterizes Van Devanter's role in politics and his relation to Senator Warren. The man quietly selected was Van Devanter, and he headed the state Republican Committee for the next four years, managing three campaigns. In addition, he acted as informal counsel and one-man drafting service to the state legislature, at least so long as it was under Republican control. In 1896, Van Devanter was Warren's chief lieutenant in securing the Wyoming delegation for William McKinley at the nominating convention of that year. As early as April 1896, Warren was informing Mark Hanna of Van Devanter's services: "Judge Willis Van Devanter represents the state's wishes and you can depend upon, and tie to him." Judge Van Devanter, Warren added, would make the best Solicitor General or even Attorney General the new administration could have.[166]

McKinley having been nominated, Van Devanter became Republican National Committeeman from Wyoming, and after McKinley was elected (with no help from Wyoming, however, which went narrowly for William Jennings Bryan), Van Devanter and Warren began campaigning hard for the Solicitor Generalship. But the Solicitor Generalship had been promised elsewhere, and Van Devanter at last, following an interview in Washington with Attorney General McKenna, reluctantly accepted appointment as Assistant Attorney General assigned to the Department of the Interior.[167] He would have much preferred to be an

---

[164] Francis Emroy Warren (1844–1929) fought with the 49th Volunteers of his native Massachusetts. He moved to Wyoming in 1868, and was governor of the territory by appointment of President Arthur in 1885–86, and, again, by appointment of President Benjamin Harrison in 1889. In 1890, he was elected first governor of the state, then went to the Senate the same year for a term that ended in 1893. He was again elected Senator in 1894 and served until his death.

[165] W. Van Devanter to F. E. War-ren, Apr. 9, 1892, Van Devanter Papers.

[166] F. E. Warren to M. A. Hanna, Apr. 24, 1896; see Hanna to W. Van Devanter, Apr. 29, 1896, Van Devanter Papers. And see L. Gould, *Wyoming* (1968).

[167] W. Van Devanter to F. E. Warren, Jan. 18, 1897; Warren to W. McKinley, Jan. 21, 1897; Van Devanter to Warren, Jan. 24, 25, 1897; Warren to Van Devanter, Mar. 12, 1897; Van Devanter to Warren, Apr. 5, 1897, Van Devanter Papers.

I: *Mr. Taft Rehabilitates the Court*

Assistant Attorney General in the Department of Justice itself—"head-quarters," as he called it—where he thought he would have not only intrinsically more challenging work, but also greater opportunity to come to the notice of the Attorney General and of other professional dignitaries, such as Supreme Court Justices. He said so to Warren, who replied, somewhat unkindly, that it was a bit early to be thinking of the Supreme Court, and struck a nerve. Van Devanter rejoined:

> I haven't had the slightest idea that I would get on the Supreme bench if I were even favored with twenty lives. The thing never crossed my mind for a moment excepting when I was deranged with my late illness. You probably wondered how I came to think of it in my delirium if I had never thought of it before, but such is the fact. . . . I realize that I have a good strong ambition, and in fact I am rather proud of it, because it usually has a good influence for one, but my ambition never reached the dizzy heights which might be suspected from your letter.[168]

The Assistant Attorney General assigned to the Department of the Interior headed a busy office, and there is no question but that Van Devanter did a superior job. When he had been in it for two years, he described it to a friend:

> Every day more decisions pass over my desk than are decided by the Supreme Court of Wyoming in months. Some of them involve rights to land in the Everglades of Florida, in Alaska, and almost everywhere, including the lake front in Chicago; while others involve matters arising in the U.S. Patent Office and other bureaus of the Interior Department. Some involve the question whether the offspring of a white man and an Indian woman are white or Indian; and quite recently a question arose as to whether a statute affecting marriages between whites and Indians included marriages also between Negroes and Indians; and so it goes. One case involves a desert claim in Arizona, a homestead in Oklahoma, a timber purchase in Minnesota or cash entry in Louisiana. While another involves some mine in Colorado, Utah, California, or Alaska, or many thousands of acres of land under some railroad grant. There is no end to the variety of matters which come and go in quick succession.[169]

---

[168] W. Van Devanter to F. E. Warren, Jan. 31, 1897; see Van Devanter to Warren, Mar. 11, 1897; Van Devanter Papers.

[169] W. Van Devanter to F. Bond, Mar. 10, 1899, Van Devanter Papers.

Van Devanter's fears that he would work unknown and without possibility of advancement proved groundless. He had sufficient contact with the regular staff in the Department of Justice, and he appeared in the Supreme Court. In the fall of 1898, he joined the faculty of the Columbian (now George Washington) University Law School, where his colleagues included Justices Harlan and Brewer, with whom Van Devanter soon developed relations of friendship and mutual respect.[170] His general standing is indicated by a public boom he enjoyed in March 1902, for appointment as Secretary of the Interior. On the occasion of an earlier, lesser boom, however, President McKinley had said he was reserving Van Devanter for judicial office, and that was what President Roosevelt gave him.[171] In March 1903, Van Devanter became a judge of the U.S. Circuit Court of Appeals for the Eighth Circuit. He now resigned not only his professorship at the Columbian Law School but also his post as Republican National Committeeman from Wyoming, which he had held throughout his service at the Interior Department.[172] And practically from this moment on, he hoped for promotion to the Supreme Court of the United States.

Van Devanter's ambition was fixed on an eventual succession to Brewer, and he advised Warren that in the meantime guarded support might be given to the candidacy for any other seat of Van Devanter's senior Eighth Circuit colleague, Walter H. Sanborn of Minnesota. At Van Devanter's urging, Warren gave Sanborn such guarded support in 1906, when Justic Brown resigned.[173] The appointment went to Moody, and that was the end of any withdrawal by Van Devanter in favor of his senior colleague. Henceforth Van Devanter was an active, even relentless, Supreme Court candidate, and he had in Senator Warren the most faithful and effective agent imaginable. But Van Devanter's colleague Sanborn was not aware that his own ambitions were past the point of possible gratification, and so from 1906 on, the two men were obvious, virtually acknowledged, rivals and relations between them were strained.

In 1907, at a time when vacancies were thought to be in the offing although none actually existed, word came to Van Devanter of inquiries made by President Roosevelt about Judge Sanborn. Roosevelt, looking ahead to future appointments, wondered whether Sanborn would not be

---

[170] W. Van Devanter to E. A. Slack, Sept. 26, 1898, to B. L. Whitman, Sept. 26, 1898, Van Devanter Papers.

[171] F. E. Warren to W. Van Devanter, June 13, 1901; Van Devanter to P. M. Chamberlain, Mar. 22, 1909, to Warren, Mar. 30, 1902, Van Devanter Papers.

[172] W. Van Devanter to M. A. Hanna, Feb. 27, 1903, Van Devanter Papers.

[173] W. Van Devanter to F. E. Warren, Nov. 16, 1903, Van Devanter Papers.

likely to take too restricted a view of the powers of Congress under the Commerce Clause. The same intelligence also reached Sanborn, and as a result, Van Devanter noted with something less than genuine amusement, Sanborn had experienced a change of views, and had "almost grown eloquent" in describing the breadth of the Commerce Clause.[174] Was Van Devanter himself affected in any way by the known requirements, so to speak, of the appointive power—requirements, he might well have thought, that would also be those of any foreseeable successor to Roosevelt? Conceivably this is the specific manner in which the Progressive movement worked its influence on the judicial process, this is the concrete way in which Roosevelt "put the fear of God into judges,"[175] and this is the reason that, as Hughes remembered, Van Devanter was not, to begin with, the inflexible conservative he became later.[176]

Van Devanter's estimate of the effect on Sanborn, however, surely carried a touch of understandable malice. As to Van Devanter himself, the truth is that he had no distinct ideological commitments in these years. Whatever had lodged in him from Wyoming was not yet developed, and he brought no commitments from the Department of the Interior or the Court of Appeals. No doubt William D. Mitchell and Chief Justice Stone were right when, after Van Devanter's death, they located the origins of his attachment to "economic freedom" and to the philosophy that the least government is the best in his experience of old Wyoming, where "men were the masters of their fate," and where "industry, character and brains earned success," the fruits of which a a man was allowed freely to enjoy. In these conditions of Van Devanter's early career, whether quite realistically perceived or somewhat idealized, we may find, if anywhere, "the seeds of his judgments," as Mitchell said.[177] But only a later hindsight enables us to do so.

Before he came to the Supreme Court, Van Devanter was, altogether and almost exclusively, a technician, a professional, "forceful,

---

[174] W. Van Devanter to J. W. Lacey, Nov. 14, 1907, Van Devanter Papers, Library of Congress. The word reached Van Devanter through another Eighth Circuit colleague. E. B. Adams to Van Devanter, Oct. 5, 1907, Van Devanter Papers. Quite probably, Van Devanter had in mind such a case as Colorado & Northwestern R.R. v. United States, 157 Fed. 321 (8th Cir. 1907), *writ of error dismissed*, 229 U.S. 605 (1913), in which San-

born held the federal Safety Appliance Acts constitutional as enforced against an intrastate railroad carrying goods destined for, or originating in, interstate commerce. There was a dissent, but Van Devanter concurred in Sanborn's opinion. Perhaps he would have liked a chance to write it.

[175] See *supra*, p. 24, n.80.
[176] See *supra*, p. 25, n.82.
[177] 316 U.S. xxi–xxii, xxxix (1942).

a brilliant and sound lawyer, adroit in politics and thoroughly loyal to his friends," as Warren said to Mark Hanna in 1896.[178] His function was more to tell his friends what was feasible and how it should be done than to tell them what to do. Thus when the silver issue split Wyoming Republicans in 1897 and the Warren faction found it prudent to favor bimetallism, Van Devanter went along, drafted a resolution on the subject, and discoursed at length to Warren on political strategy and consequences—but never on the merits of bimetallism.[179] It was some time before the ideologically committed Justice emerged alongside the skilled political and legal technician—whom, incidentally, the ideologically committed Justice was never to submerge.

At the very start of his career as a circuit judge, Van Devanter sat with three colleagues in the *Northern Securities* case[180] and evidently concurred in the judgment for the government, although for some reason he failed to sign the decree. Near the end of his tenure, he sat on the panel that gave the government its victory—which Van Devanter soon had the opportunity to help confirm—in *United States* v. *Standard Oil Co.*[181] Both Theodore Roosevelt and Taft might have thought this a good antitrust record.[182] But in 1904, Van Devanter held the Sherman Act inapplicable to a resale price maintenance agreement enforced by the holder of a patent on sales of the patented article.[183] He was following precedent in this decision[184] (as precedent might, however, have also been followed to another result in *Northern Securities*), and later went along on the Supreme Court in striking down resale price maintenance

---

[178] F. E. Warren to M. A. Hanna, Apr. 24, 1896, Van Devanter Papers.

[179] See Van Devanter Papers, Letter Press Books, 1–8.

[180] United States v. Northern Securities Co., 120 Fed. 721 (C.C.D. Minn. 1903), *affirmed,* Northern Securities Co. v. United States, 193 U.S. 197 (1904).

[181] 173 Fed. 177 (C.C.E.D. Mo. 1909), *affirmed,* 221 U.S. 1 (1911).

[182] In United States v. Union Pacific R.R., 188 Fed. 102 (C.C.D. Utah 1911), *reversed,* 226 U.S. 61 (1912), Van Devanter was a member of a three-judge majority that defeated, at the trial court level, the government's effort to rescind E. H. Harriman's purchase of the Southern Pacific Railroad. But this decision was not announced until well after Van Devanter had been appointed to the Supreme Court and had taken his seat there.

[183] National Phonograph Co. v. Schlegel, 128 Fed. 733 (8th Cir. 1904). The case is cited with approval in Lurton's opinion in Henry v. A. B. Dick Co., 224 U.S. 1, 39 (1912), in which Van Devanter concurred (heartily, one dares say), and which was eventually overruled, against Van Devanter's dissent, in Motion Picture Patents Co. v. Universal Film Co., 243 U.S. 502 (1917).

[184] Bement v. National Harrow Co., 186 U.S. 70 (1902).

agreements where no patent was involved.[185] But he later also continued to defend the position he had taken on patents.[186]

Again, Van Devanter gave some sympathetic applications as a circuit judge to federal statutes regulating railroads, particularly the Safety Appliance Act, of which he said in one case: "Obviously, the purpose of this statute is the protection of the lives and limbs of men, and such statutes, when the words fairly permit, are so construed as to prevent the mischief and advance the remedy."[187] But in the very case from which this language is quoted, Van Devanter ended up reversing a verdict against the railroad, and ordering a new trial to determine whether the injured employee might not have assumed the risk of the accident that injured him. He was generally rather a hard man to get a judgment for the plaintiff from in a negligence case, and much wedded to the doctrines of contributory negligence and assumption of risk.[188] And yet again, that was largely the technician speaking. The attitude can in some measure be traced to the later work of the Justice,[189] but Van Devanter never became, like McReynolds and then Butler, a specialist in reversing plaintiffs' judgments under the Federal Employers' Liability Act. In short, it would have taken a brave man indeed to predict, from

---

[185] Dr. Miles Medical Co. v. Park & Sons Co., 220 U.S. 373 (1911).

[186] Van Devanter joined the dissenters in Bauer v. O'Donnell, 229 U.S. 1 (1913). He was with the majority in United States v. General Electric Co., 272 U.S. 476 (1926).

[187] Chicago M. & St. P. Ry. Co. v. Voelker, 129 Fed. 522, 527 (8th Cir. 1904); see also United States v. Atchison, T. & S. F. Ry. Co., 163 Fed. 517 (8th Cir. 1908); Great Northern Ry. Co. v. United States, 155 Fed. 945 (8th Cir. 1907), *affirmed,* 208 U.S. 452 (1908); Union Stockyards Co. v. United States, 169 Fed. 404 (8th Cir. 1909). The last-mentioned opinion was later, after Van Devanter's accession, quoted with approval by Day, speaking for the Court in United States v. Union Stock Yard and Transit Co., 226 U.S. 286, 305 (1912).

[188] See Musser-Sauntry Co. v. Brown, 126 Fed. 141 (8th Cir. 1903); Chicago & N.W. Ry. Co. v. Andrews, 130 Fed. 65 (8th Cir. 1904); Chicago

Great Western Ry. Co. v. Smith, 141 Fed. 930 (8th Cir. 1905); St. Louis & S. F. R.R. v. Dewees, 153 Fed. 56 (8th Cir. 1907); Denver City Tramway Co. v. Cobb, 164 Fed. 41 (8th Cir. 1908); Great Northern Ry. Co. v. Hooker, 170 Fed. 154 (8th Cir. 1909); Chicago Great Western Ry. Co. v. Crotty, 141 Fed. 913 (8th Cir. 1905).

[189] See, e.g., N.Y. Central R.R. v. Winfield, 244 U.S. 147 (1917); Texas & Pacific Ry. v. Bigger, 239 U.S. 330 (1915) (Van Devanter, White, and McReynolds, JJ., dissenting); Seaboard Air Line Ry. v. Lorick, 243 U.S. 572 (1917) (Van Devanter and McReynolds, JJ., dissenting). But *cf.* Flannelly v. Delaware & Hudson Co., 225 U.S. 597 (1912); Chicago, Rock Island Ry. v. Wright, 239 U.S. 548 (1916). And it was Van Devanter who upheld the constitutionality of the Second Employers' Liability Act, in the cases of that name, 223 U.S. 1 (1912).

the opinions of the judge, the commitments of the Justice.[190] All that one could identify this early was the flat, sensible style.[191]

In January 1909, as Taft was forming his Cabinet while resting in Augusta, there was a considerable movement to make Van Devanter Secretary of the Treasury. Philander C. Knox, prospective Secretary of State, made the proposal to Taft, and it was supported by Senators Aldrich, Hale, and Crane, whom Van Devanter had favorably impressed

---

[190] Van Devanter's opinions as a circuit judge appear in Volumes 126–185 of the *Federal Reporter*. His luck in being affirmed or reversed by the Supreme Court was indifferent, on a slender statistical base. He was reversed twice and affirmed four times. Whitfield v. Aetna Life Insurance Co., 205 U.S. 489 (1907), *reversing* 144 Fed. 356 (8th Cir. 1906); Hunter v. Johnson, 209 U.S. 541 (1908), *reversing* 147 Fed. 133 (8th Cir. 1906); Northern Lumber Co. v. O'Brien, 204 U.S. 190 (1907), *affirming* 139 Fed. 614 (8th Cir. 1905); Lawson v. U.S. Mining Co., 207 U.S. 1 (1907), *affirming* 134 Fed. 769 (8th Cir. 1904); Great Northern Ry. v. United States, 208 U.S. 452 (1908), *affirming* 155 Fed. 945 (8th Cir. 1907); Stuart v. Union Pacific R.R., 227 U.S. 342 (1913), *affirming* 178 Fed. 753 (8th Cir. 1910). None of these direct encounters between Van Devanter and his future colleagues yields any particular insight. There is more significance in Allen v. St. Louis, Iron Mountain & Southern Ry. Co., 230 U.S. 553 (1913), *reversing* 187 Fed. 290 (8th Cir. 1911). This was a companion case to the *Minnesota Rate Cases*, 230 U.S. 352 (1913), and Hughes for the Supreme Court was reversing a judgment by the District Court in Arkansas (Trieber, J.), holding rates set by the state to be confiscatory and hence unconstitutional. But at an earlier stage of the case, Van Devanter, sitting as a trial judge, had granted the railroad a temporary injunction. *In re* Arkansas Railroad Rates, 163 Fed. 141 (C.C.E.D. Ark. 1908). Of course, the issue on a pre-

liminary injunction is not the same as the ultimate issue after trial. But Van Devanter in 1908 did express the opinion that the rates were clearly confiscatory. When the Allen case was decided in the Supreme Court, Van Devanter did not dissent.

[191] A clash between Van Devanter and his able colleague William C. Hook, who turned out to be Van Devanter's chief rival for promotion, is worth mention, as it exemplifies a capacity on Van Devanter's part to give broad readings to criminal statutes when abhorrent behavior seemed to him to fit the punishment. *Cf.* Herndon v. Lowry, 301 U.S. 242, 264 (1937) (Van Devanter, J., dissenting). Demolli v. United States, 144 Fed. 363 (8th Cir. 1906), was a prosecution for mailing obscene matter. But the defendant was the author, not the publisher, and there was no evidence of any participation by him in the mailing, except as he might naturally have surmised that the publication would be mailed. The statute punished mailing only. Van Devanter affirmed a conviction. Hook, in a dissent that, at least from a debating point of view, got much the better of the argument, pointed out that on Van Devanter's reading, the printer, the proofreader, and God knows who else might also be held. This was no way to construe a criminal statute, Hook concluded. Van Devanter's holding is to be contrasted with the strained reading favoring the defendant that he gave another statute in United States v. Dietrich, 126 Fed. 676 (C.C.D. Neb. 1904).

on a visit to Washington the previous winter. By February, many newspapers were announcing the Van Devanter appointment to the Treasury as a practical certainty. The appointment was, of course, not made, but as Knox and others discussed it with Taft, there was much talk also of Van Devanter's eligibility for the Supreme Court. The boom did no harm.[192] And in March, on what must have been virtually his first visit to the new President, Warren brought up Van Devanter's Supreme Court candidacy.[193] It was not pushed when Peckham died that fall, because Van Devanter and Warren thought the geographical factor would work against them.[194] But it was actively put forward when Brewer died.[195] And at this time, a dramatic obstacle that almost cost Van Devanter his appointment first came into view.

There is preserved in the papers left by President Taft a memorandum, undated, but filed with papers bearing dates in late November 1909, which is marked "Efficiency," and carries this notation in the President's hand: "Put this in an envelope to contain such matter as to Supreme Court Justiceships as I do not refer to A.G. [the Attorney General]." The memorandum says:

> There is no guaranty of efficiency in the future so certain as efficiency in the past. Delay in the decision of a case is often as disastrous as an adverse determination of it, and there are those who are of the opinion that the ability and disposition to dispose of judicial work with reasonable speed are desirable qualifications for a judicial position. The following statistics have been compiled from . . . the Reports of the Circuit Courts of Appeals. They disclose different degrees of efficiency in judicial positions.

Figures for the circuit judges are then tabulated by circuit. Then the judges of all the circuits are ranked together. Judge Sanborn of the Eighth Circuit comes out first, both in total number of opinions and in annual average number. Lurton of the Sixth Circuit is fourth. There follows a special comparison for the Eighth Circuit, which shows Sanborn to be far ahead of his colleague Van Devanter, with double

---

[192] P. C. Knox to W. H. Taft, Jan. 16, 1909, Taft Papers, W. Van Devanter to Knox, February 1909; Van Devanter to J. W. Lacey, Feb. 17, 1909; F. E. Warren to Van Devanter, Feb. 22, 1909; Van Devanter to Warren, Mar. 3, 1909, Van Devanter Papers.

[193] F. E. Warren to W. Van Devanter, Mar. 28, 1909, Van Devanter

Papers.

[194] W. Van Devanter to E. B. Adams, Nov. 5, 1909, Van Devanter Papers.

[195] W. Van Devanter to E. B. Adams, Mar. 30, 1910; Van Devanter to W. H. Sanborn, Apr. 2, 1910; Van Devanter to F. E. Warren, Apr. 7, 1910; Van Devanter to C. N. Bliss, Apr. 16, 1910, Van Devanter Papers.

Van Devanter's yearly average number of opinions and more than double Van Devanter's yearly average number of pages written—for pages, too, are taken into account. Sanborn is also shown to be well ahead of his colleague Hook, although not quite as spectacularly as of Van Devanter.[196]

Conceivably this memorandum was produced in Washington. In November 1909, Taft was unsuccessfully struggling against his inclination to put his friend Lurton on the Supreme Court in place of Peckham, who had died the previous month. Taft was complaining, and heard complaints, that the Court, with a majority of sick or aging Justices, was not disposing of its business. The problem of efficiency was as much in his mind as ever. It was the only problem that made him waver in his determination to appoint Lurton, and the high standing assigned to Lurton in this memorandum must have reassured Taft. Given this frame of mind, it is entirely possible that the President had ordered the memorandum prepared, presumably by the Department of Justice. But the memorandum does not read as if it had been drafted in response to a Presidential inquiry. It has a self-starting, hortatory tone. This feature of it, and the special concentration on the Eighth Circuit, give rise to the suspicion that the memorandum might be traceable to Van Devanter's Brother Sanborn.

Van Devanter so traced it, when he heard of it some months later. For the memorandum was not left and forgotten in the Presidential file once the Lurton appointment had been made. On April 16, 1910, a few weeks after Brewer's death, and one week before Taft gave this seat to Hughes, Secretary of Commerce and Labor Charles Nagel, a Van Devanter supporter, wrote Van Devanter that he was said to have produced fewer opinions than the other judges in his circuit; "also that you do not participate in the hearing of cases to the proper extent." Nobody underestimated the value of the opinions Van Devanter did write, Nagel went on, but could Van Devanter send in some explanation that Nagel could use his support?[197]

Van Devanter would always be afflicted with "pen paralysis." In later years, he became resigned to this condition, consoling himself, no doubt, with the high regard in which his colleagues held him in spite of it.[198] But in 1910, the charge of slowness seemed to him unjust and gave

---

[196] Presidential File No. IA, Folder dated Nov. 21, 22, 1909, Taft Papers.

[197] C. Nagel to W. Van Devanter, Apr. 16, 1910; see also F. E. Warren to Van Devanter, Apr. 17, 1910, Van Devanter Papers.

[198] Many years later, Hughes recalled that Van Devanter "was slow in getting out his opinions—having what one of his most intimate friends in the Court [of the 1920s and 30s] (Justice Sutherland) described as 'pen paralysis.' This difficulty increased with the years, but his careful and elaborate statements in conference, with his accurate review of authorities,

him "no little pain." He rose to the defense of his record. As to sitting at hearings in the various cities of his extremely large circuit (twelve states and one territory), he wrote Nagel, he thought he sat as often as his colleagues. As to opinionwriting, Nagel's informant failed to take account of a number of important trials, criminal and civil, over which Van Devanter had presided by special assignment, and which also involved written work. Moreover, appellate opinions were not fungible quantities. They might concern a single, simple case, or a number of cases with complicated records: "And in this connection justice to myself requires me to affirm that I have not been averse to bestowing a large amount of labor upon a single case when there has been occasion therefore [*sic*] and also to affirm that the outcome usually has justified me in so doing." Quality and accuracy, Van Devanter had assumed, were more important than quantity. Finally:

> The statement [cited by Nagel] contains an implication that I am indisposed to work and am inclined to shirk, when, no matter what my faults may be, that is the last one that will be ascribed to me by any one who really understands me, and whose criticism is genuine.
>
> There is nothing more which I properly can say at this time, save that while this letter is marked as personal you are at liberty to do with it as you think is right.[199]

In the following months, Van Devanter heard from two separate sources that Taft had him under consideration, along with his colleague William C. Hook, but was worried that Van Devanter wrote fewer opinions than the other judges and was behind in his work. "Get this impression out of his mind," was the advice of Van Devanter's friend Dennis J. Flynn, the Oklahoma Representative in the Congress, who had seen Taft.[200] During the summer and fall, Van Devanter explained to two of his close friends, his colleague Judge Elmer B. Adams and Flynn, another factor that had a bearing on the number of opinions he had been able to produce. Through the past winter and spring, Mrs. Van Devanter had been ill and had required an operation at the Mayo

---

were of the greatest value. If these statements had been taken down stenographically, they would have served with little editing as excellent opinions. His perspicacity and common sense made him a trusted advisor in all sorts of matters. Chief Justice White leaned heavily upon him and so did Chief Justice Taft, especially when the latter began to

fail in health." C. E. Hughes, *Biographical Notes,* 220–21, Hughes Papers, Library of Congress.

[199] W. Van Devanter to C. Nagel, Apr. 19, 1910, Van Devanter Papers.

[200] D. J. Flynn to W. Van Devanter, June 27, 1910; see also E. B. Adams to Van Devanter, Aug. 12, 1910, Van Devanter Papers.

Clinic. Not unnaturally, this situation interfered with Van Devanter's work.[201]

Matters came to a head in the last ten days before Taft made his appointments. On December 3, 1910, Senator Warren telegraphed Van Devanter that the President had told him that he had a list of cases decided by all the judges in the Eighth Circuit, and that it looked as if Van Devanter had not done his share. The President seemed fairly angry, and said to Warren that Van Devanter should be advised to get the other side of the case, if any, before the President.[202] Van Devanter replied immediately with the following coded wire addressed to Warren:

> It is true that I am now behind in Circuit Court of Appeals work but not to extent apparently represented. While this is to be regretted it does not arise from indolence or timidity in reaching conclusions, or hesitancy in giving effect to them. I may have given too much attention to closely contested and important cases, especially where there have been differences of opinion, and may have been too tenacious of my own views, but I have felt justified in my course because it almost always has resulted in unanimity and has tended to produce harmonious rules of decision. [This was certainly a point well calculated to appeal to Taft, who in later years, at least, exhibited a positive passion for massing unanimous courts.] I have done much important work in Circuit [trial] Courts which, if added to my appellate work, makes my total easily up to average of my associates. I emphatically protest against impressions which seem to have been created, but make no complaint of President's attitude for it is obviously reasonable. I cannot prepare and submit showing in my own behalf now without assuming attitude which would be distasteful to me. For this reason I prefer that further consideration of my name be omitted. Then at some later time when there are no appointments at stake I shall hope President will permit me personally to make full statement of my work to him and yourself. I will owe this to both because of his consideration of my name and because of your interest in presenting it.[203]

Warren sent a decoded copy of this telegram to the President, saying that he feared he had annoyed Taft in their interview of a few days back, and expressing regret. He was now asking that the President discontinue consideration of Van Devanter's name for immediate appointment to the Supreme Court.[204]

---

[201] W. Van Devanter to D. J. Flynn, Nov. 6, 1910; Van Devanter to E. B. Adams, Aug. 27, 1910, Van Devanter Papers.

[202] F. E. Warren to W. Van Devanter, Dec. 3, 1910, Van Devanter Papers.

[203] W. Van Devanter to F. E. Warren, Dec. 4, 1910, Van Devanter Papers.

[204] F. E. Warren to W. H. Taft, Dec. 5, 1910, Taft Papers.

Van Devanter meanwhile supplemented his telegram with an eight-page letter to Warren, as impassioned a document as he is known ever to have composed. Judge Sanborn had been in Washington to see the President, Van Devanter wrote, and Sanborn would not only "go a long way to accomplish his own preferment," but "would also prefer that none of his associates be appointed." Sanborn had a table prepared purporting to show the number of decisions rendered by every circuit judge in the United States. It had been prepared by an old, unreliable bailiff, and no doubt formed the basis of the President's misgivings. Van Devanter then went on to elaborate the arguments in his own defense, adding that while Sanborn was way ahead of anyone in the number of opinions written, and while Van Devanter was currently somewhat behind, he, Van Devanter, was nevertheless not out of line with the nationwide average.[205]

On December 7, Warren wrote Van Devanter that the President had sent for him and had told him that he proposed to discuss Supreme Court appointments with his Cabinet, that an early decision could be expected, and that, for himself, he had about concluded that he would appoint Judge Hook.[206] On December 9, Warren again saw Taft, and the President said that Van Devanter's telegram had made a good impression, being a dignified paper, and that Secretary Nagel had brought before the Cabinet Van Devanter's letter to him of the previous spring, which was also thought to be dignified, as well as persuasive. The Cabinet consensus favored Van Devanter, but the President himself did not appear entirely convinced. He said he feared Senator Knute Nelson of Minnesota, although far from being an Insurgent, might oppose Van Devanter on the ground that he was a railroad lawyer. Nelson was a member of the Judiciary Committee. Would Warren see about that?

Warren did, and it turned out that Nelson thought Sanborn, not Van Devanter, was a railroad servant, and was opposed also to Frank B. Kellogg of Minnesota, who had in any event taken himself out of the running in a letter to the President in August, because he was serving as special counsel to the government in the antitrust case against the Standard Oil Company.[207] Warren told the President that he had a good letter from Van Devanter and promised to get permission to give it to the President, which he did the following day. Then Warren mounted for the President's benefit the following argument against Judge Hook. If he appointed Hook, the President would be seen as engaged in pacifying the Insurgents, because both the Hook appointment and that

---

[205] W. Van Devanter to F. E. Warren, Dec. 5, 1910, Van Devanter Papers.

[206] F. E. Warren to W. Van De-

vanter, Dec. 7, 1910, Van Devanter Papers.

[207] F. B. Kellogg to W. H. Taft, Aug. 12, 1910, Taft Papers.

of Hughes would be credited to the Insurgents and against the regular Republicans. In addition, the President would be accused also of pacifying the Democrats by appointing Southerners. All of which would be rather hard on the main body of the President's Republican supporters. The argument, Warren thought, seemed to go home to Taft. And Warren left in a hopeful mood. "Let me say to you," he wrote Van Devanter, "there has been a fight, what a fight, over this matter, and nine-tenths of the time you have been one of the underdogs; but there are a few of your friends who have never let go, and I now look for success unless another one of the backsliding periods comes on."[208]

Judge Hook's reputation as the Insurgent candidate was manufactured by Senator Warren out of whole cloth for the specific and sufficient purpose of mobilizing regular Republican Senators to urge Taft, in the last moments, to appoint Van Devanter. On December 12, the nominations having just gone to the Senate, Warren exulted to Van Devanter: "I guess the fire started under Hook by claiming he was the Insurgents' candidate has spread broadly."[209] It may be doubted that Taft himself was taken in, but he is likely to have heeded the Senatorial representations which Warren was able to produce. After he made his appointments, Taft wrote to both Sanborn and Hook. To Sanborn he said, on December 15, 1910 (incidentally tending to confirm Van Devanter's allegation that it was Sanborn who had come forward with the efficiency statistics):

> I took Van Devanter only after a long investigation in which I found that he had been sick and his wife had been ill, and after a full letter of explanation from him. I think perhaps the dilatory habit in respect to turning out opinions could be corrected by close association with a court that sits all the time in the same city, and where the comparison between him and the other judges will be constant, and when he knows why it is that I seriously hesitated before taking him.[210]

To Hook on the following day:

> You know that in the selection of judges one has to make comparison . . . and it is no reflection that a man does not happen to be chosen. . . . I want to say to you that so far as Kansas was concerned there never was any question in my mind that you should be selected, and that really the choice settled down between you and Judge Van

---

[208] F. E. Warren to Van Devanter, Dec. 9, 10, 1910, Van Devanter Papers.

[209] F. E. Warren to W. Van De-vanter, Dec. 12, 1910, Van Devanter Papers.

[210] W. H. Taft to W. H. Sanborn, Dec. 15, 1910, Taft Papers.

Devanter. Judge Sanborn was excluded because of his age. You and Judge Van Devanter, it was suggested at one time, ought to be excluded because of your participation in the Standard Oil case [both Hook and Van Devanter had sat as judges on the Eighth Circuit Court of Appeals in deciding that case in favor of the government]. I thought about that and reached the conclusion that because a man had decided a case as he thought right in the course of his duty was no reason for his exclusion from the court in which the same case might come before him. The selection between you and the gentleman who was chosen was a very even matter, and fortune threw it to him.

I congratulate you upon the standing that you have in the circuit and upon the fact that I became convinced that you were Supreme Court material. It did not seem wise to take two judges from the same circuit, and for that reason the choice fell as it did; but I believe it right for me to express to you my high appreciation of the spirit in which you take the choice.[211]

Hook's spirit was indeed commendable and was soon to be even more sorely tried. He wired Van Devanter on the day of the appointments: "While my personal preference was for another, nevertheless, old man, I congratulate you."[212]

Warren had an explanation not only for Hook's defeat, but also for Taft's choice of White over Hughes. This explanation was less Machiavellian, but also entirely Senatorial. On December 13, 1910, in a sort of morning-after mood, Warren reported to Van Devanter, who was still in Cheyenne:

From all I can learn, they had a monkey-and-parrot time pretty much all day Sunday [December 11]—the President and his Cabinet—chewing the rag over the Chief Justice business. The papers had been full of Hughes, and I believe the President had fully made up his mind to make Hughes the Chief Justice; but there was a regular flare-back on the part of the Cabinet, and the high-up lawyers from New York and elsewhere reminded the President that while Hughes' original appointment was a good stroke because of public opinion, since the hoi polloi had all become convinced that Hughes was the only man, it would not be wise, the popular cry having been settled, to make Hughes the Chief Justice and thereby alienate all the strong legal minds who know that he had never had a case before the Supreme Court, and had never had but two important matters before him—one the insurance investigation—and that he was an uncertain quantity politically

---

211 W. H. Taft to W. C. Hook, Dec. 16, 1910, Taft Papers.

212 W. C. Hook to W. Van Devanter, Dec. 12, 1910, Van Devanter Papers.

and perhaps would be in jurisprudence. Of course, on the other hand, it was deemed to be pretty raw towards the Republicans, after having appointed Lurton, to then make White the Chief Justice and add Lamar or somebody from the South. But the southern Democrats, and the northern too, were red hot on the trail for having one out of the nine judges, and Bailey and Foster [Democratic Senators] and a number of others were very urgent about White. And so I think the decision was that the Insurgents, who had finally become so offensive, would receive a knock-down if neither Hughes nor Hook was appointed; but the Democrats would be right on deck to confirm and would be satisfied; and that the stalwart Republicans would prefer even a Democrat, if it were White, to Hughes. In this I think they argued wisely, for I and others would much prefer White to Hughes. I said to [Senator Elihu] Root yesterday: I am not feeling very bad about White's being made Chief Justice instead of Hughes. Root replied, I am very happy over it. White is a better Republican than Hughes. He is an old-fashioned Federalist and a straightforward, fair man. Nobody can vouch for Hughes' politics. So I think that the President, from the look of things up here, has made a ten-strike in having both stalwart Democrats and Republicans stand by him and letting the rattle-in-the-box species go farrow.[213]

On the Sunday evening of the "monkey-and-parrot time" in the White House, Hughes received a telephone call asking him to come and see the President. Within a half hour, as Hughes was dressing to go, another call came canceling the appointment. Perhaps Taft had wanted to notify Hughes privately of his decision, for he had surely made it by then. A Senatorial delegation had been to see the President, and while— no matter what Root told Warren—they did not openly object to Hughes as a Progressive, they did emphasize his youth, the fact, trivial as it may seem, that Hughes had never argued a case before the Supreme Court, which Warren mentions, and the awkward situation that might be created within the Court if so junior a member were named to preside over it.[214] The last-mentioned point, if no other, must have impressed Taft. He probably suspected White's tacit aspiration. He knew, as the Senators may not have known and as he himself had no reason to surmise when he wrote Hughes about the Chief Justiceship in April, that Harlan wanted the crowning reward. And he knew, as the Senators probably did not, that Harlan had recommended Day. He might have supposed that Day was aware of the recommendation, and that he also aspired to preside. Day would resent Hughes more than he would White, who was

---

[213] F. E. Warren to W. Van Devanter, Dec. 13, 1910, Van Devanter

Papers.
[214] See Pusey, *Hughes*, 279–80.

Day's senior, Taft might have surmised. There is no evidence that these were in fact Day's feelings, but Taft might reasonably have thought so.[215]

Moreover, there were other influences working against Hughes. In a series of letters in November and early December 1910, Amasa Thornton, a New York lawyer acquainted with both Roosevelt and Taft, argued with some vehemence that a Hughes appointment would alienate the Colonel. "I had a further interview with Mr. Roosevelt today," Thornton wrote on December 2. "He is very much opposed to the promotion of Justice Hughes . . . and I believe if you do it that it will add perplexity to a situation that is now working out for the best. . . . I know that big politics is in promoting Justice White." Not only would such a move fail to open another Rooseveltian wound, but it would stand a chance of capturing some Catholic votes.[216] That Thornton was not misrepresenting Roosevelt's feelings one may well believe on the basis of substantial other evidence, and it is certain that in the winter of 1910 Taft still had some interest in conciliating Roosevelt, and some hope that an irrevocable breach could be avoided. Governor Hughes had incurred Theodore Roosevelt's lasting displeasure over a patronage incident in 1907, and matters were not helped by a further misunderstanding in the summer of 1910, after Hughes had been appointed but while he was still in Albany.[217]

Reaction to Taft's appointments confirmed Senator Warren's impression that the President had "made a ten-strike." The President at the same time also sent in five nominations to the newly created Commerce Court, and two to the Interstate Commerce Commission. At a minimum, the general tone of opinion about the appointments as a whole may be characterized by the comment of the *Kansas City Times*, a Progressive newspaper: "Some are obviously admirable; none is obviously wrong.[218]

---

[215] *Cf. supra*, p. 37.

Speaking in 1954, Felix Frankfurter recalled that the Court as a whole was opposed to the nomination of so fresh a judge as Hughes, and that all the Justices save Holmes (and, of course, Hughes) "drew up a round robin to present to Taft" and also, "I believe," saw Taft, to inform him of their opposition to Hughes. Frankfurter gave no source for this story. His chief one would have been Holmes, but in later years, when recollection might have been uncertain. And Holmes would have been reporting the action of others, in which he did not join. He might have been privy to the expression of an intention never in fact carried out. There is no independent evidence supporting this story. F. Frankfurter, *Of Law and Men*, P. Elman, ed. (1956), 121.

[216] See Presidential Series No. 2, File 101, particularly A. Thornton to W. H. Taft, Dec. 2, 1910, Taft Papers.

[217] Harbaugh, *Power and Responsibility*, 352; M. Sullivan, *Our Times* (1930), III, 283–85, 288; Mowry, *Roosevelt and the Progressive Movement*, 136, 357.

[218] *Literary Digest*, 41:1811, Dec. 24, 1910.

There was much sober discussion of the long-range importance of the Supreme Court appointments. "In a qualified sense and yet to a very practical degree," the *New York Sun* said, "the Supreme Court is a continuous constitutional convention." Taft, it was realized, had performed one of the high functions of his office, and there was gratification that he had performed it well, as might after all have been expected, since Taft was himself a distinguished former judge.[219] The naming of White took everyone by surprise. But it was a pleasant surprise all around, not least of all for Holmes, although Holmes was still curiously rueful, and was led to reflect about retirement.[220] White's reputation was towering. Despite his dissent in the *Northern Securities* case, nobody considered him a reactionary. Even the *Philadelphia North American*, which had its doubts, thought that White's appointment was the best. The elevation by a Republican President of an ex-Confederate soldier to the headship of one of the three coordinate branches of the federal government was, of course, much noticed. "It seems to me," said Theodore Roosevelt, "that nothing could be a better augury of the future of the country than that a Republican President should appoint a former Confederate Chief Justice of the United States, and receive the unanimous applause of his countrymen."[221]

The appointment of Lamar, also a Southern Democrat, evoked in a minor key some of the same "binding-up-the-wounds-of-war" reaction as the nomination of White. The *Augusta Chronicle* was pleased to note that the South was "coming into her own—is taking her rightful place in the nation—and that at the hands of a Republican President, who is, himself, bigger and better than his party—indeed, good enough to be a Democrat."[222] If there was a complaint about Lamar, it was that he was obscure, but then he was plainly a lawyer of standing and had judicial experience. The same was true of Van Devanter, who, it was remarked, was one of the judges who had decided the *Standard Oil* antitrust case in the government's favor in the circuit court.

---

[219] *Ibid.*, 1181–83.

[220] See *Holmes-Pollock Letters*, I, 172.

[221] See *Literary Digest*, 41:1181–83, Dec. 24, 1910; see also Mowry, *Roosevelt and the Progressive Movement*, 179; *Washington Post*, Dec. 13, 1910, p. 6, col. 1.

The gesture was neither trivial nor uncontroversial. Joseph B. Foraker of Ohio, then in the Senate, recalled complaining to Taft on this score. The war was over, said Taft. But not for those who had fought in it, Foraker replied, although he had nothing but the highest regard for White himself. Foraker also recalled that the sentiments of his old comrade Justice Harlan were similar, in addition to being otherwise embittered as well. J. B. Foraker, *Notes from a Busy Life* (1916), 404–405.

[222] *Augusta Chronicle*, Dec. 13, 1910.

I: *Mr. Taft Rehabilitates the Court*

But approval was not altogether unanimous. Thus the *Philadelphia North American*:

> There is justifiable suspicion concerning Judge Van Devanter, who has participated in decisions hostile to the whole policy of railroad regulation by the federal government and indicative of undue sympathy with the railroads.[223] And this questioning spirit among progressive men in both parties is intensified by the fact that he was urged for appointment to the Supreme bench only by the politicians of known corporation affiliations. Aside from the fact that he golfed and dined with Mr. Taft in Georgia, Judge Lamar is an unknown quantity, if not a nonentity. In Georgia men are classified as "Hoke Smith Democrats" or "Joe Brown Democrats."[224] The former are Progressives. The latter are corporation-serving reactionaries. Concerning Judge Lamar all that is said at present is that he is not a "Hoke Smith Democrat" and that after leaving the Georgia Supreme Court he became counsel for the railroads.[225]

A similar note was struck about Van Devanter in the *Saturday Evening Post* a few months later, an anonymous writer pointing out that Van Devanter owed all his appointments to the Senators from Wyoming, Warren and Clarence D. Clark, who were conservative Republicans.[226] This article was brought to Van Devanter's attention, and he did not like it. He thought it "not in keeping with the dignity and surroundings of the office which I now hold."[227]

A more poignant expression of dissent came to Van Devanter about the time of the *Saturday Evening Post* article in two private letters from a boyhood friend, who was provoked to write by news of Van Devanter's elevation. L. D. Ratliff, formerly of Marion, Indiana, now of Salem, Oregon, had "had it in mind during my early formative days to be a great preacher . . . but my theology would not stay fixed, so I could not preach successfully and satisfactorily; and thus from me the years slipped by." It was interesting, Ratliff wrote, how from the same "early Republican setting you have become a defender of the rights of property, a member of perhaps the most capitalistic judicial body in the world, while I have become a rank Socialist clamoring for the complete overthrow of our whole economic system. . . . At present

---

[223] Not a very fair characterization of Van Devanter's record on the circuit court. See *supra*, pp. 50–52.

[224] This was an oversimplification of Georgia politics. See C. V. Woodward, *Tom Watson* (1931).

[225] *Philadelphia North American*, Dec. 14, 1910.

[226] *Saturday Evening Post*, Mar. 18, 1911, p. 25.

[227] W. Van Devanter to W. A. Richards, June 2, 1911, Van Devanter Papers.

in any contest between property and democracy we would expect the latter to get the worst of it. But in the coming time, when we have made our fight and won for democracy, oh, for the good old coming time!"

In a second letter, after Van Devanter had replied, Ratliff wrote:

> I see how you say you stand for the defense of every character of right that is recognized, protected or created by the laws of the land. And, theoretically, you are right, I think; but practically, as I see it, the Court is expected, and generally does represent and express the bias of the President who appoints it (so far, at least, as regards his general philosophy of government) and the spirit of the particular ruling element which he represents. If to him the prosperity of big business is the basis of good to all the people, the men he appoints . . . will be favorable to big business. . . . At this time, it seems to me, this is the philosophy that is being applied to government; and so, the idea of the superior rights of property is having its inning. . . .
>
> In all of which I am trying to say, right and things are not fixed and definite quantities in our laws and constitutions, but are the products largely of judicial rendering, and are secured and made applicable according to the bent of the Court.[228]

He was not of those, Ratliff had said in his first letter, "who believe the Court is divinely bent. Rather its members are men of like passions with ourselves, having feelings and motives entirely human." These sentiments Van Devanter must indeed have deemed "not in keeping with the dignity and surroundings" of his office. They were not the sort of thing he or his colleagues were likely to hear from people they knew, and they were out of harmony with public comment in general. This was another world impinging on Van Devanter, the world of radical agitation, of the Progressives and beyond. For over a quarter of a century, the Ratliffs of this other world would go their way, and Van Devanter his, but when Van Devanter retired, it would be "the good old coming time."

The Court at October Term 1910

White, it was reported, was notified of his nomination by a group of Senators led by Henry Cabot Lodge, who called him off the Bench to tell him. His eyes filled with tears. After he returned to his seat, the Senators, in a matter of minutes, confirmed him by acclamation.[229] The

---

[228] L. D. Ratliff to W. Van Devanter, Mar. 20, Apr. 10, 1911, Van Devanter Papers.

[229] E. G. Lowry, "The Men of the Supreme Court," *World's Work*, 629, 630, April 1914.

following Monday, he took his new oath and moved over one chair to his right from the seat immediately to the Chief Justice's left, which he had occupied since Brewer's death. Van Devanter and Lamar were confirmed with equal ease three days later, on December 15. They were sworn and took their seats on January 3, 1911, before a great audience including Mrs. Taft.[230] Van Devanter, a compact, dark-complected man of average height, must have made something of a contrast with the taller, ruddier, courtlier Lamar. The President, no doubt in view of Van Devanter's longer judicial experience, had dated his commission one day before Lamar's. Van Devanter was, therefore, senior and was seated first, in the last chair on the Chief Justice's right, next to Lurton. Lamar went to the other end of the bench, next to Hughes. And so for the first time in some years there was a full Court.

John Marshall Harlan, in his seventy-eighth year, was the great gnarled oak of this Court. He was, to shift the figure, the Court's living link with the great men who achieved its resurgence after the Civil War —Samuel F. Miller, Stephen J. Field, Joseph P. Bradley. Harlan was born into a slaveholding Whig family in Kentucky. He supported the Bell-Everett ticket in 1860, served in the Union Army, became a Republican, and was appointed to the Supreme Court by President Hayes in 1877, at age forty-four. Perhaps his chief intellectual characteristic was vigor. His mind operated with large, simple ideas in the fundamentalist tradition, and he was something of a literalist. It was on a note of literalism that he ended, not "with a swan song but the roar of an angry lion,"[231] in his spectacular dissents in the *Standard Oil* and *Tobacco* antitrust cases.[232] Holmes' judgment, often voiced, was that Harlan, "that sage," while "a man of real power, did not shine either in analysis or generalization and I never troubled myself much when he shied. I used to say that he had a powerful vise the jaws of which couldn't be got nearer than two inches to each other."[233] A kindlier but not necessarily inconsistent view was expressed by Brewer on the occasion of the twenty-fifth anniversary of Harlan's appointment. Here is a nice mixture of irony, affection, and qualified admiration:

All men are said to have their hobbies. . . . Mr. Justice Harlan has a hobby . . . and that is the Constitution of the United States. He has read and studied it so assiduously that I think he can repeat it from one end to the other, forward and backward, and perhaps with equal comprehension either way. . . .

---

[230] W. Van Devanter to R. W. Breckons, Jan. 3, 1911, Van Devanter Papers.

[231] Hughes, *Biographical Notes,* 218, Hughes Papers.

[232] See *infra,* pp. 107 *et seq.,* 113 *et seq.*

[233] *Holmes-Pollock Letters,* II, 7.

> Some mistakes a man may never regret. Brother Harlan made a mistake in holding that the civil rights bill was constitutional. The Court said so. . . . But it was a mistake on the side of equal rights, and no act done or word said in behalf of liberty and equality ever fails to touch humanity with inspiring, prophetic thrill. . . .
>
> Mr. Justice Harlan . . . believes implicitly in the Constitution. He goes to bed every night with one hand on the Constitution and the other on the Bible, and so sleeps the sweet sleep of justice and righteousness. He believes in the Constitution as it was written; that the Constitution as it was must be the Constitution as it is, and the Constitution as it shall be. . . .[234]

As his service lengthened, Harlan became a famous, picturesque figure, enjoying the warm regard of the country. Early in 1911, he was described in a popular magazine as tall, with a "grey eagle of a face, surmounted by a massive dome of a head."[235] He was bald and had an enormous voice, and there were more stories about him than about the rest of the Court combined. Hughes remembered him as "somewhat overbearing yet warm-hearted,"[236] and the warmheartedness predominated in his cordial relations with many of his colleagues. He could be attentive, remembering the birthday of so junior a colleague as Van Devanter, a bare two months after the latter's accession, with a bunch of white sweet peas placed in front of Van Devanter on the bench.[237] Lurton was an old and intimate friend, as was Day. Harlan also quickly established pleasant relations with Lamar. To Hughes he was "like a father." But Harlan never hit it off with White, and there was scarcely any intimacy with Holmes, who would fend off Harlan's assaults in debate by referring to him as "my lionhearted friend."[238]

During the summer of 1910, McKenna had the impression that Harlan was not well. "He don't write as if he was in first rate health," McKenna told Day. "There is an undertone the other way."[239] Yet he seemed to Hughes little abated in vigor as the Court convened in October. The following fall, according to Van Devanter, he returned from his vacation "looking pretty well, although thinner than usual." But he was in Court for only two days, and on the second complained

[234] D. J. Brewer in *Dinner Given by the Bar of the Supreme Court of the United States to Mr. Justice John Marshall Harlan in Recognition of the Completion of Twenty-five Years of Distinguished Service on the Bench, December 9th, 1902,* 33–37.

[235] I. F. Marcosson, "The New Supreme Court," *Munsey's Magazine,* 44:No. 6, March 1911.

[236] Hughes, *Biographical Notes,* 218, Hughes Papers.

[237] W. Van Devanter to Mrs. J. W. Lacey, Apr. 19, 1911, Van Devanter Papers.

[238] Hughes, *Biographical Notes,* 216, Hughes Papers.

[239] J. McKenna to W. R. Day, Sept. 5, 1910, Day Papers.

of a stomachache. "During the day he seemed feeble and did some muttering while on the bench." When he left, he had trouble walking. "After that he seemed to be gradually failing and at times partially delirious, although his family were reluctant to admit that he was seriously ill."[240] He died within a few days, on October 14, 1911.

Harlan, as Attorney General Wickersham said speaking in tribute to his memory, "never well learned what it was to follow a leader. . . . Where others agreed with his views he would march with them, but when they differed he marched on alone. His was not the temper of the negotiator."[241] And he did not appreciate that temper in others. Thus in the spring of 1911, he complained to Hughes about "the serenity of the Court." There were too few dissents, he said, to suit him.[242]

During the October Term 1910, Harlan added to the immense body of work he left behind twenty majority and five dissenting opinions. He also filed during that term six additional dissents without writing. He was assigned none of the great cases of the term. But he did have occasion to uphold state regulations of railroads, of grain exchanges, and of insurance rates against Commerce Clause and Due Process claims.[243] All five of his dissenting opinions hold some interest. In one case, Day, for the majority, narrowly construed a District of Columbia statute aimed at allowing married women to sue in their own names and for their own benefit, as they were not capable of doing at common law. The statute, Day held, should not be read to authorize a wife's tort action against her husband, for such family suits had long been against the policy of the common law, and the legislature had not, after all, expressly authorized them. Bringing his literalism to the service of reform, Harlan, joined by Holmes and Hughes, supported the wife's right to sue by arguing that the broad statutory language allowed no room for "mere construction," and that considerations of policy were irrelevant, since courts make no law but merely apply it.[244] Two other cases involved a complicated dispute between a railroad, claiming under

---

[240] W. Van Devanter to E. B. Adams, Oct. 14, 1910, Van Devanter Papers.

[241] 222 U.S. xxiv (1912).

[242] Hughes, *Biographical Notes*, 218, Hughes Papers.

[243] Cincinnati, I. & W. Ry. Co. v. Connersville, 218 U.S. 336 (1910); Chicago, R.I. & Pacific Ry. v. Arkansas, 219 U.S. 453 (1911); House v. Mayes, 219 U.S. 270 (1911); Brodnax v. Missouri, 219 U.S. 285 (1911); German Alliance Ins. Co. v. Hale, 219 U.S. 307 (1911). Harlan had occasion to give strict application to federal railroad regulations. Louisville & Nashville R.R. v. Mottley, 219 U.S. 467 (1911); Chicago I. & L. Ry. v. United States, 219 U.S. 486 (1911); C. B. & Q. Ry. v. United States, 220 U.S. 559 (1911); Delk v. St. Louis & San Francisco R.R., 220 U.S. 580 (1911).

[244] Thompson v. Thompson, 218 U.S. 611, 621 (1910).

a federal land grant, and settlers, claiming under the Homestead Act. In an elaborate and on the whole rather persuasive dissent, in which he was joined by Day, Harlan contended for the settlers. These cases were argued twice, once at the last term before Fuller's death, and the second time in January 1911, after reconstitution of the Court. Harlan's dissents read very much as if they had initially been prepared as majority opinions, and it is quite possible that Harlan had previously carried a majority in a closely divided Court, and had lost it owing to the recent appointments.[245] Finally, there were the two celebrated dissents in the *Standard Oil* and *American Tobacco* cases. Harlan was alone in each. The *American Tobacco* dissent, the later of the two, delivered on May 29, 1911, was—fittingly—his last opinion. Among the dissents without opinion, one was for the defendant in a double jeopardy case.[246] Another, in pursuance of his dissent in *Hurtado* v. *California*, would have required grand juries in the Philippines under the due process clause of the Organic Act.[247] In a third case, he joined with Day in Hughes' dissent against a curiously emasculating construction by Holmes of the Pure Food Act of 1906.[248]

The next senior member after Harlan was Joseph McKenna. Born of Irish immigrant parents in Philadelphia on August 14, 1843, McKenna was taken to Benicia, a new community in northern California, when he was twelve. He attended a Catholic school in Philadelphia and both public and Catholic schools in California, was admitted to the bar, shortly thereafter became District Attorney (being elected as a Republican), served also in the state Assembly, married Amanda Frances Bornemann of San Francisco in 1879, and, on a third attempt, was elected to Congress in 1884. McKenna was reelected three times. In his next to last term he became a member of the Ways and Means Committee, where a friendship with the chairman, William McKinley, ripened. Another close friend was Senator Leland Stanford. Owing perhaps to this latter friendship, and to a number of McKenna's votes in the House favoring railroads in general and the Southern Pacific in particular, McKenna acquired something of a reputation for railroad connections.

With Stanford's support, McKenna was appointed to the Court of Appeals for the Ninth Circuit by President Harrison, and took his seat in March 1892. McKinley made him Attorney General in 1897, and by then the succession to the aging and failing Justice Stephen J. Field of

---

[245] Weyerhaeuser v. Hoyt, 219 U.S. 380 (1911); Northern Pacific Ry. Co. v. Wass, 219 U.S. 426 (1911).

[246] Gavieres v. United States, 220 U.S. 338 (1911).

[247] Dowdell v. United States, 221 U.S. 325 (1911); cf. Hurtado v. California, 110 U.S. 516 (1884).

[248] United States v. Johnson, 221 U.S. 488 (1911).

California was plainly in the offing.[249] Within a year, McKenna did replace Field, taking his seat on January 26, 1898. In twelve years on the Court, McKenna had stilled the fears of those who thought him a reactionary servant of the railroads, but he had kindled no large enthusiasms anywhere. His course had been the vacillating one of the Court itself. He staked out perhaps his clearest individual position in his dissent in *Adair* v. *United States*.[250] His dissent in *De Lima* v. *Bidwell* was in line with White's concurrence in the *Insular Cases*, which McKenna joined.[251] In *Weems* v. *United States*, which dealt with the seldom-invoked Cruel and Unusual Punishment Clause of the Eighth Amendment, he took a sophisticated view of the role of language and history in constitutional construction.[252] In such celebrated great cases as the *Northern Securities* case and *Lochner* v. *New York* and *Muller* v. *Oregon*, McKenna was with the majority.[253]

McKenna was a small, bearded, birdlike man, who carried himself stiffly erect. His mother, he once said, "put a stick down my back to keep me straight."[254] In his old age, according to the recollection of Dean Acheson, who knew the Court of the early 1920s, "he always wore rubbers, a white scarf and an overcoat at all times of the year, it made no difference at all."[255] Holmes, who had his difficulties with him, and with whom McKenna engaged in a preposterous little competition of speed in opinion writing,[256] spoke of him as a "truly kind soul" and remarked on his "sweet nature."[257] Hughes remembered him as mild mannered and friendly. "He had little to say in conference—was hesitant to express a definite view, often saying that he would prefer not to vote until he could see the opinion."[258]

After Harlan's death, the spare little McKenna occupied the senior's chair to the right of the massive Chief Justice. On White's left, the contrast was symbolic rather than physical. Here, next to the ex-Confederate, sat Holmes, thrice-wounded Union veteran. At sixty-nine, Holmes was handsome, dashing, gay, vital, charming. His hair and mustache were graying, but not yet white, and his reputation was not yet what it would be. Nearly thirty years after publication of *The Common Law* and after his first judicial appointment, the public hardly

---

[249] See F. E. Warren to W. Van Devanter, Mar. 10, 1897, Van Devanter Papers.

[250] 208 U.S. 161 (1908). McKenna also joined the dissent in the First Employers' Liability Cases, 207 U.S. 463 (1908).

[251] 182 U.S. 1, 244 (1901).

[252] 217 U.S. 349 (1910).

[253] See generally M. McDevitt, Joseph McKenna (1946).

[254] McDevitt, *McKenna*, 13.

[255] D. Acheson, "Justice Is a Method," *Record of N.Y.C.B.A.*, 12: 143, 147–48, 1957.

[256] See *infra*, pp. 241 *et seq.*

[257] *Holmes-Laski Letters,* II, 896; *ibid.*, I, 693.

[258] Hughes, *Biographical Notes*, 220, Hughes Papers.

knew him. What it thought it knew was that he was aloof, a Massa-chusetts intellectual and scholar, the son of his famous father, and an old soldier with a cavalry mustache.[259] There was some slight impression abroad—despite the dissent in the *Northern Securities* case, and owing perhaps to the dissent in *Lochner* v. *New York*—that Holmes was to be classed as a progressive judge.[260] But it was a vague, ill-formed, and not widespread impression. In professional circles, to be sure, and among his colleagues, there was recognition, to a degree, of Holmes' stature. Holmes was the "best intellectual machine," said Brandeis little more than a decade later. He added that he had thought so forty years before.[261]

Yet in his seventieth year, even among his professional peers, the general acknowledgment of greatness was still to come for Holmes, and he himself felt its absence rather painfully. He was, then as now, often charged with obscurity and with a disinclination to take particular facts into account, but the charge counted more heavily then. Urging acceptance by the President's son Robert of the post of law clerk to Holmes for the year 1913–14, the renowned John Chipman Gray of the Harvard Law School wrote to Taft: "As you know, Judge Holmes' opinions seem sometimes to lack lucidity, but I have known him intimately since boyhood, and I know of no one whose talk on the law is so illuminating." Robert and the President concurred in a decision that it was better "to get started permanently at once in Cincinnati." The experience with Holmes, the President thought, would not add much to what Robert had acquired at Harvard.[262] Holmes in 1910, as we now know, was almost all that he would be, lacking only the magnificence of very great age. But no one yet was writing that to know him "was to have had a revelation of the possibilities . . . of human personality."[263] No one was yet regarding him as "a significant figure in the history of civilization and not merely a commanding American figure."[264] And Benjamin Cardozo's later judgment of Holmes as "probably the greatest legal intellect in the

[259] See E. F. Baldwin, "The Supreme Court Justices," *The Outlook*, 97:156, 158, Jan. 28, 1911; Lowry, *Men of the Supreme Court*, 631.

[260] See, e.g., D. G. Phillips, "The Treason of the Senate," *Cosmopolitan*, 41:368, August 1906; "Books and Things," *The New Republic*, 3:100, May 29, 1915; W. L. (Walter Lippmann), "Mr. Justice Holmes," *The New Republic*, 6:156, Mar. 11, 1916.

[261] Brandeis-Frankfurter Conversa-tions, Brandeis Papers, Harvard Law School Library.

[262] R. A. Taft to W. H. Taft, n.d.; J. C. Gray to W. H. Taft, Nov. 9, 1912; W. H. Taft to R. A. Taft, Nov. 19, 1912, Taft Papers.

[263] M. R. Cohen, *The New Republic*, 82:206, Apr. 3, 1935.

[264] F. Frankfurter, *Mr. Justice Holmes and the Supreme Court* (Belknap Press ed., 1961), 3.

history of the English-speaking judiciary" had not yet been rendered.[265]

Holmes was born on March 8, 1841, in Boston, descendant of a long line of Olivers and Wendells as well as Holmeses, and grandson, on his mother's side, of Charles Jackson, an Associate Justice of the Supreme Judicial Court of Massachusetts. After private schooling, he entered Harvard, and left in April 1861 to go south with the Army of the Potomac. He was wounded at Ball's Bluff, Antietam, and Fredericksburg, and returned to the Harvard Law School for a two-year course leading to an LL.B. in the fall of 1864. He then combined practice in Boston with intensive scholarship until the publication, in 1881, of *The Common Law*, which was quickly followed by appointments to the Harvard Law School faculty, and in turn to the Supreme Judicial Court of Massachusetts, where Holmes took his seat on January 3, 1883. In August 1899, he became Chief Justice of Massachusetts. Holmes had married Fanny Bowditch Dixwell, daughter of the headmaster of one of the private schools he had attended, in 1872. They were childless.

Holmes was of the Boston elite and had ties of mutual affection and esteem with the British aristocracy, but "he was a Bostonian apart."[266] And there were opinions he rendered on the Massachusetts court, particularly in a celebrated labor case,[267] that disturbed members of his caste in Boston. But although apart, a Bostonian Holmes remained. When in August 1912 President Taft was, as he said, "in the throes of giving birth to a United States District Judge in your State and Circuit," he worried about a feeling in Massachusetts that there might have been too many appointments from "the Brahmin class" of Back Bay rather than from the state at large, and he asked Holmes for advice. "So far as I know," Holmes replied, "in the state courts at least, there has been too little rather than too much [Back Bay in appointments]. Men to whom all ideas and all books come easy rarely are found outside that class, so far as I have seen."[268]

Holmes came to the Supreme Court of the United States on December 8, 1902, in succession to Horace Gray of Massachusetts. President McKinley had intended to put Alfred Hemenway of the Boston Bar in this place, but Gray's resignation was delayed, and the appointment fell to Theodore Roosevelt, who was on the lookout for a progressive judge, and was soon to be disappointed by the dissent in the *Northern Securities* case.[269] Thus fortuitously Holmes was assured

---

[265] See Frankfurter, *Holmes and the Supreme Court,* 29.

[266] *Ibid.,* 2.

[267] Vegelahn v. Guntner, 167 Mass. 92, 104 (1896).

[268] O. W. Holmes to W. H. Taft, Aug. 6, 1912, Taft Papers.

[269] See Frankfurter, *Holmes and the Supreme Court,* 18.

continuation on a larger stage of a career in the law whose "chief interest" was "the effort to show the universal in the particular. That has kept me alive. . . ."[270]

William Rufus Day, the other of Theodore Roosevelt's appointees remaining on the Court in 1910, was a thin, frail-looking, bony man with a large head. Holmes once referred to one of Day's stalwart sons as a block off the old chip.[271] Day, whom Hughes recalled as "mentally very vigorous, clear in his views and precise in his statements, while enlivening his discussions with a ready wit,"[272] was, like McKenna, a friend of William McKinley, but a friend of longer standing and more intimate involvement. When Brandeis came to know Day, he thought him a man of intense feelings, as evidenced, among other things, by his devotion to McKinley. Throughout his tenure on the Court, Day always gave each Justice a carnation on McKinley's birthday. Brandeis said of him after his death that he had found him vivid and determined in discussion.[273] On other, less guarded occasions, Brandeis called him "a fighter, a regular game cock," and again "a hot little gent."[274] Day was a public figure of some note as a former Secretary of State; and he was known also as perhaps the most avid baseball fan on the Court, a familiar fixture at Washington games.[275]

Day was born in Ravenna, Ohio, on April 17, 1849. His father was Chief Justice of Ohio. The family had New England origins and a strong antislavery tradition. Both of Day's grandfathers left the Democratic for the Republican Party on the slavery issue. Speaking in his native town in 1910, Day recalled agitation he had witnessed as a boy against the Fugitive Slave Act, which his people deemed a usurpation of federal power. No doubt the memory of this early experience predisposed him toward securing for the states a fair area of autonomy. But the antislavery tradition must have nurtured his nationalism, and it cannot be said that he ever achieved a harmonious accommodation between these two divergent tendencies in his heritage.

Day received a bachelor's degree from the University of Michigan, read law privately as well as spending a year at the law school of that university, and, being admitted to the bar in Canton, Ohio, at the age of twenty-three, practiced there continuously for a quarter of a century. It was a varied trial practice. In 1875, Day married Mary Elizabeth

---

[270] O. W. Holmes to M. R. Cohen, Aug. 31, 1920, *Journal of the History of Ideas*, 9:22, January 1948.

[271] See Hughes, *Biographical Notes*, 220, Hughes Papers.

[272] *Ibid.*

[273] See J. E. McLean, *William Rufus Day—Supreme Court Justice from Ohio* (1946), 62.

[274] Brandeis-Frankfurter Conversations.

[275] See McLean, *Day*, 62–63.

Schaefer of Canton, who had a friend who married another young lawyer in town, William McKinley. Day was McKinley's intimate in matters legal, personal, and political. For six months in 1886, Day was a judge of the Court of Common Pleas. In 1889, President Harrison appointed him to the U.S. district court, but Day declined, being then in uncertain health. McKinley's election in 1896 brought Day into the limelight. It was widely assumed that he would serve in Washington under his friend. The Solicitor Generalship would be a likely place for him, it was first thought, and in April 1897, Day received a long letter from Judge William H. Taft, of the U.S. Court of Appeals for the Sixth Circuit, himself a former Solicitor General, urging him to take that important office.

In December 1897, Day said publicly that he had declined the succession to McKenna as Attorney General. At this time, Day was First Assistant Secretary of State under the old and rather inactive John Sherman, having agreed to accept this position in April 1897, obviously out of a desire to assist McKinley in difficult circumstances. Day was to all intents and purposes the head of the department, and in April of the following year, upon Sherman's resignation, became so in name as well. At the end of the Spanish-American War, he resigned as Secretary of State but headed the U.S. delegation to the peace conference in Paris. There was scarcely a pause between his completion of this task and his appointment by McKinley, in February 1899, as a judge of the U.S. Court of Appeals for the Sixth Circuit.[276]

On February 19, 1903, Theodore Roosevelt nominated Day for the Supreme Court. To announce the nomination, Roosevelt resorted to the simple but dramatic expedient of beginning his address to a McKinley Memorial Association meeting in Canton, at which Day was present, as follows: "Mr. Toastmaster, Mr. Justice Day."[277] Day was promptly confirmed, and he was seated on March 2, 1903. The place had been vacated by the retirement of Justice George Shiras, Jr., of Pennsylvania. Roosevelt had wanted Taft for it, but the latter would not leave his post in the Philippines just then. Partly perhaps because it was McKinley's known intention to make this appointment, Day was Roosevelt's second choice.[278] And there was no cause for regret. The "good Day," as Roosevelt called him,[279] made, if anything, rather a progressive record in his first decade or so of service. It must indeed have found more favor in Roosevelt's eyes than Holmes' record, for Day not only

---

[276] *Ibid.*, 158, 13–53; W. H. Taft to W. R. Day, Apr. 22, 1897, Taft Papers.

[277] McLean, *Day,* 54. Interview with Luther Day, Apr. 26, 1960.

[278] See W. Van Devanter to F. B. Kellogg, Jan. 28, 1903, Van Devanter Papers.

[279] Pringle, *Taft,* I, 252.

joined Holmes' dissent in *Lochner* v. *New York* but was with the majority in the *Northern Securities* case.

On the "learned Sixth Circuit,"[280] as the Justices now called it with as much affection as irony, Day's tenure had briefly overlapped the first judicial career of William Howard Taft. Throughout his four years there, Day had sat with Lurton, with whom he was happily re-united early in 1910 by the appointment that their former colleague Taft made from the heart.[281] Horace Harmon Lurton was a Kentuckian by birth and an underage Confederate volunteer by conviction. He was born in Newport, Kentucky, on February 26, 1844. His father, Lycurgus L. Lurton, was a physician and Episcopal clergyman. Early in the life of Horace the family moved to Clarksville, Tennessee. From there, after private schooling, Lurton, in 1859, went north to the old University of Chicago, where the outbreak of the Civil War found him before he had obtained a degree. The young Lurton was hot with secessionist spirit. In the summer of 1861, he wrote a friend: "I am sorry to own that I am a Kentuckian. I wish I was a South Carolinian."[282] Shortly there-after, aged seventeen, he enlisted in the Confederate Army. He fought at Fort Donelson and was captured and sent north to Camp Chase, near Columbus, Ohio. At Donelson, Lurton was doubly a volunteer, for on February 4, 1862, he had been discharged from the Confederate Army for medical reasons. Donelson was a battle he wandered into from his nearby home in Clarksville, on his own, wearing his old uniform.[283] Lurton either escaped or was released from Camp Chase,[284] but only to reenlist, this time under General John H. Morgan, and to be captured once more on a raid into Ohio in 1863. His imprisonment now lasted until nearly 1865.[285]

---

[280] Hughes, *Biographical Notes,* 220, Hughes Papers.

[281] See *supra,* pp. 8–9.

[282] H. H. Lurton to "Friend Anderson," June 2, 1861, Lurton Papers.

[283] See S. B. Buckner to G. N. Cullom, Feb. 19, 1862, Lurton Papers.

[284] According to the recollection of his intimate friend Jacob M. Dickinson, Lurton escaped. It may be, however, that he was released as an underage civilian, pursuant to a written request from Confederate General S. B. Buckner, which is preserved in the Lurton Papers together with an endorsement recommending the release, dated Headquarters, District Western Tennessee, Fort Donelson, Feb. 19, 1862, and signed U. S. Grant, Brigadier General. Lurton Papers, Library of Congress. This request, with its endorsement, was sent after Lurton from Donelson to Cairo, Illinois. Perhaps it did not follow him to Camp Chase. But in that case, how did it finally come into his hand?

[285] He was set free, so at least he himself believed, pursuant to an order of President Lincoln obtained by his mother, who, after persistent effort, was able to see the President and add an incident to his legend. See 237 U.S. vii, xxiv. Efforts by Lurton to find in the War Department files the Lincoln order that released him were continual, but never successful.

I: *Mr. Taft Rehabilitates the Court*

After the war, Lurton took a law degree at Cumberland University in Lebanon, Tennessee, and in the same year—1867—married Mary Frances Owen of Lebanon. A general practice in Clarksville followed, interrupted from 1875 to 1878 by service as a chancellor in the Tennessee judiciary. In 1886, Lurton became a Justice of the Supreme Court of Tennessee, where he remained until April 1893, when he took office by appointment of President Cleveland as a judge of the United States Court of Appeals for the Sixth Circuit. During the last four months of his service in Tennessee, Lurton was Chief Justice. From 1898 until his promotion from the Sixth Circuit to the Supreme Court, Lurton was also professor of constitutional law at Vanderbilt University, and for the last five years of his tenure there, he served as dean of the Law School.[286]

Lurton sought the Supreme Court nomination, which came to him on December 13, 1909, quite actively, his chief agent being his friend Jacob M. Dickinson, who was Taft's first Secretary of War. The problem was not so much to persuade the President to make the appointment— despite his lifelong adherence to the Democratic party, Lurton had reason to be confident that his former colleague, the President, wished to appoint him—as to neutralize or forestall possible opposition in the Senate. It was necessary to counter the objections of Samuel Gompers, of the president of the Brotherhood of Railroad Trainmen, and of such a Progressive as Edward A. Moseley, Secretary of the Interstate Commerce Commission, who wrote the President that Lurton had never spoken a word "in recognition of the right of those who toil." The effort to overcome this opposition—an effort in which the services of Justice Harlan were also enlisted—was successful, and on January 3, 1910, Lurton, nearing sixty-six, the oldest man ever to be appointed an Associate Justice, took his seat on the Supreme Court.[287]

Lurton was "a chunky, grey-headed, grizzly, genial man, patently Southern," seldom ruffled, ever courteous and companionable.[288] Hughes thought him "a typical judge of the old school, solid, experienced, deliberate and conservative."[289] As a professional judge, crusty and unbending in his independence, Lurton lectured the country, in a paper published in January 1911 under the title "A Government of Law or a

---

[286] See *Dictionary of American Biography* (1933), 9:509.

[287] H. H. Lurton to J. M. Dickinson, Nov. 22, 25, 1909; E. A. Moseley to W. H. Taft, Nov. 22, 1909; W. G. Lee to Taft, Dec. 7, 1909; J. M. Harlan to Taft, Dec. 13, 1909, Lurton Papers. Lurton to W. Van Devanter, Dec. 3, 1909; Lurton to Taft, Dec. 23, 1909, Lurton Papers.

[288] Lowry, *Men of the Supreme Court,* 631. Interview of Charles Fairman with Harvey D. Jacob, June 25, 1936.

[289] Hughes, *Biographical Notes,* 220, Hughes Papers.

Government of Men," on the duty of courts not to "yield to the clamor of a temporary majority." If courts were to relax constitutional restraints, the result would be a government of men and not of laws, contrary to Montesquieu's beneficent teaching: "It is against this that I warn." The Supreme Court was not, as some thought, a continuous constitutional convention. The function of courts was to enforce the Constitution as it stood, and to engage in interpretation only when its language was doubtful, but even then only in interpretation, never in legislation.

> That this function [of judicial review] should not be understood by the millions who have come among us from lands where constitutional limitations are either unknown or are unenforceable for lack of any definite means of compelling obedience and therefore regarded as an exercise of legislative power, is not strange.

Having thus educated the great unwashed by rattling the constitutional and judicial sabre, Lurton changed course and concluded with an indication of the necessary limits of judicial power. It was as if the stern judge, after demonstrating that he was not to be intimidated, suddenly drew his audience closer, to share with it some of the difficulties of his task, and even perhaps some doubts. This portion of the paper was clearly inspired by the counsels of restraint of such commentators as James Bradley Thayer. Lurton deplored the expectation that courts existed to cure any and all vicious laws. Legislators also take a constitutional oath and have their proper responsibilities, he said, and for judges, the best way to secure the repeal of a vicious law was to enforce it. The constitutional power of the judges should be invoked only in extreme cases, when the legislature has made an egregious error.[290]

Lurton's work as a circuit judge bears out the self-portrait in his 1911 paper, just summarized, and also Hughes' characterization of him as a "judge of the old school." The style of his opinions, here as later, is plain enough, unpretentious, but not exactly unobtrusive. It is rather an assertive style, very self-assured, and sounding a note of finality, as in a military command; not a style suited to many compositions other than appellate decisions.[291] In substance, the conservatism Hughes noted

---

[290] H. H. Lurton, "A Government of Law or a Government of Men," *North American Review*, 193:9, 20, 12, 19, January 1911.

[291] The contrast, in Bleistein v. Donaldson Lithographing Co., 188 U.S. 239 (1903), *reversing* 104 Fed. 993 (6th Cir. 1900) between Circuit Judge Lurton and Mr. Justice Holmes

is instructive. In a workaday opinion, reviewing some cases and then asserting his result with the usual finality, Lurton decided that lithographs depicting for advertising purposes some of the acts in Wallace's Circus were not copyrightable. "Aside from this function as advertisements," Lurton said, "we are unable to discover that

is present without being either oppressive or unrelieved. It is a little difficult to see why Lurton in particular should have been singled out by Progressives as never having had a good word to say for the laboring man.[292] A judge like Lurton hardly ever had a good word to say for anyone—it was a stern code he saw himself as administering. Besides, reading the accusation very broadly, as it was doubtless intended, it is not altogether just.

Lurton's record in personal injury cases against railroads and the like was mixed and proves nothing,[293] but he tried—until the Supreme Court stopped him[294]—to construe a federal statute allowing suits *in*

---

they have any use whatever, or that they have any intrinsic merit or value." 104 Fed. at 994. This provoked from Holmes, reversing, an utterly Holmesian opinion in both style and substance. These lithographs, Holmes wrote, even if mere copies from life (which they weren't actually) are "the personal reaction of an individual upon nature. Personality always contains something unique . . . and a very modest grade of art has in it something irreducible, which is one man's alone." 188 U.S. at 250. It is not for judges—"persons trained only to the law," 188 U.S. at 251—to pass on artistic worth. That these lithographs have their value is proved by the desire of others to reproduce them, and "the taste of any public is not to be treated with contempt. It is an ultimate fact for the moment, whatever may be our hopes for a change." 188 U.S. at 252. The opinion bristles with references to Velásquez, Whistler, Rembrandt, Steinla's engraving of the Madonna di San Sisto, Goya, Manet. "A rule," Holmes says at one point, "cannot be laid down that would excommunicate the paintings of Degas." 188 U.S. at 251. And there is a quotation from Ruskin. The whole thing, of course, runs to no more than four pages. There follows a brief dissent by Harlan, whom McKenna joined. Harlan contents himself with quoting from Lurton's opinion below, which was concurred in also by Judge Day. This lineup of

judges speaks worlds. Of all his colleagues, Harlan and McKenna seemed to find Holmes' many-colored feathers least engaging. Now it was almost as if, calling the lower-court worthies to their aid, Harlan and McKenna were resisting what Holmes was conceding even to their "very modest grade of art"—"something irreducible, which is one man's alone"; and at the same time insisting on the power, which Holmes abjured (as perhaps just a little beneath him?), to judge with contempt and finality "the taste of any public."

[292] See *supra*, p. 75, n.287.

[293] *Compare* Chesapeake & Ohio R.R. v. Hennessey, 96 Fed. 713 (6th Cir. 1899); Louisville & Nashville R.R. v. Stuber, 108 Fed. 934 (6th Cir. 1901), *cert. denied*, 183 U.S. 698 (1901); Butts v. Cleveland, C.C. & St. L. R.R., 110 Fed. 329 (6th Cir. 1901); and Norfolk & Western Ry. Co. v. Gesswine, 144 Fed. 56 (6th Cir. 1906), *with* Cincinnati, N. O. & T. P. Ry. Co. v. Farra, 66 Fed. 496 (6th Cir. 1895); Chesapeake & Ohio Ry. Co. v. Steele, 84 Fed. 93 (6th Cir. 1898); Chesapeake & Ohio Ry. Co. v. King, 99 Fed. 251 (6th Cir. 1900); and Choctaw, O. & G. R.R. v. McDade, 112 Fed. 888 (6th Cir. 1902), *affirmed*, 191 U.S. 64 (1903).

[294] Bradford v. Southern Ry. Co., 195 U.S. 243 (1904), *answering question certified in* 139 Fed. 518 (6th Cir. 1905).

forma pauperis as applicable to appellate proceedings. These, he said, clearly bending somewhat, "are within the equity of the statute, and not excluded by its letter."[295] It is even possible to discern the thinnest trace of Populism in a series of cases involving county bonds, in which Lurton took positions against the creditors.[296] He gave some hospitable constructions to federal regulatory statutes,[297] but balked at imposing broad absolute liability on railroads under the Safety Appliance Act.[298]

Lurton applied the Sherman Antitrust Act in two private suits, one a treble-damage action,[299] the other a contract case,[300] and he concurred in Taft's landmark opinion in *United States* v. *Addyston Pipe & Steel Co.*[301] He also struck down resale price maintenance agreements in *John D. Park & Sons Co.* v. *Hartman*,[302] writing an opinion

---

[295] Reed v. Pennsylvania Co., 111 Fed. 714, 715 (6th Cir. 1901). The statute in question was the Act of July 20, 1892, 27 Stat. 252.

[296] Provident Trust Co. v. Mercer Cty., 72 Fed. 623 (6th Cir. 1896), *reversed*, 170 U.S. 593 (1898); Campbellsville Lumber Co. v. Hubbert, 112 Fed. 718 (6th Cir. 1902), *affirmed*, 191 U.S. 70 (1903); Quinlan v. Greene Cty., 157 Fed. 33, 43 (6th Cir. 1907) (Lurton, J., dissenting), *affirmed*, 211 U.S. 582 (1909); and see Greene County v. Thomas' Executor, 211 U.S. 598 (1909); *affirming* 146 Fed. 969 (6th Cir. 1906). But see Owensboro v. Cumberland Tel. Co., 230 U.S. 58 (1913).

[297] Newport News & M. V. Co. v. United States, 61 Fed. 488 (6th Cir. 1894); Coopersville Co-operative Creamery Co. v. Lemon, 163 Fed. 145 (6th Cir. 1908). And see Scranton v. Wheeler, 57 Fed. 803 (6th Cir. 1893), *reversed*, 163 U.S. 703 (1896). As to state statutes, two Commerce Clause decisions deserve notice. In Sanford v. Poe, 69 Fed. 546 (6th Cir. 1895), *affirmed sub nom.* Adams Express Co. v. Ohio State Auditor, 165 U.S. 194 (1897), Lurton upheld a property tax which White, Field, Harlan, and Brown, JJ., would have struck down. 165 U.S. at 229. In Sawrie v. Tennessee, 82 Fed. 615 (6th Cir. 1897), Lurton declared uncon-

stitutional an outright prohibition on the importation or sale of cigarettes. "I reach this conclusion," he said characteristically, "without hesitation, though reluctant to even partially [as applied to imports in the original package] strike down a statute aimed at the suppression of an evil of most pronounced character." 82 Fed. at 623.

[298] St. Louis & San Francisco R.R. v. Delk, 158 Fed. 931, 939 (6th Cir. 1908) (Lurton, J., concurring), *reversed*, 220 U.S. 580 (1911). On the Supreme Court, Lurton recused himself in this case, as in others where he had written below, e.g., Dr. Miles Medical Co. v. Park & Sons Co., *infra*, n.303, but he went along silently with the majority in a companion case holding to the same effect on the absolute liability point. Chicago, B. & Q. Ry. Co. v. United States, 220 U.S. 559 (1911).

[299] City of Atlanta v. Chattanooga Foundry & Pipe Works, 127 Fed. 23 (6th Cir. 1903), *affirmed*, 203 U.S. 390 (1906).

[300] Continental Wall Paper Co. v. Voight & Sons Co., 148 Fed. 939 (6th Cir. 1906), *affirmed*, 212 U.S. 227 (1909).

[301] 85 Fed. 271 (6th Cir. 1898), *affirmed*, 175 U.S. 211 (1899).

[302] 153 Fed. 24 (6th Cir. 1907), *dismissed*, 212 U.S. 588 (1908).

later quoted and followed by the Supreme Court in *Dr. Miles Medical Co.* v. *Park & Sons Co.*, which Lurton had also decided below.[303] But he held that the owner of a patent could impose tie-in sales as a condition on the use by anyone of the patented article, and later made a temporary majority for this position on a divided Supreme Court, and like Van Devanter, would have held also that resale price maintenance agreements were valid if they involved a patented article.[304] Finally, he sounded more than a little Confederate as he gave a grudging reading to the Fifteenth Amendment, and freely held sections of the last of the Reconstruction Civil Rights Acts unconstitutional in two cases exemplifying methods by which black people were disfranchised in his native Kentucky.[305] In one of these cases, the Supreme Court denied certiorari. But in both, Lurton reversed verdicts of guilty that had been obtained from Kentucky juries. In both, Day of the antislavery family background was on the Sixth Circuit bench and concurred without a word. Yet Day eventually went on to write *Buchanan* v. *Warley*.[306] The dates of Lurton's cases, to be sure, were 1901 and 1903, and it may be thought that Lurton, like Day for the moment, though unlike the two Kentucky juries, was merely in tune with the times. But there is later evidence,[307] though slender, indicating that this would be too charitable a view of Lurton's attitude on questions of race.[308]

White, Holmes, Harlan, McKenna, Day, Lurton, Hughes, Van Devanter, Lamar—this, then, was the Court as of January 1911, and aside from the lion-hearted Harlan, so soon to depart, it was a Court that could be expected to remain stable for some years, and to give unimpaired service. Moreover, the Chief Justiceship having been settled, the atmosphere that had seemed so strained to Hughes when he arrived in October relaxed. White, Hughes recalled, "assumed his new duties with manifest pleasure and with a most earnest desire to discharge them

---

[303] 220 U.S. 373, 399 (1911), *affirming* 164 Fed. 803 (6th Cir. 1908).

[304] Heaton-Peninsular Button-Fastener Co. v. Eureka Specialty Co., 77 Fed. 288 (6th Cir. 1896); Henry v. Dick Co., 224 U.S. 1 (1912), *overruled,* Motion Picture Co. v. Universal Film Co., 243 U.S. 502 (1917); Bauer & Cie v. O'Donnell, 229 U.S. 1 (1913) (McKenna, Holmes, Lurton, and Van Devanter, JJ., dissenting).

[305] Lackey v. United States, 107 Fed. 114 (6th Cir. 1901), *cert. denied,* 181 U.S. 621 (1901); Karem v. United States, 121 Fed. 250 (6th Cir. 1903).

[306] 245 U.S. 60 (1917).

[307] See *infra,* p. 339.

[308] Lurton's opinions as a judge of the Sixth Circuit may be found in Volumes 58–175 of the *Federal Reporter.* His judgments were affirmed by the Supreme Court fourteen times, and reversed in eight instances—not an overwhelmingly favorable record. Lurton's luck with the few of his Sixth Circuit cases still pending after he himself came to the Supreme Court was markedly worse than his prior average. He suffered three reversals and saw himself affirmed once.

well. He was no longer distant or difficult. On the contrary, he was most considerate and gracious in his dealings with every member of the Court, plainly anxious to create an atmosphere of friendliness and to promote agreement in the disposition of cases." In short, "we became a reasonably happy family."[309]

The family's material circumstances were those of genteel poverty. Its home since December 1860 was the old Senate chamber, a room capable of evoking, of course, many a great moment in the history of the Republic. For the Court, it "combined dignity with truly republican simplicity."[310] It was small, and the bench of judges stood out and dominated it. At the same time a certain intimacy was possible between the judges and their audience, especially the bar sitting immediately below the bench. A Court accustomed to frequent questioning of counsel, as this one always has been, could make the argument of a case seem, in the words of a contemporaneous observer, "like a confidential conversation."[311] Moreover, the Court had its being in the midst of the hustle and bustle of Congress, and thus appeared in closer connection with the responsible institutions of a popular government.[312] And like the Senators and Congressmen, the Justices could be observed at short range and in friendly fashion by the people who flocked through the Capitol, especially in the spring.

The courtroom was on the east side of the main corridor of the Capitol. The Clerk's office and a robing room were on the west side. The Court's sessions began at 12 o'clock sharp, to run (as has been the procedure since 1898)[313] for four hours, with a half-hour break for lunch between 2:00 and 2:30. Just before 12 o'clock, attendants would come out to separate the crowd and rope off a passageway across the corridor, through which the robed Justices then marched in a line to the courtroom, the Chief Justice at their head. This was a well-attended show. A man in the crowd of bystanders was once heard to remark, in utmost seriousness and awe, "Christ, what dignity!"[314]

The Capitol courtroom was loved by many, on and off the Court, and its location deemed an important asset. Chief Justice White always resisted any thought of a move, fearing, among other things, that the Court would be forgotten by the people if it left the Capitol.[315] This was

[309] Hughes, *Biographical Notes*, 217–18, Hughes Papers.

[310] D. Acheson, *Morning and Noon* (1965), 56.

[311] Baldwin, *Supreme Court Justices*, 159.

[312] Acheson, *Morning and Noon*, 144.

[313] See C. E. Cropley to J. C. Mc-

Reynolds, May 29, 1931, McReynolds Papers, Library of the University of Virginia (hereinafter cited as McReynolds Papers).

[314] See W. H. Taft to F. L. Bowman, Feb. 6, 1929, Taft Papers.

[315] See Hughes, *Biographical Notes*, 206–207, Hughes Papers.

obviously a groundless worry, and yet surely the judges seem more remote now, out of "that wonderful old courtroom in the Capitol, which I think," said a later Justice, "it was almost a desecration of tradition to leave."[316] But there were disadvantages also. The courtroom was badly ventilated and ill-lit. The Clerk's quarters were inadequate. There was no room provided for the bar. The library and conference room, in the basement, was small, cluttered, and extremely ill-ventilated. During long conferences, Hughes recalled years later, "the room became overheated and the air foul . . . not conducive to good humor." Hughes added: "I suppose that no high court in the country had fewer conveniences."[317]

At this time, no office space at all was made available to the Justices in Washington.[318] They all had to maintain chambers in their homes, the government providing a $2,000 furniture allowance, as well as the rudiments of a working law library,[319] for each Justice, and carrying reasonable maintenance and repair expenses.[320] Communica-

---

[316] F. Frankfurter, *Of Law and Men*, P. Elman, ed. (1956), 112.

[317] Hughes, *Biographical Notes,* 206–207, Hughes Papers.

[318] Day maintained modest office space in the post office building in Canton, where he stayed and worked in the fall, after returning from summers in Canada. But he had to fight for the space. By 1914, he was reduced to a single room. W. R. Day to G. H. Clark, Dec. 18, 24, 1912; Day to D. R. Newton, Oct. 16, 1914; Newton to Day, Oct. 28, 1914; Day to W. D. Caldwell, Nov. 3, 1914, Day Papers, Library of Congress. The office space which Day was fighting to retain had originally been assigned to him when he was a judge of the Sixth Circuit resident in Canton. There is no evidence that other Justices had any office space made available to them in their hometowns. With the later exception of Clarke, who like Day returned to Ohio from time to time, the others stayed either in Washington or at summer retreats.

[319] As late as 1921, the total annual appropriation for the purchase of books by the Marshal of the Supreme Court was $2,000. It was customary to use one-half the amount for purchases for the Conference Room library, and the other for the upkeep of the nine sets of books used by the Justices. As some of the Justices rarely made requisition on these funds, Taft at his accession as Chief Justice in 1921 was able to draw on $350 to $400 for the purchase of books for his working library. See F. K. Green to W. H. Taft, Aug. 17, 1921, Taft Papers, Library of Congress.

"You would be disappointed," Van Devanter wrote his friend District Judge Riner of Wyoming, a couple of weeks after taking his seat, "if you were to see the imperfect and dilapidated set of books which they tendered to me. Half of them were returned as utterly of no value. Even the set of the Federal Reporter is incomplete. I will have to have my library shipped here before long." W. Van Devanter to W. Riner, Jan. 16, 1911, Van Devanter Papers, Library of Congress.

[320] *Ibid.,* 207–208; see J. M. Wright to W. R. Day, July 16, 1909, Day Papers. F. J. Green to W. H. Taft, Aug. 16, 1921, Taft Papers.

tion among the Justices was by messenger, later, for some at least, by telephone, by personal calls on each other, which were not overly difficult as the homes of many were clustered in a fairly small area in northwest Washington,[321] on walks or rides to the Capitol together, and, of course, ultimately at conference. But each man's working day was spent at home.

By way of assistance, in addition to a messenger, the Justices, since 1886, were provided with $2,000 a year each to pay a secretary or clerk.[322] Most of the Justices hired male stenographic secretaries. Generally, these men were also lawyers or law students. They were expected to stay on for a few years, and many made a sort of early career of these positions, some going on to another Justice after the death or retirement of their first employer, and one serving as many as four Justices. Most of them spent most of their time doing the chores of a personal secretary, which ranged from paying bills to reading proof.[323] Others did some legal research for their Justices. Some of the abler and older ones had their salaries supplemented out of the Justices' own

---

[321] White and McKenna lived near St. Matthew's Catholic Church (now Cathedral), which is on Rhode Island Avenue. White had a massive stone Victorian town house at 1721 Rhode Island Avenue, later used as the Calvert School. McKenna was in an apartment house at 1150 Connecticut Avenue, on the corner of M Street, later a medical building. Holmes lived at 1720 Eye Street, in a house later torn down and supplanted by an office building. Lurton seems to have had an apartment at 2129 Florida Avenue. Hughes had difficulty finding a house large enough to serve as both residence and office, and after leasing unsatisfactorily, built at 2100 V Street, moving in in November 1911. The house was later occupied by the Bulgarian diplomatic mission. Van Devanter was at 1923 Sixteenth Street, which had been Brewer's house. Lamar's house was at 1751 New Hampshire Avenue. Pitney had a house at 1763 R Street. Wilson's appointees were apartment dwellers. McReynolds lived first at 815 Connecticut Avenue, and then at 2400 Sixteenth Street, where Clarke also

stayed, the more unhappily, no doubt. Brandeis was first at 1025 Connecticut Avenue (Stoneleigh Court) and then at 2205 California Street (Florence Court). Interview with Winslow B. Van Devanter, June 10, 1960; see C. E. Hughes, *Biographical Notes*, 208, Hughes Papers, Library of Congress.

[322] See 24 Stat. 254 (1886).

[323] Hughes recalled: "My secretaries (while Associate Justice I had three in succession) were fine young men who had been admitted to the bar, but as I kept them busy with dictation, hating to write in longhand, they had little or no time to devote to research and whatever was necessary in that line I did myself. Occasionally, the question of providing law clerks in addition to secretaries was raised, but nothing was done [till 1919; see *infra*, p. 83]. Some suggested that if we had experienced law clerks, it might be thought that they were writing our opinions. An exception was Chief Justice White who hired a law clerk and paid him out of his own pocket." Hughes, *Biographical Notes*, 207–208, Hughes Papers.

pockets,[324] although the judicial salary itself was far from munificent— it was raised in 1911 to $14,500, with $15,000 for the Chief Justice, and was not to reach $20,000 till 1926.[325] Holmes, as had his predecessor Gray before him, took each year a top graduate of the Harvard Law School and kept him for a year only, using him as companion and law clerk rather than as stenographer, since Holmes wrote everything in longhand. So, from his accession in 1916, did Brandeis. It is chiefly among Holmes' and Brandeis' law clerks in these years, as earlier among Gray's, that distinguished names begin to crop up.[326] Not till 1919 did Congress provide for law clerks, at a salary of $3,600, in addition to secretarial assistance.[327]

The work that the judges thus performed at home and with a minimum of assistance was by all accounts hard and absorbing. Everyone, wrote Taft some years later, testified to the "exhausting character" of the work.[328] Indeed, it often came as something of a shock to new appointees. Shortly after his accession, Day reported to his former colleague Lurton that there was a great deal more to do than on the Sixth Circuit, and a great deal more involving constitutional questions. While Day had about the same number of full opinions to prepare as on the Court of Appeals, there were "three times as many cases to consider to say nothing of the numerous applications for writs of certiorari." And "we always have the work with us." During "the term of Court from October to June there is little time for anything else but attention to its duties."[329] Hughes recalled that he "found the work very difficult."[330] Nothing that he had done previously, at the bar or as governor, so "took the 'gimp' out of him."[331] After his first week of hearing argument, Hughes thought that there was a heavy load of cases, but that within a month or so he might be ready to vote on them. Of course, he was required to vote that very Saturday at conference. And in addition to

---

[324] See, e.g., W. H. Taft to W. M. Mischler, July 12, 1921, Taft Papers.

[325] See *Judicial and Congressional Salaries,* Senate Document No. 97, 83rd Cong., 2d Sess. (1954).

[326] Gray's law clerks included Samuel Williston, Ezra Ripley Thayer, Jeremiah Smith, Jr., and John Gorham Palfrey. Among Holmes' in the decade 1910–20 were Irving S. Olds, Francis Biddle, Harvey H. Bundy, Chauncey Belknap, and Stanley Morrison. Brandeis' first clerk, for the October Term 1916, was Calvert Magruder. William A. Sutherland served from 1917 to 1919.

During the October Terms 1919 and 1920, Dean G. Acheson was law clerk.

[327] See C. A. Newland, "Personal Assistants to Supreme Court Justices: The Law Clerks," *Ore. L. Rev.,* 40: 299, 1961.

[328] W. H. Taft to M. Strauss, June 5, 1927, Taft Papers.

[329] W. R. Day to H. H. Lurton, Dec. 25, 1903, Lurton Papers.

[330] Hughes, *Biographical Notes,* 209–12, Hughes Papers.

[331] Quoted in W. H. Taft to M. Strauss, June 5, 1927, Taft Papers.

the heavy current work, Hughes found it advisable "to do a great deal of reading outside the demands of the cases in hand, in order to get a comprehensive view of the jurisprudence of the Court."[332]

Although not unaccustomed to hard work, Brandeis a few years later also found the burden of the Court's business peculiarly heavy, especially at the beginning. He was struck by the confinement that the work imposed, and by the relentless flow of it, seven days a week, every week. "It went hard with me," Brandeis said, and on another occasion he added that it takes about three years for a new judge to find himself in the movements of the Court—three years of extra-heavy labor.[333] To be sure, there were the summer vacations, and they were at this time not as cluttered with petitions for certiorari as they would later become. The Court sat normally for thirty-five weeks, eighteen of argument and seventeen of recess and opinion writing.[334] Then most if not all of the Justices scattered to various vacation spots. But that did not always seem adequate compensation, especially since the last few weeks of the term were particularly rushed and hectic. Didn't Hughes envy Brandeis' coming summer vacation, Brandeis once asked Hughes in later years, after Hughes had returned to practice? "Not at the price you have to pay for it," was the reply.[335]

As it convened at the October Term 1910, the Court was faced with a badly congested docket. The docket had been in arrears for decades, but the situation had deteriorated rapidly in the last five terms under Fuller, so that at the end of the 1909 Term, 600 cases remained undisposed of. Although it disposed of 466 cases (66 more than at the previous term), and although, as it happened, there was no appreciable rise in the number of new cases (516 as against 514 at October Term 1909), the Court ended the October Term 1910 further behind, with 650 cases left. Over any given series of terms, the number of cases docketed showed a steady increase. This had been true for some time, it was continuing, and the number had become cumulatively quite significant. Nevertheless, in a few years, the new Court, as reconstituted by Taft, and eventually aided by the Judiciary Act of 1916 which stemmed the flood a bit, made some reduction in the arrears. But to begin with, it lost more ground. It ended the October Term 1911 with 680 cases left, although it disposed of 502. At the next term, the Court strained even harder, disposed of 585 cases, and had 616 left. From

[332] Hughes, *Biographical Notes*, 87, Hughes Papers.

[333] Brandeis-Frankfurter Conversations.

[334] See F. Frankfurter and J. M. Landis, "Business of the Supreme Court at October Term, 1928," *Harv. L. Rev.*, 43:33, 36, 1929.

[335] Brandeis-Frankfurter Conversations. W. H. Taft to M. Strauss, June 5, 1927, Taft Papers.

then on there was fairly steady progress, starting with a big reduction at the October Term 1913. But no kind of mere judicial effort could bring the Court abreast of its docket. The battle was essentially hopeless, and it did not begin to be won until the radical reform instituted by the Judiciary Act of 1925 first manifested itself at the October Term 1927.[336]

Of the mass of cases on the Court's docket at October Term 1910, a number of important ones were decided while the Court was shorthanded, before the accession of Van Devanter and Lamar. But a number were held for argument to a full Bench, probably because it was on these cases that public attention chiefly centered. They were viewed as touching with particular immediacy "the main question of the day": "the regulation by law of corporate activity in its relation to the country at large."[337] These cases were *Hipolite Egg Co.* v. *United States*,[338] involving the constitutionality of the Pure Food Act of 1906; *Flint* v. *Stone Tracy Co.*,[339] testing the constitutionality of the Corporation Tax Act of 1909; the *Second Employers' Liability Cases*,[340] which involved the constitutionality of the Federal Employers' Liability Act, as amended to comply with an earlier decision, and which were argued on February 20, 1911, but not decided till the next term; and *Standard Oil Co.* v. *United States*,[341] and *United States* v. *American Tobacco Co.*,[342] calling for construction of the Sherman Antitrust Act.

These were the great cases. But the greatest of these, in the estimation of the public, were the Sherman Act cases.[343]

---

[336] "Business of the Supreme Court of the United States," in *Reports of the Attorney General* (1909–28); F. Frankfurter and J. M. Landis, "The Supreme Court under the Judiciary Act of 1925," *Harv. L. Rev.*, 42:1, 1928.

[337] Baldwin, *Supreme Court Justices*, 160.

[338] 220 U.S. 45 (1911).

[339] 220 U.S. 107 (1911).

[340] 223 U.S. 1 (1912).

[341] 221 U.S. 1 (1911).

[342] 221 U.S. 106 (1911).

[343] See Marcosson, *New Supreme Court.*

CHAPTER II

The Rule of Reason

QUITE POSSIBLY, when the Sherman Antitrust Act became law in
1890, it was for many of those who voted for it little more than
a harmless gesture. Some bill headed "A Bill to Punish Trusts" was
needed to go to the country with, said the very conservative Senator
Orville H. Platt of Connecticut, and he implied that any bill so headed
would have done as well.[1] Moreover, the movement to combine in what
could with any approach to technical accuracy be termed trusts was by
then in process of being halted by decisions in the state courts, and by
the depression of 1893.[2] Yet twenty years later, nothing so agitated the
agitated politics of the day as corporate size and the concentration of
economic power. And all the fear and the anguish evoked by the
problem of economic concentration, as well as extravagant hopes for its
solution, centered on the Sherman Act, which the Supreme Court was
about to construe, it was expected, once and for all.

It may be, as Richard Hofstadter has written, that the problem was
essentially insoluble and that the Sherman Act was merely a "ceremonial solution," which is a "temptation to the satirical intelligence."
But it cannot be said that administration of the Sherman Act had no
effect on business organization in this country, and we cannot know that
a wiser and more vigorous administration, clearer and more precise
about its aims, might not have had even greater and more enduring
consequences. Hofstadter himself concedes almost as much, and in no
respect argues the contrary.[3] At all events, whatever hindsight might

---

[1] R. Hofstadter, *The Age of Reform*
(1955), 243; but *cf.* H. B. Thorelli,
The Federal Antitrust Policy (1954),
214–21.

[2] H. R. Seager and C. A. Gulick, Jr.,

Trust and Corporation Problems
(1929), 51.

[3] Hofstadter, *Age of Reform*, 243,
253–54.

suggest, the antitrust enterprise was invested in 1910 with enormous hopes and the acutest universal interest.

Five years after the Sherman Act was passed, the Supreme Court appeared determined to ensure that it would remain no more than a gesture. In *United States* v. *E. C. Knight Co.*,[4] the Court frustrated an attempt to break up the American Sugar Refining Company, successor to the Sugar Refining Trust, which through stock acquisitions had obtained control of 98 percent of the industry. This was, held the Court, control of manufacture rather than of interstate commerce, and hence could not constitutionally be reached by the Sherman Act. A few years later, however, the Court allowed the Act to be used against rate-fixing agreements entered into by interstate railroads, and against a price-fixing and market-division arrangement by six manufacturers of cast-iron pipe.[5]

Then came Theodore Roosevelt and his dramatic assault on the holding company into which James J. Hill and J. P. Morgan had merged the Great Northern and the Northern Pacific Railways. In *Northern Securities Co.* v. *United States*,[6] the Supreme Court, dividing 5–4, ordered dissolution of the holding company. Substantial doubt was thus cast on the continued validity of the *E. C. Knight* decision. It was a famous victory, even if the great trustbuster who gained it had no intention of producing many more like it. If anyone regarded the Sherman Act as a largely "ceremonial solution," it was Theodore Roosevelt. While he intended to regulate and perhaps dissolve "bad trusts," the predators of the business world, Roosevelt came to be quite reconciled to consolidation as a fact of industrial life. He regarded the *Northern Securities* decision as important, not programmatically, but because it showed that "the most powerful men in this country were held to accountability before the law."[7] It was a victory, but a symbolic one, almost perhaps a matter of TR's self-conscious image.[8] Nevertheless, before he left office, Roosevelt also initiated proceedings against two other supposed predators, the Standard Oil Company and the American Tobacco Company.

A Standard Oil trust, when it was literally and technically that, was dissolved by a common law judgment of the state courts of Ohio in 1892. This action, and some further litigation in Ohio, led in 1899 to the creation of the Standard Oil Company of New Jersey as a holding

---

[4] 156 U.S. 1 (1895).

[5] United States v. Trans-Missouri Freight Ass'n., 166 U.S. 290 (1897); United States v. Joint Traffic Ass'n., 171 U.S. 505 (1898); Addyston Pipe & Steel Co. v. United States, 175 U.S. 211 (1899), *affirming* 85 Fed. 271

(6th Cir. 1898).

[6] 193 U.S. 197 (1904).

[7] Quoted in R. Hofstadter, "Antitrust in America," *Commentary*, 38:47, 48, August 1964.

[8] J. M. Blum, *The Republican Roosevelt* (1954), 58.

company. It was an astonishingly successful business, and the prime symbol of the bad trust. Undying, if thoroughly unwanted, fame came to the business and to its chief manager and owner, John D. Rockefeller, with publication of Ida M. Tarbell's *The History of the Standard Oil Company*, first in *McClure's* magazine in 1902–1904, and then in book form. The Bureau of Corporations, a creation of Theodore Roosevelt, investigated Standard Oil and issued generally adverse reports in 1906 and 1907. Meanwhile there was a flurry of state suits against the company, aimed at fining it and ousting it from the particular state. Some of these prosecutions succeeded at least in exacting fines, and one found its way on appeal to the Supreme Court of the United States well after *Standard Oil Co.* v. *United States* had been decided.[9] In 1907, this much

---

[9] Standard Oil Co. v. Missouri, 224 U.S. 270 (1912). This must be classified as one of the successful prosecutions, but it is also one of the prime "temptations to the satirical intelligence." For although fines were paid, and Standard Oil of Indiana was at first ousted from the state and seemed about to close down operations, the community, including ex-Governor Hadley, who as Attorney General had begun the prosecution, found in the end that it would rather keep Standard Oil than keep faith with its ideals. And perhaps it was thought sufficient, by this time, that Standard Oil should have been taught a moral lesson not only in the Missouri courts but also by the Sherman Act proceeding in the federal courts. At all events, the Missouri ouster order was suspended. S. N. Whitney, *Antitrust Policies* (1958), I, 102; H. R. Seager and C. A. Gulick, Jr., *Trust and Corporation Problems* (1929), 359–60.

State antitrust legislation is reviewed in Seager and Gulick, *Trust and Corporation Problems,* 339–66; and see "A Collection and Survey of State Anti-Trust Laws," *Colum. L. Rev.,* 32:347, 1932. A number of these statutes were tested in the Supreme Court of the United States. The Missouri statute was upheld a second time, against a more broad-gauged

attack than that mounted in the *Standard Oil* case, in International Harvester Co. v. Missouri, 234 U.S. 199 (1914); and see Armour Packing Co. v. Missouri, 265 Mo. 121 (1915), *appeal dismissed on motion of appellant,* 242 U.S. 663 (1916). But a rather curious Kentucky statute was held void for vagueness in International Harvester Co. v. Kentucky, 234 U.S. 216 (1914). And see International Harvester Co. v. Kentucky, 234 U.S. 589 (1914); Collins v. Kentucky, 234 U.S. 634 (1914); Malone v. Kentucky, 234 U.S. 639 (1914); and American Machine Co. v. Kentucky, 236 U.S. 660 (1915); *cf.* International Harvester Co. v. Kentucky, 234 U.S. 579 (1914). In Mallinckrodt Works v. Missouri, 238 U.S. 41 (1915), another provision of the Missouri statutes, this one requiring corporate officers to file with the Secretary of State an annual affidavit swearing that their corporation had not participated in any pool, trust, agreement, or combination in restraint of trade, etc., was upheld, if somewhat shakily. Finally, a Louisiana statute, using the language of antitrust, but aimed more at keeping up the price of Louisiana sugar, was held unconstitutional in 1916 in McFarland v. American Sugar Co., 241 U.S. 79. Litigation then died down,

harassed but substantially intact giant was fined $29,240,000 by Judge Kenesaw Mountain Landis for violating the Elkins Act of 1903, by receiving rebates from railroads carrying its product. The fine did not stick, but the bad publicity did.[10]

The United States filed its suit under the Sherman Act on November 15, 1906, in the Circuit Court of the United States for the Eastern District of Missouri, against the Standard Oil Company of New Jersey, some seventy other Standard Oil companies and partnerships, and John D. Rockefeller, William Rockefeller, Henry M. Flagler, and four other individuals. As was often done in these years, when the Department of Justice commanded limited personnel, the suit was put in charge of a special prosecutor, retained for a specific case, at fully adequate remuneration. The special prosecutor in this instance was Frank B. Kellogg of Minnesota, later United States Senator and Coolidge's Secretary of State. The complaint he drew up charged a conspiracy to monopolize commerce in oil by means of acquisitions and agreements fixing prices and controlling production. Control over 75 percent of the refining and marketing of petroleum was said to have been achieved by unfair methods, including price cutting, rebates, bribery, intimidation, and the like. The complaint recited the history of the Standard Oil Company in its most unfavorable light, and it asked that the control held by the Standard Oil Company of New Jersey, the holding company, be dissolved, and that all defendants be enjoined from further engaging in actions such as those charged.

Evidence was taken for nearly two years, beginning in June 1907, before an examiner appointed by the four judges who constituted the special circuit court, pursuant to the Expediting Act of 1903. The recorded testimony and the exhibits covered twenty-three very thick printed volumes. In November 1909, the circuit court decided the case. Its decree dismissed the bill as against a number of the outlying corporate defendants, but otherwise the government won.[11]

A direct appeal to the Supreme Court promptly followed, and

---

but as late as 1927, the Supreme Court, following *International Harvester Co.* v. *Kentucky,* declared a Colorado antitrust act of 1913 void for vagueness. Cline v. Frink Dairy Co., 274 U.S. 445 (1927); but *cf.* Columbus Packing Co. v. Ohio, 100 Ohio St. 285, *cert. denied,* 250 U.S. 671 (1919).

[10] S. N. Whitney, *Antitrust Policies* (1958), I, 101–103; United States v.

Standard Oil Co. of Indiana, 155 Fed. 305 (D.C. N.D. Ill. 1907); Standard Oil Co. of Indiana v. United States, 164 Fed. 376 (7th Cir. 1908). And see Standard Oil Co. of New York v. United States, 158 Fed. 536 (D.C. W.D. N.Y. 1908), *cert. denied,* 218 U.S. 681 (1910).

[11] Standard Oil Co. v. United States, 221 U.S. 1, 30–46 (1911).

Attorney General George W. Wickersham,[12] for the government, moved to have the case advanced and set for argument early in March 1910. Motions to advance were common at this time, since the Supreme Court's docket was so heavily in arrears that a case might not be reached for argument in the regular order for many, many months. There was intense public interest in the Sherman Act, the Attorney General argued in support of his motion, and the Department of Justice was called upon to enforce the Act vigorously. Together with the case against the American Tobacco Company, which had been argued in the Supreme Court early in January 1910, the *Standard Oil* case presented to the Court, Wickersham asserted, "practically the entire range of modern industrial organizations in this country, and substantially every feature of the so-called 'trust problem,' in so far as it is affected by the Sherman Act." The government needed to know what to do. It had been the policy of the government to bring test cases against great combinations. "The Standard Oil case is the most important of all these cases, affecting, as it does, the widest range of combinations and contracts which may be claimed to offend against the act of Congress." It was therefore "of momentous public importance that this court shall define and apply the act in reference to this character of organization." Finally, the *Tobacco* and *Standard Oil* cases overlapped on the issues and should be considered together.[13]

The *American Tobacco* case was initiated by the Roosevelt Administration on July 19, 1907, some sixteen months after the government had filed the Standard Oil suit. Special counsel for the government, at a compensation of $16,000 per annum, was James C. McReynolds, the future Justice, who had just moved to New York after a tour of duty as Assistant Attorney General.[14] The Tobacco combination had re-

---

[12] George Woodward Wickersham (1858–1936) was born in Pittsburgh. Following graduation from the University of Pennsylvania Law School, he practiced briefly in Philadelphia, and then in New York, both before and after his service (1909–13) as Taft's Attorney General. In 1929, President Hoover entrusted him with the chairmanship of the National Commission on Law Observance and Law Enforcement, better known as the Wickersham Commission. See *Dictionary of American Biography* (1958), XXII, Supp. 2, 713.

[13] "Additional Memorandum by the United States in Support of Applica-

tion to Advance Cause and Set Same for Argument about March 1," 2–3.

[14] C. J. Bonaparte to J. C. McReynolds, Feb. 8, 1907, McReynolds Papers, Library of the University of Virginia.

McReynolds was replacing Henry W. Taft of New York, W. H. Taft's brother, who had conducted an earlier prosecution against the Licorice Paste subsidiary of American Tobacco, and had been in charge of the initial preparation of this case, but who was now retiring. C. J. Bonaparte to J. C. McReynolds, Jan. 5, 1907, McReynolds Papers.

sulted in a more complex corporate structure than Standard Oil's. The initial consolidation was formation of the American Tobacco Company by James B. Duke out of his own and four other companies in a highly competitive market in 1890. Further consolidation along the full line of tobacco products was gradually achieved through acquisitions by the American Tobacco Company and by other companies formed and controlled for the purpose. In 1901, a holding company, the Consolidated Tobacco Company of New Jersey, was organized to hold practically the entire stock of the American and Continental Tobacco companies, the two main instruments of consolidation. Subsequently, Consolidated was replaced by a new American Tobacco Company incorporated in 1904, which was a super-holding company. In the meantime, in 1901, a cartel agreement was reached with British interests, dividing world markets. Pursuant to this agreement, two British companies, Imperial Tobacco and British-American, were to have, respectively, the British market and the export market outside Britain and the United States. Both companies bought American tobaccos. By 1910, the combine's share of the American market was 86 percent in cigarettes, 76 percent in smoking, eighty-four percent in chewing tobacco. Only in cigars was its position not similarly dominant. There had been some attempts in the states to attack the tobacco monopoly, but they had been almost wholly ineffective, even more so than the state suits against Standard Oil.[15]

Having entered the case early in February 1907, McReynolds on March 20 recommended to Attorney General Charles J. Bonaparte that James B. Duke be prosecuted criminally.[16] This sanguinary proposal was not accepted, but the civil complaint filed four months later, in the Circuit Court for the Southern District of New York, named twenty-nine individual defendants, including Duke, Oliver H. Payne, Thomas Fortune Ryan, Peter A. B. Widener and others, sixty-five American corporations, and the two British companies. It gave the history of the consolidation and charged an intent to monopolize as evidenced by such practices, aimed at driving out competitors and forcing them to consolidate, as price cutting, the use of bogus independent producers actually owned by the combine, the closing of plants of competitors after they had been bought out, and the like. The government asked that the whole combination be restrained from operating further, that specific practices and agreements be enjoined, that the two foreign companies be excluded from doing business in the United States, that the system of interlocking ownership of the various companies be dissolved,

---

[15] Whitney, *Antitrust Policies*, II, 1415; Seager and Gulick, *Trust and Corporation Problems*, 149–72.

[16] J. C. McReynolds to C. J. Bonaparte, Mar. 20, 1907, McReynolds Papers.

and that a receiver be appointed for the main group of companies, including the American Tobacco Company, to liquidate and reconstruct the business in compliance with the law.

As in the *Standard Oil* case, a special examiner was appointed to take evidence, which he did from November 1907 to March 1908. By the end of that year, the circuit court made its decision. The decree did not quite meet the government's prayer. It did declare the existence of a conspiracy in violation of the Sherman Act, and it did—subject to a stay pending appeal—enjoin the principal American companies from doing business until they could show that "reasonably competitive conditions" had been restored. But it enjoined no specific practices, and dissolved no corporate structures. Both the government and the defendants appealed.[17]

So far, under the lash of McReynolds, the case had moved with remarkable expedition. At this point, in the winter of 1908–1909, a hitch developed. On December 28, 1908, just two weeks after the decree had come down, Attorney General Bonaparte wrote McReynolds that it had been Bonaparte's intention to have the case disposed of before the close of the Roosevelt Administration:

> Some days ago, however, the President told me that he had been asked by Mr. Taft [the President-elect] to arrange, if possible, so that this case and the Standard Oil equity case should not reach the Supreme Court before October Term 1909, as he had reason to think that the chances of success would be augmented by this delay. I told him that the Standard Oil case could not, in any event, reach the Supreme Court during the present Term; that your case would be on the docket, and it had been my intention to move for its advancement; but, in view of what he says, and as the next administration was perhaps entitled to determine the question of policy involved, I should not make the motion until the matter had been further considered.

McReynolds protested. After further consultation with President Roosevelt, Bonaparte remained of the opinion that the responsibility for action was Taft's. "I think also, however, that we ought to be sure Mr. Taft fully understands the situation." He therefore asked McReynolds, on January 18, 1909, to prepare a memorandum for Taft.[18]

McReynolds did so the following day, and it was his usual crisp and uncompromising product. "The statute [the Expediting Act of 1903] seems to contemplate that suits like this should be expedited. . . . If the

---

[17] United States v. American Tobacco Co., 221 U.S. 106, 142–55 (1911).

[18] C. J. Bonaparte to J. C. McReynolds, Dec. 28, 1908, Jan. 18, 1909, McReynolds Papers.

government itself strictly observes the spirit of the law in these matters, it can with greater reason demand that others do likewise." Whatever else the circuit court may have failed to do, it declared the American Tobacco Company to be operating in violation of the Sherman Act, and directed a drastic injunction, although it suspended it while the appeal took its course. "The operation of the defendants is immensely profitable —the American Tobacco Company alone pays a million dollars a month in dividends. If, having a clear right to an advancement, the government permits the cause to go over it will be in the attitude of licensing this combination to carry on unlawful but immensely profitable operations in the teeth of the statute and to the serious detriment of the public. This might be an unfortunate position and certainly would not tend to inspire confidence in the prompt execution of the laws." Moreover, everyone was agreed that the Sherman Act needed judicial interpretation, and this was an exceedingly favorable case, from the point of view of the government, in which to obtain it. No doubt there might be strong reasons for delay "based on possible changes in the Court which must have full consideration and about which I of course know little." But mere speculation—if that was all it was—could not outweigh "the duty of the government to act with promptness in endeavoring to enforce the statute. . . ." And finally: "The defendants are rich, powerful, conspicuous, and guilty."[19]

McReynolds had his way—more or less. On February 1, 1909, Attorney General Bonaparte made the motion to advance argument of the *American Tobacco* case, but he did not suggest a date. "To avoid any misconstruction of my action, however," as he said to McReynolds, he wrote privately to Chief Justice Fuller, telling him that McReynolds desired speed, and explaining that nevertheless it was thought "inexpedient" for the government to assume responsibility for the date, since a new Attorney General might wish to participate in the argument and might need time for preparation. Bonaparte also explained to the Chief Justice that a motion to advance had not been made earlier because of a request from the President-elect, which "had been recently withdrawn." John G. Johnson, representing the American Tobacco Company, was in court when Bonaparte made his undated motion. Johnson asked that whatever date was set be no earlier than sometime in April, as he was due to try the Standard Oil case in St. Louis in March. The Chief Justice shook his head and muttered something not altogether audible but generally negative. Bonaparte thought it likely that the case would not be set down for argument before the beginning of the next

---

[19] J. C. McReynolds to C. J. Bonaparte, Jan. 19, 1909, McReynolds Papers. At the argument, McReynolds called the defendants "commercial wolves and highwaymen." See *New York Times,* Jan. 6, 1910, p. 8, col. 2.

term of Court, and it was indeed eventually set down for October 1909.[20]

Wickersham, the new Attorney General, soon found himself involved with consideration of amendments to the Interstate Commerce Act and possibly to the Sherman Act itself, and with "the critical examination of the papers relating to the Glavis charges [against Secretary of the Interior Ballinger]."[21] As fall drew near, he was unable properly to prepare for argument of the *Tobacco* case, in which he did, indeed, feel the Attorney General should participate. Moreover, when the Court convened in October 1909, Justices Moody and Peckham were both absent, and it was more than possible that neither would ever sit again. Having consulted with Secretary of State (and former Attorney General) Knox and Secretary of Commerce and Labor Nagel, Wickersham decided to ask the Court to put the case over till December. In the meantime, Peckham and Moody might be replaced and the Court strengthened. Chief Justice Fuller, as Wickersham wrote the President, "quite approved of this suggestion—i.e., of the delay—as did Justice White, both of whom I spoke to about it." The case was put over on October 13, 1909, and argued in January 1910.[22]

Further delays in the disposition of the *Standard Oil* and *American Tobacco* cases were no doing of the Taft Administration. Taft's Attorney General had held the *Tobacco* case back, but he had secured an advance of the argument in the *Standard Oil* case for March. Following the winter's arguments, Taft hoped for a decision no later than the fall of 1910. His legislative program hinged on that schedule. On January 7, 1910, the day after the argument in the *Tobacco* case had been completed, Taft sent up a message to Congress dealing with antitrust policy. In lawyerlike—and somewhat didactic—fashion, he explained what seemed to him the true meaning of the Sherman Act. The evil aimed at was not "mere bigness," but "the aggregation of capital and plants with the express or implied intent to restrain" or monopolize commerce, and thus destroy competition "utterly." A "mere incidental restraint of trade and competition" was not "within the inhibition of the act. . . ."; "absurdly unimportant combinations" were not included. And the act did not need to be amended to make this clear. "Many people," however, had "cherished a hope" that it might be possible to distinguish between "good" and "bad" trusts. It was time that the public rid itself of this idea. No such distinction was now in the statute, and it would be unwise to write one in. It had been suggested that the word "reasonable" could

---

[20] C. J. Bonaparte to J. C. McReynolds, Feb. 2, 1909, McReynolds Papers.

[21] See *infra*, p. 373.

[22] G. W. Wickersham to W. H. Taft, Oct. 13, 1909 (two letters), Taft Papers.

be made part of the statute, so that only "unreasonable" restraints and monopolies would be outlawed, but to do so would be to "thrust upon the courts a burden that they have no precedents to enable them to carry, and to give them a power approaching the arbitrary, the abuse of which might involve our whole judicial system in disaster."

Taft thus saw no need to amend the Sherman Act in any respect. But he did earnestly, if somewhat vaguely, suggest a federal incorporation statute, which might offer to "these business combinations . . . a means, without great financial disturbance, of changing the character, organization, and extent of their business into one within the lines of the law under Federal control and supervision, securing compliance with the antitrust statute." The federal government would be empowered to grant federal incorporation charters to interstate businesses, which would be prohibited from holding or purchasing stock in other corporations "(except for special reasons upon approval by the proper federal authority)." In addition to being thus prevented from becoming holding companies on the order of Northern Securities, Standard Oil, and American Tobacco, these federal corporations would also be forbidden to water their stock and be required "to file full and complete reports of their operations with the Department of Commerce and Labor at regular intervals."[23]

This message, a paper altogether characteristic of the Taft Administration, was, from the point of view of the President's political interests, altogether unfortunate. "Does the President intend by his recommendation of National incorporation for the great industrial combinations to erect a shelter under which they would be allowed to continue and perpetuate those restraints of trade, in the legal sense, of which they are now guilty under the strict interpretation of the Anti-Trust act? He protests," continued a *New York Times* editorial, "that such is not his intent." But the *Times* did not believe him.[24]

Privately, Taft was quite clear that federal incorporation was not to be "merely a soft bed for the trusts to land upon."[25] And he did not believe in "good" monopolies, nor in the innocence of preponderant size. He noted his general agreement with the following statement sent to him by Victor Morawetz, the scholarly Wall Street lawyer: "The prohibition against monopolizing trade or commerce is not applied to a simple lessening of competition leaving in existence reasonably competitive conditions; but it does apply to a concentration of control of the preponderating part of the commerce in any article, though competi-

---

[23] *Messages and Papers of the Presidents,* XV, 7441, 7449 *et seq.,* 1910.
[24] *New York Times,* Jan. 8, 1910, p. 8, col. 1.

[25] F. B. Kellogg to W. H. Taft, Oct. 5, 1910, bearing notation by Taft: "I have read this and fully concur," Taft Papers.

tion be not wholly destroyed."[26] But, more or less as usual, Taft had been misread, the more unjustly as his administration of the Sherman Act was markedly more vigorous, and less affected by "gentlemen's agreements," than Theodore Roosevelt's.[27] And so Taft was anxious to restate his policy, clarify his federal incorporation proposal, and push it through Congress, while he still had a Republican majority there. But he needed the decisions in the *Standard Oil* and *Tobacco* cases first, to prove his good faith. For Taft was proposing federal incorporation without amendment of the Sherman Act, and his good faith would be credited only if the Supreme Court confirmed Taft's assertion that the Sherman Act was effective and could be used "to break up these combinations under their present organization." Taft regretted that the delay in the disposition of these cases prevented him from "using the present Congress to put through the National Incorporation act which I believe I could get through this Congress if I have the decision of the Supreme Court as a basis. God knows what we can do with the new Congress!"[28]

The delay was caused by conditions in the Court. Peckham had died and been replaced by Lurton before the cases were argued in the winter of 1910. But the Court that heard those arguments was an eight-

---

[26] V. Morawetz to W. H. Taft, Oct. 11, 1910, Taft Papers; see V. Morawetz, "The Supreme Court and the Anti-Trust Act," *Colum. L. Rev.,* 10:687, 696, 1910.

[27] See R. H. Wiebe, *Businessmen and Reform* (1962), 81–82; R. H. Wiebe, "The House of Morgan and the Executive, 1905–1913," *Am. Hist. Rev.,* 65:49, 57, 1959.

[28] F. B. Kellogg to W. H. Taft, Oct. 5, 1910; Taft to Kellogg, Oct. 12, 1910, Taft Papers. See H. Pringle, *The Life and Times of William Howard Taft* (1939), II, 663; J. D. Clark, *The Federal Trust Policy* (1931), 142. Another annoyance to the Taft Administration during the period of delay was the introduction some ten days before the argument of the *Standard Oil* case of a bill in Congress to create the Rockefeller Foundation, which was to devote $100 million to the betterment of humanity. This proposal appalled Attorney General Wickersham, who thought that "such an indefinite scheme for perpetuating vast wealth" was against the public interest. The unrestricted power conferred by $100 million on a few men was likely to become in the highest degree corrupt in its influence, as the ancient statutes against mortmain had recognized. Moreover, Rockefeller's wealth had been achieved by illegal and indeed immoral means. "Is it, then, appropriate that, at the moment when the United States through its courts is seeking in a measure to destroy the great combination of wealth which has been built up by Mr. Rockefeller . . . the Congress of the United States should assist in the enactment of a law to create and perpetuate in his name an institution to hold and administer a large portion of this vast wealth?" Taft agreed that it was not appropriate, and the Rockefeller bill was finally withdrawn. Ultimately a charter was granted in New York. H. Pringle, *The Life and Times of William Howard Taft* (1939), II, 662–63.

man Court, owing to the absence of Moody. This circumstance might not in itself have made a decisive difference. On March 28, 1910, however, less than two weeks after the argument in the *Standard Oil* case, Brewer died. No matter how promptly his replacement might appear (in the event, it was Hughes, who did not take his seat till October), only seven Justices would have heard the argument of either the *Standard Oil* or the *Tobacco* case, and according to practice, therefore, only seven Justices could take part in the decisions. No doubt it was felt that cases of this importance should not be disposed of by so truncated a Court. Hence on April 11, 1910, an order came down setting the cases for reargument. During the summer, Chief Justice Fuller died, and in the fall Moody retired. Reargument of both cases was, therefore, held up until a full Court could be convened again, and took place January 9–17, 1911. In the interval, expectations already sufficiently high were heightened yet further.

Not only did the President's legislative program await word from the Court, but, it seems, the whole country was holding its breath. A contemporary observer noted:

> To go back over a comparatively brief period of years, the decisions of the Supreme Court have been awaited with country-wide suspense and attention in the so-called Insular cases, the determination of the validity of an income tax, and the dissolution of the Northern Securities Company. None of these cases, however, caused the markets and the whole industrial and commercial world to pause more perceptibly than have the cases of the Government against the Standard Oil Company and the American Tobacco Company. They came to be known simply as the Trust Cases. For months the financial markets have virtually stood still awaiting their settlement.[29]

A writer in the *Harvard Law Review* thought that these cases concentrated attention on the Supreme Court "to a greater extent than ever before in its history."[30] According to the *New York Tribune*, when word came to Wall Street on May 15, 1911, that the Supreme Court was about to hand down the decision in the *Standard Oil* case, the announcement

> brought a cheer that echoed in the tower of the Singer Building, so great was the delight of the waiting thousands of bankers, brokers and speculators that the uncertainty that had been hanging over the market like a black cloud was about to be swept away.

---

[29] E. G. Lowry, "The Supreme Court Speaks," *Harper's Weekly*, 55:8, June 1911.

[30] R. L. Raymond, "The Standard Oil and Tobacco Cases," *Harv. L. Rev.*, 25:31, 1911.

> Nobody seemed to care particularly what the decision would be. What was wanted was an ending of the uncertainty that for so many weary weeks had oppressed business in the Street, and whether or not it was favorable or unfavorable to the Standard Oil Company appeared to make little difference to the crowds around the tickers.[31]

The market closed, with trading virtually suspended, before the result in the case was known, and the next day stocks went up.[32]

Of course, as the *Banking Law Journal* observed shortly thereafter, the relief was so great because of the "highly exaggerated view" that had been taken "of the bearing of the question [in the *Standard Oil* case] upon business in general." In the final analysis, it should have been recognized that "the worst that could happen to the Standard Oil Company was a dissolution into its component parts, as in the case of the Northern Securities Company." The worst, which in fact happened, was a good bit less than revolutionary.[33] What the level-headed editorial writer in the *Banking Law Journal* forgot, however, was that for the public at large, and for the business world as well, the antitrust issue was never, least of all at this moment in time, merely a practical one; it was also an ideological, doctrinal issue. And antitrust doctrine seemed to stand at a momentous crossroads.

There was some concern, no doubt, and some hope in certain quarters, that the Court might reaffirm its decision in *E. C. Knight*, the Sugar Trust Case of 1895, and hold the Sherman Act altogether inapplicable. John G. Johnson of Philadelphia, who represented, though not alone, both Standard Oil and American Tobacco, spent great portions of his brief and argument pressing for this result.[34] But it must

---

[31] *New York Tribune*, May 16, 1911, p. 1, col. 5.

[32] *New York Tribune*, May 17, 1911, p. 1, col. 8.

[33] "The Standard Oil Decision," *Banking L. J.*, 28:477, June 1911.

[34] John Graver Johnson (1841–1917), a blacksmith's son who rose to leadership of the Philadelphia Bar and ownership of an art collection, had won the *E. C. Knight* case, and never got over it. "For at least twenty years," James M. Beck recalled, "as Mr. Johnson grew older . . . he seemed to fail to realize that the case as an authority was pretty dead." Quoted in B. F. Winkelman, *John G. Johnson—Lawyer and Art Collector* (1942), 177. Chief Justice White remarked in 1917 that when he first came on the Court, all the Justices regarded Johnson as "the most powerful advocate of his day." However, White added, when later Johnson argued the great antitrust cases that made him famous, the Justices thought he was no longer at his best, because he had survived into an economic era that he did not understand. G. W. Pepper, *Philadelphia Lawyer—An Autobiography* (1944), 60–61. Johnson was a big man with a big head and a Bismarckian mustache. He did not always seem to Holmes "to go to the root of the matter or quite come up to his reputation in Pennsylvania. On the other hand he delighted me by the force and brevity with which he

have been widely recognized, as Victor Morawetz wrote, that such a result could not be final. The temper of public opinion would demand that it be overturned either by legislation, or if necessary by constitutional amendment.[35] The high, almost hysterical interest in the outcome of the *Standard Oil* and *Tobacco* cases is explained, not by anxieties and hopes centering on the old *E. C. Knight* decision, but by the expectation that the Court would set out on one of two distinct paths of statutory interpretation, which supposedly led to radically diverging ideological and practical destinations.

Taft, in his message to Congress in 1910, had tried to deflate differences and state a consensus on the meeting of the Sherman Act. But he had hardly been heard. People remembered instead that in the *Trans-Missouri* and *Joint Traffic* cases of 1897–98, Justice Peckham, for a majority of the Court, had held that the Sherman Act rendered unlawful *every* restraint of trade, rather than merely "unreasonable" ones. Justice White, in dissent, had argued for a "rule of reason." As he applied it in those cases, the rule seemed to mean that only price-fixing agreements which fixed unreasonably high prices would be held unlawful. By the same token, it was widely assumed, Justice White would think that only unreasonable, or bad, trusts and combinations were unlawful, and not reasonable or good ones. In the *Northern Securities* case, the Court had divided evenly on this issue, since Justice Brewer, who had been with the majority in the *Trans-Missouri* and *Joint Traffic* cases and who made the fifth for the majority in *Northern Securities*, concurred specially, saying that he thought the Northern Securities

---

drove home what he had to say." *Ibid.* No doubt Holmes, who reported to Lewis Einstein in 1912 that he had once suggested to President Taft that instead of prosecuting John D. Rockefeller the government ought "to put up a bronze statue of him," M. DeW. Howe, *Justice Oliver Wendell Holmes —The Proving Years* (1963), 111, could take a qualified pleasure in Johnson's peroration in the first *Tobacco* argument (after much uninterrupted discourse about the *E. C. Knight* case):

In these days in America, as in India in the past times, there are men who are denounced as the Warren Hastings of trade. It may be; the pathway of great achieve-

ment is not always strewn with roses. But if you destroy the work that these men have done, who will foretell the result? They have planted our commercial flag in every part of the world. . . . You are not going to benefit the laboring classes by doing that which will deprive them of the employment that they have been given and that they would get in no other way. . . . And who will say, with any assurance, that you can safely substitute for the herculean work of the financial giants the puny efforts of the pygmies that will be left in trade?

[35] V. Morawetz, "The Supreme Court and the Anti-Trust Act," *Colum. L. Rev.,* 10:701, 1910.

combination unlawful because he deemed it unreasonable, although he had now come to think that reasonable combinations would be lawful. And so the burning questions were: If no rule of reason was introduced into the statute, would every agreement in restraint of competition, every joinder of two competitors, every acquisition of one business by another for the sake of greater efficiency, every "absurdly unimportant combination," in Taft's phrase, be unlawful? On the other hand, if the rule of reason prevailed, would only "bad" or predatory trusts, and only unreasonably high price-fixing agreements be unlawful, but not "good" trusts, no matter how big, and not "good" price-fixing agreements, no matter how destructive of competition?

This momentous doctrinal issue was a false one. The American people, wrote William B. Hornblower of the New York Bar, would not tolerate "the clamor for a literal interpretation," and for the outlawry of *every* combination, if they understood what was meant by it. "They may enjoy the slaughter of the Philistines; but they can hardly fall in love with suicide."[36] Nor was a truly literal construction of the statute possible, whether or not tolerable. Even if, repudiating the so-called rule of reason, one rested decision on the word *every,* there would still remain the terms "restraint of trade" and "monopoly" to be construed, and applied or not, in case after case. Despite his debating stance, Peckham quite likely had never meant to cover incidental or trivial restraints of trade, and had meant only that *every* combination effectively destroying competition in an entire market should be outlawed. Combinations of former competitors that left the market in which they operated substantially unaffected were, most probably for Peckham also, quite a different matter. On the other hand, regardless of what White might have had in mind before the turn of the century in the *Trans-Missouri* and *Joint Traffic* cases, the rule of reason did not necessarily imply a distinction between "good" and "bad" trusts—a distinction, as Taft's message had pointed out, that would embroil the Court in impossible and unjudicial decisions. The rule of reason could signify instead merely a candid recognition of the inevitability of judicial construction of the statute, without so much as connoting a construction different from Peckham's.[37]

Yet, however false, the rule-of-reason issue survived briefs, arguments, and opinions, and dominated initial reactions to the Court's

---

[36] W. B. Hornblower, "Antitrust Legislation and Litigation," *Colum. L. Rev.,* 11:701, 1911.

[37] See R. H. Bork, "The Rule of Reason and the Per Se Concept: Price Fixing and Market Division," *Yale L. J.,* 74:775, esp. 783–806, 1965.

judgments in the *Standard Oil* and *Tobacco* cases. It did so partly because reactions were governed more by the expectations that had risen to such a pitch than by what was in the end actually done, and partly because certain obscurities in Chief Justice White's opinions for the majority did nothing to dispel false apprehensions,[38] and the temper of Justice Harlan's dissents did everything to confirm them.[39] Parts of the briefs, however, portions of the arguments, and some colloquies between Court and counsel, as well as many passages in Chief Justice White's opinions, dealt with the real issues, and there were those, however few, who grasped the point.

The real task of the Court in these cases was to define, within the facts presented, the meaning of a restraint of trade amounting to monopoly. Whatever policies such a definition might subsume, it depended first of all on the identification of a set of economic conditions. The government's brief in the *Standard Oil* case addressed itself to the task of defining monopoly by emphasizing the charge that the consolidation of Standard Oil throughout its history was undertaken in order to secure and continue control of the market in the hands of a few men; the evidence of predatory practices was relevant as proof of the intent of this conspiracy.[40] In its *Tobacco* case brief, the government defined monopoly as a practical cessation of effective competition in a business, as the result of concentration of competing businesses not occurring as an incident to the orderly growth or development of one of them.[41]

At the first *Standard Oil* argument, and throughout the reargument of the *Tobacco* case, the Justices pressed counsel for a definition of monopoly, both in economic terms and for legal purposes, by stressing the element of intent.[42] "Generalities are very good," said Day during the second *Tobacco* argument, "but it seems to me that the Government ought to have an explanation now of what the law means by 'monopolizing.'" McReynolds, who together with Attorney General Wickersham spoke for the government, replied that control of a major part of the

---

[38] Many passages in White's opinions suggested "some of Mr. Gladstone's speeches in the House of Commons, when he seemed positively anxious not to cast light on the subject under discussion." R. L. Raymond, "The Standard Oil and Tobacco Cases," *Har. L. Rev.*, 25:31, 43, 1911.

[39] Justice Harlan's "inability to articulate his distinctions or to grasp those made by others caused considerable unnecessary confusion about both." R. H. Bork, "The Rule of Reason and the Per Se Concept: Price Fixing and Market Division," *Yale L. J.*, 74:775, 783, 1965.

[40] Brief of United States.

[41] Brief of United States.

[42] See, e.g., *Seattle Post Intelligencer*, Jan. 15, 1910, p. 1, col. 6, cont. p. 3.

business was decisive.[43] Pressed for a closer definition by McKenna, McReynolds replied: "If I may say so, I believe that the Court will make a great mistake if it attempts to decide in this case all that the Sherman Antitrust law means. There is a border land out yonder into which it is not necessary to go." But where there is a border land, there is a border, said Chief Justice White. "Where is it? What is your theory of the law, I ask you, and you respond that your theory is that we have decided this case in your favor."

So challenged, McReynolds said he was convinced the law intended to forbid interference with the free flow of competition, and that any combination that did that was illegal, although the interference had to be material and direct. "Do you maintain that it takes fifty-one per cent of the trade to effect a material obstruction?" asked Day. McReynolds replied: "Your honors have held that fifty-one per cent was sufficient to come within the law. If a combination of less is held by this Court to be sufficient, that is better. I do not believe that obstruction by two little fellows is sufficient." When Lurton tried to lure McReynolds into the debate about reasonable and unreasonable restraints, McReynolds said he thought the law meant a material and direct restraint rather than an unreasonable one. In reply to the Chief Justice, he conceded that the law distinguished between a restraint of trade by an individual commanding millions of dollars of his own, and restraint by a combination of individuals using the corporate form. But as to the case at hand, "If you

---

[43] But it was not, DeLancey Nicoll of New York had argued for the company, a single business, as charged by the government, but several, and the defendants did not control them all. Cigarettes, for example, he said, did not compete with plug tobacco, and snuff did not compete with cigars. And the snuff used by the Swedes in the Northwest was no competitor of the wintergreen or other flavored snuffs consumed by the factory girls of New England.

Holmes at this point interjected that he was wondering "who it was that consumed snuff. You hardly ever see anybody take it." "Mr. Nicoll: It is consumed in the factories, I think." The answer strained credulity: "Mr. Justice Holmes: It is consumed in the factories?" "Mr. Nicoll: Yes." (Transcript of oral argument, p. 31.)

This was not the only exchange concerning habits in the use of tobacco. When Harlan, who was in a position to know, complained that the available chewing tobacco was rotten, and that it was not possible to get any good chewing tobacco anymore, William B. Hornblower, arguing for the English companies, absolved them of responsibility. "The English people do not chew, I am told," he said, sounding more lofty than even the English people. "Personally I have no knowledge of the quality of chewing tobacco. I presume the only demand for it in Great Britain is by Americans who are abroad and demand the comforts of home." As an attempt to squelch Harlan, this cannot be said to have been a success. *Providence, Rhode Island, Evening Bulletin,* Jan. 11, 1911, p. 1, col. 4.

want size as a basis, we have it here; if you want intent, we have intent to restrain; whatever you want, we have its essential elements in this case."[44]

Once reargued, the cases were held for some four months—not a long time, considering their magnitude and importance. The Court took unusual security precautions. Ordinarily, printed proofs were distributed to the Justices by the writer of the opinion. In this instance, the Court voted not to send the opinions to the printer, but to circulate typewritten copies instead.[45] On Saturday, May 13, 1911, White's majority opinion in the *Standard Oil* case was voted on finally in conference. There was one certain dissent—Harlan. Six Justices, Van Devanter reported in confidence to a former colleague in the Eighth Circuit, were definitely with White. One—we do not know who—was still somewhat in doubt, though leaning toward concurrence.[46] Over the weekend he made up his mind, and on Monday, May 15, 1911, when the decision in *Standard Oil* was announced to a packed courtroom, the Justices stood divided 8–1.

The rule of reason was put forward gradually, with a certain caution, in White's opinion, as the last in an involved series of steps. White began with what was at the time a far from fashionable reference to legislative history: "Although debates may not be used as a means for interpreting a statute (*United States* v. *Trans-Missouri Freight Association*, 166 U.S. 318, and cases cited) that rule in the nature of things is not violated by resorting to debates as a means of ascertaining the environment at the time of the enactment of a particular law, that is, the history of the period when it was adopted." In respect of the Sherman Act, the relevant "environment" was the preexisting common law; not so much, however, any precise rules of the common law, as an evolving popular understanding of the terms the common law had used, such as restraint of trade, and the ends it had sought to achieve. The common law abhorred royal monopolies and private contractual restraints of trade because they conferred power to raise prices at will, to limit production, and to lower quality, all to the injury of the public. In this country, royal monopolies were unknown, but in the popular understanding, private actions that restrained trade were seen to have the same purposes and effects, and were condemned as monopolies. Yet the mature common law did not outlaw all contracts in restraint of trade,

---

[44] *New York Times,* Jan. 10, 1911, p. 2, col. 3.

[45] W. Van Devanter to E. B. Adams, May 14, 1911, Van Devanter Papers.

[46] W. Van Devanter to E. B. Adams, May 14, 1911, Van Devanter Papers.

for "the course of trade could not be made free by obstructing it, and
. . . an individual's right to trade could not be protected by destroying
such right." The criterion for distinguishing unreasonable and illegal
restraints of trade from reasonable and legal ones was injury to the
public. Contracts were deemed

> unreasonably restrictive of competitive conditions, either from the
> nature or character of the contract or act or where the surrounding
> circumstances were such as to justify the conclusion that they had not
> been entered into or performed with the legitimate purpose of reason-
> ably forwarding personal interest and developing trade, but on the
> contrary were of such a character as to give rise to the inference or
> presumption that they had been entered into or done with the intent
> to do wrong to the general public and to limit the right of individuals,
> thus restraining the free flow of commerce and tending to bring about
> the evils, such as enhancement of prices, which were considered to be
> against public policy.

And so the Sherman Act, read against this environmental background, prohibited not every restraint, but only "an undue restraint"
of commerce. It followed for White "inevitably"[47] that the Sherman Act
called for the exercise of judgment. The Act, moreover, called for
application of a standard which, though not specified in the statute, was
"indubitably" contemplated—"the standard of reason." The argument
was made, White continued, that the statute "embraces every contract,
combination, etc., in restraint of trade, and hence its text leaves no room
for the exercise of judgment. . . ." But the statute could not simply
apply itself. Someone, at any rate, had to decide whether a given
combination was in restraint of trade. That could only be done in "the
light of reason."

There were expressions in earlier cases—Peckham's opinion in the
Trans-Missouri Freight Association and *Joint Traffic* cases—which
seemed to look in a different direction. But, said White—and there is
more of ingenuousness than of craft in his tone—whatever the language
of the opinions, how could those cases have been decided otherwise
than "by the light of reason"? "This being inevitable," one could only
conclude that Peckham's process of judgment had been as follows: First

---

[47] "[White] moved portentously
across the thinnest ice, confident that
a lifeline of adverbs—'inevitably,'
'irresistibly,' 'clearly,' and 'necessarily'
—was supporting him in his progress."

P. A. Freund, A. E. Sutherland, M.
DeW. Howe, E. J. Brown, *Constitutional Law: Cases and Other Problems*
(2d ed., 1961), I, cxiii.

he decided, on the facts before him, that the Sherman Act was applicable. Then he went on to hold "that resort to reason was not permissible in order to allow that to be done which the statute prohibited." Restraints of trade, in other words, which are found to be within the statute are not to be exempted by judges on the ground that, in the judges' view, the statutory policy is itself unreasonable. To this position White found it possible wholeheartedly to adhere. Peckham himself, White pointed out, had held in *Hopkins* v. *United States*,[48] decided after *Trans-Missouri Freight Association* and before *Joint Traffic*, that a certain agreement was not in restraint of trade within the meaning of the Sherman Act. He spoke in the *Hopkins* case of the "direct" or "indirect" effect of an agreement upon commerce, and if this is the criterion, then "the rule of reason becomes the guide."

Having thus finally uttered the fateful phrase, White returned, if with something of a sigh, to Peckham's language in the earlier cases, which had expressly repudiated just this phrase. The matter had to be "frankly met" and "in order not in the slightest degree to be wanting in frankness, we say that in so far . . . [as] it may be conceived that the language referred to [in the *Missouri Freight Association* and *Joint Traffic* cases] conflicts with the construction which we give the statute, they [the cases] are necessarily now limited and qualified." It remained only, in the shortest of paragraphs, to dismiss any reliance on the *E. C. Knight* case as "plainly foreclosed," and to remark that the statute as construed did not delegate legislative power to the judges, or at any rate no more legislative power than many another statute, since it adequately set forth a policy in terms of the wrong to be prevented.

White then turned to the facts. The consolidation, through repeated mergers with competitors, of so much of the oil industry in Standard Oil of New Jersey, he said,

> gives rise, in and of itself, in the absence of countervailing circumstances, to say the least, to the *prima facie* presumption of intent and purpose to maintain the dominancy over the oil industry, not as a result of normal methods of industrial development, but by new means of combination which were resorted to in order that greater power might be added than would otherwise have arisen had normal methods been followed, the whole with the purpose of excluding others from the trade and thus centralizing in the combination a perpetual control of the movements of petroleum and its products in the channels of interstate commerce.

---

[48] 171 U.S. 578 (1898).

The presumption was made conclusive by the predatory conduct of the company, considered "as an aid for discovering intent and purpose."[49]

Finally, White came to the decree issued by the circuit court, which in the opinion of the prosecutor, Frank B. Kellogg, had granted all that the government had asked.[50] The decree directed Standard Oil of New Jersey—the corporation, not the individuals who controlled it—to divest itself of its holdings in all the other companies, and forbade any future exercise of control over these former subsidiaries, or receipt of dividends from them. All this White affirmed without question. The decree further enjoined all the individuals and companies named in the complaint from ever in future conspiring to restrain or monopolize trade by agreements among themselves. This provision of the decree, White held, should be construed to incorporate, in effect, the rule of reason. Not all future agreements between one or more of the former subsidiaries of Standard Oil of New Jersey need necessarily amount to a violation of the Sherman Act. Only attempts at recreating, directly or indirectly, the former illegal combination were enjoined. The decree should not be taken to mean, for instance, that any future combination of pipeline companies into a single pipeline would necessarily violate the Sherman Act, or that the tank line company might not enter into future agreements distributing its cars among the various refiners. Subject to these caveats, White affirmed this provision of the decree as well. But he modified the rest of the decree by lengthening to six months a thirty-day period of delay allowed for the execution of its provisions, and struck a clause which would have enjoined the carrying on of inter-

---

[49] The long accepted theory—embodied in the complaint in the *Standard Oil* case and accepted in White's opinion—that the company obtained its monopoly at least in part by predatory price cutting which destroyed competitors, and then maintained it in the same fashion, is refuted in J. S. McGee, "Predatory Price Cutting: The Standard Oil (N.J.) Case," *J. Law & Econ.*, 1:137, 1958. Logically, McGee argues, predatory price cutting is less profitable than simply buying out the competitor at whom it is directed. McGee's own reexamination of the record in the *Standard Oil* case persuaded him that in fact the company bought out competitors without resorting to price wars. Where there was price cutting, others started it. If Standard Oil ever did use it, it never by itself succeeded. Standard Oil rather kept buying competitors, who kept entering, or else made market-sharing agreements with them. Where Standard Oil did use price discrimination, it was because of differing market conditions. And so McGee concludes that the monopoly was the result of mergers, not of price cutting. Of course, White's opinion does not say that had he believed that predatory price cutting had not been resorted to by Standard Oil, he would have reached a different result. Nor does McGee urge that he should have.

[50] F. B. Kellogg to W. H. Taft, Nov. 20, 1909, Taft Papers.

state commerce not only by Standard Oil of New Jersey but by all of the subsidiaries, until dissolution had been accomplished.[51]

White's choice of the phrase "rule of reason" at the decisive point in his opinion was unfortunate, because he had in the past used it in quite a different sense. He meant by it now only that the statute required construction, as, of course, it plainly did. Perhaps because he hoped, as well he might have, that this much would be universally conceded, White was led to say repeatedly that this much was only good common sense—"the light of reason." There is no indication in the opinion of any drawing of distinctions between "good" and "bad" trusts. The distinction, whether or not altogether clear, was a different one, and it left open various lines of development, not excluding even condemnation of size alone. But the opinion did mark a change of position for White. Earlier, in his dissents against Peckham, White had groped for a "good" versus "bad" distinction, and he had then also used the phrase "rule of reason." It was in this context that Peckham had rejected it. And it was because he now again used the same phrase, and allowed himself to be drawn into verbal fencing, that White invited confusion and misunderstanding.[52] This invitation Harlan, not alone, but first and foremost, chose to take up. And perhaps Harlan, far from choosing, could not help it.

Harlan's opinion is part concurrence and part dissent, for he differed on the result merely in that he would have confirmed the entire decree of the circuit court without qualification. In its attack on White's construction of the Sherman Act, the opinion is all dissent, and all polemic. The Court had "not only upset the long settled interpretation of the act, but has usurped the constitutional functions of the legislative branch of the Government. With all due respect for the opinions of others, I feel bound to say that what the court has said may well cause some alarm for the integrity of our institutions." The Thirteenth Amendment having abolished human slavery, the Sherman Act was meant to abolish another kind of slavery, "the slavery that would result from aggregations of capital in the hands of a few individuals and corporations. . . ." Harlan reviewed at length Peckham's opinion in the *Trans-Missouri Freight* and *Joint Traffic* cases, showing clearly enough that Peckham considered and rejected the proposition that a rule of reason should be read into the statute. The point was therefore covered by the principle of *stare decisis*. Moreover, Congress had had full opportunity to amend the act in order

---

[51] Standard Oil Co. v. United States, 221 U.S. 1 (1911). Passages and phrases quoted are at 221 U.S. 50, 56, 58, 60, 63, 64, 65, 66, 67–68, 69, 75, 76.

[52] See R. H. Bork, "The Rule of Reason and the Per Se Concept: Price Fixing and Market Division," *Yale L. J.*, 74:775, 783–96, 801–805, 1965.

to avoid Peckham's construction, but it had never done so. The question was no longer open, and counsel should not even have been allowed to reargue it: ". . . I confess to no little surprise as to what has occurred in the present case."

Harlan's feelings had plainly been injured by White's claim that he (White) was interpreting the statute by "the light of reason" and "the rule of reason." The repetition of these phrases left a rather hard implication concerning the method that might be pursued to reach a different construction. This, said Harlan, was not nice to Peckham, "a Justice of wide experience as a judicial officer," and a man of "sagacity," let alone, one might say, reason. The Court now purported to be giving the statute, for the first time, a construction by "the light of reason," but in fact it was engaging in "judicial legislation." Better to have followed precedent. "Such a course, I am sure, would not have offended the 'rule of reason.' But my brethren, in their wisdom have deemed it best to pursue a different course." The most important aspect of the case, however, more important even than this disregard for precedent, was "the usurpation by the judicial branch of the Government of the functions of the legislative department." And it was on this note that Harlan concluded:

> I said at the outset that the action of the court in this case might well alarm thoughtful men who revered the Constitution. I meant by this that many things are intimated and said in the court's opinion which will not be regarded otherwise than as sanctioning an invasion by the judiciary of the constitutional domain of Congress—an attempt by interpretation to soften or modify what some regard as a harsh public policy. . . . The courts have nothing to do with the wisdom or policy of an act of Congress. . . .
>
> After many years of public service at the National Capital, and after a somewhat close observation of the conduct of public affairs, I am compelled to say that there is abroad, in our land, a most harmful tendency to bring about the amending of constitutions and legislative enactments by means alone of judicial construction. . . .
>
> I do not stop to discuss the merits of the policy embodied in the Anti-trust Act of 1890. . . .
>
> I dissent from that part of the judgment of this court which directs the modification of the decree of the Circuit Court, as well as from those parts of the opinion which, in effect, assert authority, in this court, to insert words in the Anti-trust Act which Congress did not put there, and which, being inserted, Congress is made to declare, as part of the public policy of the country, what it has not chosen to declare.[53]

---

[53] The dissent is at 221 U.S. 82. Passages quoted are at pp. 83, 98, 99, 100, 102, 103, 104–106.

II: *The Rule of Reason*

Harlan delivered his dissent orally, not having yet prepared and filed the opinion that now appears in the *Reports*. What he said sounded at least as harsh as what he wrote now reads, and he produced a shock effect. Hughes remembered the oral dissent as "a passionate outburst seldom if ever equaled in the annals of the Court. . . ." Harlan, Hughes thought, "went far beyond his written opinion, launching out into a bitter invective, which I thought most unseemly."[54] Hughes' recollection may be just a trifle colored, but perhaps he had in mind these passages from the oral dissent, lamenting not only the end of the Republic, but also that it was being brought about by procedures specially tailored to the purposes of the rich and powerful:

The most alarming tendency of this day, in my judgment, so far as the safety and integrity of our institutions are concerned, is the tendency to judicial legislation, so that when men having vast interests are concerned, and they cannot get to the law making power of the country which controls it to pass the legislation they desire, the next thing they do is to raise the question in some case, to get the court to so construe the Constitution or the statutes as to mean what they want it to mean. That has not been our practice.

While this happens to be a case of an overshadowing combination of such vast wealth and enormous power that it may fairly be deemed a menace to the general business interests of the country, but this difference ought not to induce us to depart from a settled, wholesome rule, which, being faithfully observed, will guard the integrity and secure the safety of the nation and of its institutions against the attacks of those who would undermine all the law and who would for the sake of present advantages and ends be willing to undo the work of the fathers. Why do I say to undo the work of the fathers? If there is any feature in our governmental system that is new among the nations of the earth it is that division of the Federal Constitution which divides the departments of government among three co-ordinate branches—legislative, executive and judicial, and neither branch has the right to encroach upon the domain of the other. Practically the decision today—I do not mean the judgment—but parts of the opinion, are to the effect practically, that the courts may by mere judicial construction amend the Constitution of the United States or an Act of Congress. That, it strikes me, is mischievous, and that is the part of the opinion that I especially object to.

I shall put my views in writing hereafter, when I get an opportunity to do so. There is much more that I wanted to say, but I cared only to emphasize that objection to the opinion of the Court.[55]

---

[54] C. E. Hughes, *Biographical Notes,* 218–19, Hughes Papers.
[55] See *Louisville Courier Journal,* May 17, 1911, p. 1, col. 2; *New York Times,* May 17, 1911, p. 6.

Attorney General Wickersham reported to the President that Harlan had delivered "a vicious, ill-tempered, old man's dissent,"[56] and Taft himself wrote his wife that Harlan's opinion was "nasty, carping and demagogic," and that it was "directed at the Chief Justice and intended to furnish La Follette and his crowd as much pabulum as possible."[57] Van Devanter, not given, ordinarily, to quick or harsh judgments, wrote privately:

> With the greatest respect for him, and with the most pronounced regret, I feel constrained to say that his [Harlan's] oral dissent was sharp, caustic, superficial, oratorical and well calculated to appeal to and stimulate the prejudice of the unthinking. It was especially calculated to be highly acceptable to Senator La Follette and others who entertain and voice his extreme views. The courtroom was filled, the Chief Justice delivered his opinion with more than the usual restraint which characterizes well considered judicial utterances. You would have commended the manner of the Chief Justice and would have inwardly condemned the manner of Justice Harlan. An unthinking and prejudiced individual would have been affected in the reverse way.[58]

On the substance of what he had joined in deciding, Van Devanter, who had been a member also of the circuit court that had tried the case, thought that White's opinion qualified "the general language and extreme expressions in prior cases, but without questioning the correctness of the ultimate decisions in them."[59] White, he thought, had not put the word "unreasonable" into the statute, "as is said in some of the press reports," but had, "by applying the rule of reason, and not by applying some arbitrary standard not founded upon reason," tried to define the term restraint of trade as used in the statute. He had construed, in normal and indeed necessary fashion, and not interpolated.[60] President Taft took much the same sensible view. He did not think that White's opinion drew a distinction between "good" and "bad" trusts, and he did not think the opinion inconsistent—except on a verbal level—with the views he himself had put forward in his message to Congress of January 7, 1910. "I was contending throughout," Taft wrote privately,

---

[56] C. D. Hilles to W. H. Taft, May 15, 1911, reporting conversation with Wickersham, Taft Papers.

[57] W. H. Taft to Mrs. Taft, May 16, 1911, Pringle, *Taft*, II, 666.

[58] W. Van Devanter to E. B. Adams, May 18, 1911, Van Devanter Papers.

[59] W. Van Devanter to E. B. Adams, May 14, 1911, Van Devanter Papers.

[60] W. Van Devanter to E. B. Adams, May 18, 1911, Van Devanter Papers.

for a reasonable construction of the act with a view to the evil aimed at. What I was criticizing [as in the message of January 7] in the word reasonable was when it was proposed to be applied to a monopoly or a partial monopoly or a restraint of trade for the purpose of enhancing prices, and it was supposed to distinguish between restraints of this character and leave it to the court to say that those in which the profits exacted by such means were moderate were lawful, and those in which they were exorbitant were to be condemned.[61]

Van Devanter entertained little hope that an understanding of the opinion similar to his own would soon come to be widely shared. Rather, within a couple of days, he noted that Harlan's view was being taken up in the press and agitated in Congress. "The agitation has produced for the moment a much greater disposition than you would expect along the line of so altering the statute as to make it a refutation of the rule of reason. Public sentiment is more or less acute on the subject and very easily arouses to speedy action."[62] Taft also knew what he could expect from "La Follette and his crowd,"[63] but even though, unlike Van Devanter, he was in a position to do something about it—as usual, he did not. He failed to seize the initiative and to impress his views on the public discussion that immediately swirled about him.

The day after the decision, the President was besieged in the White House to explain what most people took to be, and what many newspaper headlines announced as being,[64] the contradiction between the position he had taken in the message of January 7, 1910, and the decision of Chief Justice White. Had not Taft opposed reading the test of reasonableness into the Sherman Act, by amendment or otherwise, and had not Chief Justice White done precisely what Taft had opposed? The White House merely let it be known that decisions of the Supreme Court were considered by the President to be the law of the land and that citizens were supposed to bow to them. The President would be the last man to express disagreement with the Court. The President read and reread the opinions, met with his Cabinet, and indicated that prosecutions would go on, and that his proposal for a federal incorporation bill might be reexamined. But he issued neither criticism nor explanation of the decision.[65]

---

[61] W. H. Taft to J. A. Shauck, June 10, 1911, Pringle, *Taft*, II, 666.

[62] W. Van Devanter to E. B. Adams, May 18, 1911, Van Devanter Papers.

[63] W. H. Taft to Mrs. Taft, May 15, 1911, Taft Papers.

[64] See *Detroit News*, May 17, 1911, p. 11: "Taft Disagrees With Oil Decision, His Speeches Show."

[65] Lowry, "The Supreme Court Speaks," *Harper's Weekly*, 55:8, June 1911; *Detroit News*, May 17, 1911, p. 11.

While the President kept his own counsel, controversy boiled up unimpeded, and substantially dominated by Harlan's dissent. Both White's unprinted opinion and Harlan's unwritten dissent were instantly available in stenographic transcripts of the oral deliveries, and widely reported. Just about the only comments that were both relatively disinterested and unequivocally favorable to the majority's decision—so it must have seemed to the public—were made by cartoonists. On the day after the decision came down, one front page showed golfer Rockefeller hit in the head with a ball marked "Supreme Court Decision," and about to collapse on the approach to the sixth hole. The cartoon was titled "Fore."[66] On the same day, on the front page of the *Chicago Daily News*, Rockefeller was shedding tears as the dogcatcher hauled in tens of octopuses labeled "Subsidiary Oil Company." The dogcatcher was labeled "Judge," the cartoon was captioned "That Painful Moment," and underneath was the remark: "When one realizes that the dog catcher is no respecter of persons."[67]

In the news and editorial columns, the picture was otherwise. Big business was "mightily pleased," and Progressives of both parties were disappointed.[68] On May 16, Andrew Carnegie hastened to declare himself "gratified almost beyond measure," and "a happy man today."[69] Chairman E. H. Gary of United States Steel was satisfied,[70] and so were numerous other businessmen and their lawyers—a mood registered by a rising stock market.[71] But William Jennings Bryan remarked that the Supreme Court had put into the law just exactly the phrase the trusts would like to see in it.[72] Representative William C. Adamson (Democrat of Georgia), chairman of the House Committee on Interstate and Foreign Commerce, attacked the decision on the same ground, saying that the Court should not have written into the statute precisely the provision Congress had denied the trusts, despite their repeated requests.[73] That was the view also of Robert M. La Follette.[74] The

---

[66] *Providence, Rhode Island, Evening Bulletin*, May 16, 1911, p. 1.

[67] *Chicago Daily News*, May 16, 1911, p. 1.

[68] *Indianapolis News*, May 16, 1911, p. 1, col. 8.

[69] *New York Times*, May 17, 1911, p. 1.

[70] *Chicago Daily News*, May 16, 1911, p. 2, col. 3.

[71] See *New York Times*, May 17, 1911, p. 1, col. 1 ("Business Likes Oil Decision"); *Chicago Daily News*, May 16, 1911, p. 1, col. 5.

[72] *Detroit News*, May 17, 1911, p. 11; *Indianapolis News*, May 16, 1911, p. 1, col. 6.

[73] *Louisville Courier Journal*, May 17, 1911, p. 1, col. 2, cont. p. 10.
These requests had in fact been for something a good bit more complex than could possibly be read into Chief Justice White's opinion. See R. H. Wiebe, *Businessmen and Reform* (1962), 80–81.

[74] See M. Sullivan, *Our Times* (1936), IV, 577–78.

interpretation privately given, as we have seen, by Van Devanter from the inside and by Taft from the outside, that the Court had dealt with the statute, as a matter of construction, in the only way possible, that the thing that was important was the result reached, and that, of course, no emasculation of the Act had occurred—that interpretation found, to be sure, some editorial support, the *New York Tribune* even suggesting that the opinion of Chief Justice White was not inconsistent with Taft's own previously expressed views; but on the whole, the simpler and more radical reactions drowned it out.[75] The sense of emasculation was dominant and widespread among the Progressives,[76] and has survived to this day.[77]

Within two weeks, on May 29, 1911, came two more opinions by White and Harlan, in the *American Tobacco* case. They did nothing to deflect the dissent-oriented course of public discussion. Briefly, White restated the rule of reason. Peckham's opinion in the *Trans-Missouri Freight Association* and *Joint Traffic* cases were not really to the contrary, he contended once more, and the present case again demonstrated how impossible it would be to give "to the statute a narrow, unreasoning and unheard of construction." The entire tobacco combination was illegal, "not because alone of the many corporations which the proof shows were united by resort to one device or another . . . not alone because of the dominion and control over the tobacco trade which actually exists, but because we think the conclusion of wrongful purpose and illegal combination is overwhelmingly established" by the piratical conduct consistently engaged in by the combination. The upshot was "that the combination as a whole, involving all its coöperating or associated parts, in whatever form clothed, constitutes a restraint of trade within the first section, and an attempt to monopolize or a monopolization within the second section of the Antitrust Act. . . ."

It followed that the relief to be given would have to be wider than that awarded by the circuit court. To begin with, the circuit court had dismissed the complaints against the individual defendants, the United Cigars Stores Company, and the foreign corporations and their sub-

---

[75] *New York Tribune,* May 16, 1911, p. 8, col. 2; *Chicago Daily News,* May 16, 1911, p. 8, col. 2.

[76] With an occasional exception, to be sure, and having regard to the general position Theodore Roosevelt was later to take in the campaign of 1912. "I did not have a fit over the rule of reason," wrote William Allen White to President Taft in June 1911, "because I believe trusts and com-

binations are economic and industrial necessities and should be controlled rather than dismembered. I do not believe competition is a good in and of itself." White to Taft, June 20, 1911, Taft Papers, Library of Congress. For very different reasons, Louis D. Brandeis had no fit either. See *infra,* p. 136.

[77] Hofstadter, *Age of Reform,* 248–49.

sidiaries. This portion of the decree was erroneous, and had to be reversed. For the rest, the decree was vacated. In framing a new one, the circuit court should be guided by:

> 1. The duty of giving complete and efficacious effect to the prohibitions of the statute; 2, the accomplishing of this result with as little injury as possible to the interest of the general public; and, 3, a proper regard for the vast interests of private property which may have become vested in many persons as a result of the acquisition either by way of stock ownership or otherwise of interests in the stock or securities of the combination without any guilty knowledge or intent in any way to become actors or participants in the wrongs which we find to have inspired and dominated the combination from the beginning.

A mere decree of dissolution, ordering the various companies to divest themselves of their subsidiaries, would be insufficient, "since different ingredients of the combination would remain unaffected, and by the very nature and character of their organization would be able to continue the wrongful situation which it is our duty to destroy." The units resulting from a simple divestiture, White had suggested earlier in the opinion, might for one thing still be too large and powerful. The entire combination could be excluded from interstate commerce, to be sure, but such a last resort would throw out the baby with the bath-water. A receiver could be appointed to run and unscramble everything in due time, but that also would seem harsh, especially to "many innocent people," presumably stockholders. And so White ordered the circuit court to hear the parties again for the purpose of devising a plan to restore lawful and competitive conditions. He imposed a six-month deadline for the evolution of such a plan, although allowing the circuit court to extend the time if necessary. All else failing, the circuit court was authorized either to enjoin use of the channels of interstate commerce by the combination, or to appoint a receiver.[78]

When the decision was announced, Harlan's dissent was again oral:

> What I have now to say must necessarily be oral, for the court's opinion was not delivered to me until late Saturday evening, and it has been impossible for me since then to put in writing the views which I deem it necessary to express. I do not refer to this by way of complaint, for the delay in delivering to me a copy of the opinion of the

---

[78] United States v. American Tobacco Co., 221 U.S. 106 (1911). Passages and phrases quoted are, in sequence, at 221 U.S. 180, 182, 184, 185–87.

court has no doubt been unavoidable. I will hereafter prepare and file a written opinion expressing my views fully.[79]

He then proceeded to say, not at great length, substantially, and in places literally, what he later filed in writing. Why, his opinion asks, did the case need to go back to the circuit court for the issuance of a decree? The record was made, and "why cannot all necessary directions be now given as to the terms of the decree?" Then, without indicating just how he would frame a decree, Harlan went back to the rule-of-reason debate. "If I do not misapprehend the opinion just delivered," White was claiming not to be departing from the *Trans-Missouri* and *Joint Traffic* cases. "This statement surprises me quite as much as would a statement that black was white or white was black." One thing at any rate was certain, the Court's rule of reason could not "justify the perversion of the plain words of an act in order to defeat the will of Congress." And the implicit insult to Peckham's and his own methods of statutory construction still rankled:

> It is obvious from the opinions of the former cases, that the majority did not grope about in darkness, but in discharging the solemn duty put on them they stood out in the full glare of the "light of reason" and felt and said time and again that the court could not, consistently with the Constitution, and would not, usurp the functions of Congress by indulging in judicial legislation.

Finally, it was plain under any construction that the Tobacco trust was covered by the Sherman Act and was illegal. All the statements in the Court's opinion, therefore, defining and defending the rule of reason, "I say with respect, [are] *obiter dicta*, pure and simple."[80]

Unlike the Standard Oil announcement, the *Tobacco* decision was followed by a break in the stock market. There were unrelated factors at work also, but tobacco shares themselves fell most dramatically.[81] Otherwise nothing much was added to the pattern of reaction established two weeks earlier (and before too long, the price of tobacco stock came back handsomely). Attorney General Wickersham claimed another triumph for the government.[82] The *New York Tribune*, sympathetic to the Taft Administration, editorialized that the *Tobacco* decision disposed of the notion "that the interpretation of the Sherman Law 'in the light of reason' had weakened that act."[83] But the *Louisville Courier*

---

[79] *New York Times*, May 30, 1911, p. 6, col. 1.

[80] The dissent is at 221 U.S. 189. Passages quoted are at 221 U.S. 190, 191, 192, 193.

[81] *Providence, Rhode Island, Evening Bulletin*, May 31, 1911.

[82] *New York Tribune*, May 30, 1911, p. 2, col. 6.

[83] *New York Tribune*, May 30, 1911, p. 2, col. 2.

Journal, noting that the decision was hailed as "a sweeping victory for the Government," added: "Let us hope that it is, and that in the end it may prove an equal victory for the people." Meanwhile the *Courier Journal* declared itself in "general sympathy with blunt old Justice Harlan."[84]

As the year went on, professional and scholarly comment made its necessarily delayed appearance. In this literature, the Court did rather better than in the popular press and magazines. But it found vigorous critics here also.[85] The professional literature, moreover, brought forth some disaffection from the right, so to speak, manifested in complaints that the rule of reason was too vague a standard for the conduct of business affairs, and also that it might involve the Court too deeply and legislatively in the making of economic policy.[86] The net effect, therefore, of these later, calmer, and better informed comments was to add to a consensus—gathering from virtually all quarters—in favor of legislation to amend and supplement the Sherman Act.[87]

The Dissolutions and Their Consequences

The decisions in the *Standard Oil* and *Tobacco* cases had a political and a doctrinal aftermath, which we have so far held chiefly in view, and to which we must return. They affected the contest for political power, and they spawned or influenced, in time, other decisions, judicial and legislative. But they had consequences also, of course, in the oil and tobacco industries to which they were immediately addressed.

The decree in *Standard Oil* ordered the New Jersey Company, which was the holding company, to dissolve itself through a pro rata

---

[84] *Louisville Courier Journal,* May 31, 1911, p. 6, col. 2.

[85] See A. H. Walker, "A Review of the Opinions of the Chief Justice of the United States in the Standard Oil and Tobacco Cases," *Am. L. Rev.,* 45:718, 1911; H. L. Wilgus, "The Standard Oil Decision: The Rule of Reason," *Mich. L. Rev.,* 9:643, 1911. For general approval of the decisions, see "The Standard Oil Decision," *Green Bag,* 23:279, 1911; H. R. Seager, "The Recent Trust Decisions," *Political Science Quarterly,* 26:581, 1911; W. B. Hornblower, "Antitrust Legislation and Litigation," *Colum. L. Rev.,* 11:701, 1911; R. L. Raymond, "The Standard Oil and Tobacco

Cases," *Harv. L. Rev.,* 25:31 (1911); R. L. Swift, "An Interpretation of the Standard Oil and American Tobacco Cases," *Case & Com.,* 18:519, 1912.

[86] See J. M. Beck, *North American Review,* 194:55, July 1911; R. Olney, "National Judiciary and Big Business," *Boston Herald,* Sept. 24, 1911, Special Feature Section 2, col. 1.

[87] E.g., S. Untermyer, "Government Regulation of the Trusts," *Case & Com.,* 18:502, 1912; F. L. Stetson, "Control of Corporations Engaged in Interstate Commerce," *Case & Com.,* 18:512, 1912; Editorial, *Case & Com.,* 18:30, 1911. See M. Handler, *Antitrust in Perspective* (1957), 29–30.

distribution of the shares of its subsidiary corporations to its own stockholders, who would be left in direct ownership of the former subsidiaries. The principal owners of the former holding company were now the principal owners of thirty-three separate companies. But they were under an injunction as individuals not to restrain trade by agreement among themselves in violation of the Sherman Act.

The ultimate decree in the *Tobacco* case was not so simple, and not simply arrived at. When McReynolds, continuing to act for the government, first met with lawyers for the American Tobacco Company, he simply laughed off the suggestion of a reorganization into three independent companies owned, pro rata, by the same stockholders as before. He insisted, rather, on a much more massive reorganization. The ball of yarn that the trust had wound all these years, McReynolds said, must be unwound. The company's lawyers objected that they could not sell the business to anyone but those who had built it up, since no one else had enough money. That, said McReynolds, was their problem. They had better find somebody to sell to other than themselves, or the Court would appoint a receiver who would do it for them. But that, the answer came, would involve the destruction of property, confiscation. McReynolds replied: "Confiscation? What if it is! Since when has property illegally and criminally acquired come to have any rights?"[88]

Attorney General Wickersham, however, was not so uncompromising. McReynolds, he reported to the President, apparently wanted to compel a receivership. Wickersham disagreed: "I assume that the government is only concerned in breaking up a monopoly and restoring competitive conditions, and that we desire to avoid so far as is consistent with the attainment of those ends any great business disaster." And he substantially took over negotiation of the decree: "I dare not leave it entirely in the hands of Mr. MacReynolds [*sic*]," he said. "It is the most important matter I have on hand at the moment, and I am giving up everything else for it."[89] Wickersham was concerned throughout with "the effects of the proposed distribution of companies upon competition of different types of tobacco leaf, and competition with respect to the different brands of tobacco products." But he also "felt that the security of the holders of one-hundred millions of bonds was something which should be borne constantly in mind." A receivership, he thought, would be a great public misfortune. Alternative solutions all raised complex and unfamiliar business problems, and Wickersham sought the assistance of the Bureau of Corporations in the Department

---

[88] *New York Times,* Mar. 3, 1913, p. 4.

[89] G. W. Wickersham to C. D. Hilles, Aug. 29, 1911; Wickersham to W. H. Taft, Aug. 30, 1911, Taft Papers.

of Commerce and Labor. He also obtained the advice, and the concurrence with his own views, of Secretary of Commerce and Labor Charles Nagel and of Solicitor General Frederick W. Lehmann, both distinguished lawyers.[90]

On October 16, 1911, the defendants filed in the circuit court in New York a proposed plan of dissolution which Wickersham viewed, on the whole, favorably. Nine days later, having been called to a conference with the Attorney General in Washington, McReynolds handed him a fourteen-page memorandum. The disagreement between the two men remained well mannered and even friendly, but it was approaching the point of rupture. The government, McReynolds said, had insisted throughout "upon the absurdity of the claim put forward by the defendants that two corporations under one control could be competitors." The object of the decree ought to be to restore the preexisting lawful conditions of unrestrained competition so far as possible.

> In certain cases substantially the original situation can be restored and this usually should be done. It will not avail to substitute one holding company for another. Competition did not produce that situation and the statute condemns it. Generally speaking, when a corporation has been preserved as a distinct entity within a going business it should be cut loose from the other defendants and kept free from the control of any other company. This seems to have been approved by the Supreme Court when it recognized the propriety of the action of the Circuit Court so far as it went.

Under the plan proposed by the defendants,

> every company, every share of stock, every plant, every brand now under the control of those who are common stockholders of the American Tobocco Company and who have been and are bound together by contract and act in concert, will remain under their dominion, and they will still be bound together by contract as stockholders in joint ventures. Not only this, but they will be the common stockholders in the various companies whose special interests will be best subserved by the largest possible aggregate profits of all the companies. As long as such circumstances continue, manifestly there can be no hope for the public to enjoy prices made under the check of competition which necessarily requires interests substantially diverse. . . . *Consider* that if the exact situation which would result from the complete carrying out of the proposed plan had been the goal desired and labored for by those who twenty years ago formed the American

---

[90] G. W. Wickersham to W. H. Taft, Nov. 4, 7, 1911, Taft Papers.

Tobacco Company and their successors, its attainment would have been a violation of the law. If indeed, before the original bill was filed, the defendants had voluntarily done exactly what is now proposed, the resulting situation would have been contrary to law. . . .

McReynolds concluded with certain more detailed suggestions, among which were the following: The American Tobacco Company should be required to sell at once all its stock in the Imperial Company. That stock, McReynolds believed, could be sold easily enough at 175, its current quotation, which was 75 percent more than the stock had cost the American Tobacco Company in 1902. "The real reason for refraining from selling now seems to be the expectation of large dividends and perhaps a better price within the next three years." The American Tobacco Company and the Imperial Tobacco Company should be "denuded of their stock" in the British-American Tobacco Company, "and something should be done concerning the licenses to manufacture all the brands of those companies." The Connelly Foil Company "is a combination in and of itself with a monopoly. This monopoly is not properly destroyed by taking away from the company holding it less than one-third of its assets and about one-third of its annual business and giving these to another company, the ultimate control of which lies in the same individuals having control of the Connelly Foil Company. No real competition can exist under such circumstances." Much the same was true of McAndrews and Forbes Company. "The Devoe Snuff Company is a separate going business and should be entirely separated from those who control the combination. I presume the same is true and the same result should accordingly follow with respect to the National Snuff Company. The result of what is proposed in reference to the monopoly held by the American Snuff Company will be to create three concerns controlled by the same people between whom there will be no competition and against which no independent concern will probably be able successfully to compete." The American Stogie Company "should be dissolved and wound up." The American Cigar Company "should be entirely free from the dominion of any other corporation and in turn should be divided much further than is suggested." What was proposed as to Liggett and Myers Company and P. Lorillard Company, "I do not think is proper. Each one of them would become a holding company and constitute in and of itself an unlawful combination. Each of them would in fact be under the control of the same individuals who now dominate the combination and their creation would not bring about present competitive conditions. It is not improbable that the resulting conditions would be worse so far as real competition is concerned than those now existing." Finally:

It may be that by dividing the business of the combination among a much larger number of companies . . . it would be possible to bring about a condition ultimately acceptable, particularly if the stockholders in the various companies were different. But . . . the plan proposed merits the emphatic disapproval of the Government.

It has been suggested with what appears to be good reason that the distribution of brands among the proposed three principal companies will in itself result in giving to each of them an undue control over the trade, both as buyers of leaf and as sellers of manufactured goods. A satisfactory determination of this and other questions which may relate to practical operations may necessitate the introduction of proof and a material addition to the present record. Without such additional proof the Court could hardly be in a position to understand all the essentials to the solution of the problem.[91]

Wickersham, as he reported to the President, considered McReynolds' arguments "with much tribulation of spirit and perplexity of mind."[92] But he remained unconvinced, and McReynolds consequently, on October 30, 1911, handed him in New York a regretful and courteous letter of resignation. Having first, with equal courtesy, asked McReynolds to remain, Wickersham on December 1 accepted the resignation, effective December 31, 1911.[93]

The final decree, embodying some modifications suggested by Wickersham, but in the main following the defendants' proposals of October 16, was handed down on November 16, 1911, and is summarized as follows in an authoritative study:

1. The trusts' purchasing subsidiary was dissolved; nine units whose operations were nearly autonomous (e.g., The American Snuff Company) were separated by distributing their securities to American Tobacco's stockholders; and four of these nine were required to split in their turn into either two or three parts. Most of the successor companies were forbidden for five years, and the two foreign defendants (Imperial Tobacco and British-American Tobacco) permanently, to use a common leaf-buying agent. There were also permanent injunctions against owning joint subsidiaries and against certain other practices, in each instance with carefully defined exceptions. The covenants between American Tobacco and Imperial Tobacco were enjoined.

---

[91] The McReynolds memorandum is dated Oct. 24, 1911, and bears his notation about being handed to the Attorney General the following day. The notation is dated Oct. 27, 1911. The memorandum is in the McReynolds Papers.

[92] G. W. Wickersham to W. H. Taft, Oct. 26, 1911, Taft Papers.

[93] J. C. McReynolds to G. W. Wickersham, Oct. 30, 1911; J. A. Fowler to J. C. McReynolds, Dec. 1, 1911, McReynolds Papers.

2. The remaining brands and physical assets were divided among three named successor firms. A new American Tobacco Company received seventeen plants, Liggett & Myers Tobacco Company twelve, and P. Lorillard Company ten. In 1910 these thirty-nine plants had produced 80% of all cigarettes, 76% of smoking tobacco, 63% of plug chewing tobacco, and varying percentages of other products.

3. The 56% ownership of voting stock by the twenty-nine individual defendants was reduced to 35% for American Tobacco and 41% for both Liggett & Myers and Lorillard, by requiring some sales of shares and giving voting power to the preferred stock.[94]

Virtually at the eleventh hour, three national associations of independent tobacco interests—independent, that is, from the trust, and thus constituting such competition as had remained—tried to obtain modifications of the decree in the form in which the defendants and Attorney General Wickersham were settling it. On October 18, 1911, the circuit court, while not allowing them to intervene, agreed to let them be heard and file a brief.[95] Counsel for these associations, the National Cigar Leaf Tobacco Association, the Cigar Manufacturers Association, and the Independent Tobacco Salesmen's Association, were Louis D. Brandeis and Felix H. Levy. Their brief made five, as they called them, "fundamental" objections. First, they objected to the continued common ownership which would result from dissolution by distribution of stock pro rata among stockholders of the American Tobacco Company. Second, they objected that the successor companies—the three principal ones, and some of those that were being cut loose as well—were too large, and that no effective competition with any of them would be possible. The independents would be left, in the aggregate for all of them, with only 19.80 percent of the cigarette business; 21.39 percent of the smoking tobacco business; 19.05 percent of the plug tobacco business; 6.95 percent of the business in little cigars, and so forth. The third objection was that each of the three principal successor companies would be integrated, that is, "completely equipped for the conduct of a large tobacco business." None of the independents was so equipped, and all would therefore be seriously handicapped as competitors. Fourth, the injunctions prohibiting specific practices were inadequate: "It is

[94] 191 Fed. 371 (S.D. N.Y. 1911); Whitney, *Antitrust Policies*, II, 16–17.

[95] *Hearings before Committee on Interstate Commerce, United States Senate, 62nd Congress, pursuant to Senate Resolution 98, a Resolution Directing the Committee on Interstate Commerce to Investigate and Report Desirable Changes in the Laws Regulating and Controlling Corporations, Persons, and Firms Engaged in Interstate Commerce*, I, 356, Washington, Government Printing Office, 1912 (hereinafter cited as *Clapp Hearings*).

clear that for a limited period the independents should have more protection than would ordinarily be necessary in trade where one concern has not succeeded in illegally dominating the trade." And

> Fifth. The plan provides for leaving intact the United Cigars Stores Company and merely distributing among the common-stockholders of the American Tobacco Company its stockholdings in the United Cigars Stores Company. No plan can be effective to restore competition which does not provide for dividing the businesses and property of the United Cigars Stores Company among many separate concerns owned by absolutely distinct groups of individuals.

The brief urged a much more radical breakup: at least seven separate cigarette manufacturers, at least twelve separate smoking tobacco manufacturers, at least twelve separate plug tobacco manufacturers, at least seven separate manufacturers of little cigars, at least six separate manufacturers of snuff, and at least five separate manufacturers of tin foil. And it proposed also that the resulting companies not be integrated. No corporation having a plug or smoking tobacco business should be allowed to engage in cigarette or cigar manufacture, for example, and vice versa.[96]

When counsel for the independents followed up their informal brief with a motion to intervene, the Attorney General objected, and the motion was denied.[97] Thereupon, by letter and telegram on November 6 and 7, the independents went over the Attorney General's head and appealed to the President.[98] But Wickersham stood firm. He wired the President that he had taken "definite ground respecting the [defendants'] plan which I think is an honest attempt to restore competitive conditions. I cannot now without stultifying myself take any other position with the court than I have taken and I am unwilling to request it to delay its decision."[99] And that was that. After the decree was issued, some of the independents, not having standing to appeal the decree because they were not parties, sought to get the Supreme Court to issue a writ of mandamus ordering the circuit court to allow them to intervene. They were represented by Levy, and by none other than Benjamin N. Cardozo. The application was summarily denied on procedural grounds,[100] but White, at least, indicated privately that he viewed it with disfavor on the merits as well, because he was quite satisfied with the decree.[101]

---

[96] *Clapp Hearings*, I, 315.
[97] *Clapp Hearings*, I, 356–57.
[98] *Clapp Hearings*, I, 362–63.
[99] G. W. Wickersham to C. D. Hilles, Nov. 7, 1911, Taft Papers.

[100] *Ex parte* Leaf Tobacco Board of Trade, 222 U.S. 578 (1911).
[101] E. D. White to W. R. Day, Dec. 6, 1911, Day Papers.

II: *The Rule of Reason*

The decrees in both the *Standard Oil* and *Tobacco* cases had no better public reception than had been accorded White's opinions. Andrew Carnegie allowed that Standard Oil of New Jersey and the American Tobacco Company were "laughing at the government," and George W. Perkins, sometime partner of J. P. Morgan and a director of U. S. Steel, considered that "the dissolution of the Standard Oil and Tobacco companies was a great farce."[102] What were Progressives to think? The Democratic platform of 1912 condemned the Tobacco decree, and Theodore Roosevelt called it a "flagrant travesty of justice." Senator Thomas P. Gore, the Progressive Democrat from Oklahoma, thought it "a fruitless victory," "a worthless blessing," and "much ado about nearly nothing."[103] As to the Oil decree, there was, in the next few years, the mute testimony of the astronomic rise in the value of Standard Oil Company of New Jersey stock. It was left to President Taft, standing behind his Attorney General, to absorb the political damage, and declare that both decrees furnished "a useful precedent as to the proper method of dealing with the capital and property of illegal trusts," and even more explicitly and daringly, "that not in the history of American law has a decree more effective for such a purpose been entered by a court than that against the Tobacco Trust."[104]

The actual consequences of the decrees to the oil and tobacco industries—or at any rate, their practical aftermath—may seem surprising in light of their reception. In the oil industry, it was true for about the first four years or so following the decree that not much competition developed among the now separate and independent (but still Rockefeller, etc.–owned) Standard companies. These successor companies tended at first to operate within the same marketing territories that had been assigned to them when they were part of the trust. But even during this period, and starting indeed even before 1911, competition between all the Standard companies on the one hand, and independent interests entering the business (e.g., the Mellon interests: Gulf Oil Corporation) on the other, was steadily on the rise, as the oil industry in its entirety expanded dramatically with the coming of the automobile.

After about 1915, some of the old dominant stockholders having died or distributed their shares, competition among the successor Standard companies became real and even lively. By 1927, competition among these companies in what used to be each other's marketing territories was termed "considerable" by the Federal Trade Commission.

---

[102] J. A. Garraty, *Right-Hand Man —The Life of George W. Perkins* (1957), 255.

[103] Quoted in Whitney, *Antitrust Policies,* II, 16. For Senator Gore, see *Clapp Hearings,* I, 1255–56.

[104] President's Annual Message to Congress, Part I, Dec. 5, 1911, in *Messages and Papers of the Presidents,* XVIII, 8024, 8029.

It came into being, plainly, as a direct consequence of the decree. Whether the substantial and growing competition of the independents with the Standard companies was also a result of the decree or would have occurred anyway is, however, in doubt. A series of mergers (one of which was held by a federal court not to violate the provisions of the 1911 decree)[105] eventually reduced the number of Standard companies, all of them in any event grown much bigger than they had been, and in some instances bigger even than the original trust. And the business as a whole, successor companies and independents, finally settled into the condition of oligopoly which seems to be characteristic of American heavy industry. An agreement in 1923 among some of the Standard companies to pool patents in order to protect themselves against competition was upheld by the Supreme Court in 1931.[106] The industry was, of course, not free of other antitrust litigation, but none that had more than a remote connection, if any, to the original dissolution.[107]

In the tobacco industry the dominant facts during the years immediately following dissolution were the change in public taste which vastly increased the consumption of cigarettes as compared with other tobacco products, and the shift in the production of cigarettes from the use of Turkish to the use almost exclusively of domestic tobaccos. Both changes in general conditions are hardly attributable to the decree, the latter change least of all, since it was the result in part of the shortage of Turkish tobaccos which attended the First World War. But the leader in both pushing and following the new trend toward domestic-tobacco cigarettes was the R. J. Reynolds Company, which in the dissolution was given no share of the cigarette market.

Reynolds had manufactured plug tobacco. Freed of the combination, it entered cigarette production in 1912. In 1913, Reynolds introduced Camels, made of domestic tobaccos, at 10 rather than the standard 15¢ for a package of twenty, and captured 13 percent of the market by 1915, and 35 percent by 1917. In this development, the decree at least arguably played a role. Would the Reynolds initiative have been exercised by the trust, or permitted by it, if coming from the outside? The cigarette and domestic tobaccos were coming anyway, but how would the trust have dealt with these new factors?

It also seems likely that the dissolution resulted in more moderate prices for the consumer, and higher prices for the tobacco farmer. It produced—or was, at any rate, followed by—competition among the

---

[105] United States v. Standard Oil Co. of New Jersey, 47 F.2d 288 (E.D. Mo. 1931).

[106] Standard Oil Co. v. United States, 283 U.S. 163 (1931).

[107] Whitney, *Antitrust Policies,* I, 104–68; Seager and Gulick, *Trust and Corporation Problems,* 125–48.

successor companies, even if imperfect and also ultimately oligopolistic. Life for the independents, however, scarcely became easier. To survive, a number of them combined in a new company, which was nevertheless unable to last for long. Nor was entry into the cigarette market easy. And while competition affected prices till about 1923, they have been uniform since then.[108]

There is opinion which holds that if the industry had been atomized, as the independents or McReynolds demanded in 1911, the public would have been worse rather than better served, in terms of prices and quality. This is guesswork, of course. What is certain is that dissatisfaction with the Tobacco decree, more intense from the beginning than with the Oil dissolution, died hard, and that the tobacco industry, therefore, had the government on its neck, so to speak, more often than the oil industry. McReynolds, for one, did not give up his opposition to the decree. As Attorney General under Wilson, shortly after he took office he proposed the imposition of a graduated excise tax on the manufacture of tobacco, which would rise so high as to hurt the big successor companies badly and indirectly help the independents. At McReynolds' behest, and with the approval of the President and the Cabinet, such a measure was introduced in the Senate, but it raised a storm of protest, and the President finally withdrew his support, thus letting it die.[109]

Congress in 1920–21 caused the Federal Trade Commission to investigate the tobacco industry, with the result that the commission eventually issued an order against the American Tobacco Company for unlawfully combining to maintain prices with tobacco jobbers in Philadelphia. The order, however, did not stand up in court.[110] In the course of this investigation the commission also ran up against a Supreme Court decision forbidding it simply to fish around, by subpoena, in the records of the tobacco companies, "in the hope that something will turn up."[111] Another investigation by the Federal Trade Commission was made pursuant to a Senate Resolution of 1925. Finally in 1940, the government prosecuted American Tobacco, Reynolds, and Liggett and Myers criminally under the Sherman Act for collusion on prices. This attack—a second *American Tobacco* case—succeeded.[112]

---

[108] See Whitney, *Antitrust Policies,* II, 18–33; Seager and Gulick, *Trust and Corporation Problems,* 179–95; see also G. E. Hale, "Trust Dissolution," *Colum. L. Rev.,* 40:615, 618–23, 1940; E. H. Levi, "The Antitrust Laws and Monopoly," *U. Chi. L. Rev.,* 14: 153, 1947.

[109] A. S. Link, *Wilson: The New*

Freedom (1956), 417–18, 81.

[110] Federal Trade Commission v. American Tobacco Co., 274 U.S. 543 (1927).

[111] Federal Trade Commission v. American Tobacco Co., 264 U.S. 298, 306 (1924).

[112] American Tobacco Co. v. United States, 328 U.S. 781 (1946).

Aftermath—Politics, Legislation, and Doctrine

The atmospheric disturbance over the rule of reason was violent and widespread, as much so, perhaps, as any ever provoked by a decision of the Supreme Court. But it was, after all, a summer storm, and then it passed. By the end of the year, a longer-term reaction had set in, which was quite different. People talked less of what the Court had done or might do. Attention turned, rather, to industrial policy at large, and to legislative proposals. It was as if, in the 1950s, after an initial public outburst, *Brown v. Board of Education* had been followed by the most deliberate and elaborate Congressional and other public consideration of educational policy in all its aspects—everyone proceeding on the assumption that, whatever the Court had done in the past, the political process, and not the Court, must formulate policy for the future. The upshot after announcement of the rule of reason was a great national debate. It was central to the Presidential campaign of 1912, and continued into the first years of the New Freedom. The Supreme Court cannot be said to have provoked it. But, although it had been building up for some time, the debate had been awaiting disposition of the *Standard Oil* and *Tobacco* cases, and resolution of the so-called rule-of-reason issue. By its decision of those cases, therefore, the Court at least undammed the great debate.

Of course, even if largely ignored, the Court could not be entirely out of mind. Expressions of regret about the rule of reason recurred for some time, and still do, and even anger sputtered along. As late as April 1913, a bill was introduced in the Senate declaring that "the words 'unreasonable or undue' inserted by the Supreme Court of the United States on May 13, 1911, by its decision of the case entitled 'Standard Oil Company of New Jersey et al v. The United States,' between the words 'in' and 'restraint of trade or commerce,' where these words occur in Section 1 of the [Sherman Antitrust] act . . . be, and the same are hereby, stricken out and repealed, and that the said section of said statute be restored to its original form. . . ."[113]

No doubt, as a general proposition, the *Standard Oil* and *Tobacco* opinions, and particularly the *Tobacco* decree, contributed to the alienation of a portion of the Progressive movement from the Supreme Court. But the Court had merely construed a statute. It had imposed no constitutional restraints, and dissatisfaction with the decrees focused

---

[113] S. 112, 50 *Cong. Rec.* 377, 63rd Cong., 1st Sess. (1913); and see *Report of Senate Committee on Interstate Commerce* (Feb. 13, 1913), xii, quoted in G. C. Henderson, *The Federal Trade Commission* (1924), 16.

on Attorney General Wickersham, who had negotiated and accepted them, and on the lower-court judges who had issued them, more than on the Supreme Court. Hopes—false ones, there is reason to suppose—were indeed harbored that if the *Tobacco* decree could only have been brought on appeal to the Supreme Court it might have been rendered more palatable.[114]

The sum of it is, then, that for the Court, the political consequences were almost nil. These consequences were visited instead on President Taft. Initially, as we have seen, Taft kept aloof. He made no attempt to explain the rule of reason, and no effort to direct the course of early discussion, which was so heavily dominated by Harlan's dissent. By the end of the year, when the time for explanation had passed, Taft finally spoke up, but he proved quite inept in seizing a position for himself. Now he undertook not only to explain but to adopt all too firmly and, by now, gratuitously the Chief Justice's opinions, and the decrees as well. While he had something to contribute to the debate about further legislation, Taft made a great show of associating himself with the courts. And since the Supreme Court had seemed to repudiate his own prior views, he found it necessary to engage in somewhat unedifying, even if perfectly valid, verbal maneuvers to demonstrate that the Court had not done so.

The result of this performance, of all Taft did not do and of the little he eventually did, was that he became the political victim of this most striking manifestation of the Court he had reconstituted. For the Court had spoken, and even those who regretted what it said because they had somehow hoped for more, hoped for it no longer, and were willing to forget. But more was very definitely expected of the politicians, precisely because it was no longer expected of the Court. And yet the main impression left by Taft's intervention in the legislative debate was that virtually alone among all the participants, he stood pat on the Court. This was not a profitable position.

Taft's intervention came in a message to Congress on December 5, 1911. Well over half the message was devoted to defense of the *Standard Oil* and *Tobacco* decisions and decrees, and depreciation of suggestions for amending or repealing the Sherman Act. The Court, Taft said, had clarified the Act by reading it in light of common law precedents, and the result was a workable statute, sufficiently definite to guide the conduct of those who wanted to abide by it, and altogether conforming to Taft's own exposition of it, prior to the decisions, in his

---

[114] See remarks of Louis D. Brandeis, and discussion of efforts to produce an appeal by special legislation, *Clapp Hearings,* I, 1214 (Oil Decree), 1236–42 (Tobacco Decree).

message of January 7, 1910. Taft also praised the decrees extravagantly. They were admirable even though they had far from atomized either the tobacco or the oil industry, because size alone was no sin, and it was "not the purpose of the statute to confiscate the property and capital of the offending trusts."

As for new legislative proposals, Taft, without mentioning them specifically, remarked that most were "nothing but glittering generalities." There might be some advantage in proscribing in detail certain methods of unfair competition—here was a faint suggestion that some portions of a bill introduced, as we shall see, by Robert M. La Follette might be unobjectionable—but the only significant proposal Taft himself put forward recurred to the federal incorporation suggestion of his message of January 7. Federal charters of incorporation should be granted subject to rigid rules, and be supervised with extensive publicity, but should not constitute exemptions from the Sherman Act. Elaborating on his earlier message, Taft now suggested that supervision of federally chartered corporations might be entrusted to "an executive tribunal of the dignity and power of the Comptroller of the Currency or the Interstate Commerce Commission." Here again was an echo of a bill introduced in the Senate, this one by Francis G. Newlands, the Nevada Democrat. Taft proposed also—somewhat vaguely—that the "executive tribunal" he had in mind should aid the courts in framing dissolution decrees in antitrust cases.[115]

This last idea stemmed from a recommendation of Attorney General Wickersham, who had complained to the President, while negotiating the *Tobacco* decree, of "the very unsatisfactory condition of law and procedure under which I have been acting."

> It is not right that the Attorney General should be subjected to the responsibility of deciding—because the decision of the Court will almost always follow his attitude—whether or not a proposed plan of disintegration of an individual combination would restore lawful conditions. The questions involved are economic; they depend upon information which we can not have in this department; and it was a mere chance that the Bureau of Corporations had investigated the tobacco industry, and, therefore, was possessed of facts which enabled it to come to the assistance of the Department of Justice in this particular instance.

The courts, Wickersham went on, were in no better position than the Department of Justice. Decrees in such cases therefore, he suggested,

---

[115] Annual Message, *Messages and Papers of the Presidents*, XVIII, 8024–36. For a more elaborate statement of the President's position, see W. H. Taft, *The Anti-Trust Act and the Supreme Court* (1914).

ought to adjudge that a given combination is an illegal combination in restraint of trade and an attempted monopoly, and that it be enjoined from carrying on interstate commerce unless within a given time it disintegrate and remove the restraint, and abolish any chance of monopoly, pursuant to a plan submitted to and approved by the Department of Commerce, or some other appropriate executive department of the government.

The questions involved were not legal but commercial, and "should be dealt with by the Department of Commerce as economic and commercial questions, and not guessed at by the Law Department."[116]

The Congressional Hearings, 1911–12

By the time Taft's message of December 5, 1911, was sent up, the great debate about industrial policy was in full swing. It had got under way, actually, even before the decree in the *Tobacco* case was settled, in three Congressional hearings which began in the summer of 1911 and ran for several months. In the center ring was the Senate Committee on Interstate Commerce (the Clapp Committee), holding hearings pursuant to a special Senate resolution. It was flanked by a special House Committee on Investigation of the United States Steel Corporation (the Stanley Committee), which had convened in public session as early as June 7, 1911, and by the House Judiciary Committee, taking testimony on trust legislation.

The polar policies advocated in these hearings were those of George W. Perkins[117] of United States Steel, the business politician and former Morgan partner, on the one hand, and on the other, of Louis D. Brandeis, the Boston lawyer. It was through these two men that the debate gave a foretaste of the campaign of 1912, for Brandeis was to be Wilson's chief adviser on industrial policy, and Perkins, close to Theodore Roosevelt, would be the financial angel of the Progressive party.

"You may state your name, age, residence, and occupation," Senator Moses E. Clapp of Minnesota, chairman of the Senate Committee, said to Perkins on December 13, 1911. The witness replied:

---

[116] G. W. Wickersham to W. H. Taft, Nov. 4, 1911, Taft Papers.

[117] George Walbridge Perkins (1862–1920) was a self-made man. Born in Chicago, he went to public schools there, but not to college, and started as a bookkeeper for the New York Life Insurance Company. At thirty, he was a vice-president, and before he reached forty he was a partner of J. P. Morgan & Co. After nine years, in 1910, having organized the International Harvester combination and participated in other Morgan ventures, he retired, retaining only such directorships as that in U.S. Steel.

"George W. Perkins; residence, New York City; age, 49. It is pretty difficult to describe my occupation." Perkins thought that consolidation was here to stay: "I believe that you can only get that which approaches efficiency in business today by doing business on a large scale." He did not look for much benefit to the public from competition, and he did not look for much competition: "I believe . . . that we are going to be, perhaps sooner than we realize, faced with the fact that in certain lines of business the efficiency of a certain company will become so great that that will be largely the controlling element in the matter of competition." These very large, consolidated organizations, which Perkins saw as a natural consequence of modern technology, had the public for their partners, and owed a public responsibility. And so the public, through its government, should regulate them. The way to do that was by publicity: "I think that a company that had to expose its capital stock, its methods, its treatment of labor, and its treatment of its competitors and consumers, so that all who ran might read—that you would find that would be largely corrective."

The Sherman Act, even if nothing else was wrong with it,[118] was a method of regulation by lawsuit, for as a self-executing command to the responsible businessman who had no desire to engage the government in litigation it was too vague and uncertain. And so Perkins proposed the creation in the Department of Commerce and Labor of a business court or commission with power to license corporations doing interstate or foreign business. The license would be issued only if the corporation gave a credible promise to abide by regulations prescribed by the commission pursuant to Congressional mandate. The essential feature of these regulations, in turn, would look to publicity, but licensees would also be required to secure the commission's approval for all their "affairs," from "capitalization to . . . business practices." Violation of the regulations by a licensed corporation would be punished by imprisonment of the individuals responsible for the violation.

The business court or commission would be "composed largely of experienced businessmen." A commission so composed, thought Perkins, would have a most beneficial effect on business esprit. Businessmen in Europe could look forward to being knighted. Lawyers in the United

---

[118] But there was, for it aimed at a kind of destructive competition that was antisocial as well as being obsolete. Low wages and bad working conditions were the results of such competition, Perkins said elsewhere at about this same time, adding: "The Congressman who stands for literal enforcement of the Sherman Act stands for the sweat shop and child labor." Quoted in A. M. Schlesinger, Jr., *The Crisis of the Old Order* (1957), 21.

States could look forward to going on the Supreme Court or into other high government offices. Membership on this court or commission would constitute an appropriate career goal for the leaders of American business, and the agency itself, being so staffed, would command the respect of the business community.[119]

Such was Perkins' plan for what he called "immediate relief,"[120] and he had earlier put it before President Taft, urging him—quite unsuccessfully—to suspend prosecutions pending its enactment.[121] The plan had its imprecisions. Just what kind of regulations should the business court or commission lay down for the conduct of affairs from "capitalization to . . . business practices"? And would the Sherman Act remain applicable? Although he did not say it in exactly so many words, it is fairly clear that Perkins intended the commission to issue exemptions from Sherman Act prosecution.[122] By way of "prospective relief," Perkins suggested that Congress should make a study of the Sherman Act and of proposals for its amendment or repeal, and also of the possibility of a national incorporation act.[123]

Under hard cross-examination by such Senators as Albert B. Cummins, the Iowa Progressive, Perkins emerged in some confusion, and with his high-mindedness a little suspect. Yet he did speak for a kind of responsibility and statesmanship in business, and in this he was at worst ingenuous. The notion, however, of a business court staffed by businessmen was surely rather more disingenuous than naive. It was reminiscent of Richard Olney's assurance to a railroad client that the ICC need not be feared, for it could be "a sort of barrier between the railroad corporations and the people and a sort of protection against hasty and crude legislation." The railroads, said Olney, would be well advised "not to destroy the commission, but to utilize it."[124]

Far from the foolishness of wanting to destroy a commission, Perkins wanted to steal a march on "the people" and create and staff one. Through the commission there could be substituted for the annoyance of litigation the altogether different relationship with the govern-

---

[119] *Clapp Hearings*, I, 1089, 1104, 1107, 1106, 1091–92, 1122–23.

[120] *Ibid.*, 1091.

[121] See J. A. Garraty, *Right-Hand Man*, 253.

[122] He had told the Stanley Committee in August that he did not think business could well go on "under a technical enforcement of the Sherman law," by which he said he meant a "literal enforcement," by which in turn he meant, for example, "any effort to break up the United States Steel Corporation until somebody has found out whether, as you say, it, perhaps, has been successful and done good business." *Stanley Hearings*, 1533–34, 1527.

[123] *Clapp Hearings*, I, 1092.

[124] M. Josephson, *The Politicos* (1938), 526.

ment that the House of Morgan had always wanted. When the prosecution of the *Northern Securities* case was begun, J. P. Morgan complained to Theodore Roosevelt: "If we have done anything wrong . . . send your man to my man and they can fix it up."[125] Morgan sent his man to Theodore Roosevelt's man more than once, and with considerable success.[126] The men of Morgan and of others went to Taft's men with much less success, but not always in vain.[127] Perkins proposed to institutionalize this procedure, and what is more, ensure that Morgan's man did not necessarily go to Theodore Roosevelt's, but perhaps to another of Morgan's men.

Brandeis, who appeared before the Senate committee for two and a half days right after Perkins, from December 14 through December 16, 1911, took direct issue. Perkins had argued that bigness was as desirable as it was inevitable, because it was efficient. It was inefficient economically, Brandeis countered, and what was even worse, it was inefficient socially. "There used to be a certain glamor about big things. Anything big, simply because it was big, seemed to be good and great. We are coming to see that big things may be very bad and mean." An organization "which is so powerful that . . . it dominates by mere size" was "a menace to the community," even though its individual practices were lawful, and even if it brought some slight advantage in increased efficiency. A corporation could easily get "too large to be the most efficient instrument of production and of distribution." The main reason this would happen was that success in business generally depended upon one man, and "there is a limit to what one man can do well."

Trusts made money when (and only when) they were allowed to destroy competition. That was no proof of their inherent efficiency.[128] But "in the second place, whether it has exceeded the point of greatest

---

[125] Sullivan, *Our Times,* II, 414.

[126] R. H. Wiebe, "The House of Morgan and the Executive, 1905–1913," *Am. Hist. Rev.,* 65:49, 1959.

[127] Pringle, *Taft,* II, 675–77.

[128] In arguing the effectiveness and inevitability of sizeable consolidations, Perkins had pointed to Germany, which under a substantially cartelized system made great industrial strides. Asked about this, Brandeis replied that from the American point of view, Germany was a special case, if for no other reason than that the relationship between government and business there was one that was not conceivable within the American tradition. Moreover, he thought that "what success they have attained has been due to a great many other causes, and that the kartel is an incident, and I think there might be a great question whether it has advanced or retarded. I do not think the evidence, so far as it has reached me, is adequate on that point. But undoubtedly one very great factor in the German advance has been the introduction of scientific methods, and it will be found that that has contributed infinitely more than any other one thing to their extraordinary progress and advancement." *Clapp Hearings,* I, 1249.

economic efficiency or not, [a corporation] may be too large to be tolerated among the people who desire to be free."

> The real thing that "is the matter with business," Mr. Chairman and Gentlemen, is social unrest. . . .
>
> You cannot have true American citizenship, you cannot preserve political liberty, you cannot secure American standards of living unless some degree of industrial liberty accompanies it. And the United States Steel Corporation and these other trusts have stabbed industrial liberty in the back. . . . This social unrest is what is really the matter with business. Well-founded social unrest; reasoned unrest; but the manifestations of which are often unintelligent and sometimes criminal.
>
> . . . And you, gentlemen . . . who are called upon to consider questions affecting "big business," must weigh well these by-products. For by their by-products shall you know the trusts. . . .
>
> And there are still other painful by-products of the industrial trusts. Mr. Perkins has asserted that these great corporations are not private businesses, but public businesses. . . .
>
> To my mind this is a condition to be regretted. . . . Such numerous small stockholding creates in the corporation a condition of irresponsible absentee landlordism. . . .[129]
>
> Large dividends are the bribes which the managers tender the small investor for the power conferred to use other people's money.
>
> The trust problem can never be settled right for the American people by looking at it through the spectacles of bonds and stocks. You must study it through the spectacles of people's rights and people's interests; must consider the effect upon the development of the American democracy. When you do that you will realize the extraordinary perils to our institutions which attend the trusts; you will realize the danger of letting the people learn that our sacred Constitution protects not only vested rights but vested wrongs. The situation is a very serious one; unless wise legislation is enacted we shall have as a result of that social unrest a condition which will be more serious than that produced by the fall of a few points in stock exchange quotations.[130]

---

[129] There is no such thing, Brandeis added, "as an innocent purchaser of stocks." In the *Tobacco* opinion, 221 U.S. at 187, see *supra*, p. 114, White remarked that a receivership and forced sale of assets might cause loss to "many innocent people," meaning, no doubt, shareholders. Without specific reference to this remark, but mentioning shareholders of the American Tobacco Company, Brandeis went on to say that people who buy stock, and buy the chance of profit, must also share responsibility for the conduct of the business, and must take the consequences. "The idea of such persons being innocent in the sense of not letting them take the consequences of their acts is, to my mind, highly immoral. . . ." *Clapp Hearings,* I, 1177.

[130] *Clapp Hearings,* I, II, 1278, 1167–68, 1174, 1147–48, 1174, 1155–57, 1166.

The trusts stood in the way of industrial peace, and of higher wages and decent conditions of labor. In the most indignant, incendiary language, Brandeis recited to the Stanley Committee, a month after his appearance at the Senate hearings, how the U.S. Steel Corporation treated its labor force, which was largely composed of East and South European immigrants. Many men were worked twelve hours a day for seven days a week, and the pay was barely enough to subsist on, if that. This bred degeneration, physical and moral, exhaustion, alcoholism and premature ageing; derelicts in this generation and the next. It was, Brandeis and the chairman, Representative Augustus O. Stanley agreed, as a pair of Kentuckians, worse than slavery had been. And these were the conditions imposed by a corporation that had exacted huge profits from the American people. How was this possible? Because the corporation was big and powerful enough to have killed unionism in the steel industry, by a system of repression "the like of which you can not find, I believe, this side of Russia."[131] Trade unions could themselves conceivably grow large enough to endanger social and political values. (Brandeis, incidentally, was opposed to the closed shop.) But they were at the moment the only means for the achievement of labor peace. If the trusts were broken up, there could be both higher wages and shorter hours, because industrial freedom, which would thus have been gained, would vastly increase the productivity of labor.[132]

Brandeis was not advocating anarchic competition or the atomization of industry. There was a kind of efficiency in size, up to a certain point, and even consolidations (let alone natural growth) aimed at attaining it might be permitted. Congress might also well decide to permit trade agreements under certain conditions. But essentially it was competition that guaranteed efficiency, as well as being indispensable to a society wishing to secure for its members the blessings of liberty.

> The alternative which we have presented to us of "unrestricted and destructive competition on the one hand or regulated monopoly on the other" we may well reject. The real issue is, "Regulate competition or regulated monopoly." And accordingly as you want monopoly or as you want competition, your legislation should be directed—the regulation of the one or the other.[133]

Could anything be done to restore and maintain competition? "I take it," Brandeis said elsewhere in 1912, "that it is not a problem that

---

[131] *House Committee on Investigation of United States Steel Corporation, Hearings, 62nd Congress, 2nd Session* (1911), 2837, 2841–43, 2852–56, 2860 (hereinafter cited as *Stanley*

Hearings).

[132] *Clapp Hearings*, I, 1180–84, 1254.

[133] *Clapp Hearings*, I, 1245, 1250, 1285, 1162.

the American people are unable to meet, and to meet readily. We have been hearing constantly . . . that it is useless to attempt to stem the tide, that we ought to accept the Trust and undertake to regulate it. I believe that position to be absolutely unfounded. . . . Combination is not natural any more than any of the other things in life are natural which it is easier to do if you have no occasion to count the cost. The law may be made, to my mind, perfectly adequate to stem the growth of these organizations, and to say that it cannot be made adequate is to declare the law making power bankrupt. . . ."[134]

Brandeis was totally opposed to Perkins' recommendation of a business court or commission administering a system of licensing of interstate corporations. And he opposed equally all variants of this plan. No matter what the intention behind it, any sort of federal seal awarded to interstate corporations would be construed, however mistakenly, as a seal of approval. Brandeis found Taft's proposal for federal incorporation, and a bill introduced by Senator Francis G. Newlands of Nevada, which adumbrated the New Freedom's eventual Federal Trade Commission Act, almost as objectionable as Perkins' own program. He had nothing against "a commission which shall possess very broad powers of investigation and inquiry—publicity," and he was not opposed to having such a commission, with its investigative powers and with its storehouse of previously obtained information, help the courts frame decrees, as suggested by Taft upon recommendation of Attorney General Wickersham. He was not even opposed to endowing a commission with the power to initiate Sherman Act prosecutions, although he did not wish anything to be done "to relieve the Attorney General or the Department of Justice of its obligation to institute proceedings." But "in our ignorance, with our lack of authentic information with regard to practically every branch of industry except those few which have been investigated by the Bureau of Corporations," Brandeis did not think that a commission could safely be entrusted with the task of passing on various business practices and permitting them or not.

Of course, such a regulatory body as the Interstate Commerce Commission was generally deemed effective, but it had not always been so, and to the extent that it now served well (if not perfectly, even now), that was the result of the accumulation of a generation's experience and knowledge. A trade commission starting fresh would have no such benefit, would find itself involved in interminable proceedings, and would be incapable of effective regulation. Brandeis did not think that a regulatory commission was needed on the ground that the Sherman Act had been rendered unworkably vague by the *Standard Oil* and *Tobacco*

---

[134] Quoted in A. T. Mason, *Brandeis—A Free Man's Life* (1946), 352.

decisions. "The difficulty in finding out what is prohibited is, even now, far less than has been suggested." The difficulty, if any, came with businessmen who wanted to go the limit, to get as close to the illegal as possible; those who wanted merely to know how to proceed in safety under the statute had no trouble finding out.

Brandeis thoroughly approved of the rule of reason. The rule had once and for all made clear to business that there was no danger of a literal construction of the Sherman Act, which would render unlawful many ordinary business practices, and it was well that this should be clear. Under the statute as it stood following the *Standard Oil* and *Tobacco* decisions, "while in a strictly legal sense there is a realm of uncertainty opened which did not exist before, from the point of view of the practical advisor of the client's best interests, the lawyer has a comparatively simple task today."[135]

Brandeis' endorsement of the rule of reason was, however, an incidental comment only, and he was far from coming to rest on the decisions of the Court. Rather he repeatedly pressed a legislative proposal that would make the lawyer's advisory task under the Sherman Act "even simpler than it otherwise would be."[136] This was the La Follette bill, which Brandeis had collaborated in drafting.[137] The La Follette bill created no commission and no special courts. It addressed itself to the existing courts, by way of adding a number of new provisions to the Sherman Act.[138] If in a Sherman Act proceeding it was shown that a restraint of trade existed, the burden of proof for establishing its reasonableness was placed by the La Follette bill on the corporation contending that the restraint was reasonable; and any restraint of trade was to be conclusively deemed unreasonable and unlawful if accompanied by a series of practices described in detail, such as: tying conditions attached to the sale or licensing of articles (except in the case of certain patents); refusals to deal; rebates and other discriminatory price concessions; the use of bogus companies; industrial spying.

---

[135] *Clapp Hearings*, I, 1256, 1191–92, 1287, 1269–71, 1161, 1289.

[136] *Ibid.*, 1289.

[137] See Brandeis Papers, Library of the Law School of the University of Louisville, Box S.C. 1, Folder for Correspondence, 1910–13; *Hearings, House Judiciary Committee, Trust Legislation*, 62nd Cong., 2nd Sess., Ser. No. 2 (Jan. 26, 27, 1912), 9, 33, 104–105; Mason, *Brandeis*, 353.

[138] The La Follette bill, Brandeis told the House hearing on Trust Legislation the following month—or the Lenroot–La Follette bill, as it was known in the House—"rests upon the fundamental proposition which underlies the Sherman Act," and it "accepts the decisions of the Supreme Court that the law was designed merely to prohibit unreasonable restraint of trade. . . ." *Hearings, House Judiciary Committee, Trust Legislation*, 62nd Cong., 2nd Sess., Ser. No. 2 (Jan. 26, 1912), 14.

II: *The Rule of Reason*

Combinations in restraint of trade were moreover to be presumed unreasonable and unlawful if they achieved control of 40 percent of either a national or a regional market. There followed a whole series of less comprehensive provisions, all aimed at curing various defects, as La Follette and Brandeis saw them, that litigation had uncovered in the Sherman Act, including a provision that would have allowed the independents in the tobacco business to intervene in the government's suit.[139]

The La Follette bill, Brandeis argued, would not only aid greatly in making more Sherman Act prosecutions more successful, "but what would be even more potent," the bill would act "as a deterrent. . . . It would also afford to those businessmen who desired to know definitely what is illegal very many things that they should avoid. It would have the best educational effect."[140] Brandeis' position must be understood in context, in terms not only of what he proposed or accepted, but of what he opposed or feared. Plainly he feared that all proposals for regulation by commission, even if intended to defeat the designs of Perkins and company, would end by fulfilling their hopes. Undoubtedly Brandeis feared that Richard Olney's expectations about the Interstate Commerce Commission, quoted above, would come true with respect to an interstate trade commission, as Brandeis must have thought Perkins himself foresaw. Brandeis, moreover, distrusted big, overextended government as much as he distrusted big business, and even big labor. Business could grow too big for men to be able to manage it purposefully and intelligently, and so could government. Government should lay down rules, expect them to be obeyed in the vast majority of instances, enforce them when they were not—which it could do well because these instances, if the rules were well formulated, would be few—and leave the rest to private ordering.

It should be added that, as Brandeis must have known, the Newlands trade commission bill, which Brandeis opposed, though a far cry from the Perkins plan, was at best ambivalent in intention. It did not in terms or by implication blunt the force of the Sherman Act. But Senator Newlands presented it as being at any rate not inconsistent with a policy which, as Newlands said, was at the other extreme from the Sherman Act principle, namely, the policy "of freely allowing combination, both present and future, applying thereto governmental supervision and direction as the prime regulator." It was too early, Newlands believed, "to say which of these opposing tendencies [competition enforced by the Sherman Act, or regulated combination] should, or will, ultimately prevail. . . . I am urging this bill, because . . .[i]t is available

---

[139] The La Follette bill may be found in *Clapp Hearings,* II, 1778–82.

[140] *Clapp Hearings,* I, 1192.

for either tendency; it can be made to serve either principle . . . and it does not commit us permanently to either. . . ."[141] Brandeis was deliberately and permanently committed to one of the principles, and against the other.

Certain inconsistencies in Brandeis' position can thus be seen to be apparent ones only. "We have learned much about trusts and their ways in these twenty-one years," he said, "and this knowledge the La Follette bill undertakes to use."[142] Yet he denied that there was enough knowledge about business practices to enable a trade commission to regulate effectively. But that was because a commission might attempt to regulate with other ends in view than those of the La Follette bill, and would in any event have to do all the regulating, whereas a statute such as the La Follette bill would operate quite differently; a statute would ("what would be even more potent") have a deterrent, "educational" effect.

Brandeis' testimony was powerful, morally fervid, influential, but in the end, witness the Clayton and Federal Trade Commission Acts of 1914, not entirely persuasive. Of proposals other than those of Brandeis and Perkins, the most important was the bill of Senator Francis G. Newlands. The Newlands bill translated the Bureau of Corporations of the Department of Commerce and Labor into a new, bipartisan, five-member Interstate Trade Commission. Every corporation in the United States doing interstate or foreign business, with gross receipts exceeding $5 million, except for railroads falling under the jurisdiction of the Interstate Commerce Commission, was required by the Newlands bill to file with the Interstate Trade Commission a statement about its organization, financial condition, and operations, in accordance with regulations to be made by the commission. Upon the filing of such a statement, the commission was to register the filing corporation, which could then style itself as "United States registered." The commission could require further information, which it could make public, and it could revoke the registration of any corporation upon a finding that it had violated a judicial decree rendered under the Sherman Act, or, regardless of the existence of such a decree, that it had used "materially unfair or oppressive methods of competition," or of "overcapitalization." Upon revoking registration, the commission could also forbid a corporation to engage in interstate commerce. Registration once revoked could, however, be reinstated. Finally, the commission was charged with making annual reports to Congress.[143]

Another Senatorial proposal, veering more in the Brandeis direction, was that of John Sharp Williams of Mississippi, who had a bill

---

[141] *Clapp Hearings*, I, 19, 25.
[142] *Ibid.*, 1161.

[143] For text of Newlands bill, see *Clapp Hearings*, I, 1–4.

forbidding holding companies, interlocking directorates, and a number of specific competitive practices.[144] Nearer the Perkins end of the spectrum—but near it rather from the far side—was the program of Charles R. Van Hise, president of the University of Wisconsin, which exerted some influence on the evolving thought of Theodore Roosevelt.[145] Van Hise's remedy for what he saw as a serious situation was to give any corporation an option either to remain subject to the Sherman Act, or to submit itself for licensing and regulation by an Interstate Trade Commission. The commission would have the power to pass on, and approve or disapprove, prices charged by a corporation which was a natural monopoly, or which operated in restraint of trade in violation of the Sherman Act. A licensed corporation might be allowed to continue to operate in restraint of trade, in violation of the Sherman Act, for the sake of the economic advantage to be gained thereby.[146]

The Van Hise plan made precise and explicit much that Perkins had left vague or implicit, but it also went somewhat further than Perkins was willing to advocate going, at least in public. The same was true of the program put forward by Elbert H. Gary, chairman of the board of the U.S. Steel Company. Gary, who appeared before the Clapp Committee in November, before either Perkins or Brandeis, urged, like his colleague Perkins, federal licensing, publicity, and a trade commission. But as he had done also in June, at the Stanley Committee hearings in the House, he went on, startlingly enough, to propose as well federal regulation of prices "so far as necessary to prevent monopoly and restraint of trade."[147] To this Perkins was opposed.[148]

Gary's argument was that the most beneficial and important thing about prices—beneficial all the way around, to producer and consumer alike—was stability. Stability had been achieved as to steel rails, for example, as he rather candidly explained to the Stanley Committee, "more or less as a result of an interchange of opinion," for quite some time.[149] What better agency than the government to maintain price stability? Just as Brandeis distrusted big government as much as he distrusted big business, so Gary could bring himself to trust big government almost as much as he revered big business. He was thoroughly a believer, as he had occasion to tell the Senate Committee, in the I'll-send-my-man-to-see-your-man way of life. "There has never been a time since

---

[144] *Clapp Hearings,* III, 2509–15.

[145] Schlesinger, *The Crisis of the Old Order* (1957), 22.

[146] *Clapp Hearings,* III, 2524–34; see C. R. Van Hise, *Concentration and Control: A Solution of the Trust Problem in the United States* (1912).

[147] *Clapp Hearings,* I, 693–95; *Stanley Hearings,* 79.

[148] *Clapp Hearings,* I, 1103; *Stanley Hearings,* 1526.

[149] *Stanley Hearings,* 195; see also *Clapp Hearings,* I, 700–701.

our organization," he declared, "when I have not said to the powers that be in Washington—the Department of Justice, the Department of Commerce, and everyone else: 'Show us where we are wrong in any respect, and we will get right.' There has never been a time that we have not been willing to do that."

Gary also had some remarkable and revealing ideas about government, which no doubt he hoped would come true with the inevitability that had attended consolidation in the business world. Government, he believed, should be above politics. "I think the salvation of the country really is in the courts." If judges were kept sufficiently "independent of the people . . . I do not think we will have any trouble from the courts. That should be the place to which everyone might look for final satisfaction, relief, or protection." And he carefully provided in his licensing and price-fixing plan that any decisions of the trade commission which he wanted to see created should be reviewed by courts. Judges should make all final determinations. Price fixing, therefore, but judicial price fixing—that was Judge Gary's (so he was invariably called, having served on a county court in Illinois) program.

As he was describing his reliance on government by independent courts, Gary said that in that connection: "I just want to throw in a remark; it is not of any great importance in this matter." What he wished to say was that "one of the great disturbers and objections to the conditions and proceedings of this country is the frequent elections." They tended against the independence of officials. Gary would have favored a single eight-year term for the President: "I would like to see even the President of the United States, after he is elected, absolutely independent. In other words, in such a position and such a frame of mind that he has no temptation or inclination to look in any direction or toward any interest with reference to his future." One of the most harmful things to business was frequent elections and "there isn't any doubt that at the present time we are more or less affected by the approaching presidential year. I wish elections came more seldom, and I wish we could elect all the officers, National, State, and Municipal, at one time and have it over with, and not have the elections so often. That is gratis."[150]

Among other, less radical, views was that of Francis Lynde Stetson of New York, Morgan's principal lawyer. Stetson was an Edwardian cynic. He didn't think it was politically realistic to speak of repealing the Sherman Act, but he saw little value in it and thought it something of an obstacle to the conduct of business, because of its vagueness. Was it his notion then, he was asked, "that if there had been no restrictions

---

[150] *Clapp Hearings,* I, 708, 702–703, 694–95, 703.

in the form of the Sherman antitrust law that the trade conditions of the country would have worked out all right?" Stetson replied:

> Nothing ever works out all right in human affairs. I think it would have worked out as well without the law as with it. The law never does anything concretely; it never makes any money for anybody; it never provides anything except a punishment. . . . I feel very little interest in that side of human affairs.

The main point now was to clarify the Sherman Act and make it a more precise guide to business conduct. "If I could not get anything else, I would rather take Senator La Follette's bill just as it stands. I would know then what I could advise."[151]

Samuel Untermyer, also a well-known New York corporation lawyer, who thought the *Tobacco* decree a "pitiful and humiliating fiasco,"[152] had no hopes for "unrestricted competition." It was in his view "a figment of the imagination in these days." What was needed was federal permission, under rigid federal supervision, for business cooperation, agreements fixing prices, and regulating output. And so a corporation commission should be empowered to license interstate businesses, and regulate their pricing and other agreements. At the least, this would necessarily mean, as Untermyer euphemistically conceded, modification of the Sherman Act.[153] Here was a position, then, quite close to, if more politic than, Gary's.

A still more moderately stated position, put forward in very general terms, and approximating the thought of Theodore Roosevelt at this time, was that of Lyman Abbott of New York, the editor of *The Outlook*, with which Roosevelt was associated. It was no use, Abbott thought, to try to reestablish competition; no use to try to disorganize business. Brandeis' testimony, which Abbott had read, was "significant and forceful, but what it proves is not that great commercial organizations are dangerous, but that lawless commercial organizations are dangerous. . . ." The task was not to break them up, but to regulate them by federal law.[154]

The Campaign of 1912 and the Clayton and Federal Trade Commission Acts

At the opening of his campaign for the Presidency, Woodrow Wilson sounded remarkably like a sort of Democratic Lyman Abbott. "I daresay," he dared say in his acceptance speech on August 7, 1912, "we

---

[151] *Clapp Hearings*, I, 965–66.
[152] *Ibid.*, 181; see also p. 206.
[153] *Ibid.*, 182–83, 186–87, 189.
[154] *Ibid.*, 1705, 1707.

shall never return to the old order of individual competition, and that the organization of business upon a great scale of cooperation is, up to a certain point, itself normal and inevitable."[155] At this juncture, William Allen White's judgment that the programs of Wilson and Theodore Roosevelt were separated only by "that fantastic imaginary gulf that always has existed between tweedle-dum and tweedle-dee," may have been fairly accurate.[156] But White's judgment purported to apply to the campaign as a whole, and as such, it was quite inaccurate. For Wilson had merely made a false start. The issue was to become the principal one of the campaign, but as of this time, Wilson had not yet sufficiently educated himself on it. In due course, the campaign developed differences between Roosevelt and Wilson that corresponded closely to those revealed in the earlier Congressional hearings between Perkins and Brandeis. The gulf was real enough; it was Wilson's policy that prevailed in the election; and future events would surely have been affected had Roosevelt's views carried the day.

The turning point for Wilson came in a first meeting with Brandeis, held at Wilson's request on August 28, 1912. Thenceforward, with continuing help from Brandeis himself, it was a Brandeisian campaign that Wilson waged. Monopolies, Wilson argued, were "so many cars of juggernaut," and it would hardly help matters to have them "licensed and driven by commissioners of the United States. . . ." Legislation was needed, rather, to hit at the business methods by which monopoly was achieved. "Ours is a programme of liberty; theirs a programme of regulation." Nobody was "big enough to play Providence" by legalizing monopoly and then regulating it and its relations with others.

For his part, Theodore Roosevelt, advised by Perkins, resisted a proposed plank in the Progressive platform in effect endorsing the La Follette–Brandeis program for strengthening the Sherman Act by adding to it specific prohibitions of certain business methods. Like Perkins, Roosevelt argued that consolidation was here to stay, and that fully competitive conditions could not be restored. Size as such was not harmful. American business being now naturally big, big government should regulate it, overseeing its practices, and perhaps its wage and price policies. The cornerstone of the Roosevelt program was a powerful federal trade commission. The Wilsonian doctrine Roosevelt labeled "rural toryism."[157]

A common view of the outcome of this struggle—without simplify-

---

[155] A. S. Link, *Wilson: The Road to the White House* (1947), 472.

[156] *Ibid.,* 476.

[157] *Ibid.,* 488–93; A. S. Link, *Woodrow Wilson and the Progressive Era* (1954), 20–22; see G. E. Mowry, *Theodore Roosevelt and the Progressive Movement* (1946), 269–72; Blum, *Republican Roosevelt,* 116–24.

ing too much—is that Wilson and Brandeis won the battle, while Roosevelt and Perkins won the war.[158] For the Wilson Administration did create a regulatory trade commission. The President's initial recommendation to Congress, on January 20, 1914, included a near equivalent of the La Follette bill, which was the salient feature of Brandeis' program. And while Wilson also endorsed the idea of an interstate trade commission, he intended it at this stage to be a fact-finding agency only, not unlike the old Bureau of Corporations.[159] What finally emerged, however, as the Clayton Antitrust and Federal Trade Commission Acts of 1914, was in many ways something different.

Although Brandeis, testifying before the House Committee on the Judiciary in February 1914, still maintained that a fact-finding function was all "that we can safely commit to a commission today,"[160] the actual Federal Trade Commission that Congress established in 1914 had the power, subject to judicial review, to issue cease and desist orders against unfair methods of competition, which it was up to the Commission to define in the first instance, and against monopolistic practices; and power not to issue such orders. The Clayton Act, in turn, was a faint echo, if one at all, of the litany of prohibitions and presumptions contained in the La Follette bill.

Plainly, the statutes of 1914 were not quite the Brandeis program.[161] But they were not untrue to Brandeis or to the campaign. What the Wilson Administration enacted was ideologically impure. It was the product of a complicated political process, in which many influences and many counsels of moderation, many interests and many confusions played their part. Yet Brandeis was at no point excluded from this process, and in its result there was much more of Wilson and Brandeis than of Roosevelt and Perkins; and what there was of the latter was form, not substance.[162]

There was no attenuation of the Sherman Act, no licensing of combinations, no immunity from Sherman Act prosecutions, no acceptance of bigness and no compensatory effort to regulate it. There was regulation, as Brandeis had wanted it, of competition, not of monopoly.

---

[158] See, e.g., Link, *Wilson: The Road to the White House*, 444; Seager and Gulick, *Trust and Corporation Problems*, 414.

[159] 51 *Cong. Rec.* 1962–64, 63rd Cong., 2nd Sess. (1914).

[160] *Hearings, House Judiciary Committee, Trust Legislation*, 63rd Cong., 2nd Sess., Ser. No. 7, Pt. 16, 677. Compare the much more nearly Rooseveltian position put forward in the same hearings by Donald R. Richberg, *ibid.*, 416–23.

[161] Compare a memorandum by Brandeis to F. K. Lane, Dec. 12, 1913, transmitted by Lane to Attorney General McReynolds, Jan. 30, 1914, McReynolds Papers.

[162] See Link, *Wilson: The New Freedom*, 427–44; Henderson, *Federal Trade Commission*, 17–48.

Indeed, as Wilson had said in his first recommendations to Congress in January 1914, the administration did not "make terms with monopoly." And, of course, it did not remotely attempt to fix prices or wages. Looking back some six years later, in the course of a dissent against a restrictive reading of the Federal Trade Commission's powers, Brandeis himself recalled that there had been "a clear division of opinion" in the years between decision of the *Standard Oil* and *Tobacco* cases and passage of the Clayton and Trade Commission Acts. He had no doubt who won:

> Many believed that concentration (called by its opponents monopoly) was inevitable and desirable; and these desired that concentration should be recognized by law and be regulated. Others believed that concentration was a source of evil; that existing combinations could be disintegrated, if only the judicial machinery were perfected; and that further concentration could be averted by providing additional remedies, and particularly through regulating competition. The latter view prevailed in the Sixty-Third Congress. The Clayton Act . . . was framed largely with a view to making more effective the remedies given by the Sherman law. The Federal Trade Commission Act . . . created an administrative tribunal, largely with a view to regulating competition.[163]

The Steel and Harvester Prosecutions

The struggle that Brandeis briefly characterized in retrospect cannot be appreciated without taking into account two events not yet mentioned, namely, the initiation in 1911 and 1912 of prosecutions against the United States Steel Corporation and the International Harvester Company. These cases were not disposed of till many years later, in circumstances markedly different from those of the period now under discussion. But their impact, when they were brought, was great and immediate. The very act of filing both suits, and especially the suit against United States Steel, was and was taken to be a repudiation of Theodore Roosevelt's doctrine that some trusts were "good" and did not need to be broken up, but should be supervised and regulated. The suits were a repudiation of that doctrine, not in the abstract, but as Roosevelt had applied it in the past, and an identification of it, and of Roosevelt, with the names of Gary and Perkins, which carried, of course, very distinct connotations. Nor was that all. The prosecution of the Steel Corporation in particular constituted a charge that Roosevelt had been gullible.

---

[163] Federal Trade Commission v. Gratz, 253 U.S. 421, 429, 433–34 (1920).

II: *The Rule of Reason*

The government's bill of complaint against United States Steel recited—not at a disproportionate length, but with emphasis—the story of the acquisition by the Steel Corporation, in 1907, of the Tennessee Coal and Iron Company. This company, a steel producer with extensive and ideally located coal and iron properties in Alabama and Tennessee, was in a position, according to the complaint, to become "a strong probable future competitor" of United States Steel. It had received, earlier in 1907, a substantial order from E. H. Harriman for open-hearth steel rails, and was working on other orders as well.

A controlling portion of Tennessee's stock was held by a syndicate of which Grant B. Schley, of the New York brokerage firm of Moore and Schley, was a member. Moore and Schley, which had lent the syndicate funds for the purchase of Tennessee Coal and Iron, held the stock as collateral, and had, in turn, deposited it with certain banks as security against time loans amounting to upwards of $35 million. The loans were falling due, the panic of 1907 was on, Moore and Schley had no cash, and the creditors would not grant an extension with the same Tennessee stock as collateral, since they now considered it insufficient security.

At the behest of J. P. Morgan, U.S. Steel offered to buy the Tennessee Coal and Iron stock from Moore and Schley, which had to sell, since the alternative was bankruptcy. The complaint suggested that a loan in a much smaller amount than the price finally paid for the stock would have sufficed to save Moore and Schley, and would have been a measure similar to other moves made by J. P. Morgan in the course of the panic to forestall other threatened failures. It suggested also that U.S. Steel paid considerably more for the stock than, by common consent, it was worth at the time. Hence, the complaint concluded, whatever other motives may have played a part, U.S. Steel had availed itself of an opportunity, at a critical time, to take over a potentially formidable competitor.

Before the transaction was consummated, however, the directors of U.S. Steel wished to make sure that the government would not take any action against them under the Sherman Act as a result of this purchase. Consequently, Gary and another U.S. Steel director, Henry Clay Frick, paid an urgent call on President Roosevelt in Washington. The allegations of the complaint continued as follows:

> Without fully disclosing all the facts in regard to the Tennessee stock, its ownership, the amount of money estimated as necessary to relieve Moore and Schley, and the arrangements that had already been made . . . they [Gary and Frick] represented to the President that the only thing that could prevent a vicious spread of the panic was for the corporation to acquire the stock of the Tennessee company. The President recorded, in a letter to the Attorney General, written in their presence, their representations. . . . The President further said in his

letter: "Judge Gary and Mr. Frick informed me what little benefit will come to the Steel corporation from the purchase." This statement to the President was a misleading one. The property was very valuable. . . .

The President was not made fully acquainted with the state of affairs in New York, relevant to the transaction as they existed. . . . The President, taken as he was partially into confidence and moved by his appreciation of the gravity of the situation and the necessity for applying what was represented to him to be the only known remedy, stated that he did not feel it to be his duty to prevent the transaction.[164]

The filing of the complaint had an electric effect, and not alone on Colonel Roosevelt. The headlines read "Roosevelt Fooled," and the Colonel was incensed at Taft for permitting this slur on him; he was no less incensed when he learned, as was true, that Taft had not seen the complaint before it was filed. Roosevelt reacted predictably and fiercely. "I reaffirm everything," he wrote in *The Outlook*, and plunged into the campaign of 1912. Earlier hesitations about his course of action vanished. There might have been a Roosevelt candidacy and a Bull Moose party anyway, but the filing of the complaint against U.S. Steel on October 27, 1911, ensured it. And in reaffirming everything, Roosevelt also moved perceptibly, or at any rate irrevocably, nearer to Perkins and onto the ground he was to occupy with respect to the antitrust issue during the campaign.[165]

The story of the Tennessee Coal and Iron acquisition was not new. Wilson had castigated Roosevelt for his role in the transaction as early as September 1911.[166] The episode had been explored from every angle —Roosevelt himself had testified, in his own defense, so to speak— together with most aspects of the history, operations, and practices of U.S. Steel, during the previous spring and summer in hearings before the Stanley Committee of the House of Representatives, and more recently by the Clapp Committee in the Senate.[167] And yet the thrice-told tale had behind it now the authority of a Republican administration.

It was a dramatic story, easily told and easily grasped, and it symbolized a good part of what it was felt had gone awry in American business and American finance. So also, and more comprehensively,

---

[164] The text of the complaint may most conveniently be found in *Clapp Hearings*, I, 864, 877–79.

[165] *The Outlook*, 99:649, Nov. 18, 1911; Pringle, *Taft*, II, 670–75; Mowry, *Roosevelt and the Progressive Movement*, 188–98; W. H. Harbaugh, *Power and Responsibility* (1961), 405; J. M. Dickinson to W. H. Taft,

Sept. 21, 1925, and Taft to Dickinson, Sept. 29, 1925, Taft Papers. Dickinson to Attorney General Wickersham, Oct. 31, 1911, Archives, File 60–138.

[166] Link, *Wilson: The Road to the White House*, 509.

[167] For Roosevelt's testimony, see *Stanley Hearings*, 1369–92.

did the United States Steel Corporation as such, which served, in these days, as the all-purpose cynosure and horrible example that the Standard Oil Company had been before its dissolution. The profits of U.S. Steel and the manner of life of its managers, its interlocking directors and its connection with J. P. Morgan, its initial overcapitalization, its wages, its hours, its pension plan, its profit-sharing plan, its successful fight against the unionization of its workers—all were taken as the prime illustrations of what was wrong with the American social and economic system.[168] This company above all others symbolized overbearing, publicly irresponsible power, which men had gone out of their way to gather into their hands, for no other reason than that they wanted to wield it. To those who thought—and they were many—"that we cannot have democracy in politics and absolutism in industry,"[169] the Steel Corporation represented industrial absolutism.

The United States Steel Corporation was organized in 1901 by J. P. Morgan and Company. It was a venture on a heroic scale—or perhaps the better word is imperial. All the relevant statistics were outsize. The company was capitalized at nearly one and a half billion dollars. The net profit made by the organizing syndicate came to some $62,500,000. The Carnegie Steel Company alone was bought for nearly half a billion dollars, of which in turn about half went to Andrew Carnegie himself. The merger included well over one hundred other companies. It averted what might have been an epic competitive battle, provoked by Carnegie's intention to enter the manufacture of finished steel products.[170] And the final result, after further acquisitions, was the

---

[168] Testifying to the Clapp Committee on Dec. 15, 1911, Brandeis volunteered an item from the morning paper. Judge Gary, chairman of U.S. Steel, it was reported, had given his wife a $500,000 pearl necklace for Christmas. He was bringing it up, Brandeis continued,

> because it seems to me an extremely serious matter in the times of our present discontent. . . . Is it not just the same sort of thing which brought on the French Revolution, and which must suggest to everyone in this particular connection the damage which the Queen's necklace did in those days? That seems to me to be one of the horrible manifestations, the by-products, of this aggregation of

capital. And it is parading before the world the facts in regard to the unearned wealth, unearned by those who are enjoying it and taken out of the lives of the people who are toiling for them. *Clapp Hearings,* I, 1225–26; see A. Mason, *Brandeis* (1946), 361.

[169] See F. Adler to E. H. Gary, Jan. 13, 1912, and Gary to Adler, Jan. 10, 1912, transmitted by F. Frankfurter to Attorney General Wickersham, Jan. 27, 1912, Archives, File 60–138.

[170] "If I had remained in the business," Carnegie said in January 1912, "I would have had a plant at Conneaut that would have astonished the world, and which would have distanced all competition in that line." *Stanley Hearings,* 2357.

first wholly integrated manufacturer, producing everything from coal and ore to the finished article. Although even at the beginning it produced only a shade over 50 percent of finished rolled products, something over 65 percent of steel ingots and steel castings, and well under 50 percent of pig iron, and although despite all further acquisitions these percentages declined somewhat over the years, United States Steel was from its inception, as it remains today, by far the biggest single unit in the industry.[171]

The purchase of the Tennessee Coal and Iron Company was not quite what the government's complaint in the *Steel* case made it out to be. Mixed motives and uncertain purposes—more uncertain than the government in its complaint allowed—were actually in play in the transaction. The panic of 1907, which J. P. Morgan had been fighting with impressive resourcefulness and authority, was in its second week, when on Friday, November 1, the plight of Moore and Schley was called to Morgan's attention. Cash was, by this time, at a fantastic premium throughout the financial world. As Moore and Schley went, so might its creditors go. The Tennessee Coal and Iron stock was closely held and was quoted at $130, but there was no real market for it. Had it been offered by the banks that held it as collateral, acting to save themselves, it would surely have fallen fifty to sixty points before finding a buyer, and might thus not have brought enough cash to save those banks either, regardless of the fate of Moore and Schley. The failure of a major bank on top of that of an important brokerage house would probably have brought the panic to a fatal point. Hence Morgan decided that Moore and Schley had to be rescued, as he had previously decided that two trust companies which he was still supporting, and which were still in danger, had to be rescued, although he had let another, less sound one, go down.

Could Moore and Schley have been saved by a loan of United States Steel securities—since, after all, it was in the end saved by an exchange of its Tennessee Coal and Iron stock for such securities? Gary in retrospect once admitted this possibility. But Grant Schley testified to the Stanley Committee that he "should hardly have the cheek to ask" for an unsecured "bald loan" of the same U.S. Steel bonds, in the same amount, which ultimately formed the payment for the Tennessee stock. And the loan of a smaller amount would not do, for it was cash that was needed, and cash could be produced by the sale of U.S. Steel bonds that Moore and Schley and other syndicate members owned, but the same bonds would raise much less cash if loaned, and used, therefore, merely as security for further loans.

---

[171] Seager and Gulick, *Trust and Corporation Problems*, 223–24, 258;   Whitney, *Antitrust Policies*, I, 253–59.

II: *The Rule of Reason*

A loan of cash would undoubtedly have saved Moore and Schley as it did others before the Tennessee Coal and Iron transaction, and a final two trust companies after. But it is difficult to reconstruct how much cash would have been needed, although Schley at one point in his testimony indicated that $5 or $6 million might have sufficed. (And yet Gary thought that much had been offered and been found not enough.) Morgan at the same time, however, was also in need of cash to save the two trust companies that were still in danger, there being a steady run on them, and in the tight cash situation, every dollar counted.

Moore and Schley had other securities that might have been purchased by the Morgan interests, but the short of it is that there was no negotiation about these. Morgan rather convened the finance committee of U.S. Steel, which was effectively the corporation's governing body, with a view to the purchase of the Tennessee Coal and Iron stock. The idea, however, it seems clearly established, was not his own, but that of Colonel Oliver Payne, a member of the Tennessee Coal and Iron syndicate and an independent creditor of Moore and Schley, conveyed through Payne's lawyer, Lewis Cass Ledyard.

The finance committee balked. Some members feared that the transaction would provoke an antitrust suit. Henry Clay Frick was set against it on other grounds, believing that Tennessee Coal and Iron was not worth buying, since it was a high-cost producer. But its coal and ore deposits were in themselves sufficiently valuable to support the deal, Morgan argued. Finally the committee did vote an offer, but it was rejected by Moore and Schley as too low.

Morgan and George W. Perkins, his chief assistant in these dealings, had a hasty survey made of the Tennessee Coal and Iron properties, and at a second meeting of the finance committee convinced Frick, although not altogether easily, that a new rail mill which the company was building would enable it to produce more efficiently. The committee now voted to buy the Tennessee Coal and Iron stock at par, payment to be in bonds of U.S. Steel valued at eighty-four, but there were two important provisos: one, that the approval of President Roosevelt be obtained, in search of which Frick and Gary left for Washington for an appointment with the President on Monday morning, November 4; and two, that the necessary cash be raised (some of it was sought from the Rockefeller interests) to save the remaining two endangered trust companies, so that the purpose of solving the financial crisis through this deal might actually be achieved. Only when both conditions were met, was the Tennessee Coal and Iron transaction consummated.[172]

---

[172] Garraty, *Right-Hand Man*, 196–215; *Stanley Hearings*, 170–74, 190–93, 932–38, 1041, 1072–78.

The Steel Corporation, under Judge Gary's lawyerlike leadership, and the Morgan interests in general, had been casting wary glances over their shoulders at the federal government well before the episode of 1907, and they continued to do so after. As early as November 1905, at a meeting with President Roosevelt, Gary had exacted an apparent promise that an investigation, then about to be begun, of the Steel Corporation by the Bureau of Corporations would not be allowed to result in any publicity against the corporation, or in any prosecution, until such objections as the Bureau might adduce were submitted to negotiation between the Bureau and the corporation. A year later, Perkins gained an extension of the same arrangement to cover the International Harvester Company, which was also entering investigation. The expectation of Morgan, Gary, and Perkins was, as Perkins told Roosevelt in 1907, that the administration would "come to us and point out any mistakes or technical violations of any law, then give us a chance to correct them." The corporations, in turn, would keep the government advised of their own actions and intentions.

This gentlemen's agreement certainly appeared to be confirmed by the Gary-Frick-Roosevelt interview of November 1907. And the Morgan men fully expected that the relationship with the federal government would, if anything, be even more favorable to them under Taft than it had been under Roosevelt. They were disappointed.[173] The Bureau of Corporations, pressing ahead with its investigation of U.S. Steel, now ceased to exchange information with the company.[174] With President Taft's approval, although in utmost secrecy, Attorney General Wickersham appointed a special counsel—Jacob M. Dickinson of Tennessee and Chicago, who had been Secretary of War during the first two years of the Taft Administration. Dickinson spent some months in 1911 in Tennessee studying the case and preparing a complaint, his work being known, of course, to the Attorney General and generally to the President, but to scarcely anyone else even in the Department of Justice.[175]

In the meantime, Judge Gary continued to seek an accommodation. By late September, rumors of a suit or of a voluntary dissolution were rampant, and they were having a depressing effect on the price of the corporation's stock. On September 25, 1911, Gary was writing to Attorney General Wickersham that if any illegality on the part of the

---

[173] In August 1911, realizing that the administration was about to act, and that his faith in Taft had been misplaced, Gary spoke of the proceedings against U.S. Steel as "the irony of Fate." Quoted in R. H. Wiebe, "The House of Morgan and the Executive, 1905–1913," *Am. His. Rev.*, 65:49, 60, 1959.

[174] Wiebe, *Businessmen and Reform*, 46, 80–83.

[175] J. M. Dickinson to W. H. Taft, Sept. 21, 1925, Taft Papers.

U.S. Steel Corporation was thought to exist, he should wish the opportunity "of going over the whole matter with you or the Solicitor General, or both."[176] Wickersham was in New York that day for a conference on the decree in the *Tobacco* case, and under insistent questioning from newsmen, he in effect answered Gary publicly. The Steel Corporation was indeed under scrutiny, Wickersham allowed. He added that if U.S. Steel "should work out a plan of separation to avoid illegal conditions," the government would consider such a plan in an effort to avoid litigation, which of course nobody wanted.[177]

The following day, September 26, the directors of the corporation issued a statement signed by J. P. Morgan and Elbert H. Gary. The corporation, said Morgan and Gary, had engaged in no negotiations with the government. It was advised by counsel that it was "not in violation of the Sherman Act as interpreted in the recent decisions of the Supreme Court." And so the directors were anxious to set at rest rumors that they were contemplating dissolution.[178] This provoked from Wickersham a curt reply to Gary's letter of September 25: "The action taken by the directors of the United States Steel Corporation, as reported in the newspapers this morning, render it unnecessary to do more than to acknowledge the receipt of your letter."[179] But Gary pressed on:

> I do not quite agree with the conclusion stated by you.
>
> It was not intended to withdraw or modify the suggestions contained in my letter by the published statement of the Board of Directors, which, as you must realize, was made because of the great anxiety on the part of stockholders.
>
> If you and Mr. [Solicitor General] Lehmann should, after careful investigation, decide our Corporation is in any respect tainted with illegality, I should like to be informed of your conclusion and given an opportunity to go over the matter with you. It is possible I might find you were mistaken with regard to some of the facts, in which case I should like an opportunity to correct your misunderstanding; or possibly you might be able to convince me I am mistaken in some respects, and in that event I would like to have an opportunity to consider what ought to be done.
>
> I believe even the bringing of a suit for dissolution against our Corporation would result in incalculable injury to the best interests of the country.[180]

---

[176] E. H. Gary to G. W. Wickersham, Sept. 25, 1911, Archives, File 60–138.

[177] *New York Times,* Sept. 26, 1911, p. 1, col. 1.

[178] *New York Times,* Sept. 27, 1911, p. 1, col. 7.

[179] G. W. Wickersham to E. H. Gary, Sept. 27, 1911, Archives, File 60–138.

[180] E. H. Gary to G. W. Wickersham, Oct. 2, 1911, Archives, File 60–138.

A few days later, Gary was informing the Attorney General that the corporation had just decided to cancel its Hill ore lease, and also to reduce the rates on ore carried by railroads controlled by U.S. Steel in Minnesota. The recent lease of the enormously rich Hill ore deposits at high royalties was notorious. Since the Steel Corporation's ore holdings were already very large, and this lease seemed to go beyond reasonably foreseeable needs, U.S. Steel was widely accused of intending, not to supply its own needs, but to interdict these resources to potential competitors. Wickersham acknowledged receipt of Gary's letter, but made no reply.[181]

Not even the actual filing of the government's complaint caused Gary to cease behaving as if the old Roosevelt gentlemen's agreement were still in effect. Early in December, Gary wrote the Attorney General that U.S. Steel had made a verbal agreement with a minor concern, the Baltimore Bridge Company, to buy a warehouse in Baltimore for $285,000. He was informing the Attorney General, Gary said, "pursuant to my policy of trying to keep the Department of Justice advised of any action on our part in which it might be interested. . . ." This action appeared to him entirely proper, "and yet I should like to have the benefit of any suggestion you might feel disposed to offer." Although agreement had been reached with the Baltimore Bridge Company, Gary would "endeavor to rescind any action which was considered questionable by you."

It seemed to Dickinson, in charge of the case, to whom the letter had been referred, "that the United States Steel Corporation should not expect the Department of Justice to act as its advisor in regard to its future action," and that was the reply sent to Gary.[182] Thus ended the attempts to negotiate with the Taft Administration, although attempts to negotiate would be resumed at the accession of President Wilson. Taft and Wickersham had stood firm. Only when rumors reached him through the press, in February 1912, that Wickersham and Dickinson might be planning criminal indictments against officers of the Steel Corporation did Taft take alarm. The rumors, however, were groundless.[183]

The civil complaint filed by the United States named as defendants the United States Steel Corporation and its subsidiaries, and a number of

---

[181] E. H. Gary to G. W. Wickersham, Oct. 17, 1911, and Wickersham to Gary, Oct. 19, 1911, Archives, File 60–138.

[182] E. H. Gary to G. W. Wickersham, Dec. 11, 1911, J. M. Dickinson to Wickersham, Dec. 20, 1911, Assistant Attorney General J. A. Fowler to Gary, Dec. 26, 1911, Archives, File 60–138.

[183] W. H. Taft to G. W. Wickersham, Feb. 27, 1912, Wickersham to Taft, Feb. 28, 1912, Archives, File 60–138.

individuals, including J. P. Morgan, George W. Perkins, E. H. Gary, Charles M. Schwab, Andrew Carnegie, Henry C. Frick, John D. Rockefeller, and John D. Rockefeller, Jr. (some Rockefeller mining interests were included in the combination, and Rockefeller, Jr., was on the board of U.S. Steel), and P. A. B. Widener. The complaint described the rapid movement toward integration in the steel industry in the last two years of the nineteenth century, the consolidation of 1901, and the later acquisitions. It then referred to the various pools, restricting output and fixing prices, that had been prevalent in the industry prior to the turn of the century. In a section headed "Interlocking Directorates," it set forth the numerous other boards on which directors of the U.S. Steel Corporation sat. And it charged:

> Through its directors thus distributed the Corporation is in direct touch with all the large railroad and steamship companies of the United States, such powerful concerns as the Standard Oil Company, the Pullman Company, the International Harvester Company, and the Western Union Telegraph Company, and with the overwhelming majority in money and power of the banks and trust companies of the United States. The possibilities of the power and control that may thus be exerted over trade and commerce is inestimable. The power and control that have been exerted by the Corporation, largely through the grasp of its tentacles thus thrown out upon the consumer, competitors, and capital, is incompatible with the healthy commercial life of the Nation.

Finally, the complaint alleged that at meetings with its competitors (the famous Gary dinners) the corporation had succeeded, even if on a voluntary basis, in regulating output and prices more effectively than did the old pools, which were frequently broken.[184] The remedy prayed for was dissolution, to be accomplished by divesting U.S. Steel—a holding company—of its stock in its subsidiaries.

---

[184] He knew full well, Gary told the Stanley Committee, that he could not lawfully engage in price fixing. On the other hand, in a price war, U.S. Steel would necessarily bankrupt many of its competitors, which he believed would be immoral.

Now, the question was how to get between the two extremes. . . . I invited a large percentage of the steel interests of the country to meet me at dinner and then presented these views to them. . . . Then, I said that it seemed to me the only way we could lawfully prevent such demoralization and maintain a reasonable steadiness in business . . . was for steel people to come together occasionally and to tell one to the others exactly what his business was. (*Stanley Hearings,* 76–77.)

As transcripts of the proceedings at the dinners show, they were attempts, through mutual pledges of honor ("better than a contract"), to divide markets and keep up the price. (E.g., *Stanley Hearings,* 1773–98.)

As in the *Standard Oil* and *Tobacco* cases, a four-judge court was convened, and it appointed a referee to take evidence. Three years after the complaint had been filed, in November 1914, the first issue of Herbert Croly's progressive magazine, *The New Republic*, described the proceedings with some license, and yet not unfairly:

> A record of more than fifty volumes having already been produced under the bored attention of a Referee, the government dissolution suit against the U. S. Steel Corporation has at last straggled into the United States Circuit Court. Argument was begun a fortnight ago. Judges and counsel; clerks and secretaries; and stenographers who have grown up, married and settled down on the job; plaintiff, defendant and newspaper readers, all know that the decision, whatever it is, will no sooner be announced than preparations will begin for carrying the case to the Supreme Court. There the same record, built upon still more vertiginously, will appear again; the same counsel will present the same arguments; the same clerks, the same secretaries, the same stenographers, their progeny increased, will transcribe the same testimony; and Bill the Lizard, writing with his finger on the slate, may be expected to go on writing the evidence quite in the manner of the famous case of the Queen's tarts.[185]

Before Bill the Lizard had written very far, however, immediately after the inauguration in 1913, the corporation tried to open negotiations with the new President. The approach was made by Frick through Wilson's adviser, Colonel E. M. House. Frick was coldly referred to the Attorney General.[186] In May 1913, Morgan's lawyer, Francis Lynde Stetson, who was general counsel of U.S. Steel, had a conference with the new Attorney General, James C. McReynolds. A few weeks later, McReynolds stated the irreducible government position:

> l think the Government must insist that the original organization of the steel company, together with the acquisitions made at that time, constitute an unlawful combination; and, accordingly, there must be some dissection of it. Also, that subsequent acquisitions were unlawful, and that they must be dissevered.[187]

Stetson rather thought the government would win, but he found it difficult to believe that it would win a dissolution. After all, Stetson

---

[185] *The New Republic*, 1:4, Nov. 7, 1914.

[186] Link, *Wilson: The New Freedom*, 419.

[187] J. C. McReynolds to F. L. Stetson, May 31, 1913, Archives, File 60-138.

wrote McReynolds, should the government prevail, he could not but think that it would be brought face to face

> with conditions full of embarrassment and difficulties apparently insuperable. Of course, original conditions could not be restored, nor should I suppose that the restoration of those conditions, as depicted in the testimony of Judge Gary, [i.e., price-cutting competition] would be desired by the Government. Consideration of the consequences of fundamental disturbance of more than 200,000 employees and more than 100,000 stockholders, and of the general interests of the country and of the world, naturally would deter the imposition of any condition not absolutely necessary for the due protection of what justly might be regarded as an irreducible requirement of the law judicially determined.
>
> As with my previous suggestions, thus far my letter has proceeded upon the hypothesis of a determination in favor of the Government. But, of course, you will recognize that to be a conclusion by no means conceded by my clients. . . .[188]

Stetson was overly pessimistic, and he was lucky his negotiations came to nothing (as did a final attempt, through House, in September 1913).[189] Early in June 1915, the four-judge circuit court handed down its opinion, and the government lost outright. Two of the judges thought that U.S. Steel was not a combination formed with intent to monopolize, and had therefore never been in violation of the Sherman Act. The corporation, in their view, was formed to secure the economic advantages of integrated production, and for no other purpose. Two other judges thought that U.S. Steel was indeed formed with intent to monopolize, but that the intention was never realized. These judges made light of the Gary dinners, which were in any event no longer being held, and pointed out that the corporation had resorted to no unfair methods of competition—no rebates, no underselling to drive out competitors, and the like. Hence, regardless of original intent, U.S. Steel was not now a monopoly or combination forbidden by the Sherman Act, and these two judges, therefore, concurred in the dismissal of the suit.[190]

This decision, Perkins announced, was "a victory for what I term twentieth century economics. . . . It is a victory for the Roosevelt policies as against the Taft policies."[191] Dickinson, the special counsel for the government, thought that the decision "in effect renders the

---

[188] F. L. Stetson to J. C. McReynolds, June 2, 1913, Archives, File 60–138.

[189] See Link, *Wilson: The New Freedom*, 419.

[190] United States v. United States Steel Corp., 223 Fed. 55 (D.C. N.J. 1915).

[191] Quoted in Garraty, *Right-Hand Man*, 319.

Sherman Act nugatory," but he took hope from the government's earlier victory in the *International Harvester Co.* case, which he thought should, after all, control the ultimate disposition of the *Steel* case also.[192] Actually, it turned out more or less the other way around.

The Taft Administration had filed its complaint against the International Harvester Company on April 30, 1912, in the United States District Court for the District of Minnesota. International Harvester was another Morgan creation, more particularly, a creation of George W. Perkins, who as a Morgan partner had organized it in 1902 by merging the two largest competitors in the farm implement industry, the McCormick and Deering companies, and three smaller ones. Although, according to the complaint, the new combination produced 85 percent of the farm machinery sold in the United States in 1902, it was not initially the sort of financial success that U.S. Steel was.[193] Within six or seven years after its formation it did begin to return handsome profits. Yet its commanding share of what was a changing market declined steadily. The company itself entered variant markets.[194] Like U.S. Steel, it became subject to an investigation by the Bureau of Corporations during the Roosevelt Administration, and like U.S. Steel it benefited from the Roosevelt-Gary-Perkins gentlemen's agreement, and enjoyed the implied immunity from prosecution.[195] Dealing as it did in products bought by farmers, International Harvester was, however, a prime target for state antitrust actions, which resulted in some temporary ousters, and in fines and injunctions—none of substantial consequence.[196]

Under Taft, the gentlemen's agreement having been shelved, the Bureau of Corporations completed and published an adverse report. The company tried to forestall suit by negotiations begun in the fall of 1911, just as proceedings were being brought against U.S. Steel. Harvester was more cooperative than U.S. Steel, offering a good part of what the government years later accepted in a consent decree, namely, the sale of two plants and of all lines of harvesting machines except the McCormick and Deering lines. Nevertheless, Harvester was at this stage

---

[192] J. M. Dickinson to Attorney General T. W. Gregory, June 4, 1915, Archives, File 60–138.

[193] United States v. International Harvester Co., 274 U.S. 693, 695 (1927); see Garraty, *Right-Hand Man*, 126–46.

[194] See *ibid.*; Whitney, *Antitrust Policies*, II, 228.

[195] See Wiebe, *Businessmen and Reform*, 46–47; H. F. Pringle, *Theodore Roosevelt* (1931), 445.

[196] See, e.g., International Harvester Co. v. Missouri, 234 U.S. 199 (1914); International Harvester Co. v. Kentucky, 234 U.S. 216, 589 (1914); Whitney, *Antitrust Policies*, II, 228–29.

[197] *Annual Report of the Attorney General of the United States for the Year 1912*, 18; Seager and Gulick, *Trust and Corporation Problems*, 273–74; see also Whitney, *Antitrust Policies*, II, 230.

no more successful than U.S. Steel.[197] One week before suit was brought, Taft himself saw attorneys for the company. But he was not satisfied, and instructed Wickersham to proceed.[198]

The filing of the complaint against International Harvester coincided with the opening of a public counterattack by President Taft against his erstwhile mentor and friend, Theodore Roosevelt. Late in April 1912, Taft allowed correspondence to be released from government files which documented the gentlemen's agreement between Roosevelt and the Morgan interests, represented by Perkins, with particular reference to the Harvester Company. "I don't charge that there is any corruption there," Taft said in a public speech, "but I ask you . . . with your knowledge of the method by which Theodore Roosevelt has brought charges against me, what he would say if the case were reversed and George Perkins were supporting me, and I had not sued the Steel Trust and the Harvester Trust."[199]

The Harvester suit moved more expeditiously than the proceeding against U.S. Steel. Early in November 1913, Attorney General McReynolds took the unusual step of arguing the case himself to the trial court, in St. Paul, Minnesota.[200] On August 12, 1914, judgment came down for the government, one judge dissenting. The court's decree ordered dissolution of International Harvester into at least three substantially equal and independent corporations, owned by separate stockholders. In October, however, the Department of Justice agreeing, the decree was amended to provide for more flexibility, so as to require merely that International Harvester "be divided in such manner and into such number of parts of separate and distinct ownership as may be necessary to restore competitive conditions and bring about a new situation in harmony with law."[201]

The Harvester Company appealed, of course, and so when the government's own appeal from the adverse decision in *United States* v. *United States Steel Corp.* reached the Supreme Court, the *Harvester* case was there waiting. The situation of a few years earlier, when the *Standard Oil* and *Tobacco* cases were argued and decided in tandem, seemed to be repeating itself. The Supreme Court heard a first argument of the *Harvester* case in April 1915, some two months before the *Steel* case was decided by the trial court. However, on June 2, 1915, the day before the *Steel* decision, the Court set the *Harvester* case down for reargument—presumably with a view to considering the two cases

---

[198] Pringle, *Taft*, II, 675.

[199] *Ibid.*, 790–92; Garraty, *Right-Hand Man*, 257.

[200] See B. B. Schimmel, "The Judicial Policy of Mr. Justice Mc-

Reynolds" (Ph.D. diss., Yale University, 1964).

[201] United States v. International Harvester Co., 214 Fed. 987 (D.C. Minn. 1914); 274 U.S. 693 (1927).

together. Both cases were heard in March 1917. Speaking for the government, Henry B. Colton, Special Assistant to the Attorney General, called the Steel Corporation "an abnormal, illegal and grossly over-capitalized colossal super-combination of combinations," and Solicitor General John W. Davis argued that the corporation's potential power was the decisive factor in the case.[202]

But for the moment, other circumstances were decisive. While the lawyers argued, President Wilson was arming American merchant ships, and the country was moving rapidly toward war. Counsel for the Steel Corporation brought the war into the courtroom: "This is not the time," said Richard V. Lindabury, "when we are endeavoring to mobilize our industries, to disintegrate or destroy them."[203] Within two months, on May 21, 1917, the *International Harvester* case was again set down for reargument, and with it the *Steel* case, and also a number of other pending antitrust suits. No reason internal to the Court is apparent for this action,[204] and so one may credit the speculation in the press that the Justices thought it desirable to put over antitrust cases "until the country could readjust itself to war time conditions."[205] The government was soon to ask for at least this much postponement, and perhaps it had already informally indicated a wish for respite to consider what its policy should be.

The Steel Corporation, for its part, wanted no respite. It scented victory. Cousel had stressed to the Court the present need "to mobilize our industries," but this was a point intended to go to the merits, which were then being argued, not to the desirability of delay. When, shortly after the case had been docketed in the Supreme Court, the government had asked for an extension of time, the corporation had opposed the motion, even though the government's supporting reasons were entirely technical. Under the rules, a narrative record of the testimony had to be prepared. The actual transcript of testimony and the exhibits were even more extensive than they had been in the *Standard Oil* case—thirty volumes, comprising 12,151 pages, of which fourteen volumes, coming to 5,969 pages, were testimony. It was quite a task to get this original record into shape. And yet the corporation had opposed extending the time for filing a narrative record till July 1, 1916, and suggested instead that the rules be waived, and the case proceed on the original record—

---

[202] *New York Times,* Mar. 13, 1917, p. 15, col. 1; *New York Times,* Mar. 14, 1917, p. 13, col. 4.

[203] *New York Times,* Mar. 13, 1917, p. 15, col. 1.

[204] It is said in Seager and Gulick, *Trust and Corporation Problems,* 259, that "the justices who took part in the case were evenly divided." But the Justices who took part in the case numbered seven.

[205] *New York Times,* May 22, 1917, p. 15, col. 1.

the raw record, so to speak. The Supreme Court had adopted this suggestion, but had granted a short extension of time (sixty days) even so.[206]

After the order for reargument, the Steel Corporation continued to press for speed. Within two weeks counsel was writing to Solicitor General Davis:

> The Steel people are extremely anxious to have the Steel case set for re-argument at the opening of the October Term, so that it may be heard and disposed of as promptly as possible. Will you not aid us in the endeavor to bring this about? You can understand how embarrassing the present situation is to the Corporation. The Government is calling upon it for extra production that can only be accomplished by considerably enlarging some of its works at an expenditure of several million dollars. The Corporation held back from undertaking this for a time, hoping that a speedy decision would definitely determine its right to do it or not to do it. It, however, has now decided to go ahead and do the best it can, but it ought not to be required to act under the constant fear that the new and extraordinary expenditures it is making for merely patriotic purposes will result in additional embarrassment and loss in case the court should decide against it.
>
> We have been thinking of making an application to the court on the 11th inst. to set the case for hearing at as early a date as possible. It occurs to me, however, that it might be well for you and me to go together to the Chief Justice before that day and ascertain whether the court has any plan for hearing the Trust cases together or otherwise which would make unnecessary or undesirable such an application. Of course, we desire to conform to the wishes of the court.[207]

Davis answered promptly that he shared the anxiety to dispose of the *Steel* case, but the Court was rising, and nothing could be done before fall.[208]

By the next term of Court, however, the government had decided that it wished postponement. And it so moved:

> In order that the Government in this time of stress may not meet with competition from private enterprises in its financial operations and the flotation of its loans, the Treasury Department has been constrained to urge that all private financing on a large scale shall be avoided so far as at all possible. . . .
>
> It is quite clear that the dissolutions which are sought in the pending cases . . . will require financial operations on a large scale

---

[206] United States v. United States Steel Corp., 240 U.S. 442 (1916).
[207] R. V. Lindabury to J. W. Davis,

June 5, 1917, Archives, File 60–138.
[208] J. W. Davis to R. V. Lindabury, June 6, 1917, Archives, File 60–138.

if they are to be genuine and effective. Important as the remedy in these cases is believed to be, it must give place for the moment to the paramount needs of the hour.

The motion applied to both the *Harvester* and *Steel* cases.[209] And at the next term, the government again moved for postponement in the *Steel* case, without the consent of the Steel Corporation.[210] And so the *Steel* case remained to be reargued and decided in peacetime.

The *Harvester* case, with its consistently more cooperative defendant, developed differently. After the government asked for a continuance in January 1918, the Harvester Company sought settlement, and soon obtained some notable concessions from the government. It then moved to dismiss its appeal in the Supreme Court, and this motion having been granted and the case remanded to the trial court, that court, in November 1918, approved a consent decree, as agreed upon by the company and the government.

The decree provided that the company was to sell its harvesting machine lines known under the trade names of Osborn, Milwaukee, and Champion, together with the trade names themselves and the manufacturing equipment used to make these lines, as well as two out of the three plants in which they were manufactured. This degree of divestiture, which the company had also offered to undergo earlier, when it was attempting to avoid suit, but which Taft had deemed insufficient, was probably not very painful, since by far the greatest proportion of the company's output of major farm implements (as much as 85 to 95 percent in 1918) was accounted for by the two lines—McCormick and Deering—which it retained.

The consent decree also provided that the company was to be prohibited after December 31, 1911, from having more than one agent for the sale of any of its products in any city or town in the United States. This provision was designed to meet the complaint of competitors that International Harvester, maintaining as it did several agents for its various products in single towns, monopolized the best salesmen, and also tended to create monopolies for its products, since most towns could not support additional agents for competitors. But although Harvester initially rather feared the effects of this provision of the decree—this was not a concession the company had volunteered earlier—it is probable that the company in fact benefited from the resulting reduction in the number of its agents. The ones it dropped had handled very small

---

[209] *Annual Report of the Attorney General of the United States for the Year 1918*, 62; T. W. Gregory to C. A. Severance, Dec. 29, 1917, Archives, File 60–138.

[210] R. V. Lindabury to T. W. Gregory, Oct. 10, 1918, Archives, File 60–138.

percentages of its business, and yet had represented a substantial expenditure.[211]

The *Steel* case was finally reargued in October 1919, and decided against the government on March 1, 1920. The decision was that of a seven-man Court. Brandeis, who had been appointed in 1916, disqualified himself, no doubt because in the course of testimony in Congress in 1911 and 1912, he had expressed not only some rather strong sentiments about the Steel Corporation and its practices, but also what amounted to an opinion on its legality.[212] McReynolds, appointed in 1914, disqualified himself because as Attorney General he had, for a time, been in charge of the case, and because, as we shall see, he had also had an earlier involvement with it. Of the Justices who took part, the Chief Justice, Holmes, and Van Devanter formed the majority with McKenna, who spoke for the Court. Day was joined by two of the new Justices, Pitney and Clarke, in dissent. Thus the *Steel* case was decided by a portion of the majority that decided *Standard Oil* and *Tobacco*, not by new members of the Court.

McKenna's opinion for the Court started with a general acceptance of the views of the two concurring circuit judges below, who held that whatever the original intent might have been in the formation of U.S. Steel, no monopoly was actually achieved. It was in these terms that McKenna stated the decisive question, as he saw it:

> Our present purpose is not retrospect for itself, however instructive, but practical decision upon existing conditions, that we may not by their disturbance produce, or even risk, consequences of a concern that can not now be computed. In other words, our consideration should be of not what the Corporation had power to do or did, but, what it has now power to do and is doing, and what judgment shall be now pronounced. . . .

---

[211] *Annual Report of the Attorney General of the United States for the Year 1918*, 61; Whitney, *Antitrust Policies*, II, 230–32.

[212] Brandeis had said that the purchase of the Tennessee Coal and Iron Company added materially to the Steel Corporation's control of the steel business. "As a matter of fact, of course," he had continued, "this great power of the Steel Corporation has been exercised in one way and another to control the trades. It was not merely the question of percentage, but it was the huge financial power, it was the backing, it was the connections—all of these things together have given the Steel Corporation the power which would not be described simply as its power by controlling a portion of the trade—but it is the power augmented by its associations and augmented very greatly by its financial strength and its financial relations." *Hearings, House Judiciary Committee, Trust Legislation*, 62nd Cong., 2nd Sess., Ser. No. 2 (Jan. 26, 27, and Feb. 19, 1912), 19.

It was clear, said McKenna, that the Steel Corporation never had monopoly power; great power, yes, but power greater than its competitors in the aggregate, no. The very need to hold Gary dinners in order to persuade the corporation's competitors to cooperate proved as much. These dinners, McKenna added, may very well have been illegal, but they were abandoned nine months before the government brought suit, and there was no evidence that the abandonment was intended to forestall suit.

McKenna digressed here to note that the government deduced a purpose to monopolize from the various acquisitions following the consolidation of 1901. Of course, on the view of the case that McKenna had already stated, this was not a point that required discussion; McKenna was willing to assume a past unlawful purpose *arguendo*. He simply went out of his way to rehabilitate the memory of the recently deceased Theodore Roosevelt. The Tennessee Coal and Iron transaction was submitted, said McKenna, to President Roosevelt for his approval. This approval did not make it legal, to be sure, "but it gives assurance of its legality, and we know from his earnestness in the public welfare he would have approved of nothing that had even a tendency to its detriment." McKenna then quoted testimony taken from Theodore Roosevelt during the trial of the *Steel* case to the effect that Roosevelt had not been deceived, but had believed that "the Tennessee Coal and Iron people had a property which was almost worthless in their hands, nearly worthless to them, nearly worthless to the communities in which it was situated, and entirely worthless to any financial institution that had the securities the minute that any panic came, and that the only way to give value to it was to put it in the hands of people whose possession of it would be a guarantee that there was value to it." McKenna concluded that "it would seem a distempered view of purchase and result to regard them as violations of law."

Having paid his respects to TR and given the offhand lie to the charges that played so momentous a role in shaping the campaign of 1912, McKenna returned to the main line of his argument. Was the Steel Corporation, as of the present time, a combination in restraint of trade? There was testimony from some two hundred competitors and customers showing that the corporation had taken no coercive action against them. The government, on the other hand, offered merely an allegation that the corporation had the power to coerce, and the testimony of an author and teacher of economics, whose "philosophical deductions," McKenna said, may have been somewhat fortified by service as Deputy Commissioner of Corporations. But all this evidence amounted to was speculation and generalities about economic power: "We magnify the testimony by its consideration." Of course, the corporation's competitors did follow its prices. But they did so voluntarily, because it was profitable to do it. That was proof, not of power, as the government contended, but of success, and should success alone be penalized? "Are the activities [of business] to be encouraged when militant, and suppressed or regulated when triumphant because of the dominance attained? To such paternalism the Government's contention, which regards power rather than its use the determining consideration, seems to conduct." Shall we declare the law to be, McKenna asked,

> that size is an offence even though it minds its own business because what it does is imitated? The Corporation is undoubtedly of impressive size and it takes an effort of resolution not to be affected by it or to exaggerate its influence. But we must adhere to the law and the law does not make mere size an offence or the existence of unexerted power an offence. It, we repeat, requires overt acts and trusts to its prohibition of them and its power to repress or punish them. It does not compel competition nor require all that is possible.

The initial formation of the Steel Corporation may have been an illegal act, not unlike, at that stage, perhaps, the formation of the Standard Oil and American Tobacco companies. "But there are countervailing considerations. We have seen whatever there was of wrong intent could not be executed, whatever there was of evil effect, was discontinued before this suit was brought; and this, we think, determines the decree." Should a court of equity punish now, nearly twenty years later, what may have been illegal when done, but is not illegal in its present effect?

It was ten years after the formation of U.S. Steel that the government first moved against the corporation. Meanwhile many millions of dollars had been spent and invested. "And what of the foreign trade that has been developed and exists? The Government, with some inconsistency, it seems to us, would remove this from the decree of dissolution." The government, suggesting that dissolution of U.S. Steel—a holding company—would release many subsidiaries which were fully integrated in themselves and quite capable of independent operation, was asking in effect for restoration of the conditions of twenty years before, by analogy to the *Standard Oil* and *Tobacco* decrees. But in *Standard Oil* and *Tobacco*, there was persistent and systematic law breaking, masquerading under legal forms, and this illegality had to be arrested. That was not the case here. Finally:

> In conclusion we are unable to see that the public interest will be served by yielding to the contention of the Government respecting the dissolution of the company or the separation from it of some of its subsidiaries; and we do see in a contrary conclusion a risk of injury to the public interest, including a material disturbance of, and, it may

be serious detriment to, the foreign trade. And in submission to the policy of the law and its fortifying prohibitions the public interest is of paramount regard.[213]

Day's dissent stressed the initial illegal purpose of the Steel combination. Companies were bought up by the combiners at highly inflated prices, not for their value as independent producers, but for their value as parts of an illegal combination. The result was an enormous overcapitalization. This initial venture was followed by other illegal acts, including the Gary dinners. There might be no objection to size alone, but the Sherman Act did proscribe size and power obtained by illegal means, rather than by natural growth. The majority seemed to rely in part on reasons of public policy for denying relief. But:

> I know of no public policy which sanctions a violation of the law, nor of any inconvenience to trade, domestic or foreign, which should have the effect of placing combinations, which have been able thus to organize one of the greatest industries of the country in defiance of law, in an impregnable position above the control of the law forbidding such combinations.[214]

Holmes thought the disposition of the *Steel* case "very unsatisfactory." He "regretted the turn given to the opinion. . . ." But the result was the one he wanted to reach.[215] And, he wrote Felix Frankfurter, "as I said to Brandeis I couldn't change my vote (to use the odious phrase that is in use with us) because I thought that a majority of the Court, if the other two [Brandeis and McReynolds] could have taken part, would be the other way.[216] As to the opinion I did not attempt suggestions that would have been of little use."[217]

Brandeis' vote one may be sure of; Holmes was quite right. He was right too, most probably, about McReynolds, barring only the possibility that considerations of present public interest, mentioned, however vaguely, by McKenna, and changes in conditions such as the

---

[213] United States v. United States Steel Corp., 251 U.S. 417, 444, 446–47, 449, 450, 451, 452, 453, 457 (1920).

[214] United States v. United States Steel Corp., 251 U.S. at 457, 463.

[215] M. DeW. Howe, ed., *Holmes-Laski Letters* (1953), I, 248, 251.

[216] Within a month after the *Steel* decision came down, Representative Brand of Georgia offered a bill in the House to allow the President to desig-

nate circuit judges to sit on the Supreme Court in lieu of disqualified Justices. In the *Steel* case, Mr. Brand said, "four men virtually destroyed an act of Congress. . . ." Such a situation should not be allowed to recur. 59 *Cong. Rec.* 4924–25, 66th Cong., 2nd Sess. (1920).

[217] O. W. Holmes to F. Frankfurter, Mar. 10, 1920, Holmes Papers, Harvard Law School Library.

continuing decline of the Steel Corporation's percentage of the market, would have altered McReynolds' opinion from what it had been a decade earlier. For at that time, before he acquired any official responsibility for the prosecution of the case, he had expressed an opinion, and it had been a reasonably clear one.

Late in November 1911, when McReynolds, then in private practice in New York, was concluding his part-time duties as special counsel for the government in the *American Tobacco* case—duties that did not preclude private employment—he had a request from the general counsel of the Steel Corporation, Francis Lynde Stetson, for an opinion "as to the status of the Corporation under the Sherman antitrust law, and with reference especially to the suit instituted by the United States against the Corporation under that law." For a fee of $5,000, McReynolds delivered such an opinion, on December 20, 1911.[218]

The relevant law, McReynolds wrote, was not as clear as it might be. He had some unkind things to say about the opinions in the *Standard Oil* and *Tobacco* cases. They were "not easy to follow and the strange confusion of thought and language makes deductions from them uncertain. It seems fairly plain that special effort was made to rest the decisions on a basis sufficiently narrow to secure approval by the entire Court. Much said about intent, wrongful purpose, etc., probably was necessary to make them acceptable to Justice Holmes. . . ." Again: "These opinions in some respects are obscure almost to the point of incomprehensibility, and they render an entirely satisfactory conclusion concerning the full meaning of the law quite impossible." Nevertheless, it could be concluded that the Sherman Act was applicable to "an actual design, express or implied from attending circumstances, unduly to obstruct the free course of trade, or unduly to restrict a trader's liberty to engage in business, or unduly to restrict competitive conditions, provided such purpose is coupled with adequate power to create a dangerous probability of success."

Normal growth was not covered by the Act, but consolidation in a holding company of the shares of many competitors was not normal growth. Undoubtedly the Supreme Court would find, McReynolds thought, that at least one of the purposes of the initial consolidation of

---

[218] A year and a half later, in April 1913, shortly after he took office as Attorney General, McReynolds told Stetson that in view of this earlier connection, he would disqualify himself from acting for the government in the *Steel* case. Stetson, however, decided to waive any objection, and McReynolds then said he would go ahead, provided he could get President Wilson's approval. The President approved. McReynolds to Woodrow Wilson, Apr. 16, 1913, Wilson to McReynolds, Apr. 23, 1913, McReynolds Papers, Library of the University of Virginia.

1901 was "to suppress competition (actual or potential) amongst the combined companies, and to secure for the members of the syndicate large profits. . . ." Among later acquisitions, that of the Tennessee Coal and Iron Company, "if undertaken as the only way to stop a great financial panic, might be said to indicate the dominant position of the Corporation in the business of the country; if to obtain control of an important potential competitor, it would suggest a purpose further to suppress opposition."

The Steel Corporation had engaged in no unfair or oppressive competitive practices; it had sought no rebates, nor "purchased plants only to dismantle them." But the corporation's conduct, however praiseworthy, would not necessarily absolve it under the Sherman Act. "The text of the statute makes clear that it was not aimed merely at means employed, but was intended to bring about the destruction of an existing status of restraint or monopolization of trade." That was why the Standard Oil and Tobacco companies were dissolved, rather than merely having their predatory practices enjoined. However, McReynolds added, the decisive "status of restraint" must be found to exist on the basis of conditions prevailing not earlier than the time of the filing of the bill. "I am inclined to think," McReynolds wrote,

> that the Supreme Court as presently constituted would conclude, upon consideration of all the facts, that the *prima facie* presumption of purpose to dominate the industry and exclude others . . . which probably arose from the original organization and composition of the combination, has not been overcome by the course of events since that time; but strong reasons could easily be assigned for a conclusion to the contrary effect, and such a one is far from an impossibility. And the complete absence of all wicked or oppressive action towards existing competitors is a powerful circumstance in favor of the Corporation.

The mere existence of the corporation's power "has doubtless generally influenced other producers to follow its lead as regards prices and matters of trade policy, and may also have deterred others from entering." On the other hand, the corporation did have competitors.

> Which set of factors will prevail with the Court, in the present state of the decisions, no one can tell with certainty—much depends on the general economic views entertained by the Judges. But it appears to me that the probabilities are in favor of a holding that undue restriction of competition results from the unified control over so many units, such a large share of the trade, and such vast capital.[219]

---

[219] F. L. Stetson to J. C. McReynolds, Nov. 29, 1911; McReynolds to United States Steel Corporation, Dec. 20, 1911; Stetson to McReynolds, Dec. 27, 1911, McReynolds Papers.

II: *The Rule of Reason*

The opinion in the *Steel* case, George W. Perkins wired Judge Gary, "places moral conduct above legal technicalities."[220] It showed, thought the *New York Times*, that Congress and the courts had learned a lesson. Their "business education" had been "tedious and costly," but effective, if they had now learned to confine themselves to the punishment of misconduct "rather than the teaching of business men how to do business."[221] A new business era had arrived. Harold J. Laski, writing from England to his friend Holmes, regretted the "dangerous loopholes" in McKenna's opinion, which astute lawyers would know how to exploit. But recalling no doubt the events that followed the *Standard Oil* and *Tobacco* decisions nearly a decade before, he hoped that at least the *Steel* case "may lead to a concentration of public opinion on the general question and that will be worth while. . . . [O]ne feels that a serious consideration of the monopoly problem is due."[222] No concentration of public opinion occurred.[223] What did occur, with impetus from the *Steel* case, was a renewed period of concentration in business, and on business.[224]

One "dangerous loophole" in McKenna's opinion was the emphasis on U.S. Steel's innocence of predatory practices, and the corresponding stress on those portions of the opinions in the *Standard Oil* and *Tobacco* cases which discuss predatory practices. McKenna's opinion could thus be read to say that it did not matter how much market power a single combination had accumulated, so long as the power was used fairly and decently; that the Sherman Act, in Perkins' jubilant formulation, was satisfied by "moral conduct," and that everything else was a "legal technicality." The Sherman Act, then, in this view, merely enforced a

---

[220] Garraty, *Right-Hand Man,* 388.

[221] *New York Times,* Mar. 2, 1920, p. 10, col. 1.

[222] *Holmes-Laski Letters,* I, 249–50.

[223] Although to Robert M. La Follette, speaking in the Senate some two years later, the *Steel* decision still seemed one of the most "indefensible . . . ever rendered by any judicial tribunal." No man, he said, could "read it without being convinced that the remarkable doctrines which it advances, if consistently applied, would not only annihilate the Sherman Act, as Justice Day says in his dissenting opinion, but would destroy the very foundation of justice and reduce the Nation to a condition of anarchy, in which the only law would be the law of might." 62 *Cong. Rec.* 6786, 67th Cong., 2nd Sess. (May 12, 1922).

[224] E. H. Levi, "The Antitrust Laws and Monopoly," *U. Chi. L. Rev.,* 14: 153, 1947; *cf.* Senator King of Utah in 60 *Cong. Rec.* 414, 66th Cong., 3rd Sess. (1920): "The recent decision of the Supreme Court of the United States in the Steel Trust case seems to devitalize the Sherman Antitrust Law, or at least to reduce it to a rather anemic and flaccid pronouncement. That decision, in my opinion, will encourage the growth of monopolies and stimulate still further combinations in restraint of trade and conspiracies to lessen, if not destroy, competition."

code of fair business conduct. It did not necessarily prescribe competition and proscribe its suppression; in the familiar terminology, the Act sanctioned "good" trusts and punished only "bad" ones. The drawing of a distinction between "good" and "bad" trusts, in the terms that had been current a decade earlier, may not have been what McKenna had in mind. He had had occasion just a few years before to disavow just such an intention.[225] And yet the distinction could be inferred.

Of course, the natural growth of a business to the size of U.S. Steel, by internal expansion and even by acquisition plainly aimed at increasing efficiency, might not run afoul of the Sherman Act. The absence of predatory practices would serve to confirm that the process of growth had been directed at attaining greater efficiency, just as the presence of such practices in *Standard Oil* and *Tobacco* was evidence that the growth there had not been a movement toward efficiency, but an effort to monopolize the market. But as Day complained in dissent, McKenna sounded at times as if the Steel Corporation had been the outcome of a process of natural growth. Unquestionably it had grown internally, with the expansion of the entire industry, since its formation. In its origins, however, it was a combination of former competitors, and under the decisions in the *Standard Oil* and *Tobacco* cases, there was in these circumstances a presumption that the combination was aimed, not at efficiency, but at market domination and the suppression of competition. There is no mention of the presumption in McKenna's opinion. In yet another aspect, moreover, the tone of the opinion differs markedly from the tone of the *Standard Oil* and *Tobacco* decisions. As McKenna describes the government's dissolution proposals, he is incredulous—there is scarcely another word for it—to the point of being struck dumb. He rejects these proposals as impractical, as virtually inconceivable, but without ever indicating just why they could not work. Actually, dissolution might have presented difficulties less grave than those encountered in the *Tobacco* case; difficulties, indeed, more on the order of those that were met and conquered in the *Standard Oil* and *Northern Securities* decrees.

Despite all this, however, the decision in the *Steel* case was not necessarily a doctrinal departure from the *Standard Oil* and *Tobacco* opinions. It was, rather, based on a curiously—perhaps a willfully—mistaken view of the facts, and it was doctrinally a refusal to take any step beyond *Standard Oil* and *Tobacco*. Fitting the *Steel* case into the analytical framework developed in *Standard Oil* and *Tobacco*, and setting up, therefore, the presumption of illegality that McKenna failed to make explicit, one finds McKenna rebutting the presumption, and

---

[225] Thomsen v. Cayser, 243 U.S. 66(1917).

establishing present legality on the evidence of the Gary dinners, which to him indicated that U.S. Steel never achieved power to restrict production and control prices, since it was required at those dinners to invite the voluntary cooperation of its competitors. McKenna's may be thought a naive view of the dinners, giving them a perfectly perverse ultimate effect, and McKenna may be thought equally naive in his view of U.S. Steel's price leadership after the dinners were discontinued. It must count for something, after all, that the dinners were initiated and led by Gary, not by his fragmented competition, and that they achieved their purpose. And while the dinners ceased before commencement of the government's suit, they were stopped in the midst of numerous official inquiries, and in the shadow of litigation. Far from demonstrating, therefore, that monopoly power was in fact never attained, the Gary dinners are probative of power and of its use. Assuming the facts, however, to be what McKenna understood—or perhaps wished—them to be, it was no departure from the doctrine of *Standard Oil* and *Tobacco* to hold that the presumption of illegality arising from the initial merger of 1901 had been rebutted, and that the Sherman Act, which proscribes not the intention to suppress competition, as such, but the intention to do so joined to the fact of the suppression of competition, was inapplicable.

In this view of the case, there remained only the question whether a combination intended to suppress competition which has not yet succeeded in doing so may not just the same be large enough to represent effective potential power, and thus large enough to violate the Sherman Act by its size alone. This, as McKenna rightly thought, was not an issue involved in the *Standard Oil* and *Tobacco* cases, where the companies were continuously and successfully engaged in the suppression of competition. The question in this view of the *Steel* case was, rather, whether the corporation had enough inherent power to suppress competition, and perhaps indeed to do so naturally, whether it intended to or not. We have seen that at the time of consolidation, U.S. Steel produced about 43 percent of pig iron, nearly 66 percent of steel ingots and steel castings, and some 50 percent of all kinds of finished rolled products. At the time of the decision, in 1920, these percentages had declined, in one instance fairly radically, by 20 percent in steel ingot and casting production; and also by some 4 percent in pig iron production, and by nearly 9 percent in production of finished products of all kinds. But in an expanding market, the absolute size and productive capacity of U.S. Steel had increased greatly.[226] Yet on McKenna's view of the

---

[226] See Seager and Gulick, *Trust and Corporation Problems,* 258.

case, it would have been a prophylactic use of the Sherman Act to order dissolution in the circumstances, and he declined to do it.

Inferences that observers drew, and were in part invited to draw, from the opinion, its timing, and perhaps above all the symbolism that attached to the defendant—these factors, and not strictly speaking its doctrinal meaning or doctrinal consequences—are what made of the opinion in the *Steel* case a watershed in the history of the Sherman Antitrust Act. The complaint in the *Steel* case had been a repudiation of the notion that there were "good" trusts as well as "bad" ones. The failure of the *Steel* prosecution was a repudiation of the repudiation. The corporation which for so many of the most avid reformers had represented everything that the Sherman Act was meant to prevent and that progressive measures were intended to set right—this corporation had been blessed, and hence all it stood for now had, after a fashion, the sanction of law. The Tennessee Coal and Iron transaction had been vindicated, as had the Gary dinners, and the whole of Gary's policy of being "good," and gentlemanly, and polite to the government in Washington, and expecting from it in return freedom of action and equally good manners.

The *Steel* decision was the defeat and the end not only of the radicalism of the campaign for the New Freedom, but also of the relatively conservative antitrust fervor of the last Republican administration of the Progressive era. Moreover, the decision was the perfectly timed culmination of a trend. For the antitrust issue had begun to be muted some time since. In the first reforming phase of the Wilson Administration, antitrust objectives were attained in the Clayton and Federal Trade Commission Acts, and then there was a slackening of energies. The Trade Commission got off to no vigorous trust-busting start. Quite the contrary. Nor did the Justice Department undertake any spectacular prosecutions—and perhaps no really spectacular targets were left. The two biggest new cases—against the American Telephone and Telegraph Company, and against the New York, New Haven and Hartford Railroad—were settled by negotiation in 1914, even as the *Harvester* case was to be settled, and in none was the consent decree of a radical nature. Wilson and McReynolds even began to be hailed as friends and protectors of the businessman.

The second reforming surge of the New Freedom, in 1916, took other directions; it had no antitrust component. And so when the *Steel* case was decided, it must have seemed as if the decks had been finally cleared. The trust-busting adventure was over. All along, antitrust policy had depended for public support, and also for effectiveness in governing the practices of business at large, on the notorious lesson of the big case. Now the last of the big cases had failed. The country hardly expected to see its like again.[227]

Doctrinally, nevertheless, the *Steel* decision was no such watershed. Doctrine had been a good deal less than clear before, and it remained so, without being substantially affected by the decision in the *Steel* case. In the near decade between the *Standard Oil* and *Tobacco* cases and the *Steel* case, there had not been a coherent movement forward. Nor did the *Steel* case launch a coherent line of decisions in a new direction.

From May 1911, when the *Standard Oil* and *Tobacco* cases came down, to March 1, 1920, when the *Steel* case was decided, the Supreme Court wrote—exclusive of cases involving labor unions, and of cases dealing with conditions tied to the sale of patented articles, and with resale price maintenance, whether or not tied to patents, all of which need to be discussed separately—twenty-seven antitrust opinions. Of these, nine cases may be put aside as turning, in whole or in part, on procedural or otherwise peripheral issues.[228] Among the rest, one case stands out, bearing a strong resemblance to the *Steel* case in the general notoriety of the defendant, arising from the agitation between 1911 and 1914. It was decided a full two years before *Steel*, and came to the same end. This was *United States* v. *United Shoe Machinery Co.*[229]

The Shoe Machinery Cases

The United Shoe Machinery Company, which manufactured, as its name indicates, machinery used in the making of shoes, was formed by

---

[227] Link, *Wilson: The New Freedom*, 417–23; Link, *Woodrow Wilson and the Progressive Era*, 74–80, 223–30; *Washington Post*, Dec. 21, 1914, p. 4, col. 1; *Annual Report of the Attorney General of the United States for the Year 1914*, 12–15. See United States v. Great Lakes Towing Co., 217 Fed. 656 (D.C. N.D. Ohio 1914), *appeal dismissed on motion of appellant*, 245 U.S. 675 (1917) (no dissolution following Sherman Act judgment). *But cf.* Corn Products Refining Co. v. United States, 234 Fed. 964 (D.C. S.D. N.Y. 1916) (L. Hand, J.), *appeal dismissed on motion of appellant*, 249 U.S. 621 (1919) (dissolution ordered).

[228] United States v. Kissel, 218 U.S. 601 (1910); Virtue v. Creamery Package Co., 227 U.S. 8 (1913); Wilder Manufacturing Co. v. Corn Products Co., 236 U.S. 165 (1915); United States v. Hamburg-American Co., 239 U.S. 466 (1916); Fleitmann v. Welsbach Co., 240 U.S. 27 (1916); United States v. American-Asiatic S.S. Co., 242 U.S. 537 (1917); United Copper Co. v. Amalgamated Copper Co., 244 U.S. 261 (1917); People's Tobacco Co. v. American Tobacco Co., 246 U.S. 79 (1918); Buckeye Powder Co. v. DuPont Powder Co., 248 U.S. 55 (1918). See also Geddes v. Anaconda Mining Co., 254 U.S. 590 (1921). And see Frank v. Union Pacific R.R., 226 Fed. 906 (8th Cir. 1915), *appeal dismissed on motion of appellant*, 241 U.S. 694 (1916); Venner v. New York Central & Hudson River R.R., 226 N.Y. 583 (1919), *cert. denied*, 249 U.S. 617 (1919).

[229] 247 U.S. 32 (1918).

the merger in 1899 of three firms, two of which were themselves the result of prior mergers. Of the companies that combined in 1899, one made 60 percent of all lasting machines, another made 80 percent of all welt-sewing and stitching machines, as well as 10 percent of lasting machines, and the third made 70 percent of heeling and 80 percent of metallic fastening machines. The merger was thus not a combination of direct competitors, except for the 10 percent of lasting machines manufactured by one of the merging firms, which was added to the 60 percent of the same machine manufactured by another.

Following the consolidation of 1899, the United Company bought up numerous other firms, most notably, in 1910, that of Thomas G. Plant, who had invented some potentially competitive machines. Of course, even though little direct competition had existed among the initially combining companies, the consolidation effectively excluded the possibility of future competition among them, and the later acquisitions further ensured domination of the market. However, given the peculiar situation of a business in patented, complementary machines, a good argument could be made that the initial merger was necessary for more efficient operation. Improvement of all machines quite possibly depended on borrowing features of one machine for another, and thus required ownership of all outstanding patents. This argument has some plausibility as well in the case of the further acquisitions, including the acquisition of the Plant Company, whose patents may have been chiefly valuable as ideas for the improvement of the United Company's patents.

The intention, both in the origins and in the operation of the United Company, was, however, far from clear, especially in view of the highly restrictive conditions on which United leased its machines to shoe manufacturers. Leases provided that if the lessee had more work to be done than the machine leased could do, he would lease additional machinery from United and not from anyone else. Again, the lessee of any particular piece of machinery was required to use it exclusively, and also to use auxiliary machines aiding and supplementing it, and no other. Moreover, leased machines were not to be used in the manufacture of shoes on which work had been done by a machine not owned by United.

On September 19, 1911, the Taft Administration obtained a criminal indictment against S. W. Winslow, the principal figure in the United Shoe Machinery Company, some colleagues of his on the executive committee, and the company itself, for violation of the Sherman Act. And two months later, on December 12, 1911, the Taft Administration filed an equity suit, asking for dissolution of the United Company. Both actions were brought in Massachusetts, United's home state. Meanwhile, the Clapp Committee in the Senate and the Judiciary Committee of the House devoted substantial portions of their attention, in the course of their hearings on the trust problem, to the Shoe Machinery

Company. Brandeis, who had been an investor, a director, and one of counsel to the United Company in its early years, but who broke with it afterward, testified extensively, expressing the opinion that United was in flagrant violation of the antitrust laws. There were other witnesses hostile to the company, and the company defended itself. Its organization, its later acquisitions, including particularly the acquisition of the Plant Company, and its leases were examined in detail. One result, as we shall see, was a provision of the Clayton Act aimed quite specifically at the Shoe Machinery Company's restrictive leases.[230]

The criminal prosecution, which was styled *United States* v. *Winslow*, came to nothing. The trial court construed the indictment as charging violation of the Sherman Act only by the initial organization of the United Company in 1899, without reference to the later restrictive conditions tied to the leases, and without suggesting that these conditions were contemplated at the time of the initial combination. So construing the indictment, and holding that the merger of 1899 was not in itself a violation of the Sherman Act, the district court dismissed the case. On the government's direct appeal under the Criminal Appeals Act, the Supreme Court, speaking through Holmes in February 1913, unanimously affirmed. The construction of the indictment by the district court was not open for review. And looking at the matter strictly from the fixed point of view of 1899, as Holmes was thus constrained to do, he could find little to indicate that the combination had any purpose other than to achieve greater efficiency. Of course, a certain amount of competition might be suppressed, but the machines that were coming under a single ownership were in any event patented, and so, merger or no, competition had already been suppressed by law. Assuming that, after the merger, the United Company controlled 70 to 80 percent of all shoe machinery made in the United States, Holmes said, still he could see "no greater objection to one corporation manufacturing seventy per cent of three non-competing groups of patented machines collectively used for making a single product than to three corporations making the same proportion of one group each." "It is as lawful for one corporation to make every part of a steam engine and to put the machine together as for one to make the boilers and the other to make the wheels."[231]

---

[230] *Clapp Hearings,* I, 1160–61, 1164, 1957–78, 2105–21, 2154–81, 2615–25, 2652–53; *House Judiciary Hearings,* 111–29; Seager and Gulick, *Trust and Corporation Problems,* 280–303; Whitney, *Antitrust Policies,* II, 119–25; Mason, *Brandeis,* 214–29. And see for later comment by Brandeis, e.g., *Hearings Before the Committee on the Judiciary, Trust Legislation, House of Representatives.* 63rd Cong., 2nd Sess. (1915), I, 655–61.

[231] United States v. Winslow, 227 U.S. 202, 217, 218 (1913).

The suit in equity, asking for dissolution of the company, took a good bit longer to come to a conclusion. The trial court decided the case against the government in 1915, even though this time the restrictive leases as well as the initial combination were unquestionably in issue. On appeal to the Supreme Court, the case was first argued immediately after the *Steel* case, in March 1917, and set down for reargument in May of that year. But it was then reargued separately, nearly two years before the *Steel* reargument, in January 1918, and decided on May 20, 1918. As in the *Steel* case, McReynolds and Brandeis were disqualified, the latter because of his early connection with the Shoe Machinery Company, and because of the opinions he had expressed about it afterwards, and the former because of his responsibility as Attorney General during early stages of the prosecution. The seven-man Court that was thus left, and that affirmed the decision against the government, divided exactly as it would later do in the *Steel* case. McKenna, the author of the later *Steel* opinion, wrote here also, and was joined by White, Holmes, and Van Devanter. Day dissented, as he was later to do in the *Steel* case, and with him were Pitney and Clarke.

The government, McKenna wrote, asserted "somewhat fervidly" that the United Company was "absolute monarch of the industry." But the question whether the company was a monopoly in violation of the Sherman Act turned on the purpose of the initial combination and of the later acquisitions. It was doubtful, moreover, whether in any industry dominated by patents there could have been any competition for the organizers of United to intend suppressing. The trial court had found both that the original purpose was benign, and that no competition was in fact suppressed. These findings, McKenna thought, were well supported by the record. The combination of 1899, he remarked, was not disturbed by the government for a long time. Many business decisions had been made, and much money invested, "not only by the company but by the public," in reliance upon the legality of this unchallenged consolidation. And at this late date—here McKenna gave a preview of the incredulity with which he would greet suggestions of a dissolution of United States Steel—how would one go about restoring the conditions that had prevailed before 1899?

The difficulties, McKenna suggested, were virtually insuperable. The company had works at Beverly which produced in one modern factory a whole line of machines. How could these works be broken up, and if they were not to be broken up but merely sold to someone else, what was the use? Much was made of later acquisitions, particularly that of the Thomas G. Plant Company, so celebrated in the Congressional hearings. But Plant's patents, said McKenna, were not really competitive, although some were found to supplement and perfect the United Company's patents. At any rate, the acquisition was made on the basis of a business judgment. The price paid was a business price, even though large, because in combination the patents to be bought and the patents already held would have very great value, although they might not have had it separately. So as to other purchases. Some may have removed some competition, but they all proceeded in larger measure from legitimate business needs.

There remained the problem of the restrictive leases. "The company," McKenna said, "indeed, has magnitude, but it is at once the result and the cause of efficiency, and the charge that it has been oppressively used is not sustained." A line of very recent cases, culminating in *Motion Picture Co.* v. *Universal Film Co.*[232] (which overruled *Henry* v. *A. B. Dick Co.*)[233] and *Boston Store* v. *American Graphophone Co.*,[234] the last decided just a month earlier, had struck at various conditions attached to the sale of patents. These cases were not applicable here, wrote McKenna, who had dissented in the principal one, the *Motion Picture Co.* case. For the Shoe Machinery Company did not sell its patented machines, and at the same time attempt to retain the sort of control that is normally exercised by an owner. It merely leased the machines, never conveying title, and thus the situation was different. (A razor-thin distinction, if a relevant one at all.)

The government contended that all the provisions of all the leases should be viewed together, in light of the dominant position of the company. But the dominant position of the company had, on the contrary, to be put out of view, McKenna held, since it did not in itself violate the Sherman Act. Seen in isolation, one by one, the restrictive clauses were "simply bargains, based on patent rights and the conditions upon which those rights were granted." Moreover they were beneficial, helping small manufacturers and large to operate machines which they could very likely not afford to buy, and in any event releasing capital for other uses. All the machines necessarily coordinated with one another, and worked most smoothly and regularly in that way. Disregarding United's dominant position and its exclusive ownership of some machines, McKenna went on to remark that the company's lessees had the choice of leasing elsewhere or of paying a premium—which was quite a substantial one—for leases without restrictive clauses. And finally:

> Let us guard against confusion and not confound things which must be kept in distinction. A patentee is given rights to his device, but he is given no power to force it on the world. If the world buy it or use it the world will do so upon a voluntary judgment of its utility, demon-

---

[232] 243 U.S. 502 (1917).
[233] 224 U.S. 1 (1912).

[234] 246 U.S. 8 (1918).

strated, it may be, at great cost to the patentee. If its price be too high, whether in dollars or conditions, the world will refuse it; if it be worth the price, whether of dollars or conditions, the world will seek it. To say that the world is not recompensed for the price it pays is to attack the policy of the law, is to defy experience and to declare that the objects of inventive genius all around us have contributed nothing to the advancement of mankind. . . . We see nothing else in the circumstances of the parties than that which may move the transactions of men.[235]

A passage this—not in style, to be sure, but in content, although in places glancingly, even in style—of Holmesian economics.[236] But it was Holmesian economics attributed to the policy of the patent law, not necessarily imported into the Sherman Act.

There were two dissents, one by Clarke being added to Day's. Each joined the other's, Pitney joined both, and the two dissents divided the labor. Day concentrated on the restrictive leases, and Clarke on the monopolistic intent and effect of the initial combination and of the later acquisitions. The "necessary effect" of the restrictive provisions in the leases, "in view of the dominating control of the business by the lessor," said Day, "is to prevent the lessee from using similar machines, however advantageous to him it may be to do so, unless he is willing to incur the peril of losing machinery essential to his business"—the latter machinery being often in the sole control of the United Company.[237] "Keen and masterful men," S. W. Winslow and E. P. Howe, said Clarke, engineered the original combination and the later purchases. They knew what they were doing. They intended to and did achieve, and maintain by continual further acquisitions, "complete ascendancy."[238] The result was an illegal combination, and the perils and tribulations of dissolving it could be no greater than those faced by the Court in the *Northern Securities*, the *Standard Oil*, or the *Tobacco* case.

The *Shoe Machinery* case had a sequel. The Clayton Act, which became law while the *Shoe Machinery* case was being litigated in the trial court, included a provision that Congress had tailored most specifically with the United Company's leases in mind.[239] This was Section 3, forbidding any person engaged in interstate commerce to

---

[235] United States v. United Shoe Machinery Co., 247 U.S. 32, 36, 45, 56, 61, 65 (1918).

[236] "The consumer," Holmes wrote Laski at about this time (April 1919), "is the only man—a man may produce and be damned if the world doesn't want his product." *Holmes-Laski Letters*, I, 194–95.

[237] 247 U.S. at 70.

[238] 247 U.S. at 89.

[239] See United States v. United Shoe Machinery Co. of New Jersey, 247 U.S. 32, 70 (1918) (Day, J., dissenting).

The Supreme Court of the United States, 1903–1906
Rear row: Holmes, Peckham, McKenna, Day
Front row: Brown, Harlan, Fuller, Brewer, White
(The Supreme Court of the United States)

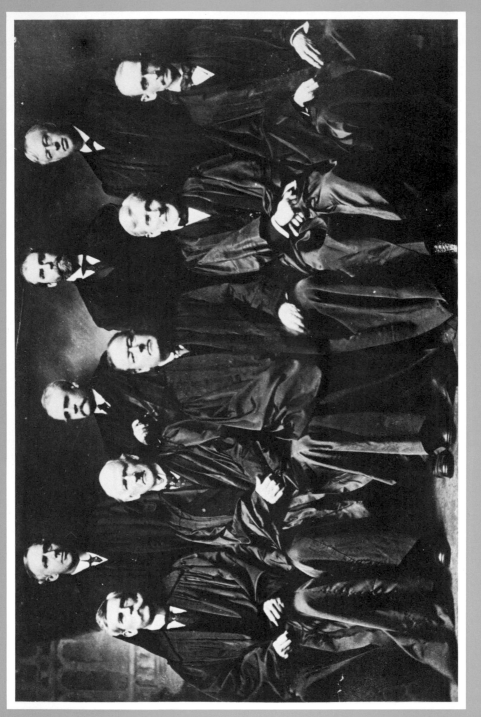

THE SUPREME COURT OF THE UNITED STATES, 1910–1912
Rear row: Van Devanter, Lurton, Hughes, Lamar
Front row: Holmes, Harlan, White, McKenna, Day
(The Supreme Court of the United States)

THE SUPREME COURT OF THE UNITED STATES, 1914–1916
Rear row: Pitney, Van Devanter, Lamar, McReynolds
Front row: Day, McKenna, White, Holmes, Hughes
(The Supreme Court of the United States)

THE SUPREME COURT OF THE UNITED STATES, 1916–1921
Rear row: Brandeis, Pitney, McReynolds, Clark
Front row: Day, McKenna, White, Holmes, Van Devanter
(*The Supreme Court of the United States*)

The Supreme Court of the United States, 1923–1925
Rear row: Butler, Brandeis, Sutherland, Sanford
Front row: Van Devanter, McKenna, Taft, Holmes, McReynolds
(The Supreme Court of the United States)

PRESIDENT THEODORE ROOSEVELT
(*Library of Congress*)

PRESIDENT WILLIAM HOWARD TAFT
(*Library of Congress*)

PRESIDENT WOODROW WILSON
(*Library of Congress*)

PRESIDENT WARREN C. HARDING
(*Library of Congress*)

MORRISON WAITE, CHIEF JUSTICE OF THE UNITED STATES, 1874–1888
(*The Supreme Court of the United States*)

MELVILLE WESTON FULLER, CHIEF JUSTICE OF THE UNITED STATES, 1888–1910
(*The Supreme Court of the United States*)

lease machinery (or supplies or other commodities), whether or not patented, on condition that the lessee should not deal in the products of a competitor, where the effect of the lease and the condition would be to substantially lessen competition or tend toward monopoly.

In October 1915, not long after the decision of the *Shoe Machinery* case in the trial court,[240] and just a year after passage of the Clayton Act, the government filed in a United States district court in Missouri a suit to enjoin most of the restrictive provisions in the Shoe Machinery Company's leases, pursuant to Section 3 of the Clayton Act. The district court promptly granted a temporary injunction, and after a trial, a final one.[241] In April 1922, four years after its decision in the first *Shoe Machinery* case, the Supreme Court affirmed. Only Brandeis disqualified himself in this instance—McReynolds having had nothing to do with this particular proceeding. McKenna dissented without opinion, but he was alone. Holmes and Van Devanter, the survivors of McKenna's four-man majority in the first *Shoe Machinery* case, went with the majority in this one as well.[242]

Day wrote for the Court. The Shoe Machinery Company, he said, was in control of roughly 95 percent of its market. Unquestionably the restrictive provisions enjoined by the court below had a tendency to monopolize. The decision in the earlier *Shoe Machinery* case could not control here, for the issue in that case had been different—whether an actual monopoly existed, rather than, as under the Clayton Act, whether there was a tendency to monopolize.[243] This second *Shoe Machinery* equity case thus used the new Clayton Act to qualify—in one aspect, to neutralize—the doctrine of the first, although it apparently made little, if any, actual difference to the dominant market position of the United Company.[244] Many years later, the government returned to the attack.[245]

The Board of Trade Case

Shortly before the first *Shoe Machinery* equity case was decided in 1918, *Chicago Board of Trade* v. *United States* came down. This was a unanimous decision (McReynolds, the former Attorney General, not

---

[240] United States v. United Shoe Machinery Co., 222 Fed. 349 (D.C. Mass.) was decided on Mar. 18, 1915.

[241] United States v. United Shoe Machinery Co., 227 Fed. 507 (E.D. Mo. 1915), 264 Fed. 138 (E.D. Mo. 1920).

[242] But not, so far as Holmes was concerned, without some private grumbling. "The record," Holmes

wrote Laski, "reaches from the floor to my middle. How I hate great cases." *Holmes-Laski Letters,* I, 319.

[243] United Shoe Machinery Co. v. United States, 258 U.S. 451 (1922).

[244] Whitney, *Antitrust Policies,* II, 125 *et seq.*

[245] United Shoe Machinery Corp. v. United States, 347 U.S. 521 (1954).

participating). It was not a merger case, and there was nothing in it to reinforce the attitude which the Court almost simultaneously displayed in the *Shoe Machinery* case, and which it was to assume also in the *Steel* case. Of this the fact that the opinion in *Chicago Board of Trade* was written by Brandeis is sufficient proof. Yet in its own ambivalent way, *Chicago Board of Trade* was something of a departure from the *Standard Oil* and *Tobacco* opinions, since it introduced criteria for judgment under the rule of reason, which it purported to be applying, other than economic ones.

The Chicago Board of Trade, the world's leading grain exchange, with sixteen hundred members, established a session for trading in grain "to arrive," known as the Call, to begin at 1:15 P.M., following the close of the regular session, and end at around 2:00 P.M. Trading at the regular sessions was in grains already in Chicago, and in "futures"—that is, grains to be delivered at stated times in the future. Sales "to arrive" were of grain in transit to Chicago from Illinois and other midwestern states, and they were obtained by mailing or wiring offers from Chicago to hundreds of country dealers, for acceptance before 9:30 A.M. on the next business day. The Board's rule establishing the Call, which was adopted in 1906, did not require members to trade in grain "to arrive" only at the Call. But it forbade members to buy, "during the period between the close of the Call and the opening of the [regular] session [at 9:30 A.M.] on the next business day, any wheat, corn, oats or rye 'to arrive' at a price other than the closing bid at the Call." The effect, as Brandeis said, was this: "Before the adoption of the rule, members fixed their bids throughout the day at such prices as they respectively saw fit; after the adoption of the rule, the bids had to be fixed at the day's closing bid. . . ."

The government attacked the rule as an illegal price-fixing agreement, and won a decree in the trial court. Reversing, Brandeis ordered dismissal of the complaint. The defendants had offered to show that the purpose of the rule was not to control prices and suppress competition, but to serve the convenience of members of the exchange by limiting the hours of trading, and to break up a stranglehold on the "to arrive" branch of the trade which four or five warehousemen in Chicago had previously obtained. This evidence was excluded as irrelevant by the trial judge, who adopted the government's theory that, whatever its purpose, the price-fixing agreement was illegal. But the meaning of the rule of reason, Brandeis held, was that

> the legality of an agreement or regulation cannot be determined by so simple a test, as whether it restrains competition. Every agreement concerning trade, every regulation of trade, restrains. To bind, to restrain, is of their very essence. The true test of legality is whether

the restraint imposed is such as merely regulates and perhaps thereby promotes competition or whether it is such as may suppress or even destroy competition. To determine that question the court must ordinarily consider the facts peculiar to the business to which the restraint is applied; its condition before and after the restraint was imposed; the nature of the restraint and its effect, actual or probable. The history of the restraint, the evil believed to exist, the reason for adopting the particular remedy, the purpose or end sought to be attained, are all relevant facts. This is not because a good intention will save an otherwise objectionable regulation or the reverse; but because knowledge of intent may help the court to interpret facts and to predict consequences.

Not only did the trial court err, therefore, in excluding evidence of "the history and purpose of the Call rule," Brandeis continued, but on the evidence that did get into the record, it was "clear that the rule was a reasonable regulation of business consistent with the provisions of the Anti-Trust Law." The rule covered only a small portion of the grain sold in Chicago, which was all that "to arrive" grain was. It was applicable only to sales made after about 2:00 P.M. In the morning, new "to arrive" prices could be set. And the rule governed only grain "to arrive" in Chicago. Members of the exchange could freely set other prices on grain "to arrive" in St. Louis, Omaha, and elsewhere, and there was a good deal of such grain. So the rule could not materially affect general market price, or the total volume of grain coming to Chicago. The advantages of the rule were that it created a public market for grain "to arrive," it distributed the business among a larger number of dealers, and eliminated risks and uncertainties. Moreover, it tended "to shorten the working day or, at least, limit the period of most exacting activity." Any board of trade and virtually all trade organizations imposed some restraints on their members' conduct of business. Restraints relating to hours of business were most common, and they made "a special appeal" when, as here, their effect was to shorten those hours.[246]

"Yes—Simply, clearly and admirably well put," Chief Justice White, author of the rule of reason, returned to Brandeis' circulated draft in the *Chicago Board of Trade* case.[247] Yet it is not quite and simply clear that the defendants' purpose, not merely in establishing the Call, but in fixing the price for the rest of the day, was anything other than to suppress the competition of a few most successful dealers in grain "to arrive." And it is not quite and simply clear what the effect

---

[246] Chicago Board of Trade v. United States, 246 U.S. 231, 237, 238, 239, 241 (1918).

[247] Brandeis Papers, University of Louisville Law School.

on general market price and on the volume of grain coming to Chicago was, or why Brandeis held the defendants' purpose lawful. Restraints ancillary to the creation of an organized exchange are one thing, and the establishment of an exclusive time period for trading would be such an ancillary restraint. But this rule also fixed prices, and Brandeis supported it, in part at least, as such, because he deemed it beneficial on the whole. That is another thing, with other implications.[248] It suggests complexities in Brandeis' view, oft-stated to Congressional committees before his accession, that the choice was between regulating competition and regulating monopoly.[249]

Brandeis favored regulating competition, and he meant it, quite literally. He feared monopoly for social and political reasons, as well as for economic ones, and he feared that wholly free competition was sometimes capable of producing monopoly. And so, as he was to make plain later, in a line of decisions dealing with trade associations, he favored restrictions of competition, even if privately imposed, which were designed to enhance the power of small business organizations, and guard against the growth of large ones. The principal significance of the *Chicago Board of Trade* case, then, is that it foreshadowed the line of decisions dealing with trade-association practices, and also the eventual, if qualified, legitimation by the Court of resale price-maintenance agreements—vertical price fixing—which Brandeis also favored, and for the same reasons.[250] To the extent that the *Chicago Board of Trade* case absolved from Sherman Act liability some horizontal price-fixing arrangements—"good" price-fixing arrangements, perhaps, rather than "bad" ones—it was soon superseded.[251]

Decisions "Sustaining" the Act

Aside from the *Shoe Machinery* cases and the rather special decision in *Chicago Board of Trade*, all of the Supreme Court's other important antitrust opinions between 1911 and the decision of the *Steel* case served, as Attorney General McReynolds said of one of them, to

---

[248] See R. H. Bork, "The Rule of Reason and the Per Se Concept: Price Fixing and Market Division," *Yale L. J.*, 74:775, 815–20, 1965.

[249] See *supra*, p. 134.

[250] See American Column & Lumber Co. v. United States, 257 U.S. 377 (1921); Maple Flooring Manufacturers Protective Ass'n v. United States, 268 U.S. 577 (1925); United States v. Colgate & Co., 250 U.S. 300 (1919); but *cf.* United States v. Schrader's Son Inc., 252 U.S. 85 (1920). *Compare* Brandeis, "Competition That Kills," in *Business—A Profession* (1913), 259, *with* Dr. Miles Medical Co. v. Park & Sons Co., 220 U.S. 373 (1911).

[251] United States v. Trenton Potteries Co., 273 U.S. 392 (1927).

sustain the Sherman Act.[252] In *Standard Sanitary Manufacturing Co.* v. *United States*,[253] a price-fixing pool, complete with penalties and market-division arrangements, which included 85 percent of manufacturers and 90 percent of jobbers in the enameled ironware (bathtubs, sinks, etc.) industry, was held to violate the Sherman Act. The Court was unanimous, McKenna writing. It is notable that the pool made a patented process, previously used only by the largest manufacturer, available to the entire industry, but tied in the pool agreement as a condition to licenses of the patented process. Patent rights, said McKenna, sounding somewhat unlike the McKenna of the *Shoe Machinery* opinion, are subject to the Sherman Act, and must be used in conformity with it.

In *United States* v. *Patten*,[254] the Court, Van Devanter writing, held over three dissents, two of which were rather closely qualified, that a corner in cotton, run by the defendants on the New York Stock Exchange, was criminally punishable under Section 1 of the Sherman Act. The corner consisted in buying all possible cotton futures contracts, so as eventually to come into ownership of the available cotton crop and be able to sell it at a freely chosen price. In *Nash* v. *United States*, another criminal prosecution, the Supreme Court, while reversing a conviction on account of an error in the trial judge's charge to the jury, held that the Sherman Act was not too vague to be enforceable as a criminal statute. Writing for the Court, Holmes said, in a passage that has become famous: "[T]he law is full of instances where a man's fate depends on his estimating rightly, that is, as the jury subsequently estimates it, some matter of degree. If his judgment is wrong, not only may he incur a fine or a short imprisonment, as here; he may incur the penalty of death."[255]

---

[252] *Washington Evening Star*, June 10, 1913, p. 5, col. 3, commenting on Nash v. United States, 229 U.S. 373 (1913).

For summary dispositions sustaining the Sherman Act see United States Telephone Co. v. Central Union Telephone Co., 202 Fed. 66 (6th Cir. 1913), *cert. denied*, 229 U.S. 620 (1913); Darius Cole Transportation Co. v. White Star Line, 186 Fed. 63 (6th Cir. 1911), *cert. denied*, 225 U.S. 704 (1912); Pulp Wood Co. v. Green Bay Paper Co., 168 Wisc. 400 (1919), *cert. denied*, 249 U.S. 610 (1919). But *cf.* Citizens Wholesale Supply Co. v. Snyder, 229 U.S. 609 (1913); United States v. Patterson, 222 Fed. 599 (6th Cir. 1915), *cert. denied*, 238 U.S. 635 (1915) (criminal conviction of officers of National Cash Register Company reversed; but a consent decree against the company followed, see *Annual Report of Attorney General for the Year 1916*, 24-25); Tillar v. Cole Motor Car Co., 228 Fed. 280 (5th Cir. 1915), *cert. denied*, 247 U.S. 511 (1918).

[253] 226 U.S. 20 (1912).

[254] 226 U.S. 525 (1913).

[255] Nash v. United States, 229 U.S. 373, 377 (1913). At the argument, Chief Justice White asked counsel for the defendant: "Do you have the crime of manslaughter in Georgia? Define it." When counsel hesitated, the Chief

In *Eastern States Lumber Association* v. *United States*,[256] the Court, Day writing, unanimously condemned a blacklist of wholesale lumber dealers who sold also at retail, directly to builders, contractors, and the like. The list was maintained by a retail lumber dealers' association, and it was held to violate the Sherman Act even though no actual agreement to use it for purposes of instituting a boycott was proven. And in *Thomsen* v. *Cayser*,[257] the Court declared an agreement by a conference of shipping lines running between New York and South Africa illegal, because it fixed uniform freight rates, which included a primage charge to be refunded to shippers who shipped exclusively on conference lines. It was in this case that McKenna, reversing a circuit court that had been misled by the opinions in the *Standard Oil* and *Tobacco* cases, pointed out that no distinction between "good" and "bad" combinations had been intended.

The decisions, however, that "sustained" the Sherman Act most consistently and with greatest impact came in a line of cases involving railroads. Sequels to some of these cases overlapped not only the *Shoe Machinery* decisions, but also the *Steel* case, and although arguably they stood apart as touching an especially sensitive and closely regulated sector of the economy, they were not written in this spirit.[258]

The first of these railroad cases was *United States* v. *St. Louis Terminal Association.*[259] Beginning in 1889, a series of rather typical robber-baron mergers, in which Jay Gould was originally involved, resulted in absolute control by a single terminal company in St. Louis of all access to the city by railroad. And the railroads which owned the Terminal Association were bound by agreement to admit no one else into the venture, except by unanimous consent. The Terminal Association's position was that other railroads could use its facilities upon payment of the same charges as were made against the proprietary railroads, and that no railroad wishing to join the venture as an owner would now be excluded. But it was quite clear that the railroads with present access

---

Justice told of an incident in New Orleans during Reconstruction, when a man shot another, while his victim was reaching for a snuff box in his hip pocket. "Now, the jury," said White, "found that in that day it was reasonable to suppose, when a man reached to his pistol pocket, he meant to pull out his pistol, and so acquitted the accused on the ground of self-defense. The jury declared the act was reasonable. How do you distinguish that case from this?" *New York Times,* Mar. 19, 1913, p. 18, col. 2.

[256] 234 U.S. 600 (1914).

[257] 243 U.S. 66 (1917).

[258] See United States v. Columbia Steel Co., 334 U.S. 495, 531 (1948); E. H. Levi, "The Antitrust Laws and Monopoly," *U. Chi. L. Rev.,* 14:153, 157, 1947; but see R. H. Bork, "Vertical Integration and the Sherman Act: The Legal History of an Economic Misconception," *U. Chi. L. Rev.,* 22: 157, 169, 1954.

[259] 224 U.S. 383 (1912).

had the power to exclude. Besides, certain of the Terminal Association's rates imposed some curious discriminations, which were much complained of in St. Louis. Thus the Association used East St. Louis as the decisive rate point, and then charged a differential between there and St. Louis proper. And it imposed an arbitrary rate on traffic originating within a certain radius of the city. For many years, the *St. Louis Post-Dispatch* had led an agitation against the Terminal Association. At last, the Roosevelt Administration began a prosecution.[260]

A four-judge trial court, dividing evenly, dismissed the suit. In April 1912, the Supreme Court, in a unanimous opinion by Lurton (Holmes taking no part for undisclosed reasons), reversed. This was not a combination of competing lines, like the *Northern Securities* case, said Lurton, but on the other hand, neither was it an instance of a terminal facility or toll bridge open to all, and subject to the possible competition of new facilities and bridges. The power to exclude, possessed by the railroads that owned the Terminal Association, may not have been used to the full, but its existence was itself intolerable, and it had in fact been used to make rates which had an adverse effect on competition.

Dissolution appeared too drastic and unnecessary a remedy, but Lurton directed that a decree be entered requiring the Terminal Association to admit on equal terms any future railroad that wanted to join in ownership and management; to extend its facilities on a fair basis to any other nonproprietary railroad; and to eliminate discriminatory and arbitrary rates. Within ninety days, a plan of reorganization was to be presented, taking account of these requirements, as well as some subsidiary ones. Failing submission of such a plan, the trial court was to order dissolution. The Supreme Court's decision was greeted with jubilation in St. Louis, as lifting a barrier to the city's progress. Cheaper coal and an influx of manufacturing were foreseen.[261] But the decree was hard fought, and not settled finally for another three years.[262]

Within the year after its decision in the *St. Louis Terminal* case, the Supreme Court, on December 2, 1912, applied the Sherman Act to what was both politically and economically a more far-reaching and more spectacular combination of railroads. The Union Pacific Railroad, controlled by E. H. Harriman, ran from the Missouri River in Iowa, and from Kansas City, to Ogden, Utah, on one main line, and to Port-

[260] See *St. Louis Post-Dispatch,* Apr. 23, 1912, p. 3, col. 1, p. 12.

[261] *St. Louis Post-Dispatch,* Apr. 23, 1912, p. 1, col. 1.

[262] United States v. St. Louis Terminal Ass'n., 236 U.S. 194 (1915). See also *Ex parte* United States, 226 U.S. 420 (1913); United States v. St. Louis Terminal Ass'n., 197 Fed. 446 (D.C. E.D. Mo. 1912), *appeal dismissed on motion of appellant,* 227 U.S. 683 (1913); Evens & Howard Fire Brick Co. v. United States, 236 U.S. 210 (1915).

land, Oregon, on another. Union Pacific also operated steamships from Portland to California, as well as out to the Orient. But it had no direct route by land to San Francisco or Los Angeles. The Southern Pacific had lines from New Orleans through to Portland, Oregon, and also from Ogden to San Francisco. At Ogden, of course, it connected with the Union Pacific. The two roads had a through rate agreement, under which Southern Pacific carried Union Pacific traffic from Ogden to the Coast. Southern Pacific also ran steamships from New York to New Orleans and from California to the Orient. In 1901, the Harriman interests bought from the estate of Collis P. Huntington and from others a controlling block of shares, amounting to 46 percent, of Southern Pacific stock. This merger was attacked by the government as being in restraint of trade under the Sherman Act.

A four-judge trial court in the Eighth Circuit dismissed the suit, one judge dissenting. The ground of decision was that the two merged railroad systems had not really been in competition, and that no competition could therefore have been suppressed by the merger. The dissenting judge, William C. Hook, took the view that the two roads were universally regarded and were in fact "parallel in a broad geographical and legal sense, for about 2,000 miles," and were in active competition for transcontinental and other traffic. His colleagues appeared to hold, wrote Hook, that two railroads could freely merge if, as in this case, the traffic they competed for entirely on their own lines on land and sea amounted to only a relatively small percentage of the total traffic of each, and if, again as in this case, transcontinental traffic that came to substantial percentages could be competed for only by moving it from the East over connecting carriers, by means of through route arrangements, so that neither road could compete without "the concurrence of its natural allies." This holding, Hook continued, "so greatly narrows the act of Congress, which, however it may be regarded, is the law of the land, that very little is left of it when applied to railroads. *Under one or both of those tests, the Union Pacific could probably have lawfully purchased control of all the great parallel systems in the United States.*"[263]

The majority opinion was by Judge Elmer B. Adams, with the concurrence of Judge Walter H. Sanborn. It was announced on June 24, 1911, well after Van Devanter had taken his place on the Supreme Court, but it noted: "Mr. Justice Van Devanter, while a Circuit Judge, participated in the hearing, deliberation, and conclusion in this case, and he now concurs in this opinion."[264] On May 18, 1911, just after the

---

[263] United States v. Union Pacific R.R., 188 Fed. 102, 120, 122–23 (June 24, 1911). Italics in original.
[264] 188 Fed. at 120.

decision in the *Standard Oil* case, Van Devanter wrote Judge Adams, who was his closest friend among his former colleagues on the Eighth Circuit, that Harlan's intemperate dissent in the *Standard Oil* case was likely to lead to a good deal of misunderstanding, and to agitation for amendment of the Sherman Act in a direction which neither Van Devanter nor Adams would favor. "In this situation," Van Devanter continued,

> I am uncertain what the effect would be of an early announcement of the contemplated decision in the Union Pacific case. In regular course the real effect of the decision in the Standard Oil case will become gradually permeated through the community, and it will be judged, as it ought to be, by a candid consideration of what is in it. Just now there is a temptation on the part of some to take advantage of such sentiment as was created by Justice Harlan's dissent. Later on, when sober second thought has its influence, that temptation will be gone. Because of this I think the announcement of the decision in the Union Pacific case after you return from your vacation in the early fall will be less likely to produce erroneous impressions than would its announcement now. . . . In all probability, although not certain, the decision in the American Tobacco Company case will be announced on the 29th instant, and the result in that case not improbably will be disappointing to those who are now engaged in immoderate and hasty criticism. That will also tend to make the second sober judgment a better and stronger one. . . .[265]

Judge Adams was evidently unable to follow Van Devanter's advice, for the decision of the circuit court in the *Union Pacific* case was announced little more than a month later. And a year and a half later, the decision was reversed by a unanimous Supreme Court, for which Day spoke. But Van Devanter recused himself. He did not do so in one other great case in which he had participated in the decision below, the *Standard Oil* case, nor in yet another case in which the Supreme Court affirmed an opinion he himself had written as circuit judge.[266] Practice varied in this respect. Lurton did recuse himself in cases in which he had written below.[267] But Van Devanter's practice was apparently to the contrary. Perhaps he distinguished the *Union Pacific* case on the ground that he had joined in the decision below

---

[265] W. Van Devanter to E. B. Adams, May 18, 1911, Van Devanter Papers. Van Devanter added: "It is not a wise thing to write letters which ought not to be preserved, and yet I feel that some of the matters before suggested might be misunderstood by

others, although not by you, so I will be glad if, after you have read this letter carefully, you will destroy it."
[266] Stuart v. Union Pacific R.R., 227 U.S. 342 (1913), *affirming* 178 Fed. 753 (8th Cir. 1910).
[267] See page 78, n.298.

while already on the Supreme Court, and perhaps his reason for recusing himself there was that he had gone farther, and had taken a hand later, in his letter to Adams on May 18, 1911.

Day's opinion for the Court acknowledged that insofar as the merger was a purchase by the Union Pacific of the connection from Ogden to the West Coast, which had previously been available on a through route basis, no competition was eliminated, but indeed the transaction carried out the Congressional purpose, expressed in the statutes that authorized the building of the Union Pacific, to have a through line of rails running to the West Coast. But the question was whether competition was otherwise eliminated, and on this question Day pretty much agreed with Judge Hook.

> A large amount of the testimony in this voluminous record was given by railroad men of wide experience, businessmen and shippers, who, with practical unanimity, expressed the view that prior to the stock purchase in question the Union Pacific and Southern Pacific systems were in competition, sharp, well-defined and vigorous, for interstate trade. . . . The Southern Pacific through its agents, advertisements and literature had undertaken to obtain transportation for its "Sunset" or southerly route across the continent, while the Union Pacific had endeavored in the same territory to have freight shipped by way of its own and connecting lines, thus securing for itself about one thousand miles of the haul to the Coast.

Moreover, "we have a right to look also to the intent and purpose of those who conducted the transactions," and this transaction was in fact a sequel to those that were frustrated in the *Northern Securities* case and in *Harriman* v. *Northern Securities Co.*,[268] and was infected with the same "intent and purpose." Turning to the decree, Day noted that at the argument in the Supreme Court, the government, in response to a question from the Court, had indicated that it would not object if the Union Pacific were permitted to retain control over the Ogden–San Francisco line. While approving this concession, Day held that in all other respects the decree would have to effectually terminate the combination. Day directed the district court to enter an immediate injunction forbidding Union Pacific to vote its Southern Pacific stock or to receive dividends from it. The district court was to proceed also to hold a hearing, and settle a final plan of dissolution.[269]

When the decision was announced, both Union Pacific and Southern Pacific stock fell a couple of points on the market, but lawyers for the Union Pacific indicated that the railroad could live with the result,

---

[268] 197 U.S. 244 (1905).
[269] United States v. Union Pacific R.R., 226 U.S. 61, 86–87, 93 (1912).

especially since the main objective of the merger, they said, had been to obtain the connection from Ogden to San Francisco.[270] Two weeks after the decision, the Union Pacific tried to make the decree even more livable. New counsel were brought in, and they were of the first rank: former Senator John C. Spooner, and John G. Milburn and Maxwell Evarts. They persuaded the Attorney General to join in a motion to clarify the decree, and in that motion they asked whether it would be satisfactory if the Union Pacific sold its Southern Pacific stock to Union Pacific shareholders, substantially in proportion to their holdings of Union Pacific stock.

The Supreme Court, Day writing again and Van Devanter still taking no part, answered promptly, on January 6, 1913. The suggested method of disposing of the Southern Pacific stock would not be satisfactory. The contention was that the distribution would be to 22,000 shareholders of the Union Pacific, and would thus so dilute and distribute control of the Southern Pacific as to accomplish the necessary dissolution. But it happened, said Day, that fewer than 400 people owned the controlling shares of Union Pacific, and that within this group, no more than 68 people were the major owners, with the other 300 having smaller holdings. A group of 68 people, then, with Harriman at its head, effectively controlled and ran the Union Pacific. If the Southern Pacific stock were distributed pro rata to the Union Pacific's shareholders, this same group would be in control of both railroads—just as if no dissolution had been decreed at all.[271]

The decree having been thus clarified, rather more than prominent new counsel may have hoped, and an early plan of dissolution that, among other provisions, would have left to the Union Pacific ownership of the Ogden–San Francisco line having been foreclosed by the opposition of the California Railroad Commission, negotiations were taken up with the new Attorney General. McReynolds, fresh from his experience in the *American Tobacco* case, was in a tough mood. By his own account, he rejected several proposals as being insufficiently "free from the fundamental defects in the plans adopted in the Standard Oil and Tobacco cases," because they did not make sure that the business would be brought out of the control of the same stockholders who controlled it when merged.

A plan McReynolds did agree to was approved by the Court on June 30, 1913. It was not simple: $38,292,400 of the $126,650,000 of Southern Pacific stock owned by the Union Pacific Company was traded to the Pennsylvania Railroad in exchange for $42,547,200 of Baltimore

---

[270] *Washington Post*, Dec. 3, 1912, p. 5, col. 3; *New York Tribune*, Dec. 3, 1912, p. 1, col. 7.

[271] United States v. Union Pacific R.R., 226 U.S. 470 (submitted Dec. 19, 1912; decided Jan. 6, 1913).

and Ohio Railroad stock. This transaction had the advantage of divesting the Pennsylvania Railroad of a significant amount of the stock of an active competitor. The Pennsylvania and the Southern Pacific were entirely noncompetitive, as were the Union Pacific and the Baltimore and Ohio. The remaining $88,357,600 of Southern Pacific stock was transferred to a trustee, with directions to collect dividends and vote the stock, for the time being, under direction of the Court. The trustee was to issue certificates of interest representing this stock. The certificates would be available for purchase to present Union Pacific stockholders, who could convert them into Southern Pacific stock upon filing an affidavit that they no longer owned any shares of Union Pacific, and were not acting in behalf of, or in concert with, any Union Pacific shareholders. Upon conversion, the holder of a certificate would get full Southern Pacific voting rights, and accumulated dividends. The whole operation was subject to a deadline. All stock represented by certificates that had not been converted by January 1, 1916, would, at the option of the Court, be ordered sold outright.

"The great advantage of the course pursued over a compulsory and immediate sale at public auction of the $126,650,000 of Southern Pacific stock," declared McReynolds, "is that, whilst as effectual in dissolving the combination, it saved the stockholders of both companies from unnecessary losses and avoided the very serious financial strain which such a sale would have entailed." The plan worked well. In its first four months, over 75 percent of the certificates issued to Union Pacific stockholders had been converted into Southern Pacific stock in accordance with the divorcement requirements of the decree. McReynolds' fixed purpose, not to "leave the separate parts of the unlawful combination under the control of the same set of men," was being met.[272]

In *United States* v. *Pacific & Arctic Co.*,[273] decided just a few months after the *Union Pacific* case, the Supreme Court, McKenna writing, unanimously upheld an indictment of a number of railroad and steamship companies for conspiracy to monopolize transportation to Alaska from the United States and Canada.[274] The rest of the antitrust

---

[272] *Annual Report of the Attorney General of the United States for the Year 1913*, 7–8. A later effort, through a stockholders' suit on antitrust grounds, to divest the Union Pacific of its St. Joseph Railway stock failed, although the Union Pacific was held to certain fiduciary obligations. Frank v. Union Pacific R.R., 226 Fed. 906 (8th Cir. 1915), *dismissed on motion*

of appellant, 241 U.S. 694 (1916).

[273] 228 U.S. 87 (1913).

[274] *Cf.* Interstate Commerce Commission v. Humboldt Steamship Co., 224 U.S. 474 (1912); Humboldt Steamship Co. v. White Pass & Yukon Route, 25 ICC 136 (1912); The Alaska Investigation, 44 ICC 680 (1917).

railroad opinions of the Supreme Court in the period under discussion concerned carriers of anthracite coal.

Anthracite is mined almost exclusively in northeastern Pennsylvania, and sold in surrounding states and in eastern Canada. As soon as railroads replaced canals in the transportation of anthracite out of Pennsylvania, they began buying up coal fields, in order to secure the sources of their traffic. Singly and in combination, the railroads bore down on the independent mine operator. The independents who survived contracted to sell their coal to the railroads at the mine, at a price which was set at a percentage of the price on the Atlantic Coast, chiefly in New York.

Congress came to the assistance of the independent operators with the Hepburn Act of 1906, forbidding any railroad to carry commodities, other than timber, which were manufactured, mined, or produced by itself or under its authority, or in which it held "any interest, direct or indirect." This provision was held constitutional in 1909, in *United States* v. *Delaware & Hudson Co.*,[275] but construed to mean that a railroad could lawfully carry coal mined by a company all of whose stock the railroad owned, provided that the railroad did not own the coal itself and was in good faith dissociated from the shipment, and provided that the mining company was a *bona fide* corporation.

Shortly after, in *United States* v. *Lehigh Valley Railroad*,[276] the Supreme Court made it clear that for the railroad to be free of the Hepburn Act prohibition, the mining company had indeed to be truly independent, and not merely a front.[277] And in *United States* v. *Delaware, Lackawanna & Western Railroad*,[278] the Supreme Court insisted further and in greater detail on the required independence of the mining company from the railroad carrying its product. Yet the net result of this course of litigation was that the provisions of the Hepburn Act were met and avoided by corporate rearrangements which did not greatly affect the reality of the situation in the anthracite industry.[279] Meanwhile, however, and against this background, the government had brought suits under the Sherman Act, the first of which, *United States* v. *Reading Co.*,[280] it successfully concluded in the Supreme Court, in December 1912, two weeks after the decision in the *Union Pacific* case.

In 1898, at a time when many of the independent mine operators' contracts for the sale of their coal to the railroads were running out,

---

[275] 213 U.S. 366 (1909).
[276] 220 U.S. 257 (1911).
[277] *Cf.* United States v. Erie R.R., 220 U.S. 275 (1911). And see Delaware, Lackawanna & Western R.R. v. United States, 231 U.S. 363 (1913).

[278] 238 U.S. 516 (1915).
[279] See Whitney, *Antitrust Policies,* II, 57–60.
[280] 226 U.S. 324, 352–53, 358–59, 365, 367 (1912).

the operators made an attempt to build and support another, independent railroad, which would compete with the six existing ones. The independent operators mined approximately 20 percent of the national supply of anthracite. The six existing railroads, the Reading, the Lehigh Valley, the Delaware, Lackawanna and Western, the Central of New Jersey, the Erie, and the New York, Susquehanna and Western, had an almost total monopoly in the transportation of anthracite, and they also produced and sold among them 75 percent of the annual national output, and controlled 90 percent of unmined reserves. Threatened by potential competition, they obtained the assistance of J. P. Morgan and Company, and bought up the principal independent anthracite producer. Thus they effectively frustrated the building of the independent railroad.

The transaction was executed through the Temple Iron Company, of which the six railroads assumed control expressly for this purpose. They owned it jointly, the interest of each being proportioned to its share of the market. In proceedings begun by the Roosevelt Administration and carried forward under Taft, with McReynolds acting as special counsel and continuing to do so even after he had resigned any further connections with th *American Tobacco* case,[281] the government obtained dissolution of the Temple Iron Company. The Supreme Court, in an opinion by Lurton, affirmed.[282] The Temple Iron Company was, said Lurton, as an entity, clearly in violation of the Sherman Act. It was suggested that the element of illegality in the Temple Company lay in the past and was beyond any present remedy; the independent railroad had "been effectively strangled," and it was idle to contemplate doing anything about that now. But the company not only had been but was still "an efficient agency for the collective activities of the defendant carriers for the purpose of preventing competition in the transportation and sale of coal. . . . The evil is in the combination." And the combination could and should be dissolved.

At about the same time as they strangled the potential competition of another railroad, the six carriers which had combined in the Temple Iron Company also concluded perpetual contracts with the independents for the purchase of their entire production, and of the product of any

---

[281] C. J. Bonaparte to J. C. McReynolds, Feb. 24, 1908; G. W. Wickersham to McReynolds, Jan. 17, 1913, McReynolds Papers.

[282] The Court was unanimous, but only six Justices participated. Day was absent from the beginning of the October Term 1911 until Jan. 18, 1912, owing to the illness of his wife, who died on Jan. 8, 1912. See 222 U.S. xxix. And so he did not hear the argument of the case on Oct. 10, 1911. Harlan was gone, of course, by the time the case was decided, and his replacement, Pitney, did not take his seat till March 1912, and so was also not present for the argument. Hughes recused himself for reasons that are not apparent.

mines to be opened by them in the future, at 65 percent of the average monthly price at which coal sold at tidewater. Such percentage contracts had been customary between the carriers and the independents for a long time, but they had previously been made at a figure less favorable to the independents, and they had not previously been perpetual. The government charged that the contracts were part of the combination in restraint of trade, but it failed to obtain an injunction against them from the trial court.

On this branch of the case, Lurton reversed. The perpetual contracts, considered singly, were not necessarily unlawful restraints of trade, he said. But they had to be viewed in context. It was the threat of effective competition from a possible independent railroad that forced the six carriers to increase the price. They paid a higher price to obtain perpetual assurance against future competitive railroads. "That they [the contracts] were designed by the defendants as a means of controlling the sale of the independent output in the market at tide-water points, thereby preventing competition with their own coal and as a plan for removing the great tonnage controlled by the independents from being used as an inducement for the entry of competing carriers into the district, is a plain deduction." Renewal of percentage contracts for short terms only "would but postpone the day of competition." By means of the perpetual contracts, the "menace of the independent output as an invitation to competing carriers and as a competing coal at tidewater would be removed forever." Lurton ordered a decree written to cancel these contracts, and enjoin future ones of the same sort.[283]

The government had attempted also, in the same suit, to attack several of the railroads, including the Reading and the Lehigh Valley, as illegal combinations in themselves, quite aside from their common venture in the Temple Iron Company, but Lurton held as a matter of good pleading that such attacks must be mounted in separate suits. The government, therefore, during McReynolds' tenure as Attorney General, brought fresh suits against the Reading and Lehigh Valley companies, charging them both with being combinations in restraint of trade under the Sherman Act, and with violation of the Hepburn Act, as well, in that they carried coal produced by companies they controlled.

Reading was a holding company formed in 1896 to own an extensive coal-carrying railroad and a large coal producer. In 1901, Reading acquired the Central of New Jersey Railroad, a coal carrier, which, in turn, controlled and brought under Reading ownership the Wilkes-Barre Coal Company, another large producer. After this acquisi-

---

[283] But some exceptions were eventually made. See United States v. Reading Co., 228 U.S. 158 (1913).

tion, Reading carried about one-third of the entire domestic production of coal; it produced somewhat less; and owned considerably greater coal reserves than it had in actual production.[284]

The trial court, a three-judge court sitting in Philadelphia, held that the merger in 1896 of the Reading Railroad and of Reading Coal into one holding company was not in violation of the Sherman Act: "The Railway and the Coal & Iron Company were not competitors; each performed its own function in putting a useful article into the hands of consumers. Although the Coal & Iron Company was a large producer of coal, and therefore a large shipper and a large seller, the size of its business was not in itself an offense."[285] The evidence showed no predatory practices, and no injury either to competitors or to competition. Both as producer and shipper, Reading met vigorous competition in the markets which it served.

The acquisition of the Central of New Jersey, and with it of the Wilkes-Barre Coal Company, was, however, a different story, for Wilkes-Barre was a substantial competitor of Reading as a producer. This transaction, therefore, suppressed competition in violation of the Sherman Act. Thus, while it dismissed the rest of the bill, including the charges of violation of the Hepburn Act, the trial court ordered that Reading divest itself of the Wilkes-Barre Coal Company.

Both parties appealed. The opinion of the Supreme Court, by Clarke, spoke for a majority of four. McReynolds was disqualified by his prosecutorial connection with the case, both earlier with the first *Reading* case, and later as Attorney General. Brandeis recused himself also. Possibly his reason was that he had been counsel for a shippers' association in an ICC proceeding that denied rate increases to Northeastern railroads, including the anthracite carriers. In this proceeding, Brandeis had delved deeply into the affairs of these railroads, and had taken public positions on many of their practices.[286]

Clarke's opinion reversed the trial court's holding that the initial organization of the Reading Company was lawful. Stressing its size,

---

[284] See Temporary National Economic Committee, *Monograph No. 38, A Study of the Construction and Enforcement of the Federal Antitrust Laws* (1941), 67 (hereinafter cited as TNEC, No. 38).

[285] United States v. Reading Co., 226 Fed. 229, 268 (D.C. E.D. Pa. 1915).

[286] See Mason, *Brandeis*, 315–34.
Curiously, the usual notation that McReynolds and Brandeis took no part is missing from the accustomed place at the foot of the opinion of the Court. This was, unquestionably, a rare clerical error. Contemporaneous reports leave no doubt that the disqualification of McReynolds and Brandeis was announced in the course of oral delivery of the opinion. See *New York Times*, Apr. 27, 1920, p. 1, col. 1; *Washington Post*, Apr. 29, 1920, p. 6, col. 1.

II: *The Rule of Reason*

Clarke wrote that Reading, at its formation in 1896, "acquired power: to increase or decrease the output of coal from very extensive mines, the supply of it in the market, and the cost of it to the consumer; to increase or lower the charge for transporting such coal to market; and to regulate car supply and other shipping conveniences, and thereby to help or hinder the operations of independent miners and shippers of coal. This constituted a combination to unduly restrain interstate commerce within the meaning of the act," citing *United States* v. *Union Pacific Railroad.*

In support of this conclusion, and presumably by way of demonstrating that the holding company had engaged in predatory practices, Clarke referred to the practices held unlawful in the first *Reading* case. Thereafter, the acquisition of the Central of New Jersey, in 1901, added substantially to the unlawful power already wielded by the Reading Company. And "this dominating power was not obtained by normal expansion to meet the demands of a business growing as a result of superior and enterprising management, but by deliberate, calculated purchase for control." Clarke, therefore, ordered dissolution of the holding company in such a way as to give each of its subsidiaries "a position in all respects independent and free from stock or other control of either of the other corporations." As an afterthought, having decided the case under the Sherman Act, Clarke added that, contrary to the trial court's holding, the Hepburn Act was also applicable. White, Holmes, and Van Devanter dissented in two paragraphs, saying that they would have reached exactly the result of the court below, for the reasons stated in the opinion of that court.[287]

The plan under which the Reading was ultimately dissolved included sale of the Wilkes-Barre Coal Company outright to third parties, and a separation of the Reading coal and railroad companies by a scheme quite like that adopted in the *Union Pacific* dissolution. The decree was not settled, however, without a second appeal to the Supreme Court. A major difficulty was a mortgage secured by the property of the holding company, the property, that is, of both the railroad and coal companies. Although the coal company was now to be spun off as a separate and independent entity, the bondholders resisted release of the coal company's property from the lien of the general mortgage, and the Attorney General feared, as the government told the Supreme Court, that the "serious financial and industrial depression accompanying the transition from the artificial stimulations of war to normal conditions of peace" might be aggravated by disruption of this important mortgage, against the wishes of the bondholders.

---

[287] United States v. Reading Co., 253 U.S. 26, 48, 57, 60 (1920).

"Grave apprehension was felt that . . . public confidence in the restoration of prosperity might be adversely affected." Hence the government agreed to provisions ensuring that the stock and property of the new coal company, as well as the property of the railroad company, would remain subject to the mortgage lien, although the coal and railroad companies would thus retain a substantial interest in each other's welfare, and a strong inducement to protect it.

In the Supreme Court, on an appeal by intervening stockholders objecting to other features of the decree, the provisions concerning the mortgage were taken up on the Court's own motion, since the issue was conformance of the decree to the Court's mandate. There was a division in conference of 5–3, Brandeis disqualifying himself,[288] against this aspect of the decree. The majority of five included Taft, the new Chief Justice (this was early in 1922), but when he came to write an opinion, Taft persuaded himself that it would be unwise to disturb the decree, barring a couple of minor modifications, "and that to do so would be to question, without warrant, the action in good faith of the Assistant Attorney General who represented both the late and the present administration in prosecuting the case, and the present Attorney General [Harry M. Daugherty]." Finally, at the suggestion of Clarke and Van Devanter, the following compromise was adopted and unanimously announced, with a bow to the Attorney General, and a reference to "a change for the better . . . in the financial situation":

> The District Court should . . . determine the respective values of the properties of the merged Reading [railroad] Company and the Coal Company which are subject to lien of the general mortgage. Then the decree should direct that the liability of each on the bonds and the pledge under the mortgage shall be modified as between the mortgagee and the mortgagors, so that the liability of the Reading [railroad] Company on the bonds outstanding, and the lien of the mortgage upon that company's property to secure them, shall be reduced to an amount proportionate to the ratio of the value of its pledged property to the value of all the property pledged including that of the Coal Company. The obligation of the Coal Company upon such bonds and the lien upon its property to secure them should be reduced in corresponding proportion. The amount that each company is to pay as interest should be similarly fixed, and specific provisions for foreclosure of these

---

[288] "I don't think McReynolds is qualified to sit," Taft wrote Clarke (W. H. Taft to J. H. Clarke, May 20, 1922, W. H. Taft Papers, Library of Congress), but McReynolds participated, and continued to do so. He had, as Attorney General, initiated the *Reading* case, but he was no longer in office when the question of the decree was dealt with, and he evidently viewed this question as separable.

separate liens on default and requisite machinery and other necessary changes to carry out the result will be made by the District Court in its discretion. By this arrangement the interests and joint obligations of the Reading [railroad] Company and the Coal Company will be completely severed and the purpose of this court carried out.[289]

Meanwhile the suit against the Lehigh Valley Railroad had been dismissed in its entirety by the trial court, and this case had also reached the Supreme Court. The Lehigh Valley was smaller than the Reading combination. It carried, in 1913, 18.84 percent of the total tonnage of anthracite coal shipped by railroad in the United States. Like its competitors, Lehigh had bought coal lands through the latter half of the nineteenth century. In 1905, it acquired the largest independent coal producer along its line. This purchase, said the opinion of the Supreme Court, again by Clarke, "was confessedly made to prevent the diversion of traffic to other lines. . . ." By 1908, the Lehigh controlled 95 percent of the tonnage moving over its line to tidewater, but its share of total production was no higher than 20 percent.[290]

Reversing the dismissal below, Clarke held that the Lehigh Railroad,

in combination with its coal company subsidiary, deliberately entered upon a policy of making extensive purchases of anthracite land tributary to the railroad company's lines, for the purpose of controlling the mining, transportation and sale of coal to be obtained therefrom and of preventing and suppressing competition, especially in the transportation and sale of such coal in interstate commerce, and that this policy was continued after the passage of the Anti-Trust Act with increasing energy and tenacity of purpose, with the result that a practical monopoly was attained of the transportation and sale of anthracite coal derived from such lands.

This was a violation of the Sherman Act, said Clarke, citing among other cases *Standard Oil, Union Pacific,* and *Reading.* It was a violation as well, he added, of the Hepburn Act. The Lehigh Valley Company was to be dissolved. White and Holmes concurred, finding themselves bound by the *Reading* case as well as by *United States* v. *Delaware, Lackawanna & Western Railroad,*[291] although, had they felt free to exercise independent judgment, they would have been for affirmance.

---

[289] Continental Insurance Co. v. United States, 259 U.S. 156, 169, 170, 172, 173 (1922); W. H. Taft to the Justices, May 12, 1922; J. H. Clarke to Taft, May 20, 1922; Taft to Clarke, May 20, 1922, Clarke to Taft, May 25, 1922, Taft Papers.

[290] TNEC, No. 38, 70.

[291] 238 U.S. 516 (1915).

Van Devanter was silent, and McReynolds and Brandeis again disqualified themselves.[292]

The second *Reading* case was argued, together with *Lehigh*, in October 1916, some months before the first argument in the *Steel* case. Both cases were then restored to the docket for reargument on the same day, in May 1917, that saw the *Steel* case similarly restored. *Reading* and *Lehigh* were reargued in November 1917, and both set down for reargument once more, owing, no doubt, to the war; antitrust policy was scarcely applicable to railroads at this time—if anything, less so than to steel manufacturers. The two cases were reargued again—although now the *Lehigh* case was merely submitted on briefs—in October 1919, together with the *Steel* case. And *Reading* was then decided just four weeks after *Steel,* on April 26, 1920, with the *Lehigh* case being set down for yet another argument, and decided several months later.

Despite this joint career, so to speak, there is a notable absence in the opinions in the *Lehigh* and *Reading* cases of any reference to the *Steel* decision. In the *Reading* case, White, Holmes, and Van Devanter, of the majority in *Steel,* dissented. Only McKenna, the writer of *Steel,* joined the dissenters there to form a majority in *Reading.* "The majority opinion in the *Anthracite cases,*" Milton Handler has written, bears an uncommonly strong resemblance to the dissenting opinion in the *Steel* case." Professor Handler remarks further:

> The percentage of control in both *Anthracite cases* was less than in the *Steel case.* The form of combination, at least in the *Reading case,* was identical. The combinations cooperated with the independents—in one case to fix prices, in the others to drive out competitors. Cooperation with competitors in all the cases had theoretically ceased at the time of suit, in one voluntarily, and in the others under compulsion of law [the first *Reading* case]. The intent to monopolize had been abandoned—or at least had proven ineffectual—in all three cases. Monopoly power was not attained by any of the defendants. Apart from combining with competitors, no defendant was guilty of predatory practices, although to be sure the anthracite companies had joined with their competitors to drive out new competition, whereas Steel had been content with price-fixing. The likelihood of potential competition was about the same; perhaps more likely in the Steel industry. All

---

[292] United States v. Lehigh Valley R.R., 254 U.S. 255, 261, 269–70 (1920). Following decision of the *Reading* and *Lehigh* cases and implementation of the decrees, the independent operators' share of the anthracite market increased greatly. But it did so in a declining market, and for reasons that had little to do with the decrees. Whitney, *Antitrust Policies,* II, 66–73.

the corporations were preeminent in their respective fields, but there was a fair number of strong independents.

About the Reading company, in its final form, after it had absorbed the Central of New Jersey, Professor Handler says that it plainly "did not stifle competition in the industry at large; at best it merely eliminated competition between two of the largest factors. Does not the case hold that a combination of giant companies doing a substantial part of the business in their fields is unlawful?" The Lehigh, in turn, had "no monopoly in any real sense other than the regional monopoly which every carrier possesses. There were many other transportation and coal companies. . . ."[293]

The *Reading* and *Lehigh* cases are, then, hardly the doctrinal children of the *Steel* decision. Not only that, but Lurton's treatment of the 65 percent contracts in the first *Reading* case, as quite likely legal, taken each individually, but as violative of the Sherman Act taken altogether and in context, contrasts with McKenna's treatment in the *Shoe Machinery* case of the restrictive lease provisions, which he insisted on viewing each as an individual lawful bargain.

It is possible to consider the second *Reading* case as being in part, and the *Lehigh* case as being wholly, vertical integration rather than horizontal monopoly cases. Seen in this way, they have little relation to the *Steel* decision, and even less to the *Shoe Machinery* case, and they also make dubious economic sense.[294] But the court that decided all these cases did not view them as unrelated. The opinions of Justice Clarke in *Reading* and *Lehigh* claim a connection back to such cases as *Standard Oil, Union Pacific,* and *Reading I.* Clarke, with his majorities made up principally of the dissenters in *Steel* and *Shoe Machinery,* simply leapfrogs those cases.

One—perhaps the only—direct doctrinal consequence of the *Steel* decision was drawn by the government itself with respect to three cases which it had also lost in the trial courts, and which it regarded as governed by the decision in the *Steel* case. On motion of the government, appeals which had been taken to the Supreme Court were voluntarily dismissed. The government evidently considered that in these cases the factor of size was alone decisive, and that on this point the *Steel* decision, rather than *Reading* and *Lehigh,* ruled. In one, the defendant controlled

---

[293] TNEC, No. 38, 71, 69, 70. *Cf.* United States v. First National Bank & Trust Co., 376 U.S. 665 (1964); United States v. Von's Grocery Co., 384 U.S. 270 (1966); but *cf.* United States v. Columbia Steel Co., 334 U.S. 495 (1948).

[294] See R. Bork, "Vertical Integration and the Sherman Act: The Legal History of an Economic Misconception," *U. Chi. L. Rev.,* 22:157, esp. 165–70, 1954.

42–47 percent of the industry, in another, 50 percent, and in the third, 70–75 percent.[295] Beyond this, the *Steel* case can be said to have spawned a dictum that control of 22 percent of a competitive industry does not violate the Sherman Act,[296] and to have influenced decision of a second *International Harvester* case.

The consent decree of 1918 in the first *International Harvester* case provided that if at any time after eighteen months the government determined that competitive conditions had not been restored, and that further relief was necessary, it could bring a new suit. Even before the consent decree had become final, the Senate by resolution, in May 1918, directed the Federal Trade Commission to study a recent rapid increase in the price of farm implements. The commission did so, and, in a report issued in May 1920, more or less absolved the International Harvester Company of any illegal practices conducing to price increases, but addressed itself also to the inadequacies of the consent decree. The commission found that the two harvesting machine lines that the company had kept—the Deering and the McCormick brands—were the successful ones, and gave it a dominating position in the industry. It recommended therefore that these two lines be separated.[297]

Pursuant to this recommendation, the government filed a petition for further relief in July 1923, alleging that the consent decree had proved inadequate, that the lines of harvester machinery that had been sold did not offer substantial competition, and that the company had actually rather increased its share of the market. And the government asked that International Harvester be divided into at least three separate and independent companies.

The government lost, both in the trial court and, in 1927, on appeal. McReynolds, Brandeis, and Justice Harlan F. Stone—the first and the last because they had had connections with the case as Attorneys General, and Brandeis because he had testified about International Harvester among others in 1911–12—were disqualified. The rest of the Court was unanimous, in an opinion by Justice Edward T. Sanford, who had been appointed in 1923. Apparently, he said, the government thought that the consent decree of 1918 meant to restore the competitive conditions that had existed prior to 1902. But that was not its purpose.

---

[295] United States v. Keystone Watch Case Co., 218 Fed. 502 (E.D. Pa. 1915), *appeal dismissed on motion of the United States,* 257 U.S. 664 (1921); United States v. American Can Co., 230 Fed. 859, 234 Fed. 1019 (D. Md. 1916), *appeal dismissed on motion of the United States,* 256 U.S. 706 (1921); United States v. Quaker Oats Co., 232 Fed. 499 (N.D. Ill. 1916), *appeal dismissed on motion of the United States,* 253 U.S. 499 (1920).

[296] Geddes v. Anaconda Mining Co., 254 U.S. 590 (1921).

[297] See Whitney, *Antitrust Policies,* II, 232–33; Seager and Gulick, *Trust and Corporation Problems,* 276–78.

II: *The Rule of Reason*

The decree, rather, meant merely to establish competitive conditions within its own terms, which it had done. The government had to be held to its agreement. Sanford indicated that it was virtually unthinkable to go back, at this late date, on a decree that had been complied with in good faith, and unthinkable to try now to restore the conditions of sixteen years before. The only substantial evidence against International Harvester was that its share of the market was around 64 percent, and that it had acted as a price leader, meaning that others followed its prices, although not necessarily all or always. But the price leadership was a voluntary affair, and neither it, nor mere size, nor the existence of unexerted power violated the Sherman Act. And here Sanford cited *United States* v. *United States Steel Corp.*[298]

While as a practical matter, then, the *Steel* decision was followed by, and no doubt influenced, a renewed merger movement, doctrinally the end result of a decade of litigation, from *Standard Oil* and *Tobacco* to *Steel*, was ambiguity. As late as 1941, Professor Handler could write that "there is today virtually as much doubt and uncertainty regarding the permissive limits of capital combinations as there was in 1890."[299] That is somewhat unjust to the opinion in the *Standard Oil* case, which did, after all, shed some light onto the prior darkness. But it tells with accuracy the story of the subsequent decisions.

---

[298] United States v. International Harvester Co., 274 U.S. 693, 709 (1927). As it turned out, the market did to International Harvester all that a different outcome of this litigation could have been expected to do. The company's share of domestic sales dropped steadily through the years, until in 1948 it was about 23 percent. (Whitney, *Antitrust Policies,* II, 234–35.)

[299] TNEC, No. 38, 74.

CHAPTER III

The Fate of Social Legislation, 1910-14

I N THE GREAT PUBLIC DEBATE that followed decision of the *Standard Oil* and *Tobacco* cases and culminated with passage of the Clayton and Federal Trade Commission Acts of 1914, antitrust policy was not viewed as a special, discrete compartment of either legislation or adjudication. Antitrust policy was part and parcel of social and economic policy at large. It was all rather a seamless web. "The real thing that 'is the matter with business,'" said Brandeis, testifying on the trust problem, ". . . is social unrest." "For by their by-products shall you know the trusts." Antitrust policy was inextricably connected with business ethics and efficiency, the wage level, conditions of labor, the union movement, the equitable distribution of the national wealth, and the survival of political democracy. To George W. Perkins also, the relationship seemed intimate, although the connections he saw were, of course, different. The Congressman, he said, who would break up industrial combinations stands for "the sweatshop and child labor."[1]

The larger concerns of which antitrust policy was an integral, if but a single, aspect were thus described by Felix Frankfurter in 1912:

> The tremendous economic and social changes of the last fifty years have inevitably reacted upon the functions of the state. More and more government is conceived as the biggest organized social effort for dealing with social problems. . . . Growing democratic sympathies, justified by the social message of modern scientists, demand to be translated into legislation for economic betterment, based upon the conviction that laws can make men better by affecting the conditions of living. We are persuaded that evils are not inevitable, and that it is the

---

[1] See *supra,* pp. 130–33.

business of statesmanship to tackle them step by step, tentatively, experimentally, not demanding perfection from social reforms anymore than from any other human efforts.[2]

These broad concerns directed attention to the courts—much more so than antitrust policy after the decision of the *Standard Oil* and *Tobacco cases*. For as Frankfurter went on to say: "Having regard to things and not words, the fate of social legislation in this country rests ultimately with our judges."[3] That same year, Dean William Draper Lewis of the University of Pennsylvania Law School wrote: "Any important act of any state legislature regulating social or industrial conditions is at the present day often little better than a patent issued by the government in a new art—of doubtful value until it has passed the gauntlet of the courts."[4]

As we saw in Chapter I, the judicial function as a whole was subject in these years to doubts, reexaminations, and outright attacks. But even though the Supreme Court was hardly the darling of the dominant political opinion, the state courts, more than the Supreme Court, were particularly distrusted and feared. With a certain segment of Progressive opinion—a segment only, but an authoritative one—the Supreme Court fared for the moment relatively well. As it faced "the main question" of the day, "the regulation by law of corporate activity in its relations to the country at large," as an article in *The Outlook* said early in 1911, the Supreme Court, freshly reconstituted, was entering upon "a new phase."[5] In 1913, in a learned and much-noted paper in the *Columbia Law Review* entitled "The Progressiveness of the United States Supreme Court," Charles Warren counted up the recent instances in which the Supreme Court had struck down social and economic legislation, and found them few.[6] "The Supreme Court," said an article in a popular magazine a year later, "in common with all the other agencies of government, has caught the present-day infection. It is progressive."[7] And as late as 1916, Frankfurter wrote in *The New Republic* that the period when "the quality of the Court was exemplified in the sturdy personalities of Justices like Brewer and Peckham" was over. "Occasionally there is a relapse, but on the whole we have entered definitely upon an epoch in which Justice Holmes has been the most

---

[2] F. Frankfurter, *Law and Politics,* E. F. Pritchard, Jr., and A. MacLeish, eds. (Capricorn ed., 1962), 4.

[3] *Ibid.*

[4] W. D. Lewis, "A New Method of Constitutional Amendment by Popular Vote," *Annals,* 43:311, 315, 1912.

[5] E. F. Baldwin, "The Supreme

Court Justices," *The Outlook,* 97:156, 160, Jan. 28, 1911.

[6] C. Warren, "The Progressiveness of the United States Supreme Court," *Colum. L. Rev.,* 13:294, 1913.

[7] E. G. Lowry, "The Men of the Supreme Court," *World's Work,* 629, April 1914.

consistent and dominating force, and to which Justices Day and Hughes have been great contributing factors."[8]

Such then, broadly described, was the main public business of the Court, as it was to remain, substantially, through the 1920s. A convenient and not altogether arbitrary period on which to focus for a first assessment of this business and of the contemporary view of its discharge is the four terms of Court from October 1910 through June 1914. Shortly after the Court rose in the summer of 1914, the First World War broke out. It was then also that the first reforming phase of the Wilson Administration ended. And for the Court, a new cycle of appointments began. Most of the cases to be examined are constitutional adjudications under the Commerce, Due Process, Equal Protection and Contract clauses. To be sure, the inquiry must not be restricted by these conceptual categories, for other cases, and even nonconstitutional ones, exemplify what is, after all, most crucial—the attitude and outlook of the judges. Some classes of cases, however, and even a few constitutional ones, need to be put aside, most of them for later consideration. These include state tax cases arising under the Commerce Clause, most cases reviewing decisions of the Interstate Commerce Commission and of the Commerce Court, cases involving state antitrust laws noted earlier,[9] and the classes of federal antitrust cases reserved for separate consideration in the discussion in the last section of Chapter II.[10] Litigation concerning labor unions and their activities, whether or not arising under the Sherman Act, also calls for separate treatment, as do the decisions involving individual liberties outside the context of economic regulation and those involving the rights of blacks and other minorities.

The Hepburn Act of 1906

First in importance judged by their nationwide practical impact, even if not first always in doctrinal importance, are a series of cases passing on federal statutes, chiefly reforms dating from the Roosevelt and Taft administrations. The earliest of these is *Atlantic Coast Line Railroad* v. *Riverside Mills*,[11] which was heard in 1910 and decided in January 1911, before the appointments of Van Devanter and Lamar and the promotion of White. The Carmack Amendment to the Hepburn Act of 1906, itself amending the Interstate Commerce Act, provided that, anything in a bill of lading to the contrary notwithstanding, an initial carrier in interstate commerce should be liable to the shipper for any loss occasioned by a connecting carrier. The loss to the shipper in

---

[8] Frankfurter, *Law and Politics,* 109.

[9] See *supra,* pp. 87–88, n.9.

[10] P. 171.

[11] 219 U.S. 186 (Jan. 3, 1911).

this case was caused by a connecting carrier, and the bill of lading expressly freed the initial carrier, the Atlantic Coast Line Railroad, of responsibility. In a suit against the Atlantic Coast Line, in which the Carmack Amendment was relied on, the shipper recovered.

The case was argued on appeal by Joseph R. Lamar, soon to ascend the Bench before which he stood. It was a small case, said Lamar in his brief,

> but the principle involved is of great and far-reaching consequence. The amount involved is so small that it forms the thinnest sort of a thin edge of a wedge.
>
> But if under the power to regulate commerce between the States and among foreign nations, Congress can require the carrier to issue a bill of lading, and then notwithstanding its express stipulation to the contrary, make the carrier responsible for the loss of goods by a connecting carrier between Richmond and New York—Congress can, in the exercise of the same power, require the carrier to issue a through bill of lading from Augusta, Georgia, to Moscow, Russia, and make the initial carrier here responsible for the loss of goods occurring in a foreign country.[12]

A unanimous Supreme Court, speaking through Lurton, affirmed the judgment for the shipper. The situation that had faced Congress, said Lurton, was that the shipper would often not know who had caused the damage to his goods. Since it was very burdensome for him to find the proper party to sue, he would accept any settlement offered. On the other hand—and here Lurton relied on information adduced in the course of debate in the House, to which he made a reference rare in opinions of this day,[13] his attention having been drawn to it in a brief for the United States as *amicus*[14]—arrangements for through routes among railroads were common, and were such that the initial carrier normally had no difficulty recovering the amount of a judgment against it from a connecting carrier with whom the real fault lay. The statute was said to violate the Due Process Clause by infringing freedom of contract. But, Lurton held, there was no such thing as absolute freedom of contract. The public interest was obvious. Congress had merely constituted connecting carrier agents of the initial carrier. The initial carrier might decline to enter through route arrangements which entailed this

---

[12] *Brief of J. R. Lamar for Atlantic Coast Line Railroad*, No. 215, at 23, Atlantic Coast Line R.R. v. Riverside Mills, 219 U.S. 186.

[13] 219 U.S. at 200–201.

[14] *Brief of the Government as Amicus Curiae in Support of the Constitutionality of Certain Portions of Section 20 of the Act to Regulate Commerce*, No. 215, at 8–9, Atlantic Coast Line R.R. v. Riverside Mills, 219 U.S. 186.

responsibility, but even if that were not so, the public interest might still justify Congress in enacting such a regulation as the Carmack Amendment.[15]

Although Congress acted again in 1915 and 1916, the effect of this decision was weakened by a construction which a now divided Court (Hughes and Pitney dissenting), again speaking through Lurton, gave to the Carmack Amendment. The Amendment, the Court held, did not forbid a limitation of liability "to a valuation agreed upon for the purpose of determining which of two alternative lawful rates shall apply to a particular shipment."[16] And the Amendment, the Court also held, thus rendering it, in a sense, counterproductive, occupied the field, and preempted efforts by the states to regulate limitations of liability in interstate commerce.[17] In the meantime, however, shortly after decision of the *Atlantic Coast Line Railroad* case, the Supreme Court, in one of the last of Harlan's opinions, upheld another provision of the Hepburn Act of 1906. Congress had outlawed all "free tickets, free passes, or free transportation for passengers" awarded by interstate carriers, viewing them as possible instruments of discrimination, rebates, and preferences.[18] Harlan applied the statute to free passes issued by a railroad before the act of Congress became effective, pursuant to a contractual arrangement that was thus perfectly valid when made. It was well within

---

[15] See also Galveston, H. & S. A. Ry. v. Wallace, 223 U.S. 481 (1912); Norfolk & Western Ry. v. Dixie Tobacco Co., 228 U.S. 593 (1913); and St. Louis & San Francisco R.R. v. Heyser, 95 Ark. 412 (1910), *writ of error dismissed on motion of plaintiff in error*, 226 U.S. 615 (1912).

[16] See *infra*, p. 417, nn.10, 11. Kansas City Southern Ry. v. Carl, 227 U.S. 639, 649 (1913); *cf.* Acts of Mar. 4, 1915, 38 Stat. 1196, and Aug. 9, 1916, 39 Stat. 441; see I. L. Sharfman, *The Interstate Commerce Commission* (1931), I, 104, n.5.

[17] Adams Express Co. v. Croninger, 226 U.S. 491 (1913).

[18] In the lower federal courts, an earlier reform, closely tied to antitrust policy and the abuses of Standard Oil, the Elkins Act of 1903, 32 Stat. 847, which made it a criminal offense for railroads to grant, or shippers to accept, rebates and like special favors, was being enforced. The Supreme Court watched benignly, but did not feel called upon to intervene. See *supra*, p. 89, n.10; Standard Oil Co. of New York v. United States, 158 Fed. 536 (D.C. W.D. N.Y. 1908), *cert. denied*, 218 U.S. 681 (1910); Hocking Valley Ry. v. United States, 210 Fed. 735 (6th Cir. 1914), *cert. denied*, 234 U.S. 757 (1914); Sunday Creek Co. v. United States, 210 Fed. 747 (6th Cir. 1914), *cert. denied*, 234 U.S. 757 (1914); Grand Rapids & Indiana Ry. v. United States, 212 Fed. 577 (6th Cir. 1914), *cert. denied*, 234 U.S. 762 (1914); Nichols & Cox Lumber Co. v. United States, 212 Fed. 588 (6th Cir. 1914), *cert. denied*, 234 U.S. 762 (1914). *But cf.* United States v. Pacific Mail Steamship Co., *writ of error dismissed on motion of plaintiff in error*, 218 U.S. 692 (1910). *Cf.* Pennsylvania R.R. v. International Coal Co., 230 U.S. 184 (1913); Mitchell Coal Co. v. Pennsylvania R.R., 230 U.S. 247 (1913); Fourche River Lumber Co. v. Bryant Lumber Co., 230 U.S. 316 (1913).

the power of Congress, said Harlan, to abrogate such contractual rights, which were necessarily entered into subject to the power of Congress to affect them.[19]

The Employers' Liability Cases

The Supreme Court also upheld other, rather more far-reaching Congressional regulations of the instrumentalities of national commerce, and of the channels along which that commerce moves. In January 1912, the Court gave its blessing to the Federal Employers' Liability Act of 1908, which imposed liability on railroads engaged in interstate and foreign commerce for injuries negligently caused to any employee "while he is employed by such carrier in such commerce."[20]

Compensating the victims of industrial accidents had been a Progressive objective of long standing, early embraced by Theodore Roosevelt. At common law, an injured employee's recovery could be defeated by a whole series of doctrines—the fellow-servant rule, the doctrine of contributory negligence, the doctrine of the assumption of risk—which not only offended against humanitarian impulses, but seemed scarcely rational as applied to modern industrial conditions. At the urging of President Roosevelt, Congress passed the Federal Employers' Liability Act of 1906, restricting the operation of these doctrines in suits brought against a railroad by its employees. Within a year and a half, however, the Supreme Court declared this statute unconstitutional because its coverage included employees of interstate railroads who were injured in intrastate commerce.[21] Three months later, Congress responded with the Act of 1908, which remedied the defect of the first statute by limiting coverage to employees injured in interstate commerce.[22]

The Act of 1908 abolished the fellow-servant rule, and substituted

---

[19] Louisville & Nashville R.R. v. Mottley, 219 U.S. 467 (1911); see also Chicago, Indianapolis & Louisville Ry. v. United States, 219 U.S. 486 (1911). *Cf.* Charleston & Western Carolina Ry. v. Thompson, 234 U.S. 576 (1914).

[20] 35 Stat. 65.

[21] First Employers' Liability Cases, 207 U.S. 463 (1908). The first Federal Employers' Liability Act was held constitutional, however, as applied in the District of Columbia. Philadelphia, Baltimore & Washington R.R. v. Tucker, 35 A.D.C. 123 (1911), *affirmed,* 220 U.S. 608 (1911). *But compare* Missouri, Kansas & Texas Ry. v. Blachley, 50 Tex. Civ. App. 141 (1908), *writ of error dismissed,* 218 U.S. 667 (1910), *with* Atchison, Topeka & Santa Fe Ry. v. Tack, 61 Tex. Civ. App. 551, 130 S.W. 596 (1910), *appeal dismissed on motion of appellant,* 226 U.S. 615 (1912).

[22] See L. P. Schoene and F. Watson, "Workmen's Compensation on Interstate Railways," *Harv. L. Rev.,* 47: 389, 392–93, 1934.

for the doctrine that contributory negligence is a bar to recovery a rule requiring the jury to reduce damages awarded to an injured employee in proportion to the amount of negligence, if any, attributable to him. It provided that whenever a violation by the railroad of the federal Safety Appliance Acts was shown, no contributory negligence could be charged to an injured employee for any purpose, nor could he be said to have assumed the risk of injury, and thus to have absolved the railroad of liability. But the doctrine of assumption of risk might otherwise operate. Attempts, through contractual arrangements between a railroad and its employees, to free the railroad of liability were declared void. The Act was to be enforceable in both state and federal courts, subject to a two-year statute of limitations, and by an amendment enacted in 1910,[23] causes of action were to survive the death of the injured employee.

The *Second Employers' Liability Cases*, as they were called, were argued in the Supreme Court in February 1911. The United States came in as *amicus curiae*, filing a brief that had been prepared by the late Solicitor General Lloyd W. Bowers, and another by James C. McReynolds, Special Assistant to the Attorney General. There was not much question that if the statute was a valid enactment under the Commerce Clause, its partial abrogation of the doctrines of contributory negligence and assumption of risk, and its abolition of the fellow-servant rule, were constitutional. The attack proceeded under the Commerce Clause, for it seemed to some, as Senator Joseph W. Bailey of Texas said in debate on the Amendment of 1910, that "they have carried that commerce clause to a point not only where it includes commerce, where it includes the instrumentalities of commerce, but they have invoked this power to regulate purely domestic control, which every state possesses, over those questions which affect the life and safety of its own people. . . . I utterly deny the power of the federal government to pass any law designed to merely ensure the safety and to protect the life and limb of those employed by these common carriers."[24] So also Charles W. Bunn,[25] arguing for one of the railroads in the *Second Employers' Liability Cases*:

> Probably the interests of the railway company, plaintiff in error, would be promoted by having the act of Congress sustained, thus securing to it at least one uniform law of liability throughout the States in lieu of the differing laws of many States. But the fact cannot be ignored

---

[23] 36 Stat. 291.

[24] 45 *Cong. Rec.* 3996, 61st Cong., 2nd Sess. (1910).

[25] Charles Wilson Bunn (1855–1941), of St. Paul, Minnesota, was general counsel of the Northern Pacific Railroad from 1896 until 1925. He was the author of a handbook on federal practice that went through several editions, and his appearances in the Supreme Court were frequent.

that for over a century it has been supposed that laws such as this fell within the exclusive power of the States, and that this view is held still by a large proportion of the bar and people.[26]

A unanimous Supreme Court, for which Van Devanter spoke, made fairly short shrift of these misgivings. Certainly they did not impress Van Devanter himself very much. "Personally," he wrote in October 1911 to his good friend Judge Elmer B. Adams, "I have no difficulty with any of the questions presented in the cases. . . ." But by then the cases had been held for over seven months. Van Devanter expected them to come down within two to three weeks, but it took three more months before the decisions were announced, and when it was all over, Van Devanter noted that he had given the cases "a good deal of attention, and the opinion received the approval of all my associates, although there had theretofore been pronounced differences of opinion in that connection."[27] So apparently there were misgivings among the Justices also, which had to be suppressed.

The Commerce power, Van Devanter's opinion declared, "is complete in itself, extends incidentally to every instrument and agent by which such commerce is carried on, may be exerted to its utmost extent over every part of such commerce, and is subject to no limitations save such as are prescribed in the Constitution." Hence it did not, in general, "admit of doubt" that Congress could regulate relations between railroads and their employees. Coming to more specific objections to the statute, Van Devanter held that no one had a property right in common law rules governing tort liability, and these could be freely changed by statute. The aim of the statute was to keep the railroads from being negligent, by imposing greater liability, and that was a purpose within the allowable discretion of Congress in dealing with interstate commerce —the limits of that discretion being assumed to be that Congress must try to further, and not impede, such commerce.

It was objected that the Act imposed liability where an employee was injured through the negligence of a fellow employee, even though that fellow employee was not himself engaged in interstate commerce. Under the earlier statute, the injured employee himself need not have been engaged in interstate commerce at the time of the accident, in order to be able to recover. This was the vice that rendered the earlier statute unconstitutional. But Congress had now cured it. The fact that a negligent fellow servant may have been in intrastate commerce was constitutionally irrelevant, because Congress was permitted to deal with

---

[26] Second Employers' Liability Cases, 223 U.S. 1, 19 (1912).

[27] W. Van Devanter to E. B. Adams, Oct. 14, 1911; Van Devanter to C. M. Potter, Feb. 24, 1912, Van Devanter Papers.

the effect of an accident on commerce, whatever its cause. The negligent fellow servant in intrastate commerce was a cause. The effect was felt by the injured employee, who was himself in interstate commerce, as was the railroad.[28]

There was objection also, on Contract Clause grounds, to the provision forbidding railroads to contract out of liability. But Congress, Van Devanter held, was merely seeing to it that rights and liabilities it had created were not evaded. Nor was there anything to the argument that the statute, by singling out railroads and not other carriers of interstate commerce, made an unreasonable classification. Finally, there was a separate point arising in one of the cases, which had been decided in the Supreme Court of Errors of Connecticut. While admitting that the causes of action created by the Act came within its general jurisdiction, the Connecticut court had declined to accept jurisdiction, because the policy of Connecticut with respect to liability was contrary to that embodied in this Act. Hence the Act could not be applied in the state courts of Connecticut, although Congress might, if it was otherwise valid, enforce it in the federal courts. "The suggestion," Van Devanter replied, "that the Act of Congress is not in harmony with the policy of the State, and therefore that the courts of the State are free to decline jurisdiction, is quite inadmissible, because it presupposes what in legal contemplation does not exist. When Congress, in the exertion of the power confided to it by the Constitution, adoped that act, it spoke for all the people and all the States, and thereby established a policy for all. That policy is as much the policy of Connecticut as if the act had emanated from its own legislature, and should be respected accordingly in the courts of the State . . . when their jurisdiction, as prescribed by local laws, is adequate to the occasion."[29]

Reaction to the decision was widespread and jubilant. An editorial in the *Chicago Daily Tribune* was characteristic:

> If what is now held constitutional by the unanimous opinion of our Court of final resort had been held constitutional ten years ago an un-

---

[28] This line of argument, while formally distinguishing the *First Employers' Liability Cases,* threw some doubt on their reasoning. For the injury to an employee engaged in intrastate commerce could also be seen as cause rather than effect. The effect was felt by the railroad, which was in interstate commerce, and might not Congress be permitted to deal with the effect, whatever the cause?

[29] Second Employers' Liability Cases, 223 U.S. 1, 47, 48, 57, 59 (1912). A few days after Van Devanter's decision came down, the Court affirmed a lower federal court's holding that the Act was constitutional. There was more emphasis in the lower court's opinion on Due Process and Equal Protection objections to the Act. St. Louis, Iron Mountain & Southern Ry. v. Watson, 169 Fed. 942 (C.C. E.D. Ark. 1909), *affirmed,* 223 U.S. 745 (1912).

just, inhumane and socially wasteful condition would have been more promptly checked and one of the chief, if not the chief, source of the present widespread popular hostility to our courts would have been obviated.

There is perhaps nothing that has bred extreme radicalism in this country so much as interpretations of our constitutional guarantees according to general theories of social and economic relations held by conservative judges and fortified by decisions of other judges of a still earlier time, but which ignore the social and economic facts of the present and the social and economic theories developed from them.

A "victory for justice as well as labor," thought the independently Republican *St. Paul Pioneer Press.* The Democratic *Philadelphia Record* considered that a reprieve had been granted to the Supreme Court "from the decision of the yellow press that it is barbaric, obsolete, fossilized, *non compos mentis*, and corrupt." The view that society should do something about industrial accidents and that the courts should not stand in the way had taken root in many quarters outside "the yellow press" as well. The desire for reform was, indeed, quite general, and so if the Court had earned a reprieve, it had earned it not only from "the yellow press."[30]

But there was irony in this triumphant conjunction, at last, of judicial action and reform objectives. For the Court had finally come around to blessing—yesterday's reform. And perhaps the Court bore some responsibility for causing Congress itself to reenact yesterday's reform, rather than aiming at new and more advanced objectives. The *Milwaukee Free Press* believed that "if there is such a thing as 'progressiveness' in a judicial decision, it is to be found in the Supreme Court's decision sustaining the Employers' Liability Law." But the *New York World*, looking ahead, pointed out that government was bound to see to it "that work-accidents are compensated promptly and automatically without the delay and money-waste of litigation."[31] People were beginning to realize, as Brandeis wrote some years later,

that no system of indemnity dependent upon fault on the employers' part could meet the situation; even if the law were perfected and its administration made exemplary. For in probably a majority of cases of injury there was no assignable fault; and in many more it must be impossible of proof. It was urged: Attention should be directed, not to the employers' fault, but to the employees' misfortune. Compensation

[30] *Chicago Daily Tribune*, Jan. 19, 1912, p. 10, col. 2; *The Literary Digest*, 44:198–200, Feb. 3, 1912; Mc-

Clure's, 35:151, June 1910; *The Outlook*, 97:809, Apr. 15, 1911.

[31] *The Literary Digest*, 44:198, Feb. 3, 1912.

should be general, not sporadic; certain, not conjectural; speedy, not delayed; definite as to amount and time of payment; and so distributed over long periods as to insure actual protection against lost or lessened earning capacity. To a system making such provision, and not to wasteful litigation, dependent for success upon the coincidence of fault and the ability to prove it, society, as well as the individual employee and his dependents, must look for adequate protection. Society needs such a protection as much as the individual; because ultimately society must bear the burden, financial and otherwise, of the heavy losses which accidents entail. And since accidents are a natural, and in part an inevitable, concomitant of industry as now practiced, society, which is served thereby, should in some way provide the protection. To attain this end, coöperative methods must be pursued; some form of insurance—that is, some form of taxation. Such was the contention which has generally prevailed.[32]

It had not yet prevailed in 1908, when Congress passed the second Federal Employers' Liability Act, but it was certainly beginning to be heard, and had the decision in the *First Employers' Liability Cases* not tended to rush Congress into curing the constitutional infirmities of its 1906 enactment, perhaps legislative energies might have been directed toward the new conception. In June 1910, Congress by joint resolution authorized the appointment by the President of a commission to investigate employers' liability and workmen's compensation. The man whom Taft appointed to serve as chairman of the commission was none other than Senator George Sutherland of Utah, and the report of the commission, submitted to the President and forwarded to Congress with his approval in February 1912, just weeks after the decision of the *Second Employers' Liability Cases*, recommended a compulsory workmen's compensation statute to take the place of federal employers' liability legislation. But Congress did not act.[33]

This was the newer "progessiveness" to which even so conservative a politician as Senator Sutherland adhered, not the statute the Court had just upheld. Nonetheless, the Court was having a good press, and the reason in part was that the decision managed to hoist the Court temporarily onto Theodore Roosevelt's bandwagon—a heady experience, almost always destined to reap some popular acclaim. It was all accidental, and the attention that was devoted to this aspect of the decision was quite unreasonably disproportionate. But there it was, just the same, and it turned on the case in which Connecticut had declined to exercise jurisdiction under the federal statute.

---

[32] Brandeis, J., dissenting, in New York Central R.R. v. Winfield, 244 U.S. 147, 154, 165 (1917).
[33] 43 *Cong. Rec.* 2228, 62nd Cong.,

2nd Sess. (1912); *Sen. Doc.* 338, 62nd Cong., 2nd Sess. (1912); see J. F. Paschal, *Mr. Justice Sutherland—A Man Against the State* (1951), 65 69.

That case, *Mondou* v. *New York, New Haven & Hartford Railroad,* had been decided in Connecticut on the authority of a somewhat earlier one, *Hoxie* v. *New York, New Haven & Hartford Railroad.*[34] As we have seen, Van Devanter dealt with the Connecticut holding very specifically, saying that it was inadmissible. Now, the Connecticut decision was the work of the redoubtable Simeon E. Baldwin, pillar of the Yale Law School, one of the founders and a former president of the American Bar Association, and at the time Chief Justice of Connecticut. In 1910, at age seventy, Baldwin retired as Chief Justice, and was promptly propelled into the Democratic nomination for governor of Connecticut. Theodore Roosevelt being on the campaign trail all over the country that fall, it was altogether natural for Baldwin to censure the former President for his assaults on courts and judges. Roosevelt's reprise was to tax Baldwin with opposition to employers' liability legislation. TR called to witness Baldwin's opinion in the *Hoxie* case, then barely a year old. Baldwin replied that he favored employers' liability and workmen's compensation, and that in the *Hoxie* case he had merely decided a jurisdictional issue. Roosevelt would have none of that. "I hit that Connecticut judge right between the eyes," he boasted. Baldwin was elected, but the controversy boiled along, Baldwin insisting that his decision had dealt, not with the merits of employers' liability, but with a jurisdictional point that Roosevelt was unable to understand, and threatening to sue Roosevelt for libel. Only when TR, without really retracting, finally declared that he had meant nothing personal, was there an end to the quarrel—and that was not till January 30, 1911. And so Van Devanter's decision, holding that Baldwin was unequivocally wrong on the so-called jurisdictional point in *Hoxie,* was widely headlined as: "Roosevelt Wins in Highest Court."[35]

Thus launched on its career, a dated reform virtually from birth, the Federal Employers' Liability Act was to be an abundant source of Supreme Court litigation. At the argument, Charles W. Bunn surmised "that railway companies have no employees who are not engaged in interstate commerce, unless indeed they carry on mining or some busi-

---

[34] 82 Conn. 352 (1909). Compare Chicago, Rock Island & Pacific Ry. v. Bradbury, 149 Iowa 51, 128 N.W. 1 (1910), *writ of error dismissed,* 223 U.S. 711 (1911), holding that the Federal Employers' Liability Act was not an exclusive grant of jurisdiction to the federal courts, and that the statute was enforceable in the courts of Iowa.

[35] See F. C. Weir, "The Social Opinions of Simeon E. Baldwin" (Ph.D. diss., Yale University, 1941), 238–55; *Chicago Daily Tribune,* Jan. 18, 1912, p. 11, col. 1. For a case reaffirming Van Devanter's holding on this point in quite a different context, see Gauthier v. Morrison, 232 U.S. 452 (1914).

ness apart from transportation."[36] But things were not to be that simple. The statute covered only employees engaged in interstate commerce at the time of their injury, and there was endless litigation over the question whether an employee carrying bolts to be used in repairing a bridge over which interstate trains passed,[37] or a fireman on a switching locomotive employed in a railroad yard,[38] or a brakeman on an interstate car in a train consisting also of intrastate cars[39] was meant to, and could constitutionally, be covered by the Act.[40] The instances mentioned arose in the first three years following decision of the *Second Employers' Liability Cases*, but there were many more to come, and it is not easy to accept that such cases, turning closely on particular facts and defying generalization, are properly of constitutional dimension, or that they ought to occupy the attention of the Supreme Court.[41]

The issue of coverage took also another form. As Van Devanter indicated, the federal statute would, under the Supremacy Clause, preempt state law, which is to say override inconsistent provisions of it. But if an inconsistent provision of state law was in question, it was first necessary to decide whether the Federal Employers' Liability Act was applicable. Was an intrastate railroad in North Carolina engaged in interstate commerce because it was operated by a lessee which was an interstate railroad? The answer was yes, since the lessee took over all the duties of the lessor, and was therefore the proper party to sue. As

---

[36] Second Employers' Liability Cases, 223 U.S. 1, 22 (1912).

[37] Pedersen v. Delaware, Lackawanna and Western R.R., 229 U.S. 146 (1913).

[38] Illinois Central R.R. v. Behrens, 233 U.S. 473 (1914). See also Central R. Co. of New Jersey v. Colasurdo, 192 Fed. 901 (2nd Cir. 1911), *affirming* 180 Fed. 832 (S.D. N.Y. 1911) (L. Hand, J.), *writ of error dismissed on motion of plaintiff in error,* 226 U.S. 617 (1912) (switch repairer in terminal yards).

[39] New York Central and Hudson River R.R. v. Carr, 238 U.S. 270 (1915).

[40] Other questions of construction and coverage also arose, of course. See, e.g., American R.R. Co. v. Birch, 224 U.S. 547 (1912); St. Louis, San Francisco & Texas Ry. v. Seale, 229 U.S. 156 (1913); Robinson v. Baltimore & Ohio R.R., 237 U.S. 84

(1915); and the Court also had to reaffirm, in 1912, the constitutionality of the provision forbidding the railroads to contract out of liability under the Act, Philadelphia, Baltimore & Washington R.R. v. Schubert, 224 U.S. 603 (1912); see also Baltimore & Ohio R.R. v. Gawinske, 197 Fed. 3 (3rd Cir. 1912), *cert. denied,* 225 U.S. 713 (1912).

[41] See Schoene and Watson, "Workmen's Compensation on Interstate Railways," *Harv. L. Rev.,* 47:389, 1934. Not until Congress amended the statute in 1939, 53 Stat. 1404 (1939), 45 U.S.C. §51, to apply to employees "any part" of whose duties are "in furtherance of interstate or foreign commerce" or "in any way directly or closely and substantially affect such commerce," if then, was the problem alleviated. See Reed v. Pennsylvania R.R., 351 U.S. 502 (1956).

for the injured employee himself, he was a fireman on an engine that was to take a train, including some cars that had come from Virginia, from one point to another within North Carolina. The Virginia cars, it turned out, placed him in interstate commerce.[42] Not infrequently, plaintiffs would try to avoid the federal statute by arguing that they were not in interstate commerce, since state law would in some respects be more liberal than the federal act.[43]

An even more incongruous strain on judicial energies were the many cases that, while occasionally raising an arguable question of statutory construction, more often depended strictly on facts, and were in no way different from run-of-the-mill negligence cases at common law.[44] The Court tried to defend itself by indicating that on questions of negligence, judgments would be reviewed only if clearly erroneous. And in *Southern Railway* v. *Gadd*,[45] the Court, holding the appeal frivolous and taken only for delay, invoked its Rule 23 and added 5 percent interest on the amount of the judgment against the appellant railroad, in addition to the interest allowed by law. But the cases kept coming. These few years, indeed, saw merely the beginning of the flood.[46]

Federal Railroad Regulation and Intrastate Commerce

Other fertile sources of litigation—in these years, while the Federal Employers' Liability Act was still quite young, even more fertile

---

[42] North Carolina R.R. v. Zachary, 232 U.S. 248 (1914).

[43] E.g., Gulf, Colorado & Santa Fe Ry. v. McGinnis, 228 U.S. 173 (1913); St. Louis, Iron Mountain & Southern Ry. v. Hesterly, 228 U.S. 702 (1913); Seaboard Airline v. Horton, 233 U.S. 492 (1914); and see Taylor v. Taylor, 232 U.S. 363 (1914); but see Missouri, Kansas & Texas Ry. v. West, 232 U.S. 682 (1914) and Chicago, Indianapolis & Louisville Ry. v. Hackett, 228 U.S. 559 (1913).

[44] E.g., Missouri, Kansas & Texas Ry. v. Wulf, 226 U.S. 570 (1913); Michigan Central R.R. v. Vreeland, 227 U.S. 59 (1913); American Railroad of Porto Rico v. Didricksen, 227 U.S. 145 (1913); Winfree v. Northern Pacific Ry., 227 U.S. 296 (1913); Troxell v. Delaware, Lackawanna & Western R.R., 227 U.S. 434 (1913); Seaboard Airline v. Moore, 228 U.S.

433 (1913); Grand Trunk Ry. v. Lindsay, 233 U.S. 42 (1914); Southern Ry. v. Bennett, 233 U.S. 80 (1914). See also Norfolk & Western Ry. v. Earnest, 229 U.S. 144 (1913); and see Shipp v. Texas & Pacific Ry., 201 Fed. 1023 (5th Cir. 1913), *cert. denied*, 229 U.S. 623 (1913); Chicago & Northwestern Ry. v. Rowlands, 149 Wisc. 51 (1912), *dismissed per stipulation*, 229 U.S. 627 (1913); Norfolk & Western Ry. v. Hauser, 211 Fed. 567 (4th Cir. 1912), *cert. denied*, 231 U.S. 749 (1913).

[45] 233 U.S. 572 (1914); and see Texas & Pacific Ry. v. Prater, 229 U.S. 177 (1913).

[46] See H. Cohen and H. M. Hart, Jr., "The Federal Employers' Liability Act in the Supreme Court" (unpublished thesis, Harvard Law School Library, 1930).

than that statute itself—were the Safety Appliance Acts of 1893, 1896, and 1903, and the Hours of Labor Act of 1907, which covered railroad employees.[47] Points, mostly very small points, of the construction of these statutes often arose in suits to recover for injuries under the Federal Employers' Liability Act. However, with respect neither to the Safety Appliance Acts nor the Hours of Labor Act did the Court put Congress or itself through a *First Employers' Liability Cases* kind of hoop. Fine constitutional questions, tied closely to particular facts, concerning the involvement of this employee or that railroad in interstate commerce at a given time, could generally be avoided, because the Court had permitted Congress to intrude rather farther into intrastate commerce with these statutes than with the first Employers' Liability Act.[48]

A comparable greater invasion of intrastate commerce by federal power was allowed also in *Interstate Commerce Commission* v. *Goodrich Transit Co.* Among the provisions of the Hepburn Act of 1906[49] was

---

[47] E.g., United States v. Atchison, Topeka & Santa Fe Ry., 220 U.S. 37 (1911); Chicago, Burlington & Quincy Ry. v. United States, 220 U.S. 559 (1911); Delk v. St. Louis & San Francisco R.R., 220 U.S. 580 (1911); Schlemmer v. Buffalo, R. & P. Ry., 220 U.S. 590 (1911); Chicago Junction Ry. v. King, 222 U.S. 222 (1911); Northern Pacific Ry. v. Washington, 222 U.S. 370 (1912); Missouri Pacific Ry. v. Castle, 224 U.S. 541 (1912); St. Louis Iron Mountain Ry. v. McWhirter, 229 U.S. 265 (1913); Chicago, Rock Island & Pacific Ry. v. Brown, 229 U.S. 317 (1913); Missouri, Kansas & Texas Ry. v. United States, 231 U.S. 112 (1913); Pennell v. Philadelphia & Reading Ry., 231 U.S. 675 (1914); Erie R.R. v. New York, 233 U.S. 671 (1914); Southern Ry. v. Crockett, 234 U.S. 725 (1914). And see Philadelphia & Reading Ry. v. United States, 162 Fed. 403 (D.C. E.D. Pa. 1908), *writ of error dismissed on motion of plaintiff in error,* 219 U.S. 590 (1911); Erie R.R. v. Russell, 183 Fed. 722 (2nd Cir. 1910), *cert. denied,* 220 U.S. 607 (1911); Illinois Central R.R. v. United States, 177 Fed. 801 (6th Cir. 1910), *writ of error dismissed on motion of plain-*

tiff in error, 223 U.S. 734 (1911); United States v. St. Louis Nat'l Stock Yards, 223 U.S. 737 (1911) (affirmed by stipulation on motion of the United States); Cincinnati Northern Ry. v. Dillon, 89 Ohio 436, 106 N.E. 1049 (1913), *affirming* 12 Ohio Law Rep. 323, 335 (Com. Pleas 1913), *affirmed,* 234 U.S. 753 (1914). See also Baltimore & Ohio Southwestern R.R. v. United States, 220 U.S. 94 (1911), which arose under the Act to Prevent Cruelty to Animals in Transit (1906).

[48] Baltimore & Ohio R.R. v. Interstate Commerce Commission, 221 U.S. 612 (1911); Southern Ry. v. United States, 222 U.S. 20 (1911). And see Belt Ry. of Chicago v. United States, 168 Fed. 542 (7th Cir. 1909), *cert. denied,* 223 U.S. 743 (1911); St. Louis Southwestern Ry. v. United States, 199 Fed. 990 (5th Cir. 1912), *cert. denied,* 229 U.S. 622 (1913); Colorado & Northwestern R.R. v. United States, 157 Fed. 321 (8th Cir. 1907), *writ of error dismissed,* 229 U.S. 605 (1912); Great Northern Ry. v. United States, 211 Fed. 309 (9th Cir. 1914), *cert. denied,* 234 U.S. 760 (1914).

[49] 34 Stat. 584.

one authorizing the Interstate Commerce Commission to require annual reports from interstate carriers on their corporate organizations, their stock, dividends, debts, numbers and salaries of employees, amounts spent on improvements, earnings and receipts from each branch of the business, balances—in short, a total picture of financial and other operations. The commission was also empowered to prescribe the accounts to be kept, to which the commission was to have access. The keeping of different forms of accounts was forbidden. The carriers involved in this case were in both interstate and foreign commerce, but did a large percentage of their business (in one case the greater part of the business) intrastate. Moreover, one of the carriers also operated amusement parks and various attendant concessions. The reporting and accounting orders issued to them by the commission covered everything. The newly created Commerce Court directed the commission to narrow its order and make it applicable only to the interstate transportation business of the carriers. The Supreme Court, Day writing, and Lurton and Lamar dissenting without opinion, reversed the Commerce Court, and reinstated the full order of the commission.

Carriers doing any amount of interstate business were subject to federal regulation, Day said. Only wholly intrastate carriers were immune. The Hepburn Act required the commission itself to report to Congress every year, the intention plainly being that Congress would rely on the information thus received for purposes of further legislation. So the commission's need to inform itself was much broader than its purely regulatory authority. To fulfill its duty toward Congress, the commission had to be knowledgeable about the entire business of the carrier.

Uniform accounting methods, in turn, were intended to preclude concealment of forbidden practices, such as rebates. And it would be impracticable to separate in a system of accounts intrastate from interstate business, the two being very often intermingled on the same train and in the use of other facilities. (As impracticable as to separate intrastate from interstate injuries to interstate railroad employees?) "We think the act should be given a practical construction, and one which will enable the Commission to perform the duties required of it by Congress. . . ." Those duties, again, related to investigation, to the collection of information, not to regulation. On this ground, somewhat lamely, Day distinguished the *First Employers' Liability Cases.*[50]

---

[50] Interstate Commerce Commission v. Goodrich Transit Co., 224 U.S. 194, 213, 214 (1912). The decision was noted as a "signal victory" for the Interstate Commerce Commission. *New York Times,* Apr. 2, 1912, p. 15, col. 3; *Chicago Daily Tribune,* Apr. 2, 1912, p. 1, col. 1. A year and a half later, the Court affirmed the power of the ICC to order a railroad

In *Houston and Texas Railway* v. *United States,* decided in 1914 and known as the *Shreveport Case,* the Court sanctioned what was perhaps not quite so deep an intrusion into intrastate commerce, but one achieved by regulation rather than investigation. Shreveport, Louisiana, is 231 miles east of Houston, Texas, on the Houston and Texas Railway, and 189 miles east of Dallas, Texas, on the Texas and Pacific line. For the trade of the territory contained in this triangle, Shreveport competed with Dallas and Houston. On intrastate traffic moving eastward from Dallas and Houston to points in Texas intermediate between Dallas and Houston and Shreveport, the railroads charged rates fixed by the Railroad Commission of Texas, which were selectively lower than rates charged for like traffic moving over like distances westward from Shreveport to the same points. It was undisputed "that the difference was substantial and injuriously affected the commerce of Shreveport."

In a proceeding initiated by the Railroad Commission of Louisiana, the Interstate Commerce Commission did two things. Finding that rates charged out of Shreveport to Texas were unreasonably high, it established new maximum rates for this traffic; and these corresponded, incidentally, to class rates generally set by the Railroad Commission of Texas for transportation over similar distances within that state— rates to which the selective lower ones from Dallas and Houston to East Texas were an exception. The Interstate Commerce Commission also found that the differential between rates from Dallas and Houston to East Texas and from Shreveport westward to Texas was an unlawful discrimination against interstate commerce moving from Shreveport, and it ordered the railroads to cease charging higher rates from Shreveport to Dallas, Houston, or intermediate points than were charged for traffic moving from Dallas and Houston eastward.

The railroads accepted the maximum rates, but objected to the portion of the order removing the differential, on the ground that it exceeded the commission's authority by attempting to regulate intrastate rates and overriding the Texas Railroad Commission's orders, since the railroads now had no choice but either to file new rates from Shreveport westward lower than those the commission had established as reasonable, or to raise their rates for traffic going east from Dallas and Houston to other points in Texas. Clearly the commission was not intending to force them—and it scarcely could find the authority to force

---

to assign a certain cost as a current expense, rather than entering it in the property account. So the control over accounting methods was to be real and close. Kansas City Southern Ry. v. United States, 231 U.S. 423 (1913). For the Court's general attitude toward the ICC—on the whole, reasonably hospitable—see *supra,* p. 216 *et seq.*

them—to lower the interstate rates which the commission itself had set as the reasonable ones. The only lawful alternative, therefore, was to raise the intrastate rates above the level fixed by the Railroad Commission of Texas.

The Interstate Commerce Commission had acted under Section 3 of the original Interstate Commerce Act of 1887,[51] which forbade undue or unreasonable preferences or advantages extended by a carrier to any person, corporation, "or locality," except that the section was inapplicable to transportation "wholly within one State." Affirming a judgment in favor of the commission's order, Hughes held[52] that the language of the statute was "certainly sweeping enough to embrace all the discriminations of the sort described which it was within the power of Congress to condemn." As for the exception, it immunized intrastate rates "as such," not the "relationship" between intrastate and interstate rates. It did not remove from federal control rates which, as in this case, were found to have an effect outside the state, because they discriminated against interstate commerce. And so the question was the constitutional one, whether such a discrimination, arising from intrastate rates, was within the power of Congress to condemn.

Congress had power to foster interstate commerce, and it had power therefore to ensure that the agencies of interstate commerce, even though they might at the same time also be instruments of intrastate commerce, were not used so "as to cripple, retard or destroy" interstate commerce. In a case in which the interstate and intrastate transactions of carriers were so related "that the government of the one involves the control of the other, it is Congress, and not the State, that is entitled to prescribe the final and dominant rule, for otherwise Congress would be denied the exercise of its constitutional authority and the State, and not the Nation, would be supreme within the national field." That was why it had been held, said Hughes, referring to *Baltimore & Ohio Railroad* v. *Interstate Commerce Commission,* decided just a couple of years earlier,[53] that the Hours of Service Act of 1907 applied not only to interstate, but also to intrastate transactions which "were so interwoven that it was

---

[51] 24 Stat. 379, 380.

[52] Lurton and Pitney noted dissent without opinion, but there was actually yet a third dissent, albeit an entirely silent one. Lamar returned: "I voted to reverse, but my views are much shaken by your opinion. The conclusion is so desirable and the reasons for unanimity so great that unless others do, I shall not dissent." He must have meant "unless others do and write," or else his views were shaken even further. Hughes' majority was an enthusiastic one. The returns are full of adjectives like "clear," "powerful," "admirable," "sound"— an opinion, said Day, "which all may comprehend." Hughes Papers, Library of Congress. See also M. J. Pusey, *Charles Evans Hughes* (1951), I, 307–308.

[53] See *supra,* p. 214, n.48.

utterly impracticable" for them to be dealt with separately. So also, in the *Second Employers' Liability Cases*, Congress had been allowed to reach injuries caused by a negligent fellow servant engaged in intrastate commerce.

To remove the injury to interstate commerce, Congress was not bound to lower interstate rates and bring them down to the level of the intrastate ones. "Otherwise, it could prevent the injury to interstate commerce only by the sacrifice of its judgment as to interstate rates. Congress is entitled to maintain its own standard as to these rates. . . ." And finally, this passage of powerful implications: "We are not unmindful of the gravity of the question that is presented when state and Federal views conflict. But it was recognized at the beginning that the Nation could not prosper if interstate and foreign trade were governed by many masters, and, where the interests of the freedom of interstate commerce are involved, the judgment of Congress and of the agencies it lawfully establishes must control."[54]

The reception accorded Hughes' decision highlighted a significant omission in the alignment of parties in the *Shreveport Case*. The real contest was between Louisiana and the railroads on one side, and Texas on the other. For in the immediate aspect, the railroad interest was adversary to that of Texas, since Texas was preventing the railroads from charging higher rates for intrastate transportation; and in the long run, the railroads surely preferred uniformity of regulation to the rule of many masters (if there was to be regulation at all, as clearly there was), and they had more to fear by way of antirailroad excesses from some states, at any rate, than from a federal commission. Richard Olney's advice to a railroad client that the ICC was to be welcomed, because it would serve as "a sort of barrier between the railroad corporations and the people and a sort of protection against hasty and crude legislation," could not so soon have been forgotten.[55]

In the real world outside the courtroom, that was in fact how the parties lined up. Railroad men and the financial community, at least once it had time to reflect, considered the decision favorable to the railroads.[56] The *Wall Street Journal* declared that the decision would "put a curb upon the radicalism which in the commissions of some western states has gone to extreme lengths." Some traders on the stock market did not quite understand this, "apparently taking it for granted that what was in favor of the Interstate Commerce Commission must be

---

[54] Houston and Texas Ry. v. United States, 234 U.S. 342, 346, 356, 351–52, 355, 359–60 (1914).

[55] See *supra*, p. 131.

[56] See *New York Times*, June 9,

1914, p. 4, col. 1, p. 12, col. 2; June 10, 1914, p. 5, col. 5, p. 10, col. 3; *New York Tribune*, June 9, 1914, p. 4, col. 3; *New York Herald*, June 9, 1914, p. 12, col. 3.

against the interests of the railroads, although in this instance it certainly was not so."[57]

So the railroads had won. But in the Supreme Court, they could only win by losing, since it was the railroads that supposedly represented the Texas side of the case. The Interstate Commerce Commission and the United States were there, of course, and Louisiana intervened and was represented. But Texas was there neither as a party nor as *amicus*. The brief for the railroads was signed by distinguished counsel— Maxwell Evarts, joined by James G. Wilson and Hiram M. Garwood— and it put the case for Texas in, apparently, the best of faith. It gamely argued the constitutional issue, as well as the question of statutory construction. But it was all rather abstract.[58] Perhaps Texas, if she had represented herself, might have offered a concrete explanation and defense of her policy of protecting local jobbers, although, to be sure, it is very unlikely that the result could have been affected.[59]

From a political point of view, the decision landed right on the principal fissure in the Progressive movement, the crack becoming more and more visible in the alliance between middle-class Progressives, on the one hand, and Jeffersonian Democrats and some agrarian populists, on the other. The decision, said the *Chicago Tribune*, was "another landmark . . . in the advance of nationalism," or, it added, "as its opponents call it, centralization."[60] Here was an issue on which the rural component of the Progressive movement could find common ground with conservatives. Francis Lynde Stetson, Morgan's lawyer, allowed that he was "a heretic among railroad men in the views I hold of the *Shreveport* case, for . . . I do not believe that the writers of our Constitution contemplated such a broadening of the central power. The decision is a logical one, but for the welfare of the country I wish it had been in favor of the State."[61]

In 1930, when Hughes was up for confirmation as Chief Justice,

---

[57] *Wall Street Journal,* June 9, 1914, p. 4, col. 1.

[58] *Brief for Appellant,* Nos. 567, 568, Houston & Texas Ry. v. United States, 234 U.S. 342 (1914).

[59] An even more extreme case in which the real party in interest—in this instance, the United States—was unrepresented was *Louisville & Nashville R.R. v. Mottley, supra,* p. 205, n.19. The railroad defending the constitutionality of the Hepburn Act provision outlawing free passes could hardly have had its heart in the argument, and indeed the case had every appearance of being contrived. Yet the brief for the railroad in support of constitutionality was thorough and vigorous, and, of course, it prevailed. These are not altogether characteristic occurrences, but neither are they isolated instances. See *infra,* pp. 552, 554, 559–63.

[60] *Chicago Tribune,* June 10, 1914, p. 8, col. 1.

[61] *New York Times,* June 10, 1914, p. 5, col. 4.

Southern Senators taxed him with the *Shreveport* decision, which "literally stripped" the states of their rights.[62] Stetson's view found expression also in an article in the *Harvard Law Review*, which charged that Hughes had rewritten the statute and the Constitution, in an orgy of "judicial legislation." If the *Shreveport* result was desired, it should have been achieved by a constitutional amendment.[63] But by far the greater number of writers in the professional journals expressed approval and support.[64]

Although both the commission and the Supreme Court proceeded with delicacy, and with full awareness of the pull exercised by the states'-rights argument, implementation of the *Shreveport* decision met with rather determined resistance. It was some time before the commission applied the decision outside Texas, and in two cases that eventually reached it from Illinois and South Dakota, the Supreme Court, while thoroughly reaffirming the *Shreveport* doctrine, cautioned the commission to move slowly and carefully. The Court emphasized the need for exquisite precision in commission orders in this area, so that only state rate structures actually discriminating against interstate commerce would be reached.[65]

In Texas itself, without any prodding from the Court, the commission showed great deliberation and restraint in taking further action. The

---

[62] See remarks of Walter George of Georgia and Carter Glass of Virginia, 72 *Cong. Rec.* 3451–52, 3585–87, 71st Cong., 2nd Sess. (1930). But the *Shreveport* decision did not entirely fail to gain Hughes a constituency, even in the South. Senator Ransdell of Louisiana, while no less a states'-rights man than the next Senator, was grateful for the removal of the competitive disadvantage under which Louisiana had labored, and hence thought that the *Shreveport* decision was "an extremely learned and fair" one. 72 *Cong. Rec.* 3381–83, 71st Cong., 2nd Sess. (1930). Memories were long: The two Senators from Louisiana voted for Hughes' confirmation, while the two from Texas voted against it. See P. Freund, "Charles Evans Hughes as Chief Justice," *Harv. L. Rev.*, 81:4, 10, 1967.

[63] W. C. Coleman, "The Evolution of Federal Regulation of Intrastate Rates: The Shreveport Rate Case,"

Harv. L. Rev., 28:34, 77–81, 1914.

[64] A. P. Matthew, "Federal Control over State Commerce When Related to Interstate Commerce," *Calif. L. Rev.*, 2:482, 1914; J. S. Sheppard, Jr., "Another Word about the Evolution of the Federal Regulation of Interstate Rates and the Shreveport Rate Cases," *Harv. L. Rev.*, 28:545, 1914; H. C. Flannery, "Constitutional and Practical Objections to the Exclusive Federal Regulation of Interstate Railroad Rates," *Minn. L. Rev.*, 2:339, 1918; C. W. Needham, "Exclusive Regulation of Railroad Rates by the Federal Government," *Minn. L. Rev.*, 2:163, 1918.

[65] American Express Co. v. Caldwell, 244 U.S. 617 (1917); Illinois Central R.R. v. Public Utilities Commission, 245 U.S. 493 (1918). And see Arkansas Railroad Commission v. Chicago, R.I. & P. R.R., 274 U.S. 597 (1927).

original order applied to only three railroads, and so, after the decision, many additional complaints were filed. The commission held more hearings, and then issued a supplemental report and order applicable to other carriers. Further hearings and orders followed before all of Texas, rather than just East Texas, could be covered, and all relevant rates affected. The Texas Railroad Commission, meanwhile, continued to contest the validity of the *Shreveport* decision itself. As late as 1917, a lower federal court had to enjoin the Texas Railroad Commission from attempting to impose penalties on the railroads involved in the original *Shreveport Case* for abiding by ICC orders.[66] But in the end, the *Shreveport* doctrine was ringingly vindicated by Congress in Section 416 of the Transportation Act, 1920, and from it grew a more comprehensive invasion, in the national interest, of state powers over transportation.[67]

Navigable Waters and the Production of Power

The most ungrudging legitimation of federal power in these years came in 1913, in *United States* v. *Chandler-Dunbar Co.*, on which, over twenty years later, the Court in large part rested its holding that the Tennessee Valley Authority was constitutional.[68] All America understands," said John Marshall in *Gibbons* v. *Ogden*, "and has uniformly understood the word 'commerce' to comprehend navigation."[69] And the Court had held as recently as 1912 that the federal power to regulate navigable waters—in this case the harbor of Pittsburgh—could brook no limitations imposed by the states, and overrode state-created private rights.[70] In *Chandler-Dunbar* the question was whether the federal power over navigation included a power to use the excess flow of a river for commercial purposes, and to exclude others from so using it. By Act of March 3, 1909,[71] Congress declared that absolute ownership by the United States of all lands and property north of St. Marys Falls Ship Canal, for its entire length up to the international boundary line at Sault Sainte Marie, Michigan, was necessary for purposes of navigation,

---

[66] Eastern Texas R.R. v. Railroad Commission of Texas, 242 Fed. 300 (1917). See Sharfman, *Interstate Commerce Commission*, II, 269–86.

[67] Wisconsin Railroad Commission v. Chicago, Burlington & Quincy R.R., 257 U.S. 563 (1922); see Sharfman, *Interstate Commerce Commission*, I, 220–25.

[68] Ashwander v. Tennessee Valley Authority, 297 U.S. 288 (1936).

[69] 9 *Wheat* 1, 190 (1824).

[70] Philadelphia Co. v. Stimson, 223 U.S. 605 (1912); and see City of New York v. United States, 188 Fed. 46 (2nd Cir. 1911), *cert. denied*, 223 U.S. 722 (1911). *Cf.* United States v. Baltimore & Ohio R.R., 229 U.S. 244 (1913). But *cf.* The Abby Dodge, 223 U.S. 166 (1912).

[71] 35 Stat. 815.

and authorized the Secretary of War to acquire such lands and property by condemnation. Congress intended to have the facilities for commerce on the Great Lakes improved through the construction of more canals and locks. Section 12 of the Act also authorized the Secretary of War to lease any excess of water power which might result from the construction of dams and locks.

The Chandler-Dunbar Water Power Company owned land alongside the river, and had constructed and was operating dams, and selling the resulting water power to commercial users. In condemnation proceedings started by the Secretary of War pursuant to the Act, an award was made to the Chandler-Dunbar Company, which included over half a million dollars for the estimated value of the water power that the company had been using commercially, and which it would now lose. The theory of the award was that riparian owners had to be compensated for exclusion from the use of water power, certainly when the flow of the river exceeded the needs of navigation. Writing for a unanimous Court, Lurton reversed on this aspect of the award.

The technical title to the bed of the river, he said, could be assumed to be in the company. The title of a riparian owner, however, was always subordinate, not only to the public right of navigation, but to all exercises by Congress of its control over navigable streams. Anything having some relation to navigation was within the control of Congress, which had plenary authority to allow or forbid all kinds of structures in or over a river as aids or hindrances to navigation. Congress might decide that the flow of a river was not in excess of the possible needs of navigation, or that if it was, it ought to be put to a certain use in the public interest, and either judgment on the part of Congress was not subject to judicial review. Here Congress had decided that the turbulent waters of the St. Marys Falls were equally a tremendous obstacle to navigation and a great source of water power, and that the wider needs of navigation would not be hindered by the presence in the river of works necessary to produce water power. All prior rights to the use of the flow of the water were always subject to the power of Congress, and therefore Congress was not now required to compensate anyone for taking the flow of water, because no one had owned it.

"Ownership of a private stream wholly upon the lands of an individual is conceivable; but that the running water in a great navigable stream is capable of private ownership is inconceivable." The company had built water works which it would now have to tear down, but it had built and operated them always subject to the power of Congress; it had never had absolute ownership in them. Nor could there be any objection to federal harnessing and commercial use of water as being beyond the power of Congress, because not properly a measure in aid of navigation. The primary purpose of Congress was to make the stream navigable, and it was in carrying out that primary purpose that in the judgment of Congress excess water would be produced. No one had a right to object to what Congress did with that excess water, for no one could claim a prior interest in it. And so the only part of the compensation award that Lurton approved was the award for land owned by the company, including islands within the river. But he disapproved any allowance for expectations of enhanced value of the land because of the water power the government would now produce. All the company was allowed to get was the present market value of its real estate.[72]

The decision was hardly noticed in the press—the only tenuous tie it seemed to have to any current political issue was to conservation[73]—but it was taken to heart in the War Department. It had seemed to Henry L. Stimson, who had been Secretary of War during the last two years of the Taft Administration, that the federal power to regulate navigation should include a power to harness surplus waters by building dams. Federal licensing of all dams built in navigable waters, and compensation to the government by the private interests which built them, should be required, Stimson believed. He persuaded President Taft to veto a bill that would have allowed a dam to be built without compensation to the government, but he did not quite obtain acceptance of the general principle he advocated—a principle on which, of course, a portion of the jurisdiction of the Federal Power Commission later rested.

When the Wilson Administration came into office, one of Stimson's principal assistants, Felix Frankfurter, remained in the Department of the Army, and had even greater difficulty persuading the Secretary of War of this more states'-rights-minded administration, Lindley M. Garrison, that the Corps of Engineers ought to control the use of water in the public interest. Secretary Garrison thought that the government lacked constitutional authority for such an enterprise, and therefore resisted ordering the Corps of Engineers to engage in country-wide planning of the location of dams. The *Chandler-Dunbar* decision clinched Frankfurter's argument—one can virtually see him sprinting into the Secretary's office, the Court's opinion triumphantly in hand. The Secretary, as Frankfurter later told the story, recognized the decision as

---

[72] United States v. Chandler-Dunbar Co., 229 U.S. 53, 69 (1913). See also Lewis Blue Point Oyster Co. v. Briggs, 229 U.S. 82 (1913); McGovern v. New York, 229 U.S. 363 (1913); Jackson v. United States, 230 U.S. 1 (1913); Hughes v. United States, 230 U.S. 24 (1913).

[73] See *New York Times,* May 27, 1913, p. 6, col. 2; *Wall Street Journal,* May 27, 1913, p. 8, col. 3.

conclusively sanctioning the extension of federal authority which Frank-furter had been urging, "though he thought the world had come to an end."[74]

The Pure Food and Drug Act of 1906

What was involved in the *Chandler-Dunbar* case was regulation of the channels of commerce, but it was a regulation having another, ulterior purpose as well. The regulation was upheld to the full breadth of its purposes, the ulterior one along with the other. This was one decision that went the limit in affirming federal power. For once the Court was willing to announce a comprehensive doctrine. But in other cases dealing with regulations of the movement of commerce in which ulterior purposes were dominant, the Court, while still hospitable, proved hesitant, and certainly shied clear of unqualified generalizations.

Such a case was *Hipolite Egg Co.* v. *United States*,[75] decided in 1911, which upheld the constitutionality of the Pure Food and Drug Act of 1906. This Act, a celebrated and hard-fought reform, was the product of some twenty-five years of agitation. Its principal backer was the redoubtable Dr. Harvey W. Wiley, long the chief chemist of the Department of Agriculture, but its parents were many, including such "muckrakers" as Edward Bok, Mark Sullivan, Samuel Hopkins Adams, and Upton Sinclair, and including also, in the end, after some doubts, Theodore Roosevelt. Sinclair's *The Jungle*, published in 1906, made a great impression on the President and on Congress, but there was a long history of other, prior revelations, chiefly about patent medicines, and in the year before publication of Sinclair's book, Charles Edward Russell, in a series of articles, castigated the "Beef Trust" (note the characteristic mingling of antitrust fervor with other reforming objectives).

By 1906, when the federal law was enacted, most states had pure food laws of one sort or another, but they could not effectively protect themselves against adulterated foods and drugs shipped in interstate commerce, since the prevailing constitutional doctrine ruled that articles shipped in interstate commerce were, while still in their original pack-ages, subject only, if at all, to federal, and immune from state, regulation.

---

[74] See E. E. Morison, *Turmoil and Tradition: A Study of the Life and Times of Henry L. Stimson* (1960), 172; H. D. Phillips, ed., *Felix Frank-furter Reminisces* (1960), 73–75.

[75] *Hipolite Egg* came down on Mar. 13, 1911, the day the decision holding the Corporation Tax Act of 1909 con-stitutional was also announced. (See *infra,* p. 242.) Probably as a result of being thus blanketed, *Hipolite Egg,* despite its importance and its poli-tical interest, went entirely unnoticed, for example, in the *New York Times* and the *Chicago Tribune*.

Again, standards adopted by the several states differed, of course, and uniform regulation was clearly desirable, both from the point of view of effectiveness, and of the least inconvenience to producers. Opposition to a federal act came from the manufacturers, but there was opposition also, voiced to the very end, by Southern Democrats, who argued that Congress had no power under the Commerce Clause to enact a regulatory measure of this sort; Congress, the argument ran, has no police powers.[76] And it was on this ground that the statute, once enacted, was attacked in litigation.

Speaking for a unanimous Court, McKenna rejected the Commerce Clause argument. The *Hipolite Egg Co.* case involved a shipment of preserved eggs from St. Louis, Missouri, to Illinois, where the eggs were stored in their original packages by the purchaser, a baking company. There they were seized as adulterated, by authority of the Pure Food and Drug Act. The seizure was said to be unconstitutional, since the eggs had passed into the general mass of property in the state, and were thus beyond the power of Congress. It would be a sufficient answer to this contention, said McKenna, that the eggs, being still in their original packages, were still in interstate commerce, had not passed into the internal commerce of the state, and were hence subject to federal, and not to state, regulation. But he preferred to rest the case on an additional ground.

In order to regulate the transportation of adulterated goods in commerce, Congress reached both the shipper and the receiver. In doing so, Congress was within its powers, since "illicit articles," at least while still in their original packages, were subject to federal authority whether or not they had completed their movement and become part of the mass of property in the state. But this holding, with its implicit promise not to restrict federal power to the regulation of goods still in their original packages, applied only to "illicit articles"—in this instance, adulterated ones. "There is here no conflict," said McKenna, "of national and state jurisdiction over property legally articles of trade. The question here is whether articles which are outlaws of commerce may be seized wherever found, and it certainly will not be contended that they are outside the jurisdiction of the National Government when they are within the borders of a State."[77]

---

[76] See C. C. Repier, "The Struggle for Federal Food and Drug Legislation," *Law & Contemp. Prob.*, 1:3, 1933; W. H. Harbaugh, *Power and Responsibility* (1961), 255–60; H. M. Hart, Jr., and A. M. Sacks, *The Legal Process* (Temp. ed., 1957), 895 *et seq.*

[77] Hipolite Egg. Co. v. United States, 220 U.S. 45, 58 (1911). The government had itself brought up on appeal another Pure Food and Drug Act case, which it had lost below. But this was an unsuitable vessel for constitutional adjudication, since it had gone off on a point of statutory construction. The appeal was dis-

What, however, was an illegitimate article, an outlaw of commerce, as contrasted with a legitimate article of commerce? And was Congress free to decide? Was McKenna saying that if Congress excluded an article from commerce, rather than merely regulating its movement, that article automatically became an outlaw, so that the power was a plenary one, which Congress had whenever it asserted it; or was something intended that was subject to closer judicial control? McKenna did not elucidate. The Court had struggled with the issue before, and it would struggle with it again, reaching the same result with respect to the Mann Act, but the opposite one later, in *Hammer* v. *Dagenhart*,[78] the child labor case of unhappy memory. The Pure Food and Drug Act had passed muster in *Hipolite Egg Co.*, but the case did not settle this vexed issue; it failed, indeed, even to take a significant step in the direction of such a settlement. And the Pure Food and Drug Act itself, although it was now constitutionally safe, was yet to suffer a setback at the hands of the Supreme Court.

In *United States* v. *Antikamnia Chemical Co.*,[79] the Court upheld regulations under the Act requiring precise descriptions on drug labels of chemical substances contained in the drug, and in *United States* v. *Lexington Mill & Elevator Co.*,[80] although the government lost, and Dr. Wiley and the *New York Times* took some alarm,[81] the Court gave a sensible construction to a section prohibiting the addition of poisonous or other ingredients that might render an article "injurious to health."[82] But in *United States* v. *Johnson*, the Court did some serious damage, which Congress had to hasten to repair. The Act punished misbranding as a criminal offense, and defined it as "any statement, design, or device regarding such article, or the ingredients or substances contained therein

---

missed early in the October Term 1910 on motion of the government. United States v. Boeckman, 176 Fed. 382 (C.C. E.D. N.Y. 1910), *appeal dismissed*, 218 U.S. 684 (1910). See also United States v. Morgan, 222 U.S. 274 (1911); Warner-Jenkinson Co. v. United States, 223 U.S. 725 (1911) (vanilla extract sold in barrels held mislabeled by invoice); Dade v. United States, 40 App. D.C. 94 (1913), *cert. denied*, 229 U.S. 610 (1913).

[78] 247 U.S. 251 (1918).

[79] 231 U.S. 654 (1914).

[80] 232 U.S. 399 (1914).

[81] See *New York Times*, Feb. 26, 1914, p. 6, col. 2; Feb. 26, 1914, p. 8,

col. 3; but *cf. New York Tribune*, Feb. 26, 1914, p. 6, col. 1.

[82] *Cf.* Weeks v. United States, 224 Fed. 69 (2nd Cir. 1915), *affirmed*, 245 U.S. 618 (1918); but *cf.* Wood Manufacturing Co. v. United States, 286 Fed. 84 (7th Cir. 1923). The relevant statutory language now reads differently, see Section 402 of the Food, Drug and Cosmetics Act of 1938, 52 Stat. 1046, 21 U.S.C. §342, but the change was neither intended to nor did it overrule the *Lexington Mill* case. See H. A. Toulmin, *A Treatise on the Law of Foods, Drugs and Cosmetics* (2nd ed., 1963), I, 244–47.

which shall be false or misleading in any particular. . . ." The articles in question in the *Johnson* case bore such labels as "Cancerine tablets," and "Dr. Johnson's Mild Combination Treatment for Cancer." Dr. Johnson was indicted for misbranding, the government alleging that the tablets were wholly worthless, and that he well knew it. In an opinion by Holmes, which Hughes found not only wrong, but as he later recalled, surprisingly so,[83] the Court affirmed a dismissal of the indictment.

Holmes construed the Act as punishing only false statements of the identity of the article or of its ingredients, but not inflated or false commendations of it. This was what the words of the Act conveyed "to an ear trained to the usages of English speech," Holmes thought. And although, he said, "the meaning of a sentence is to be felt rather than to be proved, generally and here the impression may be strengthened by argument, as we shall try to show." Following a bit of linguistic analysis, Holmes noted that liability under the Act was absolute, and that an article could be deemed misbranded even in the absence of any conscious fraud on the part of the misbrander. A purpose to impose so harsh a standard might be imputable to Congress as to questions of fact, but it seemed to Holmes hardly imputable as to matters of medical effect, on which, after all, opinions could differ.

Holmes allowed that a statement concerning medical effect could conceivably amount to a misstatement of identity, as for example, if the supposed drug had in fact been pure water. If it were pure water, then to suggest that it could cure cancer might—although Holmes forebore from so deciding—amount to a misstatement of identity. But that was not the case before the Court. Finally, and ominously: "We shall say nothing as to the limits of constitutional power, and but a word as to what Congress was likely to attempt." It was likely to attempt to deal with factual misstatements, but not "to distort the uses of its constitutional power to establish criteria in regions where opinions are far apart."

Hughes, in a dissent in which he was joined by Harlan and Day, replied in essence that Holmes' hypothetical example was the actual case before the Court. Here were labels making definite and extravagant claims about the effects on malignancies of a drug which—so the indictment alleged, and so the Court was in this posture of the case obliged to assume—was wholly worthless. The legislative history was convincing that Congress did not mean to restrict its definition of misbranding to false statements about the identity of the drug only. Should the government put in issue a label which touched on areas of opinion where no certain answer could be found, because medical opinions differed, the

---

[83] C. E. Hughes, *Biographical Notes,* Microfilm, Ac. 9943, p. 225, Hughes Papers.

indictment would have to be quashed. But that was not this case. It was readily determinable whether these medicines were wholly worthless, and the indictment charged that they were. Not opinion, but fact was misrepresented in labeling this article as a cure, when it was nothing of the sort. There was no question of the power of Congress to reach this sort of mislabeling, and none that it had intended to do so.[84]

Shortly after the decision in *United States* v. *Johnson* was announced, Secretary of Agriculture James Wilson wrote President Taft that the decision immunized fraudulent claims made for patent medicines, and created a real danger to health. The Secretary requested that the President send a special message to Congress, asking it to amend the Act as a matter of urgency. Within a month of the decision, such a message went up, informing Congress that prior to the Supreme Court's action, 100 prosecutions of the sort involved in the *Johnson* case had been concluded by pleas of guilty, and that since that decision, an additional 150 prosecutions, which were pending, would be frustrated. "Of course," the President said, "as pointed out by the Supreme Court, any attempt to legislate against mere expressions of opinion would be abortive; nevertheless, if knowingly false misstatements of fact as to the effect of the preparations be provided against, a greater part of the evil will be subject to control."

Congress responded promptly, adding to the Act a prohibition of false and fraudulent statements regarding the curative or therapeutic effect of an article. The whole course of events, from the decision of the *Johnson* case on May 29, 1911, to its overruling by Congress by the Act of August 23, 1911, consumed just under three months, and may well be considered something of a track record in the interplay between Court and Congress, although Congress took no more than three months also, as we have seen, to react to the *First Employers' Liability Cases* with the second Federal Employers' Liability Act.[85]

The Mann Act

In *Hoke* v. *United States*, decided in 1913, two years after *Hipolite Egg*, the Court, again in unanimity, and again speaking through McKenna in an opinion that had its ambivalences and obscurities, returned to the problem of the power of Congress to use the Commerce Clause for the attainment of noncommercial, ulterior ends. The Mann

---

[84] United States v. Johnson, 221 U.S. 488, 496, 498, 499 (1911).

[85] Act of Aug. 23, 1912, 37 Stat. 416; for the President's Message of June 21, 1911, see 47 *Cong. Rec.* 2379, 62nd Cong., 1st Sess. (1911). And see J. Wilson to Taft, June 14, 1911, Taft Papers.

Act,[86] or the White-Slave Traffic Act, as it called itself in its Section 8, which became law in June 1910, and passed the test of constitutionality three years later in the *Hoke* case, punished the transportation in interstate or foreign commerce of "any woman or girl for the purpose of prostitution or debauchery, or for any other immoral purpose. . . ."

The reforming impulse to which this statute answered, expressed in a large periodical literature, was a compound of late Victorian moralism, of general humanitarian revulsion at slum conditions and low wages, of feminism, and of the penchant of the New Nationalism for federal intervention to cure social ills. But there were also, in the agitation that led up to passage of the Mann Act, very distinct strains of anti-urbanism, of xenophobia and opposition to continued large-scale immigration, and even of anti-Semitism.

A series of articles in *The Forum* urged that it was "common girlhood whose moral and physical being is at stake," and concluded that today, "the World Crusade against the sex-slavery of woman . . . has become a mighty army. . . ."[87] The *Socialist New York Call* thought that an investigation of prostitution would reveal "the real nature of the wage system," and *The Literary Digest* added that the "wages of sin and the sin of wages are being connected as cause and effect just now. . . ."[88] *Current Opinion* asked, "Are Low Wages Responsible for Women's Immorality?" and answered with a qualified yes.[89] But free-floating anti-urbanism showed up in the subtitle of an article by Jane Addams in the *Ladies Home Journal*: "The Black Beast of the City."[90] And there was not a little talk about prostitution being run by foreigners.[91] *McClure's Magazine* announced in July 1910 that there were two procuring organizations of importance, "one French, the other Jewish."[92] It had earlier described a Jewish district in New York, the "leading center

---

[86] 36 Stat. 825.

[87] *The Forum*, 50:182–94, Aug. 13, 1913; see also *The Forum*, 49:276, 587, March 1913; 49:406, April 1913; and see *The Survey*, 26:699, Aug. 12, 1911; 28:593, July 27, 1912; 26:337, May 27, 1911; 26:215, May 6, 1911; 26:99, Apr. 15, 1911; 24:858, Sept. 17, 1910; 24:714, Aug. 20, 1910; 23:372, Dec. 18, 1909; and 33:81, Oct. 24, 1914 ("Anti-Vice Program of a Woman's Club"); *The Outlook*, 103:298, Feb. 8, 1913; 101:103, May 18, 1912; 101:245, June 1, 1912; *Colliers*, 50:11, Mar. 2, 1913 ("The Case of Fanny—From the Field Notes of a Settlement Worker," by Harvey J.

O'Higgins); *Harper's Weekly*, 57:4, July 4, 1913; *The Nation*, 94:76, Jan. 12, 1914. But *cf.* B. Whitlock, "The White Slave," *The Forum*, 51:193, February 1914. And see E. H. Levi, *An Introduction to Legal Reasoning* (Phoenix ed., 1962), 33–40.

[88] *The Literary Digest*, 46:621, 623, Mar. 22, 1913.

[89] *Current Opinion*, 54:402, May 1913.

[90] *Ladies' Home Journal*, 30:25, November 1913.

[91] *Current Opinion*, 54:5, January 1913.

[92] *McClure's Magazine*, 35:346, July 1910.

of the White Slave Trade of the world of Tammany Hall," where Jewish immigrant girls were led to their doom in places "plastered across their front with the weird Oriental hieroglyphics of Yiddish posters."[93] And *Current Literature* declared in December 1909: "Of late years, with our large accessions from Austrian, Russian, and Hungarian Jews, the chief source of supply in New York has been from that race, and the men who have organized the vice into a systematic business, taking it almost entirely out of the weaker hands of the 'madames,' are also of the Jewish race."[94]

To the accompaniment of sounds very much like these, the Progressive Era would end a decade later, trailing off through a Red Scare, through Prohibition, and the racially restrictive Immigration Act of 1924. Such measures did not altogether represent discontinuity with the Progressive Era, and certainly not with that expression of it which was the Mann Act. Nevertheless, as the response to the Court's decision in the *Hoke* case amply demonstrated, the statute was also in other and more commendable respects a representative Progressive reform.

Effie Hoke and Basile Economides were convicted of having, in violation of the Mann Act, induced one Annette Baden, alias Annette Hays, "a woman," to go from New Orleans to Beaumont, Texas, for the purpose of engaging in prostitution in the latter place. The constitutionality of the Mann Act was attacked on the ground that by forbidding citizens to move in interstate commerce, it deprived them of their privileges and immunities, that it violated the Ninth and Tenth amendments, that it invaded the reserved power of the states to punish for crime, and that it exceeded the power of Congress under the Commerce Clause. This last point, said McKenna, was the decisive one, for if the statute was authorized by the Commerce Clause, all other objections to it fell. The power to regulate commerce was a power to regulate transportation of people as well as of things. Congress, it was said, however —here was the argument about ulterior ends—was regulating not transportation as such, but only transportation undertaken out of certain motives and intentions, and this Congress lacked the power to do.

McKenna's answer to this contention embodied the same ambivalence as the Court's opinion sustaining the Pure Food and Drug Act. The argument, he said, confounded "things important to be distinguished. It urges a right exercised in morality to sustain a right to be exercised in immorality." (Would Congress, then, have power to prohibit transportation entered into from motives and intentions that

---

[93] *McClure's Magazine*, 34:45, 55, November 1909.

[94] *Current Literature*, 47:594, December 1909.

the Court deemed moral rather than immoral?) Taking broader ground, McKenna said also that while it was for the states to exercise primary control over morals, they were able to do so only within their own borders. Beyond the borders of each state was "a domain which the States cannot reach and over which Congress alone has power; and if such power be exerted to control what the States cannot it is an argument for—not against—its legality. Its exertion does not encroach upon the jurisdiction of the States."

But then the ambivalence returned. If Congress could forbid the facilities of interstate commerce to "the demoralization" of lotteries, "the debasement" of obscene literature, "the contagion" of diseased cattle or persons, "the impurity" of foods and drugs, it could close them also to "the systematic . . . enslavement in prostitution and debauchery of women, and, more insistently, of girls." And: "Right purpose and fair trading need no restrictive regulation, but let them be transgressed and penalties and prohibitions must be applied." Of this proposition the Pure Food and Drug Act was an apt illustration. McKenna referred to his remark in the *Hipolite Egg* case that adulterated articles were "outlaws of commerce." Women, to be sure, were "not articles of merchandise," but that did not affect the analogy. "It is misleading to say that men and women have rights."[95] If they used interstate commerce "as a facility of their wrongs, it may be forbidden to them to the extent of the act of June 25, 1910, and we need go no farther in the present case."[96]

The public and in large measure the profession read McKenna's opinion more broadly and categorically than it was written, or than, before very long, everyone was to find out it was intended. The headlines referred to it as the most progressive opinion ever, as an endorsement of the New Nationalism, and as a promise that Congress could exclude from interstate commerce goods manufactured with the aid of child labor. The Court, it seemed, had ensured that there would thenceforth no longer be any twilight zone between state and federal authority, and had construed the Constitution as a grant of national power adequate

---

[95] Holmes was much amused by this sentence, thinking that it was "delightfully distorted by taking it alone," and remarked that he had told McKenna that he, Holmes, would "make it the text of a destructive sociological discourse." Holmes to Felix Frankfurter, Dec. 19, 1915, Holmes Papers, Harvard Law School Library.

[96] Hoke v. United States, 227 U.S. 308, 321, 322, 323 (1913). See also

these companion cases: Athanasaw v. United States, 227 U.S. 326 (1913); Bennett v. United States, 227 U.S. 333 (1913); Harris v. United States, 227 U.S. 340 (1913). And see Johnson v. Hoy, 227 U.S. 245 (1913), in which decision was aborted for procedural reasons. The *Hoke* decision was reaffirmed the following year in Wilson v. United States, 232 U.S. 563 (1914).

to developing national needs.[97] "In rendering this decision," said *The Outlook*,[98] "the Supreme Court has done much to justify those who believe that, if its present tendency could characterize all our American courts, popular discontent, if not impatience, with the attitude of judges towards the problems of modern life would be greatly allayed."[99]

Those who harbored some misgivings read the opinion no less broadly than those whose hopes it seemed to fulfill. The *Central Law Journal* thought that what lay "in the womb of these *White Slave Act* cases so far as the extension of federal power over states" was concerned was that "Congress . . . can assert whatever moral view it sees fit and give it vigor in commerce legislation." Moreover, why was Congress "confined to moral views" and why could it not "reach out and promote everything it wishes under a general welfare policy?" So understood, the decision in *Hoke* was not altogether welcome. It was gratifying, to be sure, that the White-Slave Act had proved enforceable, but the declaration of "a principle, which in its potency may be destructive of much that ought to remain beyond Congressional power," was to be regretted.[100]

Holmes, McKenna, and The Pipe Line Cases

Hoke v. *United States* was not as unstinting in its enlargement of federal power as was contemporaneously supposed. But the most stinting, the least generous, endorsement of a Congressional regulation of commerce came a year and a half later, at the very end of the four-year period under discussion, in *The Pipe Line Cases*. This was an 8–1 decision. But for compromises accepted by its author, Holmes, however, it might not have gained a majority at all. The process of negotiation within the Court that finally produced the result in *The Pipe Line Cases* is the most convincing demonstration that the belief, held by many observers in these years, that the Court had turned a corner was much too sanguine. The results the Court was reaching were "progressive," to be sure, and promised much, but its opinions delivered less. Unwilling to commit itself, the Court was drifting. And it did not abandon its options

---

[97] See, e.g., *New York Tribune*, Feb. 25, 1913, p. 6, col. 4; *Chicago Tribune*, Feb. 25, 1913, p. 7, col. 4; *Indianapolis Star*, Feb. 26, 1913, p. 4, col. 1, p. 8, col. 1.

[98] *The Outlook's* contributing editor, Theodore Roosevelt, had a couple of months earlier indirectly expressed his support of the Mann Act by commending a law passed by the British Parliament, which dealt "in drastic fashion with the 'white slave' traffic." Contributing editor Roosevelt added: "One of the best features of the bill, in my judgment, is that providing for the flogging of male offenders." *The Outlook*, 103:116, Jan. 18, 1913.

[99] *The Outlook*, 103:569, 570–71, Mar. 15, 1913.

[100] *Cen. L. J.*, 76:261, 262, 1913.

to drift in the opposite direction as well. It was prepared to forgive a little, but not to forget.

The Pipe Line Cases dealt with yet another provision of the Hepburn Act of 1906, and yet another aspect of the furor over the Standard Oil trust. Standard Oil controlled most if not all the pipelines from the oil fields east of California to the Atlantic Coast, and it refused to carry any oil that had not first been sold to it. And so the Hepburn Act subjected oil pipelines to regulation by the Interstate Commerce Commission, exactly as if they had been common carriers by railroad. The commission ordered the filing of rates, the order was opposed, and the Commerce Court declared the relevant provision of the Hepburn Act unconstitutional. Holmes' opinion reversed, holding the Act constitutional, and applicable to all the pipelines involved but one.

That the transportation in question was commerce, said Holmes, was clear, since the conception of commerce "cannot be made wholly dependent upon technical questions of title, and the fact that the oils transported belonged to the owner of the pipeline is not conclusive against the transportation being such commerce." Then Holmes proceeded as follows:

> The control of Congress over commerce among the States cannot be made a means of exercising powers not entrusted to it by the Constitution, but it may require those who are common carriers in substance to become so in form. . . . [T]hose lines that we are considering are common carriers now in everything but form. They carry everybody's oil to a market, although they compel outsiders to sell it before taking it into their pipes. The answer to their objection [that they were not common carriers, but simply owners of oil doing as they wished with the oil they owned, and now being subjected by Congress to a taking] is not that they may give up the business, but that, as applied to them, the statute practically means no more than they must give up requiring a sale to themselves before carrying the oil that they now receive. The whole case is that the appellees if they carry must do it in a way that they do not like. There is no taking and it does not become necessary to consider how far Congress could subject them to pecuniary loss without compensation in order to accomplish the end in view. *Hoke v. United States*, 227 U.S. 38, 323. *Lottery Case*, 188 U.S. 321, 357. . . .

There remains to be considered only the Uncle Sam Oil Company. This company has a refinery in Kansas and oil wells in Oklahoma, with a pipeline connecting the two which it has used for the sole purpose of conducting oil from its own wells to its own refinery. It would be a perversion of language, considering the sense in which it is used in the statute, to say that a man was engaged in the transportation of water whenever he pumped a pail of water from his well to his house. So as to oil. When, as in this case, a company is simply drawing oil from its own wells across a state line to its own refinery for its own use, and that is all, we do not regard it as falling within the description of the act, the transportation being merely an incident to use at the end.[101]

In the margin on his own copy of this opinion, next to the passage in the first paragraph quoted above which says that the pipelines were common carriers in everything but form, and that Congress merely recognized that fact, Holmes noted in longhand: "I regard this as inadequate reasoning, but was compelled to strike out what I thought the real argument, and assented to prevent the case going over the Term. See first draft, post. Friday just before adjournment I had to rewrite in order to insert this notion of the majority. . . ." To his former colleague Moody, Holmes gave a further explanation on September 30, 1914. "As you say you read the reports," Holmes wrote, "vanity makes me add a few words" concerning the opinion in The Pipe Line Cases, "which causes me some discomfort as it stands." The opinion had been assigned to Holmes "vice others about a week before the end [of the term]. I shoved an opinion into the printer's hands and distributed it but heard only from two." Monday, June 22, 1914, was the last day of the term, but Thursday, Friday, Saturday, when the last Conference was held, and as late even as "Monday morning on the bench," the requests for omissions and revisions came in. "I replied to everyone that I would strike out anything between title and conclusion that would enable me to get the case off per contract. . . . I think the reasons for desiring the omissions were extra-legal—and the result is that I put my name to something that does not satisfy or represent my views. . . . I never was so disturbed but I thought it my duty to let it go as the majority was content and the case had hung along in other hands for months."

Holmes' first draft opened with the blunt statement that the pipelines had never held themselves out as common carriers, and that the statute was intended nevertheless to bring them into the category of common carriers. There followed the passage that now comes at the end of the opinion, concerning the Uncle Sam Company. But in this first draft, the exemption of the company is not put solely in terms of statutory construction. Rather Holmes says that it would be "laying down a very strong proposition" to hold in this situation that such a company as Uncle Sam was engaged in commerce when transporting its own oil. For this reason the Act should not be construed to cover the Uncle Sam Company.

Then came a paragraph, longer and more categorical than the equivalent passage in the published opinion, saying that the fact that

---

[101] The Pipe Line Cases, 234 U.S. 548, 560–62 (1914).

the pipelines gained title to the oil they transported did not affect the nature of the entire transaction as commerce. Next came an even stronger paragraph, starting, as does the first one from the actual opinion quoted above, with the concession that it might be assumed that the control of Congress over commerce could not be made a means of exercising powers not entrusted to it by the Constitution, but continuing, not with a suggestion that Congress had merely recognized as common carriers pipelines that already were such, but with the proposition that "it is too late now to deny that such control [by Congress over commerce] may be used to prevent the commerce from becoming the instrument of a monopoly that Congress deems opposed to the common weal. No one doubts, we suppose, that the amendment was passed because it was believed that the pipelines have greatly helped the Standard Oil Company towards monopolizing the business in which it was engaged. At all events to prevent or discourage monopoly was a possible reason for the statute, and this being so it is not open to doubt that the regulation so far as it contemplates future pipelines and prescribes the conditions upon which they can be established is constitutional and valid. The only ground of attack may be that it applies to private lines already engaged in transportation. . . ."

As to these existing lines, the objection was that their owners' property was being diverted to other uses than those they desired. The reply that they might, after all, give up the business did not meet the gravamen of this objection. "For that would mean the sacrifice of an expensive plant. But even a very considerable destruction of pecuniary value without compensation may be justified in cases which the phrase police power was invented to meet, *Mugler* v. *Kansas*, 123 U.S. 624, *Noble State Bank* v. *Haskell*, 219 U.S. 104, 110, and it already is established that the same is more or less true of the power to regulate commerce." Congress, Holmes went on, could make carriers answerable to shippers for losses caused by connecting carriers, citing *Atlantic Coast Line Railroad* v. *Riverside Mills*. "The power in the last case flows from the control of Congress over commerce not from the character of railroad ownership as distinguished from that of property in private use. . . . We are of opinion that just as the States may exercise what is called the police power to the serious loss of individuals without compensation, Congress can exercise its power over commerce to prevent what it regards as an abuse of such commerce, in like manner, and that the statute before us is an example of constitutional exercise of that power."

The only entirely affirmative return that Holmes got to this first draft was from Day. (If there was a second, as Holmes implied to Moody, he did not keep it.) The Chief Justice said he was much worried, and as then advised would prefer to have the cases go over to the next term. "Please do not think me overvacillating," he added. Van Devanter said:

> I should think it would require very plain words to show a purpose to make a common or public carrier out of one who never held himself out as such and desired to use his pipeline for his own purposes only. Besides, if the Act goes so far and includes existing lines I am inclined to believe it exceeds the powers of Congress. It imposes a burden and restricts the rights of the owner in a way and to an extent as to make it a taking. Suppose a buyer of oil transports it with his own teams and tank wagons—there being no pipeline—can the legislature say he must carry for others who have no teams or wagons, when he never has done so and does not wish to now? Grant that he is engaged in interstate commerce, can Congress make that a ground for making him a common carrier? Suppose he wrongfully combines with other buyers to depress the price, does that enable Congress to make him a common carrier? I doubt that it does. Granting that he can be dealt with, I doubt that it can be in this way. You will see that I am in a doubting mood and that I am hardly prepared to agree. My difficulty does not include those who were made common carriers by charter or who held themselves out as such. And I think they could not likely avoid that status when once obtained.

Then Holmes did his first revision, which, as he said in a brief memorandum to the Justices, put the Uncle Sam Company holding solely on the construction of the Act, "striking out suggestions that [the company] was not [in] interstate commerce," and eliminated references to the police power, "inserting suggestions of Justice Hughes." The substitutions for the references to the police power were all in the nature of renewed emphasis on the monopoly position of the pipelines, and on the power of Congress to deal with monopoly. In lieu of the passage citing the *Mugler* and *Noble State Bank* cases, Holmes now said that, although the sacrifice of an expensive plant was required, "when the course of business has established an instrument of commerce among the States tending to create a monopoly in the manner that we have supposed above, Congress may regulate it and in so doing may cause an appreciable pecuniary loss without compensation, under its constitutional powers." (Citing *Hoke* v. *United States*.) A similar substitution was made for the mention of the police power further on in the first draft. This time Van Devanter was mollified, and decided to "come in cheerfully," because Holmes had "done it so well from your point of view that it would be a shame to see it lost." But Van Devanter did wonder whether Holmes had not rewritten the statute: "It says nothing about monopoly and does not make it the test, although it doubtless could do so." Finally, and apparently by oral communication, this ground of

236

decision was also eliminated, and the opinion stripped down to its ultimate form.[102]

Holmes often had occasion to complain that in order to appease his colleagues, he had found it necessary to cut some of his "exuberances" out of an opinion and substitute "some pap that would not hurt an infant's stomach." He should have thought, he wrote once to Felix Frankfurter, that what he had been made to strike out was nothing but "innocuous enfantillages but my prophetic soul divined rightly that the watchers of the Ark would be down on me."[103] Holmes had early found it "a heartbreaking task to give an impression of freedom elegance and variety" in judicial opinions, and it hurt when the product was "emasculated."[104] Most frequently, matters of style were in question, or if of substance, then not essential to the decision of the case. Here, in *The Pipe Line Cases*, it was otherwise. And still, although with his paring Holmes succeeded in balancing a majority on the paring knife's edge, he could not avoid both a concurrence and a dissent.

The concurrence, brief, was by the Chief Justice, who, while agreeing with everything else, could not accept resting the result in the *Uncle Sam Oil Co.* case solely on statutory construction. The company, he thought, was engaged in interstate commerce, and was covered by the Act. But as applied to it, the Act was unconstitutional, because it took the Uncle Sam Company's property without compensation in violation of the Due Process Clause of the Fifth Amendment. Only by resorting to the power of eminent domain could Congress convert this private business into a public one without its owners' consent. Taking White's concurrence together with Van Devanter's return to Holmes' first draft, it seems clear that the difficulty Holmes encountered with his initial ground of decision in the *Uncle Sam Oil Co.* case was not that other Justices insisted on a more expansive definition of the Commerce power, but that they wished to leave no room for the inference that if the Uncle Sam Company were otherwise properly subject to federal regulation,

---

[102] Holmes Papers. See also Phillips, ed., *Felix Frankfurter Reminisces,* 298–99.

[103] He had a little case, ran another complaint by Holmes to Frankfurter, referring to Western Union Telegraph Co. v. Speight, 254 U.S. 17 (1920) (see *Holmes-Laski Letters,* I, 287, n.3), but "whether it will go or not I don't know. As originally written it had a tiny pair of testicles—but the scruples of my Brethren have caused their removal and it speaks in a very soft voice now—but whether I shall be told to let it be heard remains to be seen. I presume the castration was wise as even Brandeis who passed the original told me he had misgivings." Holmes to Felix Frankfurter, Oct. 24, 1920, Holmes Papers.

[104] *Holmes-Laski Letters,* I, 291, 486; M. DeW. Howe, ed., *Holmes-Pollock Letters* (1946), I, 131; Holmes to F. Frankfurter, Nov. 30, 1919, Holmes Papers.

Congress could turn it into a common carrier at will. Certainly in the context of Holmes' general remarks about the police power, a straight interpretation of the statute as inapplicable to the Uncle Sam Company, with no constitutional overtones of one kind or another, negative or affirmative, must have seemed more innocent of implications than Holmes' original language, although still insufficiently innocent to overcome the Chief Justice's Due Process scruples.

The dissent, by McKenna, went on at great length. This was not a case of regulation of a use to which property had been voluntarily put by its owners. Rather the oil companies were being compelled to put their pipelines to public use. "These considerations are not touched upon in the opinion of the court, and how far they affect the decision can only be conjectured. It may be not at all." What the Court did talk about, principally the circumstances out of which the Hepburn Act arose, was irrelevant. "There is quite a body of opinion which considers the individual ownership of property economically and politically wrong and insists upon a community of all that is profit-bearing. This opinion has its cause, among other causes, in the power—may I say the duress?—of wealth. If it accumulates 51% of political power, may it put its conviction into law and justify the law by the advancement of the public welfare by destroying the monopoly and mastery of individual ownership?" It was an ominous step the Court was now taking, "and projects whose shadows may even now be discerned will plead a justification by the decision in these cases."[105]

There is a vehemence to McKenna's dissent which may be taken as directed personally at Holmes, for it is a not unusual feature of his dissents against Holmes, which occurred with rather remarkable frequency. An odd and in most ways pointless little rivalry existed between the two—at least on McKenna's part, although Holmes, too, was affected by it. It was no feud. Relations were never broken, and were, indeed, not only polite but often cordial. "McKenna was on the train coming up [to New England, in June 1920]," Holmes remarked once, "and very pleasant, as usual."[106] His return to Holmes' opinion in *Federal Baseball Club of Baltimore* v. *National League* was: "I voted the other way but I have resolved on amiability and concession, so submit. I am not sure that I am not convinced."[107] And to Holmes' dissent in *Southern Pacific*

---

[105] The Pipe Line Cases, 234 U.S. at 562, 563, 567, 573, 574–75. The decision in *The Pipe Line Cases* caused no great stir, although its limits, particularly as they were made evident in the *Uncle Sam Oil Co.* case, were duly noted by the interests affected. See *New York Times*, June 23, 1914, p. 4, col. 5; *Wall Street Journal*, June 24, 1914, p. 1, col. 3.

[106] O. W. Holmes to F. Frankfurter, June 22, 1920, Holmes Papers.

[107] Federal Baseball Club of Baltimore v. National League, 259 U.S. 200 (1922), Holmes Papers.

Co. v. *Jensen*, in which he did not join, he returned with great charm and spirit, taking off only just a little bit on Holmes' now famous phrase about the law not being a brooding omnipresence in the sky: "Snappy and good but I have a brooding conviction the other way. Or to put it differently my brooding has hatched an opposite conclusion. But I like this. It gratifies my Irish heart to see heads hit even if one of them is my own."[108]

If McKenna sometimes showed a bit of strain, Holmes remained, with him as he had with Harlan, apparently unruffled and above it all. Thus in the spring of 1922, soon after Taft's accession and not long before McKenna retired, at a time when McKenna was generally rather sensitive and irritable, there was an incident in conference. McKenna lost his temper, but Holmes kept his, and even managed afterwards to be sympathetic.[109] And he continued to think of McKenna as "a truly kind soul," who left, Holmes said after McKenna retired, "affectionate memories behind him."[110] But something there was between them. They were almost the same age, although McKenna was senior in service. Holmes made references—a tad patronizing—to the kindliness of McKenna's soul. But he did not hold McKenna in high regard. When Felix Frankfurter, some time before the accession of Brandeis in 1916, told Holmes that McKenna showed some, even if not consistent, insight into the nature of problems arising under the Due Process Clause, Holmes was "utterly astounded by my estimate of McKenna." He remained essentially unconvinced, despite later, intermittent admissions that Frankfurter had opened his eyes to qualities in McKenna to which he had been blind. McKenna was "unpredictable." He had intimations "that perhaps come out oftener in his talk than in his opinions. . . ."[111] This, at most, was what Holmes would concede.[112]

McKenna for his part seemed in a number of his opinions to aspire

---

[108] Southern Pacific Co. v. Jensen, 244 U.S. 205 (1917), Holmes Papers.

[109] O. W. Holmes to W. H. Taft, Apr. 2, 1922; W. H. Taft to H. Taft, Apr. 17, 1922; W. H. Taft to H. Taft, Nov. 2, 1923, Taft Papers.

[110] *Holmes-Laski Letters,* II, 896; O. W. Holmes to F. Frankfurter, Jan. 6, 1925, Holmes Papers.

[111] F. Frankfurter to A. M. Bickel, Jan. 6, 1956. O. W. Holmes to F. Frankfurter, Apr. 30, 1921, Holmes Papers.

[112] "McKenna shrieked over the downfall of the Constitution," Holmes remarked about the dissent in Block v. Hirsch, 256 U.S. 135 (1921), which he rather resented. "Yet a few days later he said something to me about everything being a question of circumstances that showed that he understood the business as well as anyone. But he not infrequently recurs to the tyro's question: Where are you going to draw the line?—as if all life were not the marking of grades between black and white." *Holmes-Laski Letters,* I, 331. "But a Catholic perhaps does not look favorably upon so Darwinian a view." Holmes to Felix Frankfurter, Apr. 20, 1911, Holmes Papers.

to the epigrammatic dash and the economy that distinguished Holmes' writings. The attempt seldom came off, and the failure could sometimes be ludicrous.[113] McKenna had his virtues, he had his insights, as Frankfurter thought, although he surely was erratic, and he even had qualities as a writer, but he was not equal to stylistic duels with Holmes. Perhaps in frustration, McKenna turned into one of the most severe censors who, as Holmes complained, pruned his exuberances.[114] And he dissented.

In the more than fourteen years from the opening of the October Term 1910 to his retirement in January 1925, McKenna dissented or concurred separately 117 times. One-third, lacking only a fraction, of these dissents and separate concurrences—38 in number[115]—were registered against opinions of Holmes, which is a high proportion as against the 79 remaining ones distributed among McKenna's other colleagues. (In a period of twelve years from the October Term 1910 on, Day, the other most frequent pruner of Holmesian *jeux d'esprit*, dissented or concurred specially a total of 63 times, and against Holmes 18—well under a third.) And yet there is most assuredly no note of doctrinal or ideological unity running through McKenna's anti-Holmes dissents and concurrences. What they do have in common is a certain sharpness.

At least one, in *Block* v. *Hirsh*, decided in 1921 and upholding the constitutionality of the World War I emergency rent control statute in the District of Columbia, annoyed Holmes considerably. "I was content with my statement and made no changes after receiving the dissent, although it criticized my opinion, which I think bad form," Holmes said. It certainly, and most unusually, did criticize the opinion, quoting Holmes, refuting him, debating him, looking up, in despair, to the Heavens and to the text of the Constitution, disclaiming any need to "beat about" with Holmes "in generalities or grope in their indetermination in subtle search for a test. . . ."[116] Other dissents are equally acid, sometimes attempting irony, often charging Holmes with indulgence in "refined dialectics,"[117] and with other excesses.[118]

---

[113] See, e.g., United States v. Hammers, 221 U.S. 220 (1911); LeRoy Fibre Co. v. Chicago, Milwaukee & St. Paul R.R., 232 U.S. 340 (1914).

[114] *Holmes-Pollock Letters,* II, 175.

[115] Not including such cases as Hyde v. United States, 225 U.S. 347 (1912), and Brown v. Elliott, 225 U.S. 392 (1912), in which, as we know from Holmes, the Chief Justice's vacillation turned McKenna's dissents into majority opinions. See *Holmes-*

Pollock Letters, I, 193–94.

[116] Block v. Hirsch, 256 U.S. 135, 168 (1921); *Holmes-Laski Letters,* 331.

[117] Marcus Brown Co. v. Feldman, 256 U.S. 170 (1921).

[118] See, e.g., The Western Maid, 257 U.S. 419 (1922); Levinson v. United States, 258 U.S. 198 (1922); Grogan v. Walker & Sons, 259 U.S. 80 (1922); Wheeler v. New York, 233 U.S. 434 (1914).

Holmes did not take it all in silence. It was to McKenna that the following famous passage—impersonal, no doubt, but surely wounding—was directed: "I do not think we need trouble ourselves with the thought that my view depends upon differences of degree. The whole law does so as soon as it is civilized. Negligence is all degree—that of the defendant here degree of the nicest sort; and between the variations according to distance that I suppose to exist and the simple universality of the rules in the Twelve Tables or the Leges Barbarorum, there lies the culture of two thousand years."[119]

Holmes responded also to another aspect of his relationship with McKenna. It was always a point of pride with Holmes to get his opinions out in record time. "Holmes can't bear not to have a case done the day it's given to him," said Brandeis. McKenna—Taft thought, later, because he was "jealous"—tried to keep pace, and he and Holmes, Brandeis reported, "run a race of diligence in finishing an opinion assigned to either."[120] There is no question but what they did run a race, virtually all the years they sat together, and the volumes of the *Reports*, like the record of a photo finish, enable us to witness it.

At the opening of the October Term 1912, for example, the Court's first opinion was handed down by Holmes on October 28, 1912, in a case argued just thirteen days before.[121] It was the only decision that day. The next opinion day was November 11, and again Holmes alone was ready. He had two opinions in cases argued late in October.[122] A week later, McKenna weighed in with a substantial opinion, in a case argued in mid-October.[123] The other opinion that day was again by Holmes, in a case argued less than two weeks before.[124] And so it went, well into December, Holmes and McKenna vying with each other in the decision of current cases, while very few of their colleagues were ready with any recently argued ones. Thus on the first really heavy opinion day of the term, December 12, 1912, Holmes and McKenna, with seven fresh cases between them, and relatively important ones at that, far

---

[119] LeRoy Fibre Co. v. Chicago, Milwaukee & St. Paul R.R., 232 U.S. 340, 354 (1914).

[120] *Brandeis-Frankfurter Conversations*, Nov. 30, 1932, Harvard Law School Library; W. H. Taft to H. Taft, Apr. 17, 1922, Taft Papers; *Holmes-Laski Letters*, II, 684, 755; *Holmes-Pollock Letters*, I, 154.

[121] Breese v. United States, 226 U.S. 1 (1912).

[122] Harty v. Victoria, 226 U.S. 12 (1912) (argued Oct. 30, 1912); and United States v. Baltimore & Ohio Southwestern R.R., 226 U.S. 14 (1912) (argued Oct. 25, 28, 1912).

[123] Standard Sanitary Manufacturing Co. v. United States, 226 U.S. 20 (1912) (argued Oct. 15–17, 1912).

[124] Smith v. Hitchcock, 226 U.S. 53 (1912) (argued Nov. 5, 6, 1912).

outran the other Justices.[125] The story was much the same in the first few months of the October Term 1913.

The Corporation Tax Act of 1909

The great cases we have so far considered in this chapter dealt with reforms of continuing—as well as, in their day, immediate—functional importance. Doctrinally, these cases concerned the power of Congress to control commerce, and the channels and instrumentalities of commerce. Despite their equivocations, the dominant fact about them is, of course, that they all, without a break, upheld federal regulatory power. In this respect, *Flint* v. *Stone Tracy Co.*, the one remaining major case of these years that passed on federal legislation of the Progressive Era, was no exception, although it affirmed, not control over commerce, but a power to tax incomes. In *Pollock* v. *Farmers' Loan & Trust Co.*,[126] decided in 1895, the Court had denied any such power to Congress. Now the Court legitimated it, but in a decision that was entirely without doctrinal significance, and no longer of any fundamental importance.

We have seen the Court, in the *Second Employers' Liability Cases*, give its belated blessing to a dated reform—dated, but still with us. In *Flint* v. *Stone Tracy Co.*, the Court upheld a taxing statute, the Corporation Tax Act of 1909, which was obsolete on the day of its enactment. For the Sixteenth Amendment was submitted by the same Congress that passed the Act of 1909, and in 1911, when *Stone Tracy* was decided, the Amendment was winding its way through the state legislature to early ratification.

Precisely for this reason, however, *Stone Tracy* was, in a sense, a most difficult case in which to reach a result favorable to Congressional legislation. The Court was required to find a way around *Pollock* v. *Farmers' Loan & Trust Co.* at a time when it must have seemed to many of the Justices sheer gratuity to take the direct and simple course of overruling the case, since the Sixteenth Amendment was about to do that work in a fashion that made it unnecessary for the Court to admit that it had been wrong. Not only that, but Congress, after a pointed debate about its proper relationship with the Court, had decided to obey the *Pollock* decision, at least formally, not to challenge it frontally, and to go to the trouble, rather, of amending the Constitution. A great body of

---

[125] Selover, Bates & Co. v. Walsh, 226 U.S. 112 (1912) (submitted Oct. 29, 1912); Taylor v. Columbia University, 226 U.S. 126 (1912) (argued Nov. 6, 1912); Eubank v. Richmond, 226 U.S. 137 (1912) (argued Nov. 12, 13, 1912); Burnet v. Desmornes, 226 U.S. 145 (1912) (submitted Oct. 30, 1912); Jones v. Springer, 226 U.S. 148 (1912) (argued Oct. 30, 1912); Central Lumber Co. v. South Dakota, 226 U.S. 157 (1912) (argued Nov. 13, 14, 1912); Southwestern Brewery v. Schmidt, 226 U.S. 162 (1912) (argued Nov. 14, 15, 1912).

[126] 157 U.S. 429 (1895).

Congressional opinion wanted to pass a straight income tax instead of the Corporation Tax Act, and thus force the Court to face up squarely to its *Pollock* decision. President Taft persuaded Congress to compromise, while at the same time submitting the Sixteenth Amendment.[127] It would have been a poor reward for this, on the whole, respectful Congressional behavior, and a slight inducement to its repetition, if the Court had rendered the Amendment redundant just as it was being ratified. And so the Court's real choice lay between drawing thin and somewhat transparent distinctions, on the one hand, and reaffirming a highly unpopular decision, on the other, at some immediate, even if at no long-range, cost to the federal revenue.[128]

The Corporation Tax Act of 1909,[129] a section of the Payne-Aldrich tariff of that year, imposed what it defined as "a special excise tax with respect to the carrying on or doing business" by corporations, joint stock companies, or associations. The rate was 1 percent of the net income in excess of $5,000 from all sources, excluding dividends received from other corporations themselves subject to the tax. Nonprofit organizations of various sorts were exempted. In a provision that must be understood, in context of the great antitrust debate discussed in the previous chapter, as expressing the faith that corporations, however big, might be kept good if the light of publicity were but allowed to play on them, the Act required returns reporting the total paid-up capital stock outstanding, the amount of bonded debt, gross income, total expenses, losses, amounts allowed for depreciation, in the case of insurance companies, payments other than dividends on insurance contracts, interest on debts and, for banks, on deposits, taxes, and finally net income. The returns were to "constitute public records and be open to inspection as such," but in 1910, an amendment modified this language so as to allow access to the returns for inspection only "upon the order of the President under rules and regulations to be prescribed by the Secretary of the Treasury and approved by the President."

The statute was immediately attacked, and by March 1910, fifteen cases were being argued in the Supreme Court by a galaxy of eminent counsel, including John G. Johnson, Joseph B. Foraker,[130] Frederic R.

---

[127] See *supra*, pp. 22–24.

[128] See S. Ratner, *American Taxation* (1942), 271–92; R. G. Blakey and G. C. Blakey, *The Federal Income Tax* (1940), 23–52. On the Corporation Tax Act of 1909, *see generally* T. G. Frost, *A Treatise on the Federal Corporation Tax Law* (1911).

[129] 36 Stat. 112, Sect. 38 of the Tariff Act of Aug. 5, 1909.

[130] Joseph Benson Foraker of Ohio (1846–1917) was for some time the reigning Republican power in his state, serving as governor, and then as United States Senator, from 1897 to 1909. His autobiography, *Notes of a Busy Life,* was published in two volumes in 1916.

Coudert,[131] and William D. Guthrie,[132] joined by Victor Morawetz.[133] The tax in these cases and in many others had been paid under protest, and if the Supreme Court had held the Act unconstitutional, over $27,650,000 would have had to be refunded by the United States. And in that event, it was thought, a bond issue might be necessary to meet the expenses of construction at the Panama Canal.[134]

There was no decision after the first argument, the Court, under Chief Justice Fuller, being quite possibly divided. "I see," Harlan had written to Day in June 1909, "that it is seriously proposed to amend the present tariff bill by adding a tax on the gross receipts of all corporations, except, I take it charitable and religious corporations. It ought to be. Why will not such a provision raise the same question as was involved in the income tax law?"[135] Harlan, sympathetic to the objectives of the statute, saw his way clear ultimately, in the last year of his life, to go along with distinguishing the question raised by "such a provision" from that in *Pollock* v. *Farmers' Loan & Trust Co.* But did others, when the case was first argued?

There were, however, different factors in play also, having no relation to the merits,[136] the same factors that caused reargument of the *Standard Oil* and *Tobacco* cases. Moody was ill and absent, and late in March 1910, Brewer died. So, on May 31, 1910, *Flint* v. *Stone Tracy Co.* was set down for reargument, just as *Standard Oil* and *Tobacco* had been, a month earlier. When the Court reconvened in the fall, it was still shorthanded, and awaiting Taft's appointments. Reargument then took place in January 1911, right after the reargument of the *Standard Oil* and *Tobacco* cases.[137]

At the first argument, the government was represented by Solicitor General Bowers, and at the second, by his successor, Frederick W. Lehmann, who was promptly congratulated by President Taft—such was the attention this lawyer-President devoted to the progress of great

---

[131] Frederic René Coudert (1871–1955), head of the firm of Coudert Brothers, was perhaps the leading international lawyer at the New York Bar. His father once declined a seat on the Supreme Court, tendered by President Cleveland.

[132] William Dameron Guthrie of New York (1859–1935), unquestionably one of the leaders of the American Bar, appeared frequently in great cases in the Supreme Court. He also wrote and lectured widely on constitutional law. In 1907–08, he delivered the Storrs Lectures at Yale,

and from 1909 to 1922, he was Ruggles Professor of Constitutional Law at Columbia.

[133] Victor Morawetz (1859–1938) was one of the most scholarly of the prominent New York lawyers. He wrote treatises on corporations, banking and currency, and contracts.

[134] *Case & Com.,* 18:29, 30, 1911.

[135] J. M. Harlan to W. R. Day, June 13, 1909, Day Papers.

[136] See *New York Times,* Mar. 14, 1911, p. 3, col. 1.

[137] See *supra,* p. 96.

cases. Lurton, "who is not given to superlatives," had told him, wrote the President, that the whole Court was enthusiastic in praise of Lehmann, and agreed that they had not heard such an argument in many a day.[138] Lehmann replied that he had worked hard on the case, and had had his heart in it, because from the beginning, the law had appealed to him not simply as a revenue measure, nor even chiefly as such, "but more 'as the opening door to regulation which will broaden with the years.' " He had supported the law in an address as president of the American Bar Association in 1909.[139]

The Court was unanimous in *Flint* v. *Stone Tracy Co.* In a very elaborate opinion, by Day, it took up, one by one, the contentions of counsel, which as Solicitor General Bowers said at the first argument, included "every possible objection that could be made to any form of taxation under the Constitution." The Act did not impose a direct tax on property, Day held, or on individuals, but rather an excise on the privilege of doing business in corporate form. Hence the tax did not need to be apportioned—thus lightly, even if at length, was *Pollock* v. *Farmers' Loan & Trust Co.* avoided.

The tax was measured by income from property, but the measure of a valid tax was entirely within the discretion of Congress. For the same reason it did not matter that some of the income by which the tax was measured was derived, in some cases, from municipal bonds and other tax-free securities. This argument, Day said, like the main one proceeding from the *Pollock* case, confused "the measure of the tax upon the privilege, with direct taxation of the estate or thing taxed. In the *Pollock Case* . . . the tax was held unconstitutional, because it was in effect a direct tax on the property solely because of its ownership." Next it was argued that the tax fell on the exercise by the states of their power to grant corporate franchises, and hence was void as an infringement on an exclusive province of the states. Of course, Day replied, the governmental operations of the states were immune to federal taxation, but they remained so under this Act, and such a corporation as the New York Interborough Rapid Transit Company, one of the parties, could be freely taxed because it did not perform a governmental function.[140] The argument was reduced, therefore, to a claim that subjects on which the state had exerted its general regulatory police power were exempt from federal taxation. This could not be, and the contrary had often been held.

The Act, it was also maintained, by singling out corporations,

---

[138] W. H. Taft to F. W. Lehmann, marked "Personal," Jan. 22, 1911, Taft Papers.

[139] F. W. Lehmann to W. H. Taft, Jan. 23, 1911, Taft Papers.

[140] *Cf.* South Carolina v. United States, 199 U.S. 437 (1905).

made an arbitrary classification in violation of Due Process. It was of no importance, counsel had argued, that the Fifth Amendment contained no specific equal protection clause. "Congress cannot from such omission claim the right to enact laws which are unjust, unequal, oppressive and arbitrary." Tacitly conceding that the equal protection principle was applicable, Day replied that all taxation was selective, and none the worse for that.[141] But, counsel had further urged, if Congress had power thus selectively to tax corporations, it could in effect abolish them, and nullify the supposed power of the states to create them, for as Marshall had said in *McCulloch* v. *Maryland*, the power to tax was the power to destroy. This argument, Day commented, came at last to this: "That because of possible results, a power lawfully exercised may work disastrously, therefore the courts must interfere to prevent its exercise, because of the consequences feared. No such authority has ever been invested in any court. The remedy for such wrongs, if such in fact exist, is in the ability of the people to choose their own representatives, and not in the exertion of unwarranted powers by courts of justice."

Finally, there was an attack on the provision requiring detailed returns and constituting them public records. "This publicity," counsel had said, "is not required for the purpose of imposing the tax. It can in no way enhance the public revenues. It is arbitrary, visitatorial and disciplinary in its nature. It is not, in any sense, for revenue purposes." And it violated the Fourth Amendment. Day answered first with a dubious, but not altogether direct, suggestion that the Fourth Amendment was irrelevant, being merely some sort of a protection against criminal prosecutions. Coming more to the point, he said it was not to be assumed that the motive of Congress in providing for public inspection of returns was unrelated to revenue needs. Perhaps Congress thought that the possibility of public inspection would tend to assure the fullness and accuracy of returns. For the rest, returns, required as part of the tax schemes of many states, were indispensable to the enforcement of a complex taxing statute, and Congress could not be denied the necessary and proper power to require them.[142]

The decision was received in the press as a "great victory" for the government, and a triumph for Solicitor General Lehmann. And the Court, noted the *New York Times*, had preserved intact the political value of the tax, by upholding the publicity provisions. All in all, the

---

[141] "Aren't you arguing the constitutionality of a protective tariff?" Holmes had asked counsel at the reargument. The reply was, not at all, but Holmes came back with: "It struck me you were getting uncommonly close to it." *Washington Post*, Jan. 19, 1911, p. 4, col. 3.

[142] Flint v. Stone Tracy Co., 220 U.S. 107, 133, 162, 118, 169, 119 (1911).

President was delighted, and Wall Street was apathetic.[143] The periodicals, both general and professional, had been having a great deal of discussion since enactment of the statute about its constitutionality as a whole, and about the wisdom of its publicity provisions, and most of the positions taken before *Flint* v. *Stone Tracy* came down were simply reasserted now that it had been decided.

It was pointed out on many sides that there had been no thought of making corporation tax returns readily accessible to the general public—the cost of any such project would have run to some $50,000— and hence it was really only the government itself that was to be kept informed. This reassurance was necessary, since many people felt it to be quite an unjustifiable imposition on small corporations and partnerships, and very likely harmful in other ways as well, to expose their affairs to general publicity.[144] There were substantial expressions of professional opinion, both before and after the decision, that as applied to income derived from property, the Corporation Tax Act of 1909 was indistinguishable from the tax held invalid in *Pollock* v. *Farmers' Loan & Trust Co.*[145] Of course, this was not the unanimous view,[146] but over forty years later, after much water had run under the bridge of the Sixteenth Amendment, Randolph Paul's opinion of the distinction drawn by Day between *Flint* v. *Stone Tracy Co.* and *Pollock* v. *Farmers' Loan & Trust Co.* was as follows: "Thus did a few words change a tax upon income into a tax on something else measured by income. . . . Evidently the Constitution, in the view of the Supreme Court which included only two of the justices who had sat in 1895—and they dissenters—had never forbidden the thing done by the 1894 act, but only the particular way of doing it selected by the 53d Congress."[147]

The Corporation Tax Act remained in effect until March 1, 1914, when it was superseded by the first statute passed pursuant to the Sixteenth Amendment. During this time, the Act produced a total of

---

[143] *New York Times,* Mar. 14, 1911, p.3, col. 1.

[144] See *The Independent,* 68:428–29, February 1910; *The Outlook,* 94:412–13, February 1910; *ibid.,* 96:794, December 1910; *ibid.,* 97:609, March 1911; *North American Review,* 191:537, 1910; *The Nation,* 92:558–59, March 1911.

[145] See F. Goodnow, "The Constitutionality of the United States Corporation Income Tax," *Colum. L. Rev.,* 9:649, 1909; F. Bird, "Constitutional Aspects of the Federal Tax on the Income of Corporations," *Harv.* *L. Rev.,* 24:31, 1910; C. W. Pierson, *Yale L. J.,* 20:636, 1911; N. Collier, *Cent. L. J.,* 72:255, 1911.

[146] See R. Aigler, "The Constitutionality of the Federal Corporation Tax," *Mich. L. R.,* 8:206, 1910; W. Dorman, "The Federal Corporation Tax Law Constitutional?" *Green Bag,* 22:168, 1910; J. Sheppard, "Is the Federal Corporation Tax an Interference with the Sovereignty of the States?" *Harv. L. R.,* 23:380, 1910; note, *Colum. L. R.,* 11:475, 1911.

[147] R. E. Paul, *Taxation in the United States* (1954), 96.

nearly \$129,000,000 of revenue.[148] But the Supreme Court, having upheld it, proceeded to give it some quite constrained interpretations. It was almost as if the Court was a little astonished and even a little appalled by what it had wrought. In *Eliot* v. *Freeman*, decided at the same time as *Flint* v. *Stone Tracy*, Day, speaking again for a unanimous Court, held that a Massachusetts trust, in which it seems Holmes had been, but was at the time of decision no longer, a stockholder,[149] was neither a corporation nor any other kind of entity to which the Act was applicable. And in another companion case to *Stone Tracy*, *Zonne* v. *Minneapolis Syndicate*, a corporation which had leased all its property to certain trustees for a long term, and was now engaged only in receiving annual rentals, having disabled itself by amendment to its articles from undertaking any other activity, was held, also by Day, not taxable because not "doing business" within the terms of the Act.[150]

But the most damaging exercise in construction was *McCoach* v. *Minehill Railway Co.*, decided two years later.[151]

Minehill was a railroad company which in 1896 leased its road, lock, stock, and barrel, to another for a long term, and was now receiving an annual rental. But Minehill had never abandoned its full powers under its charter, even though it was not currently using them, and it maintained an office, had a board of directors, officers and employees, and its stock was bought and sold on the market. In addition to its railroad property, it also had other investments, which returned some \$24,000 annually. Pitney, for the Court, held that it was not doing

---

[148] R. G. Blakey and G. C. Blakey, *The Federal Income Tax* (1940), 58–59; S. Ratner, *American Taxation* (1942), 297, 335–36.

[149] See *Washington Post,* Mar. 14, 1911, p. 1. col. 5.

[150] Eliot v. Freeman, 220 U.S. 178 (1911); Zonne v. Minneapolis Syndicate, 220 U.S. 187 (1911). See also United States v. Whitridge, 231 U.S. 144 (1913). For a more hospitable construction, see Stratton's Independence v. Howbert, 231 U.S. 399 (1913); Von Baumbach v. Sargent Land Co., 242 U.S. 503 (1917); United States v. Biwabik Mining Co., 247 U.S. 116 (1918); Goldfield Consolidated Mines Co. v. Scott, 247 U.S. 126 (1918); Doyle v. Mitchell Bros. Co., 247 U.S. 179 (1918); Hays v. Gauley Mt. Coal Co., 247 U.S. 189 (1918); United States v. Cleveland, C., C. & St. Louis Ry. Co., 247 U.S. 195 (1918); National Bank of Commerce v. Allen, 223 Fed. 472 (8th Cir. 1915), *cert. denied,* 239 U.S. 642 (1915); Altheimer & Rawlings Co. v. Allen, 248 Fed. 688 (8th Cir. 1918), *cert. denied,* 248 U.S. 578 (1918); Nashville, Chattanooga & St. Louis Ry., 269 Fed. 351 (6th Cir. 1920), *cert. denied,* 255 U.S. 569 (1921); see also Anderson v. Forty-Two Broadway Co., 239 U.S. 69 (1915); McCoach v. Ins. Co. of North America, 244 U.S. 585 (1917); but see Herold v. Mutual Benefit Life Ins. Co., 201 Fed. 918 (3rd Cir. 1913), *cert. denied,* 231 U.S. 755 (1913); Anderson v. New York Life Ins. Co., 263 Fed. 527, 269 Fed. 1021 (2nd Cir. 1920), *cert. granted,* 255 U.S. 568, *vacated and cert. denied,* 256 U.S. 696 (1921).

[151] 228 U.S. 295 (1913).

business, and not subject to the tax. This time Day, together with Hughes and Lamar, dissented, although Pitney had tried to bring Day around before he circulated his opinion to the other Justices.[152]

The *Minehill* decision caused some consternation. It was going to result immediately in refunds by the government of taxes in the sum of some $700,000, and Attorney General McReynolds thought the opinion opened the way to wholesale evasions. Anybody, after all, could lease away his business, and thus ensure, as in *Minehill*, that neither owner nor lessee paid any tax on its earnings.[153] And a whole bushel of litigation did, indeed, spring from the decision in *Minehill*. In two further cases, the Supreme Court followed *Minehill* in one, and limited it somewhat in another.[154] But the lower courts, in the vast majority of their decisions, reached the same result, unfavorable to the government, as the Supreme Court did in *Minehill*.[155] Moreover, while the good or evil done by *Flint* v. *Stone Tracy Co.* was interred with it, and with the Corporation Tax Act of 1909 that spawned it, *McCoach* v. *Minehill Railway Co.* and other restrictive constructions of the Act had, ironically enough, something of an afterlife. For Congress carried over such language as

---

[152] M. Pitney to W. R. Day, Mar. 28, 1913, and Day to Pitney, Mar. 29, 1913, Day Papers.

[153] See *New York Times*, Apr. 8, 1913, p. 15, col. 4; May 6, 1913, p. 1, col. 4; May 13, 1913, p. 2, col. 5; *Washington Evening Star*, Apr. 7, 1913, p. 1, col. 6.

[154] United States v. Emery, 237 U.S. 28 (1915); Von Baumbach v. Sargent Land Co., 242 U.S. 503 (1917).

[155] See Abrast Realty Co. v. Maxwell, 206 Fed. 333 (E.D. N.Y. 1913), *affirmed*, 218 Fed. 457 (2nd Cir. 1914); United States v. Nipissing Mines Co., 206 Fed. 431 (2nd Cir. 1913), *cert. dismissed*, 234 U.S. 765 (1914); Anderson v. Morris & E. R.R., 216 Fed. 83 (2nd Cir. 1914); Wilkes-Barre & West Virginia Traction Co. v. Davis, 214 Fed. 511 (M.D. Pa. 1914); Bryant & May Ltd. v. Scott, 226 Fed. 875 (M.D. Calif. 1914); Miller v. Snake River Valley R.R., 223 Fed. 946 (9th Cir. 1915); New York C. & H. R.R. v. Gill, 219 Fed. 184 (1st Cir. 1913); Llewellyn v. Pittsburgh, B. & L.E. R.R., 222 Fed. 177 (3rd Cir. 1915); Traction Co. v. Collectors of Internal Revenue, 223 Fed. 984 (6th Cir. 1915); Philadelphia Traction Co. v. McCoach, 224 Fed. 800 (E.D. Pa. 1915), *affirmed*, 233 Fed. 976 (3rd Cir. 1916); Cambria Steel Co. v. McCoach, 225 Fed. 278 (E.D. Pa. 1915); Public Service Gas Co. v. Herold, 227 Fed. 496 (D. N.J. 1914); Public Service Ry. v. Herold, 227 Fed. 500 (D. N.J. 1915); Waterbury Gaslight Co. v. Walsh, 228 Fed. 54 (D. Conn. 1915); State Line & S. R.R. v. Davis, 228 Fed. 246 (M.D. Pa. 1915); Jasper & E. Ry. v. Walker, 238 Fed. 533 (5th Cir. 1917); Butterick Co. v. United States, 240 Fed. 539 (S.D. N.Y. 1917), *appeal dismissed*, 248 U.S. 587 (1918); West End Street Ry. v. Malley, 246 Fed. 625 (1st Cir. 1917), *cert. denied*, 246 U.S. 671 (1918); Public Service Ry. v. Herold, 229 Fed. 902 (3rd Cir. 1916); New York Mail & Newspaper Transportation Co. v. Anderson, 234 Fed. 590 (2nd Cir. 1916). *But cf.* Blalock v. Georgia Ry. and Electric Co., 228 Fed. 296 (5th Cir. 1915); Associated Pipe Line Co. v. United States, 258 Fed. 800 (9th Cir. 1919).

that about "doing business" from the 1909 Act into statutes implementing the Sixteenth Amendment, and the Court's construction tended to come along with the language.

Judging by the much more substantial percentage of cases the government was able to win on the "doing business" issue under later revenue acts, both the Supreme Court and the lower courts grew less and less indulgent, over time, to passive corporate recipients of income. But the *Minehill* decision exerted a significant influence just the same,[156] and events came full circle in 1949, the rule in *Minehill* having still not lost vigor, when the same company was once again held not to be doing business, and therefore not subject to federal corporation excise taxes.[157] The decision in *Eliot* v. *Freeman* that a Massachusetts trust was not an entity taxable under the 1909 Act had a somewhat less elaborate and more foreshortened, but still similar, career. It was brought forward to the Income Tax Act of 1913, and began to lapse only as the language of future statutes changed.[158]

Three years after *Stone Tracy*, William D. Guthrie brought into the Supreme Court another assault on a tax levied by the Payne-Aldrich tariff of 1909. This was a tax more piquant than productive. Like the spectacular antitrust prosecutions, it was responsive to a certain popular concern with conspicuous wealth. Congress had levied $7 per gross ton

---

[156] *Compare*, e.g., Edwards v. Chile Copper Co., 270 U.S. 452 (1926); International Salt Co. v. Phillips, 9 F. 2d 389 (3rd Cir. 1925), *reversed per curiam*, 274 U.S. 718 (1927); Conhaim Holding Co. v. Willcuts, 21 F. 2d 91 (D. Minn. 1927); Harmar Coal Co. v. Heiner, 26 F. 2d 729 (W.D. Pa. 1928), *affirmed*, 34 F. 2d 725 (3rd Cir. 1929), *cert. denied*, 280 U.S. 610 (1930); Argonaut Consolidated Mining Co. v. Anderson, 42 F. 2d 219 (S.D. N.Y. 1930), *affirmed*, 52 F. 2d 55 (2nd Cir. 1931), *cert. denied*, 284 U.S. 682 (1932); United States v. Atlantic Coastline Co., 99 F. 2d 6, 932 (4th Cir. 1938); *cert. denied*, 306 U.S. 645 (1939); *with* Three Forks Coal Co. v. United States, 9 F. 2d 946 (W.D. Pa. 1925), *affirmed*, 13 F. 2d 631 (3rd Cir. 1926); Nunnally Investment Co. v. Rose, 22 F. 2d 102 (5th Cir. 1927), *cert. denied*, 276 U.S. 628 (1928); United States

v. Hotchkiss Redwood Co., 25 F. 2d 958 (9th Cir. 1928); Hercules Mining Co. v. United States, 119 F. 2d 288 (9th Cir. 1941), *cert. denied*, 314 U.S. 658 (1941); Washington, Baltimore & Annapolis Realty Co. v. Magruder, 316 U.S. 69 (1942).

[157] United States v. Mine Hill & Schuylkill Ry. Co., 86 F. Supp. 826 (E.D. Pa. 1949).

[158] See Hecht v. Malley, 265 U.S. 144 (1924); Burk-Waggoner Ass'n v. Hopkins, 269 U.S. 110 (1925); Morrissey v. Commissioner, 296 U.S. 344 (1935); R. E. Paul and J. Mertens, *Law of Federal Income Taxation* (1934), IV, Sects. 35.18, 35.22, 35.28; C. Lyons, "Comments on the New Regulations on Associations," *Tax L.R.*, 16:441, 1916; L. M. Smith, "Associations Classified as Corporations under the Internal Revenue Code," *Calif. L.R.*, 34:461, 1946.

on the use of foreign-built yachts owned by citizens of the United States.[159] The tax was enacted, in part at least, to protect the domestic ship building industry, which complained of foreign competition,[160] but it unmistakably soaked the rich, and therein lay its interest to the public. For while Holmes was wont to say that "the crowd now has substantially all there is, that the luxuries of the few are a drop in the bucket," and that nothing significant was "withdrawn from the total by the palaces and dinners at Sherry's,"[161] the crowd itself hardly thought so.

Guthrie's clients—others similarly situated included Cornelius Vanderbilt, George J. Gould, and Lamon V. Harkness[162]—were C. K. G. Billings, Henry Clay Pierce, Mrs. Harriet Goelet, and James Gordon Bennett, the owner of the *New York Herald*.[163] The Court, speaking unanimously through Chief Justice White, found the tax constitutional, and imposed it in the cases of Messrs. Billings and Pierce. The most plausible argument against it was that it made a discriminatory classification between foreign and domestic yachts, and White did not think there was much to that. Foreign and domestic yachts were, he thought, different, and could be treated differently. In Mrs. Goelet's case there was a variable, for while an American citizen, she resided abroad, and in the absence of express language taxing overseas property of a non-resident citizen, the Court construed the statute as not applicable. In the *Bennett* case, the Court was quite satisfied that the Act meant to tax, and could constitutionally tax, a yacht owned by a resident citizen, no matter where the yacht was customarily kept, here or abroad, but left it to the lower courts to determine where Mr. Bennett was in fact domiciled.[164]

---

[159] 36 Stat. 112, Sect. 37 of the Tariff Act of Aug. 5, 1909.

[160] *House Documents,* Vol. 145, "Tariff Hearings," VII, 7515–32.

[161] *Holmes-Pollock Letters,* I, 124, 195.

[162] See *New York Herald,* Feb. 25, 1914, p. 10, col. 6.

[163] When the cases were decided, James Gordon Bennett was on his yacht, the *Lysistrata,* in the Mediterranean. It was a heavier boat than C. K. G. Billings' *Vanadis,* which, in turn, had cost half a million dollars, according to the *New York Times,* and was equipped to offer satisfaction to "the most fastidious taste for comfort and pleasure." See *New York*

Times, Mar. 18, 1914, p. 1, col. 4; Feb. 15, 1914, Rotogravure Section. Mr. Billings returned to the United States at the end of March 1914, bringing with him six dogs, obtained abroad because they were of higher quality than the American species, which he was taking with him to his Virginia estate near Richmond. See *New York Times,* Mar. 28, 1914, p. 6, col. 6.

[164] Billings v. United States, 232 U.S. 261, 289 (1914); Pierce v. United States, 232 U.S. 290, 292 (1914); United States v. Goelet, 232 U.S. 293 (1914); United States v. Bennett, 232 U.S. 299, 308 (1914). See also Rainey v. United States, 232 U.S. 310 (1914).

State Social and Economic Legislation

Aside from the decisions we have reviewed,[165] passing on the, after all, relatively few reforms of the Roosevelt and Taft administrations, the fate of social legislation was determined, with perhaps more far-reaching practical and doctrinal consequences during these years, in cases concerning state laws. And while, in the period under discussion, the cases dealing with important federal measures, whatever their equivocation, uniformly upheld federal power, the decision on state laws followed no such undeviating course. Indeed, as many relevant state enactments were held unconstitutional at the October Terms 1910–13 as at the October Terms 1922–25. The figure for both periods is thirty-five.[166] The latter terms were at a time when no one accused the Court of having turned Progressive. And yet in the earlier period, the state cases in the Supreme Court, as much as the federal ones, contributed to the temporary feeling of a segment of Progressive opinion that the Court was now in tune with its time, that it had entered "a new phase," and that the day of the

---

[165] Other federal tax litigation during the four terms under discussion was scarce, and concerned with winding up the administration of the Spanish War Revenue Act of 1898. United States v. Chamberlin, 219 U.S. 250 (1911); United States v. Fidelity Trust Co., 222 U.S. 158 (1911); and see Gill v. Austin, 157 Fed. 234 (1st Cir. 1907), cert. denied, 218 U.S. 677 (1910); Kinney v. Conant, 166 Fed. 720 (1st Cir. 1909), cert. denied, 218 U.S. 677 (1910); Gill v. Parrish, 168 Fed. 1020 (1st Cir. 1909), cert. denied, 218 U.S. 677 (1910); Eidman v. Lewisohn, 177 Fed. 1002 (2nd Cir. 1910), cert. denied, 218 U.S. 678 (1910); Sanders v. Rumsey, 169 Fed. 1022 (2nd Cir. 1909), cert. denied, 218 U.S. 678 (1910); McCoach v. Bamberger, 161 Fed. 90 (3rd Cir. 1908), cert. denied, 218 U.S. 678 (1910); Robertson v. United States, 183 Fed. 711 (7th Cir. 1910), cert. denied, 220 U.S. 616 (1911); Title Guaranty & Trust Co. v. Ward, 184 Fed. 447 (2nd Cir. 1911), cert. denied, 220 U.S. 620 (1911).

[166] In both instances, the figure covers decisions under the Commerce Clause (dealing with both regulatory and taxing measures), preemption decisions under the Supremacy Clause, but not cases of intergovernmental immunities, and decisions under the Due Process, Equal Protection, and Contract clauses, excluding civil liberties or civil rights cases. The effort is to assess comparatively, so far as numbers can do it, the fate in the two periods of what this section discusses under the loosely descriptive label of social and economic legislation. The figure includes decisions dealing with ordinances and like local legislation as well as state statutes, and it includes cases in which enactments were held invalid as applied, as well as cases in which they were held invalid on their face, in toto. But cases holding a discrete state administrative action or judicial judgment unconstitutional, when the underlying statute, if any, remains untouched, are not included, as not having, generally, a major impact.

Brewers and the Peckmans was over, not only literally, but also symbolically and ideologically.[167]

In part, the reason for this near euphoria may be found in the Hamiltonian fervor of Theodore Roosevelt's Progressivism. Those who partook of this fervor looked mainly to the federal government for reforming initiatives, often tended to view the curtailment of state powers as nothing more than an invitation to federal action, and welcomed performance by the Court of a nationalizing role. In some part, the reason was that the state cases that seemed to have the greatest practical impact, or that arrested professional attention with a striking doctrinal pronouncement—as in one Due Process opinion of Hughes that we shall examine,[168] and in another opinion, in which Holmes managed to evade his censors[169]—these most notable cases reached the right results, sustaining state reforms. From them the commentators took their cue. These, it must also be true in part, were the cases that confirmed what an influential segment of Progressive opinion wished to hear. Finally, to be sure, the numbers game of counting statutes held unconstitutional is not to be overplayed; a good majority of state measures considered by the Court were allowed to pass the judicial test, and they were, for the most part, the measures embodying reforms of some enduring importance. Just the same, it was in literal truth only that the day of the Brewers and the Peckhams was over. Doctrinally they lived on, and were to flourish again.

The first line of state cases that needs to be considered is complementary to the federal transportation cases reviewed earlier in this chapter. Aside from serving as a source of federal power, the Commerce Clause operates also—and historically, as of this time, had operated chiefly—as a restriction upon the regulatory and fiscal powers of the states. It imposes two kinds of restrictions. As was evident in the *Shreveport Case*, and also in portions of the litigation that arose from the second Federal Employers' Liability Act, the exercise of federal legislative and administrative power may preempt state regulatory measures that would otherwise be valid. But in addition, since the earliest days, the Commerce Clause of itself, without any implementation by federal legislative or administrative action, has been held to foreclose regulation and taxation when, in the judgment of the Court, maintenance of a common national market so requires.

Now, legislative centralization of economic and social regulatory power by federal statute, as in the *Shreveport Case*, is one thing. Judicial

---

[167] See *supra*, p. 201.
[168] Chicago, Burlington & Quincy R.R. v. McGuire, 219 U.S. 549 (1911).
[169] Noble State Bank v. Haskell, 219 U.S. 104 (1911).

centralization, brought about by application of the Commerce Clause itself, without waiting for a federal statute, is quite another. This latter sort of centralization often creates a regulatory no-man's-land, either because, as occasion arises, the Court turns around and also forecloses Congressional action in the same area in which it has cut off the states, or because the problem needing regulation is so fragmented that federal legislation cannot realistically be expected, and is in any event less desirable than state action. "Instances have not been wanting," Felix Frankfurter wrote some years later, "where the concept of interstate commerce has been broadened to exclude state action, and narrowed to exclude Congressional action." Even in instances where the circle of exclusion had not yet been closed, there was not infrequently ground for suspicion that, as Frankfurter also wrote, Commerce Clause decisions striking down state regulation were "not dictated by federalism; they are functions of a laissez-faire philosophy."[170] The same could sometimes be said of preemption decisions, which were not always a plain and direct function of the Supremacy Clause.

The Minnesota Rate Cases

The most widely noted Commerce Clause decision affecting the states in these years, however—and it was at once also the decision of most pervasive practical importance—did not create any no-man's-land. It sanctioned state power, and at the same time invited the exercise of federal power. This was the decision, in 1913, of the *Minnesota Rate Cases*, which foretold, and meshed perfectly with, the *Shreveport Case* of a year later. In common with the latter, it was the work of Hughes.

The *Minnesota Rate Cases* were three, and they were argued in April 1912, a little more than a year before they were decided. But their story begins with a couple of *Missouri Rate Cases*, which like them arose from protests by railroad interests against general reductions of intra-state freight and passenger rates, effected both directly by state statutes, and administratively by orders of state commissions. The railroads in Missouri—as in Minnesota and other midwestern states, too—promptly obtained from federal courts temporary, and then permanent, injunctions against enforcement of the new rates. In October 1910, appeals by Missouri were argued in the Supreme Court. But this argument was to the shorthanded Court, lacking Van Devanter and Lamar, as well as a Chief Justice, and so that spring, the *Missouri* cases were set down for reargument. Then more cases of the same sort—in a few of which,

---

[170] See F. Frankfurter, *The Commerce Clause under Marshall, Taney* and *Waite* (1937), 76.

however, the railroads had lost below—began rapidly to accumulate on the Court's docket. There were eventually to be thirty-two additional ones from Missouri, one from West Virginia, two from Oregon, two from Arkansas, and the three from Minnesota.

In October 1911, Harlan died, not to be replaced by Pitney till March 1912, and Day was absent from the beginning of the 1911 Term until January 1912, owing to the illness and then death of his wife. The Court held the *Missouri* cases, until it had collected everything it could see coming up, for argument in April 1912. The Brethren were unanimous, White wrote Day in October 1911, in the belief "that if possible the cases should be heard by the full Court,"[171] and it was equally desirable that they be grouped together.[172]

The argument for the railroads in the *Minnesota* cases—the railroads were the Northern Pacific, the Great Northern, and the Minneapolis and St. Louis—was divided between Charles W. Bunn and Pierce Butler. Bunn presented a preview of the eventual holding in the *Shreveport Case*—which others were to argue, and in which, as we have seen, railroad counsel were forced into the unnatural position of supporting the state-established rates. The lower intrastate rates had necessarily, Bunn said, to result either in a discrimination against interstate commerce, or as would happen in Minnesota owing to competitive conditions, in an adjustment of the comparable interstate rates to bring them into line. Interstate rates were established under, and subject to control by, federal authority. Both the new state rates and the old interstate rates might well be reasonable. The difference between them could be accounted for by a national preference for higher railroad profits, as opposed to a state policy favoring smaller returns on railroad property. But in such a situation, national authority should prevail.

Butler, the future Justice, was a valuation specialist, and he concentrated on the Due Process argument that the rates set by Minnesota were not reasonable, not a permissible expression of state policy favoring a low rate of return, but confiscatory. "The general rule," he contended, "is that where the property has been efficiently located, constructed and maintained and results of operation as a whole show volume of traffic and earnings sufficient to support the property, pay reasonable dividends and leave something in addition, the true value is in excess of

---

[171] Lurton wrote Day at the same time: "I do trust that you will be able to be on hand when these cases are determined. The views which I have entertained [favorable to sustaining the power of the states] have

lost a strong supporter by the death of Judge Harlan." H. H. Lurton to W. R. Day, Oct. 14, 1911, Day Papers, Library of Congress.

[172] E. D. White to W. R. Day, Oct. 10, 1911, Day Papers.

the mere cost of reproduction of the physical or tangible property." The value of railroad lands, for example, was to be calculated in light of their extraordinarily productive use by the railroad: "Railroad utility is a higher use than ordinary business, residence or farm use and makes for higher cost and therefore higher value." On their property so valued, the railroads were entitled to earn a reasonable percentage of profit, but with the new rates, they could not.

Hughes' opinion in the *Minnesota Rate Cases* spoke for a unanimous Court, except that McKenna concurred in the result without writing. The opinion ran to ninety-eight pages. Hughes had spent, he recalled, a long time at it. The cases—the *Minnesota* ones as well as the others—had not apparently been acted upon in conference immediately following the argument. Rather they had been taken for study over the summer, then presumably discussed in conference in the fall of 1912, and then assigned to Hughes late that fall.[173] The decision was finally handed down on June 9, 1913.

Hughes began with a history of the litigation. There were commission orders in Minnesota in 1906 and 1907, as well as two statutes in 1907, one fixing 2¢ per mile as the maximum fare for passengers, and another fixing certain commodity rates for cargoes of specified weight. In *Ex parte Young*,[174] the jurisdiction of the federal courts was upheld in these cases, and certain penal provisions of the statutes—separable, and now no longer relevant—were declared unconstitutional. Then the lower court appointed a master, who took evidence. On the basis of the master's findings, the court had permanently enjoined all the rates as being unconstitutional, in violation of both the Commerce and Due Process clauses.

The Commerce Clause question was whether the rates were a burden on interstate traffic. Unquestionably, the situation was such that the interstate rates had to follow the lower intrastate ones. Assuming both the lower intrastate and the higher interstate rates to be reasonable, was such an effect on the interstate rates permissible? The issue was of great importance, Hughes said. It could and did arise virtually everywhere, since the economy did not follow state lines. Thus, Hughes pointed out, in an unusual reference to briefs, the railroad commissions of eight other midwestern states, and the governors of three states, pursuant to a resolution of the Conference of Governors, all filed briefs as *amici* in support of Minnesota's position.

The authority of Congress, Hughes continued, to control intrastate

---

[173] C. E. Hughes, *Biographical Notes,* Microfilm, Ac. 9943, p. 225, Hughes Papers.

[174] 209 U.S. 123 (1908).

rates affecting interstate ones was not in question here—that would be the issue in the *Shreveport Case*. These cases arose in the absence of federal legislative or administrative action. In such circumstances, the power of the states extended "to those matters of a local nature as to which it is impossible to derive from the constitutional grant [to Congress of power over commerce] an intention that they should go uncontrolled pending Federal intervention." As these cases demonstrated, the states were thus enabled to affect interstate commerce, but: "Our system of government is a practical adjustment. . . ." Congress in such a case as this, not the Supreme Court, should be the judge of the necessity of federal action.

To be sure, interstate commerce could be protected by allowing the states to establish no intrastate rates which varied from the interstate ones. But that would be to nullify the rate-setting power of the states, and that, in turn, was for Congress to do, if at all, not for the Court. To the extent that Congress—as Hughes was to hold in the *Shreveport Case*—had in fact exercised its authority over intrastate rates in order to equalize them with interstate ones, it had delegated the function of ordering the equalization in particular cases to the Interstate Commerce Commission, which had primary jurisdiction, not in the first instance to the courts. And the extent to which Congress had in fact exercised its authority and had lodged power to act in the commission was not a question to be decided in this case, for the commission had not acted. This was the question, as Hughes said later in the *Shreveport Case*, that he was here reserving for decision subsequently, whenever it should be properly raised.

Then Hughes addressed himself to the issue whether the rates were confiscatory, as Butler had argued. Of course, under *Smyth* v. *Ames*,[175] the railroads were entitled to a fair return on the fair value of their property. But that was not a matter of formulas and artificial rules, but of reasonable judgment. The master in this case estimated the cost of reproduction of the entire railroad properties as if they were new and undepreciated, and then found that the state rates would yield a return of something a little over 6 percent, which he thought was confiscatory. But in estimating the value of land owned by the railroads he calculated the fair market value, and then added anywhere from 30 percent to double the market figure for what he called "value for railway purposes," in accordance with Butler's argument. The underlying assumption was that if a railroad were to try to buy land, it would have to pay a very substantially higher price than anyone else. This, Hughes held, was

---

[175] 169 U.S. 466 (1898).

entirely too speculative. No such excess over fair market value was allowed on condemnation by the United States of riparian lands in the *Chandler-Dunbar* case. And the railroads, after all, had power of eminent domain, just like the government.

Moreover, the master also repeatedly made allowances for legal and other expenses in arriving at the present value of railroad lands. This was totally out of the question. The railroads were entitled to the value of their lands as the market now set it, rather than merely to what they actually had paid before the properties were developed. That was fair reproduction value. But all the rest was mere conjecture, and could not be allowed. Finally, as to other property, the master had allowed the cost of reproduction without any deduction for depreciation, on the ground that the railroads so maintained their property that it was always as good as new. Nevertheless, the master also allowed certain sums for maintenance expenses. But in this fashion, the railroads were having their cake and eating it. The truth was that, no matter how well maintained, rails and other such property did depreciate, and this fact should have been reflected in a deduction from the estimated value.

Because of these major errors, as well as some additional ones, Hughes held that, so far as the Northern Pacific and Great Northern railways were concerned, the rates had not been proved confiscatory. In the case of the Minnesota and St. Louis Railroad, however, he agreed that the rates were confiscatory. This road was nearly bankrupt. The master found that for it the new rates would yield a return between 3 and 4 percent. His bases of computation were as dubious here as in the other two cases, but, without going into detail, Hughes concluded that the master's various errors did not in this instance vitiate his result. The actual earnings of the Minneapolis and St. Louis showed that it had to have higher rates. And so as to it, the injunction was affirmed.

One week later, on June 16, Hughes disposed of the rest of the cases that had been argued together. In the *Missouri* cases, a master had employed a method of valuation that was simplicity itself. He merely took the state tax assessment board's valuation of each railroad and multiplied by three. No finding of confiscation, Hughes held, could be based on this method of proof. But as to three railroads which were in the same position as the Minneapolis and St. Louis, he again reaffirmed the injunctions on the same grounds as in the case of that near-bankrupt road. In the Oregon cases, the district court had refused to issue injunctions, and Hughes affirmed. The Arkansas case was without complications and easily governed by the principal holding in the *Minnesota Rate Cases*. In the West Virginia case, the railroad had also lost below, and it presented one special argument, namely that the statute was not applicable to railroads of under fifty miles of track, which were independent and not owned by other systems, and that for this it violated the

Equal Protection Clause. The classification, Hughes held, was entirely reasonable.[176]

The Court breathed an audible sigh of relief as Hughes finished his labors. "Admirably well done," the Chief Justice returned to the opinion in the *Missouri* cases. "The Country and the Court owe you a debt. They would have to go into bankruptcy if called upon to pay." And on the opinion in the Arkansas case: "Thanks be to God you are through." Lamar wrote that the opinion in the *Minnesota* cases was "one of the greatest in our records," and that Hughes' success ought to be compensation for his "days and weeks and months of unceasing labor." The force of the argument, he thought, was "overwhelming," and the opinion not only sustained "the just rights of the states and of the United States but will be a landmark in the history of the Court." Pitney wrote that Hughes' opinions "far outclass any of the previous opinions of the Court upon subjects of this character." As Hughes was delivering the opinion in the *Minnesota* cases, Mrs. Hughes was in the courtroom, and received the following chit from Lurton: "The subject is not interesting to you and is very complex. But I would say to you, which I have already said to Judge Hughes, that his opinion now being delivered is as able and important as any opinion from this bench since the foundation of the Court. I therefore wish to congratulate you." And from Day: "Your husband has done a great work this day—the effects of which will be beneficially felt for generations to come."[177]

The various litigations that Hughes thus disposed of had been in the public eye well before they reached the stage of Supreme Court adjudication. Some Progressives, as we have seen, were nursing sanguine expectations about the Supreme Court, but the dominant note struck by the dominant opinion, in the years surrounding the campaign of 1912, was still one of disenchantment with the judiciary as a whole. And the dominant opinion, with Theodore Roosevelt in the van, cried out most violently, and on this point virtually in unison, against government by injunction, as it was called, which is to say, against the tendency of state and lower federal courts to enjoin enforcement of state social and economic legislation, readily, speedily, and it seemed almost automatically.

---

[176] The Minnesota Rate Cases, 230 U.S. 352, 369, 372–73, 402 (1913); Missouri Rate Cases, 230 U.S. 474 (1913); Knott v. St. Louis Southwestern Ry., 230 U.S. 509 (1913); Oregon Railroad & Navigation Co. v. Campbell, 230 U.S. 525 (1913); Southern Pacific Co. v. Campbell, 230 U.S. 537 (1913); Allen v. St. Louis Iron Mountain & Southern Ry., 230 U.S. 553 (1913); Chesapeake & Ohio Ry. v. Conley, 230 U.S. 513 (1913). And see Wood v. Vandalia R.R. Co., 231 U.S. 1 (1913).

[177] Hughes Papers.

State statutes were all too frequently not allowed to operate first and take their chances in litigation afterward, but were nullified at the instant of enactment, and allowed to come into effect, if at all, only years later, after a lengthy process of adjudication had run its course. Even when permitted ultimately to prevail, the legislative will had, therefore, first to undergo the penance of frustration. This, quite literally and precisely, was what Dean Lewis of the University of Pennsylvania Law School meant when he wrote that state legislation regulating social or industrial conditions was "of doubtful value until it had passed the gauntlet of the courts." And this was what Felix Frankfurter had in mind, in 1912, when he said that social legislation "must have the visé of our judiciary" to be effective.[178]

The evil of the precipitate injunction, as Progressive opinion saw it, was strikingly illustrated by the *Minnesota* and *Missouri* cases, by the Arkansas case, and by many other midwestern cases, and gave rise to angry comments in Congress. Senators and Congressmen—and not necessarily radicals, at that; they included, for example, James R. Mann of Illinois—protested that state legislation was at the mercy of "convenient and complacent courts," which postponed the operation of statutes indefinitely.[179] The federal courts, said Representative Mann, "have run wild. . . ." There were moves, foreshadowing the Norris–La Guardia Act of later years, to forbid federal courts to issue injunctions, and in the House there was even an effort—although it did not get very far—to impeach two federal judges who had almost casually, it seemed, acceded to the railroad requests for injunctions against the

---

[178] See *supra,* p. 201; Frankfurter, *Law and Politics,* 4.

[179] Remarks reported in the text date to 1910. A few years later—in 1913, shortly before the *Minnesota Rate Cases* were decided in the Supreme Court, the chairman of the House Judiciary Committee, Representative Clayton of Alabama, quoted for the benefit of his colleagues some comments of Governor Byrne of South Dakota:

It was the boast of the representatives of the railroads that in 13 minutes after the governor had signed at Pierre the act fixing passenger fares at 2 cents per mile the Federal judge at Sioux Falls had signed his sweeping order re-

straining the attorney general and all State attorneys from attempting to enforce it. Nearly four years have passed since then, but we have not yet been able to learn from the court whether or not the fares fixed are reasonable. It is now nearly six years since the order of the board fixing 2½ cents per mile as the maximum charge for passenger fares was tied up by injunctions, yet in that time the court has not said whether such order is right or wrong. . . . (49 *Cong. Rec.* 4773 (1913); see W. Pogue, "State Determination of State Law and the Judicial Code," *Harv. L. Rev.,* 41:623, 627, 1928.)

Missouri rate laws.[180] Public attention focused also on the resolution of the Governors' Conference in 1911 that led to the filing of the brief *amicus* in the Supreme Court.[181]

When the decisions came down, their importance was deemed almost as high by the press as the Justices themselves had assessed it in their returns to Hughes. And the decisions were generally welcomed. They cleared the way of rate regulation "from much of the fog of doubt that has hung over it," said the *Louisville Courier Journal*, and they affirmed "a power which but yesterday was first asserted and which has been so much obscured by shrewd quibblers and so stubbornly and ably resisted by the railroads." The *Washington Post* remarked that the Court had given a clearer definition of states' rights than the country had heard in a long time, and that its decisions galvanized into life the state commissions, "whose authority, in many instances, seemed merely nominal."[182]

But there was also ambivalence, an ambivalence characteristic of Progressive opinion on issues of federalism, as there was to be a year later in response to the *Shreveport Case*. These decisions would lead to further federal regulation, the *Detroit News* forecast, because they would demonstrate "the impracticability of state supervision of rates." The *New York Tribune* read the opinions closely—and accurately—and found in them no danger to the aspirations of the New Nationalism:

> A careful reading of Justice Hughes' opinion in the Minnesota Railroad Rate Case will show that early descriptions of it as a victory for the state rights theory were unfounded. It does not upset in favor of the states the *status quo* between them and the Nation as regulators of railroad charges. It gives back no powers which the states have lost through the steady expansion of federal control of interstate commerce. As railroad transportation has become more and more a federal concern state jurisdiction over it has been rapidly restricted. That process must continue and the decision in the Minnesota Case does not operate to stay it. With the power now left in the states through the acquiescence of Congress the Supreme Court does not interfere. But it gives notice that it will sustain any further exercise of authority which Congress may see fit to sanction for the purpose of freeing national control of interstate commerce from harassing regulations made by the states.

---

[180] 44 *Cong. Rec.* 1801–1805, 61st Cong., 1st Sess. (1909); 45 *Cong. Rec.* 7252–53, 61st Cong., 2nd Sess. (1910); 46 *Cong. Rec.* 313–16, 61st Cong., 3rd Sess. (1910).

[181] See *Indianapolis News*, Apr. 2, 1912, p. 6, col. 1.

[182] *Louisville Courier Journal*, June 11, 1913, p. 6, col. 1; *Washington Post*, June 10, 1913, p. 6, col. 1; and see *Providence, Rhode Island, Evening Bulletin*, p. 1, col. 6.

> . . . Congress has by no means exhausted its energy in federalizing the Commerce of the Nation, and as for trade purposes state lines are more and more blotted from the map, a further readjustment must take place unfavorable to the states and favorable to the Nation.
>
> That is as it should be. We have outgrown the period in which forty-eight different states could reasonably be expected to regulate commerce with beneficial results. What both the railroads and the country need is concentration of control so that it can be made uniform, equitable and effective. Congress should not hesitate to exercise the power of further unification which Justice Hughes rightly declares that it possesses.[183]

The need for federal regulation, and a certain unease with the states'-rights features of Hughes' opinions, found emphasis also in the professional journals.[184] But states'-rights sentiment was stronger in Congress and in the new Wilson Administration, and there was no inclination for the time being to take further federal action. Even Senator Newlands of Nevada thought that the accommodation Hughes had arrived at was "better than the Nation declaring itself lord paramount." Only the New Nationalism's spokesman in the House, Representative Victor Murdock, the Roosevelt Progressive floor leader, thought that the federal government should assume complete control of railroad rates.[185]

The stock market, which somehow had apparently expected a different decision, was shocked, and declined sharply.[186] The market may have been disturbed as much by the valuation aspect—the Due Process portion—of Hughes' opinions as by anything. The *New York Times* undertook to reassure it, by pointing out that confiscatory rates were still subject to federal judicial control. The Court, said the *Times*, had indicated to the railroads their means of defense, and "given them assurance of adequate protection" in the states "where the radical and adventurous spirit prevails, where parties or politicians seek their profit by harassing the corporations."[187] And valuation of railroads and other

---

[183] *Detroit News,* June 15, 1913, p. 4, col. 2; *New York Tribune,* June 11, 1913, p. 8, col. 1.

[184] See J. Bauer, "The Minnesota Rate Cases," *Political Science Quarterly,* 29:57, 1914; H. Taylor, "The Minnesota Rate Cases," *Harv. L. R.,* 27:14, 1913; Sharfman, *Interstate Commerce Commission,* II, 233.

[185] *Washington Post,* June 11, 1913, p. 3, col. 5; *Washington Star,* June 11, 1913, p. 1, col. 3.

[186] *Washington Post,* June 10, 1913, p. 1, col. 1; *Detroit News,* June 10, 1913, p. 1. col. 1; *New York Tribune,* June 11, 1913, p. 4, col. 5.

[187] *New York Times,* June 11, 1913, p. 6, col. 1; *Washington Post,* June 18, 1913, p. 14, col. 5 ("Railways Will Fight—Their Rights Preserved in Supreme Court Decisions—Books Must Show Details").

public utilities, and rate setting for them, did continue, of course, to be subjects of litigation.[188]

The railroads had fought on this front before the *Minnesota Rate Cases*,[189] and they fought on afterwards, often enough successfully. The group of cases decided together with the *Minnesota Rate Cases* themselves did not go entirely without further contest, and in at least two instances, the railroads were able subsequently to prove confiscation to the satisfaction of the Supreme Court.[190] A later attack on a 2¢ fare statute of Michigan, similar to the Minnesota one, also succeeded.[191] So did a substantial number of other claims by railroads in the Supreme Court that rates set by the states were confiscatory. The state, Hughes himself said in an opinion in 1915, holding certain North Dakota rates to be confiscatory, may regulate, "but it does not enjoy the freedom of an owner."[192] Even federal valuation of railroads by the Interstate Commerce Commission was not to be immune to attack.[193]

While, therefore, the opinion in the *Minnesota Rate Cases* resisted the more exaggerated claims made by railroads in valuation proceedings, it did not diminish judicial control over rate making, and it had little effect on the controversies over methods of valuation and standards for judicial control of rate making that were to rage through the 1920s. But

---

[188] See F. Frankfurter and H. M. Hart, Jr., "Rate Regulation," in *Encyclopedia of the Social Sciences* (1934), XIII, 104.

[189] E.g., West v. Atchison, Topeka & Santa Fe Ry., 185 Fed. 321 (8th Cir. 1910), *cert. denied,* 220 U.S. 618 (1911) (Oklahoma railroad rates enjoined as confiscatory).

[190] Rowland v. St. Louis & San Francisco R.R., 244 U.S. 106 (1917); Vandalia R.R. v. Schnull, 255 U.S. 113 (1921). And see Missouri v. Chicago, Burlington & Quincy R.R., 241 U.S. 533 (1916); Arkadelphia Co. v. St. Louis Southwestern Ry., 249 U.S. 134 (1919); and St. Louis Iron Mountain & Southern Ry. v. Hasty & Sons, 255 U.S. 252 (1921).

[191] Groesbeck v. Duluth, South Shore & Atlantic Ry., 250 U.S. 607 (1919).

[192] Northern Pacific Ry. v. North Dakota, 236 U.S. 585, 595 (1915). See also Norfolk and Western Ry. v.

West Virginia, 236 U.S. 605 (1915); Brooks-Scanlon Co. v. R.R. Commission, 251 U.S. 396 (1920); Paducah v. Paducah Ry., 261 U.S. 267 (1923); Northern Pacific Ry. v. Department of Public Works, 268 U.S. 39 (1925); Banton v. Belt Line Ry., 268 U.S. 413 (1925); Railroad Commission v. Duluth Street Ry., 273 U.S. 625 (1927); Chicago, Milwaukee & St. Paul Ry. v. Public Utilities Commission, 274 U.S. 344 (1927); and United Ry. v. West, 280 U.S. 234 (1930). And the railroads were assured, of course, access to judicial review of rate orders. See Missouri Pacific Ry. v. Tucker, 230 U.S. 340 (1913); but see Louisville & Nashville R.R. v. Garrett, 231 U.S. 298 (1913); Wadley Southern Ry. v. Georgia, 235 U.S. 651 (1915); and Detroit & Mackinac Ry. v. Paper Co., 248 U.S. 30 (1918).

[193] St. Louis & O'Fallon Ry. v. United States, 279 U.S. 461 (1929).

it did, in its Commerce Clause aspect, legitimate state control of intrastate rates, with the consequences that railroad rate setting by state commissions became a going and reasonably effective business.[194]

Other Commerce Clause and Preemption Decisions

In addition to his work in the *Minnesota* and other rate cases, Hughes, speaking for unanimous Courts, also wrote a couple of opinions sustaining other, relatively minor, state regulations of railroads in these years. There was, too, one by Harlan. Both Justices were careful to imply no denial of the supervening power of Congress, when and if that power should be exercised.[195] And in *Port Richmond Ferry* v. *Hudson County*, Hughes sustained a New Jersey statute setting rates for ferry trips from New Jersey to New York, and also for round trips on tickets sold in New Jersey. Without denying federal power, he refused, pending its exercise, and in a situation, indeed, in which its exercise was inherently unlikely, to displace state regulation. "It has never been

---

[194] See, e.g., Re Atchison, Topeka & Santa Fe Ry., 3 Mo. P.S.C. 75, P.U.R. 1916A, 594 (1915), 270 Mo. 547, 194 S.W. 287 (1917), P.U.R. 1918A, 843 (1917); Turner Creamery Co. v. Chicago, Minneapolis & St. Paul Ry., 36 S.D. 310, 154 N.W. 819 (1915); Re Missouri, K. & T. Ry. 4 Mo. P.S.C. 537 (1916); Frank Cram & Sons v. Chicago, Burlington & Quincy R.R., 39 Ann. Rep. Ia. R.C. 57 (1917); Northwestern Grain Dealers Ass'n v. Chicago, Burlington & Quincy R.R., P.U.R. 1917A, 43 (Mount. R.C. 1916); Re Southern Pacific Co., P.U.R. 1917C, 53 (Nev. R.C. 1916); Re Southern Pacific Co., P.U.R. 1920F, 725 (Nev. P.S.C. 1920); Re Northern Pacific Ry., P.U.R. 1920F, 11 (Mont. Bd. R.C. 1920); Re Chicago, Burlington & Quincy R.R., P.U.R. 1921A, 91 (Ill. P.U.C. 1920); Atchison, Topeka & Santa Fe Ry. v. State, 85 Okl. 223, 206 Pac. 236 (1922); Northern Pacific Ry. v. Department of Public Works, 25 Wash. 584, 217 Pac. 507 (1923); Re Application of Missouri Pacific R.R., 19 Ann. Rep. Neb. S.R.C. 462 (1926); Atchison, Topeka & Santa Fe Ry. v. Commerce Commission, 335 Ill. 70, 166 N.E. 466 (1929). And see United States Express Co. v. Nebraska, 85 Neb. 42 (1909), *writ of error dismissed on motion of plaintiff in error*, 226 U.S. 616 (1912); Portland Ry. Co. v. Oregon R.R. Commission, 229 U.S. 397 (1913); Portland Ry. Co. v. Oregon R.R. Commission, 229 U.S. 414 (1913); Texas & Pacific Ry. v. Louisiana R.R. Commission, 232 U.S. 338 (1914); Louisville & Nashville R.R. Co. v. Finn, 235 U.S. 601 (1915); Darnell v. Edwards, 244 U.S. 564 (1917); Pennsylvania R.R. Co. v. Towers, 245 U.S. 6 (1917); Gilchrist v. Interborough Co., 279 U.S. 159 (1929).

[195] Chicago, Milwaukee & St. Paul Ry. v. Iowa, 233 U.S. 334 (1914); Atlantic Coast Line v. Georgia, 234 U.S. 280 (1914); Chicago, Rhode Island & Pacific Ry. v. Arkansas, 219 U.S. 453 (1911); and see Pittsburgh, Cincinnati, Chicago & St. Louis Ry. v. Indiana, 172 Ind. 147, 84 N.E. 1034 (1909), *affirmed,* 223 U.S. 713 (1911).

supposed," he remarked, "that because of the absence of Federal action the public interest was unprotected from extortion and that in order to secure reasonable charges in a myriad of such different local instances, exhibiting an endless variety of circumstance, it would be necessary for Congress to act directly or to establish for that purpose a Federal agency."[196] Finally, the Court during this period also upheld certain limited state regulations of interstate communication by telegraph.[197]

In more cases than not, however, the Commerce Clause did operate to inhibit state regulatory power. Thus, on the same day on which he delivered the opinion in the *Port Richmond Ferry* case, Hughes also decided *Sault Ste. Marie* v. *International Transit Co.*,[198] holding unconstitutional a Michigan city's ordinance which forbade ferries to run between it and Canada without a $50 city license. The city, said Hughes, could not make its consent a condition precedent to navigation by ferry in interstate and foreign commerce, even though, as indicated in the *Port Richmond* case, it might in some measure have power to regulate that commerce. A similar decision, also by Hughes, was *Adams Express Co.* v. *New York*.[199] The origins of this case go back to a turbulent teamsters' strike in the fall of 1910, more than three years before the Supreme Court acted, and while in its main features, this decision, like that in the *Sault Ste. Marie* case, bespeaks the necessities of a national common market, and lies somewhere near the core of a traditional and virtually unquestioned function of the Supreme Court under the Commerce Clause, it also exemplifies judicial intervention in the handling of social problems that were themselves, at this time, the virtually unquestioned, autonomous concern of state and local government, if of any government at all.

On October 23, 1910, drivers and helpers of the United States Express Company in Jersey City and Hoboken, New Jersey, went out on strike. From its inception, the strike was fought with strikebreakers, and it was continuously violent. The issue at first was wages. Soon, however, the question of union recognition became central. Within days, the strike spread to other employers, including the Adams Express Company, and to New York City. By October 28, freight movement in

---

[196] Port Richmond Ferry v. Hudson County, 234 U.S. 317, 332 (1914).

[197] Western Union Telegraph Co. v. Commercial Milling Co., 218 U.S. 406 (1910); Western Union Telegraph Co. v. Crovo, 220 U.S. 364 (1911). Following decision of the *Crovo* case, similar cases were dismissed on motion of appellant. Western Union Telegraph Co. v. Cohn, 220 U.S. 626 (1911); and Western Union Telegraph Co. v. Tamer, 220 U.S. 627 (1911); Western Union Telegraph Co. v. Gibbs, 223 U.S. 741 (1911); Western Union Telegraph Co. v. Gilkinson, 226 U.S. 624 (1912).

[198] 234 U.S. 333 (1914).

[199] 232 U.S. 14 (1914); and see United States Express Co. v. New York, 232 U.S. 35 (1914).

New York had virtually been brought to a halt. The New York authorities refused to extend police protection to wagons driven by strikebreakers, unless they carried money or jewelry.

Early in November, Mayor Gaynor of New York began attempts at mediation. He was making progress, when the companies balked on the issue of union recognition, and it is apparent that at this stage, if not earlier, the sympathies of the city administration turned decisively toward the strikers. On November 3, a state assemblyman publicly drew Mayor Gaynor's attention to an old city ordinance which provided that the drivers of express wagons in the city had to be citizens of the United States, or have declared their intention to become such, and that they had to be licensed, at the cost of $5 each, upon applications endorsed by two reputable residents of the city, testifying to their competence. Any express company employing unlicensed drivers was subject to a fine of $10 for each offense.

The ordinance of which this provision formed a part dated back to the middle of the previous century, but it had never been vigorously or even regularly enforced. Now the mayor announced that no unlicensed wagon drivers would be permitted in the streets of New York, and the strikers were jubilant, for the effect of the new policy would plainly be to make the use of strikebreakers greatly more difficult. Some arrests followed, and some efforts by the companies to obtain licenses for nonunion drivers. But the city was carefully investigating applications for licenses, and was in no rush to grant them. Employer resistance reached the breaking point as the City Merchants Association expressed its impatience with the express companies, and Gaynor publicly castigated the express companies as lawbreakers for employing unlicensed drivers. Finally, on November 10, the companies agreed to recognize the union. Simultaneously, however, just as they were giving in, they started an action in federal court for an injunction against enforcement of the licensing ordinance. By November 14, all the men had returned to work, but the litigation continued.[200]

The express companies' attack was on the entire ordinance, which had additional provisions as well. It forbade any express business to be carried on in the city without a license issued to the business itself, and it provided for inspection and licensing of vehicles. The federal court in

---

[200] *New York Times,* Oct. 25, 1910, p. 1, col. 3; Oct. 27, 1910, p. 1, col. 3; Oct. 28, 1910, p. 3, cols. 2, 3; Oct. 29, 1910, p. 1, col. 5; Oct. 30, 1910, p. 1, col. 3, p. 2, col. 6; Nov. 4, 1910, p. 7, col. 3; Nov. 5, 1910, p. 16, col. 1; *New York Tribune,* Nov. 6, 1910, p. 3, col. 3; Nov. 7, 1910, p. 1, col. 7, p. 4, col. 4; Nov. 10, 1910, p. 1, col. 1, p. 9, col. 4; Nov. 11, 1910, p. 1, col. 7, p. 2, col. 1; Nov. 12, 1910, p. 2, col. 2; Nov. 13, 1910, p. 1, col. 7.

New York ultimately enjoined as unconstitutional enforcement of that portion of the ordinance which required the express business itself to be licensed before being allowed to enter the city, but upheld the provisions for inspection and licensing of wagons and of drivers. An appeal was argued in the Supreme Court by William D. Guthrie in December 1913, and in a unanimous decision by Hughes, delivered in January 1914, the express companies gained a total victory.

The ordinance represented, said Hughes, an attempt to condition the right to engage in interstate commerce upon local consent, and this the Commerce Clause forbade. The provision for driver's licenses might, as the court below had thought, be valid as a regulation intended to ensure safe driving in the city's streets. But it was rendered dubious as a measure so intended by its extraordinary requirements concerning citizenship and endorsement of the applicant by reputable residents of the city. These conditions would inhibit the express company from hiring its drivers elsewhere than in New York, and thus unduly burden interstate commerce. In any event, however, the provision concerning driver's licenses was not severable from the rest of the ordinance, and had to fall together with the whole—although why that was so, except as it served to avoid a head-on decision of the most difficult of the constitutional issues in the case, Hughes failed to explain.

In a number of other cases, the Court proved itself astute in guarding what it considered to be interstate traffic against imposition on it of state-established rates for intrastate traffic,[201] it followed earlier decisions in forbidding a dry state to stop importation of liquor by railroad,[202] and it even protected a railroad against a state regulation whose only sin, apparently, was that it was too rigid and pesky an attempt to enforce prompt delivery to consignees of goods brought into the state.[203] The Court frustrated a really quite impossible effort by Oklahoma to forestall government by injunction through a statute forbidding foreign corporations, including railroads, on pain of expulsion from the state, to remove into the diversity jurisdiction of the federal courts suits brought against them in the state courts. And it dealt in similar fashion with ponderous

---

[201] Ohio R.R. Commission v. Worthington, 225 U.S. 101 (1912); Texas & New Orleans R.R. Co. v. Sabine Tram Co., 227 U.S. 111 (1913); Railroad Commission v. Texas & Pacific Ry., 229 U.S. 336 (1913).

[202] Louisville & Nashville R.R. v. Cook Brewing Co., 223 U.S. 70 (1912); but cf. DeBary v. Louisiana, 227 U.S. 108 (1913); Cureton v.

Georgia, 136 Ga. 91 (1911), *writ of error dismissed on motion of plaintiff in error,* 229 U.S. 631 (1913).

[203] Yazoo & Mississippi R.R. v. Greenwood Grocery Co., 227 U.S. 1 (1913). *Compare* Minneapolis & St. Louis R.R. v. Gray, 110 Minn. 527 (1910), *writ of error dismissed on motion of plaintiff in error,* 226 U.S. 618 (1912).

reporting requirements which it perceived as relatively aimless Populist harassments of interstate corporations.[204]

In *Kansas Southern Railway* v. *Kaw Valley Drainage District*, the Court applied the Commerce Clause against local flood-control measures. The Kansas River had overflowed in 1903, and caused great damage in Kansas City. Now Kansas wanted to build levees as a safeguard for the future, and it wanted the railroad's bridges over the river raised, since it was intending to raise the shores. A state court issued an injunction requiring the railroad to comply by removing the present lower bridges, despite the railroad's protestations that it could not do so without the consent of the Secretary of War, since the Kansas River was a navigable stream. The Supreme Court reversed. The state might have validly issued an order to the railroad conditional upon its obtaining the necessary consent, but to order it in effect to stop running its trains over certain bridges was beyond the power of the state even in these rather pitched circumstances involving the elemental state interest in public safety. The state, said Holmes, coining a famous phrase, "cannot avoid the operation of this rule by simply invoking the convenient apologetics of the police power."[205]

Finally, and most dubiously, in *Oklahoma* v. *Kansas Natural Gas Co.*, the Court used the Commerce Clause to strike down an Oklahoma statute, defended as a conservation measure, which prohibited the exportation of natural gas from the state. Only domestic Oklahoma corporations were allowed to produce natural gas in the state, or lay pipelines for its transportation, and they could transmit it only to points within the state. Oklahoma, it was said in support of the statute, was a prairie state without a supply of fuel except for coal and natural gas, and would find herself without fuel for her cities if she permitted exportation. Natural gas supplies had been exhausted in other states, such as Indiana, and Oklahoma meant to ward off this fate.[206]

Over three dissents without opinion—Holmes, Lurton, and Hughes

---

[204] Harrison v. St. Louis & San Francisco R.R., 232 U.S. 318 (1914); Mercantile Trust Co. v. Texas and Pacific Ry., 223 U.S. 710 (1911) (statute similar to Oklahoma's held unconstitutional under Due Process Clause); Buck Stove Co. v. Vickers, 226 U.S. 205 (1912); Wilson-Moline Buggy Co. v. Hawkins, 80 Kan. 117, 101 Pac. 1009 (1909), *reversed*, 223 U.S. 713 (1911); International Text-book Co. v. Peterson, 133 Wisc. 302,

113 N.W. 730 (1907), *reversed*, 218 U.S. 664 (1910); International Text-book Co. v. Lynch, 81 Vt. 101, 69A. 91 (1908), reversed, 218 U.S. 664 (1910).

[205] Kansas Southern Ry. v. Kaw Valley Drainage District, 233 U.S. 75, 79 (1914).

[206] *Brief for Appellant,* No. 916, Oklahoma v. Kansas Natural Gas Co., 221 U.S. 229 (1911).

—McKenna, for the Court, held the statute unconstitutional. It might be a conservation measure, he said, but "the purpose of its conservation is in a sense commercial—the business welfare of the State, as coal might be, or timber. . . . If the States have such power a singular situation might result. Pennsylvania might keep its coal, the Northwest its timber, the mining States their minerals. And why may not the products of the field be brought within the principle? Thus enlarged, or without that enlargement, its influence on interstate commerce need not be pointed out. To what consequences does such power tend? If one State has it, all States have it; embargo may be retaliated by embargo and commerce will be halted at state lines."[207] In an earlier case, a state had been permitted to conserve its freshwater resources by prohibiting their export,[208] but that was a different matter altogether, said McKenna, since water was a natural advantage of a state.[209] (And is not natural gas?)[210]

The issue would recur, and the Court would reach the same result, even in context of a less absolute state statute, but on this later occasion over powerful written dissent.[211] So long as no national policy had been formulated by Congress, was the Court justified in displacing state efforts to fill the void, and in opting for unhindered private exploitation? The Court could not substitute national ordering for possibly less wise, and possibly separatist, local regulation; it could make a choice only between the public policy of a state and no public policy at all—for the time being, at any rate. "Our system of government," Hughes said in the *Minnesota Rate Cases*, "is a practical adjustment," and the Constitution does not require that all aspects of interstate commerce "should go uncontrolled pending federal intervention." And in the *Port Richmond Ferry* case he added that it had never been supposed "that because of

---

[207] The voice is the voice of McKenna, but the hand is the hand of counsel for the gas company, who included John G. Johnson. Their brief argued:

> Such a law, if legal in Oklahoma, would . . . be legal in every other state . . . and each state would define for itself which of its products should go into interstate commerce, and thus not only regulate interstate commerce but destroy it; it would forbid and deny to the citizen of the United States his right . . . to introduce the natural gas into interstate commerce. . . ."
> (*Brief for Appellee*, No. 916,

Oklahoma v. Kansas Natural Gas Co., 221 U.S. 229 (1911).)

[208] Hudson County Water Co. v. McCarter, 209 U.S. 349 (1908).

[209] Wildlife conservation measures were apparently also different. Booth Fisheries v. Illinois, 253 Ill. 423, 97 N.E. 837 (1912), *writ of error dismissed on motion of plaintiff in error*, 231 U.S. 763 (1913).

[210] Oklahoma v. Kansas Natural Gas Co., 221 U.S. 229, 255 (1911). Compare Ling Su Fan v. United States, 218 U.S. 302 (1910) (Philippine statute prohibiting export of silver sustained against Due Process attack).

[211] Pennsylvania v. West Virginia, 262 U.S. 553 (1923).

the absence of federal action the public interest was unprotected from extortion."

Attempts by states to block the very channels of interstate commerce—of all interstate commerce, indiscriminately—or to exclude the agents of that commerce, raised quite different problems, much more suitable to judicial resolution. And in all circumstances, if it was to perform a function under the Commerce Clause at all, the Court was entitled to assess the quality and intensity of the local interest that was invoked to justify the state regulation of interstate commerce. But there is a considerable gulf between the attitude displayed in the statements of Hughes just quoted, and that of the Court in the Oklahoma natural gas case. The temper of the Court in the latter case was made even clearer by a sequel to it.

Oklahoma asked for a modification of the decree so as to save portions of its statute which provided for inspection and licensing of pipelines, on the theory that these could validly survive even if, as the Court had held, Oklahoma must allow its natural gas to be carried out of the state. These sections, the Court answered curtly through Day a year later, were not separable. They were infected with the unconstitutional purpose of the entire statute—although no real reason was vouchsafed for this proposition. Secondly, Oklahoma argued that the decree was so broadly framed as to forbid all possible state regulation of natural gas. The Court refused to revise the language, saying that only unconstitutional measures were prohibited. But that meant that in trying to evolve future regulations, Oklahoma had to suffer the inhibition of an overly broad decree, which, conceivably, threatened to attach contempt penalties to erroneous judgments that a regulation would prove valid.[212]

The Court's temper was also predominantly, and most often, it may be thought, unnecessarily hostile to state legislation in Commerce Clause preemption cases. With great readiness, the Court would divine in federal Commerce Clause statutes a Congressional intention to occupy the field, as the phrase goes, and then it would wield the Supremacy Clause to clear the field of state law, whether or not inconsistent with federal legislation. An example of a classic sort of preemption case, to which the above description does not apply, was *Chicago, Indianapolis & Louisville Railway* v. *United States*,[213] decided by Harlan. A state statute purported to authorize the issuance of free passes by railroads in circumstances in which such passes were outlawed by the Hepburn Act.[214] Clearly the federal and state policies clashed, and there was no

---

[212] Haskell v. Kansas Natural Gas Co., 224 U.S. 217 (1912).

[213] 219 U.S. 486 (1911).

[214] See *supra*, pp. 204–205.

doubt under the Supremacy Clause which had to prevail. But such a case as this was a rare occurrence, as were, at the other end of the spectrum, cases that found room for valid state action in the interstices of federal legislation.

Among the latter, few as they were, *Savage v. Jones*,[215] written by Hughes in 1912, stands out. An Indiana statute established certain standards for animal feedstuffs, and prescribed certain labels. The statute was applied to feed brought in through interstate commerce, and the question was whether the Indiana regulatory scheme conflicted with, and was preempted by, the federal Pure Food and Drug Act. That Act, said Hughes, merely prohibited misbranding; it did not, like the Indiana statute, establish standards and prescribe labels. There was thus no conflict. The federal Act, moreover, contained no express denial of concurrent state regulatory power, and an intent to occupy the field was not lightly to be imputed to Congress. So the Indiana statute was permitted to stand.[216]

Different intimations, however, were drawn from the federal Pure Food and Drug Act in *McDermott v. Wisconsin*.[217] A Wisconsin pure food and drug statute required, subject to criminal penalties, that any syrup mixed with glucose be marked with the true name of each ingredient on the can, so that if it was over 75 percent glucose it had to be marked as glucose flavored with something else, and the statute provided that no other designation than the one prescribed by the state could appear on the label. Penalties were imposed on retailers in Wisconsin who were selling syrup brought in from Chicago labeled with such designations as "Corn Syrup with Cane Flavor." This and like designations were authorized by an administrative regulation duly made under the federal Pure Food and Drug Act. To comply with the Wisconsin statute, not only would a retailer have had to put the Wisconsin-prescribed label on, but the federally authorized label would have had to come off. Yet it would have been no violation of the federal statute or administrative order to substitute the Wisconsin label for the federal one, since the federal statute only required, and the administrative order only specified, labeling that would not mislead. The Wisconsin labels would simply mislead even less. Just the same, the Court, in an opinion by Day, held that the Wisconsin regulation conflicted with the administrative rulings made pursuant to the federal Act, if not necessarily

---

[215] 225 U.S. 501 (1912); see also Standard Stock Food Co. v. Wright, 225 U.S. 540 (1912).

[216] See also, for decisions in the same spirit, if on different subjects, Anderson v. Pacific Coast S.S. Co.,

225 U.S. 187 (1912) (also by Hughes); Missouri, Kansas and Texas Ry. v. Harris, 234 U.S. 412 (1914).

[217] 228 U.S. 115 (1913).

with the bare text of the Act itself. No federal administrative action had been in question in *Savage* v. *Jones*, which was thus distinguishable.

McDermott v. *Wisconsin* is a close case. It is surely arguable that Wisconsin's rules on top of the federal ones were too much of an administrative monstrosity to impose on manufacturers who distributed nationally or regionally. The *McDermott* case holds that a measure that might have been viewed as a valid enough state regulation of interstate commerce if there had been no federal legislation, and if the choice for the Court had been, starkly, between state regulation and none at all— such an otherwise acceptable measure became an invalid burden on commerce, both because displacing the Wisconsin statute now no longer meant that the subject would be left entirely unregulated, and because two sets of regulations operating on the same subject in the same territory were more of a literal burden than one.

Similarly close perhaps, but quite supportable, was a decision by Van Devanter protecting the primary jurisdiction of the Interstate Commerce Commission in a rate discrimination case.[218] No easily understood justification can be found, however, in the necessities of federal supremacy, or in the Court's duty to safeguard the integrity of federal policy and federal administration, for such a case as *New York Central Railroad* v. *Hudson County*,[219] which is to be compared with Hughes' decisions under the Commerce Clause itself in the *Minnesota Rate Cases* and the *Port Richmond Ferry* case.[220]

A ferry between Weehawken, New Jersey, and New York City, owned by the New York Central Railroad, carried large numbers of foot passengers commuting from one city to the other, as well as passengers coming by railroad from Albany along the west side of the Hudson and bound for New York City, and New York City passengers bound for the railroad terminal in Weehawken and traveling on. New Jersey fixed rates to be charged for foot passengers from New Jersey to New York, and on round trips from New Jersey, but not for passengers ending a railroad trip, or bound for one. Nevertheless, White, for a unanimous Court, held the New Jersey regulation to be preempted by the Interstate Commerce Act, which was applicable not only to railroads but to all bridges and ferries "used or operated in connection with any railroad." (The preemption issue did not arise in the otherwise entirely similar *Port Richmond* case, because there the ferry did not run in connection with any railroad.)

To be sure, as White said, all of the ferry's passengers were in interstate commerce. But as held in the *Port Richmond* case, regulation

---

[218] Robinson v. Baltimore & Ohio R.R., 222 U.S. 506 (1912).

[219] 227 U.S. 248 (1913).

[220] See *supra,* pp. 256–57, 264–65.

was nevertheless permitted to the state, so far as the Commerce Clause operating of its own force was concerned. Again, the Interstate Commerce Commission undoubtedly had authority to set these rates, and to set them for all the passengers, train-bound and train-arrived or no. And when the commission should act, its rates would prevail pursuant to the Supremacy Clause. But the commission had not acted. White's holding was, therefore, precisely as if Hughes had prematurely made his *Shreveport Case* ruling in the *Minnesota Rate Cases*, and had there displaced state rates affecting interstate commerce before he could rely on any administrative determination of the need to do so.

No less difficult to justify is a line of cases dealing with an apparently very common (if not very wise or attractive) kind of state statute that attempted to define duties of railroads toward shippers. The Court could not quite bring itself to hold statutes of this sort generally invalid under the Commerce Clause, or for that matter, under the Due Process and Equal Protection clauses. So the basis of decision shifted to the Supremacy Clause. The drift of the process of judgment may be observed by comparing two opinions of McKenna, *Southern Railway* v. *Reid*[221] and *Southern Railway* v. *Reid and Beam*.[222] Both concerned a North Carolina statute imposing a $50-a-day penalty for failure by a railroad promptly to receive freight tendered to it at a regular station.

In the first, the railroad explained a delay as caused by the lack of a tariff filed with the Interstate Commerce Commission to cover the route on which the shipper demanded that the freight be sent. What was involved was establishment of a point rate with a connecting carrier. The railroad took measures to establish such a rate, and to file it in accordance with the Interstate Commerce Act. Then it accepted the shipment. But not till then, for it was unlawful under the federal Act to carry any goods except at rates stated in a tariff filed with the commission. McKenna held, naturally and necessarily enough, that as so applied, the North Carolina statute was preempted, because of a direct conflict with requirements imposed on the railroad by the federal Act.

But in the second case, a delay in accepting freight for shipment was owing merely to the railroad's negligence. Tariffs duly filed with the Interstate Commerce Commission existed for the route for which shipment was tendered. So as applied here, the North Carolina statute was not in conflict with the Interstate Commerce Act. Nevertheless, McKenna reached the same result, although this time he drew a brief dissent from Lurton.[223] Also without being able to point to any conflict, and on the basis merely of a general provision in the Hepburn Act re-

---

[221] 222 U.S. 424 (1912).
[222] 222 U.S. 444 (1912).

[223] See also Southern Ry. v. Burlington Lumber Co., 225 U.S. 99 (1912).

quiring railroads to furnish transportation and to establish through routes and just reasonable rates, the Court preempted statutes imposing penalties for failure to provide cars to shippers within a reasonable period upon request.[224]

This process of preemptive judgment drifted to most serious consequences in cases dealing with the liability of carriers for loss of goods or damage to goods in transit. The Carmack Amendment to the Hepburn Act, the Court held repeatedly without any support in its language or any attempt to find support in its history, was intended to impose a uniform federal rule of liability in place of various preexisting state rules. State statutes or rules of decision, therefore, which held carriers to stricter and fuller responsibility for losses than did the Carmack Amendment as interpreted by the Supreme Court were preempted.[225] The upshot was that far from extending new and greater security to shippers, the Carmack Amendment was turned into an instrument for protecting carriers and enabling them to limit their liability virtually at will to an amount stated in small print on the back of a ticket. This might have been good or bad policy, but it was not the policy of many states, and pretty nearly the opposite of the policy announced in the Carmack Amendment itself.[226] By the same token, and by the same process of judgment, the Federal Employers' Liability

---

[224] Chicago Rock Island & Pacific Ry. v. Hardwick Farmers Elevator Co., 226 U.S. 426 (1913); St. Louis Iron Mountain & Southern Ry. v. Edwards, 227 U.S. 265 (1913); Oregon R.R. & Navigation Co. v. Martin, 58 Ore. 198 (1910), *reversed,* 229 U.S. 606 (1913); Chicago Rock Island & Pacific Ry. v. Beatty, 34 Okla. 321 (1911), *reversed,* 234 U.S. 753 (1914). And see Hampton v. St. Louis Iron Mountain & Southern Ry., 227 U.S. 456 (1913). But see Atchison, Topeka & Santa Fe Ry. v. Starr Grain & Lumber Co., 85 Kan. 281 (1911), *writ of error dismissed on motion of plaintiff in error,* 231 U.S. 762 (1913).

[225] See *supra,* pp. 202–204.

[226] Adams Express Co. v. Croninger, 226 U.S. 491 (1913); Chicago, Burlington & Quincy R.R. v. Miller, 226 U.S. 513 (1913); Chicago, St. Paul, etc. Ry. v. Latta, 226 U.S. 519 (1913); Wells Fargo & Co. v. Neiman-Marcus, 227 U.S. 469 (1913); Kansas City Southern Ry. v. Carl, 227 U.S.

639 (1913); Missouri, Kansas & Texas Ry. v. Harriman, 227 U.S. 657 (1913); Adams Express Co. v. Vervaeke, 230 Pa. 647 (1911), *reversed,* 229 U.S. 627 (1913); Adams Express Co. v. Wright, 230 Pa. 635, *reversed,* 229 U.S. 629 (1913); Chicago, Rock Island & Pacific Ry. v. Cramer, 232 U.S. 490 (1914); Great Northern Ry. v. O'Connor, 232 U.S. 508 (1914); Boston & Maine R.R. v. Hooker, 233 U.S. 97 (1914); Atchison, Topeka & Santa Fe Ry. v. Robinson, 233 U.S. 173 (1914); Atchison, Topeka & Santa Fe Ry. v. Moore, 223 U.S. 182 (1914); Seaboard Air Line Ry. v. J. M. Pace Co., 160 N.C. 215, 76 N.E. 513 (1912), *reversed,* 234 U.S. 751 (1914); Pacific Express Co. v. Rudman, 145 S.W. 268 (Tex. Civ. Appls. 1912), *reversed,* 234 U.S. 752 (1914). *But cf.* Missouri, Kansas & Texas Ry. v. Harris, 234 U.S. 412 (1914); and *cf.* Chicago, Rock Island & Pacific Ry. v. Maucher, 248 U.S. 359 (1919).

Act was in some instances turned into a statute limiting rather than extending recovery for injuries suffered by railroad employees.[227]

The Court's attitude was relatively more indulgent at this time toward state taxation rather than regulation of interstate commerce.[228] There were some important cases applying the Commerce Clause to state taxation in the period under discussion, but this intricate subject invites a longer look than can be had over a four-year span. Moreover, the Commerce Clause tax cases of these years, unlike some later ones, bear only tangentially on the Court's general approach to social and economic legislation. That approach, and the consequent impact of the Court on the Progressive movement, need now to be further explored in state cases arising under the Due Process, Equal Protection and Contract clauses, while the state taxation cases are saved for separate and detailed examination from a later perspective.

Suffice to mention here that in *Foote* v. *Maryland*,[229] argued for Maryland by a latter-day Edgar Allan Poe, who was serving as state attorney general, the Court dealt harshly with a tax which it conceived to be part of a regulatory and not a revenue-raising scheme for oyster fishing in the Chesapeake Bay; that in *Crenshaw* v. *Arkansas*,[230] striking down a license tax on peddlers, who were held to be really drummers, the Court somewhat extended the rule of *Robbins* v. *Shelby County*,[231] but that in *Browning* v. *Waycross*,[232] a tax on peddlers was duly upheld; that gross receipts taxes fell in one case, but passed muster in two;[233] that in *Baltic Mining Co.* v. *Massachusetts*,[234] which concerned a capital stock tax, a doctrine that had its origin in *Western Union Telegraph Co.* v. *Kansas*[235] was carried forward, through something of a modification of the holding of that recent case, but by no means finally settled; and that in *New York Life Insurance Co.* v. *Deer Lodge County*,[236] the proposition that insurance was not commerce, and that a tax on an

---

[227] See *supra,* pp. 211–13, and cases cited in nn.42, 43.

[228] See A. M. Bickel, *The Unpublished Opinions of Mr. Justice Brandeis* (1957), 114.

[229] 232 U.S. 494 (1914).

[230] 227 U.S. 389 (1913); see also Rogers v. Arkansas, 227 U.S. 401 (1913); and Stewart v. Michigan, 232 U.S. 665 (1914).

[231] 120 U.S. 489 (1887).

[232] 233 U.S. 16 (1914), see also Singer Sewing Machine Co. v. Brickell, 233 U.S. 304 (1914); compare also Byles v. Arkansas, 93 Ark. 612, 126 S.W. 94 (1910), *writ of error dis-*

missed on motion of plaintiff in error, 225 U.S. 717 (1912).

[233] Oklahoma v. Wells Fargo Co., 223 U.S. 298 (1912); U.S. Express Co. v. Minnesota, 223 U.S. 335 (1912); Ohio Tax Cases, 232 U.S. 576 (1914).

[234] 231 U.S. 68 (1913); see also Cudahy Packing Co. v. Denton, 79 Kan. 368, 97 Pac. 439 (1908), *writ of error dismissed by stipulation,* 223 U.S. 734 (1911); but see Atchison, Topeka & Santa Fe Ry. v. O'Connor, 223 U.S. 280 (1912).

[235] 216 U.S. 1 (1910).

[236] 231 U.S. 495, 502 (1913).

insurance company could not, therefore, be a tax on interstate commerce, was reaffirmed, having been reconsidered at all only "in deference to the earnestness of counsel," who included Roscoe Pound.

Due Process

The two cases, in these years, which permitted themselves the most striking generalizations about the Due Process Clause and the judicial function under it were *Noble State Bank* v. *Haskell* and *Chicago, Burlington & Quincy Railroad* v. *McGuire*. Both were argued to a Bench that included Hughes, but had as yet two vacancies, one of them in the Chief Justiceship. Van Devanter and Lamar had not then been seated. The decisions came down shortly after the accession of the latter two Justices, but since they had not heard the arguments, they presumably did not participate, even though a notation to that effect does not appear. To these two cases should be added, as outstanding in importance and impact among a number of other ones, *German Alliance Insurance Co.* v. *Kansas*. Of the principal two, *Noble State Bank* v. *Haskell* was the more daring, both on its facts and on its grounds of decision, and was the more widely remarked.

Oklahoma had created a depositors' guaranty fund by levying assessments of up to 5 percent on the average daily deposits of all banks. In the event of failure, depositors were to be reimbursed out of the fund. This was no isolated or idiosyncratic reform. It had been advocated in the Democratic platform of 1908, in a plank that was countered by the Republicans with a promise, later redeemed, to create a postal savings system. Similar Nebraska and Kansas statutes faced the Court in companion cases, and New York, Indiana, Ohio, Iowa, and Vermont also had such statutes.[237] The reform was attacked as taking property from solvent banks, which the Noble State Bank alleged itself to be, in order to bail out depositors of insolvent competitors. This, it was said, was a taking of property for private rather than public uses, and thus a violation of the Due Process Clause of the Fourteenth Amendment.

Holmes, for a unanimous if incomplete Court, upheld the statute in a ringing pronouncement. We must be cautious, he said,

> about pressing the broad words of the Fourteenth Amendment to a drily logical extreme. Many laws which it would be vain to ask the court to overthrow could be shown, easily enough, to transgress a scholastic interpretation of one or another of the great guarantees in the Bill of Rights. They more or less limit the liberty of the individual

---

[237] *Brief for Defendant in Error,* No. 71, Noble State Bank v. Haskell, 219 U.S. 104 (1911); *New York Times,* Jan. 4, 1911, p. 6, col. 1.

or they diminish property to a certain extent. We have few scientifically certain criteria of legislation, and as it often is difficult to mark the line where what is called the police power of the States is limited by the Constitution of the United States, judges should be slow to read into the latter a *nolumus mutare* as against the law-making power.

Unquestionably, Holmes allowed, the statute took one bank's property in order to pay the debts of another. But it did so for "an ulterior public advantage," which "may justify a comparatively insignificant taking of private property for what, in its immediate purpose, is a private use."[238] There were other cases "beside the every day one of taxation, in which the share of each party in the benefit of a scheme of mutual protection is sufficient compensation for the correlative burden that it is compelled to assume. . . . At least, if we have a case within the reasonable exercise of the police power . . . no more need be said." The police power extended "to all the great public needs." It could be exerted "in aid of what is sanctioned by usage, or held by the prevailing morality or strong and preponderant opinion to be greatly and immediately necessary to the public welfare." It could be exerted to promote commerce. Here the legislature was doing so by attempting to make the currency of checks secure, "and by the same stroke to make safe the almost compulsory resort of depositors to banks as the only available means for keeping money on hand."

The legislature had chosen, by appropriate means, to make a general panic impossible. Could it similarly require all corporations or all grocers to guarantee each other's solvency? Where was the line to be drawn? That was a futile question. "With regard to the police power, as elsewhere in the law, lines are pricked out by the gradual approach and contact of decisions on opposing sides." In denying a petition for rehearing, filed in part, no doubt, in hopes that the result might be affected by the changes that had taken place in the Court since the argument in December 1910, Holmes added a slight qualification, when he said that his general remarks about the police power had been intended to interpret what had been done in the past, "not to give a new and wider scope to the power."[239]

---

[238] Compare Eastern Oregon Land Co. v. Willow River Land & Irrigation Co., 204 Fed. 516 (9th Cir. 1913), *cert. denied*, 234 U.S. 761 (1914) (condemnation of land for purposes of building irrigation canal allowed, on the ground that the private benefit to be derived was incidental, and the public purpose predominant). But *cf.* the later Holmes of Pennsylvania Coal Co. v. Mahon, 260 U.S. 393 (1922).

[239] Noble State Bank v. Haskell, 219 U.S. 104, 110–12, 575, 578, 580 (1911). And see Shallenberger v. First State Bank, 219 U.S. 114 (1911); Assaria State Bank v. Dolley, 219 U.S. 121 (1911). See also Abilene National Bank v. Dolley, 228 U.S. 1

The disparate subject matter to the side—and the disparity is not so great—Holmes' opinion in *Noble State Bank* v. *Haskell* is the very counterpart of the opinion he was finally required to issue in *The Pipe Line Cases*.[240] This time the "fizz" (another of the words he used when complaining about his censors)[241] was left in, although not all of it apparently, and not without misgivings on the part of one or two of the Justices. Some years later, Holmes complained *"between ourselves"* to Felix Frankfurter that they had made him strike out of the *Oklahoma Bank* case "a contrast with nations with whom the Minister of Fine Arts was not less important than the Secretary of the Treasury."[242] Among Holmes' colleagues, Harlan did not like the implications in the generalities about the police power, and neither did McKenna. Both announced to Holmes that they would concur separately in the result, but not in the opinion. Yet evidently they changed their minds and went along without special notation in the end.[243]

(1913), in which the Court had earlier denied certiorari, 179 Fed. 461 (8th Cir. 1910), *cert. denied*, 218 U.S. 673 (1910).

A week after he decided Noble State Bank v. Haskell, Holmes also upheld a New York statute which, as applied, in effect made it impossible for travel agents catering to immigrants to act also as petty bankers for them, receiving and holding small deposits, many of them for ultimate transmission abroad. The business was fraught with great opportunities for dishonest practices, and in the panic of 1907, numerous losses were sustained, running into the millions, while losses in regular banks were of course much smaller. Engel v. O'Malley, 219 U.S. 128 (1911); see *Brief for Appellee*, No. 703, Engel v. O'Malley, 219 U.S. 128 (1911). Other regulations of banks were upheld in Bradley v. Richmond, 227 U.S. 477 (1913); and National Safe Deposit Company v. Illinois, 232 U.S. 58 (1914).

[240] See *supra*, pp. 232–37. Indeed, one of the things he was forced to delete out of his first draft in *The Pipe Line Cases* was a citation to Noble State Bank v. Haskell.

[241] C. E. Hughes, *Biographical Notes*, Microfilm, Ac. 9943, 224, Hughes Papers.

[242] O. W. Holmes to F. Frankfurter, Nov. 1, 1919, Holmes Papers. No doubt the remark fitted in with the passage where Holmes describes all that the police power may be used in aid of. Holmes did not let the thought go to waste. Many years later, while arguing that the police power extended to the regulation of theater ticket sales, he remarked "that theatres are as much devoted to public use as anything well can be. We have not that respect for art that is one of the glories of France. But to many people the superfluous is the necessary, and it seems to me that Government does not go beyond its sphere in attempting to make life livable for them." Tyson & Brother v. Banton, 273 U.S. 418, 445, 447 (1927) (Holmes, J., dissenting).

[243] Holmes Papers. Hughes recalled that the Justices would sometimes "squirm" at some of Holmes' generalities, and that they did so in Noble State Bank v. Haskell. C. E. Hughes, *Biographical Notes*, Microfilm, Ac. 9943, 224, Hughes Papers.

If Holmes' "fizz" was meant to educate by shocking—and to a degree, no doubt, it always was—he got the rise he wanted. Holmes reached his result, the *New York Times* reported in some astonishment, even though he "practically admitted . . . that there is a slight infringement of the Fourteenth Amendment. . . ." Deposit insurance, the *Times* went on, was part of the Bryan program, a rather poor "western" way to meet the problem of bank failures, and far from foolproof. Probably the decision would help the Democrats get deposit insurance enacted in additional states.[244] Writing in the *New York Sun*, James M. Beck, the future Solicitor General, lamented that "the door is now open wide to all manner of socialistic suggestions."[245] The decision was much noted in the professional journals, and it was prominently featured in Charles Warren's article on "The Progressiveness of the United States Supreme Court."[246] The Presidential commission headed by Senator George Sutherland of Utah, which made the abortive suggestion that Congress substitute a workmen's compensation law for the Federal Employers' Liability Act, argued the constitutionality of its proposal by quoting Holmes' passage about the reach of the police power.[247]

A few weeks after *Noble State Bank* v. *Haskell* came the opinion, also unanimous, by Hughes in *Chicago, Burlington & Quincy Railroad* v. *McGuire.* An Iowa employers' liability statute, applicable to railroads, abolished the fellow-servant rule, and invalidated contracts between a railroad and its employees by which the worker waived the right to sue. The Chicago, Burlington and Quincy, in common with a number of other major railroads,[248] had established an employee relief fund, which was fed by its own contributions as well as the workers'. Contracts between the railroad and its employees provided that any employee who accepted benefits from the fund thereby waived his right to sue the railroad in case of injury. McGuire, having been injured, accepted benefits, and the railroad claimed that he was, therefore, barred from obtaining a judgment under the state employers' liability act. The argument was that the statutory attempt to free McGuire from his obligation under his contract with the railroad was unconstitutional, as an impairment of the liberty of contract guaranteed by the Due Process Clause.

---

[244] *New York Times,* Jan. 4, 1911, p. 6, col. 1; Jan. 5, 1911, p. 8, col. 2.

[245] M. Keller, *In Defense of Yesterday—James M. Beck and the Politics of Conservatism, 1861–1936* (1958), 90.

[246] C. Warren, "The Progressiveness of the United States Supreme Court," *Colum. L. Rev.,* 12:294, 1912; Note, "State Rate Regulation and the Four-teenth Amendment," *Colum. L. Rev.,* 11:330, 1911; Note, *Colum. L. Rev.,* 11:475, 1911; Note, "Judicial Construction of the Fourteenth Amendment," *Harv. L. Rev.,* 26:9, 1913.

[247] See *supra,* p. 210, n.33.

[248] See *Brief for Plaintiff in Error,* No. 62, at 2, Chicago, Burlington & Quincy R.R. v. McGuire, 219 U.S. 549 (1911).

The railroad's reliance was in such cases as *Allgeyer* v. *Louisiana*,[249] *Lochner* v. *New York*,[250] and *Adair* v. *United States*.[251]

"Liberty," Hughes wrote, "implies the absence of arbitrary restraint, not immunity from reasonable regulations and prohibitions imposed in the interests of the community." It followed from *Munn* v. *Illinois*,[252] *Mugler* v. *Kansas*,[253] and *Muller* v. *Oregon*,[254] that only arbitrary legislative action, which had no relation to a purpose open to the government to achieve, was unconstitutional.

> The scope of judicial inquiry in deciding the question of *power* is not to be confused with the scope of legislative considerations in dealing with a matter of *policy*. Whether the enactment is wise or unwise, whether it is based on sound economic theory, whether it is the best means to achieve the desired result, whether, in short, the legislative discretion within its prescribed limits should be exercised in a particular manner, are matters for the judgment of the legislature, and the earnest conflict of serious opinion does not suffice to bring them within the range of judicial cognizance.

There could be no doubt any longer of the power of the legislature to abolish the fellow-servant rule. Invalidation of agreements obligating the employee not to sue was a measure in support of that policy, a measure insuring its efficacy, and hence also within legislative power.[255]

There was far-reaching language in Hughes' opinion, but the Holmesian *panache* was lacking, of course, and the press hardly noticed it. Commentators such as Charles Warren, who were looking for signs of movement in Supreme Court attitudes, did make something of it, but the *McGuire* opinion did not get its full due until more than a generation later, when in *West Coast Hotel Co.* v. *Parrish*, Hughes as Chief Justice declared minimum wage legislation constitutional, overruling the notorious decision in *Adkins* v. *Children's Hospital*.[256] It was the *McGuire* case, said Attorney General Robert H. Jackson in an article honoring Hughes on his retirement in 1941, that had laid the foundation for his later action in sustaining regulation of minimum wages.[257] Hughes himself thought so also.[258]

---

[249] 165 U.S. 578 (1897).

[250] 198 U.S. 45 (1905).

[251] 208 U.S. 161 (1908).

[252] 94 U.S. 113 (1877).

[253] 123 U.S. 623 (1887).

[254] 208 U.S. 412 (1908).

[255] Chicago, Burlington & Quincy R.R. v. McGuire, 219 U.S. 549, 567, 569 (1911); but *cf.* Day v. Atlantic Coast Line Ry., 179 Fed. 26 (4th Cir. 1910), *cert. denied,* 220 U.S. 617 (1911).

[256] West Coast Hotel Co. v. Parrish, 300 U.S. 379 (1937), *overruling* Adkins v. Children's Hospital, 261 U.S. 525 (1923).

[257] *A.B.A.J.,* 27:410, July 1941.

[258] C. E. Hughes, *Biographical Notes,* Microfilm, Ac. 9943, Ch. XXIII, 31–32, Hughes Papers.

In the meantime, the constitutionality, as such, of statutes abrogating the fellow-servant rule, which Hughes reasserted in the *McGuire* case, was reaffirmed once again by Van Devanter in the *Second Employers' Liability Cases.*[259] More importantly, the *McGuire* case was soon followed by a number of decisions upholding other regulations of the employment relationship—including imposition of a maximum ten-hour day for women, and prohibitions of child labor—against claims of liberty of contact.[260] *McGuire* was brigaded as a precedent with *Muller* v. *Oregon,* and it had an effect also in sustaining state regulation of contractual relationships other than the employment one.[261]

A little more than a month before *McGuire* came down, the Court, in a series of opinions by Harlan, also upheld against claims of violation of the liberty of contract state regulations of grain exchanges, and of certain rate-fixing practices of insurance companies.[262] The Court affirmed the constitutionality, as well, of state prohibition statutes, as it had done before,[263] including one that prohibited the sale of all malt liquors, whether or not in fact intoxicating. Judges must not, said Hughes, with reference to the latter statute, "substitute judicial opinion of expediency for the will of the legislature, a notion foreign to our constitutional system." The inquiry had to be "whether, considering the end in view, the statute passes the bounds of reason and assumes the character of a merely arbitrary fiat."[264] The Court even sustained an ordinance making it a crime to operate a poolroom.[265]

Other Due Process decisions upheld a conservation measure

---

[259] *Supra*, pp. 207–208. See also Aluminum Co. of America v. Ramsey, 222 U.S. 251 (1911); Missouri Pacific Ry. v. Castle, 224 U.S. 541 (1912); Lewin v. Caspar, 83 Kan. 799, 109 Pac. 657 (1910), *writ of error dismissed by stipulation,* 223 U.S. 736 (1911); Chicago, Milwaukee & St. Paul Ry. v. Kiley, 138 Wisc. 215, 119 N.W. 309 (1909), *writ of error dismissed,* 226 U.S. 621 (1912).

[260] Mutual Loan Co. v. Martell, 222 U.S. 225 (1911); Sturgis & Burn v. Beauchamp, 231 U.S. 320 (1913); Riley v. Massachusetts, 232 U.S. 671 (1914); Hawley v. Walker, 85 Ohio St. 494, 98 N.E. 1126 (1912), *affirmed,* 232 U.S. 718 (1914); Erie R.R. Co. v. Williams, 233 U.S. 685 (1914).

[261] Selover, Bates & Co. v. Walsh, 226 U.S. 112 (1912); El Paso & Southwestern R.R. v. Weikel, 226 U.S. 590 (1913).

[262] House v. Mayes, 219 U.S. 270 (1911); Brodnax v. Missouri, 219 U.S. 285 (1911); German Alliance Ins. Co. v. Hale, 219 U.S. 307 (1911). Compare Kraft v. District of Columbia, 35 App. D.C. 253 (1910), *cert. denied,* 218 U.S. 673 (1910).

[263] Mugler v. Kansas, 123 U.S. 623 (1887).

[264] Purity Extract Co. v. Lynch, 226 U.S. 192, 202, 204 (1912); Eberle v. Michigan, 232 U.S. 700 (1914); Cureton v. Georgia, 135 Ga. 660 (1911), *writ of error dismissed on motion of plaintiff in error,* 229 U.S. 630 (1913).

[265] Murphy v. California, 225 U.S. 623 (1912).

sharply restricting methods used in drilling for carbonic acid gas,[266] a variety of health and safety measures,[267] a Chicago ordinance establishing, subject to penalties for variations, standard weights for bread sold in loaves,[268] and a Milwaukee ordinance providing for summary seizure and destruction of milk produced by cows that had not been annually certified by a licensed veterinarian as free of tuberculosis.[269] But none of these cases, although they have their significance in the aggregate, are individually equal in importance to *German Alliance Insurance Co. v. Kansas.*

A Kansas statute authorized a superintendent of insurance to fix reasonable, nondiscriminatory rates for fire insurance. He did so, reducing the rates of the German Alliance Company by some 12 percent. This was a suit to enjoin enforcement of the statute, which was alleged to be unconstitutional as an arbitrary taking of private property and an interference with freedom of contract. Insurance, it was argued, was a private business, not a public utility, and the state had no constitutional warrant for regulating its rates. Only property, like a railroad, that had been voluntarily committed by its owners to a public use, said counsel for the company, who included John G. Johnson, could be subjected to price regulation. But a "general public interest" in a given business was "not equivalent to a public use."

The Court's reply, delivered by McKenna, was strong and without ambivalence; this was one of McKenna's best opinions, exhibiting that part of him which, as Holmes grudgingly conceded, "understood the business as well as anyone."[270] But it spoke for a bare majority of five,[271] and it accepted the terms of reference set out in the argument for the company. Applying the formula to which the Court had become accus-

---

[266] Lindsley v. Natural Carbonic Gas Co., 220 U.S. 61 (1911); but *cf.* Ashon v. Conservation Commission of Louisiana, 185 Fed. 221 (C.C.E.D. La. 1911), *appeal dismissed,* 229 U.S. 606 (1913) (portion of fish conservation statute struck down, but largely on procedural grounds); and *cf.* Oklahoma v. Kansas Natural Gas Co., *supra,* p. 269, n.210.

[267] Hutchinson v. Valdosta, 227 U.S. 303 (1913); Barrett v. Indiana, 229 U.S. 26 (1913); Plymouth Coal Co. v. Pennsylvania, 232 U.S. 531 (1914).

[268] Schmidinger v. Chicago, 226 U.S. 578 (1913); see also Moneyweight Scale Co. v. McBride, 199 Mass. 503, 85 N.E. 870 (1909), *writ of error dismissed on motion of plaintiff in error,* 223 U.S. 749 (1912); and see St. Louis Gunning & Advertising Co. v. St. Louis, 235 Mo. 99, 137 S.W. 929 (1911), *writ of error dismissed by stipulation,* 231 U.S. 761 (1913) (regulation of billboards).

[269] Adams v. Milwaukee, 228 U.S. 572 (1913).

[270] See *supra,* p. 239.

[271] There were only three dissenters, but it was only an eight-man Court. Lurton was ill from Dec. 3, 1913, to Apr. 6, 1914. Having not heard the argument of this case on Dec. 10, 1913, he did not participate in its decision on Apr. 20, 1914, although he was back on the Bench by then.

tomed since *Munn* v. *Illinois*, McKenna held that insurance was sufficiently affected with a public interest to be admitted, in the derisive phrase of a critic, "into the magic circle of public utilities."[272] He supported this proposition without hesitation or qualification. But he made scarcely any attempt to break out of the circle.

To a degree, said McKenna, "the public interest is concerned in every transaction between men, the sum of the transactions constituting the activities of life." But something more special was required, "something of more definite consequences," to justify regulatory legislation. It was said—by the dissenters among others—that the usual business "affected with a public interest" was a utility under a legal obligation to render service. Where no right existed in the public to demand service, the argument ran, there was no right to regulate the rates either. "Cases are cited which, it must be admitted, support the contention." But the distinction was artificial. (Indeed, it was circular. A public utility's duty to render service was imposed by law, and the question in this case, as in all such cases, was what duties and other regulations the law could impose on insurance companies.)

Many a business that was not a public utility in the common definition of the term had been subjected to regulation of one sort and another (citing *Noble State Bank* v. *Haskell*). "Against that conservatism of the mind, which puts to question every new act of regulating legislation and regards the legislation invalid or dangerous until it has become familiar, government—state and National—has pressed on in the general welfare; and our reports are full of cases where in instance after instance the exercise of regulation was resisted and yet sustained against attacks asserted to be justified by the Constitution of the United States. The dread of the moment having passed, no one is now heard to say that rights were restrained or their constitutional guarantees impaired." There were many examples of businesses that had at first been considered entirely private, but that had, over time, owing to public concern, been gradually brought under government regulation. "It would be a bold thing to say that the principle [of what was private, and what was subject to public control] is fixed, inelastic, in the precedents of the past and cannot be applied though modern economic conditions may make necessary or beneficial its application."

Fire insurance had, with the years, found itself regulated more and more, until now its rates had been set. The prior instances of regulation were evidence of a general feeling that the public welfare required it. "A conception so general cannot be without cause. The universal sense of a people cannot be accidental; its persistence saves it from the charge

---

[272] Frankfurter and Hart, "Rate Regulation," in *Encyclopedia of the* *Social Sciences,* XIII, 104, 106.

of unconsidered impulse, and its estimate of insurance certainly has substantial basis." Insurance, after all, as a way of spreading the risk of losses, was a form of taxation. The end in view was protection of the country's wealth. As such, insurance concerned the general welfare, and anything that did so could be reached by the police power (citing *Muller* v. *Oregon* and *Chicago, Burlington & Quincy Railroad* v. *McGuire*, among other cases). "What makes for the general welfare is necessarily in the first instance a matter of legislative judgment and a judicial review of such judgment is limited."

Moreover, insurance companies, holding large funds, as they did, became a financial resource of the community, and their solvency was itself crucial to the general welfare. Did this line of reasoning prove too much, and enable legislation to reach every human activity? Not at all. The decision was confined, said McKenna, to the circumstances of the insurance business. There was, finally, no infringement of the liberty of contract in insurance regulation—the liberty of insurer and insured to make their own price. "We may venture to observe that the price of insurance is not fixed over the counters of the companies by what Adam Smith calls the higgling of the market, but formed in the councils of the underwriters. . . ." The customer had to take what he got, and was powerless to negotiate. Hence to speak of liberty of contract in these circumstances was illusory.

The dissent was by Lamar, with White and Van Devanter joining. This was not, as they saw it, a statute affecting safety or morals, nor did this case concern a monopoly, or the necessities of life. Here was sheer price fixing in a strictly personal contract; a taking of property just as much as if title to it had been taken. "And if this power be as extensive as is now, for the first time, decided, then the citizen holds his property and his individual right of contract and of labor under legislative favor rather than under constitutional guaranty." Insurance, as just reasserted in *New York Life Insurance Co.* v. *Deer Lodge County*,[273] was not even considered commerce, let alone a public utility. Price fixing had in the past been generally limited to common carriers, with few exceptions. Regulation was a very different matter, there being "a distinction [so, in almost these words, counsel for the company had argued][274] between a public interest—justifying regulation—and a public use—justifying price-fixing."[275]

If *Noble State Bank* v. *Haskell* was, for Holmes, the counterpart of his sorely negotiated opinion in *The Pipe Line Cases*, *German*

---

[273] See *supra*, pp. 275–76.
[274] See *supra*, p. 282.
[275] German Alliance Ins. Co. v.

Kansas, 233 U.S. 389, 401, 406, 407, 409, 411, 412, 413–14, 416, 419, 427 (1914).

Alliance Insurance Co. v. *Kansas* was for McKenna the antithesis of his dissent there. In the dissent, he is all worry about the difficulties of line drawing and about the ultimate reach of the price-fixing power. Here he not only rises above such anxieties, but philosophizes about the repeated instances in which government regulation is at first resisted because unfamiliar, and then easily taken for granted once "the dread of the moment" has passed. And yet *The Pipe Line Cases* and *German Alliance Insurance Co.* v. *Kansas* came down within two months of each other. No one need wonder at a judgment that McKenna was erratic.

Whereas the *McGuire* case went almost unnoticed outside the professional journals, conservative opinion was quite exercised by *German Alliance Insurance Co.* v. *Kansas*, perhaps even more than by *Noble State Bank*. Price fixing caused more anxiety than virtually any other form of regulation. The issue could not be considered closed, said the *New York Times*, and in the long run, the dissent, and not McKenna's opinion, would necessarily prevail. The laws of economics could not be wished or legislated out of existence, and if states established rates that were too low, the companies would simply refuse to supply insurance; and insurance would "be added to the lengthening list of things which the people are learning they cannot supply themselves with by votes or statutes. . . . If the things are had, they must be paid for, or the supply will stop, regardless of legislation or of decisions." Missouri had tried to regulate insurance rates, and had failed and been forced to stop, because insurance companies simply refused to do business in the state. Kentucky was now having the same experience; and so would Kansas. It was a mystery what had started the epidemic of insurance regulation in certain legislatures, particularly Southern, like the contagion of railway regulation in the West, but now that—unfortunately—the judicial corrective was not forthcoming, the way to get at "the herd of wild asses" in these legislatures was by defeating them at the polls. Happily there was no prospect of similar legislation in New York, where very properly abuses of insurance companies had been dealt with, but rate setting was not contemplated.

The *New York Tribune*, more nearly in tune with current political beliefs, remarked that "the progressive spirit of the Supreme Court of the United States has again prevailed." And it thought the country would approve the decision, without, however, "accepting the radical inferences drawn from it by the minority." The Court's opinion was to be read as declaring insurance to be affected with a public interest, which indeed it was. That did not mean, however, that the country was "minded to embark on the dubious project of fixing prices and wages generally."

The insurance business itself, characteristically, like the railroads, wanted to get out from under state regulation, and be regulated by the federal government. It regretted reassertion in *New York Life Insurance Co.* v. *Deer Lodge County*, just a few months earlier, of the proposition that it was not in interstate commerce, and the head of the New York Life Insurance Company had even gone so far as to retain ex-Senator John C. Spooner of Wisconsin, a well-known lawyer with a Supreme Court practice, to draft a constitutional amendment empowering Congress to regulate insurance.[276] Among the law journals, the *Harvard Law Review* thought the majority's decision was made in the spirit of *Noble State Bank* v. *Haskell*, and *Green Bag* pointed out, with justified caution, that the majority, while it viewed the subject in broad perspective, refrained "from pressing its inferences beyond proper limits."[277]

Other forms of regulation of insurance had, as McKenna observed, and as the dissent conceded, passed muster before,[278] although the business being national, there were problems of the conflict of laws, of Due Process, and of Full Faith and Credit concerning the jurisdiction of a given state to impose its policy on a given contract of insurance, or its power to exclude a given insurance company from doing business within its borders.[279] But for many years, *German Alliance Insurance Co.* v. *Kansas* spawned no cases further enlarging or generally establishing a price-fixing power of government. Sutherland's characterization of the case, while expressly limiting it to its facts, in 1927, was quite correct. *German Alliance Insurance Co.* v. *Kansas*, he said, "marks the extreme limit to which this court thus far has gone in sustaining price fixing legislation."[280]

The *German Alliance* case was restricted to a test of the state's power to fix rates at all; it did not raise the issue, touched on earlier in the discussion of the *Minnesota Rate Cases*, whether a given rate violated the Due Process Clause because it was confiscatory.[281] As in litigation over railroad rates, so also in cases dealing with other enter-

---

[276] *New York Times*, Apr. 22, 1914, p. 14, col. 2; Apr. 25, 1914, p. 14, col. 3; May 10, 1914, p. 8, col. 1; June 13, 1914, p. 8, col. 7; July 17, 1914, p. 12, col. 7; July 23, 1914, p. 8, col. 6; *New York Tribune*, Apr. 22, 1914, p. 8, col. 2. See also *Washington Evening Star*, Apr. 20, 1914, p. 16, col. 6; *Chicago Tribune*, Apr. 21, 1914, p. 18, col. 4.

[277] Note, *Harv. L. Rev.*, 28:84, 1914; "Regulation of Fire Insurance Rates," *Green Bag*, 26:334, 1914.

[278] See, e.g., German Alliance Ins.

Co. v. Hale, 219 U.S. 307 (1911); Commercial Life Ins. Co. v. Illinois, 247 Ill. 92 (1910), *writ of error dismissed by stipulation*, 227 U.S. 681 (1913).

[279] Hunter v. Mutual Reserve Life Ins. Co., 218 U.S. 573 (1910); New York Life Ins. Co. v. Head, 234 U.S. 149 (1914); New York Life Ins. Co. v. Head, 234 U.S. 166 (1914).

[280] Tyson & Brother v. Banton, 273 U.S. 418, 434 (1927).

[281] See *supra*, pp. 257–58, 262–64.

prises that were concededly affected with a public interest, and therefore subject to price fixing, the Court, during these years, made no new departures, and decided no cases that had a measurable influence on the controversies of later years.

In *Louisville v. Cumberland Telephone & Telegraph Co.*,[282] Holmes warned that calculations of value and of probable returns were frequently endowed with a "delusive exactness." Hence experimentation, in practice, with rates set for a utility was often advisable before a finding was ventured that they were in fact confiscatory. How inconclusive, if initially indulgent, this decision was, the trial judge in the case promptly demonstrated. Holmes' opinion reversed and vacated an injunction the trial judge had issued. Shortly after the case returned to him, the trial judge, on his own motion, appointed another master and set the entire matter down for retrial. Quite evidently, the judge held strong views, and he was going to persevere in the effort to prove them correct. He had the power to persevere. The city tried by mandamus in the Supreme Court to stop him, but the Court said there was nothing in Holmes' prior opinion to prevent the judge from proceeding as he wanted to.[283]

Similarly indulgent toward state authority, and somewhat skeptical of judicial control of valuation and rate setting, was *Cedar Rapids Gas Co. v. Cedar Rapids*,[284] another Holmes decision. But in two other cases, the Court, per Lurton in one and Holmes himself in the second, insisted that the whole elaborate process of judicial control be carried through, inch by inch, delusive exactness or no. In both these cases, lower federal judges who had refused to issue injunctions and permitted ordinances setting gas and water rates to go into effect suffered reversal.[285]

The most important decision in a rate case during this period, affecting as well other cases that put into question measures of social and economic reform, dealt with a problem of federal jurisdiction, rather than with the rate-setting process itself. This was *Home Telephone &*

[282] 225 U.S. 430, 436 (1912).

[283] *In re* Louisville, 231 U.S. 639 (1914); and see *In re* Engelhard, 231 U.S. 646 (1914); Louisville v. Cumberland Telephone Co., 231 U.S. 652 (1914).

[284] 223 U.S. 655 (1912).

[285] Lincoln Gas Co. v. Lincoln, 223 U.S. 349 (1912); San Joaquin Co. v. Stanislaus County, 233 U.S. 454 (1914). And see West v. Atchison, Topeka & Santa Fe Ry., 185 Fed. 321 (8th Cir. 1910), *cert. denied*, 220 U.S. 618 (1911). *But cf.* Portland Ry. v. Oregon R.R. Commission, 229 U.S. 397 (1913); Portland Ry. v. Oregon R.R. Commission, 229 U.S. 414 (1913); Texas & Pacific Ry. v. Louisiana R.R. Commission, 232 U.S. 338 (1914).

Telegraph Co. v. *Los Angeles*,[286] in which the Court spoke unanimously through an astonished Chief Justice White, scarcely able to believe what his senses told him a lower federal court had done.

The telephone company having sought to enjoin a rate-fixing ordinance on the ground that it was confiscatory, the district court dismissed the suit for lack of federal jurisdiction, on the following reasoning. The state constitution, said the judge, also had a due process clause, and it also would be violated if the federal one was. The company had never been to the state courts to test its position under the state due process clause. If it was true that this ordinance was confiscatory and thus violated the state constitution, it could not be said to violate the Due Process Clause of the federal Constitution, since that clause applied only to state action, and action invalid under its own constitution could not be imputed to the state. Not until its own authoritative bodies, including its judiciary, had held an action to be constitutional under its own charter could the state be said to have acted. The federal court thus had no jurisdiction, there being no federal question, and in this case no basis for diversity jurisdiction. This notion—that it could not be assumed, as White summarized it, "that the State had authorized its officers to do acts in violation of the state constitution until the court of last resort of the State had determined that such acts were authorized" —struck, said White, to the root of federal supremacy. It was an error plain and of a "destructive character." Its result would be "paralysis." The true doctrine was that if an act had been done under color of state authority, it was irrelevant whether the state as a whole had sustained it. Violations by state officers of the Fourteenth Amendment could be prevented or stopped whether or not those officers also violated the law of their state.

White's alarm was exaggerated. Ways would have been found to make federal judicial power effective even if the reasoning of the district judge had prevailed. If men were angels, we would surely have to concede that his idea was right as well as logical—to let state judiciaries discipline state officers before federal power was invoked. Men being less than angels, much delay and opportunity for obstruction would unquestionably have been created in the enforcement of federal constitutional rights. But enforcement would still have been possible. Yet the exercise of federal judicial power would often have been gravely impaired, not only in cases involving social legislation at this time and through the 1920s and 1930s, but also in the racial discrimination cases of a later time. No doubt it is as well, on balance, that the federal juris-

---

[286] 227 U.S. 278, 283–84 (1913); *cf.* Memphis v. Cumberland Telegraph Co., 218 U.S. 624 (1910).

diction was saved intact. In later years, a discretionary doctrine of abstention, applied selectively, achieved something of the objectives of the district judge in this case. So did statutory law aimed at curbing the evils of government by injunction.[287]

Other state regulations of public utilities, aside from rate setting, generally fared no worse than they deserved under the Due Process Clause. (Their fate was often more uncertain, and the Court's attitude more dubious, under the Commerce Clause, as we have noted, and under the Contract Clause, as we shall see.) In *St. Louis, Iron Mountain & Southern Railway* v. *Wynne*,[288] a rather spectacular railroad-soaking statute failed, naturally enough, to pass the constitutional test. Arkansas—not apparently alone among the states—provided that a railroad that accidentally killed livestock had to pay within thirty days such compensation as the owner might demand. Should the railroad fail to pay, then upon suit, if the jury returned a verdict in an amount claimed by the owner, the railroad was liable for double the amount of the verdict. It made no difference that the amount claimed and awarded in the suit might be smaller than that originally demanded from the railroad. In this case, demand was made for $500 for two horses killed by the railroad. The railroad refused to pay, and then suit was filed for $400, which a jury awarded. Pursuant to the statute, the amount was doubled.

This, said the Court, per Van Devanter, was a taking of property without due process. Far from serving as an incentive to the prompt settlement of just claims, this statute penalized the railroad for resisting excessive claims, as it should have every lawful right to do.[289] But when the same Arkansas statute worked to double an award of damages no smaller than the demand initially made upon the railroad, the Court thought that the initial demand had thus been proved reasonable, and it held the statute constitutional as so applied, albeit against two dissents without opinion, one of them being Holmes'.[290] A similar Mississippi

---

[287] *Cf.* Snowden v. Hughes, 321 U.S. 1 (1944). And see Railroad Commission of Texas v. Pullman Co., 312 U.S. 496 (1941); but *cf.* England v. Louisiana Medical Board, 375 U.S. 411 (1964). See H. M. Hart, Jr., and H. Wechsler, *The Federal Courts and the Federal System* (1953), 846–66, 869–73.

[288] 224 U.S. 354 (1912).

[289] Hughes, in retrospect, thought it notable that even Holmes, who generally accorded great latitude to legislative action, could find some statutes so "utterly unreasonable and arbitrary" as to violate the Due Process Clause. As an example, Hughes cited Chicago, Milwaukee & St. Paul Ry. v. Polt, 232 U.S. 165 (1914), written by Holmes and applying the *Wynne* holding to a South Dakota statute. And see Chicago, Milwaukee & St. Paul Ry. v. Kennedy, 232 U.S. 626 (1914).

[290] Kansas City Ry. v. Anderson, 233 U.S. 325 (1914).

statute, similarly applied, was also upheld, as were provisions for counsel fees to be awarded to successful plantiffs.[291]

Public utility regulations upheld against Due Process attack also included requirements that overpasses, bridges, spur tracks, and like improvements be built, that certain prescribed equipment and crews be carried on all trains, and even that a railroad continue a service it wished to abandon.[292] However, a statute providing that only persons with two years of experience as brakemen on freight trains could be employed as conductors was held unconstitutional, Holmes alone dissenting. This measure touched the Court's liberty of contract nerve.[293] Lastly, in *Oregon Railroad & Navigation Co.* v. *Fairchild*,[294] in a sophisticated opinion, the Court, Lamar writing, while giving a state railroad commission all the necessary leeway to make an order requiring a railroad to lay additional trackage, held the commission to an evidentiary showing, on the record, of the public necessity justifying its action.

Among the rest of the Due Process cases decided in the years under discussion is a group testing the jurisdiction of states to tax corporations active within their borders, but incorporated and headquartered elsewhere, or to tax stock certificates, negotiable instruments, and the like owned by citizens of other states. The problems raised by these cases were analogous to those created by efforts of the states to regulate out-of-state insurance companies,[295] and indeed one of these tax cases concerned an out-of-state insurance company's accounts receivable within the taxing state.[296] A line of cases dealing with methods for

---

[291] Yazoo & Mississippi R.R. v. Jackson Vinegar Co., 226 U.S. 217 (1912); Missouri, Kansas & Texas Ry. v. Cade, 233 U.S. 642 (1914); Missouri, Kansas & Texas Ry. v. Harris, 234 U.S. 412 (1914); and see Chicago, Burlington & Quincy R.R. v. Cram, 228 U.S. 70 (1913); Chicago, Burlington & Quincy R.R. v. Kyle, 228 U.S. 85 (1913). But *cf.* Gulf, Colorado & Santa Fe Ry. v. Dennis, 224 U.S. 503 (1912).

[292] Cincinnati, I. & W. Ry. v. Connersville, 218 U.S. 336 (1910); Chicago, Rock Island & Pacific Ry. v. Arkansas, 219 U.S. 453 (1911); Consumers' Co. v. Hatch, 224 U.S. 148 (1912); Grand Trunk Ry. v. Michigan Ry. Commission, 231 U.S. 457 (1913); Chicago, Milwaukee & St. Paul Ry. v. Minneapolis, 232 U.S.

430 (1914); Union Lime Co. v. Chicago & Northwestern Ry., 233 U.S. 211 (1914); Atlantic Coast Line v. Georgia, 234 U.S. 280 (1914); Colorado & Southern Ry. v. Railroad Commission, 54 Colorado 64, 129 Pac. 506 (1912), *writ of error dismissed on motion of plaintiff in error,* 234 U.S. 767 (1914).

[293] Smith v. Texas, 233 U.S. 630 (1914); *cf.* Kotch v. Board of River Pilot Commissioners, 330 U.S. 552 (1947).

[294] 224 U.S. 510 (1912).

[295] See *supra,* p. 286, n.279.

[296] Liverpool Ins. Co. v. Orleans Assessors, 221 U.S. 346 (1911). See also, e.g., Hawley v. Malden, 232 U.S. 1 (1914); Wheeler v. New York, 233 U.S. 434 (1914).

obtaining judicial jurisdiction over a party or a *res* otherwise than by personal service of process may also be passed without comment. In each, the attempted exercise of judicial power by a state court was upheld. "Now and then," said Holmes somewhat airily in one of them, "an extraordinary case may turn up, but constitutional law, like other mortal contrivances, has to take some chances, and in the great majority of instances no doubt justice will be done."[297]

Of the miscellany of yet other cases,[298] a few give brief pause.[299] In *Chicago* v. *Sturges*,[300] the Court sustained an Illinois statute imposing absolute liability on cities to indemnify individual property owners for two-thirds of any loss suffered as a result of rioting. The statute was attacked by the city on the ground that it deprived it—the city—of due process of law. The Court, in a unanimous opinion by Lurton, held the imposition of liability without fault to be reasonable, and not to lack due process. The remarkable thing about the case is that the city was allowed, without comment, to invoke the federal Constitution against a regulation of its affairs by the state, of which it was, of course, a political sub-

---

[297] Blinn v. Nelson, 222 U.S. 1, 7 (1911). See also American Land Co. v. Zeiss, 219 U.S. 47 (1911); Venner v. Denver Union Water Co., 40 Colo. 212, 90 Pac. 623 (1907), *cert. dismissed for want of jurisdiction,* 219 U.S. 583 (1911); Jacob v. Roberts, 223 U.S. 261 (1912); St. Louis, Southwestern Ry. v. Alexander, 227 U.S. 218 (1913); Miederich v. Lauenstein, 232 U.S. 236 (1914); Grannis v. Ordean, 234 U.S. 385 (1914); Missouri, Kansas and Texas Ry. v. Goodrich, 213 Fed. 339 (8th Cir. 1914), *writ of error dismissed for want of jurisdiction,* 234 U.S. 754 (1914). Cf. Big Vein Coal Co. v. Read, 229 U.S. 31 (1913).

[298] These are cases raising plausible issues—in some instances more than plausible, even more plausible than the Court perceived. We will have a separate word to say presently about the plethora of quite implausible Due Process, as well as Equal Protection and Contract Clause, cases that the bar did not hesitate to press to the Court's attention in this period. See

infra, pp. 294 *et seq.,* 297 *et seq.,* 300 *et seq.*

[299] In addition to cases mentioned in the text, see also Provident Savings Institution v. Malone, 221 U.S. 660 (1911); Collins v. Texas, 223 U.S. 288 (1912); St. Benedict's Abbey v. Marion County, 50 Ore. 411, 93 Pac. 231 (1908), *writ of error dismissed on motion of plaintiff in error,* 218 U.S. 688 (1910); Byles v. Arkansas, 93 Ark. 612, 126 S.W. 94 (1910), *writ of error dismissed on motion of plaintiff in error,* 225 U.S. 717 (1912); St. Louis Fair Ass'n v. Gilsonite Roofing & Paving Co., 231 Mo. 589, 132 S.W. 657 (1910), *writ of error dismissed on motion of plaintiff in error,* 226 U.S. 623 (1913); O'Brien v. Schneider, 88 Neb. 479 (1911), *writ of error dismissed,* 229 U.S. 629 (1913); New Louisville Jockey Club v. Oakdale, 137 Ky. 484, 125 S.W. 1089 (1910), *writ of error dismissed for want of jurisdiction,* 231 U.S. 739 (1913); Heavner v. Elkins, 67 W. Va. 255, 71 S.E. 184 (1911), *affirmed,* 231 U.S. 743 (1913).

[300] 222 U.S. 313 (1911).

division. Seldom before,[301] and not after, despite a goodly number of attempts to have it do so,[302] did the Court undertake to pass on such relationships between states and their political subdivisions. This would have been a fertile and dubious new head of jurisdiction, if generally accepted, as it was in *Chicago* v. *Sturges.*

Rosenthal v. *New York*[303] upheld a statute punishing junk dealers for receiving, knowingly or not, certain stolen property, without first attempting by diligent inquiry to ascertain whether the person selling or delivering it had a legal right to do so. Thus the Court, giving itself little, if any, difficulty on this point, came near to permitting the imposition of criminal liability without fault. In *Preston* v. *Chicago,*[304] the Court suggested rather casually that a municipality could dismiss its employees—in this case a policeman—at will, without assigning cause, without written charges, without notice, and without an opporunity to be heard, at least so long as they were not in the tenured civil service. The problem was dealt with somewhat more deliberately in many of the highly charged cases of a later generation. *Tiaco* v. *Forbes,*[305] "not a very pleasant case," which the young Felix Frankfurter, rather to his surprise, won for the Governor-General of the Philippines, permitted a summary deportation by the Governor-General of a resident of the Philippines. No hearing was afforded, nor, indeed, was any other kind of regular procedure followed.

Preston v. *Chicago* and *Tiaco* v. *Forbes* exhibit a certain inattentiveness to a mature conception of the Court's function under the Due Process Clause. They are to be contrasted with a final pair of Due Process decisions, in which efforts to control the urban environment were held unconstitutional by unanimous Courts on narrow, qualified grounds. Both are close cases, closely decided, and one of them at least might have had large and grave consequences had the decision been placed on less discriminating grounds. *Ettor* v. *Tacoma,*[306] the less

---

[301] See, e.g., New Orleans v. New Orleans Water Works Co., 142 U.S. 79 (1891); but *cf.,* e.g., Williams v. Eggleston, 170 U.S. 304 (1898); Williams v. Parker, 188 U.S. 491 (1903).

[302] Stewart v. Kansas City, 239 U.S. 14 (1915); Pawhuska v. Pawhuska Oil Co., 250 U.S. 394 (1919); Trenton v. New Jersey, 262 U.S. 182 (1923); Newark v. New Jersey, 262 U.S. 192 (1923); Risty v. Chicago, Rock Island & Pacific Ry., 270 U.S. 378 (1926); see the *per curiam* decisions cited in Trenton v. New Jersey, *supra;* and

see De Graff v. Spokane, 143 Wash. 326, 255 Pac. 371 (1927), *dismissed for want of a federal question,* 276 U.S. 602 (1928).

[303] 226 U.S. 260 (1912).

[304] 226 U.S. 447 (1913); and see Gersch v. Chicago, 226 U.S. 451 (1913); *cf.* Brown v. Lane, 232 U.S. 598 (1914).

[305] 228 U.S. 549 (1913); see Phillips, ed., *Felix Frankfurter Reminisces,* 63–64.

[306] 228 U.S. 148 (1913).

far-reaching of the two, held the city of Tacoma strictly to an obligation to pay consequential damages to owners of property abutting on streets that the city was grading and improving. Such consequential damages had been provided for by one statute, but the promise, if such it was, was revoked by a later one. The Court held, per Lurton, that in attempting to free the city of the obligation it had previously undertaken, the later statute deprived the property owners of due process. In the absence of any statute at all, it was doubtful that consequential damages were owing. But the first statute created a substantive right, not merely a remedy; that right had vested, and it could not be defeated by subsequent legislation.

Eubank v. *Richmond*[307] concerned an ordinance of Richmond, Virginia, which provided that whenever the owners of two-thirds of the property abutting on any street requested the Committee on Streets to establish a building line on the side of the street on which their property fronted, the committee was required to do so, and that line thenceforth governed everybody, including the dissenting third. Violation of such a building line was subject to fine. McKenna, for a unanimous Court, held the ordinance unconstitutional.

Every presumption of constitutionality, he said, operated in favor of the ordinance. "Governmental power must be flexible and adaptive. Exigencies arise, or even conditions less peremptory, which may call for or suggest legislation, and it may be a struggle in judgment to decide whether it must yield to the higher considerations expressed and determined by the provisions of the Constitution" (citing *Noble State Bank* v. *Haskell*). Here the decisive consideration was that upon a vote of two-thirds of the abutting owners, the Committee on Streets of the city had no discretion. Its action then had to follow automatically. That meant that one set of property owners could quite autonomously determine the uses to which a minority of owners had to put their property. No public body weighed the public interest. No standard dealing with public safety, health, or necessity governed action. A majority of property owners could decide in their own interests, or capriciously, or on the basis of taste, which was after all arbitrary. This constituted the unreasonable feature of the legislation, violating due process. And to hold this ordinance unconstitutional on this ground, said McKenna, was not in any way to pass on the power of a city to establish a building line, or to regulate the structure or height of buildings. All that was demanded was that statutes or ordinances doing so have a more general foundation and a more general purpose. Whether right or wrong in its result, this opinion had a more permissive tone than some decisions upholding state

---

[307] 226 U.S. 137, 143 (1912).

legislation. It was in any event soon qualified, and by no means stood in the way of the validation later of a general zoning power.[308]

Equal Protection

The Court's constitutional arsenal was equipped also with two additional weapons suitable for deciding the fate of social legislation. And one of these, the Contract Clause, was put to quite active use. But the other, the Equal Protection Clause, was a sheathed sword throughout the four terms that ran from October 1910 to June 1914.[309] The opportunities to apply the clause were plentiful, but the Court consistently declined, and its language in doing so was remarkably definite and unqualified. It was, for all the world, the language of abandonment, virtually without reservation. Scarcely anything of the caution, barely discernible even in *Noble State Bank* v. *Haskell*, and plainly evident in the tone of most other Due Process cases that upheld state legislation, and of the Commerce Clause cases affirming federal power, is present here. The interment was not to be permanent, but the rhetoric at this time was of the burial service.

The chief nonmourners were Holmes and McKenna. In *Central Lumber Co.* v. *South Dakota*,[310] a statute was in question which prohibited anyone engaged in the manufacture or distribution of goods to secure a competitive advantage for himself by selling at a lower price in one city or community than in another. The measure was aimed at businesses lying close to railroad tracks, which marketed in more than one community. Hence, it was argued, it penalized size, and favored small businesses confined to their localities. Maybe so, said Holmes, upholding the statute for a unanimous Court, but if South Dakota was of the view, then generally prevailing, that some methods of competition ought to be suppressed, it did not need to strike at the same time at all

---

[308] See Cusack Co. v. Chicago, 242 U.S. 526 (1917); and see, e.g., Hadacheck v. Los Angeles, 239 U.S. 394 (1915); Euclid v. Ambler Realty Co., 272 U.S. 365 (1926).

[309] Smith v. Texas, *supra*, p. 290, n.292, presented what today would be considered an Equal Protection problem, but it was decided under the Due Process Clause, the Equal Protection point being entirely subsidiary. So it constitutes no exception. The Equal Protection Clause, as we shall see in a further section, was quiescent during these years in criminal and racial matters as well. See United States v. Heinze, 218 U.S. 532, 547 (1910); Finley v. California, 222 U.S. 28 (1911); Jones v. Jones, 234 U.S. 615 (1914); Atwater v. Hassett, 27 Okla. 292 (1910), *writ of error dismissed*, 227 U.S. 684 (1913) (grandfather clause in Oklahoma electoral law upheld); Alabama & Vicksburg Ry. v. Morris, 103 Miss. 511, 60 So. 11 (1912), *writ of error dismissed on motion of plaintiff in error*, 234 U.S. 766 (1914) (railroad passenger segregation upheld).

[310] 226 U.S. 157, 161 (1912).

such methods, or at all their practitioners. And if the legislature believed that the ability to hurt competition "usually came from great corporations whose power it deemed excessive and for that reason did more harm than good in their State, and that there was no other case of frequent occurrence where the same could be said, we cannot review their economics or their facts."

Metropolis Theater Co. v. *Chicago*[311] concerned a Chicago theater license tax which was graduated in accordance with the price of admission. Thus a theater paid a tax of $1,000 if its admission was $1 or more, $400 if it was between 50¢ and $1, and so forth. Neither seating capacity nor gross income made any difference. Holding, for a unanimous Court, that there was no lack of equal protection, McKenna said:

> To be able to find fault with a law is not to demonstrate its invalidity. It may seem unjust and oppressive, yet be free from judicial interference. The problems of government are practical ones and may justify, if they do not require, rough accommodations—illogical, it may be, and unscientific. But even such criticism should not be hastily expressed. What is best is not always discernible; the wisdom of any choice may be disputed or condemned. Mere errors of government are not subject to our judicial review. It is only its palpably arbitrary exercises which can be declared void under the Fourteenth Amendment; and such judgment cannot be pronounced of the ordinance in controversy.

In *Chicago Dock Co.* v. *Fraley*,[312] McKenna added that "the crudities or even the injustice of state laws are not redressed by the Fourteenth Amendment," which was no guarantee of perfect laws. And elsewhere he exclaimed: "If this power of classification did not exist, to what straits legislation would be brought."[313]

This being the attitude, there was no difficulty with a statute requiring building contractors to safeguard elevator openings in city buildings (but not other openings in other buildings);[314] with state antitrust laws applying only to manufacturers, and not to sellers of services;[315] with a whole congeries of tax measures;[316] with statutes

---

[311] 228 U.S. 61, 69–70 (1913).

[312] 228 U.S. 680, 686 (1913).

[313] International Harvester Co. v. Missouri, 234 U.S. 199, 213 (1914).

[314] Chicago Dock Co. v. Fraley, 228 U.S. 680 (1913).

[315] International Harvester Co. v. Missouri, 234 U.S. 199 (1914).

[316] Illinois Central R.R. v. Kentucky, 218 U.S. 551 (1910); Keeney v. New York, 222 U.S. 525 (1912); Toyota v. Hawaii, 226 U.S. 184 (1912); Citizens' Telephone Co. v. Fuller, 229 U.S. 322, 335 (1913); Baltic Mining Co. v. Massachusetts, 231 U.S. 68 (1913); Ohio Tax Cases, 232 U.S. 576 (1914); Hammond Packing Co. v. Montana, 233 U.S. 331 (1914); Webber v. Missouri, 214 Mo. 272, 113 S.W. 1054 (1908), *writ*

classifying railroads separately for purposes of abrogating the fellow-servant rule and otherwise changing the law of torts;[317] or a miscellany of other classifications.[318] And subsidiary Equal Protection points were disposed of lightly and easily in many of the Due Process cases we have discussed, including *Engel* v. *O'Malley, Chicago, Burlington & Quincy Railroad* v. *McGuire, Murphy* v. *California, Lindsley* v. *Natural Carbonic Gas Co.*, and *German Alliance Insurance Co., v. Kansas.*[319] Even a New York statute prohibiting advertising on trucks and vans, but excepting wagons engaged in the usual business of the owner, was found constitutional. The Court had a great deal more trouble reaching the same result in 1949.[320]

There were limits to the permissiveness of these cases, albeit none are apparent in the published opinions. These limits were reached as the Equal Protection and Due Process clauses seemed to some Justices to converge, with the consequence that the latter clause would become as little of a damper on legislative inventiveness as, for the moment, they were allowing the former to be. The merger of the two concepts was not resisted in federal cases arising under the Fifth rather than the Fourteenth Amendment. For here the consequence would more likely be

---

of error dismissed on motion of plaintiff in error, 220 U.S. 625 (1911); McKnight v. Hodge, 55 Wash. 289, 104 Pac. 504 (1909), *writ of error dismissed on motion of plaintiff in error,* 223 U.S. 748 (1912).

[317] Mobile, Jackson & Kansas City Ry. v. Turnipseed, 219 U.S. 35 (1910); Aluminum Co. of America v. Ramsey, 222 U.S. 251 (1911); Missouri, Kansas & Texas Ry. v. Richardson, 125 S.W. 623 (Court of Civil Appeals Texas), *affirmed,* 220 U.S. 601 (1911); New York Central & Hudson River R.R. v. Schradin, 124 App. Div. 705 (N.Y. 1908), *affirmed,* 220 U.S. 606 (1911); Missouri, Kansas & Texas Ry. v. Bailey, 53 Tex. Civ. App. 295, 115 S.W. 601 (1909), *affirmed,* 220 U.S. 608 (1911); Louisville & Nashville R.R. v. Helms, *cert. denied,* 225 U.S. 709 (1912); Missouri, Kansas & Texas Ry. v. Letot, 135 S.W. 656 (Court of Civil Appeals Texas 1911), *dismissed for want of jurisdiction,* 231 U.S. 738 (1913); and see Atchison, Topeka & Santa Fe Ry. v. Starr Grain & Lumber Co., 85 Kan. 281, 116 Pac. 906 (1911), *writ of error dismissed on motion of plaintiff in error,* 231 U.S. 762 (1913).

[318] Griffith v. Connecticut, 218 U.S. 563 (1910); Bradley v. Richmond, 227 U.S. 477 (1913); Chesapeake & Ohio Ry. v. Conley, 230 U.S. 513 (1913); Williams v. Walsh, 222 U.S. 415 (1912); Baccus v. Louisiana, 232 U.S. 334 (1914); Globe Printing Co. v. Cook, 227 Mo. 471, 127 S.W. 332 (1910), *dismissed for want of jurisdiction,* 220 U.S. 603 (1911); Swensen v. Michigan, 162 Mich. 397, 127 N.W. 302 (1910), *writ of error dismissed,* 231 U.S. 767 (1913).

[319] See *supra,* pp. 278, 279–80, 281–85, nn.265, 266.

[320] *Compare* Fifth Avenue Coach Co. v. New York, 221 U.S. 467 (1911), and St. Louis Gunning & Advertising Co. v. St. Louis, 235 Mo. 99, 137 S.W. 929 (1911), *dismissed per stipulation,* 231 U.S. 761 (1913), *with* Railway Express Co. v. New York, 336 U.S. 106 (1949). And *cf.* Morey v. Doud, 354 U.S. 457 (1957).

to shore up the Due Process Clause. Thus in *Flint* v. *Stone Tracy*, as we have seen,[321] the Court accepted without demur the argument of counsel that the Equal Protection concept bound Congress, even though Due Process was unaccompanied by an Equal Protection Clause in the Fifth Amendment. That was a shoe on another foot.

Characteristically, the threat of a contagion of permissiveness, spreading from Equal Protection to Due Process in the Fourteenth Amendment, was perceived in a couple of draft opinions of Holmes. In 1903, New York passed a statute which overruled *Roberson* v. *Rochester Folding Box Co.*,[322] and created a right of privacy. *Sperry & Hutchinson* v. *Rhodes*[323] was an award of damages and of an injunction under this statute to a plaintiff whose photograph had been used in an advertisement. "If there were any doubt as to the wide discretion belonging to a state legislature in changing the permissible uses of existing property according to its views of public policy, no room for the application of such a doubt was left here." So said Holmes in a draft of a two-paragraph opinion holding the statute perfectly constitutional against both Due Process and Equal Protection attacks. "Yes," returned Day, "but there are certain things I think better unsaid in an opinion of this Court." One of the things was this sentence, and Holmes omitted it. Another was this passage: "But even the Fourteenth Amendment does not forbid statutes and stautory changes to have a beginning. The complaint against this statute adds one more to the numberless attempts to treat the Fourteenth Amendment as having almost put an end to the possibility of change in the present condition of things." Day remarked in the margin: "Why attack our good friend in this way?" And Holmes accommodated him by substituting the following sentence, which appears in the published opinion: "But the Fourteenth Amendment does not forbid statutes and statutory changes to have a beginning and thus to discriminate between the rights of an earlier and later time." So the point was stripped of any Due Process implications, and made to sound in Equal Protection only.[324]

Keokee Consolidated Coke Co. v. *Taylor*[325] concerned a Virginia statute which forbade any person or corporation engaged in mining or manufacturing to issue to its workers scrip that was redeemable only in company stores. All scrip used to pay for labor had to be redeemable for cash, but the statute applied only to mining and manufacturing businesses. A draft opinion by Holmes sustaining the statute included the following passage:

---

[321] *Supra*, pp. 245–46.
[322] 171 N.Y. 538 (1902).
[323] 220 U.S. 502, 505 (1911).

[324] Holmes Papers.
[325] 234 U.S. 224, 227 (1914).

> Whatever freedom of contract may be deduced from the word liberty in the Amendment, it is subject to restrictions in the interest of what the legislature conceived to be the general welfare. *Chicago, Burlington & Quincy R.R. v. McGuire.* It now is recognized by legislatures and courts as well as by everyone outside of them, that as a fact freedom may disappear on the one side or the other through the power of aggregated money or men; as it long had been recognized in the case of those who deal with the great common carriers; and to suppose that every other force may exercise its compulsion at will but that government has no authority to counteract the pressure with its own is absurd. It is said that the power of duress has changed sides and now is with the United Mine Workers. But if it be admitted, as it certainly is established, that the legislature may interfere with theoretic in the interest of practical freedom, it would require a very clear case before a court could declare its judgment wrong and its enactment void.

"This is highly suggestive," Van Devanter noted in the margin next to this paragraph, "and calculated to breed all sorts of legislation on short notice." Lurton and McKenna also objected to it, and even Hughes said: "I should prefer some qualification. . . . Not that I do not think it implied, but we shall have enough from legislation without encouraging it." The passage fell, leaving again a very short opinion, in which Holmes restricted himself to dealing with the Equal Protection point by remarking that "it is established by repeated decisions that a statute aimed at what is deemed evil, and hitting it presumably where experience shows it to be most felt, is not to be upset by thinking up and enumerating other instances to which it might have been applied equally well, so far as the Court can see. That is for the legislature to judge unless the case is very clear."[326]

Holmes was allowed to pass the limits, at least as we would now see them, in two cases in which one could well wish the guardians of the Ark had guarded better. Montana imposed a $10 license fee on hand laundries, but none on steam laundries, nor on laundries run by women, when no more than two were employed. In *Quong Wing v. Kirkendall*,[327] the Court upheld the statute. "A state does not deny the equal protection of the laws," said Holmes, speaking for the majority, "merely by adjusting its revenue laws and taxing system in such a way as to favor certain industries or forms of industry." The Fourteenth Amendment did not stand in the way of the encouragement of steam laundries and the discouragement of hand laundries, nor of a policy which distinguished on the basis of sex, for the Amendment did not attempt to create "a fictitious equality where there is a real difference." Of course, if the statute was

---

[326] Holmes Papers.   [327] 223 U.S. 59, 62, 63 (1912).

aimed at the Chinese, that would be a discrimination that the Constitution forbade, citing *Yick* v. *Hopkins*.[328] And it was true that most hand laundries were operated by Chinese. But this ground of objection had not been urged, and had indeed been disavowed, when mentioned at the argument. The facts might be noticed judicially, but counsel must bring them to the attention of the Court. If counsel deliberately omitted to rely on these facts, it was no business of the Court to rest decision on them. And so the case was decided without prejudice to the racial issue.

A dissent by Lamar, alone, maintained that the statute was a revenue and not a police measure, and that taxation of smaller laundries and exemption of larger ones was arbitrary. Nor did sex make a rational difference for purposes of taxation. Hughes, without writing, concurred in the result, but not in Holmes' opinion. And there were silent dissenters. Holmes himself had his doubts. He circulated his opinion with the following memorandum: "I feel more misgiving about the facts than about our right to know them. The census shows 1,739 Chinese in Montana in 1900; 405 hand laundrymen, 445 laundry women and 45 steam laundries, but does not show the number of Chinese employed in the business." Lurton said that he had "grave doubt" and reserved his vote for the present. McKenna returned: "I doubt awfully." Chief Justice White wrote: "I am sorry to say I must dissent. May write a word but anyhow will note my dissent."[329] Lurton, McKenna, and White thought better of it.

Hughes' objection, which he did not abandon, was to the passage where Holmes reserved the racial issue. "It may or may not be that if the facts were called to our attention in a proper way the objection would prove to be real," said Holmes. Hughes thought that this went "beyond the mere reservation of the question. You may put me down as concurring in the result." But Holmes said explicitly that the decision was without prejudice to the racial question. Is it possible that Hughes' objection was that Holmes' opinion went too far in suggesting that the statute would be bad if it were attacked as a discrimination against the Chinese? That seems hardly likely, in view of the *Yick Wo* precedent, and of Hughes' own actions in other racial cases.[330] It is more probable that he considered Holmes' "it may or may not be" reservation too neutral, and a departure, however slight, from *Yick Wo*. And perhaps the case could have been disposed of by vacating the state court's judgment and remanding for reconsideration in light of the racial issue, and indeed for a trial of the facts relevant to that issue.

---

[328] 118 U.S. 356 (1886).   [329] Holmes Papers.   [330] See *infra*, pp. 775, 863.

In *Patsone* v. *Pennsylvania*,[331] in which Chief Justice White alone dissented without opinion, Holmes went a good bit, and quite regrettably, further. A Pennsylvania statute made it a misdemeanor for an unnaturalized foreign-born resident to kill any wild bird or animal except in self-defense, and "to that end" forbade such persons to own a shotgun or rifle. Upholding the statute, Holmes said that owning a shotgun or a rifle was so related to hunting and to no other purpose that the statute could be considered as an antihunting measure and no more. Thus the statute did not apply to pistols, which had uses other than hunting. (But surely it is a daring assumption that shotguns and rifles are used exclusively for hunting!)

Whether Pennsylvania could classify as she did, and single out aliens, was a matter not of abstract symmetry, but of practical experience, which might have led the state to believe that aliens were the principal source of the evil. On such a question, the Court ought to be very slow to declare that the legislature was wrong. Then the following sentence, which stands out oddly, and somewhat offensively, in this short opinion: "If we might trust popular speech in some States it [the legislature] was right—but it is enough that this court has no such knowledge of local conditions as to be able to say that it was manifestly wrong."

The Contract Clause

If the Equal Protection Clause had a tendency to merge with Due Process, so most certainly did the Contract Clause. Part of the original Constitution—Article I, Section 10—this clause forbids any state to make laws "impairing the Obligation of Contracts." It received early application at the hands of John Marshall in *Fletcher* v. *Peck* and the *Dartmouth College* case, but began to suffer a doctrinal overlap some three-quarters of a century later, as Due Process developed substantive content. Another few decades, and it was in train of being superseded.[332] Due Process, not the Contract Clause, evolved as a protection of the liberty of contract, and Due Process also took over the function of limiting the power of legislatures retroactively to alter established private contractual relationships, or to disturb "vested rights."

What was happening is illustrated perfectly by such cases, discussed earlier in this chapter,[333] as *Ettor* v. *Tacoma,* on the one hand, and

---

[331] 232 U.S. 138, 144 (1914).

[332] See B. F. Wright, *The Contract Clause of the Constitution* (1938); Note, "The Contract Clause of the Federal Constitution," *Colum. L. Rev.,* 32:476, 1932; R. T. Johnson, "The Contract Clause of the United States Constitution," *Ky. L.J.,* 16:222, 1928; J. H. Lionberger, "The Evolution of a Principle," *St. Louis L. Rev.,* 2:88, 1917.

[333] *Supra,* pp. 292–93, 279–80.

Chicago, Burlington & Quincy Railroad v. *McGuire,* on the other.[334] Both were decided under the Due Process Clause, although they concerned the impairment of preexisting contractual relationships. And when the problem of the *McGuire* case was presented in Contract Clause guise, the Supreme Court disposed of it summarily on the authority of *McGuire.*[335] Another transition from Contract to Due Process is equally instructive. The Court, as we have seen,[336] upheld under Due Process certain applications of statutes allowing penalty recoveries in tort actions against railroads. When similar statutes, applied to contractual claims against insurance companies, were attacked under the Contract Clause, the Court simply followed its Due Process holdings, even though a preexisting contractual relationship, not involved in the railroad cases, was now present, and allegedly being impaired.[337]

However, although in time, unlike Equal Protection, the Contract Clause was to lose its identity almost entirely, it had not yet done so during these years. It afforded no protection to speak of against the impairment of private contracts, but it still retained the distinct function, particularly in public utility cases, of enforcing observance by state and local governments of contracts supposedly made by them with private persons or entities. To be sure, the Contract Clause is applicable only to legislative repudiations of public contracts—by statute or ordinance—not to all ordinary breaches.[338] And a state or municipality could sometimes successfully contest the validity of the contract it was supposed to have entered into; the contract might be invalid because it was unauthorized under the state organic law.[339] Or the state or municipality might successfully contest the related issues of the proper construction of the contract,[340] or of its alleged impairment, as properly construed.[341]

---

[334] See also Selover, Bates & Co. v. Walsh, *supra,* p. 281, n.261.

[335] Atlantic Coast Line R.R. v. Miller, 231 U.S. 741 (1913); see also Quincy, Omaha & Kansas R.R. v. Shohoney, 231 Mo. 131, 132 S.W. 1059 (1910), *writ of error dismissed for want of jurisdiction,* 223 U.S. 705 (1911).

[336] *Supra,* p. 290, n.291.

[337] Fraternal Mystic Circle v. Snyder, 227 U.S. 497 (1913); see also National Surety Co. v. Architectural Decorating Co., 226 U.S. 276 (1912); Pittsburgh Steel Co. v. Baltimore Equitable Society, 226 U.S. 455 (1913); Seaboard Fire & Marine Ins. Co. v. Monteleone, 126 La. 807, 52

So. 1932 (1910), *dismissed per stipulation,* 226 U.S. 621 (1912). And see Moffitt v. Kelly. 218 U.S. 400 (1910); Grand Trunk Ry. v. Indiana R.R. Commission, 221 U.S. 400 (1911).

[338] Shawnee Sewerage & Drainage Co. v. Stearns, 220 U.S. 462 (1911).

[339] Berryman v. Whitman College, 222 U.S. 334 (1912); Wyandotte Gas Co. v. Kansas, 231 U.S. 622 (1914).

[340] J. W. Perry Co. v. Norfolk, 220 U.S. 472 (1911); Madera Water Works v. Madera, 228 U.S. 454 (1913); Trimble v. Seattle, 231 U.S. 683 (1914).

[341] Arkansas Southern Ry. v. Louisiana & Arkansas Ry., 218 U.S. 431 (1910); Pomona v. Sunset Tele-

These were all questions of state law. They were decided as federal questions under the Contract Clause, but normally with deference to a state court's view of the meaning of its own law. Moreover, the Contract Clause would also sometimes fail of application because the Supreme Court would hold either that in granting a charter or making some other public contract, the state or municipality had expressly reserved a power to amend and revoke,[342] or that the reservation was implicit, since no government could bargain away certain powers. So it was held when a railroad interposed against a statutory wrongful death action by an employee its charter from the Louisiana legislature, in which the state promised that it would exempt the railroad from liability for the death of any person in the railroad's service, even if negligently caused. No legislature, said the Court, can bargain away the police power in this fashion, and withdraw it from its successors.[343] The power of eminent domain, it was similarly held, cannot be bargained away.[344]

But there was caution, even in cases concerning the inalienable police power to guard health, safety, and morals, for the Court was not yet prepared to bargain away the Contract Clause itself.[345] And in a case in which a city was building a water works of its own in competition with a chartered water company, and the Court held that nothing in the city's contract-charter with the company prevented it from doing so, Holmes, whose attitude in Contract Clause cases of this sort was not nearly as permissive as under Due Process, felt called upon to remark that it was "impossible not to feel the force of the plaintiff's argument," and somewhat regrettable that plaintiff had to be "left to depend upon the sense of justice that the city may show."[346] Chartered public utilities threatened by the exercise of a regulatory power other than the classic, narrowly defined power to safeguard health, safety, and morals very frequently obtained more than expressions of judicial regrets. Invoked in such circumstances, the Contract Clause often afforded effective relief.

An opinion by Hughes in *Russell* v. *Sebastian*,[347] in 1914, fairly represents the Court's consensus, as well as putting the issue in a usefully large context. California, persuaded of what everyone knew, namely, that the power to grant utility franchises had led to a great deal of

---

phone Co., 224 U.S. 330 (1912); Vicksburg v. Henson, 231 U.S. 259, 739 (1913); and see German Ins. Co. v. Kentucky, 141 Ky. 606, 133 S.W. 793 (1911), *writ of error dismissed on motion of plaintiff in error*, 226 U.S. 622 (1911).

[342] Calder v. Michigan, 218 U.S. 591 (1910).

[343] Texas & New Orleans R.R. v.

Miller, 221 U.S. 408 (1911); see also Atlantic Coast Line R.R. v. Goldsboro, 232 U.S. 548 (1914).

[344] Cincinnati v. Louisville & Nashville R.R., 223 U.S. 390 (1912).

[345] Southern Pacific Co. v. Portland, 227 U.S. 559 (1913).

[346] Madera Water Works v. Madera, 228 U.S. 454, 456, 457 (1913).

[347] 233 U.S. 195 (1914).

favoritism and corruption, provided in its Constitution of 1879 that no legislature or municipality could grant such franchises, and that in a municipality which did not itself supply gas and water to the public, any individual or corporation might do so, and use the public streets to the extent necessary. The Economic Gas Company of Los Angeles availed itself of this constitutional permission, built a plant, and laid pipes in the streets. The plant was so constructed as to be capable of expanded production. In 1912, Los Angeles having grown, the company decided to lay more pipes, and was digging up the streets to do so. But the year before, the California constitution had been amended so as to revest the power to issue franchises in municipalities. Implementing this new provision, Los Angeles had passed an ordinance that forbade the laying of gas pipes without a specific charter from the city, to be obtained by purchase. Pursuant to the ordinance the Economic Gas Company was stopped from digging up streets and laying more pipes.

It was agreed all around that the Contract Clause protected the company's plant and the pipes already laid. But the argument was that the constitutional provision of 1879 extended not one, but a number of offers. Each offer could be accepted only by actually laying the pipes, did not become a contract until it was thus accepted, and safeguarded only rights actually exercised. Hence the only contract between California and this company was a contract applying to the pipes already laid, and there was no impairment of this contract by the prohibition to lay further pipes. This restrictive construction, Hughes held, was inadmissible. The Constitution of 1879 was a unitary offer of a charter to supply municipalities with gas then, and as their needs grew. The offer was accepted by the laying of the first pipe. The attempt now was to construe the state's constitution as tendering no assurance that a full utility system could be completed, so as to afford a chance of profit. The offer would not reasonably have been understood at the time in this way, or accepted as such, and the Contract Clause now forbade this reductionist construction. And so the company was held to retain its right to lay new gas pipes. A number of charters granted by various municipalities to electric, telephone, and water companies were also unanimously held to be binding.[348]

The Court went to greater and more controversial lengths in two other cases, in which it divided. *Grand Trunk Western Railway* v. *South*

---

[348] Louisville v. Cumberland Telephone Co., 224 U.S. 649 (1912); Boise Water Co. v. Boise, 230 U.S. 84, 98 (1913), see also Boise Water Co. v. Boise, 186 Fed. 705 (9th Cir. 1911), *cert. denied*, 220 U.S. 616 (1911); Old Colony Trust Co. v. Omaha, 230 U.S. 100 (1913); Omaha Electric Co. v. Omaha, 230 U.S. 123 (1913). See also Carondelet Canal Co. v. Louisiana, 233 U.S. 362 (1914).

Bend[349] involved an 1868 ordinance of the city of South Bend, Indiana, which gave the railroad the right to lay a double track over Division Street in the city. A single track was built in 1871, and a double track for part of the way in 1881. In 1892, the railroad tried to extend its double track to the full length originally authorized in 1868, but the Mayor of South Bend, using force, prevented the extension, since the ordinance that originally granted the right had been repealed insofar as it related to double tracks. Reversing the state courts, the Supreme Court, per Lamar, held that by this repealer, the city had impaired the obligation of the 1868 contract.

The city's police power extended, to be sure, to the protection of public safety, health and morals, and, therefore, franchises granting the right to sell beer or to establish gambling halls, for example, could be freely repealed. By the same token, the city could regulate grade crossings, rates of speed, signals, and the like. But unless the right to amend a public utility charter was expressly reserved, which was not the case here, the Contract Clause prevented unilateral amendments that were not regulations, but destructions of the charter. No municipality could barter away the police power, but it could make a contract as to some matters which it was able to barter away, and when it made such a contract, the federal Constitution required adherence to it. This was such a contract. If a double track along Division Street was now inconvenient, the city could regulate it, but it could not try to forbid it, for the inconvenience was assumed to have been weighed in the scales when the contract was made. It was true that the city was not requiring the previously laid double track to be torn up, but that made no difference. The ordinance was a valid contract in its entirety, and the railroad was entitled to enforce it in its entirety.

Day concurred in the result, and Hughes and Pitney dissented without opinion. At the argument, counsel for the city called the Court's attention to census figures showing the population of South Bend to have increased from 1,652 in 1850 to 53,684 in 1910. Lamar's opinion nowhere avails itself of this information. But surely it was somewhat difficult to charge the city with having foreseen in 1868 inconveniences that might arise generations later, and with having taken into account, in the bargain it made, the consequences of a half-century's growth.

Owensboro v. Cumberland Telephone Co.,[350] which divided the Court even more closely, quashed a Kentucky municipality's attempt to renegotiate a telephone charter it had granted in 1889. The charter permitted the company to maintain poles and wires on the streets. In 1909, the city, by ordinance, directed removal of the poles, unless the

---

[349] 227 U.S. 544, 551 (1913).   [350] 230 U.S. 58, 73, 74, 81 (1913).

company agreed to reopen the agreement of 1889. The question was whether the charter was a perpetual one, for it did not so provide, and if it was not, the city was, of course, well within its rights in threatening to revoke it. Such a charter, Lurton[351] held for the Court in declaring the ordinance of 1909 unconstitutional, was a valuable property right, and was assumed to be granted in perpetuity, unless expressly limited, either by its terms, or by the law of the state at the time it was made. This charter reserved to the city the right to alter and amend, but that was no more than a reservation of the normal police power, not of a right to repeal and revoke. Property rights, in reliance on which great investments were made, were not to be left "subject to the mercy of changeable city councils." Hence the reservation of a power to repeal and revoke was not to be lightly implied. "That the right may be reserved to destroy a contract may be conceded; but when such a right is claimed, it must be clear and explicit."

There was a dissent by Day, in which McKenna, Hughes, and Pitney joined, but not, notably enough, Holmes. Where Lurton took the view that a power to revoke was not lightly to be implied, the dissenters considered that it was not to be readily assumed that any municipality possessed the power to grant perpetual franchises. The reservation of the power to amend **and** alter was perhaps of uncertain meaning, but:

> If the doubt be determined in favor of the company and a grant which is not clearly in perpetuity is held to be such, the effect is to tie the hands of the municipality from obtaining revenue from the use of property held by it in trust for all its people. . . . Moreover, if limited grants are to be construed into perpetuities then the control of the streets for railway, telephone and other kindred enterprises of enormous value are granted to private corporations without compensation for the use of such valuable rights which belong to the municipality.

The Bar, the Lower Courts, and "the Possibility of Change in the Present Condition of Things"

The decisions we have reviewed under the Due Process, Equal Protection, and Contract clauses do not in themselves tell the full story of the influence of those constitutional provisions upon the life of the country. For they tell us not enough about attitudes of the bar and of some lower federal judges, or about expectations harbored by the propertied classes at which state regulatory legislation was largely aimed.

---

[351] It was Lurton, just before he was seated on the Supreme Court, who affirmed the grant of a temporary injunction in this case. See *supra*, p. 81, n.317.

And much that is effective as law is derived from such attitudes and expectations, which may lag behind current authoritative decisions, and find encouragement in selective readings of them, or in close readings that emphasize caveats and ambivalences over results.

In a sentence he was made to leave out of his opinion in *Sperry & Hutchinson* v. *Rhodes*,[352] Holmes remarked that the complaint, which the Court unanimously held to be groundless, added "one more to the numberless attempts to treat the Fourteenth Amendment as having almost put an end to the possibility of change in the present condition of things." The attempts were indeed numberless, and they reflected the confidence of a large part of the American Bar, which nothing apparently had yet succeeded in shaking, that legislative intrusions upon the present condition of things were presumptively unconstitutional, and almost invariably worth litigating about. The brief in *Noble State Bank* v. *Haskell*, for example—counsel for the bank signing the brief included Dennis T. Flynn, a major political figure in the state, for many years delegate to Congress from the Oklahoma Territory—contained the following sentence: "We, with confidence, come into court and say that our property cannot be taken from us for private use without our consent, and in support of our claim . . . we point to the history of the English-speaking people, and of every other race which has a government based on law and not in the sword."[353] This was typical. The bar and its clients had unbounded faith that anything they disliked, which was almost everything they did not themselves do, could somehow be shown to violate "the history of the English-speaking people," and thus be got rid of.

Plymouth Coal Co. v. *Pennsylvania*,[354] brought to the Supreme Court in 1914 by John G. Johnson, is illustrative. A Pennsylvania statute dating back to 1891 required owners of adjoining coal mines each to leave pillars of coal in veins worked by them along the line of the adjoining property wide enough so that, taken together with pillars on the other side, they would form barriers ensuring the safety of either mine in case the other should be abandoned and fill with water. The width of these pillars was to be determined in each case by a committee consisting of the engineers of the adjoining mines and the state mine inspector for the district, who was a regular, full-time state officer appointed by the governor.

The Plymouth Coal Company evidently decided to rid itself of the annoyance of this statute, and its lawyers thereupon developed a whole

---

352 *Supra*, p. 297, n.323.
353 *Brief for Plaintiff in Error*, No. 71, at 31, Noble State Bank v. Haskell, 219 U.S. 104 (1911).
354 232 U.S. 531 (1914).

cloud of objections to it, one more minute than the other. The chief one was that the legislature had failed to fix a uniform width for the pillars, and that for that reason the statute was arbitrary. This was an issue of delegation, if it was anything, and in the circumstances scarcely raised a federal question. For the delegation, in addition to being unexceptionable by any standard, ran, after all, from a state legislature to state officers. Then it was objected that the committee to which the decision on the width of the pillars was left seemed free under the statute to operate either by majority vote or by unanimity—the legislature had not specified which. That was perhaps too bad, although it doubtless worked out in practice, but in any event, it hardly raised a federal constitutional issue. And so forth. The Supreme Court upheld the statute, but did nothing to dissuade future litigation of this sort, since it dealt seriously with the case in an elaborate opinion taking up each of the objections on its merits.

Does it not speak worlds about the real law of the Constitution in these years that men thought they had a chance to win such a case—a chance sufficient to justify the expense and effort of litigating it all the way to the Supreme Court of the United States? And is it not a commentary on the bar? Might not one have expected counsel of the eminence of a John G. Johnson in 1914 to have advised his clients that they should try to live with such a statute, rather than undertaking to dream up ingenious points in their behalf?

Another instance of the readiness with which counsel and their clients assumed that the courts would protect them from measures they found to impinge on their interests and presuppositions is *Singer Sewing Machine Co. v. Brickell*.[355] What was involved was a classic tax on peddlers, and there was not much question of its validity under the Commerce Clause, or under the Equal Protection Clause.[356] But the case was brought up through the federal rather than state courts, and therefore questions of state law were relatively open for federal decision. The following argument, based on the state constitution, was solemnly advanced. It was claimed, as it had been under the heading of Equal Protection, too, that the tax was bad because it fell only on peddlers, and not on sellers of sewing machines by other methods. This, it was said, violated Sections 1 and 37 of the Alabama Bill of Rights, which read: Section 1: "That all men are equally free and independent; that they are endowed by their Creator with certain inalienable rights; that among these are life, liberty, and the pursuit of happiness." Section 37: "That the sole object and only legitimate end of government is to pro-

---

[355] 233 U.S. 304 (1914).   [356] See *supra*, p. 275, n.232.

tect the citizen in the enjoyment of life, liberty and property; and when the government assumes other functions, it is usurpation and oppression."

The Supreme Court of the United States spent a page and a half disposing of these contentions. And it wrote opinions as well, sometimes, to be sure, with a measure of impatience, denying that the Due Process Clause was violated where a state court, in an ordinary contract litigation, had committed alleged errors in the interpretation of the evidence and of the relevant state law; or that an ordinance requiring homeowners to connect with newly constructed sewers, to build water closets in their homes, and to cease further use of outside facilities went beyond the permissible limits of the police power; and other similarly trivial cases.[357]

The Court had to deal also with a whole clutch of Contract Clause cases which on analysis turned entirely on points of state law that were clear beyond argument, or in which the federal issue could be made to rest only on outlandishly self-serving constructions of charters.[358] There were in addition the even more frivolous efforts to engage its attention which the Court felt able to dispose of, or which sometimes disposed of themselves, without the need of full opinions, and often without the need of argument.[359]

This kind of litigation was not altogether the result of a mindless confidence that the Fourteenth Amendment had "put an end to the possibility of change in the present condition of things." Even where counsel must have recognized the high likelihood of ultimate defeat, in the Supreme Court if nowhere else, a practical purpose was often served. Litigation, albeit finally abortive, could in the meantime delay or otherwise inhibit government action. Part of the explanation, no doubt, for an occasional persistence, at some expense, in continually reframing a case so as to bring it back to the Supreme Court some three or four

---

[357] See Appleby v. Buffalo, 221 U.S. 524 (1911); Murray v. Pocatello, 226 U.S. 318 (1912); El Paso & Southwestern R.R. v. Weikel, 226 U.S. 590 (1913); Hutchinson v. Valdosta, 227 U.S. 303 (1913); Seattle & Renton Ry. v. Linhoff, 231 U.S. 568 (1913); Radford v. Myers, 231 U.S. 725 (1914); McDonald v. Oregon Navigation Co., 233 U.S. 665 (1914).

[358] Fisher v. New Orleans, 218 U.S. 438 (1910); Shawnee Sewerage & Drainage Co. v. Stearns, 220 U.S. 462 (1911); Missouri & Kansas Interurban Ry. v. City of Olanthe, 222 U.S. 187

(1911); Detroit United Ry. v. Detroit, 229 U.S. 39 (1913); Denver v. New York Trust Co., 229 U.S. 123 (1913); Vicksburg v. Henson, 231 U.S. 259 (1913); Ennis Water Works v. Ennis, 233 U.S. 652 (1914).

[359] A conservative and highly fallible count, restricted to Due Process, Equal Protection, and Contract Clause cases, and excluding summary orders in cases raising issues that were at least plausible, for the October Terms 1910–13, yields thirty-three such dismissals.

times[360] lies in a certain self-centered, self-righteous inability to accept the realities of government. But part of it must lie also in the probability that every so often the effort, although without hope of victory on the merits, would nevertheless return a profit of sorts, generally by way of delay.

This social cost inheres to a degree in any system of administering justice. But the cost was increased by prevailing attitudes at the bar toward the Due Process, Equal Protection, and Contract clauses, which the Supreme Court was insufficiently dispelling—if it meant to dispel them at all (Why attack our good friend the Fourteenth Amendment? Day admonished Holmes).[361] And the cost was heightened by the opportunities for delay that the practice of government by injunction, as its opponents called it, opened up. We have witnessed the effects of this practice in the *Minnesota* and related rate cases, and noted the outcry against it.[362] Other and varied manifestations of it are not hard to find in these years. The Supreme Court, which as head of the federal judicial system was not powerless to do so, took no reforming initiative. If anything, quite the contrary. Unquestionably it was and remained the simple truth, therefore, that a suit for an injunction against a new state regulatory measure would generally ensure some respite to the business interests concerned, regardless of ultimate outcome.

If a district judge favorably inclined on the merits could be found, the initial victory was worth quite a lot of time. In some ways, however, it was even better not to obtain a prompt, favorable initial decision, for such a decision was appealable and could be reversed, whereas a restraining order followed by a drawn-out trial and various interlocutory judgments postponed final resolution of the merits by the Supreme Court.[363] Moreover, restraining orders were quite ordinarily granted, and then continued in force pending appeal, even after a decision on the merits adverse to interests seeking to enjoin state action.

It was thus possible, not only to win before there was any decision, but also to win while losing. For example, Oklahoma passed a prohibition statute in 1908. But there was no chance of enforcing it. Some twenty different suits were immediately begun, injunctions were issued, and state officials who attempted to violate them were proceeded against for contempt. By 1911, the suits were still pending, and Oklahoma was

---

[360] See De Bearn v. De Bearn, 225 U.S. 695 (1912), 231 U.S. 741 (1913), De Bearn v. Winans, 232 U.S. 719 (1914), De Bearn v. Safe Deposit Co., 233 U.S. 24 (1914); Venner v. Chicago City Ry., 218 U.S. 669 (1910), 235 U.S. 713 (1914), 239 U.S. 657 (1915).

[361] *Supra*, p. 297.

[362] *Supra*, pp. 260–61.

[363] See, e.g., Paducah v. East Tennessee Telephone Co., 229 U.S. 476 (1913).

trying to get the Supreme Court to intervene and lift the injunctions, so that the law enacted some three years earlier could begin to operate. The Court would not interfere.[364]

In *Merrimack River Savings Bank* v. *City of Clay Center*, the city, claiming that the franchise of a light and power company had expired (in the company's view it was perpetual), forbade the company any longer to maintain poles and wires on the streets. The company sued in the United States district court, raising a Contract Clause issue, and obtained a temporary injunction. The United States circuit court then dismissed the suit for want of a federal question, but maintained the temporary injunction pending appeal to the Supreme Court. The appeal was dismissed.[365] Thereupon, the understandably impatient city officials proceeded to cut down the company's poles. They were ill advised; they should have waited for time to run out for the filing of a petition for rehearing, and for the mandate of the Supreme Court to come down. And so they were held in contempt of the Supreme Court, although since they had acted in good faith, the contempt was in effect excused.[366]

The initiation of a federal suit and the issuance of a temporary injunction could not be warded off by first conducting a litigation, with possibly more favorable prospects for the state, through the state courts, since exhaustion of state judicial remedies was no prerequisite to federal jurisdiction, as indicated in the *Home Telephone* case,[367] and made quite clear by Holmes in a later opinion.[368] In 1913, Congress tried to work a statutory change in this aspect of the situation, but it was of little consequence.[369] An earlier statutory change, providing for three-judge courts in some instances, also had little effect, except as the Supreme Court allowed it to be turned into an instrument of yet further delay.[370]

Litigation could shift from one constitutional clause to another, and strong-minded and self-willed federal judges were not unavailable. We have touched on the troubles of the city of Louisville in dealing with its telephone company. The city found first that it could not revoke the company's charter, and thus get some new leverage in its efforts to regulate it.[371] Meanwhile, the city was trying to set the company's rates,

---

[364] *Ex parte* Oklahoma, 220 U.S. 191, 210 (1911).

[365] Merrimack River Savings Bank v. City of Clay Center, 218 U.S. 665 (1910).

[366] Merrimack River Savings Bank v. City of Clay Center, 219 U.S. 527 (1911).

[367] *Supra*, p. 288, n.286.

[368] Bacon v. Rutland R.R., 232 U.S. 134 (1914).

[369] Act of Mar. 4, 1913, 37 Stat. 1013; see W. Pogue, "State Determination of State Law and the Judicial Code," *Harv. L. Rev.*, 41:623, 1928.

[370] 36 Stat. 557 (1910); *Ex parte* Metropolitan Water Co., 220 U.S. 539 (1911); see F. Frankfurter and J. M. Landis, *The Business of the Supreme Court* (1928), 143.

[371] Louisville v. Cumberland Telephone Co., *supra*, p. 303, n.348.

and was enjoined from doing so. The Supreme Court, as we saw, reversed, but the district judge promptly returned to the fray.[372] In *Columbus* v. *Mercantile Trust Co.*,[373] a water company with a thirty-year franchise was providing polluted water, and that only intermittently. So the city started building its own water plant. There was a suit to enjoin this enterprise, but a master found the facts to be as alleged by the city, and the federal district judge, agreeing, held that the water company had failed to abide by its contract, and that the city was therefore free to proceed without inhibition from the Contract Clause. Nevertheless, the judge took charge and enjoined the city from building its water works unless it agreed to pay a fair price for the water company's property, plus indemnification to its bondholders.

Reversing for a unanimous Supreme Court, Lurton quoted the remark of a Vice Chancellor in an English case: "I am not sitting here as a committee of public safety, armed with arbitrary power to prevent what it is said will be a great injury not to Birmingham only but to the whole of England; that is not my function." It was an apt text, for it did not take a recalcitrant lower federal judge, disobedient to the law that was laid down to him from on high, or intent only on vindicating his own prejudices—though there were such—to practice government by injunction. Misapprehension of the drift of doctrine or honest error were enough—and the habit of command, the executive instinct, as in this case, to take charge and impose a solution that seemed fair. These attitudes were bred by this kind of litigation and by the expectations of the bar, and they were capable of infecting, as we shall have occasion to see presently, even so distinguished a judge as William C. Hook.[374]

To be sure, examples of self-restraint can also be cited, as when a Court of Appeals declined to undertake the collection of taxes in a county that had defaulted on its bonds.[375] The most widely noted exercise of self-restraint was *Pacific Telephone Co.* v. *Oregon*,[376] decided unanimously in 1912. As permitted in its constitution, Oregon in 1906 enacted by initiative a statute taxing certain corporations. The Pacific Telephone Company resisted collection of the tax on the sole ground that the initiative, by which the tax was imposed, was a form of pure

---

[372] *Supra*, p. 287, nn.282, 283.

[373] 218 U.S. 645, 663 (1910).

[374] See Denver v. New York Trust Co., 187 Fed. 890 (8th Cir. 1911), *reversed*, 229 U.S. 123 (1913).

[375] Preston v. Sturgis Milling Co., 183 Fed. 1 (6th Cir. 1910), *cert. denied*, 220 U.S. 610 (1911); *but cf.* Hendrickson v. Apperson, 245 U.S. 105 (1917).

[376] 223 U.S. 118 (1912); see also Kiernan v. Portland, 223 U.S. 151 (1912). For another instance of denial of jurisdiction to adjudicate a claim under the Republican Form of Government Clause, see Cassidy v. Colorado, 50 Colo. 503, 117 Pac. 357 (1911), *dismissed for want of jurisdiction*, 223 U.S. 707 (1911).

democracy violating the guarantee of a republican government extended to the states by the federal Constitution. The Oregon Supreme Court upheld its own constitution, and the United States Supreme Court, the Chief Justice writing, dismissed an appeal for the want of federal jurisdiction.

The question, White held, was political and not justiciable. Congress might have power to intervene, but the federal courts did not. There was not a little jubilation in the public prints, much of it taking the romantic view that characterized the Progressive approach to structural political reforms. "The Supreme Court has restored the people to power," said the *Pittsburgh Leader*. "It has opened the way for direct legislation and actual self-government—government by the people."[377] The *New York Times*, on the other hand, was clear that the Court could not have been expected to do anything else, but it held in low esteem states "which have in mind such follies" as "destroying representative institutions and setting up what is called direct government in their place. . . ."[378] The *Times* might fairly have consoled itself and its readers by remembering that statutes enacted by the initiative were no more immune to government by injunction than legislative acts. Whether the people or the legislators proposed, the judges, for a time, at any rate, could still dispose, and certainly delay.

The Fundamental Conservatism of a Majority of Justices

It remains to examine now two cases that had little direct bearing on the fate of social legislation at the October Terms 1910–13, that constituted in themselves no particular point of contact—no convergence and no collision—of the Court's work with the main concerns of the Progressive Era. These cases are symptomatic, however, of an ominous tendency on the part of some of the Justices to share the feeling of segments of the bar that the Supreme Court should "put an end to the possibility of change in the present condition of things."

The fundamental conservatism of a majority, if a narrow one, of the Supreme Court found no better expression during these years than in *Slocum* v. *New York Life Insurance Co.* This was a diversity action on an insurance policy, and the issues on the facts were whether the insured had stopped paying premiums before he died, and whether the company had or had not agreed to take his note as an accommodation

---

[377] The *Literary Digest,* 44:411–12, Mar. 2, 1912.

[378] *New York Times,* Feb. 21, 1912, p. 10, col. 2.

of the premiums. The evidence was quite clear for the insurance company on all issues. Nevertheless, the trial judge refused a motion for a directed verdict and let the case go to the jury. Subsequently he denied a motion for a judgment notwithstanding the verdict, and let stand the jury's award of $18,000 to the plaintiff. The Court of Appeals for the Third Circuit held that the trial judge had committed error both in not directing a verdict for the insurance company and in denying the motion for judgment notwithstanding the verdict, and it remanded to the district court with direction to give judgment for the company.

The Supreme Court, by a bare majority of five, Van Devanter writing, reversed the Court of Appeals. That court was perfectly right, Van Devanter held, in vacating the judgment for the plaintiff. The evidence, with all justifiable inferences to be drawn from it, did not support the verdict, and the trial judge, therefore, committed error in failing to direct the jury to find for the defendant. But the Court of Appeals was wrong in not remanding for a new trial. It had followed the practice in the Pennsylvania state courts, which permitted appellate direction of a judgment notwithstanding, but in the federal courts, the Seventh Amendment forbade such a course of action.

That Amendment, applicable "in suits at common law, where the value in controversy shall exceed twenty dollars," guarantees the right of trial by jury, and provides that "no fact tried by a jury shall be otherwise re-examined in any Court of the United States, than according to the rules of common law." Direction of a verdict before the evidence was submitted to the jury, said Van Devanter, accorded with the rules of the common law of England, "the grand reservoir," quoting an encomium by Story, "of all our jurisprudence." But it did not so accord to direct a verdict after the case had been to the jury, and to direct it contrary to the jury's finding. The command of the Seventh Amendment was that only a jury could decide the facts. What the Court of Appeals did here was to cut off the plaintiff's opportunity, at another trial, to have a jury decide the facts on the basis, perhaps, of additional evidence or of a different presentation of it. All this, in an elaborate forty-four-page opinion, including an exhaustive review of precedents, some of which, be it said, needed to be distinguished rather gingerly.

Van Devanter was answered in a twenty-three-page dissent by Hughes, whom Holmes, Lurton, and Pitney joined. It was really too bad, said Hughes, that the majority not only prevented the federal courts in Pennsylvania from following a long established state practice, but also erected "an impassable barrier" in the way of Congressional action aimed at remedying the mischief of repeated trials, and thus diminishing the delay and expense of litigation. The result was not compelled by the Seventh Amendment. The Court conceded that the trial judge had the power to direct a verdict for the defendant after presentation of the plaintiff's evidence, and that had the judge done so, that would have been an end of the matter. It was equally conceded that the trial judge erred in not directing a verdict. The reason why the majority necessarily made these concessions was that while the jury, to be sure, must try questions of fact, the issue whether there is a question of fact for the jury to try itself presented a question of law. Precisely that question of law was what the Court of Appeals had decided. That was the substance of the matter, and "all else is form and procedure." All else, therefore, should be left to be governed by rules of practice subject to legislative control.

The Pennsylvania rule was a salutary one that had commended itself to Bench and Bar as an improvement in the administration of justice. The Seventh Amendment "does not raise forms of motions or merely modal details to the dignity of constitutional rights." If the trial court had directed a verdict, as concededly it should have done, the plaintiff would have had no opportunity to improve his case at a second trial. What was it that now entitled him to such an opportunity?[379]

There was no reasonable answer to Hughes' question, and an almost unanimous body of professional opinion so held and holds. "Few decisions rendered in recent years by the United States Supreme Court have been more generally criticized by Bench and Bar" than the *Slocum* case, said a Note in the *University of Pennsylvania Law Review* in 1913. The decision, said a writer in the *Harvard Law Review* that same year, was "a public misfortune."[380] The American Bar Association had long advocated the very procedure that was now declared unconstitutional, and had urged Congress to make it mandatory by statute. Outraged, the chairman of the association's special committee on procedural reform wrote to President Wilson to ask that Attorney General McReynolds join him in pressing the Supreme Court to grant a rehearing. The Attorney General did join, but the effort was unavailing.[381] Later

---

[379] Slocum v. New York Life Ins. Co., 228 U.S. 364, 377, 402, 408 (1913); see also Young v. Central R.R. of New Jersey, 232 U.S. 602; and see Myers v. Pittsburgh Coal Co., 233 U.S. 184 (1914). But *cf.* Becker v. Exchange Mutual Fire Ins. Co., 177 Fed. 918 (3rd Cir. 1910), *cert. denied,* 220 U.S. 611 (1911) (judgment n.o.v. held constitutional where judge reserved question of law before verdict).

[380] Note, *U. Pa. L. Rev.,* 61:673, 1913; J. L. Thorndike, "Trial by Jury in United States Courts," *Harv. L. Rev.,* 26:732, 1913. See also *Colum. L. Rev.,* 13:544, 1913; *Yale L. J.,* 23:454, 1914. But *cf.* H. Schofield, "New Trials and the Seventh Amendment—Slocum v. New York Life Insurance Co.," *Ill. L. Rev.,* 8:287, 381, 465, 1913, 1914.

[381] E. P. Wheeler to President Wilson, May 1, 1913, Archives, File 72868; *Washington, D.C., Evening Star,* May 27, 1913, p. 9, col. 3.

scholarly and general professional opinion took the same view as contemporary commentators, and current practice, under Rule 50(b) of the Federal Rules of Civil Procedure, uses a patent fiction to circumvent the *Slocum* decision.[382]

One of the notable features of *Slocum* is that the narrow majority included not only Van Devanter, but Day, thus highlighting an essential conservative strain in the makeup of these two Justices. Day at least (and in some measure also Van Devanter at this time) was perceived as a progressive judge. And not unnaturally. People reasoned from positions taken in many of the notable cases we have reviewed. It was too ready and too simple an estimate not only of Van Devanter, but of Day, as was also made clear in *Thompson* v. *Thompson*,[383] an obscure little decision on a point arising in the general jurisdiction of the District of Columbia courts.

A wife had sued her husband to recover damages in tort for several assaults he had made on her. At common law she had no legal personality and could not sue, but a statute applicable in the District of Columbia enabled married women to make contracts and sue in contract, to own real estate, and to sue "for torts committed against them, as fully and freely as if they were unmarried." But the statute, Day held for a narrow majority of four (the case was decided before the accession of Van Devanter and Lamar), should not be construed to enable women to sue their husbands. It did not in terms so provide. The common law frowned on airing family quarrels in the courts, and conceding the power of Congress to take a different approach if it saw fit to do so, "nevertheless such radical and far-reaching changes should only be wrought by language so clear and plain as to be unmistakable evidence of the legislative intention."

While this is a not illegitimate way to go about the task of statutory construction, it inevitably proceeds from a judicial value judgment, for obviously the legislature will be held to explicit, detailed statutory statements only when it impinges on conditions the judges do not wish to see too readily disturbed. Day's value judgment in this instance was highly, even rigidly, conservative. No doubt he felt freer to give vent to his conservatism on a question of common law and by the technique of statutory construction, than on larger issues of public policy and by invoking the Constitution. Harlan filed a dissent, in which Holmes and Hughes joined.[384]

---

[382] J. W. Moore, *Federal Practice* (2nd ed., 1961), 83–84, 2325–26; *cf.* Becker v. Exchange Mutual Fire Ins. Co., *supra*, n.379.

[383] 218 U.S. 611, 618 (1910).

[384] For Harlan's dissent, see *supra*, pp. 67–68.

These two decisions manifest an outlook which is perhaps as important as the many results favorable to progressive legislation that the Court was reaching at the same time. The Court may have been striving to make its peace with the dominant opinion of the day. But it could hardly be said that the Court was gaining a general capacity to accommodate itself and its law to changing social and economic conditions.

CHAPTER IV

Appointment Cycles

I N THE PERIOD 1910–30, encompassing the Chief Justiceships of
White and Taft, there were three appointment phases, three stages
of significant renewal of the institution. The first, President Taft's reconstitution of the Court, we have reviewed. The second began with the
death of Lurton in the summer of 1914, followed within a year by the
illness of Lamar, then by his death, and shortly after by the resignation
of Hughes. Wilson substituted McReynolds, Brandeis, and Clarke, and
on the whole, despite McReynolds, the Court appeared to have been
given a more progressive cast.

Actually, such movement as can be discerned was rather in the
opposite direction, owing partly to McReynolds, partly to the loss of
Hughes, at once a progressive influence and a powerfully respectable
public figure, and partly, no doubt, to the shock administered by the
Brandeis appointment. The presence of Brandeis, and the consequent
anxieties about the new radicalism he supposedly represented, tended
to bring waverers into line, and generally to cause a sharpening and
hardening of positions.[1]

The third phase consisted of Harding's appointments between the
summer of 1921 and January 1923, first of Taft as Chief Justice, and
then, in close consultation with Taft, of Sutherland, Butler, and Sanford.
Now a quite rigidly conservative majority was ensured.

These are the major cycles, due to resume under Hoover in 1930–32,
and under the second Roosevelt in 1937–39. In between, and standing
rather apart, are the appointments of Pitney by President Taft in 1912,

---

[1] See, e.g., the alignments against
early dissents by Brandeis in New
York Central R.R. v. Winfield, 244
U.S. 147 (1917); and Adams v.
Tanner, 244 U.S. 590 (1917).

and of Stone by Coolidge in 1925. The appointment of Stone was clearly an action quite separate from Harding's nominations of two years earlier. Taft's choice of Pitney in 1912 stands apart also, because the appointments of 1910 were made together, and grew out of a single political and deliberative process. The naming of Pitney, only a year later, to be sure, was an independent transaction, even though it was related to the earlier deliberations by one slender thread, or, more accurately, one broken reed.

Pitney

Harlan died on October 14, 1911, just at the beginning of the term. Taft was in no hurry, for he did not propose to act by recess appointment while Congress was out of session. And there was a dearth of rumors, even among the Justices, except, as Van Devanter reported to a friend, for "a strong inclination to suggest that the appointment will, or ought to, be made from the Third Circuit or the Seventh Circuit, neither of which is represented at this time. . . ."[2] Toward the middle of November, however, events seemed to point away from the Third and Seventh circuits. Word reached Van Devanter, through both the Chief Justice and Lurton, that two names considered in 1910 were again in the President's mind: Judge William C. Hook of the Court of Appeals for the Eighth Circuit, Van Devanter's former colleague and his chief competition in 1910, and Charles Nagel of St. Louis, the Secretary of Commerce and Labor. The President wished to have Van Devanter's opinion on the relative qualifications of the two.[3]

Taft, it seemed, had little hope of finding his man in the Third Circuit, where Pennsylvania entered the most insistent claims, although he made a firm attempt at this time. On November 29, 1911, he wrote to his Secretary of State, Philander C. Knox of Pittsburgh,[4] as follows, addressing him formally, as "Dear Mr. Secretary":

> I have been talking over with Senator [George T.] Oliver [of Pennsylvania] the regret I had that Pennsylvania did not offer a lawyer for the vacancy on the Supreme bench. He has said, Why not Knox. To which I replied that I supposed you would not accept the position. I don't

---

[2] W. Van Devanter to F. B. Kellogg, Oct. 26, 1911, Van Devanter Papers.

[3] W. Van Devanter to E. B. Adams, Nov. 20, 1911, Van Devanter Papers.

[4] Philander Chase Knox (1853–1921) was Attorney General in the cabinets of McKinley and Roosevelt from 1901 until, in June 1904, he was appointed to the Senate to fill the unexpired term of the famous Matthew S. Quay. He was elected a Senator from Pennsylvania in his own right in 1905, but resigned to become Taft's Secretary of State, serving the full four years. In 1917, he returned to the Senate and stayed until his death.

know what I could do to fill your present place if you would accept, but my interest in the Court would lead me to put aside all other considerations to secure your service on that great tribunal. I write to offer the place to you formally because if you do not accept now, as you did not when President Roosevelt offered it, you may have in writing evidence of what two Presidents have thought of your ability to fill the highest place that lawyers can aspire to. Don't for an instant think that I could fill your present place. I don't know how I could fill it. In every way your service has been most satisfying and comforting. Without you at the head of the family, the circle would be desolate; but for the reasons stated above, I wish to offer the Supreme bench to you again.[5]

Knox replied in accordance with Taft's expectation. Judicial office was not for him. But: "To be thought worthy to fill so eminent a place by one so conspicuously fitted to make discriminating choice is in itself an honor rare and distinct."[6]

In the meantime, the President had sent for the Chief Justice "to inquire about the condition in the Court so as to form some idea of the urgent and immediate necessity for action on the new appointment." White "relieved his mind of any anxiety on that subject. . . ." He was not about to urge a recess appointment.[7] By January 1912, there was still no action. "The question is, as I see it," White reported to his colleague Day, "Nagel or Hook, with the tendency of the President's mind in favor of Hook and the influences of his environment in favor of Nagel. What will come out of it I know not."[8] Hook of Kansas, it will be recalled, was the candidate under whom, the year before, Van Devanter's sponsor, Senator Francis E. Warren of Wyoming, had started a gratuitous but effective fire by claiming that he was the Insurgent candidate. Hook, as we have seen, took his defeat of 1910 bravely, like a gentleman. He would need, once more, all the spirit he could muster. For a second and fatal time, Judge Hook fell among the sharks. He was beaten now, not as an Insurgent, but as a supposed tool of the railroads, and—the rarest of disqualifications in these years—antiblack.

More markedly this time than in 1910, Hook was the beneficiary of a concerted compaign for the nomination. There was no problem now of loyalties divided between him and Van Devanter, and he had united and active support from his colleagues in the Eighth Circuit, from his bar, from conservative and moderate elements in the Congressional

---

[5] W. H. Taft to P. C. Knox, Nov. 29, 1911, Philander C. Knox Papers, Box 3, Library of Congress.

[6] P. C. Knox to W. H. Taft, Nov. 29, 1911, Taft Papers.

[7] E. D. White to W. R. Day, Dec. 6, 1911, Day Papers.

[8] E. D. White to W. R. Day, Jan. 4, 1912, Day Papers.

delegations from Eighth Circuit states, and from business and professional groups. Quite clearly the "better elements" were for him, and nothing, it was evident, could be farther from the truth than the notion that Hook was the darling of the Insurgents. About the only thing, it seemed, that Hook needed to be afraid of was the opinion of some that perhaps it was the turn of the Third Circuit to receive representation.[9]

But the thoroughly organized candidacy of Judge Hook lacked, as compared with Van Devanter's earlier one, a manager of the perseverance and in-fighting skill of Francis E. Warren. And it ran—most painful of ironies—into a Progressive opposition that might not have materialized as virulently, or been as important, in the more quiescent atmosphere of the winter of 1910, before the final break between Taft and Theodore Roosevelt, and before the Presidential race of 1912 was on in earnest. Insurgents were more insurgent now. Everyone all around was a bit bolder, a bit more ruthless. Taft for his part was both more beleaguered (and hence, perhaps, more cautious about offending) and more completely alienated from Progressive opinion (and hence, perhaps, also inclined to be more aggressive). The waters were thus more troubled, and the fishing was better.

The *Minnesota* and other rate cases were being held for argument in the Supreme Court late in 1911, and a great deal of attention centered on them. A number of Progressive governors and state railroad commissions in the West had filed *amicus* briefs, as we have seen, and they now expressed strong objection to Judge Hook more or less as part of the position they were taking in the rate cases. For there was a rate decision in a railroad case that they held against Hook.

Oklahoma, by a constitutional provision fixing passenger rates at 2¢ per mile, and by its railroad commission's orders, had reduced intrastate railroad rates in much the same fashion as Minnesota and other states. The reductions were in actual effect in Oklahoma for periods ranging up to two years, and on the basis of this experience, there was a suit to enjoin them. In *Missouri, Kansas & Topeka Railway* v. *Love*,[10] after an extended hearing, Judge Hook found the rates confiscatory as applied in intrastate commerce in Oklahoma, and issued a temporary injunction against them. Hook's error, as the Western governors and railroad commissions saw it, was that in estimating the railroad's value and operating costs, he had assigned too great a value and too high costs to the intrastate portion of the business as compared with the interstate, and had thus been led to find perfectly reasonable intrastate rates confiscatory. It is impossible now to judge, without the most detailed review of the voluminous evidence, whether the charge was at all

---

[9] Taft Papers.   [10] 177 Fed. 493 (C.C. W.D. Okla. 1910).

well taken. Hook's decision was affirmed by the Court of Appeals, and the Supreme Court refused to review it.[11]

Certainly this was not one of those out-of-hand injunctions issued minutes after a rate statute passed through a state legislature. The most that can probably be said is that Hook was all too comfortable with rules of law and methods of valuation that were fairly routine in the lower federal courts but that a more forward-looking judge might have questioned. One of Hook's supporters, a prominent Kansas City railroad lawyer who had also vocally favored Van Devanter's nomination in 1910, while taking an exaggerated and self-interested view of the opposition to the kind of law that Hook's decision represented, was probably not unfair in his protest against the singling out of Judge Hook. "The issue now presented," he complained,

> has become broader than one of personal interest in Judge Hook. It vitally affects the entire independence of the federal judiciary. If the attacks in this instance are allowed to prevail, every judge in the West hereafter, having a case before him in which state railroad commissions are directly or indirectly interested, will know beforehand that if his decision be not satisfactory to them, regardless of its merit, he will be subjected to onslaughts from their organization, which covers a large portion of the western country, and the possibility of any future promotion will be forever destroyed. There is but one step from this to organized efforts for impeachment and judicial recall.[12]

A more valid charge against Judge Hook might have been based on *Denver v. New York Trust Co.*[13] This was one of those Contract Clause cases in which the real Contract Clause issue, if any, disappeared upon analysis, but in which Judge Hook was seized with the executive instinct to take charge and see the right and proper thing done, *pro bono publico*, as he doubtless felt. He upheld a preliminary injunction that had been issued against the city of Denver to prevent it from building a new water plant, and to require it instead to buy up a water company whose franchise had expired. The Supreme Court granted certiorari— a rather rare use of the writ, as Van Devanter pointed out in an opinion

---

[11] Love v. Atchison, Topeka & Santa Fe Ry., et al., 185 Fed. 321 (8th Cir. 1911), *cert. denied sub nom.* West v. Atchison, Topeka & Santa Fe Ry., et al., 220 U.S. 618 (1911); see *supra,* p. 263, n.189.

[12] F. Hagerman to W. Van Devanter, Jan. 3, 1912, Van Devanter Papers.

[13] 187 Fed. 890 (8th Cir. 1911), *reversed,* 229 U.S. 123 (1913), *supra,* p. 308, n.358; see also Wheeler v. Denver, 229 U.S. 342 (1913); and see Wheeler v. Denver, 231 Fed. 8 (8th Cir. 1916), *appeal dismissed for want of jurisdiction,* 245 U.S. 626 (1917).

for the Court, since generally interlocutory orders were not reviewed. And Van Devanter reversed.

He could not quite understand, as he confessed to his friend and Hook's colleague, Judge Elmer B. Adams, why the Court of Appeals had come to its result. Possibly Hook "was influenced," Van Devanter speculated, "by a just wish to save a tremendous property from municipal action which was thought to be unwise from the standpoint of the public as well as of the private owners."[14] Yet that was an insufficient basis of federal judicial action. But Judge Hook's opponents made rather less of this case on its merits than of his railroad rate decision, and resorted instead to faint insinuations of venality. Judge Hook, it was whispered, or his friends, had a material interest in the water company. The allegation originated with faceless informers, it was quite probably unfounded, and it caused poor Judge Hook much pain.[15]

Another, and in context of the time most singular, objection to Judge Hook was based on the opinion of the Court of Appeals for the Eighth Circuit in *McCabe* v. *Atchison, Topeka & Santa Fe Railway*.[16] Hook was not the author of this opinion, but merely concurred silently. Judge Elmer B. Adams, Van Devanter's good friend, was the writer, while the third judge on the panel, Walter H. Sanborn, dissented. The case concerned an Oklahoma statute which required railroads in intrastate commerce to segregate white and black passengers, as the state could plainly do under *Plessy* v. *Ferguson*. But the statute allowed railroads to provide sleeping, dining, or chair cars for the exclusive use of either white or black passengers; it allowed them, in other words, not to provide such cars at all for blacks.

Five black citizens of Oklahoma attacked the statute on Equal Protection grounds among others, but they attacked it, at least arguably, too early, right after its enactment, and were not able to show that they had as yet been actually denied the accommodations in question. The suit could properly be—perhaps it had to be—dismissed on this ground, and so it was. But Judge Adams chose also to suggest that it was perfectly constitutional to permit railroads to carry sleeping cars and the like for whites only, since the legislature might well have thought, and the court judicially knew, that the two races were not equally able to afford luxuries. Hence it would amount to the imposition of a senseless expense upon the railroads to require them to carry sleeping, dining, or chair cars for blacks also, when the demand did

---

[14] W. Van Devanter to E. B. Adams, June 2, 1913, Van Devanter Papers.

[15] W. C. Hook to W. Van Devanter, Jan. 16, 1912; E. B. Adams to W. Van Devanter, June 4, 1913, Van Devanter Papers.

[16] 186 Fed. 966 (8th Cir. 1911).

not justify it. Equality of service did not necessarily mean identity of service.

These remarks of Judge Adams', in which Hook joined, the Supreme Court later, in an opinion by Hughes, went out of its way to disown, while affirming dismissal of the suit as premature.[17] Indeed, the Court declared flatly that if challenged in a properly framed case, a statute such as this would run afoul of the Fourteenth Amendment. Yet White, Holmes, Lamar, and McReynolds, the last by then having succeeded Lurton, concurred in the result, but not in Hughes' opinion— an action explicable only by their unwillingness to go along with Hughes' disapproval of Judge Adams' constitutional dicta.[18] Be that as it may, Hook's concurrence in *McCabe* apparently troubled the President, and it troubled his entourage.

The case touched on a sensitive situation for the Taft Administration, especially since it arose in Oklahoma. That state had recently disfranchised most of its blacks by writing a so-called Grandfather Clause into its constitution, which in effect applied a literacy test only to blacks. Oklahoma Republicans saw the disfranchisement as cutting heavily into the party's vote. Hence they urged that criminal proceedings be brought against state election officials in order to establish that the Grandfather Clause violated the Fifteenth Amendment. The Department of Justice resisted, taking the position—and a perfectly tenable one it was—that no criminal prosecution was proper, or likely to succeed, under the applicable federal statute. This position was cleared with the President, who approved. But party pressure was strong, and the Republican U.S. Attorney in Oklahoma, clearly insubordinate, obtained indictments anyway. Its hand having been thus forced, the Taft Administration went along. The prosecutions were partially successful in the lower courts in the spring of 1911, and ultimately attained full success in the Supreme Court.[19]

In Oklahoma, there was much agitation on the part of the whites, and much hard feeling all around, since the Department of Justice was still less than entirely forceful in pushing additional prosecutions. With a convention and an election coming on, the race issue was nothing the Taft Administration could have wished to see further stirred, least of all in Oklahoma. It was black organizations in Oklahoma, abetted by the newly founded biracial NAACP, that lodged the complaints about Judge Hook's concurrence in the *McCabe* case. Charges that the ad-

---

[17] See *infra*, pp. 929 *et seq.*

[18] McCabe v. Atchison, Topeka & Santa Fe Ry., 235 U.S. 151 (1914).

[19] Guinn v. United States, 238 U.S. 347 (1915); United States v. Mosley, 238 U.S. 383 (1915), see *infra*, pp. 775 *et seq.*

ministration's attitude toward race discrimination was ambivalent or worse could easily be substantiated—whether or not quite fairly—with evidence of its position in the matter of the Grandfather Clause. That episode, if made public, would alienate blacks and also, at the same time, inflame whites, since in the end the administration had gone along despite its better legal judgment. Altogether, an unpleasant appearance of weakness, irresolution, and lack of control would be given. It was a sleeping dog best not wakened.[20]

Late in January 1912, a Congressman active in behalf of Hook wired him: "Conferred with Attorney General this morning. Was assured speculation charges [in connection with the Denver waterworks case] were believed to be absolutely baseless and unfounded. President dined with Mr. Wickersham last night. It was agreed there to call the lawyers of the cabinet together [a practice that had been followed by Taft in 1910] Sunday or Monday to go over the Court's decisions which have been attacked. Mr. Wickersham does not like the separate car decision in which you concurred. . . . I still feel absolutely confident of final favorable result." Some three weeks later, around the middle of February, Hook was still in serious contention. But by February 19, 1912, it was all over, as the President informed the Senators from Pennsylvania. To Boise Penrose, he announced:

> I write to say to you that I expect to appoint to the Supreme Court Chancellor Pitney of New Jersey. . . . I realize . . . that as the Representative of the state of Pennsylvania, and having an interest in the proper promotion of those of her sons who are worthy of federal responsibility, you would wish to avoid anything which might prejudice in the future an opportunity for the promotion of any one of them. I want to say that this appointment is not likely to prejudice Pennsylvania in the selection of any future member of the Court, for the reason that in times past Pennsylvania and New Jersey have both been represented on the Supreme Court, the one by Mr. Justice Bradley and the other by Mr. Justice Strong; and that there is nothing in the appointment of one judge from a circuit that excludes the taking of other candidates from the same circuit if regarded as fit and strengthening to the Court; as, for instance, the Sixth Circuit has had three members of that court for fifty years, the Fifth Circuit today has two members of the Court; and so it is.
>
> While the geographical rule, with other things exactly equal, has some general influence upon an appointment to the Court, practically

---

[20] W. R. Harr to Attorney General Wickersham, Nov. 12, 1910, Feb. 11, 1911; Wickersham to J. Embry, Feb. 7, 1911; Harr to Wickersham, May 29, 1911; Harr to W. J. Gregg, Oct. 26, 1912, Archives, Taft Papers; W. C. Hook to W. Van Devanter, Jan. 19, 1912, Van Devanter Papers.

where the candidates are fit, it never prevents the selection of two from the same circuit.

This is a confidential letter, but you are at liberty to show it under a seal of confidence to any Pennsylvanian who has an interest in the matter, as indicating not only the general practice but what I should feel, were I called upon to act in the future, to be a proper rule of conduct in exercising the appointing power.

That same day, the nomination of Pitney was made public.[21]

Others who had been considered, in addition to Charles Nagel (mentioned earlier), included Judge Joseph Buffington, a Pennsylvanian, of the Court of Appeals for the Third Circuit, the candidate of Senator George T. Oliver of Pennsylvania, and of much of the Philadelphia Bar; John P. Elkins, a Justice of the Supreme Court of Pennsylvania; and perhaps Frank B. Kellogg of Minnesota, to whom the President felt called upon to write a consoling letter.[22] but the real loser was Hook. It was true, as an obituary writer said of him a decade later, that few men can have come "so near to being appointed to the Supreme Bench and not be, as Judge Hook, and that on two occasions."[23] An unquestionably able judge was lost, and because it was such a near thing, a moment's speculation on the difference he might have made is perhaps called for.

Not the Insurgent of Senator Warren's invention, he did not, on the other hand, have certain of Pitney's at least initial predispositions in labor cases, and there are indications that he would not have developed the rigid conservatism of the later Van Devanter. He was the dissenting judge, favoring the union's side of the case, in 1919, in a celebrated labor litigation, *United Mine Workers* v. *Coronado Coal Co.*[24] And his dissent, also later to be vindicated by the Supreme Court, in an important antitrust case, *United States* v. *Union Pacific Railroad*,[25] favored the government's position against the views of three colleagues, who included Van Devanter while still a circuit judge. This dissent, which was known at the time of the nomination contest in 1911–12, should have

---

[21] E. Root to W. H. Taft, Feb. 8, 1912; C. F. Amidon to Root, Feb. 3, 1912, Taft Papers. W. C. Hook to W. Van Devanter, Jan. 19, 1912, Van Devanter Papers. Taft to B. Penrose, Feb. 19, 1912, Taft Papers. See also Taft to G. T. Oliver, Feb. 19, 1912, Taft Papers, quoted in D. S. Mc-Hargue, "Appointments to the Supreme Court of the United States— The Factors That Have Affected Appointments, 1789–1932" (Ph.D. diss., University of California at Los

Angeles, May 1949), 400–408.
[22] W. H. Taft to G. T. Oliver, Feb. 19, 1912; F. B. Kellogg to Taft, Mar. 7, 1912, Taft Papers. And see *New York Times,* Feb. 19, 1912, p. 1, col. 2.
[23] J. H. Atwood, "William Cather Hook" in *A.B.A.J.,* 7:552, 555, 1921.
[24] 258 Fed. 829 (8th Cir. 1919), *reversed,* 259 U.S. 344 (1922).
[25] 188 Fed. 102, 120 (C.C. D. Utah, June 24, 1911), *reversed,* 226 U.S. 61 (1912), see *supra,* pp. 184–86.

gained Hook some needed credit with the Progressive governors and railroad commissions who were opposing him. And yet, aside from some labor cases, there is no real reason to suppose that Hook's record on the Supreme Court would have been very different from Pitney's, and if—which is a real probability—he would never have assumed some of Van Devanter's rigid positions, the fact is that the importance as well as the ultimate rigidity of Van Devanter's convictions did not become manifest until the 1920s and 1930s. Hook died on August 12, 1921.

The origins and the method of the Pitney selection are not discoverable. Given Taft's criteria, the failure of the Hook candidacy, Nagel's[26] age and lack of prior judicial experience, the Third Circuit's claims to representation and the want, after Knox's declination, of an acceptable Pennsylvania candidate, the choice of Pitney made a great deal of sense. Born in Morristown, New Jersey, on February 5, 1858, Mahlon Pitney was the son of Henry C. Pitney, a Vice Chancellor in the New Jersey equity courts. He was A.B. Princeton, 1879, a classmate of Woodrow Wilson, and thus, after Lamar, the second friend of Wilson's youth to ascend the Supreme Court.[27] Pitney read law in his father's office, and entered practice, first in nearby Dover, then back in Morristown. In 1891, he married Florence T. Shelton of Morristown. There were two sons and one daughter. He became a figure in the Republican party in New Jersey, going to Congress as a Representative in 1894, and again in 1896. After those two terms, he transferred, so to speak, to the state Senate, where he rose to be Republican floor leader, and in 1901, president of the Senate. Shortly thereafter, late in 1901, he was appointed to the state Supreme Court, and, in January 1908, was promoted Chancellor of the state.[28] He was in that high judicial office when Taft picked him.

Pitney was a tall, handsome man of distinguished appearance, and he was decent, basically open minded, honest, with even a touch of the ingenuous. He had, Brandeis said some years later, after he had come to know him well, "a great sense of justice affected by Presbyterianism, but no imagination whatever. And then he was much in-

---

[26] Charles Nagel (1849–1940), Secretary of Commerce and Labor throughout the Taft Administration, was born in Texas. He received an LL.B. from St. Louis Law School and pursued further studies at the University of Berlin. His first wife was the sister of Louis D. Brandeis. Having been widowed, Nagel married a second time in 1895. He practiced law in St. Louis for many years.

[27] "Although the relations between the governor [Wilson, by then a candidate for President] and myself," said Pitney to a newspaperman soon after his nomination, "are very cordial, I do not mean to imply that I endorse all of the principles he is advocating." *Los Angeles Examiner*, Feb. 22, 1912, p. 2, col. 6.

[28] *Dictionary of American Biography* (1934), XIV, 642.

fluenced by his experience, and he had mighty little." But, Brandeis added—and Holmes agreed—he brought "absolute concentration" to the task of judging and "real character." Beneath the imposing exterior, Pitney was a worrier. It was this part of his temperament that showed, perhaps, in his long-windedness. He was quite wordy, and for this reason at first "aggravated" Holmes and irritated the highly irritable McReynolds. But Holmes came to appreciate him. "It is hard to get a man as good as he was," Holmes wrote privately after Pitney's death, "whatever reserves one may make in superlatives."[29]

Taft had sat next to Pitney, and had an opportunity for extended conversation, at a lunch in Newark the week before the nomination.[30] This social encounter,[31] made the more pleasant, no doubt, by a common interest in golf,[32] recalls the preliminaries to the nomination of Lamar. Taft himself, writing to the Senators from Pennsylvania, Penrose and Oliver, gave what are very likely all the affirmative reasons there were for the nomination, at least all the reasons additional to the claims of the Third Circuit and the various disqualifications of other candidates. "I think that he stands so high as a judicial officer," said Taft, "with so many years before him of judicial work, that he will strengthen the Supreme Court by becoming a member of it." And: "He is a man of great personal force, of great ability and originality; he is young, that is, he is my age [fifty-two]; he has had the experience of two terms in Congress; he has had one term in the Senate of his own state, serving as President of the Senate . . . and he comes of a great lawyer stock."[33]

One aspect of the Pitney nomination demands further explanation, however. In some part, no doubt, the Hook candidacy failed because of imponderables that weighed in the balance in 1910, as well. In some small part it foundered on the presumption operating in favor of the Third Circuit. But in some part, unquestionably, Hook was defeated because Taft had no taste for the controversy that surrounded him. Yet with the Pitney nomination, Taft faced his first and only serious confirmation contest in six appointments. This was a curious way to avoid controversy. But it is quite possible that Taft never foresaw the trouble he would have with Pitney. (At least one newspaper reported

---

[29] Brandeis-Frankfurter Conversations, Harvard Law School Library; O. W. Holmes to F. Frankfurter, Dec. 9, 1924, Holmes Papers, Harvard Law School Library; M. DeW. Howe, ed., *Holmes-Pollock Letters* (1946), II, 113, 150.

[30] *New York Herald*, Feb. 19, 1912, p. 4, col. 2.

[31] One Progressive newspaper persistently referred to Pitney as a close personal friend of the President. But there is no evidence that they had even met before the Newark luncheon. See *Milwaukee Journal*, Feb. 19, 1912, p. 1, col. 3; Feb. 23, 1912, p. 2, col. 3.

[32] Taft Papers.

[33] W. H. Taft to B. Penrose, Feb. 19, 1912, and Taft to G. T. Oliver, Feb. 19, 1912, Taft Papers.

on the day the nomination was made that Taft expected no difficulty in the Senate.)[34] Pitney's was no organized candidacy, and it met, as a candidacy, no organized opposition. Taft, to be sure, was one President with the habit of studying the records of his nominees, but he was also, as President, a man of lapses. He had just been through an extended and detailed deliberative process on Hook, time was getting short, and he may have paid less attention than usual to Pitney's record. What is more likely, he may simply not have been conscious of any grounds for objection. If he examined Pitney's opinions, he examined them through his own eyes only, without benefit of an adversary process, so to speak, as in the Hook matter, which would make him aware of the impression created for others.

For himself and by himself, Taft quite probably saw nothing objectionable. On the other hand, it is possible that he simply elected to turn on his tormentors. Perhaps he realized that there was at least one case of Pitney's that Progressive opinion might object to, and decided to nominate Pitney in the teeth of the Progressives. Increasingly he was coming to identify Progressives as the enemy. The experience with Hook must have further fed this tendency. He had given in and rejected Hook, although quite likely he himself found little wrong with Hook's judicial record. But, he might have felt, he was damned if he would surrender the nominating prerogative to the opposition. He would give them instead another judge of the sort that he, Taft, valued, come what may. Pitney, Taft knew perfectly well (as he might also have known about Hook), was no reactionary. If those constant carpers and belittlers, those demagogues to whom he had finally sacrificed Hook, chose to attack Pitney as a reactionary also, why then, let them.

At any rate, there was no objection to Pitney while Taft was making his decision. The selection was unexpected, by Pitney as much as by anyone, unless we are to think Pitney capable of more disingenuousness than would have been true to character. Although "deeply sensible to the great honor," Pitney required a couple of days to think it over. "The news came as a complete surprise," he wrote Taft, "and the consideration of the interests of my wife and children has necessitated a little delay before expressing my willingness to accept."[35] And at first all was relatively smooth, compared with what was to follow. Surprise, reported *The Literary Digest*, was "in good part responsible for the brevity and reserve . . . of newspaper critics of the appointment." There seemed to be "little to awaken either enthusiasm or resentment."[36]

There was some conservative rejoicing, but it was mostly private.

---

[34] *Kansas City Star*, Feb. 19, 1912, p. 1, col. 5.

[35] M. Pitney to President Taft, Feb. 19, 1912, Feb. 21, 1912, Taft Papers.

[36] *The Literary Digest*, 44:410, Mar. 12, 1912.

IV: *Appointment Cycles*

The president of the National Association of Manufacturers, echoing a phrase Taft himself had used, wrote the President that Pitney came "from the kind of stock of which just and fearless judges are made. I doubt if you could have made a wiser selection." The secretary of the Iron and Steel Institute also communicated his pleasure to Taft.[37] Yet Insurgents in the Senate said they knew of no objection. To begin with, even the Progressive *Milwaukee Journal* remarked only that Pitney was "an unknown quantity." The *Kansas City Star*, equally Progressive and strongly anti-Taft, grumbled, but its misgivings were general, not focused on Pitney. Said the *Star*:

> Mr. Taft has named to this court a gentleman who was not known at all to a great majority of the people who are to be vitally affected by that gentleman's opinions. Chancellor Pitney may be an excellent member of the court; or he may be a most dangerous judge—speaking of course from the standpoint of public welfare. But the people who are to be *ruled* by him, more truly than they are to be ruled by Presidents and Congresses and governors and legislators for many years, know no more about him than they know about the Grand Vizier of Turkey. They had no more to do with his selection than with the Grand Vizier's selection, and they will have hardly more control over him than they will have over the Sultan's advisor.
>
> Certainly the place of the judiciary in popular government has not yet been finally and satisfactorily adjusted.

The *New York Times* suggested that Taft's action would tend to throw the influence of New Jersey Republican leaders to the President and away from Theodore Roosevelt, and that consequently the appointment might stir up a little feeling among Progressive Republicans. But there was no evidence of it as yet, and the *Times* thought it unlikely, for the Insurgents had in the past demonstrated their unwillingness to oppose the President's judicial nominations on political grounds. And no one doubted that Pitney had been selected on merit after careful consideration.[38]

One ominous voice was early raised against Pitney. A. L. Ulrick, the president of the Iowa Federation of Labor, protested to Senators Cummins and Kenyon of his state, both more or less Progressives, that Pitney was "irrevocably pledged to property rights as against human rights," and was "the consistent enemy of the working man." But he made the initial mistake of substantiating his charges with a reference to

---

[37] J. Kirby, Jr., to W. H. Taft, Mar. 15, 1912; J. T. McCleary to Taft, Feb. 20, 1912, Taft Papers.

[38] *New York Times*, Feb. 21, 1912, p. 1, col. 6; *Milwaukee Journal*, Feb. 19, 1912, p. 1, col. 3; *Kansas City Star*, Feb. 20, 1912, p. 8, col. 2; *New York Times*, Feb. 20, 1912, p. 5, col. 1.

Frask & Dugan v. *Herold*,[39] in which a sweeping injunction against picketing and other union activity had been issued, despite a New Jersey statute that attempted to legalize labor unions. If the statute was intended to immunize unions not only against certain criminal prosecutions but also against injunctions, said the court, foreshadowing the holding of a bitterly divided Supreme Court in *Truax* v. *Corrigan*[40] in 1921, it was unconstitutional. But as Pitney himself was quick to point out to newspapermen who questioned him back home in Morristown, this decision was not made by him, but by his father, Vice Chancellor Henry C. Pitney.[41]

There was poetic justice in Pitney being charged with his father's decision, since in selecting Pitney, Taft had given some weight to his judicial heritage. He comes, Taft had written Senator Oliver, "of a great lawyer stock." And as everyone would soon discover, Pitney had followed his father's decision in a later opinion of his own. Mr. Ulrick proceeded to accuse Mahlon Pitney of being "very like his father." But for a moment, the misattribution of the decision in *Frank & Dugan* to Pitney *fils* seemed to quiet any possible Senatorial opposition.[42]

On March 2, *The Outlook*, conceding that Pitney's "eminence in the legal profession is everywhere acknowledged" and that he was known "for his fair-mindedness as well as for his legal learning," contented itself with an admonition and a hope:

> The question [concerns] solely his attitude of mind toward the relation of the law with the conditions of modern industrial society. . . . In these days . . . it is highly important that judges should not only be men of integrity and of learning but also such as in the broadest sense can be called men of understanding. . . . So today the judge contributes to the well-being of his country largely as he understands the prime necessity for social justice. The whole country hopes that

---

[39] 63 N.J. Eq. 443 (Court of Chancery 1902).

[40] 257 U.S. 312 (1921).

[41] "I wish simply to deny," said Mahlon Pitney, "that I am an enemy of labor. As to the decision mentioned and whatever construction some may put on it, I have nothing to say, for the very good reason that it was not mine. The opinion was delivered orally and on the spur of the moment by my father. . . ." *Milwaukee Journal*, Feb. 23, 1912, p. 2, col. 3. Pitney also remarked: "You will have to wait until I am dead and the record is made up before you will be able to say whether or not I was the successor in any respect of John Marshall Harlan. . . . Moreover, I suspect that when the record is made up it will show that I was just a plain Pitney judge. In other words, I shall be myself. . . ." *Los Angeles Examiner*, Feb. 22, 1912, p. 2, col. 6.

[42] *New York Times*, Feb. 20, 1912, p. 5, col. 3; *Kansas City Star*, Feb. 21, 1912, p. 5, col. 2, Feb. 22, 1912, p. 3, col. 1; *Milwaukee Journal*, Feb. 20, 1912, p. 14, col. 1, Feb. 23, 1912, p. 2, col. 3; *New York Times*, Feb. 22, 1912, p. 3, col. 4, Mar. 1, 1912, p. 1, col. 6.

Chancellor Pitney understands his time and will be responsive to the educative influence of the great cases involving social injustice that are brought before the Supreme Court.[43]

On March 8, the Senate Committee on the Judiciary brought to the floor a favorable report on the nomination. Then the trouble began. Noting the sparse attendance, and expressing his desire that members of the Senate have an opportunity for further study, Senator A. O. Bacon of Georgia asked that final action be postponed. His colleague Charles A. Culberson of Texas, not then on the floor, might have something to say. And so Culberson shortly did, launching into an attack on *Jonas Glass Co.* v. *Glass Bottle Blowers' Association*, which the Senate promptly had printed for the information of other members. Debate then raged for three more days.[44]

The *Glass Bottle Blowers'* case was an opinion by Mahlon Pitney, not by his father. In 1901, the union had instituted a boycott of the Jonas Glass Company's product in an effort to unionize it. While the boycott was on, a strike began in 1902. It was, said Pitney, "a war of subjugation against the complainant corporation." The company obtained from a Vice Chancellor an enormously far-ranging injunction, which forbade the following activities: inducing any of the company's employees to quit, personal molestation of the company's workers, "addressing persons willing to be employed by complainant, against their will, and thereby causing them personal annoyance, with a view to persuade them to refrain from such employment," loitering or picketing in the streets near the premises of the company in order to annoy the company's workers, violence, threats, insults, indecent talk, "annoying language," and boycotting.

Pitney affirmed issuance of this injunction. Causing others to quit their employment, he said, either by threats or by persuasion, was unlawful, whether or not it was an interference with a binding contract of employment. "The only semblance of excuse alleged is that defendants desired to bring about 'improved labor conditions' in complainant's works; but this object did not warrant the resort to unlawful measures." There was a state statute the effect of which was to legalize labor unions, and which another judge had construed as permitting the adoption of peaceable measures for inducing workmen to quit their employment. But if the statute were to be construed so as to prevent issuance of an

---

[43] *The Outlook,* 100:477–78, Mar. 2, 1912.

[44] 48 *Cong. Rec.* 3011, 62nd Cong., 2nd Sess. (Mar. 8, 1912); *New York Times,* Mar. 9, 1912, p. 1, col. 2, Mar. 12, 1912, p. 1, col. 2, Mar. 13, 1912, p. 7, col. 3, Mar. 14, 1912, p. 8, col. 5; *New York Herald,* Mar. 9, 1912, p. 6, col. 6, Mar. 13, 1912, p. 6, col. 2, Mar. 14, 1912, p. 6, col. 3.

injunction against efforts to induce workers to quit their employment, it would be unconstitutional as an infringement upon the liberty of possessing, protecting, and acquiring property; and Pitney declined to so construe it. In all this, Pitney's heaviest reliance was on the authority of his father's decision in *Frank & Dugan* v. *Herold*. Without referring to it as his father's, of course, Pitney cited it, and followed its reasoning virutally to the letter. A dissent by four of Pitney's colleagues challenged his holding as supported only by old English cases "which bear the distinct impress of feudal law and custom.[45]

Although Pitney was guilty of no unheard-of antiunion excess in the context of that time, there was no question but that the case was an antiunion decision. And we know now, on the basis of the later record, that the decision marked an antiunion predisposition which it took many years and much argument to shake in Pitney, and which his opponents in the Senate were thoroughly justified in believing would never be shaken in him.[46]

In the end, Pitney's nomination was confirmed, by a vote of 50 to 26, on March 13, 1912. The Insurgents did not unite against him. Borah of Idaho led for his supporters. Only four Republicans voted against—Bourne, Bristow, Cummins, and Kenyon. The Democrats were mostly against, but they also were not solid, even though three of them who had voted to report the nomination favorably out of committee changed their minds upon examining the *Glass Bottle Blowers'* case.[47] After the vote, Pitney arranged to come to Washington immediately. "We are longing for your presence," Taft wired him.[48] He took his seat on March 18, 1912.

Senate contests such as the one Pitney experienced, turning on the outlook and philosophy of a Supreme Court nominee, are relatively rare; certainly Taft and Roosevelt had found them so. Four years later there was to be another, quite different, fight over Brandeis, and perhaps the Pitney episode eased the way for the later combat by making it seem not quite so unnatural.

Other cases of Pitney's in New Jersey include three additional ones relating to labor unions, but nothing much can be or was made of these.[49] In *State* v. *O'Hagan*,[50] the defendant was indicted for having published a

---

[45] Jonas Glass Co. v. Glass Bottle Blowers' Ass'n., 77 N.J. Eq. 219, 221, 222, 224, 226 (Court of Err. & App. 1908).

[46] See D. M. Levitan, "Mahlon Pitney, Labor Judge," *Va. L. Rev.*, 40:733, 1954.

[47] *New York Herald*, Mar. 14, 1912, p. 6, col. 3; *New York Times*, Mar.

14, 1912, p. 8, col. 5.

[48] W. H. Taft to M. Pitney, Mar. 13, 1912, Taft Papers.

[49] Pitney's opinions may be found in Vols. 67 through 82 of the *New Jersey Law Reports*, and in Vols. 64 through 80 of the *New Jersey Equity Reports.*

[50] 73 N.J. Law 209 (Supreme Court 1906).

libel against one Van Nimwegen, when he announced that the latter refused to recognize the Bakers' Union of Paterson, New Jersey. Pitney reversed a verdict of guilty. It was not libelous, he held, absent special circumstances, to say that a man had done something that he had a perfectly legal right to do. *Brennan* v. *United Hatters of North America*[51] was a more complicated case, involving union discipline against a member, which resulted in expulsion from the union and consequent loss of a job. Pitney affirmed a judgment against the union, but the case was close, involving among other issues a procedural one. Much the same may be said of *Levin* v. *Cosgrove*,[52] which also concerned internal union affairs.

A couple of negligence cases, in one of which he applied the fellow-servant rule where the allegedly negligent fellow servant was a supervisory employee, demonstrate how hard-nosed Pitney could be.[53] But then so were many of his judicial contemporaries. *Tomlinson* v. *Armour & Co.*,[54] a products liability case, was a forward-looking, creative common-law judgment. The plaintiff bought some canned meat from a retailer, and was made sick with ptomaine poisoning. Despite the lack of privity of contract, Pitney held the manufacturer liable.

Toward the few measures of social and economic regulation that came before him, Pitney displayed a generally hospitable attitude.[55] So he did in the one opinion of his that the Supreme Court of the United States reviewed. He upheld, in *McCarter* v. *Hudson County Water Co.*,[56] a New Jersey statute that forbade the transportation of fresh water from any lake or stream in New Jersey into another state. No one could get a vested property right in such waters, he said, and there was therefore no Due Process question. Nor was the Commerce Clause violated, since the statute applied to water in New Jersey before it could have entered interstate commerce. In an opinion by Holmes, over McKenna's dissent, the Supreme Court affirmed, emphasizing the Due Process issue, and Pitney can take credit for providing the occasion of Holmes' famous statement that all rights tend to declare themselves absolute, but are in fact limited by the neighborhood of other principles. Later analogous cases in the Supreme Court, dealing with efforts to conserve a state's

---

[51] 73 N.J. Law 729 (Court of Err. & App. 1906).

[52] 75 N.J. Law 344 (Supreme Court 1907).

[53] Knutter v. New York & New Jersey Telephone Co., 67 N.J. Law 646 (Court of Err. & App. 1902); Fielders v. North Jersey Street Ry. Co., 68 N.J. Law 343 (Court of Err. & App. 1902).

[54] 75 N.J. Law 748 (Court of Err. & App. 1908).

[55] See, e.g., Cooper Hospital v. Camden, 68 N.J. Law 691 (Court of Err. & App. 1903); New Jersey Street Ry. Co. v. Jersey City, 75 N.J. Law 349 (Supreme Court 1907).

[56] 70 N.J. Eq. 695 (Court of Err. & App. 1906).

natural gas resources, went the other way on Commerce Clause grounds in divided decisions, but Pitney did not arrive in time for one, and retired before the other.[57] Among further cases decided by Pitney, only an unremarkable holding need be noted: that execution by electrocution was not a cruel and unusual punishment.[58]

With the single exception of the *Glass Bottle Blowers'* case, which stands out quite by itself, this is an ordinary record. No wonder Taft could see nothing objectionable in it, and probably no cause to fear that anyone else would find it objectionable. Pitney hardly emerges as "a man of great personal force, of great ability and originality"—the terms in which Taft commended him to one of the Pennsylvania Senators in breaking the news of the appointment. Rather a remark of Holmes comes to mind—"He had not wings and was not a thunderbolt. . . ."[59] The tendency to be prolix is clearly evident, as is a certain lack of ease and of sophistication in dealing with arguments from principle. When he makes the attempt, even in so good a decision as *Tomlinson* v. *Armour & Co.*, Pitney sounds naive, almost callow. He is at home on a more pedestrian level, marshaling precedents, one after another after another. Altogether it was the record of a respectable judge, no doubt a good judge too, wihout sign or promise of distinction. Not the very archetype of the judge of the old school, like Lurton. Nothing of the Southern touch of style and manner as in Lamar (although Lamar's was also an undistinguished record). Rather, on the face of his opinions, like Van Devanter, but with less extra-judicial experience of affairs, and as we now know, not as able. And more verbose.

McReynolds vice Lurton

Lurton's final illness, a heart ailment, began in December 1913. He was absent from the Court from December 3, 1913, to April 6, 1914. On the latter date, he returned and sat for the rest of the term, but on July 12, 1914, he died, at the Marlborough-Blenheim Hotel in Atlantic City, New Jersey. He was taken home to Clarksville, Tennessee, for burial on July 15, Chief Justice White and several Justices attending.[60]

Lurton was seventy, and had served on the Supreme Court for just a few days over four and a half years. He had written 97 opinions of

---

[57] Oklahoma v. Kansas Natural Gas Co., 221 U.S. 229 (1911); Pennsylvania v. West Virginia, 262 U.S. 553 (1923); see *supra*, p. 269, nn.210, 211.

[58] State v. Tomassi, 75 N.J. Law 739 (Court of Err. & App. 1908).

[59] *Holmes-Pollock Letters*, II, 113.

[60] 233 U.S. i; 235 U.S. v; 237 U.S. v; *New York Tribune*, July 13, 1914, p. 1, col. 4.

the Court and recorded 19 dissents, two of them with opinion.[61] It was an abbreviated record, quantitatively and qualitatively. Of the Justices who sat with Lurton throughout his tenure, Holmes produced during these four and a half years 185 opinions of the Court and 1 concurring and 9 dissenting opinions; White 169, 3, and 4; and McKenna 144, 1, and 7. To be sure, Lurton was absent those few months near the end, Holmes' is a championship pace, and White's figure is swollen by a number of very brief memorandum opinions, of which more fell to him as Chief Justice than to others. But Day was also absent for several months during the October Term 1911, owing to the illness and then death of his wife, and yet he produced 123 opinions of the Court and 4 dissenting opinions. Lurton was a member of the committee of Justices that drafted the new equity rules of 1912, and this task took some of his time. But quite clearly he was not at the peak of his energies on the Supreme Court. His main career had been as a federal circuit judge. Volume of work to the side, he rendered, as noted in the Resolution of the Bar presented to the Court in his memory, "no startling or sensational decisions."[62]

By all odds the most important piece of work Lurton left behind was *United States* v. *Chandler-Dunbar Co.*,[63] which established the full extent of the federal power over navigable waters. Equally able, and more characteristic and more revealing, but in its consequences less enduring, was the opinion in *Henry* v. *A. B. Dick Co.*[64] Following the rule he had laid down in his best-known decision in the Sixth Circuit,[65] Lurton in the *Dick* case sustained the power of a federal patentee to impose tie-in sales as a condition upon the use of the patented article.[66] His forty-nine-page opinion, against an impassioned dissent by Chief Justice White (so impassioned that it quite annoyed Holmes),[67] Hughes and Lamar joining, is lucid, direct, forceful, and notable for the candor and freedom with which it addresses the decisive considerations.

---

[61] Attorney General Gregory, addressing the Court in his memory, managed to credit Lurton with 98 opinions of the Court, and attributed only 18 dissents to him. 237 U.S. xii, xiv. Lurton's opinions may be found in Vols. 216–34 of the *United States Reports*. The first was Wright v. Georgia R.R. & Banking Co., 216 U.S. 420 (1910), and the last, Louisiana v. McAdoo, 234 U.S. 627, decided on June 22, 1914.

[62] 237 U.S. ix.

[63] Pp. 221–23, n.72.

[64] 224 U.S. 1, 26–27 (1912).

[65] Heaton-Peninsular Button Fastener Co. v. Eureka Specialty Co., 77 Fed. 288 (6th Cir. 1896).

[66] Lurton did not always insist on positions he had taken as a circuit judge. He changed his mind, for example, when as a Justice he joined in holding that the federal Safety Appliance Acts imposed absolute liability on railroads. See *supra*, p. 78, n.299.

[67] *Holmes-Pollock Letters*, I, 190.

The issue presented itself formally as one of statutory construction, but Lurton disdained any pretense of solving it as a formal issue, by use of canons of construction, or by any exercise in grammar. The question was, he said, "with what eye shall we read meaning into [the statute]? It is a statute creating a monopoly. . . . Shall we deal with [it] . . . with the narrow scrutiny proper when a statutory right is asserted to uphold a claim which is lacking in those moral elements which appeal to the normal man? Or shall we approach it as a monopoly granted to subserve a broad public policy, by which large ends are to be obtained, and, therefore, to be construed so as to give effect to a wide and beneficial purpose." The latter was Lurton's approach, and from it flowed the result. The policy of the statute was to encourage invention by rewarding it. If the rewards exacted by the inventor amounted to abuses, the market would provide a corrective. If the market did not provide a corrective, then the supposed abuses weren't there. So he and other lower federal judges, including Van Devanter, had often held, Lurton pointed out—so often that expectations had been created which the Supreme Court, although of course free to do so, ought not now to upset.

Right or wrong, this is the opinion of a strong, creative common law judge. Lurton's economics may be thought simplistic and primitive, but no more so than Holmes' and McKenna's, for example,[68] and at least he knew that economics was what was decisive, and that while Congress in the Sherman Act may have given the courts an economic theory to go by, the patent statute was informed by a different one, which gave little guidance in such a case as *A. B. Dick*. But Lurton spoke only for a majority of four—McKenna, Holmes, and Van Devanter were with him—Day being absent, and Pitney not having heard the case. It would have gone the other way with those two, and shortly after, over Lurton's and McKenna's, Holmes' and Van Devanter's dissent, a majority departed from the decision in *A. B. Dick*,[69] and a few years later, flatly overruled it.[70]

Lurton did not import into the Sherman Act the economics that he attributed to the patent statute. He had sat with Taft in the decision of *United States* v. *Addyston Pipe & Steel Co.* in the Sixth Circuit,[71] and on the Supreme Court he rendered two stout antitrust decisions, in the *St. Louis Terminal* and first *Reading* cases.[72] His one dissent in an antitrust case, in which he was joined by White and Holmes, concerned more a point of pleading than of substance.[73] The broad-gauged attitude

[68] See *supra*, pp. 175–76.

[69] Bauer v. O'Donnell, 229 U.S. 1 (1913).

[70] Motion Picture Co. v. Universal Film Co., 243 U.S. 502 (1917).

[71] See *supra*, p. 78, n.302.

[72] See *supra*, p. 182, n.259, p. 189, n.280. See also Grenada Lumber Co. v. Mississippi, 217 U.S. 433 (1910).

[73] United States v. Patten, 226 U.S. 525 (1913).

toward problems of statutory construction, which led Lurton to seek the organizing purpose of a statute and to elaborate its policy creatively in light of that purpose—this enlightened attitude was manifest not only in the *A. B. Dick* case, but in a number of other decisions as well.[74] And there are indications that a similar approach also informed the task of constitutional construction for Lurton, since he joined Hughes' dissent in *Slocum* v. *New York Life Insurance Co.*[75]

Lurton wrote no particularly significant Due Process or Equal Protection opinions, with the sole exception of *Atlantic Coast Line Railroad* v. *Riverside Mills*, in which he upheld the constitutionality of the Carmack Amendment to the Hepburn Act of 1906.[76] But he was with the Court in *Noble State Bank* v. *Haskell* and *Chicago, Burlington & Quincy Railroad* v. *McGuire*, although he took no part, having been absent for the argument, in *German Alliance Insurance Co.* v. *Kansas*.[77] There can be little to take exception to in this general statement of his position, for which he found occasion in one minor Due Process case:

> It is a general principle of our law that there is no individual liability for an act which ordinary human care and foresight could not guard against. . . . But behind and above these general principles . . . there lies the legislative power. . . . Primarily, governments exist for the maintenance of social order . . . A recognition of this supreme obligation is found in those exertions of the legislative power which have as an end the preservation of social order and the protection of the social welfare of the public and of the individual. If such legislation be reasonably adapted to the end in view, affords a hearing before judgment, and is not forbidden by some other affirmative provision of constitutional law, it is not to be regarded as denying due process of law under the provisions of the Fourteenth Amendment.[78]

As the Due Process and Contract clauses tended to overlap, however, Lurton's attitude became considerably less permissive.[79] And it was Lurton who led a bare majority, in *Owensboro* v. *Cumberland Telephone Co.*, to the most questionable application of the Contract

---

[74] E.g., Pickett v. United States, 216 U.S. 456 (1910); Richardson v. Harmon, 222 U.S. 96 (1911); United States v. Stever, 222 U.S. 167 (1911); United States v. Munday, 222 U.S. 175 (1911).

[75] See *supra*, pp. 313–14, n.379.

[76] See *supra*, p. 202, n.11.

[77] See supra, pp. 276, 277, n.239; 279, 280, n.255; 281–82, 284, n.275.

[78] Chicago v. Sturges, 222 U.S. 313, 322 (1911), see *supra*, p. 291, n.300. See also Omaha v. Omaha Water Co., 218 U.S. 180 (1910); Mobile, Jackson & Kansas City Ry. v. Turnipseed, 219 U.S. 35 (1910); Hampton v. St. Louis Iron Mountain & Southern Ry., 227 U.S. 456 (1913); and Bradley v. Richmond, 227 U.S. 477 (1913).

[79] See Ettor v. Tacoma, *supra*, pp. 292, n.306, 300–301; Lincoln Gas Co. v. Lincoln, *supra*, p. 287, n.285.

Clause during the years of his tenure.[80] But it was Lurton also who warned that federal judges were not to sit in Contract Clause cases as committees of public safety, with arbitrary power to prevent anything that they considered injurious to the public welfare.[81] In most Commerce Clause decisions, Lurton was affected by an old-fashioned, very Southern, attachment to states' rights—by contrast to another ex-Confederate on the Bench, Chief Justice White. He was, therefore, one of the most enthusiastic supporters of the result in the *Minnesota Rate Cases*;[82] he joined Holmes and Hughes in dissent in *Oklahoma* v. *Kansas Natural Gas Co.*;[83] and he wrote a number of opinions upholding state regulation and taxation of interstate commerce.[84] The attachment to old-fashioned states'-rights doctrine also caused Lurton to dissent in *Interstate Commerce Commission* v. *Goodrich Transit Co.*[85] and in the *Shreveport Case*,[86] and to incline toward a restrictive view of the powers of the Interstate Commerce Commission,[87] although he went along silently with such decisions as the *Second Employers' Liability Cases*,[88] *Hipolite Egg Co.* v. *United States*,[89] and *Hoke* v. *United States*.[90]

Somehow, however, neither the states'-rights bias nor the fidelity to broad statutory policy in the process of interpretation extended to preemption cases under the Carmack Amendment, which Lurton had upheld, which he then very nearly emasculated by a construction that either mistook, or did willful violence to, the legislative purpose, and which, as construed, he wielded to strike down state regulation of carrier liability for loss or damage of goods in transit.[91] Of the Court's policy in construing and applying the Carmack Amendment, he was during his tenure the principal, and virtually the sole, author.

---

[80] See *supra*, p. 304, n.350; and see Boise Water Co. v. Boise City, *supra*, p. 303, n.348.

[81] Columbus v. Mercantile Trust Co., *supra*, p. 311, n.373; and see Wright v. Georgia R.R. and Banking Co., 216 U.S. 420 (1910); Cincinnati v. Louisville & Nashville R.R. Co., 223 U.S. 390 (1912).

[82] See *supra*, pp. 255, 259.

[83] See *supra*, pp. 268–69, n.210.

[84] Citizens National Bank v. Kentucky, 217 U.S. 443 (1910); Brown-Forman Co. v. Kentucky, 217 U.S. 563 (1910); Western Union Telegraph Co. v. Crovo, 220 U.S. 364 (1911); Southern Pacific Co. v. Kentucky, 222 U.S. 63 (1911). But *cf.* Louisville & Nashville R.R. Co. v. Cook Brewing

Co., 223 U.S. 70 (1912).

[85] See *supra*, p. 214, n.49.

[86] *Supra*, pp. 214–18, n.54.

[87] See Interstate Commerce Commission v. Chicago, Rock Island & Pacific Ry., 218 U.S. 88 (1910) (White, Holmes, and Lurton, JJ., dissenting); United States v. Baltimore & Ohio R.R., 231 U.S. 274 (1913).

[88] *Supra*, pp. 206–208, n.29.

[89] *Supra*, pp. 224–25, n.77.

[90] *Supra*, pp. 228–31, n.96.

[91] See *supra*, p. 204, nn.16, 17; p. 274, n.226; and see Missouri, Kansas & Texas Ry. v. Wulf, 226 U.S. 570 (1913) (Lurton, J., dissenting). But *cf.* Southern Ry. Co. v. Reid & Bean, 222 U.S. 424 (1912) (Lurton, J., dissenting).

IV: *Appointment Cycles*

The ex-Confederate left his trace also in a few cases touching on racial discrimination. But this is a judgment that has to be carefully qualified. Lurton took no extreme, nor even any isolated, positions, as his successor McReynolds would sometimes do. Of course, the statistical basis for this judgment is very slight indeed. In *Bailey* v. *Alabama*,[92] the Court, Hughes writing, held that an arrangement for forcing share-croppers, mainly blacks, to fulfill their contracts on pain of imprisonment amounted to peonage and violated the Thirteenth Amendment. Holmes and Lurton dissented. In *Creswell* v. *Knights of Pythias*,[93] a much more complicated case, presenting problems of the interaction of state and federal law, the Court, per Chief Justice White, held that the Georgia state courts could not prevent a black organization incorporated as the Knights of Pythias under federal law in the District of Columbia from using the designation in Georgia, although it was the same as that of the white Knights of Pythias. Again, Holmes and Lurton dissented. In *Jones* v. *Jones*,[94] on his last day of service, Lurton, as the spokesman for a unanimous Court, sustained the constitutionality under the Fourteenth Amendment of a Tennessee statute which provided that the estate of anyone dying intestate and without issue should pass to his brothers and sisters, but only if they had been born free. In this case, the estate was allowed to pass to the widow, because the brothers and sisters who claimed under the statute had been born slaves. Finally, there is evidence that Lurton would at the very least have joined Lamar's lone dissent in one of the Grandfather Clause cases, and it is more than possible that he would have gone even farther into wholesale opposition.[95]

Among other of Lurton's cases, the following deserve some notice.[96] In *Jordon* v. *Massachusetts*,[97] Lurton carried his states'-rights attitude into matters of criminal procedure. His opinion features this pronouncement: "When the essential elements of a court having jurisdiction in which an opportunity for a hearing is afforded are present, the power of a State over its methods of procedure is substantially unrestricted by the due process clause of the Constitution."[98] *Richardson*

---

[92] 219 U.S. 219 (1911).

[93] 225 U.S. 246 (1912).

[94] 234 U.S. 615 (1914).

[95] Guinn v. United States, 238 U.S. 347 (1915); Myers v. Anderson, 238 U.S. 368 (1915); United States v. Mosley, 238 U.S. 383 (1915); Lamar to Chief Justice White, June 10, 1915, Lamar Papers; see *supra*, p. 79.

[96] See also Charlton v. Kelly, 229 U.S. 447 (1913); Louisiana v. Mc-Adoo, 234 U.S. 627 (1914).

[97] 225 U.S. 167, 176 (1912).

[98] In federal criminal cases Lurton apparently tended to insist on strict procedural regularity. He joined Holmes, Hughes, and Lamar in dissent in Hyde v. United States, 225 U.S. 347 (1912), and Brown v. Elliott, 225 U.S. 392 (1912), and Holmes and Hughes in the dissent in Donnelly v. United States, 228 U.S. 243 (1913).

v. *McChesney*[99] was an appeal from a dismissal by the Kentucky state courts of a challenge to a statute apportioning Congressional seats. The statute, it was said, created grossly unequal districts. The Kentucky courts held that the suit raised a nonjusticiable political question. Lurton disposed of the appeal as moot, which it scarcely was, strictly speaking, and the case is notable, therefore, for the failure to deal directly with the holding of the Kentucky courts.

In *Coyle* v. *Oklahoma*,[100] a states'-rights case, Lurton held that Oklahoma was free to move its capital from Guthrie to Oklahoma City, despite a prohibition in the statehood act against so doing. When it granted statehood, Congress could not withhold any of the powers and functions that belong to states. The constitutional equality of the states, said Lurton, "is essential to the harmonious operation of the scheme upon which the Republic was organized. When that equality disappears we may remain a free people, but the Union will not be the Union of the Constitution."

Lurton's one really elaborate dissenting opinion came in *Northern Pacific Railway* v. *Boyd*,[101] in which, joined by White, Holmes, and Van Devanter, he spoke for a minority of four. The litigation grew out of the foreclosure sale and reorganization of the Northern Pacific Railroad, and *Boyd* is a leading case in the law of bankruptcy, standing for the rule that a general creditor who has been left out of a reorganization for the benefit of shareholders may treat it as a fraudulent transaction, and come in at any time to realize his debt out of the assets of the old corporation, even though they are now in the hands of a new, reorganized one.[102] Lamar wrote for the Court. Lurton protested that this was an alarming rule, threatening the stability of reorganizations undertaken in perfect good faith under judicial supervision. He was expressing, it is fair to say, the practical point of view of a circuit judge, a judicial administrator. He had been on the firing line, so to speak, and he knew the pressures to expedite a reorganization and complete it once and for all. He spoke also, perhaps, as he had to some extent in the *A. B. Dick* case too, as an admirer of the entrepreneurs who had built railroads and other economic institutions to the great benefit of the country—and more particularly, of the war-ravaged South—and who should be encouraged in their creative work. Perfect justice to creditors and investors, he may have believed, should not be sought at a sacrifice to the stability of entrepreneurial corporate structures. It is no accident, then, that he found himself in the company of Holmes in this dissent as well as in the

---

[99] 218 U.S. 487 (1910).
[100] 221 U.S. 559, 580 (1911).
[101] 228 U.S. 482 (1913).
[102] See, e.g., C. E. Nadler, *The Law of Creditor and Debtor Relations* (1956), 228, n.43; G. Glenn, *The Law Governing Liquidation* (1935), 616.

A. B. Dick opinion, for Holmes also admired the great builders, and believed that nothing they took was half so precious as the stuff they gave.

Lurton was a man of feeling and of warm friendships. He had the closest relations with Day, Harlan, and, of course, with Taft. He was, as his opinions indicate, a strong-willed and self-assured judge. But Day, speaking in his memory, emphasized his willingness, "for the sake of harmonious judgment . . . to yield something of his own convictions." And Taft, in another eulogy, remarked lovingly on Lurton's "feeling that if the Court's voice was to be useful for anything but the decision of the particular case, dissenting opinions should be avoided. If possible concessions without sacrifice of principle could reach a common ground, he sank all pride of opinion in securing for the judgment the strength of unanimity."

Lurton was also, another friend speaking in his memory pointed out, "a politician in the best sense. He was a careful student of public affairs and assisted in shaping political events in his own State, to the great benefit of its people; but he never had aspirations for office except for the Bench."[103] Discreetly and without impropriety, he never abandoned, even on the federal bench, his political interests. Thus, from the Sixth Circuit, and even in Washington, he would recommend Tennesseeans to President Taft for appointments. One of his recommendations was of J. C. Napier of Nashville for Registrar of the United States Treasury. "Aside from Booker Washington," wrote Lurton to Taft, "I believe he is the best representative of the colored race south of the Ohio River. He is in thorough accord with Booker Washington. . . . I want to be put down as very earnestly recommending him for appointment, it being one which I understand is always set apart for some member of the colored race." But it wasn't only recommendations for office that he made. From Nashville, Lurton commended the governor of Tennessee to President Taft's attention.[104] This counsel was neither importuning nor self-serving, but simply an expression of the natural interest in politics of a conservative Tennessee Democrat, and the natural helpful activity of a man to whom the affections mattered.

Lurton's successor, promptly named and seated, was a perfect replacement in point of geographic, social, and political origins. He was

---

[103] See Mr. Circuit Justice Day, in *In Memory of Horace Harmon Lurton,* United States Court of Appeals for the Sixth Circuit (Oct. 6, 1914), 16; W. H. Taft in *Proceedings of the Bar and Officers of the Supreme Court of the United States in Memory of* *Horace Harmon Lurton, March 27, 1915* (1915), 8–9; Remarks of Mr. Edmund S. Trabue, *ibid.,* 24.

[104] H. H. Lurton to W. H. Taft, Mar. 14, 1910, Mar. 25, 1909; see also Mar. 11, 1910, June 23, 1911, Taft Papers.

James Clark McReynolds, Wilson's Attorney General, like Lurton a Kentucky-born Tennesseean, long resident in Nashville, and a Grover Cleveland gold Democrat.[105] McReynolds was born in Elkton, Kentucky, near the Tennessee Border, on February 3, 1862, the second of four children of John Oliver and Ellen Reeves McReynolds. If not a member of the Southern landed aristocracy, McReynolds certainly belonged to the professional upper class.

Of Scotch-Irish stock, the McReynoldses settled first in Pennsylvania in the middle of the eighteenth century, then migrated to Virginia, and finally to Kentucky. The Reeveses had a long history in Elkton, and both James' grandfather and great-grandfather Reeves had held high political office. Dr. John O. McReynolds, James' father, who had been brought to Kentucky as a child, was a physician, like Lurton's father, but he was also quite active in business ventures. He was well-to-do, in every sense a prominent citizen, and by all accounts a formidable personage, a man of firm and wide-ranging opinions. He favored secession, served in the Confederate Army as a surgeon, and resumed civilian life a confirmed states'-rights Democrat and advocate of personal as well as public frugality. In religion, he and his wife adhered to, and impressed upon their children, the fundamentalist tenets of the Church of the Disciples of Christ. Of this church, a somewhat intolerant sect, which viewed the world in absolute terms of good and evil, James McReynolds was a member throughout his life.

McReynolds was educated at Vanderbilt University and at the University of Virginia. He received the degree of Bachelor of Science from Vanderbilt in 1882—science, not art, which is rather remarkable; but then, McReynolds was uncertain to begin with about his choice of career. There would have been nothing very broadening, anyway, in a liberal arts education at the Vanderbilt of this time. The university was under the dominion of the Southern Methodist Church, and it was characteristic of the prevailing atmosphere that the teaching of Darwin was forbidden. McReynolds had an outstanding scholastic record, and he repeated it at Virginia, where he was awarded the LL.B. in 1884, having been a favorite pupil of John B. Minor, unquestionably the leading law teacher in the South. The law at Virginia was taught out of Blackstone and other classic texts, with the addition of Professor Minor's own more recent one. It was presented by the lecture method, as a finished and closed system, approaching perfection as nearly as any product of man.

Soon after graduation from law school, McReynolds took a position as secretary to Howell E. Jackson, United States Senator from

---

[105] *Proceedings in the Supreme Court of the United States in Memory* of *Mr. Justice McReynolds,* 334 U.S. v (1948).

Tennessee, but served for a few months only, as Jackson resigned to commence his brief career on the Supreme Court. Armed with advice and a letter of recommendation from Professor Minor, McReynolds then entered practice in Nashville. It was a successful practice, running substantially to estates and trusts, and McReynolds soon combined it with business investments, in which he also prospered. In 1900, McReynolds became professor of commercial law at the Vanderbilt University Law School. Among his colleagues there was Judge Horace H. Lurton of the U.S. Court of Appeals for the Sixth Circuit, the professor of constitutional law and later dean.

In 1896, McReynolds ran for Congress as an anti-Bryan gold Democrat, and lost. The campaign put him in touch with Jacob M. Dickinson, a conservative Democrat later to be Taft's Secretary of War. The two men formed a friendship, and in 1903, Dickinson recommended McReynolds to Theodore Roosevelt's Attorney General, Philander C. Knox, whereupon McReynolds was appointed Assistant Attorney General. He held the office for four years, dealing chiefly with antitrust matters, until he left in 1907 for New York and a connection with Paul D. Cravath's firm. Within a few months he was recalled to government service, when Attorney General Charles J. Bonaparte retained him to conduct the *American Tobacco* case.[106] He managed this great and complex litigation, as well as the prosecution of the first *Reading* case. In December 1912, he resigned as special prosecutor in the *Tobacco* case because of his difference of opinion with Attorney General Wickersham over the decree, but he carried the *Reading* litigation forward even after that date.[107] Following his resignation, McReynolds set up in practice by himself in New York, mainly as a consultant in antitrust matters, and it was at this time that he wrote his opinion letter to the United States Steel Corporation, advising it that it violated the Sherman Act.[108]

McReynolds knew Colonel Edward M. House, Woodrow Wilson's intimate adviser, and in 1912 expressed to House his strong support of Wilson. As Barbara Barlin Schimmel has written, it is not surprising that McReynolds should have been drawn to Wilson: "The similarities between the two men were compelling. Both came from secure, professional families. Both grew up in a South convulsed by Civil War and Reconstruction. Both studied law at the University of Virginia, where they were students and admirers of Professor Minor. Both bolted the Bryan camp in 1896 to become Gold Democrats. Both favored states' rights and a freely competitive economy. Above all, both were earnest, compulsive, and self-exacting moralists. The crucial difference between

---

[106] See *supra,* pp. 90 *et seq.*
[107] See *supra,* pp. 117 *et seq.,* 190.

[108] See *supra,* pp. 165 *et seq.*

the two men was Wilson's capacity to change."[109] In considering the appointment of an Attorney General, Wilson's first thought was of Louis D. Brandeis. Violent opposition developed, however—a foretaste of 1916—and it was too much for Wilson. In the meantime, Colonel House was steadily urging the choice of McReynolds, whom Wilson did not know. On February 15, 1913, Wilson met McReynolds in House's apartment and a week later offered him the post.

Colonel House, and the number and virulence of Brandeis' enemies, made McReynolds Attorney General. But the appointment was logical. Just as in the early 1960s the Attorney Generalship meant civil rights, so in these years it meant antitrust. Wilson wanted "a man of experience and balance and yet a man thoroughly on the people's side." Brandeis was unfortunately out, because "I simply could not appoint a radical—that is I could not appoint a known radical." Mc-Reynolds had taken positions, most especially with respect to the *Tobacco* decree, that could be characterized as quite vigorously "on the people's side," and even radical. He had the spirit, the experience, and the admirers, but not the enemies, for even Wickersham, with whom he had differed so on the *Tobacco* decree, publicly suggested him as a fit successor. From the other side of the battle lines, Brandeis had told the Clapp Committee of the Senate in December 1911 that McReynolds displayed "a complete comprehension of the [*Tobacco*] case and of the trade and of the necessities of restoring competition, and he did a piece of work of which the country can be proud. It was an admirable professional and public performance. You cannot get a better record; you cannot find a better instance of public work in the legal line than Mr. McReynolds did in that case." And after the appointment, Brandeis congratulated McReynolds, saying that the President had made "the wisest possible choice." McReynolds' record in trust prosecutions would "assure the country," said Brandeis, "that the President's trust policy will be carried out promptly and efficiently, and business be freed at last. We are indeed to be congratulated."

Wilson's biographer, Professor Arthur S. Link, writes that "McReynolds was neither a crusader nor a distinguished public figure when he took office in March 1913." But that is a judgment somewhat colored by hindsight. McReynolds was a distinguished legal figure, and not a little of an antitrust crusader. It was an antitrust radical without enemies that Wilson wanted, and got—that was what he meant by "not . . . a known radical." What was not known about McReynolds, although it could easily have been discovered, was his conservatism on all other issues, which was also radical, and unbelievably inflexible. But

---

[109] B. B. Schimmel, "The Judicial Policy of Mr. Justice McReynolds" (Ph.D. diss., Yale University, 1964), 95.

that, perhaps, would have been deemed not very relevant, or if relevant, no disadvantage in a trustbuster.[110]

"There was," writes Professor Link,

> a large but probably a minority element in the Democratic party who wanted clean government, destruction of so-called industrial and financial monopolies, and abolition of special interest legislation. To the extent that they championed popular democracy and rebelled against a *status quo* that favored the wealthy, they were progressives. Actually, however, they were so strongly imbued with *laissez-faire* concepts that they were, strictly speaking, liberals in the nineteenth-century English tradition instead of twentieth-century progressives. They wanted impartial government with a modicum of federal regulation, rather than dynamic, positive federal intervention and participation in economic and social affairs. With their state-rights view of the Constitution, these liberal Democrats tended to suspect any attempts to commit the federal government to projects of social amelioration, because such intervention implied an invasion of the police power heretofore exercised almost exclusively by the states.

This was McReynolds' philosophy, and he was singular only in being more thoroughgoing and immovable than most. He was, in 1913, quite fully all that he would be. Indeed, he came north out of Nashville in 1903 altogether formed and finished, save only for the experience he accumulated as an antitrust prosecutor. This was no Van Devanter, a technician but otherwise an unknown quantity, whose views would develop and harden on the Supreme Court. What was said of McReynolds after his death, that he was "the supreme type of a rugged individualist," and, as Justice William O. Douglas thought, "a true representative of the old order of Southern landed aristocracy," could have been said with as much assurance and with equal justification in 1903 or in 1913. He was, then as later, entirely committed to the aristocratic principle, he seethed with contempt for grasping, newly rich businessmen (here one may find some of the seeds of his antitrust fervor), and he entertained an equal contempt for legislators. These were his sentiments in the Vanderbilt years. On such a platform he ran for Congress in 1896. To these attitudes should be added only a pronounced, if mildly paternalistic, racism—blacks were "ignorant, superstitious, immoral and with but small capacity for radical improvement"—and

---

[110] A. S. Link, *Wilson: The New Freedom* (1956), 10–15, 116; *Clapp Hearings,* I, 1215; A. T. Mason, *Brandeis—A Free Man's Life* (1946), 396; "J. C. McReynolds—The New Preceptor for the Trusts," *New York Times,* Mar. 9, 1913, p. 4; B. J. Hendrick, "James C. McReynolds—Attorney General and Believer in the Sherman Law," *World's Work,* 27:27, November 1913.

the unchangeable McReynolds, the Attorney General of 1913 and the Justice of later years, is compleat. Possibly the only element in his temperamental and intellectual makeup that is difficult to trace to the early years is the anti-Semitism to which he gave full vent later. But one may doubt that it was really after-acquired.[111]

Neither Wilson nor Progressives in general had any reason to be dissatisfied with McReynolds' performance as Attorney General. He was accessible—swallowing his distaste, for the moment—to people like Brandeis, who found him not unaccommodating.[112] And he was the trustbuster he had always been, although he showed now, perhaps, somewhat greater concern for the interests of "innocent" stockholders, and was somewhat more wary of driving a corporate defendant into bankruptcy than in his undiluted zeal as the *Tobacco* prosecutor. But he obtained a strong decree in the *Union Pacific* case, which he regarded as a model and was very proud of,[113] and he vigorously pushed the prosecutions in *United States Steel* and *International Harvester*, personally arguing and winning the latter case in the trial court.[114] He also urged, if ultimately without success, a new and indirect attack, by way of a graduated tax, on what he viewed as the still too large tobacco companies left in the wake of the antitrust decree accepted by Attorney General Wickersham.[115] In newly initiated proceedings, McReynolds exacted consent decrees from the American Telephone and Telegraph Company and the New Haven Railroad, in the latter instance after a rather spectacular fight, in the course of which he went so far as to obtain a criminal indictment, and generally displayed his usual unyielding self, although he was reluctant to drive the New Haven into receivership.[116]

With the passage of the Clayton and Federal Trade Commission Acts, and the beginning of the war, a phase in the American antitrust adventure was drawing to a close, and the Wilson Administration was engaged in an effort to make peace with the business world and regain its confidence. All this was in no way owing to any let-up in McReynolds' personal determination to enforce the Sherman Act. But it is characteristic that McReynolds, in and out of office, through the years from decision of the *Standard Oil* and *Tobacco* cases to passage in 1914 of the Clayton and Federal Trade Commission Acts, played no role in the great national debate on antitrust and general industrial policy. He held

---

[111] Link, *Wilson: The New Freedom*, 241 n.49; Schimmel, "Judicial Policy of Mr. Justice McReynolds," 16, n.48, 38, 36; *Proceedings in the Supreme Court of the United States in Memory of Mr. Justice McReynolds.*

[112] Mason, *Brandeis*, 402, 405.
[113] See *supra*, pp. 187–88.
[114] See *supra*, pp. 154 *et seq.*; 157 *et seq.*
[115] See *supra*, p. 125.
[116] Link, *Wilson: The New Freedom*, 418–23.

monopoly to be wicked, and he believed in the Sherman Act. It was as simple as that, without ramifications, implications, or complications, and that was all.[117]

Such criticism as there was of McReynolds' antitrust activities came mainly from the conservative side. His abortive proposal to further deconcentrate the tobacco industry by means of a graduated tax drew some fire,[118] for it heightened the impression that McReynolds always preferred "an axe to a pruning-knife."[119] But the only seriously embarrassing controversy he became involved in concerned, not antitrust, but a trivial and entirely justified decision he made early in his tenure. In a departure from prior administration of the Mann Act, which had theretofore been applied only to commercial vice, the U.S. Attorney in San Francisco, early in 1913, began a prosecution of two young men who had traveled from California to Nevada with two girls. Their purpose was unquestionably immoral, but in no way commercial; they had no end in view except their own gratification. Ultimately and very dubiously, after the prosecution had succeeded, a divided Supreme Court, McReynolds taking no part, held that the Mann Act was indeed applicable.[120]

One of the young defendants was the son of Anthony E. Caminetti, a Democratic leader in San Francisco, and for this reason perhaps the whole episode was a local scandal. Shortly after the indictment was handed down, Wilson's new Democratic Administration made Anthony Caminetti head of the Immigration Service in the Department of Labor. As his son's case was coming to trial, Caminetti, in June 1913, asked his superior, Secretary of Labor William B. Wilson, for a leave of absence so that he could be present in California. But the Secretary considered it a bad time from the point of view of the department's needs, and quite casually called Attorney General McReynolds to see whether the trial could not be postponed till autumn. Equally casually and routinely, McReynolds so ordered; postponements of trials for various reasons were, after all, a common occurrence.

Most startlingly, however, the U.S. attorney in San Francisco, a Republican holdover, took great umbrage, and resigned with a public statement charging a sinister conspiracy to obstruct justice. An incredible brouhaha followed. Despite many demands for McReynolds' resignation, both he and the President kept their heads; McReynolds convincingly maintained his innocence of any improper motives, and the President

---

[117] See B. J. Hendrick, "James Clark McReynolds—Attorney General and Believer in the Sherman Law," *World's Work*, 31, November 1913.

[118] E.g., *The Nation*, 96:588, June 12, 1913.

[119] *The Literary Digest*, 46:734, Mar. 29, 1913.

[120] Caminetti v. United States, 242 U.S. 470 (1917).

supported him, while ordering prosecution of the case "with the utmost diligence and energy." McReynolds was stunned, hurt, and genuinely incredulous that his integrity should have been questioned.[121]

McReynolds made no attempt to cut a political figure. He stuck to his knitting, and he took a restricted view of what his knitting was. In his first year in office, he made not a single public speech. He was stiff necked, prickly, autonomous, and aloof, then as always, and his relations with Congress and with his colleagues were none too warm.[122] One general policy recommendation that he did venture in his first year in office passed unremarked at the time, but attained notoriety a generation later, when another Attorney General and another President contrived to extract from it what became known as the Court-packing plan. Federal judges, McReynolds observed, could retire on full pay at the age of seventy, following ten years of service, and many had availed themselves of this privilege.

> Some, however, have remained upon the Bench long beyond the time that they are able to adequately discharge their duties, and in conse-quence the administration of justice has suffered. . . . I suggest an act providing that when any judge of a federal court *below the Supreme Court* fails to avail himself of the privilege of retiring now granted by law, that the President be required, with the advice and consent of the Senate, to appoint another judge, who would preside over the affairs of the court and have precedence over the older one. This will ensure at all times the presence of a judge sufficiently active to discharge promptly and adequately the duties of the court. [Italics supplied.][123]

When Lurton died, speculation that McReynolds would succeed him began immediately. There was some discussion of Taft, especially in the South, where quaintly but perhaps characteristically enough, it was felt that the first Southern-born President since the Civil War should return a courtesy to Taft, who had given the Chief Justiceship to an ex-Confederate. Taft's candidacy for the Supreme Court had begun, quite in the absence of any vacancy, virtually at the moment of his retirement from the Presidency, and there had been a flurry of Taft talk earlier in the year, when rumors were going around that Holmes was

---

[121] See Link, *Wilson: The New Freedom,* 117–19; Hendrick, "James Clark McReynolds—Attorney General and Believer in the Sherman Law," *World's Work,* 31, November 1913; "The Attorney General in Hot Water," *The Literary Digest,* 47:39, July 12, 1913.

[122] See Schimmel, "Judicial Policy of Mr. Justice McReynolds," 112–19.

[123] *Report of the Attorney General of the United States for the Fiscal Year Ending June 30, 1913,* 5; W. E. Leuchtenburg, "The Origins of Frank-lin D. Roosevelt's 'Court-Packing' Plan," *Supreme Court Rev.,* 391, 1966.

about to retire, which Holmes went so far as to deny publicly. But now, everyone could see, was not Taft's time.

Lurton had been one of only three Democrats on the Supreme Court, and it was very soon quite clear that Wilson would replace him with a Democrat. Even those who favored Taft's eventual accession, and thought that little attention should be paid to party lines in Supreme Court appointments, did not expect the elevation of a Republican to Lurton's place. Another, more seriously mentioned name was that of Franklin K. Lane of California, the Secretary of the Interior and former member of the Interstate Commerce Commission. Lane had some support; Newton D. Baker, for example, then still in Cleveland, favored him strongly. But there was word from the White House that Lane could not be spared—leaving rather an unfortunate and probably accurate implication about McReynolds. Other natural subjects of speculation were Solicitor General John W. Davis of West Virginia and former Solicitor General Frederick W. Lehmann of Missouri, but no one was surprised when on August 19, 1914, McReynolds was nominated.

No doubt Colonel House had put in a word again, and there is evidence that Postmaster General Albert S. Burleson of Texas pressed for McReynolds. Josephus Daniels, Wilson's Secretary of the Navy, in recollections many years later, remarked that McReynolds had been kicked upstairs, thus suggesting that Wilson willfully dumped on the Supreme Court an unwanted Cabinet officer. But Wilson, in September 1913, had said of McReynolds that he was "formidable, dangerously formidable, to the men who wished to act without sanction of law"— language that has faintly the ring of what Wilson was to say of his most important appointee, Brandeis, in 1916: "He knows more than how to talk about the right—he knows how to set it forward in the face of its enemies."

Wilson's mistake—and he did come to regret it—was an ignorant, not a willful one. And if he made no deep inquiry into his man on the occasion of this second appointment of him, and perhaps reflected on it too little, the explanation, and McReynolds' uncommon luck, are to be found in the events of the weeks between Lurton's death and the nomination. The Supreme Court was in its summer recess, but Congress was in session. If an appointment was made with reasonable dispatch, it could be confirmed before the Court reconvened in October. Otherwise, barring a recess appointment, there might be no new Justice for some months, for Congress would adjourn in the fall, at any rate, and so the Court would be left shorthanded for at least half the term. Clearly, therefore, speed was indicated in any responsible view of the situation. But the times were crowded and traumatic.

Lurton died on July 12, 1914. Within days, McReynolds' negotiations—ultimately successful—for a consent decree with the directors of

349

the New Haven Railroad broke down. This was front-page news. McReynolds took a most vigorous stand, recommending to the President that both civil and criminal prosecutions commence. He looked at his best. Meanwhile, also in the latter part of July, Wilson was facing a rebellion in the Senate over two nominations for the Federal Reserve Board, and he had eventually to withdraw one. On July 28, Austria, and on August 1, Germany, declared war. Mexico was erupting, and Pancho Villa was being heard from. On August 6, Mrs. Wilson died in the White House. For the next several days, the President was near the point of breakdown. Mrs. Wilson was buried in Georgia on August 11. A week later, Wilson chose McReynolds. How much of his best attention could conceivably have been concentrated on this decision? Under tremendous pressure, and needing to see to this relatively peripheral matter with some expedition, he did the obvious thing, because it was not obviously wrong.[124]

The world was busy that week, and while Lurton's death a month before had made the front pages, McReynolds' nomination did not. In the editorial columns, the radical, trust-busting image of the man predominated, and it caused some misgivings. At any rate, nowhere outside Nashville was there any enthusiasm. Every private, remarked the *New York Times* without attribution, carries a marshal's baton in his knapsack, and every lawyer has Supreme Court robes in his locker. For who would have thought just two years earlier of James Clark McReynolds for the Supreme Court? He was a lawyer of no great distinction, the *Times* went on, deprecatingly and unfairly, his one claim to fame being his stand against Attorney General Wickersham with respect to the decree in the *Tobacco* case; and this was an occasion when he was somewhat overzealous: "Possibly he will carry with him . . . some views of the relation of the Government to business more in accord with the opinions of the late Justice Harlan than . . . of the present members of the Court. . . ." But, the *Times* consoled itself, the conferences of the Justices had a way of moderating radical views: "Mr. McReynolds will come within the radiance of the light of reason [an allusion to the White

---

[124] *New York Times,* July 14, 1914, p. 9, col. 5, p. 8, col. 3, Aug. 2, 1914, p. 14, col. 3, Aug. 19, 1914, p. 9, col. 1; *New York Tribune,* July 13, 1914, p. 1, col. 4, July 14, 1914, p. 4, col. 2; *New York Times,* Jan. 9, 1913, p. 1, col. 6; *Washington Post,* Mar. 10, 1914, p. 1, col. 7; J. Daniels, *The Wilson Era—Years of Peace, 1910–17* (1944), 540–41; McHargue, "Appointments to the Supreme Court of the United States—The Factors That Have Affected Appointments, 1789–1932," 409–15; N. D. Baker to J. H. Clarke, July 21, 1914, Clarke Papers, Box No. 3, Western Reserve University Library; Link, *Wilson: The New Freedom,* 119, 452 *et seq.,* 422, 461–65; A. S. Link, *Wilson: The Struggle for Neutrality* (1960), Chs. I, VIII; A. S. Link, *Wilson: Confusions and Crises* (1964), 359.

opinions in *Standard Oil* and *Tobacco*], and the President has said that the war between Government and business is about over."

The Republican *New York Tribune* called the appointment a "serious mistake." McReynolds was "essentially a partisan and a passionate one," he had been not merely an aggressive Attorney General, which might be considered fitting enough, but had displayed "a temper for wrangling and a personal bitterness" that had marred his record. The prescient *New York World*, on the other hand, thought the choice "respectable but not ideal," and noted that "while Mr. McReynolds may not be classed as an extreme reactionary, he has repeatedly exhibited mental traits and inclinations that have given much comfort to reactionaries." It was reported that a few Progressive Senators, who had applauded McReynolds' position in the *Tobacco* case, had been disappointed in him for not pushing the New Haven Railroad prosecution uncompromisingly enough. But no serious difficulty over confirmation was expected.[125]

Colonel House couldn't have been more pleased. "Dear Mr. Justice," he wrote. "That sounds good to me. I hope it does to you. I am happy to see that the country is receiving the appointment so well. It could not be otherwise after the wonderful record you have made as Attorney General." McReynolds replied, reasonably enough as to a benefactor: "Whatever I can do that pleases you—meets in some degree your expectations, I count as doubly worth while. And won't you please know without the shadow of doubt that I never forget . . . the source of my good fortune."[126]

The opposition, such as it was, developed as expected. It consisted chiefly of George W. Norris of Nebraska, who spoke at some length, touching on the New Haven case, but emphasizing also, as did a few others, the recent replacement by McReynolds of a United States Attorney in Chicago. McReynolds, it was said, had been motivated by the overly harsh and vigorous attitude of the incumbent in matters affecting business regulation. Not at all, replied the Democratic Senator from Illinois; it was a question of making a place for a deserving Democrat. McReynolds was confirmed on August 29, in a thin chamber, by a vote of 44 to 6. Voting nay, in addition to Norris, were Moses E. Clapp, Republican of Indiana; the Iowa Insurgent Albert Cummins; the only Progressive party representative in the Senate, Miles Poindexter of

---

[125] *The Literary Digest,* 49:505–506, Sept. 5, 1914; *New York Times,* Aug. 19, 1914, p. 9, col. 1, Aug. 20, 1914, p. 10, col. 2; *New York Tribune,* Aug. 20, 1914, p. 6, col. 2; *Chicago Tribune,* Aug. 20, 1914, p. 13, col. 3.

[126] E. M. House to J. C. McReynolds, Aug. 20, 1914, McReynolds to House, Aug. 21, 1914, House Collection, Yale University Library, quoted in Schimmel, "Judicial Policy of Mr. Justice McReynolds," 121.

Washington; his colleague Wesley L. Jones, Republican of Washington; and James K. Vardaman of Mississippi, who had had a patronage quarrel with McReynolds.[127] McReynolds took the oath of office on September 5, 1914, and was seated at the start of the new term, in October.

So began the twenty-six-year career on the Supreme Court of very possibly the most difficult man ever to serve there. McReynolds was crotchety, he was prickly, he was picky, he was full of phobias. He hated smoking, he hated women lawyers, he hated Jews. He took violent dislikes to people and was brutally rude to them when he did. So he was to Pitney, to Clarke, to Brandeis, later to Cardozo and to Frankfurter. There was no telling what would govern his reaction to people, and his eccentricities were no late development; they amused Colonel House well before McReynolds arrived on the Supreme Court. Attorney General McReynolds had lunched with him, House noted in his diary.

> He discussed a vacant Federal judgeship . . . and I insisted upon his making an immediate appointment. The docket is becoming clogged and there is no reason for his delay. I had X to see him this morning in order that he might look him over. His only objection to him was that he had no chin. The two men I sent him last week as candidates for United States Marshals seemed to be all right excepting that they were too fat. I have another suggestion to make for an appointment, but the man has a large mole on the back of his ear. I shall ask him to be careful not to expose that side of his head.[128]

McReynolds had intense convictions on the pettiest of things. While in the Cabinet, he refused to allow the Treasury, which then normally supervised the construction of public buildings, to discharge this function with respect to a new building for the Department of Justice, and this led to a pitched feud with Secretary of the Treasury William G. McAdoo.[129] On the Court, he made trouble over the annual picture taking, raised a rumpus when it seemed to him that the precedence of the Justices over Cabinet officers was not adequately recognized, and worried about the manner of printing the Court's calendar. He was free to criticize opinions circulated to him by his colleagues with brusque candor, and insisted that his objections be met, though they most often concerned trivia. "Not one of his suggestions," McKenna once complained to Van Devanter, "was directed at the

---

[127] *Chicago Tribune,* Aug. 30, 1914, pt. 2, p. 1, col. 2; *Washington Post,* Aug. 30, 1914, p. 7, col. 1.

[128] C. Seymour, ed., *The Intimate Papers of Colonel House* (1926), I, 141, quoted in Schimmel, "Judicial Policy of Mr. Justice McReynolds," 116.

[129] See *ibid.,* 118.

reasoning of my opinion, and yet he said he could not concur in it, unless I accepted them."[130]

McReynolds might have amused Colonel House, but he sorely tried the patience of the normally jolly and tolerant Justice Taft—even though he did not have one of his feuds with Taft. He recurs as a painful refrain in Taft's correspondence throughout his Chief Justiceship in the 1920s. Taft complained of McReynolds' "overbearing and insulting attitude toward Clarke"; of his "masterful, domineering, inconsiderate and bitter nature" and his childishness; of his failure to sign the Court's letter of regret to Clarke upon Clarke's resignation in 1922, which was, Taft thought, "a fair sample of McReynolds' personal character and the difficulty of getting along with him"; of his being "least like a colleague," "selfish," "fuller of prejudice than any man I have known"; of his seeming "to delight in making others uncomfortable"; of his lack of a "sense of duty"; of his "continual grouch"; of his having "less of a loyal spirit to the Court than anybody"; of his being "selfish beyond everything, though full of the so-called Southern courtesy, but most inconsiderate of his colleagues and others and contemptuous of everybody."[131]

While Taft was chafing under McReynolds' idiosyncrasies, Charles S. Hamlin, an old Bostonian, who as a governor of the Federal Reserve Board was now a man about Washington, entered this telling portrait in his diaries:

> Dined at Metropolitan Club with Justice McReynolds. He talked in a rambling way attacking everything and everybody. He said that Davis could not be elected; that Judge McKenna was in thoroughly good physical condition but "there was nothing here" (touching his head); that Judge Holmes was still all right mentally, but extremely narrow and shut out from the world and should have retired long ago; that he [McReynolds] had seriously considered introducing a motion to the effect that no case should be referred to a judge, to write an opinion, who was over seventy-five years of age; that the Court must do something of this kind to preserve itself; that Brandeis, although able in a certain way, had no conception of the spirit of the common law and should never have been appointed; that he [McReynolds] distrusted all Jews, as the Oriental mind was different from the Anglo-Saxon; that Jewish lawyers looked on law as if handed down from Zion.[132]

---

[130] Taft Papers, General Correspondence, Folders for March 1924 and December 1923; J. McKenna to W. Van Devanter, Feb. 25, 1922, Van Devanter Papers.

[131] W. H. Taft to W. G. Harding, Sept. 5, 1922; Taft to E. Root, Sept. 13, 1922; Taft to R. A. Taft, Oct. 26, 1922; Taft to H. T. Manning, June 11, 1923; Taft to R. A. Taft, Feb. 1, 1925, Taft Papers.

[132] *Charles S. Hamlin Diaries*, IX, 28–29, Aug. 21, 1924, Library of Congress.

Whatever might have been meant by the remark about looking upon the law as if handed down from Zion, McReynolds' anti-Semitism was passionate and open. Did you ever think, he remarked in a return to Holmes in a case in which Holmes and Brandeis were dissenting, "that for four thousand years the Lord tried to make something out of Hebrews, then gave it up as impossible and turned them out to prey on mankind in general—like fleas on the dog for example."[133] He hoped, McReynolds wrote to Colonel House early in 1933, that the President-elect would not surround himself "with alien-minded men who have no real appreciation of our institutions. . . . Also he will fall into the ditch if he permits himself to be influenced by such men as the two Hebrews who are on our bench. The last one appointed [Cardozo], is more dangerous than the first [Brandeis]."[134]

When the mayor of Philadelphia, early in Taft's tenure, invited the Court to attend the dedication of the State House where the Supreme Court of the United States had first sat, McReynolds refused to go. "As you know," he wrote Taft, "I am not always to be found when there is a Hebrew aboard. Therefore my 'inability' to attend must not surprise you!"[135] Shortly after Taft's accession, McReynolds answered a very courteous letter from the Chief Justice inquiring about a convenient date for the Court to have dinner with the Attorney General by scrawling on its face: "Anytime, My dear Mr. Chief Justice. I do not expect to attend, as I find it hard to dine with the *Orient*."[136] When Brandeis came on the Court, McReynolds—although in time, apparently, he abandoned this rather inconvenient practice—took to leaving the conference room just as Brandeis would begin to speak and standing on the other side of the door, which he held ajar so he could come back in as soon as Brandeis finished. This behavior mortified Holmes. When the oath was being administered to Cardozo, McReynolds ostentatiously scanned a newspaper, and during the argument of *Stettler* v. *O'Hara* by Felix Frankfurter, McReynolds leaned well back in his chair and held up the other side's brief at arm's length, purporting to be reading it.[137]

McReynolds' acts of brutal discourtesy in other personal confrontations occurred as much on whim as because of the anti-Semitism he

---

[133] Evans v. Gore, 253 U.S. 245 (1920) No. 654, October Term 1919, Holmes Papers.

[134] J. C. McReynolds to E. M. House, Jan. 30, 1933, House Collection.

[135] J. H. Moore to W. H. Taft, Mar. 7, 1922, J. C. McReynolds to Taft, n.d., Taft Papers.

[136] W. H. Taft to J. C. McReynolds, Dec., 24, 1921, Taft Papers.

[137] Stettler v. O'Hara, 243 U.S. 629 (1917); see H. B. Phillips, ed., *Felix Frankfurter Reminisces* (1960), 102–103; F. Frankfurter to C. C. Burlingham, Mar. 18, 1957, Frankfurter Papers, Library of Congress.

evinced in the instances mentioned. To say that he was eccentric is to describe him, not to account for his behavior. Plainly there was a streak of sadism, of barely repressed violence in his nature. Holmes, Brandeis reported, explained McReynolds "as a savage, with all the irrational impulses of a savage. Holmes says he isn't civilized—he is a primitive man." But there was more to McReynolds, as all who knew him well and were capable of detached judgment realized. Brandeis, unbothered by McReynolds' crude hostility, was fascinated by him. "He is a *Naturmensch*," said Brandeis. "He has very tender affections and correspondingly hates." He treated Pitney "like a dog," Brandeis went on, saying "the cruelest things to him," but when Pitney sickened in his last illness, no one felt his sufferings more than McReynolds, and "not as a matter of remorse, but merely in sensitivity to pain."[138]

"Poor McReynolds," Holmes wrote in 1926, is "a man of feeling and of more secret kindliness than he would get the credit for. But as is so common with Southerners, his own personality governs him without much thought of others when an impulse comes, and I think without sufficient regard for the proprieties of the Court. . . . Formerly, according to my recollection, he was really insolent to Brandeis [a reference, presumably, to McReynolds' walking out of conference when Brandeis spoke], although now there is at least a *modus vivendi*. When I was in the hospital he wrote a charming letter to me, which I shall not soon forget."[139] The sensitivity to pain! When Taft, with whom he had no great friendship, although their relations were comparatively civil, was ill away from Washington in the summer of 1929, McReynolds wrote him: "If by any possibility I can serve, even in the least degree, send me a wire and I will go to you at once. It would be a real pleasure if I could add something to your relief or comfort."[140]

Whatever else might or might not be said of him, McReynolds was able. Holmes thought him "acute," and even Taft, at the height of his irritation, though considered him "spoiled for usefulness," acknowledged that he was "a man of real ability, and great sharpness of intellect."[141] He did himself, as Holmes also remarked, less and less justice in his opinions on the Court, being affected by a curious notion that opinions were essentially superfluities anyway, and that the less said, the better. But no one who examines the working papers, briefs, and arguments in the *American Tobacco* case or his opinion letter to the United States Steel Corporation can doubt the force of mind and high

---

[138] Brandeis-Frankfurter Conversations.

[139] *Holmes-Laski Letters*, II, 842; and see 1254.

[140] J. C. McReynolds to W. H. Taft, Sept. 6, 1929, Taft Papers.

[141] *Holmes-Laski Letters*, I, 413; W. H. Taft to R. A. Taft, Feb. 1, 1925, Taft Papers.

intelligence that were his.[142] Not only his ability, but the stiff-necked integrity—scarcely human in its proportions, a caricature, as it were, of the quality one finds and values every so often in the common run of mankind—the genuine intellectual capacity, even if often imperfectly harnessed, and the integrity, even if its manifestations were for the most part astonishing, commanded respect. Felix Frankfurter, who sat with him for two years, remembered:

> He was rude. . . . He was handsome, able, and honest. I sort of respected him. My wife can't understand that in me. I said, "I despise McReynolds, but respect him." I respected that he refused to sign a letter when Brandeis left the Court [as he had refused in Clarke's case]. There was the usual letter of farewell to a colleague, and he wouldn't sign it. I respected that, because he did not remotely feel what the letter expressed, and I despise hypocrites even more than barbarians.[143]

He was handsome, and beyond that, like Holmes in his own way, he was a striking physical presence. A six-footer, he had an athlete's build, which he kept to the end.[144] The sculptor Jo Davidson, seeing him once, exclaimed: "Look at that head! It could be a Roman Senator or a Medici Pope!"[145] His appearance was one of the things that fascinated Brandeis about him. "He would have given Balzac great joy," Brandeis said once. "I watch his face closely and at times, with his good features, he has a look of manly beauty, of intellectual beauty. . . ."[146] McReynolds was conscious of the figure he cut, and of his good features. After he retired, he gave the Marshal of the Supreme Court some instructions about funeral arrangements to be made for him. Twice he admonished that his face was not to be exposed to view. "I wish to be remembered by friends as in life," he said.[147]

McReynolds was a bachelor. There had been an Ann Rutledge in his life, and she was no legend. She was Willella Pearson, daughter of

[142] *Holmes-Laski Letters,* I, 413; J. C. McReynolds to A. E. Hollzer, Aug. 23, 1933, McReynolds Papers; J. McKenna to W. Van Devanter, Feb. 25, 1922, Van Devanter Papers.

[143] Phillips, ed., *Felix Frankfurter Reminisces,* 101.

[144] Thomas W. Gregory, Assistant Attorney General under McReynolds, and then his successor, trying to explain McReynolds' idiosyncrasies as Attorney General in judging prospective candidates for office by their appearance, said that McReynolds "is such a big, fine-looking fellow himself that he cannot get it through his head that anyone has any ability that is not built upon the same lines." B. B. Schimmel, "The Judicial Policy of Mr. Justice McReynolds" (Ph.D. diss., Yale University, 1964), 117.

[145] D. Acheson, *Morning and Noon* (1965), 70.

[146] Brandeis-Frankfurter Conversations.

[147] J. C. McReynolds to T. E. Waggaman, May 5, 1943, Feb. 11, 1946, McReynolds Papers.

the Reverend Erasmus Pearson of the Presbyterian Church in Louisiana, Missouri. Willella was at a girl's school in Nashville while McReynolds was attending Vanderbilt, and at that time apparently an attachment was formed. But in 1885, she died, at the age of twenty-four, after an illness originating in typhoid fever. McReynolds sent a long, pain-stricken letter to the local paper in Louisiana, Missouri, praising her virtues. He painted her as the ideal Victorian maiden. The letter was published, signed "An Admirer." In 1943, when he was over eighty and retired, McReynolds—again anonymously—had a tablet placed in the First Presbyterian Church of Louisiana, Missouri, commemorating Willella and her parents in tributes composed by him.[148]

Perhaps in tribute also, he never married. Brandeis thought him a lonely person, with few friends. Clarke, whom of all his colleagues he persecuted most mercilessly and who suffered most intensely under the treatment, wrote once, with the lucidity of pain, that McReynolds was "too much of a grouch to have a good opinion even of himself."[149]

Outside the circle of the Court, however, free of the almost unbearable strain that the clash of opinions and the confrontation of other independent minds and of other wills clearly caused his unbending nature, he apparently did have friends whose company he enjoyed, and whom he allowed to enjoy him. And he led a life of the mind and of the sensibilities, as well as of the affections, relatively constricted, perhaps, but yielding certain gratifications. A strange, strange man, miscast and out of time, he had no real cause to thank Woodrow Wilson, Colonel House, Brandeis' enemies, or his lucky star.[150]

Brandeis vice Lamar

When McReynolds was seated in October 1914, he joined a young and apparently vigorous Court. He and four others—Hughes, Van Devanter, Lamar, and Pitney—were in their fifties. Day was sixty-five, the Chief Justice sixty-nine, and even the two seniors, Holmes and McKenna, were only just over seventy. But by summer, Lamar, then fifty-seven, was struck down by an illness shortly to prove fatal. He was in White Sulphur Springs, West Virginia, and he told the Chief Justice about it in a heartrending letter he dictated on September 6, 1915. He had left Washington at the end of the term not feeling at all well, Lamar said, and had been under doctor's care all summer. He had

---

[148] McReynolds Papers.
[149] Brandeis-Frankfurter Conversations; J. H. Clarke to W. Van Devanter, Nov. 9, 1924, Van Devanter Papers.
[150] Acheson, *Morning and Noon*, 70–76.

not written, because he did not wish to worry the Chief. Then, "yesterday" he had a stroke that partially paralyzed his left arm and leg.

> I am now in bed and suffering great inconvenience, but no acute pain. The doctor talks more encouragingly than I feel, and says that he thinks I can be up and about within a week or two. I am not so sure as he seems to be; and am inexpressibly mortified at what seems to me to be helpless, and I fear will be useless, days for the remainder of a short life. Of course the prime regret is the fear that my incapacity will put more work upon others who are already carrying tremendously heavy burdens. I am glad to think that everybody else in the Court is in prime condition, and am trying to minimize as far as possible the reports which will go out to the public; though now so many are familiar with the facts that it cannot remain a secret longer. . . .[151]

To this anguished letter, White replied in great distress. He admonished Lamar to forget about the Court and not to worry.[152] For the rest of the month, there were many letters to Lamar and his wife from members of the Court, and from the President.[153] In October, Lamar returned to his house in Washington, and on January 2, 1916, he died there of heart failure. He was taken home to Augusta for burial, a committee of Justices consisting of Van Devanter, Pitney, and McReynolds in attendance. Lamar was fifty-eight years old, and had served five years almost to the day, although, of course, he did not sit after the close of the October Term 1914, on June 21, 1915.

In the four and a half years of his active service, Lamar wrote 113 opinions of the Court. He concurred separately without opinion twice, and dissented 24 times, writing 8 dissenting opinions.[154] This volume of production compares favorably with Lurton's record over a similar time span, and, over exactly the same period, with Van Devanter's 113 opinions of the Court and no dissenting opinions, and with Hughes' 102 majority and 4 dissenting opinions. (In total number of recorded dissents, with or without opinion, Van Devanter compares with 15 and Hughes with 28.) But Day, despite an absence of some months at the 1911 Term, wrote 123 majority and 1 concurring opinions, and filed 22 dissents, 10 of them with opinion. Among the other veterans who sat throughout Lamar's tenure, the figures are much higher. Holmes wrote 191 opinions of the Court, and 1 concurring opinion, and dis-

---

[151] J. R. Lamar to E. D. White, Sept. 6, 1915, Lamar Papers.

[152] E. D. White to J. R. Lamar, Sept. 10, 1915, Lamar Papers.

[153] Lamar Papers.

[154] Attorney General Gregory, addressing the Court in Lamar's memory, said that he participated in the decision of 1,179 cases, and credited him with 114 opinions of the Court, and 8 dissenting opinions. 241 U.S. xiv (1916). Lamar's first opinion was Baltimore & Ohio Southwestern R.R. v. United States, 220 U.S. 94 (1911), and his last was Newman v. Frizzell, 238 U.S. 537 (June 21, 1915).

sented 21 times, in 9 cases with opinion. White contributed 181 majority and 1 concurring opinions, and registered 3 dissents with opinion out of a total of 15. Finally, McKenna had 147 opinions of the Court and 1 concurring opinion, and dissented 28 times, writing 7 opinions. Altogether, the first four of President Taft's appointees turned out to be no workhorses. Taft in 1909 and 1910 had been greatly concerned with the Court's need for vigorous men to take up the slack, but the senior Justices, it is quite clear, carried much the heavier load of opinion writing.

To be sure, Lamar suffered an interruption in his judicial work. During May and June 1914, he took on a special assignment, pressed on him by his boyhood schoolmate, Woodrow Wilson. He was a member of the American delegation to the A.B.C. Conference, convened in Niagara Falls, Canada, at the behest of Argentina, Brazil, and Chile, to attempt mediation between the United States, which had occupied Veracruz, and the Mexican government of General Victoriano Huerta. Lamar's colleague on the two-man delegation, assisted by a professional diplomat as a secretary, was former Solicitor General Frederick W. Lehmann.

The conference was an inconclusive episode in the Wilson Administration's troubles with Mexico, because the President was not about to make peace with Huerta, whom he was intent upon overthrowing. However, Lamar apparently acquitted himself well. Wilson promptly tried to draft him to go to Chile to a Pan-American conference the following fall, but Lamar begged off. He had accepted this extrajudicial task, coming near the end of the term of Court, only after consultation with Chief Justice White, and had not technically absented himself from the Bench. He participated in the decision of cases during May and June, but could not take his normal share of opinions.[155] Hughes also accepted membership on a special commission, by appointment of President Taft in the summer of 1911, and devoted considerable attention to its work into the early months of 1912.[156] No doubt these extra-judicial activities cut into Lamar's and Hughes' output, as an illness of several months had cut into Lurton's, but the disparity between the

---

[155] Link, *Wilson: The New Freedom,* 405–13; C. P. Lamar, *The Life of Joseph Rucker Lamar* (1926), 249–67; W. Wilson to J. R. Lamar, May 15, 1914, W. J. Bryan to Lamar, Aug. 3, 1914, Lamar Papers; *New York Times,* May 24, 1914, p. 2, col. 1.

There was a general reassignment to others of cases in Lamar's hands in which he had not yet written, and even of at least one in which he had done a draft. W. R. Day to Mahlon Pitney, July 10, 1914, Day Papers, Library of Congress. Other cases Lamar continued to hold.

[156] C. E. Hughes, *Biographical Notes,* Microfilm, Ac. 9943, 213–15, Hughes Papers.

volume of their work and that of Holmes, White, and McKenna is too substantial to be satisfactorily explained in this fashion.

Like Lurton, and rather like Van Devanter in these initial years of a long career, but unlike Hughes, Lamar made no great mark. His most enduring contribution was in the field of administrative law. *United States* v. *Grimaud*, upholding delegation of quasi-legislative power to the administrative, is a landmark. Lamar here led to unanimity a Court that had been equally divided before his accession.[157] In *United States* v. *Midwest Oil Co.*, a hotly contested great case, Lamar, over three dissents, upheld the power of the President, acting independently, to withdraw public lands from further exploration for oil. The decision was a daring and debatable extension of Presidential power, but it was well-received.[158] In several additional cases, Lamar exhibited a sophisticated and hospitable conception of the role of administration, and a mastery of judicial techniques for, at once, enhancing, protecting, and controlling the administrative process.[159] Several times he sustained significant new orders of the Interstate Commerce Commission,[160] and he wrote some very able opinions asserting the commission's primary jurisdiction.[161] On another aspect of railroad regulation, Lamar was the author of *United States* v. *Delaware, Lackawanna & Western Railroad*, which was a rigorous—if, in practice, not ultimately adequate—implementation of the commodities clause of the Hepburn Act of 1906.[162]

Lamar perceived limits to the power of Congress under the Com-

---

[157] United States v. Grimaud, 220 U.S. 506 (1911).

[158] United States v. Midwest Oil Co., 236 U.S. 459 (1914); see W. Colby, "The New Public Land Policy with Special Reference to Oil Lands," *Calif. L. Rev.*, 3:269, 285, 1915; Notes, *Mich. L. Rev.*, 13:680, 1915; *Harv. L. Rev.*, 28:613, 1915; B. Davis, "Fifty Years of Mining Law," *Harv. L. Rev.*, 50:897, 906, 1937; *cf.* Youngstown Sheet & Tube Co. v. Sawyer, 343 U.S. 579 (1952).

[159] See, e.g., Oregon R.R. & Navigation Co. v. Fairchild, 224 U.S. 510 (1912): Degge v. Hitchcock, 229 U.S. 162 (1913); Swigart v. Baker, 229 U.S. 187 (1913); Wadley Southern Ry. v. Georgia, 235 U.S. 651 (1915).

[160] Interstate Commerce Commission v. Union Pacific R.R., 222 U.S. 541 (1912); Interstate Commerce Commission v. Louisville & Nashville R.R., 227 U.S. 88 (1913); Atchison

Ry. Co. v. United States, 232 U.S. 199 (1914); Baer Brothers v. Denver & Rio Grande R.R., 233 U.S. 479 (1914); Louisville & Nashville R.R. v. United States, 238 U.S. 1 (1915); but *cf.* Omaha Street Ry. v. Interstate Commerce Commission, 230 U.S. 324 (1913).

[161] Mitchell Coal Co. v. Pennsylvania R.R., 230 U.S. 247 (1913); Marrisdale Coal Co. v. Pennsylvania R.R., 230 U.S. 304 (1913); *cf.* Pennsylvania R.R. v. International Coal Co., 230 U.S. 184 (1913); Pennsylvania R.R. v. Puritan Coal Co., 237 U.S. 121 (1915); Eastern Ry. v. Littlefield, 237 U.S. 140 (1915); and *cf.* Fourche River Lumber Co. v. Bryant Lumber Co., 230 U.S. 316 (1913).

[162] *Supra*, p. 189, n.278; and see Delaware, Lackawanna & Western R.R. v. United States, 231 U.S. 363 (1913).

merce Clause rather sooner than most of his colleagues, joining with Lurton in dissent from the decision in *Interstate Commerce Commission* v. *Goodrich Transit Co.*[163] And although, unlike Lurton, he did not register a public dissent in the *Shreveport Case*, he did disapprove of the decision.[164] Lamar went along, however, in the other notable cases of his time upholding Congressional power.[165] He was perhaps no less quick than Lurton to find that federal statutes had occupied the field and preempted concurrent state regulation,[166] but he was more consistent, and did not compensate for this attitude with quite the states'-rights bias of Lurton in cases involving a direct application of the Commerce Clause to action by the states. Thus he was with the majority in *Oklahoma* v. *Kansas Natural Gas Co.*[167]

In Due Process, Equal Protection, and Contract Clause cases passing on state social legislation, Lamar was, on the whole, less flexible, less permissive than most of his colleagues, including Lurton. To be sure, he wrote his share of opinions upholding relatively minor state regulatory measures,[168] but he did not participate in *Noble State Bank* v. *Haskell* or *Chicago, Burlington & Quincy Railroad* v. *McGuire*, which were heard before his appointment, and in *German Alliance Insurance Co.* v. *Kansas*, he dissented.[169] So he did also in a number of other cases in which the Court found no lack of Due Process or Equal Protection, including *Quong Wing* v. *Kirkendall*, where his objection did not go to the real difficulty, concerning the possibility of racial discrimination, but was a more general and less tenable one.[170] He marshaled majorities in

---

[163] *Supra*, p. 214, n.49.

[164] *Supra*, pp. 216 *et seq.*, n.54; see also Pedersen v. Delaware, Lackawanna & Western R.R., 229 U.S. 146 (1913) (Lamar, Holmes, and Lurton, JJ., dissenting); St. Louis, San Francisco & Texas Ry. v. Seale, 229 U.S. 156 (1913) (Lamar, J., dissenting).

[165] But *cf.* Greenleaf Lumber Co. v. Garrison, 237 U.S. 251 (1915).

[166] See Chicago, Rock Island & Pacific Ry. v. Cramer, 232 U.S. 490 (1914); Great Northern Ry. v. O'Connor, 232 U.S. 508 (1914); Southern Ry. Co. v. Railroad Commission of Indiana, 236 U.S. 439 (1915).

[167] *Supra*, pp. 268–69, n.210; and see Foote v. Maryland, 232 U.S. 494 (1914) but *cf.* Banker Brothers v. Pennsylvania, 222 U.S. 210 (1911).

[168] See Provident Savings Institution v. Malone, 221 U.S. 660 (1911); Keeney v. New York, 222 U.S. 525 (1912); Standard Oil Co. v. Missouri, 224 U.S. 270 (1912); Murphy v. California, 225 U.S. 623 (1912); National Safe Deposit Co. v. Illinois, 232 U.S. 58 (1914); Eberle v. Michigan, 232 U.S. 700 (1914); and see Southern Pacific Co. v. City of Portland, 227 U.S. 559 (1913); Tennessee Coal Co. v. George, 233 U.S. 354 (1914).

[169] See *supra*, p. 284, n.275.

[170] *Supra*, p. 298, n.327; Gromer v. Standard Dredging Co., 224 U.S. 362 (1912); Kansas City Ry. v. Anderson, 233 U.S. 325 (1914); Wheeler v. New York, 233 U.S. 434 (1914); Lankford v. Platte Iron Works, 235 U.S. 461 (1915); American Water Co. v. Lankford, 235 U.S. 496 (1915); Farish v. State Banking Board, 235 U.S. 498 (1915).

divided Courts for holding two comparatively inconsequential state regulations of railroads unconstitutional,[171] and he applied the Contract Clause several times, as in *Grand Trunk Western Railway* v. *South Bend*, a quite extreme case.[172] In *Owensboro* v. *Cumberland Telephone Co.*, he was with Lurton's majority of five.[173]

Of course, Lamar seldom stood out alone, and in the case last mentioned, for example, Holmes also formed part of the majority. But it is the tendency of Lamar's actions in Due Process, Equal Protection, and Contract Clause cases viewed in bulk that is the proper foundation of judgment about him, and that tendency was toward a more rigid and solemn adherence than was common among most of his colleagues to the absolutes of *Allgeyer* v. *Louisiana, Lochner* v. *New York*, and *Adair* v. *United States*, on which he had so ringingly relied in his brief in *Atlantic Coast Line Railroad* v. *Riverside Mills*.[174] Although Lamar went along with unanimous Courts in upholding a few regulations of hours and conditions of labor,[175] he made one of six, with Pitney, White, McKenna, Van Devanter, and McReynolds, against Holmes, Day, and Hughes, when the Court divided in *Coppage* v. *Kansas*,[176] forbidding the states to outlaw the antiunion yellow-dog contract. And in *Slocum* v. *New York Life Insurance Co.*, which affords as good a test as any of basic attitudes, Lamar was with the narrow majority.[177]

Lamar came to public notice and, excepting his contribution to the development of the administrative process, did his ablest work in cases that, however spectacular one or two might have been, were peripheral or entirely unrelated to the Court's central concerns under the Commerce, Due Process, Equal Protection, and Contract clauses. Although in the end he silently joined the majority, Lamar had a crucial and conspicuous part in the disposition of *Frank* v. *Mangum*, an early and important episode in the application of the Due Process Clause to state criminal trials.

Frank, quite likely an innocent man, a Northerner and a Jew, was convicted in 1913 in Georgia of the murder of a young white girl. There

---

[171] See Smith v. Texas, 233 U.S. 630 (1914); Chicago, Milwaukee & St. Paul R.R. v. Wisconsin, 238 U.S. 491 (1915); see also Simon v. Southern Ry., 236 U.S. 115 (1915).

[172] See *supra*, pp. 303–304, n.349; and see Louisville v. Cumberland Telephone Co., 224 U.S. 649 (1912); Choate v. Trapp, 224 U.S. 665 (1912); Gleason v. Wood, 224 U.S. 679 (1912); English v. Richardson, 224 U.S. 680 (1912).

[173] See *supra*, pp. 304–305, n.350.

[174] *Supra*, p. 203.

[175] Hawley v. Walker, *supra*, p. 281, n.260; Jeffrey Manufacturing Co. v. Blagg, 235 U.S. 571 (1915); Rail and River Coal Co. v. Ohio Industrial Commission, 236 U.S. 338 (1915); Miller v. Wilson, 236 U.S. 373 (1915); Bosley v. McLaughlin, 236 U.S. 385 (1915).

[176] 236 U.S. 1 (1915).

[177] *Supra*, pp. 312–14, n.379.

was a strong showing of mob domination and other circumstances suggesting a miscarriage of justice, and the trial was a national *cause célèbre*. The state of local feeling is indicated by the short, unhappy aftermath of the case. A governor convinced of Frank's innocence commuted his death sentence to life imprisonment, and not only gave his political life in exchange, but was literally run out of Georgia. Frank himself was taken from jail and lynched in the summer before Lamar's death.

After federal questions had been raised in the case, the Supreme Court of Georgia affirmed denial of a petition for a new trial, and it declined to allow a writ of error to the Supreme Court of the United States. Application was made to Lamar as Circuit Justice of the Fifth Circuit, but finding that there was an adequate state procedural ground for the action of the Georgia Supreme Court, Lamar also refused a writ of error. So did several other Justices to whom application was made, and finally the entire Court itself. Afterward, however, new counsel brought a petition for habeas corpus in the federal district court in Georgia. This also was denied, and the district judge would not sign a certificate of probable cause for appeal, without which there could be no access to the Supreme Court of the United States. Again application was made to Lamar, and this time successfully. In a memorandum which was widely published in the press, although it is not otherwise preserved, Lamar reviewed the federal questions raised in Frank's behalf, found them to be substantial, and granted a certificate of probable cause to appeal. But when the case was decided in the Supreme Court in April 1915, Lamar was one of a majority of seven, against Holmes and Hughes, for affirmance of the denial of the petition for habeas corpus. Yet given the atmosphere surrounding the case, Lamar's action in allowing the appeal must be considered strong minded and even courageous.[178]

Probably the opinion by Lamar that had the greatest impact on the contemporary general public was *Gompers* v. *Bucks Stove & Range Co.*,[179] which brought to the Supreme Court, not for the last time,[180] the

---

[178] Frank v. Mangum, 235 U.S. 694 (1914); 237 U.S. 309 (1915); *Washington Post,* Dec. 29, 1914; *New York Times,* Dec. 29, 1914; C. Reznickoff, ed., *Louis Marshall— Champion of Liberty* (1957), I, 295–321.

There are indications that Lamar was generally sensitive to problems of procedural regularity in federal criminal trials. See Diaz v. United States, 223 U.S. 442 (1912) (Lamar, J., dis-

senting); Hyde v. United States, 225 U.S. 347 (1912) (Holmes, Lurton, Hughes, and Lamar, JJ., dissenting); Brown v. Elliott, 225 U.S. 392 (1912) (Holmes, Lurton, Hughes, and Lamar, JJ., dissenting). And see Gompers v. Buck's Stove & Range Co., *infra,* n.179.

[179] 221 U.S. 418 (1911).

[180] See Gompers v. United States, 233 U.S. 604 (1914).

contempt convictions and jail sentences of Samuel Gompers and two other labor leaders for violating an antiboycott injunction. In a very skillful opinion, Lamar, while refusing to reexamine the validity of the injunction itself, reversed the convictions on the ground that the contempts in question were criminal in nature, but had been treated by the trial court as civil ones. The opinion is notable for its adroitness in finding a narrow, but valid and dispositive, way out of a highly charged controversy that otherwise pretty well defied satisfactory resolution. A court with no aptitude for such occasional nimble *tours de force* is a Court that will suffer from self-inflicted wounds. Lamar had the necessary technical dexterity,[181] and he employed it as well in other instances, including two cases argued by eminent counsel, in one of which he was able to avoid a challenge to the Congressional investigative power, and in the other to the Presidential appointing power.[182]

Northern Pacific Railway v. *Boyd*[183] was an important decision in the law of corporate bankruptcy, overruling a number of lower-court federal cases. Lamar here spoke for a narrow majority against the dissents of Lurton, White, Holmes, and Van Devanter. His insistence on ethics over expediency in business affairs is reminiscent of the attitude he manifested as a judge of the Georgia Supreme Court many years earlier.[184] The same emphasis on the observance of personal ethical standards in business informs Lamar's opinion for a unanimous Court in *Westinghouse Electric Co.* v. *Wagner Electric Co.*,[185] another innovative decision that has had enduring significance in its own, nonconstitutional branch of the law.

Westinghouse concerned the measure of damages in patent infringement litigation, where the infringer has made some improvements on the patent he appropriated, and the portion of his profits that is attributable to his improvement is commingled with the portion properly to be allocated to the purloined patent itself. The prior rule had been that the plaintiff was required to identify profits earned by his patent which should be paid over to him, and that if he failed to identify his

---

[181] But in winding his delicate way toward disposition of the *Gompers* case, Lamar took counsel with that subtle technician, Van Devanter. It was a good opinion that Lamar had produced, Van Devanter wrote privately soon after the decision came down, adding with, perhaps, not quite the perfect tone of becoming modesty, that "while I had sufficient connection with its preparation to take some personal pride in it, it really should be credited to Lamar." Van Devanter to Elmer B. Adams, May 18, 1911, Van Devanter Papers, Library of Congress.

[182] Henry v. Henkel, 235 U.S. 219 (1914); Newman v. Frizzell, 238 U.S. 537 (1915); see also Garr, Scott & Co. v. Shannon, 223 U.S. 468 (1912).

[183] See *supra*, p. 340, n.101.

[184] See *supra*, p. 42, n.152.

[185] 225 U.S. 604 (1912).

own in a commingled mass, he had not proved his damages, and the defendant kept all. To be sure, somebody had to suffer, for the contrary rule would hand over to the plaintiff some profits that the defendant had legitimately earned. But it was the contrary rule that Lamar caused to prevail. If someone had to suffer, he reasoned, it should be the wrongdoer, not the innocent plaintiff. Characteristically, Lamar drew an analogy to a trustee who commingles his own profit with that owing to a beneficiary. Such a trustee will not be allowed unjustly to enrich himself simply because he kept careless books.[186]

Perhaps the cases last mentioned reflect the outlook on business of a member of the Southern landed gentry—an outlook that retained its decisive effect even after the many years of Lamar's experience as counsel for railroads and other corporations. The Southern gentleman manifests himself also in another aspect, that of his idealization of his womenfolk, in *United States* v. *Holte*,[187] in which Holmes held for the Court that a woman was indictable under the Mann Act for conspiring with a man to have herself transported across a state line for purposes of prostitution. Lamar, joined by Day, would have none of it. All that a woman could be under the Mann Act, he thought, was a victim, even if often a willing one. The statute was intended "to guard her against herself as well as against her slaver; against the wiles and threats, the compulsion and inducements, of those who treat her as if she was merchandise and a subject of interstate transportation. The woman, whether coerced or induced, whether willingly or unwillingly transported . . . is regarded as the victim. . . ." And Lamar added—the practical lawyer now rather than the Victorian Southerner—that if women were liable to prosecution, they would be less likely to come forward with evidence that the statute had been violated, and the upshot would thus be greater difficulty in enforcing the Mann Act.

On issues involving race, the specifically Southern attitude was less discernible in Lamar than in Lurton. Lamar was rather closer to White in this respect. He was not yet on the Court when *Bailey* v. *Alabama* was decided over the dissents of Holmes and Lurton.[188] But in *United States* v. *Reynolds*,[189] a later and perhaps aggravated peonage case, in which McReynolds took no part and Holmes concurred specially and a bit reluctantly, Lamar was with the Court. So he was also, against the dissents of Holmes and Lurton, in *Creswell* v. *Knights of Pythias*, a

---

[186] See W. Macomber, "Damages and Profits in Patent Causes," *Colum. L. Rev.*, 10:639, 642-45, 1911; G. Dike, "The Trial of Patent Account- ings in Open Court," *Harv. L. Rev.*, 36:33, 38, 43, 1922.

[187] 236 U.S. 140, 147 (1915).

[188] *Supra*, p. 339, n.92.

[189] 235 U.S. 133 (1914).

somewhat attenuated test, but relevant.[190] And in the Grandfather Clause cases, which were three in number, he dissented in only one, on a narrow and tenable, if by no means unavoidable, ground.[191] That leaves the special concurrence, with White, Holmes, and McReynolds, in *McCabe* v. *Atchison, Topeka & Santa Fe Railway*, which may be justified in part—but in part only—as taking the position that the Court should not have indulged in the discussion of matters not necessary to the decision of the case.[192]

It is quite evident that Lamar, as was said of him in a eulogy, had "a genius for friendship. It was a part of his religion; it was a part of his life."[193] He had apparently no enemies, nor even detractors, and was well loved and mourned by his colleagues among others. Hughes remembered his "gentleness and grace,"[194] and Van Devanter, more spontaneously, on the day after Lamar's death, exclaimed: "I liked him immensely."[195]

Nothing in Joseph Rucker Lamar's life was half so dramatic or consequential as what ensued upon his leaving of it. The nomination of Lamar's successor, on January 28, 1916, astonished Washington and the country. The Senate, it was reported, "simply gasped." Since the death of Lamar less than four weeks earlier, many names had been mentioned. There was great pressure for Taft, who was skeptical but receptive, not only from the South, but also from newspapers and much of the bar in the North, although Lamar, like Lurton, had been a Democrat, and his departure again left only two Democrats on the Bench. It was a more serious effort this time than in the summer of 1914, and hence provoked active opposition from Progressive and Labor supporters of the President. Early on, the White House let it be known that neither Taft nor members of the President's official family, such as the Attorney General (McReynolds' successor, Thomas W. Gregory of Texas), Solicitor General John W. Davis, and Secretary of the Interior Franklin K. Lane, would be appointed. But dozens of other names were being earnestly urged, many of them Southern. There was a whole battalion of state judges, ex-governors, ex-Senators, and sitting Senators and Congressmen. The one name hardly mentioned in public was that of Wilson's eventual choice, Louis D. Brandeis of Boston.[196]

---

[190] *Supra*, p. 339, n.93.

[191] *Supra*, p. 339, n.95.

[192] See *infra*, p. 779, n.148.

[193] Remarks of Mr. Hannis Taylor, in *Proceedings of the Bar and Officers of the Supreme Court of the United States in Memory of Joseph Rucker Lamar*, May 27, 1916, at 20.

[194] C. E. Hughes, *Biographical Notes*, Microfilm, Ac. 9943, 221, Hughes Papers.

[195] W. Van Devanter to E. B. Adams, Jan. 3, 1916, Van Devanter Papers.

[196] See Link, *Wilson: Confusions and Crises*, 325; *Washington Evening Star*, Jan. 4, 1916, p. 2, col. 2, Jan. 6, 1916, p. 1, col. 6, Jan. 7, 1916, p. 2,

IV: *Appointment Cycles*

The nomination was a surprise, but there had been other recent surprises—Pitney, White as Chief Justice. This one was also a thunder-clap, the opening of an epic struggle for confirmation. Brandeis was a Jew, and much was to be made of that, although there is good reason to believe that he was not the first Jew to be offered appointment to the Supreme Court, President Filmore having tendered a place to the fabulous Judah P. Benjamin of Louisiana in 1853.[197] Moreover, in the course of a professional and public life that for at least a quarter-century had been one relentless combat, Brandeis had gathered a whole lot of personal enemies, few of whom would now fail to be heard from. But the nomination resulted in no mere partisan engagement, nor just a skirmish over some limited issues having to do with Brandeis' personality or ethics. It provoked a fight for the soul of the Supreme Court, a deep-cutting controversy about its role in American life, a struggle to bring to bear on the Court—versus an effort to preserve it immune from—the dominant political sentiment of the time.

By 1916, the Progressive movement had touched and in some measure altered about every institution of government, save the Supreme Court. The Court, to be sure, was not in a particularly reactionary mood; it had indeed for some years acted with prudence. But nothing of the ferment, nothing of the new intellectual currents in economics, philosophy, and law, nothing even of new methods of inquiry had reached the Court. It alone was unaffected in any fundamental way. On the morrow, when the direction of the wind would change, as it was bound to, all could not be the same again in the statute book or in administration—although for the Justices, it would remain unchanged. For there were no new men among them to work basic changes in the principles, the materials, and the methods of judgment, no new men whose work would affect if not govern, influence if not dominate, the Court of the future. There was Holmes, but he was unique, an intellectual loner, beating a path that only he could follow. Besides, in basic philosophic outlook, even if not, happily, in his conception of the function of judicial review, Holmes was closer to his Brethren on the Bench than to the new men in political life. Hughes, soon to depart, was a leader, a fresh and in some ways a liberated intellect, but well within the existing, conventional mold. The rest of the Justices were lawyers and public men of the old school, some abler than others, more or less pragmatic, doctrinaire or conservative, but all of a kind.

---

col. 4; *Washington Post,* Jan. 6, 1916, p. 2, col. 3, Jan. 11, 1916, p. 3, col. 4; *New York Tribune,* Jan. 12, 1916, p. 3, col. 6, p. 4, col. 5; *Philadelphia Record,* Jan. 11, 1916, p. 11, col. 3; H. F. Pringle, *The Life and Times of William Taft* (1939), II, 951; A. L. Todd, *Justice on Trial* (1964), 27–35.

[197] See C. Warren, *The Supreme Court in United States History* (rev. ed., 1926), II, 245.

Brandeis was a man of an utterly different cast. His experience, his interests, his allegiances, his methods, everything he brought to the Court was entirely new to it. In his hands, for nearly twenty-three years —often in dissent, of course—the law of the Constitution and the function of judicial review would be put to new uses. In his opinions would be glimpsed the second half of the twentieth century. His appointment was the blow by which the Progressive movement finally toppled the last citadel of the post-Civil War Business Society. Toppled is, of course, a premature word for 1916; the citadel would stand a while longer. But when Brandeis entered, there went the Holy of Holies. This is what people sensed, and they reacted accordingly.

This, it is quite likely, was what Woodrow Wilson intended. He decided quickly, as he did on all three of his appointments, but more quickly by a couple of weeks than on the other two. Yet he may have brooded over this one for a considerably longer period, since he kept in touch about the condition of Lamar, a friend, and was aware that an appointment impended. And in this instance he knew his man, and knew him well. Wilson was in a very different frame of mind and spirit from that of a year and a half earlier, when he made the starkly contrasting nomination of McReynolds. The times were again eventful, but there was not the crashing series of climaxes that filled August of 1914. In that month, moreover, Wilson was widowed. When Lamar died, he was on his honeymoon in Hot Springs, Virginia, with the new Mrs. Wilson.

In domestic policy, Wilson stood at the threshold of what Professor Link has called "one of the most startling political developments in American history." The second phase of the New Freedom was about to be inaugurated and carried into the election of 1916. "It saw Wilson become almost a new political creature and the Democratic Party under his leadership and goad become at least momentarily transformed into an agency of advanced nationalistic reform." Of this "new orientation" the first sign was the Brandeis nomination. It was in its way a declaration of political principle, a renewed assumption of ideological leadership over the Democratic party, a battle cry.[198]

The suggestion that he nominate Brandeis had been put to Wilson, apparently, both by his friend and personal physician, Admiral Cary T. Grayson, and by Attorney General Gregory. And from the outside, though not publicly, the writer Norman Hapgood, who was very close to Brandeis and close also to Wilson, urged the appointment. But there was no need to recommend Brandeis to Wilson. Brandeis was his own man and Wilson's, no one else's. There was no gray eminence, no

---

[198] Link, *Wilson: Confusions and Crises,* 13–14, Ch. 2, 45–46, 323, 362.

EDWARD DOUGLASS WHITE, CHIEF JUSTICE OF THE UNITED STATES, 1910–1921
(*The Supreme Court of the United States*)

WILLIAM HOWARD TAFT, CHIEF JUSTICE OF THE UNITED STATES, 1921–1930
(*The Supreme Court of the United States*)

CHARLES EVANS HUGHES, CHIEF JUSTICE OF THE UNITED STATES, 1920–1941
(*The Supreme Court of the United States*)

OLIVER WENDELL HOLMES, JR.
(*The Supreme Court of the United States*)

LOUIS D. BRANDEIS
(*The Supreme Court of the United States*)

WILLIS VAN DEVANTER
(*The Supreme Court of the United States*)

WILLIAM R. DAY
(*The Supreme Court of the United States*)

JOHN MARSHALL HARLAN
(*Library of Congress*)

JAMES CLARK McREYNOLDS
(*The Supreme Court of the United States*)

JOSEPH McKENNA
(*The Supreme Court of the United States*)

MAHLON PITNEY
(*The Supreme Court of the United States*)

JOSEPH RUCKER LAMAR
(*The Supreme Court of the United States*)

HORACE HARMON LURTON
(*The Supreme Court of the United States*)

JOHN H. CLARKE
(*The Supreme Court of the United States*)

DAVID JOSIAH BREWER
(The Supreme Court of the United States)

WILLIAM HENRY MOODY
(The Supreme Court of the United States)

Colonel House, in the making of him. A year earlier, Wilson had given effective support to friends of Brandeis who were trying to get him admitted to the Cosmos Club in Washington. Brandeis was opposed as "a reformer for revenue only," and as a Jew. Most tellingly, it was feared that "he would be a disturbing element in any club of gentlemen." In proposing him now for another exclusive club of gentlemen, Wilson knew what he was about. He said so, in May 1916, at the height of the struggle over confirmation, in a public letter to the chairman of the Senate Committee on the Judiciary, which he composed on his own type-writer, with suggestions from Attorney General Gregory. Wilson wrote:

> There is probably no more important duty imposed upon the President in connection with the general administration of the Government than that of naming members of the Supreme Court; and I need hardly tell you that I named Mr. Brandeis as a member of that great tribunal only because I knew him to be singularly qualified by learning, by gifts, and by character for the position.
>
> Many charges have been made against Mr. Brandeis: the report of your sub-committee has already made it plain to you and to the country at large how unfounded these charges were. They threw a great deal more light upon the character and motives of those with whom they originated than upon the qualifications of Mr. Brandeis. I myself looked into them three years ago when I desired to make Mr. Brandeis a member of my Cabinet and found that they proceeded for the most part from those who hated Mr. Brandeis because he had refused to be serviceable to them in the promotion of their own selfish interests, and from those whom they had prejudiced and misled. The propaganda in this matter has been very extraordinary and very distressing to those who love fairness and value the dignity of the great professions.
>
> I perceived from the first that the charges were intrinsically incredible by anyone who had really known Mr. Brandeis. I have known him. I have tested him by seeking his advice upon some of the most difficult and perplexing public questions about which it was necessary for me to form a judgment. I have dealt with him in matters where nice questions of honor and fair play, as well as large questions of justice and the public benefit, were involved. In every matter in which I have made test of his judgment and point of view I have received from him counsel singularly enlightening, singularly clear-sighted and judicial, and, above all, full of moral stimulation. He is a friend of all just men and a lover of the right; and he knows more than how to talk about the right,—he knows how to set it forward in the face of its enemies. I knew from direct personal knowledge of the man what I was doing when I named him for the highest and most responsible tribunal of the nation.
>
> Of his extraordinary ability as a lawyer no man who is competent to judge can speak with anything but the highest admiration. You will remember that in the opinion of the late Chief Justice Fuller he was

the ablest man who ever appeared before the Suprem Court of the United States. "He is also," the Chief Justice added, "absolutely fearless in the discharge of his duties."

Those who have resorted to him for assistance in settling great industrial disputes can testify to his fairness and love of justice. In the troublesome controversies between the garment workers and manufacturers of New York City, for example, he gave a truly remarkable proof of his judicial temperament and had what must have been the great satisfaction of rendering decisions which both sides were willing to accept as disinterested and even-handed.

Mr. Brandeis has rendered many notable services to the city and state with which his professional life has been identified. He successfully directed the difficult campaign which resulted in obtaining cheaper gas for the City of Boston. It was chiefly under his guidance and through his efforts that legislation was secured in Massachusetts which authorized savings banks to issue insurance policies for small sums at much reduced rates. And some gentlemen who tried very hard to obtain control by the Boston Elevated Railway Company of the subways of the city for a period of ninety-nine years can probably testify as to his ability as the people's advocate when public interests called for an effective champion. He rendered these services without compensation and earned, whether he got it or not, the gratitude of every citizen of the state and city he served. These are but a few of the services of this kind he has freely rendered. It will hearten friends of community and public rights throughout the country to see his qualities signally recognized by his elevation to the Supreme Bench. For the whole country is aware of his quality and is interested in this appointment.

I did not in making choice of Mr. Brandeis ask for or depend upon "endorsements." I acted upon public knowledge and personal acquaintance with the man, and preferred to name a lawyer for this great office whose abilities and character were so widely recognized that he needed no endorsement. I did, however, personally consult many men in whose judgment I had great confidence, and am happy to say was supported in my selection by the voluntary recommendation of the Attorney General of the United States, who urged Mr. Brandeis upon my consideration independently of any suggestion from me.

Let me say by way of summing up, my dear Senator, that I nominated Mr. Brandeis for the Supreme Court because it was, and is, my deliberate judgment that, of all the men now at the bar whom it has been my privilege to observe, test, and know, he is exceptionally qualified. I cannot speak too highly of his impartial, impersonal, orderly, and constructive mind, his rare analytical powers, his deep human sympathy, his profound acquaintance with the historical roots of our institutions and insight into their spirit, or of the many evidences he has given of being imbued to the very heart with our American ideals of justice and equality of opportunity; of his knowledge of modern economic conditions and of the way they bear upon the masses of the people, or of his genius in getting persons to unite in common and harmonious action and look with frank and kindly eyes into each other's minds, who had before been heated antagonists. This friend of justice and of men will ornament the high court of which we are all so justly proud. I am glad to have had the opportunity to pay him this tribute of admiration and of confidence; and I beg that your Committee will accept this nomination as coming from me quick with a sense of public obligation and responsibility.[199]

Louis Dembitz[200] Brandeis was born in Louisville, Kentucky, on November 13, 1856. When appointed, he was thus, at fifty-nine, one year older than Lamar, the man he replaced. Brandeis was the fourth and youngest child of Adolph and Frederika Dembitz Brandeis. Adolph and Frederika, both born in Prague of comfortable and cultivated Bohemian-Jewish parents, came to the United States with their families in 1848 and 1849, respectively, in the wake of the revolution of the earlier year. Frederika was then not quite twenty and Adolph was in his middle twenties. Their families were allied, and the couple had been engaged in Prague before Adolph's departure. Their first place of American settlement was Madison, Indiana, where Adolph and Frederika were married. In 1851, the Brandeis family moved to Louisville, and by the time Louis was born, Adolph Brandeis was prospering as a grain and produce merchant.

Both Louis' father and his uncle Lewis Dembitz were abolitionists, and one of young Brandeis' earliest recollections was of his mother, during the Civil War, carrying out food and coffee to men from the North, of whom the streets seemed full. The family adhered to no formal religion, attending neither church nor synagogue. Louis went to public and private schools in Louisville, until, when he was sixteen, Adolph's business having taken a distinct turn for the worse in 1872, the family went on a three-year trip to Europe. One year was spent in Vienna, where Louis took private lessons and attended lectures at the university. For the following two years, Louis was enrolled at the Annen-Realschule in Dresden.

Having returned home, Brandeis entered the Harvard Law School in September 1875. He established there what remains one of the highest

---

[199] *Ibid.,* 323 *et seq.,* 358; Mason, *Brandeis,* 465 *et seq.;* W. Wilson to C. A. Culberson, May 5, 1916, in *Nomination of Louis D. Brandeis, Letter from the President of the United States in Response to a Letter from the Chairman of the Committee on the Judiciary,* Senate Committee Print, 64th Cong., 1st Sess. (1916).

[200] His parents named him Louis David, but early in life Brandeis substituted the middle name Dembitz, in honor of his mother's brother, Lewis Dembitz of Louisville, a well-known lawyer.

scholastic records in the annals of the institution, and received his LL.B. in 1877. The Harvard Law School, under the leadership of its dean, Christopher Columbus Langdell, a great educational innovator, had then just instituted the case system of instruction. The law was coming to be taught, not by lectures out of texts, but by discussion out of decided cases, in a spirit of intellectual egalitarianism and self-reliance. The points learned, Brandeis reported to his family, were "impressed upon the mind as they never could be by mere reading or by lectures; . . . for they occur as an integral part of the drama of life." Brandeis' teachers included John Chipman Gray and James Bradley Thayer, leading figures in American legal scholarship, and the young James Barr Ames, then at the threshold of a career that was to take him eventually to the deanship of the Harvard Law School. Brandeis also moved in intellectual circles beyond the immediate one of the law school. His father's financial fortunes were still in a precarious state, and Brandeis had to support himself in part by tutoring. But Harvard and Boston were a happy, exciting, and deeply formative experience.

Following graduation, Brandeis spent an additional year reading and studying in Cambridge. In the fall of 1878, he entered practice with an older lawyer in St. Louis, the home of his sister Fanny, who had married Charles Nagel, later Taft's Secretary of Commerce and Labor. But a year later, Brandeis returned to Boston, to form a partnership with his Harvard Law School classmate Samuel D. Warren, Jr., a well-to-do Bostonian of Bostonians. The partnership soon flourished, and Brandeis did well not only professionally but also in Boston society. He sailed, he rode, he dined out with the best people, he was even, difficult as it was for those who knew him in later life to conceive it, a member of the Dedham Polo Club. In 1882, Brandeis lectured on evidence at the Harvard Law School, and the faculty wanted him to join on a regular basis. But Brandeis preferred practice. A few years later, the association with Warren was dissolved, as the latter had to take charge of the family's paper business, but Brandeis continued with other partners. In 1891, Brandeis married Alice Goldmark of New York, a second cousin. There were two daughters.

In the early 1890s, by which time his income from the practice of law was beginning to average some $73,000 per annum, Brandeis' attention turned more and more to public issues. The events at Homestead, Pennsylvania, where a strike at a Carnegie Steel plant was broken amidst much violence, brought him up short, and highlighted for him the social and financial abuses perpetrated by business interests very much like some that he had been representing. Brandeis the reformer, the people's lawyer, was born. From these years forward, his life was markedly different, and his fame was acquired.

He testified before the House Ways and Means Committee against the Dingley tariff bill of 1897, as spokesman, in his own words, for the consumers and workingmen of New England. He fought against public transportation franchises obtained by the Boston Elevated Railway Company, and for lower utility rates. He investigated life insurance practices as counsel to a New England Policy-Holders' Protective Committee at about the same time as Charles Evans Hughes was doing it officially in New York. He invented, and did not rest until he put into effect in Massachusetts, a system of savings-bank life insurance. Over nearly a decade, he continually exposed what he considered the mismanagement of the New Haven Railroad, and fought the attempt of J. P. Morgan to establish through it a consolidated transportation system in New England. Victory finally came when Attorney General James C. McReynolds obtained a consent decree dissolving the New Haven empire.

Brandeis also denounced the monopolistic practices, as he viewed them, of the United Shoe Machinery Company, although in prior years the company had been one of his clients. In 1908, he argued and won *Muller* v. *Oregon*,[201] sustaining the constitutionality of a ten-hour law for women. His brief, which received special commendation from the Supreme Court, collected information and opinion tending to demonstrate the reasonableness of the legislation in an effort to support its constitutionality, not merely by reasoning from judicial precedents, but by bringing home to the judges the climate of fact and opinion in which it was enacted. This kind of presentation eventually became standard, and is known as the Brandeis brief. A few years later, Brandeis also obtained from the Supreme Court a *per curiam* judgment upholding another maximum-hour law for women, and just before his nomination, argued and won two more such cases.[202]

He played a central role in the investigation in 1910 of the conservation policies of Taft's first Secretary of the Interior, which ultimately drove that official from office. This was a major political event. Mediating a garment workers' strike in New York, he negotiated and gained the approval of the parties to a protocol which had far-reaching and enduring consequences in the industry, even though it remained in effect itself only for a few years. He was counsel for shippers in a general rate investigation before the Interstate Commerce Commission in 1910–11. In a subsequent, connected proceeding, he acted as counsel to the commission. And, as we have seen, he had a most prominent part between 1911 and 1914 in the various hearings on antitrust policy that followed the decision of the *Standard Oil* and *Tobacco* cases and pre-

---

[201] 208 U.S. 412 (1908).
[202] Hawley v. Walker, 232 U.S. 718 (1914); Miller v. Wilson, 236 U.S. 373 (1915); Bosley v. McLaughlin, 236 U.S. 385 (1915).

ceded passage of the Clayton and Federal Trade Commission Acts. Late in the proceedings against the American Tobacco Company, he had represented an association of independents.

For his work on most of these varied and complex matters, which increasingly took up his time, Brandeis accepted no fees. And he fought hard, very hard. He was "knocking heads right and left," he said himself rather gleefully about one episode. Nothing was spared, and Brandeis was not wary of offending. He was, in most of these controversies, not so much the people's attorney as a prosecutor in their behalf, with something of the wrath of an Old Testament prophet, and he showed no fear, no favor, and very little consideration. He was, indeed, ruthless in his righteousness. Contending with the Taft Administration over the Interior Department's conservation policy, for example, he was not loath to charge the President and the Attorney General with misrepresentation. Taft thought Brandeis' conduct unfair if not unethical. In the course of the Stanley Committee hearings on the United States Steel Corporation, Brandeis brought up a half-a-million-dollar necklace that Judge Gary had bought his wife for Christmas, and remarked that this was the sort of thing that had led to the French Revolution. Gary felt injured. "I thought," he said, that Brandeis "was a bigger man." Brandeis achieved glorious victories, but, as he would find, they were not easily forgiven.[203]

By 1910, Brandeis was a major national figure. During the next few years, his direct political involvement and activity increased, and he became even more widely known, so that in 1916, he was incomparably a more famous man than any of those recently named to the Court, saving only Hughes. Brandeis had voted for Taft in 1908, but soon became disenchanted and formed a personal and political alliance with Robert M. La Follette. Their collaboration produced the La Follette bill to supplement the Sherman Act, which Brandeis put forward at the antitrust hearings of 1911–14, and of which the Clayton Act of 1914 was a highly attenuated version.

Brandeis supported La Follette's candidacy for the Republican Presidential nomination, going on a speaking tour for him in the Middle West in 1911, and continuing to work in his behalf well into 1912. Following the collapse of the La Follette boom and the choice of Wilson by the Democrats, Brandeis, parting company with many other Progressives, who flocked to Theodore Roosevelt, publicly endorsed Wilson. Early in August 1912, Brandeis wrote Wilson commending his position on the tariff, and late that month, at Wilson's initiative, the two men held their historic first meeting, which deeply affected Wilson's antitrust views and established their relationship on an enduring basis.

---

[203] Mason, *Brandeis*, 35, 289, 361, 691, and 1–362 *passim;* Pringle, *Taft,* I, 510–14, II, 952; see *supra,* pp. 121, 132 *et seq.,* 147, n.168.

Brandeis campaigned hard for Wilson, both in the pages of *Collier's*, edited by his friend Norman Hapgood, and on the stump.

Through the winter months of 1913, before Wilson's inauguration, the newspapers were full of stories of Brandeis' imminent appointment as Attorney General or Secretary of Commerce. He was in fact Wilson's first choice for the one place and then for the other. But the published stories produced formidable opposition, seconded in Wilson's entourage by Colonel House. There was broad and passionate support for Brandeis from Progressives of both parties, but the opponents prevailed. The attacks on Brandeis were personal and ideological, with a leavening of anti-Semitism, as in this published assessment: "Brandeis is Gompers, Goldman [Emma, the anarchist], and Gyp the Blood rolled into one, and given a degree from Harvard. . . . Brandeis does not represent America." Brandeis' professional ethics were called into question, and even Ezra Ripley Thayer, the dean of the Harvard Law School, who had been an associate in Brandeis' law office for a time, wrote privately for Wilson's information: "Lots of the talk which is going about concerning him is rubbish, or worse. The most serious criticism to which he is open, *me judice*, would refer to unfair fighting. It is the adversary who has most to complain of." The entire leadership of the Democratic party in Massachusetts, in and out of office, protested to Wilson that whatever else Brandeis might or might not stand for, he did not represent the Massachusetts Democracy.

Although he succumbed to Brandeis' enemies, Wilson remained Brandeis' friend. Brandeis was one of Wilson's closest and most influential advisers, continuously called upon. He played a decisive role in formulating administration policy with respect to the Federal Reserve Act and to the Clayton Antitrust and Federal Trade Commission Acts. Meanwhile, in 1913, Brandeis began publishing in *Harper's Weekly* a series of articles called "Breaking the Money Trust," which were later put out in book form as *Other People's Money—And How the Bankers Use It*. During these years also Brandeis became actively involved in the Zionist movement.[204]

His mind made up on the daring, challenging step of nominating Brandeis, Wilson did not bother to prepare the ground by informing any Senators ahead of time, save possibly Robert M. La Follette. He made sure that Brandeis would accept, and then, no more than two or three days later, he acted. The response, public and private, was an instantaneous explosion, from friend and foe alike, but particularly from foes. The *New York Sun* considered Brandeis "utterly and even ridiculously unfit" for a place in the body that was "the stronghold of sane conserva-

---

[204] See Mason, *Brandeis*, 365–464; *supra*, pp. 136–37, 142; Link, *Wilson:*   *The New Freedom*, 10–15, 95, 212–13, 423 *et seq.*

tism, the safeguard of our institutions, the ultimate interpreter of our fundamental law." The *New York Press* thought the appointment "an insult to members of the Supreme Court." The *Wall Street Journal* could hardly believe its ears: "In all the anti-corporation agitation of the past years one name stands out conspicuous above all others. Where others were radical he was rabid; where others were extreme he was super-extreme; where others would trim he would lay the ax to the root of the tree." And now this man, "without previous judicial training," was given "the highest office in the gift of the Executive"!

The *Detroit Free Press* said: "Of all the Americans who have passed before the public view in the last ten years Louis D. Brandeis is in temperament and training perhaps the least fit for the calm, cold dispassionate work of the Supreme Court of the United States. . . . It is the solemn duty of the Senate to reject the nomination. . . ." The *New York Times* spoke more moderately, but in similar distress. Justices of the Supreme Court were appointed "for their learning, their upright-ness, and their independence, not because of their preconceived and known opinions." This nomination was an altogether deplorable attempt to "pack" the Court. "It need never be said, and cannot rightly be said that the Court needs among its members some advocate of 'social justice.' " Later on, after Brandeis was confirmed, the *Times* would lucidly state the essence of the case against him, which was that he held the wrong "preconceived and known opinions":

> The Supreme Court, by its very nature, must be a conservative body; it is the conservator of our institutions, it protects the people against the errors of their legislative servants, it is the defender of the Consti-tution itself. To place on the supreme Bench judges who hold a different view of the function of the Court, to supplant conservatism by radicalism, would be to undo the work of John Marshall and strip the Constitution of its defenses. It would introduce endless confusion where order has reigned, it would tend to give force and effect to any whim or passion of the hour, to crown with success any transitory agitation engaged in by a part of the people, overriding the mature judgment of all the people as expressed in their fundamental law.

Colonel House, off in London, was appalled. Elihu Root wrote to Senator Henry Cabot Lodge that confirmation would "be a deplorable injury to the Court, for the man is intellectually acute and morally blind. He has no moral sense." A Boston lawyer wrote to Lodge:

> I knew him some twenty-five years ago, when the influence of Sam Warren got him into the Dedham Polo Club. It was a club of gentle-men, and Brandeis was soon conspicuously left to "flock by himself" with the result that he ceased to frequent the club and his absence was

not regretted. . . . Is it not an extraordinary spectacle that is before the country? A candidate for the Supreme Court on trial, to determine whether or not he is a dishonorable, tainted knave. . . . Of course he has been clever enough to cover his tracks, and I look to see his vile face, grinning hypocrisy over his judicial gown. . . . I shall despair of the Republic if he gets the place. *Don't let him!!!*

But nobody's distress or despair quite equaled that of William Howard Taft. "I have no comment to make," said the ex-President, now Kent Professor of Constitutional Law at Yale, to reporters. However, to his good friend Gus Karger, a Washington newspaperman, he wrote:

Our worthy President has developed more qualities of Machiavelli than even I, with a full appreciation of the admirable roundness of his character, had suspected. When I think of the devilish ingenuity manifested in the selection of Brandeis, I cannot but admire his finesse. Of course, joking aside, it is one if the deepest wounds I have had as an American and a lover of the Constitution and a believer in progressive conservatism, that such a man as Brandeis could be put in the Court, as I believe he is likely to be.

He is a muckraker, an emotionalist for his own purposes, a socialist, prompted by jealousy, a hypocrite, a man who has certain high ideals in his imagination, but who is utterly unscrupulous in method in reaching them, a man of infinite cunning, of great tenacity of purpose, and, in my judgment, of much power for evil. He is only one out of nine on the Court, but one on the Court is often an important consideration; and even if the rest of the Court is against him, he has the opportunity to attack their judgments and weaken their force by insidious demagoguery, and an appeal to the restless element that can do infinite harm. . . .

When you consider Brandeis' appointment, and think that men were pressing me for the place, *es ist zum lachen.* You know me well enough to know that my judgment on this subject is not in the slightest degree colored by the fact that men had suggested me for the place. I never for one moment credited the possibility of Wilson's considering my name. The thoughts of the Judges of the Supreme Court, if they could be interpreted, would form interesting language. . . .

To his brother Henry, a lawyer in New York, Taft added: "I hope White will not end his judicial career with an apoplectic fit caused by the nomination." Some weeks later, Taft was writing to Henry Cabot Lodge:

In the last ten years of bitter attack upon the courts and the exploitation of various nostrums and hostility against our social order, it was to be expected that under an opportunist President, such as we now have, some traits of the hysteria would appear in the personnel of the Supreme Court.

I am an optimist, and therefore even Brandeis' elevation to the Court and taking part in its decisions will not discourage me. Still it is an evil and a disgrace that ought to be avoided.

Later yet, Taft found the ultimate right word for Brandeis. He was a "nightmare."

The opposition was not alone in grasping the full significance of the appointment. A Progressive newspaper in Los Angeles joyfully announced that Wilson had given the Supreme Court "its first thoroughgoing radical. . . ." It was "good to think that there will be at least one Judge on the Supreme Court Bench who sets humanity above all else and who will interpret the Constitution in terms of manhood rather than of property." Another California paper remarked: "No student of history can mistake the meaning of the first man of the Brandeis type coming to Supreme Court honors." The editors of *The Progressive Farmer*, a Southern weekly, informed Senator William E. Borah of Idaho:

> Men famous as attorneys of great trusts and monopolies, famous for their close alliance with gigantic moneyed interests, have frequently been given high judicial positions in this country, but Louis D. Brandeis is perhaps the first man ever appointed to the United States Supreme Court whose chief fame rests upon his championship of the rights of labor and the working man.

Robert La Follette, of course, rejoiced, and so did Senator Benjamin Tillman of South Carolina. Said Tillman: "Too proud to fight, is he [Wilson]? I guess this shows he isn't afraid to offend the predatory interests, which always have had too much influence in the appointment of Supreme Court Justices."[205]

In the midst of this clamor, which made it evident that confirmation would not come easily, if at all, both sides girded for battle. Within the week, the general solicitor and a member of the board of directors of the United States Steel Corporation were in Boston organizing opposition. The treasurer of the United Shoe Machinery Company had traveled to Washington and New York for the same purpose. In New

---

[205] Mason, *Brandeis*, 465–66; B. C. La Follette and F. La Follette, *Robert M. La Follette* (1953), I, 567–68; Link, *Wilson: Confusions and Crises*, 325–26; Todd, *Justice on Trial*, 69– 82, 128, 129–30, 175–76, 181, 235, 242; *The Progressive Farmer* to W. E. Borah, Feb. 5, 1916, Borah Papers, Library of Congress.

York, George W. Wickersham, Taft's Attorney General, joined in. By February 11, less than two weeks after the nomination, a Boston remonstance had been produced and published, opposing Brandeis on the ground that he lacked "judicial temperament and capacity," and that his "reputation as a lawyer is such that he has not the confidence of the people." The remonstrance was signed by fifty-five Bostonians, including A. Lawrence Lowell, the president of Harvard, Charles Francis Adams, treasurer of Harvard, a Weld, a Sargeant, a Gardner, a Peabody, a Bowditch, a Putnam, a Shattuck, and a Coolidge. Austen G. Fox, a prominent Harvard alumnus at the New York Bar, was employed to present the case against Brandeis in behalf of the remonstrators before a subcommittee of the Senate Committee on the Judiciary which had opened hearings on February 9.

Brandeis was in Washington on the day of the nomination to attend a dinner for President Wilson, given by Secretary of the Treasury William G. McAdoo. The guests included Hughes, Pitney, and, of all people, McReynolds. "I have nothing whatever to say," Brandeis told the press. "I have not said anything and will not." Three days later, in New York, a reporter for the *New York Sun* asked: "Have you heard that charges have been made to Senators concerning your relations with the United Shoe Machinery Company . . . the Lennox case, and the Warren will case?" Brandeis replied: "No, I have not. I have nothing to say about anything, and that goes for all time and to all newspapers, including both *The Sun* and the moon."

Privately, Brandeis had quite a bit to say. He sent a list of probable supporters of the nomination to Norman Hapgood. On February 2, Brandeis was back in Washington meeting with a Democratic member of the Senate subcommittee that was to hold hearings. The next day, he saw George W. Anderson, U.S. Attorney in Boston, and it was agreed, after consulting Attorney General Gregory, that Anderson would manage Brandeis' side of the case at the hearings, calling witnesses, presenting evidence, and cross-examining the opposition. Brandeis himself would return to Boston. His partner, Edward F. McClennen, would remain in Washington to represent Brandeis and assist Anderson. In Boston, another partner, George R. Nutter, would help.[206]

The Senate subcommittee hearings, which had opened before the preparations were quite complete on either side, were to run, with interruptions, for forty days, until March 8, and then resume for two more days on March 14–15. Hardly a significant aspect of Brandeis' professional career escaped scrutiny, and many an insignificant one was sub-

---

[206] Mason, *Brandeis*, 466–69, 472–73; Todd, *Justice on Trial*, 89–90, 95, 106–107, 112–13, 119.

jected to it. As John P. Frank has shown, many of the charges lodged against Brandeis were entirely without foundation. Thus an Iowa railroad commissioner who, with Brandeis, had taken part in certain railroad rate proceedings before the Interstate Commerce Commission—called the Five Percent Rate Hearings—in 1913–14, claimed that Brandeis had betrayed the interests he was supposed to represent by conceding that the railroads' net revenues were too low. But Brandeis had been retained by the commission, to act as its counsel in a quasi-judicial capacity, and he represented, therefore, no interests that he could have betrayed in this fashion. Moreover, he had suggested that railroad revenues were too low because of mismanagement and waste on the part of the railroads themselves, and had urged no rate increase.

Again, Brandeis' firm had been employed to help in a proxy fight for control of the Illinois Central Railroad. The retainer had come from New York lawyers who represented E. H. Harriman, and the charge was that Brandeis had thus, for profit, aided the very interests that he attacked in his public activities. But, of course, a lawyer need not restrict himself to the representation only of clients with whom he is in full agreement on political, social, and economic matters. In another case, in which public and private interests coincided for Brandeis, he represented a stockholder of the Boston and Maine Railroad in opposing a merger with the New Haven. Because of the coincidence of this professional activity with his public position, Brandeis declined a retainer. But, estimating his services as worth $25,000, and not wishing to deprive his partners of such a fee on account of his personal public commitments, he paid $25,000 of his own money into the firm. This perhaps quixotic act was regarded with deep suspicion by Senators who failed to understand the reasons for it.

Among further accusations utterly without substance were charges that Brandeis had represented the liquor industry in a legislative hearing in Massachusetts in 1890, and that at another time he had argued that the merger of two retail drug chains did not violate the Sherman Act. These were simply two episodes in an extensive law practice, which proved nothing except that Brandeis had practiced law.

There were some objections taken to Brandeis' conduct while at the bar that—again, as John P. Frank has well shown—had at least the appearance of seriousness, and were in one or two instances plausible, although in no instance unanswerable.

Brandeis had represented a major stockholder of the New England Railroad in bringing certain suits attacking management practices. The suits were filed in behalf of a nominal stockholder, rather than of the real party in interest. Brandeis' connection with these suits ended in 1893, and sometime later, the New Haven Railroad, interested, of course, in taking over the New England, and hoping to weaken it to that

end, began to underwrite the litigation. Brandeis, it was said, sued in
the name of a fictitious party. Moreover, he took a position in conflict
with his supposed desire to thwart a New Haven Railroad monopoly in
New England. But the practice of suing in behalf of a nominal—and as
such, real—stockholder was perfectly legal, common, and considered
ethical enough, even if perhaps unfortunate from the point of view of
public policy. Brandeis' clients were as entitled to the benefit of this
practice as anyone else. As for the New Haven interest, it entered into
the picture after Brandeis was out of it.

While Brandeis, as unpaid counsel to a Shareholder's Protective
Committee, was investigating various insurance companies, his firm
often represented one of these companies, the Equitable Life Assurance
Society, and defended it against a suit alleging mismanagement practices
very much like the ones that Brandeis was uncovering in his investigation. But the positions that a lawyer may take as a public figure need not
govern his firm's choice of clients, and even an insurance company
whose practices might on investigation appear to be questionable is
entitled to representation, and to defense in court when those practices
are attacked in a lawsuit.

In the Congressional hearings dealing with the conservation policies
of Taft's Secretary of the Interior, Brandeis, it was alleged, while appearing in the guise of a public-spirited lawyer, had in fact received
a $25,000 fee from *Collier's*, which had initially published the attacks
on the Secretary that led to the investigation. Brandeis did earn a fee,
but there had never been any dissimulation about it.

After the death of the father of Samuel D. Warren, Brandeis' first
law partner, Brandeis set up a trust agreement under which Samuel
Warren and another part-owner managed the family paper business for
the benefit of all members of the family. Later there was a squabble, and
Brandeis was counsel for the family against a dissident member. An
entirely unfounded charge was made that in the initial arrangement,
Samuel Warren and Brandeis perpetrated some sort of fraud. A second
more serious charge was that Brandeis, representing the trust, could
not properly also represent some of the beneficiaries against another.
A real problem would have arisen if in some fashion the interests of
the trust and of the beneficiaries whom Brandeis represented had
diverged. But they did not.

In the fall of 1907, the owners of a tannery in Boston, Patrick and
James Lennox, came to Brandeis, accompanied by counsel for a New
York creditor of theirs. It appeared that they were unable to satisfy
all their creditors, and Brandeis, whose advice was being sought, suggested that a solution to their difficulties, which might keep them out
of bankruptcy, would be to make an assignment of their assets to a
trustee for the benefit of creditors. This was done, and a partner of

Brandeis acted as the trustee. Eventually there was trouble. The Lennoxes sought to conceal some of their assets, Brandeis' partner, as trustee for the creditors, resisted, and bankruptcy proceedings were commenced. The charge was that Brandeis had undertaken to represent the Lennoxes and had then turned against them. But in truth he had never undertaken to represent them. He had suggested a course of action to them which they adopted. As a result, his partner undertook a fiduciary obligation, not to them, but to their creditors.

It was in connection with this case that Brandeis, at the time, struck off the famous phrase that he was acting as "counsel for the situation." Perhaps the Lennoxes had not understood Brandeis' position quite precisely enough when they agreed to an assignment for the benefit of creditors, and perhaps Brandeis was at fault in not making the position sufficiently clear to them. No doubt it is true also that to assume the role of counsel for the situation is to saddle oneself with uncommonly delicate ethical problems. And it is to invite misunderstanding. A more cautious, less self-assured, or perhaps less self-righteous man might not have wished to play such a role. But having taken it, Brandeis fell into no ethical errors.

Finally, there was the United Shoe Machinery matter. This was an old story. Whenever, in the hearings on antitrust problems between 1911 and 1914, Brandeis had dealt with the monopolistic practices, as he viewed them, of the United Shoe Machinery Company—and he had often done so—charges of inconsistencies in his position and of conflict of interest had been brought up, and Brandeis had defended himself against them. Now they were repeated. Brandeis for some years was a director of United and did some legal work for it. In a legislative hearing in Massachusetts in 1906, he defended the restrictive leases under which the company licensed use of its patented machinery. But by the end of that year, he resigned his directorship, and after 1907 had nothing further to do with the United Company. Nearly four years later, Brandeis attacked United's leases. He had changed his position because, in common with shoe manufacturers, he had come to believe that the leases were unfair and represented attempts to acquire monopoly power, because a recent lower-court decision under the Sherman Act had convinced him that the leases were in restraint of trade—even though the Supreme Court ultimately found them legal—and because, no doubt, he had simply reconsidered, and now saw United's practices in a different light.

It was intimated that Brandeis had changed sides for no reason other than that he was offered larger fees by interests adverse to United. This allegation was simply false. Was it unethical, nevertheless, to abandon a client for whatever reason, and then to enter the lists against him? There was no indication that Brandeis had used against United knowledge he had gained while in a confidential relationship with it—which would, of course, have been quite wrong. A retainer does not bind forever, although it is arguable that on the same matter it should. But when the matter is one of public importance, there is perhaps as much to be said for fidelity to a lawyer's duty and conviction, however newly formed, as a public man, as for loyalty to a private, professional connection which has been severed. Motive is crucial to the ethical judgment that is called for by the Shoe Machinery matter, and there is no reason to doubt that Brandeis' motives were selfless and pure.

Brandeis' own view of all these charges, expressed privately to McClellen, was not far off the mark. Brandeis felt "that our position is not one of apology; but on the contrary in regard to nearly every one of these transactions, we have taken a very much higher standard than ordinarily prevails, and I feel very strongly that that point of view should be emphasized and that harm has been done by allowing an attitude of apparent apology or defense when our real position is one of insisting upon a higher standard than generally prevails." It is also true that many, although not all, of those who now appeared against him had been bested by him in one or another combat, and that they could scarcely be credited with a judicious or detached attitude toward him. And quite a few of the charges worked at cross purposes. One day Brandeis violated professional ethics by being too impartial, above the adversary battle, insufficiently mindful of the interests of his clients, and another day he was too much the professional adversary, taking his clients as they came and seeking every advantage for them, regardless of his own appraisal of them and their affairs and of any clash with his own principles. He was either too much the judge and too little the lawyer, or it was precisely the other way around.

Sherman L. Whipple of the Boston Bar, who had opposed Brandeis in the later stages of the *Lennox* case, probably put his finger on one reason for the widespread ambivalence about Brandeis. If Brandeis had been "a different sort of man," said Whipple, "not so aloof, not so isolated, with more of the comradery of the Bar, gave his confidence to more men, and took their confidence, said to them when he was charged with anything that was doubtful, 'Boys, what do you think about it?' and talked it over with them—you would not have heard the things you have heard in regard to him." Brandeis, Whipple continued, rested "in the security of the purity of his own mind and the purity of his own purposes. . . . He never consults anybody; he gives little thought as to how it is going to affect the mind or minds of other men, and sometimes I have thought he took a delight in smashing a bit the traditions of the Bar, which most of us revere. . . ."

Arthur G. Hill, another Boston lawyer, at least equally perceptive, told the Senate subcommittee:

There is little question that he [Brandeis] is not generally popular with the Bar, and among a considerable proportion of lawyers here he has the reputation of not being a man with whom it is pleasant to deal in business matters, and one who is unscrupulous in regard to his professional conduct. . . . I believe that the reputation to which I have referred is not founded so much on anything that Mr. Brandeis has done as it is on other causes. He is a radical and has spent a large part, not only of his public, but of his professional career, in attacking established institutions, and this alone would, in my judgment, account for a very large part of his unpopularity. It would be very difficult, if not impossible, for a radical to be generally popular with Boston lawyers, or to escape severe adverse criticism of his motives and conduct. . . . When you add to this that Mr. Brandeis is an outsider, successful, and a Jew, you have, I think, sufficiently explained most of the feeling against him.

Privately, however, Hill added that Brandeis' unpopularity with the bar was attributable also to "a certain hard and unsympathetic quality which is largely racial."

He has no power of feeling or understanding the position of an opponent, and none of that spirit of playing the game with courtesy and good-nature which is part of the standard of the Anglo-Saxon. He fights to win, and fights up to the limit of his rights with a stern and even cruel exultation in the defeat of his adversary. It is not for nothing that in the Old Testament there isn't a word from beginning to end of admiration for a gallant enemy.

The Old Testament ruthlessness would give way somewhat once Brandeis found his bearings on the Court, but a degree of self-righteousness, a certain "pride and self-deification," in a phrase of Professor Alpheus T. Mason, would remain. In Brandeis the advocate and people's lawyer these qualities were certainly prominent, they assuredly made enemies, and however admirable in some manifestations, are not entirely attractive even in retrospect.[207] Elihu Root felt that

---

[207] In October 1911, Felix Frankfurter, in Washington as assistant to Secretary of War Henry L. Stimson, started (but soon abandoned) a diary in which he recorded his impressions of the many prominent men he was meeting. With Brandeis, Frankfurter was on the threshold of what was to become an intimate friendship. He lunched with him, on one of Brandeis' trips to Washington, on Oct. 20, 1911. Brandeis, he noted, had "depth," "great force," was "a very big man, one of the most penetrating minds I know," and had "Lincoln's fundamental sympathies." But he wished, Frankfurter added, that Brandeis also had Lincoln's "patience, his magnanimity, his humor." Frankfurter Diary, Frankfurter Papers, Library of Congress.

Brandeis had "no moral sense." But if there was a difficulty, it was precisely the opposite: he had a high moral sense, markedly individual, self-contained, and all too often brought to the forefront of daily concerns in a large practice.[208]

There can be no question but that the free-floating distrust and suspicion so well understood by Arthur G. Hill were prevalent at the Boston Bar. "What is the general professional reputation of Mr. Brandeis?" a member of the Senate subcommittee asked Hollis R. Bailey, a Boston lawyer. "First, that he is a very able lawyer," ran the answer, "that he is a man of keen intellect; that he is an able advocate; that he is not entirely trustworthy. I think that about covers it." Albert Pillsbury, also of the Boston Bar, said that Brandeis had the reputation of being "active, adroit," a "man of unbounded audacity," a "man, I should say, of duplicity, double-dealing; a man who works under cover. . . ." Brandeis, Pillsbury thought, "appeared very often in the category of a friend of the people and has very often been reputed to be under pay." Could Pillsbury point to a specific instance? That he could not. "I know nothing about the facts."

Such suspicions were further incited, although in no way substantiated, by a statement of six past presidents of the American Bar Association and the incumbent president, which Austen Fox triumphantly read on the next to last day of the Senate subcommittee hearings. From the beginning, Senator Henry Cabot Lodge had urged the bar to assert itself if it wished the nomination defeated. George W. Wickersham, in close consultation with Taft, had organized the signers. It had been a time-consuming task, and difficult. Not by any means all living past Bar Association presidents had signed. Among those who had not were Jacob M. Dickinson, Taft's Secretary of War, Alton B. Parker of New York, the Democratic Presidential candidate of 1904, Frank B. Kellogg, the *Steel* case prosecutor and future Secretary of State, and Frederick W. Lehmann, Taft's Solicitor General. But Elihu Root, the incumbent president, did sign. So, of course, did Taft, and Simeon E. Baldwin, Joseph H. Choate, Peter W. Meldrim, Francis Rawle, and Moorfield Storey. They all felt "under the painful duty to say" that "in their opinion, taking into view the reputation, character, and professional career of Mr. Louis D. Brandeis, he is not a fit person to be a member of the Supreme Court of the United States."

---

[208] J. P. Frank, "The Legal Ethics of Louis D. Brandeis," *Stanford L. Rev.*, 17:683, 1965; *Clapp Hearings*, I, 2159, 2170 *et seq.*, 2256 *et seq.*, 2615 *et seq.*, 2652–53; *Hearings, House Judiciary Committee on Trust Legislation*, 62nd Cong., 2nd Sess., Ser. No. 2 (Jan. 26, 27, Feb. 19, 1912), 111–29; Mason, *Brandeis*, 475, 478–79, 483, 487–89, 491–92; Todd, *Justice on Trial*, 87, 145.

These expressions of distrust were in some measure offset by a letter sent to the subcommittee late in the game, on May 17, 1916, by the Olympian Charles W. Eliot, aged President Emeritus of Harvard, an old acquaintance of Brandeis, who wrote of Brandeis' "quick and generous sympathies . . . gentleness, courage and joy in combat. . . ." They were offset also by warm expressions of support for Brandeis from all but one of the members of the Harvard Law School faculty. Yet the atmosphere of suspicion lingered, and it constituted the most effective argument against Brandeis' confirmation. As President Lowell of Harvard put it to Senator Lodge:

> It is difficult—perhaps impossible—to get direct evidence of any act by Brandeis that is, strictly speaking, dishonest; and yet a man who was believed by all the better part of the bar to be unscrupulous ought not to be a member of the highest court of the nation.

Even Holmes was sensitive to this point. On May 14, he wrote to Lewis Einstein:

> Brandeis' matter drags along, and I don't know what will happen. You met him at our house one night and I thought didn't fancy him, though of course you didn't say so. He always left on me the impression of a good man when he called. And I have never fully fathomed the reasons for the strong prejudice against him shown by other good men.
> Whatever happens it is a misfortune for the Court, for the time being. If he is turned down the proletariat will say only tools of the plutocrats can get in. (Though the p's don't favor me, you may bet.) If he gets in many people will think that the character of the Court no longer is above question.
> Well I always can hop off if I don't like it but having kept on a good time so far I should like to keep going until eighty.

To another friend, Holmes said of Brandeis:

> There may have been things that I should criticize. I didn't like his mode of conducting the Ballinger [Taft's Secretary of the Interior] case, and formerly he seemed to me to wish to sink the few. But we all have foibles—and the total impression that I have received, as I say, has been that of a man whom I respected and admired subject to the inquiry why it was that other good men were down on him.[209]

Brandeis' matter did drag on, and quite dangerously to his prospects. Supporters of the nomination feared that it would die of inaction,

---

[209] *Ibid.*, 86–87, 90, 92, 107, 110, 132–33, 148, 159–60, 220–21, 228–29.

without coming to a vote. Brandeis himself, for the first time in his life, was in a fight without being at the scene of battle, and he did not take easily to the novel experience. He kept in close touch, and as his detractors passed in review down in Washington, he sought to identify in his and their common past the sources of their enmity. Not unnaturally, he credited them with little, if any, good faith or capacity for detachment. He was not entirely happy, as we have seen, with the somewhat apologetic tone, as it struck him, of his defenders. He felt perfectly confident that his record must appear unassailable to any fair-minded man, and the attacks inflicted no wounds. Then, as before and later, the man's spiritual armor was a marvel. "I suppose," he wrote his brother Alfred, "eighteen centuries of Jewish persecution must have enured me to such hardships and developed the like of a duck's back."

But he did get impatient, especially when the hearings were resumed for another two days after having apparently been concluded. It was time, he thought, for Attorney General Gregory to speak out. The Attorney General had devised the strategy that kept Brandeis in Boston, supposedly aloof, but if this strategy was going to misfire into undue delay, and if Gregory was going to sit by and do nothing, then Brandeis "would rather go down and testify." But the Gregory strategy prevailed, in accord with what was the traditional practice in Supreme Court nominations.

On April 3, the subcommittee reported. The members were William E. Chilton of West Virginia, chairman, Duncan U. Fletcher of Florida, and Thomas J. Walsh of Montana, all Democrats, and Albert B. Cummins of Iowa and John D. Works of California, Republicans.[210]

The strong men among these were Walsh, one of the ablest Democrats in the Senate, later a leading figure in the Teapot Dome investigation of the early twenties, and Franklin D. Roosevelt's Attorney General-designate before his sudden death in 1933; and Cummins, formerly a Progressive governor of Iowa and an Insurgent during the Taft Administration. The subcommittee divided 3 to 2 in favor of confirmation, along strict party lines. Its report was voluminous. The majority dealt with the specific charges against Brandeis, and dismissed them one by one. Walsh, in a separate concurrence, added: "The real crime of which this man is guilty is that he has exposed the inequities of men in high places in our financial system. He has not stood in awe of the majesty of wealth. . . ." Countering the potent argument that whatever might be proved one way or the other concerning specific charges, Brandeis was a

---

[210] Clarence D. Clark of Wyoming —an acquaintance of Van Devanter, of course, but not particularly close to him—had been on the subcommittee initially, but had withdrawn.

man not above suspicion, and for that reason unfit for the Supreme Court, Walsh said:

> It is easy for a brilliant lawyer so to conduct himself as to escape calumny and vilification. All he needs to do is to drift with the time. If he never assails the doer of evil who stands high in the market place, either in court or before the public, he will have no enemies or detractors or none that he need heed.

Cummins and Works, for the minority, each filed a report, dismissing some of the charges against Brandeis, to be sure, but expressing sufficient misgivings about other ones to justify their votes. As counsel for the Interstate Commerce Commission in the Five Percent Rate Hearings, Cummins argued, Brandeis betrayed a public trust by conceding that the railroads were not earning sufficient net revenues. In the United Shoe Machinery episode, Brandeis should not have attacked a former client, and in the Lennox affair, his conduct was "an unseemly spectacle." Works covered much the same ground, and both men, while professing admiration for Brandeis' abilities and agreement with many of his positions on public policy, declared that their confidence in him was impaired.

Cummins' emphasis on the charges concerning the Five Percent Rate Hearings reflected Western suspicions that Brandeis was just another Eastern city slicker. And Cummins had special reasons for voicing these suspicions. The state railroad commissioner who first made the Five Percent Rate charges was from Iowa, and *Wallace's Farmer*, an influential weekly published in Iowa, opposed Brandeis. There was support, indeed enthusiasm, for Brandeis in the West, too, but Cummins was not alone among Progressive Republican Senators in being, at least ostensibly, troubled by the Five Percent Rate Cases, and what they might suggest. So, for example, was William E. Borah of Idaho.

To an important constituent who had urged him to support Brandeis, Borah wrote that in the Five Percent Hearings, Brandeis was supposed "to represent the public as a whole, and in my judgment there never was a time in the case when he could represent anyone except the public. If the time came when he believed that the railroads were right and were entitled to the raise of $50 million, it was his duty if he was going to change his position at all to withdraw as an attorney in the case. But the charge is that he did not withdraw but that assuming to represent the public his argument took the precise position which the railroads took." (Of course, to represent the public meant to represent the public interest, and the public interest might well call for higher railroad revenues. Moreover, Brandeis did not take the precise position which the railroads took.)

IV: *Appointment Cycles*

Borah had more general misgivings of the same sort:

> There is one other feature of the matter which I might call to your attention: I have been informed also that Mr. Brandeis is in favor of this modern scheme first formulated by some large trusts and manufacturies in the East, to-wit, the scheme of permitting all kinds of combinations, trusts and monopolies to be formed but to have some commission down here at Washington to regulate them; that he is opposed to competition, in favor of monopoly and trusts and combinations and that he is in favor of regulating them by some commission. Of course if that ever takes place in this country I need not say to you that it will not be very long until those who are supposed to be regulated will be regulating the regulators, to-wit, the commission. Now, Mr. Nichols, I have been opposing that scheme during my entire service in the Senate from time to time. I think it vicious and indefensible. I think it will destroy in time the government itself. In a very few years . . . all vital interests will be in the control of a few men and the only protection the people will have will be some commission down here at Washington which the interests have been largely instrumental in selecting. I do not know just what Mr. Brandeis' position is upon that subject but I know it is claimed that he is an earnest advocate of it. If that be true of course I would not vote for him.

The president of the Atchison, Topeka and Santa Fe Railway had once said, Borah added, that a man of Brandeis' ability could well serve the country on the Supreme Court of the United States—and what an ominous endorsement that was!

To be sure, Brandeis had never simply followed every Populist emotional current, and it was a good guess that he would not. He took a more detached and rational view of the public interest than that, he knew too much about the actual world of affairs, and he was too good a lawyer. But in his sympathies and convictions he stood with the Western antimonopoly Progressives, and it was an utter misrepresentation of his position to assimilate it to that of a George W. Perkins. Cummins, at least, who had been an active member of the Senate's Clapp Committee on antitrust policy in 1911–12, must have known as much. Borah for his part, though initially less well informed than Cummins perhaps, declined with some indignation an opportunity to meet Brandeis in the spring of 1916 and decide for himself what manner of man this was. Hence the plainly and ascertainably mistaken feeling that Brandeis was somehow not sound on the monopoly issue from the Western point of view must be regarded as a makeweight consideration.

There were other factors that led all but three of the non-Democratic Progressives in the Senate to join solid Republican opposition to Brandeis, and enabled them to persuade themselves that this man, whom the Eastern establishment attacked with such vehemence as a radical, was really a tool of big business, in the same fashion in which others could persuade themselves that this so-called political lawyer, accused of betraying his clients, was also a narrow professional who disregarded the public interest in the pursuit of advantages for the clients who employed him.

Republican Progressives were affected by the situation of their party in 1916, which was not at all what it had been four years before. Now, Theodore Roosevelt, hating Wilson's foreign policy and the man himself, was coming back into the fold, and the party was in search of a candidate who could unite it. Men were moving from both directions toward the center, where they ultimately found Hughes. Cummins himself, at this juncture, was not only moving with the general drift, but was himself seeking the nomination. The movement toward Republican unity, and a resumption of power after the Wilsonian aberration, which itself had resulted from extraordinary disunity in 1912, was not going to be allowed to founder on the issue of Brandeis. Particularly was this not going to be permitted as the Democrats themselves were making Brandeis a party issue. For the same Presidential politics that cost Brandeis Progressive votes he should have had, gained him all but one Democratic vote, in a remarkable display of party discipline and of Wilson's dominion.[211]

Nearly eight weeks passed between the action of the subcommittee and a vote in the full Senate Committee on the Judiciary, and then it was another week before the nomination finally reached the floor, a full four months after it had been made. Meanwhile all sorts of rumors circulated. One, heavily tinged with anti-Semitism, was that Wilson, before his recent marriage, had had an affair with a Mrs. Peck, and that a threatened suit for breach of promise had been settled "by Louis D. Brandeis of Boston, and Samuel Untermyer of New York, acting as Mr. Wilson's attorneys." There was, of course, not a speck of truth in the canard.

Another story which, Attorney General Gregory wrote Brandeis, was making the rounds of the Senate cloakroom, was that Brandeis did not believe in a written Constitution, and had said somewhere that the Constitution could not restrain the judges of the Supreme Court from responding to popular demands. This, Brandeis answered Gregory, was a deliberate lie. "I have not only not said any such thing, but not said

---

[211] Mason, *Brandeis*, 478, 483–87, 91–93, 501; Todd, *Justice on Trial*, 185–92; J. Holt, *Congressional Insurgents and the Party System* (1967), 155; W. E. Borah to H. C. Wallace, Feb. 1, 1916, to the *Progressive Farmer*, Feb. 7, 1916, to E. H. Berg, Feb. 9, 1916, and to L. O. Nichols, Feb. 23, 1916, William E. Borah Papers, Library of Congress.

anything which anybody could have distorted into such a statement. My views in regard to the Constitution are, as you know, very much those of Mr. Justice Holmes." Again, some Senators, having in mind *Buchanan* v. *Warley*,[212] a test of a Louisville, Kentucky, residential segregation ordinance, which had just been argued and restored to the docket for reargument in the Supreme Court, expressed fear that Brandeis would influence the Court to strike down the ordinance, although there was nothing particularly in his record to support such a surmise.

On May 8, Wilson's letter, quoted earlier, to the chairman of the Senate Committee on the Judiciary was published. George W. Anderson and other friends of Brandeis had urged that it be written, feeling in common with Brandeis that the greatest danger to confirmation was the impression of some Democratic Senators that perhaps Wilson, who had up to then kept almost entirely silent, would not really mind very much if the Senate rejected his nomination. Wilson's letter more than anything else made the Brandeis issue a party matter. It totally engaged Wilson's prestige, not only as President, but as the Democratic candidate in 1916.

On Sunday, May 14, at Norman Hapgood's apartment in Washington, Brandeis met and chatted with Senators James A. Reed, Democrat of Missouri, and Hoke Smith, Democrat of Georgia, both members of the Judiciary Committee. Reed was quite taken with Brandeis, and Hapgood thought that Smith also was "much mollified."[213] Henry Morgenthau, Sr., Wilson's former Ambassador to Turkey and a Democratic money raiser, also worked on Hoke Smith.[214] The President himself, on a trip to North Carolina, went out of his way to try to bring Senator Lee S. Overman of that state into line, and the administration brought full pressure to bear on everyone else it could reach. The upshot was that on May 24, the Judiciary Committee voted 10 to 8 for confirmation, on strict party lines, with no defections either way, and on June 1, the Senate followed suit, 47 to 22. Only one Democrat, Francis G. Newlands of Nevada, voted against Brandeis, and among the Re-

---

[212] See *infra*, pp. 789 *et seq.*

[213] Years later, running for reelection, Reed was accused of having opposed Brandeis as a Jew, and he asked the Justice to publish a denial. Brandeis would not do so in his own name, but had Norman Hapgood make a statement. "You will recall," Brandeis wrote Hapgood, "our [Reed and Brandeis] meeting at your apartment—and how handsomely he behaved after that." James A. Reed to Louis D. Brandeis, July 22, 1922, Brandeis to Norman Hapgood, July 24, 1922, Hapgood to Reed, July 27, 1922, Brandeis Papers, University of Louisville Law School Library.

[214] Earlier, just before the subcommittee reported, Morgenthau had had a brainstorm, and had dragged Brandeis down to New London to put to him the idea that he should decline the Supreme Court appointment, even if confirmed, and run for the Senate in Massachusetts against Henry Cabot Lodge. The idea was silly, and Brandeis politely rejected it. A. L. Todd, *Justice on Trial* (1964), 184–85.

publicans, only La Follette, George W. Norris of Nebraska, and Miles Poindexter, the Washington Progressive, voted for. It was a famous victory, of enduring significance. It was also, more immediately, in Professor Link's words, "the opening battle of the Presidential campaign, fought even before the party conventions had met."[215]

Brandeis took his seat on June 5, 1916. A crowded courtroom watched him stand to take the judicial oath, a lean figure just above average height, his hair graying and worn close-cropped at this time, the deep-set eyes intense. In later years it was often remarked that at certain angles the face had a Lincolnian cast, and perhaps it seemed so to friendly observers in that audience also. The Court sat once more, on June 12, during the October Term 1915, for delivery of opinions, and then adjourned. Brandeis, concerned that his considerable investments might disqualify him from taking part in some cases, had discussed his holdings with the Chief Justice, who advised him not to worry and not to make other dispositions. During the summer, which Brandeis spent as usual on Cape Cod, the President tried to draft him, as he had Lamar before, for a commission to deal with his continuing troubles with Mexico. Brandeis accepted subject to the approval of the Chief Justice, who disapproved, and so Brandeis finally declined.

Then in October, Brandeis moved to Washington, to begin a service of nearly twenty-three years, constituting unquestionably one of a very limited number of greatly influential careers on the Supreme Court since the establishment of the Republic. He was also, as even fewer of his predecessors and successors have been, one of the principal public men of his time. "His pursuit of reason and his love of beauty [this was Justice Frankfurter's assessment after Brandeis' death] were Hellenic. But Carlyle would never have said of Louis Brandeis what he said of Socrates, that Socrates was 'terribly at ease in Zion.' Justice Brandeis found it impossible to be at ease in Zion. The moral law was a goad. That was his Hebraic gift. It gave him ceaseless striving for perfection; it also gave him inner harmony."[216]

Clarke vice Hughes

The Presidential politics that played their part in the fight over the confirmation of Brandeis had begun to take shape as far back as

[215] Mason, *Brandeis,* 493–95, 497–505; Todd, *Justice on Trial,* 184–85, 202–203, 211, 224–26; Link, *Wilson: Confusions and Crises,* 356–62; A. S. Link, *Wilson: Campaigns for Progressivism and Peace* (1965), 143–44; Buchanan v. Warley, 245 U.S. 60 (1917).

[216] Mason, *Brandeis,* 511–13; I. Dilliard, ed., *Mr. Justice Brandeis—Great American* (1941), 126.

1913. Indeed, Hughes might have been nominated in 1912, had he not declared that he would under no circumstances accept. At that time, even Hughes would probably have been unable to keep Theodore Roosevelt out of the contest, and besides there was a matter of loyalty to Taft, despite the possibility that the latter would withdraw gracefully. By the summer of 1915, the talk of Hughes was incessant, privately and in the newspapers. Hughes indicated unmistakably that he would be neither an open nor a passive candidate, and when a move was made to put his name on the Nebraska preferential primary ballot, he threatened suit to have it removed.[217]

From the first, there were misgivings about making political approaches to a Justice of the Supreme Court. In 1912, Elihu Root, who as chairman of the Republican National Convention had received Hughes' declination of that year, had written Hughes: "I am clearly of the opinion that you took a wise and patriotic course. It seems to me that keeping the Supreme Court out of politics is more important than the presidency. It is a fine thing, my dear Judge, to be in a position where one is enabled to render such a service." I think, Holmes said in 1912, "a judge should extinguish such thoughts [of the Presidency] when he goes on the Bench." Taft felt much the same as late as 1914.

But as it became increasingly plain that Hughes alone among all possible candidates could reunite the Republican party, as a shared hatred of Wilson and a consequent passionate desire for victory pulled even Taft and Theodore Roosevelt somewhat together but not near enough for one to accept the other, and as the appointment of Brandeis drove Taft into a near frenzy, the misgivings receded. On April 11 and 13, 1916, Taft, in his own hand, wrote two long letters to Hughes urging his acceptance of a Republican nomination, and urging it with a fervor, as Taft himself said (he referred, actually, to his "candor," but that was a euphemism for the passion and intimacy of the letters), which seemed "unwarranted by our relations" but came "out of a full heart."

"I do not write . . . ," said Taft on April 11, "for a reply because I hope you will not send me one. I write to express a view to you contrary to that of Mr. Choate in his letter to the New York Times of yesterday.[218] I believe myself to be as anxious to keep the Supreme Court and the Supreme judges out of politics as anyone, but there are few

---

[217] "The Nebraskans who insisted on making Justice Hughes a presidential candidate," the *Washington Evening Star* commented, "probably failed to understand how any man could be indifferent to a distinction which Mr.

Bryan has so ardently sought." *Washington Evening Star,* Nov. 19, 1915, p. 6, col. 3.

[218] Joseph H. Choate, the famous lawyer and former Ambassador to Britain, believed that TR had been

general rules of polity, not involving moral considerations, to which circumstances of the country's need may not justify an exception." The country's great need was "restoration of the Republican party to power," and only Hughes could fill it. Taft listed other possible candidates, including Elihu Root and Theodore Roosevelt, and found them not equal to Hughes in respect either of qualifications or of chances of success. The Republican Convention, Taft continued, would nominate Hughes "unless you announce before the Convention acts that you will not accept the nomination under any circumstances." He realized, Taft said, that that was precisely what Hughes would probably like to do. "I know that you prefer your life on the bench and . . . that you are properly most sensitive in respect to the partisan attitude of the judges of the court and deeply deprecate making a precedent which might inspire other judges to an ambition which would demoralize them and destroy their usefulness and affect the high position of the court. But I beg of you to consider that your position in the peculiar situation of affairs is so exceptional that it cannot afford a dangerous precedent."

Two days later, on April 13, Taft returned to the fray:

> After mailing my letter last night, it occurred to me that there were certain phases of the matter I had not touched and that ought to be referred to. Of course, if you accept the nomination, your resignation must follow promptly, and an opportunity for Wilson to fill your place. His selection of Brandeis does not give hope that he will strengthen the bench by another appointment, though I think his experiences with Brandeis will make him somewhat anxious to propitiate the many whom he has shocked by that appointment. But if his filling one vacancy is to be a reason for not running, think of the vacancies he is likely to fill if he is to be reelected. He can almost destroy the court.

As for Roosevelt, his appointments, which might well include "such men as [Learned] Hand and [Samuel] Seabury and [William] Draper [Lewis] of the Pennsylvania Law School, supporters of the recall of judicial decisions, I fear would be in many ways quite as bad as Brandeis."

---

found wanting in 1912, and favored Elihu Root for 1916. As to Hughes, he said:

It should, I think, be regarded as a fatal drawback to Justice Hughes' nomination that he is a Justice of the Supreme Court, a court which must be kept forever inviolate from without or from within. Its spotless ermine should never be smirched in the muddy turmoil of politics. . . .

Besides this, Justice Hughes has never had any experience in foreign affairs . . . and what is more, no man knows what his views are on this or any other of the leading questions. . . . His judicial record is perfect; why should not he and his party and the whole people be content with that, as his one and only proper place for life? (*New York Times*, Apr. 10, 1916, p. 4, col. 3.

IV: *Appointment Cycles*

Hughes was having "a very unpleasant" year. "I am being bombarded on all sides," he wrote Day on April 16, 1916, which was shortly after Taft's letters had reached him—and gone unanswered—"my correspondence is very heavy, and the men who insist on the right 'to say a word' fill in the few crevices of time left by our work. But I refuse to be embarrassed and endeavor to plod along the straight and narrow judicial path." Not once, and not in the slightest degree, did Hughes stray from the straight and narrow. There is not the shadow of a question about that. He did absolutely nothing to enhance his availability, said not a word on public issues, and was in no way affected in his judicial work. Not only did he not cooperate in efforts to obtain the nomination for him, but he did all in his power to discourage and stop such efforts.

The only thing Hughes did not do, because he felt he could not, was to say, as he had in 1912, that he would decline the nomination if tendered. He was as conscious as anyone of the danger to the Court that inhered in the political candidacy of one of its members, but he would not put himself in a position "to fail in meeting what might be a duty to the country." Van Devanter, apparently the only colleague Hughes took the initiative in consulting, advised him that he could not rightly decline if nominated, and Chief Justice White at one point volunteered the same opinion. No one knows just when Hughes settled on it firmly, but that was his view also, well before the nomination actually came. At home, Mrs. Hughes was an outright and vigorous advocate of acceptance.

Many years later, Hughes remembered that Secretary of the Interior Franklin K. Lane hinted to him at a dinner party that if he remained on the Court, Wilson would make him Chief Justice. The same suggestion came to Hughes even more directly at about the same time from Chief Justice White, who added that he was planning retirement. There is no evidence that Wilson authorized these approaches, and it is extremely doubtful that he did. The men around Wilson quite likely shared the feeling of so many Republicans that Hughes would make the strongest possible candidate, and Lane may have been doing his loyal independent bit to keep Hughes out of the race. As for the Chief Justice, he never thought Hughes could have acted differently, and in the end he favored him over Wilson. But White was a ceaseless worrier, and saw disaster for the Court lurking around every corner. And so, no doubt, he was of two minds. He believed that Hughes could not refuse to run, and he was glad when Hughes was nominated, but he also, characteristically, feared the nomination would prove "a very great blunder [for the Court] and one from which we will be years in recovering." He might well have had a moment when it seemed to him he should take some action to forestall it.

The nomination did come, on the third ballot in Chicago, on June 10, conservative Republicans and Theodore Roosevelt's Progressives uniting to accomplish it with varying degrees of enthusiasm and resignation. Perhaps it was true, as George E. Mowry has remarked, that "no one wanted Hughes, but everyone was for him." He was inevitable. As soon as word reached him, Hughes met the newspapermen who had been besieging his house in Washington, and then immediately wrote a bleakly formal letter to the President:

> I hereby resign the office of Associate Justice of the Supreme Court of the United States.
> I am, sir, respectfully yours,
>
> *Charles Evans Hughes*

Wilson must have thought the letter curt, and he replied in kind, on the same day, June 10, 1916:

> Dear Mr. Justice Hughes:
>
> I am in receipt of your letter of resignation and feel constrained to yield to your desire.
> I, therefore, accept your resignation as Justice of the Supreme Court of the United States to take effect at once.
>
> Sincerely yours,
>
> Woodrow Wilson

Among his former colleagues, Hughes apparently left behind nothing but good will. "Unbeknownst to anybody," as the Chief Justice said, they had "arranged about our Brother Hughes" by taking four or five of his cases off his hands some time before his nomination, so he could go out "with a clean slate." Hughes, the Chief Justice thought, "bore himself admirably during those last days and I think the moment the load of the cases which he had to write were [*sic*] taken off his shoulders he rebounded and was in as fine a condition as I ever saw him. I trust in God he is going to win and hope so with all my heart." Day wrote Hughes that the office had sought the man, and that Hughes' conduct had been "honorable and dignified, in every way worthy of yourself and the great office you now resign." Day added high praise for Hughes' performance on the Court. "Your past is secure," he concluded. Holmes called at Hughes' house, and not finding him, left this note:

> Your first thought was of duty. I must confess that pretty near the first with me was the loss to the Court and especially to me. I shall miss you very much in every way, so much that I wish the needs of

the country could have been postponed until I am out of the business. As it is I shall look back with affectionate regret at the ending to the time during which we sat (and stood) side by side.

Holmes also expressed the same sentiments about Hughes to his friend Pollock, and, like White, he favored Hughes over Wilson.

Hughes' Presidential candidacy was certainly an episode full of hazards for the Court and for himself, but except for the risk of electoral defeat, they were all negotiated with singular success and luck. Neither the propriety of nominating a Justice of the Supreme Court for political office nor Hughes' record as a judge became issues in the campaign. Immediately after the nomination, a proposed constitutional amendment was introduced in the Senate to disqualify all sitting federal judges from elective office, and there were some speeches on the subject unsympathetic to Hughes, including one by Thomas J. Walsh of Montana. But Wilson would not permit condemnation of Hughes in the Democratic platform for "dragging the Supreme Court into the mire of politics," and the issue died. It well might not have, if Hughes' formidable reputation for integrity, indeed stiffness, and the impression that he was, just then, literally indispensable to the Republican party had not combined to make credible what was in fact true, namely, that Hughes neither influenced, nor was as a judge influenced by, the politics of his candidacy. Moreover, as Taft had pointed out, "the peculiar state of affairs," which included not only the need to bridge an unprecedented Republican schism, but a World War lapping at the country's shores, was in truth "so exceptional" that it rendered plausible the appeal to Hughes' conscience, and Hughes' response in terms of duty. The whole episode could be seen as affording no dangerous precedent. And yet in the perspective of time it has constituted confirmation, despite the unique circumstances, of the tradition—however individually dishonored, sometimes, in the breach—that judges must not be drawn into politics.

For Hughes himself, there were the possibilities which his life had rejected—and he apparently contemplated them, if at all, with great serenity in the interregnum before his further careers. He might have been Chief Justice in 1910, in which event he would probably have remained on the Court. His tenure would have rivaled the services of Marshall and Taney, and the history of the Court for the years leading to its confrontation with Franklin D. Roosevelt would doubtless have been different. He might have remained as a Justice, and whether or not he had reached the Chief Justiceship in lieu of Taft in 1921 or perhaps before, he would also have powerfully affected the stance of the Court in the twenties. And he might have run in 1912, when he had not yet grown somewhat remote from electoral politics and would have

397

been a different campaigner from the one he was in 1916, and thus might have won and been a two-term and a wartime President.[219]

Had Hughes never returned to the Bench, he would still enjoy a very substantial judicial reputation, one of the few important ones acquired in a short term of service.[220] Hughes served for just a couple of days short of six full terms of Court, resigning exactly five years and eight months after he was seated. Like Lurton, Van Devanter, and Lamar, among the other appointees of President Taft, he was no workhorse by comparison with his seniors. He produced 144 opinions of the Court,[221] as against Holmes' 247, White's 227, and McKenna's 190 over the same stretch. Van Devanter, seated three months later than Hughes, had 133 in the period before Hughes' resignation, and Day, who was absent from the beginning of the October Term 1911 until January 18, 1912, and again from January 3, 1916, to the end of the term in June, wrote 140.

In dissents, Hughes, with a total of 33, 5 with opinion, was second only to the erratic McKenna, who filed 39, 7 with opinion. Hughes also noted 6 separate concurrences without opinion. Holmes and Day as well as McKenna each wrote more dissenting opinions than Hughes—8 for Holmes, and 7 each for Day and McKenna—but Day's total dissents were 25 and Holmes' 24. (White dissented 18 times and Van Devanter 17.) The number of Hughes' dissents is some indication of his position on the progressive flank of the Court, as Lamar's dissenting score, also relatively high at 24 in a tenure shorter by one year and a half, tends to place him on the opposite flank.

---

[219] *Washington Evening Star,* Nov. 11, 1913, p. 1, col. 7, Nov. 12, 1913, p. 6, col. 1; Pringle, *Taft,* II, 756, 794–95, 884–86, 890–92; *Holmes-Pollock Letters,* I, 192, 237; C. E. Hughes to E. Root, June 30, 1912, Hughes Papers; *Washington Evening Star,* Jan. 25, 1916, p. 3, col. 4; W. H. Taft to Hughes, Apr. 11, 1916, Apr. 13, 1916, Hughes Papers; Hughes to W. R. Day, Apr. 16, 1916, Day Papers; C. E. Hughes, *Biographical Notes,* Microfilm, Ac. 9943, 229–32, Hughes Papers; Link, *Wilson: Campaigns for Progressivism and Peace,* 7; Lamar, *Lamar,* 179–80; G. E. Mowry, *Theodore Roosevelt and the Progressive Movement* (1946), 346; E. D. White to W. R. Day, June 15, 1916, Day Papers; Day to Hughes, June 11, 1916, Hughes Papers; O. W. Holmes to Hughes, June 11, 1916, Hughes Papers; *Holmes-Laski Letters,* I, 33; M. J. Pusey, *Charles Evans Hughes* (1951), 300–301, 315–34; 53 *Cong. Rec.* 11847–51, 64th Cong., 1st Sess. (1916); see also *ibid.,* 12121, 11853, 13204–205, and 9357–58.

[220] Hughes' achievement between 1910 and 1916 is greater than that of William H. Moody, who made a remarkable record in an active service of no more than some three years from 1906 to 1910, and at least comparable to Benjamin N. Cardozo's between 1932 and 1938.

[221] Hughes' first opinion was Kerfoot v. Farmers' and Merchants' Bank, 218 U.S. 281 (1910). For his last, see Kennedy v. Becker, 241 U.S. 556 (1916).

IV: *Appointment Cycles*

Hughes arrived on the Bench tired, without a vacation, and not in the best of health, only four days after he had resigned the governorship of New York, leaving a clean desk. He felt obliged to stay on as governor to the last possible moment, and the initial strain of the work on the Court told heavily on his nerves. He entered upon "the difficult and engrossing judicial work in October, 1910, feeling tired out instead of refreshed and full of zest. It was a long time before I was restored to my normal vigor," he recalled years later. White remembered that Hughes was often near nervous exhaustion, and that taking Hughes home one night, he (White) witnessed an electric treatment administered to Hughes. Following Saturday conferences, Hughes would often spend Sunday in bed.[222]

After his first year's labors, Hughes looked forward to a rest in the summer of 1911. But President Taft just then imposed an extra-judicial chore on him. Taft was having a hard time getting Congress to raise second-class mail rates, and so just as the session ended, he obtained a resolution setting up a commission, under the chairmanship of a Supreme Court Justice, to report on the cost to the Post Office Department of handling second-class mail. Taft named Hughes, assuring him that it was a summer's work only. After consultation with his colleagues, Hughes reluctantly accepted. It turned out to be a miserable task. The summer was taken up with public hearings, and it was only then that the work began in earnest. "I caught a severe cold," Hughes remembered, "and suffered greatly from lumbago. Through the fall while I was trying to keep up with the work of the Court I was busy over figures until late into the night. It was February 1912 before we got in our report, and it was not until the summer of 1912 that I had any opportunity for rest." Nor did the work come to anything. Taft transmitted the report to Congress, but no action followed.[223]

Many years later, after his retirement from the Chief Justiceship, Hughes touched on a reason why, in general, a newly appointed judge may find himself making a slow start:

> I plunged into the work and it was not long before I was able fairly well to keep up with it. But I found it advisable to do a great deal of reading outside of the demands of the cases in hand, in order to get a comprehensive view of the jurisprudence of the Court. . . . A new Justice is not at ease in his seat until he has made a thorough study of

---

[222] C. E. Hughes, *Biographical Notes*, 206, Hughes Papers; Brandeis-Frankfurter Conversations.

[223] C. E. Hughes to W. H. Taft, Mar. 9, 1911, Taft Papers; C. E. Hughes, *Biographical Notes*, 213–15, 227–28, Hughes Papers; Hughes to W. R. Day, Oct. 19, 1911, Day Papers; *New York Times*, Mar. 5, 1911, p. 2, col. 2, Mar. 6, 1911, p. 3, col. 2, Mar. 10, 1911, p. 15, col. 4; Pusey, *Hughes*, I, 295–96; Pringle, *Taft*, II, 624–25; *Holmes-Pollock Letters*, I, 192.

lines of cases, so that when a case is argued he at once recognizes, or by looking at a key case brings back to his memory, the jurisprudence of the Court upon the general subject and can address his mind to the particular variant now presented. That is the explanation of the ability of experienced Justices to dispose rapidly of their work, and also of the difficulties the new Justice encounters in going over ground that is more familiar to his seniors on the Bench. I spent long hours at night in close study.[224]

Brandeis once put it this way: "It takes three or four years to find oneself easily in the movements of the Court."[225] But in a period comparable to Hughes' service, Pitney, the remaining appointee of President Taft, produced nearly 180 opinions of the Court, and Brandeis himself, who in his first six terms made a contribution of majority opinions similar to Hughes—146 in number—during the same time also wrote 31 dissenting opinions. Tired to begin with, distracted by the postal commission assignment in 1911, and by the Presidential possibilities that loomed in 1912 and again from 1915 on, Hughes worked with less than his customary energy during much of his first judicial career.

Whatever Hughes' record might have lacked in volume, however, it made up in quality. It is a puzzlement of long standing whether some judges are assigned important cases, or cases become important when some judges write the opinions in them. With Hughes, both propositions were true. It was Hughes' opinions that made *Chicago, Burlington & Quincy Railroad* v. *McGuire*[226] and many of his other Due Process and Commerce Clause cases notable. And, of course, the same goes for the dissent in *Slocum* v. *New York Life Insurance Co.*[227] But the *Minnesota Rate Cases*[228] and the *Shreveport Case*[229] were remarkably important assignments to a junior judge,[230] as were also, on a somewhat lesser scale, *Dr. Miles Medical Co.* v. *Parke and Sons*, concerning the legality of retail price maintenance,[231] and *Bailey* v. *Alabama*, the peonage case.[232]

In his later careers as a very frequent advocate before the Supreme Court and the Court of Appeals in New York, and as Chief Justice, Hughes impressed all and sundry with his extraordinary command of the materials relevant to any particular judgment, and with a great force

---

[224] C. E. Hughes, *Biographical Notes*, 209–12, Hughes Papers.

[225] Brandeis-Frankfurter Conversations, see *supra*, p. 84.

[226] *Supra*, p. 280, n.255.

[227] *Supra*, pp. 313–14, n.379.

[228] *Supra*, pp. 254, 259, n.176.

[229] *Supra*, pp. 216, 218, n.54.

[230] About the only comparable assignment to a new judge in the early years of Hughes' service was the *Second Employers' Liability Cases* to Van Devanter. *Supra*, pp. 206, 208, n.29.

[231] 220 U.S. 373 (1911).

[232] *Supra*, p. 339, n.92.

and precision of statement. Those who knew him earlier also noted that he "was self-reliant and self-contained to an extraordinary degree."[233] No doubt Hughes showed his quality at the conference table even while still finding himself in the movements of the Court, and it is natural for a Chief Justice often to assign a case to that one of his colleagues who, he recalls, gave the strongest and most lucid formulation of a ground of decision persuasive to a majority. Moreover, Hughes arrived on the Court, not out of the obscurity of a Georgia law practice, or even the relative obscurity of the lower federal bench, but a famous public man. He was, as the event certainly proved, by far the most politically consequential member of the Court, a man with a following. Hence his signature on an opinion was capable of gaining the Court some credit. Deliberately or not, this must also have been a factor in bringing important cases his way, and it might have been a factor also in pulling waverers toward the results he favored.

Judged by both their contemporary and enduring influence, and as creative, original contributions, Hughes' greatest achievements were unquestionably the opinions in the *Minnesota Rate Cases* and in the *Shreveport Case*. The masterful dissent in *Slocum v. New York Life Insurance Co.* and the opinion in *Chicago, Burlington & Quincy Railroad v. McGuire* are of crucial significance as they define Hughes' attitude toward the task of constitutional construction at large, and the application of the Due Process Clause in particular. The peonage case, *Bailey v. Alabama*, stands out as the earliest indication of Hughes' approach to problems of civil rights and civil liberties.

Other opinions by Hughes exemplifying the generous view he took of the federal commerce power are *Baltimore & Ohio Railroad v. Interstate Commerce Commission*,[234] *Philadelphia Co. v. Stimson*,[235] and *Philadelphia, Baltimore & Washington Railroad v. Schubert*.[236] Moreover, starting with the dissent in *United States v. Johnson*, which Congress promptly vindicated by an amendment to the Pure Food and Drug Act, Hughes consistently gave broad, purposive constructions to

---

[233] W. H. Taft to R. A. Taft, Jan. 8, 1928, Taft Papers; F. Frankfurter, *Of Law and Men*, P. Elman, ed. (1956), 133–35, 139–50; Remarks of Mr. John Lord O'Brian, in *Proceedings of the Bar and Officers of the Supreme Court of the United States in Memory of Charles Evans Hughes* (1950), 44–45.

[234] *Supra*, pp. 213–14, n.48.

[235] *Supra*, p. 221, n.70.

[236] *Supra*, p. 212, n.40. And see Union Pacific R.R. v. Laramie Stockyards, 231 U.S. 190 (1913) (Hughes, J., dissenting); New York Life Ins. Co. v. Deer Lodge County, *supra*, p. 275, n.236 (Hughes, J., dissenting). But compare United States v. Hvoslef, 237 U.S. 1 (1915); Thames and Mersey Ins. Co. v. United States, 237 U.S. 19 (1915).

federal regulatory measures.[237] These exercises in statutory construction hang together, they form a concerted whole, because Hughes was a sophisticated lawyer, and knew exactly what he was about.

In the only major public appearance that he made, pursuant to a prior commitment, while his second Presidential boom was upon him, Hughes told the New York State Bar Association in January 1916:

> Many forget how necessary is the judicial work to the carrying out of any legislative program. I like to think of the courts as in the truest sense the expert agents of democracy—expressing deliberate judgment under conditions essential to stability, and therefore in their proper action the necessary instrumentalities of progress. . . . It is undoubtedly the duty of the courts to construe legislation according to the intent of the legislature. But the question remains, What is the intent of the legislature? The man in the street will tell you at once what it is; but when you put the case to him in its details, he hesitates. . . . [Legislative intent] is sometimes little more than a useful legal fiction,—save as it describes in a general way certain outstanding purposes which no one disputes but which are frequently of little aid in dealing with the precise points presented in the litigation. Moreover, legislative ambiguity may at times not be wholly unintentional. . . . Legislation does not execute itself; and with the legislative word, in order to make it effective, must go the judicial judgment. . . . For it is through the courts that consistency and symmetry will be given to new departments of law.

The judge, Hughes concluded, would meet his responsibility "as the interpreter of legislation in the expanding life of democracy" only through a statesmanlike appreciation of the past, present, and future of the nation.[238]

With respect to actions of administrative agencies, Hughes insisted on judicial review to ensure the legality and constitutionality of what was done,[239] but he gave ample scope to the exercise of administrative discretion.[240] Again, as in the matter of statutory construction, he was

---

[237] See *supra,* pp. 226–228, n.84; Seven Cases of Eckman's Alternative v. United States, 239 U.S. 510 (1916); United States v. Coca Cola Co., 241 U.S. 265 (1916); United States v. Jin Fuey Moy, 241 U.S. 394 (1916) (Hughes and Pitney, JJ., dissenting); McCoach v. Minehill Ry. Co., *supra,* p. 248, n.151 (Day, Hughes, and Lamar, JJ., dissenting).

[238] Hughes Papers; see *Washington Post,* Jan. 15, 1916, p. 4, col. 5.

[239] See Philadelphia Co. v. Stimson, 223 U.S. 605 (1912).

[240] The Los Angeles Switching Case, 234 U.S. 294 (1914); Interstate Commerce Commission v. Southern Pacific Co., 234 U.S. 315 (1914); Mills v. Lehigh Valley R.R., 238 U.S. 473 (1915); Interstate Commerce Commission v. Diffenbaugh, 222 U.S. 42 (1911) (McKenna and Hughes, JJ., dissenting); and see Pennsylvania R.R. v. Clark Coal Co., 238 U.S. 456 (1915).

guided by a thoughtful conception of the judicial role. Courts, he told the New York Bar Association in the speech mentioned above, should police the boundaries of administrative power, but should not be saddled with the administrative task itself. While governor, in 1907, he had warned against requiring judges to deal "with these questions of administration—questions which lie close to the public impatience, and in regard to which the people are going to insist on having administration by officers directly accountable to them. . . . Let us keep the courts for questions they were intended to consider . . . there will be abundant opportunity for review of everything that should be reviewed. But to say that all these matters of detail . . . should, at the option of the corporations, be taken into court, is to make a mockery of your regulation. And, on the other hand . . . it would swamp your courts . . . and expose them to the fire of public criticism. . . ."[241] Finally, Hughes treated cases under the Federal Employers' Liability Act in a manner consistent with both his view of the function of statutory construction and his concern for a proper division of labor between courts and other decision-making bodies. While by no means an undiscriminating plaintiff's lawyer, Hughes tended to support jury verdicts granting recovery.[242]

Overcentralized government, Hughes also told the New York Bar Association in 1916, "would break down of its own weight." And so he remained "convinced of the necessity of autonomous [local] government." It was "almost impossible even now for Congress in well-nigh continuous session to keep up with its duties, and we can readily imagine what the future may have in store in legislative concerns." His hospitality

---

[241] Pusey, *Hughes*, I, 203–205.

It was in the course of these remarks, at Elmira, New York, on May 3, 1907, that Hughes got off a phrase he was later, as Chief Justice in the 1930s, seldom allowed to forget. He did not want courts converted into administrative agencies, Hughes was saying. He had the highest regard for them, and he wanted them saved to perform the function for which they were fitted, and which was indeed a momentous one: "We are under a Constitution, but the Constitution is what the judges say it is, and the judiciary is the safeguard of our liberty and of our property under the Constitution." This sentence came to be read out of context, and quoted without its second half, as quite differ- ently intended from how in truth it was.

[242] See, e.g., Norfolk & Western Ry. v. Holbrook, 235 U.S. 625 (1915) (McKenna, Day, and Hughes, JJ., dissenting); Reese v. Philadelphia & Reading Ry., 239 U.S. 463 (1915) (Hughes and Pitney, JJ., dissenting); Illinois Central R.R. v. Skaggs, 240 U.S. 66 (1916); Illinois Central R.R. v. Messina, 240 U.S. 395 (1916) (Hughes and McKenna, JJ., dissenting); Great Northern Ry. v. Knapp, 240 U.S. 464 (1916); Osborne v. Gray, 241 U.S. 16 (1916); but see Arizona & New Mexico Ry. v. Clark, 235 U.S. 669 (1915) (Hughes and Day, JJ., dissenting); and see Chicago, Burlington & Quincy R.R. v. Harrington, 241 U.S. 177 (1916).

to the exercise of federal power was coupled, therefore, with a sensitive and pragmatic respect for the need of the states also to regulate and tax portions of the national economy. Hughes' receptivity to state regulation and taxation of commerce was manifested not only in the *Minnesota Rate Cases,* but also in such cases as *Port Richmond Ferry* v. *Hudson County.*[243] Perhaps he strayed somewhat in *Adams Express Co.* v. *New York,*[244] but he dissented in *Oklahoma* v. *Kansas Natural Gas Co.*[245]

Hughes' Due Process and Equal Protection cases, in addition to *Chicago, Burlington & Quincy Railroad* v. *McGuire,* included *Purity Extract Co.* v. *Lynch,*[246] *Sturgis and Burn* v. *Beauchamp,*[247] and *Miller* v. *Wilson*[248] and *Bosley* v. *McLaughlin,*[249] the latter two sustaining an eight-hour law for women in certain occupations.[250] In upholding, in *Price* v. *Illinois,*[251] a statute punishing the sale of unwholesome foods as applied to a preservative compound that contained boric acid, Hughes said: "It is plainly not enough that the subject should be regarded as debatable. If it be debatable, the legislature is entitled to its own judgment. . . ." Hughes was in dissent, with Holmes and Day, in *Coppage* v. *Kansas,*[252] which extended constitutional immunity to the

[243] *Supra,* pp. 264–65, n.196; *cf.* Sault Ste. Marie v. International Transit Co., *supra,* p. 265, n.198; see also Lusk v. Kansas, 240 U.S. 236 (1916); Kansas City Ry. v. Kansas, 240 U.S. 227 (1916); Wilmington Transportation Co. v. California R.R. Commission, 236 U.S. 151 (1915); Atlantic Coast Line v. Georgia, *supra,* p. 264, n.195; Chicago, Milwaukee & St. Paul Ry. v. Iowa, *supra,* p. 264, n.195; Anderson v. Pacific Coast S.S. Co., 225 U.S. 187 (1912); Bacon v. Illinois, 227 U.S. 504 (1913), and see Clement National Bank v. Vermont, 231 U.S. 120 (1913), and Savage v. Jones, *supra,* p. 271, n.215; see also Kansas City Southern Ry. v. Carl, *supra,* p. 274, n.226 (Hughes and Pitney, JJ., dissenting); Missouri, Kansas & Texas Ry. v. Harriman, *supra,* p. 274, n.226 (Hughes, J., concurring in the result).

[244] *Supra,* p. 265, n.199.
[245] *Supra,* pp. 268–69, n.210.
[246] *Supra,* p. 281, n.264.
[247] *Supra,* p. 281, n.260.
[248] 236 U.S. 373 (1915).
[249] 236 U.S. 385 (1915).

[250] See also Liverpool Ins. Co. v. Orleans Assessors, 221 U.S. 346 (1911); Heckman v. United States, 224 U.S. 413 (1912); Toyota v. Hawaii, 226 U.S. 184 (1912); Louisville and Nashville R.R. v. Garrett, 231 U.S. 298 (1913); Hawley v. Malden, 232 U.S. 1 (1914); Chicago, Milwaukee & St. Paul Ry. v. Minneapolis, 232 U.S. 430 (1914); Union Lime Co. v. Chicago and Northwestern Ry., 233 U.S. 211 (1914); Bowling v. United States, 233 U.S. 528 (1914); O'Neill v. Leamer, 239 U.S. 244 (1915); Houck v. Little River District, 239 U.S. 254 (1915); Rogers v. Hennepin County, 240 U.S. 184 (1916); but *cf.* Gromer v. Standard Dredging Co., 224 U.S. 362 (1912) (Day, Hughes, and Lamar, JJ., dissenting); Provident Savings Ass'n. v. Kentucky, 239 U.S. 103 (1915); Northern Pacific Ry. v. North Dakota, 236 U.S. 585 (1915); Norfolk & Western Ry. v. West Virginia, 236 U.S. 605 (1915).
[251] 238 U.S. 446, 452 (1915).
[252] 236 U.S. 1 (1915).

antiunion yellow-dog contract, and he favored sustaining the Oregon minimum wage statute in *Stettler* v. *O'Hara*,[253] a case disposed of without opinions by an equally divided Court, Brandeis taking no part, following reargument well after Hughes' departure. Hughes' actions in Contract Clause cases bespeak the same judicial philosophy. He made what may be regarded as a minimum obeisance to prevailing doctrine in *Russell* v. *Sebastian*,[254] but he was more consistently sparing than any of his colleagues in applying the clause. He not only joined in the dissent in *Owensboro* v. *Cumberland Telephone Co.*,[255] but dissented also in a number of other cases.[256]

Even in antitrust doctrine, although he was assigned, oddly enough, no Sherman Act opinions, Hughes made one enduring mark. Over the dissent of Holmes (and against the disapproval of Brandeis, then at the bar), Hughes held in *Dr. Miles Medical Co.* v. *Park and Sons Co.* that vertical price fixing, by means of price-maintenance contracts between wholesalers and retailers, was against public policy.[257] Still, of all the subjects of prime concern to the country and the Court in the Progressive Era, antitrust is the only one as to which Hughes did not stake out a clear and comprehensive individual position. But in another area—civil rights and civil liberties—no less interesting, if less central at the time, Hughes was about the single judge during the years of his tenure to make a record of any significance. The sole, partial exception is Holmes.

The point is not to be overstated, for the occasions offered by the Court's docket were few, and Hughes was not as alert to these issues, and did not develop as coherent a philosophy about many of them, as about problems of social and economic regulation. Yet there is not only his penetrating opinion striking down the peonage scheme in *Bailey* v. *Alabama*, but also his holding, near the end of his service, in *Truax* v.

---

[253] 243 U.S. 629 (1917); see C. E. Hughes, *Biographical Notes,* Ch. 23, p. 32, Hughes Papers.

[254] *Supra,* p. 302, n.347.

[255] *Supra,* p. 304, n.350.

[256] Southern Pacific Co. v. Portland, 227 U.S. 559 (1913) (Hughes and Pitney, JJ., dissenting); Wright v. Central of Georgia Ry., 236 U.S. 674 (1915) (Hughes, Pitney, and McReynolds, JJ., dissenting); Wright v. Louisville and Nashville R.R., 236 U.S. 687 (1915) (Hughes, Pitney, and McReynolds, JJ., dissenting); Grand Trunk Western R.R. v. South Bend, *supra,* pp. 303–304, n.349 (Hughes and Pitney, JJ., dissenting; and see New York Electric Lines Co. v. Empire City Subway, 235 U.S. 179 (1914); Louisiana Ry. and Navigation Co. v. New Orleans, 235 U.S. 164 (1914).

[257] 220 U.S. 373 (1911); R. H. Bork, "The Rule of Reason and the Per Se Concept: Price Fixing and Market Division," *Yale L. J.,* 74:775, 778, 810–11, 819–20, 1965. Hughes took the same view of price-fixing conditions tied to licenses for the use of a patented article. Henry v. A. B. Dick Co., 224 U.S. 1 (1912) (White, C. J., and Hughes and Lamar, JJ., dissenting); see also Bauer v. O'Donnell, 229 U.S. 1 (1913).

Raich,[258] that states may not exclude aliens from private employment. And in *McCabe* v. *Atchison, Topeka & Santa Fe Railway,*[259] Hughes went well out of his way to require that separate-but-equal legislation provide for as much equality as separation. He also emphasized the issue of racial discrimination that lurked just below the surface in *Quong Wing* v. *Kirkendall*[260] by concurring separately in the result. But he was silent in *Butts* v. *Merchants Transportation Co.,*[261] a decision that the Civil Rights Act of 1875 could not be saved for application to steamships running in interstate commerce between Boston and Norfolk, Virginia; in *Jones* v. *Jones,*[262] holding that a Tennessee intestate succession statute which discriminated against ex-slaves was constitutional; and in *Heim* v. *McCall,*[263] and *Crane* v. *New York,*[264] decided a few weeks after *Truax* v. *Raich,* which sustained a statute giving absolute priority of employment to citizens over aliens in the construction of public works by private contractors. Nor did he speak out for himself in two not-very-free speech cases of the day, one by McKenna and the other by Holmes.[265] Again, he enthusiastically collaborated and joined with Holmes in the dissent in *Frank* v. *Mangum* ("I shall be proud to be associated with you in this opinion"),[266] but he walked a tightrope of procedural Due Process to questionable results in *Graham* v. *West Virginia,*[267] *Tang Tun* v. *Edsell,*[268] and *Wilson* v. *United States.*[269]

Hughes' opinion-writing style was lucid and straightforward, but unafraid of the occasional generalization looking to first principles and beyond the case at hand. He was far from being the austere, distant personage of his caricatures, far even from the unadorned personality displayed in his opinions. Holmes, with whom he had a fine, warm, and bantering relationship, said of him in 1916 that he was "not only a good fellow, experienced and wise, but funny, and with doubts that open vistas through the wall of a non-conformist conscience."[270] A fuller,

---

[258] 239 U.S. 33 (1915).

[259] *Supra,* pp. 322–23, n.18.

[260] *Supra,* p. 298, n.327.

[261] 230 U.S. 126 (1913).

[262] 234 U.S. 615 (1914).

[263] 239 U.S. 175 (1915).

[264] 239 U.S. 195 (1915).

[265] Mutual Film Corp. v. Ohio Industrial Commission, 236 U.S. 230 (1915); Fox v. Washington, 236 U.S. 273 (1915).

[266] *Supra,* pp. 362–63, n.178; Pusey, *Hughes,* I, 289, and see Hyde v. United States, 225 U.S. 347 (1912)

(Holmes, Lurton, Hughes, and Lamar, JJ., dissenting); Brown v. Elliott, 225 U.S. 392 (1912) (Holmes, Lurton, Hughes, and Lamar, JJ., dissenting); Donnelly v. United States, 228 U.S. 243 (1913) (Holmes, Lurton, and Hughes, JJ., dissenting); and see United States v. Mason, 218 U.S. 517 (1910).

[267] 224 U.S. 616 (1912).

[268] 223 U.S. 673 (1912).

[269] 221 U.S. 361 (1911).

[270] *Holmes-Pollock Letters,* I, 237.

equally favorable, and, considering the source, more remarkable judgment of Hughes in 1916 was Felix Frankfurter's. Writing to his friend Morris R. Cohen, with whom he shared misgivings about Hughes as a Presidential candidate, Frankfurter said that Hughes had "ability of a high order to master the problems of statesmanship. . . . He has mastered some problems of statesmanship as to which he was completely innocent when he was Governor. He *is* subject to the impact of facts. . . . Of course Hughes carries a general stock of economic and social views with which he was inculcated at Brown thirty-odd years ago, except insofar as such views have been adjusted by specific problems of government and of life that he has had to face, but he has not a rigid, or a dull, or a commonplace mind; very much to the contrary. . . . Holmes . . . says of Hughes that while he is not prepared to say that he is a great man, he 'is a very considerable man, who has vistas.' I confess he has not allowed us to see his vistas on the stump, and what Holmes doubtless means is that he is capable of deep conceptions when his mind actually gets busy on a problem."[271]

A kind of weary amusement must have prevailed at the White House soon after the chilly letters marking Hughes' resignation had been exchanged, as voices were again raised urging Wilson to put William Howard Taft on the Supreme Court. It would be "a gracious act" and "a high service," said the *New York Times*, repeating itself. There was, of course, not a chance. More serious was New York's claim to representation, and hence the candidacy of Justice Victor J. Dowling[272] of the appellate division of the state Supreme Court, who was well connected in the Irish hierarchy of the New York Democratic party. Brandeis sent word through Norman Hapgood that an appointment from New York which would have little but geography to commend it would discourage Progressive opinion, and as for Attorney General Gregory, Solicitor General Davis, or Secretary of the Interior Lane, Wilson apparently continued reluctant to break up his official family—although, to be sure, he had brought himself to part with McReynolds. One member of that family, however, the new Secretary of War, Newton D. Baker of Cleveland, had a suggestion, and it prevailed. On July 14, 1916, the President nominated John Hessin Clarke, of Youngstown and Cleveland,

---

[271] L. C. Rosenfield, *Portrait of a Philosopher: Morris R. Cohen in Life and Letters* (1962), 247–48.

[272] Victor J. Dowling (1866–1934) was born and educated in New York (A.B. Manhattan College, LL.B. New York University), and was a Justice of

the Supreme Court of New York from 1905 to 1932, with a brief interruption. During twenty years of this service, he sat on the appellate division. Before his elevation to the bench, he had been a member of the executive committee of Tammany Hall.

judge of the United States District Court for the Northern District of Ohio.[273]

Wilson's choice, hardly known outside Ohio, was fifty-eight years old. Of Protestant Irish stock on both sides, Clarke was born in New Lisbon, Ohio, on September 18, 1857. His father had come from Ireland to New Lisbon at the age of eighteen, in 1832, and had made a substantial career there. He was a successful lawyer, a member of the small-town elite, and a prominent Democrat. Clarke's maternal grandfather, John Hessin, was also an Irish immigrant, but on his maternal grandmother's side, the ancestry traced back to a Revolutionary War chaplain.

Clarke went to Western Reserve College, then in Hudson, Ohio, where he studied the classics, and was much impressed by Walter Bagehot's *The English Constitution*. Having read law in his father's office, Clarke practiced in New Lisbon for two years, and then bought a half interest in the *Youngstown Vindicator*, a Democratic newspaper. At this time, at twenty-three, he moved to Youngstown, where in addition to sharing in the running of the paper, he also opened a law office. His first partner in the ownership of the *Vindicator* was Charles N. Vallandigham, a kinsman of Clement the Copperhead, but this partnership was of brief duration.

Both the law practice, a general corporate one, and the newspaper flourished, and Clarke was active in politics, soon acquiring a reputation for old-fashioned oratorical prowess. He was a Grover Cleveland gold Democrat. The strike at the Homestead, Pennsylvania, Carnegie steel plant, which pulled Brandeis up short in the midst of a lucrative corporate practice and turned his attention to problems of social justice, merely appalled Clarke, filling him with alarm. In 1896, Clarke opposed Bryan, and shortly thereafter, without abandoning his interest in the *Vindicator*, he left his law practice in Youngstown and joined the firm of Williamson and Cushing in Cleveland. He now had large railroad clients, and presently became general counsel of the Vanderbilt-owned Nickel Plate Railroad. Other clients were the Erie Railroad and the Pullman Company.

In the early stages of Tom L. Johnson's career as the reform mayor of Cleveland, Clarke fought his program for raising railroad taxes. But gradually Clarke evolved in a progressive direction, and by 1903, he was

---

[273] *New York Times,* June 11, 1916, p. 6, col. 1, June 12, 1916, p. 10, col. 2, July 15, 1916, p. 4, col. 2; *Washington Post,* June 12, p. 1, col. 4; *Chicago Tribune,* June 13, p. 2, col. 8, July 14, p. 9, col. 2; *New York Tri-* bune, June 13, p. 4, col. 3, July 15, p. 9, col. 4; H. L. Warner, *The Life of Mr. Justice Clarke* (1959), 63–64; Mason, *Brandeis,* 513; Todd, *Justice on Trial,* 250.

a member of the inner circle around Tom Johnson, along with Newton D. Baker. That year he ran for the Senate against Mark Hanna on a ticket on which Johnson was the candidate for governor. It was the year of a Republican sweep. In 1912, Clarke supported Judson Harmon for President, not the most progressive of the Democratic possibilities. What had been the Tom Johnson organization, now led by Baker, favored Woodrow Wilson. But at the convention, Clarke came around easily enough, and he campaigned for Wilson. He also resigned as general counsel to the Nickel Plate Railroad.

In 1914, with the support of Baker, Clarke entered the primary election for the Democratic nomination for United States Senator. He identified himself unmistakably as the Progressive candidate. The race was going badly for him when he was offered the district judgeship, and he eagerly accepted, withdrawing from the primary contest. Baker had put his name forward, but Clarke appears somehow to have gained the good opinion of James C. McReynolds, the Attorney General, although there is no indication that they had met. At any rate, it was McReynolds who effectively secured the appointment. Replying to a cordial letter of thanks, McReynolds wrote Clarke on July 18, 1914:

> After canvassing the situation with considerable care, it seemed to me much to the public interest that you should be appointed judge; and I, therefore, was very much pleased when the President sent in your nomination.
>
> If you come this way be good enough to let me have the pleasure of seeing you, and if I find myself in Cleveland, be assured that it will give me much satisfaction to be your guest at the University Club.[274]

Clarke took his seat as a district judge on July 30, 1914. His service was brief, a district judge takes a great many actions without writing opinions, and there is not much, therefore, that can be said about his record.[275] Two of Clarke's cases, however, in one of which he suffered reversal, may be noted as illustrative. The first exhibits—oddly enough for an ex-gold Democrat—a certain anticorporation, Populist bias, and a no-nonsense attempt at realistic legal analysis. The other, bearing the mark of the practiced orator, shows Clarke straining rather self-consciously for the resounding statement. Both foretell the opinions of the later Justice.

American Ball Bearing Co. v. *Adams* was a patent-infringement suit. The plaintiff was a corporation formed for the sole purpose of

---

[274] Warner, *Clarke,* 1–60; Clarke Papers, Library of Congress.
[275] Clarke's opinions as district judge may be found in Vol. 219–34 of the *Federal Reporter*.

pooling the patents of three automobile companies. On his own motion, Clarke undertook to examine the circumstances of the formation of the plaintiff, and he found it to be a dummy corporation, lacking corporate capacity to bring suit under the relevant Ohio law. It was impossible, said Clarke, to hold otherwise, "without sheer acceptance of forms and names for reality and facts." He was roundly reversed for his pains by the Court of Appeals.[276]

Rockefeller v. *O'Brien*[277] was a suit to enjoin collection of state taxes. The first sentence of Clarke's opinion reads as follows: "The controversy in this case involves a great sum of money, but this does not increase the difficulty of a just decision of it." Then Clarke went on: "The federal and state courts of the country have been in singular accord in condemning many of the methods by which Mr. [John D.] Rockefeller has acquired much of his great fortune, but the character of these methods is not involved in this suit, for the claim of the county assumes that he is the lawful owner of the $311,000,000 and more" in bonds, stocks, annuities, and the like, which the county was seeking to tax.

John D. Rockefeller had moved from Cleveland to New York in 1884. His permanent home was in New York. He retained, however, a house in East Cleveland, Ohio, and in June 1913 he came there, bringing his family and retainers with him. He had the clear intention of returning to New York, but the illness of some members of his family kept him in Ohio past a certain day in February 1914, which by the law of the state was tax listing day. And so, having caught him in this way, Ohio served Rockefeller with a bill for a tax on all his bonds, stocks, and so forth. Rockefeller resisted on the ground that he was a resident and citizen of New York, and that the personal property which Ohio sought to tax was situated and was taxed in New York. Ohio, therefore, lacked jurisdiction.

Without reaching this constitutional Due Process claim, Clarke construed the Ohio statutes to mean that a tax was not to be imposed on residents of other states who were temporarily in Ohio, whether or not the temporary stay happened to include tax listing day. Clarke concluded: "This Court is quite aware that such a decision as is here rendered will be the subject of criticism, but a judiciary which has not independence sufficient to protect the rights of rich men, when they are believed to be unjustly assailed, cannot be trusted to justly protect either the personal or property rights of the well-to-do or poor."

---

[276] American Ball Bearing Co. v. Adams, 222 Fed. 967 (D.C.N.D. Ohio 1915), *reversed sub nom.* Kardo Co. v. Adams, 231 Fed. 950 (6th Cir. 1916).

[277] 224 Fed. 541, 542, 554 (D.C.-N.D. Ohio 1915), *affirmed,* 239 Fed. 127 (6th Cir. 1917), *appeal dismissed and cert. denied,* 244 U.S. 659 (1917).

IV: *Appointment Cycles*

Judging by press comment after his Supreme Court nomination, Clarke made more of an impression by introducing ceremony into the task of naturalizing aliens—orchestral music, patriotic songs, and a speech—and by saving some hundreds of jobs when he summarily forbade the receiver of the Wheeling and Lake Erie Railroad to close certain shops, than by his opinions.[278] The action in the Wheeling and Lake Erie Railroad case was particularly remarked. An editorial in *The New Republic*, quite likely written by Felix Frankfurter, commented that Clarke had demonstrated "that no industrial issue can adequately be judged except in terms of the lives and concrete happiness of the families dependent upon it."[279]

Wilson evidently had but one doubt about Clarke, and that concerned his antitrust views, which were little known. He sent Secretary Baker to talk to Clarke, and Baker reported that Clarke's conception of antitrust policy was "correct" from the Progressive point of view—a judgment that proved to be itself quite correct.[280] Thereupon the appointment was made. The White House announced it in a statement that described Clarke as a lifelong Democrat, who had run against Mark Hanna and "been conspicuous in progressive movements in Ohio and in the country." The statement also noted Clarke's "especial interest in the naturalization and Americanization of foreign-born citizens," and added, somewhat lamely:

> He has been for some time the President of the Short Ballot League in Ohio. Judge Clark is a bachelor and has devoted the leisure of his life to wide reading, so that he is a man of broad and varied culture and probably the most gifted orator in Ohio.

The general impression, registered in most newspaper and magazine articles, was that the President had appointed "another radical" to sit beside Brandeis. And yet the reaction was remarkably, totally calm. The *Times* grumbled a little that the nomination was "likely to be viewed with some doubt and misgiving by the conservative part of the public," especially since it followed so closely upon the Brandeis appointment, and it hoped that Clarke and his colleagues would not engage in judicial legislation. There was some talk also that Ohio now had two representatives on the Supreme Court (Day and Clarke), as did Massachusetts (Holmes and Brandeis), while New York and Pennsylvania, the wealthiest and most populous states, had none. And that was all; hardly comparable to the reaction when Brandeis was named. Apparently there were radicals and there were radicals.

---

[278] See Warner, *Clarke*, 62.
[279] *The New Republic*, 7:287, July 22, 1916; *The Outlook*, 113:682, July 26, 1916; *The Literary Digest*, 53: 240, July 29, 1916.
[280] Warner, *Clarke*, 63–64.

Progressive opinion, also calm, was pleased. *The New Republic*, in the editorial mentioned earlier, felt confident that Clarke, whose name it misspelled, would line up with Holmes and Brandeis, and with Day, whom it lined up with the former two. Said *The New Republic*:

> Conventional leaders of the bar bewail the increasing embroilment in politics of the Supreme Court. That the Supreme Court is more and more concerned with issues of a political character is true. There are now pending before the Supreme Court more cases to be dealt with as questions of politics than ever before. For how can a minimum wage law, the steel trust case, or the migratory bird law avoid involving fundamental questions of statesmanship?[281] That is why the personnel of the court is watched with such concern. Partisanship on any of the pending contentious questions is not wanted. But two qualifications are fundamental, assuming of course thorough technical ability. First, a statesman's insight that the Federal Constitution is one of the means towards national life and not a limit upon it; secondly, a catholic and seasoned experience with the varied activities of the modern state. The successor to Mr. Justice Hughes named by President Wilson is endowed with these essentials. A mind naturally broad in its sympathies he has sharpened by a comprehensive legal practice and rendered publicly useful by an alert and disinterested activity in the progressive movement of recent Ohio politics. As a railroad lawyer he has become familiar with what is one of the outstanding problems before the country as well as before the court, and he has gained that experience without any subtle undermining of a passionate intellectual rectitude.

Also adding Clarke to the company of Holmes and Brandeis, *The Nation* said: "It would be hard for any ultra-conservative decision to escape from the Supreme Bench with such an array of anti-conservatives on guard." And the *New York World* thought Clarke "singularly like Justice Brandeis in having been a successful corporation lawyer whose practice served only to quicken his sympathies and activities for the causes of political and social justice." The White House had gone out of its way to emphasize the progressiveness of its nominee, it had made its point, and was drawing all the advantages and none of the dis-

---

[281] "Let me timidly suggest," wrote Holmes some years later to Felix Frankfurter, who was very probably the author of the editorial quoted in the text above, "caution in the use of the word statesmanship with regard to judges. Of course, it is true that considerations of the same class come before their minds that have or ought to be the motives of legislators, but the word suggests a more political way of thinking than is desirable and also has become *banal.* . . . When economic views affect judicial action I should prefer to give such action a different name from that which I should apply to the course of Wilson or Lodge." Holmes to Frankfurter, Sept. 9, 1923, Harvard Law School Library.

412

advantages from it. Confirmation came without a murmur on July 24, ten days after the nomination had gone up. The Chief Justice insisted on traveling from Lake Placid to Washington on August 1 to administer the constitutional oath to Clarke. The judicial oath was administered when Court opened on October 9, 1916, and Clarke was seated.[282]

Clarke was a man of just about medium height, with a full head of gray hair turning white, square jawed, rather handsome in a serious, even severe, fashion. A millionaire from the proceeds of both his newspaper and his law practice, he had never married, maintaining in Youngstown a large residence with his widowed mother, until her death, and his two sisters to whom he was much attached. The younger of the two, incidentally, was a practicing physician, not a common calling for a woman in that day. Clarke was a congenial, well-liked, but not happy person. He was given to fits of melancholy and hypochondria—it was in such a fit that he eventually resigned—and he did not wear easily the harness of the Court. He soon grew impatient with arguments, with the long conferences, and with the need to adjust opinions to the wishes of other members of a majority. It was all quite a contrast with the princely independence of a district judge.

Perhaps an inner rigidity, resembling in some degree McReynolds', rendered it difficult for Clarke to function among strong-minded equals. But McReynolds was one of the crosses Clarke had to bear, for despite McReynolds' past kindness to him, or perhaps, somehow, because of it, Clarke managed to incur one of McReynolds' open and brutal enmities. With other colleagues relations were good, ripening into intimate friendships with Van Devanter and Day. Clarke often, but not always, acted with Holmes and Brandeis, with whom he was bracketed at the time of his appointment, but no closeness developed among them. The casts of mind were altogether too different. Clarke lived to a great age after his abrupt retirement in 1922, and had he stayed on, long tenure might have lent distinction to his career, especially since he would have made a difference in the struggles of the 1930s. As it was, his premature departure gave the still living Wilson a sense of frustration about two of his three appointments.[283]

---

[282] *New York Times,* July 15, 1916, p. 8, col. 1; *The Literary Digest,* 53:240–41, July 29, 1916; *The New Republic,* 7:287, July 22, 1916; *The Nation,* 103:48, July 20, 1916; *World's Work,* 33:95, November 1916; J. H. Clarke to W. R. Day, Day Papers.

[283] Warner, *Clarke,* 11, 75–76; Register, Clarke Papers, Western Reserve University Library; Acheson, "Justice Is a Method," *Record of N.Y.C.B.A.,* 12:143–55, 1957; Acheson, *Morning and Noon,* 76–77; J. H. Clarke to W. Van Devanter, Aug. 31, 1922, Van Devanter Papers; Brandeis-Frankfurter Conversations; W. R. Day to Clarke, Nov. 5, 1922, W. Wilson to Clarke, Sept. 11, 1922, Clarke Papers, Western Reserve University Library.

CHAPTER V

The Fate of Social Legislation, 1914-21: Federal

W E HAVE SEEN that after its reconstitution by President Taft, the Supreme Court enjoyed something of a honeymoon with certain segments of Progressive opinion—the Supreme Court by itself, not the state and federal judiciaries as a whole, and with some segments, not with all of Progressive opinion; but a honeymoon of sorts just the same. At the conclusion of the four terms of Court discussed in Chapter III, Charles F. Amidon, a federal district judge in North Dakota, well known for his consistent if moderate Progressive views, expressed the judgment that "the Supreme Court has never demonstrated more fully its fitness to apply the Constitution to American life than it has done during the last seven or eight years. It seems to me," Amidon continued, "that anyone reading the opinions of the Court during this period will have his faith reassured that our constitutional government is well adapted to serve the life of the American people."[1]

Such a judgment proceeded from the Court's record in upholding federal reform legislation, and from a number of permissive pronouncements in state Due Process cases. Such a judgment was also in large part wishful thinking. If ten years later few of those who had been praising the Court from a Progressive point of view were any longer celebrating "its fitness to apply the Constitution to American life," and if twenty years later, in virtual despair, they saw the Court's failure to adapt itself "to serve the life of the American people" as gravely en-

---

[1] C. F. Amidon to W. Van Devanter, Sept. 7, 1914, Van Devanter Papers, Library of Congress.

414

dangering constitutional government in the United States, the cause was to be found in attitudes and doctrines that the Court throughout its honeymoon had done nothing effective to alter, and much to sustain.

During the first administration of Franklin D. Roosevelt, many were convinced that the choice lay between reform and a fascist or communist revolution, and that the Court would balk reform. The pitched confrontation of 1937 was the result, but its origins go back to the 1920s, when the Court, now again fully identified with the rest of the federal judiciary—it was the state courts at this time that were regarded more sympathetically—accumulated a vast reservoir of ill will. It did so by proclaiming doctrines and manifesting attitudes that had been not so much dormant (let alone abandoned) a decade before, as simply unnoticed. There is discontinuity in professional and popular reaction to the Court through the quarter century between 1910 and 1937; there is at most some vacillation, but no real discontinuity in the attitudes of a majority of the Justices, and in the doctrines they espoused.

After about 1915, there was, in general, a trend toward a hardening of lines, which culminated in the 1920s. It might have been reflected sooner in popular criticism, but for the interruption of the war, which had some impact on the Court, and, in any event, diverted attention from it. In the last seven years of White's Chief Justiceship, from the fall of 1914 to the summer of 1921, federal reform legislation was still passing muster quite regularly, but no longer uniformly. Thus by 1918, there was the striking exception of the first Federal Child Labor Act.[2] Cases dealing with state social and economic legislation went along pretty much as before. But there was a subtle change in tone. And starting with the notorious case of *Coppage* v. *Kansas*,[3] which came down in January 1915, the Court struck some heavy blows at labor unions, in both constitutional and antitrust decisions.

The recital begun in Chapter III is best taken up again with a look at the further history of federal regulatory legislation upheld by the Court in the years 1910–14.

More on the Hepburn and Employers' Liability Acts and Other Federal Railroad Regulation

The Carmack Amendment, part of the Hepburn Act of 1906, gave shippers a cause of action against the initial carrier for losses occasioned anywhere in the course of a trip. The Court sustained this statute,

---

[2] Hammer v. Dagenhart, 247 U.S. 251 (1918).

[3] 236 U.S. 1 (1915).

as we saw, and wielded it with uncommon vigor to preempt state rules of liability even more favorable to shippers.[4] The result was an impressive volume of litigation. After 1914, the Court continued to give a generous construction to the Carmack Amendment, so that its coverage extended to the full reach of the federal commerce power, in accordance with the intention of Congress.[5] But while the Carmack Amendment could ease a shipper's way to recovery, and while it did not always foreclose application of state rules favorable to shippers,[6] the Court also continued ruthlessly to enforce—state law to the contrary notwithstanding—limitations of liability imposed by carriers as part of the contract of shipment.[7] And despite some grumbling in Congress,[8] the Court was equally astute to enforce notice provisions in the contract, denying recovery unless the shipper reported his loss, often in writing, within a stated time, which might be as short as five days.[9]

[4] See *supra,* pp. 202, n.11, 204, n.16, 274.

[5] Cleveland, Cincinnati, Chicago & St. Louis Ry. v. Dettlebach, 239 U.S. 588 (1916); New York, Phila. & Norfolk R.R. v. Peninsula Exchange, 240 U.S. 34 (1916); Pennsylvania R.R. v. Olivit Bros., 243 U.S. 574 (1917); Pennsylvania R.R. v. Carr, 243 U.S. 587 (1917); Gulf, Colorado & Santa Fe Ry. v. Texas Packing Co., 244 U.S. 31 (1917); Missouri, Kansas & Texas Ry. v. Ward, 244 U.S. 383 (1917); Chicago & Eastern Illinois R.R. v. Collins Co., 249 U.S. 186 (1919); Erie R.R. v. Shuart, 250 U.S. 465 (1919).

[6] Most of the cases cited in n.5, *supra,* allowed recovery.

[7] Oregon Short Line R.R. v. Homer, 42 Utah 15, 128 Pac. 522 (1912), *reversed,* 235 U.S. 693 (1914); Pierce Co. v. Wells Fargo & Co., 236 U.S. 278 (1915); Southern Express Co. v. Stehli, 160 N.C. 493, 76 S.E. 542 (1912), *reversed,* 238 U.S. 605 (1915); Cleveland, Cincinnati, Chicago & St. Louis Ry. v. Dettlebach, 239 U.S. 588 (1916); Southern Ry. v. Prescott, 240 U.S. 632 (1916); Cincinnati, New Orleans & Texas Pacific Ry. v. Rankin, 241 U.S. 319 (1916); St. Louis & San Francisco R.R. v. Mounts, 44 Okla. 359, 144

Pac. 1036 (1914), *reversed,* 241 U.S. 654 (1916); New York Central & Hudson River R.R. v. Beaham, 242 U.S. 148 (1916); Western Transit Co. v. Leslie and Co., 242 U.S. 448 (1917); American Express Co. v. U.S. Horse Shoe Co., 244 U.S. 58 (1917); Galveston, Harrisburg & San Antonio Ry. v. Woodbury, 254 U.S. 357 (1920). And see Charleston & Western Carolina Ry. v. Varnville Co., 237 U.S. 597 (1915).

[8] See 58 *Cong. Rec.* 5916–17, 66th Cong., 1st Sess. (1919) (Mr. Jones of Texas, commenting on Erie R.R. v. Shuart, 250 U.S. 465 [1919]); but *cf. ibid.,* 5916 (Mr. Blanton of Texas).

[9] Northern Pacific Ry. v. Wall, 241 U.S. 87 (1916); Chesapeake & Ohio Ry. v. McLaughlin, 242 U.S. 142 (1916); St. Louis, Iron Mountain & Southern Ry. v. Starbird, 243 U.S. 592 (1917); Erie R.R. v. Stone, 244 U.S. 322 (1917); Southern Pacific Co. v. Stewart, 245 U.S. 359 (1917), 248 U.S. 446 (1919); Baltimore & Ohio R.R. v. Leach, 249 U.S. 217 (1919); Erie R.R. v. Shuart, 250 U.S. 465 (1919); but *cf.* Georgia, Florida & Alabama Ry. v. Blish Co., 241 U.S. 190 (1916).

Problems would sometimes arise as to the construction of the notice requirement. These would be resolved

In 1916, Congress in effect attempted to transfer from the Supreme Court to the Interstate Commerce Commission authority to regulate carriers' limitations of liability,[10] but the commission was satisfied with the status quo, and the decisive authority continued to rest in the Supreme Court.[11] And the Court deviated from its general rule only in drawing a distinction between bill-of-lading provisions limiting liability, which it enforced, and attempts at complete self-exoneration by a carrier, which it did not allow.[12] The Court also held that limitations of liability were valid only when the shipper was offered an alternate, higher rate that would subject the carrier to greater liability.[13] The carrier, however, was not necessarily required to offer an alternate rate which would subject him to full liability. So Brandeis indicated in *Western Union Telegraph Co.* v. *Esteve Brothers & Co.*[14] (The Interstate Commerce Act, including the Carmack Amendment, had been made applicable to telegraph companies in 1910.)[15]

The only Justices, apparently, who were troubled by this state of the law were Pitney and, more markedly, Clarke. Brandeis, who was not, noted that on this subject, as in Federal Employers' Liability cases, Clarke "always dilated with a wrong emotion, as Rufus Choate said. . . ." For himself, after the decision of the *Esteve Brothers* case, Brandeis thought that Court now had "the situation in fully satisfactory shape—

---

as federal questions, by compulsion, so the Court held, of the Carmack Amendment. So in Northern Pacific Ry. v. Wall, 241 U.S. 87, 98 (1916), the Court, reversing the Supreme Court of Montana, construed a notice provision in favor of the railroad. The construction placed on it by the state Supreme Court, McReynolds protested in dissent, "when sitting within surroundings designed to stimulate clear thinking, is diametrically opposed to the one now adopted. In such circumstances it appears to me hardly reasonable to say that a stockman at a wayside Montana station was bound instantly to apprehend the true interpretation, notwithstanding any mental quickening which he may have received from a 'rough wind' and a modest thermometer pointing to only 'seven or eight degrees below zero.'"

[10] See *supra*, p. 204, n.16.

[11] The commission, apparently, was at least as carrier-oriented as the Court itself. See Chicago, Milwaukee & St. Paul Ry. v. McCaull-Dinsmore Co., 253 U.S. 97 (1920).

[12] Boston & Maine R.R. v. Piper, 246 U.S. 439 (1918).

[13] Union Pacific R.R. v. Burke, 255 U.S. 317 (1921); and see Hovey v. Tankersley, 177 S.W. 153 (Ct. of Civ. Appls. Tex. 1915), *dismissed on motion of plaintiff in error,* 242 U.S. 656 (1916).

[14] 256 U.S. 566 (1921).

[15] See Postal Telegraph-Cable Co. v. Warren-Godwin Co., 251 U.S. 27 (1919); Western Union Telegraph Co. v. Boegli, 251 U.S. 315 (1920); Brewer v. Postal Telegraph-Cable Co., 204 Mo. App. 275, 223 S.W. 949 (K.C. Ct. of Appls. 1920), *cert. denied,* 254 U.S. 647 (1920); but *cf.* Postal Telegraph-Cable Co. v. Bowman & Bull Co., 290 Ill. 155, 124 N.E. 851 (1919), *cert. denied,* 251 U.S. 562 (1920).

people know where they are and it is pretty rational." So he said in conversation with Felix Frankfurter, and it was true that after 1921 the volume of litigation under the Carmack Amendment fell off measurably. But in his notes of this conversation, Frankfurter wrote in the margin, next to the remark of Brandeis just quoted: "Judicial legislation."[16] So it was, and however rational, it could be faulted for too great an insistence on nation-wide uniformity, and for giving the carriers too free a hand. After 1916, however, it is important to remember that Congress had not chosen to repudiate the Court's rules outright,[17] and that subsequent shortcomings were to be laid at least as much at the door of the Interstate Commerce Commission as at that of the Supreme Court.

If the Carmack Amendment produced a fair amount of business, the Federal Employers' Liability Act[18] inundated the docket. Until the October Term 1916, the cases came as of right, on writ of error. The Court made some feeble attempts to protect itself by imposing an occasional—very occasional—penalty for what it considered a frivolously taken appeal,[19] by indicating that only plain error would move it to reverse a judgment resting on findings of fact,[20] and by suggesting that even in cases turning on the constitutional question of whether the injured employee had been engaged in interstate commerce it would respect factual determinations made below.[21] All to little avail. Nor were these threats and declarations really credible, considering the

---

[16] Brandeis-Frankfurter Conversations, Harvard Law School Library.

[17] The new legislation did outlaw provisions absolving the carrier of liability if suit was not brought within a period shorter than two years, although the Court would have permitted carriers to require suits to be brought in a period as short as six months. See Texas & Pacific Ry. v. Leatherwood, 250 U.S. 478 (1919).

[18] See *supra*, pp. 211–13.

[19] Nashville, Chattanooga & St. Louis Ry. v. Henry, 168 Ky. 453, 182 S.W. 651 (1916), *affirmed with costs and 5 percent damages,* 243 U.S. 626 (1917); Nashville, Chattanooga & St. Louis Ry. v. Banks, 168 Ky. 579, 182 S.W. 660 (1916), *affirmed with costs and 5 percent damages,* 243 U.S. 626 (1917); Midland Valley R.R. v. Griffith, 100 Kans. 500, 166 Pac. 467

(1917), *writ of error dismissed for want of jurisdiction with 5 percent damages,* 245 U.S. 633, *cert. denied,* 245 U.S. 653 (1917); Atchison, Topeka & Santa Fe Ry. v. Cole, 97 Kans. 461, 155 Pac. 949 (1916), *affirmed with costs and 10 percent damages,* 245 U.S. 641 (1918); *cf.* Southern Ry. v. Gadd, *supra*, p. 213, n.45. And *cf.* Bruce v. Tobin, 245 U.S. 18 (1917); Chicago Great Western R.R. v. Basham, 249 U.S. 164 (1919).

[20] See Yazoo & Mississippi R.R. v. Wright, 235 U.S. 376 (1914); Great Northern Ry. v. Knapp, 240 U.S. 464 (1916); Gillis v. New York, New Haven & Hartford R.R., 249 U.S. 515 (1919).

[21] See Louisville & Nashville R.R. v. Parker, 242 U.S. 13 (1916); Erie R.R. v. Welsh, 242 U.S. 303 (1916).

number of full opinions the Court wrote in cases scarcely less trivial than those that provoked its few outbursts of impatience.

There were cases concerning the nature of the employee's activities at the time of injury (interstate or intrastate commerce).[22] Then there were points that could—often only charitably—be classified as calling for statutory construction.[23] But the great mass of cases raised factual issues of negligence, or minor questions of procedure, and nothing else. Although McReynolds made something of a specialty of reversing plaintiffs' verdicts, and Clarke—so Brandeis charged, not altogether unjustly—dilated with a misplaced emotion the other way,[24] it is not true that the Court policed the administration of the Act with a defendant's bias, as in later years, after 1940, it favored plaintiffs. If anything, plaintiffs fared slightly better than defendants at this time also.[25]

---

[22] New York Central R.R. v. Carr, 238 U.S. 260 (1915); Shanks v. Delaware, Lackawanna & Western R.R., 239 U.S. 556 (1916); Chicago, Burlington & Quincy R.R. v. Harrington, 241 U.S. 177 (1916); Illinois Central R.R. v. Peery, 242 U.S. 292 (1916); Minneapolis & St. Louis R.R. v. Winters, 242 U.S. 353 (1917); McCluskey v. Marysville & Northern Ry., 243 U.S. 36 (1917); Bay v. Merrill & Ring Logging Co., 243 U.S. 40 (1917); Raymond v. Chicago, Milwaukee & St. Paul Ry., 243 U.S. 43 (1917); Lehigh Valley R.R. v. Barlow, 244 U.S. 183 (1917); New York Central R.R. v. Porter, 249 U.S. 168 (1919); Philadelphia, Baltimore & Washington R.R. v. Smith, 250 U.S. 101 (1919); Kinzell v. Chicago, Milwaukee & St. Paul Ry., 250 U.S. 130 (1919); Southern Pacific Co. v. Industrial Accident Commission, 251 U.S. 259 (1920); Erie R.R. v. Collins, 253 U.S. 77 (1920); Erie R.R. v. Szary, 253 U.S. 86 (1920); Philadelphia & Reading Ry. v. Hancock, 253 U.S. 284 (1920); Philadelphia & Reading Ry. v. Di Donato, 256 U.S. 327 (1921); Philadelphia & Reading Ry. v. Polk, 256 U.S. 332 (1921).

[23] McGovern v. Philadelphia & Reading R.R., 235 U.S. 389 (1914); Arizona & New Mexico Ry. v. Clark,

235 U.S. 669 (1915); Robinson v. Baltimore & Ohio R.R., 237 U.S. 84 (1915); St. Louis, Iron Mountain & Southern Ry. v. Craft, 237 U.S. 648 (1915); Central Vermont Ry. v. White, 238 U.S. 507 (1915); Pecos & Northern Texas Ry. v. Rosenbloom, 240 U.S. 439 (1916); Chicago, Rock Island & Pacific Ry. v. Bond, 240 U.S. 449 (1916); Seaboard Air Line Ry. v. Kenney, 240 U.S. 489 (1916); Baltimore & Ohio R.R. v. Wilson, 242 U.S. 295 (1916); Washington Ry. & Electric Co. v. Scala, 244 U.S. 630 (1917); Great Northern Ry. v. Alexander, 246 U.S. 276 (1918); Dickinson v. Stiles, 246 U.S. 631 (1918); Hull v. Philadelphia & Reading Ry., 252 U.S. 475 (1920).

[24] "Those [Employers' Liability] cases never wearied of calling forth his long and weary dissent," Brandeis said of Clarke. "I said to him, 'Don't you see that the worse the law is the more it will stimulate unions to demand workmen's compensation laws, for the union railroad men are to blame for having resisted it.' No, he would shake his head and go on writing dissents." Brandeis-Frankfurter Conversations.

[25] In thirty-seven cases plaintiffs prevailed. In twenty-six cases the railroads prevailed.

In addition to the cases decided with full opinion, there were at least twenty-one summary affirmances and reversals in the four years from 1914 to 1918, before the jurisdictional reform of 1916 took full effect.[26] Whether disposed of summarily or with opinion, the cases were decided each within its four corners, and scarcely a general proposition ever radiated from them. A possible exception is *Southern Pacific Co.* v. *Berkshire*,[27] in which Holmes essayed formulation of a rule of tort law that may have had some influence.[28] On the issue of whether a worker was employed in interstate commerce at the time of his injury, Van Devanter, in *Shanks* v. *Delaware, Lackawanna & Western Railroad*,[29] reviewed the cases and tried to generalize. But the variables were too many. The exercise was futile. The sole decision of great consequence, to be considered in detail in the next chapter, was that so far as employees engaged in interstate commerce were concerned, the Federal Employers' Liability Act preempted and rendered inapplicable not only inconsistent state rules of tort liability, but also state workmen's compensation laws.[30]

By the Act of September 6, 1916, Congress removed Federal Employers' Liability cases from the obligatory appellate jurisdiction and made them subject only to discretionary review on certiorari.[31] The same statute also placed in the certiorari jurisdiction litigation concerning the Hours of Service Act and the Safety Appliance Acts,[32] which constituted a similar, if in volume lesser, burden.[33] The flow of full opinions was thus stemmed, and plaintiffs, who most often prevailed in

---

[26] In thirteen cases turning on factual or procedural issues, judgments for plaintiffs were affirmed. In similar cases reviewing judgments for the railroads, two were reversed and six affirmed.

[27] 254 U.S. 415 (1921).

[28] See W. Prosser, *Handbook of the Law of Torts* (2nd ed., 1955), 307–10; F. V. Harper and F. James, *The Law of Torts* (1956), § 17.1, 17.2.

[29] *Supra*, n.21.

[30] New York Central R.R. v. Winfield, 244 U.S. 147 (1917).

[31] 39 Stat. 726 (1916); F. Frankfurter and J. M. Landis, *The Business of the Supreme Court* (1928), 205–15.

[32] See *supra*, pp. 213–14.

[33] Hours of Service Act: United States v. Northern Pacific Ry., 242 U.S. 190 (1916); Atchison, Topeka & Santa Fe Ry. v. United States, 244 U.S. 336 (1917); Chicago & Northwestern Ry. Co. v. United States, 246 U.S. 512 (1918); Chicago & Alton R.R. v. United States, 247 U.S. 197 (1918); United States v. Brooklyn Eastern District Terminal, 249 U.S. 296 (1919).

Safety Appliance Acts: United States v. Erie R.R., 237 U.S. 402 (1915); United States v. Chicago, Burlington & Quincy R.R., 237 U.S. 410 (1915); Texas & Pacific Ry. v. Rigsby, 241 U.S. 33 (1916); Spokane & Inland R.R. v. United States, 241 U.S. 344 (1916); Illinois Central R.R. Co. v. Williams, 242 U.S. 462 (1917); Louisville & Jeffersonville Bridge Co. v. United States, 249 U.S. 534 (1919); Boehmer v. Pennsylvania R.R., 252 U.S. 496 (1920); United States v. Northern Pacific Ry., 254 U.S. 251 (1920).

the state courts, were in some measure advantaged, at least in that they were now more frequently saved the expense of yet another appellate proceeding. But the Court exercised its discretion to take a number of these cases each year just the same,[34] and, of course, the great mass of certiorari petitions was a considerable drain on its energies also.[35] The Federal Employers' Liability Act thus remained an institutionally as well as socially wasteful enterprise. And so it remains.

Other aspects of railroad legislation enacted by the Theodore Roosevelt and Taft administrations—aside from provisions affecting the Interstate Commerce Commission's principal regulatory activities, which are dealt with in a subsequent chapter—occupied the Court but relatively little in these years. In *Pierce* v. *United States*,[36] Brandeis allowed the government to collect a judgment under the antirebate Elkins Act of 1903 from the stockholders of a dissolved defendant corporation.[37] There were a couple of cases dealing with the Hepburn Act's prohibition of free passes,[38] and two more emphasizing the need for caution in the exercise of powers over intrastate commerce upheld in

---

[34] Philadelphia, Baltimore & Washington R.R. v. Smith, Kinzell v. Chicago, Milwaukee & St. Paul Ry., Southern Pacific Co. v. Industrial Accident Commission, Erie R.R. v. Collins, Erie R.R. v. Szary, Philadelphia & Reading Ry. v. Di Donato, Philadelphia & Reading Ry. v. Polk, *supra*, n.22; Hull v. Philadelphia & Reading Ry., *supra*, n.23; Chicago, Rock Island & Pacific Ry. v. Ward, 252 U.S. 18 (1920); Pryor v. Williams, Southern Pacific Co. v. Berkshire, Lang v. New York Central R.R., *supra*, n.27; United States v. Chicago, Burlington & Quincy R.R., Boehmer v. Pennsylvania R.R., United States v. Northern Pacific Ry., *supra*, n.33; and see all the cases arising under the Hours of Service Act cited *supra*, n.33.

[35] Between 1916 and 1920 certiorari was denied in the following classes of railroad cases: Federal Employers' Liability Act cases turning on issues of interstate vs. intrastate commerce: eighteen. Federal Employers' Liability Act cases turning on issues of statutory construction: five. Federal Employers' Liability Act cases turning on factual or procedural issues in

which judgments below were for plaintiffs: forty-one. Federal Employers' Liability Act cases turning on factual or procedural issues in which judgments below were for the railroads: twelve. Cases arising under the Hours of Service Act: three. Cases arising under the Safety Appliance Acts: seven.

[36] 255 U.S. 398 (1921).

[37] "It is stiff doctrine," Holmes returned to Brandeis, "but you make it plausible." Brandeis Papers, Harvard Law School Library. See *supra*, p. 204; see also Lehigh Coal & Navigation Co. v. United States, 250 U.S. 556 (1919); and see Vandalia R.R. v. United States, 226 Fed. 713 (7th Cir. 1915), *cert. denied*, 239 U.S. 642 (1915); Northern Central Ry. v. United States, 241 Fed. 25 (2nd Cir. 1917), *cert. denied*, 245 U.S. 645 (1917); Elgin, Joliet & Eastern Ry. v. United States, 253 Fed. 907 (7th Cir. 1918), *cert. denied*, 249 U.S. 601 (1919).

[38] See *supra*, pp. 204–205; New York Central R.R. v. Gray, 239 U.S. 583 (1916); Norfolk Southern R.R. v. Chatman, 244 U.S. 276 (1917).

the *Shreveport Case*.[39] In *United States* v. *Louisville & Nashville Railroad*,[40] the investigative and visitatorial function sustained in *Interstate Commerce Commission* v. *Goodrich Transit Co.*[41] was appreciably contracted.

The Congressional power to regulate navigable waters—also no great source of judicial business in either number or significance of cases—continued to receive hospitable and expansive treatment.[42] So did the Pure Food and Mann acts. The litigation produced by these two statutes, while again modest in volume, resulted in some quite important decisions.

Again the Pure Food and Drug Act

Seven Cases of Eckman's Alternative v. *United States*,[43] which was one wonderfully named case of a libel brought by the government against seven crates of patent medicine, sustained the constitutionality of the amendment enacted to overrule Holmes' restrictive interpretation of the Pure Food and Drug Act in *United States* v. *Johnson*.[44] Eckman's Alternative was labeled: "Effective as a preventative for pneumonia. We know it has cured and that it has and will cure tuberculosis." This claim, a unanimous Court held, Hughes writing, was false and fraudulent and violated the amended statute. It was not the sort of mere statement of opinion about therapeutic effect which Holmes, in the *Johnson* case, had doubted Congress could reach.[45]

United States v. *Coca-Cola Co.*[46] was the upshot of a long battle waged by Dr. Harvey W. Wiley, the father of the Pure Food Act. Again

---

[39] See *supra*, pp. 216 *et seq.*; American Express Co. v. Caldwell, and Illinois Central R.R. v. Public Utilities Commission, *supra,* p. 220, n.65.

[40] 236 U.S. 318 (1915); see also Ellis v. Interstate Commerce Commission, 237 U.S. 434 (1915). But *cf.* Smith v. Interstate Commerce Commission, 245 U.S. 33, 47 (1917); Jones v. Interstate Commerce Commission, 245 U.S. 48 (1917).

[41] *Supra*, p. 214, n.49.

[42] See *supra*, p. 221; Greenleaf Lumber Co. v. Garrison, 237 U.S. 251 (1915); Willink v. United States, 240 U.S. 572 (1916); Cubbins v. Mississippi River Commission, 241 U.S. 351 (1916); Economy Light &

Power Co. v. United States, 256 U.S. 113 (1921); but *cf.* United States v. Cress, 243 U.S. 316 (1917).

[43] 239 U.S. 510 (1916); see also Simpson v. United States, 241 Fed. 841 (6th Cir. 1917), *cert. denied,* 245 U.S. 664 (1917).

[44] 221 U.S. 488 (1911). See *supra*, pp. 226–28.

[45] Because it was limited to avoid Holmes' doubts, the amendment overruling the *Johnson* case, called the Sherley Amendment, was criticized as well as welcomed by Progressive writers. See, e.g., G. Creel in *Harper's Weekly,* 60:134–36, 1916; *The Outlook,* 101:992–93, August 1912.

[46] 241 U.S. 265, 277 (1916).

speaking for a unanimous Court, Hughes held that the caffeine in Coca-Cola was an adulterating added substance within the meaning of the statute, and that its name misbranded the product if, as alleged, there was neither any coca nor any cola in it. "[I]n determining the scope of specific provisions" of the statute, Hughes wrote, "the purpose to protect the public health, as an important aim of the statute, must not be ignored." But the case had been disposed of below by a directed verdict for the company, which Hughes now reversed; Dr. Wiley had by then left the government, and the will of his successors in carrying on the struggle with the Coca-Cola Company had slackened; and so the case was finally settled without being retried, the company agreeing to some slight modifications in its formula.[47]

Weeks v. *United States*,[48] another misbranding case decided for the government,[49] clarified the holding in *United States* v. *Lexington Mill & Elevator Co.*,[50] but in *Weigle* v. *Curtice Brothers Co.*,[51] Holmes, although in the end he sustained a state regulation more stringent than the federal, suggested that Congress was powerless to control the marketing in retail stores and restaurants of articles that were not sold in the original packages in which they had been shipped.

Again the Mann Act

The Mann Act, not the most attractive of Progressive reforms, was being enforced with uncommon vigor. In the first fiscal year after its effective date, there were 145 prosecutions, 76 convictions and 14 acquittals. Forty-five cases were left pending. Sentences and fines were often heavy. It was believed, Attorney General Wickersham reported, "that the act is having a salutary effect." During the following year there was a "tremendous increase" in the number of violations coming to the attention of the Department of Justice, and the Attorney General appointed a special commissioner to take charge of Mann Act enforce-

---

[47] See E. J. Kahn, Jr., "Profiles: The Universal Drink," *The New Yorker*, 35:35–36, Feb. 28, 1959; L. B. Allyn, "Pure Food in the United States," *McClure's*, 46:78, February 1916.

[48] 245 U.S. 618 (1918). For another Pure Food Act conviction of the same defendant, see Weeks v. United States, 216 Fed. 292 (2nd Cir. 1914), *cert. denied*, 235 U.S. 697 (1914).

[49] See also United States v. Schider, 246 U.S. 519 (1918); and see Goode

v. United States, 44 App. D.C. 162 (1915), *writ of error dismissed on motion of plaintiff in error*, 243 U.S. 661 (1917); and see, for cases upholding applications of the Meat Inspection Acts of 1906 and 1907, United States v. Lewis, 235 U.S. 282 (1914); Pittsburgh Melting Co. v. Totten, 248 U.S. 1 (1918); Houston v. St. Louis Packing Co., 249 U.S. 479 (1919).

[50] *Supra*, p. 226, nn.80, 82.

[51] 248 U.S. 285 (1919).

ment. There had been, from the date of enactment to October 1912, 337 convictions and 35 acquittals; 106 cases were then still pending. By October of the following year, the number of convictions had nearly doubled to 633—presumably the result of the special commissioner's efforts. Acquittals had increased to 93 and there were then 177 cases pending. A great proportion of the efforts of the Federal Bureau of Investigation was devoted to enforcement of the Mann Act. By the middle of 1916, before the war began to divert attention and energies, there had been 1,537 convictions and 238 acquittals. Sentences imposed had aggregated 2,468 years, 3 months, and 16 days, indicating an average sentence of well over a year and a half.[52]

In the pursuit of the most obvious objective of the Act—stamping out the so-called white-slave trade—the Department of Justice hardly needed the assistance of the Supreme Court, once constitutionality had been affirmed, as it had been in 1913.[53] The three decisions construing the Act that were handed down by the Court in this period dealt with cases falling only dubiously—to say the least—within the obvious purpose of the statute. But the Court swept them all in, albeit by majorities that decreased as the distance from the obvious purpose lengthened.

United States v. *Portale*[54] concerned a minor provision that required anyone harboring an immigrant woman for purposes of prostitution to report that fact to the government, subject to criminal penalties for failure to do so. A unanimous Court, per Holmes, held this provision applicable to one who, although harboring an immigrant prostitute, had had nothing to do with bringing her into the country.

In *United States* v. *Holte*,[55] Holmes held, over two dissents (Lamar, joined by Day), that a woman could be punished for conspiring with a man to have herself transported across state lines for purposes of prostitution. Holmes would have none of "the illusion that the woman always is the victim," although the legislative history might have shown, had it been examined, that Congress harbored precisely this illusion, and although punishing the travel of a willing woman raised constitutional doubts about as plausible at this time as those that troubled Holmes when it came to punishing misrepresentations on matters of medical opinion in *United States* v. *Johnson*.[56] But it was enough for Holmes here that "[t]he words of the statute punish the

---

[52] *Annual Report of the Attorney General of the United States for the Year 1911*, 25; *Ibid., for the Year 1912*, 48; *Ibid., for the Year 1913*, 50; *Ibid., for the Year 1915*, 48; *Ibid., for the Year 1916*, 52.

[53] See *supra*, pp. 228 *et seq.* See

United States v. Lombardo, 241 U.S. 73 (1916).

[54] 235 U.S. 27 (1914).

[55] 236 U.S. 140, 145 (1915); see *supra*, p. 365, n.187.

[56] See *supra*, pp. 422, 226–28. See also E. H. Levi, *An Introduction to Legal Reasoning* (1949), 24 *et seq.*

transportation of a woman for the purpose of prostitution even if she were the first to suggest the crime." This ominous insistence on the words of the statute was to have its apotheosis at the hands of Day, one of the *Holte* dissenters, in *Caminetti* v. *United States.*

Reporting on the second year's experience with the Mann Act, and predicting the great increase in prosecutions which did in fact occur, and which would continue to occur for some decades,[57] Attorney General Wickersham said that the department refrained "from instituting technical or trivial cases, or cases which more properly belong in the state courts, and has restricted itself to the class of cases at which the act was primarily directed."[58] The *Caminetti* case concerned three prosecutions not so restricted, two of which were brought by a holdover Republican U.S. Attorney in California against the son of a prominent local Democrat and his friend, and led to a brief and pointless scandal, when McReynolds as Attorney General at first delayed them.[59] If McReynolds, or anyone else with national responsibility, ever made a deliberate decision to depart from the restricted and sensible policy of Attorney General Wickersham, the fact is not apparent. It seems probable that the government slid more or less unwittingly into a policy of broader application of the Act, through occasional prosecutions started by scattered U.S. Attorneys.

Drew Caminetti, son of the Democratic leader in San Francisco, and a companion, Maury I. Diggs, transported two girls from Sacramento, California, to Reno, Nevada, intending to have sexual intercourse with them there. They were sentenced respectively to eighteen months and three years of imprisonment, and fined $1,500 and $2,000. Caminetti and Diggs had been on a common escapade. A third defendant, one Hays, whose case was now to be decided together with theirs, was involved in an entirely separate event. The charge against Hays was that he and another had "persuaded, induced, enticed and coerced a certain woman, unmarried and under the age of eighteen years," to travel from Oklahoma City to Wichita, Kansas, for purposes of prostitution and other immoral practices. No act of coercion was laid to Caminetti and Diggs. But Hays no more than Caminetti and Diggs was charged with intending to make a profit from the woman's prostitution. Hays also was procuring the woman's services for himself. None of these cases was thus, as Day pointed out at the beginning of the opinion of the Court handed down on January 15, 1917, an in-

---

[57] See Note, "Interstate Immorality: The Mann Act and the Supreme Court," *Yale L. J.,* 56:718, 725, n.48, 1947.

[58] *Annual Report of the Attorney General of the United States for the Year 1912,* 48.

[59] See *supra,* pp. 347–48. See also Note, "Interstate Immorality," 727–28.

stance of "commercialized vice." It was neither charged nor proved, Day said, "that the transportation was for gain or for the purpose of furnishing women for prostitution for hire," and it was contended in all three cases that for this reason the Mann Act was inapplicable. That was the issue.

The statute, Day wrote, punished transportation "for the purpose of prostitution or debauchery, or *'for any other immoral purpose'*. . . ." (Italics supplied.) This language was "plain" and admitted "of no more than one meaning. . . ." There was no ambiguity. Any immoral purpose would do. Under such circumstances, "the duty of interpretation does not arise and the rules which are said to aid doubtful meanings need no discussion." No doubt, where there was an "expectation of pecuniary gain," the offense was aggravated, but it was an offense just the same merely to travel with a woman in order to make her one's mistress or concubine. "To say the contrary would shock the common understanding of what constitutes an immoral purpose when those terms are applied, as here, to sexual relations."

Three years before it passed the Mann Act, Congress, in a 1907 immigration statute, had prohibited the importation of alien women and girls "for the purpose of prostitution or for any other immoral purpose,"[60] and in *United States* v. *Bitty*,[61] the Court had held this provision applicable to one who imported an alien woman, not for purposes of prostitution, but in order to live in concubinage with her. This decision, said Day, "must be presumed to have been known to Congress when it enacted the law here involved," a circumstance supporting the assumption of an awareness on the part of Congress that the phrase "any other immoral purpose" would reach more than just commercialized vice.

Congress had provided specifically in Section 8 of the statute that it was to be known as the "White-slave Traffic Act," and it was contended that this deliberately chosen title limited the application of the law. But the title of an act, Day replied, "cannot overcome the meaning of plain and unambiguous words used in its body," and it did not justify a court "to enter speculative fields in search of a different meaning." It was true also that a committee report accompanying the bill to the floor of the House assigned as the purpose of the Act the suppression of the commercialized white-slave trade. But committee reports were relevant only when there was a problem of interpretation. When the language of an act was plain and did not lead to absurd or wholly impracticable consequences, that language was "the sole evidence of the ultimate legislative intent." And if, as was argued, the statute was being

---

[60] 34 Stat. 899 (1907).   [61] 208 U.S. 393 (1908).

turned into a tool for large-scale blackmail operations, that was a consideration properly addressed to Congress, not to a court powerless to amend the law.

Nor did this construction create constitutional problems. It might be beyond the authority of Congress to punish an individual who travels in interstate commerce with intention to commit an immoral act at the end of his journey. That, although he did not mention it now, had been Day's dissenting position in the *Holte* case. But this statute punished "the movement in interstate commerce of women and girls with a view to the accomplishment of the unlawful purposes prohibited. The transportation of passengers in interstate commerce, it has long been settled, is within the regulatory power of Congress . . . and the authority of Congress to keep the channels of interstate commerce free from immoral and injurious uses has been frequently sustained, and is no longer open to question." There remained a procedural issue, concerning the trial judge's comment to the jury on defendant Diggs' failure, while on the stand, to testify to certain facts he could be presumed to have known, but Day disposed of this issue in favor of the government, and affirmed all three convictions.

Day's opinion spoke for a majority of five—himself, Holmes, Van Devanter, Pitney, and Brandeis. McReynolds was disqualified, owing, of course, to his prior connection with the case when Attorney General, and McKenna, joined by White and Clarke, dissented. The proposition, said McKenna, that the plain words of a statute must settle all questions as to its meaning "has attractive and seemingly disposing simplicity. . . ." But it could not always exempt judges "from putting ourselves in the place of the legislators." There were numerous occasions when the words might be clear in meaning, but the objects to which they were addressed were uncertain. The problem then was "to determine the uncertainty. And for this a realization of conditions that provoked the statute must inform our judgment." So here the word "immoral" could cover "every form of vice, every form of conduct that is contrary to good order." Yet it was admitted all around that as used in the Mann Act, the word "immoral" referred only to sexual acts, and once it was conceded that the word was limited at all, "that ends the imperative effect assigned to it in the opinion of the Court."

Obviously, context had to enter into the process of definition, and context meant the purpose of the statute. Hence a broader inquiry than the Court permitted itself was necessarily opened. The purpose of the statute, as indicated by its title, was to deal with "commercialized vice, immorality having a mercenary purpose. . . ." This was confirmed by the committee report that accompanied the bill when it was brought to the House of Representative James R. Mann of Illinois, its principal author. The report disclaimed any attempt to regulate the practice of

427

voluntary prostitution, and defined the bill's purpose as being to reach panderers and procurers who compelled women into vice. "In other words," McKenna summarized, "it is vice as a business at which the law is directed, using interstate commerce as a facility to procure or distribute its victims."

Attorney General Wickersham had administered the statute with this limited purpose in mind, and had explicitly so indicated in reply to an inquiry from a local U.S. Attorney. The rule that statutes are to be construed, not in rigid adherence to a supposed clear meaning of their words, but in light of their purpose,

> is a valuable one and in varying degrees has daily practice. It not only rescues legislation from absurdity . . . but it often rescues it from invalidity, a useful result in our dual form of governments and conflicting jurisdictions. It is the dictate of common sense. Language, even when most masterfully used, may miss sufficiency, and give room for dispute. Is it a wonder therefore, that when used in the haste of legislation, in view of conditions perhaps only partly seen or not seen at all, the consequences, it may be, beyond present foresight, it often becomes necessary to apply the rule? And it is a rule of prudence and highest sense. It rescues from crudities, excesses and deficiencies, making legislation adequate to its special purpose, rendering unnecessary repeated qualifications and leaving the simple and best exposition of a law the mischief it was intended to redress. Nor is this judicial legislation. It is seeking and enforcing the true sense of a law notwithstanding its imperfection or generality of expression.

The present case offered, to be sure, a strong temptation to violation of the rule, since a "measure that protects the purity of women from assault or enticement to degradation finds an instant advocate in our best emotions. . . ." But judges should not yield to emotion, nor shut their eyes "to the facts of the world and assume not to know what everybody else knows. And everybody knows that there is a difference between the occasional immoralities of men and women and that systematized and mercenary immorality epitomized in the statute's graphic phrase 'White-slave traffic.' And it was such immorality that was in the legislative mind and not the other." Finally the construction now adopted played into the hands of blackmailers, and certainly judges were entitled to reject the construction that led to mischievous consequences, if the statute was susceptible of another one. *United States* v. *Bitty* was distinguishable because the purpose of the statute there involved was different and broader.[62]

---

[62] Caminetti v. United States, 242 U.S. 470, 484–86, 488–91, 496–97, 501–502 (1917).

V: *The Fate of Social Legislation, 1914–21: Federal*

The case for Caminetti and Diggs was argued by former Senator Joseph W. Bailey of Texas,[63] with heavy reliance upon the legislative history, including portions of the vast literature exposing organized, big-city vice, which provided the impulse for passage of the statute.[64] In an able and eloquent petition for rehearing, he rehearsed many of McKenna's points. "It is a question of classification, rather than of words," Bailey wrote. "To hold that the act includes mere escapades transforms into a felony what all of the States have regarded as a misdemeanor for many years, and renders men infamous for conduct which, at its worst, might be no more than a transgression of the moral law. Our humanity revolts at the thought of punishing a moral lapse as a felony, and no law which does so can be properly enforced." The consequence could merely be the "arming" of blackmailers.

Bailey added also an insistent argument that, as construed, the statute exceeded Congressional authority to regulate interstate commerce. The women who accompanied Caminetti and Diggs were in no sense "the subject of interstate commerce." Congress was attempting to regulate the personal conduct of those who travel, and that was beyond its jurisdiction.

> I will not insult the intelligence of the court by asking whether this law, if intended to apply to other than the real white slave traffic, is designed to regulate commerce or to regulate morals. If the law means that all immorality connected in any way with interstate transportation is within this act, then it is designed to regulate morals, not commerce; and if the Congress of the United States can, under the pretense of regulating commerce, take the morals of the people under federal control, it can, under the same pretense, gradually usurp the police powers of these States and finally destroy the States themselves.[65]

Press comment on the decision generally, but not universally, regretted the result, and the opportunities for blackmail to which it would give rise. There was almost unanimous agreement, as well, that Congress had originally had no such application of the Mann Act in mind, and yet with an equal approach to unanimity it seemed to be agreed that the wording of the statute had left the Supreme Court with no choice, and that the remedy for this too-comprehensive wording lay with Congress. But Congress, it was quite apparent, would not amend

---

[63] Joseph Weldon Bailey (1863–1929) was born in Mississippi, moved to Texas in young manhood, served in the House from Texas for ten years, and for two terms in the Senate. He was a leading Democratic Congressional figure, but retired voluntarily in 1912 to resume the practice of law.

[64] See *supra,* pp. 228–32.

[65] 242 U.S. 470, 478, 480.

the statute.[66] Ten of the jurors who had convicted Caminetti and Diggs, several Democratic Senators, numerous lawyers and judges in San Francisco, and Caminetti's mother all importuned President Wilson to grant a pardon. But Wilson would not, for fear, no doubt, of provoking another scandal like the one that broke over McReynolds' head when he ordered postponement of the trial.[67]

Day had the satisfaction of receiving the following letter from the author of the statute, Representative Mann, then minority leader of the House:

> I hope it is entirely proper for me to congratulate you upon your opinion and the decision of the Supreme Court in the [Caminetti] white slave cases. While I have never thought that the writer of that Act was the one best qualified to construe the meaning of the act and hence have refrained from any expression of opinion concerning my intent and thought when I wrote the language in the white slave law, yet you have construed the law the way I intended when I very carefully considered and wrote it and while I think there probably was no public statement to that effect, yet in private statements made on the floor of the House before the bill was passed, I explained to a good many Members the bill as going fully as far as is stated in your valuable opinion.

"While of course we could not know," Day replied, "except from the language used, the purpose and intent of the framers of the law, the confirmation which you give the construction of the act is very gratifying indeed."[68] But the majority could have known, from Representative Mann's own committee report, from the debates and from other materials, what seemed then and what has seemed since unmistakably clear to others, namely, that the only publicly avowed purpose of the statute was to punish and root out commercialized vice.[69] Day's opinion represents a refusal to know. And whatever the uses of statutory construction may or may not properly be, its function is not to translate into law the private intention of a member of Congress, unacknowledged in any "public statement to that effect." It would scarcely conduce to legislative responsibility for the Court to enforce as law privately nurtured designs which do not conform to those publicly declared in debate. It is a tenable, although more than

---

[66] *The Literary Digest,* 54:178, January 1917; *Washington Post,* Jan. 19, 1917, p. 4, col. 2.

[67] See A. S. Link, *Wilson: The New Freedom* (1956), 118.

[68] J. R. Mann to W. R. Day, Jan. 29, 1917; Day to Mann, Jan. 30, 1917, Day Papers, Library of Congress.

[69] See Levi, *Introduction to Legal Reasoning,* 24 *et seq.*; Note, "Interstate Immorality," 726–27.

slightly obscurantist, position to insist on being guided only by the statutory language, in accordance with the English practice, rather than also by less formal expressions of purpose in other legislative materials. Only the statute itself is, after all, put to a vote. But there is no excuse at all for even drawing comfort from a private, undisclosed legislative intent.

Day's single admission of the relevance of anything but the so-called plain words, which came in his reference to the *Bitty* case, was all too facile. For an awareness of the *Bitty* decision could have indicated to members of Congress that bringing a woman into the country for the purpose of supporting her in a state of concubinage was considered little different from bringing her into the country for purposes of prostitution. A Congressman who received this impression of the meaning of the phrase "immoral purpose" would far from necessarily conclude that the term covered also casual instances of sexual intercourse, involving no sustained economic support by either party of the other.[70]

Day's absolute refusal to consider committee reports and debates was less extraordinary in 1917 than it would be today. When such materials were used in these years, reference to them was sometimes accompanied by a grudging statement, recalling the English tradition, to the effect that they would be examined on the assumption, taken for the sake of argument, that it was proper to resort to them; and if the reference was to debates, there might be a remark that they were notoriously of doubtful import.[71] The plain-meaning rule had and retains its attraction, from time to time, for almost all judges. Thus McKenna, whose dissent in *Caminetti* is a brilliant exposition of the true method and the proper ends of statutory interpretation, could find himself in another case contending against Day in a battle of words over what he there called "the simple service of interpretation," with no thought of context, or of "putting ourselves in the place of the legislators."[72] And yet it is easy enough to point to a sufficiency of cases decided before *Caminetti* in which use was made, sometimes decisively, of committee reports and debates.[73] Day himself was more grudging

---

[70] See Note, "Interstate Immorality," 726, n.50.

[71] See, e.g., Clark Distilling Co. v. Western Maryland Ry., 242 U.S. 311, 322 (1917); Lapina v. Williams, 232 U.S. 78, 90 (1914).

[72] Sandberg v. McDonald, 248 U.S. 185, 201–202 (1918); see A. M. Bickel, *The Unpublished Opinions of Mr. Justice Brandeis* (1957), 34–60.

[73] See, e.g., United States v. Press Publishing Co., 219 U.S. 1 (1911); Montello Salt Co. v. Utah, 221 U.S. 452 (1911); Richardson v. Harmon, 222 U.S. 96 (1911); Northern Pacific Ry. v. Washington, 222 U.S. 370 (1911); Lewis Publishing Co. v. Morgan, 229 U.S. 288 (1913); Pennsylvania R.R. v. International Coal Co., 230 U.S. 184 (1913); Lapina v. Williams, 232 U.S. 78 (1914); United States v. Midwest Oil Co., 236 U.S.

than most, but even he was not altogether without an occasional guilty knowledge of a committee report.[74]

One thing is certain, in any event. Regardless of deviations and sporadic professions that the dictionary meaning of words alone mattered and everything else was forbidden fruit for judges, statutory construction, then as now, was in fact, as it inescapably has to be, informed by purpose and context. Then as now, it was influenced by a sympathetic or unsympathetic attitude toward the legislative purpose, and affected by the judges' perception of whether one or another construction was in harmony or disharmony with the preexisting legal order, of whether it impinged on values that Congress might or might not have had in mind but that the judges deemed important, and of whether it had by-products of mischief. So White interpreted the Sherman Antitrust Act in the *Standard Oil* and *Tobacco* cases, and only Harlan was heard to wish it otherwise. So Holmes approached the Pure Food Act in *United States* v. *Johnson*.[75] And so Day himself discharged his function, according to his lights, in *Thompson* v. *Thompson*, narrowly construing a District of Columbia statute, against the plain meaning of its words, so as to preserve the common law rule that women cannot sue their husbands.[76]

Judges do not discharge their proper function when they defeat a remedial or regulatory purpose of the legislature, owing to a failure of sympathy or perception. They are often equally to be censured for carrying a statute beyond its ascertainable purpose, into an area where a fresh policy decision is called for, because a new balance must be struck between benefits expected and mischiefs risked and accepted. They are always and particularly to be censured if they disclaim responsibility for the law they make, shrugging it off upon a legislature that never addressed itself to the problem. But judges are most to be censured when in a case like *Caminetti* there can be no greater expectation of legislative revision of their decision than in constitutional adjudication itself, when therefore the only course open to the judges that is consistent with ultimate legislative responsibility is to construe the statute narrowly, and yet they construe it broadly. Of course the judges should not take into account passing political configurations. Only

---

459 (1915); Woodward v. De Graffenried, 238 U.S. 284 (1915); David v. Hildebrant, 241 U.S. 565 (1916); United States v. Pennsylvania R.R., 242 U.S. 208 (1916); Clark Distilling Co. v. Western Maryland Ry., 242 U.S. 311 (1917). But *cf.* Omaha Street Ry. v. Interstate Commerce Commission, 230 U.S. 324 (1913).

[74] See, e.g., United States v. Lexington Mill Co., 232 U.S. 399 (1914); Sandberg v. McDonald, 248 U.S. 185, 197 (1918).

[75] See *supra*, pp. 227–28, 422, 424.

[76] See *supra*, p. 315, n.383.

See also United States v. Gradwell, 243 U.S. 476 (1917); United States v. Bathgate, 246 U.S. 220 (1918).

relatively enduring institutional attributes are relevant. But the least bit of insight would have revealed that while Congress could have freely decided whether or not to overrule the opposite result in *Caminetti* and extend the coverage of the Mann Act, no legislature in our society was then capable of affirmatively legalizing debauchery.

After *Caminetti*, the *New York Tribune* reported the following comment by a leading Democratic Senator:

> No member of Congress ought to be expected to undergo the penalty that would surely follow the introduction of a bill that would restrict the present statute.
>
> Every purity league in the United States would crucify him. The trouble is, good people do not distinguish. They would mistake motives. No, the only chance of an amendment to the law would come from the Department of Justice. . . . But there is no chance of that. The law will stand as it is now written. If it benefits the blackmailers, that is bad, of course, but we can't help it.[77]

Whatever may be thought of these strictures, it is plain that Day's result was not compelled. Perhaps the constitutional doubts offered up by Senator Bailey should not have impressed themselves on the judges, as in fact they did not, although in its own terms, Day's argument does not ring true. Day conceded that Congress could not simply regulate the conduct that a traveler in interstate commerce intended to engage in once he reached his destination, and yet he affirmed a power to do precisely that in the case of a man and a woman voluntarily traveling together. And the doubts sown by Senator Bailey concerning Congress' pursuit of ulterior ends through disingenuous regulations of commerce would so powerfully affect Day and four other judges a year and a half later as to be decisive in *Hammer* v. *Dagenhart*, the first child labor case.[78] But even without harboring constitutional doubts, it was possible to be troubled by so deep an intrusion into an area of criminal jurisdiction traditionally reserved to the states, and indeed by the application of federal felony law to what Senator Bailey called "moral lapses." It was at least as possible to be bothered by this intrusion as by the imputation to Congress of a purpose to take harsh measures in matters of medical opinion, which Holmes refused to indulge in *United States* v. *Johnson*.

One is entitled, then, to find an authoritarian, puritanical streak in the judges of the majority, for they arrived at their result willingly, to say the least. They included, however, Holmes and Brandeis. How he should like "to see our people more intent on doing their job than

---

[77] *The Literary Digest,* 54:178, January 1917.   [78] 247 U.S. 251 (1918).

on pointing out grievances," Holmes wrote his friend Harold J. Laski one month before the *Caminetti* decision came down, "and oh how little I care for the upward and onward trend. I must say 'trend' that the *banalité* of the word correspond to the fact, of our legislation to make other people better, with teetotalism and white-slave laws that make felons of young men (unless our court decides they don't) for crossing a state line with a girl, and that manifest the sacredness of Woman. I think I must be an old Fogey and proud of the title."[79]

Why should Holmes have felt unable to give any effect to these sentiments in *Caminetti*, when he was astute to find room in the Sherman Act for his unsympathetic views toward antitrust policy? Perhaps, perversely, he wished the "crowd" (a favorite word) to savor the full consequences of its "upward and onward trend." As for Brandeis, when later law clerks taxed him with *Caminetti* as the one action of his they could not understand, he replied: "Holmes, you know, voted with me in *Caminetti*, and you couldn't call him a prude."[80] One might dare think of Brandeis, however, as a bit of a prude. Nothing is clearer, judging by the method of statutory interpretation that Brandeis employed in his later career, and indeed contemporaneously in such a case as *New York Central Railroad* v. *Winfield*,[81] decided four months after *Caminetti*, than that Brandeis could not have deemed himself compelled to the result by the "plain meaning" of the statutory language.

Caminetti has remained a much-discussed object lesson in how not to discharge the function of statutory construction. It has been much criticized also because the predictions that it would constitute a weapon for hosts of blackmailers have come true. And it has necessarily led to selective prosecutions, which more often than not take on the aspect of persecutions.[82] But there it stands. Congress has not touched it, of course, nor has the Court itself had any second thoughts.[83] As late

---

[79] M. DeW. Howe, ed., *Holmes-Laski Letters* (1953), I, 42.

[80] L. L. Jaffe, "An Impression of Mr. Justice Brandeis," *Harv. L. Sch. Bull.*, 8:10, 11, April 1957.

[81] 244 U.S. 147 (1917). See *supra*, pp. 420 *et seq.*

[82] See Note, "Interstate Immorality," 720, 729.

[83] Opportunities were few in any event, since prosecutions for mere debauchery rather than white slavery, strictly speaking, are sporadic, as noted. See e.g., Griffith v. United States, 261 Fed. 159 (7th Cir. 1919),

cert. denied, 252 U.S. 577 (1920); Ammerman v. United States, 262 Fed. 124 (8th Cir. 1919), *cert. denied*, 253 U.S. 495 (1920). See also Yeates v. United States, 254 Fed. 60 (5th Cir. 1918), *cert. denied*, 248 U.S. 583 (1919); Hamilton v. United States, 255 Fed. 511 (8th Cir. 1919), *cert. denied*, 249 U.S. 610 (1919); Blackstock v. United States, 261 Fed. 150 (8th Cir. 1919), *cert. denied*, 254 U.S. 634 (1920). Another case the Court declined to hear is worth mention. It is Younge v. United States, 242 Fed. 788 (4th Cir. 1917), *cert. denied*, 245

as 1946, the Supreme Court followed *Caminetti* by holding the Mann Act applicable to the practice of polygamy.[84]

Narcotics Regulation

The method of literal construction which extracted the *Caminetti* result from the Mann Act was not followed by the Court with respect to a Wilson Administration measure that raised cognate problems. The Harrison Narcotic Drug Act of 1914[85] imposed a special tax of $1 per annum on anyone who produced, imported,[86] manufactured, dispensed, sold, distributed, or otherwise dealt in opium or coca leaves, or compounds or derivatives of them. All who engaged in these activities were required to register with internal revenue collectors. Failure to register and pay the tax was made a criminal offense. Sales and exchanges of opium and coca leaves had to be recorded on order forms issued by the Bureau of Internal Revenue and were punishable if not so recorded, except in the case of doctors' prescriptions, of which less formal records were required to be kept. Use of the order forms to obtain drugs for any purpose other than lawful resale in business or dispensation in the course of legitimate professional practice was also a criminal offense. In other words, no addicts could be served, whether or not they paid the tax. Finally, Section 8 forbade "any person" who had not registered and paid the special tax to possess the drugs.

United States v. *Jin Fuey Moy*, which contrasts significantly with *Caminetti*, called for interpretation of the phrase "any person" in Section 8. Dr. Jin Fuey Moy of Pittsburgh was indicted for conspiring to give possession of the drug to one Willie Martin, a person who, as the doctor knew, had not registered and paid the tax. Unless under Section 8 possession of the drug by Martin was unlawful, there could be no punishable conspiracy, for the charge was not that the doctor himself

---

U.S. 656 (1917), a prosecution of a black man for transporting a black woman for purposes of prostitution from Parkersburg, West Virginia, to Marietta, Ohio. The Court of Appeals made quite light, as had the trial judge, of attempts by the defendant to challenge under the Fourteenth Amendment the composition of the all-white grand jury that indicted him, and the all-white petit jury that convicted him.

[84] Cleveland v. United States, 329 U.S. 14 (1946).

[85] 38 Stat. 785 (1914).

[86] The importation of opium for other than medical purposes had been forbidden by an earlier statute, Act of Feb. 9, 1909, 35 Stat. 614, and in Brolan v. United States, 236 U.S. 216 (1915), the Court held that this prohibition fell so clearly within the power of Congress to regulate foreign commerce that the question of its constitutionality was frivolous.

435

was unregistered, or that he had not demanded an order form from Martin, or had otherwise violated the Act by prescribing for him, but merely that he had conspired with Martin to give him possession. Speaking for a majority of the Court, Hughes and Pitney dissenting without opinion, Holmes held Section 8 inapplicable.

A statute, he said, must be construed "so as to avoid not only the conclusion that it is unconstitutional but also grave doubts upon that score." If the Court "could know judicially" that the only opium found in the United States was imported, then there would be no occasion for doubts, because a regulation of foreign commerce could constitutionally be effectuated by prohibiting possession.[87] But it could hardly be assumed that no opium was produced in the United States, especially since the statute itself taxed production among other things.[88] In these circumstances, "the gravest question of power would be raised by an attempt of Congress to make possession of such opium a crime." The United States, it was true, was a party to an international convention of 1912 on the opium trade, but the Harrison Act was not a measure required for the implementation of that convention, and it could not, therefore, be rested on the Treaty Clause of the Constitution. At any rate, whether the Harrison Act could benefit from the supremacy claimed for treaties would be another grave constitutional issue that ought to be avoided.

The government had argued, with somewhat surprising candor, that while the Harrison Act was formally framed as a revenue statute in order to invoke the constitutional power of Congress to levy taxes, it was in reality a police measure intended to reach all users and possessors of narcotics. Therefore Section 8 meant "all that it says, taking its words ['any person'] in their plain and literal sense." But that, of course, was just the difficulty. As a police measure, the Act raised constitutional doubts. Moreover, so construed, it was an uncommonly harsh and intrusive criminal regulation. These were "the dominant considerations," and they led to a construction of the words "any person" as limited to the classes of persons enumerated in Section 1—producers, importers, dealers, distributors, etc. "It may be assumed that the statute has a moral end as well as revenue in view," but a prohibition of possession by persons whom the statute did not tax might pass the permissible limits of a revenue measure. Possession by one such as Willie Martin was, therefore, not a crime, and the indictment of Dr. Jin Fuey Moy for

---

[87] See Ng Choy Fong v. United States, 245 Fed. 305 (9th Cir. 1917) cert. denied, 245 U.S. 669 (1918).

[88] The tax on production was upheld in Lin and Bing v. United States, 250 Fed. 694 (8th Cir. 1918), cert. denied, 247 U.S. 518 (1918).

conspiring to give Martin possession had been properly quashed by the district court.[89]

The constitutional doubts which the Court did not heed in *Caminetti* became doctrine in *Hammer* v. *Dagenhart*, the first child labor case. Doubts which Holmes avoided in *Jin Fuey Moy* became doctrine in the *Child Labor Tax Case* of 1922.[90] But they did not materialize so as to invalidate the Harrison Act itself. The constitutionality of that statute was sustained, if narrowly, in *United States* v. *Doremus*,[91] some two and one-half years after Holmes' decision in *Jin Fuey Moy*.[92] *Doremus* and a companion case, *Webb* v. *United States*,[93] were indictments of doctors for distributing narcotics to persons who had not filled out the required order forms, and who, being addicts, were allegedly not to be regarded as *bona fide* patients. The distribution of drugs to addicts, it was contended, did not fall within the exception for prescriptions by physicians to patients. Thus the government tried to avoid the pitfall of *Jin Fuey Moy*, since the transactions here were quite like Dr. Jin's. And the effort succeeded in the Supreme Court,[94] even though this prosecuting theory was also eventually to cause some trouble.[95]

The Harrison Act, said Day, purported to be an exercise of the taxing power, on which the only limitation here relevant was geographical uniformity. The motives that may impel Congress to levy a tax were

---

[89] United States v. Jin Fuey Moy, 241 U.S. 394, 401–402 (1916).

[90] 259 U.S. 20 (1922).

[91] 249 U.S. 86 (1919).

[92] Between *Jin Fuey Moy* and *Doremus* the Court consistently denied certiorari in cases in which the government had obtained convictions. See Thurston v. United States, 241 Fed. 335 (5th Cir. 1917), *cert. denied*, 245 U.S. 646 (1917); Wallace v. United States, 243 Fed. 300 (7th Cir. 1917), *cert. denied*, 245 U.S. 650 (1917); Baldwin v. United States, 238 Fed. 793 (5th Cir. 1917), *cert. denied*, 245 U.S. 664 (1917); Woe v. United States, 250 Fed. 428 (5th Cir. 1918), *cert. denied*, 248 U.S. 562 (1918).

[93] 249 U.S. 96 (1919).

[94] It succeeded also when a second attempt was made to get Dr. Jin himself, who was apparently a large-scale supplier of narcotics to addicts. A *Doremus*-type indictment did the trick. Jin Fuey Moy v. United States, 254 U.S. 189 (1920). The holding in the first *Jin Fuey Moy case* was ultimately avoided under later amendments to the Harrison Act, and the government was enabled to punish possession. United States v. Wong Sing, 260 U.S. 18 (1922).

[95] In Linder v. United States, 268 U.S. 5 (1925), a decision very much like Holmes' in *Jin Fuey Moy*, a unanimous Court held that the statute should not be construed so as to punish a doctor's judgment, "in the course of his professional practice," that an addict should get a dose of narcotics. It would raise serious constitutional questions, the Court said, if Congress were taken to have defined proper standards for professional practice. But *cf.* United States v. Behrman, 258 U.S. 280 (1922) (Holmes, McReynolds, and Brandeis, JJ., dissenting); Boyd v. United States, 271 U.S. 104 (1926).

not subject to judicial scrutiny. Nor was it relevant that the effect of the tax might be to accomplish another purpose as well. The decisive question was whether the provisions of the statute had any relation to the raising of revenue. All the regulatory provisions here were so related, as they made the traffic in narcotics visible and subject to inspection, thus facilitating tax collection. Day did not pause to note that the tax was very small, rather too small to bother with from a revenue point of view, one would have thought, nor that the provision forbidding use of the order forms by addicts forwent revenue rather than seeking it.[96] White, with the concurrence of McKenna, Van Devanter, and McReynolds, dissented in one sentence, saying that the statute was an unconstitutional attempt to exercise the police power reserved to the states.[97]

Ulterior Ends and the Commerce Clause: Liquor

The dissenters in *Doremus* were to be vindicated three years later in the *Child Labor Tax Case*, and reconsideration of *Doremus* would then briefly be in prospect. Actually the Court ended by reaffirming the constitutionality of an amended Harrison Act.[98] The power to tax had been successfully used for the attainment of ulterior ends before the Harrison Act,[99] most recently to drive colored oleomargarine out of the

---

[96] In Blunt v. United States, 255 Fed. 332 (7th Cir. 1918), in which the Court denied certiorari three weeks after *Doremus* came down, 249 U.S. 608 (1919), a conviction for unlawful use of drugs was held unconstitutional as an exercise of police, not revenue-raising, power.

[97] The *Doremus* case went back for trial, there was a conviction, and the Court refused to consider the case again. Doremus v. United States, 262 Fed. 849 (5th Cir. 1920), *cert. denied*, 253 U.S. 487 (1920). The Court also refused to take a substantial number of other cases, most of them involving doctors, or doctors and druggists.

[98] *Compare* United States v. Daugherty, 269 U.S. 360 (1926), *with* Nigro v. United States, 276 U.S. 332 (1928).

[99] Such a use of the taxing power contemporaneous with the Harrison Act was the Cotton Futures Act of 1914, 38 Stat. 693, which failed for

a most curious reason. This statute had been attached in the House as an amendment to a bill that had originated in the Senate. Being a revenue measure, its constitutionality was attacked on the ground that it had originated in the Senate, rather than in the House, as required for revenue measures, and a district court in New York (Charles M. Hough, J.) held it unconstitutional for this reason. Hubbard v. Lowe, 226 Fed. 135 (S.D.N.Y. 1915). In the Supreme Court, Solicitor General Davis accepted the ruling, and the case was dismissed on his motion. 242 U.S. 654 (1916); see also Lowe v. Weld, 242 U.S. 654 (1916). The statute was then reenacted properly, Cotton Futures Act of Aug. 11, 1916, 39 Stat. 446, but a similar Futures Trading Act fell in a case decided at the same time as the *Child Labor Tax Case*. Hill v. Wallace, 259 U.S. 44 (1922).

market,[100] and it would be used again, even after the debacle of the *Child Labor Tax Case*. A like reliance upon the Commerce Clause for remote purposes had also, as we saw, been consistently successful for some years, despite the qualifications that analysis could uncover in the interstices of various opinions, and so it proved again in 1915, in *Weber* v. *Freed*.[101] The Act of July 31, 1912,[102] a late product of the Taft Administration, prohibited bringing any film or other pictorial representation of a prize fight from abroad for public exhibition in the United States. It was contended that under the guise of regulating foreign commerce, Congress was exercising police power reserved to the states. Said Chief Justice White for a unanimous Court: "But in view of the complete power of Congress over foreign commerce and its authority to prohibit the introduction of foreign articles recognized and enforced by many previous decisions of this Court, the contentions are so devoid of merit as to cause them to be frivolous." The argument that Congress was really regulating the exhibition of films rather than their importation went to the motive of the legislature and would not be countenanced, as motives were not subject to judicial review.[103]

This attitude persisted long enough for the Court to reach the doctrinally and practically more significant result of upholding the Webb-Kenyon Act,[104] which used the Commerce Clause to enforce state prohibition policies. Webb-Kenyon was chargeable neither to the Taft nor to the Wilson Administration. It was a precursor of the Eighteenth Amendment, a victory for the Prohibitionists, who had deep roots both in the Progressive movement and in the Democratic South, and who were rapidly gathering strength, even though Taft opposed them and they could count on little more than equivocation from Wilson.

Prohibition has, of course, a long history in the American states. In 1887, in *Mugler* v. *Kansas*,[105] the Court upheld, against Due Process attack, the power of the states to forbid the manufacture and sale of liquor. Three years later, however, in *Leisy* v. *Hardin*,[106] it held that states could not, under the Commerce Clause, stop the importation of liquor in original packages. Congress immediately reacted with the Wilson Act of 1890,[107] providing that liquor brought into a state would be subject to the laws of that state upon arrival as if produced there, and would not be exempt by reason of having been imported in the

---

[100] McCray v. United States, 195 U.S. 27 (1904).

[101] 239 U.S. 325, 329 (1915).

[102] 37 Stat. 240 (1912).

[103] Although the case has an obvious free speech aspect, no point based on the First Amendment was raised or passed on. *Appellant's Brief* and *Appellant's Reply Brief*, No. 644, Weber v. Freed, 239 U.S. 325 (1915).

[104] 37 Stat. 699 (1913).

[105] 123 U.S. 623 (1887).

[106] 135 U.S. 100 (1890).

[107] 26 Stat. 313 (1890).

original package. Although this statute amounted to an exemption for liquor from a free-trade rule imposed in *Leisy* v. *Hardin* as a constitutional requirement, the Court sustained it in *In re Rahrer*.[108] But a few years later the Court said that the Wilson Act did not subject liquor to state regulation until it had arrived in the hands of a consignee within the state, so that importation could not be stopped by laws directed at the carrier, or by confiscation at the border. Hence mail-order liquor could enter.[109] This was the wetness that the Webb-Kenyon Act was intended to sop up. It declared—although without the imposition of any federal penalties—that the shipment of liquor "to be received, possessed, sold, or in any manner used, either in the original package, or otherwise, in violation of any law" of the receiving state "is hereby prohibited."

Sponsored by a Southern Democrat in the House and a Progressive Republican in the Senate, the Webb-Kenyon Act was passed in February 1913 by the lame-duck session of the 62nd Congress, and on February 28, President Taft vetoed it. He declared that the bill was unconstitutional as a delegation to the states of a power to regulate interstate commerce which belonged exclusively to Congress. In applying and construing the Wilson Act, the Supreme Court had clearly reaffirmed its view that liquor was a legitimate article of interstate commerce.[110] To be sure, there was no Supreme Court decision expressly passing on the constitutionality of a federal statute enabling the states to forbid the importation of liquor, for the Wilson Act cases had gone off, at least formally, on issues of statutory construction rather than constitutionality. But the Commerce Clause was intended to create a common national market, subject only to regulation by Congress. "Now, if to the discretion of Congress is committed the question whether in interstate commerce we shall return to the old methods [of state-imposed restrictions on commerce] prevailing before the Constitution or not, it would seem to be conferring upon Congress the power to amend the Constitution by ignoring or striking out one of its most important provisions. . . . [T]o permit the states to exercise their old authority before they became states, to interfere with commerce between them and their neighbors, is to defeat the constitutional purpose." Certainly the Webb-Kenyon Act answered to a popular wish in many states, as had the Wilson Act, as well as certain minor measures in support of the policy of that Act, which Congress had taken before Webb-Kenyon.[111] But it was different and

---

[108] 140 U.S. 545 (1891).

[109] See Vance v. Vandercook Co., 170 U.S. 438 (1897).

[110] See Louisville & Nashville R.R. v. Cook Brewing Co., *supra*, p. 267, n.202.

[111] See, e.g., United States v. Freeman, 239 U.S. 117 (1915); Danciger v. Cooley, 248 U.S. 319 (1919); Witte v. Shelton, 240 Fed. 265 (8th Cir. 1917), *cert. denied*, 244 U.S. 660 (1917).

more far-reaching for Congress now entirely to suspend interstate commerce in liquor, and thus to claim a power to do the same with respect to any other article.

Then Taft addressed himself to a most fundamental aspect of the problem facing him and the Congress:

> But it is said that this is a question with which the Executive or Members of Congress should not burden themselves to consider or decide. It is said that it should be left to the Supreme Court to say whether this proposed act violates the Constitution. I dissent utterly from this proposition. The oath which the Chief Executive takes, and which each Member of Congress takes, does not bind him any less sacredly to observe the Constitution than the oaths which the Justices of the Supreme Court take. It is questionable whether the doubtful constitutionality of a bill ought not to furnish a greater reason for voting against the bill, or vetoing it, than for the court to hold it to be invalid. The court will only declare a law invalid where its unconstitutionality is clear, while the lawmaker may very well hesitate to vote for a bill if of doubtful constitutionality because of a wisdom of keeping clearly within the fundamental law. The custom of legislators and executives having any legislative function to remit to the courts entire and ultimate responsibility as to the constitutionality of the measures which they take part in passing is an abuse which tends to put the court constantly in opposition to the legislature and executive, and, indeed, to the popular supporters of unconstitutional laws. If, however, the legislators and the executives had attempted to do their duty this burden of popular disapproval would have been lifted from the courts, or at least considerably lessened.[112]

During the Congressional debate out of which emerged both the Corporation Tax Act of 1909 and the Sixteenth Amendment, much was heard of the obligation of legislators to reach their own constitutional judgments. But at the time, this obligation was pressed by those who wanted an income tax enacted immediately, in the form of a statute rather than a constitutional amendment, on the theory that *Pollock* v. *Farmers' Loan & Trust Co.*[113] had been wrongly decided. In 1909, Taft, with Senators Elihu Root and George Sutherland, took the position that Congress should respect the constitutional decisions of the Supreme Court, and should not presume to make its own.[114] There is at most an apparent inconsistency between Taft's position in 1909 and his argument in the Webb-Kenyon veto message of 1913. It is possible, after all, for legislators both to be bound to respect the Court's decisions, and to have

---

[112] 49 *Cong. Rec.* 4291–92, 62nd Cong., 2nd Sess. (1913).

[113] 157 U.S. 429 (1895).

[114] See *supra*, pp. 21–24.

441

a responsibility to make constitutional judgments of their own on points not yet settled by the judges. But there would be little growth and little movement in the American Constitution if, in pursuance of the oath they also take, legislators and executives did not sometimes challenge constitutional determinations of the Court. And there would be equally little growth and expansion in the Constitution if, despite the oath they also take, legislators and executives did not at times respond to popular wishes by leaving questions of constitutionality to be disposed of later and elsewhere, thus generating occasions for constitutional judgments that may themselves accommodate the popular will. Such is the ambivalence about the function of judicial review and its consequences for the electorally responsible institutions that is as old as the Republic.

The essential consistency of Taft's two positions is found in their common conservatism. In 1913 as in 1909, he would have withheld legislative action, stopping constitutional movement. By the same token, there is a basic consistency on the other side in favor of movement—to overrule a decision considered wrong in one instance, and in the other to expand legislative powers with little regard for constitutional doubts. And yet a great deal is to be said for Taft's argument that the Court cannot alone sustain the whole burden of implementing constitutional guarantees and guarding the integrity of constitutional principles. Those guarantees and those principles must radiate, and affect policy, beyond the necessarily narrower confines in which the Court, clashing with Congress and the President, can effectively exert its authority. Constitutional guarantees would in many instances be less serviceable and pervasive than they ought to be if the legislature did not fulfill its own oath, independent of the judiciary's, to see to their implementation.

Congress opted for movement. The Senate overrode the President's veto hours after it was received, as did the House, three days before the inauguration, so that the Webb-Kenyon bill became the Act of March 1, 1913. Four years later, the Supreme Court also chose movement, and upheld the Act in *Clark Distilling Co.* v. *Western Maryland Railway*. The case was argued twice, and fifteen states filed a brief *amicus* in support of the Act.

West Virginia law prohibited the importation of liquor. The Clark Distilling Company sued the Western Maryland Railroad in federal court (the state being allowed to intervene as a party) to compel it to carry liquor into West Virginia. Thus the constitutionality of the Webb-Kenyon Act was put in issue. But there was first a question of construction. In *Adams Express Co.* v. *Kentucky*,[115] a year and a half earlier, the Court had held, somewhat by analogy to the cases under the Wilson Act,

---

[115] 238 U.S. 190, 199 (1915).

that the Webb-Kenyon law prohibited the shipment of liquor into a state only when the liquor "is to be dealt with" there "in violation of the local law of the State." Therefore, it was held, the Act did not apply where, as in Kentucky, state law prohibited only the transportation and sale of liquor, not personal use of it. Since the West Virginia law also did not prohibit personal use, the argument was that the *Kentucky* case governed. But White, writing for the Court, held that to construe the Webb-Kenyon Act as applicable only to shipments intended for sale where sale was forbidden, and otherwise only in states where personal use was also prohibited, would run counter to its purpose, which, after all, was to extend the earlier Wilson Act. "Assuming, for the sake of argument only, that the debates may be resorted to for the purpose of showing environment, we are of opinion they clearly establish a result directly contrary to that which they are cited to maintain."

Of course the Webb-Kenyon Act was not itself intended to interfere with personal use of liquor, yet under the construction urged, its effect would be practically to compel the states to prohibit personal use, since only in those circumstances would they be able to control all importation. But what of *Adams Express Co.* v. *Kentucky*, so recent a decision, and a unanimous one, too? With the assent of its author, Day, who was now part of his majority, White explained the *Kentucky* case away as having decided that the Webb-Kenyon Act was inapplicable where a state not only failed to prohibit personal use, but omitted also to forbid importation itself, if the importation was for personal use. But in fact—subject to a minor exception—the Kentucky statute, as much as the West Virginia law, did prohibit importation for whatever purpose, including personal use, and White's distinction was a disingenuous way of disposing of the earlier decision without quite overruling it.[116] The Court had changed its mind on the issue of construction, and had come to read the Act in a manner more consistent, no doubt, with the broad intent of Congress, because it was now prepared to reach the constitutional question it had earlier avoided.

"We are not unmindful that opinions adverse to the power of Congress to enact the law were formed and expressed in other departments of government," White began, citing Taft's veto message. "We are additionally conscious, therefore, of the responsibility of determining these issues and of their serious character." Congress could have forbidden entirely the shipment of all liquors in interstate commerce. *Hoke* v. *United States*, the Mann Act case, demonstrated as much. The question therefore was whether Congress could do a part of what it had

---

[116] See T. R. Powell, "The Validity of State Legislation under the Webb-Kenyon Law," *South. L. Q.*, 2:112, 118–22, 1917.

the power to do entirely. "The argument as to delegation to the States rests upon a mere misconception. It is true the regulation which the Webb-Kenyon Act contains permits state prohibitions to apply to movements of liquor from one State into another, but the will which causes the prohibitions to be applicable is that of Congress. . . ."

It had been settled since *Cooley* v. *Board of Wardens* "that interstate commerce is divided into two great classes, one embracing subjects which do not exact uniformity and which, although subject to the regulation of Congress, are in the absence of such regulation subject to the control of the several States, and the other embracing subjects which do require uniformity and which in the absence of regulation by Congress remain free from all state control." Consequently, it was contended, Congress can regulate the second class, the one "embracing subjects which do require uniformity," only by imposing uniformity; Congress may not, as to this second class, attempt to legitimate the sort of disparate State regulations which, absent federal legislation, would have been held unconstitutional because of their lack of uniformity. White first met the argument with a bit of sophistry that he offered without much enthusiasm. The Webb-Kenyon Act, he said, did uniformly apply "to the conditions which call its provisions into play . . . its provisions apply to all the States—so that the question really is a complaint as to the want of uniform existence of things to which the Act applies and not to an absence of uniformity in the Act itself." But then White attacked the substance of the matter, displaying his capacity, as Holmes once said, for profound thinking, "especially in the legislative direction,"[117] and his clear perception of the fundamentals of a federal system. The basic error, White said, was a confusion between the effect of the Commerce Clause in the absence of Congressional regulation, and the power conferred upon Congress to regulate. Only Congress can achieve uniformity of regulation, and as to a certain class of subjects, only Congress is competent to judge whether and in what degree uniformity can be dispensed with. Hence the states could not be allowed by the Court to exercise control over that class of subjects. But when Congress acted, it was free to impose more or less uniformity, as it chose. Congress did not transcend its regulatory power when, "in adopting a regulation," it "considered the nature and character of our dual system of government, State and Nation, and instead of absolutely prohibiting, . . . so conformed its regulation as to produce cooperation between the local and national forces of government to the end of preserving the rights of all. . . ."

Thus White encouraged the flexibility which ought to be a hallmark

---

[117] See *supra*, p. 39.

of a federal system.[118] But he concluded, in one of those circular statements which were as typical of him as his capacity for profound thinking, with an opaque qualification. It might be feared, he said, that Congress could by the same technique subject any and all articles of commerce to state control. The answer was that liquor was a subject peculiarly submitted to all kinds of special regulations, and "the exceptional nature of the subject here regulated is the basis on which the exceptional power exerted must rest and affords no ground for any fear that such power may be constitutionally extended to things which it may not, consistently with the guarantees of the Constitution, embrace."[119]

McReynolds concurred in the result, and Holmes and Van Devanter dissented without opinion. He believed, Holmes wrote Laski, "that the statute should not be construed to simply substitute the state for Congress in control of interstate commerce in intoxicants—*i.e.*, to permit a state to say although the purpose of the shipment (personal consumption) is one that we permit, we forbid the shipment in interstate commerce—the unlawfulness by state law thus consisting solely in the element of interstate commerce. And the Act of Congress was further construed to adopt any such regulation in advance—at least an extreme exercise of power. I thought the Act did not mean more than to say that if on other grounds the shipment would be illegal but for the want of

---

[118] The Court, Thomas Reed Powell commented contemporaneously, had shown "practical wisdom." It had "worked out a plan which places ultimate power over interstate commerce in a central legislative body, and yet does not require that body to foresee every possible state regulation and guard against its application. It permits Congress and the States to co-operate so that a state may be allowed to enforce its local policy without waiting till that policy receives sufficient sanction to be imposed throughout the nation. A contrary decision . . . would have been most regrettable." Powell, "Validity of State Legislation under the Webb-Kenyon Law," 138–39. But *cf.* N. T. Dowling and F. M. Hubbard, "Divesting an Article of Its Interstate Character," *Minn. L. Rev.*, 5:100, 253, 1921.

[119] Clark Distilling Co. v. Western Maryland Ry., 242 U.S. 311, 322, 325–27, 331–32 (1917). See also Beer v. American Express Co., 107 Miss. 528, 65 So. 575 (1914) (Webb-Kenyon Act held constitutional), *writ of error dismissed on motion of plaintiff in error*, 244 U.S. 662 (1917). And see Ammerman v. United States, 267 Fed. 136 (8th Cir. 1920), *cert. denied*, 254 U.S. 650 (1920).

The qualification came home to roost in another context some three years later, when a closely divided Court, holding that the Constitution required uniformity, prevented Congress from validating, and in effect adopting as its own, state workmen's compensation laws as applied to maritime accidents—just as Congress had validated and adopted state prohibition laws. Knickerbocker Ice Co. v. Stewart, 253 U.S. 149 (1920), *infra*, pp. 562 *et seq.*

power on the part of the state over interstate commerce, the fact of I.C. should not interfere. I did not intend to dissent but so disliked the C.J.'s opinion that I got stirred up—though I endeavored to assure myself that I was not dissenting solely on that ground." Writing to Felix Frankfurter, Holmes added an expression of regret "that I didn't either say a few words or shut up."[120]

The decision was widely noticed. The *New York Times* commended the Court for having "called to its aid human reason and common sense," and speculated that possibly "the great tribunal was in some measure influenced, as properly it should be influenced, by public opinion, the tide of which is setting toward prohibition." Given this tide of opinion, it was better "that prohibition laws be made effective in communities that want them than that by a federal amendment the rule of prohibition should be extended over unwilling states." That was the view as well of *The New Republic,* which thought that the decision would "deprive the agitators for a federal prohibition amendment of a strong argument in its favor," and which liked the opening of a way "for flexible cooperation between the state and national governments."

Some liquor interests consoled themselves—falsely it turned out— with the expectation that states which in the past had been content to be legally dry and actually wet would now have their sincerity tested and, finding themselves forced to be both legally and actually dry or both legally and actually wet, would choose honest wetness. "So long as the well-to-do individual was free to import liquors for his own use," said the *Boston Transcript,* indulging the same wishful prediction, "he was often inclined to favor prohibitory enactments for the 'lower classes,'" especially in the South where the classes were divided along the color line. The result now would be "a certain restraint upon the adoption of prohibitory laws," since it had become politically not practicable to adopt prohibition without attempting to make it as effective as the law now permitted. Thenceforth it would "be the 'whole hog or none,'" and hence none in many places.

Prohibition forces, free of such forebodings, were jubilant. The *New York World* saw wider implications: "It has given to the doctrine of state rights a new force and a new direction. The Webb-Kenyon Law represents the first instance since the fugitive-slave Law in which the states have appealed to the federal authority for assistance in maintaining their local legislation but it will not be the last."[121]

---

[120] *Holmes-Laski Letters,* I, 54.

[121] *New York Times,* Jan. 9, 1917, p. 6, col. 1, Jan. 10, 1917, p. 12, col. 1, col. 2, Jan. 11, p. 4, col. 2; *The New Republic,* 9:279, Jan. 13, 1917; *The Nation,* 104:64, 105, Jan. 18, 1917; *The Literary Digest,* 54:112–13, Jan. 20, 1971.

In Missouri Pacific Ry. v. Kansas, 248 U.S. 276 (1919), another attack

Ulterior Ends and the Commerce Clause: Child Labor

The progression of cases represented by *Weber* v. *Freed* and *Clark Distilling Co.* v. *Western Maryland Railway* came to a crashing halt in June 1918, with the decision of *Hammer* v. *Dagenhart*, the first child labor case. Now the Court resurrected and rendered decisive the qualifications hidden in *Hipolite Egg*, which passed on the Pure Food Act, and in *Hoke* v. *United States*, the Mann Act case.[122]

At the turn of the century, one child in six between the ages of ten and fifteen was a wage earner in the United States, often under conditions that aggravated the offense to humanitarian sensibilities. A National Child Labor Committee, founded in 1904, was instrumental in obtaining regulatory legislation in many states, but legislation was not universal, nor, of course, was it uniform, and it was largely ineffective. States willing actually to abolish the practice were put in an unfavorable competitive position, since under the Commerce Clause they could not protect themselves by excluding the cheaper child labor product of other states. Southern states, which were nurturing a new textile industry, tolerated extensive use of child labor, and the South was, therefore, a particular target of the reformers. Early in 1907, Albert Beveridge, having for the first time introduced federal anti–child labor legislation, occupied the Senate floor with a three-day speech in which he documented the pervasiveness of the practice, indicted its inhumanity, and urged the constitutionality of federal intervention. The result was an appropriation for an investigation.

In 1910, the Department of Labor began publication of a nineteen-volume report on children and women as wage earners, and in 1912, the Children's Bureau was established in the Department of Labor, with a mandate to investigate and report. The Bureau was a natural ally of the private reformers. Conditions had no doubt improved somewhat by then, but the practice was no less prevalent. The decision of *Hoke* v. *United States* in 1913 encouraged those who believed the federal government could constitutionally intervene, and definitely turned their attention to the Commerce Clause rather than the taxing power as the source of federal authority. A bill was drafted with the aid of William

---

on the constitutionality of the Webb-Kenyon Act failed. It was contended in this case that when the Act was passed over the President's veto, it was passed by a two-thirds vote of members present in each House, rather than by a constitutional two-thirds of the entire membership. Assuming for purposes of argument that the question was justiciable, White for the Court held that the Constitution required no more than the votes of a quorum in each House to override a veto.

[122] See *supra*, pp. 226, 230–31.

Draper Lewis, a well-known Progressive and the dean of the University of Pennsylvania Law School, and it was introduced in the House by A. Mitchell Palmer, Democrat of Pennsylvania and the future Attorney General, and in the Senate by Robert L. Owen, Democrat of Oklahoma.

The bill passed easily in the House in 1915, but lacking the support of the President, who was troubled by constitutional doubts, it died in the Senate. "It is very plain that you would have to go much further than most of the interpretations of the Constitution would allow if you were to give to the government general control over child labor throughout the country," said Wilson. The following year, the bill was reintroduced, by Owen in the Senate, but this time by Edward Keating, Democrat of Colorado, in the House, where it promptly prevailed, again by a very large vote. The nominating conventions intervened before action in the Senate, and both party platforms called for effective federal child labor legislation.

Whether or not Wilson had changed his mind on the constitutional issue, he was now clear that a federal child labor law was a political, and presumably a humanitarian, necessity, and he vigorously used his influence in the Senate to obtain passage. This was the Wilson, after all, who had just nominated Brandeis and fought for his confirmation. The Senate responded, and on September 1, 1916, Wilson signed the first federal measure attempting to curb the evil of child labor, as he said, "with real emotion." He knew, Wilson continued, "how long the struggle has been to secure legislation of this sort and what it is going to mean to the health and to the vigor of the country, and also to the happiness of those whom it affects. It is with genuine pride that I play my part in completing this legislation. I congratulate the country and felicitate myself." And the country reciprocated the congratulations and felicitations. Except in some quarters in the South, the acclaim was unanimous. Democratic and Republican comment alike hailed the law as a measure "of social and economic progress." If ever a statute rested on broad national consensus, it was the Keating-Owen bill, and in all the rejoicing over its passage, constitutional doubts were laid aside.[123]

Constitutional doubts, however, had dominated most of the debate since Beveridge's speech in January 1907,[124] and in the summer of 1916 they had occupied the Senate, which found itself beset once more by the same ambivalence toward its duty that had affected it with respect

---

[123] See S. B. Wood, *Constitutional Politics in the Progressive Era—Child Labor and the Law* (1968), 3–110; Link, *Wilson: The New Freedom*, 225–57; A. S. Link, *Wilson: Campaigns for Progressivism and Peace* (1965), 56–60.

[124] See R. E. Cushman, "The National Police Power under the Commerce Clause of the Constitution," *Minn. L. Rev.*, 3:452–70, 1919.

to the income tax problem, the Corporation Tax Act of 1909, and the Webb-Kenyon Act of 1913.[125] Once more proponents argued that Congress ought to enact desirable legislation despite constitutional uncertainties, which the Supreme Court could be expected to resolve in due time. At least, it was urged, this was the proper course for Senators whose doubts were not altogether grave. Opponents pressed the duty of Congress to follow its own constitutional views, and to defeat a measure, however worthy, which was constitutionally dubious. "The Supreme Court of this country," said Senator Brandegee of Connecticut, echoing the Taft of three years before, "ought to have some support," and the Congress ought not constantly "to throw upon the Supreme Court all the responsibility of setting aside acts we thought were unwise but that we passed in response to public clamor," since such a course subjected the judiciary to popular obloquy. And so again Progressives who rather feared and distrusted the Court professed great reliance upon it, and invoked its ultimate authority, while conservatives who generally praised the Court and gloried in its function held up to their colleagues a responsibility for independent constitutional judgment. And again, through the fog of ambivalence, the essential consistencies could be perceived—in favor of movement and reform, on the one side, and of stability, if not of contraction of legislative power, on the other.[126]

The Keating-Owen Act forbade shipment in interstate or foreign commerce of the product of mines where within thirty days prior to shipment sixteen-year-olds had been employed, and of the product of all other factories and establishments where within those thirty days fourteen-year-olds had been employed, or children between fourteen and sixteen had been worked longer than eight hours a day, or six days a week, or after 7 P.M. or before 6 A.M. Congress thus made no attempt directly to forbid the employment of children, but on the other hand, it did prohibit more than merely the shipment of articles actually made by children, and it enforced this prohibition with criminal penalties. The employment of children by manufacturers who produced for interstate commerce was hence severely discouraged, but, again, only by a regulation of shipment, not directly by a proscription of the practice itself of hiring children.[127]

Opposition to the Palmer-Owen and Keating-Owen bills had emanated chiefly from an organization called the Executive Committee of Southern Cotton Manufacturers, whose energizing spirit was David Clark, publisher of a textile trade journal in Charlotte, North Carolina. As soon as the Keating-Owen Act was passed, Clark started to organize

---

[125] See *supra*, pp. 21–24, 440–42.
[126] See Wood, *Constitutional Poli-*
tics in the Progressive Era, 69–75.
[127] 39 Stat. 675 (1916).

litigation to test it. He first retained John G. Johnson of Philadelphia, and upon his death, a New York firm, one of whose partners, Junius Parker, originally of North Carolina, had been general counsel to the American Tobacco Company.

Clark found one Dagenhart, who together with two minor sons was employed by the Fidelity Manufacturing Company, a small cotton mill in Charlotte. Dagenhart's older boy was fifteen, and the number of hours he would be allowed to work under the federal statute would be drastically reduced. His other boy was thirteen, and under the federal law he would not be permitted to work at all. The company notified its employees that it would observe the provisions of the Keating-Owen Act. Thereupon Clark's lawyers, in behalf of Dagenhart and his sons, sued the company and Hammer, the United States Attorney for the Western District of North Carolina, to enjoin them, respectively, from complying with and enforcing the Act. Thus a test case was launched simultaneously with enactment of the statute. The litigation was financed with money that Clark raised. The government for its part appointed special counsel, including Roscoe Pound, dean of the Harvard Law School, who served without compensation. The case was elaborately defended in the district court, although a possible suggestion that the suit was collusive and that the court should decline to hear it for that reason was not pressed. The district judge declared the Act unconstitutional.[128]

The government's brief in the Supreme Court, prepared under the immediate direction of Solicitor General Davis, who also argued the case, was Brandeisian in method. With heavy reference to nonlegal materials, Davis educated the Court in the social, economic, and medical facts of child labor in the United States. Public opinion, he said, had come to deplore child labor, just as at an earlier time it had recognized lotteries as harmful. "Neither the [lottery] ticket nor the labor is inherently bad, but the facts of life have disclosed undeniable evils in the use of both." And the problem was a national one: "In the day of steam and electricity the play of the forces of competition makes the cause operating in one State immediately felt in another." The states could not protect themselves, because they were joined in a federal union, under a Constitution that secures a common national market.

It was altogether a powerful argument, supporting Davis' reputation as one of the finest of the Solicitors General, and justifying the extraordinarily high regard in which the Justices held him.[129] But the

---

[128] See Wood, *Constitutional Politics in the Progressive Era*, 42–45, 84–85, 92–93, 96–101.

[129] "Some years ago," a Washington lawyer informed William Howard Taft, a former Solicitor General,

decision went the other way, 5 to 4. Day wrote for a majority consisting of White, Van Devanter, Pitney, and McReynolds, in addition to himself. The Congressional power over commerce, Day began, quoting a remark by Marshall in *Gibbons* v. *Ogden*, was a power to regulate, not to destroy, and decisions like *Champion* v. *Ames*,[130] the *Lottery Case, Hipolite Egg* (the Pure Food and Drug case), and *Hoke* v. *United States* (the Mann Act case), in which prohibitions destroying a branch of commerce were upheld, rested "upon the character of the particular subjects dealt with and the fact that the scope of governmental authority, State or national, possessed over them is such that the authority to prohibit is as to them but the exertion of the power to regulate."

In support of this rather question-begging assertion, Day quoted the circularity with which White had concluded the opinion in *Clark Distilling Co.* v. *Western Maryland Railway*.[131] Moreover, in each of these cases—and Day did not fail to note *Caminetti* also—"the use of interstate transportation was necessary to the accomplishment of harmful results." Not so in this instance. This statute was no regulation of transportation, but rather an attempt "to standardize the ages at which children may be employed. . . . The goods shipped are of themselves harmless. The act permits them to be freely shipped after thirty days from the time of their removal from the factory."[132] Hence the Act was a regulation of production, and production not being interstate commerce, Congress was powerless to control it.

Then Day took note of Davis' argument that federal action was justified because states willing to raise production costs by outlawing child labor could not protect themselves against competition from states where it was allowed. Many causes operating in one or another state, Day replied, bring about unfavorable competitive conditions. It was not the function of Congress to equalize them. States might put

---

early in 1921, "I met the present Chief Justice [White]. . . . [H]e paid a great compliment to John W. Davis of my state, remarking that 'with the exception of that charming and elegant gentleman and most profound lawyer, Taft, Davis, the present Solicitor General, is—and I voice the sentiment of my associates—the greatest of them all.'" R. R. McMahon to Taft, Jan. 26, 1921, Taft Papers, Library of Congress. Compare *Holmes-Laski Letters,* I, 587.

[130] 188 U.S. 321 (1903).

[131] See *supra,* pp. 444–45.

[132] This was simply a misreading of the statute. Goods made in factories where children had worked within thirty days of the date of shipment were never allowed to enter interstate commerce. The statute permitted a factory to ship its product in interstate commerce thirty days after it had abandoned the practice of child labor, but under no circumstances to ship goods made by children after any number of days "from the time of their removal." See T. R. Powell, "Child Labor, Congress, and the Constitution," *N.C. L. Rev.,* 1:61, 64, 1922.

themselves at a disadvantage by establishing maximum hours of labor and minimum wages, but "this fact does not give Congress the power to deny transportation in interstate commerce" to articles manufactured in states that choose not to regulate hours and wages. "The grant of power to Congress over the subject of interstate commerce was to enable it to regulate such commerce, and not to give it authority to control the States in their exercise of the police power over local trade and manufacture," reserved to them by the Tenth Amendment.

"That there should be limitations upon the right to employ children in mines and factories in the interest of their own and the public welfare, all will admit." And it might be desirable that they should be uniform. But there was no federal power to impose such limitations. Yet this statute was an attempt to do so. That was its "natural and reasonable affect," to which the Court could not close its eyes, although it had "neither authority nor disposition to question the motives of Congress in enacting this legislation." Judged by its necessary effect, the Act was, therefore, unconstitutional.

> The maintenance of the authority of the States over matters purely local is as essential to the preservation of our institutions as is the conservation of the supremacy of the federal power in matters entrusted to the Nation by the Federal Constitution. . . . The far reaching result of upholding the act cannot be more plainly indicated than by pointing out that if Congress can thus regulate matters entrusted to local authority by prohibition of the movement of commodities in interstate commerce, all freedom of commerce will be at an end, and the power of the States over local matters may be eliminated, and thus our system of government be practically destroyed.

The dissent was by Holmes, with McKenna, Brandeis, and Clarke joining. The objection urged against the Keating-Owen Act, said Holmes, was that "the States have exclusive control over their methods of production and that Congress cannot meddle with them, and taking the proposition in the sense of direct intermeddling I agree to it and suppose that no one denies it. But if an act is within the powers specifically conferred upon Congress, it seems to me that it is not made any less constitutional because of the indirect effects that it may have, however obvious it may be that it will have those effects, and that we are not at liberty upon such grounds to hold it void." The power to regulate commerce was given "in unqualified terms," and it included a power to prohibit, as the *Lottery Case* showed. Congress had been allowed to use the equally unlimited taxing power in order, in effect, to outlaw colored oleomargarine, and prohibitions imposed on foreign commerce had been upheld in *Weber* v. *Freed*[133] and in *Brolan* v. *United States*.[134] The Sherman Act had "been made an instrument for the breaking up of combinations in restraint of trade and monopolies, using the power to regulate commerce as a foothold, but not proceeding because that commerce was the end actually in mind. The objection that the control of the States over production was interfered with was urged again and again but always in vain." And Holmes cited as well the Pure Food and Mann Act cases, and *Clark Distilling Co.* v. *Western Maryland Railway*. He concluded with these famous passages:

> The notion that prohibition is any less prohibition when applied to things now thought evil I do not understand. But if there is any matter upon which civilized countries have agreed—far more unanimously than they have with regard to intoxicants and some other matters over which this country is now emotionally aroused—it is the evil of premature and excessive child labor. I should have thought that if we were to introduce our own moral conceptions where in my opinion they do not belong, this was preeminently a case for upholding the exercise of all its powers by the United States.
>
> But I had thought that the propriety of the exercise of a power admitted to exist in some cases was for the consideration of Congress alone and that this Court always had disavowed the right to intrude its judgment upon questions of policy or morals. It is not for this Court to pronounce when prohibition is necessary to regulation if it ever may be necessary—to say that it is permissible as against strong drink but not as against the product of ruined lives.
>
> The act does not meddle with anything belonging to the States. They may regulate their internal affairs and their domestic commerce as they like. But when they seek to send their products across the state line they are no longer within their rights. If there were no Constitution and no Congress their power to cross the line would depend upon their neighbors. Under the Constitution such commerce belongs not to the State but to Congress to regulate. It may carry out its views of public policy whatever indirect effect they may have upon the activities of the States. Instead of being encountered by a prohibitive tariff at her boundaries the State encounters the public policy of the United States which it is for Congress to express. The public policy of the United States is shaped with a view to the benefit of the nation as a whole. If, as has been the case within the memory of men still living, a State should take a different view of the propriety of sustaining a lottery from that which generally prevails, I cannot believe that the fact would require a different decision from that reached in *Champion*

---

[133] *Supra*, p. 439, n.101. [134] *Supra*, p. 435, n.86.

453

v. *Ames.* Yet in that case it would be said with quite as much force as in this that Congress was attempting to intermeddle with the State's domestic affairs. The national welfare as understood by Congress may require a different attitude within its sphere from that of some self-seeking State. It seems to me entirely constitutional for Congress to enforce its understanding by all the means at its command.[135]

The last paragraph just quoted incorporates a suggestion of McKenna. As first circulated by Holmes, the paragraph concluded with the following sentence, coming immediately after the remark about states encountering the public policy of the United States, which it was for Congress to express: "It [the State] is a good deal better off than it would be if it stood alone, but it cannot have things all its own way when it attempts to leave the domestic domain." Commenting on this sentence, McKenna returned:

You have already referred to the power of Congress as a substitute for states acting antagonistic to one another, and why emphasize it. The power over interstate commerce may have besides the inducement of a general benefit—the nation viewed as the object of legislation. This was the *raison d'être* of the cases that Day distinguishes and I take it that it makes no difference whether the evil to be suppressed or not given opportunity and facility was at the beginning or end of the transportation. Transportation is not an agency in one case more than the other.

Holmes thereupon omitted the sentence that McKenna thought superfluous, and following his suggestion, drafted the passage beginning: "The public policy of the United States is shaped with a view to the benefit of the nation. . . ." McKenna was pleased, as well he might be: "You have grasped my idea and executed it well. If you could catch another vote the opinion would be epochal. It would make the Commerce Clause truly independent, not subservient to some state purpose, or limited or restrained, as you say, by some state purpose." One of those instances, unquestionably, when the "unpredictable" McKenna "showed that he understood the business as well as anyone"![136]

The public response to the decision in *Hammer* v. *Dagenhart* was a compound of continuing support for the objectives of the Keating-Owen Act, and of shock at the rude defeat the Court had dealt to expectations of a permissive and progressive course of constitutional

---

[135] Hammer v. Dagenhart, 247 U.S. 251, 253–54, 270–74, 275–76, 277, 279, 280–81 (1918).

[136] Holmes Papers; see *supra,* p. 239.

adjudication. Few, if any, of those who had previously favored federal action against child labor were now persuaded of the error of their ways. The *New York Times*, lukewarm to begin with, came to the conclusion that perhaps child labor, like drinking, ought to be left to local control. And the *Chicago Tribune* allowed that federal regulation, if there was to be any, should be direct and straightforward, rather than being imposed "by the evasive use of laws not intended for the purpose to which they are put." But these were exceptions. The general verdict, even in relatively staid quarters, was highly adverse to the Court.

The Springfield *Republican* called the decision "a blow at social reform and economic justice which must be deeply deplored," and noted that the Court had "ignored social and national welfare. . . ." A "victory of sordidness over our little ones," said the *New York Evening Mail*, and a victory that could not "long endure. A nation that will give its blood and money on the battle-field for the freedom of mankind throughout the world will surely find a way, despite five to four decisions, to release from slavery the children of its own hearthstone." Commenting on the district court's decision in *The New Republic* in September 1917, Edward S. Corwin had characterized it as a "displaced fossil from a by-gone epoch of constitutionalism." When later it witnessed the return of the bygone epoch in the Supreme Court itself, *The New Republic's* reaction was bitter. The Supreme Court, it said, was reconverting the government into an "impotent Confederacy," by this "unwarranted distortion of the Constitution . . . largely dominated by fear of the future." With this decision, and the decision a few months earlier in *Hitchman Coal & Coke Co.* v. *Mitchell*,[137] a yelow-dog contract case, "the Supreme Court has occasioned more disquietude for the orderly working out of economic and social questions than by anything it has done in one term of court since the Dred Scott Case." And *The New Republic* concluded: "In the long run American opinion will not consent to have social legislation invalidated and its social progress retarded by the necessarily accidental and arbitrary preference of one judge in a court of nine." The *New York Tribune* agreed that it was "improbable that such a decision will stand," and what is perhaps most remarkable, such a paper as the Boston *Evening Transcript* sounded hardly less radical than *The New Republic*. The decision, said the *Transcript*, was "inimical to public health, morality and safety." It was "a national charter of injustice."[138]

---

[137] 245 U.S. 229 (1917).

[138] See *The Literary Digest*, 57:16, June 15, 1918; *The New Republic*, 12:186, Sept. 15, 1917, 15:158, June 8, 1918, 195, June 15, 1918; Wood, *Constitutional Politics in the Progressive Era*, 173–76.

William S. Kenyon of Iowa, the Progressive Republican Senator who had cosponsored the Webb-Kenyon Act, regretted the decision

> all the more because it closes the door firmly against so many of our plans. I had hoped to see Congress enact before long a bill which would deny to interstate commerce the product of factories in which women are employed more than eight hours. I had hoped to see legislation enacted which would prevent the shipment across state lines of products of factories and mines in which all necessary safety appliances have not been installed.
>
> Everyone remembers a terrible fire in New York not many years ago in which scores, if not hundreds, of girls lost their lives, due to the failure to have sufficient fire escapes. . . . I had hoped for legislation which would make a repetition of such a holocaust as that impossible. . . . As it stands, the decision of the Supreme Court denies the method by which these reforms could be enforced by the federal government.

Others in Congress and outside were not so resigned. Three days after the decision, Owen of Oklahoma complained in the Senate that one man had nullified the matured opinion of the country as expressed by Congress in his bill. One man had declared, Owen went on, "that every member of the Senate and every member of the House voting for the Act and the President of the United States violated the Constitution of the United States, which they severally lifted up their hands before Almighty God and swore to observe"—conveniently forgetting that Senators had been urged to suppress their own constitutional doubts, if any, because it was the Supreme Court's function, not theirs, to pass on constitutionality. Owen proposed to reintroduce his bill, amended so as to deprive all federal courts, including the Supreme Court, of jurisdiction to declare it unconstitutional.

Nothing came of this intemperate proposal, but many voices in and out of Congress confidently argued that Congress had power to attain the end of the Keating-Owen bill by means of a taxing rather than a Commerce Clause measure. And although other devices, such as a constitutional amendment and the technique of the Webb-Kenyon Act, were also considered, Congress within a half year after *Hammer* v. *Dagenhart* did write into the revenue act of February 24, 1919, a prohibitive tax on the product of child labor. This effort, which was eventually frustrated by the *Child Labor Tax Case* of 1922, despite all those sanguine predictions to the contrary, enjoyed, like the Keating-Owen bill, broad support, including that of Senator Henry Cabot Lodge. In the meantime, the War Labor Policies Board, whose chairman was Felix Frankfurter, inserted in all federal contracts a clause making the provisions of the Keating-Owen Act mandatory on manufacturers who sold to the government.[139]

Scholarly opinion, although also heavily partial to the views of the minority in *Hammer* v. *Dagenhart*, was somewhat more divided than lay comment. There had been expressions of opinion before the decision that a statute such as the Keating-Owen Act would strain the Commerce Clause, and a few writers subsequently supported Day.[140] But the weight of opinion was very much the other way.[141]

Compared with the tone that was to be increasingly taken against the Court in the space of a very few years, the criticism evoked by *Hammer* v. *Dagenhart* in the professional journals, for the most part in the press, and—barring Senator Owen's outburst—in Congress was marked by a certain restraint, which was the product chiefly of incredulity. Many observers had convinced themselves that the Court was heading in a quite different direction, and *Hammer* v. *Dagenhart* seemed like an aberration. Hence the repeated predictions that it would be overruled, and that in any event the same end could be attained by use of the taxing power. Hence also admonitions that until overruled, the decision was law, could claim respect as such, and should not serve as a pretext for a general attack upon the Court and its function.[142] And yet in the harshness of some of the comment, the Court was having a foretaste of what was soon to come in great volume. It got such a foretaste, for example, from Thomas Reed Powell, then on the Columbia political science faculty, soon to go to the Harvard Law School, who

---

[139] See *Survey*, 40:283, June 8, 1918; 56 *Cong. Rec.* 7431–35, 65th Cong., 2nd Sess. (1918) (Senator Owen of Oklahoma); T. R. Powell, "The Child-Labor Decision," *The Nation*, 106:730, and 730–31, June 22, 1918; Wood, *Constitutional Politics in the Progressive Era*, 177 et seq., 199–216; R. E. Cushman, "The National Police Power under the Taxing Clause of the Constitution," *Minn. L. Rev.*, 4:247, 248, 1920.

[140] See, e.g., H. Hull, "The Federal Child Labor Law," *Political Science Quarterly*, 31:519, 1916; and see Cushman, "National Police Power under the Commerce Clause," 452, 456, n.11.

[141] See, e.g., T. R. Powell, "The Child Labor Law, the Tenth Amend-

ment, and the Commerce Clause," *South. L. Q.*, 3:175, 1918; H. W. Bikle, "The Commerce Power and Hammer v. Dagenhart," *U. Pa. L. Rev.*, 67:21, 1919; W. C. Jones, "The Child Labor Decision," *Cal. L. Rev.*, 6:395, 1918; T.M. Gordon, "The Child Labor Law Case," *Harv. L. Rev.*, 32:45, 1918; Note, *Yale L. J.*, 27:1092, 1918; Note, *Mich. L. Rev.*, 17:83, 1918; Cushman, "National Police Power under the Commerce Clause," 471, n.52.

[142] See Wood, *Constitutional Politics in the Progressive Era*, 180–84; *The Outlook*, 119:245, June 12, 1918; J. A. Ryan, "The Supreme Court and Child Labor," *Catholic World*, 108:212, 223, November 1918; Powell, "Child-Labor Decision," 730, 731.

during the 1920s and 1930s would be one of the Court's most acerbic and effecitve academic critics.[143]

Writing in August 1918, Powell allowed that his criticism did not necessarily "extend to withholding confidence or respect. A realistic investigation of the working of our institutions would disclose that there must be judicial authority to make mistakes." But he did say of Day's opinion that it neglected "history, logic and judicial precedents"; that it dealt in "loose conceptions with halos over them," thereby creating confusion; that it was "obviously in error," its errors including at least one palpable non sequitur; that it displayed "a narrow and myopic vision"; that once all its "confused and erroneous thinking" was brushed aside, there was left only "fiat"; and that the result was "wretchedly supported" and "obviously unfounded." It was, Powell wrote, "unfortunate for the position of the judiciary that the narrow margin by which the decision was reached invites the inference that the judges who composed the majority were influenced by their personal predilections on a question of policy."[144]

When Powell returned to *Hammer* v. *Dagenhart* four years later, in connection with a critique of the *Child Labor Tax Case* of 1922, his language was somewhat heightened, but the difference is one of degree. In 1922, Powell referred to "Mr. Justice Day's crucial blunder," and remarked that it was "pitifully obvious that he is wrong."[145] An escalation had occurred during these four years, but the open warfare is plainly seen to have commenced in 1918.[146]

---

[143] "He did great service . . . in his vigorous analysis of language, in his exposure of the emptiness in and beneath phrases, the illogicalities. . . . A lot of things were taken for granted. Powell was the fellow who pierced them. He lanced all these pretensions. . . ." H. Phillips, ed., *Felix Frankfurter Reminisces* (1960), 292–93.

[144] Powell, "Child Labor Law, Tenth Amendment, and Commerce Clause," 175, 188, 189, 191, 197, 198, 199, 202.

[145] Powell, "Child Labor, Commerce, and the Constitution," 62–64.

[146] A fully matured sample of Powell's style of criticism is worth extracting from the 1922 article. Powell refers to Day's "hypothetical vaticination" in *Hammer* v. *Dagenhart* that "the far-reaching result of

upholding the act cannot be more plainly indicated than by pointing out that if Congress can thus regulate matters entrusted to local authority by prohibition of the movement of commodities in interstate commerce, all freedom of commerce will be at an end, and the power of the states over local matters may be eliminated, and thus our system of government be practically destroyed." Powell comments:

This would have been true enough had the condition which made the goods nontransportable been one to which transportation in no way contributed. No one would have the hardihood to argue in favor of the constitutionality of congressional prohibition of interstate transportation of all goods

V: *The Fate of Social Legislation, 1914–21: Federal*

The only other decision in the years under discussion which tended toward a contraction of the Congressional power to regulate commerce was *Blumenstock Brothers* v. *Curtis Publishing Co.*,[147] a treble-damage action by a Chicago advertising agency against the *Saturday Evening Post* and other magazines, charging a violation of the Sherman Act in that the magazines refused to accept the plaintiff's advertising unless he reduced the advertising that he offered to competitive publications. A unanimous Court, Day writing, affirmed a dismissal of the suit on the ground that while the circulation and distribution of the magazines did quite probably constitute interstate commerce, the advertising contracts did not. But aside from *Blumenstock*, the trend that had impressed itself on observers since Taft's reconstitution of the Court appeared to continue after *Hammer* v. *Dagenhart*, thus confirming the impression that that decision was an aberration.

Again Liquor

When Congress, in the penultimate stages of total prohibitionist fervor, took a step beyond the Webb-Kenyon Act, the Court followed, striding lightly and easily beyond *Clark Distilling Co.* v. *Western Maryland Railway*. The Reed "Bone-Dry" Amendment, tacked on incongruously to the Post Office Appropriation Act of 1917,[148] imposed criminal penalties on the transportation of liquor in interstate com-

---

from states in which divorce is allowed or of all persons who beat their wives. Such interdictions of interstate transit would brow-beat the states not to permit divorce and brow-beat husbands not to brow-beat their wives. They would wield the commerce power as a club to control local enterprises in no way dependent upon interstate commerce. Intramarital pugilism would be dissuaded, not because belligerent husbands need interstate commerce for the achievement of this particular aim, but because for other reasons they are sufficiently eager for interstate wanderings to be willing to comply with the independent and unrelated condition which Congress selects as the criterion whether such wanderings may take place. This would partake of the nature of brigandage or blackmail. There would be no appropriate connection between the transportation and the conduct which makes it licit or illicit. Such a supposed statute should rightly be held to transcend the commerce power because of its intended and necessary effect to which interstate transportation has no necessary relation. No such situation is presented by a congressional prohibition of goods made by children. By such a statute the harmful results of child labor are forfended only to the extent that interstate transportation is economically necessary to their fruition. Here, then, is Mr. Justice Day's crucial blunder. Powell, "Child Labor, Congress and the Constitution," *N.C. L. Rev.*, 1:61, 63–64, 1922.

[147] 252 U.S. 436 (1920).

[148] 39 Stat. 1058 (1917).

merce, "except for scientific, sacramental, medicinal, and mechanical purposes, into any state or territory the laws of which state or territory prohibit the manufacture or sale therein of intoxicating liquors for beverage purposes. . . ." It thus not only equipped the Webb-Kenyon Act with federal teeth, but imposed a federal policy rather than merely supporting state prohibition. For it forbade the shipment of liquor into states which, while prohibiting manufacture or sale, did not necessarily prohibit use or even shipment.

The Webb-Kenyon Act, as construed in the *Clark Distilling Co.* case, enabled a state which prohibited importation to make its prohibition effective against liquor shipped in interstate commerce. The Reed Amendment, however, applied regardless of the will of the state, and invoked the federal criminal law against transactions which the state might be willing to allow or ignore. As Robert E. Cushman, then of the University of Minnesota, later of the Cornell Political Science Department, commented contemporaneously in some puzzlement, the Reed Amendment proceeded "upon the somewhat curious theory that Congress ought to impose its own brand of prohibition not upon all the states but only upon those states which have seen fit to adopt another sort of prohibition."[149] A half a year after *Hammer* v. *Dagenhart*, in *United States* v. *Hill*,[150] the Court upheld the Reed Amendment as a commonplace exercise of Congressional authority to regulate movement in interstate commerce, which included authority to prohibit movement.

The *Hill* case involved the transportation of one quart-bottle of liquor for personal use from Kentucky into West Virginia, which state, although it prohibited the sale, manufacture, and commercial importation of liquor, did not prohibit importation of one quart a month per individual for personal use. Day of all people wrote for the Court, and he cited *Hammer* v. *Dagenhart*, of all cases. But perhaps it was not so extraordinary that the author of *Caminetti* should sanction a progression by Congress from the Webb-Kenyon Act to the Reed Amendment that was very much like the Court's own progression, in construing the Mann Act, from the *Hoke* case to *Caminetti*.

Day drew a dissent from McReynolds, in which Clarke joined. The Reed Amendment, said McReynolds, "in no proper sense regulates interstate commerce, but is a direct intermeddling with the State's internal affairs." And he asked: "If Congress may deny liquor to those

---

[149] Cushman, "National Police Power under the Commerce Clause," 381, 412.

[150] 248 U.S. 420, 428 (1919); and see United States v. Simpson, 252 U.S. 465 (1920); Williams v. United States, 255 U.S. 336 (1921); see also Lindsey v. United States, 264 Fed. 94 (4th Cir. 1920), *cert. denied,* 252 U.S. 583 (1920); Ciafirdini v. United States, 266 Fed. 471 (4th Cir. 1920), *cert. denied,* 254 U.S. 634 (1920).

who live in a state simply because its manufacture is not permitted there, why may not this be done for any suggested reason, *e.g.*, because the roads are bad, or men are hanged for murder or coals are dug. Where is the limit?"

This extension of the commerce power, hardly consistent with *Hammer* v. *Dagenhart*, was received complacently enough in the law reviews, although as we have seen, it did puzzle Robert E. Cushman, and it struck Thomas Reed Powell as curious also. McReynolds' dissenting query, thought Powell, required an answer. "There must be some limit to the power of Congress to make its prohibitions of interstate commerce dependent upon legislation in the state of destination where the congressional prohibition is not in furtherance of that state legislation. The sound basis for the decision must be the reasonableness of the relation between the congressional prohibition and the state laws upon which it is made contingent."[151]

In *United States* v. *Ferger*,[152] decided over one silent dissent (Pitney) one year after *Hammer* v. *Dagenhart*, the Court sustained the Act of August 29, 1916,[153] which punished forgery of an interstate bill of lading. Of course, when a bill of lading is forged, there is no interstate shipment which Congress may be said to be regulating, and this troubled the trial court. The power of Congress, White said quite sensibly for the Supreme Court, did not depend on the "intrinsic existence of commerce in the particular subject dealt with." It rested on "the relation of that subject to commerce and its effect upon it." But the greatest and most spectacular, if precariously achieved, triumph of the federal commerce power, also emphasizing the relation of the particular subject dealt with to commerce and its effect upon it, had preceded *Hammer* v. *Dagenhart*.

Ulterior Ends and the Commercial Clause: the Railroad Labor Troubles of 1917

Wilson v. *New*, decided in March 1917, upheld the Adamson Eight-Hour Law hastily enacted by Congress the previous summer to avert a general railroad strike. It was a costly victory. The bare majority,

---

[151] T. R. Powell, "Constitutional Law 1918–19," *American Political Science Review*, 13:607, 608, 1919; but see Notes, *Harv. L. Rev.*, 32:733, 1919; *Colum. L. Rev.*, 19:79, 1919; *Mich. L. Rev.*, 17:511, 1919; *Yale L. J.*, 28:501, 1919, but *cf. Cent. L. J.*, 88:97, 1919.

[152] 250 U.S. 199, 203 (1919); see also United States v. Ferger No. 2, 250 U.S. 207 (1919); and see LeMore v. United States, 253 Fed. 887 (5th Cir. 1918), *cert. denied*, 248 U.S. 586 (1919); Jackson v. United States, 266 Fed. 770 (9th Cir. 1920), *cert. denied*, 254 U.S. 649 (1920).

[153] 39 Stat. 538 (1916).

for which Chief Justice White spoke, and which could not have been formed without him, was not only narrow but in his person reluctant.[154] It is altogether possible that White, in a sense, exacted a price for *Wilson* v. *New* by also forming the later majority in *Hammer* v. *Dagenhart*. There is excellent reason to believe, moreover, that the conditions which gave rise to the Adamson Law and the manner of its enactment so alarmed Day as to permanently and adversely affect his attitude toward social legislation. Day had been counted a progressive judge, bracketed with Holmes and Hughes by sanguine observers such as Felix Frankfurter in the first few years after Taft's reconstitution of the Court.[155] The Adamson Act, Frankfurter came later to conclude, marked a turning point for Day. When Brandeis once remarked how odd it was for Day "of all people" to have written that "terrible decision" in *Hammer* v. *Dagenhart*—Day, "who was so hot for federal power in other cases"—Frankfurter said that the Adamson Act had roused terrible fears in Day, who had spoken of it in this sense to Dr. Alice Hamilton during a summer vacation on Mackinac Island in Canada. From that time on, said Frankfurter, Day was turned against social legislation. "No," replied Brandeis, "not social legislation. It did not affect his attitude on white slavery and narcotic drugs, but only where property was involved." Frankfurter agreed: "Yes, the fear of the power of labor and the redistribution of economic power."[156]

National concern with labor relations in the railroad industry had long been manifested by a series of statutes providing for mediation and voluntary arbitration. Early in 1916, these loose arrangements broke down utterly. The four railroad brotherhoods—engineers, conductors, firemen, and trainmen—united in a demand for the eight-hour day and time-and-a-half for overtime. The railroads were then operating on a ten-hour-day or one-hundred-mile-run basis, which meant that the men were paid for a day's work after ten hours, or after completing a one-hundred-mile run in less than ten hours. The unions complained that management was increasing the length and weight of trains, thus

---

[154] Writing to Justice Sutherland some six years later, on the occasion of the decision of *Adkins* v. *Children's Hospital*, which declared wage regulation unconstitutional, Henry W. Anderson of Richmond, Virginia, a prominent lawyer well acquainted with a number of the Justices, recalled: "I had a long talk with the late Chief Justice White just following his decision in [*Wilson* v. *New*], and he convinced me in defending the opinion for the majority, that he was not sure of its correctness. I think the circumstances and conditions surrounding the country at the time largely influenced that judgment." H. W. Anderson to George Sutherland, Apr. 10, 1923, Sutherland Papers, Library of Congress.

[155] See *supra*, pp. 201–202.

[156] Brandeis-Frankfurter Conversations.

slowing them down while making them more profitable, and that the men were not getting their share of this increased productivity. And they firmly refused to submit their demands to arbitration.

Mediation failed, and by August 13 a strike appeared inevitable. On that day, President Wilson called both sides to the White House. The crisis was widely regarded as comparable only to the Civil War. The President could make no headway toward a settlement, and so he proposed his own terms, which were the eight-hour day, pro rata pay for overtime rather than time-and-a-half, and appointment, by authority of Congress, of a commission to assess operational consequences of the eight-hour day and report to the parties without making recommendations. This amounted to a substantial concession to the unions, but not a total one. The unions accepted, but management did not, even when the President added a proposal that the Interstate Commerce Commission be explicitly authorized to grant rate increases to compensate the railroads for additional wage costs, and that two more members be added to the commission so that rate cases could be expedited.

The union leaders informed the President that the strike would begin on the morning of September 4, and that they had no way to rescind the strike call. Having told the railroad representatives that the responsibility for the disaster would be theirs, and having consulted Democratic leaders in the Senate, Wilson, at 2:30 P.M. on August 29, 1916, went before a joint session of Congress and called for enactment of his settlement terms, including the provisions for rate increases. And he added proposals for compulsory arbitration of railroad labor disputes, and for Presidential authority in case of military necessity to seize the railroads and draft into the army such crews and management personnel as might be needed to run them. Wilson said:

> It has seemed to me, in considering the subject matter of the controversy, that the whole spirit of the time and the preponderant evidence of recent economic experience spoke for the eight-hour day. It had been adjudged by the thought and experience of recent years a thing upon which society is justified in insisting as in the interest of health, efficiency, contentment, and a general increase of economic vigor. The whole presumption of modern experience would, it seemed to me, be in its favor, whether there was arbitration or not, and the debatable points to settle were those which affected its establishment.

He was as much in favor of arbitration, Wilson added, as were the railroad managers, but he faced conditions in which arbitration was unobtainable. The only alternative was a strike threatening the life of the nation. Something had to be done. Existing statutes offered no way to avert the strike, and so he was proposing a law that would do so.

Later that evening, the House leadership told Wilson that his full program could not be enacted quickly, and so Representative William C. Adamson of Georgia, chairman of the Interstate Commerce Committee, and majority leader Claude Kitchin of North Carolina drafted a short statute providing only for the eight-hour day with time-and-a-half for overtime and the investigative commission. Two days later, Wilson having pointed out that the unions had agreed to accept pro rata rather than time-and-a-half pay for overtime, the bill was changed accordingly, and introduced in the House at five o'clock in the afternoon of August 31. The next day the House passed it by a large majority after short debate. On September 2, it went through the Senate by a somewhat smaller but still substantial majority. Being assured that the President would sign it, the union leaders called off the strike.

The bill provided that as of January 1, 1917, eight hours would be the standard of a day's work and pay in the operation of trains in interstate commerce, that the President would appoint a three-member study commission, and that pending the report of that commission and for thirty days thereafter, the compensation of railroad workers would not be reduced below the present day's wage, but that they would receive for all time worked in excess of eight hours pro rata pay. Violation of the act was made a misdemeanor punishable by fine and imprisonment.

This was the Adamson Act, and no one was really happy or even quite comfortable with it. Wilson expected Congress to deal with his other recommendations at the next session, and in the meantime he was clear that the eight-hour day was right. What was more important, he was clear that the federal government had the duty to avert a strike. "The business of government," he said defending his action, "is to see that no other organization is as strong as itself; to see that no body or group of men, no matter what their private interest is, may come into competition with the authority of society." Majority leader Kitchin believed that the strike would have been "the greatest catastrophe that ever befell our country," and that but for the Adamson Act, "the present Administration would have been destroyed." *The New Republic*, perhaps Wilson's chief nonpartisan defender, said that the Adamson Act "was a small price to pay for the prevention of a terrible national calamity." But it admitted that the measure, enacted speedily under heavy pressure, had caused bitterness.

The acrimony started in the brief debates in the House and Senate. "Oh, for an hour of Grover Cleveland or Theodore Roosevelt," cried Representative Gillette of Massachusetts, the future Republican Speaker. Wilson, it was widely charged in the same vein, had surrendered to threats and sacrificed principle. "We have cringed and crawled," said William E. Borah of Idaho, "we have humiliated ourselves, debauched our Government, discredited union labor, and settled nothing." For the first time in American history, said the *Chicago Tribune*, Congress had "enacted a law under duress." Much was made of the presence of union leaders in the Ways and Means Committee room just off the House floor, and of continual consultations with them. Not surprisingly, the *Railway Age Gazette* spoke of the manner in which the Adamson bill was "jammed through" as "outrageous," "the triumph of Mobocracy," "the most shameful performance in American history." But *The Nation* was also of the view that Congress had been "the submissive victim of a hold-up," and asked whether "averting of the strike was worth such a sacrifice of the nation's dignity." Hughes, out on the hustings, mounted a vigorous attack. The Adamson Act, he said, would not achieve the eight-hour day, but amounted merely to an indirect wage increase for the standard hundred-mile run, which the *Journal of Commerce* estimated—quite accurately—at $60 million a year on the pro rata basis.[157]

The Adamson Act was not put into effect. The railroads claimed that the eight-hour day was an administrative impossibility, given their methods of operation. Through the fall numerous suits were filed to enjoin enforcement. Attorney General Gregory appointed Frank Hagerman of Kansas City, a well-known railroad lawyer, to take charge of all these cases for the government, and by late November agreement was obtained with the railroads that one of the cases should be expedited to an early decision in the Supreme Court. The government picked a suit filed by the receiver of the Missouri, Oklahoma and Gulf Railway (New) against the U.S. Attorney in the Western District of Missouri (Wilson).

The case came before Circuit Judge William C. Hook, sitting in district court in Kansas City, because Hook had jurisdiction in bankruptcy over the railroad's reorganization, and over all aspects of the receiver's conduct of its affairs. At Hagerman's urging, and making it

---

[157] See E. Berman, *Labor Disputes and the President of the United States* (1924), 106–17; Link, *Wilson: Campaigns for Progressivism and Peace*, 83–92, 103–104; F. H. Dixon, *Railroads and Government* (1922), 103; P. Taft, *Organized Labor in American History* (1964), 263–69; T. R. Fisher, *Industrial Disputes and Federal Legislation* (1940), 162; W. J. Lauck, "The Case of Railroad Employees for an Eight-Hour Day," *Annals of the American Academy of Political and Social Science*, 13:69– 70, 1917; *The New Republic*, 8:130, 208, 209, Sept. 9, Sept. 30, 1916; *New York Times*, Sept. 2, 1916, p. 1, col. 8, Sept. 3, 1916, p. 1, col. 8; E. J. Clapp, "The Adamson Law," *Yale Rev.*, 6:259, 270–72, January 1917; *Am. Rev. of Reviews*, 54:362, 363, October 1916; *American Industries*, 17:9, September 1916; *The Literary Digest*, 53:651–52, 718, Sept. 16, 1916, 875–76, Oct. 7, 1916; *Railway Age Gazette*, 61:394, Sept. 8, 1916, 531, Sept. 29, 1916; *The Nation*, 103:213, Sept. 7, 1916.

clear that his decision was not based on full consideration of the merits of the case, but was intended merely to expedite final adjudication, Hook on November 22, 1916, acted on motions, without oral argument, and issued a final decree holding the Adamson Act unconstitutional. Nevertheless, by agreement, he ordered the railroad to keep accounts of wages that would have been earned if the Act had been enforced, so as to make possible payment of these wages should the Act ultimately be held valid. Other railroads were also keeping such accounts.[158]

The aim of these proceedings was to obtain a decision in the Supreme Court by January 1, the effective date of the Act. But it was January 8, 1917, before *Wilson* v. *New* even came on to be heard in the Supreme Court. The argument consumed the better part of three days.[159] Solicitor General Davis opened for the government, defending the Act conservatively as a protection of commerce through the regulation of hours of labor and the settlement of a strike. But when asked by the Chief Justice whether he claimed "the same power in fixing wages as in fixing rates," Davis, who had indeed claimed it at length in his brief, answered in the affirmative. "I can't follow that argument," said White. "The subject is regulating hours of service. The government has regulated commerce for ages, so to speak. It was held in the case of the Employers' Liability Act that that regulation was valid. That was no decision that the government has the power to regulate wages." When Davis replied that that was what the government was contending for, White repeated: "That's the logic I can't follow."

Davis pressed the point. If the government could regulate other elements of the relationship of master and servant in the railroad industry, it could regulate wages for many of the same reasons. Wages were the most vital part of the master-servant relationship. "If underpaid and discontented, safety of commerce in charge of employees is affected. Also, wages have a direct relation to rates, investment and expense of service." Could Congress then regulate the wages of all persons making goods for shipment in interstate commerce, White asked? The argument did not go that far, said Davis. McReynolds then intervened. "Has Congress the power to prescribe what railroads shall pay for various things—locomotives, land?" Davis said he was not sure Congress lacked that power—"all authority is dependent upon its reasonable and not arbitrary use." Congress moreover had power to

---

[158] See *Traffic World*, 18:722, Oct. 7, 1916; *Journal of Political Economy*, 25:387, 388, 1917; *New York Times*, Nov. 16, 1916, p. 1, col. 1, p. 4, col. 4, Nov. 23, 1916, p. 1, col. 1; *Railway Age Gazette*, 61:994–95, Dec. 1, 1916.

[159] "I humbly think," Holmes wrote to Harold J. Laski, "that an hour to a side was all that was needed—but we had some old-fashioned roaring." *Holmes-Laski Letters*, I, 55.

prevent railroad strikes and obstruction of interstate commerce (citing *In re Debs*),[160] and had exercised it. The contention that the Adamson law was administratively unworkable was an afterthought.

For the railroads, Walker D. Hines, general counsel of the Santa Fe Railroad, said:

> The primary purpose of the act was arbitrary regulation of private contracts. It sets aside legitimate methods, substituting an unworkable speculative arrangement. Its classifications give benefit only to the four brotherhoods who were demanding the changes—all for the benefit of a special, high-paid class. In all aspects it is of unconstitutional and bewildering unworkability, without relation to any substantial promotion of commerce.

"Can Congress," asked Day, "authorize the Interstate Commerce Commission to fix railroad wages?" Hines thought not, unless wages were abnormally low and could be deemed to interfere with commerce. Having ascertained that the wage contracts of the brotherhoods had been made before 1913, Brandeis said: "Shouldn't this Court take judicial notice of the fact that there has been a great increase in the cost of living since these wages were fixed?" Hines, quite politely and elaborately, answered in effect, so what? And the Chief Justice chimed in: "If there is no power there can be no justification for its attempted exercise."

Wages, Hines continued, had no substantial relation to safety and efficiency in this case. "Then you argue that this is a regulation of wages and of private relations between employers and employees remote from service," said Pitney. "It is a most remote regulation of commerce," Hines replied. And it was misnamed an eight-hour law, he continued, because it was really a wage-fixing measure. "Isn't it a historical fact," asked Brandeis, "that in the introduction of the legislative policy of reducing the hours of labor many of the states began in fixing what number of hours should be a standard day, and later, in the progress of legislation, there came an actual prohibition of more?" Perhaps so, said Hines. "And isn't it a fact," Brandeis pursued, "when [the Adamson Act] was introduced there never was a suggestion that the purpose of the legislation was to fix wages and not to reduce hours?" "They did not increase wages much," Hines replied, emphasizing that no penalty pay was provided for overtime.

The other argument for the railroads was made by John G. Johnson, then seventy-five, and in the last few months of his life. Said Johnson:

---

[160] 158 U.S. 564 (1895).

There is nothing in the Adamson Act for protection of the public. The brotherhoods have the honesty not to pretend they were protecting the public, but stood upon their own selfish ends. . . . Have we come to that? Have we reached the period when the men who threaten a strike shall be rewarded? I'm not comparing men, only methods, but we might as well buy off a gang of highwaymen with a bribe to prevent interference with commerce.

Frank Hagerman concluded for the government. If Congress could raise wages for a limited period, could it do it for an unlimited period, Pitney wanted to know. "Where do you draw the line between private operation and public management?" "I don't draw the line," Hagerman replied. "But it may be necessary for the purposes of this argument," said Pitney. Chief Justice White then attempted a statement of the government's case:

Here is a question of a strike. More pay is asked. The other side says more pay means higher rates. Congress says, "We haven't had a chance to investigate this matter, but we'll put a temporary arrangement into effect and give an opportunity for full investigation, with a temporary increase of wages and also an increase of rates." Now that's your proposition, isn't it?

Hagerman assented. And in support of the proposition he launched into a recital of the course of negotiations. "The carriers were pretending that they wanted arbitration, but they refused to arbitrate the eight-hour day demand unless all other questions were also arbitrated." "What's this got to do with the law question?" White asked. "I don't want to interrupt you, but we have a question of law and you are discussing things we have no cognizance of." Hagerman very reasonably replied: "I didn't start it, your Honor." "I know that," White conceded, "but I suggest that you conclude it."

The following day, as Hagerman was nearing the end, McReynolds said: "Is there no limit to what Congress can do to stop a strike? In the Debs case, could Congress have ordered the railroads to pay Mr. Debs $50,000 to stop a strike?" "That's putting it pretty fierce, but I believe Congress could," said Hagerman. He was not persuading Van Devanter, who remarked: "Oh, you don't mean that. That minimizes and detracts from everything you've said." Holmes apparently agreed that Hagerman was overdoing it: "I think that you are very wise in dealing with this question to be precise and not consider the degree the matter can be pushed."[161]

---

[161] *Commercial and Financial Chronicle,* 104:126–28, Jan. 13, 1917; *New York Times,* Jan. 9, 1917, p. 1, col. 4, Jan. 10, 1917, p. 1, col. 2.

V: *The Fate of Social Legislation, 1914–21: Federal*

The Socratic interplay at the argument did not augur particularly well for the fate of the Adamson Act, even though in retrospect one can see Chief Justice White's opinion—limited and cautious, but favorable—in the process of formation. But "the degree the matter can be pushed," in Holmes' phrase, was plainly worrying many of the Justices, and the outlines of dissenting positions, particularly Pitney's and McReynolds', emerged more obviously than White's ultimate decision. The full extent of the government's strongly stated claims can hardly be said to have been accepted any earlier than 1937.[162]

The brotherhoods grew restless, and by March, there having been no decision yet, they notified the railroads that unless a settlement was reached, they would strike on March 17. The railroads, sharing the expectation of a Supreme Court decision adverse to the Adamson Act, refused to move before the Supreme Court acted. Wilson, who in December had asked Congress to enact those parts of his program which had been left pending in the summer, publicly informed the parties that a strike was "inconceivable." After all, American merchantmen were being armed just then. The President appointed a mediation committee, which included two Cabinet members, and in response, the union leaders on March 17 postponed the strike for forty-eight hours.

Through the night of March 18, no progress was made in talks in New York, and Wilson wired the parties that in view of the international situation he would under no circumstances permit a strike. Early in the morning of March 19, the railroads gave in, and settled on the basis of the Adamson Act. The eight-hour day was accepted with certain adjustments to fit existing schedules, and pro rata pay for overtime. A commission representing both employers and the unions would resolve further disputes concerning application of the eight-hour principle. In Washington a few hours later, Chief Justice White delivered the Court's opinion in *Wilson* v. *New*. It amounted to a ratification of a settlement which by then the Court was powerless to disturb, although a few days earlier its judgment might have been decisive.[163]

White began by describing in some detail the events of the spring and summer of 1916. The Act which resulted was, he said, both an hours-of-labor and a wage statute. But while the eight-hour day was permanently fixed, wages were only temporarily regulated, "leaving the employers and employees free as to the subject of wages to govern their relations by their own agreements after the specified time." He went on: "[W]e put the question as to the eight-hour standard entirely out

---

[162] See NLRB v. Jones & Laughlin Steel Corp., 301 U.S. 1 (1937).

[163] See Berman, *Labor Disputes and the President*, 117–24; Link, *Wilson:* *Campaigns for Progressivism and Peace*, 207, 292–93; *Railway Review*, 60:100, Jan. 20, 1917; *Traffic World*, 19:597, Mar. 24, 1917.

of view on the ground that the authority to permanently establish it is so clearly sustained as to render the subject not disputable," citing cases on the Hours of Service Acts. The business of common carriers by rail was in large measure a public business, and Congress had regulated it in numerous and extensive ways. It was equally true, however, that the right of a carrier and its employees to fix a standard of wages was beyond the control of public authority. Thus White posed a dilemma, from which he sought escape in three marathon sentences:

> But taking all these propositions as undoubted, if the situation which we have described and with which the act of Congress dealt be taken into view, that is, the dispute between the employers and the employees as to a standard of wages, their failure to agree, the resulting absence of such standard, the entire interruption of interstate commerce which was threatened, and the infinite injury to the public interest which was imminent, it would seem inevitably to result that the power to regulate necessarily obtained and was subject to be applied to the extent necessary to provide a remedy for the situation, which included the power to deal with the dispute, to provide by appropriate action for a standard of wages to fill the want of one caused by the failure to exert the private right on the subject and to give effect by appropriate legislation to the regulations thus adopted. This must be unless it can be said that the right to so regulate as to save and protect the public interest did not apply to a case where the destruction of the public right was imminent as the result of a dispute between the parties and their consequent failure to establish by private agreement the standard of wages which was essential; in other words that the existence of the public right and the public power to preserve it was wholly under the control of the private right to establish a standard by agreement. . . . If acts which, if done, would interrupt, if not destroy, interstate commerce may be by anticipation legislatively prevented, by the same token the power to regulate may be exercised to guard against the cessation of interstate commerce threatened by a failure of employers and employees to agree as to the standard of wages, such standard being an essential prerequisite to the uninterrupted flow of interstate commerce.

Whatever else this highly adjectival and adverbial prose may fail to communicate, it makes clear that White was upholding a power of Congress, not to fix wages, but to prevent or settle a strike. In general, he said, Congress may prophylactically protect interstate commerce from interruption, and it may *a fortiori* act against the event itself. But Congress may foresee that wage disputes will cause strikes interrupting commerce, and may wish to apply the prophylaxis of a wage regulation well in advance of a strike, and regardless of privately negotiated employment contracts. So it applied the prophylaxis of an Hours of Service or Safety Appliance Act regardless of disputes or private agreements. Why with respect to wages Congress must wait for a dispute to exist and the actual interruption to impend, White did not say. But he clearly meant for Congress to wait. He was upholding, he repeated later on, an authority "to fix wages where by reason of the dispute there had been a failure to fix by agreement."

The prose is what it is, and the logic is shaky, but the intention is plain. This was an ad hoc validation of an ad hoc strike settlement in exigent circumstances. It was more only in that White suggested that Congress could prospectively provide for compulsory arbitration of such disputes. What Congress had done here, White said, "amounted to an exertion of its authority . . . to compulsorily arbitrate the dispute . . .—a power none the less efficaciously exerted because exercised by direct [ad hoc] legislative act instead of by enactment of other and appropriate means. . . ."

Addressing himself to the manner rather than the substance of the settlement, which, it was urged, amounted "to a decision without a hearing and to a mere arbitrary bestowal of millions by way of wages upon employees," White pointed out that the settlement adopted by Congress was not one-sided. Congress had rejected the unions' demand for time-and-a-half pay for overtime. And so "the statute certainly affords no ground for the proposition that it arbitrarily considered only one side of the dispute to the absolute and total disregard of the rights of the other. . . ." The objection on this score boiled down, therefore, to the assertion that the Adamson Act was "an unwise exertion of legislative power begotten either from some misconception or some mistaken economic view or partiality for the rights of one disputant over the other or some unstated motive which should not have been permitted to influence action. But to state such considerations is to state also the entire want of judicial power to consider them"—except as White would a short time hence join the *Hammer* v. *Dagenhart* majority in considering the motives behind the Child Labor Act. Finally, White refused briefly to credit the argument that the eight-hour day was an administrative impossibility. As the opinion was delivered only hours after the railroads had agreed in New York to put the eight-hour day into effect, this passage had greater authority than could have been claimed for it when White committed it to paper.

McKenna, while joining the opinion of the Court, filed a brief concurrence. The Adamson Act, he said, was intended to be and was a regulation of hours of service, not of wages. "Of course, in a sense, the two things are related." But regulation of one is not necessarily to be regarded as regulation of the other, else cases such as *Muller* v. *Oregon*, and similar decisions upholding state and federal regulations of hours of labor in certain occupations or for certain employees, would have to be read as also upholding the power to regulate wages. Yet McKenna added, somewhat enigmatically, that so far as railroads were concerned, he thought anyway that wages could be regulated: "I speak only of intention; of the power I have no doubt."

The four dissenters had three voices. Day was "not prepared to deny to Congress, in view of its constitutional authority to regulate commerce among the States, the right to fix by lawful enactment the wages to be paid to those engaged in such commerce in the operation of trains carrying passengers and freight. While the railroads of the country are privately owned, they are engaged in a public service, and because of that are subject in a large measure to governmental control." Congress, Day said, going well beyond the limits of White's position, may ensure reasonable rates and proper service, and to that end regulate wages. But this Commerce Clause power was subject to the restraint of the Due Process Clause of the Fifth Amendment. Congress could fix a just wage, but the Adamson Act made an arbitrary award, which confiscated the property of the railroads. Congress upon the face of the statute had expressed its inability to fix a just wage prior to an investigation which it proposed to undertake. Instead, by legislative edict, it instituted an experiment the cost of which was to fall, not on both parties to the labor dispute, nor on the public, but entirely on the railroads. There was no provision for compensation should the investigation prove that the wage Congress had temporarily established was unjust, and Congress had not followed the President's recommendation that the Interstate Commerce Commission be explicitly authorized to grant a rate increase commensurate with the increased wages. The railroads were, of course, not free to adjust rates on their own. Due Process was also a guarantee of fair procedure. Yet Congress had undertaken no investigation, and had not even deliberated, before "speedily" enacting the Adamson Act. Congress had acted "in violation of the spirit of fair play and equal right. . . ."

Pitney, joined by Van Devanter, dissented in some fifteen pages. The Adamson Act was a regulation of wages, not hours. Unlike the Hours of Service Act, for example, it in no way prohibited work for longer than eight hours, but merely increased the pay. Consequently the Adamson Act could not be sustained as a regulation of commerce. It removed no impediment, prescribed no service, imposed no safeguards. "In short, it has no substantial relation to or connection with commerce —no closer relation [echoing a question of McReynolds at the argument] than has the price which the carrier pays for its engines and cars or for the coal used in propelling them." While it was "true in fact" that the purpose of Congress was to prevent a threatened strike, and thus to remove an obstruction to commerce, it was "immaterial in law." "The suggestion that an increase in the wages of trainmen will increase their contentment, encourage prompt and efficient service, and thus facilitate the movement of commerce, is altogether fanciful. The increase effected is not at all conditioned upon contented or efficient service." So much for one of Solicitor General Davis' arguments. With regard to procedural objections under the Due Process Clause, Pitney simply expressed concurrence in Day's opinion.

The last of the dissenters, McReynolds, spoke for himself in three short paragraphs. The Act was a regulation of wages. McReynolds had not theretofore believed that the Commerce Clause authorized the fixing of wages, "and the argument advanced in support of the contrary view is unsatisfactory to my mind." It followed from "the doctrine now affirmed by a majority of the Court" that Congress could fix a maximum as well as a minimum wage, could require compulsory arbitration, and could protect the free flow of commerce against workers, owners, or strangers.[164]

Replying to a comment by Felix Frankfurter on the Chief Justice's limitation of federal power over wages to cases where the parties had themselves been unable to reach agreement, Holmes wrote a kind of private concurring opinion:

> I am disturbed at the point to which you advert in the Adamson case. I told the C.J. that I went the whole unicorn as to the power of Congress and I understood that he wouldn't do more than assume for the sake of argument that Congress couldn't meddle when the parties agreed. But the opinion looks very much like a direct denial of power in that case. I take no stock in the distinction (this is all entre nous of course). My impression was that Day had the most rational dissent, although I thought it manifestly wrong to say that property is taken, etc. when a rate is fixed as presumptively just unless and until shown otherwise by experience. If absolute certainty is the condition of constitutional power, God help us. I hear rumors that we came near universal anarchy if the strike had gone on. I don't know, but it is getting to be time to find out who is the governing power in this country. . . . Patriotism is the demand of the territorial club for priority, and as much priority as it needs for vital purposes, over such tribal groups as the churches and trade unions. I go the whole hog for the territorial club—and I don't care a damn if it interferes with some of the spontaneities of the other groups.[165]

---

[164] Wilson v. New, 243 U.S. 332, 345–46, 347–48, 351–52, 355, 357, 358–59, 361, 364–65, 367, 369, 370, 371, 372, 376, 380, 387, 388, 389 (1917).

[165] O. W. Holmes to F. Frankfurter, Mar. 27, 1917, Holmes Papers. To Harold J. Laski, Holmes wrote: "My opinion goes the whole hog with none of the C.J.'s squeams— but I don't care to say more than is necessary. As I put it after the argument, I think if Congress can weave the cloth it can spin the thread." *Holmes-Laski Letters,* I, 69.

Public reactions to the decision were fairly predictable. The Chief Justice's opinion was a surprise to all intelligent people, declared the *Railway Review*. There were those, reported *The Nation*, who were saying "bitterly in their haste that the Court's decision sweeps away the foundation of private rights in respect of railway property." The *New York Times* stayed cool, and welcomed the strike settlement, in which "the real victors were the railroad managers, for they let the national feeling conquer self-interest. They have nothing to be ashamed of. The Brotherhood chiefs have nothing to be proud of." The *Railway Wage Gazette* believed that the unions had won a battle, but lost a campaign, and the *New York World*, although it saw the matter from a very different point of view, rather agreed, predicting that the workers had "given new life at Washington to a power that will surely regulate them as it long has regulated their employers." Samuel Gompers, president of the American Federation of Labor, focused on the same aspect of the opinion. He protested against the Chief Justice's dictum that compulsory arbitration would be constitutional.

The New Republic hailed "a statesmanlike decision," and *The Outlook* thought that the country would be left with the belief "that both the President and Congress pursued a wise course when a universal strike was threatened in September." The decision, moreover, greatly strengthened "the principle of government regulation." But *Survey* regretted that the case established "no precedent that can be depended on to justify legislation carefully and thoroughly drafted for the purpose of destroying industrial evils or promoting social progress. It merely establishes the right of Congress to act in an emergency and for no social purpose except to save the public from inconvenience. Whatever precedents are established may prove disquieting, not only to the unions and their friends, but to employing corporations as well."[166]

In the law journals, Thomas Reed Powell in February 1917 accurately predicted the outcome. A few months later, he wrote:

> In essence [the] judgment whether the statute was a regulation of commerce was simply a determination of the effect of the statute on a practical situation. Any other answer to the particular problem before the Court than that given by the majority would have been so devoid of simple common sense that it would inevitably have shaken the confidence which our supreme judicial tribunal deservedly enjoys.

[166] See *Railway Review*, 60:428, Mar. 24, 1917; *The Nation*, 104:360, Mar. 29, 1917; *New York Times*, Mar. 24, 1917, p. 10, col. 4; *Railway Age Gazette*, 62:612, Mar. 23, 1917; *The Literary Digest*, 54:887, Mar. 31, 1917; *Commercial and Financial Chronicle*, 104:1102, Mar. 24, 1917; *The New Republic*, 10:217, Mar. 24, 1917; *The Outlook*, 115:543, Mar. 28, 1917; *Survey*, 37:737, Mar. 31, 1917.

By implication, Powell charged McReynolds and Pitney among the dissenters with lack of "simple common sense." He was critical also of Day, especially of his insistence on some form of procedural due process in Congress, which, said Powell, was a matter not subject to judicial review, since under the Constitution "each House may determine the rules of its proceedings." On the whole, the doctrine for which *Wilson* v. *New* stood seemed to Powell a limited one.

Robert E. Cushman viewed the decision as rather more significant. It struck him as important that in considering whether or not the Adamson Act was a regulation of commerce, "the Court paid practically no attention to what the law was about. The mind of the Court was fixed upon what would happen if the law was not passed." The decisive factors were the threat of a strike and the consequences of a strike:

> If this is true, then it would seem to follow that any legislation which forms the subject matter of the demands of a body of individuals possessing the power to bring interstate commerce to a standstill if those demands are not granted, must be regarded as a legitimate exercise of the power of Congress to regulate commerce, provided such legislation does not violate the due process of law clause or any other specific constitutional prohibition. This startling doctrine without doubt opens up some rather interesting possibilities in the way of broadening the scope of the national police power under the commerce clause.[167]

The strike settlement and later awards by the federal director general after the wartime takeover of the railroads, and not the Adamson Act, governed wages and conditions of labor in the railroad industry, but the Adamson Act did have a judicial sequel. A bankrupt railroad, barely able to continue in operation, had succeeded in making an agreement with its men for a wage scale lower than that frozen by the Adamson Act. All parties were content to proceed under their agreement, but the receiver feared that he was subject to the Adamson Act and required to pay higher wages in conformance with it. Of course, the period for which the Adamson Act fixed wages was a temporary one, and it had expired by the time this case was argued in December 1917, but the issue was live nevertheless, since if the Act was applicable, back wages would be due. The case was kept in the Supreme Court for

---

[167] See T. R. Powell, "Due Process and the Adamson Law," *Colum. L. Rev.,* 17:114, February 1917; T. R. Powell, "The Supreme Court and the Adamson Law," *U. Pa. L. Rev.,* 65: 607, May 1917; Cushman, "National Police Power under the Commerce Clause," 289, 317; see also H. T. Smith, "The Eight-Hour Railway Wage Law," *Va. L. Rev.,* 4:83, 1916; but *cf.* M. H. Lauchheimer, "The Constitutionality of the Eight-Hour Railroad Law," *Colum. L. Rev.,* 16:554, 1916.

some two and one-half years after argument, causing difficulties, perhaps, because it precisely fit the situation in which, according to White's opinion, the Act could not constitutionally apply—the situation of a federal attempt to fix wages where the parties themselves were not in disagreement, but had settled on a different wage scale. Finally, in June 1920, the Court, per Holmes, held the Act inapplicable as a matter of statutory construction: "To break up such a bargain would be at least unjust and impolitic, and not at all within the ends that the Adamson Law had in view. We think it reasonable to assume that the circumstances in which, and the purposes for which, the law was passed, import an exception in a case like this."[168]

Day, Van Devanter, Pitney, and McReynolds noted their concurrence with the decision, but also their adherence to the views they had expressed in *Wilson* v. *New*. Van Devanter had written Holmes: "I am in full accord with the result and the construction put on the statute in reaching it. What was decided in the earlier case was so much in conflict with my views of the subject, and is so still, that it is hard, very hard, to assent to it even indirectly. Perhaps I must; but let me think about it before giving a full or limited concurrence." Day knew immediately what he had to do. He wrote Holmes: "In the Adamson Law case, written by you for the C.J. [thus indicating that the Chief Justice had initially assigned the opinion to himself, and then reassigned it to Holmes, either, as was not unusual toward the end of his tenure, because he was unable to get through with his work, or because he had been converted to a statutory, rather than a constitutional, disposition of the case and preferred to have someone who had favored this disposition from the beginning formulate it], I agree with what you say as to the former decision, and with your disposition of the case just written. I do not wish to be estopped if another 'hold-up' statute is passed. Please say for me that I concur in the result."[169]

The Treaty and Foreign Relations Powers

An emergency had expanded the federal commerce power in *Wilson* v. *New*. The same office could be performed by a treaty. Congress, in a provision of the Department of Agriculture Appropriation Act of 1913,[170] invoked the commerce power to protect migratory birds from indiscriminate extermination. The provision was held unconstitutional by two district courts as an invasion of state functions.[171] The

---

[168] Fort Smith & Western R.R. v. Mills, 253 U.S. 206, 209 (1920).
[169] Holmes Papers.
[170] 37 Stat. 847 (1913).

[171] United States v. Shauver, 214 Fed. 154 (E.D. Ark. 1914); United States v. McCullagh, 221 Fed. 288 (D.C. Kan. 1915).

government brought up one of these cases, *United States* v. *Shauver*, on writ of error, but lacking confidence in the result, delayed it. The case was kept in the Supreme Court, undisposed of even after argument, while efforts were made to provide another and firmer constitutional basis for federal regulation of migratory birds.

The supporters of the 1913 provision, who included Senators George P. McLean of Connecticut and Elihu Root of New York, first toyed with the notion of a constitutional amendment, and then settled on a resolution calling for a migratory bird treaty. A treaty was concluded with Great Britain, which pledged the parties to protect birds migrating between the United States and Canada by specifying close seasons for hunting and by other means. Despite some protests that a disingenuous end run was being made around the Commerce Clause and the Tenth Amendment, the treaty was ratified and, after a wartime delay, implemented by the Migratory Bird Treaty Act of 1918.[172] Thereupon, on motion of the Solicitor General, the writ of error in *United States* v. *Shauver* was dismissed.[173] The 1918 Act was held constitutional in *Missouri* v. *Holland*, in April 1920.

In this train of events, Chief Justice White played a remarkable role. According to the recollection of Edwin M. Borchard, then Librarian of the Supreme Court, later professor of law at Yale, the Chief Justice was very anxious to reverse the lower court in *United States* v. *Shauver* and uphold the constitutionality of the 1913 attempt at migratory bird regulation. In common with many conservationists, he felt that the birds were a great natural resource, essential to agriculture, since they preyed on insects that destroyed crops and forests. The states, he thought, were unreliable as protectors of the birds:

> But the Court stood divided 3 to 3, three judges being ill or absent. The Chief Justice thereupon held [*United States* v. *Shauver*] undecided upon until a full bench could sit, but in the meantime engaged the writer, then librarian of the Supreme Court, to make an exhaustive study of the law, from Roman times until the present to endeavor to show that the Federal Government must possess the power of bird regulation. The study, which occupied several months, reached the conclusion that the states alone were the repositories of the power to regulate migratory birds, since by no possibility could this migratory resource be called interstate commerce, which depends on the acts of man. In the conversations with the Chief Justice and Dr. Holmes of the Bureau of Animal Industry, there developed an idea, earlier sug-

---

[172] 39 Stat. 1702 (1916); 40 Stat. 755 (1918); see J. P. Boyd, "The Expanding Treaty Power," *N.C. L. Rev.*, 6:428, 441–44, 1928; and see 55 *Cong.* Rec. 5546–48, 65th Cong., 1st Sess. (1917); 56 *Cong. Rec.* 7449, 65th Cong., 2nd Sess. (1918).

[173] 248 U.S. 594 (Jan. 7, 1919).

gested in a resolution introduced by Senator McLean of Connecticut, that a treaty with Canada might be concluded, whereupon the legislation could be enacted again and rest for its constitutional justification upon the implementation of a treaty.[174]

Borchard's story is confirmed and enlarged upon in a letter to the Chief Justice, dated November 3, 1915, from Louis Marshall, the well-known New York lawyer who appeared often before the Court, and who was to file a brief *amicus* in behalf of the Association for the Protection of the Adirondacks in *Missouri* v. *Holland*. "In conformity with the promise which I made to you last week," wrote Marshall, "when you discussed . . . [the migratory bird law] with Senator [Philander C.] Knox [of Pennsylvania] and me, I take the liberty of calling to your attention the state of the law in New York relating to the migratory fish of the sea." Apparently the prevailing opinion in New York was that only federal authority could regulate migratory fish. "Having thus called your attention to the legislation of New York," Marshall continued, "in view of your expressed desire for my views on the general subject I venture to make the following additional comments." There followed a brief of several pages presenting a novel argument for overturning the decision in *United States* v. *Shauver*. Marshall thought that the United States could regulate migratory birds in order to safeguard the vast areas of timberlands which it owned. Congress had undoubted power to protect federal property, insects destroyed trees, and Marshall cited expert evidence of the importance of birds in keeping the insect population within bounds.[175]

What thus emerges is a most extraordinary performance on the part of White, who was normally scrupulous to a fault in observing the judicial proprieties.[176] "It is a great place, Judge," said White in 1916, in welcoming Clarke, "but we live in a cave." Under Taft, a committee of the Court officially cooperated with Congress in putting through the Judiciary Act of 1925, which was known as the Judges' bill. This much-needed measure might well have been enacted earlier but for White's

---

[174] See E. M. Borchard, "Treaties and Executive Agreements—A Reply," *Yale L. J.*, 54:616, 632–33, 1945.

[175] C. Reznikoff, ed., *Louis Marshall —Champion of Liberty* (1957), II, 1068–74.

[176] An earlier lapse of White's was a letter of June 24, 1912, to Elihu Root expressing "admiration for and appreciation of" Root's controversial service as presiding officer at the Republican Convention in Chicago. "To an outsider," wrote White, "it seemed we were possibly near a great crisis. The dignity, intelligence, the firmness, the patriotism so well, so superbly manifested by you in the discharge of your duty was at once felt all over the country and begot hope and confidence! You have rendered another great public service for which every self-respecting American owes you a debt of gratitude. . . ." Quoted in P. C. Jessup, *Elihu Root* (1938), II, 204.

exquisite scruples about the wall of separation, as he evidently viewed it, between Court and Congress. White was "unalterably opposed"—the phrase is Van Devanter's in a letter a decade later to Taft—to any lobbying by judges even with respect to technical jurisdictional bills. The Judiciary Act of 1915, modifying the Court's appellate jurisdiction, was drafted by Van Devanter. White approved of it, but insisted that neither the Court nor any member be in any way perceived as being connected. with it. White himself would not venture even privately a direct expression of opinion about it to a Senator. He disclosed, Van Devanter noted contemporaneously, the most acute "reluctance to being understood as acting or promoting any particular legislation, even relating to the Court. . . ." The Judiciary Act of 1916, again altering the appellate jurisdiction, was drafted by McReynolds, Van Devanter recalled for Taft in 1927, with the assistance of Day and himself. It was introduced and passed while the Court was in summer recess. "When Chief Justice White returned in the fall he was much disappointed in what had been done—so much so that he never became reconciled to that act."[177] And yet here was White, at the very time he was welcoming Clarke into the cave and keeping hands off the Acts of 1915 and 1916, deep in consultations about migratory bird legislation.

Everyone who has power is likely at one time or another to find some cause that seems greater than the restraints he normally acknowledges, and it can turn out to be something like human neutrality in the war among the birds, the insects, and the trees. White, moreover, maneuvered to keeep *United States* v. *Shauver* from being decided. Perhaps it was this episode that Holmes had in mind when, some years later, in "timidly" suggesting to Felix Frankfurter "caution in the use of the word statesmanship with regard to judges," he remarked: "I didn't think the late Chief Justice [White] shone most when he was political." A statesman, Holmes went on, "would consider whether it was wise to bring to the mind of Congress what it might do in this or that direction— but it seems to me wrong to modify or delay a decision upon such grounds."[178] Not the least curious aspect of White's behavior was his readiness to receive what amounted to an *ex parte* brief from an interested lawyer in a case then on the Court's docket.

Missouri v. *Holland* was a suit by the state in the United States District Court for the Western District of Missouri to enjoin the federal game warden from enforcing the Migratory Bird Act of 918. The district

---

[177] J. H. Clarke to N. D. Baker, Jan. 21, 1925, quoted in H. L. Warner, *The Life of Mr. Justice Clarke* (1959), 112, n.6; W. Van Devanter to W. R. Day, July 4, 1914, and Van Devanter

to W. H. Taft, May 11, 1927, Van Devanter Papers.

[178] O. W. Holmes to F. Frankfurter, Sept. 9, 1923, Holmes Papers. *See supra*, p. 412.

court sustained the Act, and so on appeal did the Supreme Court, per Holmes, with Van Devanter and Pitney dissenting without opinion. There was at the threshold an issue of the state's standing to sue, which on full consideration, in not easily distinguishable circumstances some three years later, the Court decided against the state.[179]

Holmes, who as Brandeis once said, cared little about problems of jurisdiction and liked to decide cases that interested him,[180] dealt with the standing issue lightly and quite unsatisfactorily. He was helped along by the government's failure to press it, which in turn may be accounted for by the earlier efforts to ward off decision of the first migratory bird law. It may have seemed a little difficult for the government to be avoiding constitutional adjudication once more. Holmes noted that Missouri argued the unconstitutionality of the Act under the Tenth Amendment, as an invasion of its sovereign right. He then disposed of the standing problem in the following sentence, which embodied all he had to say about it: "The State also alleges a pecuniary interest, as owner of the wild birds within its borders and otherwise, admitted by the Government to be sufficient, but it is enough that the bill is a reasonable and proper means to assert the alleged quasi sovereign rights of a State."

The argument on the merits, Holmes went on, was that the federal government cannot do by treaty what it could not do otherwise. Lower courts had indeed held the earlier migratory bird law unconstitutional as exceeding the normal powers of Congress, Holmes replied, but whether those cases "were decided rightly or not they cannot be accepted as a test of the treaty power. Acts of Congress are the supreme law of the land only when made in pursuance of the Constitution, while treaties are declared to be so when made under the authority of the United States."[181] He was not suggesting, Holmes said, that there were no quali-

---

[179] Massachusetts v. Mellon, 262 U.S. 447 (1923).

[180] Brandeis' remark, made in the early summer of 1923, was as follows: "Few of them realize that questions of jurisdiction are really questions of power between states and nation. Holmes and Taft for different reasons know little about it because they don't care—Taft because he likes to decide questions as a matter of expediency, where controversies arise; Holmes cares nothing about expediency, but likes to decide cases where interesting questions are raised. ["I have a case," Holmes wrote Laski late in March

1920, referring almost certainly to *Missouri* v. *Holland,* "that interested me very much and on which I worked fiercely." *Holmes-Laski Letters,* I, 254.] Holmes is beginning to learn—intellectually he is beginning to appreciate our responsibility, though not emotionally. I tell him, 'The most important thing we do is not doing.' Van Devanter knows as much about jurisdiction as anyone, more than anyone. But when he wants to decide, all his jurisdictional scruples go." Brandeis-Frankfurter Conversations.

[181] Some four years earlier, in *United States* v. *Jin Fuey Moy,* the Narcotics

fications on the treaty-making power; merely that whatever they might be they could not be taken over literally from the limitations that governed the exercise of normal powers. But it was "obvious that there may be matters of the sharpest exigency for the national well being that an act of Congress could not deal with but that a treaty followed by such an act could. . . ."[182] Then, these famous words:

> With regard to that we may add that when we are dealing with words that also are a constituent act, like the Constitution of the United States, we must realize that they have called into life a being the development of which could not have been foreseen completely by the most gifted of its begetters. It was enough for them to realize or to hope that they had created an organism; it has taken a century and has cost their successors much sweat and blood to prove that they created a nation. The case before us must be considered in the light of our whole experience and not merely in that of what was said a hundred years ago. The treaty in question does not contravene any prohibitory words to be found in the Constitution. The only question is whether it is forbidden by some invisible radiation from the general terms of the Tenth Amendment. We must consider what this country has become in deciding what that Amendment has reserved.

The argument that state sovereignty had been unlawfully invaded rested on a claim by the state to title in migratory birds. That claim was sound enough against the state's own inhabitants, but to put the claim of the state upon title as against the federal government "is to lean upon a slender reed." The whole foundation of the asserted right of the state was the presence there "of birds that yesterday had not arrived, tomorrow may be in another state, and in a week a thousand miles away." This was not much, and it was not enough: "No doubt the great body of private relations usually fall within the control of the State, but a treaty may override its power." So it had been held with respect to the escheat of land and jurisdiction over foreign consuls in earlier cases. "But for the treaty and the statute there soon might be no birds for any powers to deal with. We see nothing in the Constitution that

---

Tax Act case, Holmes had indicated that the extent to which treaties could under the Supremacy Clause enlarge Congressional powers was an open question. See *supra*, pp. 435–36, 437, n.89.

[182] The phrase "a treaty followed by such an act" in this passage does not quite meet a suggestion in Brandeis' return, which read as follows: "Yes. It's fine. May it not be well to suggest that a treaty *plus* an act of Congress may perhaps do what a treaty alone could not? It might allay fears." Holmes Papers, Harvard Law School Library.

compels the Government to sit by while a food supply is cut off and the protectors of our forests and our crops are destroyed."[183]

In dealing with other treaties in the decade 1910–20, the Court had been concerned with construction, not with constitutional issues.[184] *Missouri* v. *Holland*, therefore, drew considerable notice from scholarly commentators, as having, in the words of one writer, brought the treaty power to "political maturity." And there was speculation about possible future uses of the treaty power, particularly its potentiality for the solution of such problems as child labor, night work by women, the eight-hour day, and workmen's compensation. There might be international agreements concerning these subjects, it was thought, on which domestic legislation of otherwise dubious constitutionality might then be rested.[185]

Aside from *Missouri* v. *Holland*, the treaty cases of the decade that came to any sort of public notice and that continue to hold—lightly —a certain interest involved extraditions. Thus one Porter Charlton, an American citizen, son of a Yale classmate of William Howard Taft, was wanted in Italy on charges that he had murdered his wife, whose body was found in the waters of Lake Como. The Supreme Court permitted the government to extradite Charlton.[186] In another case, a contractor was wanted by Canada for frauds connected with the construction of new parliament buildings in Winnipeg. Kelly, the man in question, had first been illegally arrested in Chicago, and then, while still in custody, validly rearrested under a fresh warrant. "It was not even argued," Holmes took occasion to remark, "that the appellant was entitled to a chance to escape before either of the warrants could be executed. This proceeding is not a fox hunt."[187] And *Collins* v. *Miller*,[188]

---

[183] Missouri v. Holland, 252 U.S. 416, 431, 433, 434, 435 (1920).

[184] See, e.g., Rocca v. Thompson, 223 U.S. 317 (1912) (and compare In the Matter of Paul Bukva, *motion for leave to file petition for writ of mandamus denied*, 241 U.S. 647 [1916]); Petersen v. Iowa, 245 U.S. 170 (1917); Duus v. Brown, 245 U.S. 176 (1917); Sullivan v. Kidd, 254 U.S. 433 (1921). See also Cameron Septic Tank Co. v. Knoxville, 227 U.S. 39 (1913); dePass v. United States, 49 Ct. Cl. 382 (1914), 52 Ct. Cl. 517 (1917), *affirmed*, 243 U.S. 625 (1917).

[185] See, e.g., E. S. Corwin, "Constitutional Law in 1919–1920," *American Political Science Review*, 15:52,

1921; C. K. Burdick, "The Treaty Making Power and the Control of International Relations," *Cornell L. Q.*, 7:34, 1921; J. P. Chamberlain, "Migratory Bird Treaty Decision and Its Relation to Labor Treaties," *Am. Lab. Leg. Rev.*, 10:133, 1920; J. P. Boyd, "The Expanding Treaty Power," *N.C. L. Rev.*, 6:428, 448, 1928; T. R. Powell, "The Supreme Court and the Constitution, 1919–1920," *Political Science Quarterly*, 35:411, 417, 1920.

[186] Charlton v. Kelly, 229 U.S. 447 (1913); see *Washington Post*, June 11, 1913, p. 2, col. 1.

[187] Kelly v. Griffin, 241 U.S. 6, 13 (1916).

[188] 252 U.S. 364 (1920).

which went off on jurisdictional grounds, saw the beginning of proceedings, not to end for another three years,[189] to extradite a dashing British officer, a Sandhurst man and veteran of the Boer War and World War I, to India on charges of having there obtained a $32,000 diamond necklace by false pretenses.[190] The foreign relations power, as well as occasionally a treaty, was touched on also in a miscellany of cases raising tariff questions, but none of these controversies was of any particular moment.[191]

Litigation of some consequence flowed, however, from another measure involving the foreign relations of the United States, the Seamen's Act of 1915.[192] This statute shed an ironic light on expectations, then current and soon to be heightened by *Missouri* v. *Holland*, that the treaty power might be used to ease the way for domestic reforms. For the Seaman's Act showed, quite to the contrary, that treaties could present serious obstacles to the attainment of progressive social purposes at home.

The Seamen's Act prescribed detailed safety requirements for ships sailing into American ports. In the following provisions, among others, it also regulated conditions of labor for seamen. Section 11 made it

---

[189] See Collins v. Loisel, 259 U.S. 309 (1922); Collins v. Loisel, 262 U.S. 426 (1923).

[190] See *New York Times*, June 19, 1923, p. 4, col. 2. Other extradition cases of the decade 1910–20 were: Glucksman v. Henkel, 221 U.S. 508 (1911); McNamara v. Henkel, 226 U.S. 520 (1913); Bingham v. Bradley, 241 U.S. 511 (1916).

[191] See Faber v. United States, 221 U.S. 649 (1911); Altman and Co. v. United States, 224 U.S. 583 (1912); The Five Percent Discount Cases, 243 U.S. 97 (1917); Struckmann and Waege v. United States, 44 Ct. Cl. 202 (1909), *affirmed*, 223 U.S. 712 (1911); Eighteen Packages of Dental Instruments v. United States, 230 Fed. 564 (3rd Cir. 1916), *appeal dismissed for want of jurisdiction*, 242 U.S. 617 (1916).

For other tariff cases in the decade 1910–20 see: United States v. Eckstein, 222 U.S. 130 (1911); United States v. Baruch, 223 U.S. 191 (1912); United States v. Citroen, 223 U.S. 407 (1912) (and see United States v.

Tiffany, 178 Fed. 1006, *cert. denied*, 218 U.S. 675 [1910]); Latimer v. United States, 223 U.S. 501 (1912); Louisiana v. McAdoo, 234 U.S. 627 (1914); United States v. Salen, 235 U.S. 237 (1914); United States v. Sherman, 237 U.S. 146 (1915); *Ex parte* Park and Tilford, 245 U.S. 82 (1917); Waite v. Macy, 246 U.S. 606 (1918); Nicholas & Co. v. United States, 249 U.S. 34 (1919); Vitelli & Son v. United States, 250 U.S. 355 (1919); National Lead Co. v. United States, 252 U.S. 140 (1920); United States v. Aetna Explosives Co., 256 U.S. 402 (1921). And see Marks and Rawolle v. United States, *cert. denied*, 220 U.S. 623 (1911), 225 U.S. 709 (1912); Garramone v. United States, *cert. denied*, 223 U.S. 722 (1911); Goodman & Co. v. United States, *cert. denied*, 225 U.S. 699 (1912); Quaintance v. United States, *cert. denied*, 225 U.S. 711 (1912); Bache v. United States, 4 Ct. Cust. Appls. 414 (1913), *cert. denied*, 235 U.S. 702 (1914).

[192] 38 Stat. 1164 (1915).

unlawful, subject to criminal penalties, to pay any advance wages to a seaman or to a seaman's employment agent. Such advances, if previously made, could not be deducted from the final payment of wages earned. The section was applicable "as well to foreign vessels while in waters of the United States, as to vessels of the United States." Section 4 entitled seamen to receive on demand one-half of the wages then earned at every port at which a vessel called to load or deliver cargo before the voyage ended. A refusal by a master to comply with a demand for half wages in accordance with this section released the seaman from his contract, thus enabling him to leave the ship, and gave him the right to full payment of wages earned up to that time. This section also was applicable not only to American ships, but "to seamen on foreign vessels while in harbors of the United States."

The Seamen's Act was the culmination of a lifelong campaign by Andrew Furuseth, president of the International Seamen's Union. A fascinating and inspiring man, Viking and prophet, a moral force of the first magnitude, Furuseth was altogether an original. Born in Norway, he went to sea as a boy. In the 1880s he jumped ship and took up residence in the United States. Furuseth was dedicated to abolishing the appalling bondage in which seamen were held the world over. He meant to get one great maritime nation to provide by law a haven where the oppressed seaman could desert and seek justice. Thus Furuseth hoped to spearhead worldwide reform. He chose the United States. Here he organized his fellows, and he lobbied. But the returns on his efforts before 1915 were slender.[193]

The Act of 1915 was sponsored in the Senate by Robert M. La Follette, with whom Furuseth had formed a warm friendship. It passed there in October 1913, with the support of President Wilson. Then complications set in. Germany, Great Britain, and other maritime powers protested. The United States was bound by many treaties to arrest and surrender seamen deserting from the ships of foreign nations. Moreover, an international conference on safety at sea was to open in London in November 1913 with American participation, and it seemed inappropriate to prejudice agreements that might be reached there with unilateral safety requirements. So the Wilson Administration used its influence to hold up House action on the La Follette bill.

The American delegation to the London conference included Andrew Furuseth, who before long resigned in protest against the relative weakness of the safety standards there agreed, which conflicted with the more stringent ones of the Seamen's bill. Nevertheless, the

---

[193] E.g., Act of Dec. 21, 1898, 30 Stat. 755; see Pacific Mail S.S. Co. v. Schmidt, 241 U.S. 245 (1916).

Wilson Administration submitted the London Convention for unconditional ratification. The Senate, however, in December 1914, added to
the instrument of ratification a proviso reserving to the United States
the right to abrogate treaties that called for the arrest of deserting seamen, and to impose upon foreign vessels in United States waters higher
standards of safety than those of the London Convention. The Seamen's
bill was then pushed to final passage. But the State Department advised
a veto. The integrity of the London Convention, of many commercial
and maritime treaties, and of American foreign relations in general, it
was urged, should not be put in hazard.

Secretary of State Bryan and the President were initially so persuaded, but at this point La Follette, with Furuseth in tow—Furuseth,
as La Follette said, "a great soul speaking through his face, the set
purpose of his life shining in his eyes"—called on both Wilson and
Bryan. There were emotional pleas, and they prevailed. Wilson signed.
He earned due credit from Samuel Gompers on behalf of organized
labor. From Furuseth he got something more. Wrote Furuseth: "In
signing the Seamen's Bill, you gave back to the seamen, so far as the
United States can do it, the ownership of their bodies, and thus wiped
out the last bondage existing under the American flag. The soil of the
United States will be holy ground henceforth to the world's seamen."[194]

By 1918, four cases dealing with the Seamen's Act were awaiting
decision in the Supreme Court. One concerned a marginal procedural
point. It was disposed of unsympathetically, over a dissent by Brandeis
and Clarke.[195] *Sandberg* v. *McDonald*[196] and *Neilson* v. *Rhine Shipping
Co.*[197] called for construction of Section 11, prohibiting advances, and
Dillon v. *Strathearn S.S. Co.*[198] of Section 4, providing for payment of
half wages. Sandberg, not an American citizen, had signed on a British
ship in Liverpool and received an advance. The ship eventually put in at
Mobile, Alabama, where Sandberg asked for payment of half wages
earned. He received a sum from which the amount advanced him in
Liverpool had been deducted, and he claimed that the deduction was a
violation of Section 11 of the Seamen's Act. For a majority of five, Day
held the Act inapplicable.

The question was whether the prohibition of advances was intended

---

[194] See Link, *Wilson: The New Freedom,* 269–73; B. C. La Follette and F.
La Follette, *Robert M. La Follette*
(1953), I, 521–36; S. B. Axtell, ed.,
A Symposium on Andrew Furuseth
(n.d.); P. S. Taylor, *The Sailors'
Union of the Pacific* (1923).

[195] *Ex parte* Abdu, 247 U.S. 27

(1918); and see Abdu v. S.S. Nigretia,
249 Fed. 348 (2nd Cir. 1918), 255
Fed. 56 (2nd Cir. 1918), *cert. denied,*
249 U.S. 612 (1919).

[196] 248 U.S. 185 (1918).

[197] 248 U.S. 205 (1918).

[198] 248 U.S. 182 (1918).

to apply to foreign vessels taking on seamen in foreign ports, and Day went about answering it by the same method of statutory construction he had used in the *Caminetti* case.[199] He looked at the language of Section 11, which spoke of application to vessels "while in waters of the United States." The advance in this case, he said, had been made in Liverpool, not in the United States, and was therefore unaffected by the Act.[200] Employing the same literal approach, a dissent by McKenna came to the opposite conclusion. The Act was applicable to ships in the waters of the United States, said McKenna, and all Sandberg was asking was that it be applied to a ship in those waters. It was as simple as that— and it was neither more nor less persuasive than Day's view. Holmes, Brandeis, and Clarke joined McKenna's dissent.

In the *Neilson* case, against the same dissenters, Day held the Act inapplicable as well to an advance made by an American ship to a seaman hired in a foreign port, even though, Day noted regretfully, the advance had been actually paid not to the seaman, but to an agent. "This 'Seamen's' Act is no ordinary act of Congress!" said one of the briefs in *Sandberg* v. *McDonald*, in a passage quite possibly written by Furuseth; it rings true, and Furuseth often worked with counsel in seamen's cases. "The pages of the Federal Reporter . . . are full of stories of how, under the cloak of the advance, had hidden the assassins of [the seaman's] character and his wages. Societies sprang up in the name of humanity to protect him. Years pass and at last through the long night there flashes for the seaman the light of the 'Seamen's' Act!" But not for Seaman Neilson![201] *Dillon*, the fourth of the cases, had come up on a certificate which was technically faulty, and it had to be dismissed.

A year later the *Dillon* case was back on certiorari, all proper jurisdictionally now, and in what otherwise also turned out to be surprisingly more favorable circumstances. New counsel now appeared for the seaman—George Sutherland, the future Justice, who while in the Senate had been one of the men reached by Furuseth's passion.[202] As at the earlier argument, Frederic R. Coudert of New York appeared for the British Embassy, contending against application of the Seamen's

---

[199] See *supra*, pp. 430–31.

[200] Accord: Nellemenn v. Steamship London, 241 Fed. 863 (3rd Cir. 1917), *cert. denied*, 245 U.S. 652 (1917); Sandgren v. Ulster S.S. Co., 262 Fed. 751 (5th Cir. 1920), *cert. denied*, 252 U.S. 585 (1920). See also Gordon v. Steamship Cubadist, 256 Fed. 203 (5th Cir. 1919), *cert. denied*, 249 U.S. 618 (1919).

[201] *Petition for Writ of Certiorari and Brief in Support of Petition*, No. 392, at 11, Sandberg v. McDonald, 248 U.S. 185 (1918).

[202] See J. F. Paschal, *Mr. Justice Sutherland* (1951), 71–72.

Sutherland had his moments, of which his response to Furuseth was only one. He also favored workmen's compensation. See *supra*, p. 210.

Act. By March 1919, some three months after the second argument, Brandeis had prepared an elaborate opinion. It was entitled "Memorandum," and printed up in enough copies to be shown to some of his colleagues, even though, as Brandeis noted on his copy, it was not generally circulated.

The issue, said Brandeis, was whether foreign seamen who had signed on to a foreign vessel abroad, under articles providing for payment of wages at termination of the voyage and not before, must receive half wages earned when making an intermediate call at an American port. It was necessary to consider "the nature, the occasion, and the purpose" of the Seamen's Act. That Act was intended not only to emancipate the American seaman, but also to restore American shipping to a position of full participation in the foreign carrying trade. Emancipation of the American seaman would raise the labor costs of American vessels. Congress meant, therefore, to impose similar costs on foreign merchantmen as well. Congress concluded that if seamen on foreign vessels were freed from liability to arrest for desertion in American ports, and if in addition they were enabled to obtain part payment of wages here, foreign vessels entering the American trade would be compelled to raise wages and improve working conditions to a level of practical equality with those prevailing on American vessels; else they would lose their seamen upon landing here, and could take on new crews only by adopting American standards. As conditions were equalized, American bottoms would be in a better position to compete for the foreign carrying trade. All this Congress had ample authority to do. Treaties did not stand in the way, since the Seamen's Act abrogated inconsistent ones. And the power of the United States to establish conditions for entry into its ports was clear. It was argued that the statute should be construed so as to require the payment by foreign vessels only of wages earned by a seaman while actually in an American port, but that would mean payment of trivial amounts, and not serve the general purpose of the Act. That more than trivial payments were intended was shown by the legislative history, from which Brandeis proceeded to quote copiously. Among other documents, a House report stated explicitly that the provisions as to half wages were to be applicable to foreign ships in American ports, so that seamen could jump ship here, if they wished, with sufficient funds in their pockets to enable them to survive. It remained to distinguish the decisions in *Sandberg* v. *McDonald* and *Neilson* v. *Rhine Shipping Co.* Advances were in question there, Brandeis said lamely, not payments of half wages in American ports, and the place where the advance was made "was deemed decisive."

What happened as a consequence of this draft opinion is told with notable economy of language in a notation that Brandeis' law clerk,

Dean G. Acheson, a quarter century later President Truman's Secretary of State, attached to the opinion in Brandeis' file:

> This opinion was prepared at a time when it appeared that the decision might have gone against the interpretation of the Act which is here advocated. The Chief Justice was wavering, Pitney, Van Devanter, Day and McKenna were contra. I don't remember whether a copy was sent to the Chief or not. But eventually it was decided according to this view and Judge Day wrote a poor opinion.
>
> This took the Justice two weeks of hard work while Court was sitting.[203]

White, Pitney, and Van Devanter had been with Day in the *Sandberg* case. McKenna, the author of the *Sandberg* dissent, might now have taken one of his erratic turns, or he might very reasonably have thought that *Sandberg* ruled *Dillon*, and that as no persuasive distinction was possible, there was little point in dissenting again. For the considerations that Brandeis adduced, cutting through the verbalism of both Day and McKenna in the *Sandberg* case, certainly ruled *Sandberg* as well as *Dillon*—either both or neither. To be sure, it was not lightly to be presumed that Congress meant to reach out and make criminally punishable the payment of advances in foreign ports. But Congress provided that half wages earned be paid foreign seamen in American ports, and for the reasons Brandeis recited, it would have wished to ensure that those half wages were not diminished, and diminished perhaps to the vanishing point, by deductions of advances made earlier. Quite like *Dillon*, *Sandberg* had demanded his half wages. His case differed only in that he had protested deductions for prior advances. Like Dillon's, Sandberg's articles were signed abroad. The claim was that those articles, and whatever was done under them abroad, could not prevail against the purposes of American law in an American port. Brandeis' argument decided both cases, and it is not unreasonable to speculate that the argument might have decided the *Sandberg* case the other way had Brandeis mounted it a year earlier. He could not have failed to do so then because of a lack of familiarity with the materials he now adduced. Although there is no evidence that Brandeis helped draft the Seamen's Act, he was a friend of its sponsor, Senator La Follette, and was well acquainted also with Andrew Furuseth, who was often a guest at his table.[204] The reason for Brandeis' earlier silence may perhaps be found

---

[203] See Bickel, *Unpublished Opinions of Brandeis*, 34–60.

[204] See Axtell, ed., *A Symposium on Andrew Furuseth*, 35–37; P. A. Freund, "Mr. Justice Brandeis," in A. Dunham and P. B. Kurland, eds., *Mr. Justice* (1956), 97–101.

in the condition of his personal docket the year before. *Sandberg* came down on December 23, 1918, about a month and a half after it had been argued. In these six weeks, Brandeis delivered five opinions of the Court[205] and one important dissent.[206] He received also other assignments. There may simply have been no time for what Acheson later called "two weeks of hard work."

That it was Day who finally wrote the opinion in the *Dillon* case may be explained simply by an initial assignment to him, which continued in effect after Brandeis converted him. It may be explained also as a subsequent assignment, since Day as the author of *Sandberg* was the logical candidate. Day's opinion, relatively brief, and speaking for a unanimous Court, rested on the language of the statute with the same bland assurance as in the *Sandberg* case. The only visible mark it bears of the Brandeis memorandum is a passage asserting almost entirely without documentation that, "[a]part from the text, which we think plain," the purpose of Congress to equalize conditions among American and foreign seamen would be defeated by a construction other than the one adopted.[207] *Sandberg* was mechanically distinguished. It stood, and continued to stand a decade later, despite a Congressional attempt to overrule it.[208]

Banks and the Currency

The New Freedom, like all federal legislative programs, functioned for the most part under the Commerce Clause, the amplest repository of federal power, which can either find further amplification in treaties,

---

[205] Iowa v. Slimmer, 248 U.S. 115 (Dec. 9, 1918); Tempel v. United States, 248 U.S. 121 (Dec. 9, 1918); United States v. Spearin, 248 U.S. 132 (Dec. 9, 1918); Luckenbach v. W. J. McCahan Sugar Refining Co., 248 U.S. 139 (Dec. 9, 1918); MacMath v. United States, 248 U.S. 151 (Dec. 9, 1918).

[206] International News Service v. Associated Press, 248 U.S. 215, 248 (Dec. 23, 1918).

[207] Strathearn S.S. Co. v. Dillon, 252 U.S. 348, 354 (1920); see also Thompson v. Lucas, 252 U.S. 358 (1920).

This was the passage that caught the attention of Thomas Reed Powell, who was of course unaware of its origins. He referred to it—with eyebrows somewhat raised, perhaps considering the apparent source—as offering a "moral justification for the statute." And he added: "The principle of the decision suggests interesting possibilities in the way of closing our ports to foreign vessels whose hospitality on the high seas is not to our liking." T. R. Powell, "The Supreme Court and the Constitution, 1919–1920," *Political Science Quarterly*, 35: 411, 419, 1920.

[208] Jackson v. S.S. Archimedes, 275 U.S. 463 (1928). See 69 *Cong. Rec.* 7080–81, 70th Cong., 1st Sess. (1928).

as *Missouri* v. *Holland* showed, or can override them, as it did by the Seamen's Act. But the federal government has available, of course, other means as well for affecting social and economic conditions in the country. We have touched here and in a prior chapter on the powers to tax and spend, and we will return presently to taxing measures under the new Sixteenth Amendment. In the Federal Reserve Act of 1913, the Wilson Administration engaged in a notable exercise of the federal power to regulate the currency and establish banks.

The Federal Reserve Act gave rise to a constitutional issue, but one that was marginal to its central scheme.[209] Among its many provisions reorganizing the existing system of federally chartered national banks under a central coordinating agency was one authorizing national banks to act as trustees, executors, administrators, and registrars of stocks and bonds.[210] This provision was challenged in *First National Bank* v. *Union Trust Co.*,[211] and sustained on the basis of the classic doctrine of implied powers enunciated by John Marshall in *McCulloch* v. *Maryland*. Marshall had inferred the power to charter a national bank from the fiscal functions of Congress expressly mentioned in the Constitution. If there is power to establish a bank, said White for the Court now, taking Marshall's reasoning one step further, there is power to enable it to do the things that banks do. It had been held below, by the Michigan Supreme Court, that while there might be a natural connection, as Marshall had said, between the business of banking and the exercise of expressly granted federal fiscal powers, there was none between the business of running estates, or acting as trustee for bondholders, and the federal fiscal power. But this was fallacious, White replied. The connection to be sought was that between running estates, etc., and the business of banking. Thus White confirmed, as Marshall had before him, Jefferson's fear of the possible reach of implied powers. "Congress are authorized to defend the Nation," said Jefferson. "Ships are necessary for defense; copper is necessary for ships; mines, necessary for copper; a company necessary to work the mines; and who can doubt this reasoning who has ever played at 'This is the House that Jack Built'?"[212]

There was a dissent by Van Devanter, with Day, going not to the substance of White's holding, but to the form in which the suit arose. The Attorney General of Michigan, for the state, brought a *quo warranto*

---

[209] See Link, *Wilson: The New Freedom*, 199–240.

[210] 38 Stat. 251, 262 (1913).

[211] 244 U.S. 416 (1917).

[212] C. Warren, *The Supreme Court in United States History* (1926), I, 501.

proceeding in the Michigan courts seeking, in effect, to enjoin the First National Bank of Bay City, Michigan, from acting as trustee, executor, etc. (The Attorney General was suing on the relation, which is to say, upon the complaint, of the Union Trust Company, a competitor state bank.) The contention was that the exercise of these functions by a national bank was in contravention of the laws of the state, and invalid under the federal Constitution. The Michigan Supreme Court held against the Attorney General on the state law point, but for him on the federal constitutional issue.

A national bank, said Van Devanter, is an instrumentality of the United States, performing a federal function, and analogizable to a federal officer discharging his duties. As such, a national bank was not subject to suit in state courts, but only in federal ones. There was exclusive federal protective jurisdiction in such cases. White's answer was that this was generally true, but that in providing in the Federal Reserve Act that national banks should exercise the functions in question only "when not in contravention of state or local law," Congress had impliedly authorized suits in the state courts. Van Devanter thought that no such extraordinary concession of state jurisdiction should be lightly implied from the phrase White relied on. Day, who had urged Van Devanter to file this dissent, had wished to deny not only the intention, but also any power of Congress to confer jurisdiction upon state courts in proceedings of this sort against a federal corporation.[213] But Van Devanter refrained from pressing the argument that far, and Day went along silently.

Both before and after the Federal Reserve Act, national banks provided a fairly steady, although moderate and not very significant, flow of Supreme Court business. Since national banks are federal instrumentalities, state taxation or regulation of them is subject to Congressional control, and there were cases testing the limits of Congressional permission or prohibition of state regulation and taxation.[214] There were cases questioning, as in the *First National Bank* case, but without constitutional overtones, the exercise of one or another function by national

---

[213] W. R. Day to W. Van Devanter, May 30, 1917, Van Devanter Papers.

[214] See McCarthy v. First National Bank, 223 U.S. 493 (1912); Holden Land Co. v. Inter-State Trading Co., 233 U.S. 536 (1914); Clement National Bank v. Vermont, 231 U.S. 120 (1913); Bank of California v. Richardson, 248 U.S. 476 (1919); Bank of California v. Roberts, 248 U.S. 497 (1919); Merchants' National Bank v. Richmond, 256 U.S. 635 (1921); State National Bank v. Richardson, 135 Ky. 772, 123 S.W. 294, 1189 (1909); *writ of error dismissed for want of jurisdiction,* 225 U.S. 696 (1912).

banks,[215] and in greatest number, cases concerning the rights and liabilities of shareholders and directors.[216]

In *American Bank and Trust Co. v. Federal Bank*,[217] an attempt by a federal reserve bank to extend its power and functions administratively, not pursuant to explicit statutory authorization, was stopped by the Court. The Federal Reserve Bank in Georgia had tried to get country banks to deposit their reserves in the federal system by collecting large numbers of checks drawn on the country banks and then presenting them together as a sort of run on the banks. It had a right, the federal bank contended, just as did anyone else, to present checks for payment. "But the word 'right,' " said Holmes for a unanimous Court, "is one of the most deceptive of pitfalls; it is so easy to slip from a qualified meaning in the premise to an unqualified one in the conclusion. Most rights are qualified. A man has at least as absolute a right to give his own money as he has to demand money from a party that has made no promise to him; yet if he gives it to induce another to steal or murder the purpose of the act makes it a crime." It was unlikely that a private party would be entitled to organize a run on a bank—the antitrust laws, at any rate, might have something to say about that—and it was unthinkable that Congress had meant to authorize its federal banking instrumentalities to do so.

A later exercise by the Wilson Administration of federal financial power was attacked more centrally than the Federal Reserve Act. The Farm Loan Act of 1916[218] created Federal Land and Joint Stock Land Banks, which after the initial process of capitalization, itself assisted by the federal government, were authorized to write farm mortgages, and

---

[215] See Kerfoot v. Farmers' and Merchants' Bank, 218 U.S. 281 (1910); Miller v. King, 223 U.S. 505 (1912); Wingert v. First National Bank, 223 U.S. 670 (1912); Evans v. National Bank of Savannah, 251 U.S. 108 (1919); Barron v. McKinnon, 196 Fed. 933 (1st Cir. 1912), *writ of error dismissed per stipulation,* 229 U.S. 630 (1913).

[216] See Apsey v. Kimball, 221 U.S. 514 (1911); Thomas v. Taylor; 224 U.S. 73 (1912); Jones National Bank v. Yates, 240 U.S. 541 (1916); Chesbrough v. Woodworth, 244 U.S. 72 (1917); Korbly v. Springfield Institution for Savings, 245 U.S. 330 (1917); Williams v. Vreeland, 250 U.S. 295 (1919); Bowerman v. Hamner, 250 U.S. 504 (1919); Corsicana National Bank v. Johnson, 251 U.S. 68 (1919); Bates v. Dresser, 251 U.S. 524 (1920); Chesbrough v. Northern Trust Co., 252 U.S. 83 (1920); Wallach v. Billings, 277 Ill. 218, 115 N.E. 382 (1917), *cert. denied,* 244 U.S. 659 (1917). *Cf.* Herrmann v. Edwards, 238 U.S. 107 (1915); see also United States v. Weitzel, 246 U.S. 533 (1918); Harriman National Bank v. Seldomridge, 249 U.S. 1 (1919); United States v. Chase National Bank, 252 U.S. 485 (1920); Keyser v. Milton, 228 Fed. 594 (5th Cir. 1916), *cert. denied,* 241 U.S. 661 (1916).

[217] 256 U.S. 350, 358 (1921).

[218] 39 Stat. 360 (1916); see A. S. Link, *Wilson: Confusions and Crises* (1964), 345–50.

on the security of these mortgages to issue bonds exempt from both federal and state taxation. *Smith* v. *Kansas City Title Co.*[219] was a suit brought in federal court by a shareholder of a Missouri corporation against the corporation and its officers to enjoin them from investing corporate funds in these bonds, on the ground that the statute authorizing issuance of the bonds was unconstitutional, and the bonds themselves, therefore, worthless.

The case brought a galaxy of counsel to the bar of the Court: William Marshall Bullitt of Kentucky, Taft's last Solicitor General, and Frank Hagerman, the well-known railroad lawyer from Kansas City, for Smith, the shareholder; and Charles E. Hughes and George W. Wickersham, the former Attorney General, with whom William G. McAdoo, Wilson's former Secretary of the Treasury, was on the brief, for the Federal Land and Joint Stock Land Banks that defended the case. The Farm Loan Act was attacked as a constitutionally unjustified invasion of state sovereignty. Hughes, who had earlier given an opinion to some brokerage houses that bonds issued under the Act were good, defended it on the broad ground that Congress had power to spend for the general welfare. This power was not limited by the express enumeration of other Congressional powers, and it could therefore be used to stimulate agricultural development. Congress did, to be sure, labor under some restrictions. The purpose of an expenditure had to be public and national. But it could "hardly be disputed that the agricultural interests of the country, broadly considered, are of National and not merely State concern. Any view that would treat the food supply of the people as not a matter directly related to the common defense and general welfare of the United States would be so narrow as to be quite inadmissible."

No one had questioned analogous expenditures, Hughes continued, as when Congress set up a Bureau of Education, or the Agriculture Department itself, or passed the Land Grant College Act of 1862. In providing for the general welfare, Congress could either spend federal money or seek to generate credit. In this instance it had done both, through the instrumentality of the Land and Joint Stock Banks and their bonds. These bonds were, therefore, themselves valid federal instrumentalities, and as such they could, of course, be made tax exempt.[220] Wickersham rested the argument for constitutionality on the narrower

[219] 255 U.S. 180, 210, 201, 213–14 (1921).

[220] *Supplemental Brief for Appellee, Federal Land Bank of Wichita, Kan., on Reargument,* No. 199, at 28, 45–47, Smith v. Kansas City Title Co., 255 U.S. 180 (1921); see C. E. Hughes, *Biographical Notes,* Microfilm, Ac. 9943, 246–48, Hughes Papers, Library of Congress; *cf.* United States v. Butler, 297 U.S. 1 (1936); Helvering v. Davis, 301 U.S. 619 (1937).

ground, alluded to also by Hughes, on which *First National Bank* v. *Union Trust Co.* had been placed. The federal government, he said, may establish banks, and then enable them to do things that banks do.

Upholding the Farm Loan Act in the *Smith* case, Day, for the Court, occupied the narrower ground. Congress had set up some banks, he said, and that was well within its power, as was demonstrated by a provision making these banks possible depositories of public monies. It was precisely because the expressly granted federal power to raise money naturally created the need for a place to keep it that Marshall in *McCulloch* v. *Maryland* had inferred the power to establish banks. The Land and Joint Stock Banks had not, with a minor exception, actually been used as federal depositories. But this was a constitutionally irrelevant circumstance, for it could lead only into an inquiry concerning the true motives of Congress—was "the attempt . . . to make these banks . . . public depositaries . . . but a pretext"?—and that, said Day, the author of *Hammer* v. *Dagenhart*, was no proper judicial inquiry. Nothing was "better settled."[221]

Smith v. *Kansas City Title Co.* was first argued in January 1920, then reargued at the following term in October 1920, and not decided until February 1921.[222] At neither argument were jurisdictional questions touched on by the parties. But after the first argument, Holmes did pose a jurisdictional problem in a memorandum of two paragraphs that he circulated to the Court. Jurisdiction was based on the existence of a federal question, not on diversity of citizenship. The applicable statute, using the very language of Article III of the Constitution, then as now extended federal-question jurisdiction only to suits "arising under" the Constitution or laws of the United States. This suit, Holmes contended, arose under Missouri law. The stockholder claimed a right to prevent the directors of his corporation from making an investment which, in his view, was contrary to their duty. But the duties of these directors,

---

[221] Still, thought Edward S. Corwin, Day's reasoning made of the Farm Loan Act an instance of "the tail wagging the dog." Much better, Corwin concluded, to have adopted Hughes' broader argument. "Apparently, however, the Court did not like to face the socialistic implications of such reasoning, and so it took the more roundabout route." E. S. Corwin, "Constitutional Law in 1920–21, I," *American Political Science Review*, 16:22, 25–27, 1922; cf. T. R. Powell, "The Supreme Court's Construction of the Federal Constitution in 1920–21," *Mich. L. Rev.*, 20: 1, 18–19, 1921.

[222] In the meantime, action on applications for farm mortgages had been suspended. In the meantime also, the agricultural crisis of the 1920s came upon the country. There was, therefore, considerable displeasure in Congress with the Court's delay. See, e.g., 60 *Cong. Rec.* 2967–83, 66th Cong., 3rd Sess. (1921). See also *The Outlook*, 127:410, Mar. 16, 1921; *The Literary Digest*, 68:14, Mar. 26, 1921.

as also the rights of stockholders, were defined by the law of Missouri, not of the United States. Even if Missouri law could be read to authorize investment only in securities valid under the Constitution and laws of the United States, and it thus became material to determine the legality of the bonds by federal standards, still the issue of federal law would be material only as Missouri had chosen to make it so. That choice would be the law of Missouri, which thus, again, would give rise to the suit. "The whole foundation of the duty," said Holmes, the positivist who did not believe in law as "a brooding omnipresence in the sky,"[223] "would be Missouri law, which at its sole will incorporated the other law as it might incorporate a document. The other law or the document would depend for its relevance and effect not on its own force but upon the law that took it up." Only a few years before, the Court had held squarely that a suit "arises under the law that creates the cause of action," and it seemed to Holmes that the Court had meant that a suit arises *only* under that law.[224] If so, this suit could not be maintained.

McReynolds agreed with Holmes—if agree is strong enough a word. "How on earth," McReynolds wrote Holmes, "can such a proceeding involve the Court? It is beyond me!"—although it was Mc-Reynolds above all others who failed elsewhere to heed the implications of the positivistic view of law which influenced Holmes.[225] The Court as a whole was moved only to the extent that it noted the point, even though it had not been argued. The stockholder's claim, said Day, was that the bonds were invalid because the Farm Loan Act was unconstitutional, and since under Missouri law the company was authorized to invest in *legal* securities only, it was "apparent that the controversy concerns the constitutional validity of an act of Congress which is directly drawn in question." The debate was at a standstill, and has hardly been resolved since.[226]

Holmes expanded his memorandum into a two-page dissent, in

---

[223] *Cf.* Southern Pacific Co. v. Jensen, 244 U.S. 205, 218, 222 (1917) (Holmes, J., dissenting).

[224] American Well Works Co. v. Layne, 241 U.S. 257, 260 (1916). Alleging that it owned a valid patent, and that the defendant was maliciously slandering that patent by claiming that it infringed one of its own, and thus by its propaganda and by threatening suit interfering with the successful conduct of plaintiff's business, plaintiff sued for damages. Over the solitary dissent of McKenna, Holmes for the Court held that this suit arose under

the state law of torts, and not under the federal patent law, even though the question of the validity of plaintiff's patent would eventually be involved. There was, therefore, Holmes held, no federal jurisdiction.

[225] See *ibid.*

[226] See Puerto Rico v. Russell and Co., 288 U.S. 476 (1933); Gully v. First National Bank, 299 U.S. 109 (1936); H. M. Hart, Jr., and H. Wechsler, *The Federal Courts and the Federal System* (1953), 763–69; C. A. Wright, *Federal Courts* (1963), 48, 51.

which McReynolds joined. Holmes included with slight modifications the passage quoted above. Egged on perhaps by McReynolds' exclamations, he went so far as to declare himself "unable to deem even debatable" the issue whether the cause of action arose under Missouri or federal law. In reply to a citation by Day of *Brushaber* v. *Union Pacific Railroad*, the first Sixteenth Amendment income tax case (decided a few years before and presently to be discussed), Holmes conceded that his objection might have been taken there also, since *Brushaber* was a stockholder's action to prevent the railroad from complying with the income tax law. But, he said, the point was not raised by the parties, and hardly considered by the Court. Holmes' dissent began with the following sentence: "No doubt it is desirable that the question raised in this case should be set at rest, but that can be done by the Courts of the United States only within the limits of the jurisdiction conferred upon them by the Constitution and the laws of the United States."

Brandeis returned that the dissent was forceful and that he was glad Holmes had written it.[227] But for reasons that are not evident—perhaps he was connected with one of the parties through an investment—Brandeis did not participate in *Smith* v. *Kansas City Title Co.* Particularly in view of its first sentence, he surely considered this dissent evidence, as he said later, that although Holmes cared little about jurisdictional issues, he was "beginning to learn—intellectually he is beginning to appreciate our responsibility. . . ."[228] Yet it is as likely that Holmes saw in the jurisdictional issue one of those questions that interested him and that he liked to decide, namely, the question of the sources of law, on which he had very definite views. At any rate, many years later, in his great statement on jurisdictional problems in *Ashwander* v. *Tennessee Valley Authority*,[229] Brandeis expressed hearty approval of Holmes' position in *Smith* v. *Kansas City Title Co.*

The Income Tax

Revenue, mainly tariff revision but also implementation of the Sixteenth Amendment, was the first legislative concern of the Wilson Administration, with priority even over establishment of the Federal Reserve System. The Sixteenth Amendment became effective in February 1913. By October, an Income Tax Act was on the books, part of the Underwood-Simmons Tariff Act of 1913.[230] The work chiefly

---

227 Holmes Papers.
228 See *supra*, p. 480, n.180.
229 297 U.S. 288 (1936).
230 38 Stat. 114 (1913).

of Representative Cordell Hull of Tennessee, the future Secretary of State, it came out of the House incorporating the principle of progressive taxation, but at very low rates. A Populist-Progressive revolt in the Senate increased the rates a bit.

The act imposed a "normal" tax of 1 percent on personal income, with exemptions of $3,000 per individual, and an additional $1,000 for married taxpayers. A surtax was levied on incomes exceeding $20,000 a year, which rose as high as 6 percent (it had gone no higher than 3 percent in the House bill) on incomes over $500,000, plus the normal 1 percent. Taxable income was defined as "gains, profits, and income derived from salaries, wages, or compensation for personal services . . . or from professions, vocations, business, trades, commerce, or sales or dealings in property, whether real or personal . . . also from interest, rent, dividends, securities, or the transaction of any lawful business carried on for gain or profit, or gains or profits and income derived from any source whatever, including the income from but not the value of property acquired by gift, bequest, devise, or descent." Proceeds of life insurance and interest on state and United States bonds were exempt. Allowable deductions included necessary business expenses, interest, federal, state, and local taxes, losses not compensated by insurance, bad debts, and depreciation and depletion. The salaries of the President of the United States and of federal judges then in office were not taxed. The corporate income tax, from which certain nonprofit corporations were exempted, was 1 percent of net income. The tax was retroactive to March 1, 1913, and so far as possible it was collected at the source, employers and corporations being required to deduct it from salaries and from interest payable on bonds and the like. The Commissioner of Internal Revenue had broad authority to make regulations.[231]

In the Supreme Court, during the years 1914–21, a fair amount of tax litigation still arose under the Corporation Tax Act of 1909,[232] and even under the War Revenue Act of 1898,[233] a provision of which was held unconstitutional in *United States* v. *Hvoslef*,[234] as applied to goods leaving a state for a foreign port, since it collided with Article I, Section 9, of the Constitution, which prohibited taxes on articles ex-

---

[231] See Link, *Wilson: The New Freedom*, 182, 191–93; R. G. Blakey and G. C. Blakey, *The Federal Income Tax* (1940), 71–100; S. Ratner, *American Taxation* (1942), 323–36.

[232] See *supra*, pp. 248–49, nn.150, 155; see also Rock Island, Arkansas &

Louisiana R.R. v. United States, 254 U.S. 141 (1920).

[233] 30 Stat. 448 (1898).

[234] 237 U.S. 1 (1915); see also Thames & Mersey Ins. Co. v. United States, 237 U.S. 19 (1915); *cf.* Peck & Co. v. Lowe, 247 U.S. 165 (1918).

ported from any state.[235] But the significant tax business stemmed from the Act of 1913 and subsequent statutes.

The stockholder's action in *Brushaber* v. *Union Pacific Railroad*, begun in the U.S. District Court for the Southern District of New York, reached the Supreme Court in 1915, and was decided in January 1916. The defendant railroad entered no appearance, and the case was briefed and argued by the Solicitor General, technically as *amicus*. Speaking for a unanimous Court, Chief Justice White addressed himself first to arguments purportedly derived from the text of the Sixteenth Amendment,[236] such as that the power to tax incomes implied a requirement of uniformity, which Congress violated by exempting some classes of income, and that no retroactive tax of any sort was authorized. White concisely reviewed the history of the taxation of incomes prior to *Pollock* v. *Farmers' Loan & Trust Co.* That case, in which he had himself, of course, filed a notable dissent, held, he said, that an income tax really fell on property, was therefore direct, and would have to be apportioned. To this holding the Sixteenth Amendment was directed. It did not create, and newly circumscribe and shackle, a power to tax incomes, but rather freed an ample preexisting power from the apportionment limitation imposed in the *Pollock* case. White's reading of the Sixteenth Amendment was, in context, intended to have liberating consequences, and so ultimately it did. But in the short term the effect was restrictive, directing attention to definitions of "income," and preserving the authority of the *Pollock* decision as applied to taxes that did not fit a judicial definition of "income."

White then turned to "numerous and minute, not to say in many respects hypercritical, contentions," most of which were claims of violation of the Due Process Clause of the Fifth Amendment. Retroactivity to the date of effectiveness of the Sixteenth Amendment was unobjectionable. So were the various discriminations, by way of allowances of deductions and of exemptions, which inhered in any system of taxation, and the provisions for collection at the source. The Constitution would not be held to "conflict with itself by conferring upon the one hand a taxing power and taking the same power away on the other

---

[235] For other cases concerning the War Revenue Act of 1898 see United States v. Jones, 236 U.S. 106 (1915); McCoach v. Pratt, 236 U.S. 562 (1915); Uterhart v. United States, 240 U.S. 598 (1916); Rand v. United States, 249 U.S. 503 (1919); Coleman v. United States, 250 U.S. 30 (1919); Sage v. United States, 250 U.S. 33 (1919); Henry v. United States, 251 U.S. 393 (1920); Simpson v. United States, 252 U.S. 547 (1920); Cochran v. United States, 254 U.S. 387 (1921).

[236] "The Congress shall have power to lay and collect taxes on incomes, from whatever source derived, without apportionment among the several States, and without regard to any census or enumeration."

by the limitations of the due process clause." For this—rather capacious —reason, the progressive feature of the tax was also not subject to attack. "In this situation it is of course superfluous to say that arguments as to the expediency of levying such taxes or of the economic mistake or wrong involved in their imposition are beyond judicial cognizance." As to the argument that the authority conferred by the Act to make administrative regulations was void because it delegated a legislative function—in a characteristic phrase, "to state the proposition is to answer it."[237]

The *Brushaber* decision received some exegesis in the legal journals,[238] but drew little discussion in the press and the periodical literature. It was rather submerged in a continuing debate on the policy and administration of the 1913 Act. The high exemptions allowed by that Act were widely regarded as excluding too large a segment of the population from the tax base.[239] The complexity of regulations, and in general of administration of the income tax, were also much noted.[240] Receipts under the 1913 Act were disappointing, as was the number of people who filed returns showing taxable income—no more than some 367,000 in the first year. And so just as *Brushaber* came down in January 1916, a new bill was being considered in the Ways and Means Committee of the House. The decision encouraged proponents of the

[237] Brushaber v. Union Pacific R.R., 240 U.S. 1, 24, 25, 26 (1916); see also Stanton v. Baltic Mining Co., 240 U.S. 103 (1916); Tyee Realty Co. v. Anderson, 240 U.S. 115 (1916); Dodge v. Osborn, 240 U.S. 118 (1916); Dodge v. Brady, 240 U.S. 122 (1916). See also Edwards v. Keith, 231 Fed. 110 (2nd Cir. 1916), *cert. denied*, 243 U.S. 638 (1917); Brady v. Anderson, 240 Fed. 665 (2nd Cir. 1917), *cert. denied*, 244 U.S. 654 (1917).

[238] See, e.g., Note, *Harv. L. Rev.*, 29:536, 1916; Comment, *Cal. L. Rev.*, 4:333, 1916; Comment, *Yale L. J.*, 25:585, 1916; J. H. Riddle, "The Supreme Court's Theory of a Direct Tax," *Mich. L. Rev.*, 15:566, 1917; F. W. Hackett, "The Constitutionality of the Graduated Income Tax Law," *Yale L. J.*, 25:427, 1916; H. Hubbard, "From Whatever Source Derived," *A.B.A.J.*, 6:202, 1920.

[239] See, e.g., *Bench & Bar*, 11:97, 1916; T. G. Frost, "Inequities of the Federal Income Tax," *Case & Com.*, 23:818, 1917; H. C. Black, "Sociological Aspects of Income Tax," *Case & Com.*, 23:789, 1917; *Independent*, 74:1038, May 8, 1913; *The Literary Digest*, 47:407, Sept. 13, 1913; *The Nation*, 96:432, May 1, 1913, 97:199, Sept. 4, 1913, 224, Sept. 11, 1913, 299, Oct. 2, 1913, 102:91, Jan. 27, 1916; *The New Republic*, 4:111–12, Sept. 4, 1915, 8:82, Aug. 26, 1916; *The Outlook*, 103:886, Apr. 26, 1913, 105:163, Sept. 27, 1913, 106:256, Jan. 31, 1914.

[240] See, e.g., *Journal of Political Economy*, 27:313, 1919; *Mass. L. Q.*, 6:5, 1920; A. C. Kelley, "Federal Taxation of Income from Production of Minerals," *Journal of Political Economy*, 29:265, 1921; *Independent*, 77:191, Feb. 9, 1914; *The New Republic*, 5:107, Dec. 4, 1915, 317, Jan. 29, 1916, 8:31, Aug. 12, 1916; *The Outlook*, 105:559, Nov. 15, 1913, 106:299, Feb. 7, 1914, 338, Feb. 14, 1914.

new bill. Said Representative Cordell Hull: "The Supreme Court . . . has unfettered the income tax . . . all doubt is removed and Congress is left much freer" to achieve a higher yield.[241]

What emerged now as the Revenue Act of 1916, spurred by a general defense preparedness drive, but also as part of the preelection reforming surge of the New Freedom, was a statute marking for the first time a real shift toward progressive income taxation as the main source of federal revenue. Personal exemptions remained the same, but the normal tax was raised to 2 percent for both individuals and corporations, and the individual surtax rose to a maximum of 13 percent on very high incomes, in addition to the regular 2 percent. A special tax of 12½ percent was imposed on the net income of munitions manufacturers, and stock dividends issued by all corporations were specifically taxed "to the amount of their cash value." A permanent estate tax—so it proved to be—was enacted, running from 1 percent on estates exceeding a $50,000 exemption by $50,000, to 10 percent on estates exceeding the exemption by $5 million or more. Salaries of the President and of judges continued not to be taxed.[242]

The Supreme Court held the estate tax of 1916 constitutional in *New York Trust Co.* v. *Eisner.*[243] The taxpayer (represented by George Sutherland) argued that the tax was direct and void for want of apportionment, since it fell unavoidably on the estate, rather than on the privilege of receiving a legacy which could be declined. Holmes for a unanimous Court replied, "not by an attempt to make some scientific distinction, which would be at least difficult, but . . . on the practical and historical ground that this kind of tax always has been regarded as the antithesis of a direct tax. . . ." And for the anthologies, he added: "Upon this point a page of history is worth a volume of logic."

The Court dealt also with a variety of issues under the Acts of 1913 and 1916, and under subsequent statutes, which began to come with annual regularity.[244] Deserving of more note, and receiving more

---

[241] Blakey and Blakey, *Federal Income Tax,* 102–103, 111.

[242] 39 Stat. 756 (1916); Link, *Wilson: The New Freedom,* 60–65; Blakey and Blakey, *Federal Income Tax,* 104–21; Ratner, *American Taxation,* 341–61.

[243] 256 U.S. 345, 349 (1921).

[244] See Gould v. Gould, 245 U.S. 151 (1917) (alimony not income); Peck and Co. v. Lowe, 247 U.S. 165 (1918) (tax on income from exports not direct tax on exports and valid

under Art. I, Sec. 9); Crocker v. Malley, 249 U.S. 223 (1919) (Massachusetts trust held not subject to tax on dividends received from other corporations, see Paul and Mertens [1934], *Law of Federal Income Taxation,* IV: sec. 35.18); DeGanay v. Lederer, 250 U.S. 376 (1919); Maryland Casualty Co. v. United States, 251 U.S. 342 (1920); Carbon Steel Co. v. Lewellyn, 251 U.S. 501 (1920) (application of 12½ percent tax on munitions manufacturers under Act of

notice from contemporaries, although in the long term also not of great consequence, were a series of cases, culminating in a constitutional decision in *Eisner* v. *Macomber*, which attempted to give legal definition to the economic concept "income."

In *Towne* v. *Eisner*, a corporation, on December 17, 1913, had transferred $1,500,000 of profits earned before January 1, 1913, from its surplus to its capital account, and issued 15,000 shares as a stock dividend to shareholders of record on December 26. Towne in due course received upwards of 4,000 shares, worth more than $400,000. They were taxed as income, Towne sued for a refund, and lost in the District Court for the Southern District of New York, Judge Augustus N. Hand holding that the stock dividend was, indeed, income within the terms of the 1913 Act, and was constitutionally taxable under the Sixteenth Amendment. The shareholder, said Judge Hand, did "have something different before and after receiving the additional stock." In lieu of a mere chance that he might receive his share of a surplus in cash, he now had "a permanent interest in the capitalized surplus. . . . This interest is derived from earnings, and may really be of much greater advantage . . . than the possibility . . . which he has lost. It becomes capital of the corporation, but in his hands it is income, and in many respects resembles the common extraordinary cash dividend, accompanied by a right to subscribe for additional stock at par to an amount equivalent to the dividend in cash. To say that this distribution is not income, because he [the taxpayer] received no cash, and the intermediate step is not taken, is, to my mind, quite to disregard the real nature of the transaction."[245]

The case came to the Supreme Court on writ of error, because the taxpayer contended that as construed below and applied to him, the 1913 Act was unconstitutional. The government moved to dismiss on the ground that the decision turned on an issue of construction rather than constitutionality, since the word "income" appeared both in the Sixteenth Amendment and in the statute, and any holding that the stock dividend was not income would be a holding that the statute did not apply, making resort to the constitutional issue unnecessary. But the Court, per Holmes, overruled the motion to dismiss. It did not

---

1916); Worth Brothers Co. v. Lederer, 251 U.S. 507 (1920) (application of 12½ percent tax on munitions manufacturers under Act of 1916); Forged Steel Wheel Co. v. Lewellyn, 251 U.S. 511 (1920) (application of 12½ percent tax on munitions manufacturers under Act of 1916); Penn Mutual Life Ins. Co. v. Lederer, 252 U.S. 523 (1920); United States v. Field, 255 U.S. 257 (1921); LaBelle Iron Works v. United States, 256 U.S. 377 (1921); United States v. American Chicle Co., 256 U.S. 446 (1921); United States v. Woodward, 256 U.S. 632 (1921).

[245] Towne v. Eisner, 242 Fed. 702, 706 (S.D. N.Y. 1917).

follow that what "income" meant in the Constitution it would also have to mean in the statute, said Holmes. "A word is not a crystal, transparent and unchanged, it is the skin of a living thought and may vary greatly in color and content according to the circumstances and the time in which it is used."

On the merits, Charles E. Hughes had argued for the taxpayer that a stock dividend was not in any sense income, "but is a mere readjustment of the evidence of the stockholder's interest already owned. The 'stock dividend' takes nothing from the property of the corporation and adds nothing to the interests of the stockholders. The only change in substance is that, instead of the property represented thereby being distributed to stockholders, it is permanently fixed as capital so that it cannot be distributed." Hence the tax here levied was a direct tax on property, and unconstitutional because not apportioned. Moreover, even if a stock dividend could ever be considered income, that would be so only when it represented a real gain, subject to taxation when earned. But the surplus from which this stock was issued had all been accumulated prior to the adoption of the Sixteenth Amendment, at a time when it could not be taxed without apportionment. When Congress in the 1916 Act undertook specifically to tax stock dividends, it excluded those based on accumulations of surplus existing prior to March 1, 1913. Solicitor General Davis argued that the term "income" was not restricted to cash, but covered any advantage or service that was subject to monetary appraisal. And he described the advantage derived by the stockholder from this distribution as Judge Hand had done.

For a unanimous Court, McKenna concurring in the result without opinion, Holmes very briefly reversed in favor of the taxpayer. Although jurisdiction was based on the presence of a constitutional issue, it was open to the Court to construe the statute, and Holmes put the case on the statutory ground. "Notwithstanding the thoughtful discussion that the case received below," he said, "we cannot doubt that the dividend was capital. . . . In short, the corporation is no poorer and the stockholder is no richer than they were before." Whatever small benefit the taxpayer may have gained surely did not amount to the upwards of $400,000 on which he was taxed. His old stock plus his new were worth no more than his old was alone. If the corporation had simply carried the million and a half involved from surplus to capital on its books, without any distribution, or if stock of the par value of $1,000 had been recalled, and ten shares worth $100 each had been issued instead, all would admit that there had been no income. That was, in effect, what had happened.[246]

---

[246] Towne v. Eisner, 245 U.S. 418, 419, 425, 426 (1918).

Brandeis' return to Holmes in *Towne* v. *Eisner* was: "Yes, but I should think that the opinion ought to be held until the other cases involving the income tax submitted or advanced for hearing are decided." McKenna apparently had similar worries, and he made them more explicit. He marked the passage, since become famous, "A word is not a crystal . . ." "Good," and generally approved on the jurisdictional issue. "On the other ground," he went on, however, "I am afraid you put too much stress upon the contract of gain or loss of the stockholder and the corporation. . . ." He referred to the place where Holmes said that the corporation was no poorer and the stockholder no richer than they were before. "In Number 452 [*Southern Pacific Co.* v. *Lowe*], a case yet to be heard," said McKenna, where by a bookkeeping entry, the Central Pacific Railroad, a wholly owned subsidiary of the Southern Pacific, paid its parent a dividend from surplus, it could hardly be contended that the Southern Pacific was any the richer. "So," McKenna went on, "in Number 705, *Peabody* v. *Eisner*, also a case yet to be heard," in which stock dividends were involved.[247]

That Brandeis had reason to be uncomfortable with *Towne* v. *Eisner* will presently be clear. Just what McKenna had in mind, other than the obvious bearing of these cases upon one another, is quite obscure, and nothing in the further positions he took explains why he noted concurrence in the result in *Towne* v. *Eisner*. If he meant to suggest that the case had as well been put on constitutional grounds, or that he was ready to put it on such grounds, he gave no indication of it to Holmes.

Holmes, at any rate, was not one to hold an opinion that he had ready, and *Towne* v. *Eisner* was announced on January 7, 1918. *Southern Pacific Co.* v. *Lowe*[248] and *Peabody* v. *Eisner*[249] were heard in March and decided in June 1918, together with two other cases, all on grounds of statutory construction. In *Southern Pacific*, the payment from surplus was held not taxable under the Act of 1913, but Pitney took care to say that the case turned upon its "very peculiar facts." In *Peabody* v. *Eisner*, the taxpayer received from the Union Pacific Railroad an extra dividend consisting in part of cash and in part of stock owned by the Union Pacific in the Baltimore and Ohio Railroad.[250] The Court allowed a tax under the 1913 Act, saying that *Towne* v. *Eisner* was not applicable because the portion of the dividend consisting of Baltimore and Ohio shares was not a stock dividend but a distribution of some of the Union Pacific's assets.

It was claimed in the *Peabody* case that the distribution was from

---

[247] Holmes Papers.
[248] 247 U.S. 330, 338 (1918); and see Gulf Oil Corp. v. Lewellyn, 248

U.S. 71 (1918).
[249] 247 U.S. 347 (1918).
[250] See *supra*, pp. 187–88.

surplus accumulated before the effective date of the Act of 1913—a point argued by Hughes in *Towne* v. *Eisner*, although not passed on by Holmes there. The point was centrally involved in *Lynch* v. *Hornby*,[251] argued and decided at the same time as *Peabody* and *Southern Pacific*, where a cash dividend was paid out of surplus accumulated before the effective date of the 1913 Act. The Court held that cash dividends were taxable whether paid from surplus accumulated at any time or from current earnings. But in *Lynch* v. *Turrish*,[252] which had been treated in the court below as indistinguishable from the *Hornby* case, the Supreme Court reached a different result. In question here was the liquidation of a company whose assets had appreciated to double the par value of its shares before the effective date of the Act of 1913. The company's assets were sold and final distribution was made to shareholders after the effective date of the Act, but there had in the meantime been no further increase in value. The gain was not taxable to shareholders as income, the Court held, because of its accrual prior to the effective date of the Act. It was not subject to income taxation when it accrued. The distribution now was, therefore, treated as a distribution of capital, not of a gain, and hence could not be taxed as income. This holding, like the others, was rested on construction of the statute, and *Turrish* and *Southern Pacific* were distinguished in *Lynch* v. *Hornby* as restricted to their special facts. *Lynch* v. *Turrish* was written by McKenna and was unanimous, Brandeis and Clarke concurring in the result without opinion. The other three cases were all written by Pitney, and two were unanimous, Clarke dissenting without opinion in *Southern Pacific Co.* v. *Lowe*.[253]

The upshot was that stock dividends paid from surplus were not taxable even if they represented economic gain, but dividends in cash or in the stock of another corporation, equally paid from surplus, were taxable even if they did not represent economic gain. Yet payments from a subsidiary to a parent corporation, and final distributions of assets to shareholders, were not taxable if no real gain had accrued. It was not, as McKenna probably sensed, just a question of whether the corporation was any poorer and the shareholder any richer. With this not altogether lucid preparation, the Court approached the task of giving constitutional definition to the term income, and now it divided 5 to 4.

In 1916, the Standard Oil Company of California had some $50 million worth of shares outstanding. It also had a surplus amounting to some $45 million, of which a little less than half had been earned prior to the effective date of the Income Tax Act of 1913, the rest later.

[251] 247 U.S. 339 (1918).
[252] 247 U.S. 221 (1918).
[253] See also Miller v. Gearin, 258

Fed. 225 (9th Cir. 1919), *cert. denied,* 250 U.S. 667 (1919).

The company decided to issue a stock dividend of 50 percent of the outstanding stock, transferring the value of the new issue from the surplus account to the capital stock account. Mrs. Macomber, a shareholder, received her portion of the stock dividend, and the government taxed it as income under the Revenue Act of 1916, which explicitly provided that stock dividends be so treated. Mrs. Macomber resisted, and won below on the authority of *Towne* v. *Eisner*. The case was argued twice in the Supreme Court, by an Assistant Attorney General for the government (Solicitor General Davis had resigned in November 1918, and his successor, Alexander C. King of Georgia, did not choose to argue this case himself) and by Charles E. Hughes for the taxpayer. There was an *amicus* brief on the taxpayer's side by George W. Wickersham.

Towne v. *Eisner*, said the government, was not controlling, as it merely construed an earlier statute. Of course, it was true that a stock dividend did not enrich the shareholder. But that was irrelevant; it could be equally true of a cash dividend, which could be paid out of capital rather than profit. This stock dividend was paid out of profits accumulated after the effective date of the 1913 Act, and hence taxable when earned. There was no question that profits could be taxed to the shareholder if distributed to him when earned. What this corporation had done instead was to reinvest these profits, wait some years, and then distribute them in the form of stock dividends. "If the constitutional power exists to tax corporate earnings when they are passed to the stockholder by means of a cash dividend, no reason is perceived why the same power does not exist to tax the same earnings when they are passed to him, in an equally concrete form, by means of a stock dividend."

Hughes met these arguments by insisting on the distinction—it was "not a form or technicality [but] vital"—between the corporation and the taxpayer, as the Court itself had done in *Lynch* v. *Hornby* and in *Peabody* v. *Eisner*, when it taxed to the shareholder dividends paid from funds on which the corporation itself could not have been taxed. But, to be sure, the Court had failed to take the distinction, and had merged the shareholder and the corporation, in *Lynch* v. *Turrish* and in *Southern Pacific Co.* v. *Lowe*. It was not relevant, said Hughes, to inquire whether the stock dividend was paid out of corporate profits. The question was whether it was income, not to the corporation, but to the shareholder. Undivided corporate profits were corporate income, all right, but it was a separate question whether they were income to the shareholder. Now it was "of the essence of income that it should be realized. Potentiality is not enough. Book entries or opinions of increase are not income. Income necessarily implies separation and realization. The increase of the forest is not income until it is cut. . . . Income is the gain, come to fruition, from capital, from labor, or from both combined. This is sound doctrine both in law and in economics."

For the majority, which in addition to himself included White, McKenna, Van Devanter, and McReynolds, Pitney held first that *Towne* v. *Eisner* was controlling, for it rested on a judgment of the essential nature of a stock dividend. Nevertheless, "in view of the importance of the matter," Pitney proceeded to reexamine the essential nature of a stock dividend. The inquiry was crucial, since if a stock dividend was not income within the meaning of the Sixteenth Amendment, then under the remaining authority of *Pollock* v. *Farmers' Loan & Trust Co.*— overruled, as was said in *Brushaber* v. *Union Pacific Railroad*, only so far as "income" was concerned—any tax falling on stock dividends was direct, and void unless apportioned. Wrote Pitney:

> The fundamental relation of "capital" to "income" has been much discussed by economists, the former being likened to the tree or the land, the latter to the fruit or the crop; the former depicted as a reservoir supplied from springs, the latter as the outlet stream, to be measured by its flow during a period of time. For the present purpose we require only a clear definition of the term "income," as used in common speech, in order to determine its meaning in the Amendment; and, having formed also a correct judgment as to the nature of a stock dividend, we shall find it easy to decide the matter at issue.

Income had to be gain, but the crucial element in the definition was that income had to be severed from capital. A corporation was an entity distinct from the shareholder. When it issued a stock dividend, it made a book adjustment, but did not sever any part of its assets for distribution to the shareholder. The stockholder merely got a new piece of evidence of his preexisting proportionate interest in the corporation. The stock dividend might indicate that the shareholder was, or had for some time been, richer than before, but it also showed that "he has not realized or received any income." The stockholder might sell the new shares, and be taxed on his profit, if any, but exactly the same was true of his old shares. Moreover, the stock dividend was an indication that the shareholder was richer only if he had held the stock for a sufficient period of time. It was no such indication if he bought after the surplus had been accumulated. Market quotations might or might not reflect the true nature of a stock dividend, but they were in any event "an unsafe criterion in an inquiry such as the present, when the question must be, not what will the thing sell for, but what is it in truth and in essence." The government in effect argued that the Act of 1916 imposed a tax not so much on income to the shareholder, as on his proportionate interest in the undivided profits of the corporation. But if so construed, the 1916 Act would still be unconstitutional, since it would impose a tax on property, which required apportionment. *Collector* v. *Hubbard*[254] was to the contrary, but it was overruled by *Pollock* v. *Farmers' Loan & Trust Co.*, and that case, except as itself narrowly overruled by the Sixteenth Amendment, continued to state the constitutional position.

Holmes, joined by Day, dissented in a paragraph. *Towne* v. *Eisner*, he continued to think, was right, but it did not decide the constitutional issue. "The known purpose of [the Sixteenth] Amendment was to get rid of nice questions as to what might be direct taxes, and I cannot doubt that most people not lawyers would suppose when they voted for it that they put a question like the present to rest. I am of the opinion that the Amendment justifies the tax."

Brandeis filed a much more elaborate dissent, in which Clarke joined. There were two well-known methods, he said (rehearsing at some length a point made by Judge Augustus Hand in *Towne* v. *Eisner*), of in effect distributing accumulated corporate profits to stockholders without increasing corporate indebtedness. One method was the stock dividend, and if the stockholder wanted to turn it into cash, he could readily do so by selling it. The other method was to issue a cash dividend, at the same time giving the stockholder the privilege of buying new stock at a price below the market. Again, as under the first method, the shareholder had his option whether to realize cash or not. These methods had long been recognized equivalents, as Brandeis demonstrated by reviewing some of the history of other Standard Oil companies. What the Court was now doing was drawing an artificial legal distinction between them. For it was clear, Brandeis thought, that if the second method had been used, and a cash dividend issued with rights to buy new stock, Mrs. Macomber would be considered to have derived taxable income.

Powers conferred upon Congress were to be liberally construed. Was there anything in the nature of the Sixteenth Amendment that should lead to a narrow construction of the power there conferred? The reason, if any, could not be that the term "income" had some plain and exclusive meaning as applied to dividends. Dividends could be paid out of capital, out of surplus, or out of borrowed funds, and they could equally be paid in cash or in some other medium. These were, throughout, simply options raising questions of financial management. Suppose a corporation bought some of its own outstanding common stock, and then in due time, instead of paying a regular cash dividend, paid a dividend in this stock. Could anyone doubt that that would be income to the taxpayer? It was said that the taxpayer was made no richer by the stock dividend, but that was commonly true of cash dividends also,

---

[254] 12 Wall. 1 (1870).

which upon payment out of corporate assets depressed for a time the value of the shareholder's stock.

Perhaps the main insistence of the majority was that in issuing a stock dividend, the corporation did not part with any physical asset, it segregated no asset for realization by the stockholder. But such segregation and realization, Brandeis asserted, were not essential to a definition of income. And the Court had previously demonstrated that a dividend in whatever form need not represent actual gain to the shareholder in order to qualify as income. Finally:

> If stock dividends representing profits are held exempt from taxation under the Sixteenth Amendment, the owners of the most successful businesses in America will, as the facts in this case illustrate, be able to escape taxation on a large part of what is actually their income. So far as their profits are represented by stock received as dividends they will pay these taxes not upon their income but only upon the income of their income. That such a result was intended by the people of the United States when adopting the Sixteenth Amendment is inconceivable. . . . It seems to me clear, therefore, that Congress possesses the power which it exercised to make dividends representing profits, taxable as income, whether the medium in which the dividend is paid be cash or stock, and that it may define, as it has done, what dividends representing profits shall be deemed income. It surely is not clear that the enactment exceeds the power granted by the Sixteenth Amendment. And, as this court has so often said, the high prerogative of declaring an act of Congress invalid, should never be exercised except in a clear case.[255]

Eisner v. *Macomber* caused a stockmarket depression on the day it came down, which although momentary, did involve losses in the thousands. The opinion of the Court made clear, of course, that the Court was affirming the judgment for the taxpayer below, but in the very second sentence of the opinion, Pitney curiously went out of his way to remark that the Revenue Act of 1916 "evinces the purpose of Congress to tax stock dividends as income." Whether because he took his clue from this sentence, or because, as was reported, Pitney spoke throughout "in a low and mumbling tone," an agent of Dow Jones hastened to wire a report that stock dividends had been held taxable, and Wall Street, which in common with most observers had been expecting the actual result, promptly went into a decline.

---

[255] Eisner v. Macomber, 252 U.S. 189, 193, 195, 198, 200, 205, 206–207, 212, 215, 220, 237–38 (1920). At this point, in a footnote, Brandeis cited James B. Thayer, "American Doctrine of Constitutional Law," *Harv. L. Rev.*, 7:129, 142, 1893.

V: *The Fate of Social Legislation, 1914–21: Federal*

When shortly thereafter the false report was corrected, the market recovered more than it had lost. Yet there was no jubilation. Despite Brandeis' warning, informed observers did not believe that much opportunity had been created for the distribution of tax-free profits, and emotional estimates of the prospective loss of federal revenue were discounted.[256] After all, when stock dividends, or any other stocks, were sold, the increase in value over the original investment, representing profit, was taxed as income. If there was any doubt of that, the Supreme Court within the year dispelled it by expressly holding that capital gains were so taxable.[257] And the other way around, the response to the opposite result in *Eisner* v. *Macomber* would doubtless have been the substitution for stock dividends of stock splits accompanied by increases in par value, and if this device had brought on taxation, then the creation of a market in fractions of shares would have followed, enabling stockholders to sell fractions as their interests appreciated in value.[258]

The decision was soon recognized, then, for what it was—a tempest in a teacup. Congress, despite some grumbling,[259] reconciled itself to it, and did not repeat the attempt of the 1916 Act.[260] And the Supreme Court, although unquestionably ready in the next generation to overrule *Eisner* v. *Macomber*, could not find the occasion to do so.[261] But the case did give rise to a voluminous literature, virtually all of it approving the position of the majority. The consensus of the economists was stated by Edwin R. A. Seligman of Columbia, in a paper entitled "Are Stock Dividends Income?" which he published in September 1919, after the first but before the second argument of *Eisner* v. *Macomber*, and which was heavily relied on by Hughes at the reargument and by Pitney in his opinion. "Realization," Seligman contended, "is a necessary attribute of income." The next characteristic was that income was "something dis-

---

[256] See *New York Times*, Mar. 9, 1920, p. 1, col. 1, col. 2, col. 3; *The Independent*, 101:437, Mar. 20, 1920; *New York Tribune*, Mar. 10, 1920, p. 12, col. 1; *The Outlook*, 124:455, Mar. 17, 1920; *The Literary Digest*, 65:160–61, Apr. 17, 1920.

[257] Merchants' Loan & Trust Co. v. Smietanka, 255 U.S. 509 (1921); Eldorado Coal Co. v. Mager, 255 U.S. 522 (1921); Goodrich v. Edwards, 255 U.S. 527 (1921); Walsh v. Brewster, 255 U.S. 536 (1921); Darlington v. Mager, *affirmed*, 256 U.S. 682 (1921).

[258] See B. I. Bittker, *Federal Income Taxation of Corporations and*

Shareholders (1966), 199.

[259] See, e.g., *New York Times*, Mar. 9, 1920, p. 1, col. 3 (Cordell Hull); 59 *Cong. Rec.* 7759–62, 66th Cong., 2nd Sess. (1920); 61 *Cong. Rec.* 5176–77, 67th Cong., 1st Sess. (1921); 64 *Cong. Rec.* 1255–57, 67th Cong., 4th Sess. (1923); 65 *Cong. Rec.* 2794, 2797, 68th Cong., 1st Sess. (1924).

[260] See B. W. Kanter, "The Present Tax Status of Stock Dividends," *Taxes*, 31:418, 1953; Bittker, *Federal Income Taxation of Corporations and Shareholders*, 195–208.

[261] Helvering v. Griffiths, 318 U.S. 371 (1943).

tinct and separate from the person or thing that affords the income. . . . Separation is of the essence of the enjoyment." And he gave the example, alluded to by both Hughes and Pitney, of the growing forest which could produce income only when the timber was cut.[262]

Among lawyers and laymen, Brandeis also found few adherents, and finds few to this day. Plainly *Lynch* v. *Hornby* and *Peabody* v. *Eisner*, as well as *United States* v. *Phellis*[263] and *Rockefeller* v. *United States*,[264] decided two terms thence, after Taft's accession, showed that there could be taxable income without gain, some of Pitney's remarks in *Eisner* v. *Macomber* notwithstanding. Yet that was scarcely a reason for allowing a tax where there may or may not have been gain, but there was certainly no realization. *Lynch* v. *Hornby* and like cases, as Thomas Reed Powell pointed out, were a matter of "the practical convenience of treating the corporation as an economic unit distinct from the stockholders. When a corporation parts with assets, it would be confusing to insist on a nice appraisal of what the stockholder gains." An appraisal is, therefore, not undertaken, and "the stockholder has to pay an income tax on what in whole or in part is not a gain to him but merely a change in the form of his capital." This was an excellent place to stop. True enough, the cash dividend that was taxed in *Lynch* v. *Hornby* was no more genuine income than one or another stock dividend. And yet a cash dividend is severed from corporate assets, while a stock dividend is not, and "this will do for a legal line between them."[265]

The New Republic, essaying almost alone a full-fledged defense of Brandeis, thought that an investor in a soundly financed company—

---

[262] E. R. A. Seligman, "Are Stock Dividends Income?" *American Economics Review*, 9:517, 519, 524, 1919.

Even the irrascible Henry C. Simons, who, writing in the 1930s, considered the majority opinion in *Eisner* v. *Macomber* "an engaging metaphysical treatise on the quiddity of income," who was equally unimpressed with the economics of Edwin R. A. Seligman and his attempts to define income, and who for this reason regretted that "an utterly trivial issue was made the occasion for injecting into our fundamental law a mass of rhetorical confusion which no orderly mind can contemplate respectfully"—even Simons did not for a moment maintain that stock dividends should be taxed as income, or that the realization criterion was anything but sensible and convenient. See H. C. Simons, *Personal Income Taxation* (1938), especially at 198–99.

[263] 257 U.S. 156 (1921).

[264] 257 U.S. 176 (1921).

[265] See T. R. Powell, "Stock Dividends, Direct Taxes, and the Sixteenth Amendment," *Colum. L. Rev.*, 20:536, 546, 1920; T. R. Powell, "Income from Corporate Dividends," *Harv. L. Rev.*, 35:363, 1922; E. H. Warren, "Taxability of Stock Dividends as Income," *Harv. L. Rev.*, 33:885, 1920; R. Magill, *Taxable Income* (2nd ed., 1945), 24–80. For comments on Towne v. Eisner, see Comment, *Yale L. J.*, 27:553, 1918; Note, *Colum. L. Rev.*, 18:63, 1918; R. E. More, "Stock Dividends as Income," *Mich. L. Rev.*, 16:521, 1918.

even if not in one where "capital is openly and shamelessly watered"—received an increment of real value when a stock dividend was declared. His original shares did not decline in price upon the issue of such a dividend, or at least not in a proportionate measure. Hence the effect upon the interest of the investor was "identical with the effect of the declaration of an extra cash dividend out of the accumulated surplus. If such extra cash dividends are taxable, stock dividends ought to be taxable as well." Whether cash or stock dividends were issued was merely, as Brandeis had said, "a question of internal corporate management." But under assault from Professors Charles E. Clark of Yale Law School and Edward S. Corwin of Princeton, who pressed the realization criterion, even *The New Republic* retreated, admitting that there were of course "technical grounds for supporting the decision."[266]

Such support as the dissenters gathered and retained was of two sorts. There were those, like Charles E. Clark, who although he considered *Eisner* v. *Macomber* "quite simply correct," believed also that if the decision was a harbinger of a continuing judicial effort to define income and to supervise federal taxation, Congress would be unduly hampered and the result would be unfortunate.[267] Other commentators focused on Holmes' dissent and on the last paragraph of Brandeis', rather than on Brandeis' economic reasoning. For *The New Republic*, in an editorial probably written by Felix Frankfurter, *Eisner* v. *Macomber* was a "challenge" to the "wisdom of leaving the ultimate law-making power of the nation to nine men."

> The influences of . . . two radically different types of mind, the imaginative and the unimaginative, are revealed in all judicial history, and have played their part since the foundation of the Supreme Court. Naturally, the less imaginative the mind, the more it is subject to the undertow of its own habits, its own experiences, its own sense of what is right. Inevitably, therefore, intellectual limitations of the individual become constitutional limitations imposed on the entire country.
>
> The Supreme Court's power as the ultimate law-giver puts too heavy a strain upon ordinary men. . . . We shall never face the issues until there is general recognition of the fact that the Supreme Court in cases of public concern is not exercising ordinary judicial powers but powers that demand qualities deeper and different from those possessed by ordinary judges. . . . [T]he question which the recent

---

[266] See *The New Republic*, 13:326, Jan. 19, 1918, 22:237, Apr. 21, 1920, 23:59, 60, 61, June 9, 1920.

[267] See C. E. Clark, "Eisner v. Macomber and Some Income Tax Problems," *Yale L. J.*, 29:735, 1920. See also E. Seligman, "Implications and Effects of the Stock Dividend Decision," *Colum. L. Rev.*, 21:313, 1921; T. D. Zuckerman, "Are Stock Dividends Income?" *Journal of Political Economy*, 28:591, 1920.

Supreme Court decisions insistently raise sooner or later face all institutions—Does it work? Is it worth more than it costs?

After Professors Clark and Corwin forced it to renege somewhat on its defense of Brandeis' economics, *The New Republic* maintained that the issue before the Court had not been whether stock dividends were income, but whether Congress violated the Constitution in treating them as income—and that was an issue "not to be decided by technical niceties."[268] So also Thomas Reed Powell:

> So far as *Eisner* v. *Macomber* turns on economic issues, the majority has much the better of the argument. . . . Mr. Justice Holmes has found the solider ground for dissent. . . . As Marshall bids us remember, it is a Constitution we are expounding. Must every word be restricted to its nicest meaning, or shall Congress be allowed reasonable latitude? . . . No answer to these questions can be given by philologists and economists. The answer which the Supreme Court should give depends upon its conception of its function.[269]

And this, after all, not the taxability of stock dividends, was the issue that determined people's attitudes toward the Court for the next two decades.

The Court had one further constitutional encounter with the income tax, and it was peculiarly embarrassing. Congress, in the Revenue Act of 1919, specifically taxed the salaries of the incumbent President and sitting federal judges.[270] It was widely felt to be both inequitable and impolitic to persist in exempting federal officials from taxation. Article III of the Constitution forbids Congress to diminish the compensation of federal judges during their terms of office, and Article II similarly safeguards the salary of the President. Yet it was questionable whether these provisions limited the power to tax, and as with the Corporation Tax Act of 1909, and later with Webb-Kenyon and the first Child Labor Acts, Congress found itself caught up in the familiar ambivalence concerning its duty to construe and apply the Constitution. Once again Congress opted for movement, adopting the theory that the duty of constitutional interpretation belonged alone to the Supreme Court, which could exercise it only if Congress acted without regard to constitutional doubts.[271]

---

[268] *The New Republic*, 22:235, 238, Apr. 21, 1920, 23:61, June 9, 1920.

[269] Powell, "Stock Dividends, Direct Taxes, and the Sixteenth Amendment," 549.

[270] 40 Stat. 1062 (1919).

[271] See *House Report No. 767*, at 29, 65th Cong., 2nd Sess. (1918); *Senate Report No. 617*, at 6, 65th Cong., 3rd Sess. (1919); 56 *Cong. Rec.* 10366–370, 65th Cong., 2nd Sess. (1918). Cf. *supra*, pp. 21–24, 448–49.

V: *The Fate of Social Legislation, 1914–21: Federal*

The action of Congress caused quite a flurry among federal judges. On the day the Revenue Act of 1919 was passed, Van Devanter's old colleague, and more or less friendly rival for promotion to the Supreme Court, Judge Walter H. Sanborn of the Court of Appeals for the Eighth Circuit, wrote him:

> Now I am inclined to think that the circuit and district judges in this matter should follow the lead of the Justices of the Supreme Court. So far as the amount of money to be paid under the revenue bill is concerned, while I am not delighted to be required to pay it, I am willing to pay it if the government needs it, but there is a great principle at stake, and I should like to know what course you, the Chief Justice, and the other Justices of the Supreme Court intend to pursue. Do you intend to protest against the payment and get the question before the Attorney General or any other law officer of the United States before paying it? Or do you intend to pay it in silence? I shall be glad to receive any suggestions you may see fit to make, and I should like to know whether I may communicate any of the suggestions you make, and if so what ones, to the other judges who make inquiries of me on this subject.

Van Devanter was as undelighted as anyone to be required to pay. The tax on his salary came to $1,580, and he very much felt the consequences of the general rise in prices that had accompanied the war. The rent on his house had been considerably increased. The wages of his three servants had gone up more than 50 percent, so that any one of the three now got more than any two of them had received when Van Devanter first came to Washington in 1911, and all other expenses had similarly risen. Salaries, however, had not. Supreme Court Justices received the same $14,500 that they were paid in 1911. Van Devanter had been supplementing his secretary's meager $2,000-a-year salary with an allowance out of his own pocket, which he was finding it difficult to continue, let alone increase. He was personally lobbying through Congress a bill to provide $3,600 a year per Justice for a secretary–law clerk, and it was not until late in 1919 that he was successful in this endeavor. That would enable him without personal expense to pay a living wage to a secretary–law clerk for the first time.

Van Devanter answered Sanborn that he had consulted his colleagues and that they entertained "widely divergent views." One factor was that the Justices were under an obligation "to maintain an attitude which will enable me to participate in the consideration and decision of any case involving the question which may come before the Court in regular course." This, Van Devanter thought, meant that he should not try to decide for himself whether the tax was valid or not, but include his salary in his tax return and pay without protest. In fact, that was soon to be what all the Justices in concert did. But Van Devanter very carefully warned Sanborn, as he had orally warned another circuit judge, that what the Justices did should constitute no precedent for lower-court judges. Van Devanter was not about to have any part in foreclosing the possibility of litigation. His advice to lower-court judges was to "examine into the matter carefully" and then conform their action to whatever conclusion they had reached respecting the validity or invalidity of the tax; in other words, raise the issue, and make a case, if like Sanborn they deemed the tax unconstitutional.[272]

District Judge Walter Evans of the United States District Court for the Western District of Kentucky—there is no evidence that Van Devanter had been in touch with him, and he was not in Van Devanter's old Eighth Circuit—did what Van Devanter thought was proper for lower federal judges. He paid the tax under protest, and then sued the government for a refund. Another district judge held against him. In the Supreme Court, William Marshall Bullitt, a friend of Evans, argued for the judge together with another Kentucky lawyer. Both were, Van Devanter thought, "not at all equal to the occasion." They "had not gone to the bottom." At the first conference, it seemed that five Justices were prepared to hold the tax valid, but further discussion produced a majority the other way, and the opinion was assigned to Van Devanter. "Being thoroughly impressed with the merit of my view I gave it my best attention, and I have taken some satisfaction in the outcome."[273]

It was a matter of regret, Van Devanter began, that the solution of this problem had to fall to the Justices; "and this although each member [of the Court] has been paying the tax in respect of his salary voluntarily and in regular course." But there was no alternative to the assumption of jurisdiction. "Moreover, it appears that, when this taxing provision was adopted, Congress regarded it as of uncertain constitutionality, and both contemplated and intended that the question should be settled by us in a case like this." The issue was the independence of the judges, which was provided by the Founders not for their benefit, but "to promote the public weal." The importance of that independence had been attested to by Hamilton, Marshall, Washington, Story, and by "Mr. Wilson, now the President," in his book, *Constitutional Government in the United States.* The power to tax was "the power to embarrass and

---

[272] W. H. Sanborn to W. Van Devanter, Feb. 24, 1919; Van Devanter to Sanborn, Mar. 3, 1919; Van Devanter to E. Bierer, Jr., June 14, 1919, Oct. 3, 1919; F. E. Warren to Van Devanter, June 30, 1919, July 2, 1919, Van Devanter Papers. See Act of July 19, 1919, 41 Stat. 209; C. A. Newland, "Personal Assistants to Supreme Court Justices: The Law Clerks," *Ore. L. Rev.,* 40:299, 302–303, 1961.

[273] Van Devanter to W. H. Sanborn, June 18, 1920, Van Devanter Papers.

destroy," and a tax diminished the judicial salary as much as would any other requirement to pay back part of it.

When the Income Tax Act of 1862 was applied to judicial salaries, Chief Justice Taney protested in a letter to the Secretary of the Treasury, which the Court ordered printed in its *Reports*.[274] Taney's influence—although Van Devanter did not say so—was at a rather low ebb during the Civil War, and his letter had no effect, but in 1869, a ruling by the Attorney General stopped the taxation of judges' salaries. That was the proper constitutional position prior to passage of the Sixteenth Amendment, and it was not changed now, because the Amendment, as held in *Brushaber* v. *Union Pacific Railroad*, did not enhance the preexisting power to tax.

> Apart from his salary, a Federal judge is as much within the taxing power as other men are. If he has a home or other property, it may be taxed. . . . If he has an income other than his salary, it also may be taxed. . . . And, speaking generally, his duties and obligations as a citizen are not different from those of his neighbors. But for the common good—to render him, in the words of John Marshall, "perfectly and completely independent, with nothing to influence or control him but God and his conscience"—his compensation is protected from diminution in any form, whether by a tax or otherwise, and is assured to him in its entirety for his support.

For Holmes, Van Devanter's opinion was "the recrudescence of an old problem."

> Whether to dissent as to the judge's salaries being included in the income tax, was the occasion and the problem whether to allow other considerations than those of the detached intellect to count. The subject didn't interest me particularly—I wasn't at all in love with what I had written and I hadn't got the blood of controversy in my neck. In fact I thought that Van Devanter put his side rather nobly. So when another (not he) suggested that I helped to make the position of the majority embarrassing—as deciding in their own interest, I hesitated. But I reflected that if my opinion were the unpopular one I should be but a poor creature if I held back—and that philosophically the reasons were the same when I was on the other side. And anyhow you get lost in morasses if you think of anything except the question, the answer, and whether the public interest is that both sides should be stated.[275]

The tax, Holmes wrote, would have been valid under the original Constitution, and even if not, was made lawful by the Sixteenth Amendment. There was no reason to exonerate a judge from the ordinary duties of a citizen, and a requirement that he pay his taxes could not possibly

---

[274] 157 U.S. 701.   [275] *Holmes-Laski Letters*, I, 266.

be construed as an attack on his independence. Surely the Constitution had not intended to make judges a privileged class "free from bearing their share of the cost of the institutions upon which their well-being if not their life, depends." In any event, the Sixteenth Amendment gave power to tax income from whatever source derived, and that language covered the income of judges, from whatever source they derived it.[276]

Brandeis alone joined in Holmes' dissent—"eagerly," as he said in his return. McReynolds, quite likely the judge who urged Holmes to withhold the dissent, returned, "Sorry to see *you* go wrong!" It was on this return—no doubt suspecting Brandeis of having egged Holmes on—that McReynolds added his remark that the Lord tried to make something out of the Hebrews for centuries, but finally gave up and turned them out to prey on mankind, "like fleas on the dog for example."[277] The decision was certainly a financial help to the judges. Holmes reported privately in February 1921 that the exclusion of his salary "made an amazing difference" in his income tax.[278] But the authority of the case was good for less than a generation. Congress did ultimately succeed in taxing judicial salaries.[279]

Inter Arma

The United States declared war on April 6, 1917, and although this date marks the effective end of the New Freedom, the war produced as great an expansion of federal power as the reforming measures of the entire Progressive Era.

As early as the summer of 1916, Congress had authorized the President to take over the railroads in time of war.[280] In the summer and fall of 1917, the country experienced a severe railroad traffic jam on the East Coast, and it became clear as well that the railroads could not very well finance privately the great, exigent new needs for equipment.[281] By proclamation dated December 26, 1917, the President, therefore, took possession of the railroads, naming the Secretary of the Treasury, his son-in-law, William G. McAdoo, Director General. On March 21, 1918, Congress by statute ratified and codified the takeover.[282]

The owners of the roads were to be compensated for the use made of them, but all earnings were to be property of the United States during

---

[276] Evans v. Gore, 253 U.S. 245, 247–48, 263, 265 (1920).

[277] Holmes Papers. See *supra*, p. 354.

[278] O. W. Holmes to F. Frankfurter, Feb. 5, 1921, Holmes Papers; see also *Holmes-Laski Letters*, I, 335–36.

[279] *Compare* Miles v. Graham, 268 U.S. 501 (1925), *with* O'Malley v. Woodrough, 307 U.S. 277 (1939).

[280] 39 Stat. 645 (1916).

[281] See F. H. Dixon, *Railroads and Government* (1922), 119–22.

[282] 40 Stat. 451 (1918).

the period of federal operation. The President was authorized to establish rates, which the Interstate Commerce Commission could pass on, but not suspend pending adjudication. In passing on these rates, the commission was to consider the changed circumstances, and the President's recommendations. It was, in other words, to give a weight to Presidential rates that it was not otherwise required to give to rates set by the railroads themselves. The power of the states to tax the railroads was saved by the Act, as were "the lawful police regulations of the several states."

The Director General promulgated rates covering all classes of service, intrastate as well as interstate. The new intrastate rates were generally higher than those previously prevailing, but the Director General most distinctly declined to submit himself to the jurisdiction of state rate-making commissions.[283] The North Dakota Utilities Commission thereupon filed suit in the state courts against the Director General and the Northern Pacific Railway to enjoin them from interfering with state-established intrastate rates. The suit succeeded in the state courts. In the Supreme Court of the United States, an *amicus* brief was filed in support of North Dakota's position by thirty-seven other states and the National Association of Railway and Utility Commissions. Upholding the authority of the President, the Supreme Court reversed, in an opinion by Chief Justice White. In taking over the railroads, said the Chief Justice, the President exercised more than the federal commerce power, and he labored under no such restrictions as limit that power. The railroads were being operated pursuant to the war power of the United States which, White indicated, reached as far as it needed to reach. The United States had obligated itself to pay just compensation to the owners of the railroads, and it had naturally assumed commensurate authority to set all rates.[284]

In July 1918, Congress also authorized the President to take possession and control of "any telegraph, telephone, marine cable, or radio system or systems."[285] The President did so on July 22, putting the Postmaster General in charge, and the latter, like the Director General of the railroads, also fixed both intrastate and interstate rates. In a series of cases argued and decided together with the North Dakota railroad litigation, the Supreme Court upheld the full measure of Presidential authority in this instance as well.[286] Brandeis, who had concurred in the result, alone and without opinion, in the railroad case, now dissented alone without opinion.

---

[283] See Dixon, *Railroads and Government,* 174.

[284] Northern Pacific Ry. v. North Dakota, 250 U.S. 135 (1919).

[285] 40 Stat. 904 (1918).

[286] Dakota Central Telephone Co. v. South Dakota, 250 U.S. 163 (1919); Kansas v. Burleson, 250 U.S. 188 (1919); Burleson v. Dempcy, 250 U.S. 191 (1919); MacLeod v. New England Telephone Co., 250 U.S. 195 (1919).

Brandeis had been consulted, by Wilson himself among others, about the railroad takeover, and he had been mentioned as a possible Director General.[287] It might have been as well if he had remained aloof from an executive concern so likely, in this or that aspect, to be transformed into a judicial one. Yet evidently the detachment of his judgment was not affected. Although Brandeis agreed that Congress had given the President authority to set intrastate railroad rates without submitting them to state regulatory commissions, he must have been put off by the sweeping tone of White's opinion. In the telephone cases, the statutory reservation of state taxing and police power was word for word the same as in the railroad case, but in the telephone legislation, Congress had failed to make an express grant of authority to set rates at all. Such an express grant was included in the statute ratifying the railroad takeover, and this may have made the difference for Brandeis. In neither instance, presumably, did he see a constitutional issue, but he was perhaps prepared to infer from a bare authorization to take possession and control, with no mention of rates, only a power to set interstate telephone rates, not intrastate. If this was the distinction that Brandeis drew, it was not one that commended itself to scholarly commentators.[288] Yet the refusal to be carried along, even in an emergency, by the urge to take shortcuts in order "to get things done" was entirely characteristic of Brandeis, as the New Dealers who were to consult him in the early 1930s would discover.[289]

These cases, themselves argued and decided after the Armistice, were the only significant contests over federal control of railroads and telephones, although Brandeis, as White told him in a return, "worked out in a very satisfying way," in favor of the exercise of federal authority, a further conflict with state law, and there were two or three other minor controversies.[290]

---

[287] See G. W. Anderson to L. D. Brandeis, Dec. 21, 1917; F. Frankfurter to Brandeis, Dec. 12, 1917, Box World War, No. 2, Brandeis Papers, University of Louisville Law School Library; A. T. Mason, *Brandeis—A Free Man's Life* (1946), 520–23.

[288] See, e.g., H. W. Biklé, "State Power over Intrastate Railroad Rates during Federal Control," *Harv. L. Rev.*, 32:299, 1919; Note, *Harv. L. Rev.*, 33:94, 1919.

[289] See Mason, *Brandeis*, 520–21, 613 *et seq.*

[290] Missouri Pacific R.R. v. Ault, 256 U.S. 554 (1921) (for White's return, see the Ault case in Brandeis Papers); see also United States v. Union Pacific R.R., 249 U.S. 354 (1919); Atchison, Topeka & Santa Fe Ry. v. United States, 256 U.S. 205 (1921); Norfolk-Southern R.R. v. Owens, 256 U.S. 565 (1921); Western Union Telegraph Co. v. Poston, 256 U.S. 662 (1921); and see Commercial Cable Co. v. Burleson, 250 U.S. 360 (1919); United States v. Alaska S.S. Co., 253 U.S. 113 (1920); Director General v. Viscose Co., 254 U.S. 498 (1921); Krichman v. United States, 256 U.S. 363 (1921).

V: *The Fate of Social Legislation, 1914–21: Federal*

Before seizing its railroads, the United States drafted its men, by act of May 18, 1917.[291] Despite the prevalent, and increasingly exaggerated and undiscriminating, patriotic fervor, the constitutionality of the draft was promptly attacked. It was very promptly and almost summarily sustained by a unanimous Supreme Court, Chief Justice White writing. Argument was had in the Supreme Court on December 13 and 14, 1917, and the Court's opinion came down on January 7. It dealt with the subject in broad terms, finding federal authority in the provisions of Article I of the Constitution, which empower Congress to declare war and to raise and support armies. "As the mind cannot conceive an army without the men to compose it, on the face of the Constitution the objection that it does not give power to provide for such men would seem to be too frivolous for further notice." To the argument that the Constitution empowered Congress to raise a volunteer army, but that compulsory military service was in conflict with guarantees of individual liberty, White replied that "the very conception of a just government and its duty to the citizen includes the reciprocal obligation of the citizen to render military service in case of need and the right to compel it." Many of the colonies exacted compulsory service, as did most civilized nations at present, and as the United States itself had done during the Civil War on both sides.

Having thus disposed of the fundamental attack upon the draft, White dealt in a paragraph with two more particular objections. One was that the Selective Service Act made an unconstitutionally broad delegation of power to the President and to local draft boards to select the men who would actually serve. White simply cited a number of cases that had held other delegations constitutional in other circumstances. The second particular objection was that the complete exemption provided for ordained ministers and theological students, and the exemption from combatant service for members of religious sects whose tenets did not permit engaging in war amounted to an establishment of religion or an interference with its free exercise. White replied that the "unsoundness" of this contention was "too apparent to require" an answer. The claim, finally, that the draft was an imposition of involuntary servitude in violation of the Thirteenth Amendment rose to an even higher stage of unsoundness. It was "refuted by its mere statement."[292]

The Court's unanimous legitimation of the draft was widely regarded as a matter of course, so much so as to suggest that the contrary result would simply not have been accepted. "Every patriotic citizen expected" the decision, said the *New York Times*. The *Chicago*

---

[291] 40 Stat. 76 (1917).
[292] Selective Draft Law Cases, 245 U.S. 366, 377, 378, 390 (1918).

Tribune thought that there was "never any danger that compulsory service would not be upheld by any court not composed of philosophical or other anarchists." *The Nation*, a less virile publication, agreed that the Court had delivered a verdict "for which the country was hardly waiting with bated breath," but declared that it was well, nevertheless, to have "a clear-cut pronouncement on the legality of a state of facts which, otherwise, there would have been a few subtle or discontented minds to make a subject of debate."

Much that was written bore a distinct tone of impatience with any opposition, and of readiness to attribute an unpatriotic if not treasonous cast to what *The Nation*, more politely than most of its contemporaries, called "subtle or discontented minds." *The Outlook* found it "difficult . . . to conceive how any other view [than that taken by the Court in upholding the draft] could ever have been seriously argued by anyone familiar with constitutional law or the Anglo-Saxon principles of free institutions." A writer in the *Michigan Law Review* characterized the objections raised against the draft as "obviously flimsy if not wholly insincere," and added that "an examination of the names of the score or more contestants [in the cases that reached the Supreme Court, and in a few additional ones in the lower courts] would cause one to suspect that in some cases at least their obstructing efforts were part of that treacherous hostile propaganda with which we now know our country has been menacingly infiltrated, both before and since the beginning of the war."[293]

In *Cox* v. *Wood*,[294] four months later, the Court dismissed out of hand the further claim that while the United States might have power to conscript men for the defense of the homeland, it could not constitutionally send them into an overseas war. Counsel for the draftee in *Cox* v. *Wood* was Hannis Taylor, of Washington, D.C., a lawyer of some distinction with pretensions to scholarship,[295] author of books on international law, on the American and English constitutions, and on

---

[293] *New York Times,* Jan. 9, 1917, p. 12, col. 3; *Chicago Tribune,* Jan. 9, 1917, p. 6, col. 2; *The Nation,* 106: 52, Jan. 17, 1918; *The Outlook,* 118: 81, Jan. 16, 1918; H. M. Bates, "The National Army Act and the Administration of the Draft," *Mich. L. Rev.,* 16:376, 377, 379, 1918.

[294] 247 U.S. 3 (1918).

[295] Of which Holmes did not think much. "I don't believe he has anything whatever to say," Holmes wrote to Sir Frederick Pollock after dutifully reading one of Taylor's books, "except to repeat what is well known. But he swaggers and poses, and if he loses a case before us, I believe that he writes articles pitching into the Court, or has been known to. . . . He is a pushing man." M. DeW. Howe, ed., *Holmes-Pollock Letters* (1946), I, 143–44; see also *Holmes-Laski Letters,* I, 46–47.

the jurisdiction and procedures of the Supreme Court, and United States Minister to Spain in the second Cleveland Administration. For some years, Taylor had made frequent appearances before the Supreme Court. In his brief, he permitted himself to remark that the Selective Service Act and other war measures (including price-control legislation, presently to be discussed) had put the country under "autocratic Executive control" more far-reaching than any "assumed by the monarchy in France, even in the darkest days that preceded the French Revolution." Conditions were "alarming . . . unprecedented in English and American constitutional history"; there was an "existing Dictatorship." Solicitor General Davis, in the government's brief, suggested that these passages, being "a gross attack before this court upon the coordinate legislative and executive branches of the Government," were "impertinent and scandalous" and should be stricken from the records of the Court.

"Considering the passages referred to and making every allowance for intensity of zeal and an extreme of earnestness on the part of counsel, we are nevertheless constrained to the conclusion," Chief Justice White was constrained to conclude, "that the passages justify the terms of censure by which they are characterized in the suggestion made by the Government. But despite this conclusion, which we regretfully reach, we see no useful purpose to be subserved by granting the motion to strike. On the contrary, we think the passages on their face are so obviously intemperate and so patently unwarranted that if, as a result of permitting the passages to remain on the files, they should come under future observation, they would but serve to indicate to what intemperance of statement an absence of self-restraint or forgetfulness of decorum will lead, and would therefore admonish of the duty to be sedulous to obey and respect the limitations which an adhesion to them must exact."[296]

"Here is wisdom which many lesser folk would do well to emulate," said *The Nation* of Chief Justice White's ponderous treatment of Mr. Taylor's transgression. "Yet for such statements men have been sent to prison for long terms, when at most they should be rebuked or sent to a psychopathic hospital for observation. But the passion for heresy

---

[296] Cox v. Wood, 247 U.S. 3, 6–7 (1918); *Brief and Argument for Appellant,* No. 833, O.T. 1917, at 53–55, and *Brief for Appellee,* No. 833, O.T. 1917, at 3–4, Cox v. Wood, 247 U.S. 3, 6–7 (1918).

Holmes thought that Taylor had made "a pompous row." *Holmes-Pollock Letters,* I, 267. "Reading some

of his [Taylor's] anarchist manifestos in [*Cox v. Wood*]," Holmes wrote Harold J. Laski, "I relieved my mind to my neighbor Vandevanter [*sic!*] by whispering 'I do despise a martyr. He is a pigheaded adherent of an inadequate idea'—and then I felt better." *Holmes-Laski Letters,* I, 119.

hunting still lives."[297] No mere rebuke or psychopathic hospital (the latter itself a hysterical notion) awaited defendants in the first of the wartime sedition cases, also arising under the Selective Service Act, which were argued at the same time as the cases dealing with the constitutionality of the draft, and were decided one week later.[298]

After the constitutional challenges had failed, enforcement of the draft as such, aside from the provisions punishing seditious speech, produced no great volume of litigation.[299] The Court upheld the constitutionality of a section of the Selective Service Act forbidding maintenance of houses of prostitution within five miles of military posts.[300] Another section of the Act guarding the morals of servicemen, this time by forbidding the sale of liquor to them, led to some litigation in the lower federal courts, but not to any adjudication in the Supreme Court, which several times denied certiorari.[301] Nor did the exercise of court-martial jurisdiction in a vastly expanded army give rise to much business.[302]

In *Caldwell* v. *Parker*,[303] the Court upheld the jurisdiction of a state court to try a soldier stationed in an army camp in wartime for the murder of a civilian outside the camp. There had been no demand by military authorities to surrender the accused soldier to them, but the argument was made, and seconded in behalf of the United States by the Solicitor General in an *amicus* brief, that under the Articles of War as reenacted in 1916, military authorities had exclusive jurisdiction, whether or not they insisted upon it, and state courts had none. It was unnecessary to decide, Chief Justice White said for the Court, whether exclusive military jurisdiction could constitutionally exist in such a

---

[297] *The Nation,* 106:697, June 15, 1918.

[298] Goldman v. United States, 245 U.S. 474 (1918); Kramer v. United States, 245 U.S. 478 (1918); Ruthenberg v. United States, 245 U.S. 480 (1918).

[299] See O'Connell v. United States, 253 U.S. 142 (1920); In the Matter of Kitzerow, 252 Fed. 865 (E.D. Wisc. 1918), *motion for leave to file petition of mandamus denied,* 247 U.S. 505 (1918); Brown v. United States, 257 Fed. 703 (9th Cir. 1919), *cert. denied,* 251 U.S. 554 (1919).

[300] McKinley v. United States, 249 U.S. 397 (1919); see also Pollard v. United States, 261 Fed. 336 (5th Cir.

1919), *cert. denied,* 252 U.S. 577 (1920); Nakano v. United States, 262 Fed. 761 (9th Cir. 1920), *cert. denied,* 254 U.S. 632 (1920).

[301] O'Sullivan v. United States, 249 Fed. 935 (6th Cir. 1918), *cert. denied,* 247 U.S. 514 (1918); Fetters v. United States, 260 Fed. 142 (9th Cir. 1919), *cert. denied,* 251 U.S. 554 (1919); Laughter v. United States, 261 Fed. 68 (5th Cir. 1919), *cert. denied,* 251 U.S. 561 (1920).

[302] See Kahn v. Anderson, 255 U.S. 1 (1921); Givens v. Zerbst, 255 U.S. 11 (1921); Mikell v. Hines, 259 Fed. 28 (4th Cir. 1919), *cert. denied,* 250 U.S. 645 (1919).

[303] 252 U.S. 376 (1920).

case.[304] The Chief Justice merely held that, given the American tradition of general preference for civil jurisdiction, the Articles of War should, in the circumstances, be construed to permit its exercise, there being no express Congressional command to the contrary.

Beginning in the period of American neutrality and after, a variety of cases turning on the war power and the executive foreign relations power, as conceived both in municipal and international law, claimed the attention of the Court. There were questions of the rights and duties of a neutral, and the effect of American neutrality laws;[305] issues of the immunity of public vessels from suit—domestic ones requisitioned by the United States, and foreign ones;[306] ordinary admiralty litigation, now affected by the conditions of war;[307] and cases concerning the property of alien enemies, embargoes, and application of the Trading with the Enemy Act.[308]

The most notable of the Court's decisions dealing with the laws of war, or the silence of laws in war, arose not out of the European conflict, but out of the decade's strife in Mexico. *Oetjen* v. *Central Leather Co.*[309] was a suit begun in the state courts of New Jersey to recover possession of hides confiscated from their owner in Mexico by General Francisco Villa (otherwise known as Pancho) in January 1914, when Villa was in the service of General Carranza. The latter was conducting a revolution against the provisional government of General Huerta, who had himself assumed office after the assassination of President Madero. Villa confiscated the hides in the course of military operations.

For a unanimous Court, Clarke affirmed a dismissal of the suit. Since the trial of the case, the United States had recognized Carranza as the *de facto* government of Mexico, and in August 1917, as the *de jure* government. The conduct of foreign relations, said Clarke, and particularly the function of recognizing foreign governments, belonged ex-

---

[304] *Cf.* O'Callahan v. Parker, 395 U.S. 258 (1969).

[305] The Steamship Appam, 243 U.S. 124 (1917); Horn v. Mitchell, 243 U.S. 247 (1917); Gayon v. McCarthy, 252 U.S. 171 (1920).

[306] The Lake Monroe, 250 U.S. 246 (1919); *Ex parte* Muir, 254 U.S. 522 (1921); The Pesaro, 255 U.S. 216 (1921); The Carlo Poma, 255 U.S. 219 (1921); *Ex parte* Hussein Lutfi Bey, 256 U.S. 616 (1921).

[307] The Kronprinzessin Cecilie, 244 U.S. 12 (1917); Watts, Watts, and Co. v. Unione Austriaca, 248 U.S. 9 (1918); Allanwilde Corp. v. Vacuum Oil Co., 248 U.S. 377 (1919); International Paper Co. v. The Gracie D. Chambers, 248 U.S. 387 (1919); Standard Varnish Works v. The Bris, 248 U.S. 392 (1919).

[308] United States v. Chavez, 228 U.S. 525 (1913); United States v. Mesa, 228 U.S. 533 (1913); Birge-Forbes Co. v. Heye, 251 U.S. 317 (1920); Central Trust Co. v. Garvan, 254 U.S. 554 (1921); Stoehr v. Wallace, 255 U.S. 239 (1921).

[309] 246 U.S. 297 (1918).

clusively to the political branches of government, and the legitimacy of a foreign government recognized by the United States was not subject to judicial review. Recognition of a foreign government was, moreover, retroactive, and validated in the eyes of the United States that government's previous actions. The seizure of the hides was, therefore, an action by the legitimate government of Mexico, and under international law was not to be questioned in the courts of another country. In a companion case, Clarke added that the rule that some questions were political and not justiciable "does not deprive the courts of jurisdiction once acquired over a case. It requires only that, when it is made to appear that the foreign government has acted in a given way on the subject-matter of the litigation, the details of such action or the merit of the results cannot be questioned but must be accepted by our courts as a rule for their decision. To accept a ruling authority and to decide accordingly is not a surrender or abandonment of jurisdiction but is an exercise of it."[310]

Price Controls

The one war measure that ran afoul of the Supreme Court—although not in such a way as to put the war power or any portion of it basically in doubt—was the Lever Act of 1917.[311] This statute vested a great deal of authority in the President over those portions of the economy—and extensive they were—which were seen as relating to the war effort. Subject to the eventual payment of just compensation, the President was empowered to requisition foods, feeds, fuels, and all manner of war supplies together with storage facilities.[312] But the chief concern of the statute was with food (it was known also as the Food Control Act), and to implement it, President Wilson created a Food Administration, under Herbert Hoover.

In addition to various provisions aimed at maintaining an adequate food supply, the Act contained this section:

> That it is hereby made unlawful for any person willfully . . . to make any unjust or unreasonable rate or charge in handling or dealing in or with any necessaries; to conspire, combine, agree, or arrange with any other person . . . to exact excessive prices for any necessaries. . . . Any person violating any of the provisions of this Section upon conviction thereof shall be fined not exceeding $5,000 or be imprisoned for not more than two years, or both. . . .

[310] Ricaud v. American Metal Co., 246 U.S. 304, 309 (1918). But cf. MacLeod v. United States, 229 U.S. 416 (1913).

[311] 40 Stat. 276 (1917), as amended, 41 Stat. 297 (1919).

[312] See United States v. Pfitsch, 256 U.S. 547 (1921).

In a group of cases argued and decided well after the Armistice, but before the state of war had officially ended, and while the Lever Act was still in effect, this provision was held invalid.

In the main case, *United States* v. *Cohen Grocery*,[313] the Cohen Grocery Company was charged with violating the Act by "wilfully and feloniously making an unjust and unreasonable rate or charge in handling and dealing in a certain necessary." The specifications were that the company had sold in St. Louis, Missouri, fifty pounds of sugar for $10.07, and a hundred-pound bag for $19.50. Affirming the trial court, the Supreme Court, Chief Justice White writing, quashed the indictment.

The question, said the Chief Justice, was whether the language quoted above "constituted a fixing by Congress of an ascertainable standard of guilt . . . adequate to inform persons accused of violation thereof of the nature and cause of the accusation against them." That the statutory language did not discharge this constitutionally essential office (under the Fifth and Sixth amendments) was so clear from its "mere statement as to render elaboration on the subject wholly unnecessary." Although quite often when convinced that to state a question was to answer it, White took himself at his own word and stopped right there, he did in this instance offer some elaboration. The statute left open, he said, "the widest conceivable inquiry, the scope of which no one can foresee and the result of which no one can foreshadow or adequately guard against. In fact, we see no reason to doubt the soundness of the observation of the court below, in its opinion, to the effect that, to attempt to enforce the section would be the exact equivalent of an effort to carry out a statute which in terms merely penalized and punished all acts detrimental to the public interest when unjust and unreasonable in the estimation of the court and jury." In a footnote, White cited the varying standards that trial judges in other cases had attempted to read into the Act. Nor, he added, had administrative officers been more successful in their efforts to find a firm standard.

Pitney, whom Brandeis joined, concurred in the result only, on narrower grounds, although for related reasons. The statute, Pitney held, did not have to be construed so as to cover the Cohen Grocery Company's sales in St. Louis, or similar retail sales, and in order to avoid the constitutional issue reached by the Court, should not be so construed. Rather it should be read to punish the making of unjust or unreasonable rates, literally, "in handling or dealing in or with any

---

[313] 255 U.S. 81, 86, 89, 95 (1921); see also Tedrow v. Lewis and Son Co., 255 U.S. 98 (1921); Kennington v. Palmer, 255 U.S. 100 (1921); Kinnane v. Detroit Creamery Co., 255 U.S. 102 (1921); Weed and Co. v. Lockwood, 255 U.S. 104 (1921); Willard Co. v. Palmer, 255 U.S. 106 (1921); Oglesby Grocery Co. v. United States, 255 U.S. 108 (1921); Merritt v. United States, 255 U.S. 567 (1921).

necessaries," meaning, said Pitney, "the fixing of compensation for services, rather than the price at which goods are to be sold." So construed, the statute would deal with fees for hauling, handling, storage, or the like; and would otherwise punish only conspiracies "to exact excessive prices," thus applying to a sale of sugar or other necessaries only if the price at which the sale was made had been set by a conspiracy "to exact excessive prices." No conspiracy was charged to the Cohen Grocery Company.

In *Weeds, Inc.* v. *United States*,[314] a companion case decided on the same day, a conspiracy to exact "excessive prices" was charged, but White reversed a conviction on the ground that that phrase was no less vague than the phrase "unjust or unreasonable rate" used in the *Cohen Grocery* indictment. Pitney, again joined by Brandeis, now held that the excessive-price clause was not vague, because there was implicit in it a standard, namely, fair market value, in relation to which prices would be deemed excessive or not.[315] However, the trial court had rejected evidence offered by the defendants showing the market value of the goods they were charged with having sold at excessive prices. On Pitney's theory, such evidence was of course crucial, and its exclusion was an error. Therefore, he concurred in reversal of the conviction.

Chief Justice White's opinion persuaded most editorial writers that the price-control provisions of the Lever Act were indeed badly drawn and deserved to fall.[316] In the more progressive segment of public opinion, there were regrets that profiteers would now go unpunished, and some bitterness in recollecting how, despite assurances previously given that the Act had no application to labor disputes, it had been used to fight a strike. When the coal miners walked out late in 1919, Attorney General A. Mitchell Palmer obtained an injunction against them in the United States district court in Indiana on the ground that the strike violated the Lever Act, and Acting United Mine Workers President John L. Lewis said, "We cannot fight the government." His men did not agree, but the strike was soon settled just the same.[317] It was interesting to note, *The Nation* now remarked, that the Lever Act was used successfully in the courts against the coal strike, "and met defeat only when it

---

[314] 255 U.S. 109 (1921).

[315] *Cf.* Note, "Constitutionality of Lever Act under the Sixth Amendment," *Minn. L. Rev.*, 5:298, 1921; Comment, *Mich. L. Rev.*, 19:336, 337, 1921.

[316] See *The Literary Digest*, 68:17, Mar. 19, 1921; *New York Times*, Mar. 1, 1921, p. 1, col. 3; *Boston Evening Transcript*, Mar. 1, 1921, p.

12, col. 2; *Washington Post*, Mar. 2, 1921, p. 6, col. 2; *New York Herald*, Mar. 2, 1921, p. 8, col. 2; *The Nation*, 112:360, Mar. 9, 1921; *The New Republic*, 26:54, Mar. 16, 1921.

[317] See P. Taft, *Organized Labor in American History* (1964), 349–50; S. Gompers, "The Broken Pledge," *American Federationist*, 27:41–50, January, 1920.

attempted to deal with profiteers. . . . The Act achieved the unintended goal, but its unconstitutionality was discovered when it attempted the goal intended. Such a sequence of events, whether it be proper legal process or not, inevitably tends to discredit the courts and leads wide circles of our people to believe that the courts are used as tools of business interests."[318]

Other commentators, less concerned about the coal strike of over a year before, consoled themselves with the thought that despite the Act's failure "to prevent extortion, it may be held that its short existence has been of value to the public in deterring evildoers."[319] And indeed, without use of the provisions ultimately struck down in the *Cohen Grocery* case, but perhaps under their overhanging threat, Herbert Hoover's Food Administration achieved a good deal of price control by administrative means, chiefly by obtaining consent agreements from various trade associations.[320] So at this late date, the only damage the Supreme Court did was to cause many prosecutions to be dropped and indictments to be quashed, and perhaps a half a million dollars in fines that the government had collected in unappealed cases to be returned.[321] Moreover, as it turned out, where ill-advised defendants made little contest and pleaded *nolo contendere* rather than not guilty, the government was in the end not obliged to return fines.[322]

Litigation concerning wartime rent-control laws went off on no such side issue as proved decisive in *United States* v. *Cohen Grocery*, the Lever Act case. The Court met a fundamental constitutional challenge to rent control head on, and although closely divided, it sustained the power of government to act in war-caused emergency conditions.

By Act of October 22, 1919,[323] Congress provided that occupancy of rental premises in the District of Columbia under leases then in effect should continue at the option of the tenant at the rents then obtaining, subject to regulation by a commission. Provision was made to assure landlords of a reasonable return on their investments, and a landlord could regain possession for purposes of occupancy by himself or his

---

[318] *The Nation,* 112:360, Mar. 9, 1921; see also *The New Republic,* 26:54, Mar. 16, 1921.

[319] *The Outlook,* 127:410, Mar. 16, 1921; see also *Boston Evening Transcript,* Mar. 1, 1921, p. 12, col. 2; *Washington Post,* Mar. 2, 1921, p. 6, col. 2.

[320] See W. F. Gephart, Provisions of the Food Act and Activities Which Should Be Made Permanent," Supple-

ment, *American Economic Review,* 9:61, 63 *et seq.,* March 1919; L. C. Gray, "Price-Fixing Policies of the Food Administration," Supplement, *American Economic Review,* 9:252, March 1919.

[321] *The Literary Digest,* 68:17, Mar. 19, 1921.

[322] United States v. Gettinger, 272 U.S. 734 (1927).

[323] 41 Stat. 297 (1919).

family upon giving thirty days' notice in writing. One Hirsch, averring that he wished to occupy certain premises himself, sought to evict a tenant, Block, whose lease had expired, but who continued in occupancy pursuant to the statute. Claiming that the statute was unconstitutional *in toto*, Hirsch did not give the required thirty days' notice. His constitutional argument was upheld by the Court of Appeals for the District of Columbia, which held that Hirsch was entitled to occupancy, but Holmes, speaking for a majority of five including also Day, Pitney, Brandeis, and Clarke, reversed.[324]

Congress formally declared in the statute that rent control was made necessary by an emergency growing out of the war. A housing shortage in the District of Columbia was dangerous to the public health, and otherwise burdened the federal government in the conduct of its business in the national capital. The statute was enacted for a limited emergency period of two years only. The Congressional declaration, said Holmes, was entitled to respect, especially as it stated "a publicly notorious and almost world-wide fact." The question thus was "whether Congress was incompetent to meet [the emergency] in the way in which it has been met by most of the civilized countries of the world." In the circumstances, the business of renting buildings in the District of Columbia has been clothed "with a public interest so great as to justify regulation by law." And here, reaching back to the cluster of decisions of a few years earlier that had sustained state regulatory measures, Holmes cited *German Alliance Insurance Co.* v. *Lewis* and *Noble State Bank* v. *Haskell*.[325]

To be sure, tangible property was involved in this case, Holmes went on, but the fact that it "is also visible tends to give a rigidity to our conception of our rights in it that we do not attach to others less concretely clothed." Yet the doctrine of eminent domain as well as zoning regulations was sufficient indication that tangible property is not "exempt from the legislative modification required from time to time in civilized life." There was no good reason in general why, if the need arose, a legislature should be empowered to limit the height of buildings, but should be incompetent, in the presence of some other exigent need, to limit the rent that may be charged for them. "Housing is a necessary of life. All the elements of a public interest justifying some degree of public control are present. The only matter that seems to us open to debate is whether the statute goes too far." And that was a matter for judicial determination from time to time.

It was also a matter not really ripe for decision in this case, for

---

[324] The litigation was a private one, but the United States appeared as *amicus,* in support of the rent-control statute.

[325] See *supra,* pp. 276 *et seq.*

as Holmes was frank to remark, Hirsch had put in issue only the requirement of thirty days' notice. Moreover, Hirsch alleged, to be sure, that he wanted the premises for his own occupancy, but Block denied this, and had this issue of fact been tried, Block might have prevailed. But the narrowing of the field of vision in a case in this fashion was a practice that Holmes had little patience with. "The general question to which we have adverted must be decided," he said, "if not in this then in the next case, and it should be disposed of now." The statute guaranteed reasonable rents, and provided machinery for determining their reasonableness. To keep rents down to a level where they provided no more than a reasonable return went "little if at all farther than the restriction put upon the rights of the owner of money by the more debatable usury laws." It might be "unjust" to pursue high profits derived by landlords or others "from a national misfortune with sweeping denunciations," but the policy of restricting such profits was embodied in taxation, for example, and was readily accepted.[326]

The dissent, in which White, Van Devanter, and McReynolds joined, was by McKenna. It was a diatribe, a continuation of the debate, if that is the word, between Holmes and McKenna in The Pipe Line Cases, and it annoyed Holmes.[327] The grounds of dissent, said McKenna, were "the explicit provisions of the Constitution of the United States," and it was to wonder that argument was needed, so plain was their application. Whatever the excuse, and it did not matter that in this instance it was war, a violation of the Constitution was "an evil—an evil in the circumstance of violation, of greater evil because of its example and malign instruction." Housing was scarce, it was said, and therefore it could be taken from those who had it. "If such exercise of government be legal, what exercise of government is illegal? Houses are a necessary of life, but other things are as necessary. May they too be taken from the direction of their owners and disposed of by the Government?" There was intimation in the opinion that Congress in the rent-control statute had "imitated the laws of other countries." Had conditions then, here and in the rest of the world, come to the point that they were "not

---

[326] Brandeis exulted over Holmes' opinion: "Yes. This is in every way worthy. I do not recall when you have ever done better." Day also approved: "This is a long stride, but you have taken it with clearness and force, and I march with you." Holmes Papers.

[327] See *supra,* pp. 237 *et seq.,* 239. Holmes recognized that McKenna was "very much disturbed by the de-

cision." As to the other dissenters, "I doubt if the Chief was so much— but am not sure. Van Devanter in spots is a very stout conservative and I think McReynolds is generally for holding a pretty tight rein." But the dissent "criticized the opinion as such, which I think bad form." O. W. Holmes to F. Frankfurter, Apr. 20, 1921, Holmes Papers.

amenable to passing palliatives, so that socialism, or some form of socialism, is the only permanent corrective or accommodation? It is indeed strange that this court, in effect, is called upon to make way for it. . . ." "The wonder comes to us, What will the country do with its new freedom?" The decision just rendered could only cause "dread" and "take away assurance of security."[328]

In a companion case, *Marcus Brown Co.* v. *Feldman*, which presented the unusual spectacle of William D. Guthrie of the New York Bar, who had been retained by the state, arguing in favor of a measure of social and economic regulation, Holmes summarily upheld, on the authority of *Block* v. *Hirsch*, a New York statute similar to the District of Columbia rent-control law. McKenna added another page and a half of dissent, concluding harshly that in his view it was "safer, saner, and more consonant with constitutional preëminence and its purposes to regard the declaration of the Constitution as paramount, and not to weaken it by refined dialectics, or bend it to some impulse or emergency 'because of some accident of immediate overwhelming interest which appeals to the feeling, and distorts the judgment.'"[329] The phrase "refined dialectics" was aimed at Holmes and intended, presumably, to wound. The language concerning "some accident of immediate overwhelming interest" certainly was so aimed and intended; it was taken from Holmes' dissent in *Northern Securities Co.* v. *United States*.[330]

McKenna was not alone in his lament. Commenting on the New York statute involved in the *Marcus Brown* case, George W. Wickersham remarked that "the age of individualism is passed and the era of collectivism [has] arrived."[331] Even Edward S. Corwin found it "impossible not to sympathize a good deal with Justice McKenna in his dismay, though he has hardly defined the problem. . . . Indeed, we can do more, and protest against the too careless embodiment in our constitutional jurisprudence of the assumption that because government has the power to meet emergencies, anything which it may do to that end is necessarily constitutional."[332] In July 1921, the Maryland State Bar Association heard a full-scale assault, later published in the *Massachusetts Law Quarterly*, by a prominent practitioner upon the author of the opinions in *Block* v. *Hirsch* and *Marcus Brown Co.* v. *Feldman*. Skeptic and fatalist, Holmes was wedded to the idea, "in no sense juristic," that

[328] Block v. Hirsch, 256 U.S. 135, 154, 155, 156–57, 159, 160, 161, 162, 168, 169 (1921).

[329] Marcus Brown Co. v. Feldman, 256 U.S. 170, 200–201 (1921).

[330] 193 U.S. 197, 400 (1904).

[331] G. W. Wickersham, "The Police Power and the New York Emergency Rent Laws," *U. Pa. L. Rev.*, 69:301, 1921; but *cf.* J. H. Wigmore, "A Constitutional Way to Reach the Housing Profiteer," *Ill. L. Rev.*, 15:359, 1921.

[332] E. S. Corwin, "Constitutional Law in 1920–21," *American Political Science Review*, 16:22, 35, 1922.

constitutionality should turn on the imaginary conclusion of a hypothetical "reasonable man." Abjuring "the notion of a fixed constitution," Holmes, "the most notable non-conformist who has ever sat as a member of the Supreme Court of the United States," was hailed by a "company of young radicals," including "Mr. Harold Laski." Would the author of *Block* v. *Hirsch* make the same answer with respect to a fixed constitution as was made by La Place to Napoleon's inquiry concerning the part played by God in La Place's nebula theory: "Sire, I have managed without that hypothesis"?[333] The alarms were, of course, premature. Though Congress extended the Rent Control Act of 1919 beyond its original two-year limit, neither Holmes nor certainly a majority of his colleagues were willing to assume the existence of a permanent emergency, and the consequent permanent validity of rent control.[334]

Prohibition

In most respects, the war-swelled tide of government receded in the 1920s. The tide of Prohibition, which crested during the war, was an exception. It had been running in the states for some time. In 1913, the Webb-Kenyon Act had attempted to make state prohibition laws more effective by closing the channels of interstate commerce to liquor destined for a state where its sale or use was forbidden. It was widely expected that demands for a constitutional amendment decreeing national prohibition would now subside. Not the Webb-Kenyon Act, however, nor the Reed "Bone-Dry" Amendment which followed it, had any such effect. Within nine months after passage of the Webb-Kenyon Act, the Anti-Saloon League resolved to agitate for a national constitutional amendment.[335]

The war was a great help. It did, wrote Charles Merz, "three things for prohibition. It centralized authority in Washington; it stressed the importance of saving food; and it outlawed all things German [e.g., beer]."[336] In the Selective Service Act, Congress forbade the sale of liquor to servicemen. The Lever Act, aimed at conserving food, included a provision that prohibited the use, after September 9, 1917, of food materials in the production of distilled spirits for beverage purposes, and authorized the President to limit or forbid their use in the production of malt or vinous liquors.[337] From December 1917 through September 1918, President Wilson issued a series of proclamations restricting the

---

[333] See F. Johnston, "Some Modern Aspects of the Police Power," *Mass. L. Q.*, 8:50, 52, 57, 58, 59, 1923.

[334] See Chastleton Corp. v. Sinclair, 264 U.S. 543 (1924).

[335] See C. Merz, *The Dry Decade* (1932), 15.

[336] *Ibid.*, 25.

[345] See *supra*, p. 439.

production of all sorts of drinks, including near-beer. Beginning in January 1919, he relaxed some of the earlier proclamations so as to end up prohibiting only the manufacture of intoxicating beverages.[338]

But Congress was in no mood to relax. On November 21, 1918, ten days after the Armistice, it enacted the War-Time Prohibition Act.[339] For purposes, as it said, of conserving manpower and increasing efficiency in war production, this statute outlawed the sale of distilled spirits, or their removal from bond except for export, from June 30, 1919, until the war had come to an end and demobilization was complete. From May 1, 1919, until the end of demobilization, the War-Time Prohibition Act forbade the use of food products in the manufacture of beer, wine, or other intoxicating liquors. And from June 30, 1919, to the end of demobilization it also prohibited the sale of beer, wine, or other intoxicating malt or vinous liquors, except for export. The date on which the war was to be decreed ended and demobilization considered complete, within the intent of the War-Time Prohibition Act, was to be determined by Presidential proclamation.

There was, virtually from the day of enactment, controversy over the meaning of the word "intoxicating" in the Act. Almost a full year later, on October 28, 1919, well after the Eighteenth Amendment had been ratified and shortly before it entered into effect,[340] Congress in the Volstead Act (over a Presidential veto) provided that the War-Time Act's prohibition of intoxicating liquors applied to any beverage with a content of 0.5 percent or more of alcohol by volume.[341] Only at this time, and not before (laws and administrative orders had been following one upon the other at a pace to distract and overwhelm prospective litigants), did cases testing the War-Time Prohibition Act reach the Supreme Court.

On November 20 and 21, 1919, two months before the Eighteenth Amendment and the Volstead Act were to come into full force, three cases were argued in the Supreme Court. Two, decided under the title *Hamilton* v. *Kentucky Distilleries Co.*, were suits against Collectors of Internal Revenue, who administered the War-Time Prohibition Act, to enjoin them from interfering with the withdrawal, distribution, and

---

[338] See United States v. Standard Brewery, 251 U.S. 210, 215–16 (1920); Jacob Ruppert v. Caffey, 251 U.S. 264, 278–80 (1920).

[339] 40 Stat. 1045 (1918).

[340] Congress proposed the Eighteenth Amendment on Dec. 18, 1917. It was ratified on Jan. 16, 1919, becoming effective on Jan. 16, 1920—by

its own terms, one year after ratification. There was, thus, a period of one year during which the War-Time Prohibition Act, and not the Eighteenth Amendment, was the governing federal law.

[341] See Jacob Ruppert v. Caffey, 251 U.S. 280 (1920).

sale of whisky held in bond in warehouses. The third, *Jacob Ruppert* v. *Caffey*, challenged the provision of the Volstead Act of October 28, 1919, which supplemented the War-Time Prohibition Act so as to outlaw beer containing 0.5 percent or more of alcohol by volume. *Ruppert* v. *Caffey* was a suit to enjoin enforcement against the plaintiff brewer of the criminal penalties of the War-Time Act, as supplemented.

In a preface to a memorandum he circulated to his colleagues on the *Ruppert* case, Brandeis had occasion to explain just what was at stake in *Hamilton* v. *Kentucky Distilleries Co.* The controversy concerned bonded whisky in the physical possession of the government, which, acting under the War-Time Prohibition Act, refused to release it, except for export. The owners were attacking the Act in order to gain possession of their whisky. Should they succeed in time, they could move and market the whisky before January 16, 1920, when the Eighteenth Amendment would come into effect.[342] Large amounts were therefore in play,[343] and the Court was urged to, and did, act expeditiously so as not, in effect, to moot the case. The decision, Brandeis writing for a unanimous Court, came down on December 15, 1919, less than a month after the argument.

Speed and unanimity were achieved despite difficulties and divisions within the Court. At first, Brandeis reported to Felix Frankfurter a couple of years later, the decision at conference had gone 5 to 4 in favor of holding the War-Time Prohibition Act invalid. The Chief Justice was with Brandeis in the minority. Holmes was with the majority. "Then White met Holmes on the street," Brandeis recalled. "Holmes told him he had doubts about his vote and he was ready to have it written the other way and to see how it would go. White then came to see me and asked me to write it because he thought I could get Holmes more easily." Holmes, Brandeis went on, balked at the War-Time Prohibition Act on Due Process grounds—"the thing that prevailed with him in Mahon [*Pennsylvania Coal Co.* v. *Mahon*][344] later. I told him the Mugler case governed [*Mugler* v. *Kansas*, upholding, in 1887, the power of the states to forbid the manufacture and sale of liquor],[345] but he never has liked that case. Undoubtedly his impatience with Prohibition explains this. I then wrote and gradually they all came with me—McReynolds and Pitney and others kicked—I said 'let Pitney

---

[342] See Brandeis Papers, Harvard Law School Library, file for Jacob Ruppert v. Caffey, 251 U.S. 264, 278–80 (1920).

[343] To wit, as was reported in the press after *Hamilton* v. *Kentucky Distilleries* was decided, liquor

"valued in the neighborhood of a billion dollars." See *The Literary Digest*, 63:15, Dec. 27, 1919.

[344] 260 U.S. 393 (1922); see Bickel, *Unpublished Opinions of Brandeis*, 227–29.

[345] See *supra*, p. 439.

go over my opinion,' and Pitney worked hard for a few days and we agreed. It was then that I began to know Pitney closely."[346]

The Due Process argument against the War-Time Prohibition Act was that, while in the exercise of the war power Congress might temporarily regulate the sale of liquor in order to promote the efficiency of its servicemen and of workers engaged in arms production and the like, the prohibition of the War-Time Act amounted to an uncompensated taking of property. Brandeis held that there had been no taking. A period of seven months and nine days was provided by the Act from its passage to the time when its restrictions on sales became effective, and during that period the liquor in question could have been disposed of. Even afterward, sale for export was permitted. This was a regulation, therefore, not a taking, and a regulation, if anything, less severe than states had been allowed to impose (citing *Mugler* v. *Kansas*).

The Due Process point to the side, it was conceded that the Act was a valid exercise of the war power when passed, even though hostilities had even then ceased, because the war power reaches to the period of demobilization. The argument, however, was that by the time this suit was brought, demobilization was complete, and the emergency was over, since it was evident that hostilities were not about to be resumed. Hence the statute had ceased to be valid. Statements by the President that the war was over were cited by plaintiffs. Brandeis noted that in many respects Congress had treated the war as continuing, for example in supplementing the War-Time Prohibition Act on October 28, 1919, and in refusing to ratify the treaty of peace with Germany. The President also was still operating many wartime controls. Parts of the army were, moreover, being kept in occupied enemy territory and in Siberia. And the President had issued no such proclamation declaring the termination of demobilization as the War-Time Prohibition Act contemplated.

The motives of Congress, as also the wisdom of legislation, were not subject to judicial review. Congress, moreover, in the exercise of any of its powers, and particularly of the war power, must have a wide latitude of discretion. No doubt there might be circumstances in which the Court would say that the war power no longer supported a statute such as this, but "it would require a clear case to justify a court in declaring that such an act, passed for such a purpose, had ceased to have force because the power of Congress no longer continued." This was not that case. It was contended, finally, that during the year's period of grace provided by the Eighteenth Amendment, Congress was necessarily foreclosed from enforcing other Prohibition legislation, else

---

[346] Brandeis-Frankfurter Conversations.

the intended period of grace would be illusory. Brandeis found the contention quite unsound, as it reached, he thought, too far, abrogating by implication not only exercises of the federal war power, but also exercises of the police power of the states, to which, after all, the Eighteenth Amendment also applied.[347]

Ruppert v. *Caffey*, having been argued at the same time as *Hamilton* v. *Kentucky Distilleries Co.*, was undoubtedly considered at the same conference, and initially decided against the government, as Brandeis reported the *Kentucky Distilleries* case was. The mission Chief Justice White gave Brandeis, to construct a majority the other way, covered *Ruppert* v. *Caffey* as well. On its merits, *Ruppert* was the more difficult case in which to sustain Brandeis' position. Brandeis' task of persuasion was more arduous, and he took longer to prepare a very elaborate opinion. In the meantime, just before *Hamilton* v. *Kentucky Distilleries Co.* came down, two more cases testing the War-Time Prohibition Act were argued.[348] Indictments had been brought under the original War-Time Prohibition Act, before it was supplemented by the Volstead Act, for manufacturing beer with a content of as much as 0.5 percent of alcohol. The district courts had dismissed the indictments on demurrer. The Supreme Court unanimously affirmed dismissal of the indictments, and Day was assigned to write a single opinion, to be entitled *United States* v. *Standard Brewery*.

The original War-Time Prohibition Act, as we have seen, forbade production of "beer, wine, or other intoxicating" beverages, and did not mention alcoholic content. Plainly, Day held, the operative word was "intoxicating." It was the government's theory that beer containing 0.5 percent of alcohol by volume was intoxicating, but the Court could not so hold as a matter of law, and indeed the indictments in these cases did not so charge—they charged only the alcoholic content of the beer, not its intoxicating quality. *Hamilton* v. *Kentucky Distilleries Co.*, which had come down by the time the *Standard Brewery* case was announced, had decided that Congress could under the war power prohibit the sale of intoxicating liquor. "But the question was neither made nor decided as to whether Congress could prohibit even in time of war the manufacture and sale of non-intoxicating beverages." This constitutional question, which would have to be settled in order to sustain the indictments,

---

[347] Hamilton v. Kentucky Distilleries Co., 251 U.S. 146 (1919).

[348] The Kentucky Distilleries Company was represented by distinguished Midwestern counsel, Levy Mayer and William Marshall Bullitt. The cases just mentioned and the *Ruppert* case brought in, among others, stellar Eastern counsel, Elihu Root and William D. Guthrie. The two groups were later to join in attacking the validity of the Eighteenth Amendment itself.

ought surely to be avoided. A natural construction of the statute made such avoidance possible.[349]

Day delivered the opinion in *Standard Brewery* on January 5, 1920. There was pressure on Brandeis to be ready with *Ruppert* v. *Caffey* on the same date. Just before Christmas 1919, Brandeis circulated a draft of an opinion in the *Ruppert* case, titled "Memorandum by Mr. Justice Brandeis," and in a prefatory note said: "I am wholly unable to understand why it is deemed important that this case be decided on January 5, 1920." There appeared to be a belief that a decision favorable to the plaintiff could be of financial value to brewers, but only if rendered very promptly, so that beer with a higher alcoholic content than 0.5 percent—in fact, in this case, just under 2.75 percent by weight and 3.4 percent by volume—could be marketed before January 16, 1920, when the Eighteenth Amendment took effect. But this belief rested on a misapprehension.

The situation of the brewers was quite different from that of the owners of whisky in *Hamilton* v. *Kentucky Distilleries Co.*, and certainly different now that that case had been decided so as to uphold the War-Time Prohibition Act. Beer was not held in bond under the control of the government. Brewers were entirely free to dispose of their stocks, subject only to the risk of prosecution. If the War-Time Act had been struck down in the *Kentucky Distilleries* case, brewers, like distillers, could have sold their product until January 16, 1920, without later being held liable for having done so. But the actual decision did not remove the risk of prosecution. Nor would *Standard Brewery*. The question in the *Ruppert* case was the validity of the Volstead Act supplementing the War-Time Prohibition Act so as to proscribe beer with a content of 0.5 percent alcohol, whether or not held to be intoxicating. *Ruppert* was a suit to enjoin prosecution. Even if Ruppert won, and the Supreme Court reversed the dismissal by the court below of the prayer for an injunction, and held the Volstead Act invalid, the case would have to go back, under the original War-Time Act, for trial on the issue whether beer such as Ruppert's was in fact intoxicating; and even if the Supreme Court handed down its decision by January 5, there was no chance that the trial of this issue could be concluded before January 16, 1920, so as to give Ruppert any opportunity to market his beer. As of that date, under other provisions of the Volstead Act implementing the Eighteenth Amendment, beer with a content of 0.5 percent of alcohol would be illegal. So no amount of expedition could help the brewers at all. The only real question in the case, which gave it the nature of a controversy (although Brandeis did not bother to go on to

---

[349] United States v. Standard Brewery, 251 U.S. 210, 220 (1920).

this point), was whether the brewers could be prosecuted for past sales.[350]

Brandeis apparently did not succeed in abating the pressure for speed. The opinion in *Ruppert* v. *Caffey* came down on January 5, on the same day as the *Standard Brewery* case. Brandeis held the 0.5 percent provision added by the Volstead Act to the War-Time law valid. The legislation and decisions of the highest courts of nearly all the states established, he said, "that it is deemed impossible to effectively enforce either prohibitory laws or other laws merely regulating the manufacture and sale of intoxicating liquors, if liability or inclusion within the law is made to depend upon the issuable fact whether or not a particular liquor made or sold as a beverage is intoxicating. In other words, it clearly appears that a liquor law, to be capable of effective enforcement must, in the opinion of the legislatures and courts of the several States, be made to apply either to all liquors of the species enumerated, like beer, ale or wine, regardless of the presence or degree of alcoholic content; or if a more general description is used, such as distilled, rectified, spirituous, fermented, malt or brewed liquors, to all liquors within that general description regardless of alcoholic content; or to such of these liquors as contain a named percentage of alcohol; and often several such standards are combined. . . ." The named percentage was very often 0.5 percent.

These propositions concerning state laws and practices, elaborated in somewhat greater descriptive detail in the text, were supported by nine long footnotes, covering most of fifteen pages, which classified and listed relevant state statutes and decisions.[351] "The decisions of the

---

[350] See Brandeis-Frankfurter Conversations.

[351] This massive Brandeis brief within the opinion was the work of Brandeis' law clerk, Dean Acheson. "The idea of footnotes," Mr. Acheson has recollected, "was the Justice's, but the compilation of them was mine. They established a world's record in footnotes to that time and constituted 57 percentum of the opinion by volume. They were a noble work, worthy of a better cause." Mr. Acheson recalls also that at one stage the vast collection of cases contained two that had crept in by mistake. The error did not escape the Justice, who called it to his law clerk's attention. When Acheson "expressed chagrin and regret," however,

Brandeis "dismissed the matter with a sentence—'Please remember that your function is to correct my errors, not to introduce errors of your own.' " Mr. Acheson adds: "I remembered."

As Mr. Acheson tells the story, the opinion was ready for delivery on a Monday. While other Justices were reading other opinions, Mr. Acheson noticed that a page kept bringing volumes of reports to Brandeis, which "seemed strange and vaguely ominous." Then when the Chief Justice nodded to Brandeis to start delivering his opinion, Brandeis shook him off, and later, in chambers at home, pointed out to Acheson the erroneous inclusion of the two inapposite cases. This embellishment on the story is too good not to be true. Yet most

courts as well as the action of the legislatures make it clear—or, at least, furnish ground upon which Congress reasonably might conclude—" said Brandeis, driving the point home, "that a rigid classification of beverages is an essential of either effective regulation or effective prohibition of intoxicating liquors."

That such a rigid classification and prohibition of beverages, whether or not in fact intoxicating, may constitutionally be imposed by the states, Brandeis continued, had been decided some years earlier, in a thorough and well-considered opinion (written, incidentally, by Hughes).[352] It was maintained that Congress could not go this far because it was exercising not an express, but an implied power, and further powers may not be implied from powers themselves implied. The argument, said Brandeis, was "a mere matter of words." Finally it was contended that the manufacture and sale of beverages with 0.5 percent alcoholic content could not constitutionally be prohibited if no period of grace was granted in which to dispose of existing stocks. There was hardship no doubt, said Brandeis, and hardship also in that facilities of production, whether with or without a period of grace, would become useless, but that the hardship was not unconstitutional followed necessarily "from the principle acted upon in *Mugler* v. *Kansas. . . .*"[353]

As Brandeis later told Frankfurter, Pitney was commissioned to go over his opinion with a fine-tooth comb. Pitney returned a draft saying that he had "suggested numerous changes . . . but none, I think, that impairs in the least the substance of your very able argument." Indeed, the only substantive suggestion concerned a concluding passage in which Brandeis argued, by way of makeweight, that since Ruppert's beer was almost certainly in fact intoxicating, given its relatively high alcoholic content, Ruppert should not be granted standing to raise the issue whether beer of a much smaller alcoholic content may be prohibited even though not intoxicating. He was claiming another's constitutional rights. Pitney thought this additional point might be omitted, and it was. He also conveyed McKenna's view that the nine footnotes detailing state statutes and decisions were a kind of objectionable particularization. "I do not share in this objection," said Pitney, "but do not oppose your acceding to it." It was an objection in which Holmes would have joined on general principles,[354] but McKenna, who,

---

probably the error was discovered in less dramatic circumstances, for given the Christmas recess, the only possible other opinion day before Jan. 5, 1920, when *Ruppert* v. *Caffey* was in fact handed down, was Dec. 22, 1919, and Brandeis did not have the opinion in *Ruppert* v. *Caffey* ready by then,

nor was there pressure on him to deliver it that early. See D. Acheson, *Morning and Noon* (1965), 79–80.

[352] See *supra*, p. 281, n.264.

[353] Jacob Ruppert v. Caffey, 251 U.S. 264, 282–84, 288–89, 299, 301 (1920).

[354] See *Holmes-Laski Letters*, I, 128.

as Brandeis noted on the face of this draft, concurred in Pitney's suggestions, withdrew his objection to the footnotes.

Elsewhere on the draft, Pitney made some highly complimentary remarks. He thought Brandeis' answer that the argument concerning the difference between implied and express powers was a mere matter of words hit the bull's-eye. And he marked the passages immediately following: "Good!" Holmes returned, "Yes," but added: "Incidentally, I think *Mugler* v. *Kansas* a mighty fishy decision." But he was merely whispering in Brandeis' ear, he said, not suggesting any changes. "You have done nobly and I felicitate you on getting away with it." Not a hearty or entirely convinced concurrence, but assent just the same.[355]

Holmes, McKenna, and Pitney were thus in again, as they had come in also in *Hamilton* v. *Kentucky Distilleries Co.*, but this time there were Justices who had not been rounded up. And Holmes with his razor-thin assent was the swing-man. For the decision went by the narrowest margin. Clarke dissented alone without opinion. McReynolds, joined by Day and Van Devanter, dissented with opinion. If a power to prohibit the sale of nonintoxicating beer could arise from what was itself the implied power established in the *Kentucky Distilleries* case, asked McReynolds, "why may not the second implied power engender a third under which Congress may forbid the planting of barley or hops, the manufacture of bottles or kegs, etc., etc.?" *Ex parte Milligan*,[356] the famous Civil War habeas corpus case, exemplified the kind of protection that the Court was duty-bound to extend in wartime to rights guaranteed by the Constitution. "The doctrines then clearly—I may add, courageously—announced, conflict with the novel and hurtful theory now promulgated." After quoting at some length from *Ex parte Milligan*, McReynolds noted that the entire edifice erected in Brandeis' opinion rested on the assumption of a Congressional power to deal with a wartime emergency. "Can it be truthfully said," he asked, "in view of the well-known facts existing on October 28, 1919, that general prohibition immediately after that day of the sale of non-intoxicating beer theretofore lawfully manufactured, could afford any direct and appreciable aid in respect of the war declared against Germany and Austria?"[357]

Reaction in the press to *Hamilton* v. *Kentucky Distilleries* and *Ruppert* v. *Caffey* showed the extent to which the Prohibition experiment had gained public acceptance. There would be relief, said *The* unanimous decision of the highest court." The opinion was strong and *Outlook*, that Prohibition would be maintained without a lapse between

---

[355] See Brandeis Papers, Harvard Law School Library; see also *Holmes-Laski Letters*, I, 473.

[356] 4 Wall. 2 (1866).
[357] Jacob Ruppert v. Caffey, 251 U.S. 264, 306, 309 (1920).

the wartime statutes and the coming into effect of the Eighteenth Amendment. The *New York Times*, previously no supporter of Prohibition, remarked how fortunate and salutary it was that *Hamilton* v. *Kentucky Distilleries* had been decided unanimously. Bitter as was the disappointment of the Wets, they could not "murmur against the clear, and even those who had been opposed to Prohibition "will be glad that a wild Bacchic explosion, a New Year's Eve of wastrels, is not to be." Only the *Chicago Tribune* expressed a serious, if qualified, doubt. The reasoning of *Hamilton* v. *Kentucky Distilleries* was that the country was still at war, which plainly the country was not. "Inherently it is wrong and harmful to base laws upon reasons which do not exist. . . . Inherently it is wrong to have a prohibition law based on the assumption that grains and men and money must be conserved to fight a war when the war is not being fought."[358]

Ruppert v. *Caffey* was greeted as finally disposing of all significant issues that might still have been in doubt, not only about wartime prohibition, but also about the Eighteenth Amendment. The brewers had entertained hopes that near-beer might still be allowed, and these had now been finally dashed. But counsel for the brewers pointed out that neither the validity of the Eighteenth Amendment itself, nor of various provisions of the Volstead Act under the Amendment, had yet been adjudicated, and even Wayne B. Wheeler, counsel for the Anti-Saloon League, agreed that the question, and only that question, whether the Eighteenth Amendment had been properly adopted remained open.[359] The Department of Justice announced that the government intended to pursue a vigorous program of prosecuting violators of the War-Time Prohibition Act.[360]

The brewers who held out the prospect of further litigation were not bluffing. A case embodying the first attempt to put the validity of the Eighteenth Amendment in issue was argued in the Supreme Court on January 5, 1920, the day the decision in *Ruppert* v. *Caffey* came down. This attempt was met by a jurisdictional objection, and failed within the week.[361] But issue was joined no more than two months later in the *National Prohibition Cases*.

The Eighteenth Amendment provided as follows:

---

[358] *The Outlook,* 123:527, Dec. 24, 1919; *New York Times,* Dec. 16, 1919, p. 12, col. 1; *Chicago Tribune,* Dec. 17, 1919, p. 8, col. 1.

[359] See *The Outlook,* 124:54, Jan. 14, 1920; *New York Times,* Jan. 6, 1920, p. 1, col. 1, p. 3, col. 3.

[360] See *New York Times,* Jan. 6, 1920, p. 1, col. 1; see, e.g., Vincenti v. United States, 272 Fed. 114 (4th Cir. 1921), *cert. denied,* 256 U.S. 700, 257 U.S. 634 (1921); see also Goldsmith-Grant Co. v. United States, 254 U.S. 505; but *cf.* United States v. Yuginovich, 256 U.S. 450 (1921).

[361] Duhne v. New Jersey, 251 U.S. 311 (1920).

V: *The Fate of Social Legislation, 1914–21: Federal*

Section 1. After one year from the ratification of this article the manufacture, sale, or transportation of intoxicating liquors within, the importation thereof into, or the exportation thereof from the United States and all territory subject to the jurisdiction thereof for beverage purposes is hereby prohibited.

Section 2. The Congress and the several States shall have concurrent power to enforce this article by appropriate legislation.

Counsel for the brewers and distillers who attacked the Eighteenth Amendment in the *National Prohibition Cases*—Elihu Root and William D. Guthrie, among others—relied chiefly on two contentions. One, the more fundamental and far-reaching, was that even aside from its guarantee to each state of an equal vote in the Senate, Article V of the Constitution did not create an unlimited amending power, and that the Eighteenth Amendment passed the limits implicit in Article V. The other contention turned on Section 2, and its novel provision for concurrent enforcement by the federal government and the states.

Unlike other constitutional provisions and amendments, the Eighteenth Amendment did not relate to the powers or organization of government, said Root. On the contrary, it was "itself an exercise of the legislative power of government, and a direct act of legislation regulating the conduct of life of the individual." The question was whether Article V of the Constitution authorized an amendment "which in substance and effect is merely a police regulation or statute." The genius of the American government was that majorities could both enact police regulations and repeal them at will. When such a regulation was put in the form of a constitutional amendment, a minority, and in our system a very tiny minority at that, was granted a veto over any repealer. Had the Eighteenth Amendment merely conferred power on Congress to deal with the manufacture and sale of liquor, the rule of legislative majorities would have been preserved; but it was not under the Amendment as written.

At first blush, it might seem that the Eighteenth Amendment did nothing different from what was done by the Thirteenth. But that was not so. The Thirteenth Amendment was not directly a police regulation; it dealt rather, in true constitutional fashion, with questions of power. The existence of slavery represented an exercise of governmental power, and this power the Thirteenth Amendment withdrew. Article V of the Constitution could not be construed to permit amendments dealing with "mere sumptuary laws which are not constitutional amendments in truth or essence." If no limitations were to be deemed implicit in Article V, then the Congress and three-fourths of the state legislatures could by amendment "establish a state religion, or oppress or discriminate against any denomination, or authorize the taking away of life, liberty and property, without due process of law, etc., etc. This would destroy the most essential limitation upon power under the American system of government. . . ."

Moreover, Article V should not be read to authorize destruction of the federal system, which was at the heart of the American constitutional scheme. Yet the Eighteenth Amendment, by "*directly*" invading the police powers of the states, began their destruction. "The Civil War amendments afford no justification for the Eighteenth Amendment. Their primary purpose was to crystalize into the Constitution some of the essentials of a free Republican government, and it was expressly made the constitutional duty of the Federal Government to guarantee to the States such a form of government. This federal duty the Civil War amendments helped to realize; and the fact that, as an incident and indirectly, they interfered to some extent with the States is of no consequence. They are not like the Eighteenth Amendment, which is germane to no original federal duty, and which directly, primarily and deliberately invades the right of the States to govern themselves."[362]

Guthrie's argument was that under Section 2 of the Eighteenth

---

[362] Brandeis' clerk this year, as we have noted, was Dean Acheson. Mr. Acheson has recalled:

The Chief Justice would often be brought and left at Stoneleigh Court [Brandeis' residence] by his chauffeur to talk with Justice Brandeis. It fell to me to walk him home the two blocks to Rhode Island Avenue, for his eyesight was too bad to permit crossing streets alone. His talk, easy to start, made these walks a delight. One day we were walking home along Connecticut Avenue, soon after Mr. Elihu Root's argument in the *National Prohibition Cases.* . . .

Whatever their differences . . . no member of the Court was persuaded by Mr. Root. I hoped to draw out the Chief Justice on one aspect of his argument. Mr. Root drew a long bow, nothing less than that the Eighteenth Amendment to the Constitution was itself unconstitutional. His argument employed the "entering wedge" or "slippery slope" technique. . . . I reminded the Chief Justice that, when he had

pressed Mr. Root on the similarity of prohibiting slavery and prohibiting liquor, Mr. Root thought that the pressure of war had, perhaps, distorted the symmetry and logic of our governmental system. The Chief Justice had inquired whether the pressure of war was not as valid a factor as symmetry or logic? After recalling this exchange, I mused that the Chief Justice's position had been a most "interesting" one.

The old gentleman came to a full and palpitating stop. "Young man," he bellowed, his jowls quivering, "I know what you're thinking." So did I, and feared that I had imposed too far on his good nature by hinting that the old Confederate soldier had come a long way. But his quivering ended in a chuckle. "Remember this," he added. "You'll be lucky when you're my age if you've only been a damned fool once." I am not so far as I should like from that age now, and already not that lucky. Acheson, *Morning and Noon*, 60–61.

Amendment, each state was authorized to enforce prohibition within its own borders, while Congress was empowered to do so in interstate and foreign commerce, and in the District of Columbia and territories and possessions. But if Congress enacted a regulation with intrastate as well as interstate effect, or if a state law concerned interstate as well as intrastate commerce, then the concurrence of the states in the Congressional legislation, or of Congress in the state statute, was necessary to make either effective. The Volstead Act thus required the concurrence of the states. Section 2 was "unique and unprecedented" and must have been intended, if it was to have any meaning at all, to suspend the normal operation of the Supremacy Clause of Article VI of the Constitution, under which valid Congressional legislation was supreme over state law.

This construction of Section 2 was worked out by Guthrie and Root in cooperation with George Sutherland, the former Senator, now in private practice and soon to be appointed to the Court. In March 1920, Guthrie wrote Sutherland that "Senator Root and I would be grateful if you could dictate your own views as to the meaning of the 'concurrent power' clause. . . . We believe . . . that it would be of great help to us if we could have the benefit of such suggestions as occurred to you, since the matter came before you for action when you were in the Senate, and you may be able to give us some idea of what was really intended, if indeed there was any clear idea at that time."

Sutherland replied that he did not think anybody had "the slightest idea what was intended." Section 2 seemed "an anomaly," and so far as Sutherland knew, "the purpose of the provision was never stated to any committee or upon the floor of either House." It seemed to Sutherland that Section 2 had to be construed so as to avoid conflicts between state and federal legislation—conflicts that would normally, in other contexts, be avoided by means of the Supremacy Clause, which was, however, presumably not applicable in this instance. The only way to achieve this end was to restrict the power of Congress to the regulation of liquor in interstate commerce, and the power of the states to internal enforcement of the Eighteenth Amendment.[363]

Solicitor General Alexander C. King presented the government's argument that the Eighteenth Amendment was as valid as the Thirteenth, Fourteenth, or Fifteenth, and that Congressional legislation under it was as supreme as any other valid federal law, the states merely being granted by Section 2 power to pass and enforce prohibition legis-

---

[363] W. D. Guthrie to G. Sutherland, Mar. 11, 1920; Sutherland to Guthrie, Mar. 15, 1920; Guthrie to Sutherland, Mar. 17, 1920; Sutherland to Guthrie, Mar. 18, 1920; Guthrie to Sutherland, Mar. 25, 1920, Sutherland Papers, Library of Congress.

lation that was not in conflict with acts of Congress. An *amicus* brief supporting the Amendment was filed by Charles E. Hughes in behalf of twenty-one state attorneys general. Hughes had refused a retainer from the liquor interests. "While I thought the Amendment unwise as a matter of policy," he later recalled, "I took not the slightest stock in the view advanced by Mr. Root that the people had no power to adopt such a constitutional amendment if they saw fit. . . ."[364]

The Court's decision, which came down on June 7, 1920, was as unique and anomalous in its way as Section 2 of the Eighteenth Amendment. The Court issued something that was a cross between a *per curiam* order and an opinion: eleven "conclusions of the court," announced by Van Devanter. Root's contention was disposed of in conclusions four and five, which in their entirety read as follows: "The prohibition of the manufacture, sale, transportation, importation and exportation of intoxicating liquors for beverage purposes, as embodied in the Eighteenth Amendment, is within the power to amend reserved by Article V of the Constitution. That Amendment, by lawful proposal and ratification, has become a part of the Constitution and must be respected and given effect the same as other provisions of that instrument."

Guthrie's argument fared no better. With equal brevity the Court said that Section 2 did not require Congressional legislation to be concurred in by the states. The section in no fashion divided the enforcement power between Congress and the states along the lines separating foreign and interstate commerce from intrastate. Rather Congressional power under Section 2 was plenary, reaching both interstate and intrastate traffic and manufacture. Taking account of some additional contentions, Van Devanter declared also that the Amendment was equally applicable to liquor manufactured before it became effective as to liquor that might be manufactured after, and that while there were, no doubt, limits "beyond which Congress cannot go in treating beverages as within its power of enforcement, we think those limits are not transcended by the provision of the Volstead Act (Title II, Section 1), wherein liquors containing as much as one-half of one per cent of alcohol by volume and fit for use for beverage purposes are treated as within that power. *Jacob Ruppert* v. *Caffey*, 251 U.S. 264."

Van Devanter's bare statement of conclusions sufficed for a majority, but not for all of the Justices. "I profoundly regret," White began a concurring opinion, "that in a case of this magnitude . . . the court has deemed it proper to state only ultimate conclusions without an exposition of the reasoning by which they have been reached." White agreed with the propositions announced by the Court, and he appreciated

---

[364] C. E. Hughes, *Biographical Notes,* Microfilm, Ac. 9943, 245–56,   Hughes Papers.

that the issues were difficult, but it seemed to him "that the greater the perplexities the greater the duty devolving upon me to express the reasons which have led me to [my] conclusion. . . ." And so he proceeded to give some reasons for rejecting Guthrie's proposed construction of Section 2 of the Eighteenth Amendment. That construction would in large measure nullify the first section of the Amendment. For a failure by a state to concur in Congressional legislation or pass any of its own would render Prohibition ineffective within that state. White was not prepared to assume that the framers of the Amendment wished to invite even partial defeat of its purpose (although it might be countered that such was often the nature of legislative compromises). Section 2 should, therefore, be read merely as an effort to enlist the states in the enforcement of the Amendment and of Congressional legislation enacted pursuant to it. Root's contention that the Amendment as a whole was unconstitutional White ignored. In a paragraph, McReynolds also concurred, saying simply that he accepted the result—dismissal of the suits—reached by the Court, but wished at this point to express no view on the construction to be given to the Eighteenth Amendment. He preferred to consider issues of construction as enforcement cases arose in the future.

McKenna and Clarke filed dissenting opinions. The Court's statement of conclusions established a precedent, said McKenna, that would "undoubtedly decrease the literature of the court if it does not increase lucidity." That, contrary to Root's argument, the Eighteenth Amendment was now validly a part of the Constitution, McKenna agreed. But as to Section 2, he accepted essentially Guthrie's construction. It seemed to him required by the language of the section. Under other provisions of the Constitution, Congressional legislation was supreme. But this provision spoke of concurrent power. Its framers, McKenna believed, "meant what they said" and "must be taken at their word." The notion "that words were made to conceal thoughts" had not yet "been erected into a legal maxim of constitutional construction." Section 2 called for "united action between the States and Congress, or, at any rate, concordant and harmonious action; and will not such action promote better the purpose of the Amendment—will it not bring to the enforcement of prohibition the power of the States and the power of Congress, make all the instrumentalities of the States . . . agencies of the enforcement, as well as the instrumentalities of the United States . . . ? Will it not bring to the States as well, or preserve to them, a partial autonomy, satisfying, if you will, their prejudices, or better say, their predilections?—and it is not too much to say that our dual system of government is based upon them. And this predilection for self-government the Eighteenth Amendment regards and respects, and by doing so, sacrifices nothing of the policy of prohibition."

Clarke's dissent also concerned Section 2, and Clarke also agreed essentially with Guthrie. The concurrence of the states in Congressional legislation was needed, and would prove beneficial, Clarke thought, because "to a great extent" it would "relieve Congress of the burden and the general government of the odium to be derived from the antagonism which would certainly spring from enforcing, within States, federal laws which must touch the daily life of the people very intimately and often very irritatingly." Clarke also dissented from the conclusion that liquor containing no more than 0.5 percent of alcohol by volume could be brought within the prohibition of the Eighteenth Amendment.[365]

White and McKenna, Holmes wrote Frankfurter shortly after the decision came down, had set a "bad example" in censuring the Court "for not giving reasons for [its] conclusions as to the 18th Amendment. There were good reasons for not giving them, but personally I think that the validity of the amendment needed none. The attack seems to me like what I said about so-called great cases in the Northern Securities matter—bringing hydraulic pressure to bear upon first principles to see if they couldn't be made doubtful. There was a lot of money and they took a sporting chance. But of course the decision opens vistas. And although it seemed to me plain it appeared that there could be a difference of opinion about the meaning of the 'concurrent' power given to Congress and the States. . . . The poor Chief was heroic this Term but dreadfully hampered and my last news was that the operation on his eyes must be postponed to the autumn. He seemed very sad as we said goodbye. . . . Van Devanter also showed a deal of grit. He was suffering badly from lumbago etc. but put through the 18th Amendment. . . .[366]

The reasons for not giving reasons that Holmes alluded to remain

---

[365] National Prohibition Cases, 253 U.S. 350, 361–62, 364, 367, 370, 386, 387–88, 393, 398, 403, 405–406, 408 (1920); see also New Jersey v. Palmer, 252 U.S. 570 (1920); and see Dillon v. Gloss, 256 U.S. 368 (1921).

A week before it decided the *National Prohibition Cases,* the Court also resolved in favor of the validity of the Eighteenth Amendment a dispute concerning its ratification. The Ohio Constitution, as amended in 1918, provided that proposed amendments to the federal Constitution were to be ratified in Ohio by referendum. The Eighteenth Amendment called for ratification by legislatures, and it was

ratified by the Ohio legislature. Pursuant to the constitution of the state, however, the Ohio secretary of state proposed to submit the Eighteenth Amendment to a referendum. The Supreme Court ordered him enjoined from doing so on the ground that no state could change the ratification method provided by Congress for an amendment to the federal Constitution. Hawke v. Smith, 253 U.S. 221 (1920). See also Hawke v. Smith, 253 U.S. 231 (1920) (Nineteenth Amendment).

[366] O. W. Holmes to F. Frankfurter, June 22, 1920, Holmes Papers.

obscure, but White's and McKenna's "bad example" in objecting to the absence of reasons was not much emulated. The result was taken as a matter of course. John Barleycorn was in his coffin, sealed and buried, and Prohibition was an accomplished fact.[367] All that the future held now was enforcement, but that was the next decade's problem. In the first year after it put the stamp of legitimacy on the Eighteenth Amendment and the Volstead Act, the Court was presented with only one enforcement case, in which it sought to safeguard a right to continued private use of liquor in private dwellings.[368]

---

[367] See, e.g., *The Literary Digest,* 65:22–23, June 19, 1920.

[368] Street v. Lincoln Safe Deposit Co., 254 U.S. 88 (1920).

CHAPTER VI

The Fate of Social
Legislation, 1914-21: State

O NE LOOKS IN VAIN through the mass of decisions dealing with state measures of social and economic regulation during the last seven years of the White Court for new doctrinal departures, or for authoritative clarifications of the doctrinal ambiguities of earlier years. A markedly conservative settlement of doctrine may be detected if decisions dealing with the activities of labor unions are taken into account. But the great bulk of cases passing on social and economic regulation went along very much as before, which is to say, most often erratically. So they appear, viewed in the aggregate or examined in detail, judged qualitatively or quantitatively.

It is possible to discern a certain difference in tone, an occasional hardening of positions, especially in the face of early Brandeis dissents. But even this difference is as much a matter of what was not there as of what was, as much the absence of a certain strain in the melody as its replacement by another, as much the muted sound of certain notes as the dominance of other ones. It comes down to little more than the observation that there were, through these seven years, no *Minnesota Rate Cases*,[1] no *Noble State Bank* v. *Haskell*, and no *Chicago, Burlington & Quincy Railroad* v. *McGuire*.[2]

---

[1] See *supra*, pp. 254 *et seq.*   [2] See *supra*, p. 276.

Commerce Clause and Preemption Decisions

A small group of decisions, made in the spirit of the *Minnesota Rate Cases*, upheld state regulation of railroads under the Commerce Clause.[3] Something of the spirit of the *Minnesota Rate Cases* also informed *Hendrick* v. *Maryland*,[4] in which, in January 1915, the Court had its first encounter with the automobile as an instrument of interstate commerce. A unanimous opinion, written by McReynolds, upheld requirements of local licensing for out-of-state drivers and local registration for out-of-state cars, as well as the exaction of appropriate fees. A state's interest in safety and in collecting funds for building its roads justified the imposition of a reasonable burden on interstate commerce, the Court said, so long as the burden was not discriminatory. In *Kane* v. *New Jersey*,[5] shortly thereafter, the Court, again unanimously, this time through Brandeis, extended the holding of *Hendrick* v. *Maryland*, and sustained a statute that required nonresident interstate drivers to appoint an agent for the service of process within the state. Dealing with another subject of rising practical importance, the Court allowed states to fix rates for natural gas sold to consumers, whether it came to the consumer directly through an interstate pipeline, or entered intrastate commerce first through an intermediate sale from the pipeline to a local company.[6]

There were decisions, however, in which a very different attitude reigned. In 1910 and 1911, the Court had permitted states to regulate interstate telegraph messages originating within their jurisdiction by enforcing liability for negligent transmission.[7] Now, through Holmes, who had dissented alone in one of the earlier cases, the Court pretty well insulated the transmission of interstate telegraph messages from regulation by any state. In *Western Union Telegraph Co.* v. *Foster* (called the *Ticker Cases*),[8] Holmes held that the transmission of stock exchange quotations by telegraph constituted interstate commerce until completed in a subscriber's office, and was "a business generically withdrawn from state control." There could be no state regulation, said Holmes, although he seemingly left room for "some incidental con-

---

[3] See Wilmington Transportation Co. v. California R.R. Commission, 236 U.S. 151 (1915); Chicago, Milwaukee & St. Paul Ry. v. Public Utilities Commission, 242 U.S. 333 (1917); Missouri Pacific Ry. v. McGrew Coal Co., 244 U.S. 191 (1917), 256 U.S. 134 (1921).

[4] 235 U.S. 610 (1915).

[5] 242 U.S. 160 (1916).

[6] Public Utilities Commission v. Landon, 249 U.S. 236, 590 (1919); Pennsylvania Gas Co. v. Public Service Commission, 252 U.S. 23 (1920).

[7] Western Union Telegraph Co. v. Commercial Milling Co., 218 U.S. 406 (1910); Western Union Telegraph Co. v. Crovo, 220 U.S. 364 (1911); see *supra*, p. 265, n.197.

[8] 247 U.S. 105, 114 (1918).

venience that can be afforded [by state regulation] without seriously impeding the interstate work."[9]

The opening thus left to state regulation was only apparent. In *Foster*, Massachusetts had attempted to prevent the transmittal of stock exchange quotations by telegraph to a person who, the state had determined, ran an illegal bucket shop. This was an attempt, said Holmes, to affect the business "in its very vitals." But in *Western Union Telegraph Co.* v. *Speight*,[10] Holmes forbade imposition by the state of liability for negligence in the transmission of a message, thus silently overruling, if without deigning to mention them, the decisions of 1910 and 1911. The badly transmitted message in *Speight* had actually gone from one point to another in North Carolina. Following its habitual practice, however, the company had sent the message through another point outside the state, this being the most convenient and economical route. That, Holmes held, placed the message in interstate commerce, and withdrew it from the authority of the state.[11]

---

[9] While it came down unanimously, *Western Union Telegraph Co.* v. *Foster* really stood otherwise. At best, it was decided 6 to 3, being one of those cases in which the dissenters forewent expression of their views. "At the present I think I shall not dissent," Clarke returned to Holmes, "but I cannot agree." Day wrote Holmes: "I am disposed to say no more, reserving the right to join in a dissent if one be written." Brandeis' first return was: "Please note my dissent." Then, on the very morning of the day the decision was announced, Brandeis wrote Holmes: "In your ticker cases I have concluded that dissent would only aggravate the harm. Hence shall not dissent." Holmes Papers, Harvard Law School Library. And see M. DeW. Howe, ed., *Holmes-Pollock Letters* (1946), I, 265.

[10] 254 U.S. 17 (1920); see also Gardner v. Western Union Telegraph Co., 231 Fed. 405 (8th Cir. 1916), cert. denied, 243 U.S. 644 (1917).

[11] The *Speight* case was Holmes' first opinion for the October Term 1920. He thought it "an easy one," as he wrote Harold Laski, but the argument that the message was really intrastate, and that the routing of it through an out-of-state point was merely a way of evading state regulation, presented him with the opportunity "to put in a line, if it is not stricken out, about that bastard notion *evading* a law—when it is evaded either it is broken according to its true construction and implications or care has been taken to keep on the right side of the line. The very meaning of a line in the law is that you may walk up to it if you don't pass it." M. DeW. Howe, ed., *Holmes-Laski Letters* (1953), I, 287. The line was stricken out, and still the day before the case came down Holmes was not quite certain it would go. (In the end the decision was unanimous, Pitney alone concurring in the result without opinion.) This was the opinion of which Holmes wrote Frankfurter on Oct. 24, 1920—the day before it was announced—that it had "had a tiny pair of testicles." They had been removed, the opinion spoke "in a very soft voice now," and yet it remained to be seen "whether I shall be told to let it be heard." Even Brandeis "who passed the original told me he had misgivings." Holmes Papers; see *supra*, p. 237.

VI: *The Fate of Social Legislation, 1914–21: State*

The high-church nationalism of Holmes' telegraph cases was not by any means, as we have seen, the only stance assumed by the Court in Commerce Clause decisions during these years. The judges judged, assessing and balancing in varying conditions the imperatives of a common market, and the quality and intensity of the local interest that claimed protection at the hands of state government. Sometimes what a common market necessarily called for was fairly clear. Thus the Court continued to forbid dry states from stopping the importation of liquor,[12] except as the Webb-Kenyon Act came to their assistance.[13] And the Court forbade the imposition of requirements on foreign corporations which amounted in practice to excluding them from interstate commerce within the state, although varieties of conditions could be attached to the privilege of coming into the state to do intrastate business.[14] But the judges judged, and their ultimate criterion was whether a state measure burdened interstate commerce unduly and unreasonably. McReynolds' decisive sentence in upholding the Maryland automobile and driver registration law in the *Hendrick* case was: "The prescribed regulations upon their face do not appear to be either unnecessary or unreasonable."[15] Decisions turning on a judgment of necessity and reasonableness were quite often dictated, as Felix Frankfurter remarked, not by federalism, but by "a laissez-faire philosophy."[16]

Here was the point of contact, conscious or not, between Commerce Clause and Due Process decisions. Sometimes there would be deference to a legislature's notion of necessity and reasonableness, as when the Court upheld a Florida statute punishing the shipment of immature or otherwise unfit citrus fruits out of the state.[17] This was a regulation of interstate commerce, to be sure, said the Court, but it was reasonable for the state to wish thus to protect the reputation of its citrus industry.[18] Similarly, though not without dissent, the Court sus-

---

[12] Kirmeyer v. Kansas, 236 U.S. 568 (1915); Rossi v. Pennsylvania, 238 U.S. 62 (1915); Adams Express Co. v. Kentucky, 238 U.S. 190 (1915), *supra*, p. 442, n.115; Rosenberg v. Pacific Express Co., 241 U.S. 48 (1916). *Cf.* Taft Co. v. Iowa, 183 Iowa 548, 167 N.W. 467 (1918), *writ of error dismissed for want of jurisdiction*, 252 U.S. 569 (1920). See *supra*, pp. 439 *et seq.*

[13] Seaboard Air Line Ry. v. North Carolina, 245 U.S. 298 (1917).

[14] Sioux Remedy Co. v. Cope, 235 U.S. 197 (1914); Wisconsin v. Philadelphia & Reading Coal Co., 241 U.S.

329 (1916); York Manufacturing Co. v. Colley, 247 U.S. 21 (1918); *cf. supra*, p. 268, n.204. But *cf.* Dalton Adding Machine Co. v. Virginia, 246 U.S. 498 (1918); Munday v. Wisconsin Trust Co., 252 U.S. 499 (1920); and see American Distributing Co. v. Hayes Wheel Co., 257 Fed. 881 (6th Cir. 1919), *cert. denied*, 250 U.S. 672 (1919).

[15] *Supra*, n.4, 235 U.S. at 623.

[16] See *supra*, p. 254.

[17] *Cf. supra*, pp. 268 *et seq.*

[18] Sligh v. Kirkwood, 237 U.S. 52 (1915).

tained a requirement that interstate railroads stop at all county seats on their route through a state.[19] And, again over dissent, the Court in *South Covington & Cincinnati Street Railway* v. *Kentucky* upheld the imposition by Kentucky of its separate-but-equal passenger segregation rule in interstate traffic.[20] The Court summarily approved application of a state workmen's compensation law to workers who were engaged in interstate transportation, but not in railroading, and who were thus not affected by the Federal Employers' Liability Act.[21]

But the Court found many exercises of state power unreasonable. Thus while *South Covington & Cincinnati Street Railway* v. *Kentucky* permitted Kentucky to segregate interstate passengers traveling on a trolley line between Covington, Kentucky, and Cincinnati, Ohio, Kentucky was not allowed to regulate the number of standees to be carried on any car of the same trolley line, or to require that a sufficient number of cars be operated at all times to accommodate the public, or that the temperature in the cars be kept at not less than fifty degrees Fahrenheit. "Commerce cannot flourish in the midst of such embarrassments," said the Court.[22] And *Seaboard Air Line Railway* v. *Blackwell*[23] held unconstitutional, over a short dissent by White, Pitney, and Brandeis, a Georgia statute that required all trains, including interstate ones, to slow down before public road crossings in the state. The contention was that along the 123-mile trip within Georgia from Atlanta to the South Carolina line there were 124 public road crossings at grade, so that an interstate train abiding by the statute would add six hours to its run.

Perhaps this law was indeed unworkable, but then perhaps the Georgia legislature would have soon so discovered. At any rate, it is notable that the constitutionality of the Georgia law was adjudicated in a tort suit in which there had been a verdict for damages in favor of one Blackwell, whose son had been killed at a grade crossing. The statute provided that in such circumstances no negligence beyond viola-

---

[19] Gulf, Colorado & Santa Fe Ry. v. Texas, 246 U.S. 58 (1918); see also International & Great Northern Ry. v. Anderson County, 246 U.S. 424 (1918).

[20] 252 U.S. 399 (1920); see also Cincinnati, Covington & Erlanger Ry. v. Kentucky, 252 U.S. 408 (1920); *cf.* Butts v. Merchants Transportation Co., 230 U.S. 126 (1913).

[21] Valley Steamship Co. v. Wattawa, 244 U.S. 202 (1917).

[22] South Covington & Cincinnati Street Ry. v. Covington, 235 U.S. 537, 548 (1915). See also Illinois Central R.R. v. Louisiana R.R. Commission, 236 U.S. 157 (1915); Chicago, Burlington & Quincy R.R. v. Wisconsin R.R. Commission, 237 U.S. 220 (1915); Missouri, Kansas & Texas Ry. v. Texas 245 U.S. 484 (1918); St. Louis & San Francisco Ry. v. Public Service Commission, 254 U.S. 535 (1921); but *cf.* Pittsburgh, Cincinnati, Chicago & St. Louis Ry. v. Indiana, 180 Ind. 245, 102 N.E. 25 (1913), *writ of error dismissed per stipulation,* 235 U.S. 710 (1914).

[23] 244 U.S. 310 (1917).

tion of the statute needed to be proved against the railroad. The state of Georgia was not represented and had no opportunity to argue in favor of the validity of its law. Not only that, but as happened all too often in tort actions against railroads which reached the Court, there was no appearance for Blackwell, and so nobody argued in the Supreme Court in favor of the constitutionality of the Georgia statute.[24]

The judgment of reasonableness—the wild card in the Commerce Clause deck—was in play also in preemption cases.[25] There were, to be sure, a number of decisions in the period 1914–21 sustaining state regulations that ventured into the neighborhood of a federal statute, most notably in a pure food and drug case in which the Court followed Hughes' opinion of 1912 in *Savage* v. *Jones*.[26] And in a few instances in which state action was preempted, the decisions of the Court could be viewed as flowing inevitably, or at least unexceptionably, from the relevant federal statute.[27] Many decisions were highly dubious, however; for example, two invoking the Carmack Amendment and the Safety Appliance Acts, in which Holmes, as he would say, got a couple of phrases past "the watchers of the Ark,"[28] who let them go because they threatened no Ark the watchers were watching. Good phrases they were, and Holmes liked them, no doubt, but they reached for, and caused mischief.

"When Congress has taken the particular subject matter in hand," said Holmes in *Charleston & Western Carolina Railway* v. *Varnville Co.*,[29] "coincidence is as ineffective as opposition, and a state law is not to be declared a help because it attempts to go farther than Congress has seen fit to go." Four years later, in *Pennsylvania Railroad* v. *Public Service Commission*, he said it again: "But when the United States has exercised its exclusive powers over interstate commerce so far as to take possession of the field, the States no more can supplement its requirements than they can annul them."[30]

Nothing was more dubious, or had greater impact, than two groups of decisions—the principal cases were *New York Central Railroad* v. *Winfield* and *Southern Pacific Co.* v. *Jensen*—restricting application of state workmen's compensation laws. Here the wild card really came up, and led the Court into excess.

James Winfield lost an eye while engaged in interstate commerce

---

[24] *Cf. supra*, p. 219; *infra*, pp. 554, 559, 563.

[25] *Cf. supra*, pp. 270 *et seq.*

[26] Corn Products Refining Co. v. Eddy, 249 U.S. 427 (1919). See *supra*, p. 272, n.215.

[27] See Essex v. New England Telephone Co., 239 U.S. 313 (1916); Louisville & Nashville R.R. Co. v. Ohio Valley Tie Co., 242 U.S. 288 (1916); Northern Pacific Ry. v. Solum, 247 U.S. 477 (1918).

[28] See *supra*, p. 237.

[29] 237 U.S. 597, 604 (1915); see *supra*, p. 416, n.7.

[30] 250 U.S. 566, 569 (1919).

as an employee of the New York Central Railroad. He was part of a track-repairing crew, and as he tamped down some cross ties, he struck a pebble, which bounced up and hit him in the eye. No negligence could be attributed to the railroad. The accident was just that, pure and simple. Therefore, although engaged in interstate commerce as a railroad employee, and covered by the Federal Employers' Liability Act, Winfield could not recover under it, since the Act rendered a railroad liable only if some form of negligence could be proved against it. But New York had a workmen's compensation law which established various groups of hazardous employments, including railroad work, and required every employer whose business was hazardous according to the meaning of the statute to provide compensation to workers injured on the job. The amount of compensation was prescribed in a schedule, and awards were to be made without regard to fault—that is to say, with no need for the worker to prove negligence on the part of the employer. This statute, as we shall see, had been upheld by the Supreme Court against a Due Process attack just a couple of months earlier.[31] And as noted, it survived a Commerce Clause attack when applied to nonrailroad employees in interstate commerce who were not covered by any federal statute.[32] The question now, in *New York Central Railroad* v. *Winfield*, was whether the New York statute could be applied where the Federal Employers' Liability Act also applied in general, but afforded no recovery in the particular case. The Court decided this question in the negative.

Although not disposed of until May 21, 1917, *New York Central Railroad* v. *Winfield* had first been argued early in 1916, and then reargued a year later on February 1, 1917.[33] The delay in disposing of the case is no doubt accounted for by the condition of the Court during the October Term 1915. Lamar died on January 2, 1916, more than a month before the first argument in the *Winfield* case, and his replacement, Brandeis, did not take his seat for some time. Day was ill, and did not attend Court from January 3, 1916, to the end of the term.[34] So it

---

[31] New York Central R.R. v. White, 243 U.S. 188 (1917).

[32] Valley Steamship Co. v. Wattawa, *supra*, p. 552, n.21. The decision in this case was announced on the same day as *New York Central R.R.* v. *Winfield*.

[33] *New York Central R.R.* v. *Winfield* was another of those cases which tested the constitutionality of a state law in a suit between private parties. But the state in this instance appeared in support of one of the parties, no doubt viewing the litigation as a test case. Argument was by counsel for the parties, but the Attorney General of New York participated in framing the brief for Winfield, and signed it.

[34] See 241 U.S. iii; W. Van Devanter to E. B. Adams, Jan. 12, 1916, Van Devanter Papers, Library of Congress; E. D. White to W. R. Day, Feb. 18, 1916, Mar. 9, 1916, Day Papers, Library of Congress.

was a seven-man Court. Moreover, during the spring, as the prospect of Hughes' Presidential nomination became stronger, his colleagues contrived to lighten his burden somewhat, thus adding further to their own.[35] If it had been just a matter of the inability of a very shorthanded Court to complete the opinion in *Winfield*, however, the case might have been carried over but not reargued. Yet without Day, without Hughes or his replacement, and without Lamar's replacement, the decision could have been made by only the remaining six Justices who had heard argument—a bare quorum. That was clearly undesirable.[36]

The eventual opinion of the Court was by Van Devanter. It was settled, Van Devanter began, that when Congress acts on any given subject, "all state laws covering the same field are necessarily superseded by reason of the supremacy of the national authority." The question was, therefore, what subject had Congress acted upon, what field had it covered? The argument for Winfield was that Congress had provided for accidents caused by the negligence of the employer, and had not covered injuries occurring without fault. The counterargument, which Van Devanter adopted, was that the Federal Employers' Liability Act had a broader scope, and made negligence "a test,—not of the applicability of the act, but of the carrier's duty or obligation to respond pecuniarily for the injury." Congress, Van Devanter said, intended the law concerning compensation for injuries to railroad employees engaged in interstate commerce to be national and uniform. There had previously been much variation in the laws of the several states, and the House and Senate committee reports which brought the Federal Employers' Liability Act to the floor for enactment stressed—Van Devanter quoted them—the desirability of fixing "a uniform rule of liability throughout the Union." The new federal statute, the committee reports declared, would "supplant the numerous State statutes on the subject so far as they relate to interstate commerce." And Van Devanter concluded: "thus the Act is as comprehensive of injuries occurring without negligence, as to which class it impliedly excludes liability, as it is of those as to which it imposes liability. In other words, it is a regulation of the carriers' duty or obligation as to both."

There was a dissenting opinion by Brandeis in which Clarke joined.

---

[35] See *supra*, p. 396.

[36] Compare, e.g., Rowland v. St. Louis & San Francisco R.R., 244 U.S. 106 (argued February 1916, reargued May 1917, decided May 21, 1917); Five Per Cent Discount Cases, 243 U.S. 97 (argued February 1916, reargued February 1917, decided Mar. 6, 1917); New York Central R.R. v. White, 243 U.S. 188 (argued February 1916, at the same time as the *Winfield* case, reargued again with *Winfield*, reargued February 1917, decided Mar. 6, 1917); Bunting v. Oregon, 243 U.S. 426 (argued April 1916, reargued January 1917, decided Apr. 9, 1917).

It was the first dissenting opinion of Brandeis' career. "That case laid me low," he said of it to Felix Frankfurter somewhat later.[37] The dissent was massive and elaborately documented, running sixteen printed pages. Brandeis summarized its theme in his subsequent conversation with Frankfurter: "What those fellows don't understand is that recognition of federal powers does not mean denial of state powers. I have not been against increase of federal power, but curtailment of state powers."[38]

No doubt, Brandeis wrote, Congress could have forbidden the states—as the Court now did—to exact from railroads any compensation for their employees' injuries additional to that exacted by the Federal Employers' Liability Act. But the question was, had Congress done so? Congress in fact had made no provision for compensation for injuries not caused by the negligence of the employer. The Court had previously held—here Brandeis quoted from Hughes' opinion in *Savage v. Jones*,[39] and then added a compilation of other cases in a two-page footnote—that the intent of Congress to supersede state legislation was not to be inferred unless what Congress had done was in actual conflict with the law of a state. Conflict meant that the federal statute and the state law could not be reconciled or stand together.

The difference beween Brandeis and the majority was thus quite clear from the beginning. Van Devanter, without the epigrammatic flair of Holmes, took the same premise as Holmes,[40] who joined him in the majority in this case:[41] when Congress acts on a given subject, state laws attempting to supplement or complement the action must fall, regardless of whether they conflict with it. Brandeis thought that only conflicting state statutes fell, unless Congress went out of its way to forbid also supplementary and complementary regulation by the states. Starting with these different premises, no wonder Van Devanter and Brandeis looked for and found different intents of Congress.

There was also an additional difference, one of method, between Van Devanter and Brandeis, which was more pervasive, affecting their approaches to a wider range of cases than the one at hand. Van Devanter went so far as to look at legislative history, strictly speaking— the reports of committees. Finding these ambiguous, Brandeis looked also "at the circumstances under which the Employers' Liability Act

---

[37] Brandeis-Frankfurter Conversations, Harvard Law School Library.

[38] *Ibid.*

[39] *Supra*, p. 272, n.215.

[40] See *supra*, p. 553, nn.29, 30.

[41] And who told Brandeis (so he reported to Laski) that Brandeis' "long essay on the development of employers' liability"—see *infra*—was "out of place and irrelevant to the only question: whether Congress had dealt with the matter so far as to exclude state action." *Holmes-Laski Letters*, I, 128.

was passed; look, on the one hand, at its origin, scope and purpose; and, on the other, at the nature, methods and means of state Workmen's Compensation Laws. If the will is not clearly expressed in words we must consider all these in order to determine what Congress intended." The Court at this time had barely begun to examine committee reports and debates.[42] For Brandeis, examination of such materials was a matter of course. But the relevant inquiry was much broader. It was a full-scale historical investigation of the social and economic conditions that gave rise to a statute.

At common law, Brandeis wrote, defenses such as contributory negligence and the fellow-servant rule often defeated the worker's attempt to get compensation for his injuries. "The wrongs suffered were flagrant; the demand for redress insistent; and the efforts to secure remedial legislation widespread. But the opponents were alert, potent and securely entrenched." The states did little to remedy the situation, while the number of accidents rose appallingly. In 1905–1906, 3,807 railroad employees were killed while on duty, and 55,524 were injured. The resultant pressure produced the Federal Employers' Liability Act— an emergency relief measure, not in any sense a scheme to promote safety or secure uniformity.

The Act was a specific remedy for a specific thing. Far from demonstrating a purpose to achieve uniformity, the limited coverage of the Act showed that it was not intended as a comprehensive treatment of the problem of industrial accidents on interstate railroads. "The scope of the Act is so narrow as to preclude the belief that thereby Congress intended to deny to the States the power to provide compensation or relief for injuries not covered by it." The Act was intended to take out of play a number of the defenses available to the employer at common law; it was not intended to deny to the states the power to create a wholly new remedy. Workmen's compensation acts were a wholly new remedy, a radically different remedy, as Brandeis explained in a famous passage quoted in a previous chapter.[43] When Congress passed the Federal Employers' Liability Act, the idea of social insurance embodied in workmen's compensation laws had not yet gained its later currency. Not one of the thirty-seven states and territories that now had such laws had them then. Nonetheless the idea was not unknown to Congress. In these circumstances, how could it be concluded that Congress, by simply passing the Employers' Liability Act, had not only decided against the workmen's compensation idea for itself, but had meant to foreclose its application to railroad employees by the states,

---

[42] See *supra*, pp. 430–31, 485–89.

[43] See *supra*, pp. 209–210; see also *supra*, pp. 205 *et seq.*

which after all had the prime responsibility of caring for the maimed and injured?

"Upon the State," Brandeis wrote, "falls the financial burden of dependency, if provision be not otherwise made. Upon the State falls directly the far heavier burden of the demoralization of its citizenry, and of the social unrest, which attend destitution and the denial of opportunity. Upon the State also rests under our dual system of government the duty owed to the individual to avert misery and promote happiness so far as possible. Surely we may not impute to Congress the will to deny to the States the power to perform either this duty to humanity or their fundamental duty of self-preservation." And if the states were free to make compensation under a scheme such as New York had adopted, what was there in the Employers' Liability Act that could demonstrate an intent of Congress to deny the states the power to raise the money necessary for this compensation through the employer? The social insurance idea of workmen's compensation statutes was carried out in numerous and varied ways in the several states. The compensation might come either out of general tax revenues or out of employer contributions, which were then passed on to the public through pricing of the employer's product. No uniformity existed, and it was difficult to see why any was necessary or why Congress should be thought to have imposed it. There was no conflict between workmen's compensation laws and the Federal Employers' Liability Act, and no reason to impute to Congress an intention to preempt the former by the latter.[44]

"All Cases of Admiralty and Maritime Jurisdiction"

On the same day on which it decided the *Winfield* case, the Court, as we have noted, also held in *Valley Steamship Co. v. Wattawa*[45] that a state workmen's compensation law could constitutionally be applied to workmen engaged in interstate commerce who were not covered by the Federal Employers' Liability Act. The employer in this case, as its name indicates, was in fact a steamship company. It was argued, therefore, that the company was subject to exclusive federal admiralty jurisdiction, and that for this reason state workmen's compensation laws could not be applied to it. But this point had not been timely raised in the state courts, and McReynolds, in a brief opinion for the Supreme Court, declined to consider it. The point was, however, open for

---

[44] New York Central R.R. v. Winfield, 244 U.S. 147, 148, 149, 150, 153, 158, 160, 163–64, 166 (1917); see also Erie R.R. v. Winfield, 244 U.S. 170 (1917); New York Central R.R. v. Tonsellito, 244 U.S. 360 (1917).

[45] See *supra*, pp. 552, n.21; 554.

decision in *Southern Pacific Co.* v. *Jensen,* which was argued and re-argued together with and immediately preceding *New York Central Railroad* v. *Winfield,* and also decided on the same day with it.

The issue was not quite the preemption issue of the *Winfield* case. It arose, not under a federal regulatory statute, but under Article III of the Constitution, which extends the judicial power of the United States, among other matters, "to all Cases of admiralty and maritime Jurisdiction," and under the Judiciary Act of 1789 which, in imple-menting Article III in a provision still in effect, gave to the district courts of the United States "exclusive original cognizance of all civil causes of admiralty and maritime jurisdiction; . . . saving to suitors, in all cases, the right of a common-law remedy where the common law is competent to give it." Yet despite this difference, the *Jensen* and *Winfield* cases are united, not only by their common subject matter, but also by common attitudes displayed by a majority of the Justices, and by the concept of uniformity they employed to give effect to those attitudes. That concept as used in *Jensen* is either the same as that employed in *Winfield,* or a very near blood relative. Not for nothing did the Court group these cases together for argument and reargument, and consider them at the same time, for decision on the same day.[46]

The Southern Pacific Company, the employer, appeared in *Jensen* not as a railroad, but as the operator of a steamship running between Galveston, Texas, and New York. Jensen, a stevedore employed to unload the ship in New York, was killed while trying to cross from it to the pier on a gangplank some ten feet long. There was an award under the New York workmen's compensation law, which the New York Court of Appeals affirmed. The Supreme Court of the United States, McReynolds writing, reversed. The Federal Employers' Liability Act, said McReynolds, was not in issue. It applied only to railroad operations, not to steamships, even if operated by a railroad company. "It is unreasonable to suppose that Congress intended to change long-established rules applicable to maritime matters merely because the ocean-going ship concerned happened to be owned and operated by a company also a common carrier by railroad." (Yet it had been reason-able to suppose, and McReynolds had joined in supposing, simply supposing, in the *Winfield* case that Congress had intended to displace state workmen's compensation laws.)

---

[46] New York Central R.R. v. White, 243 U.S. 188 (1917), testing the con-stitutionality of the New York work-men's compensation law under the Due Process Clause, was also argued at the same time.

Like *Winfield,* *Jensen* and *White* were suits between private parties. As in *Winfield,* the Attorney General of New York was on the briefs in *Jensen* and also in *White,* defending the con-stitutionality of the law of his state.

The "long-established rules applicable to maritime matters" had been developed by federal courts exercising the jurisdiction conferred on them by Article III of the Constitution. But Congress could, if it wished, change them, McReynolds pointed out. Congress had "paramount power to fix and determine the maritime law which shall prevail throughout the country." In the absence of Congressional action, the maritime law had been developed by the federal courts, but was no less supreme national law than if Congress had written it. Yet since the Judiciary Act saved to suitors their common law remedies, state legislation could "to some extent" also change the maritime law. Thus, notably, in *The Hamilton*,[47] a 1907 opinion by Holmes, a state statute which grafted onto the maritime law a cause of action for wrongful death was sustained as not in conflict with the provision of Article III establishing the federal admiralty jurisdiction.

But there were distinct limits, said McReynolds, to what could be done by state legislation. No state statute could be allowed to modify the general maritime law "if it contravenes the essential purpose expressed by an act of Congress or works material prejudice to the characteristic features of the general maritime law or interferes with the proper harmony and uniformity of that law in its international and interstate relations. This limitation, at the least, is essential to the effective operation of the fundamental purposes for which such law was incorporated into our national laws by the Constitution itself." Just so, the Commerce Clause had been interpreted to foreclose certain state regulations whether or not Congress had exerted its own regulatory power under it.

Now, the work of a stevedore was a maritime employment. If New York could affect it by legislation, so could every other state, and freedom of navigation would be seriously impeded. "The necessary consequence would be the destruction of the very uniformity in respect to maritime matters which the Constitution was designed to establish. . . ." Common law remedies were saved by the Judiciary Act, to be sure, but a workmen's compensation statute was no common law remedy; it was a scheme wholly unknown to the common law.

The *Jensen* and *Winfield* decisions were joined together in attitude and concept. Not for Holmes, however, who was with the majority in *Winfield*, but in *Jensen* filed one of his most celebrated dissenting opinions, which Brandeis and Clarke also signed. If it was constitutional for a state to create by its own statute a cause of action for wrongful death in admiralty, to create, in other words, a right to a money

---

[47] 207 U.S. 398 (1907).

judgment for a negligently caused death, there was no earthly reason, wrote Holmes, why a state could not equally create, as New York had done, a cause of action in admiralty for death caused by an accident rather than by negligence. "No doubt there sometimes has been an air of benevolent gratuity in the admiralty's attitude about enforcing state laws. But of course there is no gratuity about it. Courts cannot give or withhold at pleasure." State laws were enforced in admiralty because the state had constitutional power to pass them. There was no superior law emanating from the United States, such as an Act of Congress, which took away this power. The general maritime law could not do so. It was not a superior law emanating from the United States and invalidating state laws. It was, rather, a limited body of customs, which in recent times had itself undergone change. New rights had been created in the maritime law. From what source, asked Holmes, were such new rights derived? He answered in one of the most famous passages in judicial literature, reflecting his positivistic view of law:

> I recognize without hesitation that judges do and must legislate, but they can do so only interstitially; they are confied from molar to molecular motions. A common-law judge could not say I think the doctrine of consideration a bit of historical nonsense and shall not enforce it in my court. No more could a judge exercising the limited jurisdiction of admiralty say I think well of the common-law rules of master and servant and propose to introduce them here *en bloc.* Certainly he could not in that way enlarge the exclusive jurisdiction of the District Courts and cut down the power of the States. If admiralty adopts common-law rules without an act of Congress it cannot extend the maritime law as understood by the Constitution. It must take the rights of the parties from a different authority, just as it does when it enforces a lien created by a State. The only authority available is the common law or statutes of a State. . . . The common law is not a brooding omnipresence in the sky but the articulate voice of some sovereign or quasi-sovereign that can be identified; although some decisions with which I have disagreed seem to me to have forgotten the fact.[48] It always is the law of some State, and if the Distict Courts adopt the common law of torts, as they have shown a tendency to do, they thereby assume that a law not of maritime origin and deriving its authority in that territory only from some particular State of this

---

[48] This is a reference, no doubt, to the federal common law of commercial transactions which the courts were then still spinning, over Holmes' opposition, pursuant to the decision in Swift v. Tyson, 16 Pet. 1 (1842), which in turn was not overruled till some twenty years later, by Brandeis, in Erie R.R. v. Tompkins, 304 U.S. 64 (1938).

Union also governs maritime torts in that territory—and if the common law, the statute law has at least equal force. . . .[49]

Pitney, who chose not to join in Holmes' dissent, wrote a dissenting opinion of his own, in which Brandeis and Clarke—but not Holmes—also joined. "While concurring substantially in the dissenting opinion of Mr. Justice Holmes," said Pitney, "I deem it proper, in view of the momentous consequences of the decision, to present some additional considerations." He did, in some twenty-two printed pages. Yet what he added was worth saying. The Constitution, in Pitney's view, established federal power. It did not prescribe a particular code of maritime law. So much was clear on the face of the Constitution, and from the debates of the Philadelphia Convention. The clause of the Judiciary Act of 1789 which saved common law remedies was not restricted to those existing at the time. Admiralty courts were at liberty to lay hold of common law principles and of state statutes, even as courts of common law were at liberty to adopt maritime rules. "This eclectic method had been practiced by the courts of each jurisdiction prior to the Constitution, and there is nothing in that instrument to constrain them to abandon it." Until this decision, Pitney had never supposed otherwise. As to a need for uniformity, it could be no greater in admiralty, surely, than under the Commerce Clause, and if there was such a need, it was for Congress to declare it.[50]

Congress responded promptly to the decision in *Jensen*. Within five months, it passed, and the President on October 6, 1917, approved, an amendment adding a clause to the section of the Judiciary Act of 1789 which conferred the admiralty jurisdiction on the federal courts, while saving a common law remedy; so that the section now gave to the federal courts exclusive original cognizance "of all civil causes of admiralty and maritime jurisdiction, saving to suitors, in all cases, the right of a common-law remedy where the common law is competent to give it, *and to claimants the rights and remedies under the workmen's compensation law of any State.*" (Added language in italics.)[51] It took a couple of years for this new statutory language to come to judgment,

---

[49] Holmes' dissent drew two returns from members of the majority—not a common practice. Day wrote: "As an old sailor I stand for a uniform rule of liability on the high seas—hence I cannot agree with your view." Holmes Papers. And it was to this dissent that McKenna made the witty return saying that he liked it, playing on Holmes' now famous phrase by noting his own "brooding conviction the other way," and ending with the declaration that it gratified his "Irish heart to see heads hit even if one of them is my own." See *supra*, p. 239.

[50] Southern Pacific Co. v. Jensen, 244 U.S. 205, 213, 215, 216, 217, 220, 221–22, 223, 237 (1917).

[51] 40 Stat. 395 (1917).

but in *Knickerbocker Ice Co.* v. *Stewart*, decided in May 1920, it did so, and fell before the five-man majority that decided *Jensen*, a majority held together once more by the urge to uniformity.

Like *Winfield* and *Jensen, Knickerbocker Ice Co.* was also a suit between private parties. But this time, neither the state of New York nor the United States was heard, however indirectly, to defend the constitutionality of their laws; and again, as in the *Blackwell* case noted earlier and in too many other instances,[52] the employee himself was not represented in the Supreme Court either. Thus, although it had two *amicus* briefs before it, the Court effectively decided the case *ex parte*. In more recent years, the Court has appointed counsel for indigent parties who were otherwise unrepresented, particularly in criminal cases. And it has often invited submissions by interested states and by the United States. Since 1937, the United States has had an absolute right to intervene in any private action in which the constitutionality "of any Act of Congress affecting the public interest" is drawn in question.[53] And under the Court's Rule 24(b), as revised, states may intervene in suits in which their statutes or other actions are attacked. But of these later reforms there was as yet no intimation in 1920.

Knickerbocker Ice Co. v. *Stewart* dealt with federal social legislation, to be sure, and is indeed one of the few cases in which the White Court held such federal legislation unconstitutional. It is treated here rather than in the previous chapter, however, so that it may be seen in the full context of the Court's preemption of state workmen's compensation statutes.[54]

William M. Stewart was accidentally killed while working on a barge in the Hudson River. Compensation was awarded his widow under the New York law, and the award was upheld by the state courts despite *Jensen,* in view of the Act of October 6, 1917. The Supreme Court reversed, McReynolds again writing for the majority. The Constitution, he conceded again, gave Congress power to legislate with respect to maritime matters. What was more important, however, "it took from the States all power, by legislation or judicial decision, to contravene the essential purposes of, or to work material injury to, characteristic features of [maritime] law or to interfere with its proper harmony and uniformity in its international and interstate relations."

The Act of October 6, 1917, McReynolds noted, had been passed somewhat in haste and with little debate. Nonetheless he was satisfied, on the basis of a brief report of the Senate Judiciary Committee, that Congress intended to save state workmen's compensation statutes as

---

[52] *Cf. supra,* pp. 219, 553, 554, 559.
[53] 28 U.S.C. Sec. 2403 (1958); see

United States v. Johnson, 319 U.S. 302 (1943).
[54] See *supra,* pp. 444–45.

applied to maritime injuries from "the objections pointed out by *Southern Pacific Co. v. Jensen.* It sought to authorize and sanction action by the States in prescribing and enforcing, as to all parties concerned, rights, obligations, liabilities and remedies designed to provide compensation for injuries suffered by employees engaged in maritime work." But, as so construed, "we think the enactment is beyond the power of Congress."

The power conferred upon Congress by the Constitution in maritime matters, McReynolds held, was a power "to establish, so far as practicable, harmonious and uniform rules applicable throughout every part of the Union"—that and nothing else. The subject of maritime law was entrusted to Congress "to be dealt with according to its discretion—not for delegation to others. To say that because Congress could have enacted a compensation act applicable to maritime injuries it could authorize States to do so as they might desire is false reasoning. Moreover, such an authorization would inevitably destroy the harmony and uniformity which the Constitution not only contemplated but actually established. . . ." It was true that the decision in *Clark Distilling Co. v. Western Maryland Railway*[55] in a sense allowed Congress to delegate to the states its regulatory authority under the Commerce Clause. But by the Webb-Kenyon Act, which was there in question, Congress did exercise its own will—it prohibited importation of liquor.[56] In any event, the *Clark Distilling Co.* case was explained by the exceptional nature of the subject—liquor. And it arose under the Commerce Clause, not in admiralty.

The dissent was by Holmes, this time joined not only by Brandeis and Clarke, but also by Pitney, who did not write separately. It could hardly be, Holmes began, reverting to his point in *Jensen*, that the simple constitutional provision conferring admiralty and maritime jurisdiction on the federal courts "enacted a whole code for master and servant at sea, that could be modified only by a constitutional amendment." Somehow or other, something like such a code had been developed. If Holmes' explanation that its source was the common law of the states was not accepted, "I can only say, I do not know how [the code was developed], unless by the fiat of the judges. But surely the power that imposed the liability can change it, and I suppose that Congress can do as much as the judges who introduced the rules. For we know that they were introduced and cannot have been elicited by logic alone from the medieval sea laws."

Congress had legislated. Should it be thought necessary, for purposes of receiving the Act as a true expression of the will of Congress,

---

[55] See *supra,* pp. 442–45, n.119.   [56] But only where state law prohibited it.

to construe it as validating only existing, and not future, state workmen's compensation laws, then this construction ought plainly to be adopted to save the constitutionality of the Act, and it would not change the result Holmes contended for in this case. Uniformity would not be achieved, but nothing in the Constitution commanded it. To read into Article III "a requirement of uniformity more mechanical than is educed from the express requirement of equality in the Fourteenth Amendment seems to me extravagant." He had thought, Holmes added, that *Clark Distilling Co.* v. *Western Maryland Railway* "went pretty far in justifying the adoption of state legislation in advance, as I cannot for a moment believe that apart from the Eighteenth Amendment special Constitutional principles exist against strong drink. The fathers of the Constitution so far as I know approved it."[57]

Neither the *Jensen* case nor *Knickerbocker Ice Co.* v. *Stewart* caused any stir in the press, although *The New Republic*, to which Felix Frankfurter was a contributor and adviser, did take notice. Prompt relief from Congress was called for, said the editors, by way of a nationwide workmen's compensation law. But the evil of such decisions as *Knickerbocker Ice Co.*, they continued, "lives after their rectification. One wonders if the venerable Chief Justice and his colleagues realize how they sap confidence in the 'law' which they administer and in the Constitution of which they are the special guardians. 'Petty decisions' make a petty Constitution and swell the tide of discontent against its petty and rigid restrictions more than all the diatribes of 'agitators.' "[58] A generation later, the leading admiralty text looked back on *Jensen* as a prime contender for "the distinction of being the most ill-advised admiralty decision ever handed down by the Supreme Court."[59]

Knickerbocker Ice Co. v. *Stewart* by no means disposed of the problem. It produced rather several judicial and legislative sequels.[60] Brandeis' final judgment on *Jensen* and *Knickerbocker*, given in conver-

---

[57] Knickerbocker Ice Co. v. Stewart, 253 U.S. 149, 160, 163–64, 167, 168, 169 (1920).

This remark was an effort, Holmes told Harold Laski, "(as Rufus Choate put it about a witness who was seen amusing himself with a lady on a haycock) to mitigate the asperities of haymaking. . . ." For his pains, he got "a long anonymous letter in pencil (frequent in anonymous communications) . . . referring me copiously to the Old Testament. . . ." "Rum lot, the anonymous," Holmes concluded.

Holmes-Laski Letters, I, 264.

[58] *The New Republic,* 23:37–38, June 9, 1920.

[59] G. Gilmore and C. L. Black, Jr., *Admiralty* (1957), 526.

[60] See Grant Smith-Porter Ship Co. v. Rhode, 257 U.S. 469 (1922); Washington v. Dawson & Co., 264 U.S. 219 (1924); Crowell v. Benson, 285 U.S. 22 (1932); Longshoremen's & Harbor Workers' Compensation Act of 1927, 44 Stat. 1424 (1927), 33 U.S.C. Sec. 901 (1958).

sation with Felix Frankfurter in the early 1920s, was that its fault lay in its absolutist rigidity, in the abandonment, so to speak, of the function of judgment. In a sense, it was not so much that the judges had played the wild card, as that for once they had failed to play it. And Brandeis thought that by then (the early 1920s) McReynolds was beginning to see where he had gone wrong. What he had done was to turn "specific questions of fact into 'law.' Of course, where uniformity is required, you want uniformity—but it is absurd by an *ipse dixit* to determine what does and what does not require uniformity, as they did in the Jensen and Knickerbocker cases."[61]

State Taxation

In passing on state measures regulating interstate commerce, the Supreme Court has not tolerated discrimination in favor of local business, and it has generally resisted attempts to exclude articles or instrumentalities of interstate commerce from a state. Faced with non-discriminatory regulations that fell short of outright exclusion, the Court has sought to project the kind of burden on interstate commerce, or impediment to it, that a given regulation would impose if multiplied. The Court has tested any single regulation by regarding it as if it had been enacted in all states, with variations in detail from state to state. On the other hand, the Court has weighed in favor of the state, and from the state's point of view, the magnitude and particularity to itself of the interest that it was trying to protect, and has tended to look most favorably upon regulations that got closest to the core of state police power, as when they concerned the health, safety, or morals of the state's population.

Even so, as we have seen, the Court has somewhat independently assessed the claimed state interest, and has often subjected it to a value judgment of the Court's own. This—the Court's own judgment of reasonableness or necessity—has been the wild card in the Commerce Clause deck, or to change the figure, the point of contact between the Commerce and Due Process clauses.

When judging the validity of state taxation rather than regulation of interstate commerce, the Court has again been quick to forbid provincial discrimination. Finding no discrimination, overt or covert, the Court has been equally concerned to project a given tax by multiplying it, so as to test its effect in burdening or impeding the movement of goods and services within a national common market. The state interest sought to be vindicated by a tax, however, is not so readily particularized as the interest to be protected by a regulation. There is,

---

[61] Brandeis-Frankfurter Conversations.

to be sure, the very large interest in keeping state governments solvent and thus alive. But this is not an interest that can help the Court differentiate between one tax and another. Every so often a tax is enacted specifically for the purpose of reimbursing a state for the expense of administering a given regulation, and then, as we shall see, to the extent that the tax covers this expense and produces no further revenue, it is judged quite as the regulation which it supports would be. So, for example, a tax may cover the expenses of inspecting foodstuffs or other products for cleanliness or safety. On the whole, however, there are seldom distinct state interests that can be identified as justifying a given tax. Hence in tax cases the point of contact between the Commerce and Due Process clauses—the judgment of reasonableness and necessity—is not so soon or so often or so obviously reached.

The option of simply determining whether something is or is not interstate commerce, and disallowing a tax on it if it is—this option has long been effectively foreclosed. For intrastate and interstate business are all too often intermingled, and the latter has come increasingly to predominate. It was never intended, by encouraging the free flow of commerce, to impair the existence of the states as viable units of government. Yet that would have been the result of the successful operation of the Commerce Clause, if in promoting the rise of a national economy the clause had been permitted to withdraw more and more and finally nearly all wealth-producing activity from the taxing jurisdiction of the states. And so it soon became clear, as Thomas Reed Powell once wrote, that "in plain, economic fact the states can tax interstate commerce if they go about it in the right way. The problem then reduces itself to one of drawing the lines between the right ways and the wrong ways of taxing interstate commerce."[62]

The lines between right and wrong as often as not find expression in rule-of-thumb formulas, and these are infected with a considerable element of the arbitrary. Formal aspects of the tax, which do not seem to have much connection with its actual economic incidence, were often emphasized. Thus it made a difference whether interstate commerce was taxed as such, or whether the tax fell on property or on a corporate franchise, even though ultimately interstate commerce pays the tax anyway. This stress on the formality of labels can lead to absurd results, and yet focusing on the label is an attempt to magnify the tax, to see the generality of its applications. One form of tax more than another may in the generality of cases lend itself to discriminatory application against interstate commerce, or result in the imposition of crippling, multiple burdens.

---

[62] T. R. Powell, "Contemporary Commerce Clause Controversies over State Taxation," *U. Pa. L. Rev.,* 76: 773, 774, 1928.

The state tax cases decided in the ten and a half years of the White Chief Justiceship have not so far been examined.[63] They are substantial in volume, and they struggle with the imponderables suggested above. Surveying an important segment of them in 1919, Thomas Reed Powell concluded that they could be doctrinally explained and fitted together only by "the principle of 'some, but not too much.' " The Court, he remarked, was "evidently feeling its way and hampering its future action as little as possible." On analysis, theories expressed in various opinions turned out to work at cross purposes, and yet practical considerations could be perceived which did harmonize the decisions.[64]

Fees that covered with some precision the cost of safety inspection of goods coming into the state, as for example, oil products,[65] were the taxes most indulgently treated by the Supreme Court. But if a fee exceeded the cost of the inspection undertaken by the state, it lost its justification as such. The Court was no respecter of disguise.[66] The Court was almost as tolerant of taxes falling directly on property held within a state, or on sales made there. In property tax cases, the chief question was whether the property was indeed held in the taxing state; whether it had come to rest there, rather than being in transit. As an opinion by Hughes explained, the property—for example, grain held in an elevator in Chicago—might have arrived through interstate commerce and be again destined for it, and yet be at rest in the taxing state, under the control of a resident.[67]

Hughes' sensible criterion—sensible, although as usual in these matters, depending on variables—was briefly thrown into doubt in two decisions by Day in 1919 and 1920.[68] Harking back to a formula proposed by John Marshall himself for foreign imports in *Brown* v. *Maryland*,[69] Day held that property could not be said to have come to rest in a state and to have become taxable there if it had arrived in

---

[63] See *supra,* pp. 275–76.

[64] See Powell, *State Excises on Foreign Corporations,* 17, 32.

[65] See Red "C" Oil Co. v. North Carolina, 222 U.S. 380 (1912); Pure Oil Co. v. Minnesota, 248 U.S. 158 (1918).

[66] See Foote v. Maryland, 232 U.S. 494 (1914); Standard Oil Co. v. Graves, 249 U.S. 389 (1919); Askren v. Continental Oil Co., 252 U.S. 444 (1920).

[67] Bacon v. Illinois, 227 U.S. 504 (1913); see also Susquehanna Coal Co. v. South Amboy, 228 U.S. 665 (1913). See also Darnell v. Indiana, 226 U.S. 390 (1912); Mackay Telegraph Co. v. Little Rock, 250 U.S. 94 (1919). *Cf.* Brodnax v. Missouri, 219 U.S. 285 (1911). And *cf.* Dawson v. Kentucky Distilleries Co., 255 U.S. 288 (1921).

[68] Standard Oil Co. v. Graves, *supra,* n.66; Askren v. Continental Oil Co., *supra,* n.66; but *cf.* Wagner v. City of Covington, 251 U.S. 95 (1919).

[69] 12 Wheat. 419 (1827).

interstate commerce and was still in the package in which it had been shipped. The formula solved the problem of variables less than it seemed to—for, after all, what is an original package, especially as the concept is applied to products that are shipped in bulk?—and it often led to excessively arbitrary results. It had been abandoned by the Court for interstate commerce before the turn of the century, and despite Day's attempt to revive it, it was soon discarded once more, shortly after Taft's accession.[70]

During its short afterlife, however, the original-package doctrine threatened to apply, not only in property tax cases, but to sales taxes as well, which also depended for their validity on the article taxed having come to rest in the state.[71] But the validity of a sales tax turned more often on a related inquiry, not affected by the original-package doctrine. The question was whether the contract of sale was concluded in the taxing state. This was the issue often raised by flat-fee license taxes imposed on the seller for the privilege of doing business, which were a common alternative to the direct sales tax, although they were smaller in amount if the volume of sales was substantial.

A peddler, the Court had long held, carrying the goods he sold with him, and selling them as he traveled, could be subjected to a license tax; he was assimilated to a competitive local establishment. A drummer, however, soliciting orders which he sent out of state to be filled, could not be taxed, because the sales in which he was instrumental were made by contracts concluded outside the state. But who peddled and who, marching to the beat of a more distant contract, drummed—this depended on numerous factual variables. Thus the Browning of *Browning* v. *Waycross*[72] was in the business of erecting lightning rods in the city of Waycross, Georgia. The rods were manufactured and shipped into Waycross by a St. Louis, Missouri, concern. Browning solicited orders, which he sent to St. Louis to be filled. The contract of sale, completed in St. Louis, stipulated an obligation on the part of the seller to install the rods, and when they arrived in Waycross, Browning installed them. The city imposed an annual license tax on him for the privilege of doing so, and the Supreme Court upheld it. Installation of the rod was a local business, the Court said. The sale of the rod was a transaction that had been completed by the time Browning came around to install it. To be sure, the installation was provided for in the contract of sale, but that did not alter the true nature of things. Cases where the obligation of the

---

70 Sonneborn Bros. v. Cureton, 262 U.S. 506 (1923).

71 *Compare* Banker Brothers v. Pennsylvania, 222 U.S. 210 (1911), *with* Bowman v. Continental Oil Co., 256 U.S. 642 (1921).

72 233 U.S. 16 (1914).

seller to install the article he had sold arose because of some peculiar quality or inherent complexity of the article were different. Those were cases in which possibly the installation could be deemed essential to the accomplishment of the sale, and part of it. Not so with lightning rods, however.

Yet the Court, in a cursory opinion by Holmes just a few years earlier—unanimous, as was the opinion in *Browning* v. *Waycross*—had held that where orders were solicited under a form contract which provided that upon delivery of the portrait the buyer would have the option to purchase a frame from the delivery agent, the sale of the portrait and its installation in the frame were part of a single interstate transaction, and could not be subjected to a license tax.[73] A slight factual variation in a somewhat later case—clear testimony by the purchaser that the frame was sold to him separately by an agent who carried a supply of frames—resulted in an affirmance by an equally divided Court of a holding that the agent selling the frames was a peddler and could be made to pay a license tax.[74] A few years later, the Court, speaking once more unanimously through Holmes, reaffirmed the earlier proposition that the sale of the frame was part of a single, nontaxable interstate transaction.[75]

This illustration of the minute factual variables on which decision often depended, and of the fluctuation of decision, is by no means unique. Another oft-cited state tax case of the decade was *Crenshaw* v. *Arkansas*.[76] It concerned sales of ranges in Arkansas by a Missouri corporation which had a regional agent in the state, who in turn employed two types of subagents. One subagent went out with a sample range, traveling about and soliciting orders, which were filled on credit within sixty days. The ranges were then shipped from Missouri to the regional agent. Another subagent made the delivery to the purchaser. The solicitors never delivered, and the deliverers never solicited. The sales, the Court held, were made at the home office in Missouri, and neither type of subagent, deliverer nor solicitor, could be subjected to an annual license tax. The entire operation was a drumming, not a peddling operation. Now, it required a real act of will to keep in focus the possible aggregate effect of the taxes dealt with in such cases, and

---

[73] Dozier v. Alabama, 218 U.S. 124 (1910).

[74] Roselle v. Virginia, 110 Va. 235, 65 S.E. 526 (1909), *affirmed by an equally divided Court*, 223 U.S. 716 (1912). The case was heard at the October Term 1911, following Harlan's death, and before Pitney was seated on March 18, 1912. Hence the eight-man Court.

[75] Davis v. Virginia, 236 U.S. 697 (1915).

[76] 227 U.S. 389 (1913); see also Rogers v. Arkansas, 227 U.S. 401 (1913).

thus to maintain any sense of the importance of deciding each case one way or the other.[77]

The Court was considerably more lenient with license taxes imposed on concerns that maintained facilities in the taxing state and engaged in intrastate business there, so long as there was no dispute about the intrastate character of that business. Flat license fees would be upheld in such circumstances even though the taxpayer conducted an interstate business as well, and no one could be sure that some of the burden of the tax did not fall on the interstate segment of the enterprise;[78] indeed, sometimes even if quite apparently it did so fall, as when the intrastate business lost money.[79] The Court was satisfied if the tax was not nominally levied on the interstate business, and if the tax was reasonable in amount, so that it could, in theory at any rate, be absorbed by the intrastate portion of the enterprise. But the Court was alert to any possibility that the tax actually discriminated against the interstate business.[80] And when Pennsylvania measured a license tax not by a flat fee but by a small percentage of gross receipts from all sales, and the taxpayer, who maintained warehouses in the state, sold $47,000 worth of goods within it, and $430,000 worth outside it, the Court held that the portion of the tax consisting of a percentage of the interstate sales fell on interstate commerce directly, taxed it as such, and was unconstitutional.[81]

---

[77] In addition to the cases referred to in the text, *compare* Stewart v. Michigan, 232 U.S. 665 (1914); Heyman v. Hays, 236 U.S. 178 (1915); Southern Operating Co. v. Hays, 236 U.S. 188 (1915); Western Oil Refining Co. v. Lipscomb, 244 U.S. 346 (1917); and Bowman v. Continental Oil Co., 256 U.S. 642 (1921), *with* Singer Sewing Machine Co. v. Brickell, 233 U.S. 304 (1914); Armour & Co. v. Virginia, 246 U.S. 1 (1918); Wagner v. City of Covington, 251 U.S. 95 (1919); and Newport v. Heckerman, 254 U.S. 614 (1920). See also Dalton Machine Co. v. Virginia, 236 U.S. 699 (1915).

[78] See Ewing v. City of Leavenworth, 226 U.S. 464 (1913); U.S. Fidelity Co. v. Kentucky, 231 U.S. 394 (1913); Cornell Steamboat Co. v. Sohmer, 235 U.S. 549 (1915); Postal Telegraph-Cable Co. v. Richmond, 249 U.S. 252 (1919); Ameri-

can Manufacturing Co. v. St. Louis, 250 U.S. 459 (1919). See also General Electric Co. v. Alderson, 49 Mont. 29, 140 P. 82 (1914), *writ of error dismissed on motion of plaintiff in error,* 238 U.S. 644 (1915); Postal Telegraph Co. v. City of Portland, 228 Fed. 254 (D. Ore. 1915), *appeal dismissed on motion of appellant,* 241 U.S. 693 (1916); Evansville & Bowling Green Packet Co. v. Logan, 180 Ky. 216, 202 S.W. 492 (1918), *writ of error dismissed for want of jurisdiction,* 251 U.S. 543 (1920); but *cf.* International Textbook Co. v. Lynch, 218 U.S. 664 (1910).

[79] See Postal Telegraph-Cable Co. v. Fremont, 255 U.S. 124 (1921); *cf.* Ohio Tax Cases, 232 U.S. 576 (1914).

[80] See Bethlehem Motors Co. v. Flynt, 256 U.S. 421 (1921).

[81] Crew Levick Co. v. Pennsylvania, 245 U.S. 292 (1917).

Yet gross receipts were not necessarily an impermissible measure of a license tax under all circumstances. Thus Wisconsin, as the headquarters state and state of incorporation of an insurance company which kept huge amounts of securities in the state, was allowed to impose an annual license tax measured by 3 percent of gross income earned in the state.[82] Of course, much of the income earned in the state—on securities held there, for example—came from outside. Only premiums actually collected outside the state on policies held by nonresidents, and rents from real estate, which was separately taxed, were excluded from the measure of the license tax. But the license tax was levied in lieu of all other taxes, such as, for example, property taxes on securities, aside from the separate real estate tax, and this commutation feature of the license tax weighed heavily with the Court. Moreover, in deciding this case, the Court assumed for purposes of argument that insurance was commerce in the first place. The latter issue had been decided in the negative in 1868,[83] and the decision was reaffirmed by a divided Court in 1913, Hughes and Van Devanter dissenting without opinion, in *New York Life Insurance Co.* v. *Deer Lodge County*,[84] which held once again that far from being an article of commerce, a policy of insurance was "a personal contract, a mere indemnity, for a consideration, against the happening of some contingent event. . . ." For the insurance company, which plainly preferred being regulated, if at all, by Congress rather than being subject to varieties of state control, Professor Roscoe Pound of the Harvard Law School had argued the contrary.

Again, Ohio was permitted to levy, against railroads among other utilities, an annual tax for the privilege of doing intrastate business, the measure of which was 4 percent of gross receipts, excluding earnings derived wholly from interstate business.[85] The case is a striking illustration of Thomas Reed Powell's remark that the question the Court was concerned with was not so much whether a state was taxing interstate commerce, but how it was doing it.[86] By an act of March 10, 1910, Ohio had measured this same tax by 1 percent of gross receipts in the state from all business, with no exclusion for receipts from interstate commerce. Fearing that the tax so measured might be constitutionally vulnerable, the legislature a year later amended it to exclude earnings derived wholly from interstate commerce. But at the same time, it raised the rate to 4 percent. The legislature evidently calculated that

[82] Northwestern Mutual Life Ins. Co. v. Wisconsin, 247 U.S. 132 (1918).

[83] Paul v. Virginia, 8 Wall. 168 (1868).

[84] 231 U.S. 495, 508 (1913).

[85] Ohio Tax Cases, 232 U.S. 576 (1914); see also Northern Express Co. v. Washington, 80 Wash. 309 (1914), *writ of error dismissed on motion of plaintiff in error*, 241 U.S. 686 (1916).

[86] See *supra*, p. 567.

this device would keep the returns from the tax stable. The calculation was not far wrong.[87] The selectivity of the taxable subjects was an important factor in making such a scheme politically feasible—and legally suspect.

Property taxes, whose generality caused them to be viewed favorably, became suspect if they were levied on property not permanently within the state, or if the tax, though falling on property, was measured by the value attaching to that property on account of its use in interstate commerce.

In *Union Tank Line Co.* v. *Wright*, tank cars owned by the company had moved in and out of Georgia, the taxing state, in the year for which a property tax was levied on them. Fifty-seven cars, the company claimed, were the daily average in the state. The fair market value of the fifty-seven cars was conceded to be about $47,000. The state in fact valued them at $291,000, because it used a formula under which the company's property was valued as a whole, and the valuation assigned to property in Georgia was in the same proportion as the track mileage in Georgia bore to the mileage everywhere. This "unit rule" and apportionment formula had been approved by the Supreme Court in *Pullman Palace Car Co.* v. *Pennsylvania*.[88] Nevertheless, in the *Union Tank Line Co.* case, the Court, per McReynolds, held the Georgia tax unconstitutional as applied. The apportionment formula had previously been held valid, said McReynolds, because it had achieved results that corresponded approximately to the market value of the property employed there on a daily average. Here the formula had produced a grossly excessive valuation.

McReynolds wrote for a majority of five. Day concurred in the result without opinion, "in view of the undisputed facts of this case." Pitney, joined by Brandeis and Clarke, dissented. The assumption that an average of fifty-seven cars were in Georgia during the taxable year, said Pitney, was arbitrary, not necessarily accurate, because if the state were actually to check the average number of cars used, "the cost of administration easily might consume the tax." Hence the statement that the tax was based on a grossly excessive valuation was a guess. The state should not be foreclosed from taxing the actual, going-concern value of the company's property. The majority was departing from the holding of the *Pullman Palace Car Co.* case, which had long been deemed authoritative, and been followed in the tax laws of many states.[89]

---

[87] See *Ohio Railroads, Report of the Railroad Commission of Ohio 1909* (Springfield, Ohio: 1910).

[88] 141 U.S. 18 (1891).

[89] Union Tank Line Co. v. Wright, 249 U.S. 275, 286, 290 (1919). Compare Germania Refining Co. v. Fuller, 184 Mich. 618, 151 N.W. 605 (1915), *affirmed*, 245 U.S. 632 (1917); Wells, Fargo & Co. v. Nevada, 248 U.S. 165

In *United States Express Co.* v. *Minnesota*[90] and *Cudahy Packing Co.* v. *Minnesota*,[91] a property tax measured by gross earnings within the state was upheld. The receipts that were the measure of the tax were earned from interstate as well as intrastate business, indeed in major part from interstate business, but they were earned within the taxing state, and the tax that was imposed fell on them indirectly only, being in fact a property tax on wagons and cars used in the state. These decisions exemplify the somewhat uncertain distinction made by the Court between taxation that burdened interstate commerce indirectly, and any sort of tariff falling on it directly, as such. Thus the Court held unconstitutional a tax which was not a property tax, but was levied in addition to property taxes, and fell directly on gross receipts from both intrastate and interstate commerce. The tax was apportioned. Only that fraction of gross receipts was taxable which bore the same relation to total gross receipts as the portion of the company's business done within the state bore to the whole of its business. What was nevertheless decisive against this tax was that it was not levied on property, and did not use gross receipts merely as a measure of the true, going-concern value of property, but rather was levied on gross receipts as such.[92]

Taxes, however, falling on net rather than gross receipts were upheld, at least so long as they employed some sort of a formula for arriving at a portion of total net receipts attributable to business— whether intra- or interstate—done within the taxing state. Net income taxes, Pitney held in *United States Glue Co.* v. *Oak Creek*, are only an indirect burden on interstate commerce. A tax on gross receipts fell regardless of whether there was any profit, and could make the difference between profit and loss, thus perhaps tending to discourage the conduct of the commerce. A tax on net receipts had no such deterrent effect. It was not payable unless there had been a profit, and could not be heavy unless the profit was large. "Such a tax, when imposed upon net incomes from whatever source arising, is but a method of distributing the cost of government, like a tax upon property, or upon franchises treated as property, and if there be no discrimination against interstate commerce, either in the admeasurement of the tax or in the means adopted for enforcing it, it constitutes one of the ordinary and general burdens of government, from which persons and corporations otherwise subject to the jurisdiction of the States are not exempted by the Federal Constitu-

(1918); St. Louis & East St. Louis Ry. v. Hagerman, 256 U.S. 314 (1921). See also Northern Pacific Ry. v. King County, Washington, 196 Fed. 323 (9th Cir. 1912), *appeal dismissed per stipulation*, 231 U.S. 758 (1913).

[90] 223 U.S. 335 (1912).

[91] 246 U.S. 450 (1918).

[92] Oklahoma v. Wells, Fargo & Co., 223 U.S. 298 (1912).

tion because they happen to be engaged in commerce among the States."[93]

Very much the same sort of problem raised by taxes on gross and net receipts was presented to the Court also by taxes which, while falling nominally on the privilege of doing intrastate business, were measured by a proportion of issued capital stock. In 1910, a divided Court held that unapportioned capital stock taxes, imposed on railroad and telegraph companies incorporated elsewhere and doing both interstate and intrastate business in the taxing state, and imposed without any effort to reach only that proportion of the capital stock which bore a relation to the amount of business done in the taxing state, were unconstitutional.[94] But that was not the last word. Three years later, in *Baltic Mining Co.* v. *Massachusetts,*[95] the Court upheld an unapportioned capital stock tax, which was different in that it rose to a maximum of $2,000 a year, and did not in any circumstances go beyond. This compromise was then reaffirmed in 1918, although in the two decades following it had a most unstable existence.[96]

Where there was no maximum, unapportioned capital stock taxes were held unconstitutional.[97] But apportioned ones, as when Arkansas fixed its tax at a percentage of "the proportion of the outstanding capital stock of the corporation represented by property owned and used in business transacted in this State," were upheld whether or not they had a stated maximum.[98] The caution represented by *Union Tank Line Co.* v. *Wright*, however, in which the property tax that was struck down was also apportioned, had to be taken into account. An apportionment formula for taxing capital stock was held invalid when, as applied, it resulted in a gross overassessment.[99]

---

[93] United States Glue Co. v. Oak Creek, 247 U.S. 321, 329 (1918); see also Underwood Typewriter Co. v. Chamberlain, 254 U.S. 113 (1920).

[94] Western Union Telegraph Co. v. Kansas, 216 U.S. 1 (1910); Pullman Co. v. Kansas, 216 U.S. 56 (1910); Ludwig v. Western Union Telegraph Co., 216 U.S. 146 (1910). See also Atchison, Topeka & Santa Fe Ry. v. O'Connor, 223 U.S. 280 (1912).

[95] 231 U.S. 68 (1913).

[96] See Cheney Brothers Co. v. Massachusetts, 246 U.S. 147 (1918); General Ry. Signal Co. v. Virginia, 246 U.S. 500 (1918). Compare Cudahy Packing Co. v. Hinkle, 278 U.S. 460 (1929); Atlantic Refining Co. v. Virginia, 302 U.S. 22 (1937).

[97] Looney v. Crane Co., 245 U.S. 178 (1917); International Paper Co. v. Massachusetts, 246 U.S. 135 (1918); Locomobile Co. v. Massachusetts, 246 U.S. 146 (1918); Union Pacific R.R. v. Public Service Commission, 248 U.S. 67 (1918); see also Massachusetts v. Liquid Carbonic Co., 232 Mass. 19 (1919), *cert. denied,* 249 U.S. 603 (1919).

[98] St. Louis, Southwestern Ry. v. Arkansas, 235 U.S. 350, 360 (1914). See also Chicago, Rock Island & Pacific Ry. v. Kansas, 95 Kan. 272, 147 P. 789 (1915) (*sub nom.* Dawson v. Sessions), *affirmed,* 245 U.S. 627 (1917).

[99] Wallace v. Hines, 253 U.S. 66 (1920).

All these convolutions and fine distinctions concerned the taxation of corporations incorporated elsewhere than in the taxing state. So-called domestic corporations, taxed by the state of their incorporation, could be subjected to capital stock taxes without apportionment and without a minimum, at least so long as the circumstances were such, the Court said, "as to indicate no purpose or necessary effect in the tax imposed to burden commerce...."[100]

Taxes measured by gross receipts and by capital stock, and even taxes measured by net receipts, raised a Due Process as well as a Commerce Clause problem, insofar as they reached assets outside the taxing state. But the two problems coincided. If the state was exceeding its jurisdiction in taxing assets outside its borders, it was almost certainly also violating the Commerce Clause by imposing a direct burden on interstate commerce. And so the Due Process point was incidental, although often raised. But there was a category of state tax cases in which the Due Process point was primary, and a Commerce Clause argument, if any, was secondary. Through the decade under discussion, most such cases were easily disposed of in favor of the state. The Due Process contentions, generally lacking much weight, turned on issues of the sufficiency of contact between the taxing state and the business or transaction taxed, and on questions of the situs of intangible property.[101]

Three decisions that were of some consequence concerned the imposition of state income and estate taxes on nonresidents. *Shaffer* v. *Carter*[102] upheld the authority of the states, which had been subject to some doubt, to tax income earned within a state by nonresidents—in this case, the yield of gas and mining leases held in Oklahoma by a resident of Illinois. In *Travis* v. *Yale & Towne Manufacturing Co.*,[103] the Court,

---

[100] Kansas City, Memphis & Burmington R.R. v. Stiles, 242 U.S. 111, 119 (1916). Compare Kansas City Ry. v. Kansas, 240 U.S. 227 (1916); Lusk v. Kansas, 240 U.S. 236 (1916); Albert Pick & Co. v. Jordan, 169 Calif. 1, 145 Pac. 506 (1914), *affirmed,* 244 U.S. 647 (1917) (but *cf.* Perkins Manufacturing Co. v. Jordan, 200 Calif. 667, 254 Pac. 551 [1927]); St. Louis-San Francisco Ry. v. Middlekamp, 256 U.S. 226 (1921).

[101] See Liverpool Ins. Co. v. Orleans Assessors, 221 U.S. 346 (1911); Southern Pacific Co. v. Kentucky, 222 U.S. 63 (1911); Hawley v. Malden, 232 U.S. 1 (1914); Equitable Life Society v. Pennsylvania, 238 U.S. 143 (1915); Rogers v. Hennepin County, 240 U.S. 184 (1916); Fidelity & Columbia Trust Co. v. Louisville, 245 U.S. 54 (1917); Maguire v. Trefry, 253 U.S. 12 (1920); Cream of Wheat Co. v. Grand Forks, 253 U.S. 325 (1920). But *cf.* Provident Savings Ass'n. v. Kentucky, 239 U.S. 103 (1915). See also Illinois Central R.R. v. Kentucky, 218 U.S. 551 (1910); Pullman Co. v. Knott, 235 U.S. 23 (1914); Bullen v. Wisconsin, 240 U.S. 625 (1916).

[102] 252 U.S. 37 (1920); *cf.* Hendenskoy v. Alaska Packers' Ass'n., 267 Fed. 154 (9th Cir. 1920), *cert. denied,* 254 U.S. 652 (1920). See *Colum. L. Rev.,* 20:457, 1920; *Yale L. J.,* 29: 799, 1920.

[103] 252 U.S. 60 (1920).

reaching an issue scarcely ripe in the posture of the case, struck down a provision of New York's income tax law that treated nonresidents differently from residents. Exemptions were granted to residents for themselves and their dependents, but not to nonresidents, who for their part were entitled to a credit in the amount of a tax paid in another state on income earned in New York. Using what was very much a Commerce Clause analysis, Pitney for a unanimous Court held that this discrimination against nonresidents violated the Privileges and Immunities Clause of Article IV of the Constitution. Yet in *Maxwell* v. *Bugbee*,[104] a divided Court held constitutional under both the Privileges and Immunities and Due Process clauses a New Jersey estate tax which, by a formula that took account of property outside the state in measuring the tax on property left within it, fell more heavily on the estates in New Jersey of nonresident decedents than resident ones.

The estates thus discriminatorily taxed in this case were those of James McDonald of Washington, D.C., and James J. Hill of Minnesota (*the* James J. Hill, who was worth some $54 million, but died intestate), both of whom left substantial shareholdings in the Standard Oil Company, a New Jersey corporation. The devolution of these shares to the heirs of McDonald and Hill was taxed in New Jersey. Day, for the Court, held that New Jersey had denied neither due process nor equal protection, and had violated neither the Privileges and Immunities nor the Commerce Clause. Holmes, joined by White, Van Devanter, and McReynolds, dissented on Due Process grounds. "Many things," he said, "that a legislature may do if it does them with no ulterior purpose, it cannot do as a means to reach what is beyond its constitutional power." New Jersey could not tax the property of McDonald or Hill outside the state, and no matter what the form of words used, that was what the New Jersey formula, which took account of the out-of-state portion of their estates, had attempted to accomplish indirectly.

Another restraint on state taxation arose from the Supremacy Clause of the federal Constitution and was analogous to the preemption doctrine applicable to state regulatory measures. States could not tax, at least they could not discriminatorily tax, the federal government and its instrumentalities, Marshall had held rather obviously in *McCulloch* v. *Maryland*,[105] remarking too offhandedly that "the power of taxing . . . may be exercised so as to destroy. . . ." In time, the Court spun out a variety of rules forbidding perfectly nondiscriminatory taxation by the states—not only direct, but often quite indirect and even remote—of federally chartered banks, of public lands and other public property held

---

[104] 250 U.S. 525, 543 (1919); see also Skarderud v. Tax Commission, 36 N.D. 471, 162 N.W. 704 (1917)

(*sub nom.* Moody v. Hagen), *affirmed*, 245 U.S. 633 (1917).

[105] 4 Wheat. 316, 427 (1819).

by private parties under various arrangements with the United States and of activities carried on under contract with the United States, of earnings from federal bonds, and of land and mineral properties (and earnings from them) of which the United States was trustee for its Indian wards, but which were often held and operated by private business interests. The Court in these years tended to bestow immunity rather liberally.[106] But it did also, at times, find the nexus to the United States too tenuous to sustain immunity, as for example, in an early opinion by Brandeis in *McCurdy* v. *United States*.[107] The Secretary of the Interior had tried to keep Oklahoma from taxing land bought by an Indian with the income from oil leases held in trust by the United States. Brandeis held that the applicable statute authorized no such immunity as the Secretary had attempted to create.[108]

Two closely related cases should be mentioned here even though they did not concern state taxation. In *Johnson* v. *Maryland*,[109] Holmes relied on *McCulloch* v. *Maryland* to hold that the state could not require an employee of the U.S. Post Office driving a mail truck from Maryland to Washington, D.C., to have a state driver's license. *Ruddy* v. *Rossi*[110] turned on the following provision of the Homestead Act: "No lands

---

[106] See Sargent & Lahr v. Herrick & Stevens, 221 U.S. 404 (1911); Williams v. Talladega, 226 U.S. 404 (1912); Farmers Bank v. Minnesota, 232 U.S. 516 (1914); Choctaw & Gulf R.R. v. Harrison, 235 U.S. 292 (1914); Indian Oil Co. v. Oklahoma, 240 U.S. 522 (1916); Howard v. Gypsy Oil Co., 247 U.S. 503 (1918); Bank of California v. Richardson, 248 U.S. 476 (1919); Bank of California v. Roberts, 248 U.S. 497 (1919); Merchants' National Bank v. Richmond, 256 U.S. 635 (1921); Large Oil Co. v. Howard, 63 Okla. 143, 163 Pac. 537 (1917), *reversed*, 248 U.S. 549 (1919). *Cf.* Choate v. Trapp, 224 U.S. 665 (1912); Ward v. Love County, 253 U.S. 17 (1920); Broadwell v. Carter County, 253 U.S. 25 (1920).

[107] 246 U.S. 263 (1918). See also Choctaw, Oklahoma & Gulf R.R. v. Mackey, 256 U.S. 531 (1921). And see Clement National Bank v. Vermont, 231 U.S. 120 (1913); Amoskeag Savings Bank v. Purdy, 231 U.S. 373 (1913); Bothwell v. Bingham County,

237 U.S. 642 (1915); Fidelity & Deposit Co. v. Pennsylvania, 240 U.S. 319 (1916); see also State National Bank v. Richardson, 135 Ky. 772, 123 S.W. 294, 1189 (1909), *writ of error dismissed for want of jurisdiction*, 225 U.S. 696 (1912); Union Sand & Material Co. v. Arkansas, 127 Ark. 456, 192 S.W. 380 (1917), *cert. denied*, 243 U.S. 652 (1917).

[108] The opinion was a learned document, and Brandeis set forth some appropriate references at the bottom of the page. He drew from Holmes the following admonition, which Brandeis never heeded, in this case or later, although it represented a minor but firm conviction of Holmes: "Yes. Forcibly put—but I can't think it good form to treat an opinion as an essay and put in footnotes." McCurdy v. United States, 246 U.S. 263 (1918), Brandeis Papers, University of Louisville Law School Library; *cf. Holmes-Laski Letters,* I, 128.

[109] 254 U.S. 51 (1920).

[110] 248 U.S. 104, 105, 108, 110–11 (1918).

acquired under the provisions of this Act shall in any event become liable to the satisfaction of any debt or debts contracted prior to the issuing of the patent [i.e., title] therefor." A settler had made an entry on a plot of land in 1903, and finally got his patent in 1912. He was sued on debts that arose before 1912, and the state courts granted recovery and issued executions which were levied on the land. The Supreme Court reversed. The statute, the Court held, immunized the land. It did so clearly, and was within the power of Congress as defined in *McCulloch* v. *Maryland*. In a dubitante dissent, Holmes said: "My question is this: When land has left the ownership and control of the United States and is part of the territory of a state not different from any other privately owned land within the jurisdiction and no more subject to legislation on the part of the United States than any other land, on what ground is a previous law of Congress supposed any longer to affect it in a way that a subsequent one could not?" As the majority construed and applied the statute, it amounted to nothing but an attempt to regulate the alienability of land with which the United States no longer had any nexus. Holmes continued:

> I am aware that my doubts are contrary to manifest destiny and to a number of decisions in the State Courts. I know also that when common understanding and practice have established a way it is a waste of time to wander in bypaths of logic. But as I have a real difficulty in understanding how the congressional restriction is held to govern this case—a question which nothing that I have heard as yet appears to me to answer—I think it worthwhile to mention my misgivings, if only to show that they have been considered and are not shared.

In the 1920s and early 1930s, the liberality with which the Court had been granting immunity from state taxation became even more marked, as was also an equal liberality in granting reciprocal immunity from federal taxation to states and their instrumentalities. The Court's decisions gave rise increasingly to the sort of misgivings Holmes had voiced in *Ruddy* v. *Rossi*, and ultimately these misgivings led to substantial retrenchment.[111]

---

[111] *Compare*, e.g., Gillespie v. Oklahoma, 257 U.S. 501 (1922); Panhandle Oil Co. v. Mississippi, 277 U.S. 218 (1928); Indian Motorcycle Co. v. United States, 283 U.S. 570 (1931); Burnet v. Coronado Oil & Gas Co., 285 U.S. 393 (1932), *with* James V. Dravo Contracting Co., 302 U.S. 134 (1937); Helvering v. Mountain Producers Corp., 303 U.S. 376 (1938); Oklahoma Tax Commission v. United States, 319 U.S. 598 (1943); New York v. United States, 326 U.S. 572 (1946).

Due Process

During the October Terms 1914 to 1920, as in the four terms preceding, and for some terms to come, litigation testing state measures of social and economic regulation under the Due Process Clause was the single largest category of constitutional business coming before the Court. Out of the great number of cases, a few groups of decisions require detailed treatment, because of their practical significance or because of holdings or dicta of particular doctrinal interest.

BLUE-SKY LAWS

In *Hall* v. *Geiger-Jones Co.*, the Court sustained the first, and not very successful, statutory efforts to regulate the sale of corporate securities—a subject, of course, taken in hand by the federal government in the 1930s.[112] An Ohio statute required each dealer in securities to obtain a license from the state upon a showing of good character. Licenses had to be renewed annually, and the state superintendent of banks and banking was authorized to revoke a license if he found that a dealer no longer enjoyed good business repute, or had engaged in illegitimate or fraudulent transactions. *Hall* v. *Geiger-Jones Co.* was a suit to enjoin enforcement of this statute.[113]

In the Supreme Court, the Attorneys General of Iowa and Wisconsin filed an *amicus* brief in behalf of the National Association of Attorneys General, supporting the constitutionality of blue-sky laws, and former Attorney General George W. Wickersham filed an *amicus* brief on the other side in behalf of the Investment Bankers' Association of America. (In one of the companion cases, Wickersham represented a dealer.) The Court upheld the constitutionality of the statute, vacating an injunction that had been granted below. McKenna wrote for the majority, McReynolds alone dissenting without opinion.

The applicable principles, said McKenna, had become "platitudes." They were that rights of acquisition, disposition, and enjoyment of property were protected by the Constitution, and yet that reasonable

---

[112] See M. E. Parrish, *Securities Regulations and the New Deal* (1970), 5 *et seq.*

[113] South Dakota and Michigan had similar acts, challenged in companion cases, and altogether twenty-six states, beginning with Kansas in 1911, had enacted such statutes. They were called "blue-sky" laws because, as McKenna remarked in the opinion in the *Hall* case, *infra*, n.114, 242 U.S. at 550, they were aimed at "speculative schemes which have no more basis than so many feet of 'blue sky' "; or as was perhaps more commonly thought, because they were directed at promoters whose promises were "as limitless as the blue sky." See *The Literary Digest,* 54:325, Feb. 10, 1917.

state regulations could impair these rights. The Ohio statute gave the superintendent of banks and banking a good deal of discretion, but his discretion was "qualified by his duty, and besides, as we have seen, the statute gives judicial review of his action." Opposition to the statute was based essentially on the notion that because the business of dealing in securities could not be constitutionally prohibited, it could not be regulated. That, of course, did not by any means follow. No doubt, McKenna added in the companion case from Michigan, the efficacy of blue-sky laws was subject to differences of opinion. But it was for the state to resolve such differences in a manner satisfactory to itself. The statute "burdens honest business, it is true, but burdens it only that under its forms dishonest business may not be done. . . . Expense may thereby be caused and inconvenience, but to arrest the power of the State by such considerations would make it impotent to discharge its function. It costs something to be governed."[114]

WORKMEN'S COMPENSATION

A group of significant decisions dealt with the problem of industrial accidents. After the *Second Employers' Liability Cases*, the Supreme Court routinely upheld state statutes abrogating the fellow-servant rule and like common law defenses, and otherwise changing the relevant common law, often selectively, with application to some industries only.[115] But the trend in state legislation was toward adoption of the more radical solution of workmen's compensation programs, which established liability without regard to fault, and awarded compensation in accordance with a prescribed schedule.[116]

---

[114] Hall v. Geiger-Jones Co., 242 U.S. 539, 549, 550, 554 (1971); Caldwell v. Sioux Falls Stockyards Co., 242 U.S. 559 (1917); Merrick v. Halsey & Co. 242 U.S. 568, 587 (1917).

An argument was also put forward that blue-sky laws imposed a burden on interstate commerce and thus violated the Commerce Clause, but McKenna made short shrift of it.

The subject was a live one in January 1917, when *Hall* v. *Geiger-Jones Co.* came down, and the decision had a good reception. See *The Literary Digest*, 54:325, Feb. 10, 1917. Even the president of the Investment Bankers' Association, which had con-

tended for the opposite result, let it be known that his organization was not opposed to the general purpose of blue-sky legislation. See *New York Times*, Jan. 24, 1917, p. 15, col. 2.

[115] See *supra*, pp. 208, n.29, 294–96, n.317; Easterling Lumber Co. v. Pierce, 235 U.S. 380 (1914); Halifax Tonopah Mining Co. v. Lawson, 36 Nev. 591 (1913), *affirmed*, 239 U.S. 632 (1915); Bowersock v. Smith, 243 U.S. 29 (1917); Cincinnati, Hamilton & Dayton Ry. v. McCollum, 183 Ind. 556, 109 N.E. 206 (1915), *affirmed*, 245 U.S. 632 (1917). See also *supra*, pp. 279–81.

[116] See *supra*, pp. 209, 553–55.

The constitutionality of such statutes was first raised in the Supreme Court, if only indirectly, in 1915, in *Jeffrey Manufacturing Co.* v. *Blagg*.[117] The Ohio workmen's compensation statute in question in the *Blagg* case applied only to employers of five or more persons, and acceptance of the workmen's compensation scheme was voluntary even on the part of such employers. However, employers of five or more who did not enter the workmen's compensation system were deprived of the fellow-servant, assumed-risk, and contributory-negligence defenses in suits against them at common law. Employers of fewer than five persons continued to have such defenses available to them. In upholding this classification by size as reasonable and constitutional under the Equal Protection Clause, Day for a unanimous Court gave a benign description of the workmen's compensation scheme as aiming "to substitute a method of compensation by means of investigation and hearings before a board, for what was regarded as an unfair and inadequate system, based upon statutes or the common law."

This was a good omen, and its promise was kept by the Court two years later, in *New York Central Railroad* v. *White*, which was argued and reargued, with two companion cases, at the same time as *New York Central Railroad* v. *Winfield*, although decided a couple of months earlier.[118] New York, whose statute was in issue in the *White* case, had had to amend its constitution in order to enact a workmen's compensation law. An earlier statute had been held unconstitutional by the New York Court of Appeals in 1911, in the notorious case of *Ives* v. *South Buffalo Railway*, which had been a major target of Theodore Roosevelt in his Progressive campaign of 1912, when he sought to put the fear of God into judges.[119] The new statute, enacted in December 1913, was applicable to employees engaged in so-called hazardous occupations, of which a very large number were listed. Whether or not the employer was at fault, the statute scheduled awards for industrial injuries, to be made by an administrative board. The awards were designed to compensate for medical expenses and loss of earning power. The remedy so provided was exclusive; employees were not free to resort to trial by jury in lieu of it. Employers were offered insurance by the state against the liability so imposed on them, but were left the option of seeking private insurance or of not insuring at all. If they failed to insure, however, they could be required to deposit securities as a guarantee of payment of possible future awards.

---

[117] 235 U.S. 571, 574 (1915). See also Vandalia R.R. v. Stilwell, 181 Ind. 267, 104 N.E. 289 (1914), *affirmed*, 239 U.S. 637, 241 U.S. 638 (1916).

[118] See *supra*, pp. 553–55.

[119] See *supra*, pp. 13–14, n.39. The decision of the Court of Appeals rested partly on state constitutional grounds, and partly on federal ones, the latter remaining unreviewed by the Supreme Court.

"The scheme of the act is so wide a departure from common-law standards respecting the responsibility of employer to employee," said Pitney in the opinion of a unanimous Court, "that doubts naturally have been raised respecting its constitutional validity." The contention was advanced that "both employer and employee are deprived of their liberty to acquire property by being prevented from making such agreements as they choose respecting the terms of the employment." But it was argued on the other hand that in modern industry, "the causes of accident are often so obscure and complex" that fault could not be readily assigned. The existing system put the burden of loss chiefly on the workman, who was least able to bear it. The heart of the matter, Pitney held, was that common law rules had to be subject to alteration. "No person has a vested interest in any rule of law entitling him to insist that it shall remain unchanged for his benefit."

But this was not an unqualified proposition. He was not deciding, said Pitney, that a state could "suddenly set aside all common-law rules respecting liability as between employer and employee, without providing a reasonably just substitute." New York had provided a substitute. "Of course, we cannot ignore the question whether the new arrangement is arbitrary and unreasonable, from the standpoint of natural justice." Yet accidents were a cost attributable to the operation of a business, "as truly as the cost of repairing broken machinery or any other expense that ordinarily is paid by the employer." It was reasonable, "on grounds of natural justice," to impose on the employer liability in a limited and predictable amount, while freeing him of the risk of large verdicts in suits at common law.

The new liability was not dependent on fault, but liability without fault was no novelty in the law, and workmen's compensation acts in effect simply disregarded the proximate cause of the accident, and looked to a cause "more remote—the primary cause, as it may be deemed—and that is, the employment itself." Nonetheless, this was "not to say that any scale of compensation, however insignificant on the one hand or onerous on the other, would be supportable." The Court was referred to two recent decisions upholding freedom of contract in the relations between employer and employee, *Coppage* v. *Kansas* and *Truax* v. *Raich*.[120] "It is not our purpose to qualify or weaken either of these declarations in the least," said Pitney. But workmen's compensation statutes, although impinging on the employment contract, were a reasonable, and therefore valid, exercise of state police power.[121]

A companion case from Iowa, presenting a statute that hardly

---

[120] 236 U.S. 1 (1915), and 239 U.S. 33 (1915).
[121] New York Central R.R. v.

White, 243 U.S. 188, 196–98, 201–203, 205–206 (1917).

differed from the New York one, was also disposed of unanimously in accordance with the decision in *New York Central Railroad* v. *White*.[122] But a Washington statute involved in a second companion case, *Mountain Timber Co.* v. *Washington*, did not get by so easily. This statute differed in that it required employers to contribute to a state liability insurance fund, and did not leave them the option, open under the New York statute, to forego insuring themselves. Thus an employer who judged that his conduct of his own business was prudent enough to justify the risk of not insuring could not act upon his judgment; he was taxed, rather, for the imprudence of others. Still, Pitney for a majority upheld the Washington statute as well. The compulsory insurance premiums, he said, could be viewed at their worst as an occupation tax of the sort that the state could have chosen to levy for some other reasonable purpose. And Pitney cited Holmes' opinion in *Noble State Bank* v. *Haskell*, which had sustained a compulsory deposit insurance scheme for banks.[123]

White, McKenna, Van Devanter, and McReynolds dissented without opinion in *Mountain Timber Co.* v. *Washington*.[124] One could understand, Thomas Reed Powell pointed out contemporaneously, that the dissenters did not feel bound by *Noble State Bank* v. *Haskell*, since a premise of the decision in that case was that the state could have taken the whole business of banking under its control, and could thus regulate it in lesser ways, whereas it was not to be assumed that industries covered by workmen's compensation statutes could likewise be fully taken under state control. But the distinction between the New York and Iowa cases, in which these dissenters were with the majority, and the Washington case was nevertheless, Powell went on, a distinction without much difference. Employers who elected not to join the state insurance system under the New York law were, after all, required to deposit securities, and thus also to incur an expense willy-nilly. And it was in any event the commonest sort of business practice to insure against liability. Why should the Constitution guarantee "a liberty to run a risk which most businessmen regard as a liberty to commit folly"? If an employer could be compelled to pay compensation for accidents in his factory not his fault, Powell thought, it was "but a slight step further to compel him to join in a cooperative plan for providing payment, so long as the plan corresponds with the business practices

---

[122] Hawkins v. Bleakly, 243 U.S. 210 (1917). See also Middleton v. Texas Power & Light Co., 249 U.S. 152 (1919).

[123] See *supra*, p. 276.

[124] Mountain Timber Co. v. Washington, 243 U.S. 219 (1917); see also Thornton v. Duffy, 254 U.S. 361 (1920).

followed by sensible men."[125] But a slight step further can be impossible if the first one was difficult and distasteful, and so there is the hint in the narrow division in the Washington case that the unanimity of *New York Central Railroad* v. *White* was delusive.

The hint was confirmed some few years later by Brandeis in private conversation with Frankfurter. "But for Pitney," said Brandeis, "we would have had no workmen's compensation laws." Pitney, Brandeis said on another occasion, "came around upon study, though he had been the other way."[126] Without Pitney there would have been no majority in the Washington case, and quite possibly not in the other two cases either. But what Pitney came around to was a narrow and particular ground of decision. "The reasonableness of other statutes than the one before the court," was Powell's accurate assessment, "cannot be predicated on any general pronouncements abstracted from the opinion in the [*White*] case." This did Powell's realist heart good. The Supreme Court, he wrote, offered no comfort "to those in search of a complete definition of the concept of due process. . . . Men may differ as to the wisdom of the specific judgments which the Court from time to time may form. But only those who are ignorant that law is an instrument for regulating practical affairs will have anything but praise for the method by which the judgments are reached."[127]

It may have been nice to know that the Court would not strike down such legislation as workmen's compensation laws out of hand, in doctrinaire fashion. But at the same time the Court was reserving the power to do so, which was less pleasing to know. The Court was continuing to arrogate to itself, and to deny to the legislatures, the ultimate judgment of reasonableness—not rationality, but reasonableness—and necessity. The Court was taking no such principled leap forward as Holmes had been allowed to make in *Noble State Bank* v. *Haskell*.

Despite the notoriety of the *Ives* case no more than five or six years earlier, the decisions in the *White* and companion cases in March 1917 received little notice in the press. Perhaps it was that they occasioned no surprise; they were expected. If so, the expectations were more sanguine than was quite justified. The subsurface division, or at least incipient division, in *New York Central Railroad* v. *White* itself was confirmed within the year in the *Arizona Employers' Liability Cases*.

In Arizona, while workers in hazardous occupations—chiefly mining—were covered by a workmen's compensation statute, they were

---

[125] See T. R. Powell, "The Workmen's Compensation Cases," *Political Science Quarterly*, 32:542, 563–65, 1917.

[126] Brandeis-Frankfurter Conversations.

[127] Powell, "Workmen's Compensation Cases," 560, 568.

also given the choice of trial by jury under an employer's liability act, and thus the opportunity to recover damages in amounts set by the jury and not limited by the prescribed scale of the workmen's compensation law. Having elected trial by jury, as he could freely do (although irrevocably, once he did it), the injured employee might be barred from recovery if the employer was able to prove that the injury had in fact been due to the employee's own negligence. But no other defenses, such as the fellow-servant rule and assumption of risk, could be made by the employer, and what was most important, liability was imposed regardless of fault by Arizona employer's liability act as well as by its workmen's compensation statute.

The *Arizona Employers' Liability Cases* were several private suits in which verdicts had been recovered after trial by jury and without proof of negligence on the part of the employer.[128] The difficulty, such as it was, in these cases stemmed from Pitney's argument in *New York Central Railroad* v. *White* that while the New York statute created a new head of liability, it also conferred upon the employer a counter-vailing benefit, by freeing him from the risk of large verdicts in cases in which, at common law, he had been subject to suit. The Arizona scheme did no such thing. Rather, Arizona had extended the risk of large verdicts to a new class of cases, in which the injured workman need not prove the employer's negligence. Nevertheless, the five-man majority Pitney had led when the Court divided in the Washington case held together again—but not easily, nor quickly. Indeed, although it appears that initially the majority won over Chief Justice White, one of the dissenters in the Washington case, there may have been a stage also at which there was no majority at all for holding the Arizona system constitutional.

The Arizona cases were first argued in January 1918. There was a decision in conference (we don't know what the division was) to uphold the statute, and the writing of the opinion was assigned to Holmes. If a later notation by Holmes on his copy of the opinion is correct, as it almost certainly is, the assignment was made by the Chief Justice, which would mean that at this point he favored upholding the statute, since when the Chief Justice is in a minority, not he, but the senior Justice of the majority assigns the writing of the majority opinion. The senior Justice—McKenna being in dissent—would have been Holmes, and we may assume that he would have remembered having

---

[128] The state of Arizona was not a party, and was in no fashion repre-sented, as *amicus* or otherwise, in any of these cases. In one of them there was no appearance at all for the em- ployee in the Supreme Court, and in two, counsel for the employees sub-mitted on briefs, without oral argu-ment.

assigned the opinion to himself. So the Chief Justice had joined the majority at this point.

Holmes wrote and circulated the opinion which now appears as a concurrence joined in by Brandeis and Clarke. It reached its result in just a few long strides, reminiscent of the opinion in *Noble State Bank* v. *Haskell*. There was "some argument made for the general proposition that immunity from liability when not in fault is a right inherent in free government. . . ." Holmes' answer was: "But if it is thought to be public policy to put certain voluntary conduct at the peril of those pursuing it, whether in the interest of safety or upon economic or other grounds, I know of nothing to hinder." Even the criminal law in some instances required a man "to know facts at his peril. Indeed, the criterion which is thought to be free from constitutional objection, the criterion of fault, is the application of an external standard, the conduct of a prudent man in the known circumstances, that is, in doubtful cases, the opinion of the jury, which the defendant had to satisfy at his peril and which he may miss after giving the matter his best thought." So much, Holmes concluded "without further amplification," could be taken to have been established by *New York Central Railroad* v. *White* and its companion cases—although quite plainly Holmes was establishing a proposition free from the cautions and qualifications Pitney had surrounded it with in those cases.

Damages recoverable by the injured worker, though limited by the judge's control over the jury, were not limited as in workmen's compensation statutes. But that seemed a scarcely tenable objection. Holmes was no economist, and he was not brought up on "externalities," but he had an insight into the costs rightly chargeable to an enterprise. "If a business is unsuccessful," he said, "it means that the public does not care enough for it to make it pay. If it is successful the public pays its expenses and something more. It is reasonable that the public should pay the whole cost of producing what it wants and a part of that cost is the pain and mutilation incident to production. By throwing that loss upon the employer in the first instance we throw it upon the public in the long run and that is just. If a legislature should reason in this way and act accordingly it seems to me that it is within constitutional bounds."

That was fine, but the Court was in no frame of mind to hand down another *Noble State Bank* v. *Haskell*. After the decision had been finally announced, Holmes noted what had happened in a letter to his friend Pollock:

> My last opinion was in favor of the constitutionality of a state law throwing all the risks of damage to employees on the employers in hazardous businesses. To my wonder four were the other way, and my opinion was thought too strong by some of the majority, so that Pitney

spoke for the Court and I concurred, with what I had to say—Brandeis and Clarke only with me. I pointed out that even in what was supposed to be the Constitutional principle of basing liability on fault it meant that a man had to take the risk of deciding the way the jury would decide—in doubtful cases. But already [this was on June 17, 1919, after adjournment] law grows remote and as soon as I feel a little brisker I expect to forget it altogether.[129]

On a slip sheet of his opinion, Holmes wrote this: "This case originally was written by me as assigned by the C. J. D[ay] and P[itney] thought there was danger in this op. and P wrote what none of his majority could disagree with and so I suggested that his op. should be the op. of the Court to avoid a majority with one op. by 3 JJ. and another by 2."[130]

It is easy to see why Day and Pitney would have been concerned. Holmes was not forming one of those discrete practical judgments that Powell so admired, pursuant to which "the reasonableness of other statutes than the one before the court cannot be predicated on any general pronouncements abstracted from the opinion in the case." He was doing the exact opposite. He was stating a general principle, capable of life and growth and application to other cases, and he was stating it boldly, without fear of its implications. All Holmes accomplished, apparently, was to dissolve the majority. The cases went over, and during the summer, Brandeis wrote a dissent—which would indicate that there was now a majority the other way, prepared to hold the Arizona statute unconstitutional.

Brandeis' dissent, which remained unpublished, although preserved in his papers in a print bearing the date October 1918, was a very different document from Holmes'. Brandeis recognized and dealt with the problems that such members of the shaky majority as Pitney and Day might have, given their premises and their anxieties. "If we were permitted to express an opinion upon the wisdom of the statute," Brandeis began, "the arguments urged against it might prove persuasive." (This was not merely a concession to such colleagues as Pitney and Day; Brandeis himself very likely saw things this way.) It was wasteful to preserve the employee's right to "unprofitable and demoralizing lawsuits." But the wisdom of the act was no concern of the Court. The constitutional difficulty, if any, could not be simply that the statute created liability without fault, for *New York Central Railroad* v. *White* had established that, in some circumstances at least, the creation of such liability was constitutional. Was it then arbitrary and unreasonable to allow the amount of compensation to be determined by a jury, rather

---

[129] *Holmes-Pollock Letters,* II, 15.　　[130] Holmes Papers.

than to be set in a statutory schedule as in the New York law? The damages that a jury might grant were not unlimited. They were restricted, as at common law, to reasonable compensation for the injuries suffered. There was no allowance of punitive damages. Finally Brandeis discussed, with care and in detail, certain particular and relatively minor objections that were made to the Arizona scheme, and disposed of each of them.[131]

We may surmise that Brandeis' opinion played some role in reconstituting a majority in favor of the constitutionality of the Arizona law. The decision was finally announced on June 9, 1919, in an opinion by Pitney, which went on at great length. Like Brandeis, Pitney remarked that the Court had no business considering the wisdom of the Arizona scheme. *New York Central Railroad* v. *White* made clear that the common law rules of employers' liability were subject to change by legislation. Liability without fault was not unconstitutional so long as it was not imposed unreasonably, and the question was whether imposing it, as Arizona had done, without any equivalent protection to the employer was unreasonable. It was not. A burden was put on the employer, but—here Pitney borrowed Holmes' thought—he could reflect this new burden in the wages he paid and the prices he charged. The employer was not being punished without fault. "That, we may concede, would be contrary to natural justice." But only compensatory damages were exacted by the Arizona statute, not punitive ones. The reasoning behind the statute might have been that injuries to workmen were inevitable, and that the employer, who took in the gross income of the industry, was in the best position to bear and distribute the cost of injuries. "Whether this or similar reasoning was employed, we have no means of knowing; whether, if employed, it ought to have been accepted as convincing, is not for us to decide. It being incumbent upon the opponents of the law to demonstrate that it is clearly unreasonable and arbitrary, it is sufficient for us to declare, as we do, that such reasoning would be pertinent to the subject and not so unfounded or irrational as to permit us to say that the State, if it accepted it as a basis for changing the law in a matter so closely related to the public welfare, exceeded the restrictions placed upon its action by the Fourteenth Amendment."

The four dissenters produced two opinions, one by McKenna, joined in by White, Van Devanter, and McReynolds, and the other by

---

[131] See A. M. Bickel, *The Unpublished Opinions of Mr. Justice Brandeis* (1957), 69–70; see also *ibid.*, 61–76. In discussing the Arizona Employers' Liability Cases, and in some measure also New York Central R.R. v. White and its companion cases, I have followed substantially my treatment of them in this book.

McReynolds, joined in again by White and Van Devanter, and also by McKenna. The earlier workmen's compensation cases, McKenna wrote (he had dissented in the Washington case), had not been easy to decide "against the contentions and conservatism which opposed them, and there was, at least to me, no prophecy of their extent, and therefore to me the present case is a step beyond them. I hope it is something more than timidity, dread of the new, that makes me fear that it is a step from the deck to the sea—the metaphor suggests a peril in the consequences." This further step could be justified only on the basis of a generalization such as Holmes had formulated. "Of this there can be no disguise. It may be confused by argument and attempt at historical analogies and deductions, but to that comprehensive principle the case must come at last."

It seemed to McKenna "to be of the very foundation of right— of the essence of liberty as it is of morals—to be free from liability if one is free from fault." Yet if this statute did not "punish without fault what does it do?" The statute was an interference with "precepts of constitutional law . . . [and] precepts of moral law that reach the conviction of aphorisms and are immediately accepted by all who understand them. . . . I say this, not in dogmatism, but in expression of my vision of things, and I say it with deference to the contrary judgments of my brethren of the majority." Of course, pretexts could always be found for the violation of rights. "Tyranny even may find pretexts and seldom boldly bids its will avouch its acts. . . ." What could be the limits of the infringement of rights here validated? Would it extend to nonhazardous employments, and if not, why not? The New York statute involved in the *White* case listed forty-two groups of hazardous occupations. The "drift of opinion and legislation" currently favored labor and set it apart so as to withdraw it from the action of economic forces and their consequences, giving it "immunity from the pitilessness of life. And there are appealing considerations for this drift of opinion and inevitable sympathy with it as with many other conditions, but which the law cannot relieve by a sacrifice of constitutional rights." Holmes' argument, taken up also by Pitney, that the cost of industrial accidents, being imposed upon the employer, was passed on to the consumer had an "attractive speciousness" about it. If valid it could justify the imposition of any and all burdens upon employers. It was "certainly facile and comprehensive." Here, in short, was the McKenna of the *Pipe Line Cases*.[132]

McReynolds' dissent ran nearly fourteen pages, an extraordinarily long opinion for him, even though he took up considerable space by printing both the Arizona employers' liability and workmen's compensa-

---

[132] See *supra,* pp. 232 *et seq.*

tion laws in the margin. It was for the Court to determine what was oppressive and contrary to justice under the Constitution—not for the legislature and not for the people—"otherwise constitutional inhibitions would be futile. And plainly, I think, the individual's fundamental rights are not proper subjects for experimentation; they ought not to be sacrificed to questionable theorization." Until now McReynolds "had supposed that a man's liberty and property—with their essential incidents—were under the protection of our charter and not subordinate to whims or caprices or fanciful ideas of those who happen for the day to constitute the legislative majority. The contrary doctrine is revolutionary and leads straight toward destruction of our well-tried and successful system of government. Perhaps another system may be better—I do not happen to think so—but it is the duty of the courts to uphold the old one unless and until superseded through orderly methods." *New York Central Railroad* v. *White* and its companion cases were decided on their facts. The facts that made for constitutionality were clearly laid out in the opinions. Without them, "the result, necessarily, would have been otherwise unless we were merely indulging in harmful chatter." Here the facts were different. The employer was given "no *quid pro quo* for his new burdens." Therefore: "As a measure to stifle enterprise, produce discontent, strife, idleness and pauperism the outlook for the enactment seems much too good." He was unable to see, McReynolds concluded, "any rational basis for saying that the act is a proper exercise of the State's police power. It is unreasonable and oppressive upon both employer and employee. . . ." This was *echt* McReynolds, the man himself, rough, direct, and utterly unyielding, as his colleagues saw him, and as later, particularly in the late 1930s, he would be more generally perceived. He did not often have occasion thus to reveal himself, fully and publicly, in these years.[133]

"I thought the dissent amazing," Holmes wrote Pollock when it was all over, "and that the opinion, which I agreed to make the opinion of the Court in order to get something that could be called that, was but a flabby performance."[134] Harold J. Laski, then at Harvard, wrote Holmes: "Felix [Frankfurter] has just shown me your colleague McReynolds's opinion in the Arizona case and I did not conceive that such stuff could be got out from your court. Was it meant seriously? Is it just a bad joke? It is really an unbelievable thing from any point of view."[135] It was no joke, and neither was McKenna's. Both dissents

[133] Arizona Employers' Liability Cases, 250 U.S. 400, 431–33, 422, 425–26, 434–39, 450–53 (1919); see also Chicago, Rock Island & Pacific Ry. v. Cole, 251 U.S. 54 (1919); Superior Pittsburgh Copper Co. v. Davidovitch, 19 Ariz. 402, 171 Pac. 127 (1918), *affirmed*, 251 U.S. 544 (1920).

[134] *Holmes-Pollock Letters*, II, 22.

[135] *Holmes-Laski Letters*, I, 225.

were clear indication of the limits governing the formation of the sort of "practical judgments" that T. R. Powell was seeking in the Court of these years.

MAXIMUM HOURS AND MINIMUM WAGES

These same limits were at least equally apparent in decisions passing on hours-of-labor and minimum-wage laws. *Muller* v. *Oregon*, decided in 1908, had upheld a ten-hour law for women, and its general authority had been enhanced by the tone and outlook of Hughes' opinion in *Chicago, Burlington & Quincy Railroad* v. *McGuire*.[136] Similar statutes were subsequently upheld,[137] and in 1915, in *Miller* v. *Wilson*[138] and *Bosley* v. *McLaughlin*,[139] Hughes sustained eight-hour laws for women in certain occupations. "As the liberty of contract guaranteed by the Constitution is freedom from arbitrary restraint—not immunity from reasonable regulation to safeguard the public interest," said Hughes in the *Miller* case, "the question is whether the restrictions of the statute have reasonable relation to a proper purpose." And that question virtually answered itself in these cases—certainly with the aid of briefs filed by Brandeis, who defended the statutes in both *Miller* v. *Wilson* and *Bosley* v. *McLaughlin*.[140]

The questions left over concerned maximum-hour laws applicable to men as well as to women, and minimum-wage laws. Litigation on these issues, as on maximum-hour laws for women since and including *Muller* v. *Oregon*, was energized and supported, if not altogether organized and directed, by the National Consumers' League, whose role in these cases resembles, though it was not an initiating role, and was

---

[136] See *supra*, pp. 373, n.201, 280–81.

[137] See *supra*, p. 281, n.260.

[138] 236 U.S. 373, 380 (1915).

[139] 236 U.S. 385 (1915); see also Wathen v. Jackson Oil Co., 235 U.S. 635 (1915); Charles Schweinler Press v. New York, 214 N.Y. 395, 108 N.E. 639 (1915), *writ of error dismissed for want of jurisdiction*, 242 U.S. 618 (1915).

[140] For example, the eight-hour law in *Bosley* v. *McLaughlin* applied to student but not to graduate nurses, and the distinction was attacked as unreasonable. Upholding it, Hughes relied on a pamphlet entitled *Educa-*

tional Status of Nursing, by M. Adelaide Nutting, director of the Department of Nursing and Health, Teachers College, Columbia University, issued by the United States Bureau of Education (Bulletin, 1912, No. 7). The pamphlet had been brought to the Court's attention as an appendix to Brandeis' brief. It pointed to special abuses in the conditions of labor of student nurses, and argued particularly for a reduction in their hours of work. See *Brief for Appellee*, Nos. 362 and 363, October Term 1914, Bosley v. McLaughlin, 236 U.S. 385 (1915).

RUFUS W. PECKHAM
(Library of Congress)

CHARLES J. BONAPARTE
Attorney General, 1906–1909
(Library of Congress)

GEORGE W. WICKERSHAM
Attorney General, 1909–1913
(Library of Congress)

JOHN D. ROCKEFELLER
(Library of Congress)

J. P. MORGAN
(Library of Congress)

JAMES CLARK McREYNOLDS
Attorney General, 1913–1914
(Culver Pictures)

THOMAS W. GREGORY
Attorney General
(Library of Congress)

IDA TARBELL
(Library of Congress)

GEORGE W. PERKINS
(Library of Congress)

A. MITCHELL PALMER
Attorney General, 1919–1921
(Library of Congress)

FELIX FRANKFURTER
(Harvard Law Art Collection)

Dear Judge,

I return herewith your memorandum in No. 15 — *McCabe v. Atchison etc R'y Co.* — I cannot construe the statute as requiring the carrier to give equal, though separate, accommodations so far as sleeping cars, dining cars and chair cars are concerned. All agree — both parties and the Attorney General — that such cars may be provided exclusively for whites — that a

Letter from Hughes to Holmes concerning the *McCabe* case
(*Library of Congress*)

black man must sit up all night just because he is black, unless there are enough blacks to make a 'black sleeping-car' pay.

I don't see that it is a case calling for 'logical exactness' in enforcing equal rights, but rather as it seems to me it is a bald, wholly unjustified, discrimination against a passenger solely on account of race.

Faithfully,

Charles E. Hughes

To Mr. Justice Holmes

SUPREME COURT OF THE UNITED STATES.

No. 231.—OCTOBER TERM, 1916.

Charles H. Buchanan, Plaintiff in Error, *vs.* William Warley.	In Error to the Court of Appeals of the State of Kentucky.

[   ]

Mr. Justice HOLMES dissenting.

This is a bill brought by the owner of a parcel of land in Louisville, Kentucky, for specific performance of a contract to purchase the same for $250. It is stated in the contract that the defendant is buying the lot for the purpose of having a house built on it for his residence and it is agreed therein that he is not to be bound unless he has a right under the laws of the State of Kentucky and the City of Louisville to occupy the property as a residence. The defendant is colored, and sets up an ordinance of the City by which he would be forbidden to occupy the property as proposed, if, as is the fact, the greater number of the houses in the block in which the property is situated are occupied by whites. The plaintiff replies that the ordinance is bad under the Fourteenth Amendment. A demurrer to the reply was sustained by the Courts of the State and the plaintiff brings the case here.

The contract sounds so very like a wager upon the constitutionality of the ordinance that I cannot but feel a doubt whether the suit should be entertained without some evidence that this is not a manufactured case. But however that may be I think that the plaintiff shows no such interest as entitles him to complain under the Fourteenth Amendment. It is possible that the ordinance unduly abridges the constitutional rights of the blacks, but that question is not before us. The plaintiff is a white man and cannot avail himself of this collateral mode of attack, on the ground of a wrong to some one else. *Hendrick* v. *Maryland*, 235 U. S. 610, 621. *Missouri, Kansas & Texas Ry. Co.* v. *Cade*, 233 U. S. 642, 648. *Hatch* v. *Reardon*, 204 U. S. 152, 160. The general effect of the ordinance is supposed to be beneficial to the whites for

Holmes's undelivered dissent in *Buchanan* v. *Warley*

the same reasons that make it bad for the blacks. The only ground available to the plaintiff is in respect of his property. His claim in regard to that is that his market for a lot, valued by him at $250, is diminished by diminishing the inducements of a small minority of possible buyers to make the purchase. It is alleged, to be sure, that the lot has no value except for a residence of a colored person, but that obviously sounds too much in prophecy to be regarded as an allegation of fact. Either white or black may buy the land subject to this single restriction upon its use.

The restriction is very remote from a taking of property as that phrase commonly is understood. The value of property may be diminished in many ways by ordinary legislation as well as by the police power properly so called without any constitutional obligation to pay the owner, *Northern Pacific Ry. Co.* v. *Duluth,* 208 U. S. 583, 596, unless the diminution reaches such a magnitude as to necessitate the exercise of eminent domain. *Camfield* v. *United States,* 167 U. S. 518, 524. *Martin* v. *District of Columbia,* 205 U. S. 135, 139. *Welch* v. *Swasey,* 214 U. S. 91, 107. I should think it plain that the injury inflicted in this case was not so grave that it must be paid for, when the only ground for a claim to compensation was the greatness of the harm. If I am right, and the ordinance is valid so far as the plaintiff's property rights are concerned, he cannot alter his case by making a contract in the teeth of it. *Manigault* v. *Springs,* 199 U. S. 473, 480. *Hudson County Water Co.* v. *McCarter,* 209 U. S. 349, 357. *Louisville & Nashville R. R. Co.* v. *Mottley,* 219 U. S. 467, 480.

I think that the writ of error should be dismissed or the judgment affirmed.

FRANK B. KELLOGG
(*Library of Congress*)

BOOKER T. WASHINGTON
(*Library of Congress*)

RAY STANNARD BAKER
(*Library of Congress*)

MOORFIELD STOREY
(*Harvard Law Art Collection*)

otherwise also less central and crucial, that of the NAACP Legal Defense Fund in suits attacking racial discrimination before and after the decision in *Brown* v. *Board of Education* in 1954. Counsel for the League, and in its behalf, and by arrangement with the appropriate attorneys general, for the states, was Louis D. Brandeis, whose service began with *Muller* v. *Oregon* and ended upon his appointment to the Court.[141] Brandeis—not by plan, since he had no control over the sequence in which statutes were attacked in the state courts, and might have preferred a strategy of first concluding maximum-hour litigation—found himself with two minimum-wage cases in the Supreme Court before he could take the next and conclusive step on the subject of maximum-hour statutes. *Stettler* v. *O'Hara* and *Simpson* v. *O'Hara* put in issue an Oregon law pursuant to which a minimum wage ($8.64 per week) was set for women workers, who were also not allowed to work longer than fifty hours a week or nine hours a day.

Brandeis argued these cases on December 16 and 17, 1914. Nine states, said Brandeis, had minimum-wage laws, and more were enacting them. The Oregon statute was modeled on legislation that had worked successfully in the Australian state of Victoria for eighteen years and been adopted in other British colonies, including New Zealand, and in Great Britain itself in 1909. Oregon had found that large numbers of women in the state were employed at below-subsistence wages and were consequently underfed or ill-housed, or else supplemented their inadequate income with "contributions from 'gentlemen friends.'" The consequences of low wages were thus "a reduction of vitality . . . ill health, and . . . immorality and the corruption of the community." Unhealthy women, moreover, did not "as a rule have healthy children," and "degeneration" was found, therefore, to "threaten the people of Oregon." In the face of these conditions, the legislature of Oregon had declined "to fold their arms in despair and say, 'The resulting unhappiness of our people and the ruin of our commonwealth must be accepted as one of the crosses that man and states must bear.'" In seeking a remedy, Oregon might have relied on education. For low wages are uneconomical, depressing productivity. To be productive, horses and cows must be well fed and also have "humane treatment in other respects," and so must women. "There is also a law of ethics that man shall not advance his own interests by exploiting his weaker fellows or through casting burdens upon the community."

All this could be made clear in time. But Oregon was not satisfied

---

[141] See C. E. Vose, "The National Consumers' League and the Brandeis Brief," *Midwest Journal of Political Science*, 1:267, 1957; A. T. Mason, *Brandeis—A Free Man's Life* (1946), 245–53.

to await the fruits of slow processes of education. "For people have been slow to recognize the wrongs of low wages as they have been slow in recognizing—or at least delinquent in acting upon—the great truth that 'the wages of sin is death.' " Nor did Oregon, like Massachusetts—"our small, once homogeneous community, with its Puritan traditions, [in which] the sense of duty was so potent that men could be relied upon to do in important relations of life what they ought to do, if only the facts were made clear to them and publicly disclosed"—choose to be content with the sanction of publicity. (Brandeis was not sure that publicity would prove to be effective in Massachusetts itself.) Rather Oregon elected to follow the Australian example, and institute an experiment which had worked there and in England.

The minimum wage had come to be enacted gradually, after other regulations of the employment relationship. "The legislatures have certainly not been guilty of precipitate action. Our marvel is at the patience with which widespread evils have been borne as if they were inevitable. How potent the forces of conservatism that could have prevented our learning that, like animals, men and women must be properly fed and properly housed, if they are to be useful workers and survive!"

Only in the last quarter of his argument did Brandeis "discuss for a moment the question of constitutionality." The applicable legal principles were well settled. The test was whether the legislature had "reasonable cause to believe" that a desired effect on health, safety, or morals would be achieved by the act in question. The burden of proof was on those who attacked the law. "In answer to the question, whether [Brandeis'] brief contains also all the data opposed to minimum-wage laws, I want to say this: I conceive it to be absolutely immaterial what may be said against such laws. Each one of these statements contained in the brief in support of the contention that this is wise legislation, might upon further investigation be found to be erroneous, each conclusion of fact may be found afterwards to be unsound—and yet the constitutionality of the act would not be affected thereby. This court is not burdened with the duty of passing upon the disputed question whether the legislature of Oregon was wise or unwise, or probably wise or unwise, in enacting this law. The question is merely whether, as has been stated, you can see that the legislators had no ground on which they could, as reasonable men, deem this legislation appropriate to abolish or mitigate the evils believed to exist or apprehended. If you cannot find that, the law must stand." Nothing, Brandeis concluded, "could be more revolutionary than to close the door to social experimentation. The whole subject of women's entry into industry is an experiment. And surely the federal constitution—itself perhaps the greatest of human experiments—does not prohibit such modest attempts as the woman's minimum-wage act to reconcile the existing industrial

594

system with our striving for social justice and the preservation of the race."[142]

William Hitz, then a government lawyer, soon to become a Justice of the District of Columbia Supreme Court, a sympathetic but independent and certainly competent observer, recorded the impression made on him:

> I have just heard Mr. Brandeis make one of the greatest arguments I have ever listened to. . . . [T]he reception which he wrested from that citadel of the past was very moving and impressive to one who knows the Court. . . . When Brandeis began to speak, the Court showed all the inertia and elemental hostility which courts cherish for a new thought, or a new right, or even a new remedy for an old wrong, but he visibly lifted all this burden, and without orationizing or chewing the rag he reached them all and held even Pitney quiet.
>
> He not only *reached* the Court, but he *dwarfed* the Court, because it was clear that here stood a man who knew infinitely more, and who cared infinitely more, for the vital daily rights of the people than the men who sat there sworn to protect them. It was so clear that something had happened in the Court today that even Charles Henry Butler [the Court's Reporter of Decisions, to use the present title of his office] saw it and he stopped me afterwards on the coldest corner in town to say that no man this winter had received such close attention from the Court as Brandeis got today, while one of the oldest members of the clerk's office remarked to me that "that fellow Brandeez has got the impudence of the Devil to bring his socialism into the Supreme Court."[143]

Brandeis might have held Pitney quiet, and in later years as a colleague he could reach him on occasion, but standing at the bar this time he did not convince him. Yet Brandeis needed to convince Pitney in order to win. The decision went against Brandeis, the majority for holding the statute unconstitutional consisting almost certainly of Chief Justice White, and Van Devanter, Lamar, Pitney, and McReynolds. Hughes, who recalled many years later that he "had expressed in conference my view in support" of the statute,[144] was the other way, as was Holmes, and probably also McKenna and Day. The writing of a majority opinion must have been assigned to one of the Justices in the majority, for Holmes prepared and circulated a dissent. It was as follows:

---

[142] L. D. Brandeis, *The Curse of Bigness*, O. K. Fraenkel, ed. (1934), 52–69.

[143] Quoted in Mason, *Brandeis*, 253; Vose, "National Consumers' League," 280.

[144] See C. E. Hughes, *Biographical Notes*, Microfilm, Ac. 9943, Ch. 23, p. 32, Hughes Papers, Library of Congress.

The single question is whether the Fourteenth Amendment takes away the power of the states to prohibit certain contracts that they deem contrary to public welfare. To answer it I see no need to mention the police power. The police power is a conciliatory phrase invented to cover certain interferences with the full enjoyment of property without payment, which constitutions seem to forbid. If the uncompensated taking in this sense is small as compared with a complete appropriation and if the Court cannot say that a reasonable man might not believe it to be required by some considerable form of public welfare, it may be upheld, on the general principle that it is absurd and impossible to press the great constitutional safeguards to literal and logical extremes. But in the present case there is no taking of property at all, and I see no advantage in sugarcoating the act of the state with a special name. If it runs against the Constitution of the United States the name will not save it and short of that the state may do what it likes.

In deciding whether it does run against the Constitution the thing most carefully to be guarded against is erecting upon general phrases in Bills of Rights structures of particular belief not required by the language and not shared by half the world. In this case we are concerned with the provision that no state shall deprive any person of life, liberty, or property, without due process of law. It appears to me that upon these words we have built a Tower of Babel that already has been followed by confusion. I think that neither grammatical nor historical interpretation can deduce from them any dogma as to the prohibition or allowance of contracts. The earlier decisions on the Fourteenth Amendment began within the time of some Justices still upon the Bench and went no further than an unpretentious assertion of the liberty to follow the ordinary callings. I think that the expansion of that platitude into the dogma of liberty of contract is extravagant and mistaken. This dogma has been repeated in deciding cases that I should have decided differently; but a dogma hardly can be established by judicial decision and this one is shown not to be established by its uselessness for the decision of any particular case. For without enumerating all the restrictive laws that have been upheld it is obvious that among them there have been quite as serious and direct interferences with liberty of contract as any that can come from this present law.

Usury laws prohibit contracts by which a man receives more than so much interest for the money that he lends. Statutes of frauds restrict many contracts to certain forms. Some Sunday laws prohibit practically all contracts during one-seventh of our whole life. Insurance rates may be regulated. *German-Alliance Insurance Company* v. *Kansas*, 233 U.S. 389.[145] Railroads may be required to pay their employees fortnightly in cash. *Erie Railroad Company* v. *Williams*, 233 U.S. 685.[146] Employers of miners may be required to pay for coal by

---

[145] See *supra*, pp. 281 *et seq.*   [146] See *supra*, p. 281, n.260.

weight before screening. *McLaine* v. *Arkansas,* 211 U.S. 539. Payment of sailors in advance may be forbidden. *Patterson* v. *Bark Eudora,* 190 U.S. 169. The size of a loaf of bread may be established. *Schmidinger* v. *Chicago,* 226 U.S. 578.[147] Women's hours of labor may be fixed. *Muller* v. *Oregon,* 208 U.S. 412. *Riley* v. *Massachusetts,* 232 U.S. 671, 679. *Hawley* v. *Walker,* 232 U.S. 718. *Miller* v. *Wilson,* 236 U.S. 373. *Bosley* v. *McLaughlin,* 236 U.S. 385. I confess I do not understand the principle on which the power to fix a minimum for wages of women can be denied by those who admit the power to fix a maximum for their hours of work. One appears to me to meddle with freedom of contract as directly as the other. Certainly, in view of the varied limitations that have been put upon the right to contract, no mere generality about that right being embraced in the word liberty of the Fourteenth Amendment is enough to decide the matter. That liberty has been cut down on all sides and I seek for a criterion by which to limit the right of states to cut it down.

If, as some decisions say, there is a limit, I know of no criterion, apart from history or common usage, unless it be whether the law is one that a reasonable man could believe to be for the public good. Certainly the criterion is not whether we believe the law to be for the public good. I have done my share without a qualm to enforce laws that I devoutly believe to be as evil as laws well can be.[148] It never can be emphasized too much that one's own opinion about the wisdom of the law should be excluded altogether when one is doing one's duty on the Bench. The only opinion of our own, even looking in that direction, that is material, is, as I have suggested, our opinion whether a reasonable man could believe the law wise. But we certainly cannot be prepared to deny that a reasonable man might have that belief about this law in view of the legislation in Great Britain, Australia and a number of the United States. Skeptically as I regard such attempts I should much more confidently deny the wisdom of the other types of legislation that I have referred to and that irrespective of my personal convictions I have done my part to uphold.

---

[147] See *supra,* p. 282, n.268.

[148] About a year later, just before *Stettler* v. *O'Hara* and *Simpson* v. *O'Hara* were to be reargued, Holmes wrote to Harold J. Laski:

On the economic side I am mighty sceptical of hours of labor and minimum wage regulations, but it may be that a somewhat monotonous standardized mode of life is coming. Of course it only means shifting the burden to a different point of incidence, if I be right, as I think I be, that every community rests on the death of men. If the people who can't get the minimum are to be supported you take out of one pocket to put into the other. I think the courageous thing to say to the crowd, though perhaps the Brandeis school don't believe it, is, you now have all there is—and you'd better face it instead of trying to lift yourselves by the slack of your own breeches. But all our present teaching is hate and envy for those who have any luxury, as social wrongdoers.

Holmes-Laski Letters, I, 51–52.

In Australia the power to fix a minimum for wages in the case of industrial disputes extending beyond the limits of any one state is given to a court, and its president recently has given a most interesting account of its operation. 29 *Harvard Law Review* 13. If a legislature should adopt what he thinks the doctrine of modern economists of all schools, that "freedom of contract is a misnomer as applied to a contract between an employer and an ordinary individual employee," *ibid.* 25, I could not pronounce an opinion with which I agree impossible to be entertained by reasonable men. If the same legislature should accept his further opinion that industrial peace was best attained by the device of a court having the above powers, I should not feel myself able to contradict it, or to deny that the end justifies restrictive legislation quite as adequately as beliefs concerning Sunday or exploded theories about usury. I should have my doubts—but they would be whether the bill that has to be paid for every gain, although hidden as interstitial detriments, was not greater than the gain was worth; a matter that is not for me to decide.

If, however, I were at liberty to entertain considerations of what seem to me expediency and practical statesmanship I should think that the possible unwisdom of the law in question was far outweighed by the benefit of having social experiments made upon a limited scale. That advantage is made possible by this being a Union of States. It is a very precious one and no such experiment honestly attempted should be balked by an outside power unless it is one that the Constitution of the United States clearly forbids. I am wholly convinced that nothing in the Fourteenth Amendment directly or indirectly forbids this one to be tried.

This dissent, which if issued would undoubtedly have taken its place among the great, well-remembered opinions of Holmes, never saw the light of day. For the rest of this term—the October Term 1914—and during the next, nothing happened. Either the writer of the majority opinion was not ready to deliver it, or he found his majority shaky. The first is the more likely supposition, and it seems therefore that mere chance—the working habits, the schedule, the state of health of one Justice—kept a decision from being announced which would undoubtedly have had a major impact, telescoping some of the history of the Court by bringing the twenties back into the teens, so to speak.[149]

During the summer of 1915, Lamar, a member of the majority, sickened. He did not return to sit in October, and by January 1916 he was dead. At this point the Court was very likely in stalemate. Brandeis, who replaced Lamar, was not seated till June, and in the same month, Hughes resigned. There being two new Justices, even though it was quite evident that one of them, Brandeis, could not take part in the

---

[149] Compare Adkins v. Children's Hospital, 261 U.S. 525 (1923).

decision, *Stettler* v. *O'Hara* and *Simpson* v. *O'Hara* were restored to the docket on June 12, 1916, in order to be reargued.

Felix Frankfurter succeeded Brandeis as counsel for the Consumers' League. (The attorney of record for Oregon, which was being sued in each case, remained its attorney general.) Frankfurter submitted a new brief, on the Brandeis model, prepared, as were Brandeis' briefs, with the help of Josephine Goldmark of the Consumers' League, a first-class researcher, and incidentally Brandeis' sister-in-law. The brief contained tables showing the cost of living for women working in factories in Oregon and in other states, and the inadequacy of wages paid them to cover the cost of living. These data supported the stated purpose of the Oregon minimum-wage law to protect women and children from the effects of low wages on their health and morals. As usual in a brief on the Brandeis model, voluminous evidence was collected to demonstrate that there was much opinion favoring minimum-wage legislation as a remedy for the evils that attended below-subsistence wages. The brief also cited opinion to the effect that higher wages enforced by the state did not constitute a net cost to the employer, since they often stimulated higher productivity.

All these materials were adduced to bolster the argument that the statute was not an arbitrary and unreasonable regulation. Frankfurter then justified the restriction on freedom of contract that was undoubtedly embodied in the statute by maintaining that the employer was simply required to pay—if indeed a net cost was imposed on him at all—for benefits he enjoyed, and in the enjoyment of which the state would otherwise be subsidizing him. In other words, the contention was that by being required to pay subsistence wages, the employer paid for the labor he got, whereas if he paid a wage below subsistence, someone else would have to subsidize the workers, and thus indirectly the employer. The statute furthermore prevented unfair competition by forcing everyone to pay a living wage, as some employers were doing voluntarily anyway, and it redressed the imbalance of inherently unequal bargaining power between employers and employees. Thus, Frankfurter contended, the statute established rather than impaired true freedom of contract. Inequality of bargaining power was what impaired it. With this argument Frankfurter necessarily drew an analogy to collective bargaining cases such as *Coppage* v. *Kansas*. The analogy was perfectly valid, but given the mood of a majority of the Justices, it was not likely to work out in Frankfurter's favor.[150]

---

[150] Not many briefs filed in court, even in the Supreme Court, are reviewed in the learned journals as original contributions to the literature of their subject. This one was. See T. R. Powell, "The Oregon Minimum Wage Cases," *Political Science Quarterly,* 32:296, 1917.

The attorney general of Oregon, thinking perhaps that Brandeis' presentation some two years earlier had sufficed, almost deprived Frankfurter of the opportunity to make his own oral argument. Without informing Frankfurter, the attorney general of Oregon moved to have *Stettler* v. *O'Hara* and *Simpson* v. *O'Hara* submitted on briefs this second time around. Frankfurter, however, hurried down to Washington from Cambridge, where he was on the faculty of the Harvard Law School, and at an interview with the Chief Justice succeeded in persuading the latter that oral argument should be heard. The Court consequently denied the motion to have the cases submitted on briefs, and Frankfurter did argue them on January 18 and 19, 1917.[151] By then, a case that was to conclude the course of litigation on hours-of-labor statutes was also before the Court. This was *Bunting* v. *Oregon*, and Frankfurter argued it the day before he argued the minimum-wage cases.[152]

The law involved in the *Bunting* case, also an Oregon statute, established a maximum ten-hour day for everyone, men as well as

---

[151] See Phillips, ed., *Felix Frankfurter Reminisces*, 94–101.

The Nation published a vignette of "that august tribunal," the Supreme Court, "intently listening to the plea of a small, dark, smooth-faced lawyer, mostly head, eyes, and glasses, who looked as if he might have stepped out of the sophomore classroom of a neighboring college. As a matter of fact, he had just stepped out of a classroom for he was Professor Felix Frankfurter of the Harvard Law School, and his mode of address indicated that he had merely exchanged one group of pupils for another. He lectured the Court quietly, but with a due sense of its indebtedness to him for setting it right where it had been wrong, and giving it positive opinions where uncertainty had been clouding its mental vision. He was becomingly tolerant when the gray-haired learners asked questions which seemed to him unnecessary, and gentle when he had to correct a mistaken assumption." *The Nation*, 104:320, Mar. 15, 1917. It was at this time that McReynolds committed the ostentatious rudeness of leaning well back in his chair during Frankfurter's argument and holding up the other side's brief at arm's length, as if he were reading it. See *supra*, p. 354. "A childish form of sadism," Frankfurter called it many years later, remembering that he was delighted at the time because he thought, "Gee, this is swell. You're out. I don't have to pay any attention to you. I can't possibly reach your mind anyhow so you might as well leave the chair empty, and that suits me down to the ground." See H. B. Phillips, ed., *Felix Frankfurter Reminisces* (1960), 103.

[152] The Court, in the meantime, following earlier precedent, had sustained the fixing of both an eight-hour day and a minimum wage for employees of the city of Baltimore and of its contractors. Regulation of such public and quasi-public employment was a different matter. Elkan v. Maryland, 122 Md. 642, 90 Atl. 183 (1914), *affirmed*, 239 U.S. 634 (1915); *cf.* Atkin v. Kansas, 191 U.S. 207 (1903); and *cf.* e.g., United States v. Garbish, 222 U.S. 257 (1911) (eight-hour law applicable to federal contractors).

women, working in any mill, factory, or manufacturing establishment. The only exceptions allowed applied to watchmen and employees engaged in making necessary repairs, or in cases of emergency, where life or property were in imminent danger. The statute also limited overtime work to three hours a day, and required overtime to be compensated at the rate of time-and-a-half of regular wages. The proper standard of judgment, Frankfurter told the Court—he dared to tell the Justices, he said later, even though two of them, White and McKenna, were Catholics—was indicated in Cromwell's famous remark: "Ye may be right and I may be wrong. But by the bowels of Christ I suffer ye to concede it possible that ye may be wrong." That was what the Court should tell itself. McReynolds, "in his snarling, sneering way," Frankfurter remembered, asked: "Ten hours! Ten hours! Ten! Why not four?" As Frankfurter recalled it: "I paused, synthetically, self-consciously, dramatically, just said nothing. Then I moved down towards him and said, 'Your honor, if by chance I may make such a hypothesis, if your physician should find that you're eating too much meat, it isn't necessary for him to urge you to become a vegetarian.' Holmes said, 'Good for you!' very embarrassingly right from the bench. He loathed these arguments that if you go this far you must go further. 'Good for you!' Loud. Embarrassingly."[153]

On April 7, 1917, Frankfurter won all three of his cases, *Bunting* v. *Oregon* and the two minimum-wage cases. The opinion in *Bunting* was by McKenna. White, Van Devanter, and McReynolds dissented without opinion, and Brandeis, of course, who had been involved at the earliest stages of the case, before Frankfurter replaced him, took no part. It was virtually conceded, and McKenna simply assumed, that maximum-hour laws were as valid in their general application to male workers, regardless of whether a particular occupation was especially hazardous or wearing, as to female workers. That might have seemed a considerable leap some years earlier, but it was not by now.

The main point of the attack upon the statute, and the point that chiefly occupied McKenna, although his opinion was quite brief, centered on the overtime wage provision. It was argued that this was not a ten-hour statute, but rather a thirteen-hour statute, with a wage regulation added. This argument, said McKenna, was to some extent an attack on the motives of the legislature, since the legislature purported to be regulating hours, not wages, and had said so in the preamble to its statute. Now, motives of legislatures were not properly subject to judicial scrutiny. Moreover, it did not follow from the overtime provision that the aim was really to regulate wages. It might have been neither possible nor wise to make the ten-hour day a rigid requirement.

---

[153] *Ibid.,* 102.

The legislature might have deemed it wiser to impose a tentative restraint rather than an absolute one, and to achieve its purpose through the interest of those affected, whom it deterred from exceeding the ten-hour day. "New policies are usually tentative in their beginnings, advance in firmness as they advance in acceptance. They do not at a particular moment of time spring full-perfect in extent or means from the legislative brain. Time may be necessary to fashion them to precedent customs and conditions and as they justify themselves or otherwise they pass from militancy to triumph or from question to repeal."[154] Here was not the McKenna of the *Pipe Line Cases* or of the *Arizona Employers' Liability Cases*, but the other McKenna. This too he was capable of.

In *Stettler* v. *O'Hara* and *Simpson* v. *O'Hara*, the judgments below, which had upheld the statute, were affirmed by an equally divided Supreme Court.[155] Quite plainly, White, Van Devanter, Pitney, and McReynolds had held together for reversal, while McKenna, Holmes, Day, and Clarke had been for affirmance, and Brandeis, of course, had taken no part.[156] McKenna or Day may have vacillated, however, for in the course of the 1916 Term, presumably after the reargument, Holmes reprinted and recirculated his dissent. He omitted a couple of flourishes that might have been found unduly offensive. The following sentence was left out: "It appears to me that upon these words [the Fourteenth Amendment] we have built a Tower of Babel that already has been followed by confusion." Also omitted was the reference three sentences further to the extravagant and mistaken expansion of the platitude that the Fourteenth Amendment guaranteed an unpretentious right to follow the ordinary callings into the dogma of liberty of contract. But on the copy of this second circulation preserved in his files, Holmes added the following paragraph in longhand, and we may presume that it would have been included had the dissent ultimately been published:

> I have stated my opinion that it is superfluous to refer to the police power, in the sense in which I understand that phrase. Most certainly the liberty of contract evolved under the Fourteenth Amendment is not more protected than property, which the Amendment protects in express words. When the value of a manufacture may be destroyed without compensation upon modern conceptions of public policy, as in *Mugler* v. *Kansas*, 123 U.S. 623,[157] I cannot understand why, as

---

[154] Bunting v. Oregon, 243 U.S. 426, 438 (1917); see also Rail & River Coal Co. v. Ohio Industrial Commission, 236 U.S. 338 (1915).

[155] 243 U.S. 629 (1917), *affirming* 69 Ore. 519, 139 Pac. 743 (1914), and 70 Ore. 261, 141 Pac. 158 (1914).

[156] See T. R. Powell, "The Constitutional Issue in Minimum-Wage Legislation," *Minn. L. Rev.*, 2:3, 1917.

[157] Holding state prohibition statutes constitutional (see *supra*, p. 439), a particular *bête noire* of Holmes.

always has been the practice through the whole history of our commerce laws, the making of contracts may not be restricted upon the ground of an equally strong and I think, at least equally plausible conviction, that the restraint is required by the future welfare of our race.[158]

The decisions were not widely noted in the press, but *The New Republic*, reflecting no doubt its contributor Frankfurter's own reaction, pointed out that if by chance the minimum-wage law had been declared invalid in the Oregon state courts, the evenly divided Supreme Court would have affirmed a judgment of its unconstitutionality. "Nothing could bring more strikingly to light the constant peril of leaving to the courts their present power of reviewing legislation under the Fifth and Fourteenth Amendments." *The New Republic* also pointed with chagrin to the delay that the lengthy litigation had imposed before maximum-hour and minimum-wage laws could become effective.[159] Law journal opinion, much of it following a classic article by Frankfurter himself,[160] had long been heavily in favor of upholding the constitutionality of maximum-hour and minimum-wage laws.[161]

THE STANDARD OF RATIONALITY

The standard of judgment that Brandeis had pressed on the Court in his brief in *Muller* v. *Oregon* and in his argument in *Stettler* v. *O'Hara*, that Frankfurter urged in the *Bunting*, *Stettler*, and *Simpson* cases, and that Holmes and Hughes were applying with some consistency was the standard of rationality. The question under this standard was not whether social and economic legislation was of dubious worth, or even, as Holmes often thought, positively evil. The question was whether legislation was rational in the sense of being supported by reasoned and informed opinion. If it was, it benefited from a presumption of constitutionality that could not easily be rebutted. Hence the great bulk of it was sustained.[162] A statute would be struck down only if it clashed with some fundamental principle, which was itself found

---

[158] Holmes Papers.

[159] *The New Republic*, 10:305, Apr. 14, 1917.

[160] F. Frankfurter, "Hours of Labor and Realism in Constitutional Law," *Harv. L. Rev.*, 29:353, 1916.

[161] See, e.g., J. G. Palfrey, "The Constitutionality of Statutes Limiting Hours of Labor for Men," *Mass. L. Q.*, 1:52, 1916; W. L. Owens, Note, *Mich. L. Rev.*, 15:584, 1917. But *cf.*

R. G. Brown, "Oregon Minimum Wage Cases," *Minn. L. Rev.*, 1:471, 1916.

[162] The great bulk, but not all. The standard has positive content. The test of rationality is a test. See, e.g., McFarland v. American Sugar Co., 241 U.S. 79 (1916), *supra*, p. 88, and Gast Realty Co. v. Schneider Granite Co., *infra*, p. 638, n.236, both opinions by Holmes.

in or deduced from the Constitution, and was fit for application without reference to the Court's own assessment of the worthiness—the reasonableness and necessity—of any particular legislative policy.[163]

An ambivalent approximation of the presumption that rational legislation is constitutional prevailed in *Muller* v. *Oregon*, in *Bunting* v. *Oregon*, and in the workmen's compensation cases. In these years, as earlier,[164] the presumption was fully operative and was most boldly proclaimed in cases testing laws that could be related to a state's concern with the health and morals of its population. Thus, upholding an Illinois statute that forbade the use of boric acid in canned foods, Hughes for a unanimous Court said that the question concerning a law of this sort was whether it was "palpably unreasonable and arbitrary." The statute, he went on, could be declared unconstitutional only if it appeared that "by a consensus of opinion . . . [boric acid] was unquestionably harmless with respect to its contemplated uses. . . . It is plainly not enough that the subject should be regarded as debatable. If it be debatable, the legislature is entitled to its own judgment. . . . [I]t is sufficient to say, without passing upon the opinions of others adduced in argument, that the action of the legislature cannot be considered to be arbitrary. Its judgment appears to have sufficient support to be taken out of that category."[165]

Brandeis' very first opinion was on a similar point, similarly disposed of. He held in *Hutchinson Ice Cream Co.* v. *Iowa*[166] that a state could require that ice cream contain a fixed percentage of butterfat.[167] If a statute aimed at relieving certain evils was not arbitrary, said the ever unpredictable McKenna in another such case in 1916, "we cannot measure . . . [the] extent [of the evils] against the estimate of the legislature, and there is no impeachment of such estimate in differences of opinion, however strongly sustained. And by evils . . . [is] not necessarily meant some definite injury but obstacles to a greater public welfare. Nor do the courts have to be sure of the precise reasons for the legislation or certainly know them or be convinced of the wisdom or adequacy of the laws."[168]

---

[163] *Cf.* H. Wechsler, "Toward Neutral Principles of Constitutional Law," in H. Wechsler, *Principles, Politics and Fundamental Law* (1961).

[164] See *supra*, p. 000.

[165] Price v. Illinois, 238 U.S. 446, 452, 453 (1915); see also Hebe Co. v. Shaw, 248 U.S. 297 (1919); and see Curtice Brothers Co. v. Barnard, 209 Fed. 589 (7th Cir. 1913), *appeal* dismissed *per stipulation*, 241 U.S. 686 (1916).

[166] 242 U.S. 153 (1916).

[167] The Chief Justice's return was: "Yes E.D.W. *Very* well *done*. Indeed fine!" Brandeis Papers, University of Louisville Law School Library.

[168] Armour & Co. v. North Dakota, 240 U.S. 510, 513 (1916); see also Jones v. City of Portland, 245 U.S. 217 (1917).

On occasion, the presumption of the constitutionality of rational legislation was allowed to have decisive effect even in cases where the commercial aspect of a regulation predominated over any concern with health and morals. Thus again McKenna, in *Rast* v. *Van Deman & Lewis Co.*, sustaining a statute that in effect forbade retail sales promotion schemes involving redeemable coupons or other premiums: "It is established that a distinction in legislation is not arbitrary, if any state of facts reasonably can be conceived that would sustain it, and the existence of that state of facts at the time the law was enacted must be assumed. It makes no difference that the facts may be disputed or their effect opposed by argument and opinion of serious strength. It is not within the competency of the courts to arbitrate in such contrariety."[169] And in *Green* v. *Frazier*,[170] the presumption was sufficient for a unanimous Court, speaking through Day, to uphold North Dakota legislation that put the state in the business of manufacturing and marketing farm products, authorized it to build homes, and created a state banking system. This North Dakota scheme was thought by some, as T. R. Powell remarked, "to have a strong flavor of state socialism. If they are right, the federal Constitution appears to allow more room for socialistic experiments than a number of its most fervent eulogists would lead us to infer."[171] Yet Day was content to say: "Whether it [the North Dakota program] will result in ultimate good or harm is not within our province to inquire."

A majority of the Justices, however, unhesitatingly reneged on the presumption of constitutionality whenever it threatened to be erected into a principle of general application. It was permitted to do service in reaching a result otherwise acceptable to a majority, even if reluctantly or marginally so; but it was not allowed to command, of its own force, results that were not otherwise acceptable. Those who used the presumption to justify a result had to take care not to generalize from it too much, not to phrase it in terms that would foreclose future escapes from it. This was borne in on Brandeis (almost as if, as a freshman, he needed to be taught the lesson right off) during his first term, even while *Bunting* v. *Oregon* was being decided, first through the indirection of a Commerce Clause preemption judgment in *New York Central Railroad* v. *Winfield*,[172] and then head-on in *Adams* v. *Tanner*.

The statute in the *Adams* case, passed as an initiative measure in

[169] 240 U.S. 342, 357 (1916); see also Tanner v. Little, 240 U.S. 369 (1916); Pitney v. Washington, 240 U.S. 387 (1916).

[170] 253 U.S. 233, 240 (1920); and see Scott v. Frazier, 253 U.S. 243 (1920). See also Walls v. Midland Carbon Co., 254 U.S. 300 (1920).

[171] T. R. Powell, "Constitutional Law in 1919–1920, II," *Mich. L. Rev.*, 19:117, 136, 1920; see A. A. Bruce, "The Tyranny of the Taxing Power," *Mich. L. Rev.*, 18:508, 1920.

[172] See *supra*, pp. 553 *et seq.*

a general election in the state of Washington, forbade employment agencies to accept any fee from persons for whom they obtained employment, although fees could be charged to the employer. It was contended that the statute thus in effect abolished employment agencies conducted for profit, since collecting fees from employers was not feasible. The Court through these years approved a good many measures licensing, and sometimes quite closely and onerously regulating, various callings and professions.[173] In *Adams* v. *Tanner*, however, a majority of the Court, through McReynolds, treated the Washington statute as prohibiting rather than regulating employment agencies, and as a prohibitory measure held it unconstitutional.

"You take my house," McReynolds recited, "when you do take the prop that doth sustain my house; you take my life when you do take the means whereby I live." Now, he continued, it was plain that there was nothing "inherently immoral or dangerous to public welfare in acting as paid representatives of another to find a position in which he can earn an honest living. On the contrary, such service is useful, commendable, and in great demand." The state maintained that while employment agencies might be beneficial to some people, they compelled the needy and unfortunate to pay for what they ought to have as of right—namely, a job. This argument, said McReynolds, might indicate the purpose that the framers of the statute had in mind, but "in reason," such an argument could not support the statute. No doubt abuses grew up in connection with employment agencies. That was reason enough to regulate them, but not to abolish them; it did not "justify destruction of one's right to follow a distinctly useful calling in an upright way." All professions and businesses certainly offered opportunities for bad practices, "and as to every one of them, no doubt, some can be found quite ready earnestly to maintain that its suppression would be in the public interest. Skillfully directed agitation might also bring about apparent condemnation of any one of them by the public. Happily for all, the fundamental guaranties of the Constitution cannot be freely submerged if and whenever some ostensible justification is advanced and the police power invoked."

McKenna dissented in a sentence, "upon the ground that under the decisions of this court—some of them so late as to require no citation or review—the law in question is a valid exercise of the police

---

[173] See Brazee v. Michigan, 241 U.S. 340 (1916); Lehon v. Atlanta, 242 U.S. 53 (1916); Crane v. Johnson, 242 U.S. 339 (1917); McNaughton v. Johnson, 242 U.S. 344 (1917); Nikell and Burke v. Stephens, 245 U.S. 640 (1918); McNaughton v. Stephens, 245 U.S. 640 (1918); Medcraf v. Hodge, 245 U.S. 630 (1917); Payne v. Kansas, 248 U.S. 112 (1918); LaTourette v. McMaster, 248 U.S. 465 (1919); McCloskey v. Tobin, 252 U.S. 107 (1920); but *cf.* Craig v. Kentucky, 241 U.S. 692 (1916).

power of the State, directed against a demonstrated evil." Brandeis, joined by Holmes and Clarke—but not by McKenna—dissented in an elaborate opinion, nineteen pages long. This was the second dissenting opinion of Brandeis' career, the first having been delivered three weeks earlier in *New York Central Railroad* v. *Winfield.*

It was a serious thing, Brandeis began, to declare the statute of a state invalid under the Fourteenth Amendment—and, he implied, a trifle disingenuously, not a common occurrence. Hence he proposed to state the reasons for his dissent. Assuming that, as plaintiffs alleged and as the Court had assumed, the Washington statute amounted to a prohibition of a business, not a regulation, yet the Court had in the past allowed various prohibitory measures, relating not only to liquor, but most recently, in *Rast* v. *Van Deman & Lewis Co.,* to the sale of trading stamps. It was thus clear that the police power extended to prohibition as well as regulation, and not only to "the promotion of health, safety or morals," but also to "the prevention of fraud or the prevention of general demoralization." The constitutional question always—the only constitutional question—was whether legislation was clearly arbitrary or unreasonable, or lacked any real or substantial relation to the object sought to be attained.

Brandeis used the word "unreasonable" as indicating irrationality. For he went on: "Whether a measure relating to the public welfare is arbitrary or unreasonable, whether it has no substantial relation to the end proposed is obviously not to be determined by assumptions or by *a priori* reasoning. The judgment should be based upon a consideration of relevant facts, actual or possible—*Ex facto jus oritur.* That ancient rule must prevail in order that we may have a system of living law." It was therefore necessary—and by inference, in such a case as this, entirely sufficient—to inquire what the evil was to which the statute was addressed, why the particular statutory remedy was adopted, and, "incidentally," what had been the relevant experience, if any, in other states or countries. "But these enquiries are entered upon, not for the purpose of determining whether the remedy adopted was wise or even for the purpose of determining what the facts actually were. The decision of such questions lies with the legislative branch of the government. The sole purpose of the enquiries is to enable this court to decide, whether in view of the facts, actual or possible, the action of the State of Washington was so clearly arbitrary or so unreasonable" as to violate the Fourteenth Amendment.

Having thus, in language and cadences that were to recur in his opinions,[174] projected during this first year of his service the premise

---

[174] See New State Ice Co. v. Liebmann, 285 U.S. 262 (1932); Liggett Co. v. Lee, 288 U.S. 517 (1933).

and the method of the generation of judges that would succeed him, Brandeis turned to the facts from which the law ought to have spoken in the case at hand. Private employment agencies, as reports of the United States Bureau of Labor and of a Commission on Industrial Relations that Congress had created showed, led to many abuses, including fraud and extortion. Moreover, they tended to clog the labor market, and to increase rather than alleviate irregularity of employment, since they were interested in job changes, from which they earned their fees. And they erected barriers to employment rather than removing them, since their fees were low when jobs were plentiful, and high when jobs were scarce. The costs of the service, such as it was, provided by employment agencies fell on those least able to bear them; not only the workers rather than the employers, but the neediest among the workers. "The weakest and poorest classes of wage earners are therefore made to pay the largest share for a service rendered to employers, to workers, and to the public as well."

The remedies that had been applied in the various states had in the past been chiefly regulation, and competition by state employment agencies. They were largely ineffective.

> The problem which confronted the people of Washington was far more comprehensive and fundamental than that of protecting workers applying to the private agencies. It was the chronic problem of unemployment—perhaps the gravest and most difficult problem of modern industry—the problem which, owing to business depression, was the most acute in America during the years 1913 to 1915. In the State of Washington the suffering from unemployment was accentuated by the lack of staple industries operating continuously throughout the year and by unusual fluctuations in the demand for labor with consequent reduction of wages and increase of social unrest. Students of the larger problem of unemployment appear to agree that establishment of an adequate system of employment offices or labor exchanges is an indispensable first step toward its solution. There is reason to believe that the people of Washington not only considered the collection by the private employment offices of fees from employees a social injustice; but that they considered the elimination of the practice a necessary preliminary to the establishment of a constructive policy for dealing with the subject of unemployment.

All of this was supported by extensive documentation contained in twenty-four footnotes.[175]

Brandeis circulated his dissent before the majority opinion had

---

[175] Adams v. Tanner, 244 U.S. 590, 593, 594–95, 597, 599, 600, 605, 613–15 (1917).

been approved, in the hope presumably of persuading some members of the majority. He did not, but he evoked enthusiastic responses from Clarke and Holmes. "Only the Lord can so harden their heads as well as their hearts," wrote Clarke, "as to prevent their confessing their sin of ignorance when voting in so grave a matter. No matter what decision is rendered this will soon be the law of the case. Your selections are admirable and the restraint of comment discreet, having regard to your purposes. The authority attaching to such a statement from a member of this Court will make it a great public service. I am glad you are circulating it in advance. The experiment is worth trying." And Holmes: "Note me as agreeing with you vehemently."[176] In the law journals, Brandeis' dissent was noted as novel in content and particularly in method, and as indicating "the new spirit of rational approach."[177] So Brandeis had his impact, even though newspapers outside the state of Washington hardly noticed the decision.

THE BEN AVON DOCTRINE

Brandeis was brought up short also and, as it were, taught a similar lesson by his conservative seniors on another subject of due process adjudication—the constitutionality of rates fixed by the state for public utilities, and of procedures for fixing them. The vehicle for teaching Brandeis his lesson was *Ohio Valley Water Co.* v. *Ben Avon Borough*, decided after two arguments in 1920. The majority's chosen schoolmaster, as in *Adams* v. *Tanner*, was McReynolds.

Aside from the *Ben Avon* case, of which more presently, decisions on rate fixing for public utilities were substantial in number and a mixed bag. A handful of cases raised the issue of *German Alliance Insurance Co.* v. *Kansas*: whether a business sufficiently affected public interest to be admitted "into the magic circle of public utilities,"[178] so that the rates it charged would be at all subject to regulation by the state. In *Terminal Taxicab Co.* v. *District of Columbia*,[179] Holmes held for a unanimous Court, following *German Alliance Insurance Co.*, that the business of providing taxicabs to the public pursuant to contracts with the railroad terminal and various hotels in Washington, D.C., was a public utility. But Holmes was required to distinguish that portion of the same company's business which consisted of furnishing automobiles from a central

---

[176] Mason, *Brandeis*, 517–18.

[177] *Cal. L. Rev.*, 5:494, 495, 1917. See also *Cent. L. J.*, 85:111, 1917; *Yale L. J.*, 27:134, 1917; *Ill. L. Rev.*, 12:428, 1918; *cf. Harv. L. Rev.*, 31:490, 1918.

[178] *Supra*, p. 283, n.272; see *supra*, pp. 282 *et seq.*

[179] 241 U.S. 252, 256 (1916).

garage on individual orders rather than pursuant to an overall contractual arrangement.

"Although I have not been able to free my mind from doubt," wrote Holmes, "the Court is of opinion that this part of the business is not to be regarded as a public utility. It is true that all business, and for the matter of that, every life in all its details, has a public aspect, some bearing upon the welfare of the community in which it is passed. But however it may have been in earlier days as to the common callings, it is assumed in our time that an invitation to the public to buy does not necessarily entail an obligation to sell. It is assumed that an ordinary shop keeper may refuse his wares arbitrarily to a customer whom he dislikes, and although that consideration is not conclusive [citing the *German Alliance Insurance Co.* case] it is assumed that such a calling is not public as the word is used. In the absence of clear language to the contrary it would be assumed that an ordinary livery stable stood on the same footing as a common shop, and there seems to be no difference between the plaintiff's service from its garage and that of a livery stable." In *Van Dyke* v. *Geary*,[180] however, Brandeis was allowed to hold, McReynolds alone dissenting without opinion, that a water system established by the owner of a large tract of land, constituting the better part of a town, to sell water to purchasers of lots was a public utility.

It was also claimed in *Van Dyke* v. *Geary* that the rates fixed for the water by the state public service commission, although supposedly resulting in a 10 percent return on invested capital, were actually confiscatory, because the value of the water system and the cost of operating it had been grossly underestimated. Property valuation and operating costs, Brandeis remarked briefly, were largely matters of fact and opinion. Both had been thoroughly looked into by the public service commission, as well as by the federal district court, which had sustained the judgment of the commission, and from which the case had been appealed to the Supreme Court. The question on appeal was not whether every factual issue had been correctly resolved in the Supreme Court's view, but whether a fair-minded inquiry could have established these rates. The answer to this question, Brandeis held, was yes. Moreover, the district court had retained jurisdiction, and if the rates turned out in practice to be confiscatory, the owners of the water system could return for appropriate relief.

Very frequently, now as earlier, rate cases were indeed decided this simply, the Court guarding, in a phrase of Holmes, against the attribution of "delusive exactness" to calculations of value, costs, and

---

[180] 244 U.S. 39 (1917). And see Producers Transportation Co. v. Railroad Commission, 251 U.S. 228 (1920).

probable returns.[181] Although Brandeis, applying the method of *Van Dyke v. Geary* in exactly the same spirit, held in another case that a railroad passenger fare set by statute was confiscatory,[182] this method worked out in most instances to uphold the orders of state commissions. Thus in *New York & Queens Gas Co. v. McCall*, Clarke for a unanimous Supreme Court affirmed a judgment of the New York Court of Appeals sustaining an order of the state public service commission. The order was attacked as confiscatory on the ground that it allowed too low a rate of return on investment. The New York Court of Appeals, Clarke noted, had held that in reviewing an action of the commission, it had no authority to substitute its judgment of what was reasonable in a given case for that of the commission, but was limited to determining whether the commission had acted arbitrarily and capriciously, in which event— but in which event only—the commission's action was unlawful. The Supreme Court similarly, Clarke said, had no business substituting its conception of the wisdom of an order for that of a state commission; it was not the task of the Court to analyze the evidence, balance it, and decide whether it preponderated for or against the order. Rather the Court would examine the record only so far as necessary to determine whether there had been "a want of hearing or such arbitrary or capricious action on the part of the Commission as to violate the due process clause of the Constitution."[183]

There had been departures from this method, even by Holmes,[184] and in some cases the method was inapplicable, and was neither followed nor rejected, the issues being in the full sense issues of law, such as whether a railroad could be required to carry on some part of its business at a loss or marginal profit.[185] But in *Ohio Valley Water Co. v. Ben Avon Borough*, the method itself was called into question, and to the extent that it assigned, as it did, great weight to the determinations of state rate-fixing commissions on matters of fact and opinion, it was repudiated. It must have appeared to a majority of the Justices that, like the presumption of constitutionality, this method, acceptable enough in many rate cases, threatened to entrench itself as a generalization

---

[181] See *supra,* p. 287.

[182] Groesbeck v. Duluth, South Shore & Atlantic Ry., 250 U.S. 607 (1919); see *supra,* p. 263, n.191; and see Rowland v. St. Louis & San Francisco R.R., 244 U.S. 106 (1917), *supra,* p. 263, n.190.

[183] 245 U.S. 345, 348–49 (1917).

[184] See *supra,* p. 287, n.285.

[185] See Northern Pacific Ry. v. North Dakota, 236 U.S. 585 (1915), *supra,* p. 263, n.192; Norfolk & Western Ry. v. West Virginia, 236 U.S. 605 (1915), *supra,* p. 263, n.192; Denver v. Denver Water Co., 246 U.S. 178 (1918); Detroit United Ry. v. Detroit, 248 U.S. 429 (1919) (*cf.* Detroit United Ry. v. Michigan, 242 U.S. 238 [1916]; Detroit United Ry. v. Detroit, 255 U.S. 171 [1921]; Vandalia R.R. v. Schnull, 255 U.S. 113 (1921), *supra,* p. 263, n.190.

from which there could be no escape. And that would not do, for the result would be to insulate the vast bulk of state rate-fixing orders from effective federal judicial control. It was not perhaps that the majority wished to exercise such control on a continuous basis, but that it wished to retain the option to do so. Again Brandeis somehow made the threat real and present, although as we shall see, his own position was by no means as clear as it had been in *Adams* v. *Tanner*.

The *Ben Avon* case came up from the Supreme Court of Pennsylvania. Following an adversary hearing held on complaint of the borough of Ben Avon, the state public service commission arrived at a valuation of the Water Company's property, and fixed rates for the water sold by the company to consumers. The company appealed to the Superior Court of Pennsylvania, which modified the order of the commission, holding that the commission had undervalued the property of the company in several respects. On further appeal, the Supreme Court of Pennsylvania reversed the judgment of the Superior Court, and reinstated the original order of the commission. The commission's valuation of the company's property, said the Supreme Court, was supported by competent evidence and was reasonable. Where the Superior Court had differed with the commission's valuation, it had merely substituted its own judgment for the commission's. In so doing, the Superior Court had exceeded the authority conferred upon it by Pennsylvania law.

In the Supreme Court of the United States, the company contended that the commission's rate-fixing order was a purely legislative act, of which the company was entitled to have judicial review, else the order took its property without due process, in violation of the Fourteenth Amendment; that the company's right to judicial review was denied, and the Fourteenth Amendment violated, when the Supreme Court of Pennsylvania held that neither it nor the Superior Court had authority to decide whether the commission's order was in accord with the weight of the evidence, but only whether it was supported by competent evidence and was reasonable; and that the order as reinstated by the Supreme Court of Pennsylvania was in fact not in accord with the weight of the evidence, in that it undervalued the company's property and fixed rates which were confiscatory. For the borough of Ben Avon it was argued that the Supreme Court of Pennsylvania had reviewed the evidence and had found no undervaluation, and that its finding was correct.

It was clear by the time the *Ben Avon* case was argued in the Supreme Court of the United States, as it is clear now, that the Constitution guarantees a judicial review somewhere, in some court, of public utility rates fixed either by statute, as they sometimes used to be, or by order of a commission. Thus in *Oklahoma Operating Co.* v.

Love,[186] decided while *Ben Avon* was under consideration in the Supreme Court, Brandeis held unconstitutional a statute that required orders of a commission to be obeyed, subject to heavy penalties, without prior opportunity for judicial review. Only by disobeying the order, inviting contempt proceedings, and then raising issues of the legality of the order while defending itself against a finding of contempt could a utility obtain judicial review. If it lost, it was subject to the heavy penalties provided for having disobeyed. "Obviously," said Brandeis, "a judicial review beset by such deterrents does not satisfy the constitutional requirements. . . ."[187] But the deterrents against judicial review in Oklahoma barred effective access to federal as well as state courts. There was no way other than the contempt proceeding for a utility to reach the Supreme Court of the United States on appeal from the state courts, and the penalties would presumably accrue while an attempt was made in a lower federal court to enjoin enforcement of a rate order. Indeed, *Oklahoma Operating Co.* v. *Love* was a suit for an injunction in a lower federal court, begun with a prayer for a preliminary injunction against imposition of the penalties, and it was this prayer that Brandeis granted.

While it was clear, therefore, and reaffirmed in *Oklahoma Operating Co.* v. *Love*, that review in some judicial forum—a lower federal court, if no other—was constitutionally required, it did not necessarily follow that the federal Constitution required that a *state* judicial forum be provided for review. The states, after all, so far as the federal Constitution is generally concerned, "may distribute the powers of government as they choose,"[188] among such institutions as they choose to set up. And at any rate, to say that judicial review was required was not to say anything about its necessary scope. A review limited to a determination that the order of the commission had been reasonable and neither arbitrary nor capricious was the practice of the Supreme

---

[186] 252 U.S. 331, 337 (1920); and see Oklahoma Gin Co. v. Oklahoma, 252 U.S. 339 (1920). *Cf.* Wadley Southern Ry. v. Georgia, 235 U.S. 651 (1915); Detroit & Mackinac Ry. v. Fletcher Paper Co., 248 U.S. 30 (1918).

[187] In so holding, Brandeis avoided what (as Terminal Taxicab Co. v. District of Columbia, *supra*, n.179, demonstrated) would have been a difficult question: whether laundries, declared by the state to be a virtual monopoly in Oklahoma, could constitutionally be treated as public utilities for purposes of rate fixing. *Cf.* New State Ice Co. v. Liebmann, *supra*, n.174. *Oklahoma Operating Co.* v. *Love* and a companion case were argued twice, the Court indeed refusing to accept a submission on briefs in lieu of a second argument, but ordering oral reargument. The reason may have been that while the case was in the Supreme Court, Oklahoma changed the law that was under attack. But the change had no bearing on the disposition of these cases.

[188] L. L. Jaffe, *Judicial Control of Administrative Action* (1965), 637.

Court of the United States, and had been held to suffice in state courts as well in such a case as *New York & Queens Gas Co.* v. *McCall*.

Ben Avon is thus seen—not in hindsight, but contemporaneously— as a simple case, run of the mill. So apparently the Justices saw it at first. The decision in conference after the first argument in October 1919—whether unanimously or by a divided Court, we do not know— was to affirm, upholding the judgment of the Supreme Court of Pennsylvania and the order of the commission. The opinion was assigned to Brandeis. But difficulties did lurk in *Ben Avon*, raising doubts that Brandeis at this time shared, and called to his colleagues' attention. Having done so, he lost control of the case, which the majority then used to reassert judicial dominion over the process of rate making.

The question of the necessary scope of the constitutionally required judicial review of rate making was not squarely raised in *New York & Queens Gas Co.* v. *McCall* or in like earlier cases. The parties merely tendered the ultimate substantive issue of confiscation, arguing not that the state courts had improperly exercised the function of review, but that they had reached a wrong result. The Supreme Court then applied its own method of review, examining the reasonableness of the rate-making order but nothing more, and of course at least inferentially approving use of the same method in state courts. But the issue of a constitutionally required scope of judicial review in state courts, not having been tendered as such, could be said not to have been met head-on. Moreover, the force of *New York & Queens Gas Co.* v. *McCall* and of earlier precedents to the same effect, such as *Oregon Railroad & Navigation Co.* v. *Fairchild*,[189] was weakened by Holmes' opinion in *Prentis* v. *Atlantic Coast Line*,[190] a well-remembered great case, then little more than a decade old.

Prentis v. *Atlantic Coast Line* was a suit in a lower federal court to enjoin the Virginia rate-making commission from enforcing railroad passenger fares which it had fixed, and which were claimed to be confiscatory. The commission was set up by Virginia law as a court. It held hearings before fixing rates, and an appeal lay from it to the Supreme Court of Virginia, which was given full authority to reexamine the facts and revise the rates. If a rate order was disobeyed, the commission was empowered to conduct enforcement proceedings, in which penalties for disobedience could be imposed, and from which an appeal could again be taken to the Supreme Court of Virginia. In *Prentis*, a rate order had been issued by the commission, but no appeal

---

[189] 224 U.S. 510 (1912), *supra*, p. 290, n.294; and see Louisville & Nashville R.R. v. Garrett, 231 U.S. 298 (1913).

[190] 211 U.S. 210, 226, 228 (1908); see H. M. Hart, Jr., and H. Wechsler, *The Federal Courts and the Federal System* (1953), 858–61.

to the Supreme Court of Virginia had been taken, and the enforcement stage had by no means been reached. The railroads had gone into federal court first. The state's defense against the federal suit rested on the proposition that proceedings before the commission were judicial in nature. Under *Revised Statutes*, Section 720, the federal courts were without jurisdiction to enjoin state judicial proceedings, which were *res judicata*. The commission's action, the state contended, could be appealed to the Supreme Court of Virginia and presumably thence to the Supreme Court of the United States, but it was proof against collateral attack.

Holmes assumed that the commission would be sitting as a judicial body when it enforced an order and punished for violation of it. But when it fixed rates, Holmes said, the commission acted as a legislative body. "A judicial inquiry investigates, declares and enforces liabilities as they stand on present or past facts and under laws supposed already to exist. That is its purpose and end. Legislation on the other hand looks to the future and changes existing conditions by making a new rule to be applied thereafter to all or some part of those subject to its power. The establishment of a rate is the making of a rule for the future, and therefore is an act legislative not judicial in kind. . . ." To be sure, the commission held hearings, but the question was, to what end, a legislative or a judicial end? "Legislation cannot bolster itself up in that way [by holding hearings and making itself seem like a judicial proceeeding]. Litigation cannot arise until the moment of legislation is past." It followed that a lower federal court had jurisdiction to enjoin a rate-making order. The proceedings resulting in the order were not judicial, but legislative, and the order was not *res judicata*.

Nonetheless, Holmes did not let the federal suit for an injunction go forward. Considerations of comity between the state and federal governments counseled, he held, that the railroads be required to pursue their appellate remedy in the Supreme Court of Virginia first. State judicial remedies, as was soon to be quite definitely settled, did not have to be exhausted before one could seek vindication of federal constitutional rights in a federal court.[191] But the remedy to be had in the Supreme Court of Virginia at this stage in the rate-making process was not judicial. The court had full revisory authority over the commission's order, and its function, therefore, was also legislative. That being so, the railroads would retain their right of access to the federal court after an adverse decision in the Supreme Court of Virginia. There was no call to fear being met by a plea of Section 720 and of *res judicata*. Nor would the railroads be stopped by the argument that the only way they could

---

[191] See *supra*, pp. 287–88; Bacon v. Rutland R.R., 232 U.S. 134 (1914), *supra*, p. 310, n.368.

get into a federal court was to wait for enforcement proceedings, under the overhanging threat of punishment, and then appeal from such proceedings to the Supreme Court of the United States. To confine the railroads to this particular remedy "for the assertion of their rights," said Holmes, "would be to deprive them of a part of those rights."

So Brandeis was to hold in *Oklahoma Operating Co. v. Love*, on the ground that "a judicial review beset by such deterrents" was obviously deficient. But Holmes in the *Prentis* case went on to give a very different reason. "If the railroads were required to take no active steps," said Holmes, "until they could bring a writ of error from this court to the Supreme Court . . . [of Virginia] after a final judgment [to enforce the rate and punish them for violating it] they would come here with the facts already found against them. But the determination as to their rights turns almost wholly upon the facts to be found. Whether their property was taken unconstitutionally depends upon the valuation of the property, the income to be derived from the proposed rate and the proportion between the two—pure matters of fact. When those are settled the law is tolerably plain. All their constitutional rights, we repeat, depend upon what the facts are found to be. They are not to be forbidden to try those facts before a court of their own choosing if otherwise competent."

The purpose for which Holmes distinguished the function of the rate-making commission in Virginia from that of a court was to allow a federal equity suit in the face of *Revised Statutes*, Section 720. That was why he called the function of the commission legislative rather than judicial. In the same context, and for the purpose both of requiring recourse to the Supreme Court of Virginia and of leaving the way open to the federal court after such recourse had been had, Holmes said that the Supreme Court of Virginia also exercised a legislative function. Unless Holmes of all people had suddenly accepted the tyranny of labels and started thinking words and not things, he should have been implying nothing at all about a constitutionally required scope of judicial review. But he did end with a gratuitous generalization about a constitutional right to have the facts judicially determined. In this generalization, a great deal that needs to be sorted out was jumbled together.

A proceeding may be legislative rather than judicial in the sense that its result could as well and as constitutionally be achieved by legislation, with no need for a prior adversary hearing, even though the Due Process Clause requires that obligations and other burdens be imposed specifically on individuals or corporations only after an adversary hearing. It was taken for granted at the time of *Prentis* that rates to be charged in the future could be fixed directly by legislation; using a commission was optional. But it does not follow that all rate making had to be considered legislation. Rate making looks to the future. As it is based on valuation and costs, however, it also adjudicates the past;

that is why the issue of confiscation is always imminent, and it is of course a judicial issue. Not the result but the process and the purpose for which the question is asked determine whether rate making is legislative or judicial.[192]

To be sure, a hearing purporting to be judicial may be found not to be. It may not have the attributes of an adversary proceeding necessary to satisfy the Due Process Clause. This may conceivably have been true of the hearing afforded by the Virginia commission. The commission operated by announcing a proposed rate and then hearing objections to it. If the commission did not itself come forward with evidence to support its proposed rate, which the railroads could refute, then the hearing was not the adversary one required by the Due Process Clause; the proceeding was legislative, not because in the nature of things, given its intended end, it always had to be, but because in fact it was, even though it called itself judicial.

Now, in any case in which a full adversary hearing must constitutionally be granted, as it must be on the issue of confiscation, but was not afforded before a commission or like body,[193] it must be made available somewhere, and may be provided *de novo* by a reviewing court.[194] And even if an adequate adversary hearing—whether called legislative or judicial for one or another purpose—was had, there is still in addition a constitutional right to judicial review of questions of law. "The supremacy of law demands," said Brandeis in a celebrated opinion of the 1930s, "that there shall be opportunity to have some court decide whether an erroneous rule of law was applied [by a commission or like body]; and whether the proceeding in which facts were adjudicated was conducted regularly. To that extent, the person asserting a right, whatever its source, should be entitled to the independent judgment of a court. . . ."[195] But this right to a judicial review of the legal consequences to be drawn from facts is different from a right to have the facts established in an adversary hearing, and the two rights together do not amount to a right to have those facts established by a court.

Holmes blurred, indeed obliterated, these crucial distinctions by setting up his apparently mutually exclusive categories of legislative and judicial hearings, from which then sprung a third category, called administrative hearings, located somewhere in between, but nearer the judicial than the legislative end. *Oregon Railroad & Navigation Co.* v. *Fairchild* and *New York & Queens Gas Co.* v. *McCall* were classified

---

[192] *Cf.,* e.g., Securities & Exchange Commission v. Chenery Corp., 332 U.S. 194 (1947).

[193] *Compare* Londoner v. Denver, 210 U.S. 373 (1908), *with* Bi-Metallic Co. v. Colorado, 239 U.S. 441 (1915).

[194] See, e.g., Oregon R.R. & Navigation Co. v. Fairchild, *supra,* n.189; Jordan v. American Eagle Fire Ins. Co., 169 F. 2d 281 (D.C. Cir. 1948).

[195] St. Joseph Stock Yards Co. v. United States, 298 U.S. 38, 84 (1936).

as cases dealing with administrative rather than legislative hearings, since neither involved rate fixing alone. In *Fairchild*, a commission, following a hearing, ordered a railroad to lay additional trackage and sidings to connect to various localities. The order, obviously imposing costs, was attacked as confiscatory. In *McCall*, a commission, again after a hearing, ordered a gas company to extend its lines and offer service in a new community, and the company claimed that at the established rates it would get too small a return on its investment.

It was under the shadow, then, of Holmes' pronouncements in the *Prentis* case, and of a nomenclature and assumptions which had grown up around these pronouncements, that Brandeis and his law clerk at that time, who was Dean Acheson, began work on *Ohio Valley Water Co.* v. *Borough of Ben Avon*. There are preserved in Brandeis' file two typewritten memoranda, which although unsigned, bear corrections in Acheson's hand and are certainly his work. Counsel had not raised the point, wrote Acheson, but it appeared that under the law of Pennsylvania a judicial review in which the issue of confiscation could be raised and decided was available in a proceeding other than the one that the company had initiated in this case. Instead of appealing from the commission's rate order to the Superior and then to the Supreme Court of Pennsylvania, the company could have brought an original suit in equity to enjoin enforcement of the order—either in a state court, as specifically allowed by Pennsylvania law, or Acheson pointed out interestingly enough, in a lower federal court. The Pennsylvania law provided that no penalties would accrue for failure to obey the order while such a suit was pending.[196]

The route to judicial review that the company took in this case was thus one of two available to it; and along the other, the route equally available though not taken, the company would plainly have been accorded every constitutional right to judicial review it could possibly claim. Yet the route it did choose also enabled the company to raise the issue of confiscation. That issue was actually passed on by both the Superior and the Supreme Court of Pennsylvania on the basis of the factual record made in the hearing before the commission. Since the company could have had another and fuller judicial review, but had elected not to avail itself of it, it might be thought that there was no need to go into the adequacy of the judicial review actually afforded. But, Acheson went on, "a party may not be denied its constitutional

---

[196] In Oklahoma Operating Co. v. Love, *supra*, n.186, 252 U.S. at 336, the state did make the argument that judicial review was available otherwise than merely in contempt proceed-ings, namely by means of mandamus or prohibition. But Brandeis held that on a fair reading of the state law, that was not so.

right to a judicial review because it elected to pursue a remedy which, though restricted to an existing record, purported to offer a review of the law, if that remedy did not in fact provide a review of the law according to accepted appellate practice." The company contended that the review it received in the Supreme Court of Pennsylvania did not accord with accepted appellate practice, and the question whether or not it did had to be faced.

Acheson began with the proposition, which he took to have been established by *Prentis* v. *Atlantic Coast Line*, and which nobody now controverted, that "the hearing had before the Commission, although conducted with notice and an opportunity to examine witnesses, was a legislative hearing and not the judicial one required by law." The Supreme Court of Pennsylvania reviewed the findings of the commission after the fashion of a trial court reviewing the findings of a master, or an appellate court those of a trial judge sitting in equity. It accepted findings that were supported by evidence and led to a reasonable result. This was customary and adequate appellate practice. The company's contention to the contrary failed, therefore. But there remained another question: "whether the hearing before the Commission was a sufficient base upon which to build the judicial proceedings required by the Constitution—did that hearing correspond to the proceedings in a trial court or before a master; is the right to judicial review simply the right to appellate review of any record?" This question the company did not raise. The company in effect waived whatever right it might have claimed to have the facts proved afresh, and attacked instead the appellate review it had received. The question was nonetheless crucial. Addressing it, Acheson posited three premises which at first blush seemed to answer it very nicely, although as we shall see, in the end Acheson felt they did not quite.

The premises were these: that the company had a constitutional right to a judicial determination on the issue of confiscation; that such a judicial determination need involve only questions of law, the facts being examined merely to determine whether a reasonable commission could have found them to be as stated; and that pure findings of fact by the commission were to be accepted as final. "At a time when the idea of a government of laws and not of men had resulted in a practical paralysis of administration," said Acheson, "the conception of the fitting judicial review was one in which the matter was tried de novo before a court, a complete, new record established by a reintroduction of all the evidence, and in general the proceedings before the Commission regarded with cold aloofness." But that time had passed. In *Oregon Railroad & Navigation Co.* v. *Fairchild*, the Court had indicated that no trial *de novo* was necessary if there had been a proper quasi-judicial proceeding before the commission (with notice, and right to present evidence and to cross-examine adverse witnesses), and that judicial review on the record made in such a proceeding was sufficient. So the Court had also held in cases coming to it through lower federal courts from the Interstate Commerce Commission,[197] and so it had held again in a state case in *New York & Queens Gas Co. v. McCall*. On this particular point, said Acheson, *Ben Avon* was "on all fours with *New York & Queens Gas Co. v. McCall*."

Yet there was a rub, and it was *Prentis*. *Oregon Railroad & Navigation Co. v. Fairchild, New York & Queens Gas Co. v. McCall*, and like cases came up on appeal from administrative hearings, whereas in *Ben Avon* the Court was confronted with a legislative hearing. *Prentis* had held that a hearing before a legislative body constituted no part of the constitutionally required judicial review. "Litigation," Acheson quoted Holmes, "cannot arise until the moment of legislation is past." The issue of confiscation was first of all and above all a factual issue, as Holmes had said in *Prentis*. Acheson quoted the passage in which Holmes remarked that all the constitutional rights of the railroads in *Prentis* depended "upon what the facts are found to be. They [the railroads] are not to be forbidden to try those facts before a court of their own choosing if otherwise competent." That was undoubtedly the law, said Acheson, and the facts in *Ben Avon* had not been tried in a court, but had been found in a legislative proceeding. A judicial review accepting facts so found would not do.

Having thus exploded the premises he had posited, Acheson returned to his original escape hatch. The company was given by Pennsylvania law an opportunity for a judicial review that did include a judicial trial of facts. This opportunity the company did not take, and it could not now be heard to complain that the alternate judicial review it did seek failed to afford it a judicial trial of the facts. Whether a suit in equity and a judicial trial of the facts were now still open to the company under Pennsylvania law, and whether the disposition of the *Ben Avon* case he was suggesting could be supported only if such a suit were still open, Acheson did not make clear, although he did say that in his view the Pennsylvania Supreme Court had not held the commission's findings of fact to be conclusive, or even in accord with the weight of the evidence, but merely reasonable, from which the inference might be drawn that the court's decision would not be *res judicata* against the company in an equity suit. Yet Acheson also said that the court had reviewed the findings of the commission as if they were those of a lower court, from which the opposite inference might be drawn. At any rate, Acheson closed with a brief discussion of the substantive issue of confiscation itself. It would take a great deal, he said, to cause the Supreme

---

[197] See *infra*, pp. 650–61.

Court of the United States to overrule the decision of the highest court of a state that the valuation arrived at by a commission was reasonable, and the necessary showing had not been made in *Ben Avon.*

Brandeis at first took a less complicated view of the case than did his law clerk. Whether before or after he received Acheson's memoranda, Brandeis drafted a brief opinion, printed in November 1919. The order of the commission, he said, was a legislative act, and on the issue of confiscation, the company was "of course, entitled . . . to a judicial determination." Since the order was legislative, rather than, as in *Oregon Railroad & Navigation Co.* v. *Fairchild* and *New York & Queens Gas Co.* v. *McCall,* administrative, "the hearing which preceded the order, although it appears to have been entered upon after due notice, to have been conducted according to judicial practice and to have been participated in throughout by the Company does not satisfy the requirements of a judicial review." Here Brandeis cited *Prentis* v. *Atlantic Coast Line.* An order of the commission fixing rates, even though affirmed on appeal in the Pennsylvania courts, was not under Pennsylvania law "conclusive of the question whether those rates are confiscatory"—the implication being that proceedings on appeal in the Pennsylvania courts were also not judicial, just as review by the Virginia Supreme Court had been held not to be judicial in *Prentis.* (But Brandeis did not say this in so many words, perhaps because it might have raised a question of the jurisdiction of the Supreme Court of the United States to hear the case at all at this stage, on writ of error to the Supreme Court of Pennsylvania.) In any event, the point was that the company could attack the commission's order in a suit in equity, affording all the judicial review anyone could want.

Brandeis ended thus: "As the Supreme Court of Pennsylvania did not hold that the order of the Commission was conclusive and did not pass otherwise upon the question whether the rates were confiscatory [the court, Brandeis had said, held only that the rates were supported by competent evidence and were reasonable], but merely determined the jurisdiction of the Superior Court [which it held to be narrower than that court had assumed], a matter wholly of state concern, the constitutional right of the Company asserted was not denied." The inference was plainly to be drawn—by analogy to what Holmes had said the situation would be in *Prentis* after an appeal to the Supreme Court of Virginia—that the company retained its right to bring an equity suit in the Pennsylvania courts and thus get the judicial review to which it was entitled, and which it had not received.

It is altogether possible that this disposition of the *Ben Avon* case, patterned essentially on *Prentis* v. *Atlantic Coast Line,* would have been satisfactory to a majority of the Justices. Something like it was apparently favored by a majority till virtually the very last moment. But it was not satisfactory to Brandeis in the simplicity and directness of this first draft opinion, which he did not circulate to the Court. What the Supreme Court of Pennsylvania had actually done was oversimplified, and too much else was passed over in silence. So while the first draft might have done well enough, Brandeis did not let it alone. He went through three more drafts, and produced a substantially longer opinion, which he did circulate in January 1920.

Now Brandeis took account of all the issues stirred in Acheson's memoranda. The company, he said as before, could have obtained judicial review by bringing a bill in equity in the state courts, or, Brandeis now added following Acheson, in a lower federal court. (This is significant because it suggests, of course, that so long as federal courts are accessible, the Constitution does not require that judicial review be provided in the state courts; it suggests that what was decisive in *Oklahoma Operating Co.* v. *Love* was that Oklahoma had deterred litigation in federal as well as state courts.) It was not necessary to decide, therefore, Brandeis went on, whether the appeals to the Superior and Supreme Courts of Pennsylvania from what had been a legislative hearing before the commission satisfied "the constitutional requirements of a judicial review." But then, as he had not done in the earlier draft, Brandeis added: "It is true, however, that an additional or alternative remedy [the review in the Superior and Supreme Courts of Pennsylvania] may deny the constitutional right to due process of law because of its nature or the course of the proceeding." And it was the company's contention that due process had been denied it in this fashion, because the Supreme Court of Pennsylvania did not weigh the evidence and did not allow the Superior Court to do so. On the other side, it was argued for the borough of Ben Avon that the review provided in the Supreme Court of Pennsylvania was a full judicial review which satisfied the constitutional requirement.

Neither contention, Brandeis said, was wholly correct. The Supreme Court of Pennsylvania held that the Superior Court should not have exercised revisionary power, but only the power to review questions of law. The Supreme Court held further that the valuation arrived at by the commission was reasonable. Without weighing the evidence, the Supreme Court examined it in order to determine whether it supported the findings of the commission. But it did not by any means follow that the company had been denied due process. The method of review employed by the Supreme Court of Pennsylvania was the established method for reviewing administrative orders. And Brandeis cited the *McCall* case, as well as the practice of the Supreme Court of the United States in reviewing orders of the Interstate Commerce Commission, without now drawing any distinction between "legislative" and "administrative" proceedings. It remained to decide only whether the Supreme Court of the United States must itself weigh the evidence on the issue of confiscation. Brandeis thought not. In this Court also the issue was the reasonableness of the commission's order, and this Court no more than the Supreme Court of Pennsylvania, said Brandeis, should substitute its judgment of the facts for that of the commission. The commission's order was supported by evidence, and was, therefore, as upheld by the Supreme Court of Pennsylvania, "conclusive upon this court"—which sounded rather as if, having once elected not to bring an original suit in equity, the company might now be stuck.

Brandeis circulated this opinion to the Court together with the following typewritten memorandum:

> This opinion is in accord with the vote of the Conference, but I suggest that the record and briefs be examined in connection with it for this reason:
>
> The opinion rests primarily upon the existence of an alternative remedy. That such a remedy exists was not referred to at the Conference, nor in the argument, nor in any of the briefs—although these were evidently prepared with much care—, nor were the sections of the Statutes which show the existence of the remedy referred to. The reasoning of the opinion departs also in minor respects from contentions made by the parties.
>
> The ground upon which the opinion is rested made it unnecessary to consider another question—also not raised in argument or briefs— on which I feel some doubt, namely: whether a judicial review of a legislative order satisfies the constitutional requirements where the evidence on which the order is to be reviewed is necessarily limited to that introduced at the legislative hearing which preceded the entry of the order.

One would take it from this memorandum that the initial decision in conference in October was based on acceptance of the argument, made in behalf of the borough of Ben Avon, that the Supreme Court of Pennsylvania had satisfied the company's constitutional right to a judicial review by weighing the evidence and concluding that the commission's view of it, rather than that of the Superior Court, was correct. And it may be that an opinion similar in tone and substance to Clarke's opinion in *New York & Queens Gas Co.* v. *McCall*, and stirring no other issues, would have been acceptable to a majority of the Justices, or even the whole Court. Brandeis did not write it because of his own doubt, of which he gave notice in his memorandum. He had a few paragraphs expressing the doubt printed up, perhaps for inclusion in the opinion, though he ultimately omitted them, and contented himself with the summary statement in the memorandum to the Court. These paragraphs derived substantially, but not entirely, from Acheson's work. Brandeis wrote in part:

> The doubt does not arise from the fact that the order was entered by a commission as distinguished from a court; for a state may, consistently with the Federal Constitution, commit the decision of judicial questions to a tribunal other than a court. And as the opportunity to review a judicial decision by appeal is not an essential of due process, a limited review is clearly not open to constitutional objection. The court recently sustained a like limited review of an administrative order in *New York & Queens Gas Co.* v. *McCall.* Nor does any serious doubt arise from the fact that the Supreme Court, instead of rendering its decision upon the weight of the evidence, followed the common practice by which appellate courts refuse to reverse findings of the tribunal which heard the witnesses where there was ample evidence and no manifest error is shown. Due process is not ordinarily denied by a statute fixing the burden of proof or prescribing that a presumption shall attach to a particular fact. . . . [P]ractically all appellate courts recognize that a presumption of correctness attaches to findings under review. The mere fact that the Supreme Court of Pennsylvania gave such effect to the order and findings of the Commission is therefore not inconsistent with the constitutional requirements of judicial review.
>
> The real difficulty lies in the fact that the order here in question is a legislative act. It rests upon evidence; but the evidence was introduced at a hearing which preceded the entry of the order. Because the hearing preceded the order, it cannot itself constitute a judicial review, although entered upon after due notice [this and the following two phrases appeared also in Brandeis' short draft opinion dated November 1919], conducted according to judicial practice; and participated in throughout by the Company. *Prentis* v. *Atlantic Coast Line.* Can a hearing by another tribunal which is necessarily limited to the consideration of evidence introduced before the entry of the legislative order satisfy the constitutional requirements of a judicial review? Whether it could do so, if such hearing were the only opportunity for judicial review afforded, we need not now determine; for the Company was not so limited in its remedy.

But the doubt was not so easily laid. For Brandeis himself was saying in his opinion of January 1920, that even though the judicial review actually afforded the company was not the sole opportunity for judicial review that was available, it could nevertheless "deny the constitutional right to due process of law because of its nature or the course of the proceeding." He then said that the review in the Supreme Court of Pennsylvania did not deny due process because it was a proper appellate review. But the doubt he raised was not that. It was not whether the Pennsylvania Supreme Court followed good appellate practice. It was whether appellate review on the record made before the commission was constitutionally sufficient. If there was substance to this doubt, then the review in the Supreme Court of Pennsylvania could deny "the constitutional right to due process of law because of its nature or the course of the proceeding," and could do so, by Brandeis' own reasoning, regardless of whether it constituted the sole opportunity for judicial review.

Brandeis might have disposed of *Ben Avon* after the fashion of the *McCall* decision, and there is indication that this is what he was assigned to do. He did not, because of a doubt arising from the opinion in *Prentis*, which the company had not emphasized in its argument and the Justices had apparently not discussed in conference, but which troubled him. Initially, in his November draft, Brandeis proposed a disposition that would have avoided this doubt; or perhaps the doubt had then not yet fully impressed itself on him. Now, however, he raised it, and having raised it, proposed a disposition that did not, on analysis, avoid it. He said he was avoiding it in his memorandum to the Court, and the statement was undoubtedly ingenuous, for if he had not been trying to be candid Brandeis would not have needed to go this far in fully exposing his view of the case. But in truth his disposition did not make it "unnecessary to consider" the doubt he was calling to the brethren's attention.

There are preserved three returns to Brandeis' opinion of January 1920, and probably that was all Brandeis got. Holmes sent a note saying that the opinion sounded convincing, "and only your exhortation to examine the record and briefs leads me to retain it for the chance of doing so." Thus the author of *Prentis*, and hence the real author of all the trouble in *Ben Avon*, washing his hands, as it were. Clarke said: "I accept your concern as to alternative remedy, but it's a bold outsider who gives an opinion on Penn statutory law especially as to practice. They have a way there of amending an act without repealing the one amended which renders it so difficult to know what the statutory law really is that we Ohio lawyers—just across the line—never risked an opinion, and I have often had conflicting opinions as to the same question on the same day from the best lawyers in Western Penn. This simply by way of caution. I can't go into it and should have little confidence in the result if I should do so." The most important, and in view of the final outcome the most surprising, return was from McReynolds: "I concur in the result only." In the result only, but he concurred.

Within a very few days, on January 12, 1920, the Court issued an order restoring the case to the docket for reargument, and indicating what it wanted reargued: "The attention of counsel is directed," said the Court, "to the question of whether under the state law the right to review the action of the Commission was limited by the state statutes to the particular remedy which was here resorted to, or whether such statutes left open the right to invoke judicial power by way of independent suit for the purpose of redressing wrongs deemed to have resulted from action taken by the Commission."[198] Reargument was had early in March 1920, and apparently it satisfied the Court that the alternative remedy did in fact exist. The decision again was to affirm. Brandeis' suggested disposition was accepted. But the opinion was reassigned, withdrawn from Brandeis and given to McReynolds. Issues of the scope of judicial review, to which Brandeis had called attention, would not be confronted. They would be avoided in accordance with his suggestion. But they might at least have to be stated, and this was not a task to be entrusted to Brandeis.

Some six weeks later, McReynolds circulated the opinion which, with minor changes, now appears in the *Reports*. With it went the following note from McReynolds to the Court:

> The attached is not according to the vote.
>
> The conference seemed to accept the suggestion, at least I did, that if the judgment of the court below were affirmed it might work out proper relief through Section 31 [the section in the Pennsylvania law providing for the alternate remedy of a bill in equity].
>
> Investigation has convinced me that the better way is to reverse and leave that court to deal with the situation. I have spoken with some who voted to affirm and they now seem to favor the course suggested.
>
> The Chief Justice recommends that I circulate what has been written as a memorandum rather than return the cause to the conference.

McReynolds was brief. The Court, he said, was "compelled to conclude" that as the Supreme Court of Pennsylvania interpreted the law of the state, neither it nor the Superior Court had power to "determine the question of confiscation according to their own independent judgment when considering action by the Commission on appeal." The order of the commission was a legislative act. Whenever it was claimed that such an act was confiscatory, the Due Process Clause required the state to "provide a fair opportunity for submitting [the issue of confiscation] to a judicial tribunal for determination upon its own independent judgment as to both law and facts. . . ." Now, it was possible that the required review could be obtained by means of a bill in equity. The Supreme Court of Pennsylvania had not construed the statute providing this alternate means of review. Hence there was some legitimate

---

[198] 251 U.S. 542 (1920).

doubt about it. On the other hand, before *Ben Avon* itself was decided, the company could reasonably have supposed that an appeal to the Supreme Court of Pennsylvania would afford it a full judicial review, including an independent determination of the issue of confiscation. As distinguished from the Supreme Court of Virginia in the *Prentis* case, the Supreme Court of Pennsylvania performed a judicial, not a legislative, function in reviewing rate-making orders. This was not disputed. Judicial review in the Supreme Court of Pennsylvania turned out to be truncated and insufficient, but the company could reasonably have expected otherwise.

The case could not be disposed of, therefore, by holding that the company had chosen not to avail itself of a notoriously open alternate method of judicial review (by bill in equity), but had elected to seek a remedy known to be more restricted, and should now sleep in the bed it had made. The existence of the alternate remedy and the scope of the one chosen were, rather, both questionable at the time the company made its election. In the event, the company had not received the judicial review to which it was constitutionally entitled. If it was indeed open to the company to bring a bill in equity, and if this remedy was still available, the Supreme Court of Pennsylvania could so indicate, and could presumably relegate the company to this remedy. But until that was done, the order of the commission could not stand, and the judgment upholding it had to be reversed.

McReynolds' holding was a compromise of sorts, a cross between Brandeis' conclusion that the appellate review actually afforded the company in the Pennsylvania Supreme Court had been adequate as such, and his doubt whether the constitutionally required judicial review could be allowed to proceed on the factual record made in a "legislative" hearing. An "independent judgment as to both law and facts" might or might not call for a trial *de novo* of the facts. McReynolds' willingness to assume that the Pennsylvania Supreme Court could have given the company the judicial review to which it was entitled certainly suggested that such a review, including the required independent judgment, could be had without a trial *de novo*. Given McReynolds' holding, his disposition of the case was more logical and made more practical sense than an affirmance. For McReynolds would seem to have been right in suggesting that the company's election to follow the route of an appeal rather than filing a bill in equity (in a state or even a federal court) could not be regarded as a knowing waiver of the constitutional right, as McReynolds was now establishing it, to an independent judicial judgment.

Brandeis filed his opinion of January 1920 as a dissent, changing it only by the addition of a paragraph to refute the company's contention on the reargument that dicta in certain Pennsylvania cases indicated the unavailability of judicial review in an original equity suit. The doubt about review on the record made before the commission, raising the possibility that a trial *de novo* might be constitutionally required, which Brandeis mentioned in his memorandum to the Court in January, went unmentioned in the dissent. The result, as in January, was an ambivalent and not very compelling document. As much as McReynolds, Brandeis continued to characterize the proceedings before the commission as legislative. Unlike McReynolds, he considered the review in the Pennsylvania Supreme Court adequate as an appellate review, but he was obviously of two, or at least one and a half, minds about it, else he would not have placed so much emphasis on the availability of another and fuller review by bill in equity. And if the availability of this fuller review had some decisive importance, Brandeis should not have been content, as he was, to leave unanswered the question whether it would still be available after affirmance of the judgment of the Supreme Court of Pennsylvania. If on the other hand the review actually given by the Supreme Court of Pennsylvania met constitutional requirements, the availability also of another mode of review by bill in equity in the state courts and, as always of course, in the federal courts was scarcely relevant. It was relevant because Brandeis' real worry was the possibility of a constitutional right to a trial *de novo*. But of this there was no hint in the opinion.[199]

Brandeis not only lost his majority in *Ben Avon*, he also had a bit of trouble holding his companions in dissent. Holmes, still withdrawn and enigmatic despite his authorship of *Prentis*, returned that he inclined with Brandeis and against McReynolds, but hesitated. Clarke groped for a way to dissociate himself from Brandeis' pronouncements about the availability under Pennsylvania law of review by bill in equity. Both Holmes and Clarke, however, finally joined in Brandeis' dissent.[200]

"Probably no administrative law decision ever gave rise to more instant, voluminous, or steadily critical comment by legal writers," said a standard text, speaking of *Ben Avon* fifty years later.[201] The *Ben Avon* doctrine, wrote Felix Frankfurter and Henry M. Hart, Jr., in the early 1930s, was accounted for "by judicial distrust of the non-judicial determination, even indirectly, of issues of constitutional right . . . and above all by the vast interests that are at stake and the distrust of governmental curbs to big business at the time a divided court rendered the decision.

---

[199] Ohio Valley Water Co. v. Borough of Ben Avon, 253 U.S. 287, 289 (1920).

[200] See Brandeis Papers, Harvard Law School Library.

[201] See W. Gellhorn and C. Byse, *Administrative Law—Cases and Comments* (1970), 362; see, e.g., E. F. Albertsworth, "Judicial Review of Administrative Action by the Federal Supreme Court," *Harv. L. Rev.*, 35: 127, 1921.

In practice a genuinely independent judgment by the court is almost impossible by reason of the multitudinous details and their recondite significance; yet the *Ben Avon* case remains a sword of Damocles hanging over the regulatory systems, especially those of the states."[202] It remains so still, although since the Court has permitted the use of simpler methods of rate setting, putting less stress on valuation, its importance is greatly diminished.[203]

How did the *Ben Avon* decision come to pass, Felix Frankfurter asked Brandeis a couple of years later, considering that the result was unwarranted by the prior state of the law, and was wrong on grounds of policy? "That came to pass, as so much is to be explained," Brandeis answered, "on two grounds: First, it wasn't adequately considered— they didn't understand what they pretended to do—'an independent inquiry into the facts in confiscation cases'; and secondly and largely on personal grounds, they didn't propose to follow my views." That wasn't so much true now, under Taft, Brandeis said, but "it was very consistently true under the old Chief. I could have had my views prevail in cases of public importance if I had been willing to play politics. But I made up my mind I wouldn't—I would have had to sin against my light, and I would have hated myself, and I decided that the price was too large for the doubtful gain to the country's welfare. But you must constantly bear in mind the large part played by personal considerations and by inadequacy of consideration."[204]

It is not likely that Brandeis meant that his relations with White were bad, or were worse than his relations with Taft, and that this was the reason that his views had less chance to prevail under White. The point was that White was less effective than Taft in marshaling the Court. There was consequently more individual politicking by other Justices under White than later, when Taft tended to take charge of such politicking as was necessary. Taft would on occasion undertake to push through an opinion by Brandeis. White would not, and Brandeis himself didn't or couldn't, or both. Brandeis was also undoubtedly perceived by a majority of his colleagues as more of a menace, because a more unknown menace, in his early years than in the 1920s. There was more generalized distrust and fear of Brandeis now than later, and therefore more caution in accepting anything from him.

Even so, Brandeis' explanation of the *Ben Avon* decision, while perhaps sufficient, was not full. Brandeis omitted to mention the unresolved ambivalence in his own approach to *Ben Avon*. He made clear

---

[202] F. Frankfurter and H. M. Hart, Jr., "Rate Regulation," *Encyclopedia of the Social Sciences*, 13:104, 108, 1934.

[203] See Jaffe, *Judicial Control of Administrative Action*, 648–53.

[204] Brandeis-Frankfurter Conversations.

in opinions in later years[205] that there could be no effective rate regulation if courts, state or federal, attempted independently to redetermine the matters of fact and opinion that were the substance of questions of valuation, costs, and returns—whether by taking evidence *de novo* or by purporting to render a fresh judgment on a record made in administrative hearings. The exactness that would thus be sought under constitutional compulsion was, in truth, as Holmes remarked, delusive. And burdened with the effort to attain it, rate making would break down. Yet if this was as clear to Brandeis at the time of *Ben Avon* as later, he failed to make it clear. Nor could he very well, without dispelling the doubt whether judicial review might, consistently with the Due Process Clause, be restricted to a record made in a "legislative" hearing. Brandeis succeeded in repressing this doubt in future rate-making cases, but it surfaced again, and was decisive for him, in a case concerning citizenship. A proper judicial review on that issue, he held, was constitutionally required to include a judicial trial *de novo* of facts that had previously been found in a quasi-judicial and adequately adversary administrative hearing. It didn't even help that the hearing in this instance had been "administrative," rather than "legislative," as in *Prentis* and *Ben Avon*.[206]

PROCEDURE, SUBSTANCE, AND A WELTER OF CASES

Public utilities, and especially railroads, raised the due process complaint that their property was being arbitrarily confiscated not only in rate-fixing controversies, but very often also against statutory or administrative requirements that they make improvements, employ specified equipment and crews, or maintain or extend service.[207] But it was a rare case in which a public utility was able to persuade the Supreme Court to strike down requirements of this sort.[208] "Intelligent

---

[205] See Crowell v. Benson, 285 U.S. 22 (1932); St. Joseph Stock Yards Co. v. United States, 298 U.S. 38 (1936).

[206] Ng Fung Ho v. White, 259 U.S. 276 (1922).

[207] See *supra,* p. 290.

[208] *Compare* Great Northern Ry. v. Minnesota, 238 U.S. 340 (1915); Chicago, Milwaukee & St. Paul R.R. v. Wisconsin, 238 U.S. 491 (1915); Mississippi R.R. Commission v. Mobile & Ohio R.R., 244 U.S. 388 (1917); Brooks-Scanlon Co. v. Railroad Commission, 251 U.S. 396 (1920); Great Northern Ry. v. Cahill, 253 U.S. 71 (1920), *with* Missouri Pacific Ry. v. Omaha, 235 U.S. 121 (1914); Michigan Central R.R. v. Michigan R.R. Commission, 236 U.S. 615 (1915); Chicago & Alton R.R. v. Tranbarger, 238 U.S. 67 (1915); Phoenix Ry. v. Geary, 239 U.S. 277 (1915); Atlantic Coast Line v. Glenn, 239 U.S. 388 (1915); St. Louis, Iron Mountain & Southern Ry. v. Arkansas,

VI: *The Fate of Social Legislation, 1914–21: State*

self-interest," Holmes remarked in one opinion, "should lead to a careful consideration of what the [utility] is able to do without ruin, but this is not a constitutional duty."[209] One demand that states sometimes made of railroads—a requirement to continue operating at a loss, despite the owner's wish to abandon the enterprise—gave even Holmes trouble, however. It seemed to him to drive to the point of ruin and beyond, although Brandeis thought that Holmes' forebodings of ruin were premature.[210]

Holmes' attitude became evident as the Court considered *Bullock v. Railroad Commission of Florida*,[211] decided in 1921. At lower court in Florida had issued a decree authorizing the foreclosure sale of a bankrupt railroad to a purchaser who proposed to dismantle it for its scrap value. The state thereupon obtained from the Supreme Court of Florida a writ of prohibition voiding so much of the lower court's decree as authorized the dismantling. In the Supreme Court of the United States, the railroad asked that this writ of prohibition be vacated because it forced the railroad to continue operations at a loss, and thus confiscated its property arbitrarily in violation of the Due Process Clause. Holmes for a unanimous Court affirmed the judgment of the Supreme Court of Florida on the ground that the writ of prohibition did no such thing as the railroad claimed.

Whatever future rights to dismantle a purchaser might have, said Holmes, he retained; the writ of prohibition did not take them away. The Supreme Court of Florida had simply said that under Florida law the foreclosure sale as such could not enlarge the purchaser's rights over what they would otherwise be, and over what the bankrupt railroad's were. But Holmes took great pains to point out that generally people who had put their money into a railroad had no obligation to go

---

240 U.S. 518 (1916); Chicago, Terre Haute & Southeastern Ry. v. Anderson, 242 U.S. 283 (1916); Lake Shore & Michigan Southern Ry. v. Clough, 242 U.S. 375 (1917); Chesapeake & Ohio Ry. v. Public Service Commission, 242 U.S. 603 (1917); Sutton v. New Jersey, 244 U.S. 258 (1917); Great Northern Ry. v. Clara City, 246 U.S. 434 (1918); Chicago & Northwestern Ry. v. Ochs, 249 U.S. 416 (1919); Lake Erie & Western R.R. v. Public Utilities Commission, 249 U.S. 422 (1919); Pacific Gas Co. v. Police Court, 251 U.S. 22 (1919); St. Louis, Iron Mountain & Southern Ry. v.

Williams, 251 U.S. 63 (1919); Sullivan v. City of Shreveport, 251 U.S. 169 (1919).

[209] Erie R.R. v. Public Utility Commissioners, 254 U.S. 394, 411 (1921).

[210] A "heightened respect for property," Brandeis remarked to Felix Frankfurter in the early 1920s, seemed to be part of Holmes' growing old. Holmes had said to him recently, Brandeis reported: "I suppose miserliness is a legitimate incidence of age." This "a propos of accumulating and buying bonds." Brandeis-Frankfurter Conversations.

[211] 254 U.S. 513, 521 (1921).

on running it at a loss. Rather they had a right to stop. "Without previous statute or contract, to compel the company to keep on at a loss would be an unconstitutional taking of its property." It was just that this particular case reduced itself to the point that the Supreme Court of Florida's writ of prohibition did not compel the railroad to keep on, but simply excluded from the foreclosure decree an illusory grant of authority to dismantle. Under Florida law, whether and when the railroad could be dismantled had to be decided in another proceeding, not by the foreclosure court.[212]

In the first version of this opinion, however, Holmes, disdaining the point of Florida law which in the end he allowed to be decisive, reversed on the ground that the railroad's property was being confiscated. Brandeis disagreed both with the disposition of the case and with Holmes' reasoning. "There is no right to compel operation at a loss," he returned to this version of Holmes' opinion, "because that involves putting in new money. But it does not follow that because it [the railroad] cannot be operated today, except at a loss, the judgment (a prophecy) of the wise may not be that in a reasonable time it will not [sic!] be possible to operate at a profit. The mere fact that, at public sale, X will not buy charged with the obligation to operate now—is not proof." It could not be stated as an absolute right, Brandeis went on, that a bankrupt railroad, operating at a loss, was entitled to stop without the consent of the state.

Having indicated to Holmes the grounds of his disagreement, Brandeis proceeded to draft a dissent. Holmes held, he wrote, "that although those who construct a railroad under a state charter thereby devote the property to a public use, the Federal Constitution implies . . . a condition, paramount to the right of the State, to the effect that the owners may dismantle the railroad and dispose of the junked material" whenever they find that they are operating at a loss. But there was nothing in the federal Constitution that gave the railroad such a right, and there was "much in the common law to the contrary." At common law, by an appropriate expression of intent, an owner of property could irrevocably devote it to public use, as for example when he built a highway. Railroads were a form of highway. The owner of a highway right-of-way was under no obligation at common law to keep it in repair. Nor, however, could he remove the material with which it was fitted for use. By the same token, a railroad could not be dismantled without the consent of the state.

To be sure, the owner could not be required "to operate the property at a loss . . . and where it is clear that there is no prospect of

---

212 *Cf.* Detroit and Mackinac Ry. v. Michigan Railroad Commission, 240 U.S. 564 (1916).

being [able] to operate it without incurring a loss a Court may well apply the principle by which land is held to revert to the dedicator when the intended use becomes impossible . . . or the use is abandoned by the public." (This was the "prophecy" which Brandeis had mentioned in his return to Holmes.) "But it is for the courts of a State, not for this Court, to determine how and by what tribunal it shall be determined that a further use has become impossible." In a further draft of his dissent, Brandeis went on to show that Holmes in his first opinion had misread what the Supreme Court of Florida had actually done, and he suggested the disposition that Holmes and the Court then in the end accepted.[213]

Aside from the main groups of decisions discussed so far in this section, there was a welter of additional due process litigation. A sizeable number of cases dealt with the right to an adversary hearing, whether judicial or administrative, to establish the facts on which an individual's or a corporation's legal obligations might be based. This is the elemental procedural guarantee of the Due Process Clause that Holmes in *Prentis* v. *Atlantic Coast Line* and Brandeis as well as the Court in *Ohio Valley Water Co.* v. *Borough of Ben Avon* did not sufficiently distinguish from the right to a judicial review on issues of law.

In a few cases, notably *Coe* v. *Armour Fertilizer Works*,[214] the court held that hearings were constitutionally required. But in *Bi-Metallic Co.* v. *Colorado*,[215] a decision still often cited as drawing the classic distinction between rule making, which can be accomplished without a prior hearing, and adjudication, which must include a hearing, Holmes held that an administrative order increasing the valuation of all taxable property in the city of Denver by 40 percent was lawfully issued without a hearing.[216] Holmes assumed that any individual property owner who was peculiarly affected because his situation differed factually from the common one, (as for example, if his property had been previously overvalued) would at some stage be entitled to a hearing in which he could prove the facts that rendered his situation exceptional. But all to whom the order applied equally, as a simple doubling of the tax rate might have done, could not complain that the enactment of what amounted to legislation had taken place without a prior hearing. "Where a rule of conduct applies to more than a few people it is impracticable

---

[213] See Bickel, *Unpublished Opinions of Brandeis,* 222–26, 232–36.

[214] 237 U.S. 413 (1915); see also Saunders v. Shaw, 244 U.S. 317 (1917); Postal Telegraph Cable Co. v. Newport, 247 U.S. 464 (1918); Turner v. Wade, 254 U.S. 64 (1920).

[215] 239 U.S. 441, 445 (1915).

[216] See also St. Louis Land Co. v. Kansas City, 241 U.S. 419 (1916); Hancock v. City of Muskogee, 250 U.S. 454 (1919); Farncomb v. Denver, 252 U.S. 7 (1920).

633

that everyone should have a direct voice in its adoption," said Holmes.
"The Constitution does not require all public acts to be done in town
meeting or an assembly of the whole." People's rights against general
statutes were protected "in the only way that they can be in a complex
society, by their power, immediate or remote, over those who make the
rule. . . . There must be a limit to individual argument in such matters
if government is to go on."

Bi-Metallic Co. v. *Colorado* came down unanimously, but there
had been doubters among the Justices. Pitney returned to Holmes: "I
say nothing." Obviously he had something he might have said. And
Chief Justice White returned: "It is to me a very doubtful case. Yes,
provisionally. If there is a dissent I may retract."[217] A few years later,
White, joined by Clarke, dissented without opinion when the Court held
that a hearing could be dispensed with under circumstances that were
greatly more questionable.

Ownbey v. *Morgan*[218] was a suit against Ownbey, a citizen of
Colorado, in the Delaware state courts by Morgan as executor of his
father, J. P. Morgan, the banker, on a debt stated at $200,000. The
suit was begun by attachment of shares of stock held by Ownbey in a
Delaware corporation. Under the law of Delaware, Ownbey could come
in and defend only if he provided a bond in the amount stated in the
complaint. Ownbey was unable to procure the bond because the shares
that were seized were his entire property, and the corporation that had
issued the shares was at the moment in the hands of a receiver. Consequently no money could be raised on the security of these attached
shares. Ownbey tried to appear and defend anyway, alleging prior payment of the debt, but under the Delaware law he was prevented from
doing so because he had not filed the required bond. A default judgment
of something over $200,000 was rendered, and collected against the
attached shares.

This proceeding, the Court held, Pitney writing, did not constitute
a denial of due process, even though judgment was rendered without a
hearing. The requirement for posting bond dated back to colonial days,
tracing even farther than that to a "custom of London." It worked out
harshly in the peculiar circumstances of this case, but should be judged
only in its general operation, and generally, one who had property to be
attached could raise the money for a bond. "The due process clause,"
said Pitney, "does not impose upon the States a duty to establish ideal
systems for the administration of justice, with every modern improvement and with provision against every possible hardship that may
befall. . . . However desirable it is that the old forms of procedure be
improved with the progress of time, it cannot rightly be said that the

---

[217] Holmes Papers.   [218] 256 U.S. 94, 110–11, 112 (1921).

Fourteenth Amendment furnishes a universal and self-executing remedy. Its function is negative, not affirmative, and it carries no mandate for particular measures of reform."[219]

The procedural aspect of the Due Process Clause was highlighted as well in a series of cases dealing with efforts by the states to obtain jurisdiction for their courts over persons and corporations otherwise than by personal service. Earlier in the White Chief Justiceship, the Court had taken a permissive and even perhaps rather casual attitude in such cases.[220] Now, while there was still, of course, no absolute insistence on personal service under all circumstances,[221] and while corporations doing business in a state could be served constructively,[222] occasions were found for indicating limits. Thus constructive service on corporations was not allowed where the business done in the state, if any, was trivial.[223] And in *Simon v. Southern Railway*,[224] Lamar, writing for a unanimous Court and calling "upon principles of natural justice" as well as invoking the Due Process Clause, held that constructive service on a corporation in a state in which it was doing business would be allowed only for causes of action arising within that state.

In the well-known case of *McDonald* v. *Mabee*,[225] Holmes, also for a unanimous Court, insisted that only under closely defined, quite exceptional conditions could an individual defendant be deprived of what was otherwise a constitutional right to personal service of process. The defendant in *McDonald* v. *Mabee* had been a resident of Texas but had moved to Missouri, even though his family still resided in Texas. The plaintiff claimed that Texas had obtained jurisdiction over the

---

[219] The case brought distinguished counsel to the bar of the Court. Ownbey was represented by Louis Marshall, and the Morgan interests by Harlan F. Stone. Stone's representation of the Morgan interests in this case was held against him in the controversy over his nomination to the Supreme Court a few years later. See J. P. Frank, "The Appointment of Supreme Court Justices: III," *Wis. L. Rev.*, 1941, pp. 461, 489–91, 495; A. T. Mason, *Harlan Fiske Stone: Pillar of the Law* (1956), 185–88. The ancient Delaware practice that was in question in *Ownbey* v. *Morgan* has since been modernized. See J. W. Moore, *Cases on Debtors' and Creditors' Rights* (1955), 47.

[220] See *supra*, pp. 290–91.

[221] See Kryger v. Wilson, 242 U.S. 171 (1916); Pennington v. Fourth National Bank, 243 U.S. 269 (1917); Taylor & Kirby v. Drainage District, 167 Iowa 42, 148 N.W. 1040 (1914), *affirmed*, 244 U.S. 644 (1917); *cf.* Chicago Life Ins. Co. v. Cherry, 244 U.S. 25 (1917).

[222] See Pennsylvania Fire Ins. Co. v. Gold Issue Mining Co., 243 U.S. 93 (1917); *cf.* Washington-Virginia Ry. v. Real Estate Trust, 238 U.S. 185 (1915).

[223] See Riverside & Dan River Mills v. Menefee, 237 U.S. 189 (1915); Philadelphia & Reading Ry. v. McKibbin, 243 U.S. 264 (1917); Toledo Rys. & Light Co. v. Hill, 244 U.S. 49 (1917).

[224] 236 U.S. 115, 122 (1915).

[225] 243 U.S. 90, 91, 92 (1917).

defendant in a suit on a promissory note by publication of notice in a newspaper in Texas once a week for four successive weeks after the defendant had left the state. This notice, Holmes held, was constitutionally deficient. Holmes wrote:

> The foundation of jurisdiction is physical power, although in civilized times it is not necessary to maintain that power throughout proceedings properly begun, and although submission to the jurisdiction by appearance may take the place of service upon the person. No doubt there may be some extension of the means of acquiring jurisdiction beyond service or appearance, but the foundation should be borne in mind. Subject to its conception of sovereignty even the common law required a judgment not to be contrary to natural justice. And in States bound together by a Constitution and subject to the Fourteenth Amendment, great caution should be used not to let fiction deny the fair play that can be secured only by a pretty close adhesion to fact.

Perhaps, Holmes conceded, since the defendant's family was still in Texas, service at his last usual place of residence might have been enough. But "an advertisement in a local newspaper is not sufficient notice to bind a person who has left a State intending not to return. To dispense with personal service the substitute that is most likely to reach the defendant is the least that ought to be required if substantial justice is to be done." It was "going to the extreme" even to suggest that service at a last usual place of residence would suffice.

The jurisdiction of states, in the substantive rather than procedural sense, to regulate business done within their borders which had incidents also in other states was put in issue in *New York Life Insurance Co.* v. *Dodge*.[226] Missouri law declared null a portion of an insurance contract between a resident of Missouri and a New York insurance company doing business in Missouri, which was valid under the law of New York. As McReynolds viewed it, writing for a bare majority, the portion of the contract that was in question had been concluded in New York, under the law of that state. To refuse to give it effect, McReynolds held, was to violate the liberty of contract guaranteed by the Due Process Clause and most recently reaffirmed in *Adams* v. *Tanner*. Brandeis, joined by Day, Pitney, and Clarke, but notably not by Holmes, who made the fifth for the majority, dissented. But the point decided in the case, as Holmes was to demonstrate just a few years later, was quite narrow.[227]

---

[226] 246 U.S. 357 (1918); *cf.* New York Life Ins. Co. v. Head, 234 U.S. 149 (1914), *supra,* p. 286, n.279.

[227] See Mutual Life Ins. Co. v. Liebing, 259 U.S. 209 (1922).

A handful of decisions upheld early zoning regulations. In *Cusack Co. v. Chicago*,[228] the Court, McKenna alone dissenting without opinion, heavily qualified McKenna's 1912 decision in *Eubank v. Richmond*[229] that a power to zone could not be delegated to a majority of property owners in a given area. In *Hadacheck v. Los Angeles*,[230] McKenna himself upheld a zoning ordinance. "There must be progress, and if in its march private interests are in the way they must yield to the good of the community," McKenna ringingly pronounced.

Difficulties closely related to the problem in zoning cases were presented by controversies concerning the formation of road improvement, drainage, and similar special districts with power to make assessments against property owners. Like the zoning problem, these difficulties were also to recur through the 1920s,[231] but they were more baffling. They raised ultimately the question—by no means answered, and perhaps unanswerable—whether any constitutional criteria apply to the process of constituency formation. A drainage district, for example, having been formed, and having made assessments for the improvements that were the purpose of its existence, would be attacked by a minority which either did not wish to be improved, or conceived that the improvement would not benefit it at all, or not benefit it to a degree commensurate with the expense forced upon it. If the district was formed by the vote of a majority of property owners in a given area, the minority's contention would be, as in *Eubank v. Richmond* and *Cusack Co. v. Chicago*, that an improper delegation of governmental power to a private group had taken place. As in the *Cusack* case, the Court did not intervene on this ground.[232] But the Court did hold, although to do so was scarcely to meet the issue, that the dissenting property owners were entitled to an adversary hearing to determine whether they would benefit from the improvement for which the district taxed them. Van Devanter, so holding, got off what for him was a rare epigram: "That there is an inseparable union between the public good and due regard for private rights should not be forgotten."[233]

If a dissenting owner was indeed not benefited, he might prevail

---

[228] 242 U.S. 526 (1917).

[229] 226 U.S. 137 (1912), *supra*, p. 293, n.307.

[230] 239 U.S. 394, 410 (1915); see also Reinman v. Little Rock, 237 U.S. 171 (1915); St. Louis Poster Advertising Co. v. St. Louis, 249 U.S. 269 (1919); and see also Pacific States Supply Co. v. San Francisco, 171 Fed. 727 (N.D. Calif. 1909), *appeal dismissed on motion of appellant*, 235 U.S. 709 (1914); Broussard v. Baker, 74 Tex. Crim. Appls. 333, 169 S.W. 660 (1913), *writ of error dismissed for want of jurisdiction*, 241 U.S. 639 (1916).

[231] See Browning v. Hooper, 269 U.S. 396 (1926); Cole v. Norborne Drainage District, 270 U.S. 45 (1926).

[232] See O'Neill v. Leamer, 239 U.S. 244 (1915).

[233] Embree v. Kansas City Road District, 240 U.S. 242, 248 (1916).

on the ground that his property was being arbitrarily taken, in violation of the Due Process Clause, for a private (the other owners' benefit), rather than a public use,[234] even though, of course, as a general proposition, it is no defense against imposition of a tax—local, state, or federal —that the purpose to which the tax money is to be put will not directly benefit the taxpayer. At other times, this general proposition prevailed against the dissenting property owner.[235] Relatively insignificant as these cases are, they exposed rather spectacularly an absence of standards in the application of the Due Process Clause. In one instance, however, Holmes found a tenable ground for decision. Whatever else the Due Process Clause might or might not require, it did impose the obligation to make classifications that are not palpably irrational. Taxing districts might be created more or less at discretion. But the Constitution was violated where a street improvement district was defined by "a farrago of irrational irregularities."[236]

Among a goodly miscellany of remaining Due Process cases,[237] *Mt. Vernon Cotton Co.* v. *Alabama Power Co.*[238] should be mentioned because it connects with an aspect of the drainage and street improvement controversies just discussed, and because the opinion features a characteristic Holmes passage. A statute of Alabama provided for the condemnation of private property needed in the manufacture of water

---

[234] See Myles Salt Co. v. Iberia Drainage District, 239 U.S. 478 (1916).

[235] See Wagner v. Baltimore, 239 U.S. 207 (1915); Houck v. Little River District, 239 U.S. 254 (1915).

[236] Gast Realty Co. v. Schneider Granite Co., 240 U.S. 55, 59 (1916); and see Withnell v. Bush Construction Co., 185 Mo. App. 408, 170 S.W. 361 (1914), 190 Mo. App. 33, 175 S.W. 260 (1915), *affirmed*, 243 U.S. 633 (1917); but see also Schneider Granite Co. v. Gast Realty Co., 245 U.S. 288 (1917); Withnell v. Ruecking Construction Co., 249 U.S. 63 (1919). *Cf.* Gomillion v. Lightfoot, 364 U.S. 339 (1960).

[237] See Grant Timber Co. v. Gray, 236 U.S. 133 (1915); Booth v. Indiana, 237 U.S. 391 (1915); Southwestern Telephone Co. v. Danaher, 238 U.S. 482 (1915); Brand v. Union Elevated R.R., 238 U.S. 586 (1915); Stewart v. Kansas City, 239 U.S. 14

(1915), *supra*, p. 292, n.302 (see also City of Chelsea v. Boston, 221 Mass. 468, 109 N.E. 389 [1915], *writ of error dismissed for want of jurisdiction*, 245 U.S. 626 [1917]); Miller v. Strahl, 239 U.S. 426 (1915); Northwestern Laundry v. Des Moines, 239 U.S. 486 (1916); Farmers Irrigation District v. O'Shea, 244 U.S. 325 (1917); Union Pacific R.R. v. Laughlin, 247 U.S. 204 (1918); Merchants Exchange v. Missouri, 248 U.S. 365 (1919), see *supra*, p. 282, n.268; Pierce Oil Corporation v. City of Hope, 248 U.S. 498 (1919); Mount St. Mary's Cemetery v. Mullins, 248 U.S. 501 (1919); Perley v. North Carolina, 249 U.S. 510 (1919); Standard Scale Co. v. Farrell, 249 U.S. 571 (1919); American Fire Ins. Co. v. King Lumber Co., 250 U.S. 2 (1919); Nicchia v. New York, 254 U.S. 228 (1920); Nickel v. Cole, 256 U.S. 222 (1921).

[238] 240 U.S. 30, 32 (1916).

power to be supplied to the public. Holmes held the statute constitutional as a taking of private property for a public use. "In the organic relations of modern society," Holmes wrote, "it may sometimes be hard to draw the line that is supposed to limit the authority of the legislature to exercise or delegate the power of eminent domain. But to gather the streams from waste and to draw from them energy, labor without brains, and so to save mankind from toil that it can be spared, is to supply what, next to intellect, is the very foundation of all our achievements and all our welfare. If that purpose is not public we should be at a loss to say what is."

One or two other cases, not seen as having any significance contemporaneously, are suggestive of the live issues of another day. In sustaining, as it had consistently done before,[239] state prohibition statutes, the Court allowed mere possession of liquor for personal use to be made a crime, even though the consequence was, of course, a very considerable invasion of privacy.[240] The Court also sustained a statute that gave a wife a right of action against any person who sold intoxicating liquors to her husband. The theory was that such a person injured the wife by diminishing her means of support.[241] A decision by a state court holding constitutional a statute that prohibited the sale of snuff was brought up on writ of error, but did not reach the stage of adjudication.[242] *Waugh v. Mississippi University*[243] concerned a state that abolished Greek-letter fraternities in the state universities. The law was attacked by a student as depriving him of due process in an argument that McKenna, writing for the Court, characterized as "elaborate and somewhat fervid," but to no avail. A writ of error attempting to get the Supreme Court to review the conviction under New York law of Margaret Sanger for disseminating birth-control information was argued, but dismissed for want of jurisdiction.[244] And an effort to obtain review of a decision by the Supreme Court of Illinois upholding a Sunday closing law against due process challenge was met with a denial of certiorari.[245]

[239] See *supra*, p. 281, nn.263, 264.

[240] Crane v. Campbell, 245 U.S. 304 (1917); Barbour v. Georgia, 249 U.S. 454 (1919). *Cf. supra*, p. 547, n.368. And *cf.* Stanley v. Georgia, 394 U.S. 557 (1969).

[241] Eiger v. Garrity, 246 U.S. 97 (1918).

[242] Olson v. North Dakota, 26 N.D. 304, 144 N.W. 661 (1913), *writ of error dismissed*, 245 U.S. 676 (1917).

[243] 237 U.S. 589, 596 (1915).

[244] Sanger v. New York, 222 N.Y. 192, 118 N.E. 637 (1918), *writ of error dismissed for want of jurisdiction*, 251 U.S. 537 (1919); *cf.* Griswold v. Connecticut, 381 U.S. 479 (1965).

[245] Boerner v. Thompson, 278 Ill. 153, 115 N.E. 866 (1917), *cert. denied*, 245 U.S. 669 (1918); see McGowan v. Maryland, 366 U.S. 420 (1961).

Equal Protection

So dormant at the 1910–14 Terms that Holmes and McKenna once or twice read burial services over it, the Equal Protection Clause was alive and well again during the last seven years of the White Chief Justiceship.[246] To be sure, most legislative classifications still passed muster, whether the objection on equal protection grounds was subsidiary, as in some of the due process cases treated in the previous section,[247] or the main or sole constitutional argument. Holmes, when he got the chance, now as earlier, used the most broadly dispositive language. "The Fourteenth Amendment," he said in one case, "is not a pedagogical requirement of the impracticable." A state, therefore, should be permitted to "do what it can to prevent what is deemed an evil and stop short of those cases in which the harm to the few concerned is thought less important than the harm to the public that would ensue if the rule laid down were made mathematically exact." Once a classification had been laid down, and a line drawn, "the fact that some cases, including the plaintiff's, are very near to the line makes it none the worse. That is the inevitable result of drawing a line where the distinctions are distinctions of degree; and the constant business of the law is to draw such lines."[248]

Holmes, in short, did not see how classification could be avoided, and how—putting aside instances of racial and perhaps other invidious discriminations which might be deemed unconstitutional as such—the Equal Protection Clause could hold legislative classifications to any standard additional to that of rationality. Brandeis, of course, consistently took the same view. Their colleagues were no better able to formulate standards under the Equal Protection Clause, and most often reached the same result as Holmes and Brandeis.[249] But their language

---

[246] As we shall see in later chapters, the Equal Protection Clause was successfully invoked during these years in important racial cases.

[247] See, e.g., Jeffrey Manufacturing Co. v. Blagg, *supra,* n.117; Rast v. Van Deman & Lewis Co., *supra,* n.169.

[248] Dominion Hotel v. Arizona, 249 U.S. 265, 268, 269 (1919); see also Fort Smith Lumber Co. v. Arkansas, 251 U.S. 532 (1920); Alaska Fish Co. v. Smith, 255 U.S. 44 (1921).

[249] See Phoenix Inc. Co. v. McMaster, 237 U.S. 63 (1915); Crane v. Johnson, 242 U.S. 339 (1917); Pennsylvania Tunnel & Terminal R.R. v. Hendrickson, 87 N.J.L. 239, 93 A. 589 (1915), *affirmed,* 243 U.S. 633 (1917); Cincinnati, Hamilton & Dayton Ry. v. McCollum, 183 Ind. 556, 109 N.E. 206 (1915), *affirmed,* 245 U.S. 632 (1917); Nickell & Burke v. Stevens, 245 U.S. 640 (1918); Omaechevarria v. Idaho, 246 U.S. 343 (1918) (Van Devanter and McReynolds, JJ., dissenting without opinion); Sunday Lake Iron Co. v. Wakefield, 247 U.S. 350 (1918); McCoy v. Union Elevated R.R., 247 U.S. 354 (1918); Branson v. Bush,

was much more guarded. And in these years, in a few notably dubious instances, led each time by Pitney and McReynolds, they managed to drive to the opposite result.

Atchison, Topeka & Santa Fe Railway v. *Vosburg*[250] concerned a statute that required railroads to furnish cars to shippers of freight on demand, and imposing a countervailing duty on shippers to use cars placed at their disposal. Violation by a railroad or by a shipper of his statutory duty incurred a daily penalty. But a railroad was liable also for attorney's fees in a suit to collect the statutory penalty, while shippers were not. This difference was alleged to deny equal protection, and Pitney, somehow managing to get a unanimous Court to go along with him, so held. He could perceive, he wrote, no reason why shippers should be exempted from liability for attorney's fees. The suit to collect the penalty seemed equally onerous to prosecute on either side. Hence the classification was arbitrary. Yet, rather obviously, the legislature might have thought that railroads regularly employed house counsel, whereas many shippers did not. And a statute imposing a duty on railroads to furnish cars without creating any countervailing obligation on the part of shippers would presumably not have been a violation of equal protection.

In *Greene* v. *Louisville & Interurban Railroad*,[251] railroad property (capital stock, as it happened; but no attack was made on this ground) was assessed for taxation at 75 percent of actual value. Different kinds of property in the same state were assessed by another board, operating under another statute, at 52 percent of actual value. The Supreme Court of the state had held that this disparity in taxation by

---

251 U.S. 182 (1919) (McReynolds, J., dissenting without opinion); Goldsmith v. Prendergast Construction Co., 252 U.S. 12 (1920); Watson v. State Comptroller, 254 U.S. 122 (1920); Lower Vein Coal Co. v. Industrial Board, 255 U.S. 144 (1921).

Among the cases sustaining state legislation against equal protection attack one, and one only, would have a familiar ring in the latter part of the century, and perhaps even raise a question concerning the result. A Washington statute of 1915 granted what it called a pension, what we would now call a welfare payment, to indigent mothers, at the same time repealing a prior statute that had granted such a pension to abandoned

wives. In a suit by a claimant, the Washington Supreme Court, denying the claim, held the classification constitutional. The state, said the court, was distributing a bounty, and following a public policy that it deemed suitable in the distribution. Such a policy was not assailable in court. The Supreme Court of the United States summarily affirmed the decision. Snyder v. King County, 93 Wash. 59 (1916), *affirmed*, 248 U.S. 539 (1918).

250 238 U.S. 56 (1915).

251 244 U.S. 499 (1917); see also Louisville & Nashville R.R. v. Greene, 244 U.S. 522 (1917); Illinois Central R.R. v. Greene, 244 U.S. 555 (1917).

two separate assessment bodies violated the state constitution, but that there was no state judicial remedy for it, presumably because the appropriate remedy would have been to bring down the higher assessment rather than to raise the lower one, and the real illegality was in the lower assessment, not in the higher. The Louisville and Interurban Railroad consequently went into federal court, claiming a violation of the federal Equal Protection Clause. Pitney, for the Supreme Court, on review of the lower federal court's judgment, could not quite bring himself to hold that the Equal Protection Clause had been violated— and no wonder, since in the end the case amounted to no more than an instance of taxation of different kinds of property at different rates, a practice to which the Court quite consistently found no impediment in the Equal Protection Clause.[252] But Pitney did hold that federal jurisdiction having been properly invoked on the basis of the equal protection claim, all other issues in the case, including those of state law, were open for decision. He held further that the Supreme Court of the United States was not bound by the state court's view that no judicial remedy could be provided for what the state court had conceded was a violation of the state constitution. And Pitney ended by enjoining collection of the higher tax assessed against the railroad on the ground that the assessment violated the state constitution. Holmes, Brandeis, and Clarke dissented without opinion.

Finally, *Royster Guano Co.* v. *Virginia*,[253] another tax case, was an attack on a Virginia statute under which corporations incorporated in Virginia that did business both within and outside the state were taxed on their total income derived from business both within and outside, but corporations incorporated in Virginia that did no business within the state, but only outside, were not taxed on their outside business, and thus not taxed at all. This discrimination, Pitney held, constituted a lack of equal protection. It was arbitrary, had no rational basis, and was indeed probably an inadvertence, since a later Virginia statute had corrected it. Brandeis, joined by Holmes, dissented. The Equal Protection Clause, he wrote, forbade only "inequality which is the result of clearly arbitrary action and, particularly, of action attributable to hostile discrimination against particular persons or classes." The Court held the discrimination involved in this case to be arbitrary because unsupported by any rational reason. "I can conceive of a reason for differentiating in respect to taxation between the two classes of domestic corporations," Brandeis said.

The chartering of companies which did business outside the state of incorporation was an important source of revenue for the states.

---

[252] *Cf.* Sunday Lake Iron Co. v. Wakefield, *supra,* n.249.

[253] 253 U.S. 412, 417–18, 420 (1920).

There were organization fees and franchise taxes, and they amounted to something. Here Brandeis gave some statistics. For this revenue, the states competed with one another. A state which taxed the business done by a corporation that had come in merely to be chartered would lose applicants for its charters to other states which imposed no such taxes. Companies, on the other hand, that engaged in business within the chartering state could be supposed to wish to be chartered for this reason, and the chance of their fleeing to incorporate themselves elsewhere was considerably less. Hence Virginia felt free to tax corporations that did business within its borders also on the business done outside. The fact that the Virginia statute had been changed for the future, far from showing that the earlier classification was an inadvertence, demonstrated rather that "the legislatures of the several States may safely be entrusted with the duty of legislation."[254]

The Contract Clause

Now as earlier, the Contract Clause afforded little protection against the impairment of private contracts,[255] although in *Bank of Minden* v. *Clement*,[256] the Court held that an attempt by statute to nullify retroactively a contract valid when made was unconstitutional. Again, now as earlier,[257] appeals to the Contract Clause in cases setting

---

[254] The last paragraph of Brandeis' dissent reads as follows:

I cannot doubt that the classification for purposes of taxation made by the Act of 1916 [the Virginia statute in question] was within the power of the State. But if I did not think the matter clear, I should, for the reasons stated by me fully elsewhere, feel constrained to resolve the doubt in favor of the constitutionality of the act.

In an earlier draft, which he circulated to the Court, Brandeis referred not to "reasons stated by me fully elsewhere," but rather to "the reasons stated by me in *Eisner v. Macomber*, decided March 8, 1919," just a little more than a year earlier. See *supra*, pp. 500 *et seq.* Holmes' return was: "I agree to everything except the incorporation of Eisner v. Macomber. I think it excellent." So *Eisner v.*

Macomber came out, and a blind reference was left in its stead. Brandeis Papers, Harvard Law School Library. Presumably Holmes objected because Brandeis' dissent in *Eisner v. Macomber* was an opinion in which Holmes had not joined. But on the point to which Brandeis now cited it, the dissent surely stated nothing that Holmes ought to have found objectionable.

[255] See Menasha Wooden Ware Co. v. Minneapolis, St. Paul & Sault Ste. Marie Ry., 159 Wisc. 130, 150 N.W. 411 (1914), *affirmed*, 245 U.S. 633 (1917); Union Dry Goods Co. v. Georgia Public Service Corp., 248 U.S. 372 (1919); Kansas City Bolt & Nut Co. v. Kansas City Light & Power Co., 275 Mo. 529, 204 S.W. 1074 (1918), *affirmed*, 252 U.S. 571 (1920).

[256] 256 U.S. 126 (1921).

[257] See *supra*, p. 301.

up agreements with public authorities might fail because a state or municipality would be held to have explicitly[258] or implicity[259] reserved the right to revoke or amend the contract relied on, or to have lacked power to bargain away the right to revoke,[260] or most frequently because, properly construed, the contract was inapplicable, or nonexistent, or otherwise not impaired.

In *Interborough Transit Co.* v. *Sohmer*,[261] the contract with the builder of the New York subway provided that his rolling stock and equipment were to be exempt from taxation. Yet Holmes, affirming a decision of the New York courts, and with a bow to the "great force" of George W. Wickersham's argument to the contrary, upheld collection of a franchise tax. The contract, the New York courts had held, included no exemption from franchise taxes. "As a literal interpretation [this conclusion] is undeniably correct," said Holmes, "and we should not feel warranted in overruling it because of a certain perfume of general exemption. We must accept the words used in their strict sense."

Again in *Port of Seattle* v. *Oregon & Washington Railroad*,[262] Brandeis held a public contract not to have been infringed. Brandeis dealt with all possible implications of the contract in light of the surrounding state law, which he examined and explained exhaustively. He got a churlish assenting return from McReynolds, for whom Brandeis' labors amounted to no more than a confirmation of his own view that "the case involves no substantial fed. question and should have been dismissed. The opinion is devoted to a discussion of state law much of which I think is unnecessary." But what seemed unnecessary to McReynolds was precisely what persuaded the Chief Justice. "I voted the other way," White returned, "but in view of your statement of the Washington cases I was wrong and hence say, Yes." Clarke wrote: "I like this," and added, very justly, "but you must be working night and day."[263] And from the outside, Roscoe Pound, the dean of the Harvard

---

[258] See Ramapo Water Co. v. New York, 236 U.S. 579 (1915); Dunham v. Kauffman, 90 Ohio St. 419, 108 N.E. 1118 (1914), *writ of error dismissed for want of jurisdiction,* 241 U.S. 653 (1916).

[259] See Milwaukee Electric Ry. v. Wisconsin R.R. Commission, 238 U.S. 174 (1915); Louisville Bridge Co. v. United States, 242 U.S. 409 (1917); Englewood v. Denver & South Platte Ry., 248 U.S. 294 (1919); Darling v. Newport News, 249 U.S. 540 (1919); Armour & Co. v. Dallas, 255 U.S. 280 (1921); and see New York Electric Lines Co. v. Gaynor, 218 N.Y. 417, *writ of error denied,* 242 U.S. 617 (1916).

[260] See Pennsylvania Hospital v. Philadelphia, 245 U.S. 20 (1917).

[261] 237 U.S. 276, 284 (1915).

[262] 255 U.S. 56 (1921).

[263] In another one of these cases, and a relatively simple one, although

Law School, wrote his former student, now Brandeis' law clerk, Dean Acheson:

> I was much interested in the opinion in the Port of Seattle case which you sent me. When once these things get into law sheep binding they are on the high road to become part of the law. Hence I can feel that progress is making.
>
> What pleases me specially about the decision in that case is that it appreciates and gives effect to the local situation. A good many decisions of the Supreme Court of the United States upon the questions arising west of the Missouri River have seemed to the population of that part of the country to quite ignore the local conditions which have made the local law of those regions appear strange to the common-law lawyer.[264]

But the Contract Clause was by no means fading away as yet. *Owensboro v. Cumberland Telephone Co.*[265] remained an influential precedent, and in a series of cases, decided over the impassioned dissents of Clarke, joined by Brandeis, but notably not by Holmes, the clause was given effect to protect public utilities against municipal and state regulation and taxation. "It may be," wrote Clarke in one of his dissents, "that the settled conviction which I have that no legislator, congressman or councilman would knowingly consent to grant perpetual rights in public streets to a private corporation has so darkened my understanding that I cannot properly appreciate the point of view of my associates. . . ."[266]

Holmes himself, in a hotly contested litigation that evoked three opinions from him in four years, forbade Georgia to tax a railroad to which, he held, the promise of freedom from taxation had been made

---

it drew the dissents, without opinion, of Pitney and McReynolds, Brandeis ended as follows: "As we conclude that there was a contractual duty to repave arising from the acceptance of the franchise, we have no occasion to consider whether there was, as contended, also a statutory duty to do so. . . ." Milwaukee Electric Ry. v. Milwaukee, *infra*, n.264, 252 U.S. at 106. Holmes returned: "Good. Yes. I believe [John Chipman] Gray [of the Harvard Law School, and a life-long acquaintance of Holmes] used to object to 'contractual' and I don't use it. But the Century Dict. cites the Encyc. Brit. and Sir H. Maine (a good

writer) for the word." It stayed in. Brandeis Papers, Harvard Law School Library.

[264] Brandeis Papers, Harvard Law School Library.

[265] *Supra,* p. 304, n.350.

[266] Owensboro v. Owensboro Waterworks Co., 243 U.S. 166, 187 (1917). See also Cincinnati v. Cincinnati & Hamilton Traction Co., 245 U.S. 446 (1918); Northern Ohio Traction Co. v. Ohio, 245 U.S. 574 (1918); Covington v. South Covington Street Ry., 246 U.S. 413 (1918). *Cf.* Georgia v. Cincinnati Southern Ry., 248 U.S. 26 (1918); Los Angeles v. Los Angeles Gas Corp., 251 U.S. 32 (1919).

in an early-nineteenth-century charter.[267] But when in *Denver* v. *Denver Union Water Co.*,[268] Pitney for the Court construed an ordinance that simply permitted a water company to operate in Denver as constituting a franchise the value of which had to be calculated as part of the company's property for purposes of arriving at a nonconfiscatory rate of return, Holmes, joined by Brandeis and Clarke, dissented. There was no franchise, he said. The city could oust the company at will. To be sure, the city was not likely to do so, since it needed the water supplied by the company, and so Holmes conceded that to hold there was no franchise was to make a judgment about rights *in vacuo*. But, he added, it was "not quite as tautologous as it seems, that the law knows nothing but legal rights." And in another protracted litigation in which franchise rights were interposed against attempts by Detroit to regulate trolley fares, Holmes at one stage joined Clarke and Brandeis in a dissent that relied on the views he had expressed in *Denver* v. *Union Water Co.*[269]

A final pair of Contract Clause cases are of interest in light of a later Court's struggle with recalcitrant local authorities in the implementation of school desegregation.[270] When Dallas County, Missouri, defaulted on some bonds, the bondholders sued in federal court in the diversity jurisdiction, and recovered a judgment of $1 million against the county. Under the law of Missouri in force when the bonds were issued, it was the duty of county officers to levy and collect annually a tax of 30 percent of the amount of defaulted bonds for the purpose of paying them off. The federal court issued writs of mandamus to the county officers ordering them to perform the ministerial act of levying the re-

---

[267] Wright v. Central of Georgia Ry., 236 U.S. 674 (1915); Wright v. Louisville & Nashville Ry., 236 U.S. 687 (1915); Central of Georgia Ry. v. Wright, 248 U.S. 525, 249 U.S. 590, 250 U.S. 519 (1919).

In Central of Georgia Ry. v. Wright, the only one of these opinions that went through with no dissents recorded, Brandeis returned to Holmes: "I think this case, like [Wright v. Central of Georgia Ry.] 236 U.S. 674, is wrongly decided, and have no sympathy with any of the cases bartering away the right of taxation. But you have restricted the opinion so closely to the facts of this case that I am inclined to think it will do less harm to let it pass unnoticed by dissent." Clarke and Pitney also suppressed dis-

sents. Holmes Papers. But within two months, a rehearing was granted, and when Holmes in a final opinion stuck to his guns, McKenna, Pitney, Brandeis, and Clarke recorded their dissents without opinion.

[268] 246 U.S. 178, 197 (1918).

[269] Detroit United Ry. v. Michigan, 242 U.S. 238 (1916) (Clarke and Brandeis, JJ., dissenting), 245 U.S. 673 (1917), 248 U.S. 429 (1919) (Clarke, Holmes, and Brandeis, JJ., dissenting). *Cf.* Columbus Ry. & Power Co. v. Columbus, 249 U.S. 399 (1919); Burr v. Columbus, 249 U.S. 415 (1919). But *cf.* Detroit United Ry. v. Detroit, 255 U.S. 171 (1921).

[270] See Griffin v. School Board of Prince Edward County, 377 U.S. 218 (1964).

quired tax, but these officers refused to do so, avoided service of process, and in general defied the orders of the court. The bondholders thereupon asked the court to appoint a commissioner to levy the taxes. Holmes (McKenna and Pitney dissenting without opinion) affirmed a judgment refusing this request. The extent of the obligation, he said, which the federal district court could enforce was the extent given it by the law of Missouri. No less, but no more. And the law of Missouri created a right for the bondholders to have the tax levied by county officers, not by commissioners appointed by a federal court.[271]

Yet in *Hendrickson* v. *Apperson*,[272] a unanimous Supreme Court, McReynolds writing, reached a different result. This was a suit by bondholders to enforce a long-standing judgment against Taylor County, Kentucky. The county had a remarkable record of avoiding judgments against it. It did so by taking advantage of a state statute authorizing the appointment of more than one collector of taxes by the executive of a county, and the assignment to each of these collectors of specific taxes to collect. The county would thus appoint a collector to collect the taxes it needed to keep it going. It would also appoint a collector to collect the taxes to pay its judgment debts. But the latter collector would never file a bond, never qualify for office, and never collect a cent. In this way, the county avoided satisfying judgments against it, while seeming to do what the judgments required of it. A lower federal court consequently issued a decree requiring the county executive to appoint a collector who would at the same time collect both the county's operational taxes and the taxes for the payment of the judgment in favor of the bondholders. The decree was resisted as an unwarranted interference with the lawful discretion of the county executive to appoint collectors as he saw fit, and to charge each of them with collection of those taxes he assigned to him. McReynolds affirmed the decree. If the discretion that was claimed were held to exist, he said, it would impair the obligation of the contract on which the judgment was issued. The county's "notable and repeated successful efforts to avoid payment of adjudicated indebtedness" had to be taken into consideration. "Actual conditions cannot be ignored, and certainly we ought not, through assumptions out of harmony with patent facts and over-nice refinements, to facilitate the practical destruction of admitted legal obligations."

It was quite evident at the end of the White Chief Justiceship that the Contract Clause had not yet descended into obsolescence. Never-

---

[271] Yost v. Dallas County, 236 U.S. 50 (1915).

[272] 245 U.S. 105, 113–14 (1917); see also Hendrickson v. Creager, 245 U.S. 115 (1917); and see Montezuma Valley Irrigation District v. Norris, 248 Fed. 369 (8th Cir. 1918), *cert. denied*, 248 U.S. 569 (1918).

theless, compared with the Due Process Clause, the Contract Clause, as also in some measure the Equal Protection Clause,[273] was something of a last resort. The bar continued to be sanguine and quick to litigate almost any new measure of social and economic regulation,[274] and much that came up for adjudication under the Due Process Clause was trivial and should never have been brought up, or into litigation in the first place. One must, of course, guard against what is for these purposes the false wisdom of hindsight, but even in terms of the contemporary understanding and expectations, it does appear that a greater proportion of Contract Clause cases were utterly without merit. Several, though disposed of with opinion by the Court, were dismissed as raising insubstantial federal questions.[275]

---

[273] See *supra,* n.249.
[274] See *supra,* pp. 305 *et seq.*

[275] See, e.g., Ramapo Water Co. v. New York, *supra,* n.258.

CHAPTER VII

Federal Administration and the Federal Specialties

THROUGH THE NINETEENTH CENTURY, although the Supreme Court came into the public eye chiefly on account of its constitutional and other public business, the issues that were the grist of the Court's mill were "predominantly common law topics and federal specialties like admiralty, bankruptcy, patents, claims against the government and legislation concerning the public domain."[1] The Court's unique function, then as ever, was to declare and enforce the Constitution, and to elaborate and harmonize the public policies of the federal government as formulated in statute law. But in the nineteenth century, performance of this function claimed only a fraction of judicial energies, and the bulk of the Court's business consisted of "ordinary private litigation."[2] In the first third of the twentieth century, a change set in. It was gradual, but it gathered momentum, so that by 1928, Felix Frankfurter and James M. Landis could write: "The Supreme Court has ceased to be a common law court. . . . The issues which normally come before the Supreme Court are not the ordinary legal questions in the multitudinous lawsuits of *Smith* v. *Jones* before other courts. The Supreme Court is the final authority in adjusting the relationships of the individual to the separate states, of the individual to the United States, of the forty-eight states to one another, and of the state to the United States. It mediates between the individual and government; it marks the boundaries between state and national action."[3]

---

[1] F. Frankfurter and J. M. Landis, *The Business of the Supreme Court* (1927), 301.

[2] *Ibid.*, 303.
[3] *Ibid.*, 307–308.

649

The second decade of the twentieth century, with which this volume is concerned, was a transitional period. Constitutional and federal statutory litigation was on the rise, as we have seen. Cases calling for review of orders of the Interstate Commerce Commission, which we are about to examine, were making a respectable showing on the Supreme Court's docket. Even the much newer Federal Trade Commission surfaced in the Court for the first time. But the administrative process, that "dynamo of the modern social service state," as one scholar has called it,[4] was still more or less aborning, and the major reform in the Court's jurisdiction, which was to remove the bulk of "ordinary private litigation," lay in the future; it was the work of the next decade. As of this period, the federal specialties still loomed quite large, and the Supreme Court had by no means ceased to be a common law court.

The Interstate Commerce Commission

Acheson in his memorandum and Brandeis in what ultimately became his dissent in *Ohio Valley Water Co.* v. *Ben Avon Borough* were entirely justified in arguing, as they did, that on review of orders of the Interstate Commerce Commission, the Court examined the facts only to the extent of determining whether an order was supported by substantial evidence; and that the Court's decision in the *Ben Avon* case ran counter to an established practice.[5]

In *Interstate Commerce Commission* v. *Delaware, Lackawanna & Western Railroad*, decided in 1911, White, having disposed of a question of statutory construction, went on to hold that a finding by the commission that its order would prevent preferences and discriminations "embodies a conclusion of fact beyond our competency to re-examine."[6] Of course, the commission's orders had not in the past always met with so hospitable a reception in the courts, but as I. L. Sharfman noted in his authoritative study published in 1931, after the Interstate Commerce Act amendments of 1906 and 1910[7] "the scope of judicial interference progressively narrowed."[8]

---

[4] L. L. Jaffe, "An Essay on Delegation of Legislative Power: II," *Colum. L. Rev.*, 47:561, 592, 1947.

[5] See *supra*, pp. 620, 622; Ohio Valley Water Co. v. Ben Avon Borough, *supra*, p. 628, n.199, 253 U.S. at 297.

[6] 220 U.S. 235, 255 (1911); see also Southern Pacific Terminal Co. v. Interstate Commerce Commission, 219 U.S. 498 (1911); Interstate Commerce Commission v. Baltimore & Ohio R.R., 225 U.S. 326 (1912); and see Interstate Commerce Commission v. Illinois Central R.R., 215 U.S. 452 (1910).

[7] Hepburn Act, 34 Stat. 584 (1906); Mann-Elkins Act, 36 Stat. 539 (1910).

[8] I. L. Sharfman, *The Interstate Commerce Commission*, 2:424 (1931).

VII: *Federal Administration and the Federal Specialties*

Interstate Commerce Commission v. *Union Pacific Railroad,*[9] decided in the Supreme Court in 1912, concerned a rate fixed by the commission, after hearing, for lumber moving from the West Coast to St. Paul, Minnesota. Having recited some of the evidence taken by the commission, Lamar wrote:

> With that sort of evidence before them, rate experts of acknowledged ability and fairness, and each acting independently of the other, may not have reached identically the same conclusion. We do not know whether the results would have been approximately the same. For there is no possibility of solving the question as though it were a mathematical problem to which there could only be one correct answer. Still there was in this mass of facts that out of which experts could have named a rate. The law makes the Commission's findings on such facts conclusive.

A year later, in an elaborate and very able opinion (again, as before, for a unanimous Court), in *Interstate Commerce Commission* v. *Louisville & Nashville Railroad,*[10] Lamar gave the commission great leeway, while at the same time reserving a reviewing function to the courts. The commission had found certain rates charged by the railroad between New Orleans and Montgomery, Alabama, to be unreasonable, and had ordered that they be reduced. At the argument, rather large claims were entered in behalf of the commission. It was contended, in effect, that rate orders were not subject to judicial review at all. This contention Lamar rejected. Under the statute, there was a right to a full hearing. Findings by the commission had to be based on evidence, else they would be arbitrary, no more than capricious administrative fiats beyond the authority of any officer of government to issue, because they would be "inconsistent with rational justice," and would come "under the Constitution's condemnation of all arbitrary exercise of power." It was, to be sure, not the province of courts to adjudicate afresh facts found by the commission. "But the legal effect of evidence is a question of law. A finding without evidence is beyond the power of the Commission." Findings could not be based simply on the commission's expert knowledge, or on background information not introduced in the record. The commission could not reach its conclusions in the manner of "jurors in primitive days." Coming to the facts in the record before him, however, Lamar held that the weight to be given to any item of evidence was "peculiarly" to be determined by "the body experienced in such matters and familiar with the complexities, intricacies and history

---

[9] 222 U.S. 541, 550 (1912).   [10] 227 U.S. 88, 91, 92, 93, 98, 100 (1913).

of rate-making in each section of the country." The commission's order was "not arbitrary but sustained by substantial, though conflicting, evidence. The courts cannot settle the conflict nor put their judgment against that of the rate-making body. . . ."

A number of other decisions through the decade were to the same effect,[11] the Court even going out of its way on occasion to classify a finding by the commission as one of fact, so that it could more readily be upheld.[12] And even when the commission's order was based on findings that were at best of mixed law and fact, and acknowledged to be such, the Court in a series of cases upheld what Chief Justice White called "a certain latitude of judgment and discretion" on the part of the commission. This phrase the Chief Justice got off in the hotly contested *Intermountain Rate Cases* of 1914,[13] in which the commission exercised authority granted to it in 1910 by the Mann-Elkins Act to allow rate variations between long and shorter hauls. The railroads were dissatisfied with the commission's order, which allowed some variations but not other ones, and they claimed among other things that the Mann-Elkins Act vested too much discretion in the commission, and amounted, therefore, to an unconstitutional delegation of legislative power. White, having none of this, upheld the commission.[14] The commission, said White in another long-and-short-haul case, was brought into being to exercise its expertise in the performance of a function for which it was peculiarly fitted. It was not meant to be, and should not be allowed to become, "a mere instrument for the purpose of taking testimony to be submitted to the courts for their ultimate action."[15] And Pitney a few years later: "It may be conceded that the evidence [before the commission] would have warranted a different finding; indeed the first report

---

[11] See The Los Angeles Switching Case, 234 U.S. 294 (1914); Interstate Commerce Commission v. Southern Pacific Co., 234 U.S. 315 (1914); Louisville & Nashville R.R. v. United States, 238 U.S. 1 (1915); Louisville & Nashville R.R. v. United States, 245 U.S. 463 (1918) (*cf. ibid.*, 207 Fed. 591 [Commerce Court 1913], *reversed*, 238 U.S. 642 [1915]); Seaboard Air Line Ry. v. United States, 254 U.S. 57 (1920).

[12] See, e.g., Pennsylvania Co. v. United States, 236 U.S. 351 (1915).

[13] 234 U.S. 476, 488 (1914); see also United States v. Union Pacific R.R., 234 U.S. 495 (1914); and see United States v. Merchants and Manu-

facturers Traffic Ass'n., 242 U.S. 178 (1916).

[14] It was easy to criticize the decision in its details, said the *New York Times* somewhat grudgingly, but the railroads were not complaining "as loudly as the Stock Exchange operators." The country was "coming to understand that it and the railways are in the same boat and that neither can thrive at the expense of the other." *New York Times*, June 24, 1914, p. 10, cols. 1 and 2.

[15] United States v. Louisville & Nashville R.R., 235 U.S. 3214, 321 (1914); see also Skinner & Eddy Corp. v. United States, 249 U.S. 557 (1919).

of the Commission was to the contrary; but to annul the Commission's order on this ground would be to substitute the judgment of a court for the judgment of the Commission upon a matter purely administrative, and this can not be done."[16] Earlier, in upholding an order of the commission that prescribed uniform methods of accounting for the railroads, Pitney allowed that the commission's prescribed method was by no means the inevitable one, perhaps not even the one the Court might have preferred. But so long as the commission had acted on a tenable theory of accounting, as it had done, the courts were not authorized to override its judgment.[17]

The decisions just discussed, wrote Gerard C. Henderson in 1924, rested "on a statesmanlike comprehension of the purpose and function of administrative enforcement, and of the importance of expert decision upon questions of great economic importance."[18] This was doubly true of another series of decisions, starting with White's famous opinion, before his accession to the Chief Justiceship, in *Texas & Pacific Railway v. Abilene Cotton Oil Co.*,[19] which shored up the authority of the Interstate Commerce Commission by safeguarding its primary or original jurisdiction. The opinions in *Abilene Cotton Oil* and in cases following it were notable, said I. L. Sharfman, for their "recognition that the exercise of administrative discretion inheres in the enforcement of the principal provisions of the Interstate Commerce Act, and that the exclusion of courts from the entertainment of suits as an original matter is essential to the preservation of this discretionary authority."[20]

The doctrine of *Abilene Cotton Oil* was readily applied in opinions written by several of the Justices,[21] but it was most ably reaffirmed during this decade by Lamar. Suits for damages by shippers against railroads based on allegations of discrimination, whether in the form of rebates granted to some but not all shippers, or by way of other discriminatory treatment, would not be allowed to proceed in the courts,

---

[16] Manufacturers Ry. v. United States, 246 U.S. 457, 482 (1918).

[17] Kansas City Southern Ry. v. United States, 231 U.S. 423 (1913). See also, as upholding discretionary judgments of the Interstate Commerce Commission, Atchison, Topeka & Santa Fe Ry. v. United States, 204 Fed. 647 (Commerce Court 1913), *affirmed,* 231 U.S. 736 (1913); Atchison Ry. v. United States, 232 U.S. 199 (1914); O'Keefe v. United States, 240 U.S. 294 (1916); St. Louis Southwestern Ry. v. United States, 245 U.S. 136 (1917).

[18] G. C. Henderson, *The Federal Trade Commission* (1924), 98.

[19] 204 U.S. 426 (1907).

[20] Sharfman, *Interstate Commerce Commission,* 2:404.

[21] See Robinson v. Baltimore & Ohio R.R., 222 U.S. 506 (1912); Texas & Pacific Ry. v. American Tie Co., 234 U.S. 138 (1914); Pennsylvania R.R. v. Clark Coal Co., 238 U.S. 456 (1915); Loomis v. Lehigh Valley R.R., 240 U.S. 43 (1916); Northern Pacific Ry. v. Solum, 247 U.S. 477 (1918); Director General v. Viscose Co., 254 U.S. 498 (1921).

Lamar held in *Mitchell Coal Co.* v. *Pennsylvania Railroad*[22] and *Morrisdale Coal Co.* v. *Pennsylvania Railroad*,[23] so long as there was any question concerning the lawfulness of the alleged discrimination under applicable provisions of the Interstate Commerce Act. Rather, such suits were to be stayed until the shipper could obtain a ruling from the Interstate Commerce Commission on the reasonableness or unreasonableness, and consequent lawfulness or unlawfulness, of the practice complained of. It was not merely, as White had emphasized in the *Abilene Cotton Oil* case, that the primary jurisdiction of the commission had to be safeguarded in order to ensure uniformity of application of the Interstate Commerce Act. It was also that the problem of what was a reasonable practice under the Act called for resolution in light of the specialized knowledge of the rate-setting tribunal. In the *Morrisdale* case, Lamar went so far as to hold that even where the commission had previously promulgated a general rule applicable to the practices in question, it was nevertheless for the commission to decide in the first instance what the application of that general rule would be to the special circumstances of an unusual case. Where, however, in a case decided at the same time, the allegation was that the railroad departed from its published tariff, which the Interstate Commerce Act plainly and specifically forbade it to do, Lamar held that a suit for damages might proceed without prior recourse to the Interstate Commerce Commission, since no occasion was offered for the exercise of the expert administrative judgment.[24] Earlier, in *Procter & Gamble* v. *United States*, White had strained the doctrine of primary jurisdiction so as to insulate negative orders by the Interstate Commerce Commission—refusals by the commission to grant relief—from judicial review altogether. To undertake to review a refusal by the commission to act, said White, would amount to a substitution of the discretionary judgment of judges for that of the commission—although he failed to explain why, if a properly narrow scope of judicial review was exercised, judges would be any more guilty of an overintrusion when reviewing negative orders than when they reviewed affirmative ones.[25]

---

[22] 230 U.S. 247 (1913).

[23] 230 U.S. 304 (1913).

[24] Pennsylvania R.R. v. International Coal Co., 230 U.S. 184 (1913); see also Pennsylvania R.R. v. Puritan Coal Co., 237 U.S. 121 (1915) (and see Illinois Central R.R. v. Mulberry Coal Co., 238 U.S. 275 [1917]); Eastern Ry. v. Littlefield, 237 U.S. 140 (1915); Louisville & Nashville R.R. v. Cook Brewing Co., 223 U.S. 70 (1912); Pennsylvania R.R. v. Sonman Coal Co., 242 U.S. 120 (1916); Pennsylvania R.R. v. Stineman Coal Co., 242 U.S. 298 (1916).

[25] See Procter & Gamble v. United States, 225 U.S. 282 (1912); Hooker v. Knapp, 225 U.S. 302 (1912); Lehigh Valley R.R. v. United States, 243 U.S. 412 (1917). *Cf.* United States v. Illinois Central R.R., 244 U.S. 82 (1917). But *cf.* Louisville & Nashville

Also supportive of the Interstate Commerce Commission were a number of decisions upholding judgments for reparations against railroads based on commission findings. Such judgments, obtained after trial by jury, in which the commission's findings constituted *prima facie* evidence, compensated shippers for past charges which the commission had held excessive.[26] Court and commission cooperated for the most part harmoniously as well, if to a dubious end, in limiting the liability of carriers for loss or damage to goods in transit.[27] Again, the exercise by the commission of a broad, if not limitless, investigative power was upheld.[28] And in cases coming to it independently of any proceedings before the Interstate Commerce Commission, the Court generally construed the Interstate Commerce Act, as amended in 1903, 1906, and 1910, with fidelity to the ascertainable reforming purposes of Congress. Provisions embodying antitrust and antirebate policies, as well as less dramatic provisions, benefited from this attitude.[29]

Yet despite the generally sympathetic approach to the Interstate Commerce Act, and despite the affirmations of administrative competence and the many disclaimers of judicial authority to pass on administrative determinations of fact or exercises of discretion, the Court, as Sharfman has written, still left itself "ample room for judicial interference, without precise definition as to its scope. . . ."[30] The Interstate Commerce Commission was by no means cut loose entirely without leading strings. It suffered a fair number of reversals on questions of

---

R.R. v. United States, 207 Fed. 591 (Commerce Court 1913), *reversed on confession of error by the Solicitor General*, 238 U.S. 642 (1915) (see *ibid.*, 245 U.S. 463 [1918], *supra*, n.11. The negative-order doctrine was overruled in Rochester Telephone Corp. v. United States, 307 U.S. 125 (1939).

[26] See Baer Brothers v. Denver & Rio Grande R.R., 233 U.S. 479 (1914); Meeker & Co. v. Lehigh Valley R.R., 236 U.S. 412 (1915); Meeker v. Lehigh Valley R.R., 236 U.S. 434 (1915); Mills v. Lehigh Valley R.R., 238 U.S. 473 (1915); Southern Pacific Co. v. Darnell-Taenzer Co., 245 U.S. 531 (1918); Spiller v. Atchison, Topeka & Santa Fe Ry., 253 U.S. 117 (1920); Vicksburg, Shreveport & Pacific Ry. v. Anderson-Tully Co., 256 U.S. 408 (1921). *Cf.* Phillips v. Grand Trunk Ry., 236 U.S. 662 (1915).

[27] See *supra*, pp. 274, n.226, 415–17; but *cf.* Chicago, Milwaukee & St. Paul Ry. v. McCaull-Dinsmore Co., 253 U.S. 97 (1920), *supra*, p. 417, n.11.

[28] Interstate Commerce Commission v. Goodrich Transit Co., 224 U.S. 194 (1912), see *supra*, pp. 214–15, 422; Smith v. Interstate Commerce Commission, 245 U.S. 33, 47 (1917); Jones v. Interstate Commerce Commission, 245 U.S. 48 (1917), see *supra*, p. 422, n.40. But *cf.* United States v. Louisville & Nashville R.R., 236 U.S. 318 (1915); Ellis v. Interstate Commerce Commission, 237 U.S. 434 (1915), see *supra*, p. 422, n.40.

[29] See *supra*, pp. 189, nn.276, 277, 278; 195–96, n.292.

[30] Sharfman, *Interstate Commerce Commission*, 2:392.

law, only some of which called for an answer to be derived by a process of statutory construction.[31] It was even subjected once or twice, despite the decision in the *Procter & Gamble* case, to writs of mandamus requiring it to assume a jurisdiction it had declined to exercise, because it had, as the Court thought, misread the law.[32] Finally and most seriously, there were also instances in which the Court, covertly or explicitly, overrode the commission's discretionary judgments.

In *Florida East Coast Line* v. *United States*,[33] the commission ordered the railroad to reduce certain rates that the commission had itself at an earlier time held reasonable. Conditions had changed, said the commission. The shipments in question were now being handled on a more economical basis by the railroads, with the shippers doing more of the packing. White, for a unanimous Court, held that the commission's order should be enjoined. The evidence of new methods of shipment, he said, related to other railroads, not to the Florida East Coast Line itself. As to this railroad, there was no specific proof in the record. The question was whether an inference was justified that the same conditions shown to prevail in shipments by other railroads prevailed (or perhaps could prevail) also in shipments by the Florida East Coast Line. There was no basis in the record for making this inference, White held. Formally this was a decision that the commission's findings were unsupported by evidence of record. But it surely came close to denying the authority of the commission to draw inferences from its experience. The decision, therefore, amounted to an assumption of control over the exercise of the commission's discretion on a question of mixed law and fact.

Not frequently, but in several notable instances, the Court quite explicitly overrode exercises of administrative discretion by the commission. Thus in the *Tap Line Cases*,[34] the commission forbade railroads to enter into through-route and joint-rate arrangements with producers of lumber who owned their own tap lines running from their plants to the main line. The commission found that such arrangements, which reduced rates for the lumber shipped by owners of tap lines, constituted a discrimination in their favor. The tap lines, the commis-

---

[31] *Ibid.*, 1:236–43.

[32] See Interstate Commerce Commission v. Humboldt Steamship Co., 224 U.S. 474 (1912); Louisville Cement Co. v. Interstate Commerce Commission, 246 U.S. 638 (1918); and see Kansas City Southern Ry. v. Interstate Commerce Commission, 252 U.S. 178 (1920).

[33] 234 U.S. 167 (1914); and see United States v. St. Louis, Iron Mountain & Southern Ry., 217 Fed. 80 (E.D. Ill. 1914), *appeal dismissed on motion of the Solicitor General*, 241 U.S. 693 (1916).

[34] 234 U.S. 1 (1914); see also United States v. Butler County R.R., 234 U.S. 29 (1914); *cf.* O'Keefe v. United States, *supra*, n.17.

sion held, should be classified as plant facilities, not as common carriers to be accommodated by joint rates. For a unanimous Court, Day reversed. The tap lines were considered common carriers in the state in which they were located, and they should be so held, said Day. The commission was free to regulate them, and it was free to find that a particular division of joint rates between a railroad and the owner of a tap line had a discriminatory effect, or amounted to a rebate. But the commission could not flatly forbid through-route and joint-rate arrangements. "It would be a strained construction of the situation, . . ." Sharfman has written, "to assume that the Commission and the Court were but seeking the same end, through the application of different methods. In reality, legal concepts prevailed over administrative wisdom, and the policy of regulation was substituted for the policy of prohibition." The former policy, in Sharfman's judgment, proved in many instances inadequate.[35]

In *Louisville & Nashville Railroad* v. *United States*,[36] the commission ordered two railroads which had joined in putting together a union terminal in Nashville to make switching services available on equal terms to competing traffic of a third railroad. Holmes for a minimal majority, over a dissent by Pitney joined in by Day, Brandeis, and Clarke, held that the commission had exceeded its authority. Under the statute, a single railroad owning terminal facilities was not obliged to make them available to a competing railroad. Hence in this case, said Holmes, if either carrier had owned the terminal by itself, it could not have been forced to open it to anyone else. The same, he reasoned, ought to be true of joint owners. The commission's argument was that the joint owners extended switching services to each other, and for that reason ought not to be allowed to refuse them to a third railroad. They were in a different position from that of a single owner of a terminal which switched its own cars only. The distinction, sensible and practically necessary though it struck the commission as being, did not impress Holmes, who replied with one of his favorite generalizations about the nature of line drawing in the law: "What is done seems to us not reciprocal switching but the use of a joint terminal in the natural and practical way. It is objected that upon this view a way is open to get beyond the reach of the statute and the Commission. But the very meaning of a line in the law is that right and wrong touch each other and that anyone may get as close to the line as he can if he keeps on the right side."[37]

---

[35] Sharfman, *Interstate Commerce Commission*, 2:164–65.

[36] 242 U.S. 60, 74 (1916).

[37] See Sharfman, *Interstate Commerce Commission*, 3A:412–13. Other cases in which the commission was reversed on issues touching its exercise of administrative discretion are Inter-

The degree of judicial interference represented by such cases as these gave rise to no particular furor in the press or in Congress. But the decade was one in which a great deal of public attention played on the railroad problem. The dominant opinion both in and out of Congress favored an increase in the power and freedom of the Interstate Commerce Commission, which was trusted to exercise strong control over the railroads. The memory and the premonition, even if not the present sense, of active and overbearing judicial interference were keen. They caused the virtual stillbirth of an experiment with a specialized Commerce Court, intended to expedite and render uniform judicial review of commission orders. The idea of a specialized court, expert like the commission itself, unburdened by other business, and subject only to the authority of the Supreme Court, was not new.[38] But the Taft Administration pushed it to realization. It was neither a pro- nor an anti-railroad idea, and it did not cover a purpose to impede vigorous regulation. As Attorney General Wickersham wrote the President in September 1909:

> Every carrier affected by an order of the Commission has a constitutional right to appeal to a court to protect it from the enforcement of the order, upon the ground that it is either confiscatory or unjustly discriminative; and as this right may now be exercised in any one of the many courts of the United States, not only does delay result, but great uncertainty, resulting from contrariety of decision. It is impossible to meet this condition effectively except by concentrating the judicial review in one court, so organized as to be able to deal speedily and effectively with the questions presented. The analogy furnished by the Customs Court of Appeals is very pertinent.[39]

The proposal to set up a specialized Commerce Court, having exclusive jurisdiction to review orders of the Interstate Commerce Commission, though exercising a scope of review no broader than had prevailed up to then in the several circuit courts, was enacted in 1910 because the administration succeeded in tying it into what became the Mann-Elkins Act of that year. But it was strongly opposed in Congress by Democrats and Insurgents, the principal sponsors of the Mann-Elkins

---

state Commerce Commission v. Diffenbaugh, 222 U.S. 42 (1911); Union Pacific R.R. v. Updike Grain Co., 222 U.S. 215 (1911); United States v. Baltimore & Ohio R.R., 231 U.S. 274 (1913) (see also United States v. Baltimore & Ohio R.R., 225 U.S. 306 [1912]).

[38] See Frankfurter and Landis, *Business of the Supreme Court*, 153–56.

[39] G. W. Wickersham to W. H. Taft, Sept. 2, 1909, Taft Papers, Library of Congress; *cf.* 45 *Cong. Rec.* 378, 379, 61st Cong., 2nd Sess. (1910) (President Taft's Message to Congress, Jan. 7, 1910), quoted in Frankfurter and Landis, *Business of the Supreme Court,* 156.

Act. The opposition feared that a specialized court would be railroad-minded and would impose its preferences on the commission. No sooner was the five-judge Commerce Court established, than Insurgent Republicans and Democrats in Congress began efforts to abolish it. In this atmosphere, the Commerce Court took up its task, and came on strong, "not wisely but too well." The Commerce Court, wrote Frankfurter and Landis in reviewing the experience, "entered an environment partial to the Commission and distrustful of courts. With undoubted courage and disinterestedness the Court, heedless of the public temper, promptly began to reverse the Commission and to curb its activity. But its legal wisdom was not equal to its indifference to popular sentiment. For the Commerce Court was itself promptly reversed and curbed by the Supreme Court."[40]

The week of January 9, 1912, was, as one newspaper reported, interstate commerce week in the Supreme Court.[41] *Interstate Commerce Commission* v. *Union Pacific Railroad*,[42] which struck an important blow for the freedom of the commission, was decided on January 9, and on January 11, 12, 15, and 16, the first four cases appealed from the Commerce Court were argued in the Supreme Court.[43] At this time a legislative movement to abolish the Commerce Court had been set afoot. It was to succeed in Congress, only to be met that summer with a Presidential veto.[44] The first of the cases argued was *Procter & Gamble* v. *United States*,[45] and the argument had not gone on for long before Van Devanter from the Bench raised the ominous question whether the Commerce Court might not have exceeded its jurisdiction in undertaking to review a negative order of the commission.[46] On April 1, 1912, the Supreme Court rendered its first decision in a case appealed from the Commerce Court. This was *Interstate Commerce Commission* v. *Goodrich Transit Co.*,[47] which was argued in February 1912, and in which the Commerce Court had undertaken to limit the commission's investigatory powers. The Supreme Court restored those powers to the commission, reversing the decision of the Commerce Court. On June 7, 1912, followed three more reversals, in *Procter & Gamble* v. *United States* and a companion case, and in *Interstate Commerce Commission* v. *Baltimore & Ohio Railroad*,[48] in which the commission had found

---

[40] Frankfurter and Landis, *Business of the Supreme Court*, 165.

[41] See *Washington Times*, Jan. 12, 1912, p. 6, col. 1.

[42] *Supra*, p. 651, n.9.

[43] Procter & Gamble v. United States, *supra*, n.25; Hooker v. Knapp, *supra*, n.25; United States v. Baltimore & Ohio R.R., 225 U.S. 306 (1912);

Interstate Commerce Commission v. Baltimore & Ohio R.R., *supra*, n.6.

[44] Frankfurter and Landis, *Business of the Supreme Court*, 166–70.

[45] *Supra*, p. 654, n.25.

[46] See *Washington Post*, Jan. 12, 1912, p. 12, col. 4.

[47] *Supra*, n.28.

[48] *Supra*, n.6.

that certain rates were discriminatory and had changed them, and the Commerce Court had enjoined enforcement of the commission's order. On June 10, 1912, the Commerce Court finally achieved an affirmance at the hands of the Supreme Court in *United States* v. *Baltimore & Ohio Railroad*.[49] But the affirmance was on a minor point—the authority of the Commerce Court to issue a temporary injunction *pendente lite* against an order of the commission. The Supreme Court did not reach the merits of the case (although when it finally did, a year and a half later, it affirmed a permanent injunction issued by the Commerce Court).[50] So in four out of the first five of its cases to reach the Supreme Court, the Commerce Court suffered reversal.

Much notice was taken in the press, which was also closely following proceedings in Congress aimed at abolishing the Commerce Court. The occasion was reported as "a black day for the Commerce Court," in which it received "blow after blow."[51] The worst apprehensions of those who had opposed creation of the Commerce Court seemed to be confirmed. The court seemed bent on hobbling the commission, even to the point of usurping power. It hardly mattered that in the *Procter & Gamble* case, at least, the question was a very close one, and that the decision of the Commerce Court could not fairly be characterized as prorailroad, or that of the commission and of the Supreme Court as antirailroad. Its opponents in Congress were all too ready to seize on these reversals, and the Commerce Court was certainly put in a bad light.

In all, twenty-two appeals were taken from the Commerce Court to the Supreme Court.[52] Fourteen resulted in reversals of judgments of the Commerce Court.[53] But in two of these reversals, *Florida East Coast Line* v. *United States* and *Omaha Street Railway* v. *Interstate Commerce Commission*, the Commerce Court had upheld orders of the Interstate

---

[49] 225 U.S. 306 (1912).

[50] United States v. Baltimore & Ohio R.R., 231 U.S. 274 (1913).

[51] *New York Tribune,* June 8, 1912, p. 5, col. 1; *New York World,* June 8, 1912, p. 7, col. 1.

[52] *Cf.* Frankfurter and Landis, *Business of the Supreme Court,* 165, n.95; Sharfman, *Interstate Commerce Commission,* 2:64–65, n.71.

[53] In addition to the four mentioned earlier, the reversals were: Interstate Commerce Commission v. Louisville & Nashville R.R., *supra,* n.10; Omaha Street Ry v. Interstate Commerce Commission, 230 U.S. 324 (1913); Florida East Coast Line v. United States, *supra,* n.33; The Los Angeles Switching Case, *supra,* n.11; Interstate Commerce Commission v. Southern Pacific Co., *supra,* n.11; Intermountain Rate Cases, *supra,* n.13; United States v. Union Pacific R.R., *supra,* n.13; The Pipe Line Cases, *supra,* p. 238, n.105; United States v. Louisville & Nashville R.R., *supra,* n.15; Louisville & Nashville R.R. v. United States, 207 Fed. 591 (Commerce Court 1913), *reversed on confession of error by the Solicitor General,* 238 U.S. 642 (1915); *cf. ibid., supra,* n.11.

Commerce Commission. The Supreme Court thought these orders should be enjoined. In nine cases, the decisions of the Commerce Court were affirmed. In four of these, the Commerce Court had itself upheld orders of the commission.[54] In five, orders of the commission had been enjoined.[55] In one case, the judgment of the Commerce Court was modified,[56] and in another, in which the Commerce Court had upheld the commission, the appeal was dismissed on motion of the railroad.[57]

It was not unfair to conclude that the Commerce Court was holding somewhat too tight a rein on the commission. But the court was allowed to make all too brief a record. It might have performed differently in the longer run. Its luck was abominable. Thus on January 13, 1913, one of its judges, Robert W. Archbald, having been impeached by the House, was convicted by the Senate of corrupt conduct while a Commerce Court judge and removed from office. The case cast no reflection on the court as a whole, but it assuredly added no luster to its reputation.[58] On October 22, 1913, after less than three years of existence, the court was abolished by Congress, and President Wilson, now in office, did not protect it with his veto.[59] The court actually closed its doors two months later, its judges being retained as floating circuit judges.

The Federal Trade Commission

It was a generation after the birth of the Interstate Commerce Commission that the next major federal administrative agency came into being. This was the Federal Trade Commission, a product of the extended national debate on antitrust policy that followed decision of the *Standard Oil* and *American Tobacco* cases. Established in 1914, it was modeled substantially on the Interstate Commerce Commission. The Trade Commission got off to a slow start. Then, as soon as it was in motion, it collided with the First World War. Antitrust is a peacetime

---

[54] Kansas City Southern Ry. v. United States, *supra*, n.17; Atchison, Topeka & Santa Fe Ry. v. United States, *supra*, n.17; Atchison Ry. v. United States, *supra*, n.17; Houston & Texas Ry. v. United States, *supra*, p. 218, n.54.

[55] United States v. Baltimore & Ohio R.R., 225 U.S. 306 (1912); United States v. Baltimore & Ohio Southwestern Ry., 226 U.S. 14 (1912); United States v. Baltimore & Ohio R.R., 231 U.S. 274 (1913); Tap Line

Cases, *supra*, n.34; United States v. Butler County R.R., *supra*, n.34.

[56] United States v. Union Stock Yard, 226 U.S. 286 (1912).

[57] Pennsylvania R.R. v. Interstate Commerce Commission, 193 Fed. 81 (Commerce Court 1911), *appeal dismissed on motion of appellant*, 235 U.S. 708 (1914).

[58] See Sharfman, *Interstate Commerce Commission*, 1:70, n.80; Frankfurter and Landis, *Business of the Supreme Court*, 171.

[59] 38 Stat. 208, 219 (1913).

idea, unwanted on a war voyage. The commission flourished briefly after the war, but soon encountered the Harding-Coolidge era, when the politics and policies of the Progressives seemed as ancient and distant, for the moment, as the earliest days of the Republic.[60]

Among the other troubles which beset the Federal Trade Commission was a restrictive attitude on the part of the Supreme Court, contrasting markedly with the treatment accorded by the Court to the Interstate Commerce Commission. A cluster of Federal Trade Commission cases came to the Supreme Court early in the Chief Justiceship of William Howard Taft. Only one such case, *Federal Trade Commission* v. *Gratz*, the first to reach the Supreme Court, was decided under White, in June 1920. It augured ill indeed.

The commission had issued a complaint against Gratz, a partnership, for allegedly engaging in unfair competition in violation of Section 5 of the Federal Trade Commission Act. Gratz sold steel ties used for binding bales of cotton. The cotton was bound in bags, and Gratz, the commission charged, refused to sell any of its ties unless the prospective purchaser also agreed to buy the bagging to be used with the ties; that is, Gratz would insist that for each six ties that the buyer wished to purchase, he would have to buy also six yards of bagging. After a hearing, the commission found the facts as charged and ordered Gratz to cease and desist. The United States Court of Appeals for the Second Circuit then vacated the order on the ground that it was unsupported by the evidence. Without examining the evidence, but on the basis of the complaint alone, McReynolds[61] for a majority of the Supreme Court affirmed the judgment of the Court of Appeals.

The commission's complaint, McReynolds held, was insufficient to charge the offense of unfair competition within the meaning of the Federal Trade Commission Act. As a matter of law, the practice charged could not constitute unfair competition. The statute itself did not define that phrase, and the task of defining it fell, therefore, to the courts— not, McReynolds was distinctly implying, to the commission in the exercise of its administrative discretion. There could be no basis for a charge of unfair competition in "practices never heretofore regarded as opposed to good morals because characterized by deception, bad faith, fraud or oppression, or as against public policy because of their

---

[60] See G. C. Davis, "The Transformation of the Federal Trade Commission, 1914–1929," *Miss. Valley Hist. Rev.*, 49:437, 1962.

[61] The Federal Trade Commission soon developed into one of McReynolds' pet peeves. He and it were to have a prolonged hate affair. See, e.g., Federal Trade Commission v. Curtis Publishing Co., 260 U.S. 568 (1923); Federal Trade Commission v. Klesner, 274 U.S. 145 (1927); Federal Trade Commission v. Claire Co., 274 U.S. 160 (1927).

dangerous tendency unduly to hinder competition or create monopoly." There was no allegation that Gratz had monopoly power. Its customers were free not to accept the bags which Gratz wanted them to buy together with the ties; they were free to buy neither.

Pitney concurred in the result without opinion, but Brandeis, joined by Clarke, dissented at length. It was preposterous, he began, to purport to decide this case on the pleadings. The commission had compiled a record of four hundred pages, and it was incumbent upon the Court to examine this record and to decide whether the evidence supported the commission's findings. The complaint did not have to set out the reasons why the practice charged constituted unfair competition. The evidence would do that. Never had the Interstate Commerce Commission been required to go farther in its pleadings than the Federal Trade Commission had gone in this case. The nature of the proceeding before the commission had to be given its setting. Here Brandeis recited the history of the evolution of antitrust policy following decision of the *Standard Oil* and *American Tobacco* cases, and defined the purpose which the Federal Trade Commission was created to serve.[62] "The belief was widespread," he wrote, "that the great trusts had acquired their power, in the main, through destroying or overreaching their weaker rivals by resort to unfair practices." With these the commission was to deal, not by inflicting punishment for past misdeeds, but by fostering competition "through supervisory action." It was not intended that the commission would lock the barn door after the horses had fled. "The potency of accomplished facts had already been demonstrated. The task of the Commission was to protect competitive business from *further* inroads by monopoly. It was to be ever vigilant. . . . Its action was to be prophylactic. Its purpose in respect to restraints of trade was prevention of diseased business conditions, not cure."

In deciding what practices were to be deemed unfairly competitive, the commission was to have discretion and to let its judgment be governed by varying conditions in different businesses. The discretionary power confided to the Federal Trade Commission, subject to limited judicial review on questions of law, was modeled on that exercised by the Interstate Commerce Commission. It had been validly exercised in this case. Obviously the practice in question was not necessarily an unfair method of competition under the usual conditions of a competitive trade. The situation was different, however, when the seller had preponderant power. The evidence showed that Gratz was the Carnegie Company's sole agent for selling and distributing steel ties, which Carnegie, a subsidiary of United States Steel, manufactured in so large a proportion that it dominated the market. Gratz was also the sole

---

[62] See *supra*, p. 144.

agent west of the Mississippi for the company which manufactured some 45 percent of all bagging used for cotton baling. Gratz was thus in a position, and had good reason, to force prospective purchasers of ties to buy their bagging from him. Under these conditions, Gratz's practice could well be viewed as an unfair method of competition.[63]

A Federal Common Law of Administrative Power

Quite apparently, the Supreme Court conceived its function when reviewing orders of the Federal Trade Commission differently from that when it reviewed actions of the Interstate Commerce Commission. Such differences in judicial attitudes toward various administrative agencies have persisted, with or without foundation, in markedly different statutory provisions. But the differences came in time to be fewer and less important than the unities, and there developed something that could fairly be called a common law of judicial review of administrative action. It was beginning to emerge in the years 1910–21, but barely, just barely, being essentially limited as yet to a judicial acceptance of delegation of discretionary, quasi-legislative power to administrators and administrative agencies. Any other generalization about judicial review of administrative action was still extremely risky. A common law of administrative power would have been relevant chiefly to cases, to be discussed presently, dealing with public lands, with Indian affairs, with government contracts and other claims against the government, with patents, and with aliens; and in all such cases, the variables predominated and the unities were immanent at best. Even on so fundamental a question as the right to any judicial review of administrative action—review of any sort, whatever its scope—no coherent principle could at this stage be extracted which would be applicable across the board.[64]

On the issue of the delegation of a measure of legislative power to administrators, however, coherent and authoritative statements can be found in decisions dating to the White Chief Justiceship. The leading

---

[63] Federal Trade Commission v. Gratz, 253 U.S. 421, 427, 434, 435 (1920). It took some years, but ultimately Brandeis' dissent became law. See Federal Trade Commission v. R. F. Keppel & Brothers, Inc., 291 U.S. 304, 310 (1934); Federal Trade Commission v. Cement Institute, 333 U.S. 683, 693 (1948); Atlantic Refining Co. v. Federal Trade Commis-

sion, 381 U.S. 357, 367 (1965); Federal Trade Commission v. Brown Shoe Co., 384 U.S. 316 (1966).

[64] Compare, e.g., Reaves v. Ainsworth, 219 U.S. 296 (1911), with Philadelphia Co. v. Stimson, 223 U.S. 605 (1912), supra, p. 221, n.70. Cf. Tang Tum v. Edsell, 223 U.S. 673 (1912).

case is *United States* v. *Grimaud.*[65] Congress had authorized the Secretary of Agriculture to make regulations governing sheep grazing on forest reserve lands, and had imposed criminal penalties for violation of the Secretary's regulations. A lower federal court held the statute unconstitutional because of excessive delegation of the legislative function. This decision was affirmed by an equally divided Supreme Court— without opinion, as had been the custom—in March 1910, under Fuller. The case was then set down for reargument after Brewer's death, which opened the possibility that the deadlock could be broken. It was reargued to a full Court in March 1911, and decided in May in a notable opinion by Lamar for a unanimous Court. Lamar upheld the delegation. Plainly, said Lamar, Congress had wanted to allow some grazing on forest reserve lands, but not on all, or always, and it was impracticable for Congress itself to determine just when and where grazing would be allowed under such a policy. Hence the decision was delegated to the Secretary, but the delegation was, properly speaking, of administrative power to fill up the details in the legislation. It was not a delegation of the power of the legislature itself to settle on an overall policy. Thus it was Congress itself which had decided to enforce the regulations to be made by the Secretary through the criminal process, and it was Congress which had fixed the penalties. The Secretary had not been empowered to decide when to render certain behavior criminal. This reasoning persuaded the remaining doubters at least to acquiesce. The *Grimaud* doctrine, which had its antecedents, of course, as Lamar's opinion demonstrates, was reaffirmed in other decisions, and remains fully authoritative.[66]

Public Lands and Water Rights

In *United States* v. *Midwest Oil Co.*, decided some four years after *United States* v. *Grimaud*, Lamar for a divided Court went a substantial distance beyond his holding in *Grimaud*. By act of February 11, 1897,[67] Congress opened public lands valuable chiefly for petroleum and other

---

[65] 220 U.S. 506 (1911); see also Light v. United States, 220 U.S. 523 (1911).

[66] See, e.g., Roughton v. Knight, 219 U.S. 537 (1911); Hannibal Bridge Co. v. United States, 221 U.S. 194 (1911); United States v. Morehead, 243 U.S. 607 (1917); The Mail Divisor Cases, 251 U.S. 326 (1920); *cf.* Curtin v. Benson, 222 U.S. 78 (1911);

Cochnower v. United States, 248 U.S. 405, 249 U.S. 588 (1919). In context of a rather singular argument raising the delegation issue, Holmes had occasion in Western Union Telegraph Co. v. Richmond, 224 U.S. 160 (1912), to reaffirm the doctrine of the *Grimaud* case as applied to state administrative officials.

[67] 29 Stat. 526 (1897).

mineral deposits (which were excluded, as we shall see, from other grants, and from the Homestead Act) to "free and open . . . occupation, exploration and purchase by citizens of the United States . . . under regulations prescribed by law." Very considerable acreages of oil-producing land passed into private hands under this statute, especially in California. Oil deposits were in consequence being rapidly depleted, and in 1909, the Department of the Interior, concerned that the low cost of oil lands was encouraging overproduction, and that while the navy was becoming increasingly dependent on oil as a fuel, publicly owned oil lands were rapidly vanishing, conducted an investigation and recommended to the President that he, in effect, suspend operation of the Act of February 11, 1897. Accordingly, on September 27, 1909, President Taft, by proclamation, withdrew over three million acres of public lands in California and Wyoming from further entry by private persons, pending action by Congress. The President's order was without statutory authority, was denounced as illegal by oil interests, and was widely ignored.[68]

Having issued his proclamation, the President asked Congress to ratify it. Congress met him halfway. By act of June 25, 1910,[69] it authorized future withdrawals like the one the President had made, but provided that preexisting rights were to be neither abridged nor enlarged. Thus the President's proclamation was neither ratified nor overruled. Meanwhile, six months after the proclamation but before Congress acted, one Henshaw entered some of the withdrawn lands, discovered oil, and assigned his claim to the Midwest Oil Company. Henshaw was one of many who were undeterred by the President's proclamation, and the government chose his as a test case, bringing suit against the company to recover the land and for an accounting of the oil removed. Since the Act of June 25, 1910, explicitly preserved, though it did not enlarge, claims valid prior to its passage, the President's power to make the withdrawal was put squarely in issue. A federal district court held the proclamation invalid, and dismissed the government's suit. The government appealed to the Court of Appeals for the Eighth Circuit, which certified certain questions to the Supreme Court. That Court thereupon directed that the entire record be sent to it, and the case was argued in January 1914 while Lurton was ill, then reargued in May 1914 after Lurton's return. Although he heard the reargument, however, Lurton did not survive to take part in the decision, which was rendered by an eight-man Court in February 1915, after Lurton's death, McReynolds, his replacement, taking no part.

---

[68] See W. E. Colby, "The New Public Land Policy with Special Reference to Oil Lands," *Cal. L. Rev.*, 3:269, 276–77, 1915.

[69] 36 Stat. 847 (1910).

Reversing, Lamar upheld the authority of the President to issue his proclamation of withdrawal. The practice of withdrawing lands from public entry by Presidential proclamation was of long standing, said Lamar. It grew up in connection with land-grant statutes which, like the Act of February 11, 1897, neither called for nor forbade the exercise of Presidential authority. The President's action in the past, as in this instance, was always prospective, not retroactive, and thus did not have the effect of defeating any individual rights. Usage, it was argued, could not establish validity. "But government," Lamar answered, "is a practical affair intended for practical men." For this reason there was and ought to be a presumption in favor of the validity of a usage, as "a wise and quieting rule." Granted that in the Act of June 25, 1910, Congress had not ratified the President's action. Yet Congress had also not disturbed it, and assuming it was valid when taken, it remained so.

Day, joined by McKenna and Van Devanter, dissented at length. The withdrawal of lands from public entry by Presidential action had in the past been restricted to instances where the lands were to be put to a use explicitly sanctioned by Congress, as in the case of lands earmarked for military or Indian reservations, or instances where several grants made by Congress were in conflict with each other, so that the true legislative purpose could not be discovered, and withdrawal was necessary to give Congress a chance to resolve the ambiguity in its laws. Here, however, Congress had clearly expressed its will in the Act of 1897. And when the President asked for ratification, Congress refused it to him. "It is one of the great functions of this court," Day concluded, "to keep, so far as judicial decisions can subserve that purpose, each branch of the Government within the sphere of its legitimate action, and to prevent encroachments of one branch upon the authority of another."[70]

Lamar, it must be noted, drove to his conclusion, "wise and quieting" though it may have been, rather by main force. Though the decision was well received,[71] the dissent, joined in by Van Devanter, an appointee of Taft and the Court's acknowledged expert on the law of public lands, had the better of the argument. In 1952, when another President, having undertaken another daring extension of Presidential power, was treated less indulgently by the Supreme Court, Justice Robert H. Jackson took occasion to point out that Taft's own later view of the reach of Presidential power was more conservative than the conception embodied in the oil-lands withdrawal proclamation.[72]

Litigation dealing with public lands came to the Supreme Court in

---

[70] United States v. Midwest Oil Co., 236 U.S. 459, 472, 473, 511 (1915).

[71] See *supra*, p. 360, n.158.

[72] See Youngstown Sheet and Tube Co. v. Sawyer, 343 U.S. 579, 635, n.1 (1952) (Jackson, J., concurring).

very substantial volume throughout the White Chief Justiceship. In addition to the Homestead Act, which of course opened up vast acreages to private settlement, numerous statutes made grants of land to railroads, as also to states in aid of public schools, or to encourage reclamation projects. All these statutes, including the Homestead Act, were administered by the Land Office of the Department of the Interior. None of them actually passed title to anyone. Rather Congress would grant alternate sections of land along its track to a railroad, for example, at a time when only its starting and terminal points were known, if indeed the railroad was ever going to be built. In due time, the railroad filed with the Land Office a map describing its claim, and affidavits averring that the land claimed fell within the terms of the grant. Upon approval, commonly given on the strength of the affidavits without inspection of the lands in question, patents issued, passing title. Essentially by this method, the United States, over several decades ending in 1871, granted some 129 million acres of public lands to the railroads.[73]

In *Burke* v. *Southern Pacific Railroad*,[74] a unanimous Court, speaking through Van Devanter, held that a patent so granted was not subject to collateral attack, and could be questioned, if at all, only in a suit by the United States to cancel it for fraud or other illegality—except even then, presumably the rights of purchasers in good faith might stand in the way. The case concerned the grant in 1866 to the Southern Pacific Railroad of alternate sections along its track by a statute which expressly excluded mineral lands from the grant. The Southern Pacific, in other words, was given the right to select, and perfect title in the usual way to, alternate sections, but it was expressly enjoined not to select, and could not be given title to, sections of land that contained mineral deposits.[75] In 1892, oil was discovered on land within the general area of the grant. The Southern Pacific thereupon presented fraudulent affidavits to the Land Office averring that these lands were nonmineral, and selected sections within them. Patents were issued, but the Land Office took the precaution of including in the patents a saving clause stating that no title would vest in lands that were mineral.[76] Some years later, Burke entered land to which the Southern Pacific had thus obtained title, and eventually sued to establish his own title and oust the Southern Pacific.

Van Devanter held that the exclusion in the 1866 statute of

---

[73] See A. Chandler, *Land Title Origins* (1945), 503–509; B. Hibbard, *A History of Public Land Policies* (1924), 242–67.

[74] 234 U.S. 669 (1914); see also Spokane & British Columbia Ry. v. Washington & Great Northern Ry., 219 U.S. 166 (1911); and see Work Mining & Milling Co. v. Dr. Jack Pot Mining Co., 194 Fed. 620 (8th Cir. 1912), *cert. denied*, 226 U.S. 610 (1912).

[75] 14 Stat. 292 (1866).

[76] See United States v. Southern Pacific R.R., 251 U.S. 1 (1919).

mineral lands was applicable to oil-bearing lands such as these, but that the issuance of the patent on the basis of affidavits that the lands were within the grant and were not mineral vested title in the Southern Pacific conclusively as against third parties, the saving clause in the patent notwithstanding. That saving clause, Van Devanter held, was void. The issuance of the patent constituted a determination that the lands were not mineral, and were within the terms of the grant. It was the function of the Land Office to make that factual determination at the time of issuing the patent, and no saving clause in the patent could substitute for performance of the function, or deny what the patent, by virtue of having been issued, affirmed. The patent was proof against collateral attack. The government itself could sue the Southern Pacific to cancel such patents. But the government must allege fraud or other illegality in suing its grantee, as in fact it ultimately did—and successfully.[77] The saving clause as such would not avail the government any more than it could a third party.

Burke was a hard case, of course, but Van Devanter was confident that it had made good law, although he was a touch defensive about it. He thought, he wrote his former colleague on the Eighth Circuit Court of Appeals, Elmer B. Adams, that the question of the validity of the saving clause in the Southern Pacific patents was "of the greatest possible importance to the western country." If the saving clause were valid,

there would be no such thing as a bona fide purchase, because every purchaser under such a patent would necessarily take with notice of [the saving clause], and the discovery of minerals at any time in the land would automatically demonstrate that the land was not covered by the patent but excepted from it. No doubt there will be those who will not understand the decision and will be disposed to criticize it as one which favors the land grant railroads. It hardly is a railroad question any more, for four fifths of the land has long since passed into the hands of others, and the real question is between the present holders and the Government. True, the case in hand was against a railroad company, but even in the oil district of California the great bulk of the alternate odd numbered railroad sections have long since passed into the hands of individuals, and are much more frequently held in tracts of less than 160 acres than in tracts exceeding that acreage. . . . What is here said is permissible in a letter to you, and may serve to give you an accurate impression of the real character of the question involved and how far-reaching any disposition of it would be.[78]

---

[77] See *ibid.*

[78] W. Van Devanter to E. B. Adams, July 5, 1914, Van Devanter Papers, Library of Congress.

In many other cases as well, the Court showed its concern for the stability of titles derived from railroad land grants, despite irregularities and sharp dealings that were not uncommon in the pell-mell rush of westward railroad building. The Court was also on occasion more disposed than were post-land-grant Congresses and administrations to construe in favor of the railroads what McKenna in one case referred to as "rights conveyed to aid that great enterprise."[79] Said McKenna, again, in another case, even while reaching a result ultimately unfavorable to the railroad: "Empire was given a path westward and prosperous commonwealths took the place of the wilderness." It was not, in niggardly hindsight, to be forgotten, he implied, that such was the purpose of the railroad land grants. They were not rash gifts, but the instruments of a policy whose success was now evident, but had not always been assured.[80] Of course, irregularities did sometimes result in a railroad or its assignee losing its claim to a parcel of land, or being ousted from it,[81] especially where fraud was involved.[82]

Most suits seeking to divest fraudulently obtained titles to public lands, however, concerned patents issued, not under railroad land grant statutes, but under more general ones, notably the Homestead Act. *Diamond Coal Co.* v. *United States*[83] is illustrative. Believing that certain tracts of land could be profitably mined for coal, the company caused an agent to obtain title in his own name under the "soldiers' additional entries" section of the Homestead Act.[84] The agent then transferred his patents to the company. The Homestead Act, however, like the Southern Pacific land grant and many others, excluded mineral lands.[85] This difficulty was circumvented by the presentation of fraudulent affidavits

---

[79] Union Pacific R.R. v. Laramie Stock Yards, 231 U.S. 190, 203 (1913); see also Union Pacific R.R. v. Snow, 231 U.S. 204 (1913); Union Pacific R.R. v. Sides, 231 U.S. 213 (1913).

[80] Oregon & California R.R. v. United States, 238 U.S. 393, 416 (1915); and see *ibid.*, 243 U.S. 549 (1917).

[81] See Southern Pacific R.R. v. United States, 223 U.S. 560 (1912); Svor v. Morris, 227 U.S. 524 (1913); Northern Pacific Ry. v. Trodick, 221 U.S. 208 (1911); Chicago, Milwaukee & St. Paul Ry. v. United States, 244 U.S. 351 (1917); United States v. New Orleans Pacific Ry., 248 U.S. 507 (1919); Caldwell v. United States,

250 U.S. 14 (1919). *Cf.* Oregon & California R.R. v. United States, *supra,* n.80 (and see 39 Stat. 218 [1916]).

[82] See Krueger v. United States, 246 U.S. 69 (1918); United States v. St. Paul, Minneapolis & Manitoba Ry., 247 U.S. 310 (1918); United States v. Southern Pacific R.R., *supra,* n.76. See also Northern Pacific Ry. v. United States, 176 Fed. 706 (9th Cir. 1910), *appeal dismissed on motion of appellant,* 223 U.S. 746 (1912).

[83] 233 U.S. 236 (1914); see also United States v. Diamond Coal Co., 255 U.S. 323 (1921).

[84] 17 Stat. 333 (1872).

[85] 12 Stat. 392 (1862), as amended, 26 Stat. 1095 (1891).

averring that the land was not mineral. The United States brought and won a suit to cancel the patents thus obtained.[86]

Another category of public land cases concerned conflicts between alleged rights derived from the federal law making a grant to private parties, and the general law of the state in which the land was held. The issue in such cases—*Ruddy* v. *Rossi*[87] was one—is referable ultimately to the Supremacy Clause. But the question initially is of the construction of the statute making the grant, and of the nature of the supposed federal right that was conveyed. *Buchser* v. *Buchser*[88] is a good example, worth mention additionally because it provided the occasion for a Holmesian *tour de force*. Buchser had acquired title to land in the state of Washington under the Homestead Act. At the time title vested in him, he was married. Washington being a community property state, and Buchser's wife having died, his children now claimed a share in the land derived from their mother's half. Buchser sued to quiet title, and Holmes, who had dissented in *Ruddy* v. *Rossi*, upheld the community property right, speaking now for a unanimous court. Of course, he said, federal law controlled until the instant when title passed, and conceivably the United States could have provided against the incidence of community property, imposing "a peculiar character upon land within a state after parting with all title to it." But the clearest kind of expression of legislative intent would be necessary to reach such a result, and in any event Congress had done nothing of the sort. And so, once title had passed under the Homestead Act, the state law of community property controlled the manner in which the land was held. "The only semblance of difficulty," Holmes was pleased to add, "is due to the coincidence in time of the acquisition of a separate right by the settler and the beginning of a community right in the wife. But this is by no means an extreme illustration of the division of an indivisible instant that is practiced by the law whenever it is necessary. A statute may give a man a right of action against another for causing his death, that accrues to him at the instant that he is *vivus et mortuus*," citing a Massachusetts case.[89]

There was finally an almost unending miscellany of the kind of case

---

[86] See also United States v. Hammers, 221 U.S. 220 (1911); Gilson v. United States, 234 U.S. 380 (1914); Wright-Blodgett Co. v. United States, 236 U.S. 397 (1915); United States v. Smull, 236 U.S. 405 (1915); Linn Timber Co. v. United States, 236 U.S. 574 (1915); Booth-Kelly Co. v. United States, 237 U.S. 481 (1915); Causey v. United States, 240 U.S. 399 (1916); United States v. Whited & Wheless, 246 U.S. 552 (1918); Exploration Co. v. United States, 247 U.S. 435 (1918). *Cf.* Waskey v. Hammer, 223 U.S. 85 (1912); United States v. Poland, 251 U.S. 221 (1920).

[87] *Supra,* p. 578, n.110; see *supra,* pp. 577–78, nn.106, 107.

[88] 231 U.S. 157, 162 (1913).

[89] Higgins v. Central New England & Western R.R., 155 Mass. 176, 179, 29 N.E. 534 (1892).

that, as Van Devanter reported when he was Assistant Attorney General assigned to the Department of the Interior, crossed his desk every day.[90] Such cases constituted a very considerable and for the most part wholly unjustifiable burden on the Supreme Court, of which Van Devanter bore much more than his proportionate share. The Court limited the scope of its review in many cases in which it was, in effect, being asked to pass on decisions of the Land Office. Thus in *Ness v. Fisher*,[91] Van Devanter held that an administrative construction of a requirement contained in the land grant statute, though debatable, was not to be overriden by the Supreme Court, since it constituted the exercise of a discretionary function confided to the Land Office. And factual determinations by the Land Office were generally held to be conclusive if supported by plausible evidence.[92] But nothing stemmed the flood of cases.[93]

A much smaller number of cases brought to the Court questions of water rights in the arid states and territories. "The doctrine of appropriation," said Holmes in one of these cases in which he applied it, "has prevailed in these [Western] regions probably from the first moment that they knew of any law. . . ." Hence Holmes assumed that the doctrine prevailed in Montana, and concluded that it was "unnecessary to consider whether Morris [the plaintiff, who had sued one Bean to prevent him from diverting in Montana waters which would normally flow to Morris in Wyoming and be his by appropriation] is not protected by the Constitution; for it seems superfluous to fall back upon the citadel until some attack drives him to that retreat."[94]

Indian Affairs

Litigation arising from Indian affairs, which was voluminous through the decade of the White Chief Justiceship, also frequently concerned rights in land. Indian lands are not public. Though with undoubted and often shameful deviations, the United States did from the first recognize Indian title, and generally obtained Indian lands by exchange or purchase. Felix S. Cohen, an outstanding and sympathetic student of American Indian law, has written: "The notion that America was stolen from the Indians is one of the myths by which we Americans are prone to hide our real virtues. . . ."[95] But the United States acted as

---

[90] See *supra*, p. 47.

[91] 223 U.S. 683 (1912).

[92] See Bailey v. Sanders, 228 U.S. 603 (1913); Logan v. Davis, 233 U.S. 613 (1914).

[93] In 1910–20, at least sixty such cases were decided.

[94] Bean v. Morris, 221 U.S. 485, 487, 488 (1911). See also, e.g., Rickey Land & Cattle Co. v. Miller & Lux, 218 U.S. 258 (1910).

[95] F. S. Cohen, "Original Indian Title," *Minn. L. Rev.*, 32:28, 34, 1947.

trustee of land retained by the Indians or obtained by them from the United States in exchange for ancestral lands as the Indians were moved westward. The land belonged to the Indians, but they in turn were wards of the United States. As trustee, the United States exercised very substantial control, short of having and exerting the rights of an owner.[96] In principle at least—a commendable if paternalistic principle—the United States had an obligation to protect its wards, and controlled their holdings in order to fulfill this obligation.

The starting point of most arrangements between the United States and Indians concerning land was a treaty, and the Supreme Court early held that ambiguities in such treaties were to be resolved in favor of the Indians.[97] This attitude continued to prevail. *Northern Pacific Railway* v. *United States*, for example, was a suit by the United States to cancel certain patents obtained under a railroad land grant. The government argued that the patents were issued by mistake, since the land in question had previously, by treaty, been constituted an Indian reservation. The issue in the case concerned the boundary of the reservation, ambiguously defined by the treaty in terms of the traditional Indian understanding of the contours of their land. Upholding the government's contention, McKenna said for a unanimous Court: "It [the government] yields to the rule which this court has declared—that it will construe a treaty with the Indians as 'that unlettered people' understood it, and 'as justice and reason demand in all cases where power is exerted by the strong over those whom they owe care and protection,' and counterpoise the inequality 'by the superior justice which looks only to the substance of the right without regard to technical rules.' "[98]

Indian treaties, like other treaties, could be repealed by act of Congress. Similarly, having made some statutory arrangement in the exercise of its power of control over Indian lands, Congress could and not infrequently did change its mind and rearrange matters differently. Moreover, the doctrine of sovereign immunity made it difficult for Indians, as for anyone else, to hold the United States to account directly.

---

[96] See F. S. Cohen, *Handbook of Federal Indian Law* (1942), 94–97; R. A. Brown, "The Indian Problem and the Law," *Yale L. J.*, 39:307, 319–23, 1930.

[97] See Cohen, *Federal Indian Law*, 37.

[98] Northern Pacific Ry. v. United States, 227 U.S. 355, 366–67 (1913). See also Missouri, Kansas & Texas Ry. v. United States, 235 U.S. 37 (1914); Northern Pacific Ry. v. Wis-mer, 246 U.S. 283 (1918); Seufert Brothers v. United States, 249 U.S. 194 (1919); see also United States v. Omaha Indians, 253 U.S. 275 (1920). And see Alaska Pacific Fisheries v. United States, 248 U.S. 78 (1918); Lane v. Pueblo of Santa Rosa, 249 U.S. 110 (1919). *Cf.* Kindred v. Union Pacific R.R., 225 U.S. 582 (1912); Williams v. Chicago, 242 U.S. 434 (1917); Nadeau v. Union Pacific R.R., 253 U.S. 442 (1920).

In order for the United States to be directly held to its obligations, the Congress had to consent to suit against the United States. But Congress frequently did so, and when it did, the United States became liable for violating, through subsequent Congressional action, rights that had vested under an Indian treaty, or under an earlier act of Congress. So the Supreme Court held, Van Devanter writing, in *United States* v. *Mille Lac Chippewas.*[99] What is equally important, Indian rights could be put in issue in suits to which the United States was not a party. A case of far-reaching effect, not directly involving the United States, which upheld Indian rights was *Choate* v. *Trapp*, handed down in 1912, in a unanimous opinion by Lamar.

When it organized Oklahoma as a state, Congress found it desirable to break up the large communal landholdings and tribal governments in the Indian territory encompassed in what was to become Oklahoma. A commission was appointed to negotiate with the tribes. It ran into great difficulties because the Indians, as the commission reported, held passionately to their customs and institutions, as well as to the more concrete privileges they enjoyed. But an agreement of sorts was finally reached, and embodied in the Curtis Act of 1898.[100] The communal holdings were to be divided, and allotted to individual members of the tribes. Individual holdings were subjected to restraints on alienation, and exempted from any taxation so long as title remained in the original allottee, up to a maximum period of twenty-one years. In 1908, after Oklahoma's admission, Congress by statute removed the restraints on alienation, as well as the exemption from taxation.[101] And so Oklahoma attempted to tax these lands. *Choate* v. *Trapp* was a suit by large numbers of Indians against the Oklahoma taxing authorities to enjoin collection of taxes on Indian lands. The Indians lost in the Oklahoma courts, which held that Congress could change the law applicable to its Indian wards at will. The privilege not to be taxed was a gratuity, said the Oklahoma courts, and could be withdrawn.

The Supreme Court, through Justice Lamar, reversed. Congress had plenary power over the Indians, no doubt, he wrote, and could repeal statutes, treaties, and agreements by later statutes. But, Lamar went on, "there is a broad distinction between tribal property and private property, and between the power to abrogate a statute and the authority to destroy rights acquired under . . . law." The freedom from taxation granted by the Curtis Act, which Congress had full power to grant, was a property right, and it had vested. It was a right arising out of a contractual relationship with the United States, since the arrangement embodied in the Curtis Act consisted of an offer to the Indians of the

---

[99] 229 U.S. 498 (1913).   [100] 30 Stat. 505 (1898).   [101] 35 Stat. 312 (1908)

674

lands allotted and of their freedom from taxation, in exchange for relinquishment by the Indians of claims to other lands. This offer was accepted by the Indians. The result was a contract binding on the United States. Congress had now lifted the restraints on alienation which had also been a part of the arrangement. To lift restraints on alienation was to remove an obligation resting on the Indians. Freedom from taxation, however, was a benefit, which had vested as a right. The Due Process and Contract clauses forbade Congress to take back such a right, particularly from "a weak and defenseless people, who are wards of the nation, and dependent wholly upon its protection and good faith."[102]

"The decision in *Choate* v. *Trapp*," wrote Felix S. Cohen in 1940, "stands as a landmark in the history of judicial protection of Indian rights. . . . To this day, Congress has never again enacted a statute that withdrew from Indian hands property rights lawfully vested, and every piece of proposed legislation that falls within this description is analyzed today in terms of the Court's opinion in that case."[103] It bears emphasis, however, that *Choate* v. *Trapp* applied only to rights that could be held to have vested. Otherwise, Congress retained power to change or revoke previously made arrangements, including arrangements that called for individual allotments of land.[104] And Congress could and did in other circumstances end the immunity of Indian lands from state taxation.[105]

The breakup of tribal land holdings into individually allotted tracts, exemplified in *Choate* v. *Trapp*, had become the guiding Indian lands policy of the federal government with passage of the General Allotment Act of 1887.[106] The policy originated in mixed motives. An ideological objective to assimilate the Indian to the white man's individualized property system played its role, and it was high-minded, whether right or wrong. But it was also undoubtedly true that the policy of dividing massive tribal holdings into personal ones, and purchasing, and incorporating into the public domain, what was left after personal allotments had been made, suited the movement of railroads and people in the western country.

---

[102] Choate v. Trapp, 224 U.S. 665, 671, 675 (1912); see also Gleason v. Wood, 224 U.S. 679 (1912); English v. Richardson, 224 U.S. 680 (1912); Ward v. Love County, 253 U.S. 17 (1920); Broadwell v. Carter County, 253 U.S. 25 (1920).

[103] F. S. Cohen, "Indian Rights and the Federal Courts," *Minn. L. Rev.*, 24:145, 199, 1940.

[104] See United States v. Roswell, 243 U.S. 464 (1917); Chase, Jr., v. United States, 256 U.S. 1 (1921); Gilpin v. United States, 256 U.S. 10 (1921).

[105] Sweet v. Schock, 245 U.S. 192 (1917); Fink v. County Commissioners, 248 U.S. 399 (1919); see also Hudson v. Hopkins, 75 Okla. 260, 183 P. 507 (1919), *writ of error dismissed for want of jurisdiction*, 256 U.S. 681 (1921). *Cf. supra*, p. 578, n.107.

[106] 24 Stat. 388 (1887).

The effects of the policy were also mixed. The hope had been that it would result in emancipation of the Indian from his status as a ward of the federal government. But owing in part to the enormity of the administrative task, and in part to resistance by Indians attached to their tribal ways, the hope was not soon realized. Indians who did become individual owners, moreover, were often prey to white settlers hungry for their land. Total Indian holdings diminished as the government purchased and distributed to settlers tribal lands that remained after individual allotments had been made. Yet much wealth did come into Indian hands. And Congress guarded against Indians being overreached by white settlers. It did so by forbidding alienation of land allotted to individual Indians for fixed periods of time, which could be either extended or shortened by Congress itself or by administrative action.[107] These restrictions gave rise to a great deal of litigation. For the aggregate pressure on Indians to sell to white settlers was great and, as it came to bear on the individual Indian, very often effective.

Suit would be brought either by an Indian or a white buyer to quiet title which was clouded by a statutory restraint on alienation. Or Indians who had been overborne in a bargain would sue to rescind a transaction or declare it void, on the ground that the Indian had no valid title to pass. *Tiger* v. *Western Investment Co.*[108] established the proposition that Congress had plenary power to extend periods during which alienation of lands allotted to Indians would be restricted, and that nothing in the Due Process Clause limited this power to protect the wards of the United States, even after citizenship had been conferred upon them. In the great majority of cases, the Court construed provisions imposing restraints on alienation broadly, in light of the policy they embodied to protect individual Indians against their own improvidence and against fraud.[109] The Court held further, per Hughes, Lurton dissenting without

---

[107] See Cohen, *Federal Indian Law,* 206–23; Brown, "Indian Problem and the Law," 320–21.

[108] 221 U.S. 286 (1911); see also Williams v. Johnson 239 U.S. 414 (1915); Brader v. James, 246 U.S. 88 (1918).

[109] See Park Rapids Lumber Co. v. United States, 226 U.S. 605 (1913); Starr v. Long Jim, 227 U.S. 613 (1913); Monson v. Simonson, 231 U.S. 341 (1913); Franklin v. Lynch, 233 U.S. 269 (1914); Taylor v. Parker, 235 U.S. 42 (1914); Sage v. Hampe, 235 U.S. 99 (1914); Gannon v. Johnston, 243 U.S. 108 (1917); Sunday v. Mallory, 237 Fed. 526 (8th Cir. 1916), *reversed in part,* 248 U.S. 545 (1919); Kenny v. Miles, 250 U.S. 58 (1919); Parker v. Riley, 250 U.S. 66 (1919); Parker v. Richard, 250 U.S. 235 (1919); Privett v. United States, 256 U.S. 201 (1921); Anchor Oil Co. v. Gray, 256 U.S. 519 (1921). *Cf.* United States v. Bartlett, 235 U.S. 72 (1914); Skelton v. Dill, 235 U.S. 206 (1914); Adkins v. Arnold, 235 U.S. 417 (1914). But *cf.* United States v. First National Bank, 234 U.S. 245 (1914); Henkel v. United States, 237 U.S. 43 (1915).

opinion, in *Heckman* v. *United States*,[110] that the Attorney General of the United States had standing, without specific statutory authorization, to bring suit in behalf of individual Indians to cancel conveyances made by them in violation of statutory restrictions on alienation. The government's interest, said Hughes, while not pecuniary, was an interest in the enforcement of its laws. There were many such suits. *Heckman* itself was one of several hundred. The government, to be sure, did not always win,[111] and its authority to sue at all was not unlimited, standing being denied the Attorney General when he tried to cancel for fraud a deed to land held by an Indian in unrestricted fee simple.[112] But the decision in *Heckman* v. *United States* had great significance, in its own context and beyond.

Its later significance is most plainly foreshadowed by *United States* v. *Osage County*,[113] decided in 1919, and *LaMotte* v. *United States,*[114] decided in 1921. In the *Osage County* case, the Attorney General was permitted to sue in federal court—thus circumventing the more cumbersome remedies afforded to individual plaintiffs under state law— as guardian for Osage Indian allottees, to enjoin state taxation of their lands which was alleged to be arbitrary, excessive, and discriminatory, and imposed in systematic disregard of the state's own laws. State taxation—but of the ordinary, nondiscriminatory sort—was permitted under the applicable federal statute. In the *LaMotte* case, the Attorney General was granted standing, again as guardian of the Osage Indians, and again without specific statutory authorization, in a suit to enjoin assertion of alleged rights by private parties under lawful leases obtained from the Indians, allegedly in violation of applicable restrictions on alienation. During the decade between the decision of *Brown* v. *Board of Education* and passage of Title III of the Civil Rights Act of 1964, the United States, if somewhat hesitantly, had occasion again to assert its inherent authority to invoke the jurisdiction of its own courts to protect other wards of the nation—using the term now, with reference to blacks, in a loose sense, not the technical one in which it was applied to Indians —against both official and private assaults on their federal rights.[115]

---

[110] 224 U.S. 413 (1912); see also Goat v. United States, 224 U.S. 458 (1912); Deming Investment Co. v. United States, 224 U.S. 471 (1912); Bowling v. United States, 223 U.S. 528 (1914); United States v. Noble, 237 U.S. 74 (1915).

[111] See Mullen v. United States, 224 U.S. 448 (1912); United States v. First National Bank, *supra*, n.109; United States v. Bartlett, *supra*, n.109;

Henkel v. United States, *supra*, n.109.

[112] United States v. Waller, 243 U.S. 452 (1917).

[113] 244 U.S. 663 (1917), 251 U.S. 128 (1919).

[114] 254 U.S. 570 (1921).

[115] See, e.g., Simkin v. Moses H. Cone Memorial Hospital, 232 F.2nd 959 (4th Cir. 1963), *cert. denied,* 376 U.S. 938 (1964); United States v. U.S. Klans, 194 F. Supp. 897 (M.D.

Problems of the descent and distribution of Indian lands, mostly as they had been parceled out under allotment statutes, came up in numerous cases. The governing law was federal, but it often referred to tribal custom or to a specific state law adopted for the purpose, and the complications were many.[116] Other complexities abounded, but treaties and statutes commonly placed great reliance in the Bureau of Indian Affairs and the Secretary of the Interior for the resolution of controversies and the filling in of details. The Supreme Court availed itself of the opportunity so offered to limit its own role. It held that findings of fact made by the Secretary and his subordinates were conclusive unless shown to be arbitrary, and that there would be no judicial interference with the exercise by the Secretary of discretion conferred on him in applicable statutes or treaties. Generally, the Court was as supportive of the Secretary's administration of Indian affairs as of any other administrative process in these years, and more supportive than of most.[117] In one or two instances, indeed, the Court went farther than due regard for the integrity of the administrative process would have required.[118]

Congress also not infrequently used the Court of Claims, partly as a court, partly as an administrative agency, to untangle details or clear up contradictions left in the wake of a series of Indian treaties and statutes. Congress would consent to suit against the United States, and give the Court of Claims jurisdiction to straighten out whatever mess had occurred, with a right of appeal to the Supreme Court of the United States. The technique worked well enough,[119] both before and after Congress ran into a notable jurisdictional snag in the well-known case of *Muskrat* v. *United States*.[120] This was an effort by Congress to obtain

---

Ala. 1961); see W. Taylor, "Actions in Equity by the United States to Enforce School Desegregation," *Geo. Wash. L. Rev.*, 29:539, 1961.

[116] See, e.g., Washington v. Miller, 235 U.S. 422 (1914); Blanset v. Cardin, 256 U.S. 319 (1921).

[117] See Jacobs v. Prichard, 223 U.S. 200 (1912); Gritts v. Fisher, 224 U.S. 640 (1912); Ross v. Stewart, 227 U.S. 530 (1913); Knight v. Lane, 228 U.S. 6 (1913); Ross v. Day, 232 U.S. 110 (1914); La Roque v. United States, 239 U.S. 62 (1915); Johnson v. Riddle, 240 U.S. 467 (1916); Lane v. Mickadiet, 241 U.S. 201 (1916); Hill v. Reynolds, 242 U.S. 361 (1917); Harnage v. Martin, 242 U.S. 386

(1917); Wellsville Oil Co. v. Miller, 243 U.S. 6 (1917); Anicker v. Gunsburg, 246 U.S. 110 (1918); United States v. Ferguson, 247 U.S. 175 (1918); Johnson v. Payne, 252 U.S. 209 (1920); United States v. Bowling, 256 U.S. 484 (1921). *Cf.* Lowe v. Fisher, 223 U.S. 95 (1912); Cherokee Nation v. Whitmire, 223 U.S. 108 (1912). But *cf.* United States v. Wildcat, 244 U.S. 111 (1917).

[118] See Brown v. Lane, 232 U.S. 598 (1914); Hallowell v. Commons, 239 U.S. 506 (1916); see also Turner v. Fisher, 222 U.S. 204 (1911).

[119] See, e.g., The Sac and Fox Indians, 220 U.S. 481 (1911).

[120] 219 U.S. 346 (1911).

adjudication in the Court of Claims of, among other issues, the constitutional question that the Court answered a few months later, when it upheld extension by Congress of the duration of restraints on alienation in *Tiger* v. *Western Investment Co.*[121] The jurisdictional act authorizing the *Muskrat* suit, the Court held, amounted to an attempt to obtain an advisory opinion from the Supreme Court, because *Muskrat* did not constitute the sort of case and controversy necessary for invoking the Court's jurisdiction under Article III of the Constitution. Whatever the explanation or justification for the *Muskrat* holding, it stands out as an aberration among the many adjudications of Indian affairs in this period.

Aside from a miscellany of odds and ends,[122] the Court dealt also with a range of specially protected or specially defined positions of Indians under federal law. The largest single category of such cases had to do with the prohibition by Congress, subject to criminal penalties, of the importation of liquor by Indians as well as white men into Indian country—a term that did not refer only to Indian reservations, but covered rather more generally, if somewhat vaguely, areas of Indian settlement. The Court was firm in construing the prohibition liberally, and upholding the constitutional power of Congress to impose it as so construed. The Justices even found it necessary in 1916 explicitly to overrule a decision then a decade old which had taken a somewhat more restrictive view of the power of Congress.[123] The Court's attitude was disinterested and high-minded, but it was based on an unpleasantly patronizing (even if possibly realistic) view of the Indians and their culture. Thus in *United States* v. *Sandoval*, Van Devanter, expert, and frequently called upon to write, on Indian affairs as well as the law of public lands, upheld application of the prohibition against importation of liquor to Indian pueblos in New Mexico, which were not reservations but were held by the Indians in fee simple under Spanish grants confirmed by Congress. These Indians, said Van Devanter, though sedentary and possibly citizens, lived in relative isolation, "adhering to primitive modes of life, largely influenced by superstition and fetishism, and chiefly governed according to the crude customs inherited from their ancestors." They were "essentially a simple, uninformed and inferior people." Van Devanter cited at length reports of Indian agents who had visited the pueblos. These reports showed that the pueblo Indians were "dependent upon the fostering care and protection of the Government, like reservation Indians in general; that, although industrially superior, they are intellectually and morally inferior to many of them; and that they are

---

[121] *Supra*, p. 676, n.108.

[122] See, e.g., Matter of Eastern Cherokees, 220 U.S. 83 (1911); Heirs of Garland v. Choctaw Nation, 256

U.S. 439 (1921).

[123] United States v. Nice, 241 U.S. 591 (1916), *overruling* Matter of Heff, 197 U.S. 488 (1905).

easy victims to the evils and debasing influence of intoxicants." Among their old customs, one agent reported, was a "secret dance, from which all whites are excluded," and which was "perhaps one of the greatest evils. What goes on at this time I will not attempt to say, but I firmly believe that it is little less than a ribald system of debauchery." The information about pueblo customs brought forth by Indian agents "finds strong corroboration," Van Devanter went on, "in the writings of ethnologists, such as Bandelier and Stevenson, who, in prosecuting their work, have lived among the pueblos and closely observed them." Indian communities of this sort had long been subjected to guardianship and protection by the United States. There was no explicit constitutional authority for this practice, except as Congress was authorized to regulate commerce with the Indian tribes, but it was a long-continued and judicially sanctioned legislative and executive usage. The power had been implied because it had to exist somewhere, and had never existed anywhere but in the federal government. The only qualification was this: it was not intended "that Congress may bring a community or body of people within the range of this power by arbitrarily calling them an Indian tribe, but only that in respect of distinctly Indian communities the question whether, to what extent, and for what time they shall be recognized and dealt with as dependent tribes requiring the guardianship and protection of the United States are to be determined by Congress, and not by the Courts."[124]

Think of it what one will, and it is easy enough to be repelled by Van Devanter's tone, *United States* v. *Sandoval* is in method a Brandeisian opinion, demonstrating the attractiveness of Brandeis' method to any judge, no matter what his general outlook, when the subject of the legislative regulation he dealt with was one of which he had had experience.

Other special positions of the Indian under federal law which manifested themselves in Supreme Court litigation[125] included the establishment of federal jurisdiction (exclusive of that of the states) in cases of major crimes, such as murder, committed on an Indian reservation by or against an Indian;[126] exemption of Indians from laws incompatible

---

[124] United States v. Sandoval, 231 U.S. 28, 39, 41, 42, 44, 46 (1913). See also Hallowell v. United States, 221 U.S. 317 (1911); *Ex parte* Webb, 225 U.S. 663 (1912); United States v. Wright, 229 U.S. 226 (1913); Perrin v. United States, 232 U.S. 478 (1914); Pronovost v. United States, 232 U.S. 487 (1914); Johnson v. Gearlds, 234 U.S. 422 (1914); Joplin Mercantile Co. v. United States, 236 U.S. 531 (1915); United States v. Soldana, 246 U.S. 530 (1918).

[125] See also *supra,* pp. 577–78.

[126] See Donnelly v. United States, 228 U.S. 243, 708 (1913); United States v. Pelican, 232 U.S. 442 (1914); Apapas v. United States, 233 U.S. 587 (1914); Louie v. United States, 254 U.S. 548 (1921); Hendrix v. United States, 219 U.S. 79 (1911).

with their customs, such as the penal law forbidding adultery;[127] the applicability of tribal custom, not the civil law, to Indian marriages;[128] protection by special federal laws of Indian property and of Indians in their commercial relations with non-Indians;[129] and exemption of inalienable Indian land from liability for satisfaction of a tort judgment.[130]

Claims Against the United States and Government Contracts

A heavy flow of heavily trivial cases, augmented by World War I and destined to be stemmed only by the jurisdictional reform of 1925, brought to the Supreme Court monetary claims against and by the United States, and issues concerning contracts with the United States. The great bulk of these cases arose under the Court of Claims Act of 1863[131] and the Tucker Act of 1887.[132] Both statutes provided for appeals as of right to the Supreme Court.[133]

The Court's burden was only slightly alleviated by reliance on fact findings made in the Court of Claims, which were held to be conclusive,[134] but were not always as helpful as they might be,[135] and by an occasional decision vesting broad discretion in administrative officers. The most notable of the latter was *The Mail Divisor Cases*,[136] in which Holmes, in a plurality opinion for himself, White, Brandeis, and Clarke, in effect upheld discretionary authority in the Postmaster General to change the compensation awarded to railroads for carrying the mail.[137]

---

[127] See United States v. Quiver, 241 U.S. 602 (1916); *cf.* Southern Surety Co. v. Oklahoma, 241 U.S. 582 (1916).

[128] See Carney v. Chapman, 247 U.S. 102 (1918); *cf.* Thomas v. Thomas, 220 U.S. 607 (1911).

[129] See United States v. Anderson, 228 U.S. 52 (1913); Ash Sheep Co. v. United States, 252 U.S. 159 (1920); Tinker v. Midland Valley Co., 231 U.S. 681 (1914). See also Turner v. United States, 248 U.S. 354 (1919); United States v. Hutto, 256 U.S. 524, 530 (1921). But *cf.* Kennedy v. Becker, 241 U.S. 556 (1916).

[130] See Mullen v. Simmons, 234 U.S. 192 (1914).

[131] 12 Stat. 765 (1863), as amended in 1866, 14 Stat. 9 (1866); see Gordon v. United States, 2 Wall. 561 (1864); Thurston v. United States, 232 U.S. 469 (1914).

[132] 24 Stat. 505 (1887).

[133] *Cf.* Frankfurter and Landis, *Business of the Supreme Court,* 110–12.

[134] See Cramp v. United States, 239 U.S. 221 (1915).

[135] See Ripley v. United States, 220 U.S. 491, 222 U.S. 144 (1911); United States v. Archer, 241 U.S. 119 (1916), *after remand, affirmed by an equally divided Court,* 251 U.S. 548 (1920).

[136] 251 U.S. 326 (1920).

[137] For other cases upholding the exercise of administrative discretion, see also Smith v. Hitchcock, 226 U.S. 53 (1912); Plumley v. United States, 226 U.S. 545 (1913); United States v. Ross, 239 U.S. 530 (1916); United States v. Babcock, 250 U.S. 328 (1919); *cf.* Degge v. Hitchcock, 229 U.S. 162 (1913); Reaves v. Ainsworth, 219 U.S. 296 (1911). But *cf.*

But other controversies concerning the rates at which railroads and others serviced the mail and carried United States military personnel and equipment were plentiful.[138] The flow of cases included also military pay controversies,[139] and disputes over government building, dredging, and other contracts, over subcontractors' and materialmen's claims, and over the obligations of sureties on contractors' bonds,[140] not to speak of a miscellany of yet additional litigation.[141]

A miscellaneous claim to recover one or another small amount of money from the government, trivial as measured against the central function of the "one supreme Court" created by Article III of the Constitution, is neither trivial, of course, nor miscellaneous in the eyes of the claimant. And it deserves full and careful adjudication. It is, after all, a claim to justice. The Supreme Court, one might suppose, would have difficulty summoning the attention and care called for in the adjudication of such claims, trivial or no, and that would be one reason why mandatory appellate jurisdiction over these cases should not be lodged in the Supreme Court. Another reason would be that, far from treating such cases as trivial, the Court might give them full and painstaking consideration—and that would have to be regarded as a misallocation of the nation's judicial resources. Time, effort, and serious attention were, in truth, lavished on cases of this sort. One particularly well-documented example is *Burnap* v. *United States.*[142]

Title Guaranty and Trust Co. v. Crane Co., 219 U.S. 24 (1910); United States v. O'Brien, 220 U.S. 321 (1911); Cochnower v. United States, 248 U.S. 405, 249 U.S. 588 (1919).

[138] See, e.g., Huse v. United States, 222 U.S. 496 (1912); Grand Trunk Western Ry. v. United States, 252 U.S. 112 (1920). In Grand Trunk Western Ry. v. United States, holding for the government, Brandeis, who was not prone to attacks of sentiment, was moved to remark that the case was "one of apparent hardship." 252 U.S. at 120. The decision was unanimous. The Chief Justice, however, had returned: "It is admirably well done. But the case is indeed a hard one." McReynolds had noted: "I suppose it must be, but it should not." And McKenna, with candor, but giving indication that he was failing in these, his last years: "This is well reasoned and seems conclusive, but

I have never understood the case so I reserve opinion." Brandeis Papers, Harvard Law School Library.

[139] See Wood v. United States, 224 U.S. 132 (1912); Plummer v. United States, 224 U.S. 137 (1912); McLean v. United States, 226 U.S. 374 (1912); Hannum v. United States, 226 U.S. 436 (1913); United States v. Mason, 227 U.S. 486 (1913); Morse v. United States, 229 U.S. 208 (1913); Pennington v. United States, 231 U.S. 631 (1914); United States v. Vulte, 233 U.S. 509 (1914); Dwight v. United States, 239 U.S. 608 (1916); United States v. Andrews, 240 U.S. 90 (1916).

[140] In 1910–20, more than fifty such cases were decided.

[141] See, e.g., Herrera v. United States, 222 U.S. 558 (1912); Seaboard Air Line Ry. v. United States, 256 U.S. 655 (1921).

[142] 252 U.S. 512 (1920).

VII: *Federal Administration and the Federal Specialties*

In 1910, the Secretary of War appointed Burnap to a position as landscape architect in the Office of Public Buildings and Grounds at a salary of $2,400 a year. Five years later, Burnap was suspended, some charges having been filed against him, and in August 1916, he was discharged. Burnap contended that the suspension and discharge were illegal, and brought suit in the Court of Claims for back salary. His argument was that since he had been appointed by the Secretary of War, only the Secretary could remove him, whereas he was in fact removed by the Chief of Engineers acting as head of the Office of Public Buildings and Grounds. The Court of Claims held against Burnap, and the Supreme Court, in a unanimous opinion by Brandeis, affirmed. The opinion ran to some seven pages. Brandeis reviewed numerous statutes, cases, and opinions of the Attorney General dealing with the power to appoint and remove civil servants. He concluded that it had been error for Burnap to be appointed by the Secretary of War. Appointments to the position of landscape architect should properly be made by the Chief of Engineers. The Chief of Engineers would therefore have had full power to remove Burnap if he had appointed him. The fact that the appointment had inadvertently been made by the Secretary of War did not materially alter the situation, Brandeis held, because the defect was cured by the acquiescence of the Chief of Engineers in the appointment over a period of years, which amounted to a ratification of it. Since the Court was not being asked to review the discharge as having been made without adequate cause, but merely to decide whether the proper officer had made it, that was an end of the matter.

But the end was not lightly arrived at. Brandeis' opinion had gone through several drafts. Moreover, Brandeis and his law clerk, Dean Acheson, looked beyond the record for relevant materials which could appropriately be relied on within the Court's judicial notice. Thus Brandeis' file in the case contains a carbon copy of a typewritten opinion dated September 27, 1916, by W. W. Warwick, the Comptroller of the Treasury, who reviewed and approved the War Department action in discharging Burnap. Not only that, but there is a memorandum by Acheson indicating that he had asked the Chief of Engineers to make a thorough search for any regulations that might affect the conduct of the Office of Public Buildings and Grounds. The search failed to reveal anything new. A copy of the published regulations applicable to the Chief of Engineers is in the file. Acheson also interviewed Mr. Warwick and made a memorandum of his conversation with him for Brandeis. It was quite favorable to Burnap's cause, but plainly dealt with facts of which it would not have been appropriate to take judicial note. Warwick told Acheson that his personal opinion, despite the legal opinion he had given officially, was that Burnap was in the right. Burnap's immediate superior, at whose behest he was discharged, was an officer of somewhat ill repute. At the time the case was being decided in the Supreme Court, this officer was appearing before a Congressional committee, having been charged with brutal treatment of soldiers while provost marshal of Paris during the war. Warwick had also somewhat changed his mind on the law. He now believed that it would be salutary to hold that the error in making the appointment through the Secretary of War was decisive in Burnap's favor. Overcentralization of the appointment function in the heads of departments was on the increase, Acheson reported Warwick as saying, and it was undesirable—a thought, Acheson might rightly have believed, that Brandeis would find congenial. But Brandeis, unsentimental as ever, and intent only on the legal issue and on materials relevant to it, was unmoved. Yet he made this notation on Acheson's memorandum: "To be preserved carefully in file." It was.

Other Justices did not let the decision slip by in reliance on Brandeis' opinion. Both Pitney and Holmes questioned the categorical statement that the original appointment by the Secretary of War rather than the Chief of Engineers was without authority of law. Brandeis was sure of it, however, and it stayed in the opinion. Clarke said he was approving "on trust," and even Holmes remarked: "This has your usual thoroughness and I presume is right." But such expressions of modesty and deference to the writer of the opinion were common in all manner of cases. The fact is that claims against the government, however trivial in the larger view, were not treated as trivial, and often made no less demand on the energies of the Justices than important causes.[143]

Another illustration, as striking in its way as the *Burnap* case, and demonstrating, not only Brandeis' unsentimental meticulousness, but the pains taken by the Court as a whole, was *Tempel* v. *United States*.[144]

Tempel was a suit for compensation for submerged land in the Chicago River owned by the plaintiff, which the United States had dredged in order to improve navigation in the harbor of Chicago. The lower court held for the government on the ground that the owner having for long failed to complain of the use by the public of the stream in front of his property for navigation, he could not now claim any rights in the submerged land over which this navigable stream flowed. The case was argued in the Supreme Court in November 1917, and the indications are that the decision was to affirm the judgment for the government. But in March 1918, Pitney, who had evidently shared the majority, or as it likely was, the unanimous view, circulated a memorandum saying that while he could accept part of the lower court's reasoning, he did not agree that the government owed no compensation

---

[143] Brandeis Papers, Harvard Law School Library. [144] 248 U.S. 121 (1918).

at all. Hence he thought there ought to be a reversal. There followed, undoubtedly, further discussion at conference, with the result that the case was held over to the following term, and, if it had been Pitney's to begin with, reassigned to Brandeis.

In October 1918, Brandeis circulated in memorandum form a slightly longer version of the opinion that now appears in the Reports. The government had no reason to believe it was dredging land to which the plaintiff asserted ownership. Therefore, Brandeis held, on the face of the pleadings and on the basis of uncontroverted facts, a contractual obligation on the part of the government to compensate the owner of the dredged land could not be implied. But the Tucker Act, under which this suit was brought, waived sovereign immunity and consented to a suit such as this against the United States only "upon any contract, express or implied." Hence the suit should have been dismissed for lack of jurisdiction.

Pitney replied in a long memorandum, which drew an eight-page rejoinder from Brandeis in November 1918. Whatever the plaintiff's omissions to make timely claims, and whatever the government's mis-apprehensions, the plaintiff did own the dredged land, and Pitney thought it "inconsistent with the honor and dignity of the United States as with the principles of justice and equity to refuse compensation. . . ." Brandeis replied: "It is for Congress, not for this court, to determine in what cases honor and dignity or justice and equity require that the United States submit to being sued." Congress had consented to suits founded on contract, but not generally to suits for torts (and would not for nearly forty years more).[145] "If we were at liberty to discuss the question of justice," Brandeis went on, however, "others might reasonably believe that the Government should not be compelled to pay for an innocent invasion of the petitioner's land; since it was misled into making important expenditures for dredging thereon, because of petitioner's failure, extending over many years, to look after his property. . . . For aught that appears the Government might and would (had it been apprised of the situation) have narrowed the dredged channel or have dredged further out in the stream, thereby avoiding the invasion of any possible private property right. But, however great the hardship to petitioner, relief under the Tucker Act must be denied."

Mincing no words, Brandeis had started his memorandum by saying that he had considered Pitney's, and had not found in it "reference to any fact, argument, or case which had not been considered by me." He now proceeded in detail to deal with Pitney's facts, arguments, and

---

[145] See Act of August 2, 1946, 60 Stat. 812, 842 (1946).

cases.[146] And he apparently persuaded all, perhaps even Pitney, for his opinion came down without dissent. But then, as Brandeis had discovered the previous year, in connection with the workmen's compensation cases, Pitney could come around upon study, and did not stick to earlier conclusions out of vanity.[147] Brandeis gave no quarter in argument, nor did he embellish his points with little courtesies to soothe his opponent. Such a memorandum as he wrote in *Tempel* in reply to Pitney would have hurt his cause with a man given to vanity of opinion.

A limited number of cases involving claims against the government were decided on constitutional grounds. These were cases of taking of property by the United States for which just compensation was alleged to be owing under the Fifth Amendment, and a couple in which statutory provisions restricting the fees recoverable by attorneys who litigated claims were challenged under the Due Process Clause.

In *United States* v. *Grizzard*,[148] the government took a strip of privately owned farmland and flooded it for purposes of building a dam. The Court allowed compensation not only for the land taken, but also for the decrease in value of adjoining land, itself not taken, resulting from loss of the owner's access to a road that led to outbuildings and the like. But in other cases of alleged takings, the Court was more niggardly. Thus in *Peabody* v. *United States*,[149] the government installed an artillery battery in Maine, positioned to defend Portsmouth, not far from a summer resort hotel. Prospective customers of the hotel thought that it would be within the practice firing range. In fact, it was not. Shells had been fired over the land of the hotel only twice in over ten years. Yet the location of the battery did ruin the business of the hotel. Nonetheless, a unanimous Court, per Hughes, held that there had been no taking, and that no compensation was due. Six years later, after some additional, but still not persistent, firing over the grounds of the hotel, the Court, declining to reconsider this decision, still found no taking.[150]

The attorneys' fees problem had its origin in the Omnibus Claims Act of 1915,[151] which appropriated money for the payment of over a thousand claims arising out of the Civil War. For some decades, these

---

[146] Brandeis Papers, Harvard Law School Library.

[147] See *supra,* p. 585.

[148] 219 U.S. 180 (1911); see also United States v. Heyward, 52 Ct. of Cl. 87 (1917), *affirmed by an equally divided Court,* 250 U.S. 633 (1919); United States v. Wayne County, 53 Ct. of Cl. 417 (1918), *affirmed,* 252 U.S. 574 (1920).

[149] 231 U.S. 530 (1913); and see Bothwell v. United States, 254 U.S. 231 (1920); Great Western Serum Co. v. United States, 254 U.S. 240 (1920); United States v. North American Co., 253 U.S. 330 (1920).

[150] Portsmouth Harbour Land & Hotel Co. v. United States, 250 U.S. 1 (1919).

[151] 38 Stat. 962 (1915).

claims had been referred by Congress to the Court of Claims for advisory opinions (rendered by that court in its capacity as a legislative court, and not reviewable by the Supreme Court), and now Congress was making payment on claims on which the court had recommended favorably. Section 4 of the Act provided that no more than 20 percent of the monies appropriated to satisfy any of the claims covered by the Act could be paid to any agent or attorney for services rendered in connection with a claim. In addition, it was made unlawful—a misdemeanor punishable by a $1,000 fine—for any agent or attorney to exact or receive any sum which in the aggregate exceeded 20 percent of the amount of recovery on a claim, "any contract to the contrary notwithstanding."

In *Capital Trust Co.* v. *Calhoun*,[152] decided in June 1919, McKenna held these provisions of Section 4 of the Act constitutional as applied to prevent recovery by an attorney of more than 20 percent of the monies paid by the United States in satisfaction of a claim. By way of a dictum, however, McKenna remarked that if a demand for a fee in excess of 20 percent of the amount of recovery were made, not against money appropriated by Congress, but against other assets of the claimant, the limitation embodied in Section 4 would not apply. The decision was unanimous, although Holmes concurred in the result without opinion, and McReynolds took no part.

Less than a year later, McKenna's dictum was called into question in *Calhoun* v. *Massie*.[153] In this case, Calhoun, the attorney, accepted payment of his maximum 20 percent out of the money appropriated by Congress and paid out by the Treasury on Massie's claim. But he then sued Massie in a state court, seeking to recover an amount equal to an additional 30 percent of the recovery, pursuant to a preexisting contract between him and Massie, under which he was entitled to a fee of 50 percent of any payment on Massie's claim. In an opinion that spoke for a bare majority of five, Brandeis held Section 4 applicable so as to foreclose recovery by Calhoun, and constitutional as applied. Congress, he said, in this and in earlier statutes, had "manifested its belief that the causes which gave rise to laws against champerty and maintenance are persistent." Congress had ample power to act on such a belief. Neither the Fifth Amendment nor the Contract Clause stood in the way. Brandeis made no mention of the dictum in *Capital Trust Co.* v. *Calhoun*. Rather he ended with two somewhat makeweight arguments. There were "special reasons" in this case, he said, why Calhoun's prior contract with Massie "cannot prevail over the statute enacted later." It was clear

---

[152] 250 U.S. 208 (1919).   [153] 253 U.S. 170, 174, 176, 177, 179, 180 (1920).

at the time the contract was made that payment of Massie's claim could eventually come only under a statute, and enough prior limitations on attorney's fees had been enacted by Congress for Calhoun to have been on notice that a limitation on his fee was possible in this instance also. An expectation that the contract might be overriden could, therefore, be imputed to Calhoun. Secondly, Calhoun had accepted payment directly from the Treasury of his maximum 20 percent fee. He thus received payment under the very Act which prohibited the payment of any further fee. "Calhoun cannot take under the act and repudiate its provisions."

In his return to Brandeis' circulation of this opinion, Holmes marked these passages: "Hm!?" In the margin Holmes wrote: "I think Congress could do as it damn chose in regulating compensation of lawyers in C. Cl. for past as well as future cases. I think the passages above are fishy, but if they make this result easy to swallow I close my potato trap."[154] These passages were not let off so easily, however, in an extremely sharp dissent by McReynolds, concurred in by McKenna, Van Devanter, and Pitney, in which the knowing, at least, could detect public ventilation of McReynolds' private animus against Brandeis, and of his view, not untinged with anti-Semitism, that Brandeis was un-ethically crafty. In two paragraphs under the heading "As to certain 'special reasons why the contract cannot prevail over the statute enacted later'"—which was Brandeis' language in introducing these passages— McReynolds said that to impute to Calhoun the expectation that his contract with Massie might be overridden by a later statute and to hold him barred from recovery on this ground was to assume Brandeis' own construction of Section 4, which McReynolds contested, and to assume that as so construed Section 4 was constitutional. "If these two assumptions are correct," McReynolds rather tellingly went on, "of course there is no right to recover. This special reason can only serve to mislead." Again, to say that because Calhoun received 20 percent under the Omnibus Claim Statute he could not repudiate the provisions which barred recovery of anything more was to assume Brandeis' construction of the Act and its constitutionality as such. "If these assumptions are correct no further discussion is needed. This special reason lacks substance and can serve no good purpose." Brandeis' opinion, McReynolds wrote further, ran squarely counter to the dictum of the previous year in *Capital Trust Co.* v. *Calhoun*. Brandeis now held this dictum to be "obviously erroneous" without so much as mentioning it. "The result is necessarily injurious both to the court and the public." The dictum

---

[154] Brandeis Papers, Harvard Law School Library.

in *Capital Trust Co.* v. *Calhoun* accorded with the command of the Fifth Amendment, McReynolds insisted, and should have been decisive in this case.[155]

Patents, Copyright, Trademarks, Unfair Competition, Tying, and Price Maintenance

Patents constitute the most technical, and often a downright impenetrable, "federal specialty."[156] The ordinary patent case is a suit by the holder of a patent against an alleged infringer to enjoin him from infringing and require him to account for profits made by infringing. With the creation of the Circuit Courts of Appeals in 1891,[157] such cases could no longer be brought to the Supreme Court as of right, but only on certiorari.[158] The reform came just in time, as the industrial growth of the country led to an enormous increase in the number of patents issued after 1870.[159] Certiorari was, on occasion, granted for reasons not readily apparent.[160] But most often, cases were taken because of a conflict between circuits, a patent having been held valid in one circuit and invalid in another.[161] Aside from the usual infringement suit, direct

---

[155] A comparison case, Newman v. Moyers, 253 U.S. 182 (1920), raised no substantive difficulties, calling simply for application of the holding in *Capital Trust Co.* v. *Calhoun.* The opinion was therefore assigned to McKenna, the author of *Capital Trust Co.* v. *Calhoun.* But the case was entangled in some procedural difficulties, which, when he circulated an opinion, it became evident McKenna did not understand and had failed to unravel. Brandeis thereupon circulated a memorandum to the Court dealing with the procedural problem. This memorandum then became the opinion of the Court, all Justices going along, including McKenna. Brandeis Papers, Harvard Law School Library.

[156] See Frankfurter and Landis, *Business of the Supreme Court,* 175.

[157] 26 Stat. 826 (1891).

[158] See Chott v. Ewing, 237 U.S. 197 (1915) (and see United States *ex rel.* Chott v. Ewing, 40 App. D.C. 591 [1913], *cert. denied,* 238 U.S. 630

[1915]); *cf.* New Marshall Co. v. Marshall Engine Co., 223 U.S. 473 (1912); Briggs v. United Shoe Co., 239 U.S. 48 (1915); American Well Works Co. v. Layne, 241 U.S. 257 (1916); Odell v. Farnsworth Co., 250 U.S. 501 (1919).

[159] Frankfurter and Landis, *Business of the Supreme Court,* 176.

[160] See Minerals Separation, Ltd. v. Hyde, 242 U.S. 261 (1916) (and see Minerals Separation, Ltd. v. Butte & Superior Mining Co., 250 U.S. 336 [1919]); Goshen Manufacturing Co. v. Myers Manufacturing Co., 242 U.S. 202 (1916); Railroad Supply Co. v. Elyria Iron Co., 244 U.S. 285 (1917); Werk v. Parker, 249 U.S. 130 (1919).

[161] See Fireball Gas Co. v. Commercial Acetylene Co., 239 U.S. 156 (1915); Abercrombie & Fitch Co. v. Baldwin, 245 U.S. 198 (1917); Grinnel Washing Machine Co. v. E. E. Johnson Co., 247 U.S. 426 (1918); Symington Co. v. National Castings Co., 250 U.S. 383 (1919); Bone v. Marrion County, 251 U.S. 134 (1919);

review of actions of the Commissioner of Patents in passing on applications was possible, mostly in the Court of Appeals for the District of Columbia, but it was relatively rare, partly, no doubt, because the Commissioner's discretion was in the vast majority of cases upheld. Such cases almost never reached the Supreme Court.[162]

Sometimes the Court would miss a direct conflict between circuits.[163] The problem was a serious one. Conflicts could lead to awful tangles.[164] *Res judicata* could help where possible,[165] but other devices short of ultimate decision in the Supreme Court were few.[166] Yet the Court managed to keep the volume of patent cases it accepted within severe limits, despite the very great mass of certiorari, which themselves constituted a not inconsiderable burden.[167] For with rare exceptions, nothing but unique factual issues were raised.

The only case concerning patentability decided by the Supreme Court during the White Chief Justiceship that was of any enduring doctrinal significance was *Diamond Rubber Co. v. Consolidated Tire Co.*[168] This was an opinion by McKenna, the Court's leading specialist on the subject, to whom, along with Clarke, the bulk of these cases was assigned. The patent in *Diamond Rubber* was for the first rubber tire not cemented to the wheel, but inserted in a rim. McKenna showed

---

Meccano, Ltd. v. John Wanamaker, 253 U.S. 136 (1920) (and see *ibid.,* 249 U.S. 594 [1919]; 250 U.S. 647 [1919]); New York Scaffolding Co. v. Liebel-Binney Co., 254 U.S. 23 (1920); New York Scaffolding Co. v. Chain Belt Co., 254 U.S. 32 (1920).

[162] Review was denied in more than a dozen such cases.

[163] *Compare* Telefunken Wireless Telegraph Co. v. National Electric Signalling Co., 208 Fed. 679 (3rd Cir. 1913), *cert. denied,* 234 U.S. 760 (1914), *with* Kintner v. Atlantic Communication Co., 240 Fed. 716 (2nd Cir. 1917) (Hough, J., at 240 Fed. 721: the evidence "renders the result reached in 208 Fed. impossible, by the reasoning there used"), *cert. denied,* 244 U.S. 661 (1917).

[164] See Rubber Tire Co. v. Goodyear Co., 223 U.S. 724 (1911), 232 U.S. 413 (1914); Seim v. Hurd, 232 U.S. 420 (1914); Woodward Co. v. Hurd, 232 U.S. 428 (1914); *cf.* Diamond Rubber Co. v. Consolidated

Tire Co., *infra,* n.168; and see B. F. Goodrich Rubber Co. v. Consolidated Tire Co., 251 Fed. 617 (7th Cir. 1918), *cert. denied,* 247 U.S. 519 (1918); Republic Rubber Co. v. Consolidated Tire Co., 251 Fed. 625 (7th Cir. 1918), *cert. denied,* 247 U.S. 519 (1918).

[165] See Hart Steel Co. v. Railroad Supply Co., 244 U.S. 294 (1917); Marshall v. Bryant Electric Co., 185 Fed. 499 (1st Cir. 1911), *cert. denied,* 220 U.S. 622 (1911).

[166] See National Brake Co. v. Christensen, 229 Fed. 564 (7th Cir. 1915), *cert. denied,* 241 U.S. 659 (1916); *ibid.,* 254 U.S. 425 (1921).

[167] In cases where patents had been held valid and infringed, review was denied in more than fifty. In cases where patents had been held valid, review was denied in thirty-five. In cases construing patents narrowly and holding them not infringed, review was denied in twenty-one.

[168] 220 U.S. 428, 437 (1911).

himself rather indulgent on the question of invention when judged against the background of the prior art, and on the issue of the utility of the invention. ("His success," he said of the inventor, "is his title to consideration.") But no general conclusions are to be drawn from McKenna's attitude in this case. Statistically, on a fairly narrow base, to be sure, the Court appeared neither friendly nor unfriendly to patent claims. The same judgment can be made about the lower federal courts, resting on the broader statistical base of the cases in which certiorari was denied.[169]

On the question of the measure of damages owing to the patent holder from an infringer, which produced a much lower volume of petitions for certiorari than the issue of patentability,[170] the Court made an important new departure in *Westinghouse Electric Co.* v. *Wagner Electric Co.*[171] Where an infringer's profits are attributable both to the patent he infringed and to noninfringing improvements made by him, and efforts by the patent holder to arrive at an apportionment of the commingled profits prove fruitless, the burden of proof on the issue of damages, the Court held, should shift to the infringer. If the infringer is unable to segregate the profits attributable to his noninfringing improvement, he must pay over his entire profits. The rule had been, and in general remained, that the patent holder had the burden of proof. But application of that rule might result in the award of merely nominal damages where the patent holder could not prove which profits in a commingled mass were directly attributable to the infringement; and such a result would be unjust. Hence the rule was modified.

Aside from a decision about the effect of an international agreement on the duration of patents registered in more than one country,[172] the only additional patent cases the Court had to deal with concerned the problem, brought especially to the fore by military procurement activity during World War I, of use and infringement by the government and its contractors.[173]

Copyright cases—which like patent litigation originate in the provision of Article I, Section 8, of the Constitution empowering Congress to "promote the Progress of Science and useful Arts, by securing for limited Times to Authors and Inventors the exclusive Right to

---

[169] See *supra*, n.167.

[170] Review was denied in thirteen such cases.

[171] 225 U.S. 604 (1912), 233 Fed. 752 (8th Cir. 1916), *cert. denied*, 242 U.S. 640 (1916); see also Dowagiac Manufacturing Co. v. Minnesota Plow Co., 235 U.S. 641 (1915). See G. P.

Dike, "The Trial of Patent Accountings in Open Court," *Harv. L. Rev.*, 36:33, 1922. See *supra*, p. 364.

[172] Cameron Septic Tank Co. v. Knoxville, 227 U.S. 39 (1913).

[173] See K. Fenning, "Patent Infringement by the Government," *Yale L. J.*, 37:773, 776, 1928.

their respective Writings and Discoveries"—were fewer than patent cases, so many fewer that one is tempted to draw conclusions about the relative progress of "Authors and Inventors." Still, two or three decisions were notable, making for a higher proportion of signficant copyright than patent cases. In *Kalem* v. *Harper Brothers*,[174] Holmes held that the producer of a silent movie based on the novel *Ben Hur* had infringed the author's copyright. A movie, said Holmes, is a "dramatization" within the terms of the Copyright Act.[175] *Ferris* v. *Frohman*[176] was a suit by Charles Frohman, the New York producer, who bought the rights to a British play, but omitted to copyright it, and then found Ferris, a rival producer, stealing a march on him by pirating the play, copyrighting his version, and having it performed. Frohman sued at common law in a state court to vindicate his and the author's property rights in the play, on the theory that it was unpublished, and therefore neither copyrightable nor in the public domain. Ferris' defense was that his copyright was valid. Frohman won below, and the Supreme Court, per Hughes, affirmed. The play had been previously performed, but a visual or auditory performance of a work, Hughes held, was not publication. It did not divest a work of its common law protection as the property of its author, nor did it constitute the sort of publication which was a prerequisite to protection under the Copyright Act.[177] Finally, *Herbert* v. *Shanley Co.*[178] was a decision, again by Holmes, that performance of a copyrighted musical composition in a restaurant, without charging admission, but as an incident of serving dinner to the public, infringed the exclusive right of the owner of the copyright to perform the work publicly for profit.

There were only a few additional and less notable copyright cases,[179] including a dismissal of an appeal per stipulation in a controversy over commercial publication of the Reports of the Court itself,[180]

---

[174] 222 U.S. 55 (1911); *cf.* Manners v. Morosco, 252 U.S. 317 (1920); Street & Smith v. Atlas Manufacturing Co., 204 Fed. 398 (8th Cir. 1913), *appeal dismissed,* 231 U.S. 348 (1913), *cert. denied,* 231 U.S. 755 (1913), 232 U.S. 724 (1914).

[175] See B. Kaplan, *An Unhurried View of Copyright* (1967), 35–36.

[176] 233 U.S. 424 (1912).

[177] See B. Kaplan, "Publication in Copyright Law: "The Question of Phonograph Records," *U. Pa. L. Rev.,* 103:469, 474–75, 1955.

[178] 242 U.S. 591 (1917).

[179] See Hills & Co. v. Hoover, 220 U.S. 329 (1911); American Lithographic Co. v. Werckmeister, 221 U.S. 603 (1911); Westermann Co. v. Dispatch Co., 249 U.S. 100 (1919); DeJonge v. Breuker & Kessler, 235 U.S. 33 (1914).

[180] Banks Law Publishing Co. v. Lawyers' Cooperative Publishing Co., 169 Fed. 386 (2nd Cir. 1909), *appeal dismissed per stipulation,* 223 U.S. 738 (1911).

which aborted a decision that might have provided a sequel to *Wheaton v. Peters*.[181]

Trademark and unfair competition cases constituted a greater volume of business than copyright, though not as great as patent cases. Trademarks are a federal specialty because of statutes providing for their registration, which Congress has enacted under its power to regulate interstate commerce. But trademark protection stems from the common law, and it was common law doctrine that the Court elaborated and developed in trademark cases. The law of trademarks, moreover, is closely allied to the common law tort of unfair competition or palming off, which could independently give rise to a cause of action in the federal courts only in the diversity jurisdiction, but which not infrequently did so, and was in any event often alleged together with claims of trademark infringement.

Although not, like patents, the field of expertise of any Justice in particular, trademarks and unfair competition, perhaps because of their high common law content, were a subject on which Holmes wrote with some frequency and some relish. Thus in *Jacobs v. Beecham*,[182] Holmes took to task a "modern advertiser," as he called him, who had palmed off a product of his own as Beecham's Pills, and attempted to justify his conduct by claiming that he had guessed and reproduced Beecham's secret formula.[183] *Straus v. Notaseme Co.*[184] involved the use by Macy's of a design that the Notaseme Company had previously employed to identify its own product. Holmes held that Macy's should be enjoined. But there had been no intent to deceive. The duplication was unwitting on Macy's part, a result perhaps, Holmes suggested, of "the poverty of the designer's invention." Hence no damages were to be awarded. In *Coca-Cola Co. v. Koke Co.*,[185] Holmes enjoined use of the term "Koke" as in infringement on the Coca-Cola mark. But he declined to enjoin the use of the word "dope." That word, wrote Holmes, was "one of the most featureless known even to the language of those who are incapable of discriminating speech." In some places it might be used to ask for a Coca-Cola. It might equally be used to ask for almost anything. But to imitate the word "Coke" was to perpetrate a deception.

---

[181] 8 Pet. 591 (1834).

[182] 221 U.S. 263, 272 (1911).

[183] "Yes," Van Devanter returned, "but with the remark in passing that it is in more of a partisan vein than I have ever noticed in your writing." Holmes Papers, Harvard Law School Library.

[184] 240 U.S. 179, 181 (1916).

[185] 254 U.S. 143, 147 (1920); see also Gay-Ola Co. v. Coca-Cola Co., 200 Fed. 720 (6th Cir. 1912), *cert. denied*, 229 U.S. 613 (1913); Old Dominion Beverage Corp. v. Coca-Cola Co., 256 U.S. 703 (1921).

Holmes ended the *Coca-Cola* opinion with the following sentence: "The product including the coloring matter is free to all who can make it if no extrinsic deceiving element is present." This remark stifled a doubt, which Holmes noted on the draft of the opinion he circulated to the Court, saying that it was "probably best passed in silence, but as it is gnawing away at the bottom of my opinion I state it." Judging by his own familiarity with the name Coca-Cola, Holmes noted, "and ignorance of and indifference to the question who made it, I think it probable that the public generally are in the same condition. The product of course is free to all who can compound it or anything like it, and I hesitate to create a rather fishy monopoly with no limit of time. On the other hand, we have the agreement of two courts and the registration of the mark. I should be glad if I could hear from the Brethren in time to embody the majority view." On his own copy of the opinion, Holmes added in longhand: "I find the same doubt present in other cases [of which there were a number, decided in lower courts] when the plaintiff succeeded." Day made light of Holmes' difficulty: "The doubt suggested at the foot of your opinion," he wrote him, "should not hinder, as I view it, the granting of a decree. Forget it." Holmes did.[186]

In *Hanover Milling Co.* v. *Metcalf*,[187] dealing with the difficult question of the territorial coverage of a trademark, in which Pitney spoke for the Court, Holmes wrote a concurring opinion urging that trademarks valid under the law of a state be valid throughout it, without regard to market definitions, and achieve validity in other states only under the law of such other states. Additional cases,[188] including one that presented an aspect of an international controversy over the

---

[186] Holmes circulated the opinion to McReynolds with a special notation saying that he knew McReynolds did not agree, but merely wanted him to see the prevailing opinion. McReynolds answered: "Perhaps after all it is a mere question as to which ought to hang first. I am content with the one you choose." And there was no dissent. Holmes Papers.

Other Holmes opinions on trademarks and unfair competition, not mentioned in the text, are: Waterman Co. v. Modern Pen Co., 235 U.S. 88 (1914); Schlitz Brewing Co. v. Houston Ice Co., 250 U.S. 28 (1919); Stark Brothers Co. v. Stark, 255 U.S. 50 (1921).

[187] 240 U.S. 403 (1916); see also United Drug Co. v. Rectanus Co., 248 U.S. 90 (1918); *cf.* 15 U.S.C. Sec. 1072 (1958).

[188] See, e.g., Hamilton-Brown Shoe Co. v. Wolf Brothers, 240 U.S. 251 (1916); Rock Spring Co. v. Gaines & Co., 246 U.S. 312 (1918); Beckwith v. Commissioner of Patents, 252 U.S. 538 (1920); Baldwin Co. v. Howard Co., 256 U.S. 35 (1921) (and see R. S. Howard v. Baldwin Co., 328 Fed. 154 [2nd Cir. 1916], *cert. denied,* 243 U.S. 636 [1917]; see also Baldwin Co. v. Robertson, 265 U.S. 168 [1924]); American Steel Foundries v. Whitehead, 256 U.S. 40 (1921).

Chartreuse mark following the expulsion from France of the Carthusian monks who made the liqueur,[189] hold little interest. Nor are there cases of any note among the many denials of certiorari and the few summary dismissals of appeals.[190]

Some interest attaches to *Creswell* v. *Knights of Pythias,* however.[191] This was a suit by the white Knights of Pythias to prevent a similar black organization from using the same name. The suit succeeded in the state courts of Georgia against a defense of laches, and on writ of error, White for a majority of the Court went to great lengths to find a federal ground on which to rest the jurisdiction of the Supreme Court, and thus enable himself to reverse the judgment below. Holmes and Lurton dissented. The black organization was represented, incidentally, by Alton B. Parker of New York, the former Chief Justice of the New York Court of Appeals and Democratic Presidential candidate in 1904.

Finally, a great deal of interest attaches to *International News Service* v. *Associated Press,* an unfair competition case that stirred issues ranging well beyond the law of tortious palming off.

Even though he was a member of the Associated Press, William Randolph Hearst also owned a similar but smaller news-gathering organization, the International News Service, which supplied news to several hundred papers, including some of his own, that did not have membership in the Associated Press. Being considerably weaker, the International News Service shored up its competitive position by systematically pirating Associated Press dispatches and transmitting them to its subscribers as its own, without attribution to Associated Press. The practice had been going on for some time, to the great annoyance of the Associated Press management, but it became strikingly evident late in 1916, when the British government in effect expelled the International News Service from Europe, denying it the use of cables from Britain, as punishment for past violations of British censorship. Despite being thus barred, the International News Service continued to supply European

---

[189] Baglin v. Cusenier Co., 221 U.S. 580 (1911).

[190] These numbered thirty.

[191] See 225 U.S. 246 (1912); cf. Knights of Pythias v. Mims, 241 U.S. 574 (1916); Knights of Pythias v. Smyth, 245 U.S. 594 (1918); see also Grand Lodge Knights of Pythias v. Supreme Lodge Knights of Pythias, 2 Tenn. Civ. App. 429 (1911), *reversed on confession of error by defendants in error,* 231 U.S. 768 (1913); but *cf.* Faisin v. Adair, 148 Ga. 403, 96 S.E. 871 (1918), *cert. denied,* 248 U.S. 583 (1919); National Order of the Daughters of Isabella v. National Circle, Daughters of Isabella, 270 Fed. 723 (2nd Cir. 1920), *cert. denied,* 255 U.S. 571 (1921).

news regularly and promptly.[192] Associated Press thereupon brought suit in federal court, on the basis of diversity of citizenship, alleging that International News accomplished its pirating by bribing employees of newspapers that subscribed to the Associated Press, by otherwise inducing Associated Press members to violate its bylaws and permit International News Service to obtain dispatches before publication, and by copying news from the bulletin boards and early editions of Associated Press newspapers in the East, and then transmitting the news to Western papers, which often reached the streets with it earlier than the Eastern papers themselves. All this was alleged to constitute theft of Associated Press property.

In the lower courts, an injunction was issued against all three practices. As the case reached the Supreme Court, no contest was made over that part of the injunction which forbade bribing or otherwise influencing members of the Associated Press and their employees to supply the International News Service with Associated Press dispatches before publication. The only issue was the order against copying and transmitting news from bulletin boards and early editions.

Arguing that this portion of the decree below should be reversed, Samuel Untermyer for the International News Service maintained that facts cannot constitute private property, that news cannot be copyrighted, and that any common law right in it is extinguished upon publication on bulletin boards or in early editions. Such publication, he contended, amounts to a dedication of the published matter to the public, and confers a universal right of reproduction and use. The tort of unfair competition was not made out. International News had not palmed off its wares as if they were those of the Associated Press, as in the conventional case of unfair competition. Quite the contrary was alleged. The Associated Press, Untermyer said, had tried to get Congress to create a copyright in news for a limited period, and had failed. The courts should not confer a right that Congress had seen fit to withhold. To admit ownership in the Associated Press of the news supplied by it to its members, and by its member papers to it, "would result in assuring to that organization absolute dominion over the news of the country. Its service is not available to any newspaper that may desire to avail itself of it or to anyone not a member who may wish to embark in the newspaper business."

For the Associated Press, Frederick W. Lehmann argued that news was indeed property, as the court below had held, in the sense that it could be owned by the organization that had gone to the expense of gathering it. There was no exclusive right, of course, to the event that

---

[192] See O. Gramling, *AP—The Story of the News* (1940), 263, 285– 86; K. Cooper, *Kent Cooper and the Associated Press* (1959), 197–98.

constituted the news. Any one else could discover and report it. Nor, however, was there a right to appropriate the discovery and report of another organization. Lehmann relied heavily on cases that had protected against unauthorized appropriation of stock market quotations sent over a ticker. These were known as the *Ticker Cases*.[193] The principle of these cases, he argued, had also been recognized in England.

The opinion of the Supreme Court, by Pitney, upheld the injunction against pirating from bulletin boards and early editions. A report of news as such—"the history of the day"—could not be copyrighted, Pitney wrote. But it was not important whether news was in any sense property, since the case turned on the question of unfair competition, which did not depend on any property right analogous to the common law right of a proprietor of an unpublished work. The news itself might be regarded as common property. But this case concerned "the business of making [the news] known to the world, in which both parties to the present suit are engaged." Although "we may and do assume that neither party has any remaining property interest as against the public in uncopyrighted news matter after the moment of its first publication, it by no means follows that there is no remaining property interest in it as between themselves." As between the parties, news reports were to be regarded as "*quasi* property, irrespective of the rights of either as against the public." The *Ticker Cases* had sustained a right in stock market quotations, analogous to a right in a trade secret, and strangers were restrained from obtaining the quotations by inducing a breach of the contract under which they were made available to receivers, who were bound not to make them public. Of course the purchaser of a newspaper can communicate the information in it to anyone, but that was quite different from transmitting the news for commercial purposes in competition with its initial gatherer.

The Associated Press, Pitney continued, was being given no right to monopolize either the gathering or the distribution of news, or even to prevent reproduction of its articles. It was given the right merely to prevent a competitor from reaping the fruits of its efforts and expenditure. Untermyer had argued that the elements of unfair competition were lacking because International News Service had not tried to palm off its dispatches as those of the Associated Press. This sort of palming off was, said Pitney, the most familiar case of unfair competition. But if the fraudulent practices of International News Service were not the characteristic ones, they were no less fraudulent for that. Instead of misrepresenting, International News Service had misappropriated. An element of false pretense was involved, since International News Service

---

[193] See Hunt v. New York Cotton Exchange, 205 U.S. 322 (1907); Board of Trade v. Christie Grain & Stock Co., 198 U.S. 236 (1905).

never made attribution to the Associated Press, but transmitted A.P. dispatches as if they had been gathered by its own efforts. But this false pretense, "although accentuating the wrong," was not the essence of the matter. "It is something more than the advantage of celebrity of which complainant is being deprived." The practice of using a competitor's news as a tip and the basis of an independent investigation was engaged in by the Associated Press itself and by all newspapers, and was distinguishable. It had been distinguished in English cases. Pirating was something else.

Pitney spoke for a majority of five. Clarke, very probably because of his interest in a newspaper, the *Youngstown Vindicator*,[194] took no part. Holmes, joined by McKenna, wrote a separate opinion, in substantial but not total agreement with the majority. There was no property right in uncopyrighted news stories, said Holmes. The question was purely one of unfair competition, of which the ordinary case was the reverse of the present one. Here, the falsehood was "a little more subtle, the injury a little more indirect . . . but I think that the principle that condemns the one condemns the other. It is a question of how strong an infusion of fraud is necessary to turn a flavor into a poison. The dose seems to me strong enough here to need a remedy from the law." But in this view, the only wrong was the implied misstatement, and it could be corrected with a suitable acknowledgement stating the truth about the source of the news. And so Holmes thought that the injunction should be changed to forbid International News Service to publish news obtained from the Associated Press for a given period of time after publication, "unless it gives express credit to the Associated Press. . . ."

Brandeis alone dissented, and at length. He saw the case in an altogether different light. The *Ticker Cases* and all other analogies were imprecise, said Brandeis. "The question presented for decision is new; and it is important." Property meant the right to exclude others; absolutely, if the property was private, qualifiedly, if the property was affected with a public interest. "But the fact that a product of the mind has cost its producer money and labor, and has a value for which others are willing to pay, is not sufficient to ensure to it this legal attribute of property. The general rule of law is, that the noblest of human productions—knowledge, truths ascertained, conceptions, and ideas—become, after voluntary communication to others, free as the air to common use." Only in certain classes of cases, involving creation, invention or discovery, and not always then, was it the policy of the law to confer the attribute of property on "incorporeal productions." These

---

[194] See *supra,* p. 408.

were cases covered by copyright and patent statutes. Aside from the statutes, protection was sometimes extended at common law against breach of contract or of trust, and against palming off. Thus the ticker cases rested not upon the existence of a property right in news, but on a finding of a breach of contract. They were really trade secret cases, and inapposite here, as was also the rule against palming off.

"To appropriate and use for profit, knowledge and ideas produced by other men, without making compensation or even acknowledgement, may be inconsistent with a finer sense of propriety," but in a case such as this, and altogether with very few exceptions, none of which were applicable, the law sanctioned the practice. "That competition is not unfair in a legal sense, merely because the profits gained are unearned, even if made at the expense of a rival, is shown by many cases. . . . He who follows the pioneer into a new market, or who engages in the manufacture of an article newly introduced by another, seeks profits due largely to the labor and expense of the first adventurer; but the law sanctions, indeed encourages, the pursuit. He who makes a city known through his product, must submit to sharing the resultant trade with others who, perhaps for that reason, locate there later." Nothing that International News Service had done was illegal or fraudulent or intended to injure the Associated Press. There was an obvious injustice just the same, but to give relief would require the making of a new rule of law, better left, in the circumstances, to the legislative.

> The unwritten law possesses capacity for growth; and has often satisfied new demands for justice by invoking analogies or by expanding a rule or principle. This process has been in the main wisely applied and should not be discontinued. Where the problem is relatively simple, as it is apt to be when private interests only are involved, it generally proves adequate. But with the increasing complexity of society, the public interest tends to become omnipresent; and the problems presented by new demands for justice cease to be simple. Then the creation or recognition by courts of a new private right may work serious injury to the general public, unless the boundaries of the right are definitely established and wisely guarded. In order to reconcile the new private right with the public interest, it may be necessary to prescribe limitations and rules for its enjoyment; and also to provide administrative machinery for enforcing the rules. It is largely for this reason that, in the effort to meet the many new demands for justice incident to a rapidly changing civilization, resort to legislation has latterly been had with increasing frequency.
>
> The rule for which the plaintiff contends would effect an important extension of property rights and a corresponding curtailment of the free use of knowledge and of ideas; and the facts of this case admonish us of the danger involved in recognizing such a property

right in news, without imposing upon news-gatherers corresponding obligations.

Perhaps half the newspaper readers in the country, Brandeis continued, were dependent on news gatherers other than the Associated Press. It happened that the channel through which the International News Service supplied its four hundred newspapers with news of the European war was suddenly shut off to it by the action of a foreign government. For all that was known, the expulsion of International News Service was wholly undeserved, and in any event, the four hundred newspapers served by the International News Service and their readers were certainly innocent. It might be that these newspapers would gladly have availed themselves of the services of the Associated Press. But under the bylaws of that organization, election to membership required the affirmative vote of at least four-fifths of the members. In addition, individual members had an effective right to protest.[195] And so the deprivation that these four hundred newspapers suffered might not have been curable.

A legislature urged to enact a law to protect news-gathering agencies would likely consider the possibility and the consequences of such an occurrence as the exclusion of the International News Service from Europe. "Legislators might conclude that it was impossible to put an end to the obvious injustice involved in such appropriation of news [as practiced by I.N.S.], without opening the door to other evils, greater than that sought to be remedied. Such appears to have been the opinion of our Senate which reported unfavorably a bill to give news a few hours protection. . . ." And such was the view that denied to news the privilege of copyright. "Or legislators dealing with the subject might conclude, that the right to news values should be protected to the extent of permitting recovery of damages for any unauthorized use, but that protection by injunction should be denied, just as courts of equity ordinarily refuse (perhaps in the interest of free speech) to restrain actionable libels, and for other reasons decline to protect by injunction mere political rights. . . ." Or again, a legislature might conclude that

news-gathering is a business affected with a public interest . . . [and that] news should be protected against appropriation, only if the

---

[195] Not many years later, none other than William Randolph Hearst himself, whom the Associated Press never got around to expelling, despite what his International News Service was doing, exercised his right of protest to exclude from Associated Press membership Baltimore and Rochester newspapers that were in competition with papers of his own. See *The Nation*, 119:230, Sept. 3, 1924.

gatherer assumed the obligation of supplying it, at reasonable rates and without discrimination, to all papers which applied therefor. If legislators reached that conclusion, they would probably go further, and prescribe the conditions under which and the extent to which the protection should be afforded; and they might also provide the administrative machinery necessary for ensuring to the public, the press, and the news agencies, full enjoyment of the rights so conferred.

Courts are ill-equipped to make the investigations which should precede a determination of the limitations which should be set upon any property right in news or of the circumstances under which news gathered by a private agency should be deemed affected with a public interest. Courts would be powerless to prescribe the detailed regulations essential to full enjoyment of the rights conferred or to introduce the machinery required for enforcement of such regulations. Considerations such as these should lead us to decline to establish a new rule of law in the effort to redress a newly-disclosed wrong, although the propriety of some remedy appears to be clear.[196]

The opinion of the Court, undoubtedly one of Pitney's best, including even an unusual turn of phrase ("it is something more than the advantage of celebrity of which complainant is being deprived") could be viewed, as Professor Paul Freund has written, as "a high example of progressivism in the law."[197] And it evoked general approval in contemporaneous law review comment. The case, said one writer, showed "the adaptability of the courts to meet new conditions. . . ." It demonstrated that the Supreme Court "keeps pace."[198] Even the occasional doubter, while doubting, more or less approved. The decision was right, wrote Albert Kocourek, but should have been based on a property concept as applied to news. For it seemed to Kocourek "impossible in the present state of our legal system to introduce a new rule of unfair competition based solely on lawful appropriation, systematic or otherwise, of another's ideas."[199]

Time has been with the doubter. After fifty years, Professor Benjamin Kaplan has written, "the peculiarly strong sympathetic appeal of the facts for A.P. comes through undimmed, but we see also the

---

196 International News Service v. Associated Press, 248 U.S. 215, 219, 234, 235, 236, 242, 247–48, 249, 250, 257, 259, 262–63, 264–65, 266, 267 (1918).

197 P. A. Freund, "Mr. Justice Brandeis," in A. Dunham and P. B. Kurland, eds., *Mr. Justice* (1956), 97, 113.

198 E. S. Rogers, "Unfair Competition," *Mich. L. Rev.*, 17:490, 491,

494, 1919; and see Note, *Harv. L. Rev.*, 32:566, 1919; W. W. Cook, "The Associated Press Case," *Yale L. J.*, 28:387, 1919; see also Note, *Colum. L. Rev.*, 18:257, 1918. Cf. B. Pepper, Note, *Cornell L. Q.*, 4:223, 1919; W. H. Loyd, Note, *U. Pa. L. Rev.*, 67:191, 1919.

199 A. Kocourek, Comment, *Ill. L. Rev.*, 13:708, 719, 1919.

wisdom of Professor Kocourek's objection at the time that the limits, which is to say the exact policy justifications, of the new doctrine were so hard to describe that the well-wishing adventurer might pause before setting forth."[200] The decision, Judge Learned Hand held in 1929, should be restricted closely to its exact facts, and not followed beyond them. "The difficulties of understanding it otherwise are insuperable. We are to suppose that the court meant to create a common-law patent or copyright for reasons of justice. Either would flagrantly conflict with the scheme which Congress has for more than a century devised to cover the subject-matter."[201] By and large, Judge Hand's view has prevailed.[202]

And so Brandeis' dissent, proceeding from so utterly different a vantage point from that of the majority, has had its vindication. Pitney approached the common law in a progressive and creative spirit, certainly more so than Van Devanter in *Slocum* v. *Life Insurance Co.*,[203] or Day in *Thompson* v. *Thompson*.[204] But Brandeis added another dimension. He opened another window to another world. His lateral vision took in First Amendment values and institutional considerations. A kind of ultimate, if tacit, vindication came to him in 1971, in the decision of the heated and hurried Pentagon Papers controversy. The argument for the United States, urging the propriety of an injunction to stop unauthorized publication of classified government documents, attempted to make something of the decision in *International News Service* v. *Associated Press*. But the case is nowhere so much as noticed in the seriatim opinions of the Justices, concurring or dissenting.[205]

The question, central to Brandeis' dissent in *International News Service* v. *Associated Press*, whether courts should continue to evolve a common law of unfair competition or, having regard to imponderables of social and economic policy, should leave the task to legislatures—this fundamental question arose as well in a group of cases concerning yet other variants of unfair competition. Like *International News Service* v. *Associated Press*, these cases stirred issues ranging well beyond the law of tortious palming off. Although the First Amendment was not involved, even marginally, general antitrust policy was, and very much

---

[200] Kaplan, *Unhurried View of Copyright*, 87.

[201] Cheney Brothers v. Doris Silk Corp., 35 F.2nd 279, 280 (2nd Cir. 1929).

[202] See Sears, Roebuck & Co. v. Stiffel Co., 376 U.S. 225 (1964); Compco Corp. v. Day-Brite Lighting, Inc., 376 U.S. 234 (1964); Columbia Broadcasting System v. DeCosta, 377 F.2nd 315 (1st Cir. 1967); *cf.* W. E. Sell, "The Doctrine of Misappropriation in Unfair Competition," *Vand. L. Rev.*, 11:483, 1958.

[203] See *supra*, pp. 312–14, n.379.

[204] See *supra*, p. 315, n.383.

[205] Brief for the United States and Transcript of Argument, No. 1873, O.T. 1970, New York Times Co. v. United States, 403 U.S. 713 (1971).

so. The problem stemmed from attempts by the seller of a patented, trademarked, or otherwise unique article to tie to his sale of it conditions governing use by the buyer, or more frequently, binding the buyer to resell only at a stated price, and not below.

In 1911, while it was considering the *Standard Oil* and *Tobacco* antitrust cases, but before handing down its rule-of-reason opinions, the Court decided *Dr. Miles Medical Co.* v. *Park & Sons Co.* The Dr. Miles Company manufactured a patent medicine by a secret process. The company marketed it through wholesalers who sold to retail druggists. When department stores started selling the product at reduced prices, Dr. Miles found that its regular retailers, who had difficulty competing at those prices, either stopped stocking the product or did not sell it aggressively. Dr. Miles, therefore, concluded minimum price-maintenance agreements with both wholesalers and retailers, and sold its product only upon signature of such agreements. Park and Sons, a wholesale drug concern, refused to sign. But, it was alleged, Park and Sons nevertheless obtained the product illicitly from other wholesalers, and then sold it at cut-rate prices. This was a suit to enjoin Park and Sons from so doing, on the ground that the conduct engaged in by Park and Sons constituted the common law tort of malicious interference with a contractual relationship. Jurisdiction was based on diversity of citizenship. The suit was dismissed below in an opinion by Lurton, while on the Sixth Circuit.[206]

Affirming the dismissal, Hughes for the Court held first that even the contract with the wholesalers, let alone that with the retailers, was not a true agency contract, and that the allegations properly construed did not make out a case of inducing breach of trust by an agent. Viewing the contracts as sale, not agency contracts, Hughes concluded that they were obviously aimed at fixing the price ultimately paid by the consumer and "eliminating all competition." That had been the conclusion reached as well in an elaborate opinion in a similar case by Lurton on the Sixth Circuit a year before the *Dr. Miles* case was decided there, and from this opinion Hughes quoted at some length. The case was *John D. Park & Sons.* v. *Hartman.*[207] So it was obvious, Hughes continued, that the contracts restrained trade. The argument was that they were not invalid either at common law or under the Sherman Act because they related to proprietary medicines manufactured by a secret process, and because, in any event, a manufacturer was entitled to control the price at which he sold his product.

---

[206] 164 Fed. 803 (6th Cir. 1908), see *supra,* p. 78, n.302. Having written the opinion below, Lurton now recused himself. Alton B. Parker of New York represented Park and Sons in the Supreme Court.

[207] 153 Fed. 24 (6th Cir. 1907), see *supra,* p. 78, n.301.

As to the first argument, Hughes replied that whatever the rights of a patentee might be, they were derived from a statutory grant provided for in the Constitution. Dr. Miles had no such grant, had not made the disclosure of his process which was a prerequisite to receiving such a grant, and was altogether outside the policy of the patent law. Dr. Miles was entitled at common law to protection against invasion by fraud or otherwise of his right to his secret, but no such invasion had occurred. Undoubtedly Dr. Miles had a production monopoly, and might simply refuse to sell to anyone. But if Dr. Miles did sell, it became subject to the general public policy against the imposition of restraints on alienation, and against price fixing. Dr. Miles' price fixing might be viewed as intended to protect the interest of the retailers who were hurt by cut-rate competition. But if those retailers were to maintain prices by an agreement among themselves, that would be an illegal restraint of trade. The situation was no different when the restraint was imposed by the manufacturer. "The complainant having sold its product at prices satisfactory to itself, the public is entitled to whatever advantage may be derived from competition in the subsequent traffic." The issue, Hughes concluded, was "carefully considered and the decisions reviewed by Judge Lurton in delivering the opinion of the Circuit Court of Appeals in *Park* v. *Hartman, supra,* and, in following that case, it was concluded below that the restrictions sought to be enforced by the bill were invalid both at common law and under the act of Congress of July 2, 1890 [the Sherman Act]. We think that the court was right."

Presented with an opportunity to explode what he viewed as economic delusions without needing to worry overmuch whether his disbelief in the Sherman Act was affecting his application of it,[208] since the case did not, strictly speaking, arise under the statute, Holmes dissented with a will. In the case of a single object such as a painting, Holmes supposed, a contract between the original seller and his buyer setting the price for any further resales could not be held bad. This case differed only in that the contract here was part of a scheme of numerous such contracts. Yet a slight change in the form of the contract would

---

[208] "I hope and believe that I am not influenced by my opinion that it [the Sherman Act] is a foolish law. I have little doubt that the country likes it and I always say, as you know, that if my fellow citizens want to go to Hell I will help them. It's my job." M. DeW. Howe, ed., *Holmes-Laski Letters* (1953), I, 249. "I always used to say about the Sherman Act, if you want to go to that show and have the money to buy a ticket I have nothing to say, except that I don't think you would want to if you did not entertain economic delusions." *Ibid.,* 335. "I don't mean to let my disbelief in the Sherman Act affect my application of it—but I think it has been enlarged by construction in ways that I regret." *Ibid.,* 719.

avoid the result reached by the Court. All the owner of an article needed to do was to make the retail dealers his actual agents by retaining title until the goods left their hands, and then, said Holmes, "I cannot conceive that even the present enthusiasm for regulating the prices to be charged by other people would deny that the owner was acting within his rights." But, Holmes added, "I go farther. There is no statute covering the case; there is no body of precedent that by ineluctable logic requires the conclusion to which the court has come.[209] The conclusion is reached by extending a certain conception of public policy to a new sphere. On such matters we are in perilous country."

Judges should not interfere with people running their own business unless the reason for interfering was very clear. What then was the reason? Protection of the consumer? "On that point I confess," wrote Holmes, "that I am in a minority as to larger issues than are concerned here. I think that we greatly exaggerated the value and importance to the public of competition in the production or distribution of an article (here it is only distribution), as fixing a fair price. What really fixes that is the competition of conflicting desires. We, none of us, can have as much as we want of all the things that we want. Therefore, we have to choose. As soon as the price of something that we want goes above the point at which we are willing to give up other things to have that, we cease to buy it and buy something else. Of course, I am speaking of things that we can get along without." Aside from necessaries, it was "the point of most profitable returns" that marked "the equilibrium of social desires and determines the fair price in the only sense in which I can find meaning in those words." That was what served the public best. "I cannot believe that in the long run the public will profit by this court permitting knaves to cut reasonable prices for some ulterior

---

[209] In this Holmes was right, having had a hand himself in establishing the existing precedents. Before Lurton's decision in *Park* v. *Hartman,* the cases had generally gone the other way. See, e.g., Garst v. Harris, 177 Mass. 72, 58 N.E. 174 (1900); Dr. Miles Medical Co. v. Jaynes Drug Co., 149 Fed. 838 (1906).

After the decision, Pollock wrote Holmes:

> Either your dissenting opinion in the *Miles Medical Co.'s* case is right or much of our recent authority here is wrong. . . .

It seems to me that the majority of your Honourable Court are being led into an archaic reaction by their anti-monopolist zeal: and I cannot think that any sound doctrine of public policy requires you to favor the cheapening of Dr. Miles's medicines to the citizens of the United States.

The rule that you can't make a covenant run with goods has obviously nothing to do with the case, but seems to have introduced some confusion. M. DeW. Howe, ed., *Holmes-Pollock Letters* (1946), I, 178.

purpose of their own and thus to impair, if not to destroy, the production and sale of articles which it is assumed to be desirable that the public should be able to get."

The defendant had acted fraudulently, and should be stopped. The analogy relied upon to establish an evil effect in the price maintenance contract and thus to justify failure to enforce it was "that of combinations in restraint of trade. I believe that we have some superstitions on that head, as I have said; but those combinations are entered into with intent to exclude others from a business naturally open to them, and we unhappily have become familiar with the methods by which they are carried out. I venture to say that there is no likeness between them and this case. . . . I think also that the importance of the question and the popularity of what I deem mistaken notions makes it my duty to express my view in this dissent."[210]

Dr. Miles did not, as we saw, arise under the Sherman Act. Nor was Hughes' opinion based on the statute. But in his summary statement at the end, Hughes did adopt Lurton's conclusion below that the price-fixing contracts were invalid both at common law and under the Sherman Act, and subsequent decisions under the Sherman Act have consistently maintained the position that attempts at vertical resale price fixing are as much a *per se* violation of the statute as horizontal price fixing. The position has not escaped criticism—from Brandeis contemporaneously, as we shall see, and from others[211]—and by amendment to the Sherman Act and to the Federal Trade Commission Act, states were allowed to enforce certain fair-trade laws, which in turn provided for retail price fixing.[212] Otherwise, however, the *Dr. Miles* view generally prevailed, and resale price-fixing contracts were held invalid whether they dealt with general articles of trade or with patented, copyrighted, trademarked, or branded articles.[213]

---

[210] Dr. Miles Medical Co. v. Park & Sons Co., 220 U.S. 373, 399, 409, 411–12, 413 (1911).

[211] See, e.g., R. H. Bork, "Vertical Integration and the Sherman Act: The Legal History of an Economic Misconception," *U. Chi. L. Rev.*, 22: 157, 160–63, 1954.

[212] See Note, "The Operation of Fair-Trade Programs," *Harv. L. Rev.*, 69:316, 1956.

[213] Bauer & Cie v. O'Donnell, 229 U.S. 1 (1913); Straus v. American Publishers' Ass'n, 231 U.S. 222 (1913); Straus v. Victor Talking Ma-

chine Co., 243 U.S. 490 (1917); Boston Store v. American Graphophone Co., 246 U.S. 8 (1918); United States v. Schrader's Son, Inc., 252 U.S. 85 (1920); Frey & Son v. Cudahy Packing Co., 256 U.S. 208 (1921) (but *cf.* Frey & Son v. Welch Grape Juice Co., 261 Fed. 68 [4th Cir. 1919], *cert. denied*, 251 U.S. 551 [1919]). See also Waltham Watch Co. v. Keene, 209 Fed. 1007 (2nd Cir. 1913), *cert. denied*, 232 U.S. 724 (1914). And see Standard Sanitary Manufacturing Co. v. United States, 226 U.S. 20 (1912), *supra*, p. 181, n.253.

Brandeis' first judicial encounter with the problem of retail price maintenance came in *Boston Store* v. *American Graphophone Co.*[214] The price maintenance contract in this case concerned a patented article, and was tied to the license to use the patent. The Court, Chief Justice White writing and Van Devanter and Holmes dissenting, followed *Dr. Miles*. Brandeis concurred as follows:

> Whether a producer of goods should be permitted to fix by contract, express or implied, the price at which the purchaser may resell them, and if so, under what conditions, is an economic question. To decide it wisely it is necessary to consider the relevant facts, industrial and commercial, rather than established legal principles. On that question I have expressed elsewhere views which differ apparently from those entertained by a majority of my brethren. I concur, however . . . because I consider that the series of cases referred to in the opinion settles the law for this court. If the rule so declared is believed to be harmful in its operation, the remedy may be found, as it has been sought, through application to the Congress or relief may possibly be given by the Federal Trade Commission which has also been applied to.

The last sentence of this brief opinion, handed down in March 1918, was a preview of the position Brandeis was to elaborate in December of the same year in *International News Service* v. *Associated Press*. Legislative relief was in this instance found, as we have noted, both in Congress and in state legislatures. The views which differed— more than apparently—from those of a majority of his brethren Brandeis had expressed in 1913 in *Harper's Weekly*. He had deplored the decision in *Dr. Miles*, called cutthroat prices "the most potent weapon of monopoly," urged, as Wilson had done on Brandeis' advice during the campaign, that Congress regulate competition rather than accept and then regulate monopoly, and contended that Congress and the courts should permit the voluntary private regulation of competition by those engaged in business.[215] In this way the independent retailers could be saved from the practice of loss leaders by the giant chains.

These views Brandeis never abandoned. He pressed them on the Wilson Administration,[216] and he found other occasions to give effect to them in decisions of the Court. So he did in the *Chicago Board of Trade* case, in which he handed down an opinion of the Court on the

---

[214] *Supra*, n.213, 246 U.S. at 27–28 (Brandeis, J., concurring).

[215] L. D. Brandeis, "Competition That Kills," in *Business—A Profession* (1914), 236.

[216] See L. D. Brandeis to F. K. Lane, Dec. 12, 1913; Lane to J. C. McReynolds, Jan. 30, 1914, McReynolds Papers, University of Virginia Library.

same day on which the concurrence in *Boston Store* was announced.[217] But he never succeeded in shaking the *Dr. Miles* doctrine.

In 1919, in *United States* v. *Colgate & Co.*,[218] an escape hatch of uncertain dimensions from *Dr. Miles* was opened up. Interestingly enough, it was Hughes, the author of *Dr. Miles*, now in private practice, who was counsel for the Colgate Company and who drew the distinctions from *Dr. Miles* that persuaded the Court. *Colgate* had some practical effect, but it began to be qualified by the Court within months after having been handed down.

The government indicted the Colgate Company under the Sherman Act, alleging that it had combined with its wholesale and retail dealers to fix resale prices and thus suppress competition among wholesalers and retailers. Various letters and communications from the company to its dealers were cited, which urged the dealers to maintain a fixed price. The company, it was further alleged, also refused to deal with price cutters. Hughes, ever careful not to contend against his former judicial self,[219] argued in the Supreme Court that there was in this case no agreement imposing any restraint on alienation or on a dealer's freedom to sell. *Dr. Miles* had dealt with an attempted restraint upon the dealer's right of alienation, whereas this case was concerned with the right of a manufacturer to refuse to sell, Hughes contended. There were no agreements or contracts in this case, no combination, no monopoly, and no monopolizing intent.[220]

The indictment had been dismissed in the district court, and the case was in the Supreme Court on direct appeal. For a unanimous Supreme Court, McReynolds affirmed. On a direct appeal such as this, the Supreme Court was required to accept the district court's construction of the indictment. There was some doubt about that— more than McReynolds allowed[221]—but McReynolds construed the district court's construction to be that the indictment alleged no contract or agreement, but merely unilateral action by the company in refusing to deal with wholesalers and retailers who did not maintain the fixed

---

[217] See *supra*, p. 179, n.246; p. 180, n.250; M. Handler, *Antitrust in Perspective* (1957), 20–21.

[218] 250 U.S. 300 (1919).

[219] Nor would he pit Hughes the lawyer against Hughes the judge. If a case required arguments at variance with legal principles he had enunciated as Associate Justice, he declined it. This self-imposed rule did not, however, prevent him from arguing a case if he saw an honest distinction between the principle he had laid down for the court and the new point at issue." M. J. Pusey, *Charles Evans Hughes*, (1951), II, 634.

[220] Brief for Defendant-in-Error, United States v. Colgate & Co., 250 U.S. 300 (1919), No. 828, October Term 1918; see E. H. Levi, "The Parke, Davis-Colgate Doctrine: The Ban on Resale Price Maintenance," *The Supreme Court Review*, 1960: 258, 276, 292–93.

[221] See Levi, "Parke, Davis-Colgate Doctrine," 284 *et seq.*

price. As so construed, McReynolds went on to hold, the indictment stated no offense under the Sherman Act. In the absence of agreements and of a purpose to monopolize, a manufacturer had a right to decide whom he wished to sell to. And that was all that the indictment, as construed, alleged that Colgate had done. *Dr. Miles* was a case of an unlawful combination effected through contracts with dealers which forbade them to set their own prices.

District judges had considerable difficulty accepting the distinction between *Colgate* and *Dr. Miles*.[222] But they thought they had been told something in *Colgate*, and they obeyed it as best they could understand it. The upshot was confusion, followed by an irritable reaction on the part of McReynolds. In *United States v. Schrader's Son, Inc.*,[223] the government charged a violation of the Sherman Act by a manufacturer who refused to sell to any dealer not willing to enter into a price-maintenance contract. The indictment was dismissed below on the authority of *Colgate*, and on March 1, 1920, eight months after *Colgate*, McReynolds for the Supreme Court reversed. The author of the opaque, heavily quotation-laden opinion in *Colgate* now remarked loftily: "It seems unnecessary to dwell upon the obvious difference between the situation presented when a manufacturer merely indicates his wishes concerning prices and declines further dealings with all who fail to observe them, and one where he enters into agreements—whether expressed or implied from a course of dealing or other circumstances—with all customers throughout the different States which undertake to bind them to observe fixed resale prices." Clarke concurred in the result, and Holmes and Brandeis dissented—all without opinion.

McReynolds took pride in the brevity of his opinions, and had a theory to justify it, although its real source was probably sheer impatience. "When a judge fully appreciates that every unnecessary word in an opinion hurts it," McReynolds declared privately in 1933, "he may be relied upon to write with a good effect. But when vanity, or an itch to throw off new and striking phrases and shine in the books [did McReynolds have Holmes and Brandeis in mind?], troubles him, his outgivings are apt to be noxious."[224] There was no unnecessary word in the *Colgate* opinion, nor enough of the necessary ones. The surface of a complex problem was barely scratched.

One year after *Schrader's Son*, McReynolds' vaunted brevity came home to roost once more in *Frey & Son v. Cudahy Packing Co.*[225] Here the Court of Appeals had reversed a verdict for the plaintiff in a

---

[222] See *ibid.*, 294 *et seq.*

[223] *Supra*, n.213, 252 U.S. at 99.

[224] J. C. McReynolds to H. A. Hollzer, Aug. 23, 1933, McReynolds Papers.

[225] *Supra*, n.213, 252 U.S. at 210; *cf.* Frey & Son v. Welch Grape Juice Co., *supra*, n.213.

treble-damage suit on the ground that there was no case to go to the jury under *Colgate*. This was done before the decision in the Supreme Court of *Schrader's Son*, and it was error, McReynolds now held. "Apparently the former case [*Colgate*] was misapprehended," he said. Apparently there can be such a thing, McReynolds explained, as an agreement or combination implied from a course of dealing, rather than embodied in a written contract. Nevertheless, McReynolds affirmed the judgment for the defendant in the Court of Appeals, because in his view the trial court had also erred when it instructed the jury that it could find defendant guilty if the jury believed that defendant had a sales plan calling for fixed resale prices, that defendant brought the plan to the attention of wholesalers on frequent occasions, and that the wholesalers in fact cooperated. Standing alone, said McReynolds, this was not sufficient to make out an offense under the Sherman Act— citing *Colgate*. Pitney, joined by Day and Clarke, dissented, professing not to understand the basis of McReynolds's holding—and not unjustly.

Colgate and its progeny gave rise to a literature of major proportions.[226] The decision, whatever its intended meaning, continued to be eroded, in later years to the vanishing point.[227] Meanwhile, in patent cases, a short-lived threat had developed to the flank of the *Dr. Miles* doctrine.

The A. B. Dick Company held a patent on a mimeograph machine. In accordance with its practice, it sold the machine to a customer subject to a license restriction that the machine could be used only with stencils, paper, ink, and other supplies made by the Dick Company. One Henry sold the customer some ink of his own for use in the machine, and the Dick Company sued Henry in a federal court for contributory patent infringement. *Henry v. A. B. Dick Co.*[228] was argued in the Supreme Court in October 1911, and decided on March 11, 1912. Harlan was gone, and Day was absent at the time of the argument owing to the illness of his wife.[229] So it was a seven-man Court, and it divided 4 to 3 in favor of the validity of the condition attached to the Dick Company's patent.[230]

---

[226] See, e.g., C. W. Dunn, "Resale Price Maintenance," *Yale L. J.*, 32: 676, 1923; F. F. Nesbit, "The Legality of Resale Price Fixing," *Georgetown L. J.*, 11:26, 1923; C. T. Murchison, "Resale Price Maintenance," *N. Car. L. Rev.*, 1:37, 1922; Z. Chafee, "Equitable Servitudes on Chattels," *Harv. L. Rev.*, 41:945, 1928.

[227] See Levi, "Parke, Davis-Colgate Doctrine," 258.

[228] 224 U.S. 1 (1912).

[229] See 222 U.S. xxix.

[230] "The far-reaching importance of the decision would seem to suggest," T. R. Powell commented a few years later, "the propriety of adopting for such cases some canon similar to the one that a statute will not be declared unconstitutional except by a majority of the full bench." T. R. Powell, "The Nature of a Patent Right," *Colum. L. Rev.*, 17:663, 664, n.10, 1917.

The opinion for the majority was by Lurton.[231] It relied heavily on his own well-known Sixth Circuit opinion in 1896 in *Heaton-Peninsular Button-Fastner Co.* v. *Eureka Specialty Co.*,[232] and on a later opinion to the same effect by Van Devanter in the Eighth Circuit.[233] The Dick Company's complaint, Lurton held, stated a claim under the patent law, and properly construed, that law gave a patentee the right to attach conditions such as the Dick Company's to the sale of a license to use the patented article. So the lower federal courts had held. Business had been done in reliance on these decisions, and if there was to be a change now, Congress ought to make it. *Dr. Miles* was distinguishable because it did not arise under the patent law.

With Lurton were McKenna, Holmes, and Van Devanter. The dissent was by White, Hughes and Lamar joining. The Court, said White, was allowing the owner of a patent to establish a monopoly in nonpatented articles. White's opinion is vigorous, if often somewhat question begging.[234] It parades horribles, it speaks of evil consequences, and it calls upon Congress to amend the patent law so as to overrule the majority decision. As delivered orally, the dissent was apparently even more vigorous, and it annoyed Holmes, who was not easily quite so annoyed, and hardly ever by White, whom after all he admired. Holmes complained to his friend Pollock:

> I am weary with work and some slightly worrying incident of the job, *e.g.*, a week ago Monday the C. J. dissented with Hughes & Lamar from a decision by Lurton under the patent law. I didn't care a straw about the case one way or t'other and thought I could have written a better opinion on either side. But the Chief has Irish blood—he is naturally a politician and a speaker—and much as he abhorred the outbreak of Harlan in the Oil and Tobacco cases,[235] I thought he made a stump speech that was no better and that had more tendency to hurt the Court. The result was that while the point decided had been accepted as law in the Circuits for ten years, the newspapers have been flaming and it has been suggested that if the recall of judicial opinions were in operation the majority might get the benefit of it. I am too near the time when I can hop off, if I want to, to care personally, but I regretted the performance very much, especially as I thought it not only bad in tone but very thin and beside the point in the reasoning. The printed dissent is more moderate and gives no idea of his oral discourse, though I think it very poor work. All this of course just between ourselves.[236]

---

[231] See *supra*, pp. 335–37.

[232] 77 Fed. 288 (6th Cir. 1896), *supra*, p. 79, n.304.

[233] National Phonograph Co. v. Schlegel, 128 Fed. 733 (8th Cir. 1904), *supra*, p. 50.

[234] See Powell, "Nature of a Patent Right," 663.

[235] See *supra*, pp. 107 *et seq.*, 113 *et seq.*

[236] *Holmes-Pollock Letters*, I, 190.

The reaction in Congress, on the part of the Department of Justice, and in the press was, as Holmes reported, one of considerable excitement and hostility.[237] Attorney General Wickersham was naturally concerned with the effect of the decision on the litigation the government had begun against the United Shoe Machinery Company.[238] Day having returned to the Court on January 18, following the death of his wife, and Pitney having been confirmed for Harlan's place on March 13, the government therefore joined in a petition for rehearing of the *Dick* case before a full Bench. This petition was denied, as is set forth in an unusual note appended to the report of the case.[239] But Congress, impressed with White's dissent, and having an eye to the *Shoe Machinery* litigation, wrote a provision into the Clayton Act of 1914 forbidding conditions in leases of patented or unpatented articles which required the lessee not to deal in the products of a competitor, if the effect was to lessen competition or tend toward monopoly.[240]

Within the year, indications began to appear that had Day and Pitney sat, the *Dick* case would, indeed, have gone the other way. In *Bauer & Cie* v. *O'Donnell*,[241] a full Court, Day writing and McKenna, Holmes, Lurton, and Van Devanter dissenting, held that a retail price maintenance condition tied to the sale of a patented article was invalid. *Dr. Miles* was followed, and the *Dick* case distinguished on the ground that it applied only to conditions having to do with the use of the article. Then in 1917, in *Motion Picture Co.* v. *Universal Film Co.*,[242] the *Dick* case was expressly overruled—a rare event in the Court of these years.

Motion Picture Co. v. *Universal Film Co.* concerned a patent for the only available machine that exhibited motion pictures by feeding the film through the machine in a regular and accurate movement. The patent was licensed to a manufacturer on condition that he attach to every sale of the machine a license requiring that the machine be used only to exhibit certain films and no other. This was a suit for infringement. There were, noted Clarke for the Court, some forty thousand such machines in use. The tying condition, Clarke held, was invalid. The patent statute protected only the patented article, and the films here in ques-

---

[237] See, e.g., *New York Daily Tribune*, Mar. 12, 1912, p. 5, col. 5, Mar. 13, 1912, p. 7, col. 2; *Wall Street Journal*, Mar. 12, 1912, p. 7, col. 2, Mar. 13, 1912, p. 6, col. 1; *The Financial World*, Mar. 16, 1912, p. 1, col. 1.

[238] See *supra*, pp. 171 *et seq.*

[239] 224 U.S. at 1.

[240] See *supra*, p. 176, n.239; 51 *Cong. Rec.* 14093, 16274, 63rd Cong., 2nd Sess. (1914).

[241] *Supra*, n.213.

[242] 243 U.S. 502, 513, 515, 519, 521 (1917); and see Motion Picture Patents Co. v. United States, 225 Fed. 800 (D.C.E.D. Pa. 1915), *appeal dismissed per stipulation*, 247 U.S. 524 (1918).

tion were obviously no part of it. This was plain on the language of the statute. "It is so plain that to argue it would obscure it."[243] Moreover, tying arrangements were a "perfect instrument of favoritism and oppression." Congress would not likely have wished to sanction them, and courts should not. The court below had relied on the Clayton Act, but Clarke had no need to do so, since he was prepared to overrule the *Dick* case anyway. Yet the Clayton Act supported him in the view, concurred in by Congress, that tying conditions were "gravely injurious to that public interest, which we have seen is more a favorite of the law than is the promotion of private fortunes."

The dissent was by Holmes. The patentee, he wrote, need not sell his invention at all, and that being so, Holmes could not understand why the patentee may not sell his invention on one or another condition. Some predominant public interest might prevent, but Holmes perceived none in the circumstances. If tying sales led to domination of the market, it was a domination only insofar as the need for the patented article permitted. Moreover, the rule of the *Dick* case had prevailed for a good many years, and no doubt important transactions had taken place in reliance upon it. It should not be overruled. Brandeis was disqualified in the *Shoe Machinery* litigation, as was McReynolds. They would have changed the result. Both were with the majority in the *Motion Picture* case, Brandeis viewing conditions tied to the lease or sale of patented articles quite differently from resale price maintenance agreements.

Bankruptcy

In 1898, Congress enacted the fourth and most comprehensive statute carrying out the power granted in Article I of the Constitution to establish "uniform Laws on the subject of Bankruptcies throughout the United States."[244] The statute authorized voluntary and involuntary

---

[243] T. R. Powell argued it, and showed that it was possible to shed a great deal of light on it. The question, he concluded as so often, was not one "to be resolved by any inexorable logic. The tool to be used was not the syllogism but a practical judgment about practical consequences. . . . But with the issue clearly drawn, there is ample room for disagreement as to which side of the line any particular case may fall." Powell, *Colum. L. Rev.,* 17:684, 1917; and see W. F. Baxter, "Legal Restric-

tions on Exploitation of the Patent Monopoly: An Economic Analysis," *Yale L. J.,* 76:267, 276–77, 1966; D. F. Turner, "The Validity of Tying Arrangements Under the Antitrust Laws," *Harv. L. Rev.,* 72:50, 1958; W. S. Bowman, Jr., "Tying Arrangements and the Leverage Problem," *Yale L. J.,* 67:19, 1957.

[244] 30 Stat. 544 (1898). The Bankruptcy Act of 1898 has often been amended, and in 1938, it was extensively revised by the Chandler Act, 52 Stat. 875.

proceedings for almost all debtors, observed state exemptions, and contained liberal discharge provisions. And it produced a great volume of federal judicial business, especially with the onset of the panic of 1907.

Until 1915, much of this business—though not all; there were some restrictions[245]—could find its way to the Supreme Court of the United States on writ of error or on appeal. In addition, there were cases from state courts in which a right under the Bankruptcy Act, or one or another conflict with the Act or with bankruptcy proceedings, was alleged.[246] (The Bankruptcy Act also had criminal provisions, but cases arising under these were rare in the Supreme Court.)[247] Relief came with the Judiciary Act of 1915,[248] which substituted certiorari for appellate jurisdiction in bankruptcy cases brought up from federal courts of appeals, and so far as state cases were concerned, also with the Act of 1916,[249] which substantially restricted review by writ of error from state courts.[250] But there remained a great many petitions for certiorari, more than under the Federal Employers' Liability and the Hours of Service Acts[251] taken together.[252]

Aside from denials of certiorari and dismissals of appeals, summary dispositions were very few,[253] even in cases that turned out to involve little more than factual issues.[254] Altogether, the bulk of the business was a throwback to the docket of the nineteenth century. It belonged to the time when ordinary private litigation was the grist of the Court's mill. In the emerging Court of the twentieth century, it was

---

[245] Writ of error or appeal was dismissed in more than twenty of these cases, generally "for want of jurisdiction."

[246] Fifteen of these cases were decided on the merits; in another ten writ of error was dismissed.

[247] See United States v. Rabinowich, 238 U.S. 78 (1915).

[248] 38 Stat. 803 (1915).

[249] 39 Stat. 532 (1916).

[250] After 1915, appeals and writs of error were dismissed in ten cases.

[251] See *supra*, p. 421, n.35.

[252] In 1910–20, more than two hundred petitions were denied in these cases.

[253] See Miller v. First National Bank, 16 N.M. 497, 121 Pac. 31 (1911), *affirmed*, 235 U.S. 689 (1914); Bergdoll v. Harrigan, 217 Fed. 943 (3rd Cir. 1914), *affirmed*, 238 U.S. 609 (1915); Hopkins v. United States *ex rel*. Ellington & Guy, Inc., 238 Fed. 840 (E.D.N.C. 1917), *affirmed*, 246 U.S. 655 (1918); and see *infra*, n.260.

[254] *Compare*, e.g., First National Bank v. Littlefield, 226 U.S. 110 (1912); Miller v. Guasti, 226 U.S. 170 (1912); Merchants Bank v. Sexton, 228 U.S. 634 (1913); Greey v. Dockendorff, 231 U.S. 513 (1913); Home Bond Co. v. McChesney, 239 U.S. 568 (1916); and Stowe v. Harvey, 241 U.S. 199 (1916), *with* Andrews v. Osborn, 209 Fed. 148 (3rd Cir. 1913), *affirmed*, 239 U.S. 629 (1915); and Farmers & Merchants State Bank v. Park, 209 Fed. 613 (5th Cir. 1913), *affirmed*, 241 U.S. 645 (1916).

an anomaly.[255] Yet there were, of course, a few cases that dealt with large, recurring issues in the administration of the bankruptcy laws, or that merited the Court's attention because they arose at the intersection between this federal speciality and other branches of law. And one or two cases are of interest for extrinsic reasons.

Chicago, Burlington, & Quincy Railroad v. *Hall*[256] held that the Bankruptcy Act dissolved liens obtained against exempt property of an insolvent within four months of bankruptcy. In this case, the wages of a bankrupt had been attached in garnishment proceedings, and he was allowed to recover them from his employer, so that he might be enabled, said the Court, "to start afresh with the property set apart to him as exempt." The rule of the *Hall* case was codified by Congress in a subsequent revision of the Bankruptcy Act.[257] *Burlingham* v. *Crouse*[258] decided that only the cash surrender value of life insurance policies, not their ultimate proceeds, formed part of a bankrupt's estate held by the trustee in bankruptcy for the benefit of creditors. *Francis* v. *McNeal*,[259] an opinion by Holmes, established the proposition that when a partnership is declared bankrupt, the trustee in bankruptcy may draw on the private holdings of one of the partners to discharge the obligations of the firm.

Four cases, three decided with full opinion and one disposed of by summary reversal, dealt with the interplay between applicable state law and the provisions of the Bankruptcy Act voiding preferential payments to some creditors made within a time certain before bankruptcy.[260] *Dean* v. *Davis*,[261] an opinion by Brandeis, added important elements

---

[255] In 1910–20, more than sixty such cases were decided on the merits. See *supra*, p. 649.

[256] 229 U.S. 511, 515 (1913).

[257] See *Collier on Bankruptcy* (14th ed., 1978), 4:142; *ibid.*, 1:860, n.12.

[258] 228 U.S. 459 (1913); see also Everett v. Judson, 228 U.S. 474 (1913); Andrews v. Partridge, 228 U.S. 479 (1913); and see Cohen v. Samuels, 245 U.S. 50 (1917); Frederick v. Fidelity Ins. Co., 256 U.S. 395 (1921) (but *cf.* Lake v. New York Life Ins. Co., 218 F.2nd [4th Cir. 1955], *cert. denied*, 349 U.S. 917 [1955]); see I. H. Cohen, "Life Insurance as an Asset in Bankruptcy: Part I," *Va. L. Rev.*, 28:211, 227–30, 1941; S. A. Riesenfeld, "Life Insurance and Creditors Remedies in the United States," *U.C.L.A. L. Rev.*, 4:583, 1957.

[259] 228 U.S. 695 (1913); *cf.* Liberty National Bank v. Bear, 276 U.S. 215 (1928).

[260] Bailey v. Baker Heights Machine Co., 239 U.S. 268 (1915); Carey v. Donohue, 240 U.S. 430 (1916); Martin v. Commercial National Bank, 245 U.S. 513 (1918); Bunch v. Maloney, 233 Fed. 967 (8th Cir. 1916), *reversed*, 246 U.S. 658 (1918).

[261] 242 U.S. 438 (1917); see C. E. Corker, "Hazards of Doing Business with an Insolvent: The Dean v. Davis Amendment in the Chandler Act," *Stan. L. Rev.*, 1:189, 1949; J. E. Mulder, "Ambiguities in the Chandler Act," *U. Pa. L. Rev.*, 89:10, 26–30, 1940.

to the definition of those transfers of property by an insolvent on the verge of bankruptcy which are deemed fraudulent and voidable. *Central Trust Co.* v. *Chicago Auditorium*[262] held that bankruptcy, even though involuntary, could constitute a breach of contract, and that provable damages for the breach were valid claims, no different from the claims of other creditors, against the estate in the hands of the trustee in bankruptcy. *Schall* v. *Camors*[263] held on the other hand that tort claims were not recoverable. *Gratiot State Bank* v. *Johnson*,[264] another Brandeis opinion, was a significant procedural decision affecting the rights of creditors who were not parties to the original adjudication of insolvency.

The most complex and drawn-out of bankruptcy litigations were those involving railroad reorganizations, of which *Northern Pacific Railway* v. *Boyd*[265] was an important example. Enormous interests were in play, and eminent counsel appeared—Francis Lynde Stetson for the Northern Pacific Company in the *Boyd* case, Charles Evans Hughes, Samuel Untermyer, and Frederick W. Lehmann in other cases.[266] Simply mastering the facts in such cases was a considerable challenge, although at times, as Holmes remarked in *Kansas City Railway* v. *Guardian Trust Co.*,[267] the facts were "less complicated than the proceedings that have grown out of them."

Two additional cases may be mentioned for their extrinsic interest. *Sexton* v. *Kessler*[268] concerned stock placed in escrow by the bankrupt as security for a loan. In November of 1907, in the midst of the panic of that year, when the bankrupt in the case was already insolvent but four months before the filing of a petition in bankruptcy, he handed the stock over to the creditor. A unanimous Supreme Court, Holmes writing, held that the transaction did not constitute an illegal preference and was not voidable. *Sexton* v. *Kessler* was overruled by Congress in the revision of the Bankruptcy Act of 1938.[269] But it provided a noted writer on bankruptcy with an opportunity for a remarkable critique of Holmes. "In view of the high regard in which this Justice is held," wrote Professor James MacLachlan in 1956, "it may seem graceless to record

---

[262] 240 U.S. 581 (1916).

[263] 251 U.S. 239 (1920); see G. Glenn, "Basic Considerations in Court Claims in Bankruptcy and Reorganization," *N.Y.U. L. Q. Rev.*, 18:367, 1941.

[264] 249 U.S. 246 (1919).

[265] See *supra*, p. 340, nn.101, 102; 364.

[266] See Kansas City Ry. v. Guardian Trust Co., 240 U.S. 166 (1916) (Untermyer and Lehmann); Southern Pacific Co. v. Bogert, 250 U.S. 483 (1919) (Hughes).

[267] 240 U.S. at 172–73.

[268] 225 U.S. 90 (1912); see also Gorman v. Littlefield, 229 U.S. 19 (1913); National City Bank v. Hotchkiss, 231 U.S. 50 (1913); Mechanics' Bank v. Ernst, 231 U.S. 60 (1913); Duel v. Hollins, 241 U.S. 523 (1916).

[269] See *Collier on Bankruptcy*, 3: 900, 905.

the opinion that in commercial law and several related fields he made a disproportionate number of decisions open to challenge as technically unsound or unrealistic. . . . His fine brief literary style helped him to evade or to elide brilliantly the considerations that should have controlled the case. . . . Those who ignore his technical decisions and attack his philosophy attack him where his reputation rests upon a far firmer foundation. . . ."[270]

Gleason v. *Thaw*[271] held that the professional services of an attorney fraudulently obtained by false pretenses, did not constitute the sort of property that could be recaptured from a bankrupt. The attorney was simply a creditor like other creditors. The case was an episode in the extraordinary story of Harry K. Thaw, the deranged Pittsburgh heir, who murdered the architect Stanford White in New York over the affections of the showgirl Evelyn Nesbit.[272] The Supreme Court had had another encounter with this celebrated *crime passionnel* in *Drew* v. *Thaw*,[273] when it ordered the extradition of Thaw back to New York after his escape from the state hospital for the insane to which he had been committed following his acquittal on the ground of insanity. Gleason had been Thaw's chief counsel, and it had been represented to him that his fee would be paid out of Thaw's income from his father's estate and his expectation from the estate of his mother. But in fact Thaw's money had been tied up in a spendthrift trust by his father, and his mother declined to die. He went into bankruptcy, and Gleason got no more than $20,000 out of the $80,000 he considered his proper fee. Following his defeat in the Supreme Court, Gleason turned to a suit against the mother on a contract and then on a tort theory. He lost again.[274]

A series of cases whose implications transcend the administration of the Bankruptcy Act dealt with the question of a bankrupt's Fifth Amendment privilege not to be forced to incriminate himself. In two cases in 1911 and 1913, Holmes held for unanimous Courts that the bankrupt was not protected by the Fifth Amendment against delivering his books to the trustee in bankruptcy, even though the books might contain incriminating matter. In *Matter of Harris*,[275] the order requiring the books to be turned over provided that the trustee would give the bankrupt his chance to plead the Fifth Amendment as occasion might arise. No immunity was extended, however, and no assurance against

---

[270] J. MacLachlan, *Bankruptcy* (1956), 331, n.1.

[271] 236 U.S. 558 (1915).

[272] See G. Langford, *The Murder of Stanford White* (1962); E. Nesbit, *Prodigal Days* (1934).

[273] 235 U.S. 432 (1914).

[274] Gleason v. Thaw, 234 Fed. 570 (2nd Cir. 1916), *cert. denied*, 243 U.S. 656 (1917).

[275] 221 U.S. 274, 279–80 (1911).

the use of leads and other information in the development of evidence. But the Fifth Amendment, Holmes held, did not apply at all, because it protects only against forced testimony, and does not protect a bankrupt against yielding possession of books that under the law he may no longer keep. There would have been nothing to prevent Congress from simply giving the trustee title to the bankrupt's books as well as to his other property. "That is one of the misfortunes of bankruptcy if it follows crime. The right not to be compelled to be a witness against one's self is not a right to appropriate property that may tell one's story." In *Johnson* v. *United States*,[276] in which the bankrupt's books were introduced in evidence against him in a criminal proceeding for concealing funds, Holmes added: "A party is privileged from producing the evidence but not from its production. The transfer by bankruptcy is no different from a transfer by execution of a volume with a confession written on the fly leaf."[277]

The bankruptcy statute does extend immunity to the bankrupt in respect of incriminating statements made by him in an examination to which he is required to submit. In *Glickstein* v. *United States*,[278] a unanimous Court, White writing, held that the grant of immunity did not protect the bankrupt from a prosecution for perjury committed in the course of such an examination. Finally, *Arndstein* v. *McCarthy*,[279] a cryptic opinion by McReynolds, held that where Fifth Amendment protection is available to a bankrupt despite the limited statutory grant of immunity, the filing by the bankrupt of certain schedules without objection pursuant to court order did not constitute a waiver of the privilege.

---

[276] 228 U.S. 457, 458 (1913).

[277] See also Kaplan v. Leech, 213 Fed. 753 (3rd Cir. 1914), *cert. denied,* 234 U.S. 765 (1914).

[278] 222 U.S. 139 (1911); *cf.* Cameron v. United States, 231 U.S. 710 (1914).

[279] 254 U.S. 71, 379 (1920); and see McCarthy v. Arndstein, 262 U.S. 356 (1923), *reaffirmed on rehearing,* 266 U.S. 34 (1924). *Cf.* Kastigar v. United States, 406 U.S. 441 (1972).

PART TWO

By Benno C. Schmidt, Jr.

Acknowledgments

ALEXANDER M. BICKEL DIED on November 7, 1974, at the height
of his extraordinary powers. At his death, he left virtually complete the seven chapters that comprise Part One of this volume, devoted
to the history of the Supreme Court during the Chief Justiceship of
Edward Douglass White, Confederate veteran, former Democratic
Senator from Louisiana, and Associate Justice from 1894 to 1910. White
remained in the center seat from December 19, 1910, until his death on
May 19, 1921, shortly after the end of the 1920 Term of the Court.

The period 1910–21 was almost as eventful in the life of the
Supreme Court as it was for the nation. The gathering momentum of
Progressive reform energies, massive immigration, the despair and hope
of race relations, the cataclysm of World War, and the frenzied pace of
change in industry and labor relations are only a few of the tremendous
forces during this period that gave new shape to American society,
politics, and law. Rarely has there been a decade in our modern history
when questions about the proper role and performance of the Supreme
Court were posed with such divisive intensity. The aggressive doctrines
of laissez-faire constitutionalism coexisted in uneasy balance alongside
quickened judicial sympathy, or at least tolerance, for progressive
regulation to ameliorate the hard lot of working men, women, and, it
must be added, children. The White Court saw the beginnings of a
modern constitutional jurisprudence of civil liberties: decisions giving
unprecedented scope to all three of the Civil War amendments in relation
to black people's rights, decisions concerning the rights of aliens,
decisions construing for the first time the meaning of freedom of expression in relation to the juggernaut of national security in wartime,
decisions reflecting the first glimmerings of concern for the probity of
state criminal processes. And in many nonconstitutional decisions con-

struing the growing body of federal, social, and economic legislation, the White Court was faced with legal questions hardly less important to our nation's development and no less charged with political controversy at the time. Three of the most imposing personalities in our history—Oliver Wendell Holmes, Jr., Charles Evans Hughes, and Louis Dembitz Brandeis—shaped the White Court by the force of their extraordinary intellects and characters. It was a Court that included also the most difficult person ever to sit on the Supreme Court, James C. McReynolds, and one of the modern Court's most careful craftsmen, Willis Van Devanter. And it was a Court whose stature and dynamics reflected the towering reputation, devotion to duty, and the genial integrity of its admirable Chief Justice. In short, in substance and in character, the history of the White Court cannot be assayed without an effort, in the words of the first report of the Permanent Committee for the Oliver Wendell Holmes Devise, to "reach far into collateral fields, in order to set the Court at all stages firmly in the political, economic, and intellectual context of the moment."

Professor Bickel stated the guiding principles that governed his work on this volume in a letter to the general editor of the Holmes Devise History, Professor Paul A. Freund:

> I understood that this was to be a lawyer's history, tracing doctrine, as well as a history for the general reader; that it was to place the work of the Court in context, political, social and economic, intellectual, so far as possible; that it was to treat great cases not as isolated episodes, but as part of a process, thus emphasizing the background and the consequences as well as the decision; and that it was to be an authoritative work, standing on its own two feet, readable independently of other materials, and certainly readable by someone without access, and without the wish for access, to the official reports. Finally, I understood that the inner life of the Court was to be emphasized also, so far as available materials permitted.

And Professor Bickel added, with modest understatement about his prodigious efforts, "Many years of work have gone into trying to meet, as best I knew how, those objectives. . . ."[1]

How successfully Professor Bickel carried out his purposes is attested by the seven imposing chapters that constitute his legacy to the Holmes Devise project. They demonstrate, in the opinion of one who has worked through them carefully and sought to follow their lead, that the most brilliant and influential constitutional scholar of the generation that came of age during the era of the Warren Court was also a historian

---

[1] A. M. Bickel to P. A. Freund, Nov. 10, 1967.

of great gifts, one capable not only of probing analysis of the evolution of legal doctrine and judicial practice but of bringing to vivid life the legal struggles, the great characters, the political contests, and the social thought of the Progressive era.

Professor Bickel's chapters are presented essentially as he left them. It was only necessary for me to respond to minor editorial needs, complete, track down, and correct some footnotes, and make stylistic changes not involving substance that I am sure Professor Bickel would have wanted.

Professor Bickel left no interpretive writings or outlines covering the portion of the volume not completed at his death, beyond his copious case notes and the fruits of his research in the personal papers of the Justices, Justice Department files, and newspapers and periodicals of the Progressive era. Thus, Professor Bickel should not be held responsible for the interpretations advanced in Part Two of this volume, nor can I enlist the weight of his authority for anything I say.

Professor Bickel's research has been of tremendous value in my efforts to put the White Court's work in historical perspective, and I want to record my boundless indebtedness to him and to his work. But the vicarious enlightenment to be derived from another's research is spotty and faint, and I have had to immerse myself in the rich and elusive political, social, and intellectual history of the United States since Reconstruction to try to make historical sense of the Supreme Court's work and influence in the later stages of the Progressive era. This has proven to be a time-consuming task for one who comes to history as an unlicensed practitioner. In addition, I have been notably unsuccessful in trying to restrict my focus to the period of the White Court as such, and I am grateful for the tolerance shown by the general editor and the publisher for my penchant to stray into other periods of the Court's work and the country's history. In the midst of other scholarly and academic obligations, my completion of this volume has taken considerably more time than I anticipated, and I regret that my delays have for several years kept Professor Bickel's work from the wide audience it deserves.

Professor Bickel and I have been the beneficiaries of the support and kindness of many libraries and manuscript collections. The Library of Congress is the repository for most of the personal papers that have been consulted in the preparation of this volume. We have also made extensive use of the libraries of Yale and Columbia universities, the Oral History Collection of Columbia University, the New York Public Library, the Library of the Association of the Bar of the City of New York, the Massachusetts Historical Society, the Library of the United States Supreme Court, the National Archives, and the libraries of the University of Louisville and the University of Georgia. We owe a special debt to Mrs. Erika Chadbourne, Curator of Manuscript Collections at the Harvard Law School Library, for her helpfulness with research in the Holmes Papers, the Brandeis Court Files, the Hand Papers, and the Brandeis-Frankfurter Conversations.

Throughout the period in which work on this volume proceeded, Professor Bickel and I have benefited from the support and counsel of the Permanent Committee for the Oliver Wendell Holmes Devise and its administrative officers, especially the late Dr. Joseph P. Blickensderfer, the late Lloyd A. Dunlap, Mrs. Elizabeth E. Hamer, Mrs. Jean D. Allaway, and Dr. James Hutson.

I believe that Professor Bickel would want to record his special indebtedness to Justice Felix Frankfurter, his mentor and cherished friend, who was the proximate cause of Professor Bickel's original appointment to write this volume by the Permanent Committee of the Holmes Devise, as he was the guiding force behind the inception of the Supreme Court History Series as a whole. In addition, I know that Professor Bickel would want to thank Mrs. Isabel Poludnewycz who typed his manuscript with great care. Many students at Yale Law School helped Professor Bickel with various research chores and they will know how grateful he was for their assistance. Finally, I am sure Professor Bickel would want to express his gratitude to Professor Paul A. Freund for his encouragement, his insights, and his valuable editorial assistance.

My thanks also go to a large number of student research assistants at Columbia Law School, to Mrs. Gloria Kourie who has typed portions of this volume with great care, and to many colleagues and friends who have read drafts of my part of this manuscript and offered countless constructive suggestions, especially William Leuchtenburg, Kent Greenawalt, Harold Edgar, Peter Strauss, Bruce Ackerman, and Telford Taylor. Finally, I wish to express my great debt to Paul Freund for his encouragement, editorial assistance, and patient prodding.

Preface

Herein lie buried many things which if read with patience may show the strange meaning of being black here at the dawning of the Twentieth Century. This meaning is not without interest . . . for the problem of the Twentieth Century is the problem of the color line.

W. E. B. Du Bois[1]

THE SUPREME COURT'S race relations decisions between 1910, when Associate Justice Edward Douglass White, veteran of the Confederate Army and a leader of the opposition to Reconstruction in Louisiana, became Chief Justice, and 1921, when White died, constitute one of the Progressive era's most notable, and in some ways surprising, constitutional developments. Each of the Civil War amendments was given unprecedented application. For the first time, in the *Grandfather Clause Cases* in 1915, the Supreme Court applied the Fifteenth Amendment and what was left of the federal civil rights statutes to strike down state laws calculated to deny blacks the right to vote.[2] For the first time, in *Bailey* v. *Alabama*[3] in 1911 and *United States* v. *Reynolds*[4] in 1914, it used the Thirteeenth Amendment to strike down state laws that supported peonage by treating breach of labor contracts as criminal fraud and by encouraging indigent defendants to avoid the chain gang by having employers pay their fines in return for commitments to involuntary servitude. For the first time, in *Buchanan* v. *Warley*[5] in 1917,

---

[1] W. E. B. Du Bois, *The Souls of Black Folk* (1903), 1.

[2] See, e.g., Guinn & Beal v. United States, 238 U.S. 347 (1915); Myers v. Anderson, 238 U.S. 368 (1915).

[3] 219 U.S. 219 (1911).

[4] 235 U.S. 133 (1914).

[5] 245 U.S. 60 (1917). See *infra*, text accompanying notes 181–300.

it found in the Fourteenth Amendment constitutional limits on the spread of laws requiring racial separation, and, also for the first time, in *McCabe* v. *Atchison, Topeka & Santa Fe Railway*[6] in 1914, it put some teeth in the equality side of the "separate but equal" doctrine.

To be sure, only with respect to peonage could the White Court be said to have dismantled the legal structure of racism in any fundamental way. After the White Court passed into history in 1921, blacks in the South remained segregated and stigmatized by Jim Crow laws; disfranchised by invidiously administered literacy tests, white primaries, and poll taxes; and victimized by a criminal process from whose juries and other positions of power they were wholly excluded. But if the White Court did not blunt the newly aggressive and self-confident ideology of racism inundating America in the Progressive era, neither did it put its power and prestige behind the flood, as had the Waite and Fuller Courts that preceded it, and, at critical points, it resisted.[7] The White Court's principled countercurrents were more symbols of hope than effective bulwarks against the racial prejudice that permeated American law. But the decisions taken together mark the first time in American history that the Supreme Court opened itself in more than a passing way to the promises of the Civil War amendments.

This development is usually passed over by students of constitutional law and by historians of the Progressive era, and it raises questions about two entrenched assumptions about race relations after the Civil War. In the first place, the thesis that the Progressive era was the worst of times for black people since Reconstruction, a thesis whose powerful truth is still not firmly enough anchored in our optimistic historical consciousness about the Progressive era, needs an important qualification. In the Supreme Court in the second decade of the twentieth century, it was the best of times black people had as yet seen. In the

---

[6] 235 U.S. 151 (1914).

[7] It is true that the Waite Court handed down two decisions, Strauder v. West Virginia, 100 U.S. 303 (1880), and Yick Wo v. Hopkins, 118 U.S. 356 (1886), that altogether held considerable promise for the rights of black people. *Strauder* struck down a state law limiting jury service to white males, and *Yick Wo* invalidated a conviction of a Chinese alien for operating a wooden laundry without a permit in violation of a San Francisco ordinance, where officials had granted permits to all but one non-Chinese applicant but to none of the approxi-

mately two hundred Chinese applicants. Although the *Strauder* principle did bar states from excluding blacks altogether on the face of state laws from the exercise of civil rights, it did not reach either racial separation laws or exclusion achieved by biased administration. The *Yick Wo* principle fell into disuse in the hands of the Fuller Court because that Court refused to recognize the systematic administrative exclusion of blacks in the South from jury service and from the right to vote. See generally, Chapter XI, *infra*.

second place, the leveling tendency of our constitutional memory, pre-occupied with fundamental shifts of doctrine rather than interstitial change, has tended to see the period from *Plessy* v. *Ferguson* in 1896 to the dismantling of separate but equal that began in earnest around 1940 as one long, relatively undifferentiated slough of despond for the constitutional rights of black people. One consequence of this has been that extremely important decisions, both historically and in current doctrinal implication, have been all but forgotten. The *Peonage Cases* and *McCabe* are the prime examples. Another has been that certain decisions that have stuck in our memory, such as *Buchanan* v. *Warley* and the *Grandfather Clause Cases*, have been misunderstood both in the doctrinal and social impulses behind them and in the striking shifts of judicial attitude they entailed. The accepted view of *Buchanan* is that concerns for property protection, and not concerns about the core rights of black people, lay behind the decision. The accepted view is that the *Grandfather Clause Cases* were preordained, the inevitable reaction of even a Court committed to segregation and political exclusion of black people. Neither of these views stands up very well when measured in historical perspective.

The fact of the matter is that the White Court breathed life into Reconstruction principles that had been left for dead by the Waite and Fuller Courts for three decades. The promise of these decisions was not realized in the decade of reaction and anxiety that set in after World War I, but the decisions remained a constitutional foundation for the belated recognition of principles of racial justice that gathered momentum after World War II. The challenge for constitutional historians is to understand why these decisions occurred at a time when race relations in law, politics, and general social contemplation hit rock-bottom levels of injustice and callousness.

CHAPTER VIII

The Heyday of Jim Crow

Introduction: The Apotheosis of Jim Crow

At the turn of the twentieth century, the only school or college in Kentucky that admitted blacks and whites to the same classroom was Berea College in the Eastern mountains, near the former estates of Cassius M. Clay, the abolitionist. Founded in the 1850s to "promote the cause of Christ by instructing all youths of good moral character," Berea had opened its doors to blacks after the Civil War, and it offered in the final third of the nineteenth century, as one observer put it, "the spectacle of both races studying in the same institution in completest harmony."[1] Most of the white students were from the mountain areas of Kentucky, Tennessee, Virginia, and the Carolinas, and although about half left when blacks were first admitted, most returned shortly. The white students maintained friendly relations with the local Ku Klux Klan, and the college escaped harassment.

The early twentieth century was not hospitable to such peculiar methods of promoting the cause of Christ, however. In 1904, the Kentucky legislature, riding the aggressive drive to separate the races then sweeping the South, prohibited any person, corporation, or association from operating any educational institution "where persons of the white and negro races are both received as pupils," and likewise barred students from attending interracial classes, all under threat of a heavy fine.[2] The statute did permit institutions to operate separate and distinct

---

[1] E. King, *The Great South* (1972), 605. *Cf.* generally G. Stephenson, *Race Distinctions in American Law* (1910), 154–59.

[2] Act of March 22, 1904, ch. 85, 1904 Ky. Acts 181.

branches for each race, so long as they were at least twenty-five miles apart. When, in the shadow of this statute, Berea closed its doors to the 174 black students previously admitted, its white students sent a poignant farewell message to their black former schoolmates:

> Friends and Fellow-Students: As we meet for the first time under new conditions to enjoy the great privileges of Berea College, we think at once of you who are now deprived of these privileges. Our sense of justice shows us that others have the same rights as ourselves, and the teaching of Christ leads us to "remember them that are in bonds as bound with them."
>
> We realize that you are excluded from the class rooms of Berea College, which we so highly prize, by no fault of your own, and that this hardship is a part of a long line of deprivations under which you live. Because you were born in a race long oppressed and largely un-taught and undeveloped, heartless people feel more free to do you wrong, and thoughtless people meet your attempts at self-improvement with indifference or scorn. Even good people sometimes fear to recognize your worth, or take your part in a neighborly way because of the violences and prejudices around us.
>
> We are glad that we have known you, or known about you, and that we know you are rising above all discouragements, and showing a capacity and a character that give promise for your people. . . .[3]

The students' plaintive but hopeful "sense of justice" found no satisfaction when the college challenged the Kentucky law in the state courts. The trial court upheld the statute in a long, self-confident opinion that concluded, "[n]o well-informed person in any section of the country will now deny the position of the Southern people that 'segregation in school, church and society is in the interest of racial integrity, and racial progress.' "[4] The Kentucky Court of Appeals saw righteous principles at work. "[T]he purity of racial blood" was something "deeper and more important than the matter of choice."[5] There was no higher obligation of social welfare than to prevent "the mixing of the races in cross-breeding,"[6] and "[t]he natural law which forbids their intermarriage, and that social amalgamation which leads to a corruption of the races, is as clearly divine as that which imparted to them different natures. . . . From social amalgamation it is but a step to illicit intercourse, and but

---

[3] The letter is quoted in Stephenson, *Race Distinctions,* 156–57.

[4] The trial court opinion was not reported, but appears in the record of the cases in the Supreme Court.

[5] Berea College v. Commonwealth, 123 Ky. 209, 220–21, 94 S.W. 623, 626 (1906).

[6] *Ibid.,* at 221, 94 S.W. at 626.

another to intermarriage."[7] On top of these arguments for upholding the state statute across the board, and rather in passing, the Court of Appeals added, "[b]esides, appellant as a corporation created by this State has no natural right to teach at all. Its right to teach is such as the State sees fit to give to it."[8]

When the case made its way to the United States Supreme Court in 1908, the college had ground for hope. The right to pursue a lawful calling, such as private school teaching, without unreasonable interference could find considerable support in *Lochner* v. *New York*,[9] the seminal decision of three years before upholding occupational freedom and freedom of contract in the baking business from the "meddlesome interference" of maximum-hours legislation. A private school, the college argued, "stands upon exactly the same footing as any other private business."[10] True, *Plessy* v. *Ferguson* in 1896 had upheld a state law mandating segregation in railroad cars, but that decision had concerned "commingling of the two races upon terms unsatisfactorily to either," as the *Plessy* Court had put it, further remarking that "[i]f the two races are to meet upon terms of social equality, it must be the result of natural affinities . . . and a voluntary consent of individuals."[11] Also, to convene a private school, to associate privately and freely for purposes not only innocent but suffused with religious charity, to teach and learn with whomever one chose, these might have been viewed as legal interests of greater weight than where one had a right to sit in a railroad car.

The promised collision in the Supreme Court between principles of occupational liberty and free association and Kentucky's sweeping imperative of racial separation made the *Berea College* case one of great public interest. The Court, however, managed to skirt the problem. Kentucky was upheld, but on the very narrow ground of control of corporations so casually superimposed by the Kentucky Court of

---

[7] *Ibid.*, at 225–26, 94 S.W. at 628.

[8] *Ibid.*, at 228, 94 S.W. at 628–29.

[9] 198 U.S. 45 (1905).

[10] *Brief for Plaintiff in Error*, 10, Berea College v. Kentucky, 211 U.S. 45, 48 (1908). Berea College's argument anticipated the Supreme Court's application of occupational liberty concepts to protect freedom of choice in academic settings in Meyer v. Nebraska, 262 U.S. 390 (1923), and Pierce v. Society of Sisters, 268 U.S. 510 (1925). The state met these arguments in an extraordinary brief that leapt from pseudo-scientific data about racial differences in cranial size, brain weights, and the theory of evolution to claims about the "almightiness of heredity" and the "omnipotence of the transmitted germ plasma," in upholding the reasonableness of the statute's purpose to "preserve race identity, the purity of blood, and prevent an amalgamation." *Brief for Defendant in Error*, 4, 38–42, Berea College v. Kentucky, 211 U.S. 45 (1908).

[11] Plessy v. Ferguson, 163 U.S. 537, 544, 551 (1896).

Appeals. The opportunity to put principled limits on the reach of Jim Crow laws was not taken up; but neither did the Court embrace the state courts' paean to white supremacy. As Justice Josiah David Brewer wrote for the majority, a state's decision as to the powers conferred on one of its corporations was a purely local matter. Corporations could be denied powers that individuals or groups might have a constitutional right to exercise. That the Kentucky statute covered persons and groups as well as corporations, that it prohibited students and teachers from attending interracial schools, incorporated or not, was no barrier to dealing only with the restriction on corporate activity. Brewer surmised that the Kentucky legislature probably would have wanted to restrict interracial education by corporations, even if it could not prohibit the same activity by individuals and groups. The prohibitions on corporations and on individuals were not interdependent logically or as a practical matter. Accordingly, the Court need not consider whether individuals might have a constitutional right to associate in private, voluntary interracial education, but only whether the restriction on Berea College impaired the object of its original corporate charter, which was "the education of all persons who may attend." The college could still educate all persons, Brewer pointed out, although blacks and whites would have to be separated.[12]

This circumvention did not sit well with Justice John Marshall Harlan, a Kentuckian personally familiar with Berea College, who seized the occasion for his last great dissent in a race relations case. When Brewer felt the blast of Harlan's righteous indignation, he might well have thought back six years to his affectionately ironic celebration of Harlan's twenty-fifth anniversary on the Court. For no case could illustrate better than *Berea College* Brewer's point that Harlan had "one hand on the Constitution and the other on the Bible."[13] Obviously, it was the education of the races together that Kentucky sought to prevent, Harlan pointed out, no matter who did the educating. This was clear on the face of the statute, and it was a "reflection upon the common sense of legislators"[14] to suppose that they would have prohibited only corporations from teaching blacks and whites together if all others could do so. The state courts had sustained the statute on the broadest principles of racial separation, and the point about state control of its

---

[12] 211 U.S. at 54, 56. Fuller, White, Peckham, and McKenna joined in Brewer's opinion. Holmes and Moody concurred in the judgment only. Harlan wrote a dissent, and Day dissented without opinion.

[13] Address of D. J. Brewer, *Dinner Given by the Bar of the Supreme Court of the United States to Mr. Justice John Marshall Harlan in Recognition of the Completion of Twenty-five Years of Distinguished Service on the Bench, December 9th, 1902*, 35.

[14] 211 U.S. at 62 (Harlan, J., dissenting).

corporations was "merely incidental" and "a make-weight." As the Kentucky legislature and the state courts had done, Harlan insisted, the Supreme Court should face the basic question of principle raised by the segregation mandate.

On that question, Harlan was adamant. "The capacity to impart instruction to others is given by the Almighty for beneficent purposes," he wrote, "and its use may not be forbidden or interfered with by Government. . . .[15] If Kentucky could prevent white and black children from gathering together in private institutions of learning, it could forbid whites and blacks from sitting together in churches. No government should be allowed to "lay unholy hands on the religious faith of the people"; and yet, the right of free association for purposes of religious belief is "no more sacred nor more fully or distinctly recognized than is the right to impart and receive instruction not harmful to the public."[16] Harlan concluded with a passionate outburst that was, to borrow Hughes' words about another of his dissents, "not a swan song but the roar of an angry lion."[17]

> Have we become so inoculated with prejudice of race that an American government, professedly based on the principle of freedom, and charged with the protection of all citizens alike, can make distinctions between such citizens in the matter of their voluntary meeting for innocent purposes simply because of their respective races?[18]

Widespread press coverage confirmed Harlan's sense that the Court would be seen as having upheld a sweeping application of Jim Crow. The *New York Times* reported that the Supreme Court had held that the states could "prevent the co-education of the white and black races."[19] The *Chicago Tribune* began its editorial: "Berea College loses. That is the fact which has more interest to people in many parts of the country than the exact bearing of the decision. . . ."[20] "Statute Against Mixed Schools Constitutional" was the *Washington Post's* headline.[21] The view from below the Mason-Dixon line was the same. "A Far Reaching Decision" headlined the *Daily Picayune* in New Orleans, over

---

[15] *Ibid.,* at 65 (Harlan, J., dissenting).

[16] *Ibid.,* at 68 (Harlan, J., dissenting).

[17] This is how Hughes described Harlan's partial dissent in the *Standard Oil* antitrust case. C. E. Hughes, *Autobiographical Notes,* D. Danelski and J. Tulchin, eds. (1973), 170.

Harlan's dissent in *Standard Oil* is at 221 U.S. 1, 82–106 (1911).

[18] 221 U.S. at 69 (Harlan, J., dissenting).

[19] *New York Times,* Nov. 10, 1908, p. 1, col. 4.

[20] *Chicago Tribune,* Nov. 11, 1908, p. 8, cols. 1–2.

[21] *Washington Post,* Nov. 10, 1908, p. 11, col. 3.

a story that said the Supreme Court had held that the states could constitutionally prevent coeducation of the races.[22] The *Atlanta Constitution* was smugly reassured, and its editorial caught the sense of Southern comfort with the nation's mood about race relations in the last year of Theodore Roosevelt's Presidency:

> The soundness of the decision will nowhere be questioned except in a few remote corners where prejudice may outweigh judgmnt.
>
> It was the only decision which, in reason or justice, could have been rendered. Its vast and far-reaching importance minimizes any rebuke it contains to Berea College. . . .
>
> Radical racial differences and natural antagonisms can be overcome neither by legislative enactment nor court decision.
>
> Recognition of these differences by the highest judicial tribunal in the country will prove a far step in the direction of that better understanding which will conduce to a thoroughly peaceful and orderly solution of the great national problem involved. . . .
>
> Conservative and able thinkers of the negro race are as strenuously opposed to coeducation as are those of Caucasian blood. They know not only that attempt to enforce it would result in interminable discord and strife, freshening the fires of an antagonism now, happily, almost quenched, but they know also that the educational and industrial development and progress of their own race as well as that of the whites, will be subserved and more rapidly advanced by separation. . . .
>
> The court's decision must, therefore, be viewed as the finding most favorable to the negro race.[23]

Northern opinion seemed as little stirred by the decision as the *Atlanta Constitution* supposed, although there were a few pockets of outrage. Harlan's dissent stirred the *New York Evening Post* to editorialize, "these are noble words, and they go to the root of the matter"; and the *Philadelphia Inquirer* wondered "[w]hat American would have dreamed forty years ago that the Supreme Court of the United States would make it illegal to teach colored children and white children under the same roof."[24] But a more characteristic Northern reaction had been earlier reflected in a widely publicized statement of Charles W. Eliot, president of Harvard. At a meeting of the Twentieth Century Club of Boston to consider Berea College's situation in February 1907, after the state court decision but before the Supreme Court had acted, Eliot remarked:

---

[22] *Daily Picayune*, Nov. 21, 1908, p. 3, col. 3.

[23] *Atlanta Constitution*, Nov. 11, 1908, p. 6, cols. 2–3.

[24] *Literary Digest* (1908), 752.

Perhaps if there were as many Negroes here as there we might think it better for them to be in separate schools. At present Harvard has about five thousand white students and about thirty of the colored race. The latter are hidden in the great mass and are not noticeable. If they were equal in numbers or in a majority, we might deem a separation necessary.[25]

Along the same lines, *The Outlook*, whose editor Lyman Abbott was a stout friend of blacks on such issues as peonage and lawless violence, approved the *Berea College* decision because education of the races together "is neither a natural right nor a right guaranteed by the Constitution. Whether whites and blacks should be educated in the same school at the same time is a question to be decided by considerations of expediency or public welfare."[26]

The law reviews also lined up in support of the state. The *Harvard Law Review*, for example, thought the Court's holding on separability was strained but viewed the state's policy of segregating private schools as even more justified than segregating public transportation because "the experience of children in school has deeper relation to the morals and health of the community." The right to prohibit miscegenation being clear, "to prohibit joint education is not much more of a step."[27] The *Virginia Law Register* was lyrical: "[T]he Supreme . . . Court occasionally lets a star shine, which arouses hopes in the breast of the faithful watchers who have not entirely abandoned the doctrine of States Rights. We hail the decision in the case of Berea. . . ."[28]

The *Berea College* case was the last of the critical race-relations decisions handed down by the Supreme Court during the Chief Justiceship of Melville Weston Fuller, and it is a revelation of the state of racism under law in the United States in the first decade of the twentieth century. The drive to separate the races had swept over the private prerogatives of an institution that had opened its doors to both races to "promote the cause of Christ." In support of this aggression, the Kentucky courts relied more on divine than temporal authority, while the state's submissions to the Supreme Court mixed religious precepts and eugenic pseudo-science in an unabashed exaltation of racism. The Supreme Court permitted this far-flung extension of Jim Crow.

---

[25] Quoted in Stephenson, *Race Distinctions,* 164.

[26] *The Outlook,* 90:757–58, 1908.

[27] Note, "Constitutionality of a Statute Compelling the Color Line in Private Schools," *Harv. L. Rev.,* 22:217, 218, 1909.

[28] Editorial, "The Berea College Case," *Va. L. Reg.,* 14:643, 1908. *Cf.* generally *Central L. J.,* 68:137, 1909 (defending the decision); *Law Notes,* 12:163, 1908 (reviewing the decision and the *New York Evening Post's* criticism of it as "almost . . . a latter-day Dred Scott decision").

And yet, alongside the very heights of racism sustained in the Supreme Court's handling of the *Berea College* episode was carried a hint of constitutional dialectic. The Court strained not to have to embrace the principle of state power to subordinate the right of voluntary private association to the commands of racial separation. Kentucky was upheld on the narrowest possible ground. The Court declined the invitation it had taken up in *Plessy* v. *Ferguson* twelve years before to discourse on the constitutional irrelevance of "social equality" for blacks, and on the impotence of law to alter racial prejudice. There was no judicial indulgence of the pretense that enforced segregation does not stigmatize blacks. Instead there was an awkward tactic of avoidance, the very unpersuasiveness of which suggested that in *Berea College* the Supreme Court felt the beginning of misgivings about how far Jim Crow should be permitted to go, and perhaps even the beginning of embarrassment with the duplicity and judicial passivity reflected in *Plessy*.

The constitutional landscape surrounding racism had changed since 1896, when *Plessy* was handed down. The years between *Plessy* and *Berea College* were also roughly the years between the measured judicial restraint of *Holden* v. *Hardy*[29] and the aggressive activism of *Lochner* v. *New York*.[30] A hands-off attitude by the Court to segregation legislation that overrode principles of free association, occupational liberty, freedom of contract, and property rights posed a serious problem of consistency in the era of freewheeling, laissez-faire constitutionalism. It is not reaching far to surmise that Justice Brewer, who wrote the *Berea College* opinion and whose most memorable judicial utterance was that "[t]he paternal theory of government is to me odious," must have felt the pinch.[31] Perhaps if the decision stood alone, this would be reading a lot into the Court's retreat from adjudication on the merits in *Berea College*. But it is surely not reading too much into the decade that followed, a decade in which the Court, under the leadership of a Chief Justice from the deep South, began a halting recognition of the promises of justice for black people contained in the Thirteenth, Fourteenth, and Fifteenth amendments.

During the Progressive era, racism took deeper roots in American society than at any time since the Civil War. Many forces came together around the turn of the century to encourage racism, or at least to disable the restraining forces that since Reconstruction had held racism somewhat in check. The death of Frederick Douglass in 1895 marked the end of an era of aggressive black leadership, and in the same year at

---

[29] 169 U.S. 366 (1898).
[30] 198 U.S. 45 (1905).

[31] See Brewer's deeply felt dissent in Budd v. New York, 143 U.S. 517, 551 (1892).

the Cotton States and International Exposition in Atlanta, a little-known black educator named Booker T. Washington electrified the whites in the crowd by a brilliant oration that exhorted his people to "cast down your bucket where you are" and look to self-help in manual labor, while affirming that "[i]n all things that are purely social we can be as separate as the fingers, yet one as the hand in all things essential to mutual progress." "The wisest among my race," Washington intoned, "understand that the agitation of questions of social equality is the extremist folly. . . ."[32] As Republicans and Progressives rallied behind imperialist adventures abroad that brought eight million nonwhites under force of American arms, they took up characteristic Southern attitudes toward black people.[33] Imperialism bolstered a broad movement toward national reconciliation that tended to gloss over old sectional grievances, especially the divisive issue of race, as both major political parties sought a national base that could tap the growing sense of economic and cultural community and manifest destiny. At the same time, growing apprehension about waves of immigrants from southern and eastern Europe found an outlet in crude racial antipathies that led many among the Northern urban middle classes to look with quickened sympathy on the racial anxieties of Southern whites.[34]

Perhaps the most important impetus for the hardening of Northern attitudes toward black people was the vogue of Darwinism. The theory of evolution had a revolutionary effect on racist thinking in the United States. The subtitle of Darwin's *The Origin of the Species* was "The Preservation of Favoured Races in the Struggle for Life," and although he had initially been writing about pigeons, Darwin himself wrote in 1871 in *The Descent of Man:* "At some future period, not very distant as measured by centuries, the civilized races of man will almost certainly exterminate and replace the savage races throughout the world."[35] The intellectual currents loosed by Darwin tended to galvanize the mishmash of romantic, superstitious, and crassly exploitative modes of racist thought into a rationalized, unsentimental pseudo-scientific ideology positing the gross and innate inferiority of black people. By the 1890s, tough-minded racial Darwinists were seeing in census statistics showing

---

[32] B. T. Washington, "The Atlanta Address, September 18, 1895," in A. Blaustein and R. Zangrando, eds., *Civil Rights and the American Negro: A Documentary History* (1968), 289, 290–92.

[33] C. V. Woodward, *The Strange Career of Jim Crow* (1955), 72–74 (rev. ed., 1957), 54. For a probing discussion of the relation to imperialism of various streaks of racist thought in the United States during the Progressive era, see G. Fredrickson, *The Black Image in the White Mind* (1971), 305–11.

[34] K. Stampp, *The Era of Reconstruction 1865–1877* (1965), 19.

[35] Quoted in Fredrickson, *Black Image in the White Mind,* 230.

higher black mortality and a lower black birthrate than those of whites a demonstration of the futility of egalitarian or even traditionally paternalistic approaches to black economic, social, and political participation. As George M. Fredrickson had written:

> If the blacks were a degenerating race with no future, the problem ceased to be one of how to prepare them for citizenship or even how to make them more productive and useful members of the community. The new prognosis pointed rather to the need to segregate or quarantine a race liable to be a source of contamination and social danger to the white community, as it sank even deeper into the slough of disease, vice, and criminality.[36]

Charles Francis Adams was gripped by the new thinking when in 1908 he condemned his former naive commitment to Reconstruction principles as resting on "utter ignorance of ethnological law." He urged that race relations be approached in less of a theocratic and humanitarian, and more of a scientific spirit, bottomed on the Darwinian hypothesis that blacks were lower on the scale of evolution than whites.[37] As sociologists, psychologists, and anthropologists inundated American opinion with eugenic suppositions of the innate inferiority of black people, one Northern railroad executive summed up the prevailing views in 1910 when he described Southern attitudes toward black people as "not race prejudice but race knowledge."[38] Even Jane Addams had to concede in 1913 that "the old abolitionist arguments now seem flat and stale."[39]

On top of all this, the psychology of mass paranoia that feeds the scapegoating function of racism was amply nurtured around the turn of the century, especially in the South, by the unsettling effects of rapid industrialization and urbanization, the emergence of bitter class conflicts, the United States' entry into the exhilarating, frightening arena of world affairs, and the specter of radicalism and violence that spread beyond race relations to engulf labor disputes across the country. An awful sense of social disintegration and chaos that gripped many Americans in the late nineteenth century was fertile ground for the growth of the most hideous of all the modes of racist thinking around the turn of the century, what George M. Fredrickson has called the stereotype of the "Negro as beast," a lustful brute with raging sexual appetites for white women.[40]

[36] *Ibid.,* 255.

[37] C. Adams, *The Solid South and the Afro-American Race Problem* (1908), 16–18.

[38] R. Wiebe, *Businessmen and Reform: A Study of the Progressive Movement* (1962), 182.

[39] J. Addams," Has the Emancipation Act Been Nullified by National Indifference?" *Survey,* 29:565–66, 1913.

[40] Fredrickson, *Black Image in the White Mind,* 276 et seq.

VIII: *The Heyday of Jim Crow*

The law and politics of racism fed on itself. At the state level in the 1890s, the movement to deny black people the vote turned from sporadic violence and unsystematic official derelictions to a wholesale constitutional machinery of disfranchisement, which by the first decade of the twentieth century had managed to remove black people almost completely from political power in the South. At the same time, the totalitarian tendency of the ideology of racial separation asserted itself after Jim Crow's relatively restricted beginnings on public transportation in the South, and white politicians in the South vied with one another and their anxious constituencies in pressing the requirement of segregation into every corner of Southern life. As the main force damping potentially explosive class divisions among Southern whites, race hatred was stoked by the political interests that profited from white solidarity. The quality of white political leadership in the South went into desperate decline at about the midpoint of the Progressive era. Flamboyant demagogues like Cole Blease, Theodore Bilbo, and, in his tragic later years, Tom Watson rallied their mobs of frustrated white supporters with incendiary racial slanders of astonishing malevolence. In 1912, Cole Blease scandalized the Governor's Conference by praising lynchers and threatening to "wipe the inferior race from the face of the earth." The disapproval of respectable elements only goaded this generation of grotesque race baiters to more violent tirades.[41]

On the level of national politics as well, the Progressive era was a time of deepening gloom for black hopes. Theodore Roosevelt reflected a reasonably benevolent paternalism toward black people that, although bottomed on the notion, as Roosevelt put it in a 1906 letter to the novelist Owen Wister, that blacks "as a race and as a man . . . are altogether inferior to the whites," had faith in the long-range potential of "racial uplift" and the prospects for constructive accommodation between whites and blacks.[42] As President, Roosevelt made a few token black appointments and risked the outrage of Southern demagogues by hosting Booker T. Washington at the White House. But Roosevelt's

---

[41] As Professor Woodward has written: "Abuse by the city press was grist to [the demagogue's] mill, and the more he was badgered and set upon by respectable politicians, reforming parsons, and Northern liberals, the more readily and joyfully did a slandered, misunderstood, and frustrated following uphold his cause and identify themselves with the persecuted leader." C. V. Woodward, *Origins of the New South, 1877–1913* (1971),

393. In 1910, the Mississippi Senate resolved 25 to 1 that Bilbo was "unfit to sit with honest upright men in a respectable legislative body." *Ibid.*, 394–95.

[42] Quoted in Fredrickson, *Black Image in the White Mind*, 299–300. For an account of the racial views of Presidents Roosevelt, Taft, and Wilson, see R. Logan, *The Betrayal of the Negro* (1965), 347.

paternalism did not cause him to question segregation or political exclusion, although he did mount an aggressive campaign against peonage. By 1912, as the Progressive candidate, Roosevelt disavowed the traditional Republican commitment to federal protection for black civil and political rights.

William Howard Taft was considerably more dubious about black rights than even Roosevelt, committed as he was to sectional reconciliation and to Republican inroads in the solid South. In 1908, Taft was the first Republican candidate to campaign through the South; "Winning the South" was a favorite campaign address, the themes of which were that Southern whites were the black man's best friends and that the South need have no fear of Republican efforts to enforce "social equality." In office, however, Taft's Administration maintained the policy of investigating and prosecuting peonage and even allowed itself to be forced by an insubordinate United States Attorney in Oklahoma into prosecuting the *Grandfather Clause Cases*. Taft did nothing, however, to cast doubt on the rightness of the expanding principle of racial separation, nor did he use his party position to bring black people in the South into politics.

The election of Woodrow Wilson brought a Southern paternalist of the old school to the White House. During Wilson's Administration, segregation policies for the first time took hold in the federal government, and even the modest tradition of token high-level black appointments was largely eradicated. Blacks and whites alike saw in the Wilson Administration the vindication at the federal level of the South's policies toward black people of segregation, political exclusion, and economic dependency.

But the Progressive era saw other developments that laid the foundation for the White Court's limited recognition of rights under the Civil War amendments, and that set in motion undercurrents that would eventually end the era of Jim Crow. The growth of judicial activism in support of constitutional rights of property, occupational liberty, and freedom of contract in the first decade of the twentieth century helped to set the stage for judicial recognition of black people's civil rights in at least four ways. First, laissez-faire constitutionalism was a doctrinal structure that could, and in several key cases did, confront judicial deference to racist ideology and states' rights with a powerful counterweight. Second, apart from the particular content of the rights embraced in the heyday of substantive due process, the doctrinal by-product was a conception of constitutional rights as having a core that was hard, qualitative, and not to be trammeled by legislative majorities marching to the tune of current fashions in public policy. Third was the complex phenomenon of institutional conviction and confidence whose mysteries are buried in the phrase "judicial activism." In part, this is an explicit attitude toward the Constitution: that its commands must be respected, that it should not be circumvented by legislative verbalisms and pretexts, that forms must not overtake constitutional substance. In part, it is an implicit attitude about the institutional capacities of the Supreme Court: that the Court can hold to its assessment of social reality in the face of legislative contradiction, that the real purpose and obvious effects of legislation must be given more weight than the verbalisms of statutory language or the pretentions of legislative motivation, and that the Court, not the political institutions, is the custodian of constitutional values. Fourth, one of the central premises of laissez-faire constitutionalism, especially in the freedom of contract cases, was that rights must be appraised from the perspective of individuals rather than that of the classes or groups of which they were a part. This approach underlies the *McCabe* decision in an obvious way, but it played an important part in *Buchanan* v. *Warley* as well. Less obviously, the *Peonage Cases* reflect a sturdy individualist perspective on the rights and wrongs of contract breach by agricultural laborers.

The relationship between the recognition of black people's constitutional rights in the Progressive era and laissez-faire constitutionalism is central, but much more subtle than has commonly been supposed. To view the judicial recognition of black claims in *Buchanan* v. *Warley* or in the *Peonage Cases* as a simple doctrinal by-product of laissez-faire constitutionalism both exaggerates the hold of property rights and freedom of contract theory in constitutional law during this period, and underestimates the Court's commitment to baseline principles of individual liberty for all, blacks as well as whites. But the aggressive concepts of constitutional law and institutional role that developed between 1890 and 1910 laid the groundwork for the recognition of Reconstruction principles in the decade that followed.

The judicial process in race cases was also importantly affected by events outside the courtroom. The promise of black people to rise above discouragement, which the students at Berea College saw, was given voice by the Niagara Movement which, joined by a number of prominent white supporters of black people's rights, led in 1910 to the formation of the National Association for the Advancement of Colored People, the most significant of the many reform organizations that came into being in the Progressive era. The NAACP soon became a major voice in the Supreme Court, and for the first time, black people were given systematic litigation support in key cases, most of which were pleaded by the association's first president, the gifted, indomitable Moorfield Storey. Beyond the four corners of the judicial process, the Progressive era saw impressive gains in black mobility, economic self-sufficiency, and literacy, all contributing to unprecedented levels of black assertiveness by 1920. In 1913, fifty years after emancipation, only three out of ten black adults could not read, compared with five out of ten at the turn of the century. The Census Bureau reported in the same year that there were 128,557 black farm owners in the South, and some 38,000 black owners of businesses and 550,000 black owners of houses. To the 350,000 Southern-born blacks living north of the Mason-Dixon line in 1900 were added about 100,000 in the first decade of the twentieth century. Floods, agricultural depression, the boll weevil disasters of 1915 and 1916, and above all, World War I triggered a massive exodus of blacks from the South. By 1920, almost 800,000 Southern-born blacks lived in the North, attracted by the economic opportunities of the war economy and the access to industrial jobs opened by drastic falloffs in immigration.[43] More than 360,000 black men were drafted to serve in the armed forces during World War I, and many felt on their return, as W. E. B. Du Bois wrote in 1919: "Make way for Democracy! We saved it in France, and by the great Jehovah, we will save it in the United States of America, or know the reason why."[44] One measure of the tensions produced by new levels of black assertiveness is that the year 1919 saw race riots in many parts of the country, North and South, that, measured by loss of life, reflected the highest levels of interracial violence in American history.[45]

The Progressive era was thus the worst of times and the best of times for the freedmen. In 1913, Moorfield Storey captured both the despair and the hope of black people in protesting the Harvard Club of Philadelphia's plan to exclude blacks from its annual dinner:

> Consider for a moment the situation. There are in this country some ten millions of colored people, who are our fellow citizens, entitled to all the rights that any of us can claim under the Constitution and the law. Their ancestors were torn from their homes, brought to this country against their will, and were held as slaves until they were freed by the Civil War. The people of this country who countenanced those crimes and protected the system of slavery did these helpless Negroes the greatest possible injury, and certainly we owe them all the reparation that it is in our power to make. We have given them liberty, and, starting as emancipated slaves without property or education, they are gradually and bravely struggling upward. Their path is blocked by every kind of obstruction that ignorance and prejudice can interpose.

---

[43] See generally N. Weiss, *The National Urban League 1910–1940* (1974). Immigration fell from 1,218,-480 in 1914 to 326,700 in 1915 and continued to decrease to 110,618 in 1918. M. Ellison, *The Black Experience: American Blacks Since 1865*

(1974), 81–82.

[44] Blaustein and Zangrando, eds., *Civil Rights and the American Negro*, 334.

[45] See generally A. Waskow, *From Race Riot to Sit-In, 1919 and the 1960's* (1966).

They find themselves denied employment for which they are fitted, they are denied justice in the courts, and even in the Northern States like Pennsylvania and Illinois they are cruelly lynched and their property destroyed, as at Coatesville and Springfield, while no perpetrator of wrong against them is brought to justice. They are flouted, insulted, and despised on account of their color. . . .[46]

In the same year, in a letter seeking to encourage black editor William Munroe Trotter in the face of the segregation policies of the Wilson Administration, Storey wrote:

The mills of the Gods grind slowly and patience does its perfect work. It is only fifty years since slavery was abolished in this country, and the colored man was made free, but left poor, ignorant, and well-nigh helpless. There was and could be no organization among the former slaves for mutual defence. The States reconstructed by Andrew Johnson passed inhuman statutes of every kind framed for the purpose of re-establishing slavery in fact if not in name. Colored men were forbidden to leave their plantations, forbidden to assemble in public meetings, and denied all the rights which belong to freemen. The great organization known as the Ku Klux Klan murdered, robbed, and terrorized them, and all that their white neighbors could do to keep them down was done faithfully. Now the Ku Klux Klan seems as barbarous as the Inquisition, and in spite of every obstacle the race has forced its way upward until colored men pay taxes on $700,000,000 worth of property, own 20,000,000 acres of land, own banks and are engaged successfully in business of every kind. They have many colleges and schools, newspapers, eloquent, educated, and able leaders, and in every walk of life are proving their ability to compete with anybody. No race in the history of the world to my knowledge has made such progress from such beginnings in so short a time, and now you colored men are encountering opposition created by your very success. Instead of insisting that colored men will not work except under the lash, that they are and always must remain hewers of wood and drawers of water because they are incapable of anything else, as was claimed fifty years ago, the cry now is that there is danger of racial equality, that colored men will sit at the table with white men and may marry white men's daughters. This is not the fear of an inferior race; it is the fear that a race, though inferior, is proving its right to equality. The very arguments of those who would discriminate against you are admissions of your ability to rise, and of the fact that you have risen and are rising.[47]

Somewhere between the pathos of the students at Berea College in 1904 and the fighting faith of Moorfield Storey lies the achievement

---

[46] M. DeW. Howe, *Portrait of an Independent: Moorfield Storey* (1932), 258.

[47] *Ibid.*, 263–64.

of the Supreme Court in race cases during the Chief Justiceship of Edward Douglass White. Before 1910, only the distraught dissents of John Marshall Harlan had for thirty years kept abroad the hope that the Civil War amendments might protect the claims of black people to equality and justice. By 1910, race relations seemed immutable; blacks were segregated, out of politics except as targets for paranoid fears, and excluded from any roles in the legal system other than victim or supplicant. The White Court shook the illusion that this arrangement was permanent, giving black people in the second decade of the twentieth century more important constitutional victories than had been seen before, or would be seen again until World War II administered a shock to Jim Crow that eventually brought down the American age of racism under law.

The ambivalence so characteristic of developments in the Progressive era pervades the White Court's accomplishments in race cases. Its decisions upholding the constitutional rights of black people can be viewed as the first serious judicial commitment to Reconstruction principles, a commitment that after almost a half century of neglect kept the promises of the Civil War amendments from languishing into very deep depths of repose. It is even possible to see in these decisions the seeds of doctrines and judicial attitudes that would lead to the end of Jim Crow and disfranchisement a generation later. As against both past and future, in short, the race cases of the second decade of the twentieth century can bear a large significance. It is also possible to take a much more modest view: that the White Court happened along when the momentum of racism in American society produced laws so blatantly, even absurdly, unconstitutional that even a Court prepared to countenance racial segregation and the exclusion of black people from politics and the judicial process, so long as these aims were not proclaimed on the surface of state laws, was shamed into standing behind the formal validity of the Civil War amendments. In this view, the decision in *Buchanan* v. *Warley* striking down residential segregation could conceivably have been handed down by the same Court that approved segregation in public transportation in *Plessy* v. *Ferguson* twenty-one years before. The Grandfather Clause might have been regarded as a mechanism too explicitly calculated to deny blacks the vote, even by the Court that turned its back on wholesale disfranchisement by invidiously administered literacy and other tests.[48] And the *Peonage Cases* might be thought to be decisions that could have come down any time after Reconstruction, reflecting as they did the more or

---

[48] Guinn v. United States, 238 U.S. 347 (1915); Myers v. Anderson, 238 U.S. 368 (1915).

less accepted core principle of the Thirteenth Amendment that there must be an end of involuntary servitude.[49]

Edward Douglass White himself exemplifies this dilemma of interpretation. As Associate Justice from 1894 to 1910, White joined in every opinion denying constitutional protection to black people, including the invitations to black segregation and disfranchisement of *Plessy* v. *Ferguson* and *Williams* v. *Mississippi*. The former Confederate's promotion as the first Chief Justice from the deep South, a Southern Democrat elevated by the Northern Republican William Howard Taft, was itself one of the most conspicuous of the acts of sectional reconciliation that marked Republican subordination of concerns for racial justice. Yet as Chief Justice, White wrote for the Court in the *Grandfather Clause Cases* decisions that were considerably less preordained than they have seemed in retrospect, and joined in the *Peonage Cases* and in *Buchanan* v. *Warley*. Is it plausible to suppose that White's outlook changed when he took the center seat, reflecting in reverse the tendency to sectional reconciliation that in the political branches worked against the hopes of black people? Did events of the decade that saw the semicentennial of the Emancipation Proclamation and Appomattox, the terrible conflagration of World War I, and the massive northward migration of black people cause White and his colleagues to lengthen their view?

If one looks at the race relations decisions handed down by the Court between 1910 and 1921 with attention to the litigation history of the cases, to the way the decisions were understood by contemporary observers, and to the style of the opinions, there is much that points to an important change in the receptivity of the Supreme Court to black claims. Several of the most important decisions favoring black claims presented either serious problems of justiciability or involved non-constitutional questions whose resolution could easily have led the Court to avoid the central constitutional issues. Indeed, it is not too much to say that in several cases, the White Court reached out to protect claims of racial justice. But the essential ambivalence of the White Court's position in race cases cannot be gainsaid. None of the decisions, except possibly the *Peonage Cases*, attacked the basic structure of legalized racism in any fundamental way, and none had much practical consequence in alleviating the desperate legal and political situation of black people in this period.

The White Court's mediations of principle and prejudice in race cases in the later stages of the Progressive era are a revealing chapter

---

[49] United States v. Reynolds, 235 U.S. 133 (1914); Bailey v. Alabama, 219 U.S. 219 (1911).

in the schizophrenia inflicted on American constitutionalism by the exploitation of black people in the United States. W. E. B. Du Bois wrote in 1903 of the "double consciousness" of the black person in America: "One ever feels his twoness,—an American, a Negro; two souls, two thoughts, two unreconciled strivings; two warring ideals in one dark body, whose dogged strength alone keeps it from being torn asunder."[50] The collision between the promises of the Reconstruction amendments and the reality of American law's treatment of black people projected a comparable judicial dualism on the White Court. In casting a few shafts of constitutional principle into the legacy of prejudice left by the Fuller Court, the White Court grappled with basic contradictions between principle and prejudice in American law.

II.   The Supreme Court and Racial Segregation

A.   THE HISTORICAL CONTEXT

The Supreme Court's involvement in racial segregation during the first two decades of the twentieth century was rooted in the last two decades of the nineteenth, when the Court turned away from the constitutional claims of Reconstruction. Among the many nineteenth-century decisions that played a role, two carried the main burden of repudiation: the *Civil Rights Cases*, decided in 1883, and *Plessy* v. *Ferguson*,[51] decided in 1896. These cases dealt with racial segregation in railroads or other public accommodations; the first involved the constitutionality of a federal statute prohibiting it, the second a state statute requiring it.

Segregation first became a major political issue in the 1870s as many private railroads and streetcar companies, theaters, hotels, and restaurants excluded blacks altogether or set them apart in Jim Crow areas. The practice was not much more extensive in the South than in the North. The concerted and much-publicized resistance of blacks to these insults helped [Sumner had died by then] drive congressional Republicans to what was both the crowning achievement and the last gasp of the Radical effort to enshrine the principle of equality in American law. "Whereas it is essential to just government we recognize the equality of all men before the law," the Civil Rights Act of 1875 began, "all persons within the jurisdiction of the United States shall be entitled to the full and equal enjoyment of the accommodations . . . in inns, public conveyances on land or water, theaters and other places of public amusement . . . applicable alike to citizens of every race and color. . . ."[52]

---

[50] Du Bois, *Souls of Black Folk*, 4.
[51] The Civil Rights Cases, 109 U.S. 3 (1883); Plessy v. Ferguson, 163 U.S. 537 (1896).
[52] Act of March 1, 1875, ch. 114, 18 Stat. 335.

In 1883, when the Supreme Court finally decided the dozens of cases dealing with the Act's constitutionality, the Court's opinion was authored by Justice Joseph P. Bradley, who had cast the deciding vote in the Electoral Commission which threw the election of 1876 to Rutherford B. Hayes, and set in place the complex series of political events that historians have termed the Compromise of 1877, marking the end of the Reconstruction period. An ardent Unionist from New Jersey, a supporter of Lincoln and Grant, a backer of the Civil War amendments, Bradley now was joined by seven colleagues—only one from the South (William Woods of Georgia), all but one Republican, and the only Democrat (Stephen J. Field), appointed by Lincoln—in carrying out the first installment of the Court's contribution to the end of Reconstruction. Treating complex questions simply, the Court found the Civil Rights Act of 1875 beyond Congress' enforcement powers under the Thirteenth and Fourteenth amendments. "It would be running the slavery argument into the ground," Bradley wrote, to view acts of private discrimination as badges of slavery that Congress could prohibit under its power to enforce the abolition of slavery.[53] As for the Fourteenth Amendment, it only permitted Congress to deal with state, not private, action. Bradley drew support from assumed requirements of state law that common carriers, innkeepers, and the like not discriminate, and in a muddy passage, he invited Congress to counteract any state laws which required, or perhaps even countenanced, discrimination. But private discrimination by railroads, inns, theaters, and the like was beyond Congress' reach. In treating racial discriminations by inns, public carriers, and the like as private action, Bradley ignored the long legal tradition of imposing special duties and privileges on such public instrumentalities, extensively documented six years before in *Munn* v. *Illinois*.[54] Likewise passed over was the point that the clearest sense, as a matter of language, in which a state could deny equal protection was by inaction in protecting one group while acting to protect another, as by requiring certain businesses to serve the public generally but not black people.

To be sure, a state's inaction against private discrimination is different from refusal to enforce impartially the criminal law, but to conceive of discrimination by inns, public conveyances, and the like as "private discrimination" begged a central question. The question of Congress' power to prohibit discrimination in public accommodations was genuinely difficult, but Bradley's failure even to contend with the arguments for such power suggests that the key to his and the majority's thinking lay in this statement toward the end of the opinion: "When a

---

[53] 109 U.S. at 24.   [54] 94 U.S. 113 (1877).

man has emerged from slavery . . . there must be some stage in the progress of his elevation when he takes the rank of a mere citizen, and ceases to be the special favorite of the laws. . . ."[55]

Only Justice Harlan, a Southerner, and a former slaveholder at that, offered a lonely and, as it seemed, eccentric voice of protest. *The Civil Rights Cases* mirrored the basic elements of the Compromise of 1877 and the dominant mood of the country. In striking down Congress' power to protect blacks from the stigma of segregation in public accommodations, the Court provided a constitutional footing for the Republican party's readiness to turn its back on the issue of equal treatment for the freedmen. The opinion's vacuous references to the presumed protections of state law paralleled Republican rationalizations about the presumed paternal care the New South would extend to blacks, rationalizations that helped the successors of Lincoln abjure responsibility for the withdrawal of federal protection.[56] The Court even gave voice to the country's petulant air of illusion in its defensive posturing that blacks should no longer be "the special favorite of the laws."[57]

The Supreme Court gave its full constitutional blessings to Jim Crow in the 1890s when racial separation matured from a matter of private prejudice to a mandate of state law. The first batch of Jim Crow laws after the Civil War covered railroad cars. The "separate car law" was a fitting legal symbol for a Southern society in motion, losing its roots in the solid earth of feudal agricultural arrangements that had kept blacks in their place without the need for a legal structure specifically enforcing racial separation. Segregation laws had been originally a Northern contrivance, commonplace above the Mason-Dixon line before the Civil War,[58] and they were revived by Southern legislatures when emancipation, new conditions of personal mobility, and urbanization threatened the heritage of caste that had managed to coexist in the old South with rather relaxed and close associations between the

---

[55] 109 U.S. at 25.

[56] On the country's mood in this period see P. Buck, *The Road to Reunion* (1962); on the Republican commitment to Reconstruction principles see S. Hirshson, *Farewell to the Bloody Shirt: Northern Republicans and the Southern Negro 1873–1893* (1962).

[57] Another 1883 decision, hardly noticed at the time, helped lay the foundation for the acceptability of segregation. In Pace v. Alabama, 106 U.S. 583 (1883), a unanimous Court, in an offhand opinion of little more than a page, saw nothing wrong with an Alabama statute punishing more severely adultery and fornication between whites and blacks than the same offenses between persons of the same race. This was not racial discrimination, Justice Field explained, because the same punishment was applied to whites and blacks for the same offense.

[58] C. V. Woodward, "The Case of the Louisiana Traveler," in J. A. Garraty, ed., *Quarrels That Have Shaped the Constitution* (1966) 145.

races.[59] Aside from a few short-lived statutes after the Civil War, lasting Jim Crow legislation began in Florida in 1887 with a requirement that railroads put blacks in separate cars or in separate compartments.[60] Ironically, this was the same year that the Interstate Commerce Act barred railroads from causing customers "undue or unreasonable prejudice or disadvantage." But the ICA was concerned with economic favoritism, and it was the impulse of the state laws to segregate, not the federal statute's ban on discrimination, that carried the nation's dominant convictions on race relations.[61] Riding the crest of Democratic

---

[59] White Southerners, Ray Stannard Baker wrote in 1906, "want the New South but the old Negro. That Negro is disappearing forever along with the old feudalism and the old-time exclusively agricultural life." R. S. Baker, *Following the Color Line* (1964), 44. Baker saw the Jim Crow car as the symbol of white insistence on projecting the heritage of caste into the future: "In their homes and in ordinary employment, they meet as master and servant; but in the street cars they touch as free citizens, each paying for the right to ride, the white not in a place of command, the Negro without an obligation of servitude." *Ibid.,* 30. Of all the abundant discriminations and disabilities with which they had to deal, separation in trains and streetcars was the most bitter pill for Southern blacks, Baker reported. *Ibid.,* 31.

[60] Although railroad companies commonly discriminated against blacks in the South after the Civil War, the usual arrangement was to exclude blacks from the first-class, or "ladies," cars, but to allow them to sit with whites in the second-class "smokers." In the seaboard South, blacks were allowed in first-class cars alongside whites. In no state before the 1880s was segregation required by law. There was a brief period of statutory Jim Crow immediately after the Civil War as Mississippi, Florida, and Texas in 1865 and 1866 adopted laws requiring segregation on the railroad. All of these laws were quickly aborted

during Reconstruction. Woodward, *Strange Career of Jim Crow,* xv.

Although the legal regime of Jim Crow did not become systematic until the 1890s, the general attitude that blacks and whites should be segregated had its origins in attitudes toward free blacks that were commonplace before the Civil War. These attitudes were revealed in a number of important judicial statements about segregation before the war, e.g., Roberts v. City of Boston, 5 Cush. (59 Mass.) 198, 206–209 (1848) (Shaw, C. J., sustaining the constitutionality under the Massachusetts Constitution of separate public schools for whites and blacks in Boston); Crandall v. State, 10 Conn. 340 (1934); Dred Scott v. Sandford, 19 How. (60 U.S.) 393, 407 (1857): Fisher's Negroes v. Dabbs, 6 Yerger 119 (Tenn. Sup. Ct., 1934).

[61] The Interstate Commerce Act was read as consistent with the Jim Crow policies expressed in these state statutes. Racial discrimination was not adverted to in the congressional hearings or debates which led to the Act: the impulse behind the antidiscrimination provision was prevention of economic favoritism by carriers to preferred shippers. See, e.g., *Report of the Senate Select Comm. on Interstate Commerce,* S. Rep. No. 46, 49th Cong., 1st Sess. (1886), 215. Nonetheless, challenges to racial separation on railroads came to the Interstate Commerce Commission almost imme-

radicalism, the Jim Crow car entered the law books of Mississippi the next year; Texas in 1889; Louisiana in 1890; Alabama, Arkansas, Georgia, and Tennessee in 1891; and Kentucky in 1892.[62]

An obvious constitutional problem with these laws was that railroads were instrumentalities of interstate transportation, and a recent case had squarely held that state commands going to racial seating arrangements on such instrumentalities interfered with interstate commerce. In 1878 in *Hall* v. *DeCuir*,[63] a unanimous Court had held invalid as applied to interstate carriers a provision of a Louisiana Reconstruction Constitution and an implementing statute that gave "equal rights and privileges" to all passengers on public conveyances.[64] A riverboat plying between New Orleans and Vicksburg, Mississippi, was held by the state courts to have violated this law by segregating a black passenger traveling between two points in Louisiana on a segment of the Mississippi River that flowed wholly within that state. The Supreme Court thought such rules governing passenger disposition within Louisiana would affect the carrier's conduct throughout the voyage. If each state regulated such matters within its borders, a carrier might have to change passenger arrangements from one side of the Mississippi River to the other. "Commerce cannot flourish in the midst of such embarrassments,"[65] Chief Justice Waite wrote. Uniformity of regulation in such matters was a necessity, and thus Congress must have exclusive power to act.

Because the case arose before 1875, the Civil Rights Act of 1875 did not apply, and no other congressional statute was relevant. Congress' inaction meant that interstate commerce must be left " 'free and untrammelled,' "[66] a principle the Court applied in *Hall* as meaning the carrier was free to adopt reasonable rules for the comfort of passengers. Segregation of passengers was thought to be so obviously a reasonable regulation that Waite's majority opinion did not discuss the point, although Justice Clifford, concurring, cited chapter and verse from the

---

diately, and in a series of decisions, the commission held that the Act permitted racial separation, although it did require strict equality in accommodations. Councill v. Western & Atlantic R.R., 1 I.C.C. 339 (1887); Heard v. Georgia R.R., 1 I.C.C. 428 (1888); Heard v. Georgia R.R., 3 I.C.C. 111 (1889). In the first three cases that came before it, the commission ruled that accommodations for blacks were not equal and violated

the Act. Later, the commission would loosen considerably the obligation of equality in the provision of separate accommodations for blacks.

[62] Woodward, *Strange Career of Jim Crow*, 146.

[63] 95 U.S. 485 (1878).

[64] La. Const. of 1869, Art. 13.

[65] 95 U.S. at 489.

[66] *Ibid.*, at 490 (quoting Welton v. Missouri, 91 U.S. 275, 282 (1875).

Northern law of school segregation to support his view that the Louisiana statute was an unreasonable interference.[67]

When the first of the railroad segregation statutes reached the Supreme Court in *Louisville, New Orleans & Texas Railway* v. *Mississippi*[68] in 1890, the Court revealed a greater commitment to the flourishing of segregation than to the flourishing of commerce. The Mississippi separate car law of 1888 was the reverse of the Louisiana law struck down in *Hall*, but the impact on interstate commerce looked similarly "embarrassing." Seeking to avoid the rule of *Hall*, the Mississippi courts had construed the law to affect commerce within the state only, a feeble effort at distinction since the Louisiana court in *Hall* had applied the integration requirement only to the Louisiana segment of an interstate voyage at the instance of a passenger traveling within the state only. But the Louisiana courts in *Hall* had recognized that they were dealing with a piece of an interstate voyage, whereas the Mississippi courts refused to recognize this obvious fact about railroads. On these conclusory verbalisms of the state courts, the Supreme Court managed to distinguish the cases. The operative effect on an interstate railroad was the same: a railroad with integrated seating coming from outside the state would have to add a Jim Crow car for the Mississippi portion of its run. But what the *Hall* decision deemed an embarrassment to interstate commerce when the state required integration was now discovered to be little or no trouble. Justice Harlan, joined in this case by Bradley, found it "difficult to understand how a state enactment, requiring the separation of the white and black races on interstate carriers of passengers, is [not] a regulation of commerce among the states, while a similar enactment forbidding such separation is a regulation of that character."[69] But the Court was prepared to subordinate the consistency of the commerce principle to the consistency of the segregation result.

In upholding the Mississippi statute in the *Louisville* decision, Justice Brewer stressed that the only question before the Court was whether railroads had to install segregated facilities, hinting that whether black passengers could be forced to use them would pose questions of personal rights not decided. This was a common style in the Court's decisions dealing with the rights of black people around the turn of the

---

[67] According to Waite's biographer, Justices Miller, Strong, and Hunt supported the Louisiana law in conference but decided not to register their dissent. Justice Harlan did not participate. C. Magrath, *Morrison R.* *Waite: The Triumph of Character* (1963), 140.

[68] 133 U.S. 587 (1890).

[69] *Ibid.*, at 594 (Harlan, J., dissenting). Harlan carelessly reversed the *Hall* and *Louisville* holdings.

century. A state law of broad effect would be upheld gingerly in its particular application, with the Court ducking the legitimacy of the law's broader impact or even casting vague doubts. But the doubts drifted on such looseness of reasoning that the lower courts were not encouraged to evolve any doctrinal counterpoint. The laws were left intact and operated in life with their full breadth. Thus, state and lower federal courts routinely upheld state laws segregating interstate transportation facilities, despite the implications of *Hall* v. *DeCuir* and the reservations of *Louisville*.[70]

In 1896, when *Plessy* v. *Ferguson* posed the issue the Court had left open in *Louisville*, whether a black passenger could be forced by law to submit to segregation, the Court at least had the courage to bare its doctrinal convictions. The result was a decision that was one of the cornerstones of the law of race relations through the Progressive era and beyond. *Plessy* was a case arranged by Louisiana railroads and a committee of blacks in New Orleans to challenge the constitutionality of an "Act to promote the comfort of passengers" enacted in Louisiana in 1890 requiring railroads to provide "equal but separate accommodations for the white and colored races."[71] There was a revealing exception: "nurses attending children of the other race" were not covered. The railroads wanted no part of the law because of the expense entailed and because it obliged them to assign passengers to their proper racial places, a ticklish business in Louisiana. Blacks' objections were forcefully put in the Supreme Court brief of their lawyer, Albion W. Tourgee, the colorful Reconstruction carpetbagger in North Carolina and sometime novelist:

> The exemption of nurses shows that the real evil lies not in the color of the skin but in the relation the colored person sustains to the white. If he is a dependent, it may be endured: if he is not, his presence is insufferable. Instead of being intended to promote the *general* comfort and moral well-being, this act is plainly and evidently intended to promote the happiness of one class by asserting its supremacy and the

---

[70] S. M. Lemmon, "Transportation Segregation in the Federal Courts Since 1865," *J. Negro Hist.*, 38:174, 1953. The *Louisville* decision also left open the question whether *interstate* passengers traveling on an interstate conveyance could be forced by state law to submit to segregation while traveling through a state requiring it. In 1900, the Supreme Court made clear that passengers in the midst of interstate journeys could not be forced

to submit to state Jim Crow laws. In Chesapeake & Ohio Ry. v. Kentucky, 179 U.S. 388 (1900), the Court held that a state law applicable in its terms to all railroad traffic within the state must be construed to cover only passengers traveling within the state. For the state law to apply to interstate passengers, the Court held, was clearly unconstitutional.

[71] 1890 La. Acts no. 111.

inferiority of another class. Justice is pictured blind and her daughter, the Law, ought at least to be color-blind.[72]

The Supreme Court's response to Tourgee's indignation was in tune with the times. Politics and public opinion had turned decisively against Reconstruction's opaque commitment to equal protection. Alabama and Mississippi had already disfranchised blacks, as agrarian radicalism in the 1890s in the South had led anxious moderates to bolster their shaky leadership by fanning the flames of white supremacy. In 1891, Congress had defeated the Lodge Bill, which would have broadened federal protection to blacks seeking to vote in federal elections, and three years later it had wiped from the books virtually all the explicit Reconstruction statutory protections for black voting rights. In 1895, the year before *Plessy*, Booker T. Washington had embraced racial separation, at least "in all things social," in his hugely publicized Atlanta address.

The *Plessy* opinion, by Justice Henry Billings Brown, was an untroubled endorsement of racial separation. The Fourteenth Amendment "could not have been intended to abolish distinctions based upon color, or to enforce social, as distinguished from political, equality, or a commingling of the two races upon terms unsatisfactory to either." Laws requiring separation of the races in public schools had long existed in states like Massachusetts, New York, and Ohio, where the political rights of the colored race have been longest and most earnestly enforced.[73] Even Congress had authorized segregated schools in the District of Columbia, Brown pointed out. The question was whether

---

[72] Quoted in Woodward, *Strange Career of Jim Crow*, 152–53. Tourgee scoffed at the semblance of equality and impartial treatment that the state courts had perceived in the law. It was designed to debase the "inferior race," to gratify "the sentiment of white superiority and white supremacy of right and power." He asked the Justices to imagine being put in a Jim Crow car: "What humiliation, what rage would then fill the judicial mind." *Ibid.*, 153.

[73] 163 U.S. 537, 545 (1896). The state cases on which Brown relied, including preeminently Chief Justice Lemuel Shaw's Massachusetts ruling in Roberts v. Boston, 59 Mass. (1 Cush.) 198 (1850), were decided before the Fourteenth Amendment was

adopted, and Brown has been chastised for using them as evidence of what Northern states thought was permissible after the Fourteenth Amendment. However, Brown was not citing them as implicit precedents on the meaning of the Fourteenth Amendment, but rather as evidence of the widespread acceptance of segregation in areas where the legal rights of blacks were most extensively recognized before the Civil War. Brown might have added that most of the Northern states with any significant black population required school segregation when they ratified the Fourteenth Amendment. See generally A. M. Bickel, "The Original Understanding and the Segregation Decision," *Harv. L. Rev.*, 69:1, 1955.

the Louisiana law was reasonable, and the state legislature must be able to act in accord with "the established usages, customs, and traditions of the people."

Brown had a leg to stand on in his appeal to original intent and prevailing practices, but he slipped into absurdity when he tried to supply reasons apart from historical momentum for upholding the Louisiana statute.

> We consider the underlying fallacy of the plaintiff's argument to consist in the assumption that the enforced separation of the two races stamps the colored race with a badge of inferiority. If this be so, it is not by reason of anything found in the act, but solely because the colored race chooses to put that construction upon it. . . . The argument also assumes that social prejudice may be overcome by legislation, and that equal rights cannot be secured to the negro except by an enforced commingling of the two races. . . . If the two races are to meet upon terms of social equality, it must be the result of natural affinities, a mutual appreciation of each other's merits and a voluntary consent of individuals. . . . Legislation is powerless to eradicate racial instincts or to abolish distinctions based upon physical differences, and the attempt to do so can only result in accentuating the difficulties of the present situation. If the civil and political rights of both races be equal one cannot be inferior to the other civilly or politically. If one race be inferior to the other socially, the Constitution of the United States cannot put them upon the same plane.[74]

Alone in dissent, Justice Harlan addressed the bygone convictions of Reconstruction to the conscience of posterity.[75] It was the greatest of his many great dissents, and, elevated to prevailing doctrine in the second half of the twentieth century, stands as one of the most majestic utterances in the whole course of American law. It was also, in its day, shouting into the wind. Harlan, a Southerner, had had no truck with the "underlying fallacy" on which Brown had pinned his argument. "Every one knows" that the segregation law had the purpose of compelling black citizens to keep to themselves, and "[n]o one would be so wanting in candor as to assert the contrary," Harlan claimed, although this was precisely what the Court's opinion had just asserted. The "thin disguise of 'equal' accommodations for passengers in railroad coaches will not mislead anyone, or atone for the wrong this day done." The decision would permit the races to be forced apart in jury boxes, on

---

[74] 163 U.S. at 551–52.

[75] Justice Brewer did not participate, but in view of his opinion in *Louisville* upholding the Mississippi railroad segregation law of 1888, and his later decision in *Berea College,* there is little doubt that he would have stood with the majority in *Plessy.*

the streets, in legislative halls, and at public gatherings, Harlan protested, even though such separation was "conceived in hostility to, and enacted for the purpose of humiliating," black citizens. But Harlan did not stop to rest only on the claim of bad purpose: "[I]n view of the Constitution, in the eye of the law, there is in this country no superior, dominant ruling class of citizens. There is no caste here. Our Constitution is color-blind, and neither knows nor tolerates classes among citizens."[76] The decision, he feared, would "stimulate aggressions, more or less brutal and irritating, upon the admitted rights of colored citizens," and "encourage the belief that it is possible, by means of state enactments, to defeat the beneficent purposes . . . of the Constitution." Harlan concluded with prophetic words:

> Sixty millions of whites are in no danger from the presence of eight millions of blacks. The destinies of the two races, in this country, are indissolubly linked together, and the interests of both require that the common government of all shall not permit the seeds of race hate to be planted under the sanction of law. What can more certainly arouse race hate, what more certainly create and perpetuate a feeling of distrust between these races, than state enactments, which, in fact proceed on the ground that colored citizens are so inferior and degraded that they cannot be allowed to sit in public coaches occupied by white citizens? That, as all will admit, is the real meaning of such legislation as was enacted in Louisiana.[77]

Plessy is rich in surprise. "The most fascinating paradox in American jurisprudence," Professor C. Vann Woodward has written, "is that the opinions of two sons of Massachusetts, Shaw and Brown, should have bridged the gap between the radical equalitarian commitment of 1868 and the reactionary repudiation of that commitment in 1896; and that a Southerner [Harlan] should have bridged the greater gap between the repudiation of 1896 and the radical rededication of the equalitarian idealism of Reconstruction days in 1954."[78] There is surprise on the level of doctrine, as well. This bedrock decision of the "separate but equal" principle said nothing about equality, and indeed, in its reasoning, seemed to reject equality as a condition to the constitu-

---

[76] 163 U.S. at 557, 562, 563, 559. Just before that, Harlan had written:

The white race deems itself to be the dominant race in this country. And so it is, in prestige, in achievements, in education, in wealth, and in power. So, I doubt not, it will continue to be for all time, if it remains true to its great heritage and holds fast to the principles of constitutional liberty.

Ibid., at 559.

[77] *Ibid.,* at 560.

[78] Woodward, *Strange Career of Jim Crow,* 155.

tionality of Jim Crow. The ruse of the segregation statutes, including the one upheld in *Plessy*, was to require "equal but separate" accommodations, a verbalism designed to dovetail with the requirement of equal protection in the Fourteenth Amendment. But the *Plessy* Court did not indulge the fiction of equality; its rationale was that railroad seating belonged to the domain of social relations rather than political rights, and the opinion expressly stated that the purpose of the Fourteenth Amendment "in the nature of things" could not have been to enforce social, as distinguished from political and civil, equality. Separation of the races in "social relations" was the principle announced; "separate but equal" was the style of the later apologetics of constitutional racism, but it cannot be found in the rationale of *Plessy* v. *Ferguson*.

Another surprise about *Plessy* is that this most momentous decision concerning the rights of blacks was greeted by the nation with hardly a ripple of notice. The *Civil Rights Cases* thirteen years before had set off waves of press reaction, congressional agitation, and public clamor. So closely did *Plessy* mirror the spirit of the age, however, that the country hardly noticed.

Although *Plessy* set the Court and the country firmly on the path of Jim Crow, the decision left many questions for the future. First, the absence of concern with equality in the opinion, but its presence in the statute upheld, left unclear whether inequality of treatment might cast doubt on the validity of racial separation. Obviously, inequality would not be a rigorous condition. In many settings, insistence on anything approaching real equality would have crushed the separate but equal principle under the impossible economic burden of true redundancy, and also would have worked at cross purposes with the plain motivation of such laws to degrade blacks as inferiors. Since equality was patently a fiction in the law of segregation as it operated in life, the question was how the judicial role would be played in the constitutional charade, and whether anything short of absolute deprivation, naked on the face of a statute, or even that, would be deemed so unequal as to upset the validity of segregation. Second, what was the distinction between "the political equality of the negro," which the Constitution was said to ensure, and "social equality," which it did not?[79] Brown gave

---

[79] Brown's repeated use of the term "political equality," which the Fourteenth Amendment was said to protect, to contrast with "social equality," which the Amendment did not protect, was a curious breach with the constitutional tradition. During and after Reconstruction, it was routinely asserted that the Fourteenth Amendment did not protect political equality, since voting rights were generally assumed not to be covered by the Equal Protection Clause, in view of the explicit remedy of reduced congressional

two entirely unhelpful examples of what he meant by political equality: the right of blacks not to be excluded from juries and the right of blacks to integrated accommodations on railroads where local law required such integration. The first example dealt with exclusion, not separation, and the second turned on local law, not the Fourteenth Amendment. Would residential segregation fall on the political or social side of the line? Would required segregation of private schools be deemed to interfere with "political rights" of voluntary association?

The obscure line between political and social equality was not Brown's only hint of doctrinal limits as to how far racial separation could be taken. Harlan's dissent paraded such seemingly farfetched horribles as separation in public streets, on streetcars, in the courtrooms, or in legislative galleries. "The reply to all this," responded Brown airily, "is that every exercise of the police power must be reasonable, and extend only to such laws as are enacted in good faith for the promotion of the public good, and not for the annoyance or oppression of a particular class."[80] By this language, the Court set aside the antidiscrimination principle of *Strauder* v. *West Virginia*[81] as the governing constitutional principle for laws embodying racial classifications and replaced it with a vague rule of reason. The future would tell whether this "rule of reason" reflected some diffuse sense of limits on the spread of segregation, or whether it was merely the lame rejoinder of a judge who did not care to confront the reach of his *ratio decidendi*.

Finally, built into the majority's reasoning was the possibility of a third limiting principle. Brown referred to the purpose of the Louisiana law as being the prevention of "an enforced commingling of the two races." Freedom of choice was a dubious justification for a law mandating segregation, but the weight given this argument in the Court's reasoning implied a different approach to noncompulsory settings, as Brown seemed to recognize: "If the two races are to meet upon terms of social equality, it must then be the result of natural affinities, a mutual appreciation of each other's merits and a voluntary consent of individuals." How far "the voluntary consent of individuals" might be secure from the state's impulse to segregate was left unclear. Brown pointed out that laws forbidding whites and blacks to marry were "universally recognized as within the police power of the State," even though he allowed that such laws "may be said in a technical sense to interfere with the freedom of contract."[82] But marriage was a relation-

---

representation specified in Section 2. The usual claim made about the Fourteenth Amendment was that it protected "civil equality," as opposed to both political and social equality.

Brown appears to have used the terms political and civil interchangeably.

[80] 163 U.S. at 550.
[81] 100 U.S. 303 (1880).
[82] 163 U.S. at 545, 551.

ship grounded in state law, and miscegenation laws had unquestioning acceptance in almost all quarters. Brown's reasoning suggested that other occasions for voluntary association between the races, in private educational institutions, for example, might be beyond the reach of state interference. The *Berea College Case* would test the Court on this issue, and the Court would shy away.

Elements of paradox in *Plessy* were not restricted to the majority opinion. In tracing out the logical extremities of racial separation, Justice Harlan undoubtedly thought that he had enlisted the force of the absurd in his resistance to Jim Crow. But the absurdity in retrospect is that what Harlan himself probably thought farfetched extensions of the separation principle became reality in the South within a decade. The Supreme Court stood by as the South took *Plessy* as authority for drawing the color line into the most improbable corners of Southern life. But the ultimate irony of Harlan's position in *Plessy*, one of which he was surely unconscious, was that the next important judicial sanctification of segregation would come three years later in an opinion by himself, in which the Court laid the foundation for half a century of segregation in public education, the very area of public law in which Harlan's approach in *Plessy* would ultimately be vindicated half a century later.

Perhaps more has been made of *Cumming* v. *Richmond County Board of Education*[83] than is justified, since the case was mishandled by counsel and since the particular official decision under review was not in itself unfriendly to blacks. But Harlan's opinion in *Cumming* would eventually be seen as upholding not only the principle of segregation in public schools but also blatant inequality. The Board of Education in Richmond County, Georgia, had closed the only public high school for blacks after deciding that the building could be put to better use as a primary school for a larger number of younger black children who were without any school to attend. The Board promised to open a new black high school when it could afford to, and it claimed that three church-affiliated high schools were open to blacks at no greater expense than the annual $10 fee that had been charged to blacks attending the public high school. In the meantime, the Board continued to support a public high school for white girls, allegedly because a large gift for the maintenance at that particular high school depended on its continuation, and although no public high school for white boys existed in the county, the Board did appropriate public funds to assist a Baptist high school that would take all white male high school students for $15 per year.

The black taxpayers and parents who challenged this situation in the Georgia courts did not think to question the principle of segregation in

---

[83] 175 U.S. 528 (1899).

public education, but they asked that the tax collector be enjoined from levying taxes for the support of the white high schools so long as no high school for blacks was given public support. The Board obviously was puzzled by their ingratitude. The Board answered that it had given black high school patrons "every respect and consideration," and had explained to them that four hundred black children in the county were without any elementary schools. The black high school served only sixty students, but could, if converted, accommodate many more of the black children. It would be unconscionable "to keep up a high school for 60 pupils and turn away 300 little negroes who are asking to be taught their alphabet and to read and write."[84]

When the case reached the Supreme Court, the complainants' approach backfired. But even had they pleaded the case well, the Supreme Court almost certainly would not have granted relief. First, the complainants changed their tactics and sought to challenge squarely the county's system of segregated education, but since they had not raised this contention below, the Court refused to consider it. This was not their only misjudgment. The Court found fault also with the relief they sought, which would have deprived the white students without giving blacks additional high school opportunities. In any event, Justice Harlan wrote, the Board's decision was "in the interest of the greater number of colored children." The evidence did not show that the Board had sought to harm the black students, but even if it had, Harlan indicated, the proper relief for a court of equity would have been to require schooling for blacks, not the withholding of education from whites. Harlan added that, although the burdens and benefits of taxation must be shared by all citizens, "the education of the people in schools maintained by state taxation is a matter belonging to the respective States," and interference by the federal courts would require "clear and unmistakable disregard of rights secured by the supreme law of the land."[85]

Thus, it was reasonably clear after *Cumming* that even Justice Harlan took for granted the authority of the state to segregate public schools. *Cumming* indicates that the essence of Harlan's conception of an equal protection violation was a hostile purpose to degrade blacks on account of their race, not the mere use of a racial classification. Moreover, Harlan apparently thought that public education was virtually an autonomous state function. So Chief Justice Taft viewed *Cumming* in 1927 when he drew from the decision the unqualified conclusion that the Supreme Court had settled the power of states to segregate public education.[86] And so Harlan would himself make clear in 1908 in his

---

[84] The Board's answer was quoted in Justice Harlan's statement of the case, 175 U.S. 528, 533 (1899).

[85] *Ibid.*, at 544–45.
[86] Gong Lum v. Rice, 275 U.S. 78 (1927).

759

dissent to the *Berea College* decision. It is virtually certain, moreover, that Harlan's approval of segregated public education reflected his own sense of constitutional principle, and not a reluctant observance of the force of the *Plessy* precedent. Harlan was no respecter of precedent, particularly one he disagreed with as vehemently as *Plessy* v. *Ferguson*.

Alongside and after *Cumming*, segregation swept through the laws of the Southern states and beyond. The turn of the century marked a turning point for Jim Crow. The first wave of railroad segregation laws had encountered stiff resistance in the Southern seaboard, but as Virignia, the last holdout, fell in 1900, the Richmond *Times* sounded the theme for the new century: "It is necessary that this principle be applied in every relation of Southern life. God Almighty drew the color line and it cannot be obliterated. The negro must stay on his side of the line. . . ."[87] The first radiations touched points of nearest contagion. After 1900, all the Southern states quickly required segregated waiting rooms in railway stations. Streetcars were next, as Jim Crow swept aside the last effective conservative resistance in the cities of the South. Streetcar companies opposed these laws nearly everywhere, citing the expense and practical difficulty, and blacks responded with boycotts in more than twenty-five Southern cities. But when blacks looked to white conservatives for help, the paternalistic commitments of the late nineteenth century had withered. After a few initial successes, the boycotts failed. The victory of Jim Crow on the trolleys of cities across the South set the stage for rigid, ubiquitous segregation.[88]

B. Southern Society Under Jim Crow

In *The Mind of the South*, W. J. Cash wrote of the scene in 1914, "There is an atmosphere here, an air, shining from every word and deed. And the key to this atmosphere . . . is that familiar word without which it would be impossible to tell the story of the Old South, that familiar word 'extravagant.' "[89] Few features of Southern life after the turn of the century would better fit Cash's thesis than the law and practice of racial separation. "After I had begun to trace the coloured line I found evidences of it everywhere—literally in every department of life," wrote Ray Stannard Baker of his 1906 tour of the South.[90] "In the theaters, Negroes never sit downstairs, but the galleries are black

[87] Woodward, *Strange Career of Jim Crow*, 158.

[88] A. Meier and E. Rudwick, "The Boycott Movement Against Jim Crow Streetcars in the South, 1900–1909," *J. Am. Hist.*, 55:756–57, 1969. C. V. Woodward, *American Counterpoint* (1964), 257–58.

[89] Quoted *ibid.*, 282.

[90] Baker, *Following the Color Line*, 34.

with them. Of course, white hotels and restaurants are entirely barred to Negroes, with the result that coloured people have their own eating and sleeping places, many of them inexpressibly dilapidated and unclean. . . . No good public accommodations exist for the educated or well-to-do Negro in Atlanta."[91] Baker perceived a profound movement in the first decade of the century, the "rapid flying apart of the races. . . ."

> Negroes crowd into "coloured quarters" in the cities. More and more they are becoming a people wholly apart—separate in their churches, separate in their schools, separate in cars, conveyances, hotels, restaurants, with separate professional men.[92]

In Atlanta, Jim Crow rode building elevators, presided over toilets and drinking fountains, and swore to tell the truth on separate but equal Bibles in the municipal courtrooms. Prisons and mental hospitals were segregated by force of state law in most of the South, and private hospitals were segregated by law or custom. Not content with separation in life, Jim Crow extended his hegemony beyond by segregating cemeteries, the practice of undertakers, and medical school cadavers. Public recreation was not an occasion for his relaxation. Blacks were pushed out of municipal parks throughout the South. Louisiana tent shows had to have separate entrances, exits, and ticket windows at least twenty-five feet apart. There were even separate but equal telephone booths in Oklahoma.

Segregation statutes penetrated private preserves as well. Residential segregation gripped the imagination of municipal lawmakers in Southern cities from 1910, when Baltimore first designated all-white and all-black blocks, to 1917, when the Supreme Court in *Buchanan* v. *Warley*[93] struck down a Louisville ordinance forbidding a person from purchasing residential property in a block in which he or she would not be in the racial majority. A number of states imposed on private employers and employees rigid and elaborate codes of segregation in the work place. Whites and blacks could not work in the same rooms, use the same entrances, stairs, or exits, be paid from the same windows, drink from the same bucket, use the same toilets.[94] Two states forbade fraternal societies that allowed blacks and whites to call each other brother. Florida, not satisfied with segregating its public schools and with requiring not only separate textbooks for the use of each race[95] but even separate storage of those books when not in use, prohibited

---

[91] *Ibid.*, 34–35.
[92] *Ibid.*, 299–300.
[93] 245 U.S. 60 (1917).

[94] Woodward, *Strange Career of Jim Crow,* 83.
[95] *Ibid.*, 87.

private schools from educating blacks and whites in the same building.[96] Kentucky followed suit with the law that stopped Berea College's tendencies toward amalgamation, as did Tennessee and Oklahoma. Georgia and Texas denied state aid to any school that educated whites and blacks.

Although the law books, of course, do not nearly register the extent of segregation in the South, law was the foundation of the structure of racial separation, from the informal practices of sheriffs and judges, to the ordinances of Southern cities and towns, to statewide statutes, up to the supreme law of the United States Constitution which, after *Plessy* v. *Ferguson*,[97] grounded the structure in pseudo-legitimacy.[98] William Graham Sumner's dictum that "stateways cannot change folkways" was embraced in *Plessy* and echoed in countless refrains of judicial abnegation, but Southern lawmakers had a more generous view of the effectiveness of law. As Professor Woodward put it: "Whether railways qualify as folkways or stateways, black man and white man once rode them together and without a partition between them. Later on the stateways apparently changed the folkways—or at any rate the railways—for the partitions and Jim Crow cars became universal."[99]

The doctrine of racial separation was coupled to the principle of equality only in the verbal tissue of statutes and judicial apologetics. Equality was no concern of the law of racial separation in life. But the charge of hypocrisy misses the point. Jim Crow reflected a society that felt itself under no constraint to treat blacks equally, not even the formal constraint of legal fiction. In the new railroad depot in Atlanta, "one of the finest railroad stations in this country," Ray Stannard Baker found

> the whole front was given up to white people, and the Negroes were assigned a side entrance, and a small waiting-room. Prominent coloured men regarded it as a new evidence of the crowding out of the Negro, the further attempt to give him unequal accommodations, to handicap him in his struggle for survival.[100]

On the streetcars, blacks sat in the back; in the theaters, in the galleries; on the trains, in the rear of smoky combination coach and baggage cars. Even blacks prepared to pay first-class fares were often

---

[96] Stephenson, *Race Distinctions*, 190.

[97] 163 U.S. 537 (1896).

[98] L. Pollak, "Emancipation and Law: A Century of Progress," in R. Goldwin, ed., *One Hundred Years of Emancipation* (1964), 170.

[99] Woodward, *Strange Career of Jim Crow*, 92.

[100] Baker, *Following the Color Line*, 34.

put in second-class accommodations. Baker reported that "[w]ell-to-do Negroes who can afford to travel, also complain that they are not permitted to engage sleeping-car berths." When Booker T. Washington wanted first-class sleeping accommodations on his travels, he would usually have to pay for an entire car.[101]

That inequality was an unabashed feature of the regime of racial separation was nowhere more systematically evident than in the field of public education. Improvement of public education was one of the South's greatest achievements in the Progressive era, but the reform of Southern education was fueled by racism. There is no better demonstration of Professor Woodward's thesis that Southern Progressivism was "For Whites Only." Inequality deepened dramatically in the period of Progressive educational reform.[102] By "determined effort," wrote Du Bois in 1907, black schools had been made less efficient than twenty years before.[103] Edgar Gardner Murphy agreed, writing in the same year that "[p]assionate and rapidly developing enthusiasm for white education is bearing sharply and adversely upon the opportunities of the negro." The educational situation of blacks "is steadily growing worse, and their schools upon every sort of pretext, are being hampered and impoverished where they are not actually abandoned."[104] John Hope, president of Atlanta's Morehouse College, said in 1917 that since the turn of the century, "Atlanta had gone backward in public school facilities for the Negro. There is no Negro high school in Atlanta . . . and only about three in the state of Georgia."[105] In 1900, the average black child in South Carolina got about one-sixth of what was spent

---

[101] *Ibid.*, 33.

[102] *Cf.* generally L. Harlan, *Separate and Unequal* (1968), 250–69 (discussing low educational expenditures in South for schools generally, and particularly for black schools).

The word "unequal" is simply inapposite to describe the radical deprivation of black public schools in the South in the Progressive era. White teachers were paid on the average two and one-half times as much as their black counterparts. Compulsory attendance laws in the Southern states were unenforced for black children; 37.7 percent of the black children of grade school age attended regularly in the Southern seaboard states, in 1915, compared to 58.2 percent of the white. *Ibid.*, 258. For high schools, the disparities were drastically greater.

In 1916, there were 29 times as many white high school students as black, *ibid.*, 250, although white children were only 20 percent more numerous, *ibid.*, 256. In 1916, an investigator for the federal Bureau of Education found that the Southern states as a whole appropriated annually \$6,429,991 for white high schools and only about \$350,000 for black high schools. *Ibid.*, 261. For every white teacher, there were 44.6 white children; for every black teacher, 95 black students. *Ibid.*, 258. Moreover, school terms were shorter in black schools, typically by as much as a month. Black schools, being fewer, were of course farther apart and harder to get to.

[103] *Ibid.*, 13–14.

[104] *Ibid.*, 254.

[105] *Ibid.*, 263.

for a white child's education; by 1915, black children received only one-twelfth.

Blacks were worst off where they were most numerous. A 1916 study of black education in counties across the South by an investigator of the federal Bureau of Education found that expenditures for black students were nearly equal to those for whites in counties where blacks made up less than 10 percent of the population, were about half where blacks were 10 to 25 percent, were about one-fifth where blacks were half the population, and dropped to less than one-twelfth where blacks made up 75 percent or more of the population. State education funds were apportioned to counties based upon total school enrollment without regard to race, but county officials controlled the apportionment of state funds between white and black schools. The larger the proportion of blacks in the population, the more relatively few white pupils could benefit at the expense of the greater number of blacks. In the "black-belt," rural counties where the tradition of white paternalism supposedly had deepest roots, the inequality of education was most glaring.[106] The white minorities in lowland areas deprived the large black school populations of money in order to better their own white schools relative to the white schools in up-country counties where the whites had a larger share of the population. It is sometimes said that whites were willing to shoulder substantial costs to sustain the system of racial separation. This is almost certainly a myth taking the system overall, but in the field of public education it is patently false. The segregation of public education was not a financial burden where white and black schools were significantly unequal; on the contrary, discrimination against black schools represented tremendous fiscal savings for whites, compared to the costs of a unitary system.

The white power structure that provided black public education with a fraction of what was given to white schools did so with an air of magnanimity or resentful self-sacrifice.[107] So pronounced was their com-

---

[106] *Ibid.,* 261.

[107] *Ibid.,* 259. The attitude is illustrated by this statement of Thomas Nelson Page, a white supremacist of reasonably good will toward blacks and author of *The Negro: The Southerner's Problem,* a widely read book published in 1940:

The South has faithfully applied itself during all these years to giving Negroes all the opportunities possible for attaining an education, and it is one of the most creditable pages in her history that in face of the horror of Negro-domination during the Reconstruction period; of the disappointment at the small results; in face of the fact that the education of Negroes has appeared to be used by them only as a weapon with which to oppose the white race, the latter should have persistently given so largely of its store to provide this misused education.

Quoted in G. Myrdal, *An American Dilemma* (1944), 2:888.

placency that Gunnar Myrdal could write: "The great wonder is that the principle of the Negroes' right to public education was not renounced altogether."[108] Southern politics in the Progressive era was punctuated by repeated demands that white men's taxes should not be spent on black education. Governor Hoke Smith of Georgia said in 1908 that "Negro education should have reference to the Negro's future work . . . really the training for farm labor. If it is given this direction it will not be necessary to tax the white men's property for the purpose."[109] Governor Vardaman of Mississippi in the same year pronounced that "[m]oney spent to-day for the maintenance of the public school for negroes is robbery of the white man and a waste upon the negro." This was not only the cant of politicians. Thomas Nelson Page wrote in 1904 that the great majority of Southern whites thought black education was without benefit.[110] In particular, this was the resentful cry of up-country whites who were penalized relative to lowland whites in the black counties by the racially neutral state allocation formulae. But a more pervasive theme in the deprivation of black education was resolve to maintain an economic underclass. When Governor Vardaman cut off an $8,000 appropriation for Alcorn College, he said: "I am not anxious even to see the Negro turned into a skilled mechanic. God Almighty intended him to till the soil under the direction of the white man and that is what we are going to teach him down there at Alcorn College."[111] Of philanthropic assistance to black education, Vardaman was candid enough to say: "What the North is sending South is not money but dynamite; this education is ruining our Negroes. They're demanding equality."[112] Shortly before his death in 1915, Booker T. Washington echoed this theme with a pragmatic assessment of how to seek modest improvements in black education: "We are trying to instill into the Negro mind that if education does not make the Negro humble, simple, and of service to the community, then it will not be encouraged."[113]

By 1915, what Ray Stannard Baker had called the "rapid flying apart of the races" had proceeded so far that an English visitor to the southern United States from South Africa could write: "How often the very conditions I had left were reproduced before my eyes, the thousands of miles melted away, and Africa was before me."[114] Another Englishman who traveled through the South in this time wrote that racial adjustment was one of the world's most urgent problems, and that the

---

[108] Myrdal, *American Dilemma*, 2: 888.

[109] A. B. Hart, *The Southern South* (1910), 329.

[110] *Ibid.*, 327.

[111] *Ibid.*, 248.

[112] *Ibid.*

[113] *Ibid.*, 247.

[114] Quoted in Woodward, *Strange Career of Jim Crow*, 97–98.

problem was nowhere in the world more acute than in the southern United States. He called his book, published in 1910, *Through Afro-America*.[115] The mutually supporting systems of segregation, disfranchisement, the lily-white legal system, and involuntary servitude looked to the maintenance of a caste system in the South that one would have had to travel to the tip of Africa to replicate.

III. Transportation Segregation and the Supreme Court Under Chief Justice White

As Jim Crow laws first made their way into Southern statute books in the 1880s as regulations of railroads and other public carriers, so in the Supreme Court of the United States the process of bending the Constitution to accommodate them was dominated by cases involving public transportation. In this area of race relations, the Supreme Court during the Progressive era did little to cast doubt on the sway of *Plessy* and *Louisville*, and even the *Civil Rights Cases* had a final approving echo. There was, however, one intriguing decision, *McCabe* v. *Atchison, Topeka & Santa Fe Railway*,[116] handed down in 1914, which for the first time put some constitutional teeth in the equality side of the separate but equal formula, and in the process carried a hint of the doctrine's demise. Otherwise, the White Court was content to leave matters where the Fuller Court had left them.

A. *Chiles* v. *Chesapeake & Ohio Railway:* NO QUESTIONS ASKED

On the last day of Melville Weston Fuller's Chief Justiceship, a brief and untroubled decision came down, one in a rush of decisions handed down on that final day of the 1909 Term, that broadened the Court's invitation to interstate carriers to segregate their passengers. J. Alexander Chiles, a black graduate of the University of Michigan Law School, had bought a first-class ticket from Washington, D.C., to Lexington, Kentucky, and took his seat in the first-class car set aside for whites. He was ordered to go into one of the two black areas of another car that was divided into three sections: one for white smokers, one for black smokers, and one for blacks generally. When Chiles refused, saying, "I am an interstate passenger; I am a lawyer and I know my rights," this brought a policeman, and Chiles moved to the Jim Crow car under protest. The railroad was wise enough not to rely

---

[115] W. Archer, *Through Afro-America* (1910).   [116] 235 U.S. 151 (1914).

on the Kentucky law requiring it to segregate passengers; rather, the railroad claimed the right to make its own reasonable rules for the safety and comfort of its passengers. Chiles disputed that the railroad had any such rule, but the jury, all white of course, found against him on this point. He also contended that, unlike the first-class car, the black compartment lacked a washroom and was innundated with smoke from the engine and from the adjacent smoking compartments. The state courts, however, found the Jim Crow car accommodations substantially equal.

The Supreme Court followed the Kentucky court's approach without difficulty. The outcome was controlled by *Hall* and *Plessy*, Justice McKenna thought. In *Hall*, McKenna said, the Court had viewed Congress' inaction as "equivalent to the declaration that a carrier could by regulation separate colored and white interstate passengers." That the railroad's policy was reasonable was established not only by *Hall*, McKenna thought, but also by *Plessy*, which "not only sustained the [segregation] law but justified as reasonable the distinction between the races on account of which the statute was passed and enforced."[117] McKenna had not complicated his thinking with the teachings of James Bradley Thayer, and seemed to think that in upholding the Louisiana Jim Crow law as reasonable, the Court had consulted its own notions of sound policy.[118] One can understand why. Justice Harlan dissented alone, without opinion.

A Court sympathetic to Chiles' claim that "the ticket and not the color of the skin [should] determine the carriage of the passenger"[119] might have found complexities in the case that McKenna ignored. The congressional silence which *Hall* had treated as a "declaration that a carrier could, by regulation, separate colored and white passengers" had, since *Hall* was decided, been breached by the Interstate Commerce Act of 1887, section 3 of which made it unlawful for any common carrier operating in interstate commerce "to subject any particular person . . . to any undue or unreasonable prejudice or disadvantage in

---

[117] Chiles v. Chesapeake & Ohio Ry., 218 U.S. 71, 77 (1910).

[118] In 1893, Thayer's famous article "The Origin and Scope of the American Doctrine of Constitutional Law" had argued that legislation should be held unconstitutional only "when those who have the right to make laws have not merely made a mistake, but have made a very clear one—so clear that it is not open to rational question." *Harv. L. Rev.*, 7:129, 144,

1893. Precisely the point of the doctrine was to distinguish between the open discretion of legislative policy making and the function of judicial review which, Thayer thought, did not invite the judges to take a free vote on their sense of sound policy. See generally A. M. Bickel, *The Least Dangerous Branch* (1962).

[119] *Brief for Plaintiff in Error*, Chiles v. Chesapeake & Ohio Ry., 218 U.S. 71 (1910).

any respect whatsoever."[120] Since Chiles was an interstate passenger, the case presented at least the question whether section 3 was compatible with racial separation and, even if it was, whether it drew tighter prohibitions around inequalities in accommodations than did the "substantial equality" apologetics that grew up after *Plessy*. Years later, in 1941, in an opinion by Chief Justice Hughes, the Court held that although this provision of the Interstate Commerce Act permitted segregation, it required precise equality of accommodations,[121] and that inequalities like those *Chiles* alleged and undoubtedly could have proved violated the Act. Moreover, a different Court might have paused before accepting that the railroad's internal policy could be divorced from state law requiring separate accommodations. At the very least the state statute encouraged railroads to segregate all passengers, since that would avoid having to distinguish blacks traveling interstate from those moving intrastate who were required by the state law to be segregated. A half century later, a Supreme Court that was as determined to find state involvement in an allegedly private choice to discriminate as the *Chiles* Court was eager not to, held that a state law requiring separate toilets for blacks and whites in restaurants so burdened service to both races that the decision to serve only whites should be judged as state action under the Fourteenth Amendment.[122] But such outcomes as these are the product of judicial doubts about, if not abhorrence of, the discriminatory choice, and *Chiles* may be taken to show the absence of any such concern about the Jim Crow car in the Supreme Court of the United States in 1910.

Although *Chiles* was a routine decision on the level of doctrine, it did clear away any lingering doubts about whether interstate travel might be a reprieve for blacks from racial separation on the railroad. As the *Virginia Law Register* put it, "[T]he Supreme Court of the United States has definitely pointed out a way to carriers of passengers, by which they may conform to enlightened public sentiment with regard to an intermixture of the two races even on interstate coaches, without fear of rendering themselves liable for damages."[123] Like the railroad that sent Chiles into the Jim Crow car, the Supreme Court in 1910 was in step with "enlightened public sentiment."

---

[120] 24 Stat. 380 (1887).

[121] Mitchell v. United States, 313 U.S. 80 (1941). See generally J. S. Ransmeier, "The Fourteenth Amendment and the Separate But Equal Doctrine," *Mich. L. Rev.*, 50:203, 215, n.64, 1951.

[122] Robinson v. Florida, 378 U.S. 153 (1964).

[123] *Va. L. Reg.*, 16:387, 1910. For another contemporaneous comment on *Chiles* and the other transportation discrimination cases, see J. N. Baker, "The Segregation of White and Colored Passengers of Interstate Trains," *Yale L. J.*, 19:445, 1910.

B. *Butts* v. *Merchants & Miners Transportation Co.:*
The "Ghost of the Old Civil Rights Act"

The mood of untroubled acquiescence in the Jim Crow temper of the times was also evident in the first case involving segregation in public transportation to be decided by the Court in the tenure of Chief Justice White.[124]

Mary F. Butts' complaint against a vessel plying between Boston and Norfolk, Virginia, gave the Supreme Court an opportunity in 1913 to lay to rest the ultimate achievement of Reconstruction. The public accommodation provisions of the Civil Rights Act of 1875 had not been entirely dispatched by the *Civil Rights Cases* of 1883, which in nullifying applications of the Act within the states had left open whether the Act would apply "to cases arising in the Territories or the District of Columbia, which are subject to the plenary legislation of Congress. . . ."[125] The high seas were another area of plenary jurisdiction where the Act might have been thought to remain in force. Butts had a first-class ticket from Boston to Norfolk. All white first-class passengers were given rooms on the upper deck but Butts, who was black, had been given a lower deck stateroom; she had been assigned to the second meal-sitting, along with the second-class passengers, using, as she alleged, the soiled table linen left after the first sitting. The district court in Massachusetts agreed with the ship owner that the Act was entirely invalid and dismissed her complaint.

The final hour of what Senator Charles Sumner had hoped would be the "final protection" for the freedman[126] reflected none of the idealism or controversy that had attended both the Civil Rights Act's passage and its first encounter with the Supreme Court. *Butts* was a remembrance of what had come to pass four decades before, not because it represented a renewal of past ardor, but because it posed the slightly disagreeable task of final interment. Justice Van Devanter's precise, muted opinion hardly broke the silence of an era in which Reconstruction clamor was the faintest echo.

Although his statement of the case made no mention of dirty linen, Van Devanter did not flinch from full quotation of the Act, including the majestic preamble: "Whereas, it is essential to just government we recognize the equality of all men before the law, and hold that it is the

---

[124] Butts v. Merchants & Miners Transportation Co., 230 U.S. 126 (1913).

[125] The Civil Rights Cases, 109 U.S. 3, 19 (1883). Of course, neither the *Civil Rights Cases* nor *Butts* touched the jury discrimination provisions of the Civil Rights Act of 1875.

[126] A. Westin, "The Case of the Prejudiced Doorkeeper," in J. Garraty, ed., *Quarrels That Have Shaped the Constitution* (1966), 132.

duty of government in its dealings with the people to mete out equal and exact justice to all, of whatever nativity, race, color, or persuasion, religious or political; and it being the appropriate object of legislation to enact great fundamental principles into law. . . ."[127] The statute embodied its "great fundamental principle" by protecting "all persons within the jurisdiction of the United States,"[128] words aiming, as Van Devanter recognized, to abolish discrimination on public carriers uniformly throughout the United States. But since the *Civil Rights Cases*, a decision that "has stood unchallenged for almost thirty years,"[129] had voided the Act as applied to discrimination occurring within the states, the major part of the legislative purpose had failed. Was the Act separably effective in the territories, the District of Columbia, and on the high seas? Van Devanter thought not. "How can the use of general terms denoting an intention to enact a law which should be applicable alike in all places within that jurisdiction be said to indicate a purpose to make a law which should be applicable to a minor part of that jurisdiction and inapplicable to the major part?"[130] He found support in a long quote from *United States* v. *Reese*,[131] the 1876 decision which had struck down the Civil Rights Act of 1870 because it prohibited interference with the right to vote in general terms while the Fifteenth Amendment only authorized protection of the franchise against abridgement on account of race. The indictments in *Reese* alleged refusal to count the vote of a black man, a matter within Congress' power to condemn, but the Court had refused "to reject a part which is unconstitutional, and retain the remainder," because that would be "to make a new law, not to enforce an old one."[132] An even more analogous decision, *El Paso & Northeastern Railway* v. *Gutierrez*,[133] did not point the other way, Van Devanter thought. That case had applied the Federal Employers' Liability Act (FELA) in the District of Columbia and in the territories, even though that Act had been held unconstitutional as to accidents occurring within the states in the *First Employers' Liability Case*.[134] But the FELA had a separate provision applying to the District of Columbia and the terri-

---

[127] 18 (Part 3) Stat. 335 (1875).

[128] *Ibid.*, at 336.

[129] *Butts,* 230 U.S. at 132.

[130] *Ibid.*, at 133.

[131] 92 U.S. 214 (1876).

[132] *Ibid.*, at 221. The Court in *Reese* went on to say:

It would certainly be dangerous if the legislature could set a net large enough to catch all possible offenders, and leave it to the courts to step inside and say who could be rightfully detained and who should be set at large. This would, to some extent, substitute the judicial for the legislative department of the government.

[133] 215 U.S. 87 (1909).

[134] Howard v. Illinois Central R.R., 207 U.S. 463 (1908).

tories, whereas the Civil Rights Act of 1875 simply applied throughout the United States, with no differentiation. Moreover, the Civil Rights Act was a penal statute, and must be strictly construed. Since it is not possible, Van Devanter concluded, to separate "that which is constitutional from that which is not," when both "are dependent upon the same general words . . . which alone indicate where the sections are to be operative," the Civil Rights Act of 1875 was adjudged "altogether invalid," even as to places where Congress had clear power to impose it.[135]

Van Devanter's opinion in *Butts* has a considerable air of insecurity, with its redundant use of long quotes to support simple, even mechanical, principles of statutory construction. But the insecurity was of style, a reflection of Van Devanter's writing difficulty, not of result. The decision was treated as virtually a foregone conclusion, and with Harlan having died, no dissents were recorded.

Holmes, however, was not persuaded and probably failed to register his dissent only because exhaustion and preparations for a European trip had removed him from Washington before the end of the 1912 Term.[136] One June 17, 1913, the day after *Butts* came down, Van Devanter wrote to Holmes at Beverly Farms in Massachusetts:

> I am enclosing a copy of the opinion prepared by me and announced yesterday in No. 131, *Butts* v. *Merchants & Miners Transportation Co.* It is the civil rights case. You will recall that there were differences of opinion in conference and that there was a division in the vote. The opinion was prepared in conformity to the vote of the majority, and when prepared received the approval of the eight who were present. The opinion is not in accordance with your vote, and I do not know what course you would wish to take after considering it. It seemed to me that in the circumstances, you having heard the argument and participated in the consideration of the case in conference, it was due to you that an opportunity be given for you to indicate your action on

---

[135] *Butts,* 230 U.S. at 131, 132, 133, 135, 138 (1913).

[136] On June 5, 1913, Holmes wrote from the Supreme Court to his friend Mrs. John Chipman Gray: "I have been working very hard—I believe I have delivered 40 decisions this term and I have some more up my sleeve and I suppose I am tired—my wife decided so and turned me toward Europe." Holmes reported that he had twisted his knee ("I beat Turner for colors from there to the sole of my foot"), but that he had finished his Court work and was ready to go. He apologized for not being able to see Mrs. Gray before he left and explained, "the Court sits so late that if I was to go at all it seemed advisable to get off as soon as might be." O. W. Holmes to Mrs. J. C. Gray, June 5, 1913, Holmes Papers, Harvard Law School Library. Sometime between June 5 and June 16, when *Butts* came down, Holmes left Washington to prepare for his European trip.

the opinion. To let it go as though you were concurring would not be right, to put you down as dissenting without having seen the opinion would not be justified, and to put you down as not participating might not be according to your wish. This did not occur to me at first, but I presented it yesterday morning at the final conference, and the view generally expressed was that it would be better to send the opinion to you and to ask you to indicate your action in the matter, which I now do. I inquired of the reporter when the opinion would be published, and he said that it would not be reached for three or four weeks; so, if you will indicate to me your wishes they will be carried out.

I hope you had a good voyage and that you will have an agreeable sojourn on the other side.[137]

Why Holmes disagreed, and whether, as Van Devanter's note implies, others initially had shared his doubts in conference, is a matter for speculation, for there is no record of any reply by Holmes. Perhaps Holmes wanted to save the Civil Rights Act in areas of Congress' plenary jurisdiction out of sympathy with its aims, although that does not seem too likely in view of his position in other cases involving the rights of black people. Or perhaps it was his general desire to preserve the force of federal statutes to whatever extent possible. He may have thought that the presumption of constitutionality ought to override the Court's rather mechanical rule of nonseparability, keeping in force the lesser coverage of a statute whose major part had been struck down. But the presumption of constitutionality operates perversely, if at all, in a case like *Butts*. The scope of Congress' constitutional authority was not in issue; no one doubted Congress' power to forbid discrimination in areas of plenary jurisdiction. The question was one of statutory construction. Van Devanter's mechanical approach, as distinguished from the result it produced, in one case was highly deferential, because it reduced the element of judgment to virtually nothing. If a statute's scope was defined in a single set of general words, when the major coverage fell, so would the lesser. Van Devanter may have invited Holmes' resistance by a poor choice of words in stating that the Act was "adjudged altogether invalid." He might better have characterized the decision as one of statutory interpretation only, reflecting Congress's presumed policy judgment, and defended his flat rule of interpretation on the ground that courts were not competent to assess whether the lesser coverage made sense in terms of the legislative policies underlying the overall coverage, whether full breadth and uniformity of application was necessary to effectuate the antidiscrimination policies involved, or what Congress might have thought about the lesser coverage without the

---

[137] Van Devanter Papers, Library of Congress.

larger if it had considered the question. And Van Devanter might have emphasized what he did not mention: that Congress was free after *Butts* to act against Jim Crow in the areas of its plenary jurisdiction if it wanted to.

Still, Holmes might well have remained unpersuaded. Of course, Congress' power to act its will on the Jim Crow question in areas of general sovereignty could equally well have been enlisted against the *Butts* result. Were it a mistake to keep the statute, on the books, Congress could remove it. Moreover, had the Court looked beyond the Act's words of coverage to its general purposes as revealed in all its words, the Court could easily have made the case for maintaining the statute within the areas of Congress' plenary jurisdiction. If "it is essential to just government to recognize the equality of all men before the law," there would have been considerable force in arguing that the Act should be preserved to the extent of the sovereignty of the government whose "duty" it was, in the words of the Act, "to mete out equal and exact justice" and "to enact great fundamental principles into law." These high purposes were in no way undermined in theory by the holding of the *Civil Rights Cases*. Had the court in *Butts* been willing to look beneath the literal terms of coverage of the statute to its broader purposes, it would still have had to consider whether the nondiscrimination principle made practical sense as a rule of limited territorial application. But since uniformity on the Jim Crow question was long lost in the wake of the *Louisville* decision, as many states variously imposed either segregation or integration requirements on the intrastate portions of interstate carriers' activities, to add a federal rule of nondiscrimination in the District of Columbia, the territories, and on the high seas would not have been much of a further embarrassment.

Since either holding would have left the question for Congress to resolve if it cared to, the issue in *Butts* may be conceived as where to put the weight of legislative inertia. Where a mechanical rule of construction pointed one way and an extrapolation of overall purpose the other, should the Justices have tried to take the temper of current legislative preferences? There is no indication that Van Devanter or any other Justice did this, but if the current mood was an appropriate guide, we may surely view the Court's opinion as sufficient unto the day, for few speculations about congressional consensus at that time could have been on firmer ground than that the commitments embodied in the Civil Rights Act of 1875 were as lost as dreams. On the other hand, if the Justices had glimpsed the future, and seen the need for a symbolic counterpoint in the heyday of Jim Crow, or if they had consulted their own sense of justice, surely a less controversial referent in deciding a closely balanced question of statutory construction than in the exercise of constitutional review, there would have been much to be said for putting the burden of legislative inertia on the forces of apartheid, maintaining the grand principle of the Civil Rights Act of 1875 as the rule for areas of plenary federal jurisdiction. The practical impact of such a determination would have been modest indeed, and no issue of state sovereignty was involved. Thus, the decision was largely of symbolic significance either way. The principle of equality could have been served at little cost.

Van Devanter's simple rule of statutory construction was a retreat from such considerations, and aside from the special symbolic and moral significance of the Civil Rights Act of 1875, his mechanical approach has much to recommend it. It promotes fairness to those who might be caught in the tattered remains of a torn statutory web, predictability for the legal system, tidiness in the statute books, and continuing legislative assessment of the costs and benefits of particular legislative policies. Thus *Butts* has been much relied on for the basic proposition that a statute framed in terms of a general application that is partially unconstitutional will not be reframed to operate within a narrower, constitutional compass. Oddly, over time, *Butts* has also evolved into a precedent supposedly supporting the notion that separability should be pursued by the routes both of statutory interpretation and of legislative intent, seen as distinct, if usually parallel, paths to judgment.[138] Van Devanter's opinion in *Butts* does not really invite the recourse either to congressional motivation or to judicial attribution of overall statutory

---

[138] For example, to take only three well-known later instances, the Court in *Dorchy* v. *Kansas* relied on *Butts* in conceiving of separability as "a question of interpretation and of legislative intent." 264 U.S. 286, 290 (1924). *Williams* v. *Standard Oil Co.* more clearly separates the two in finding in *Butts* a presumption against "mutilation" of a statute when the Court seeks to discover the legislature's intent. 278 U.S. 235, 242 (1929). And in *Carter* v. *Carter Coal Co.,* in refusing to separate the labor regulations and the price-control provisions of the Bituminous Coal Conservation Act of 1935, the majority used *Butts* this way:

Paraphrasing the words of this court in *Butts* . . . we inquire— What authority has this court, by

construction, to convert the manifest purpose of Congress to regulate production by the mutual operation and interaction of the latter alone? Are we at liberty to say from the fact that Congress has adopted an entire integrated system that it probably would have enacted a doubtfully effective fraction of the system?

298 U.S. 238, 316 (1936). Other Supreme Court opinions relying on *Butts* in dealing with separability issues are: United States v. Raines, 326 U.S. 17 (1960); Yu Cong Eng v. Trinidad, 271 U.S. 500 (1926); United States v. Walter, 263 U.S. 15 (1923); Hill v. Wallace, 259 U.S. 44 (1922). See generally, H. P. Monaghan, "Overbreadth," *Sup. Ct. Rev.* 1, 1981.

purpose that later cases have purported to find in it. For Van Devanter it was the precise words of coverage in the statute—the absence of any direct reference to the high seas, the District of Columbia, and the territories—and nothing more capacious, from which it followed that the Civil Rights Act of 1875 was "altogether invalid."

The *Butts* decision was greeted with indifference in the press, although there was an occasional flash of interest in the discovery that a historic relic had a spark of life sufficient for one last judicial *coup de grace*. The *Christian Science Monitor*'s brief report noted that the Civil Rights Act "has generally been regarded as constitutionally null for a generation."[139] The inevitability of the decision was likewise reflected in two comments in legal periodicals, but with differences in historical resonance. The *Virginia Law Register* opened its account of the case with this flight:

> Reminiscences of the Reconstruction days and of legislation passed at that time, or very soon after, are never pleasant, but occasionally as a ghost of one of these old acts is summoned by some witch of Endor or Saul-like lawyer from the shades to which it has been relegated for so many years, the case is not without interest. The case of Butts . . . finally and forever lays the ghost of the old Civil Rights Act of 1875.[140]

The *California Law Review*, on the other hand, struck a poignant note: "As a result of the decision in the principal case, which seems unquestionably sound, we note the passing from the statute book of one of the great landmarks of American political history."[141]

C. *McCabe* v. *Atchison, Topeka & Santa Fe Railway:* AN INTIMATION OF THINGS TO COME

By contrast to the casual acceptance of Jim Crow in *Chiles*, and the demise of Reconstruction principles symbolized by *Butts*, the next case concerning segregation on railroads seems to have been dropped into the Progressive era from three or four decades in the future. *McCabe* v. *Atchison, Topeka & Santa Fe Railway*[142] was the first decision dealing with state Jim Crow laws in the tenure of Chief Justice White and after the death of Harlan, but more important, *McCabe* reflected the arrival of its author, Charles Evans Hughes. Hughes approached race issues not

---

[139] *Christian Science Monitor,* Jan. 22, 1913, p. 4, col. 3. Two of the three main newspapers in Richmond failed to menion the decision at all, and the other simply noted the decision in a straightforward, brief account. *Richmond News Leader,* June 17, 1913, p. 8, col. 6. The *Washington Evening Star* also briefly noted the case, June 16, 1913, p. 2, col. 6. Otherwise, the newspapers took no notice.

[140] *Va. L. Reg.,* 19:307, 1913.

[141] *Cal. L. Rev.,* 1:541, 543, 1913.

[142] 235 U.S. 151 (1914).

from the radical dissenting position of Harlan, but from the disarming position of one who, without flourish, simply cast the light of accepted tools of legal analysis and principle on a body of law that could only exist behind judicial winks and shrugs. The effect in *McCabe* was to give an intimation of things to come when Hughes would return to the Court as Chief Justice in the 1930s. And Hughes went out of his way to do it.

The Oklahoma separate coach law of 1907 was a typical Jim Crow statute with an atypical proviso. The railroads' obligation to "provide separate coaches or compartments, for the accommodation of the white and negro races . . . equal in all points of comfort and convenience" did not cover sleeping, dining, or parlor cars, which could "be used exclusively by either white or negro passengers, separately but not jointly."[143] What this awkward language meant was that the limited demand of black passengers for luxury cars should relieve the railroad of the burden of duplicating an expensive accommodation used mainly by whites. For luxuries, in other words, the rule of law was "exclusive and not joint," rather than "separate but equal."

A few days before this statute took effect, five black plaintiffs tried to enjoin several railroads from making any racial distinctions in their service, adding to their broad attack on the separate coach law a narrower challenge to the luxury car proviso. The federal circuit court denied relief and the eighth Circuit Court of Appeals affirmed in a decision that would touch the Supreme Court not only in its appellate function, but also in its personnel. In the Court of Appeals, *McCabe* set at odds two leading candidates for promotion to the Supreme Court. Judge William C. Hook, Van Devanter's rival in 1910 and a serious candidate to replace Harlan in 1911 and 1912, joined an opinion by Judge Elmer B. Adams upholding the Oklahoma law, while Judge Walter H. Sanborn, the perennial prospect, filed a vigorous dissent. *Plessy* "foreclosed further discussion" of the broad argument against racial separation, Adams and Hook thought, and as for the proviso, the legislature no doubt had in mind "what we judicially know, that the ability of the two races to indulge in luxuries, comforts, and conveniences, was so dissimilar that sleeping and dining cars which would be well patronized by one race might be very little if at all by the other. . . ." The principle of equality did not call for "equal service, irrespective of the demand for it. No mere question of abstract or theoretical right can require the constant and regular equipment and hauling of substantially empty dining, sleeping or chair cars for either race."[144]

---

[143] Okla. Comp. Laws Sec. 860 (1910).
[144] McCabe v. Atchison, Topeka & Santa Fe Ry., 186 F. 966, 969–70 (8th Cir. 1911), *affirmed*, 235 U.S. 151 (1914).

VIII: *The Heyday of Jim Crow*

When Hook was under consideration for the Supreme Court in 1912, his concurrence in *McCabe* played a modest but significant role in Progressive objections and hurt him with Taft, and doubtless the pungency of Sanborn's able dissent helped to stir the objections. How could anyone think, Sanborn asked, that the requirements of equal protection were met when whites were given luxury cars and blacks were not? The question "bears its own answer" and Sanborn was not able to "wink so hard as not to perceive" it. Railroads need not provide luxury cars for whites if separate but equal cars for blacks were unprofitable. In any event, talk of the impracticability of separate Pullmans for blacks was beside the point, since separate compartments in the same car would meet the Oklahoma law.

In the Supreme Court, the railroads and the state took a "let's be reasonable" approach. The railroads' brief asked the Court to recognize that "separation of the races in public places and especially in transportation facilities is vital to the people of the Southern states. It is a practical condition with them and not a theoretical question. It is a situation that can be dealt with only from a practical standpoint." The brief developed the "practical standpoint" this way:

Practically, persons of African descent had found no reason to complain of the Pullman car and dining service for the white race. In Judge

---

The plaintiffs also contended that the separate coach law violated the Commerce Clause and the Enabling Act by which Oklahoma was admitted to the Union. The lower federal courts rejected the Commerce attack on the basis of Louisville, New Orleans & Texas Ry. v. Mississippi, 133 U.S. 587 (1890), assuming that the statute would be construed by the state courts only to apply to intrastate commerce. The Enabling Act claim was summarily rejected. The Court of Appeals' willingness to allow demand to set limits on the obligation of the quality of accommodations was supported by recent decisions of the Interstate Commerce Commission construing the statutory requirement of equality under the antidiscrimination provision of the Interstate Commerce Act. After initial insistence on a rigorous standard of equality, the commission loos-ened up from 1909 on. In Cozart v. Southern Ry., 16 I.C.C. 226 (1909), the commission sustained differences in accommodations for whites and blacks by emphasizing that the Act barred only "undue prejudice." *Ibid.*, at 230. In Gaines v. Seaboard Air Line Ry., 16 I.C.C. 471 (1909), the commission took into account the limited demand for certain accommodations by blacks in defining the scope of "undue prejudice." *Ibid.*, at 472–74. This was an explicit shift in rationale. Before *Gaines,* the commission had refused to consider limited black demand as a relevant factor. The loose standard of equality ushered in by *Cozart* and *Gaines* would prevail in the ICC until 1941 when the Supreme Court, in an opinion by Chief Justice Hughes, required strict equality under the Act. Mitchell v. United States, 313 U.S. 80 (1941).

777

Sanborn's dissenting opinion they found a theoretical basis for such complaint. This is said without any disrespect for Judge Sanborn. . . . From his environment [Sanborn was originally from Concord, Massachusetts] he has come in contact only with the theoretical side of this extremely practical question.[145]

The Oklahoma attorney general depicted the black plaintiffs as spoilsports. "[W]hat the habits, uses, quantities, quality and expenditure of white travel justify and get, by way of passengers' luxuries, this other race demands shall be enjoyed along with them or not at all, at the same time confessing that the density and expenditures of the travel of the blacks cannot demand the like in their own right. . . . It is the old story of the lure of the fruit,—sweet because it is forbidden."[146]

Justice Hughes' response to this situation, for a slim majority of the Court, was thought by the *Harvard Law Review* to usher in "[a] new phase of the Jim Crow question."[147] There was an element of exaggeration in this, but it captured an important shift, not so much on the surface of doctrine as in judicial attitudes. Hughes' brisk opinion took pains to avoid crediting the separation principle of *Plessy* or *Louisville*, while it insisted on an uncompromising equality principle. He dealt with *Plessy* and *Louisville* merely by listing the conclusions of the Court of Appeals, and said only "there is no reason to doubt the correctness . . . of these conclusions." But Hughes rejected out of hand the argument that if luxury cars were provided for whites they need not be provided for blacks if the volume of black traffic did not amount to a substantial demand.

It makes the constitutional right depend upon the number of persons who may be discriminated against, whereas the essence of the consti-

---

[145] *Brief for Appellees*, 22, McCabe v. Atchison, Topeka & Santa Fe Ry., 235 U.S. 151 (1914).

[146] *Brief for State*, 4, McCabe v. Atchison, Topeka & Santa Fe Ry., 235 U.S. 151 (1914). Later the brief contended that "[t]he federal constitution did not guarantee the Negro man chair cars, diners, nor sleepers, unless he was traveling ordinarily in such numbers and such wise as to reasonably use and reasonably demand separate accommodations of that character." *Ibid.*

The rambling brief of the five black challengers was no more uplifting. After a drawn-out argument which

failed to mention *Plessy*, and contended that the luxury car proviso was "passed from the sinister motive of annoying or oppressing a particular person or class," the brief put this bizarre objection: "The Indian . . . who is far more vicious as well as unclean and unhealthy, is thereby made a member of the white race and entitled to enjoy as a white man . . . the Italian fresh from the slums of Italy, who cannot speak our language nor understand our customs, manners, habits or life, is a white man." *Brief for Appellants*, 50–51.

[147] Note, *Harv. L. Rev.*, 28:417, 1915.

tutional right is that it is a personal one. . . . [i]f facilities are provided, substantial equality of treatment of persons traveling under like conditions cannot be refused. It is the individual who is entitled to the equal protection of the laws. . . .[148]

That was it; there was no suggestion that principle and practicality were in tension, no concession that there was anything to be said on the other side.

After establishing the unconstitutionality of the proviso, Hughes' opinion moved to the surprising announcement that there was "an insuperable obstacle" to the granting of relief. The complainants had brought suit before the law went into effect, and had not alleged that they had requested nor had been denied any accommodations by any of the railroads they had sued. They had made general allegations of hardships to their race, but that could not establish their right to relief as individuals, and in any event the extraordinary relief of an injunction depended not only on their demonstration of an injury but on the absence of an adequate remedy at law. The lower federal courts had missed the point and proceeded to the merits, but there was no standing, and no ripe controversy between the parties. Accordingly, no relief was possible, and so, quite anticlimactically, the judgment of the Court of Appeals was affirmed.

White, Holmes, Lamar, and McReynolds concurred only in the affirmance, thereby disassociating themselves from Hughes' opinion. One can be pretty sure that the four were in disagreement with Hughes' position on the invalidity of the luxury car proviso, and were not merely reflecting unwillingness that the Court should express a position on the merits in the absence of a case or controversy. Lamar consistently opposed the aspirations to constitutional equality of black persons in his tenure on the Court, and McReynolds would in time become the Court's leading protester against the application of the unbending equality principle of *McCabe*. McReynolds, usually the unbending constitutional ideologue, found ample play for considerations of practical expediency in the constitutional law of racial separation.[149] The other Southerner on the Court, Chief Justice White, is less certainly to be put in opposition to Hughes' position on the merits. White was with the majority in *Plessy*

---

[148] McCabe v. Atchison, Topeka & Santa Fe Ry., 235 U.S. 151, 160, 161–62 (1914).

[149] In Missouri *ex rel.* Gaines v. Canada, 305 U.S. 337 (1938), McReynolds, dissenting, echoed Oklahoma's brief in *McCabe* in his position on whether the state must admit a black to the University of Missouri Law School: "The problem presented obviously is a difficult and highly practical one. . . . The State should not be unduly hampered through theorization inadequately restrained by experience." *Ibid.*, at 354.

and *Berea College*, but he would soon write for the Court in the *Grandfather Clause Cases* and he joined in *Buchanan* v. *Warley*. That was a unanimous opinion, however, and it seems likely that *Plessy* provides a better indication of White's thinking in *McCabe*.

As for Holmes' refusal to go along with Hughes, there is evidence, though hardly conclusive, of a difference of view on the merits. In Holmes' papers is preserved a note from Hughes responding to a memorandum Holmes apparently sent to Hughes on the case. Holmes' memorandum has not survived, and his position must therefore be derived from Hughes' somewhat murky response to it. (See insert following page 592.)

> Dear Judge,
>
> I return herewith your memorandum in No. 15—*McCabe* v. *Atchison etc. Rwy Co.*—I cannot construe the statute as requiring the carriers to give equal, though separate, accommodations so far as sleeping cars, dining cars and chair cars are concerned. All agree— both parties and the Attorney General—that such cars may be provided exclusively for whites—that a black man must sit up all night just because he is black, unless there are enough blacks to make a "black sleeping-car" pay.
>
> I don't see that it is a case calling for "logical exactness" in enforcing equal rights, but rather as it seems to me it is a bald, wholly unjustified, discrimination against a passenger solely on account of race.
>
> Faithfully,
Charles E. Hughes
>
> To Mr. Justice Holmes

Holmes evidently had suggested that the provision be construed to require equal, but completely separate, rather than partitioned, luxury cars for blacks and whites. Such a strained construction was possible because the state courts had not had occasion to pass on the meaning of the statute. But although this construction would have avoided the constitutional problem, it would have given the provision a meaning its words could not easily bear and that everyone knew it did not have. What Hughes was responding to in his second paragraph is harder to discern. Possibly this was further response on the same point, with Hughes denying that the statute could be construed with "logical exactness" to require equality of accommodations. But it seems more likely, in view of Holmes' general attitudes toward law and his general record in opposition to the claims of black people in constitutional cases, that Hughes' second paragraph was replying to what would have been a typical Holmes criticism of Hughes' "logical exactness" in insisting on equality in an unbending way, rather than applying the principle of separate but equal with a realistic awareness of the need for flexibility in the life of the law in practical experience. One can almost hear the epigrams. The strong tone of Hughes' response at the end of the second paragraph suggests that this might well have been Holmes' objection. Certainly it would have been entirely in character for Holmes to see eye to eye with the state on the need for a "practical" rather than a "theoretical" approach, though perhaps not for the same reasons.[150]

The difference between Hughes and Holmes highlighted in Hughes' letter suggests a final feature of the *McCabe* decision that, with the benefit of hindsight, was instinct with challenge to the flaccid conception of constitutional rights that permitted the victimization of blacks in the heyday of Jim Crow. Holmes may have caught an echo of *Lochner v. New York* in the uncompromising individualist perspective Hughes took toward the question of equal rights; such an approach to rights was a central tenet of laissez-faire constitutionalism, especially the freedom of contract decisions such as *Lochner, Adair* v. *United States*, and *Coppage* v. *Kansas*.[151] These and similar decisions assessed rights from a starkly individualistic point of view and not in the context of economic relations between groups such as employers and employees. One of the most trenchant criticisms of laissez-faire constitutionalism was that the Court's individualist perspective produced a romantic conception of contractual relations as being a product of bargaining between autonomous individuals unaffected by the necessities of group dynamics in the marketplace. The collision between the legislative branch and the Court reflected in a case like *Lochner* was as much a difference on whether to view the employment relation in the baking trade as an individual or a group interaction as it was a difference in the weight to be given values of individual autonomy as against the various welfare values served by maximum-hours legislation. *McCabe*'s rejection of the Oklahoma legislature's approach to the issue of reciprocal rights to luxury accommodations as a matter of group rather than individual demand may have seemed to Holmes an instance of the contagious vigor of the individualist premises of the substantive due process decisions, and to be resisted on that account.

McCabe was a rare case where poor lawyering probably helped the cause of civil rights. When William Harrison, the black attorney who brought the case in Oklahoma, approached the NAACP for help in appealing to the Supreme Court, Moorfield Storey, on the basis of Judge Sanborn's dissent, at first wanted to take the case up, though he thought it probably would be lost. Storey saw to it that the association advanced

---

150 C. E. Hughes to O. W. Holmes, Nov. 29, 1914, Holmes Papers.

151 Lochner v. New York, 198 U.S. 45 (1905); Adair v. United States, 208 U.S. 161 (1908); Coppage v. Kansas, 236 U.S. 1 (1915).

the cost of printing the record,[152] but once he saw the record he realized that the plaintiffs had no standing, and he refused to take the appeal because that would "weaken his influence with the Court in other cases . . . of greater importance to the colored race."[153] So the NAACP withdrew.

Harrison went ahead undaunted, and in appealing a case not ripe for decision he managed, paradoxically, to get the Supreme Court effectively to strike down the Oklahoma proviso without expressed dissent. Had the case been ripe, the four concurring Justices would almost certainly have dissented on the merits, and the rejection of Oklahoma's luxury car law would have been by the slimmest margin. As it was, the rejection of the Oklahoma proviso was perceived, wrongly but widely, as unanimous. This is not to say that Harrison's strategy was sound, for he could not have known that Hughes would seize the occasion to pronounce on the merits of a nonjusticiable claim, much less that such a tactic would command a majority.[154]

In later years, *McCabe* would be treated as a major precedent, the basis for holding unconstitutional variations of separate accommodations based on differences in demand by whites and blacks.[155] *McCabe* was the first time the Court gave weight to the equality side of the separate

---

[152] Storey insisted that the money be treated as a loan because "the responsibility of protecting Negro rights should be assumed and paid for by the colored man." Black lawyers and plaintiffs must be self-reliant and not turn to whites, in the form of the NAACP, for help. C. Kellogg, *NAACP* (1967), 1:203.

[153] *Ibid.*

[154] Harrison was criticized for his handling of the case by Du Bois. Black lawyers often appeared in court only half prepared, Du Bois complained, and Harrison had been warned about the inadequacy of his case but chose to take it to the Supreme Court anyway. This sort of thing happened in case after case, Du Bois said, because black lawyers found it hard to get adequate training or useful experience. Because of Harrison's mistake, the work of challenging the Oklahoma law would have to begin all over again. W. E. B. DuBois, "In Court," *Crisis,* 9:133, 133–34, 1915.

[155] Hughes as Chief Justice would in 1938 carry the *McCabe* principle forward in Missouri *ex rel.* Gaines v. Canada, 305 U.S. 337 (1938), in holding that Missouri denied equal protection by not admitting an aspiring black law student to the only state law school, even though the state was prepared to pay his tuition at an out-of-state school and claimed that if a sufficient number of blacks wished to attend law school it would establish a state law school for them. Hughes insisted that the University of Missouri Law School was uniquely suited to students who wished to practice in Missouri, and that the state owed equal treatment to each individual black law student, even if he were the first and only black student to apply. To the state's argument that limited demand among blacks for legal education justified it in failing to provide equal facilities, Hughes responded that in *McCabe* "[w]e found that argument to be without merit."

but equal equation. In view of *Plessy's* ambivalence as to whether equality was part of the Jim Crow principle at all, and the later cases' inattention to the question, and in view of the open and notorious conditions of inequality in the law of Jim Crow as it actually operated, *McCabe* must be viewed as a significant departure in the law of race relations. That Hughes should lead the Court to insist in such uncompromising fashion on equality in the face of the state's plea for a "practical" solution signaled a fundamental shift in the Court's attitude toward Jim Crow, if not a change on the verbal surface of doctrine. Since "separate but equal" would be in jeopardy if the Courts insisted on "separate but really equal," *McCabe's* refusal to wink at inequality was a challenge to the entire structure of Jim Crow law built up since the 1880s. And as if to amplify the signal of change, the majority had reached out to pronounce it in a case not ripe for adjudication.[156] Those willing to open their imagination to the future could see in *McCabe* not only "a new phase of the Jim Crow question," but the beginnings of corrosion in the constitutional mandate for racial separation.[157]

McCabe was thus a breach in the aura of permanency that surrounded the regime of Jim Crow in the second decade of the twentieth century.[158] It was not so from any explicit doctrinal innovation, for the

---

Ibid., at 351. McReynolds' dissent in *Gaines* also echoed *McCabe.* Another decision in which Chief Justice Hughes relied on *McCabe* as having established the principle of a personal right to equality regardless of overall demand was Mitchell v. United States, 313 U.S. 80, 97 (1941).

[156] More subtly reinforcing the challenge was Hughes' careful refusal to put the majority on record as affirming the rightness of either *Plessy* or *Louisville.*

[157] A letter to the *New York Times* by one Cleveland G. Allen saw "the great decision" in *McCabe* as one of a number of "growing signs" that "[r]ace prejudice and discrimination is now tottering on its last leg." "A new birth of freedom is sweeping over the land," Allen thought. *New York Times,* Dec. 6, 1914, Sec. 4, p. 2, col. 5. And *The Nation* wrote that the *McCabe* doctrine "is as cheering as it is sound; and it leaves no doubt that, in the end, the Supreme Court

will not consent to the setting up in this country, and under our Constitution, of a 'Jim Crow' government." *The Nation,* 99:645, Dec. 3, 1914. "In the end" would prove to be somewhat farther off than these writers hoped.

[158] For the *Harvard Law Review,* *McCabe* invited speculation that the changeable concept of unconstitutional discrimination "at any given time" was mostly determined "by an equally unstable public opinion." *Harv. L. Rev.,* 28:417, 418, 1915. After the Civil War, it recalled, mere segregation in public conveyances was thought to be unconstitutional. Later, Jim Crow was accepted.

Yet it is questionable whether this kind of equality is that which the Fourteenth Amendment was intended to secure. In practice, these classifications are always imposed by the white race; and the motive is admittedly the avoidance of the black race. Since this purpose is

decision was not inconsistent on its face with the doctrine of separate but equal. However, by insisting on principled adherence to the equality side of the doctrine, *McCabe* revealed a judicial attitude which cast doubt on the future of the doctrine itself, because realistically, the separate but equal doctrine was incompatible with itself, and if courts approached the doctrine in a rigorous rather than in an excusing way, it could not long survive.

The foregoing reads a lot into *McCabe*, and it may be a reading that is too much influenced by the frontal challenge to segregation into which the equality principal grew in the hands of the Hughes and Vinson Courts two and three decades later. *McCabe* may also be read as a decision of rather modest significance for the future of Jim Crow. If the issue were viewed as the relatively easy one of absolute deprivation of service to blacks, not relative inequality, then *McCabe* was not inconsistent with the loose, substantial equality standard with which the courts could wink at inequalities in accommodations for blacks not amounting to categorical deprivations. Moreover, the practical consequence of the decision—to force the partitioning of Pullmans—hardly struck at the roots of Jim Crow. Also, as a number of the law reviews pointed out, the principle stated was dictum.[159] *McCabe* thus embodies the duality characteristic of all the decisions upholding the claims of black people handed down by the Supreme Court under Chief Justice White. Which way one leans will depend more on the aggregate significance of all the decisions than on the inferences that can be drawn from any single decision alone. Still, one feature of the case stands out: it was not a justiciable controversy. In 1914, when blacks politically and in contemplation of law were at their lowest point since the Black Codes, a majority of the Supreme Court went out of its way to denounce the outright imposition of inequalities in public transportation on the face of state law. Against the momentum of *Louisville, Plessy, Cumming,* and *Berea College,* this was a signal event.[160]

---

accomplished, the technical equality before the law held out to the negro partakes somewhat of the nature of a sop.

Ibid. After this speculative relativity, the article paralleled the anticlimax of *McCabe* with the conclusion that the only practical effect of the decision would be that railroads would partition their Pullmans. *Ibid.,* 419.

[159] See, e.g., *Central L.J.,* 80:43, 1915; *Va. L. Reg.,* 20:781, 1915; *Law*

Notes, 18:182, 1915.

[160] After *McCabe,* the NAACP went to work to challenge the Oklahoma proviso law in a justiciable case. Joel Spingarn went to Oklahoma and was involved in preparing two test cases when the issues of war preparedness and the draft precipitated a struggle over the place of blacks in the military that refocused the energy of the NAACP and brought Spingarn back to New York. The railroads were brought under closer government reg-

D.   *South Covington & Cincinnati Street Railway* v.
      Kentucky: THE CLOSING OF A CIRCLE

The third and final decision of the White Court involving segregation on public transportation was *South Covington & Cincinnati Street
Railway* v. *Kentucky,* handed down in April 1920.[161] *South Covington*
was the last of the long series of decisions involving Jim Crow on railroads and other carriers stretching back to *Hall* v. *DeCuir*[162] in 1880.
It was an appropriate reflection of the progression of Jim Crow in
forty years that this final case involved single streetcars holding about
thirty-two passengers that carried persons for a 5¢ fare on a six-mile
route through Cincinnati across the Ohio River into Covington,
Kentucky, and back. About 80 percent of the line's passengers traveled
across the river; about 5 percent were black.

When Kentucky charged this streetcar company with violating the
state's separate coach law,[163] the company claimed that the state was
interfering with interstate commerce. Since Ohio had a law prohibiting
racial separation in public transportation within that state, on the same
trip a streetcar would be subject to conflicting regulations. The Kentucky
state courts upheld the applicability of the separate coach law as to
passengers traveling between points within Kentucky, although application to interstate passengers was disavowed.

The South Covington and Cincinnati Street Railway had been to
the Supreme Court a few years before.[164] In 1915, the line had challenged Covington's power to regulate it in various ways. By ordinance,
the city had required the line to provide sufficient cars to meet passenger
demand; to limit the number of passengers in any car; to prevent
passengers from standing on the front and rear platforms, unless certain

---

ulation, calling for a reconsideration
of strategy, and the Oklahoma follow-
up cases were never brought.

Another, broader effort to challenge
Jim Crow conditions on railroads also
was stymied by World War I. Florence Kelley, one of the founders of
the NAACP and the force behind the
National Consumers' League, approached Louis Brandeis who advised
that extensive facts should be gathered
about concrete instances of discriminatory conditions to be presented to
the Interstate Commerce Commission.
As an extensive factual record was
in the final stages of preparation,

Brandeis was appointed to the Court
in January 1916. This plan also fell
to the preoccupation with the railroads' war preparedness before World
War I. The ICC challenge was abandoned, and the NAACP eventually
settled on an open letter of protest to
President Wilson. Kellogg, *NAACP,*
1:204–205.

   [161] 252 U.S. 399 (1920).
   [162] 95 U.S. 485 (1877).
   [163] 1915 Ky. Acts 795.
   [164] South Covington & Cincinnati
Street Ry. v. Covington, 235 U.S. 537
(1915).

safety devices were installed; to keep the cars clean and ventilated and fumigated weekly; and to keep the temperature in the cars above fifty degrees. The company objected that these regulations burdened interstate commerce and deprived it of property without due process.

In the 1915 decision, a unanimous Court, Justice Day writing, struck down several of the ordinance's provisions. That the company was a Kentucky corporation whose Kentucky facilities connected with those of a separate, jointly owned Ohio corporation across the river did not matter. Whether commerce was interstate was determined by "what is actually done," and where there was an uninterrupted transportation of passeners between states, on the same cars, under the same operation, and for a single fare, there was interstate commerce, without doubt. Therefore, the question was whether the requirements burdened inter-state commerce or were reasonable health and safety measures that affected commerce only incidentally. The passenger limits and the require-ment that demand be accommodated were struck down. The line would have had to put on many more cars to meet demand in Covington, which necessarily would have increased its traffic in Cincinnati, beyond the number of cars permitted by that city's regulations. "On one side of the river one set of regulations might be enforced, and on the other side quite a different set, and both seeking to control a practically continuous movement of cars." On the other hand, the safety requirements on the front and rear platforms were found to affect interstate commerce only incidentally and were upheld. As to these, there was no evidence of conflicting regulations in Cincinnati. The temperature requirement was struck down offhandedly as "unreasonable" and a violation of due process. It was "impossible" and "impracticable," Justice Day thought he knew, to keep the cars to the minimum temperature owing to the frequent opening of doors.[165]

The square holding five years before that this very line was operating in interstate commerce and should not be subjected to con-flicting regulations about passenger accommodations was a bit awkward for the Court when the applicability of Kentucky's separate coach law came before it. Justice McKenna, however, writing for the Court, man-aged to perceive "a distinct operation in Kentucky." The company de-rived its powers to operate in Kentucky from the state and should not be permitted to escape its obligations to the state. The Jim Crow regulation "affects interstate business incidentally and does not subject it to un-reasonable demands." It was of equal importance to preserve the sovereignty of the states within their boundaries as it was to prevent

---

[165] *Ibid.*, at 545, 548, 549.

states from burdening interstate commerce. "[W]e need not extend the discussion," McKenna concluded, claiming that the earlier *South Covington* case made clear that segregation for Kentucky travelers on the Kentucky side of the river was not an unreasonable burden on interstate commerce.[166]

McKenna's reluctance to elaborate was understandable. His level of abstraction obscured the burdens imposed by the Kentucky statute, realities spelled out in detail in the streetcar company's brief. A map of the line's route was part of the record and showed a web crossing three bridges between Cincinnati and Covington. The company could not feasibly add a Jim Crow car when its cars came across the river from Cincinnati, because the area on the Kentucky side of the bridges was "in the heart of the business and residence district of Covington." To maintain switching facilities in that area was unreasonable since the "very essence of the street car travel is speed, cars at frequent intervals, and low fares."[167] Even if a Jim Crow partition was built into each car, segregation would still be impractical, the company argued. The single motorman who operated the streetcars could not distinguish between interstate and intrastate passengers, since tickets were not bought for any destination. Ohio law did not permit passengers going from point to point within Cincinnati to be segregated. Kentucky travelers would have to be segregated. Interstate passengers were subject to neither law. Thus, one group of whites and blacks would have to be allowed to sit wherever they wanted, and a second group would have to be segregated, with no ready way to distinguish one group from another. A black traveler within Kentucky would be forced to the Jim Crow section even though interstate blacks could remain in the white section and interstate whites could sit in the black area. "[T]he process would be a farce and would be attended with constant difficulty and danger of race antagonism and disorder," contended the company.[168]

As the author of the earlier *South Covington* decision from which McKenna and the majority purported to find guidance, Justice Day, joined by Van Devanter and Pitney, registered a vigorous dissent that was a good deal more candid about the absurd situation created by the conflicting Ohio and Kentucky statutes and the freedom of interstate

---

[166] South Covington & Cincinnati Street Ry. v. Kentucky, 252 U.S. 399, 403–404 (1920). A comparison case turning on nearly identical facts and producing the same division within the Court was Cincinnati, Covington & Erlanger Ry. v. Kentucky, 252 U.S. 408 (1920).

[167] *Brief for Plaintiff in Error*, 24, South Covington & Cincinnati Street Ry. v. Kentucky, 252 U.S. 399 (1920).

[168] *Reply Brief of Plaintiff in Error*, 5, *ibid*.

passengers from either.[169] That three Justices dissented calls attention to the roles of Holmes and Brandeis, who by switching sides could have swung the Court to Day's position. But McKenna had probably spoken to their overriding concerns in his final paragraph when he pointed to "the equal necessity, under our system of government, to preserve the power of the states within their sovereignties as to prevent the power from intrusive exercise within the National sovereignty."[170] Emanations from the interstate commerce clause that would bar the application of state Jim Crow laws to interstate business could be the basis for barring other state regulations as well. For Holmes and Brandeis, *South Covington* was an occasion for affirming state power to regulate interstate enterprises.

Not until 1941 would the Supreme Court again confront Jim Crow on the railroads, and by then Hughes would be in the center seat, to lead a reconstituted Supreme Court in a new direction that would take it back to "the one pervading purpose" of the Civil War amendments, "the protection of the newly-made freeman and citizen from the oppressions of those who had formerly exercised unlimited dominion over him."[171]

The series of cases of which *South Covington* was the final complacent statement ended as it began, with the question of embarrassments to interstate commerce. It started in *Hall* v. *DeCuir* with a riverboat passenger traveling on a separately ticketed, discrete journey within a state unable to claim the protection of the state's antisegregation law. It ended with a streetcar traveling an undifferentiated loop across two states' borders unable to free itself from the absurd inconveniences of compliance with one of those states' segregation statutes. *Hall* and *South Covington* represent opposite extremes converging on the same result, two incongruous buttresses supporting for a half century one of the monuments of Southern distinctiveness, the Jim Crow car.[172] It is

---

[169] 252 U.S. 399, 404 (1920). Without difficulty, Day distinguished *Chesapeake & Ohio Ry.* v. *Kentucky,* the 1900 decision sustaining the Kentucky separate coach law as applied to the intrastate part of an interstate train's run. 179 U.S. 388 (1900). In that case, the Court had concluded that the Kentucky law applied only to intrastate passengers and that the obligation to add a Jim Crow car for travelers within Kentucky was not an unreasonable burden on interstate commerce. Day thought the streetcar

line involved in the *South Covington* case was quite different because of the impracticality of adding a car at the Kentucky line and the confusion of trying to sort out intrastate passengers on so short a run. 252 U.S. at 407–408.

[170] 252 U.S. at 404.

[171] Slaughterhouse Cases, 83 U.S. (16 Wall.) 36, 71 (1873).

[172] The phrase is from C. V. Woodward, *The Burden of Southern History* (1968), 18.

fitting that the cycle should begin and end with attention to the interstate commerce aspects of state legislation concerning Jim Crow in public transportation. The problem of equality was an afterthought in these cases. It intruded in the period between *Hall* and *South Covington* momentarily in *McCabe*; otherwise public transportation cases between *Hall* and *South Covington* were a solid phalanx of support for Jim Crow in public transportation.

IV.   The Curious Case of Buchanan v. Warley

Buchanan v. *Warley*[173] was an awkward case contrived to test the constitutionality of an ordinance adopted in May 1914 in Louisville, Kentucky, that forbade "any colored person to move into and occupy as a residence . . . any house upon any block upon which a greater number of houses are occupied . . . by white people than are occupied . . . by colored people."[174] With the usual reciprocity, the ordinance also stood in the way of any whites wanting to move to blocks occupied mainly by blacks. The occupancy rights of existing owners were not disturbed, and there was an exception for servants. When the Louisville chapter of the NAACP organized itself to challenge this law, its head, William Warley, who was black, arranged a deal with Charles H. Buchanan, a white real-estate agent friendly to the NAACP, for the sale of an unoccupied end lot on a block containing ten residences, eight occupied by whites and two, those nearest Buchanan's lot, by blacks. The contract looked to litigation. Warley withheld $100 of the $250 purchase price, reciting in the contract that "I am purchasing the . . . property for the purpose of having erected thereon a house which I propose to make my residence. . . . I shall not be required to . . . pay for said property unless I have the right under the laws of the state of Kentucky and the City of Louisville to occupy said property as a residence."[175] When Warley set up the ordinance as his excuse for not performing, the state courts refused Buchanan's plea for specific performance, holding that the ordinance was constitutional and a full defense for Warley.[176] By writ of error, the case then went on to its intended destination, the Supreme Court of the United States.

When *Buchanan* was first argued on April 10 and 11, 1916, Justice Day lay ill in Ohio, and the vacancy left by the passing of Justice Lamar

---

[173] 245 U.S. 60 (1917).

[174] The ordinance is quoted in the Court's opinion. *Ibid.,* at 70–72.

[175] The clause is quoted in the Court's opinion, *ibid.,* at 60–70; see also W. B. Hixson, Jr., *Moorfield Storey and the Abolitionist Tradition* (1972), 139. A good account of the factual background of the case is R. L. Rice, "Residential Segregation by Law, 1910–1917," *J. South. Hist.,* 34:179, 1968.

[176] Harris v. City of Louisville, 165 Ky. 559, 177 S.W. 422 (1917).

was not yet filled by Brandeis, then in the final throes of confirmation.[177] But Day and Brandeis would catch up with the case. "Some big things are going over to next term to be tackled by a full Court," a distracted but cordial Hughes wrote to the absent Day a few days after the argument. "It will be a great term—that next term," he continued, almost as if he anticipated regret for his coming absence. "We have just added to its importance by restoring to the docket for reargument the Louisville Segregation case."[178] By the time *Buchanan* was reargued in late April 1917, Hughes had left the Bench to run for President and had been replaced by Clarke. Day was well again and Brandeis had taken his seat.[179] Thus, the Bench that heard *Buchanan* the second time included

---

[177] Several Southern Senators adverted to the *Buchanan* case as a reason for opposing Brandeis in the confirmation fight because they predicted his opposition to the ordinance, a surmise that was correct though not based on anything in particular in Brandeis' record. See discussion, *supra*, pp. 391, 371.

[178] The letter gives evidence of the distractions that beset Hughes at that eventful time:

But the run of the mine gives us plenty to do, and there is no spare time. So far as I am personally concerned, the year has been a very unpleasant one. I am bombarded on all sides, my correspondence is very heavy, and the men who insist on the right "to say a word" fill in the few crevices of time left by our work. But I refuse to be embarrassed and endeavor to plod along the straight and narrow judicial path. The "boys" are all in good form, particularly young Holmes who sparkles ever with the fire of an endless youth. If you haven't seen it, get the April number of the Harvard Law Review—an extraordinary tribute to him on his seventy-fifth birthday.

I understand that we shall hear argument for only three weeks longer. Apparently no cases will be ready after that time. And then the usual mad whirl of opinions!

C. E. Hughes to W. R. Day, Apr. 17, 1916, Day Papers, Library of Congress. On June 10, 1916, Hughes resigned from the Court to accept the Republican nomination for President.

[179] At either the first or second argument, the shadow of World War I intruded in the person of Rene Viviani, former Premier of France, who observed the proceedings as the guest of the Chief Justice. Kelly Miller, one of the most articulate and passionate advocates of black civil rights, was also in the courtroom and recalls Viviani's presence:

It so happened that M. Vivian [*sic*], Ex-Premier of France, member of the French High Commission sent from the democracy of France to make an appeal to the democracy of America, was a guest of the Chief Justice on this occasion. This gallant representative of the gallant French Republic was confronted by the ridiculous anomaly of witnessing the highest tribunal in the dominant democracy of the world trying to determine whether or not the rights of an American citizen at home to buy and occupy property should be limited by race and color. Great indeed was the triumph of democracy when a right decision was reached on this issue.

K. Miller, *An Appeal to Conscience* (1918), 57.

two Southerners (not counting Brandeis), White and McReynolds, and was, despite the departure of Hughes, perhaps somewhat more sympathetic to claims of racial justice than it had been a few years before. The decision to hold *Buchanan* for a full Bench—and for decision after the Presidential election of 1916—reflected the Court's and the country's sense of the case's vast significance. It was and was understood to be the most important race relations case since *Plessy* twenty years before.

A. THE SPREAD OF RESIDENTIAL SEGREGATION

The controversy that came to the Court from Louisville might have come from other cities, most in border states unsettled by the influx of blacks moving northward and to the cities. The first municipal ordinance requiring residential segregation came in 1910 in Baltimore, and the idea quickly spread. As *The Chautauquan* reported:

> Segregation of the Negro in railroad cars, in schools and colleges, in hotels and restaurants, has long been practiced in many of our states and cities, and the "Jim Crow" statues are familiar enough. But segregation by law of colored inhabitants in a northern city, and one so near the national capital, is a new thing.[180]

Mooresville and Winston-Salem in North Carolina passed residential segregation ordinances in 1912. Asheville followed the next year. Three Virginia cities, Richmond, Norfolk, and Roanoke, passed such laws in 1913, as did Atlanta, Georgia, Madisonville, Kentucky, and Greenville, South Carolina. In 1914, Louisville adopted the ordinance that came to the Supreme Court. Birmingham, Alabama, and St. Louis, Missouri, were next, and the wave moved into Texas in 1916.[181]

That residential segregation should have been spawned in the border states in the second decade of the twentieth century reflected the evolution of race relations in the Progressive era. As the Jim Crow railroad car was a symbol of white supremacy for a society in motion, so residential segregation was both racism's ultimate expression and its desperate response to the great twin movements of the black race in the Progressive era, the migration from country to city and from the deep South to points north. In 1915, but for Atlanta and Greenville, all of the dozen or so residential segregation ordinances in effect had been enacted in cities in border states. "Right here in Alabama nobody is thinking or talking about land and home segregation," wrote Booker T.

---

[180] *The Chautauquan*, 62:11, 1911.   [181] Kellogg, *NAACP*, 1:184.

Washington in December 1915, in one of his last public utterances.[182] Washington thought it "remarkable that in the very heart of the Black Belt where the black man is most ignorant the white people should not find him so repulsive as to set him away off to himself." But he should not have been surprised. Traditional forms of caste that prevailed in the deep South needed to take on new contours as Jim Crow was exported to the North along with the northward, urban movement of hundreds of thousands of blacks after 1910.

Washington undoubtedly engaged in some wishful exaggeration about conditions in Alabama, for the Baltimore idea had appeal in the deep South, particularly in cities like Atlanta that felt the pinch of black influx and changing racial patterns common in cities in the border areas. Any extensions of Jim Crow that were remotely practicable, and many that were not, were difficult for white politicians to resist. Once cities like Baltimore, St. Louis, and Louisville had pointed the way, it was, as Washington pointed out, "always difficult, in the present state of public opinion in the South, to have any considerable body of white people oppose them, because their attitude is likely to be misrepresented as favoring Negroes against white people."[183] Thus, it was not hard to foretell, as *The Chautauquan* saw as early as 1911, "that the 'Baltimore idea' may spread and that the cry that negroes are invading white streets and causing property to depreciate may lead to 'black ghetto' ordinances by the score."[184]

Knowledge that the Louisville ordinance was headed for challenge in the Supreme Court checked the spread. "News has come from Birmingham," reported the *Survey* in 1914, "that the City Council, after announcing its intention of passing a segregation ordinance, has decided to await the results of the Louisville and Richmond cases."[185] What was explicit in Birmingham was implicit elsewhere; cities around the country stood on the brink of residential apartheid as the nation awaited the response of the Supreme Court. The *Survey* did not much exaggerate when it wrote that *Buchanan* would not only affect the forty-two thousand black people living in Louisville, but "may, in fact, largely determine if the Negro is to be segregated in the United States."[186]

---

[182] B. T. Washington, "My View of the Segregation Laws," *The New Republic*, 113, Dec. 4, 1915. Washington attacked residential segregation as unnecessary and degrading. His main argument was that segregation ordinances would relegate blacks to the poorest, most crime-ridden, and generally disreputable parts of cities. Blacks would thereby lose the beneficial example of contact with white neighbors and fail to get this most useful type of education in self-improvement.

[183] *Ibid.*

[184] *The Chautauquan*, 62:11, 12, 1911.

[185] *Survey*, 33:72, 1914.

[186] *Ibid.*

Indeed, it was not only the cities that stood poised over residential segregation. There was considerable agitation about the awesomely impractical notion of rural property segregation as well. This idea would have commended itself anyway to those inclined to press racial separation to the limit, but its leading exponent seems to have been inspired by the South African brand of territorial apartheid.[187] In 1914, the North Carolinian Clarence Poe, editor of the *Progressive Farmer*, an influential agricultural journal, following the lead of Maurice S. Evans, a leading South African politician and theorist of "native segregation," whom Poe met in England, advocated that farm areas be segregated in the South. The North Carolina Farmer's Union unanimously endorsed such a plan at its convention that year.[188] The typical suggestion was that counties where one race owned most of the acreage could, by referendum, opt to prevent the purchase of land by a member of any other race. Since blacks were disfranchised most uncompromisingly in areas where they were most populous, this would have been, like all of Jim Crow as a practical matter, a one-way exclusionary device.[189]

Residential segregation was the one type of Jim Crow law that met with a mixed reception in the state courts.[190] The first Baltimore ordinance, which provided that blacks could not move into blocks occupied exclusively by whites and vice versa, was struck down by the Maryland Supreme Court in a confused opinion which finally settled on the objection that the ordinance could have prevented current owners from occupying their own property.[191] More confidently, the Supreme Court of North Carolina threw out the Winston-Salem ordinance of 1912 forbidding persons to live in blocks where the majority was of another race, because it thought that basic property rights must permit an owner to sell to whomever he or she wished. The North Carolina court cited

---

[187] See C. M. Fredrickson, *White Supremacy* (1981), 253.

[188] Woodward, *Strange Career of Jim Crow*, 86.

[189] W. D. Weatherford, "Race Segregation in the Rural South," *Survey*, 33:375, 1915.

[190] In 1890, a federal circuit court had struck down a San Francisco ordinance that required Chinese to live only in designated areas. Chinese living in other areas within the city were required to relocate within sixty days. A disgusted federal circuit judge could not "comprehend how this discrimination and inequality . . . can fail to be apparent to the mind of every intelligent person, be he lawyer or layman." *In re* Lee Sing, 43 Fed. 359, 360 (N.D. Cal. 1890). Of all the residential segregation ordinances, this was the most extreme, applying only to one race, requiring present property owners to relocate, and segregating in designated sectors rather than in currently occupied areas.

[191] State v. Gurry, 121 Md. 534, 88 A. 546 (1913). The history of the Baltimore residential segregation ordinance is illuminated in G. Power, "Apartheid Baltimore Style: The Residential Segregation Ordinances of 1910–1913," *Mary. L. Rev.*, 42:289, 1982.

the sad history of Celtic pales in Ireland and Jewish ghettoes in Russia to bolster its conclusion that the state could not be presumed to have authorized its cities to pursue "so revolutionary a public policy."[192] At first, the Georgia Supreme Court struck down a complicated Atlanta ordinance that not only prohibited blacks from moving into blocks inhabited exclusively by whites and vice versa, but went on to provide that on mixed blocks a black could not move into a house previously occupied by a white if any whites living on adjoining lots objected, and vice versa. The court thought the effect of this "was to destroy the right of the individual to acquire, enjoy, and dispose of his property."[193] Two years later, however, the same court reversed itself and upheld a second Atlanta segregation ordinance.[194] The Virginia Court of Appeals, in a paean to judicial restraint and progressive breadth for the police power, sustained the ordinances of Richmond and Ashland, except in their application to current property holders, treating *Plessy* and the later cases upholding racial segregation in public transportation and in schools as conclusive on the equal protection question.[195] Virginia indeed went farther than any state in authorizing its cities to divide whole areas, even entire towns or cities, into "segregation districts" where only one race could live.[196]

The Kentucky courts in the *Buchanan* case itself sustained residential segregation in a burst of progressive spirit. As the Kentucky Court of Appeals put it:

> The advance of civilization and the consequent extension of governmental activities along lines having their objective in better living conditions, saner social conditions, and a higher standard of human character has resulted in a gradual lessening of the dominion of the individual over private property and a corresponding strengthening of the regulative power of the state in respect thereof. . . .

Kentucky was "fully committed to the principle of the separation of the races whenever and wherever practicable and expedient for the public welfare. . . .[197]

---

[192] State v. Darnell, 166 N.C. 300, 303, 81 S.E. 338, 339 (1914).

[193] Carey v. City of Atlanta, 143 Ga. 192, 202, 84 S.E. 456, 460 (1915).

[194] Harden v. City of Atlanta, 147 Ga. 248, 93 S.E. 401 (1917).

[195] Hopkins v. City of Richmond, 117 Va. 692, 86 S.E. 139 (1915).

[196] Fredrickson, *White Supremacy*, 254.

[197] Harris v. City of Louisville, 165 Ky. 559, 569, 572, 177 S.W. 472, 476,

477 (1916). The concern of the North Carolina Supreme Court that residential segregation of blacks could lead to separation of other groups was dismissed as

the time-worn sophistry (always advanced when legislation of this character is being attacked), that if the power exist to segregate whites and blacks, then the power must likewise exist to segregate Re-

B. THE NAACP CHALLENGE

The unrestrained commitment to the principle of racial separation reflected in residential segregation laws helped bring into play a counter-vailing commitment to racial equality that not only would bring down residential segregation, at least in its *de jure* aspect, but would, in the fullness of time, put the axe to the principle of racial separation root and branch. For the wave of ordinances that began in Baltimore fueled the emergence of the NAACP, and, in particular, galvanized local chapters which pressed court challenges across the country. The Baltimore branch successfully challenged that city's ordinance in the Maryland Supreme Court in 1910, and did so again with a second segregation ordinance passed in 1911. When Baltimore persisted with a third ordinance, which also was challenged, the Maryland courts deferred decision until *Buchanan* was resolved. Although the Baltimore branch of the NAACP had planned to carry its challenge to residential segregation to the Supreme Court, its victories in the state courts permitted that role to be played instead by the NAACP branch in Louisville, Kentucky, also organized especially to challenge that city's segregation ordinance.[198]

The NAACP had able counsel locally and in the Supreme Court. W. Ashbie Hawkins led the efforts in Baltimore. One of Louisville's leading lawyers, Clayton B. Blakey, a graduate of the University of Michigan Law School, took charge of the litigation in Kentucky. Charles Nagel, Louis D. Brandeis' brother-in-law and a former Secretary of Commerce and Labor in the Taft Administration, headed a group of eminent St. Louis attorneys, including Frederick W. Lehmann and

---

publican and Democrat, persons of Irish descent and those of German descent. . . . To give ear to this kind of reasoning is to close one's mind to the gravity of the race problem as it exists in our country today, and especially to those phases of it most intimately con-cerned with congested municipal conditions.

Ibid., at 566–67.

[198] Mary White Ovington, one of the NAACP's founders and later its chairman, states, without affording de-tails, that the organization was assisted by real estate brokers in challenging residential segregation:

But the realtor knew that prop-erty depreciated as the well-to-do moved into a new section of city, more open and attractive than the old. He knew that if the laboring class—which happened to be black —might not acquire the property, it would remain unoccupied and bring disaster to the owner. Old neighborhoods that become unfash-ionable do best with freedom of sale and get more rent from Ne-groes than from whites.

When the NAACP brought its test case before the Supreme Court, it was not without some support from real estate operators.

M. W. Ovington, *The Walls Came Tumbling Down* (1947), 115–16.

Wells H. Blodgett, who challenged that city's ordinance and submitted an *amicus* brief in *Buchanan*. Moorfield Storey, first president of the NAACP, who had early recognized the initial Baltimore ordinance as a "most inauspicious" interference with the right of blacks to acquire desirable property, and who saw early in 1911 that the movement would spread, took the lead in the Supreme Court.[199]

By the time *Buchanan* v. *Warley* reached the Supreme Court, the significance of the case could be measured in the heavy weight of many briefs and a voluminous record. In addition to the main briefs by Storey and Blakey and that of the city attorneys of Louisville, *amicus* briefs on both sides were submitted concerning the Baltimore, St. Louis, and Richmond ordinances. Altogether, twelve briefs were submitted. Elaborate street maps dividing white and black sections of the various cities were included in the record as both sides sought to support their contentions about the impact of residential segregation on property values and living conditions for whites and blacks. Pages of photographs of mansions, tidy bungalows, shanties, and slums competed to show the Justices the high and low living standards of black, integrated, and white neighborhoods.[200]

Moorfield Storey concentrated his constitutional argument on the hostile purpose of residential segregation—to confine blacks to the least desirable sections of the city—and on the fundamental nature of the property rights of buyers and sellers that were infringed by the Louisville ordinance. To help establish that the ordinance's purpose was to stigmatize and degrade blacks, Storey quoted with evident relish the brief of the Louisville city attorney in the Kentucky Court of Appeals: "It is notorious that in a community such as Louisville only the most degraded and vicious element among the white would be willing to live in a normally negro section."[201] Storey dismissed as absurd the claim that residential segregation operated equally on blacks and whites. "A law which forbids a Negro to rise is not made just because it forbids a white man to fall."[202] He equally stressed that the "common law right of every landowner is to occupy his own house or to sell or let it to whomever

---

[199] M. Storey to E. Mason, Mar. 17, 1911, quoted in Howe, *Moorfield Storey*, 254.

[200] "A unique feature of the supreme court presentation was a booklet of photographs of the Louisville negro residence districts showing costly and beautiful homes and public buildings." *Atlanta Constitution*, Apr. 28, 1917, p. 4, col. 5.

[201] *Brief for Plaintiff in Error on Rehearing*, 25, Buchanan v. Warley, 245 U.S. 60 (1917).

[202] *Ibid.*, at 33. It would be "[t]he same sort of equality . . . as would exist were the General Council of New York to prohibit all Jews from engaging in business on Fifth Avenue, and all Gentiles from engaging in business on Mott Street." *Ibid.*, at 25.

he pleases."[203] One of the "first essentials of a free government is the right of every citizen to establish his residence where he sees fit. . . ."[204] In his pursuit of doctrinal support from the principles of laissez-faire constitutionalism, Storey went so far as to liken blacks to employers as classes whose property rights were the victims of increasingly frequent statutory assaults. On this basis, he distinguished residential segregation from the accepted Jim Crow laws in transportation and education by stressing the vital character of the property rights affected although he insisted that all forms of segregation were invalid.[205]

Louisville met these arguments in the currency of unalloyed racism. "It is shown by philosophy, experience and legal decisions, to say nothing of Divine Writ, that . . . the races of the earth shall preserve

---

[203] *Brief for Plaintiff in Error*, 25, Buchanan v. Warley, 245 U.S. 60 (1917).

[204] *Ibid.*, at 27.

[205] Newspaper reports of the first argument indicate that the Justices asked many questions, including this exchange: "Justice McReynolds asked Storey if under his argument race segregation of all forms were not a disregard of rights. The Boston man held that it was, and then Justice McReynolds asked if the attorney believed it possible to segregate without violating someone's rights. 'No,' said Storey." *St. Louis Post Dispatch*, Apr. 11, 1916, Sec. 1, p. 13, col. 3.

Amicus submissions on behalf of the NAACP chapters in Baltimore, Richmond, and St. Louis generally tracked the arguments made by Storey, although the NAACP brief from Baltimore added that "[t]he notion at the basis of all their segregation ordinances is the preservation of property values." *Amicus Brief for Baltimore Branch of the NAACP*, 31, Buchanan v. Warley, 245 U.S. 60 (1917). The Richmond NAACP brief pointed out that such ordinances "could not have been passed with as much facility before as after the Constitution of Virginia of 1902, since which time the colored man neglected politics and failed to qualify for the electorate." *Amicus Brief for Richmond Branch*

of the *NAACP*, 14, Buchanan v. Warley, 245 U.S. 60 (1917). But the most eloquent arguments against residential segregation were put in the brief of the St. Louis Branch of the NAACP, by Wells H. Blodgett, Frederick W. Lehmann, and Charles Nagel, among others:

> When lines of race, or nationality or religion, are drawn, it is in the spirit of bigotry and prejudice— never in the spirit of charity and equity. . . . It does not answer to say that pride may be met with equal pride. . . . No prouder people lived than the Jews, none more self-reliant or resourceful. . . . [But] they knew that . . . the ghetto was the open door to the pogrom.

Amicus Brief for St. Louis Branch of the NAACP, 9, Buchanan v. Warley, 245 U.S. 60 (1917).

The repeated references in the NAACP briefs to the potential for residential segregation to spread beyond its initial victims, the blacks, to other groups, especially Jews, reflected real alarm. In 1916, Louisville officials felt the need to assure local Jewish leaders that no segregation of Jews was in prospect. J. R. Pole, *The Pursuit of Equality in American History* (1978), 258.

their racial integrity by living socially by themselves."[206] If black parts of town were undesirable, it was only because "the shiftless, the improvident, the ignorant and the criminal carry their moral and economic condition with them wherever they go."[207]

C. A LANDMARK OPINION IN MODEST DRESS

After the collision of sweeping theories in the briefs, the intense scrutiny of the press, and the general sense all around that Jim Crow was being tested at its farthest reaches, the matter-of-fact recital of the facts and proceedings below with which Day began his opinion for a unanimous Court had an air of incongruous modesty. It was in keeping with this approach that the first question Day posed had nothing to do with the merits, but rather was the question of Buchanan's standing to assert that the Louisville ordinance violated the rights of blacks. The awkwardness of this problem was highlighted by the irony that Warley, the head of the Louisville NAACP, was represented by counsel for the city of Louisville upholding the ordinance that would excuse Warley from the contract he had entered into for the sole reason of having the ordinance declared invalid. Moorfield Storey by the same token was led to posture on behalf of the white man Buchanan that he "is not complaining of discrimination against the colored race. He is not trying to enforce their rights but to enforce his own."[208] But the burden of Storey's argument, of course, was precisely that the ordinance denied the rights of blacks, and he thought he had good reason to worry that the Court might avoid the case on the standing ground. "[Y]ou know how ingenious the Court sometimes is in finding a method of avoiding a disagreeable question,"[209] he had written to Wells Blodgett before the argument. Holmes would indeed press this position in a dissent that he decided ultimately not to deliver.

---

[206] *Brief for Defendant in Error*, 7, Buchanan v. Warley, 245 U.S. 60 (1917).

[207] *Ibid.*, at 12. Not satisfied with attacking Storey's "worn-out sophistries," Louisville's lawyers accused him of advocating intermarriage, though not for himself. "We do not for a moment believe that Mr. Storey, or any member of his family practices what he preaches." *Supplemental Reply Brief for Defendant in Error on Rehearing*, 143, Buchanan v. Warley, 245 U.S. 60 (1917). This nasty dig at Storey may have been calculated to twit him about the racial views of his own wife, the former Gertrude Cutts, of Virginia ancestry, who adamantly refused to associate with blacks in social or professional gatherings, causing Storey no little embarrassment. Hixson, *Moorfield Storey and the Abolitionist Tradition*, 111.

[208] *Brief for Plaintiff in Error on Rehearing*, 11, Buchanan v. Warley, 245 U.S. 60 (1917).

[209] Quoted in Hixson, *Moorfield Storey and the Abolitionist Tradition*, 110.

VIII: *The Heyday of Jim Crow*

Day affirmed at the outset the principle that a litigant may assert only personal rights. The city of Louisville insisted that this principle required the case to be dismissed for want of standing. Day denied this in come confusion. Buchanan's property rights were "directly involved and necessarily impaired"[210] by the ordinance because he could not sell his lot to a willing and contractually bound black purchaser. Thus, the case was not of the sort "wherein this court has held that where one seeks to avoid the enforcement of a law or ordinance he must present a grievance of his own, and not rest the attack upon the alleged violation of another's rights."[211] That was all Day had to say on the point, and as we shall see presently, it did not persuade all the Justices, despite the recorded unanimity.

Coming to the merits, Day noted that this "drastic measure" was "based wholly upon color; simply that, and nothing more,"[212] its justification being to prevent racial conflicts, maintain racial purity, and protect the value of property owned by whites. But the Fourteenth Amendment protected property, including "the right to acquire, use, and dispose of it."[213] Certain uses of property, Day recognized, could be controlled in the interest of health and safety, as in the cases of restrictions on brickyards or livery stables. But could the transfers of property be inhibited "solely because of the color of the proposed occupant of the premises"?

Day's answer to this question, evoking the great constitutional changes brought on by the Civil War, introduced an abrupt shift of tone and perspective, not only from the first half of his own opinion, but from the entire corpus of Jim Crow law that had grown out of *Plessy* v. *Ferguson*. The Civil War amendments were an integral part of the Constitution, Day reminded the country, having as their central purpose, as Justice Miller had said in the *Slaughterhouse Cases*, to raise the colored race "to the dignity of citizenship and equality of civil rights."[214] Day admitted that "the question of color has not been involved."[215] in many of the Fourteenth Amendment cases decided by the Court, but he insisted that the core purpose of the Amendment was "to extend federal protection to the recently emancipated race from unfriendly and discriminating legislation by the states."[216] There followed strong statements from *Strauder* v. *West Virginia* ("What is this but declaring that the law in the states shall be the same for the black as for the white"),[217]

---

[210] Buchanan v. Warley, 245 U.S. 60, 73 (1917).
[211] *Ibid.*
[212] *Ibid.*
[213] *Ibid.,* at 74.

[214] *Ibid.,* at 76.
[215] *Ibid.*
[216] *Ibid.*
[217] *Ibid.,* at 77.

and from the Civil Right Act of 1866[218] and 1870,[219] granting all persons the same rights enjoyed by white citizens to purchase or sell property and to make and enforce contracts. These enactments dealt not with "social rights," Day contended, but with "those fundamental rights in property which it was intended to secure upon the same terms to citizens of every race and color."[220]

Only after this resolute sounding of Reconstruction principle did Day take passing notice of *Plessy*, and then only in the course of reciting Louisville's arguments. *Plessy* was no justification for residential segregation, Day asserted cryptically, because it did not permit blacks to be deprived of public transportation, and "the express requirements were for equal though separate accommodations."[221] He then quoted the distinction drawn by the Georgia Supreme Court in striking down the Atlanta residential segregation ordinance:

> In each instance the complaining person was afforded the opportunity to ride, or to attend institutions of learning. . . . In none of them was he denied the right to use, control, or dispose of his property, as in this case.[222]

Day allowed that "there exists a serious and difficult problem arising from a feeling of race hostility which the law is powerless to control," but this problem could not be solved "by depriving citizens of their constitutional rights and privileges."[223] Nor could residential segregation be justified by analogy to antimiscegenation laws as prohibiting "the amalgamation of the races."[224] Rather it was a restriction on "the civil right of a white man to dispose of his property if he saw fit to do so to a person of color and of a colored person to make such a disposition to a white person."[225] Thus, the Louisville ordinance violated the

---

[218] "All citizens of the United States shall have the same right in every State and Territory, as is enjoyed by the white citizens thereof to inherit, purchase, lease, sell, hold and convey real and personal property." Act of Apr. 9, 1866, 14 Stat. 27 (1866).

[219] All persons within the jurisdiction of the United States shall have the same right in every State and Territory to make and enforce contracts, to sue, be parties, give evidence and to the full and equal benefit of all laws and proceedings for the security of persons and property as is enjoyed by white citizens, and shall be subject to like punishment, pains, penalties, taxes, licenses, and exactions of every kind, and no other. 16 Stat. 144 (1870).

[220] *Buchanan*, 245 U.S. at 79.

[221] Day dismissed *Berea College* as having rested solely on the power of the state to amend corporate charters.

[222] *Buchanan*, 245 U.S. at 80 (quoting Carey v. Atlanta, 143 Ga. 192, 201, 84 S.E. 456 [1915]).

[223] *Buchanan*, 245 U.S. at 80–81.

[224] *Ibid.*, at 81.

[225] *Ibid.*

"fundamental law" of the Fourteenth Amendment "preventing state interference with property rights except by due process of law."[226] The limits of Jim Crow had been drawn, and for the first time in a case involving racial segregation, the Supreme Court had spoken with one voice.

1. *The Reaction to Buchanan.* Immediate reaction to the *Buchanan* decision in the press was somewhat dampened in the excitement of local elections and news from the front.[227] But the black press exulted in the decision. To the *New York Age*, a black newspaper, *Buchanan* "proves that the instrument devised by the Fathers of the Republic has not yet become 'a scrap of paper,' "[228] and a black newspaper in Richmond, the *Planet*, could think of nothing with "a greater tendency to restore the confidence of the colored people in the integrity of the courts and the sense of fair play in the nation."[229] *The Guardian*, the black weekly in Boston, rejoiced at the invalidation of "the most outrageous of all civil discriminations against the negro race."[230] A "hopeful and optimistic" *Journal and Guide*, a black newspaper published in Norfolk, Virginia, noted that the decision was handed down by a Court that was mainly Democratic and whose Chief was a Southerner, and was "unique and remarkable also for the reason that never before in the history of the Supreme Court has that tribunal reached a unanimous decision upon any question upholding the rights of the Negro."[231]

General periodicals soon grasped the large significance of what the Court had done. "A Momentous Decision" was the title of *The Nation's* story,[232] which saw in the decision "cause for no little satisfaction in this period of flux that we have this remarkable demonstration of the value of a written Constitution."[233] Linking *Buchanan* with other decisions, *The Nation* saw a major shift in judicial attitudes. "[A]s in the case of the 'grandfather-clause' laws to disfranchise colored men, the Supreme Court has again shown itself a true bulwark of the liberties and rights of the colored population of the United States."[234] Only nine

---

[226] *Ibid.*, at 82.

[227] The *New York Times* mentioned the decision in passing and the *Chicago Tribune* failed to cover it at all. *New York Times*, Nov. 6, 1917, p. 18, col. 1.

[228] "The Negro's Right of Residence," *Literary Digest*, 55:17, 18, Nov. 24, 1917.

[229] *Ibid.*

[230] *Ibid.*

[231] *Ibid.* The Baltimore *Afro-Amer-*

ican wrote: "The joy in Bunkville [*sic*] when home run Casey came to bat . . . is nothing compared with the rejoicing in Baltimore, Richmond, St. Louis and other Southern towns over the outcome of the Louisville Segregation decision." Quoted in Rice, "Residential Segregation by Law," 179, 194.

[232] *The Nation*, 105:526, 1917.

[233] *Ibid.*

[234] *Ibid.*

years before, when the *Berea College* decision came down, "it seemed as if this great tribunal had definitely placed itself on the side of those who degrade and depress our colored citizenship."[235] But "there are millions to-day giving profound thanks and taking new hope as they bear the heavy burdens of the disadvantaged."[236] William H. Baldwin, writing in the *Survey*, thought the decision opened vistas to the end of racial separation: "[I]t does seem logical that if a Negro is sustained in his right to buy, sell and use property—and therefore to reside—where he will, he ought also to have full right to choose his own seat in a public conveyance."[237] This prospect, Baldwin suggested, was reinforced by "the new sense of value which has come to every individual as a result of war production, economy and financing, and which is accentuated in the Negro by reason of the great emigration from the South."[238] Even if that were speculation, Baldwin concluded, the decision "is a distinct end in itself,"[239] because it came "when several northern industrial centers are becoming restive under the great influx of Negroes from the South."[240] Thus, the decision stopped the spread of Jim Crow into the North at the point of its greatest expansive potential.[241]

Southern newspapers noticed the decision in editorials that by and large minimized its practical effects. The Richmond *News-Leader*, for example, reassured its readers that race segregation remains "a fit principle in the South"[242] and that what the city was prevented from doing by formal enactment "can be maintained by custom, if not by law."[243] In Louisville, the *Post* also thought the invalidation of the segregation ordinance would not change residential patterns in that city.[244]

By contrast to most of the popular press, law reviews from all parts of the country generally registered surprise and disapproval. And by further contrast, the law reviews saw the decision as mainly about property rights rather than about a bedrock principle of nondiscrimination. The most pungent criticism came in the *Virginia Law Review* from S. S. Field,[245] city solicitor of Baltimore, who had defended that city's residential segregation ordinances in the Maryland courts and had submitted a forceful *amicus* brief to the Supreme Court in *Buchanan*. The decision rested entirely on the right to sell property to whomever one

---

[235] *Ibid.*

[236] *Ibid.*

[237] W. H. Baldwin, 3d, "Erasing the Color Line," *Survey*, 39:185, 1917.

[238] *Ibid.*

[239] *Ibid.*

[240] *Ibid.*, 186.

[241] *Ibid.* For other comments, see "No Race Segregation by Law," *The*

Outlook, 117:548, 1917.

[242] "The Negro's Right of Residence," *Literary Digest*, 55:17, Nov. 24, 1917.

[243] *Ibid.*, 18.

[244] *Ibid.*

[245] S. S. Field, "The Constitutionality of Segregation Ordinances," *Va. L. Rev.*, 5:81, 1917.

wished for any reason, Field thought, and he could not understand how property rights were infringed by a prohibition on selling to a person of the wrong race but not by a prohibition on sale for use as a saloon or livery stable. There was "not a paragraph; not even a sentence; of discussion of the race question which has engaged the profound attention of thinkers and statesmen. . . ." The Court seemed to think that the case involved "nothing more important than a few dollars of difference" between the price Warley contracted to pay and what a white purchaser would have been willing to pay. "It is a striking illustration of the modern tendency to look upon property rights as more sacred than personal rights."[246] Law review comments from less partisan pens were, on the whole, in agreement. The *Yale Law Journal* shared Mr. Field's puzzlement about why residential segregation was a more stringent deprivation than other restrictions on the use of property. If the location of certain businesses could be controlled, why not the location of the races? It concluded that the Court unfortunately had given greater weight to landowners' powers of alienation than to the public interest in race segregation.[247] *Law Notes* regretted the decision in an editorial which remarked: "It was generally believed by the profession that the federal Supreme Court would consider the matter of residential segregation to be wholly a question of state policy."[248] Neither the *Michigan Law Review* nor the *Central Law Journal* could see how segregation could be reasonable in public transportation and education and not in residential location.[249] From a lofty perspective, the *Harvard Law Review* objected that the "result is reached by one of those anomalous and objectionable devices which characterize our methods of solving fundamental questions. . . . [T]he primary, the real, interests involved in the ordinance are certain civil rights of the negro race . . . and yet . . . the invalidity of the ordinance was determined professedly solely with reference to the property rights of a white man." The decision was thus another example of a "system which permits

---

[246] *Ibid.*, 83. Field was sensitive enough to note the chary way Justice Day had handled the decisions upholding segregation in public transportation and public education, and since Field thought it clear that a better case could be made for residential segregation than in transportation or education, he thought "[t]he opinion is alarming in that it possibly jeopardizes the laws requiring separate coaches for white passengers, and, what is more important, separate schools for white children." *Ibid.*, 87. How, Field wondered, could the Louisville ordinance have been thought unreasonable if traditions and customs counted for more than logic?

[247] Comment, "Unconstitutionality of Segregation Ordinances," *Yale L.J.*, 27:393, 1918.

[248] "Residential Segregation of Races," *Law Notes*, 21:162–63, 1917.

[249] Note, "Constitutionality of Segregation Ordinances," *Mich. L. Rev.*, 16:109, 111, 1917.

of the entertaining and determination of legal and political questions of the most profound importance to the entire country, upon such a casual, oblique and unscientific presentation of the real interests involved." On the merits, the *Harvard Law Review* doubted that the Louisville ordinance "was so clearly lacking in reasonableness as to be unconstitutional," and wished that the social facts about residential integration could have been presented to the Court as they were in the briefs "filed by Mr. Brandeis and Professor Frankfurter in the Oregon cases."[250] Only Thomas Reed Powell in the *Columbia Law Review* broke with this chorus, although he did take Justice Day to task for not stating persuasive reasons in support of the Court's holding. Powell thought it plain that the choice of residence was "materially and legally" more important than discrimination in public transportation or schools. He stressed that the Court had upheld racial separation only in passing, intermittent situations or in laws specifically aimed against miscegenation, but "when steps are taken to impose continuous and permanent barriers to the freedom of the members of either race to settle their abode where they will and can, the Supreme Court has wisely refused to accept fictions of equality in the face of the obvious fact of inequality."[251]

2. *Holmes' Dissent Not Made.* One of the themes that ran through the contemporaneous reaction to *Buchanan* was surprise that the Court was unanimous. *The Nation* quoted an unnamed "distinguished member of the bar" (in fact, Moorfield Storey) as having supposed " 'that the prejudice of some judges might lead them to dissent from the conclusion, but the unanimous opinion of the Court is a great victory for the cause.' "[252] The magazine continued: "When it is recalled that the Chief Justice is from Louisiana and that Mr. Justice McReynolds is a Tennessean, the significance of the unanimity of the Court is apparent."[253] That there were no dissents is indeed surprising, but the further surprise is that the Justice who came closest to dissenting was neither of those two sons of the Confederacy, but rather Mr. Justice Holmes. There is

---

[250] *Harv. L. Rev.*, 31:475, 476, 477, 479, 1917. This is a reference, of course, to Bunting v. Oregon, 243 U.S. 426 (1917), in which Brandeis, assisted by Frankfurter, prepared a very long, factual brief in support of Oregon's law establishing a ten-hour day for manufacturing work, but permitting up to three hours overtime at time-and-a-half rates. Since Brandeis was appointed to the Court before the argument, Frankfurter submitted the brief. A divided Court upheld the law.

[251] T. R. Powell, "Constitutionality of Race Segregation," *Colum. L. Rev.*, 18:147, 152, 1918. But *cf. Colum. L. Rev.*, 15:545, 1915 (nuisance concepts an adequate basis for upholding residential segregation).

[252] "A Momentous Decision," *The Nation*, 105:526, 1917.

[253] *Ibid.*

a printed dissent, revised in Holmes' hand, in the back of his Volume for the October Term 1917, noted as "Dissent. Not delivered."[254] It points up the problems of justiciability in *Buchanan* v. *Warley*, and reflects Holmes' view that the decision was grounded in untenable notions of property rights. What it reflects about Holmes' opinion of residential segregation is less certain, but his reluctance to go along with the Court in drawing bounds to racial separation is of a piece with most of his work in the area of race relations. The dissent, with corrections in Holmes' hand, is reproduced in this book (see insert following page 592) and is well worth reading.[255]

Evaluation of Holmes' near dissent, and of Day's opinion for the Court, can begin with the question whether *Buchanan* v. *Warley* was fit for adjudication. Holmes' suggestion that the case should not be entertained without evidence that it was not manufactured might have troubled the Court had it cared to look, because the case was far from the "honest and actual antagonistic assertion of rights" that the Supreme Court has many times, before and since *Buchanan*, held to be requisite to the adjudication of constitutional questions.[256] Warley had helped establish the Louisville chapter of the NAACP, of which he was head, for the specific purpose of getting rid of the ordinance and had entered into the contract with Buchanan to contrive a case that would accomplish that result. On the other hand, there was no question about the enthusiastic antagonism of counsel, or that the Louisville ordinance was in fact adversely affecting personal rights. Warley had invited the city attorneys of Louisville to intervene in his behalf in the state courts, and these lawyers appeared in the Supreme Court in earnest support of the ordinance. In addition, the *Buchanan* record itself revealed that the Louisville ordinance had given rise to real disputes. In a case argued and decided with *Buchanan* in the state courts, the Kentucky courts had

---

[254] Holmes Papers.

[255] *Ibid.* Why Holmes chose not to record this dissent is not clear. As late as Oct. 25, 1917, six months after the second *Buchanan* argument and only eleven days before the decision came down, Holmes wrote to Day, "I am debating whether to adhere to my dissent in [*Buchanan*] and therefore retain it." O. W. Holmes to W. R. Day, Oct. 25, 1917, Day Papers. Probably, Holmes abandoned it for the reason that he suppressed many dissents: because he was unable to attract support from at least one other Justice and decided his solitary difference was not important enough to make public. But his note to Day indicates that the question was a close one.

[256] E.g., United States v. Johnson, 319 U.S. 302 (1943); Chicago & Grand Trunk Ry. v. Wellman, 143 U.S. 339 (1892). Compare, Fletcher v. Peck, 6 Cranch 87 (1810). See generally H. Hart, Jr., and H. Wechsler, *The Federal Courts and the Federal System* (1953), 14–26.

upheld a fine under the ordinance, and the record of that case was submitted along with *Buchanan* to the Supreme Court.[257] But neither government counsel's intervention in feigned private disputes, nor parallel cases of real adversity, has been deemed sufficient to cure the problem of collusion.[258]

Holmes' avoidance instinct may well have been sound, therefore. Certainly Day's opinion offered no argument for treating the case as a real controversy. Perhaps Day was silent because no one raised the collusion issue, and the record revealed no arrangements for one party to bear the other's expenses, to provide counsel, or show other solid evidence of collusion. Moreover, partly because of the difficulty of discovering when a controversy is indeed feigned, the Court's rulings on this particular problem of justiciability have a rather haphazard quality. Holmes did not press the point in his unpublished dissent, and in view of his reputation for indifference to justiciability problems, Day might have dismissed his concern as reflecting more a desire to duck the merits than a wish to uphold the requisite of true adversity in constitutional cases.

The justiciability problem Holmes did press—his objection to Buchanan's standing to assert that the ordinance abridged the rights of blacks—was an extremely complex one that tended to highlight the collusion issue, although Holmes did not probe it very deeply. Holmes insisted that Buchanan, as a white man, could not avail himself of this "collateral mode of attack."[259] For Day, on the other hand, it was enough that the ordinance affected Buchanan's contract with Warley. Each dispatched the issue in a sentence or two, their opposite conclusions rooted in the confusion that, then as now, surrounded the capacity of litigants to press the claims of parties not before the Court.

None of the three cases that Holmes relied on was on point. In *Hatch* v. *Reardon*[260] and *Missouri, Kansas & Texas Railway* v. *Cade*,[261] state laws had been applied validly to intrastate transactions, and those affected had tried to assert that the laws in question would violate the Constitution if applied to other parties transacting in interstate commerce. In those cases, the third-party claims were entirely hypothetical, involving applications of the state laws that were not before the Court, had not been pressed by state authorities, had not been countenanced by the state courts, and were separable from the issues presented in the

---

[257] Harris v. City of Louisville, 165 Ky. 559, 177 S.W. 472 (1915), *reversed sub nom.* Buchanan v. Warley, 245 U.S. 60 (1917).

[258] United States v. Johnson, 319 U.S. 302 (1943).

[259] Unpublished dissent, Holmes Papers.

[260] 204 U.S. 152 (1907).

[261] 233 U.S. 642 (1914).

cases at bar.[262] Holmes' third citation, *Hendrick* v. *Maryland*, was more complicated, but, again, the claim Hendrick was not allowed to assert was that of an entirely hypothetical third party in a situation not presented in the application of state law before the Court.[263] In *Buchanan*, by contrast, the impact of the Louisville ordinance on Warley was revealed in the transaction at the heart of the case, albeit that its effect was to excuse him from performance, and the Kentucky courts had unburdened themselves of a ringing affirmation of precisely this impact. There was no separability in the ordinance's impact on buyer and seller.

---

[262] There were many other decisions in the years immediately preceding *Buchanan* denying standing to parties asserting possible unconstitutional applications of laws to other parties in other circumstances. See, e.g., Jeffrey Manufacturing Co. v. Blagg, 235 U.S. 571, 576 (1915); Plymouth Coal Co. v. Pennsylvania, 232 U.S. 531, 544–45 (1914); Rosenthal v. New York, 226 U.S. 260 (1912) (junk dealer responsible to inquire as to proper title to certain types of goods sold to him, cannot assert discrimination against owners of other types of property, where plaintiff's own interest was to prove the burdens imposed were unreasonable); Yazoo & Mississippi Valley R.R. v. Jackson Vinegar Co., 226 U.S. 217 (1912) (where penalty imposed on intrastate carriers for tardy settlement of claims, plaintiff could not assert unconstitutional application if statute imposed penalties where claims were frivolous or excessive since in this case no such claim was involved); Standard Stock Food Co. v. Wright, 225 U.S. 540 (1912) (where flat inspection fee charged to all businesses under a statute, an admittedly large business has no standing to challenge fee as discriminating against small businesses); Seaboard Air Line Ry. v. Seegers, 207 U.S. 73 (1907) (where statute upheld as valid regulation of an intrastate activity, claimants do not have standing to assert invalidity if it were applied to interstate activity); Lee v. New Jersey, 207 U.S. 67 (1907) (where state statute regulating oyster industry deemed valid as to claimants, claimants do not have standing to allege invalidity if it were applied to interstate activities).

[263] 235 U.S. 610 (1915). *Hendrick* dealt with a Maryland automobile license scheme that allowed nonresidents with licenses from their home states to obtain a special nonresidents' license permitting temporary use in Maryland, but denied this privilege to residents of the District of Columbia, who had to submit to the same procedures as Maryland residents. Hendrick had neither a license from the District of Columbia, nor a temporary or permanent license in Maryland. When he was charged with driving a car in Maryland without a license, he challenged the Maryland law, claiming that the exclusion of District of Columbia residents from the temporary Maryland license privilege denied equal protection. The Supreme Court refused to allow Hendrick to assert the rights of licensed District of Columbia residents to be treated equally with licensed drivers from other states. Since the Maryland courts had not reviewed the exclusion of licensed District of Columbia drivers from the Maryland temporary license scheme, in Hendrick's own case or any other, the reaction of the state courts to the hypothetical claim was also hypothetical.

Holmes asserted an unqualified version of the *jus tertii* principle: that a litigant may not put in question the effect of a law on others, even where the litigant is injured by that law in a way that necessarily reveals its impact on the rights of others he is seeking to assert. In other words, if the limitation on Buchanan's rights was reasonable, viewed in itself, Buchanan should not be permitted to complain that the limit was invalid because of its effects on others. Such a purist notion can be defended on the theory that courts should only assess those particular constitutional objections to laws that a litigant's own flesh-and-blood experience reveals. But the Supreme Court has not, before *Buchanan* or after, insisted on any such unqualified version of the *jus tertii* principle. Where a litigant is in fact injured by the impact of a law, and where part and parcel of that very impact also burdens persons not party to the litigation, the Court generally considers the third party's rights in passing on the validity of the law. Indeed, the Court has regarded rules against assertion of third party interests only as discretionary policies to prevent unnecessary adjudication of hypothetical problems, policies routinely set aside when some special relationship—whether transactional, contractual, familial, or associational—existed between the litigant who was injured in fact and the third party.[264] Of course, there was a special relationship between Buchanan and Warley of the sort that would usually suffice to permit Buchanan to assert Warley's rights as well as his own. But the problem was whether the fact that Buchanan and Warley had a collusion of interest in the very litigation before the Court should break the nexus that ordinarily would permit Buchanan to assert Warley's rights. Neither Day's majority opinion nor Holmes' unpublished dissent dealt with this.

Even if Holmes' purist version of the *jus tertii* doctrine had been accepted by the Court, it should not have barred Buchanan's assertion of his own rights, which could easily have been viewed as coincident with Warley's rights. Buchanan was not asserting a third person's rights, but his own rights under the contract. Buchanan's contract with Warley contained a condition precedent to Warley's obligation to perform: that Warley have the legal right to occupy Buchanan's lot. Buchanan thus had a direct and primary interest in establishing this condition precedent. For Buchanan to press Warley's right to occupy was simply an assertion of his personal interest in the effectiveness of his contract. Thus, the central issue of justiciability was whether this was a real and not a collusive case. That decided, there cannot be a serious question

---

[264] See generally R. A. Sedler, "Standing to Assert Constitutional Jus Tertii in the Supreme Court," *Yale* *L.J.*, 71:599, 1962; Note, "Standing to Assert Constitutional Jus Tertii," *Harv. L. Rev.*, 88:423, 1974.

whether one party to a contract has standing to contest the constitutionality of a law that, if valid, would discharge the other party.[265] Holmes missed this point, which seems plain, because he failed to bring the broad *jus tertii* principle he asserted to the level of the facts of the case.

The problem with this line of analysis is that *Buchanan* was unlike the usual *jus tertii* case in the bizarre respect that the third party was actually in the case as the nominal defendant and was seeking to have the law upheld that the plaintiff would have wished to assert was a violation of the defendant's rights. Whether this should bar the *jus tertii* assertion, where the state court had dealt with the asserted rights on the merits, and where attorneys for Louisville intervened to provide actual adversariness before the Supreme Court, is a debatable question.[266] That such an awkward situation should present itself certainly calls attention to the problem of collusion. Perhaps this is what Holmes, in his elliptical way, was trying to get at. The whole confusion could have been avoided had the Louisville litigants not tried to be so cute about structuring the lawsuit so that a white man was challenging the segregation ordinance. This cuteness very nearly cost the NAACP its unanimous Court.

Justice Day might have taken another approach to the case that would have eliminated the *jus tertii* problem entirely, had he and the Court been prepared to expand the scope of the constitutional guaranty involved, whether based on property rights or racial equality concerns, to protect white property owners from the harms, economic and associational, caused by unconstitutional segregation. But 1917 was too early in the day for the Court to perceive that racial segregation could hurt whites as well as blacks. As late as 1953, in *Barrows* v. *Jackson*,[267] the Court assumed that the Fourteenth Amendment did not protect whites from the impact of racial discrimination. This approach seems dubious. As a general proposition, unconstitutional laws should be subject to challenge by anyone hurt by them, even if an identical injury could be imposed by a constitutional law, assuming, of course, that the law in

---

[265] See Terrace v. Thompson, 263 U.S. 197 (1923) (a landowner was given standing to assert that a law forbidding certain aliens to own or lease land violated the alien's rights, although the Court upheld the law on the merits).

[266] For discussion of this problem, see M. Rohr, "Fighting for the Rights of Others: The Troubled Law of Third-Party Standing and Mootness in the Federal Courts," *Miami L. Rev.,* 35:393, 456, 1981. On the question of collusion, *Buchanan* raises the question whether state cases should be treated differently from federal cases. Compare, United States v. Johnson, 319 U.S. 302 (1943).

[267] 346 U.S. 249 (1953).

question is not separable so that only its constitutional impacts can be upheld. Certainly, the Louisville segregation ordinance was not separable in its impact on whites and blacks.[268]

Justice Day's opinion was not of much help to Holmes in explaining why Buchanan should be able to assert Warley's rights. Collusion aside, Day was correct, but seemed none too sure why.[269] He simply blurred the distinction between Buchanan's rights as seller and the rights of black purchasers. Since Buchanan's contract rights had been diminished because of the race of his purchaser, the Court had "to enquire into the constitutional right of the white man to sell his property to a colored man, having in view the legal status of the purchaser and occupant."[270] This cryptic collapse of the sellers' property rights and the rights of black purchasers into an undifferentiated issue of state police power exceeded even Holmes' developed capacities of innuendo, and it probably indicates that Day himself was left with a residue of doubt about Buchanan's standing.

3. Buchanan *as a Property Rights Decision.* The view that each Justice took of the standing question shaped his approach to the merits.

---

[268] See generally, H. P. Monaghan, "Overbreadth," *Sup. Ct. Rev.* 1, 1981.

[269] The Court did not have the benefit of cogent argument on the standing question from either Storey or the Louisville city attorneys. The Louisville brief simply asserted, without elaboration, that the "plaintiff in error is a *white* man and therefore neither can nor does make any claim that *he* is being discriminated against because of his color." *Brief for Defendant in Error,* 80, Buchanan v. Warley, 245 U.S. 60 (1917).

Storey responded to this objection as follows in his brief at the second argument:

[The plaintiff] is not complaining of discrimination against the colored race. He is not trying to enforce their rights but to enforce his own. He is seeking to make the defendant pay for land which the latter has agreed to buy provided he can legally occupy it as a residence. The plaintiff tenders the deed and asks the defendant to accept and pay for it. The defendant replies that he is not bound to do so, because the ordinance prevents his occupying the lot as a residence. The plaintiff replies that the ordinance is void. If he is right, he recovers; if not, the defendant prevails.

The question, therefore, is whether the ordinance is or is not valid.

Upon the answer to this question depends the plaintiff's right to enforce his contract with the defendant.

For the validity of the ordinance depends on whether it is or is not in violation of the Fourteenth Amendment and therefore that is the question which the case presents. As in Truax v. Raich, 239 U.S. 33, 39, it is "idle to call the injury [suffered by the plaintiff] indirect or remote."

Rehearing Brief for Plaintiff in Error, 11–12, Buchanan v. Warley, 245 U.S. 60 (1917).

[270] 245 U.S. at 75.

Holmes' view of the standing question narrowed the merits to a scope he could easily dismiss. Seeing the impact on Buchanan only as a speculative diminution of his property interest—to the extent that the prohibition on black occupancy dissuaded some possible buyers—Holmes found Buchanan's objection to the ordinance no more substantial than any other owner's objection to a restriction on a particular use of property, where the restriction fell well short of constituting a taking, and indeed probably conferred reciprocal advantages on all property owners in white areas.[271] Day's apparent doubts about Buchanan's standing to assert the invalidity of the ordinance's impact on Warley may well have contributed to the emphasis he gave to property rights of sellers, thus in turn shaping the central question lawyers and historians have puzzled over concerning *Buchanan v. Warley*: whether the decision should be viewed as a constitutional victory for rights of property or for rights of black people. The question demands attention even if it has no certain answer, and even if it reflects a somewhat artificial distinction. For on the tendency of the answer will turn much of one's assessment of the Supreme Court's work in the law of race relations in the Progressive era. How the question was answered at the time, or rather the different ways it was answered, tells a good deal about how the Court was perceived in the heyday of Jim Crow.

Both at the time and later, most legal scholars have seen *Buchanan* as a decision about property rights. Field's article and the *Harvard Law Review* comment discussed previously are samples of the consensus in the law reviews at the time of the decision. Later accounts have tended in the same direction. Louis Pollak explains *Buchanan* this way:

> The trouble with the ordinance was not, however, that the racial division of the city contravened the equal protection clause. The trouble with the ordinance was that it unduly interfered with the white seller's 'liberty' to sell to whom he chose—a substantive economic 'liberty' protected by the due process clause under the latitudinarian, business-oriented reading of the clause which was then fashionable.[272]

---

[271] Because Buchanan's was a corner lot, with blacks as the two nearest neighbors, Buchanan claimed that no white person would want to occupy it, and that the Louisville ordinance was therefore, in effect, a taking. Holmes thought the claim that the lot had no value except as a residence for a black person could not be credited. For a contrast with Holmes' view of the property rights question in *Buchanan,* see his famous opinion in Pennsylvania Coal Co. v. Mahon, 260

U.S. 393 (1922).

[272] L. Pollak, *Emancipation and Law: A Century of Progress* in R. Goldwin, ed., *One Hundred Years of Emancipation* (1964), 158, 171. Professor Pollak had given fuller expression to this view in a well-known article: *Buchanan* "was apparently put upon due process grounds rather than upon equal protection," because the Equal Protection Clause's separate but equal gloss might have been thought to support "the even-handed

Paul Brest believes the decision "probably is best explained in terms of the supposed uniqueness of real property and the then-prevailing doctrine of economic due process."[273] And George M. Frederickson has written that the "Louisville residential segregation law was unconstitutional because it interfered with the legal right of an owner to dispose of his real estate as he saw fit."[274] Robert Cover has gone so far as to claim that the racial discrimination element in *Buchanan* actually had the effect of bolstering the constitutionality of the ordinance.[275]

It is easy to see why this view of *Buchanan* has taken hold. Day's opinion makes no mention of equal protection, other than in the course of general recitals of the Fourteenth Amendment. He focuses throughout either on the Amendment at large or on the due process clause and rights of property. Moreover, there is the offhand, disengaged way

---

injustice of the ordinance," because the white plaintiff might have lacked standing to assert equal protection claims, and because the judicial climate was receptive to challenges to economic regulations. Thus, he concludes, "[f]or perhaps the wrong reasons [*Buchanan*] rightly decided that the fourteenth amendment barred states from establishing Negro ghettos." L. Pollak, "Racial Discrimination and Judicial Integrity: A Reply to Professor Wechsler," *U. Pa. L. Rev.*, 108:1, 10–11 1959.

John E. Nowak, Ronald D. Rotunda, and J. Nelson Young write: "The ordinance violated the due process clause because it was an unwarranted interference with property rights. The Court felt constrained to use the due process clause to protect property rights in the civil rights area as it had done in the business area." J. Nowak, R. Rotunda, and J. Young, *Handbook on Constitutional Law* (1978), 403.

Laurence Tribe, on the other hand, finds the *Buchanan* opinion "ambiguous: although framing its analysis in terms of substantive due process doctrine, at a critical juncture the opinion invoked equal protection notions in order to explain why the challenged ordinance did not fall within the police

power." L. Tribe, *American Constitutional Law* (1978), 1154.

The Supreme Court has treated the *Buchanan* rationale variously, to suit its purposes. In Shelley v. Kraemer, 334 U.S. 1, 11–12 (1948), Chief Justice Vinson's opinion for the Court described *Buchanan* as protecting the right of blacks to occupy and purchase property, that is to say, in equal protection terms. In Bolling v. Sharpe, 347 U.S. 497, 499 (1954), Chief Justice Warren's opinion for the Court described *Buchanan* as resting on the due process rights of property owners.

[273] P. Brest, *Processes of Constitutional Decisionmaking* (1975), 450.

[274] Fredrickson, *White Supremacy,* 254.

[275] The basis for the decision, Cover has written, was "substantive due process . . . protecting rights held by any and all individuals from a form of prohibited state interference. It just happened . . . that the probable motive or precipitating factor for the interference was a scheme of persecution against a 'minority group.' Strictly speaking, in each case that fact was legally irrelevant." R. M. Cover, "The Origins of Judicial Activism in the Protection of Minorities," *Yale L.J.,* 91:1287, 1295, n.22, 1982.

Day handled the equal protection precedents dealing with racial segregation. *Plessy* was not said to control because in that case blacks were not deprived of public transportation and were ensured of equal accommodations. On the other hand, the effect of the Louisville ordinance was supposedly "to destroy the right of the individual to acquire, enjoy, and dispose of his property."[276] Of course, this unelaborated characterization is not persuasive. On its face, the Louisville ordinance no more deprived blacks of the right to own and enjoy property than separate car laws deprived them of the right to public transportation. Perhaps Day had in mind a notion of the uniqueness of real property, with respect to which separate but equal would be a contradiction in terms. Or he might have been swayed by Storey's contention that residential segregation tended to restrict blacks to the least desirable areas, with the result that residential segregation was grossly unequal in reality. But Day did not bother to say so, and whatever might be interpolated to shore up his effort to distinguish *Plessy*, the fact remains that the opinion makes no serious effort to reconcile its holding with *Plessy* or to suggest a coherent theory of equal protection principles in relation to racial segregation. Thus, both Day's characterization of the ordinance and his handling of the precedents point to a property-rights reading.

Moreover, to see *Buchanan* as a decision about property rights helps accommodate it to the view, common among historians and constitutional scholars, that the period from *Plessy* through the decade of the 1920s was one of gathering momentum for racism, in the Supreme Court as well as in the country at large. *Buchanan* can be rendered less aberrational if it is seen as resting on property-rights concerns, rather than on concern for the civil rights of blacks. Certainly the Court's unanimity, and especially McReynolds' support for the decision, becomes less puzzling on this view. In all other cases involving segregation, McReynolds embraced a relaxed *Plessy* standard of reasonableness that invariably condoned Jim Crow.

Buchanan can be and was read differently, however. Much of the popular press, we have seen, greeted the decision as a momentous victory for the civil rights of blacks, in line with the perceptions of the NAACP, Booker T. Washington, and Moorfield Storey, that residential segregation was the most egregious type of discrimination against blacks. The NAACP briefs in the Supreme Court concentrated on social and constitutional principles of race relations, although, to be sure, Storey focused on the importance of property rights, in emphasizing the radical nature of the racial injustice done by the Louisville ordinance. The state courts' response to residential segregation, whether approving or

---

[276] *Buchanan,* 245 U.S. at 80.

not, was mainly concerned with the appropriate limits to racial separation, if any. When the state courts focused on property rights, they mostly affirmed "progressive" principles of police power regulation. And the rhetorical thrust of Justice Day's opinion, as distinguished from its imprecise analytic framework, was attuned more to the basic rights of blacks than to the essential elements of property. Indeed, measured against Day's generally flat style, the *Buchanan* opinion is a resounding statement of Reconstruction principles, statutory and constitutional. Day not only took pains to affirm that the central purpose of the Fourteenth Amendment was "protection for the recently emancipated race," but he defined the essence of this protection by a long statement of the uncompromising antidiscrimination principles found in *Strauder* v. *West Virginia*. The Civil Rights Acts of 1866 and 1870 were treated not as a hollow echo of bygone convictions but as statements of enduring principle. And Day's answer to the "serious and difficult problem arising from . . . race hostility" was that citizens cannot be deprived of constitutional rights, a flat repudiation of the vague and flaccid *Plessy* standard of reasonableness as the governing constitutional sanction for legalized racism.

Day's overall record certainly supports an understanding of *Buchanan* v. *Warley* as a decision directed by its author to concerns about racial justice rather than general concerns about property rights. William R. Day was descended from strong antislavery forebears in Ohio and Connecticut, and late in life he often recalled childhood memories of antislavery agitation and protest against the Fugitive Slave Law in his hometown, Ravenna, Ohio.[277] After he came on the Supreme Court in 1903, Day was a sturdy friend of black legal aspirations. He joined Harlan in dissent in *Berea College*[278] and dissented ably in *South Covington & Cincinnati Street Railway*.[279] He joined Hughes in reaching out to overturn the luxury car proviso to the Oklahoma Separate Car Law,[280] and in the first great peonage decision in *Bailey* v. *Alabama*,[281] after having dissented with Harlan against the Court's initial dismissal of that appeal on jurisdictional grounds.[282] He authored the opinion striking down the Alabama criminal surety system in the other great peonage decision of the White Court.[283] Although he did

---

[277] J. E. McLean, *William Rufus Day: Supreme Court Justice from Ohio* (1946), 13 *et seq*. As Secretary of State, Day had opposed the expansionist tide then favoring annexation of the Philippines.

[278] See *supra*, text accompanying notes 8–25.

[279] See *supra*, text accompanying notes 168–79.

[280] See *supra*, text accompanying notes 149–67.

[281] 219 U.S. 219 (1911).

[282] Bailey v. Alabama, 211 U.S. 452 (1908).

[283] United States v. Reynolds, 235 U.S. 133 (1914).

write one of the key decisions permitting blatant discrimination in the administration of voter qualifications,[284] he was part of the unanimous Court that struck down the Grandfather Clause.[285] Day's is indeed a record in race cases that lacks only passionate intensity of expression and the occasion to have dissented from *Plessy* and the *Civil Rights Cases*, to compare to the great achievement of Harlan. Moreover, Day's record in cases involving contract and property rights was almost invariably to uphold a broad construction of state police power, as his dissents in *Lochner* and *Coppage* exemplify. Day took an increasingly dim view of national economic regulation, as distinguished from regulation of morals and health, but it is clear that this reflected federalism concerns and not a commitment to laissez-faire constitutionalism.[286] Day may well have included the statements about property rights, as well as the affirmation of Reconstruction principles, to capture Justices of both views for his unanimous Court.

The historical context of *Buchanan* suggests further doubts about an exclusive property rights perspective on the decision. *Buchanan* was decided in the same year as *Bunting* v. *Oregon*,[287] the year of American entry into World War I, and a year after Felix Frankfurter's somewhat overconfident assessment in the *Harvard Law Review* that *Muller* v. *Oregon*[288] in 1908 marked a turning point away from the laissez-faire individualism of *Lochner* v. *New York*[289] toward a sympathetic awareness of community interests in the regulation of property and employment contracts.[290] It is true that substantive due process protection of property rights was not dead, but only on the wane until its reinvigoration in the 1920s, and it might be thought that *Buchanan* was a harbinger of the enhanced commitment to property rights of the next decade. But apart from its racial aspect, the type of property regulation that the Louisville ordinance represented—a restriction on property use to promote neighborhood homogeneity and prevent uses thought to be noxious or out of keeping with community character—was one the Supreme

---

[284] Giles v. Teasley, 193 U.S. 146 (1904).

[285] Guinn & Beal v. United States, 238 U.S. 347 (1915).

[286] See generally the discussion in McLean, *William Rufus Day*, 114.

[287] 243 U.S. 426 (1917).

[288] 208 U.S. 412 (1908).

[289] 198 U.S. 45 (1905).

[290] F. Frankfurter, "Hours of Labor and Realism in Constitutional Law," *Harv. L. Rev.*, 29:353, 369–70, 1916. It is true that the year after *Buchanan*

brought the decision in Hammer v. Dagenhart, 247 U.S. 251 (1918), striking down the federal child labor statute, and that Day wrote the majority decision. However, Day combined a restrictive view of federal legislative power under the Commerce Clause, at least where economic, rather than health or morals, regulation was at issue, with an ample view of state police power. And *Buchanan* was, of course, a question of state police power.

Court affirmed nine years after *Buchanan*, in the midst of its heightened judicial commitment to laissez-faire.[291] The *Euclid* v. *Ambler Realty Co.* decision thus tends to indicate that it was the element of racial discrimination touching property rights and not a neutral conception of property rights that produced the decision in *Buchanan* v. *Warley*.

These emanations of text and context do not show that *Buchanan* was a case about racial justice rather than rights of property, but they do tend to undermine the converse proposition. However, just as *Buchanan* cannot be viewed as upholding some general notion of property rights, so it obviously cannot be viewed as invalidating racial segregation apart from the basic property rights infringed. It was the combination of racial discrimination touching on an important right that produced the decision. For Booker T. Washington and Moorfield Storey, residential segregation was a particularly galling and disabling racial injustice, because freedom to acquire and live on desirable property was the reward for hard accomplishment and the avenue to further progress. Full and equal rights of property were for them, as for the Reconstruction Congress, an essential requisite to racial justice. To see *Buchanan* as an opinion about property rights, rather than about the rights of blacks, separates a seamless concept of baseline constitutional protection against racial discrimination and misjudges the thrust of the Court's action. In this respect, the popular press understood *Buchanan*'s significance better than the law review commentaries of the day, excepting the discerning realism of Thomas Reed Powell in the pages of the *Columbia Law Review*. The decision called a halt to the spread of Jim Crow laws, and found in the Fourteenth Amendment and the Civil Rights Acts of 1866 and 1870 an antidiscrimination principle different in kind from the relaxed judicial deference of the *Plessy* opinion. "I cannot help thinking," Moorfield Storey wrote to Oswald Garrison Villard after the *Buchanan* decision came down, "it is the most important decision that has been made since the *Dred Scott* case, and happily this time it is the right way."[292] Twenty years later, though Jim Crow remained entrenched in public education, transportation, and elsewhere, W. E. B. Du Bois would look back on *Buchanan* as "the breaking of the backbone of segregation."[293]

Notwithstanding *Buchanan*, and although the Supreme Court struck down in the next decade two thinly disguised ordinances from New Orleans and Richmond designed to circumvent the rule of

---

[291] 272 U.S. 365 (1926).
[292] Hixson, *Moorfield Storey and the Abolitionist Tradition*, 142.

[293] P. S. Foner, ed., *W. E. B. Du Bois Speaks, Speeches and Addresses 1890–1919* (1970), 52.

Department of Justice.
Washington.

August 10, 1910

The President.

Sir:

I inclose herewith certain correspondence between myself, as Acting Attorney General, and Mr. James A. Harris, Chairman of the Republican State Central Committee of Oklahoma, in regard to the adoption by the people of Oklahoma on the 2nd instant of an amendment to the State constitution designed to exclude the negro population of the State from the right of suffrage, contrary to the provisions of the Fifteenth Amendment and of the Oklahoma Enabling Act (34 Stat. 267, chap. 3335, sec. 3.).

The amendment in question provides:

> No person shall be registered as an elector of this State, or be allowed to vote in any election held herein, unless he be able to read and write any section of the constitution of the State of Oklahoma; but no person who was, on January 1st, 1866, or at any time prior thereto, entitled to vote under any form of government, or who at that time resided in some foreign nation and no lineal descendant of such person shall be denied the right to register and vote because of his inability to so read and write sections of such constitutions.
> Precinct election inspectors having in charge the registration of electors shall enforce the provisions of this section at the time of registration provided registration be required. Should

Letter from Acting Attorney General W. R. Harr to President Taft
concerning the Grandfather Clause in Oklahoma,
containing Taft's response *(upper right corner)*:
"Aug. 14, 1910—Read—
I concur in the view of the A. G. that the Executive has no power
to intervene or a U.S. Court by equitable proceeding.
W. H. Taft."

LOUIS D. BRANDEIS
(*New York Public Library Picture Collection*)

JOHN G. JOHNSON
(*Harvard Law Art Collection*)

JOHN W. DAVIS
(Culver Pictures)

OLIVER WENDELL HOLMES, JR.
(Harvard Law Art Collection)

Cosmopolitan Magazine

Vol. XLII   MARCH, 1907   No. 5

RAWHIDE LASH USED DAILY BY AN OVERSEER IN ONE OF THE FLORIDA LUMBER-CAMPS FOR
WHIPPING WHITES AND BLACKS INTO SUBJECTION. THIS CAT-O'-NINE-
TAILS IS IN THE POSSESSION OF THE AUTHOR

Slavery in the South To~Day

A REVELATION OF APPALLING CONDITIONS IN FLORIDA AND OTHER STATES, WHICH MAKE POSSIBLE THE ACTUAL ENSLAVE- MENT OF WHITES AND BLACKS UNDER TRUST DOMINATION

By Richard Barry

Author of "Port Arthur—A Monster Heroism"

  Editor's Note.--Like an infamy resurrected from the Dark Ages, a condition of slavery exists to-day, the horrors of which would strain credulity were they not sub- stantiated by most copious and exact facts. The hoary institution of chattel slavery has reappeared in our day and generation to add its fresh budget to the sufferings and crimes of centuries. Torrents of the noblest blood have drenched the earth that no man should have the right to hold another in servitude. Civilization has assured itself that this iniquity was forever abolished. The recesses of Africa, it is true, still resound with the cry of massacre, and the lash and bullet are there the potent allies of slave-snatchers and a crowned butcher. But we were confident that within our borders, in the vast expanse of our own enlightened country, slavery in every form except that of industrial slavery had been crushed, never to rise again. As a shattered, obsolete condition of the receding past we had read about it with wonderment, and contemplated it as an historical abomination which could not be repeated.

  In a new and sinister guise, however, slavery has again reared its hideous head, a monster suddenly emerging from the slimy sordid depths of an inferno peopled by brutes and taskmasters in human semblance. Whites and blacks are to-day being indiscrim- inately held as chattel slaves, and the manacle, lash, bloodhound, and bullet are teaching them submission without partiality to color. So often have we heard fine discourses on the superiority of the whites and the bestial inferiority of other races that we buckramed ourselves with a lofty race pride, and spoke down with a spirit of splendid condescension. Like a galvanic shock it undermines our self-importance to find that this new form of slavery places white and black on a plane of perfect equality, and enslaves them both with generous disregard of ancestry or complexion. But where in negro slavery there was often sentiment, a marked exchange of affection between

A Pawn in the Struggle for Freedom

By

Ray Stannard Baker

Author of "Following the Color Line," etc.

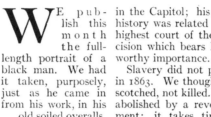

WE pub-lish this month the full-length portrait of a black man. We had it taken, purposely, just as he came in from his work, in his old soiled overalls, his old greasy hat, his old shoes, the stub of a half-smoked cigarette in his fingers. We wanted to show him exactly as he is. However you will probably not be able to distinguish him from a thousand—or a million—other black men whose backs are bent daily to the heaviest burdens of the South. Look well at the dull black face and you will see there the unmistakable marks of ignorance, inertia, irresponsibility. If you are given to reflec-tion, you may well ask:

Is this the thing the Lord God made and gave to
   have dominion over sea and land?
Is this the dream He dreamed who shaped the
   suns
And pillared the blue firmament with light?

And yet, curiously—or not at all curiously, as you happen to look at such matters—this thing which the Lord God made, he has used in dreaming his greatest dream—the dream of human freedom.

A few months ago the name of this appar-ently inconsequential black man resounded in the Capitol; his apparently unimportant history was related and discussed before the highest court of the land, and the legal de-cision which bears his name is one of note-worthy importance.

Slavery did not perish from off the earth in 1863. We thought it did, but it was only scotched, not killed. No evil is ever instantly abolished by a revolution or a legal enact-ment: it takes time and training and a deeper revolution in the human soul. The name was changed but the thing itself—in-voluntary servitude—has continued to this day. Under the guise of a contract for labor many negroes, and, indeed, some white men have been held—and legally held—in a form of peonage not essentially different from slavery.

See how it worked out in Alabama in the case of the negro Alonzo Bailey. In 1908 Bailey signed a contract to work for a white planter for one year at twelve dollars a month. He got an advance payment of fifteen dollars in cash.

After working for a little over one month, Bailey left the plantation. It is not in evi-dence why he left, whether he was himself sick or lazy, or whether the master was cruel. It matters little; the point is, he broke his contract to work for an entire year. Ordi-narily when a man breaks a contract which he has with you, you may sue him and get damages. But the negro is penniless, and besides that, what the planter wants is not his money, he wants the service of those black hands and that bent back.

Bailey was not sued but arrested. For the Alabama Statute at that time said that any person who received money under such a contract and stopped before it was worked out, the presumption was that he *intended to defraud* the employer, and therefore that he was criminally punishable. Moreover, when he came into court the law said he might not even testify to what his own intent was, the contract being made *primà facie* evidence of the intent to defraud. In short, the workman had the law loaded against him. No matter how honest he might have been in signing the contract, no matter what might have arisen afterwards—death or illness or marriage—when he stopped work the law presumed him guilty of fraud and made him criminally punishable.

Well, Bailey was tried, and of course punished. He was sentenced to serve one hundred and thirty-six days at hard labor—absolutely without a hearing, the only witness against him being his white employer with the contract in his hand—which, by the way, was an unacknowledged and unwitnessed contract.

This meant that Bailey would have to go to the chain gang—a criminal—unless, perchance, some white man would pay his fine and get him out. But in that event he would have to work for the white man under new and more difficult obligations, for the debt now would include lawyer's charges and court fees. Under such conditions it might take him years to work free again, as indeed, it has taken many a Southern negro. But in the end the white man would get what he wanted—the enforced labor of the black man.

When Bailey was arrested his wife sought out Edward S. Watts, an able young white attorney, and asked him if he could not free her husband. Now, there are many public-spirited white men in the South who have long seen the rank injustice of such a system of peonage as this. One of these is a just judge, William H. Thomas, of Montgomery, who had already decided, in another case, that the contract labor law was unconstitutional. His decision, fought by the planters to the highest court of the State, was finally reversed. Mr. Watts, however, believing in spite of what the Supreme Court of Alabama had said that the system was wrong, carried the case into the federal courts, where, assisted by Fred S. Ball, one of the leading lawyers of Alabama, they fought the case of Bailey through the Supreme Court of the United States. Here in a decision written by Justice Hughes, the Alabama law is overturned. "The State,"

Photograph by Chambers   *Photograph by Coleman*

EDWARD S. WATTS   FRED S. BALL

Able Southern lawyers who believe that peonage is wrong. They handled the negro's case and carried it to the Supreme Court of the United States where Alabama's bad law was overthrown

IS THE FIFTEENTH AMENDMENT VOID?

NEARLY forty years have elapsed since the Fifteenth Amendment was proclaimed by the Secretary of State to be part of the Constitution of the United States. During that time, it has been hated with a deadly hatred by the section of the country it was designed chiefly to affect. It has been despised, flouted, nullified, evaded. Nevertheless, the Supreme Court of the United States, the lawful guardian of the Constitution, has in no single instance held any state or federal statute or the act of any state or federal officer to be in conflict with the Amendment; and no case in that court can be found which would have been decided differently if the Amendment had never existed.

In a number of cases, it is true, the Supreme Court has decided that the Amendment does *not* do this and does *not* do the other; but if the student of constitutional law, not content with such negative information as to what the Amendment does not do, seeks to ascertain affirmatively what, if anything, it has accomplished, he must find his way by the pure light of reason unaided by the binding authority of any actual decision of our highest court.

Confronted by these remarkable circumstances, the student of constitutional law not unnaturally asks himself: "Can it be that an enactment which has thus borne the slings and arrows of outrageous fortune for nearly forty years and yet during all that time has never affected the result in a single decided case in the court of last resort — can it be that such an enactment is indeed part of the fundamental law of the United States?" To consider one aspect of that question is the object of this article.

The assumptions will be indulged that the Amendment was proposed in a constitutional manner by two thirds of both Houses of Congress and was duly ratified by legislatures in three fourths of the states. Attention will be concentrated upon the question whether, assuming the Amendment to have been proposed and ratified in the manner prescribed for constitutional amendments, it is within the express and implied limitations on the power of three fourths of

Title page of an article by Arthur W. Machen, Jr.,
Harvard Law Review 23:169 (1910)
(*Courtesy of the* Harvard Law Review)

VIII: *The Heyday of Jim Crow*

Buchanan,[294] residential segregation in the nation's cities maintained its momentum, just as the *Richmond News-Leader* had predicted. It was not only economic constraints, social pressures, and mob violence that reinforced segregation generally. Private rights of property and contract would provide an adequate substitute, in practical terms, for the positive regulation that the White Court had set aside in *Buchanan.* The legal system played an important role in cementing the patterns of segregation through the creation and enforcement of racially restrictive covenants that limited the sale of property to, in the usual phrase, "Caucasians only." Since the courts not only enforced these covenants against the owners who had agreed to them but also held that they "ran with the land," thus binding subsequent purchasers as well, the way was open through persuasive covenanting to reserve whole neighborhoods to whites.[295] The NAACP challenged the judicial enforcement of these covenants as "state action" tantamount to residential segregation by judicial decree, but in 1926, the Supreme Court unanimously rejected the challenge on the ground that only discrimination by individuals was involved.[296] It was the first time the NAACP lost a major case in the Supreme Court, and it permitted private agreement to accomplish what the White Court had declared in 1917 statutes could not. Not until the aftermath of World War II, with all the shocks to the foundations of racism that cataclysm entailed, would the Supreme Court strike down judicial enforcement of racially restrictive covenants[297] and complete the dismantling of state-enforced residential segregaiton begun in the shadow of the previous World War.

---

[294] See Richmond v. Deans, 281 U.S. 704 (1930) (*per curiam*); Harmon v. Tyler, 273 U.S. 668 (1927) (*per curiam*). See also Jackson v. Maryland, 132 Md. 311, 103 A.2nd 910 (1918), in which Maryland's highest court struck down the last Baltimore ordinance attempting residential segregation. In the *Harmon* case, there is evidence that the Louisiana courts were encouraged by the onslaught of law review criticism of *Buchanan* to hope that the Supreme Court would retract. H. Shulsky and W. B. Carmen, Jr., "Per Curiam Decisions of the Supreme Court" (thesis,

Harvard Law School Library, May 1, 1919), 23. During the 1920s, Norfolk, Dallas, and Indianapolis all passed residential segregation ordinances that were struck down by state courts. As late as 1940, Winston-Salem passed such an ordinance, and it too was struck down by state courts. Rice, "Residential Segregation by Law," 179, 196.

[295] See generally C. Vose, *Caucasians Only* (1959).

[296] Corrigan v. Buckley, 271 U.S. 323 (1926).

[297] See Shelley v. Kraemer, 334 U.S. 1 (1948).

The Supreme Court and Jim Crow in the Progressive Era: An Interim Summing Up

The effort to gauge the significance of the victories the White Court gave for the first time to black claims in segregation cases, as well as the defeats, must await a consideration of the Supreme Court's decisions in other types of race relations cases during the Progressive era. Nonetheless, one or two conclusions are warranted at this stage. The White Court did not repudiate the essential principles of Jim Crow laid down by the Fuller Court in *Plessy* v. *Ferguson* and *Louisville, New Orleans & Texas Railway* v. *Mississippi*. But it prevented the radical spread of racial separation laws into enforced territorial apartheid, which, had it been legitimated by the Supreme Court, would surely have swept through the cities and towns of the South and probably beyond into the countryside. Had such a totalitarian form of racism sunk its roots into American law in the second decade of the twentieth century, the consequences are formidable to contemplate. *Buchanan* v. *Warley* did not put an end to the many forces, including law, that buttressed residential segregation in American cities. But we cannot know how far the momentum of racism would have carried territorial separation, or what colossal problems would have been encountered in American law in the effort at extirpation, had *Buchanan* approved the concept as a matter of law.

In measuring the White Court's achievement in *Buchanan* v. *Warley*, it must be allowed that the case might have been decided the same way by the Fuller Court, and almost certainly would have been by the Taft Court. White himself had joined *Plessy* twenty-one years before, and the presence of McReynolds on the unanimous *Buchanan* Court cautions against viewing the decision as a substantial repudiation of Jim Crow. Nonetheless, *Buchanan* remains a landmark: the first decision putting constitutional limits on the expansion of the doctrine of separate but equal in race relations. The Fuller Court had a ripe opportunity to seize this achievement in the *Berea College* case a decade before, but it backed away. Greatness consists in part in being there, and in *Buchanan* v. *Warley*, the White Court seized the occasion.

McCabe v. *Atchison, Topeka & Santa Fe Railway* is a less significant step in the law of race relations, and the Court was divided in taking it. Yet the majority had to reach far even to accept the case, and the doctrinal cast of the decision had potentially monumental consequences. *McCabe* insisted on equality as a personally held right with respect to all areas of racial separation law, a potentially destructive challenge to Jim Crow, whereas *Buchanan* covered only one type of Jim Crow law. But because the blatant inequality in *McCabe* was one that could hardly be missed, the principle *McCabe* announced did not carry very far, at least for the next two decades.[298]

The White Court's failure to disapprove racial separation in *Butts v. Merchants & Miners Transportation Co.* and *South Covington & Cincinnati Street Railway* v. *Kentucky* is solid evidence that its sympathy for the rights of black people did not go so far as to embrace any broad willingness to strike at Jim Crow whenever the opportunity was presented. *Butts* and *South Covington* were both decisions that could have gone the other way, and probably should have, quite apart from any predisposition one way or the other toward Jim Crow. *Butts* and *South Covington* indicate that *McCabe* and *Buchanan* were, to the Court that rendered them, decisions about the appropriate limits of the doctrine of separate but equal, both in terms of internal logic and external reach, and not signals of fundamental displeasure with the doctrine itself.

Apart from the particular ambit of their holdings, moreover, and equally important in constitutional effect, *McCabe* and *Buchanan* introduced elements of principle into the trackless landscape of judicial deference, self-induced blindness to social and doctrinal realities, and avoidance of decision that made up the constitutional law of race relations by 1910. The notion that principle was abroad in the Supreme Court to contend with the racial prejudice permeating American law was itself a striking departure from the legacy of the Fuller Court. That the principles of *McCabe* and *Buchanan* were modestly limiting rather than destructive to Jim Crow in his heyday must be allowed, and yet their very presence as serious contestants on the constitutional stage ushered in a new phase for "the problem of the twentieth century." *McCabe* and *Buchanan* stand as twin signals of the White Court that in the second decade of the twentieth century Jim Crow no longer had a casual apologist in the Supreme Court of the United States.

---

[298] I am grateful to Professor Mark Tushnet for pointing out that in 1930, the Atchison, Topeka & Santa Fe Ry. refused to provide Pullman service for George Washington Carver, citing the economic consideration of general lack of demand by black passengers for luxury accommodations. L. McMurry, *George Washington Carver* (1981), 229–31.

CHAPTER IX

The Peonage Cases:
The Supreme Court
and the "Wheel of Servitude"

THE *Peonage Cases—Bailey* v. *Alabama,*[1] handed down only two weeks after Edward Douglass White became Chief Justice early in 1911, and *United States* v. *Reynolds,*[2] decided three years later—lay at the juncture of race and economic arrangements that fixed the distinctive character of the South during the Progressive era. They were the most lasting of the White Court's contributions to justice for black people, and among its greatest achievements. Yet the decisions reveal in a striking way the ambivalence of the Court's approach to constitutional issues affecting blacks during the Progressive era. Although the Supreme Court purported not to notice, the *Peonage Cases* peeled back a corner of the system of forced labor for black people that continued in the South into the twentieth century. The Court advanced the rights of blacks and gave realistic scope to the Thirteenth Amendment's protection against involuntary servitude, even as it denied that its decision was attuned in any way to race relations. It was in the name of property rights and an imaginative variant on freedom of contract that the Court gave constitutional support to the most wretched of the South's black agricultural laborers. Holmes, at least, thought the Court's protestations of race blindness had a distinctly hollow ring. Dissenting vigorously in *Bailey* and going along only grudgingly in *Reynolds*, Holmes believed that the *Peonage Cases* made no sense as elaborations of positive, race-

---

[1] 219 U.S. 219 (1911).   [2] 235 U.S. 133 (1914).

neutral constitutional rights, and were dubious even as decisions addressed to the reality of racial exploitation. One must ask whether the majority's reasoning in *Bailey* and *Reynolds* is explicable except as reflecting the very concern the Court disavowed, a concern for the discrimination against blacks in the South's agricultural economy and lily-white system of law enforcement.

Although the social reality of peonage was unquestionably an aspect of race relations, the legal framework of the condition encouraged the Court to turn away from an antidiscrimination perspective toward a theory of positive right. None of the statutes that supported peonage were cast in racial terms, and accordingly an antidiscrimination approach would have required the Court to root the doctrine of the *Peonage Cases* in the racial animus and impact of the state laws under review, or in the reality or likelihood of invidious administration by the system of Southern law enforcement. But in other areas of race relations, the Supreme Court had refused to measure the constitutionality of state laws by racist purpose or administration. In 1898, in *Williams* v. *Mississippi*,[3] the Court disregarded discriminatory legislative motivation in upholding property, literacy, and other voting qualifications passed for the open purpose of disfranchising black voters. The doctrine that bad purpose was not a ground for invalidating a law proper on its face was reaffirmed by the White Court in another context in the oleomargarine tax decision, *McCray* v. *United States*.[4] Moreover, although the Supreme Court never disavowed the 1886 decision of *Yick Wo* v. *Hopkins*,[5] that racially discriminatory administration "with an evil eye and an unjust hand" was unconstitutional, its decisions in voting rights cases after *Williams* and in cases challenging the discriminatory administration of jury selection procedures reflected extreme unreceptivity to such claims. Thus, the state of race relations law generally under the Fourteenth and Fifteenth Amendments did not encourage an antidiscrimination approach to state forced labor laws.

The Thirteenth Amendment might have been taken as an invitation for the Court to weigh racially discriminatory purpose and patterns of administration in the limited context of involuntary servitude, even though such approaches had otherwise been eschewed. For one thing, the Court might have thought that the problem of peonage in the South presented a relatively easy case for attribution to the states of a purpose hostile to the ends of the Thirteenth Amendment, in view of the unbroken succession of forced labor laws for black people from slavery through

---

[3] 170 U.S. 213 (1898). *Williams* and other decisions dealing with black disfranchisement are discussed in chapter 10, *infra*.

[4] 195 U.S. 27 (1904).

[5] 118 U.S. 356 (1886).

the Black Codes and down to the contract fraud and criminal surety statutes involved in *Bailey* and *Reynolds*. In a strict historical sense, the shadow of unconstitutionality fell over these twentieth century laws more obviously than was the case with the segregation laws or disfranchisement measures coming before the Supreme Court around this time. Second, the Court had the support of a vague federal statute outlawing peonage and all state laws maintaining it, and this statute might have been taken as a congressional mandate to look at the purpose and administrative reality of laws putting criminal penalties behind breaches of contracts to labor. Third, in dealing with peonage, the Court had the benefit of Justice Department investigations and submissions which underscored that the purpose and effect of forced labor laws was the subjugation of black laborers. This window on enforcement reality was not provided by the executive branch in any other area of race relations law during this time.

The White Court's election to approach the *Peonage Cases* not as problems essentially of race relations in the South, and not as issues of discrimination, but rather in terms of constitutional limits on legal sanctions for breach of labor contracts, has had important consequences for our constitutional law. On one hand, with respect to race relations, avoidance of the tests of discriminatory purpose and evil-eyed administration in the *Peonage Cases* kept out of constitutional law in the Progressive era principles that could have been deployed to challenge disfranchisement and jury exclusion, and even to expose the contradiction in practice within the doctrine of separate but equal. On the other hand, the positive-right approach of the *Peonage Cases* established a limited right to breach contracts as a fundamental freedom, and in so doing revealed that the central principle of laissez-faire constitutionalism, freedom of contract, embraced a free labor value that shielded workers from the harshest power an unscrupulous employer could exercise: the power to force continued labor on pain of criminal punishment for quitting.

The judgment of posterity has tended to affirm the validity, if not necessarily the wisdom, of the White Court's doctrinal choice. However strained the Court's color-blind approach may appear in light of the facts of the *Bailey* and *Reynolds* cases or the social reality of the day, the free-labor principle of the *Peonage Cases* has become thoroughly embedded in the bedrock of our constitutional and contract law. The *Peonage Cases* were an important step in the evolution of constitutional principles under the Civil War amendments, they shed light on the nature of Progressivism in the South, and they reflected a little-noted element of reciprocity and concern for labor in the theory of laissez-faire constitutionalism.

Although the *Peonage Cases* stand for undoubted progress in their impact on civil rights, they also exemplify the resistance of race relations to change. The Court pierced the gloom of racial and labor arrangements in the South largely as a result of executive initiative, and much of the practical impact of the *Peonage Cases* on Southern labor practices depended on executive enforcement. The Roosevelt and Taft administrations had their differences in approaching peonage, but both were committed to active investigation and prosecution. During the Wilson Administration, however, executive energy on this matter that mainly victimized black people was blunted by complacency about racial injustice and preoccupation with matters thought to be more pressing. And so the Supreme Court's invalidation of the most blatant legal arrangements underlying black economic servitude in the South probably left matters pretty much unchanged in the fields and lumber camps.

In part, this was because forced labor in the South was supported by a web of state laws too complex and varied for the Supreme Court and other courts to disarm. Assistant Attorney General Charles W. Russell, the Justice Department's roving special investigator and prosecutor of peonage, wrote in his *Report on Peonage* in 1908: "I have no doubt, from my investigation and experiences, that the chief support of peonage is the peculiar system of State laws prevailing in the South, intended evidently to compel services on the part of the workingman."[6] Russell was not only speaking about laws simply making breach of contract by laborers a criminal offense, which even Southern state courts tended to invalidate, but he was also alluding to more subtle and defensible laws: those making breach of contract without repaying an advance presumptive evidence of an intent to gain money by false pretenses, which the Supreme Court would strike down in *Bailey*; criminal-surety laws under which indigent convicts avoided the chain gang by contracting themselves into servitude for employers who would put up their fines, which would be struck down in *Reynolds*; and enticement laws prohibiting the hiring of a laborer already under contract to work for another, which some state and lower federal courts threw out. But Russell also pointed to other laws supporting the system of black forced labor in the South that eluded the doctrinal grasp of the courts. Vagrancy laws, for example, so open-ended that any person without a job or means of support was fair game for arrest and conviction, were a potent threat to black laborers who fled from contractual promises, real or claimed, or who dawdled before committing themselves to labor obligations. A Florida statute adopted in 1905 defined as vagrants subject to a $250 fine or six months on the chain gang a motley multitude of persons, beginning with "[r]ogues and vagabonds, idle or

---

[6] C. W. Russell, *Report on Peonage* (1908), 7.

dissolute persons," including "common night walkers," "[p]ersons who neglect their calling," and winding up with "all able-bodied male persons over eighteen years of age who are without means of support."[7] This law, Russell wrote, was "admirably adapted to adjust itself to the case of a workingman whom it is sought to place or keep in servitude. . . . If a State can make a crime . . . whatever it chooses to call a crime, it can nullify the [Thirteenth] amendment and establish all the involuntary servitude it may see fit."[8]

An even more pervasive problem, Russell reported, was the web of law and custom in the South that "result[s] in making the petty officers of the law—deputy sheriffs, constables, justices of the peace, and the like—an outer cordon of guards to hold the peons in slavery, and also cause[s] the neighbors to acquiesce in what they would otherwise regard as outrages."[9] Doubtless the most potent support for all manner of black subjection to the will of whites, of which forced labor was only the most pronounced aspect, was a system of criminal justice administered by, for, and all too often only in the interest of, whites. Blacks who offended whites risked entrapment in a law enforcement process in which the occasions for justice depended on the good will of white police, white lawyers, white judges, and white juries. Too many of these believed that forced labor was the appropriate lot of black men. The threat, even unspoken, of legal recourse by white against black was a potent weapon of duress, in view of the terrible consequences of conviction and assignment to the chain gang.

I.   Black Forced Labor from Reconstruction to the Progressive Era

A more or less unbroken momentum of law and history carried peonage into the twentieth century. Despite the Thirteenth Amendment's command that "[n]either slavery nor involuntary servitude, except as a punishment for crime . . . shall exist within the United States," forcing blacks to work was the paramount concern of the Black Codes passed in the relaxed period of Presidential Reconstruction following the Civil War. Under the Codes, black males who did not enter employment could be charged as criminal vagrants. Those who quit jobs for which they had contracted could be arrested and returned to their employers. Enticement laws prohibited other employers from hiring laborers already under contract. Black children could be "apprenticed" to their former masters by order of the probate courts. Indigents fined for petty offenses

---

[7] 1905 Fla. Laws Secs. 3370, 3571, quoted in Russell, *Report on Peonage,* 30.

[8] C. Russell, *Report on Peonage,* 30–31.

[9] *Ibid.,* 31.

such as vagrancy avoided harsh punishment by contracting to work for private employers who paid their fines, and the force of the state's criminal law fell behind the employment obligation.[10]

The Freedmen's Bureau and the Union Army sought to give some measure of political rights and personal security to the freedman, but these agencies of Reconstruction generally tried to keep the freedmen working on the land of their former owners. The labor contract was to take the place of slavery, but was to be surrounded by what General O. O. Howard, head of the Freedman's Bureau during the early stages of Reconstruction, called a "wholesome compulsion."[11] In Mississippi, for example, one of the bureau's typical early orders required freedmen to sign labor contracts or be arrested for vagrancy. Bureau officials believed that the former slaves lacked the self-reliance and stability to work in a system of freedom of contract. The planters, of course, had little experience with a free market system in agricultural labor, and resisted the notion that blacks could work reliably as freemen. Howard instructed his agents to secure a steady labor force by enforcing specific performance of blacks' labor contracts. To hold planters to their duty, the bureau gave laborers a lien on the crop they worked to produce. Each side "would have a duty to perform and be held to it."[12]

When Congress took charge of Reconstruction, the radical program centered not on forced labor, but on voting rights, equal access to courts and education, and desegregation. If blacks had equal rights under state law and participated in the political process, they would protect themselves through state government and the state courts, radicals hoped.[13] Although the most egregious forced labor provisions of the Black Codes, such as the "apprenticeship laws," were repealed, legal compulsions surrounding black labor were left largely intact. Even radical South Carolina enacted a statute in 1869 that made criminal simple breaches of labor contracts. Other states, such as Mississippi and Georgia, which during Reconstruction did away with laws punishing contract breaches, used open-ended fraud and false-pretenses laws to punish laborers and sharecroppers who had received advances and then breached contracts without repayment.[14] Such laws gained momentum after Reconstruction, as similar statutes were enacted in

---

[10] See generally D. Novak, *The Wheel of Servitude: Black Forced Labor After Slavery* (1978), ch. 1; W. Cohen, "Negro Involuntary Servitude in the South, 1865–1940: A Preliminary Analysis," *J. South. Hist.*, 42:31, 1976.

[11] Novak, *Wheel of Servitude*, 9.

[12] D. Nieman, *To Set the Law in Motion* (1979), 60. This book contains an excellent, balanced discussion of the bureau's policies toward black labor.

[13] *Ibid.*, 196.

[14] Novak, *Wheel of Servitude*, 23.

Alabama in 1885, North Carolina in 1889 and 1891, and Florida in 1891.[15]

The pinnacle of the system of servitude during Reconstruction and after was convict labor. The convicts were leased to private interests by the state, toiled on state or county chain gangs, or were forced into criminal-surety contracts under which a period of servitude for a private employer was exchanged for the wherewithal to pay a fine, levied as a result of a criminal conviction often based on petty or trumped-up charges. The practice of leasing convicts began during Reconstruction when large numbers of blacks became convicts for the first time.

Leased convict labor was the shame of the South. "One reason for the large number of arrests—in Georgia particularly—lies in the fact that the state and the counties make a profit out of their prison system," reported Ray Stannard Baker in 1908. Baker found that "[s]ome of the large fortunes in Atlanta have come chiefly from the labour of chain-gangs of convicts leased from the state." Because the "demand for convicts by rich sawmill operators, owners of brick-yards, large farmers, and others is far in advance of the supply," Baker went on, the "natural tendency is to convict as many men as possible."[16] Russell concluded that the convict-lease system in Georgia and Florida "is largely a system of involuntary servitude—that is to say, persons are held to labor as convicts under those laws who have committed no crime."[17] Alabama Governor Thomas E. Kilby in 1919 declared his state's convict-lease system "a relic of barbarism . . . a form of human slavery."[18]

The cruelty of many convict-lease arrangements amounted to virtual disregard for human life. Annual death rates for prisoners were staggering—typically around 20 percent and in some places approaching 50 percent.[19]

Almost all the convicts caught in this lethal system were blacks. In 1890, in the Southern states there were about four and a half times as many black prisoners compared to the black population as there were white prisoners, and by 1904 about five and a half times as many.[20] No wonder that Professor C. Vann Woodward has concluded that

[15] Cohen, "Negro Involuntary Servitude," 42.

[16] R. S. Baker, *Following the Color Line* (1964), 50.

[17] Russell, *Report on Peonage*, 17.

[18] Quoted in G. Tindall, *The Emergence of the New South, 1913–1945* (1967), 213.

[19] F. Green, "Some Aspects of the Convict Lease System in the Southern States," *The James Sprunt Studies in History and Political Science: Essays in Southern History* (1949), 31:119. Mississippi abandoned the convict lease in 1890, Tennessee in 1895, Georgia in 1908, Florida in 1924, and North Carolina in 1933. *Ibid.*, 121.

[20] The statistics are given in an interesting entry titled "Negroes in the United States" in the *Encyclopaedia Britannica* (eleventh ed.) 19:349 (1910).

IX: *The Peonage Cases*

"[t]he convict lease did greater violence to the moral authority of the Redeemers than did anything else. For it was upon the tradition of paternalism that the Redeemer regimes claimed authority to settle the race problem. . . ."[21] No aspect of race relations better demonstrated the sordid interplay of paternalism and coercion.

Convicts who served their time on state and county chain gangs suffered hardships as severe as those inflicted on convicts leased to private interests. Federal District Judge Emory Speer made the following findings of fact about the miserable throng in the Bibb County chain gang in Georgia in 1904:

> The sufferers wear the typical striped clothing of the penitentiary convict. Iron manacles are riveted upon their legs. These can be removed only by the use of the cold chisel. The irons on each leg are connected by chains. The coarse stripes, thick with the dust and grime of long torrid days of a semi-tropical summer, or incrusted with the icy mud of winter, are their sleeping clothes when they throw themselves on their pallets of straw in the common stockades at night. They wake, toil, rest, eat, and sleep to the never-ceasing clanking of the manacles and chains of this involuntary slavery. Their progress to and from their work is public, and from dawn to dark, with brief intermission, they toil on the public roads and before the public eye. About them, as they sleep, journey, and labor, watch the convict guards, armed with rifle and shotgun. This is to at once make escape impossible, and to make sure the swift thudding of the picks and the rapid flight of the shovels shall never cease. If the guards would hesitate to promptly kill one sentenced for petty violations of city law should he attempt to escape, the evidence does not disclose the fact. And the fact more baleful and more ignominious than all—with each gang stands the whipping boss, with the badge of his authority. This the evidence discloses to be a heavy leather strap about 2½ or 3 feet long, with solid hand grasp and with broad, heavy, and flexible lash. From the evidence, we may judge the agony inflicted by this implement of torture is not surpassed by the Russian Knout, the synonym the world around for merciless corporal punishment. If we may also accept the uncontradicted evidence of the witnesses, it is true that on the Bibb County chain gang for no day is the strap wholly idle, and not infrequently it is fiercely active. One witness, who served many months, testified that if the gang does not work like "fighting fire," to use his simile, the whipping boss runs down the line, striking with apparent indiscrimination the convicts as they bend to their tasks. Often the whipping is more prolonged and deliberate. At times, according to another witness, also uncontradicted, the convicts, when at the stockade, are called into the "dog lot." All present, the whipping boss selects the victims in his judgment worthy

---

[21] C. V. Woodward, *Origins of the New South* (1951), 215.

of punishment. They are called to the stable door, made to lie face downward across the sill, a strong convict holds down the head and shoulders, and the boss lays on the lash on the naked body until he thinks the sufferer has been whipped enough.[22]

A report issued in 1877 by the United States Commission of Labor found chain-gang convicts in Georgia "barbarously treated . . . the death rate is very high." Tennessee's convicts faced "wretched surroundings . . . [and an] appalling death rate."[23] Throughout the South, annual death rates among prisoners in state custody averaged from 16 to 25 percent. The Southern penal system lends credence to W. J. Cash's assessment that the South after Reconstruction embraced "the savage ideal as it had not been established in any Western people since the decay of medieval feudalism."[24]

The South's brutal treatment of its primarily black prison population was reinforced by the Progressive era's prevailing conception of blacks as innately inferior, essentially animal-like beings. In 1905, Simeon E. Baldwin of Connecticut, the noted constitutional law professor at Yale, president of the American Bar Association, and one of the great legal figures of his time, offered this defense of whipping:

> Of late years there has been a decided movement in the United States toward a return to the penalty of whipping for atrocious cases of assault or offenses by boys. It is probable that it will find more favor hereafter in the South as a punishment for negroes. Most of their criminals are of that race. The jails have no great terrors for them. They find them the only ground where they can mingle with their white fellow citizens on terms of social equality. But they are sensitive to physical pain. A flogging they dread just as a boy dreads a whipping from his father, because it hurts.[25]

A review of this suggestion in the *Yale Law Journal* commented that although whipping would remind some "sentimentalists" of the tortures of the Middle Ages:

> . . . [c]ertainly it is not inhuman that some such retrogression should be resorted to in the case of the negro. Metaphorically, he has cut across a long corner in his journey toward civilization. He is lost in his environment because he has not arrived by a natural route. The very crimes for which the negro of the lower class is so notorious, are largely

---

[22] Jamison v. Wimbish, 130 F. 351, 355–56 (W.D. Ga. 1904).

[23] Novak, *Wheel of Servitude*, 33.

[24] Quoted in Tindall, *Emergence of New South*, 184.

[25] S. E. Baldwin, *The American Judiciary* (1905), 246. I am grateful to Professor Yale Kamisar for calling this and the succeeding reference to my attention.

due to his forced growth along some lines and, perhaps, stagnation in others—they are not the crimes which were common to him in Africa. So that, in the face of so many unwise gifts forced upon him, there could be, in our opinion, no more salutary measure than to reduce his punishment to the level of his comprehension.[26]

The exhausting cruelty of the penal system made almost any private servitude preferable. To avoid the chain gang, black convicts signed up with private employers who would pay their fines in return for much longer periods of forced labor. But the chain gang buttressed the system of involuntary servitude even with regard to those blacks never caught in the toils of Southern justice. Contract breaches, switching jobs, failure to pay debts, and simple idleness were surrounded with the threat of false accusations and criminal sanctions—a potent weapon in the hands of white employers who sought to bend blacks to their bidding.

Unlike the other legal arrangements defining the place of the freedmen in the South, such as voting rights and segregation laws, which ebbed and flowed with the energies of Reconstruction and the volatile changes in Southern politics in the last quarter of the nineteenth century, the laws supporting involuntary servitude show a stubborn continuity from the days of the Black Codes through the various stages of Reconstruction and beyond. Booker T. Washington could observe in 1888 that in the cycle of debt and obligation, "colored people on these plantations are held in a kind of slavery that is in one sense as bad as the slavery of ante bellum days."[27] A half century later, W. E. B. Du Bois echoed this assessment: "It was the policy of the state to keep the Negro laborer poor, to confine him as far as possible to menial occupations, to make him a surplus labor reservoir and to force him into peonage and unpaid toil."[28]

Peonage maintained its grip after the Civil War despite the federal government's ample power to combat forced labor practices. The Thirteenth Amendment, the Supreme Court said in its first interpretation, forbids not only "all shades and conditions of African slavery," but also such practices as "apprenticeship for long terms" or "reducing the slaves to the condition of serfs," by which the prohibition on slavery

---

[26] *Yale L.J.*, 15:204, 1906. The review is signed G.S.A., undoubtedly referring to G. S. Arnold, Chairman of the Editorial Board for volume 15.

[27] Quoted in P. Daniel, *The Shadow of Slavery: Peonage in the South 1901–1969* (1972), ix. See the eloquent, moving account of an anonymous black peon in "A Negro Speaks, 1905," H. Aptheker, ed., *A Documentary History of the Negro People in the United States* (1951), 832 *et seq.*

[28] W. E. B. Du Bois, *Black Reconstruction in America* (1939), 696.

might have been evaded.[29] Moreover, in 1867, Congress passed a statute which was vague in concept and definition, but focused in its aim to destroy the system of vassalage that had evolved under Spanish rule in the New Mexico Territory. The statute declared unlawful "the holding of any person to service or labor under the system known as peonage," nullified all laws and practices maintaining "the voluntary or involuntary service or labor of any persons as peons, in liquidation of any debt or obligation, or otherwise," and punished anyone "who shall hold, arrest, or return . . . any person . . . to a condition of peonage. . . ."[30] Thus, as Justice Jackson was later to say, federal armor against peonage raised both sword and shield.[31] Federal prosecutions might have been launched against those holding peons in servitude, and state efforts to enforce peonage conditions (for example, by criminal punishment for breach of labor contracts) could have been blocked by pleading a federal defense under the statute and the Thirteenth Amendment.

Neither federal sword nor shield was engaged against peonage before 1900. After the Compromise of 1877, federal authorities probably shared the views of their predecessors during Reconstruction that legal sanctions to force blacks to work and to stick to their obligations

---

[29] Slaughter-House Cases, 83 U.S. (16 Wall.) 36, 69 (1873). The Court continued:

Undoubtedly, while negro slavery alone was in the mind of the Congress which proposed the thirteenth article, it forbids any other kind of slavery, now or hereafter. If Mexican peonage or the Chinese coolie labor system shall develop slavery of the Mexican or Chinese race within our territory, this amendment may safely be trusted to make it void.

Ibid., at 72. Justice Field's dissent stated that the prohibition on "involuntary servitude" included "serfage, vassalage, villenage, peonage, and all other forms of compulsory service for the mere benefit or pleasure of others." Ibid., at 90.

[30] 14 Stat. 546 (1847). The declaratory portion of the statute is now codified at 43 U.S.C. Sec. 1994 (1976), the criminal prohibition at

18 U.S.C. Sec. 1581 (1976). In the Revised Statutes, the first two clauses appeared as Sec. 1990 under the title "Civil Rights" and the third as Sec. 5526 under the title "Crimes." The legislative history of the peonage statutes is ably traced by Judge Henry Friendly in United States v. Shackney, 333 F.2nd 475 (2nd Cir. 1964). At the time the statute was enacted, the most extensive discussion of peonage in the New Mexico Territory was Jaremillo v. Romero, 1 N.M. 190 (1857), a decision of the New Mexico Supreme Court handed down in 1857. The opinion recounts that when the United States occupied New Mexico in 1846, it found a large class of persons called peons who had one common characteristic, "all were indebted to their masters." Ibid., at 194. Once in debt, a peon could be held in servitude, and other masters could purchase the debt and debtor.

[31] Pollock v. Williams, 322 U.S. 4, 8 (1944).

were necessary for economic and social stability. In any event, with respect to peonage as in other respects, Southern blacks were left in the hands of the Southern Redeemers by a careless federal establishment. Even if some United States Attorneys had wanted to prosecute peonage in the nineteenth century, the pervasiveness of the condition and the resistance of Southern juries must have dampened their interest. Even after the turn of the century, when the peonage reform movement got underway, the record of peonage prosecutions in the South is replete with jury nullification of efforts by frustrated federal prosecutors and judges. The all-white juries of the South were easily convinced that some black laborers required coercion to force them to live up to their alleged contractual obligations, or that, in any event, federal intervention ought to be resisted. The Attorney General reported in 1908: "It is notoriously difficult to secure convictions in peonage cases, owing to . . . strong local sympathy for the defendants."[32] And in 1910, a South Carolina newspaper reported that the acquittal of a man charged with peonage "was not at all surprising, for while everybody knows that he is guilty it is equally well known that he is not any more guilty than scores or perhaps hundreds of other men."[33] But inaction by the Justice Department cannot wholly account for the failure of any case involving peonage to reach the Supreme Court before 1900 in which federal law was asserted as a defense to state judicial action. One explanation for the absence of Supreme Court review is the fact that peonage victimized the helpless, who had neither knowledge nor money with which to assert their rights. Moreover, the confusing welter of pseudo-legalities which supported peonage practices in the South must have made constitutional challenge seem a dim hope. The *Bailey* case would reveal the substantial network of support, financial and otherwise, that was needed to propel a peonage case to the Supreme Court. In the last quarter of the nineteenth century, the conditions for the development of such a network were not present.

II. *Peonage Reform in the Progressive Era: Not "For Whites Only"*

Why peonage became a serious concern after 1900 in the Justice Department and in the federal and state courts in the South is easier to understand. Progressive impulses, political advantage, and emerging judicial concerns for freedom of contract and freedom to labor made

---

[32] *Report of the Attorney General* (1908), 6.

[33] *Anderson Daily Mail*, Apr. 29, 1910, quoted in Daniel, *Shadow of Slavery*, 23.

peonage an attractive target for investigation and reform. A typical Progressive blend of muckraking journalism that exposed peonage conditions to shocked urban audiences, investigation and prosecution by the executive branch, and judicial intervention emerged. Characteristically, too, the reformist impulse petered out before moving beyond declarations of principle in landmark cases to the systematic work of law enforcement that would have been needed to eradicate peonage practices in the South.

The Progressive era delighted in throwing the light of publicity on hidden horrors in American life, especially if they could be regarded as anachronisms outside the mainstream.[34] To the urban, middle-class reformers whose energies and humanitarian instincts fueled the Progressive movement, peonage was an exotic, cruel, and pathetic condition hidden in rural cotton fields, backwoods turpentine camps, and work gangs laying railroad tracks or roads in dark swamps or under a blazing sun. Urban newspapers and leading magazines had a journalistic field day with the characters and melodrama of peonage: sinister overseers, baleful whipping bosses, pathetic victims, conniving officials, desperate midnight dashes for freedom, frantic chases, horseback captures, and all the antebellum paraphernalia of bondage—whips, chains, guns, hounds, clubs, and filthy, overcrowded stockades.[35] Northern newspapers, and some Southern papers as well, sent correspondents to cover several of the more sensational peonage trials. Peonage reformers like Booker T. Washington and Alabama Federal Judge Thomas Goode Jones orchestrated press publicity to goad grand juries and prosecutors, to raise money for legal fees, and to push the Department of Justice.

Peonage affronted broadly held Progressive notions about fair and enlightened economic arrangements. Progressives tended to stress economic individualism and freedom of choice for workers, and exploitation of labor was the central concern of a movement whose humanitarian energy was most characteristically revealed in the crusade against child labor.[36] It was crucial that peonage was viewed as undermining

---

[34] R. Hofstadter, *The Age of Reform* (1955), 5.

[35] Typical works by muckrakers concerned with involuntary servitude in the South were Baker, *Following the Color Line*; C. Keeler, *The Crime of Crimes; or, The Convict System Unmasked* (1907); and R. Barry, "Slavery in the South To-Day," *Cosmopolitan Magazine*, 42:481, March 1907. Childhood remembrances of the terrible spectacles of peonage are colorfully sketched in W. H. Hugg,

"Peonage or Debt Slavery in the Land of the Free," *Nat'l. Bar J.*, 3:43, 1945.

[36] Stephen Wood refers to the federal child labor statute enacted in 1916 as the "crowning achievement" of progressivism. In the decade from 1904 to 1914, forty-six of the forty-eight states improved their protective laws against child labor or increased educational opportunities for children. See generally S. Wood, *Constitutional Politics in the Progressive Era: Child Labor and the Law* (1968), 23, 78.

rather than upholding the values of freedom of contract. This view is obviously correct as to the baldest type of involuntary servitude: physically coercing laborers to work without contracts. But it was not necessary in principle with respect to criminal laws that bound laborers to the tenor of their contractual obligations, especially those that purported only to punish fraud. These laws could have been regarded as upholding the sanctity of contractual promises, and thereby enhancing a system of freedom of contract, with the result that laborers would be able to get higher advances and even higher wages because employers would not have to discount for the possibility of unremedied breach. This was a point that Holmes stressed in his dissent in the *Bailey* case. The fact that forcing contractual performance by criminal laws was seen as an infringement on, rather than a reinforcement of, freedom to labor tells us much about the values underlying laissez-faire constitutionalism.

The peonage reform movement was not concerned with explaining the relationship of its aims to principles of freedom of contract. If it had been, it might have argued that laws treating breach of labor contracts as a crime amounted to the enforcement of contracts to go into slavery. A laborer's freedom to contract, the argument would maintain, necessarily included two precious, though necessarily limited, freedoms: the freedom to change jobs or move on in search of a better one, and the freedom to respond to abusive or unreasonable demands by walking off the job. True, under conventional principles of contract law these "freedoms" were subject to the imposition of civil liability for breach of contract in the form of money damages, but this was not much of a restraint on a Southern agricultural laborer's mobility. Moreover, in historical context, and in the context of Southern custom and law enforcement, in which forced labor continued to be viewed by many whites as the appropriate lot of black males, one had to have severe doubts about the fairness of the legal system in enforcing labor contracts by criminal sanctions. If the system was likely to be skewed in favor of employers in deciding such questions as whether contracts existed, whether unreasonable demands by employers relieved laborers of the duty of continuing performance, or whether events excusing performance had occurred, then criminal liability for breach was indeed a one-way device for forced labor. This was especially so in view of the terrible consequences of conviction in the South.

Although peonage reformers were not concerned with thinking through the implications of freedom of contract theory, they tended to embrace freedom of contract as their guiding ideology. This view meant that in the case of peonage, unlike most other labor concerns, reformist revulsion at brutal and coercive labor arrangements did not collide with laissez-faire individualism. Along with humanitarian concerns for work-

833

ers and hopes for racial justice, the words of Adam Smith, quoted by Justice Field at the end of his dissent in the *Slaughter-House Cases* (as in the official reports), echo through the movement for peonage reform: "The property which every man has in his own labor, as it is the original foundation of all other property, so it is the most sacred and inviolable."[37]

Reinforcing these powerful appeals to Progressive sympathies was the widespread sense among Progressive Southerners that peonage exacerbated the shortage of labor in the South; laborers, white as well as black, were thought to be deterred by the threat of involuntary servitude from remaining in or coming to the South to work on the farms, lumber camps, and railroads. A typical expression of this view was uttered in 1907 by United States District Judge William H. Brawley of South Carolina, when he struck down that state's law punishing breach of labor contract by one who had received an advance:

> [T]his legislation is as economically unwise as it is constitutionally illegal. Our state, through public appropriations and private contributions, is now actively and earnestly engaged in promoting immigration. Those efforts will be unavailing so long as our statute books hold legislation tending to create a system of forced labor, which in its essentials is as degrading as that of slavery. Desirable immigrants from foreign lands look for a land of freedom, where labor is respected and protected, and all the allurements of soil and climate will be vain to tempt them to a state where they will be in competition with forced labor. Although in its practicable application this legislation affects the negro only, in its terms it is directed against all laborers on farm lands, and constitutes a menace surely calculated to repel the coming of white men.[38]

Many Southern newspapers welcomed the Supreme Court's decisions in *Bailey* and *Reynolds* for similar reasons. Promoting economic growth was not by any means the most important impetus to peonage reform, but almost all the reformers were convinced that peonage reform would benefit the South economically.

It is significant that the legal challenge to peonage, though carried out for the most part in federal courts, was largely the work of native Southerners. The resourceful work of such federal judges as Thomas Goode Jones, Emory Speer, and Brawley, all Confederate veterans and successful politicians before going on the bench, added to the momentum for peonage reform that eventually brought *Bailey* and *Reynolds* to the

---

[37] 83 U.S. (16 Wall.) at 110 (quoting A. Smith, *The Wealth of Nations* [1776], b.1, ch. 10, pt. 2 at 151).

[38] *Ex parte* Drayton, 153 F. 986, 996 (D.S.C. 1907).

IX: *The Peonage Cases*

Supreme Court. A number of Southern United States Attorneys in Florida, Alabama, and Georgia undertook special efforts against peonage. In the Justice Department, the burden of special investigations and prosecutions was carried by Charles W. Russell, a Virginian. Even the xenophobic Tennessean James C. McReynolds, Wilson's first Attorney General, pressed for the prosecution that led to the *Reynolds* decision and to the invalidation of Alabama's criminal surety system. Perhaps most striking, the state courts in the South played a modest role in attacking peonage. Peonage reform did not altogether escape the sectional recriminations that were triggered by any effort to uplift the status of blacks, but it provoked no storm of resistance and no closing of ranks in the South. It was one reform effort, at least, where the fruits of Southern Progressivism were not, in Professor Woodward's phrase, "For Whites Only."[39]

Some of the energy that gathered behind peonage reform and distinguished it from other efforts to improve the status of blacks stemmed from the tendency of peonage to escape racial boundaries. It was concern as much about immigrants held in peonage, especially Italians, as about black victims that spurred Theodore Roosevelt to press the Justice Department to send Russell south on his mission of investigation and prosecution. The tendency of peonage to victimize whites as well as blacks helped to pique the sympathetic imagination of Southern reformers. "What hope can the respectable negro have," asked Judge Emory Speer of Georgia,

> What incentive to better effort or better life—if he, his wife, his daughters, or his sons, may in a moment be snatched from his humble home and sold into peonage? Let us for a moment put ourselves in his place, and imagine our furious indignation or hopeless despair if our loved ones or ourselves could be subjected to such a condition of involuntary servitude. Nor, if conditions like these described in the indictment shall continue, will the negro remain the sole victim of peonage. Crime is ever progressive. Very many poor and ignorant white people are scarcely less hapless than negroes, and cases are already reported where white men have been made in this way the victims of powerful and unscrupulous neighbors.[40]

If peonage tended to ensnare some whites, it netted a far greater number of blacks; it was in origin, official contemplation, and public consciousness overwhelmingly an aspect of the victimization of blacks. But in contrast to resistance to segregation or to the disfranchisement of blacks, the effort to reform peonage was able to draw on the

---

[39] Woodward, *Origins of New South*, 369–95.

[40] United States v. McClellan, 127 F. 971, 978–79 (S.D. Ga. 1904).

paternalistic views about directions for progress in race relations that dominated the thinking of Southern Progressives.[41] Nor was it an accident that Booker T. Washington lent his prestige and fund-raising powers to the reform effort. How could black laborers "cast down your bucket where you are" and "prosper in proportion as we learn to dignify and glorify common labor" if their freedom to contract, employment mobility, and working conditions were jeopardized by legal coercion, debt servitude, and physical terror?[42] The struggle to eliminate peonage was not a fight about whether the black laborer's place was indeed "in the cornfield," but rather about the conditions of freedom when he was there.[43] Peonage reform did not threaten the laws and customs of racial segregation, nor did it concern such controversial problems of political equality as the right to vote or to participate in the administration of justice. At the same time, it drew squarely on the considerable vestiges of abolitionist sentiment that survived into the Progressive era. Peonage was viewed as twentieth-century slavery, in some ways even more heedless in its victimization of blacks than antebellum conditions of servitude. Washington organized financial and editorial support for the *Bailey* case from Oswald Garrison Villard, Lyman Abbott, and other descendants, lineally and ideologically, of the New England abolitionists.

Most important in accounting for the success of the reform movement, peonage affronted the vague sense of responsibility and moderation toward blacks felt by anti-Populist, patrician Southern Bourbons. "[T]here are many public-spirited white men in the South who have long seen the rank injustice of such a system of peonage as this," wrote Ray Stannard Baker after the *Bailey* decision came down.[44] He had in mind solid white supremacists, but they tended to think of blacks in a protective, rather custodial frame of reference. A preeminent example of this type was Thomas Goode Jones, Confederate war hero and twice governor of Alabama in the 1890s, who led the fight against peonage in Alabama after his appointment as federal district judge by President Roosevelt. "The Negro race is under us," Jones had said at the Alabama suffrage convention in 1901. "He is in our power. We are his custodians. . . . If we do not lift them up, they will drag us down."[45] Another federal judge active against peonage, Emory Speer of Georgia, was the famed orator whose "main" address at the Atlanta Exposition of

---

[41] See generally G. Fredrickson, *The Black Image in the White Mind* (1971), 283–304.

[42] L. R. Harlan, ed., *Booker T. Washington Papers* (1974), 3, 584.

[43] A. S. Link, *Wilson: The New Freedom* (1956), 246.

[44] R. S. Baker, "A Pawn in the Struggle for Freedom," *American Magazine*, 72:608, 609, September 1911.

[45] Quoted in Novak, *Wheel of Servitude*, 47–48.

1895 (where Booker T. Washington stole the show) coupled his paean to "the imperious and commanding nature of the Anglo-Saxon race" with this responsibility: "[w]e are the trustees for humanity."[46] Southerners, albeit in various federally appointed roles, advocated peonage reform for a decade before the *Bailey* case made its way to the Supreme Court in 1911. As Attorney General William H. Moody put it in 1904 in arguing the first peonage conviction to reach the Supreme Court: "The verdict in this case, and other like cases, resulted from the combined action of southern judges, southern prosecuting officers, and southern grand and petit juries."[47]

III.   *Peonage Prosecution in the Federal Courts*

A.   THE CLYATT CASE

The first major peonage prosecution began in 1901 after Samuel M. Clyatt had led a party of three armed men from Georgia into the turpentine stills of northern Florida to look for former employees who he claimed had left his still without repaying money they owed him. Aided by a local deputy sheriff, Clyatt dragged at gunpoint two black men in handcuffs back to Georgia. The United States Attorney in northern Florida, John Eagan, had been troubled by reports of blacks forced by beating and death threats to work in turpentine stills, logging camps, and farms, and he chose the Clyatt episode to test the legality of forced labor by persons under contract and in debt.[48]

Clyatt saw nothing illegal in his actions. A Florida statute, passed in 1891, provided for the imprisonment of a laborer who entered a contract with fraudulent intent and then left a job in breach of contract and owing money.[49] Florida sheriffs did not bother with court proceedings, Eagan explained in a letter to Attorney General Moody; they simply got warrants from local justices of the peace. Armed with these warrants, they would "forcibly deliver [the] laborer to the possession of the employer who made the complaint, and the employer held him in his service until his claim, including all costs and charges of the proceedings, [was] worked out."[50] Clyatt claimed that he had such a warrant for the

---

[46] Quoted in R. Logan, *Betrayal of the Negro* (1965), 303–304.

[47] *Supplemental Brief for the Respondent*, 38, Clyatt v. United States, 197 U.S. 207 (1905).

[48] There had been one isolated and abortive peonage prosecution in the federal courts in 1899, United States v. Eberhart, 127 F. 252 (C.C.N.D. Ga. 1899). Along with the prosecu-

tion of Clyatt, Eagan secured the indictment of Robert W. Lewis for forcing a black laborer to return to Lewis' farm to work off a debt. *In re* Lewis, 114 F. 963 (C.C.N.D. Fla. 1902).

[49] 1891 Fla. Laws ch. 4032.

[50] J. Eagen to W. Moody, July 13, 1901, quoted in Daniel, *Shadow of Slavery*, 6.

return of the men he seized, issued by a Georgia justice of the peace and, as the county sheriff testified, "It has been the universal custom and practice of the turpentine men in Georgia and Florida to go and take negroes whenever they wanted to in this way." Nevertheless, the jury in the Tallahassee federal court found Clyatt guilty and Judge Charles Swayne sentenced him to four years in federal prison.

Operators of turpentine stills and lumber mills in Georgia and northern Florida pooled their resources and retained two eminent Georgia lawyers and politicians, Senator Augustus O. Bacon and Congressman William G. Brantley, to appeal Clyatt's conviction to the Supreme Court. The operators believed, the United States Attorney from Georgia wrote Moody, that unless they "were permitted to control their labor as they saw fit, without any interference from the federal authorities, they would be unable to carry on the sawmill business."[51]

The *Clyatt* appeal was also taken seriously by the government. It was one of only four cases that Moody argued personally in the Supreme Court in his two-and-a-half-year tenure as Attorney General. Moody told the Court that its judgment would not only determine the outcome of more than one hundred peonage prosecutions undertaken since Clyatt's conviction in 1901, but beyond that, "we may truthfully say that upon the decision of this case hangs the liberty of thousands of persons, mostly colored, it is true, who are now being held in a condition of involuntary servitude, in many cases worse than slavery itself. . . ."[52]

Bacon and Brantley argued that the Thirteenth Amendment did not empower Congress to punish individuals acting privately, unsupported by state law or official action. By definition, they contended, neither slavery nor involuntary servitude could exist except as an embodiment of state law. The federal peonage statute, they claimed, reflected this view. In declaring unlawful "the holding of any person to service or labor under the system known as peonage," and in nullifying "all acts, laws, resolutions, or usages" by which peonage was maintained, the statute spoke only to practices supported by state authority.[53] This was a problematic argument given the extent of official involvement in

---

[51] A. Akerman to W. Moody, Apr. 14, 1904, quoted in Daniel, *Shadow of Slavery,* 9.

[52] *Brief for Respondent,* 2–3, Clyatt v. United States, 197 U.S. 207 (1905).

[53] This argument had been accepted in 1899 by District Judge William T. Newman in United States v. Eberhart, 127 F. 252 (C.C.N.D. Ga. 1899). Newman held that the federal peonage statute intended to abolish only sys-

tems of peonage supported by state authority, such as had existed in New Mexico. "No such system as this ever existed in Georgia. . . . It would be the merest perversion of this act to attempt to apply it to an ordinary case of restraint of personal liberty." *Ibid.* The question was expressly left undecided *In re* Lewis, 114 F. 963 (C.C.N.D. Fla. 1902).

the Clyatt case, but had the Court accepted Bacon's and Brantley's constructions either of the Thirteenth Amendment or of the statute, peonage practices could have been largely insulated from federal attack.

Moody carried all of the Justices.[54] "The Amendment denounces a status or condition, irrespective of the manner or authority by which it is created," wrote Justice Brewer for the Court.[55] "We entertain no doubt of the validity of this legislation, or its applicability to the case of any person holding another in a state of peonage, and this whether there be a municipal ordinance or state law sanctioning such holding."[56] However, in passing, the Court defined peonage rather narrowly. Although the statute spoke of involuntary service "in liquidation of any debt or obligation," the Court appeared to restrict the statute's coverage to forced servitude for debt, or at least that is how lower courts and the Justice Department in later years read this language from Brewer's opinion:

> What is peonage? It may be defined as a status or condition of compulsory service, based upon the indebtedness of the peon, to the master. The basal fact is indebtedness. . . . Peonage is sometimes classified as voluntary or involuntary; but this implies simply a difference in the mode of origin, but none in the character of the servitude.[57]

A debtor could voluntarily contract to labor to pay off a debt, but "[t]he debtor, through contracting to pay his indebtedness by labor or service, and subject like any other contractor to an action for damages for breach of that contract, can elect at any time to break it, and no law or force compels performance or a continuance of the service."[58]

---

[54] It was Moody's usual impressive performance. After the oral argument in *Clyatt,* Justice Harlan wrote Solicitor General Henry M. Hoyt: "Of course I cannot say anything about the merits of the case, but I can say that the case of the Government was magnificently presented by the Attorney General. It was an argument of rare power and eloquence." P. Hefron, "Profile of a Public Man," *Supreme Court Historical Society Yearbook 1980* (1981), 30, 33. Moody was an impressive oral advocate. In his first argument in Massachusetts before the Supreme Judicial Court at the age of twenty-six, he so impressed Chief Justice Horace Gray that Gray personally congratulated the young lawyer at the end of the argument, in a rare gesture. A few years later, Holmes remarked to his colleagues on the Massachusetts bench that Moody was one of the two ablest men of his age in the state. *Ibid.,* 31.

[55] Clyatt v. United States, 197 U.S. at 216.

[56] *Ibid.,* at 218.

[57] *Ibid.,* at 215.

[58] *Ibid.* The Court took note of possible exceptions, such as sailors jumping ship, the obligation of apprentices, or workers walking off the job in dangerous circumstances. In Robertson v. Baldwin, 165 U.S. 275 (1897), the Court had upheld the constitutionality of a federal statute passed in 1790 which provided that if a seaman left a vessel in breach of a contract to serve through a voyage,

The rejection of Bacon's and Brantley's arguments did not seal Clyatt's fate, however. He had been indicted for "returning" two blacks to a condition of peonage, but the government had neglected to prove anything about the victims' condition before Clyatt abducted them. It had not proved the charge of "returning" them to peonage. Brewer conceded that the evidence left little doubt, and that Clyatt had not even objected during the trial to the variance between indictment and proof. But in "a matter so vital to the defendant," the Court must recognize this

---

the seaman could be jailed until the vessel was ready to proceed and then delivered to the master of the vessel to complete the promised performance. Justice Brown's majority opinion offered two justifications, one of which was obviously wrong. The first was that if a seaman voluntarily agreed to serve throughout a voyage, and was forced by law to complete his service, the resulting servitude could not be deemed involuntary within the meaning of the Thirteenth Amendment. *Ibid.,* at 280–81. But this reasoning would allow enforcement of a voluntary contract to become a slave, Justice Harlan rightly protested in dissent. *Ibid.,* at 292 (Harlan, J., dissenting). A servitude is involuntary whenever one is compelled to serve against his or her will, whether the service was voluntarily assumed or not. On this point, the Supreme Court in *Clyatt,* with Brown in the majority, came into agreement with Harlan.

Brown's second justification in *Robertson* was more substantial. The individual liberties protected by the Bill of Rights were "not intended to lay down any novel principles of government, but simply to embody certain guaranties and immunities which we had inherited from our English ancestors, and which had from time immemorial been subject to certain well-recognized exceptions arising from the necessities of the case." *Ibid.,* at 281. So, too, the Thirteenth Amendment's prohibition of involuntary servitude was adopted to prevent revivals of slavery in various guises and not

to bar certain types of compulsory service, such as military enlistments, recognized from time immemorial. Brown went on to show that under the laws of ancient Greece, medieval England, the Hanseatic League, the *ancien regime,* and the United States from the colonies down to the present, seamen were compelled by law to finish voyages. *Ibid.,* at 282–87.

"Under this view of the Constitution," puffed Harlan, "we may now look for advertisements, not for runaway servants as in the days of slavery, but for runaway seamen." *Ibid.,* at 303 (Harlan, J., dissenting). He was willing to grant the constitutionality of compulsory military service, or compelled apprenticeship for minors, but viewed the Thirteenth Amendment as barring compelled service by any adult for any private person or enterprise. As for the ancient law respecting seamen, they were enacted "when human life and human liberty were regarded as of little value, and when the powers of government were employed to gratify the ambition and the pleasures of despotic rulers rather than promote the welfare of the people." *Ibid.,* at 293 (Harlan, J., dissenting).

In 1911, in a long article summarizing Harlan's career, the *New York Times* called this dissent "one of his most memorable and most powerful dissenting opinions," and "a masterpiece of destructive criticism." *New York Times,* June 4, 1911, sec. 5, p. 2, col. 2.

"plain error." So Clyatt's conviction was reversed.[59] This pattern, in broad outline, was characteristic of peonage prosecutions in the federal courts. Few defendants served time. Where convictions were had, lenient sentences usually followed. Many of those jailed were pardoned. Clarification of law, public education, and show trials were the goals of the reformers, not punishment.

Justice Harlan rebelled from this exactitude, although he agreed with the majority's reading of the Thirteenth Amendment and the peonage statute. "[I]t is going very far to hold in a case like this, disclosing barbarities of the worst kind against these negroes, that the trial court erred in sending the case to the jury."[60] Interestingly, this remark of Harlan's was the only mention of the fact that Clyatt's victims were black. Aside from some general discussion of the Thirteenth Amendment's prohibition of slavery, Brewer's opinion carries no suggestion that the case had anything to do with race relations. The majority in *Clyatt* thus turned away from Attorney General Moody's observation that "thousands of persons, mostly colored . . . are now being held in a condition of involuntary servitude, in many cases worse than slavery itself. . . ."[61] In the Supreme Court, this aloof perspective would persist, and it contrasted with that of the Northern press, of the Justice Department, and of the federal judges and prosecutors who grappled with peonage at the local level.

B. PEONAGE IN THE LOWER FEDERAL COURTS

Of the "more than a hundred cases" that the federal government prosecuted between Clyatt's conviction in 1901 and the Supreme Court's decision in 1905, the most significant were the multiple prosecutions known as the *Alabama Peonage Cases,* a product of the energetic social conscience of Thomas Goode Jones.[62] Jones was a Southern paradigm.

---

[59] Clyatt v. United States, 197 U.S. at 216, 218, 215, 222.

[60] *Ibid.,* at 223 (Harlan, J., dissenting in part).

[61] *Brief for United States,* 2–3, Clyatt v. United States, 197 U.S. 207 (1904).

[62] Thomas Goode Jones (1844–1914) was the well-to-do son of one of the South's earliest railroad entrepreneurs. He rose to the rank of major in the Confederate Army, serving as an aide to Generals Early and Gordon, was wounded four times, and participated in many decisive battles

in Virginia. He carried one of the flags of truce at Appomattox. Jones was a dogged foe of the Populists in Alabama politics in the 1890s. As governor, Jones gained the reputation of a foe of organized labor by calling out the state militia to join with Pinkertons to crush a series of strikes in 1894. In private life, Jones was an attorney for the Louisville and Nashville Railroad, and was elected president of the Alabama Bar Association in 1901, the same year he was appointed to the federal bench. He held in *Ex parte* Riggins, 134 F. 404

A Civil War hero who in the 1890s led Alabama's conservative Democratic party against the populist Farmers' Alliance, he was twice elected governor of Alabama in the stormy campaigns of 1890 and 1892, his victories due in part to sweeping, and allegedly fraudulent, majorities in predominantly black counties.[63] He unsuccessfully championed voting rights for blacks in the Alabama suffrage convention of 1901, and afterwards, with the support of Booker T. Washington, was appointed United States district judge by Theodore Roosevelt in 1901.[64] In 1903, Jones induced agents of the United States Secret Service to investigate peonage in Alabama. Their report startled even lifelong natives of the state,[65] and stimulated President Roosevelt to press Attorney General Philander C. Knox to look into the peonage problem. Knox promised "vigorous and uncompromising prosecutions."[66]

Jones convened federal grand juries in Birmingham and Montgomery and saw to it that the trials that followed went forward in a glare of publicity, orchestrated mainly behind the scenes by Booker T. Washington. Prompted by Washington, Oswald Garrison Villard sent a correspondent to Alabama and publicized the most lurid peonage practices in the *New York Evening Post*. Lyman Abbott, editor of *The Outlook*, who also received information about peonage from Washington

---

(C.C.N.D. Ala. 1907), that Congress was empowered under the Fourteenth Amendment to punish private action, such as lynching, that interfered with the state's duty to afford due process, and that the predecessor provision to 18 U.S.C. Sec. 241 reached such conduct. Jones was forced to abandon this view after the Supreme Court held in Hodges v. United States, 203 U.S. 1 (1906), that the Fourteenth Amendment did not apply to private action. See United States v. Powell, 151 F. 648 (C.C.N.D. Ala. 1907), *affirmed,* 212 U.S. 564 (1909). After the infamous burning of two blacks in the Huntsville lynching of 1904, Jones managed the indictment of several mob members in his district court. Baker, *Following the Color Line,* 199. Jones was also known for upholding the constitutional rights of railroads and other corporations to appeal the legality of rate regulation to federal courts, a position that put him in conflict, once again, with Populist attitudes in Alabama. *Dictionary of*

American Biography (1943), X, 202; R. Sobel and J. Raimo, eds., *Biographical Directory of the Governors of the United States 1789-1978* (1978), I, 24.

[63] On the role of black voting in the political warfare between agrarian Populists and Southern conservatives in the 1890s, see chapter 10, *infra.*

[64] Washington had written the President: "I do not believe that in all the South you could select a better man through whom to emphasize your idea of the character of a man to hold office than you can do through Ex-Gov. Jones," Daniel, *Shadow of Slavery,* 45, n.5.

[65] Warren S. Reese, Jr., the U.S. Attorney for the Middle District of Alabama, wrote to the Attorney General that although he had spent all of his thirty-seven years in Alabama, "I never comprehended until now the extent of the present method of slavery through this peonage system." *Ibid.,* 44.

[66] *Ibid.,* 46, 52.

on a confidential basis, editorialized against "a revolting system of enslaving helpless negro laborers." *The Nation* told its readers that "these new Alabama slaves are sometimes worked naked and barely kept from starvation." The drama of peonage was not underplayed. One ghoulish peonage master indicted by grand jury in Montgomery was John W. Pace, an awesome 275-pounder in a homespun shirt and broad-brimmed black hat, depicted in the *Evening Post* as "a combination of feudal baron and wholesale slavedriver," "a grave, animal-like person, with two feet almost eaten off with disease, with fingers which are expected to drop away within a year . . . quite like the slave-whipping characters of 'Uncle Tom's Cabin.' " Pace led a parade through the press of conniving sheriffs who sold to the highest bidders blacks arrested on trumped-up charges, corrupt judges who used fines and the threat of the chain gang to indenture blacks, and peon masters who brutally maltreated their imprisoned workers.[67]

Judge Jones' charge to the Alabama grand juries, issued on June 16, 1903, a year before the Supreme Court handed down the *Clyatt* decision, is the most impressive statement on the problem of peonage ever formulated by an American judge. After tracing the path of peonage from Spain into the New Mexico Territory and into its myriad forms in the South after the Civil War, Jones concluded that the federal statute of 1867 punished private acts of peonage as well as abuse of authority by officials. He defined peonage not only as involuntary service in pay-ment of a debt, but as coerced service in performance of any obligation, real or concocted. Whether or not the initial debt or obligation was voluntarily incurred, peonage arises "the moment the person desires to withdraw, and then is coerced to remain and perform service against his will," whether by physical force, threats of false accusations, or recourse to the criminal process to force an indigent convict to hire out to a surety who would pay his fine in return for involuntary labor.[68]

---

[67] *Ibid.*, 49–54.

[68] Peonage Cases, 123 F. 671 (M.D. Ala. 1903). Jones did not view a bona fide surety system of the sort that came before the Supreme Court in 1914 in *Reynolds* as peonage. Accord-ing to Jones, if one who is convicted and fined contracts with a surety in open court with the written approval of the judge, "the law of the state treats him as a convict who has re-signed himself to the custody of his surety to escape that of the state, and the surety may restrain him of his liberty, and invoke the aid of the state law to compel the service." 123 F. at 683. The involuntary perform-ance, however, could not extend be-yond that contracted to secure the fine; any additional advances could not be the basis for further involun-tary performance. Moreover, a surety could not transfer the obligation with-out the convict's consent because "such an agreement involves personal trust and confidence on the part of the convict in the selection of a keeper. . . ." *Ibid.*

In the course of his charge, Judge Jones pronounced two Alabama statutes unconstitutional, although, interestingly, he upheld the statute that would eventually come to the Supreme Court in the *Bailey* case. One of the laws Jones struck down punished anyone who had contracted in writing to cultivate land, abandoned the contract without the consent of the employer or owner, and then took similar employment without notifying the new employer of the prior contract. The other punished persons employing a laborer under contract to another. "Courts are always reluctant to exercise the delicate power of declaring a statute unconstitutional, and will avoid passing upon such questions when possible," Jones told the grand jury, evidencing not the slightest reluctance, but "the issue stares the court in the face, and must be met, unless the court abdicates its duty." The statutes were "a coercive weapon" with which an employer could compel performance. Breach of contract could only be treated as a crime, Jones declared, when it might endanger life or seriously inconvenience the public, as in the case of a train switcher. "One of the most valuable liberties of man is to work where he pleases, and to quit one employment and go to another, subject, of course, to civil liability for breach of contract obligations."[69]

Jones expressed some sympathy for the policy behind the statutes he struck down: "Every reflecting man recognizes the great evils resulting from the abandonment of farms by laborers and renters, without justifiable excuse, after obtaining advances and incurring indebtedness to the employer, sometimes leaving the crops when it is almost impossible to secure other labor to save them." In addressing this evil, the state had reached the limit of its power by enacting a statute punishing the obtaining of money by contract with intent to defraud. Jones thought this statute was constitutional because it did not "coerce the performance of civil obligations by criminal penalties."[70] As *Bailey* was later to show, however, the power to treat fraud as a crime left considerable room for the enforcement of peonage.

After the immense publicity generated by the Alabama grand juries' investigations, the net result of eighteen indictments seemed

---

[69] The statute was invalid for the further reason that it was "a vicious species of class legislation." It applied only to contracts for farm labor or sharecropping, and was designed solely in the interest of the employer or landlord. Jones contended that "[t]he right to pursue any lawful calling, unfettered and unvexed by exactions not made of other men in like occupations," was a fundamental right and could not be subjected to unequal burdens and penalties. The statute was inconsistent with several Alabama Supreme Court decisions invalidating "unequal, partial and discriminatory legislation," and also violated the Equal Protection Clause of the Fourteenth Amendment and the federal statute against peonage. 123 F. at 688–89.

[70] 123 F. at 680, 685, 686.

modest. The *Montgomery Advertiser* noted with relief that peonage had been found to exist "in but two counties and involving only eighteen persons," and called this a "triumphant refutation" of the distortions in "certain newspapers."[71] But Jones put his faith in public education through investigation, publicity, and a few exemplary convictions, rather than in deterrence by large-scale prosecutions.

A critical question for Jones and the other reformers was whether Southern juries would convict whites for holding blacks in peonage. The answer of the *Alabama Peonage Cases* was mixed. In the first prosecution, John W. Pace frustrated the press' appetite for a sensational trial by pleading guilty.[72] In a second prosecution, trial also was avoided because of a guilty plea.[73] The willingness of Southern juries to convict was finally tested by the prosecution of a sawmill owner named Fletcher Turner, who was accused of buying and abusing black laborers arrested for vagrancy from a local marshal who admitted on the stand to selling victims to Turner and Pace. The jury was pulled between Turner's lawyer—"Are you going to brand Fletch Turner as a convict on such testimony from three negroes and one sorry white man?"—and Judge Jones—"The question between us and God and our consciences is can we rise above our prejudices, if we have them, so far that we as white men are able and willing to do a negro justice." The jury hung, because, as Jones saw it, "for no other reason than the base one that the defendant was a white man and the victim of the law he violated is a negro boy."[74] But in the other case to go to trial in the summer of 1903, Robert Franklin, dubbed by the press "the kipnapping constable," was convicted. The *Montgomery Advertiser* made much of the willingness of a Southern jury to convict, saying that the state "stands today without a stain upon her escutcheon," and "we have witnessed the passing of peonage in Alabama."[75]

Judge Jones was also sanguine. He wrote to Booker T. Washington defending his lenient sentences, and even suggested that Washington should recommend pardons to President Roosevelt:

> The object of all good men now is to lessen the friction between the races and to put the blacks especially on as high a plane as possible. Would or would it not confound those who are filled with low hates, if the representatives of the negro race, should publicly take the ground that it had no desire, now that the system was broken up, for vengeance,

---

[71] Quoted in Daniel, *Shadow of Slavery,* 49.

[72] *Ibid.,* 52.

[73] The defendants in the second trial were sentenced to a year and a day.

[74] Daniel, *Shadow of Slavery,* 54–

55. On retrial, Turner pleaded guilty and Jones fined him $1,000, the lightest sentence possible.

[75] *Ibid.,* 57. Judge Jones again imposed the lightest sentence possible, a $1,000 fine.

or to subject the families of the men who are now in prison, to the suffering that they inflicted on others.[76]

A month later, President Roosevelt pardoned two of the peonage defendants, and, according to the *Montgomery Advertiser*, told a visitor that the pardons were issued "wholly on the advice of Judge Jones."[77] The most notorious peonage master, John W. Pace, was also eventually pardoned.

Four years later, Jones' efforts seemed ineffectual to Assistant Attorney General Charles W. Russell. Four persons had served a total of five months in jail, and the sum of the fines paid was $500. From the vantage of Russell's investigations of widespread peonage through the South, Jones' approach of "pardoning everyone on a promise of good behavior was a failure."[78] Russell's frustration with the stubborn resilience of peonage colored his judgment. Jones' grand jury charge supplied a broad rationale for a neglected statute enacted to end Spanish peonage in the New Mexico Territory. Under Jones' reading, the statute's coverage would extend to the patterns of servitude that had evolved in the South. He grounded his reading in general themes of personal and economic liberty current in the day and broadened the appeal of the reform effort beyond concern for blacks. A Southerner to his roots, Jones helped counter the South's defensive tendency to view the legal assault on peonage as neo-abolitionist meddling from above the Mason-Dixon line. His example gave strength to other Southern moderates. He pushed Booker T. Washington into an active, though always covert, posture against peonage. Although his lenient approach to the peonage offenders may have seemed niggling to Russell, it was surely a defensible approach to initial prosecutions for a customary, widespread practice. More important, Jones created a momentum against peonage that reached into the White House itself, stirred the Justice Department, galvanized public interest, and led directly to the great peonage decisions of the United States Supreme Court.

A number of other federal district judges in the South brought Confederate credentials and eloquent indignation to the effort against peonage.[79] William H. Brawley,[80] a veteran of the attack on Fort Sumter

---

[76] *Ibid.*, 62.

[77] *Ibid.*

[78] *Ibid.*, 63–64.

[79] Henry Clay Niles, district judge for Mississippi, advised a federal grand jury in Vicksburg in January 1907 that a Mississippi statute, which treated the breach of a labor contract after securing an advance as *prima* *facie* evidence of fraud, was unconstitutional: "A State law calculated to compel a man, by threat of imprisonment to remain in servitude, and making him prima facie guilty of a crime upon evidence showing only a breach of contract, violates the letter and spirit of the Constitution." Russell, *Report on Peonage,* 34. The

who lost his left arm at Seven Pines, struck down as "legalized thraldom" a South Carolina law passed in 1904 that punished breach of contract after receiving an advance,[81] in a wide-ranging opinion that drew support from such laissez-faire staples as *Allgeyer* v. *Louisiana*[82] and Justice Field's dissent in the *Slaughter-House Cases*,[83] along with the writings of such as Adam Smith, Thomas Cooley, and Christopher Tiedemann: "The right of every citizen to work where he will, and for whom he will, to select not only his employer, but his associates, to follow any of the common avocations of life, is one of those inalienable rights formulated in the Declaration of Independence, and in the Bill of Rights. . . ." The racial element was not downplayed in Brawley's court. Indeed, the state attorney general justified the statute because the "great body of such laborers, as is well known, are negroes, and . . . being without any financial responsibility the ordinary remedies by judgment and execution for breaches of contract would be utterly futile." The state also pressed an argument that was, as Brawley put it, "not without its force, and not

---

similar Alabama statute had been up-held by Judge Jones, but would be struck down by the Supreme Court in *Bailey.*

Niles (1850–1918) was born in Mississippi, was admitted to the bar in 1872 after reading law in his father's office, and served two terms in the Mississippi legislature, in 1878 and 1886. In 1880, he was a delegate at the Republican National Convention, and he was named United States District Attorney for the Northern District of Mississippi in 1880. Two years later, he was appointed United States District Judge for the Northern and Southern Districts of Mississippi. *Who Was Who in America 1897–1942* (1943), I, 899.

[80] William Hiram Brawley (1841–1916) was born in Chester, South Carolina, graduated from the University of South Carolina and, after the amputation of his left arm in 1862, ran the blockade to England where he studied law and literature. He returned home at the close of the Civil War, was admitted to the bar in 1886, and practiced in Chester until 1874 when he moved to Charleston. Brawley served in the state legislature from 1882 to 1890, where his chairmanship

of the judiciary committee and his great oratorical ability made him the leading figure in that body. He was elected to the House of Representatives in 1890, where his most important contribution was his opposition to the Free Silver movement. He was the only Southern Representative to vote against the Bland Silver Bill, and he supported repeal of the Sherman Silver Purchase Act. President Cleveland appointed him federal district judge for South Carolina in 1892. *Dictionary of American Biography* (1943), II, 609.

[81] Act of Feb. 25, 1904, ch. 243, 1904 S.C. Acts 428, 429: "Any laborer working on shares of crop or for wages . . . under a verbal or written contract to labor on farm lands, who shall receive advances, either in money or supplies and thereafter wilfully and without just cause fail to perform . . . shall be liable to prosecution for a misdemeanor. . . ." An unusual feature of the South Carolina laws was that conviction did not discharge the obligation, which had to be performed after release from the chain gang.

[82] 165 U.S. 578 (1897).

[83] 83 U.S. (16 Wall.) 36, 83 (1872).

without its appeal to state pride, and to those race instincts, which, doubtless, for some wise purpose, are ineradicable."[84] This was that "the white people of the state, now charged with the responsibility of its government, being better acquainted with the negro, his capacities and limitations, can determine better than those outside of it what policy will best subserve his interest and their own." Brawley's powerful answer evoked the strains that beset Southern federal judges in these cases:

> In much of this contention the writer of this opinion fully concurs. Other men's devotion to the state may require proofs. The marks of his are written in the lead of its enemies on his person. . . . [B]elonging by birth and by associations of a lifetime to that class of slave owners and land holders in whose supposed interest this legislation is enacted, and in whose many virtues he has a just pride, and fully conscious of the trials and difficulties which still encompass them, and having shared the adverse fortune which overwhelmed them all in a common calamity, it is not without profound sympathy that he has looked upon every effort made to surmount the uparalleled difficulties which environ two races so dissimilar, bound to live on the same soil and under the same laws. The question presented does not permit of brief treatment, and the problem presented is possibly beyond any human solution. The one sufficient answer to the argument is that the question of human liberty is not one of merely local concern. It rests upon the Constitution of the United States. . . .[85]

Another federal district judge celebrated and reviled for his efforts to stamp out peonage was Emory Speer of Georgia.[86] Aside from

---

[84] *Ex parte* Drayton, 153 F. 986, 989, 988, 996 (D.S.C. 1907).

[85] 153 F. at 996.

[86] Emory Speer (1848–1918) was born in Culloden, Georgia, son and grandson of Methodist divines, whose inherited evangelical eloquence made itself felt in his forceful judicial decisions. At the age of fifteen, Speer joined Lewis' Kentucky brigade during its fighting retreat before Sherman's advance through Georgia. After the war, Speer graduated from the University of Georgia in 1869, was admitted to the bar, and served as Solicitor General of the Western Circuit of Georgia from 1873 to 1876. Initially a Democratic champion of Georgia's mountain whites, Speer was elected as an Independent to the House of Representatives in 1878, was reelected in 1880, and became a Republican before the close of his second term. He was appointed United States Attorney for the North Circuit of Georgia in 1883, and managed to secure a conviction of the Banks County White Cappers that was affirmed by the Supreme Court in *Ex parte* Yarborough, 110 U.S. 651 (1884). Over intense Democratic opposition, in the last days of Chester A. Arthur's Presidency, Speer was appointed United States District Judge for the Southern District of Georgia, an office he held until he died. Speer was controversial for his expansive views of federal powers, particularly

Jones, Speer was the federal judge in the South most engaged against peonage. The most notable of the numerous peonage cases over which he presided was *United States* v. *McClellan*,[87] a prosecution of a sheriff and a lawyer for selling blacks into involuntary servitude. The roster of counsel for the defendants included the chairman of the Georgia senate committee dealing with penal institutions, a Georgia congressman on the House Judiciary Committee, and the state prosecutor who would have had jurisdiction to prosecute peonage under state law. That such an array should turn out, Speer noted,

> is somewhat persuasive of the conclusion that if there is no system of peonage de jure, to which the statute applies, there is yet a de facto system of some equivalent sort, which has evoked the liveliest apprehensions of those who participate in its operation and emoluments.[88]

Speer denounced the defendants as "lawless and violent men who would seize helpless and pathetic negroes, and for their own selfish purposes consign them to a life of involuntary servitude, compared to which the slavery of ante bellum days was a paradise."[89] To Speer, peonage was not an isolated anachronism found on backwoods farms; it was big business:

> How can the plain farmer, or manufacturer of turpentine or lumber, who labors for himself, with the assistance of his sons or hired help, hope for fair play in the market, when a huge sawmill in the vicinity, or an unscrupulous planter, with a stockade full of unpaid hands, can underbid his prices? Why should one man, through lawless methods, be permitted to grow rich, while his neighbors, who piously respect the law and the rights of their fellow man, however humble, shall forever toil on, perhaps in poverty and want? The demoralization of the spectacle to the plastic mind of youth, the incalculable harm flowing from the

---

concerning peonage and the antitrust laws. In 1913, in the first year of the Wilson Administration, a House committee was appointed to conduct an investigation as a prelude to possible impeachment proceedings, but the committee recommended against impeachment and the proceedings were dropped. Speer was appointed dean of Mercer University Law School in 1893, and in 1897, he published his Lectures on the Constitution of the United States. He lectured at Yale in 1906. He was renowned for his eloquent addresses on public occasions, and a selection of these was published in 1909 in *Lincoln, Lee, Grant and Other Biographical Addresses. Dictionary of American Biography* (1943), XVII, 441; O. A. Park, "Judge Emory Speer: Biographical Sketch," in *Report of the Thirty-Sixth Annual Session of the Georgia Bar Ass'n.* (1919), 101–20.

[87] 127 F. 971 (S.D. Ga. 1904).
[88] *Ibid.,* at 973.
[89] *Ibid.,* at 977.

triumphant defiance of law, the reproach to the fair fame of our beloved state, all are involved in this supreme question.[90]

When Speer's enemies sought to have him impeached in 1913, a member of the House Judiciary Subcommittee that investigated the charges and recommended against impeachment stated: "The one thing above all others that stirred sentiment against Judge Speer is his conduct in trying peonage cases. . . ."[91]

C. THE RUSSELL REPORTS

A similar sense that peonage was a burgeoning enterprise in the South led the Justice Department, under prodding from Roosevelt, to revamp its approach to peonage in 1906. In that summer, complained the *Birmingham News*, south Alabama "was swarmed by federal secret service agents, yellow magazine writers and reformers from the North. Their advent was caused by reports that hundreds of white men were being held in actual bondage. . . ."[92] Rather than rely on local United States Attorneys, Attorney General Charles J. Bonaparte appointed Assistant Attorney General Charles W. Russell as a special investigator and prosecutor to coordinate federal action against peonage.[93] Russell was to investigate the extent of peonage and report to the Attorney General; he was to seek indictments, manage prosecutions, and spur United States Attorneys in their enforcement efforts. The upshot was a

---

[90] *Ibid.*, at 978.

[91] Remarks of A. Volstead, 52 *Cong. Rec.* app. S 548, 63rd Cong., 3rd Sess. (1915).

[92] *Birmingham News*, Nov. 29, 1910.

[93] Charles Wells Russell (1856–1927) was born in Wheeling in what is now West Virginia but was then Virginia. He received an LL.B. from Georgetown University in 1883 and an LL.M. in 1884. He married Lucy Ford Mosby in 1879 and, after her death, her sister Lelia James Mosby. He served in various positions in the Justice Department starting in 1886 and from 1893 to 1895 was legal adviser of the joint congressional committee headed by Alexander M. Dockery, Democratic Representative from Missouri, investigating the organization of the executive departments.

From 1897 to 1902, he engaged in private practice in Washington, D.C. He rejoined the Justice Department in 1902 to investigate the title of the French Panama Canal Company and arranged the transfer of the Canal property to the United States. In 1905, he became Assistant Attorney General in charge of insular and territorial affairs and served in this capacity until 1910. During this period, Russell was charged with investigating peonage. From 1910 to 1914, he served as U.S. Minister to Persia and helped secure American aid to protect Persian independence during the tense years preceding World War I. Russell edited *The Memoirs of Colonel John S. Mosby* (1917). He also published several volumes of poetry. *Dictionary of American Biography* (1943), XVI, 241.

series of reports that are small classics in the history of race relations in the United States. "I had been selected as being a southern man and a Democrat," Russell wrote in his first *Report*.[94] Born in Virginia in 1856, and married in turn to two sisters of the famous Confederate Ranger John S. Mosby, Russell's Southern credentials were indeed in good order. Russell was designated after two highly publicized personal appeals to President Roosevelt. In October 1906, a Florida woman had complained to Roosevelt about peonage in her state, and, as Russell recalled, "[u]nfortunately, the newspaper men about the White House filled the next day's papers with startling details of her statements, likely to prove irritating to the Florida people and get them into a mood unfavorable to the discovery by me of the real facts."[95] Shortly after, another visitor introduced a new dimension to what had been thought to be mainly an aspect of race relations. Mary Grace Quackenbos, a New York City lawyer, had discovered that labor agents in New York were sending large numbers of immigrant laborers to work in Southern turpentine camps, sawmills, and railroad construction crews. Stimulated by a complaint of the Italian Ambassador that immigrants from that country were being held to forced labor in Mississippi, her well-publicized investigations revealed that hundreds of these unfortunates were held in servitude.

Russell's measured descriptions of what he encountered as he traveled through the South made his *Report on Peonage* an extraordinarily forceful document. Of Knoxville, Tennessee: "Negroes were held in slavery and brutally beaten by foremen at railroad construction camps . . . in a mountain gorge through which runs a small river, down which the bodies of negroes occasionally floated from this or some of the construction camps (there were 11 in all)." Of Pensacola, Florida: "The brutality of the treatment of these laborers, both in Alabama and Florida, lacked none of the picturesque accessories of peonage—dogs to chase the escaping slaves, guns, whipping, etc." In Florida, where Russell's principal object was "to get at the truth about the alleged peonage of thousands of persons on the Florida Keys, where the Flagler people are building a railroad from the vicinity of Miami to Key West," Russell found that "[h]undreds and hundreds of men were shipped from New York and found themselves upon the little islands, where even to get a drink of water depended on the company's will. . . . [T]o get away on any boat was a question of the company's consent, and when any indebtedness remained this consent could not be obtained." If any escaped, they would be arrested and "were soon in debt and back on the islands." The workmen "were largely Italians and negroes, the former

---

[94] Russell, *Report on Peonage*, 20.   [95] *Ibid.*

shipped from New York to the delights of 'the land where it never snows,' as the advertisement said, the land of flowers and fruits."

The peonage Russell encountered in Florida was an economic arrangement supported by an extensive alliance of private interests:

> We have henceforth a fight in the open with those who have combined to thwart our purposes through the ownership of the principal Florida newspaper, the *Jacksonville Times-Union*, which has suppressed and misrepresented the truth and sought by the most extraordinary methods to influence juries and public opinion and to drive us out of the State. Flagler, the millionaire lord of the east coast . . . the turpentine association, the United Groceries Concern, the newspapers which take their cues largely and their news from the Times-Union, and whatever else can be organized, all these are organizing for this principal struggle, so far as Florida is concerned.

From the time Russell began his investigations in October 1906 to the filing of his third and final *Report* two years later, one can trace a growing sense that peonage was not only a device for forcing blacks into servitude. Russell's first *Report* mainly concerned black peonage, but by the fall of 1908 he wrote:

> [T]hese laws have become a trap for the enslavement of white workmen as well as black, and ought to be repealed, or amended with that fact in view. Some of them are considered to have been passed to force negro laborers to work; but if so, they are now affecting other persons, and the States formerly depending upon negro laborers exclusively need twice as many hands, and are resorting to every means to obtain them from Europe, directly or indirectly.

By this time, Russell saw peonage as "rather a mining, lumbering, construction and manufacturing than an agricultural phenomenon," and immigrants received even more attention than blacks. On one plantation in Arkansas, Russell found seven hundred Italians, and he concluded: "[u]ntil we began our work in October, 1906, the chief supply of peons came from the slums—*i.e.*, foreign quarters of New York and from Ellis Island."[96]

Daniel A. Novak suggests that it was large-scale peonage of immigrant whites that triggered the Roosevelt Administration's commitment to prosecute peonage in the first decade of the twentieth century.[97] There is no doubt that immigrant peonage spurred executive interest. But immigrant peonage reinforced a concern about the peonage of black

---

[96] *Ibid.*, at 22, 23, 13, 24, 31, 19, 15, 17.

[97] Novak, *Wheel of Servitude*, 47.

people that had been building since the turn of the century. The roots of heightened federal involvement lay in Judge Jones' investigations of black peonage, in the celebrated prosecutions in his and other federal courts in the South (virtually all of which involved peonage of black people), in the shocking revelations by the press of peonage practices, and in Attorney General Moody's success in *Clyatt* in establishing broad federal constitutional and statutory powers to move against peonage. Russell's growing emphasis on immigrants reflected his surprise that peonage was not only a feature of race relations in the agrarian South, but that it also entrapped white workers in railroad construction, sawmills, and turpentine plants.[98] No doubt he felt, with Judge Speer, that emphasizing the victimization of whites alleviated the political liabilities of federal intervention. But the emergence of concern about immigrant peonage does not conclusively show that without it the federal executive would not have moved strongly against black involuntary servitude in the Progressive era. And the Southern reform effort that brought the *Bailey* and *Reynolds* cases to the Supreme Court was dominated by a concern about black peonage.

As with Jones' efforts a few years before, Russell's prosecutions harvested more publicity than prisoners. A major failure concerned one O'Hara, who had first attracted Mrs. Quackenbos' concern as the superintendent of a sawmill and a turpentine still where large numbers of Eastern European and Russian immigrants, mostly Jews, were held in servitude. Russell tried O'Hara twice, putting on elaborate cases with over fifty witnesses documenting extraordinary cruelties. But the juries returned not guilty verdicts in both trials in a matter of minutes.[99] Even more press coverage focused on the successful prosecution of William S. Harlan, manager of the Jackson Lumber Company, because one of his victims, a Hungarian immigrant named Mike Trudics, published his story in *The Independent*.[100] Harlan was convicted of conspiring to

---

[98] See also Barry, "Slavery in the South To-Day," 481. ("Like a galvanic shock it undermines our self-importance to find that this new form of slavery places white and black on a plane of perfect equality, and enslaves them both with generous disregard of ancestry or complexion.")

[99] Daniel, *Shadow of Slavery*, 85.

[100] Shortly after his arrival in America in 1906, Trudics signed with a labor agent in New York to work in an Alabama sawmill for $1.50 a day. The transportation fee of $18.00 was to be repaid at the rate of $3.00

a month. He was transported to the Jackson Lumber Company operation near the Florida-Alabama border and put to work logging in the forest. "The work in the woods sawing logs was hot, too hot and too heavy for me," and he was paid only $1.00 a day. Trudics tried to flee, was tracked down with hounds, brutally whipped, and driven back to camp at gunpoint. Armed men kept him and the other laborers cooped up in boxcars at night. M. Trudics (as told to A. Irvine), "The Life Story of a Hungarian Peon," *The Independent*, 63:

operate a peonage system, and was sentenced to eighteen months imprisonment and fined $5,000. After unsuccessful appeal and habeas proceedings,[101] Harlan sought a pardon from President Taft, and appealed for help to Booker T. Washington. The *Bailey* case was then pending in the Supreme Court and Washington was reluctant to intercede. One day after the *Bailey* decision came down, however, showing the same instinct for leniency he demonstrated in the *Alabama Peonage Cases,* Washington wrote to President Taft on behalf of Harlan: "There are few men anywhere in the South who have stood higher than Mr. Harlan. . . . Sixty-five percent of the people employed at his mill plant are colored, and without exception they tell me that he has treated them with the greatest degree of kindness."[102] A fine should be sufficient punishment, Washington urged. Taft was not moved: "Fines are not effective against men of wealth. Imprisonment is necessary." To pardon Harlan, Taft felt, "would give real ground for contention so often heard that it is only the poor criminals who are really punished."[103] Harlan served four months in jail.

D. THE TANGLED WEB OF STATE LAW

The state courts reacted ambivalently to state laws supporting involuntary servitude. Only in Louisiana was breach of contract for personal employment by itself a crime. The courts in other Southern states viewed punishment for simple breach, even where money was advanced and not repaid, as a violation of the provisions of their state constitutions barring imprisonment for debt.[104] "The criminal feature

---

557, 559, 561–63, Sept. 5, 1907. In his report, Russell refers to Trudics as Trudics Mihaley. Russell, *Report on Peonage,* 4 et seq.

[101] Harlan sought habeas corpus in Alabama before Judge Jones. Jones denied the petition and the Supreme Court affirmed. 180 F. 119 (1909), *affirmed,* 218 U.S. 442 (1910).

[102] Daniel, *Shadow of Slavery,* 93.

[103] *Ibid.,* 93–94.

[104] The Georgia Supreme Court insisted that mere breach of contract could not be punished, although it too approved the power of the state to punish fraudulent procurement of an advance by a promise to labor. Brown v. State, 8 Ga. App. 211 (1910); Young v. State, 4 Ga. App. 827 (1908); Lamar v. State, 120 Ga.

312 (1904). The Supreme Court of South Carolina followed Judge Brawley's lead by striking down in 1907 a statute which treated as a crime the mere breach of a contract to labor on a farm after receiving an advance, on the ground that this constituted imprisonment for debt. Again, however, that court made clear that fraud could be punished. *Ex parte* Hollman, 790 S.C. 9 (1907). In 1909, the Supreme Court of North Carolina insisted that proof of fraud was essential to make out a crime even under a statute that clearly attempted to punish mere breach after procuring an advance. State v. Williams, 150 N.C. 802 (1909). Only in Louisiana, the single Southern state that did not have a prohibition in its constitution

of the transaction is wanting," the Alabama Supreme Court wrote in a typical decision, "unless the accused entered into the contract with intent to injure or defraud his employer, and unless his refusal to perform was with like intent and without just cause."[105] In other cases, that court insisted that the fraudulent intent "must be ascertained by means of inferences from the facts and circumstances developed by the proof." The jury was not allowed to indulge in "mere unsupported conjectures, speculations, or suspicions as to intentions which were not disclosed by any visible or tangible act, expression or circumstance."[106]

Southern legislatures, on the other hand, were anything but ambivalent. The Alabama legislature in 1903 dealt with its highest court's insistence on clear proof of fraudulent intent by making breach and failure to repay an advance *prima facie* evidence of intent to defraud. North Carolina enacted a similar law in 1905, as did Florida in 1907. Between 1903 and 1908, Georgia, Mississippi, Arkansas, and South Carolina for the first time passed false pretenses laws specifically applicable to contract breaches and followed Alabama's lead by making breach and failure to repay advances presumptive evidence of fraud.[107] In addition, all the Southern states except Tennessee enacted new and sweeping vagrancy laws between 1893 and 1909.[108] Enticement laws remained on the books in all the Southern states.

Legislative support of peonage practices went beyond the state houses. In Congress, Southern Senators and Representatives were joined

---

against imprisonment for debt, did the state Supreme Court uphold a statute punishing the simple breach of a contract when an advance was obtained and not repaid, although the circumstances of the case gave rise to a strong inference of fraud, and the court's rather confused opinion made much of this. State v. Murray, 116 La. 655 (1906). This decision was overruled by the Louisiana Supreme Court in 1918. State v. Oliva, 144 La. 51 (1918).

[105] *Ex parte* Riley, 94 Ala. 82, 83 (1891).

[106] *Ibid.,* at 83–84. See also Dorsey v. State, 111 Ala. 40 (1895). The Alabama court also struck down in 1904 the state law that Jones had declared invalid the year before. The invalidated statute provided for punishment of one who abandoned a

contract to cultivate lands without consent or excuse, and entered a similar contract without giving the second party notice of the first contract. The state court agreed with Jones' "forceful opinion opposed to the constitutionality of the act," because it violated the property right of disposing of one's labor by contract, citing *Allgeyer* and Justice Bradley's *Slaughter-House* opinion. Toney v. State, 141 Ala. 120, 125 (1904). In 1912, the Mississippi Supreme Court struck down a similar law. State v. Armstead, 103 Miss. 790 (1912).

[107] See generally Cohen, "Negro Involuntary Servitude," 43.

[108] Recall Russell's discussion of the Florida vagrancy law passed in 1905. Russell, *Report on Peonage,* 30.

by several Northern colleagues in heaping abuse on Quackenbos, Russell, and Attorney General Bonaparte.[109] Congressman Frank Clark of Florida called Russell "a dirty bird that fouls its own nest," and complained to the *Washington Post* on January 18, 1907: "[t]he Government witnesses in these so-called peonage cases are, as a rule, riff-raff scum from the large cities and loafing negroes and neither class will work."[110] Congress refused the Justice Department's requests for broadening amendments to the federal peonage statute to cover involuntary servitude without the element of indebtedness, so that simple enslavement could be punished.[111] Moreover, to deflect concern away from black victims of peonage, Southern Congressmen managed in 1908 to divert the responsibility for studying and reporting on peonage from the Justice Department to the Immigration Commission, and to limit its mandate to peonage but only among immigrants. When the Immigration Commission published its forty-two-volume report in 1911, the year of the *Bailey* decision, a mere seven pages concerned peonage. There had been some peonage in the Southern states in 1906 and 1907, the report said, "but these were only sporadic instances and the Commission found no general system of peonage anywhere." Congress thus managed to head off the embarrassment of further Russell reports, but it could not keep the momentum of peonage reform from reaching the Supreme Court.

IV. Bailey *v.* Alabama: *"One of the Great and Memorable Acts of Our Progressive Period"*

It was not an accident that the state of Alabama gave the Supreme Court its historic opportunity to strike at peonage. Alabama was the home of Judge Jones and Booker T. Washington, the area of the most

---

[109] See generally, Daniel, *Shadow of Slavery*, 100 et seq.

[110] 42 *Cong. Rec.* 2750, 50th Cong., 1st Sess. (1908); *Washington Post*, Jan. 18, 1907, p. 5, col. 4. Russell made reference to this change in his first report:

The published statement of Congressman Clark, of the Jacksonville district, that there is no peonage in Florida after these convictions by Florida juries at Pensacola and many indictments found by its own neighbors at Jacksonville shows the intensity of the feelings artificially worked up in his district. Without such feeling, so absurd an announcement would have subjected him to ridicule among his own constituents. Instead, many of them (chiefly those directly or indirectly interested in enslaving labor) consider him the author of a patriotic falsehood, and imagine that the ruse of the ostrich who desires concealment will be successful.

Russell, *Report on Peonage*, 22–23.

[111] *Report of the Attorney General of the United States: 1911* (1911), 27.

extensive legal action against peonage and the focus (along with Florida) of most of the muckraking publicity about peonage, the state that contrived the most ingenious web of statutes supporting peonage and provided the legislative example for other Southern states, and the last state to abolish the brutal practice of convict leasing.[112]

After the Alabama Supreme Court had held in the *Riley* case that a conviction under the state's contract-fraud law required clear proof of the laborer's fraudulent intent both at the time the contract was entered into and when it was breached, the legislature in 1903 provided that breach "shall be prima facie evidence of the intent to injure or defraud his employer."[113] This amendment was at first declared unconstitutional by Judge William H. Thomas of the Montgomery City Court, a committed opponent of peonage who was to play a major role in the *Bailey* case. However, the Alabama Supreme Court upheld it,[114] reasoning that so long as the statute did not treat breach as conclusive proof of fraud, and did not bar a defendant's right to present evidence in rebuttal, it could create evidentiary presumptions when the facts bore a reasonable relation to the inference drawn. On top of this, a state rule of evidence prevented testimony "as to his uncommunicated motives, purpose, or intention."[115] The statutory presumption and the bar on testimony, Booker T. Washington protested in a letter to Oswald Garrison Villard, "simply means that any white man, who cares to charge that a Colored man has promised to work for him and has not done so, or who has gotten money from him and not paid it back, can have the Colored man sent to the chain gang."[116]

Washington and his white allies found their opportunity to test the

---

[112] Alabama abolished convict leasing in 1928. Cohen, "Negro Involuntary Servitude," 57.

[113] 1903 Ala. Acts 345–46. Before 1903, the Alabama contract-fraud law read as follows:

Any person, who with intent to injure or defraud his employer, enters into a contract in writing for the performance of any act of service, and thereby obtains money or other personal property from such employer, and with like intent, and without just cause, and without refunding such money, or paying for such property, refuses to perform such act or service, must on conviction be punished as if he had stolen it.

Ala. Crim. Code Sec. 4930 (1896).

The 1903 Amendment added the following proviso: "And the refusal or failure of any person who enters into such a contract to perform such act or service, or refund such money or pay for such property, without just cause, shall be prima facie evidence of the intent to injure or defraud his employer." *Ibid.*

[114] State v. Thomas, 144 Ala. 77 (1906). The facts of the *Thomas* case are not given in the state court opinion, but are described in Baker, *Following the Color Line*, 95.

[115] Bailey v. State, 161 Ala. 75, 77 (1909).

[116] Quoted in Daniel, *Shadow of Slavery*, 67.

Alabama law when a black farm laborer named Alonzo Bailey contracted on December 26, 1907, to work for a year and was paid an advance of $15.00. He was to earn $12.00 a month and repay the advance by deductions of $1.25 from each month's pay. When Bailey left the job after working for a little over a month without repaying the advance, he was arrested and held in jail pending trial. Bailey's wife managed to secure the services of a young white Montgomery lawyer, Edward S. Watts, who petitioned for habeas corpus before Judge Thomas on the theory that Bailey was being held for trial under a law that was unconstitutional, since the presumption allowed conviction on the basis of breach alone. Thomas denied the writ on authority of the Alabama Supreme Court's reversal of his earlier ruling, but privately urged Booker T. Washington to organize an appeal to the United States Supreme Court.

Even before the Alabama Supreme Court affirmed the denial of habeas, on the ground that the law, even with the *prima facie* provision, punished fraud, not breach,[117] Washington and Thomas worked behind the scenes to organize support for Bailey's appeal to the Supreme Court. Thomas' former law partner, Fred Ball, also a white man needless to say, was recruited to join the inexperienced Watts on Bailey's behalf. To mobilize Justice Department support, Judge Jones was enlisted to write letters to President Roosevelt emphasizing the case's importance, letters which incidentally revealed that Jones had, behind the scenes, helped Watts and Ball draft their appeal papers and briefs. Washington sought money from his Northern supporters. Villard said he was "squeezed dry" but offered to help by publicizing the cause in the *New York Evening Post*. *Bailey* was "precisely the kind of a case for which I want my endowed 'Committee for the Advancement of the Negro Race,' " Villard wrote Washington. "Sooner or later we must get that committee going."[118] Washington also appealed to Attorney General Bonaparte, already instructed by the President to look into the case and back the efforts of "philanthropic white men of this state."[119] Bonaparte agreed to file an *amicus* brief challenging the constitutionality of the Alabama statute.

But the Supreme Court was not prepared to decide. "[T]he trouble with the whole case is that it is brought here prematurely by an attempt to take a short cut," wrote Justice Holmes for the Court. The record showed only that Bailey was charged with having obtained money under a written contract with intent to defraud. Without doubt, such conduct

---

[117] Bailey v. State, 158 Ala. 18 (1908).

[118] The activities of Thomas, Washington, and others in supporting Bailey's appeal are set out in detail in Daniel, *Shadow of Slavery*, 68 et seq.

[119] *Ibid.*, 71.

could be made a crime, Holmes reasoned, and the Alabama law was therefore valid apart from the presumption. Moreover, that provision was separable, since the statute originally stood without it. If the state at Bailey's trial offered satisfactory proof of fraud, the *prima facie* evidence rule would be superfluous, mooting the claim that it in effect punished a mere breach of contract. It was true that the state had relied only on the fact of breach in the preliminary hearing which bound Bailey over for trial, but "it hardly will be contended that this court should require the state courts to release all persons held for trial, where in its opinion the evidence fails to show probable cause." It was true also that the state court had gone farther than necessary and in denying habeas upheld the presumption, but Holmes thought the "unsatisfactoriness of such attempts to take a short cut" was apparent.[120]

It was not apparent to Justice Harlan.[121] The state courts had upheld Bailey's custody and denied a right claimed under the United States Constitution, namely not to be tried under a statute that was, on its face, unconstitutional. The judgment was final. Whether the state courts should decide the merits of Bailey's challenge to the Alabama statute in advance of trial was a matter of local law, but since the state courts had done so, how could the Supreme Court avoid ruling on the constitutionality of the state's judgment? "The course pursued in the disposition of this case by the court has not, so far as I am aware, any precedent in its history," Harlan fumed.[122]

Harlan's impatience is understandable and entirely in character, though Holmes had the better of the argument. Surely if Alabama properly could punish demonstrated fraud in contracting for an advance, and if the charge against Bailey embraced this legitimate potential application of the Alabama statute at trial, then a ruling on possible unconstitutional reliance on the statutory presumption should await trial and the development of a factual record. How could the Supreme Court know whether the state had evidence of fraud other than the breach until Bailey was tried? Moreover, whether the Alabama courts would require evidence of fraud beyond the simple fact of breach was unclear at this point. Certainly the state statute could bear that construction. Thus, a constitutional challenge to the state law as punishing breach alone was premature. Perhaps Harlan found Holmes' ripeness

---

[120] Bailey v. Alabama, 211 U.S. 452, 454–55 (1908).

[121] Without opinion, Justice Day also dissented, 211 U.S. at 459.

[122] 211 U.S. at 458. Harlan recognized that if Bailey had sought habeas before trial in a lower federal court, it should have been denied as premature. But since the state courts had decided that a challenge to the validity of the statute was ripe, he thought the Supreme Court was bound to consider the question on the merits.

concerns hard to credit, as he might have if he shared Brandeis' later-developed judgment that Holmes cared little for such niceties.[123] Also, Harlan may have taken a stronger view of the *prima facie* evidence provision than Holmes. When *Bailey* came back to the Supreme Court, Holmes made clear his understanding that the presumption permitted, but did not compel, the jury to infer fraud from breach. Harlan may have thought that the statute created a mandatory presumption requiring conviction if unrebutted, or that that was how it would work with Alabama juries. Confusion on this point would not be surprising.[124]

When the case went back to Alabama for trial before Judge Thomas, Bailey demurred to the indictment and offered no evidence. The state showed only that he had entered the contract, received an advance, and failed to perform or repay. The only point Bailey's lawyer established on cross-examination of the state's only witness, Bailey's employer, was that Bailey was black. Thomas refused to charge that the contract-fraud law was unconstitutional, or that as a matter of law the state's evidence did not show fraudulent intent. The jury was told that it was permitted but not compelled to infer fraudulent intent from Bailey's breach. It found Bailey guilty. He was fined $30.00 and assessed court costs of $46.40,[125] translated, since he could not pay, into 136 days of imprisonment at hard labor.[126]

Once again, Bailey's supporters organized for the Supreme Court. Thomas and other whites in Alabama contributed $200, and Ray Stannard Baker took charge of fund raising in the North. Washington's friend William J. Schieffelin put up $150. Lyman Abbott contributed

---

[123] See Brandeis-Frankfurter Conversations, June 28, 1923, Harvard Law School Library.

[124] "One ventures the assertion that 'presumption' is the slipperiest member of the family of legal terms," Charles T. McCormick has written, and no question is more confused than whether a statutory presumption merely permits a jury to infer or compels it to find, in the absence of contrary proof. C. McCormick, *Handbook of the Law of Evidence* (1954), 639.

[125] Under the statute, punishment on conviction was limited to a fine set at double the damage suffered by the injured party, with half the fine to be paid to the injured party.

[126] In their second appeal to the Alabama Supreme Court, Bailey's lawyers added a due process argument: that the rule barring testimony as to uncommunicated motives prevented Bailey from rebutting the presumption of fraud and denied him the right to present evidence in defense. Not so, the state court held. The defendant could testify as to facts surrounding his breach, and establish motive circumstantially. Other witnesses could testify to the defendant's motives. And even if the defendant offered no evidence at all, the statute did not require the jury to find fraudulent intent from the mere fact of breach. The jury was free to determine guilt or innocence "by the whole evidence." Bailey v. State, 161 Ala. 75, 78, 79 (1909).

$100 in return for Judge Thomas' promise to supply information to his magazine about the operation of the contract-fraud law in Alabama and other Southern states. The Justice Department, now under Taft's Attorney General, George W. Wickersham, agreed to appear as *amicus* in Bailey's behalf.

The second *Bailey* appeal was argued on October 20 and 21, 1910, before a Supreme Court recently and substantially changed by deaths and new appointments. Justice Harlan presided over a Court of seven Justices. Chief Justice Fuller had died the previous July 4, and White had not yet been named his successor, although White would be in the center seat by the time the second *Bailey* opinion was handed down on January 3, 1911. Peckham and Brewer had also died since the first *Bailey* decision. Horace H. Lurton, who had come on the Court on January 3, 1910, in place of Peckham, did not promise much sympathy for the legal rights of blacks in the South. But Charles E. Hughes, as he preferred to be called, the son of an abolitionist minister,[127] took his seat ten days before the *Bailey* arguments, and must have seemed a favorable prospect to Bailey's lawyers. Both the dissenters in the previous *Bailey* appeal, Harlan and Day, remained on the Bench and must have seemed likely to view the Alabama contract-fraud law as invalid. Justice Holmes' majority opinion in the first *Bailey* decision contained words both of deference to the state and of encouragement to Bailey's supporters. Justices Van Devanter and Lamar, who filled the side seats of White and Moody respectively, would not join the Court until January 3, 1911, the day the second *Bailey* decision was handed down. The absent but as yet unretired Moody, who as Attorney General had argued the *Clyatt* case, was a strong opponent of peonage. But as his concurrence in the *Berea College* decision had indicated, he was also deferential to state legislative judgments.[128]

Bailey's lawyers and the Justice Department pressed on the Court the racial impact of the Alabama statute. Watts' brief asserted that the statute applied only to "service rendered by the commonest laborer or the poorest tenant of the farmlands. . . . [A]s a matter of common knowledge in Alabama, such laborers and such tenants are, as a class, negroes. . . ."[129] Watts pointed out that many such laborers were virtually compelled to take advances because they had been convicted of some misdemeanor, fined, and had to enter a contract to pay the fine if they

---

[127] D. Fehrenbacher, *The Dred Scott Case: Its Significance in American Law and Politics* (1978), 590.

[128] Although Moody did not retire until Nov. 20, 1910, he did not sit

during the 1909 Term or participate in any of the Court's work.

[129] *Brief by Edward S. Watts and Daniel W. Troy for Plaintiff in Error*, 7, Bailey v. Alabama, 219 U.S. 219 (1911).

were to escape the chain gang. Bailey's brief thus previewed for the Court the type of criminal-surety arrangement that was to come before it in *United States* v. *Reynolds* in 1914. The brief for the United States by Attorney General Wickersham asserted similar points. "It is common knowledge that Alabama is chiefly an agricultural state and that the majority of laborers upon the farms and plantations are negroes." Every reported conviction under the Alabama statute involved a farm laborer. The law in effect coerced "a particular class of laborers" into performing labor contracts, thereby violating the rule of *Yick Wo* v. *Hopkins* against imposing legal burdens on a particular class "with an evil eye and an unequal hand."[130] Florida, Mississippi, North Carolina, and Louisiana had similar statutes, and the Attorney General shared with the Court what the United States Attorney for the Western District of Louisiana had written to the Justice Department: " 'I do not believe that there is a well-advised man in the State, lawyer or layman, that does not know that this act was passed in order to give the large planters of the State absolute dominion over the negro laborer.' " Finally, the Attorney General argued that the statutory presumption of fraud stripped Bailey of the presumption of innocence, "the foundation of the criminal law," and became conclusive because of Bailey's inability to testify to his intent.[131] This was said to violate due process.

The Alabama attorney general defended Bailey's conviction as an instance of the established crime of taking property by false pretenses, an altogether different matter from compelling the performance of contracts. The presumption of fraud was a reasonable extrapolation from breach and nonpayment, and, in any event, the right of legislatures to create such *prima facie* rules was established. In punishing employees and not employers, the legislature simply attacked the problem of fraud where it existed, and the statute was neutral with regard to race. As for the due process attacks, *Twining* v. *New Jersey*,[132] the seminal decision of two terms previous, had made clear that due process required only

---

[130] 118 U.S. 356, 373–74 (1886).

[131] *Brief for United States as Amicus Curiae,* 10, 19, 20–21, 26, 30, Bailey v. Alabama, 219 U.S. 219 (1911). A separate brief filed by Fred S. Ball argued that in view of the Alabama bar to testimony about uncommunicated motives, the "artificial presumption . . . is practically conclusive because the defendant cannot testify in his own behalf as to his unexpressed intent." *Brief of Fred S. Ball for Plaintiff in Error,* 20, Bailey

v. Alabama, 219 U.S. (1911). Ball offered a parade of dubious horribles in his brief claiming that the presumption and testimonial bar would allow conviction where a laborer's wife became sick and he had to take her away for treatment, where he left for a better job, etc. But in such cases, the Alabama rule would permit the defendant to show these circumstances and rebut the presumption effectively. *Ibid.,* at 14–15.

[132] 211 U.S. 78 (1908).

notice and an opportunity to be heard. Aside from these two fundamental prescriptions, as *Twining* stated, "this court has up to this time
sustained all state laws, statutory or judicially declared, regulating
procedure, evidence, and methods of trial."[133]

The Supreme Court's response to these arguments was written by
Justice Hughes, and it is interesting to speculate why the opinion in the
first major case decided by the seven-person Court in the 1910 Term
should have been assigned to the newest member. Almost certainly, the
assignment was Harlan's to make.[134] Harlan, of course, had great expectations for Hughes. "Taft did a great thing to appoint [Hughes]," wrote
Harlan to Lurton during the summer of 1910, "The more I see of him
the better satisfied I am of his eminent fitness for the bench."[135] But in
view of Harlan's many heartfelt dissents to Supreme Court opinions that
turned a deaf ear to the aspirations of blacks, his concern about the
"barbarities" of peonage in *Clyatt*, and his dissent in the first *Bailey* decision, why he should have foregone the chance to write the Court's
opinion is a puzzle. Had the assignment been made by anyone less frac-
tious than the Senior Justice, one might guess that the opinion went to
the newest arrival to deflect the divisions about race that had troubled
the Court in previous cases involving the Civil War amendments. But
this is an unlikely motive to ascribe to the Court's most indomitable
controversialist, unless, of course, Harlan thought that he might not be
able to hold the majority if he wrote the opinion himself. This possibility
cannot be dismissed, although only two, Holmes and Lurton, dissented
from the majority's position, and there is no evidence that anyone in the

---

[133] *Ibid.*, at 111; *Brief for Defendant in Error,* Bailey v. Alabama, 219
U.S. 219 (1911). It is interesting that
Alabama did not attempt to justify its
statute by arguing that agricultural
labor was within the class of jobs
which, when unexpectedly terminated,
caused special hardship and loss, because of the critical timing of planting, harvesting, haying, and so forth,
and because agricultural laborers
would typically be unable to pay damages for such losses.

[134] Hughes' biographer has written
that Chief Justice White assigned
Bailey to Hughes because "Hughes
emerged in conference as the ablest
champion of the view that the Alabama law was unconstitutional." M.
Pusey, *Charles Evans Hughes* (1951),
I, 288. But White did not become

Chief Justice until Dec. 19, 1910,
two months after the oral argument.
Harlan presided from the opening of
the term until then. In all probability,
the majority opinion was assigned
while Harlan presided. Hughes later
recalled that during this period of
vacancy in the Chief Justiceship, "Justice White, I am sure, felt that he
was entitled to the place, and through
the fall he was plainly out of sorts.
At that time, while Justice Harlan
was presiding as Senior Justice, Justice
White had little to say in conference
and seemed offish." C. E. Hughes,
*Autobiographical Notes of Charles E.
Hughes,* D. Danelski and J. Tulchin,
eds. (1973), 170.

[135] J. M. Harlan to H. H. Lurton,
July 3, 1910, Lurton Papers, Library
of Congress.

five-person majority was shaky. If Harlan thought the majority in *Bailey* was firm, it is likely that the choice of Hughes was a tactic designed to press rather than to dampen Harlan's warm sense of rivalry and division within the Court. Recalling the 1910 Term, Hughes later wrote, "Justice Harlan was antipathetic to Justice Holmes, and Holmes to Harlan, though each respected the soldierly qualities of the other. When in conference Justice Harlan would express himself rather sharply in answer to what Justice Holmes would say, the latter, always urbane, would refer to Justice Harlan as 'my lion-hearted friend.' "[136] The conference discussion about *Bailey* probably produced one of the confrontations Hughes later remembered; Holmes and Harlan had been in opposition in the first *Bailey* decision. Harlan may have chosen Hughes to enlist the eminent newcomer in his first important decision in opposition to Holmes.[137] On the other hand, Harlan may have thought that his own majority opinion would be understood as directed to the reform of race relations, whereas Hughes could more credibly cast the opinion in less controversial freedom of contract terms.

In light of the whole background of peonage reform in the South, of the legal lineage of the Alabama statute before the Court, and of the treatment of peonage in past cases in the lower federal courts, the opening of Hughes' opinion is a surprise: "We at once dismiss from consideration the fact that the plaintiff in error is a black man."[138] A few lines later: "No question of a sectional character is presented, and we may view the legislation in the same manner as if it had been enacted in New York or Idaho."[139] Hughes followed this with a reproving dismissal of the Attorney General's contention that the Alabama law had been administered in a racially discriminatory manner. "Opportunity for coercion and oppression, in varying circumstances, exists in all parts of the Union, and the citizens of all the States are interested in the maintenance of the constitutional guarantees, the consideration of which is here involved."[140]

Hughes granted that Alabama could punish contracting for an advance with intent to defraud, but since the statute treated breach without repayment alone as *prima facie* evidence of fraud, and thereby permitted a jury to convict on no other evidence, its "natural operation and effect"[141] was to punish mere breach. It did not matter that the jury was not required by the presumption to convict; Bailey's conviction

---

[136] Hughes, *Autobiographical Notes,* 168.

[137] Hughes' first opinion for the Court, unanimous in conformity with tradition, was in a little case called Kerfoot v. Farmers' & Merchants' Bank, 218 U.S. 281 (1910), involving the effectiveness of a trust conveyance to a national bank.

[138] Bailey v. Alabama, 219 U.S. 219, 231 (1911).

[139] *Ibid.*

[140] *Ibid.*

[141] *Ibid.,* at 235.

rested entirely on the presumption. At this point, Hughes flirted with the due process argument. Under the presumption and the bar against testifying as to uncommunicated motives, unless Bailey could adduce circumstances affirmatively showing good faith, "he was helpless. He stood, stripped by the statute of the presumption of innocence, and exposed to conviction for fraud upon evidence only of breach of contract and failure to pay."[142] A legislature could establish presumptions so long as "there shall be some rational connection between the fact proved and the ultimate fact presumed" and the statute "does not shut out from the party affected a reasonable opportunity to submit . . . all of the facts bearing upon the issue."[143] But this was true only "where the entire subject-matter of the legislation is otherwise within state control," because the "power to create presumptions is not a means of escape from constitutional restrictions."[144]

Once seen as punishing mere breach of contract, Hughes had no difficulty in striking down the Alabama statute. The plain intent of the Thirteenth Amendment was "to render impossible any state of bondage; to make labor free, by prohibiting that control by which the personal service of one man is disposed of or coerced for another's benefit."[145] Congress was well within the authority of the Amendment in prohibiting peonage, which Hughes defined, following *Clyatt*, as compulsory service for a creditor until a debt is paid. If the state could not directly punish refusal to labor for a creditor, it could not do the same thing indirectly by a statutory presumption allowing conviction without proof of any fact other than refusal. Hughes summed up on a note combining realism and an echo of Adam Smith:

> Without imputing any actual motive to oppress, we must consider the natural operation of the statute here in question . . . and it is apparent that it furnishes a convenient instrument for the coercion which the Constitution and the act of Congress forbid; an instrument of compulsion peculiarly effective as against the poor and the ignorant, its most likely victims. There is no more important concern than to safeguard the freedom of labor upon which alone can enduring prosperity be based.[146]

From Harlan and White, who had become Chief Justice by the time the opinion came down, came reactions that must have gratified

---

[142] *Ibid.*, at 236.

[143] *Ibid.*, at 238–39 (quoting Justice Lurton's opinion for the Court in Mobile, Jackson & Kansas City R.R. v. Turnipseed, 219 U.S. 35, 43 (1910), decided two weeks before *Bailey*, which upheld a presumption of evidence of negligence in certain tort actions).

[144] Bailey v. Alabama, 219 U.S. 219, 239 (1911).

[145] *Ibid.*, at 241.

[146] *Ibid.*, at 244–45.

Hughes in his first major effort. Hughes took his draft to White's home and read it to him, as White's eyesight was already very poor. White, Hughes later recalled, was delighted. "Cannot be improved on—clear, convincing and in my opinion unanswerable," returned the Chief Justice. On his copy, Harlan wrote: "I am with you 'through & through.' . . . You may well be proud of this opinion," and returned Hughes' draft without change.[147] Notwithstanding Harlan's evident satisfaction with Hughes' effort, it is intriguing to imagine what the *Bailey* opinion might have looked like had Harlan retained it for himself. Harlan shared Hughes' concern for "the freedom of labor," as his opinion in *Adair* v. *United States*,[148] striking down a federal law against "yellow dog" contracts on interstate railroads, made clear. But it is hard to imagine a Harlan opinion in *Bailey* that would have subordinated the racial aspect of the case so completely.

A.   JUSTICE HOLMES' "INTELLECTUAL DISTILLATION"

From Justice Holmes, however, came one of his longest dissents, joined by Lurton, and it was a classic example of his pursuit of the general, aloof from the operational dimension of a case.[149] "We all agree that this case is to be considered and decided in the same way as if it arose in Idaho or New York," began Holmes with a trace of impatience for Hughes' *politesse*. "The fact that in Alabama it mainly concerns the blacks does not matter."[150] Holmes disagreed with Hughes' major premise. Even if the Alabama law had in substance treated simple breach of contract as a crime, which Holmes denied but was willing to assume for argument, it would not violate the Thirteenth Amendment. Any type of liability for breach was "a disagreeable consequence which tends to make the contractor do as he said he would." To add criminal liability to the usual civil action for damages "simply intensifies the legal motive for doing right, it does not make the laborer a slave."[151] If the laborer is sent to jail for breach, Holmes argued, he is not forced to work for

---

[147] Pusey, *Hughes,* 1:289; Returns, No. 300, 1910 Term. White also provided his new colleague with the correct form of judgment at the end of the opinion. Hughes had written: *"Judgment reversed and cause remanded for new trial."* White corrected this to the proper *"Reversed and cause remanded for further proceedings not inconsistent with this opinion."* (Italics in original.) Hughes Papers, Library of Congress.

[148] 208 U.S. 161 (1908).

[149] Compare Holmes' reluctant acquiescence to human nature in his concurrence in *United States* v. *Reynolds,* the next peonage case. See *infra,* text accompanying notes 215–17.

[150] Bailey v. Alabama, 219 U.S. at 245–46 (Holmes, J., dissenting).

[151] *Ibid.,* at 246.

a private master in peonage. Of course, the criminal penalty will make the laborer less likely to quit in the first place, but "it does not strike me as an objection to a law that it is effective. If the contract is one that ought not to be made, prohibit it. But if it is a perfectly fair and proper contract, I can see no reason why the State should not throw its weight on the side of performance."[152] But all this went further than necessary, Holmes insisted, because the Alabama law did not punish breach. It punished fraud, and breach was merely evidence that a jury might or might not find determinative. "Is it not evidence that a man had a fraudulent intent if he receives an advance upon a contract overnight and leaves in the morning?"[153] The presumption was general and covered breaches at any time, "but that does no harm except on a tacit assumption that this law is not administered as it would be in New York, and that juries will act with prejudice against the laboring man."[154] When breach did not indicate fraud, a fair jury would acquit. "[T]heir experience as men of the world"[155] would tell jurors when fraudulent intent was a fair inference from breach. The presumption merely allowed the jury to draw the inference when warranted. "In my opinion the statute embodies little if anything more than what I should have told the jury was the law without it." The bar against testifying as to uncommunicated motives merely prevented "a naked denial." If the laborer had an "excuse for breaking the contract it will be found in external circumstances, and can be proved."[156]

"I was surprised by [Holmes'] dissent from my opinion in the peonage case," recalled Hughes three decades later in his *Autobiographical Notes*.[157] One can understand why. Perhaps the best-known feature of Holmes' well-known theory of contract law was that contractual liability was not, as he put it in *The Common Law*, a kind of "limited slavery":

---

[152] *Ibid.*, at 247.

[153] *Ibid.*, at 248.

[154] *Ibid.* Compare Holmes' discussion in *The Common Law:*

Whenever it is said that a certain thing is essential to liability, but that it is conclusively presumed from something else, there is always ground for suspicion that the essential element is to be found in that something else, and not in what is said to be presumed from it.

O. W. Holmes, *The Common Law,*

M. DeW. Howe, ed. (1963), 235–36.

[155] Bailey v. Alabama, 219 U.S. at 248 (Holmes, J., dissenting).

[156] *Ibid.*, at 249.

[157] Hughes took pains to add: "We did not always agree but there was never any unfriendliness in our disagreement." The only other surprise Hughes mentioned was Holmes' opinion in United States v. Johnson, 221 U.S. 488 (1911), narrowly construing the Food and Drug Act and prompting a strong dissent by Hughes. 221 U.S. at 499. See Hughes, *Autobiographical Notes*, 174.

It might be so regarded if the law compelled men to perform their contracts, or if it allowed promises [*sic*?] to exercise such compulsion. If, when a man promised to labor for another, the law made him do it, his relation to his promisee might be called a servitude *ad hoc* with some truth. But that is what the law never does. . . . The only universal consequence of a legally binding promise is, that the law makes the promisor pay damages if the promised event does not come to pass. In every case it leaves him free from interference until the time for fulfillment has gone by, and therefore free to break his contract if he chooses.[158]

Beyond the incongruity with his general ideas about contracts, Holmes' dissent is virtually an exhibition of juristic attitudes he derided in his lectures and essays. The detached logic of the dissent seems amazing in view of Holmes' preachments that law must be judged as experience. In words that might have stung their target a little,[159] *The Outlook* said of Holmes' position: "Those who wish to see how ingenious reasoning can lead an acute mind to disregard simple facts of human experience will do well to read the dissenting opinion. . . ."[160] Expanding on this theme, Max Lerner, Holmes' devoted, but clear-eyed, admirer, was later to write:

Holmes's dissent has struck many commentators as legalistic in the worst sense of legalism. While he goes through a rigorous train of reasoning (as, in his own way, Justice Hughes does also), it is of the sort which pays homage to the forms without going beyond them to the

---

[158] O. W. Holmes, *Common Law,* 235–36. Holmes granted that equity sometimes compelled specific performance, but this was an exceptional remedy. *Ibid.* In his lecture, "The Path of the Law," delivered in 1897, Holmes noted that his way of looking at contractual liability "stinks in the nostrils of those who think it advantageous to get as much ethics into the law as they can. It was good enough for Lord Coke, however, and here as in many other cases, I am content to abide with him." O. W. Holmes, *Collected Legal Papers* (1921), 175.

Holmes had not altered these views of the nature of contractual liability when he wrote in *Bailey.* Two months after *Bailey,* but not apropos of the decision, he wrote to Pollock: "I stick to my paradox as to what a contract was at common law: not a *promise*

to pay damages or, etc., but an act imposing a liability to damages *nisi.*" (Emphasis in original.) M. DeW. Howe, ed., *Holmes-Pollock Letters* (1941), I, 177. Pollock's *Principles of Contract* (8th ed., 1911), 192 n.k., had criticized Holmes' position as a "brilliant paradox," inconsistent both with the existence of equitable remedies and the doctrine of anticipatory breach.

[159] Holmes boasted that he never read the newspaper, though sometimes his letters complained about criticisms of his work in the press. See, e.g., O. W. Holmes to H. Croly, May 12, 1919, in M. DeW. Howe, ed., *Holmes-Laski Letters* (1953), 202.

[160] "The Case of Alonzo Bailey," *The Outlook,* 97:101, 103, Jan. 21, 1911.

social reality. Holmes's insistence that the *prima facie* assumption of intent to defraud need not be the determining factor with a jury has a hollow sound in the known context of class and race relations in the South; and his reliance on the "men of the world" who compose such a jury has an element of unconscious humor.[161]

Along the same lines, Holmes' most indefatigable admirer, Felix Frankfurter, wrote in a letter to Morris Cohen in 1916:

> Read his [Hughes'] opinion in *Bailey* v. *Alabama* (219 U.S.) and see how much better a nose he had for the actual operation of peonage laws in the South than Holmes, whose opinion is much more brilliant as an intellectual distillation, but considerably removed from the realities of a modern commercial or agricultural community.[162]

As it skims without a hitch from the existence of civil liability for breach of contract to the legitimacy of criminal sanctions for breach, without a hint of concern for the practical consequences of such an extension, Holmes' dissent is also oblivious to questions of degree, which he liked to say were pretty much all of law. Such seamless logical extensions were almost as common a feature of Holmes' judicial performance as they were a favorite target of his nonjudicial utterances.

Finally, Hughes must have been surprised by the moralistic tone of Holmes' dissent.[163] Holmes made much of his belief in divorcing morals and ethics from law, and yet a cold Puritan passion for obligation glints through this bleak statement: "Breach of a legal contract without excuse is wrong conduct, even if the contract is for labor, and if a State adds to civil liability a criminal liability to fine, it simply intensifies the legal motive for doing right. . . ."[164]

Holmes' position in *Bailey* is less surprising when measured against his work on the Massachusetts bench. In 1899, Holmes had upheld, with apparent relish, the constitutionality of a state law which allowed debtors to be held in contempt for failure to repay creditors if the

---

[161] M. Lerner, *The Mind and Faith of Justice Holmes* (1943), 338.

[162] F. Frankfurter to M. Cohen, Oct. 3, 1916, Frankfurter Papers, Library of Congress. This letter is an acute defense of Hughes' "native ability of high order to master the problems of statesmanship" because he was "subject to the impact of facts."

[163] The *American Law Review* wrote in defense of Holmes that the dissent "appeals to us as based on a higher plane of morality than that of the majority opinion." It also thought that "if an employer does not know that an agreement with an employee was more than a debt of honor, the bargains he would make would be less favorable than the ones he makes now. . . ." *Am. L. Rev.*, 45:278, 279, 1911.

[164] Bailey v. Alabama, 219 U.S. 219, 246 (1911) (Holmes, J., dissenting).

creditors had furnished "necessaries" and a court had established a schedule of repayment. Massachusetts was one of a few states that did not have a constitutional bar against imprisonment for debt, and although the statute authorized contempt only if the judge was satisfied that the debtor was able to pay, Holmes' opinion for the Supreme Judicial Court made clear his view that the legislature "might have revived unconditional imprisonment in case of failure to pay."[165] Imprisonment for debt was not hard for Holmes to stomach. Moreover, the Alabama law's presumption of fraudulent intent fit in with Holmes' abiding stress on the primacy of external conduct, rather than state of mind, as the basis of liability.[166] In addition, deference to jurors, "men of the world," who ought necessarily to decide most legal questions, since most are questions of degree, runs through Holmes' writings on and off the Bench.[167]

In his *Autobiographical Notes*, shortly after noting his surprise at Holmes' dissent in *Bailey*, Hughes spoke of Holmes' willingness to sustain statutes he did not like: "[H]e would say that in his epitaph should be written, 'Here lies the supple tool of power.' "[168] Perhaps, implicitly, Hughes thought that Holmes' position in *Bailey* was an instance of his detached deference to legislative regulation of economic arrangements, to legislative experimentation, and to local responses to

---

[165] Brown's Case, 173 Mass. 498, 500 (1899). Characteristically, Holmes treated the state law as a benefit, not a burden, to debtors: "We know of nothing to prevent the Legislature making the purchase of the necessaries of life easier by giving special remedies against those who willfully try to avoid paying for them." *Ibid.*

Compare Holmes' view of the Alabama law in *Bailey*: "For it certainly would affect the terms of the bargain unfavorably for the laboring man if it were understood that the employer could do nothing in case the laborer saw fit to break his word." 219 U.S. at 246.

[166] In Commonwealth v. Rubin, 165 Mass. 453, 455–56 (1896), in the course of a virtuoso discussion of the difference between larceny and conversion in a case of horse stealing, Holmes elaborated on the many instances when "the original intent was presumed conclusively from the sub-

sequent conduct." As English law became "less extreme and more rational," the significance of subsequent conduct in determining intent was given increasing prominence and increasingly left to the jury. Later, in First Amendment cases, Holmes would come to see the need for a strictly subjective concept of intent in order to protect the free expression rights of critics of government policy. *Compare*, Debs v. United States, 249 U.S. 211 (1919); *with*, Abrams v. United States, 250 U.S. 616 (1919).

[167] See, e.g., Pinney v. Hall, 156 Mass. 225 (1892). *Cf. Holmes-Pollock Letters*, I, 74. ("I think there is a growing disbelief in the jury as an instrument for the discovery of truth. The use of it is to let a little popular prejudice into the administration of law. . . .")

[168] Hughes, *Autobiographical Notes*, 175

local problems. But one can sometimes sense a difference in Holmes' thinking, however elusive, between a "duty of enforcing laws that I believe to embody economic mistakes,"[169] and a committed defense of a legislative prerogative in which he believed. The *Bailey* dissent falls on the commitment side of the line. Like General Howard, Holmes was willing to tolerate a dose of "wholesome compulsion" for black laborers in the South whom he viewed, as he was to make clear in *Reynolds*, the next peonage decision, as impulsive and unreliable.

B. The Aftermath of *Bailey*

The press regarded *Bailey* as a major Progressive advance. "One of the most important decisions of the Supreme Court in recent years,"[170] said *The Outlook* with understandable enthusiasm, since its editor Lyman Abbott had helped finance the appeal and had been fed publicity about the case from Booker T. Washington. The magazine ranked Alonzo Bailey with Onesimus and Dred Scott as historic symbols of "that sense of human brotherhood that was inevitably to render slavery unbearable."[171] *The Nation* thought the decision "will cause rejoicing North and South. . . . [The Alabama law] was a long step toward reenslaving the negro." It took up the theme of the Southern federal judges that peonage was bad business for the South: "The Supreme Court's decision will be heartily welcomed by broad-minded Southerners everywhere; for they understand that vexing as the labor problem is, the solution lies in other directions than involuntary servitude."[172] As if to prove *The Nation*'s point, the *Birmingham News* inaccurately headlined: "Decision Wipes Out One of the Relics of Carpet Bag Days." "The law had fallen into disrepute," that newspaper explained, forgetting that it had been enacted only eight years before, and "[t]he decision . . . in the opinion of many, will have the immediate effect of inviting a higher class of labor to the state. . . ."[173] The *Montgomery Advertiser*, on the other hand, agreed with Holmes that the same law in New York would have passed muster with the Court. *The Advertiser* predicted that black laborers would suffer from the decision because advances would no longer be offered.[174]

Over many of the laudatory press comments was draped the theme of national harmony. After opening with "[o]ne is inclined to clap his

---

169 *Holmes-Pollock Letters*, I, 167.

170 *The Outlook*, 97:47, Jan. 14, 1911.

171 "The Case of Alonzo Bailey," *The Outlook*, 97:101, Jan. 21, 1911.

172 *The Nation*, 92:25, 26, Jan. 12, 1911.

173 *Birmingham News*, Jan. 3, 1911, p. 1.

174 Daniel, *Shadow of Slavery*, 78–79.

hands at this decision," *The Independent* found "the brightest side" of the case to be "a disinterested love for justice."

> In the Supreme Court there were several Justices whose sympathies undoubtedly would have dictated another ruling, being both Democrats and Southerners, while from Alabama's point of view the case was fought out from beginning to end by Southern men. As far as can be learned, no negro or Northern man took a hand in the fight, but Southern lawyers, backed by some unknown Southern private citizens, fought the battle through to the end.[175]

All in all *The Chautauquan* did not overstate the matter when it wrote: "This decision has been hailed as one of the great and memorable acts of our progressive period."[176]

The official reaction to *Bailey* in the Southern states reflected the different readings of the decision that were possible. The Alabama legislature swiftly passed a new contract-fraud law without the provision making breach without repayment *prima facie* evidence of fraud.[177] Pending criminal prosecutions under the law struck down in *Bailey* were apparently abandoned by Alabama authorities after the decision.[178] The Georgia Supreme Court, on the other hand, insisted on the constitutionality of that state's false pretenses statute, which treated breach as presumptive evidence of fraudulent intent, because Georgia had no

---

[175] *The Independent*, 70:213, 214, Jan. 26, 1911. Since *The Independent*'s editor, William Hayes Ward, learned of the case from Booker T. Washington, the concluding comment presumably means that Washington was still at pains to hide his close involvement with the case, along with the involvement of Ray Stannard Baker and other Northern liberals. The great accommodator might have been viewed as somewhat less accommodating had his central role in *Bailey* come out.

[176] "The Suppression of the 'New Slavery,'" *The Chautauquan*, 62:14, 16, 1911. *Bailey* was widely but not very intelligently commented on in the law reviews, which on the whole tended to support Holmes' position. See, e.g., "Current Topics and Notes," *Am. L. Rev.*, 45:278, 1911; Notes, *Colum. L. Rev.*, 11:363, 1911; Notes, *Harv. L. Rev.*, 24:391, 1911; Notes,

U. Pa. L. Rev., 60:336, 1912; Editorial, *Va. L. Reg.*, 16:781, 782, 1911.

[177] 1911 Ala. Laws, No. 98, at 93–94. The Alabama Court of Appeals sustained the constitutionality of the new statute in Thomas v. State, 13 Ala. App. 431 (1915).

[178] A letter to Attorney General McReynolds from Oliver D. Street, the Special Assistant U.S. Attorney retained to handle the Justice Department's challenge to Alabama's criminal-surety laws in the *Reynolds* case, says this of the Alabama attorney general and other state officials: "They say, and I am of the opinion that such is the case, that prosecutions under section 6845 of the Code of Alabama have been altogether abandoned by the criminal authorities in the State of Alabama. . . ." O. Street to J. C. McReynolds, Feb. 11, 1914, National Archives Record Group No. 60, File 50–106.

rule barring the accused from making a statement as to uncommunicated motives.[179] This statute, and the narrow reading of *Bailey* that sustained it, remained undisturbed until 1942 when the Supreme Court struck it down in *Taylor* v. *Georgia*.[180] Florida acquiesced at first and then reverted. In 1913, the legislature struck out the *prima facie* evidence clause in its contract-fraud law. Then in 1919, Florida reenacted a statute with such a clause.[181] This law, despite its evident unconstitutionality, remained in effect until the Supreme Court struck it down in 1944 in Justice Jackson's forceful opinion in *Pollock* v. *Williams*.[182]

Beyond its significance in altering legal relations of black and immigrant laborers to their employers in the South, *Bailey* was a reassuring symbol of the progressive tendencies of constitutional law in the Progressive era. The new Supreme Court, rehabilitated by President Taft with an ex-Confederate as its Chief, in one of its first utterances remembered the promise of the Thirteenth Amendment on the crucial question of freedom to labor. Eschewing sectional recrimination and elevating the new court above the quagmire of race relations, the newest member had issued a magisterial opinion which extended the hand of federal protection to America's most wretched black workers. And it all came under the rubric of freedom to labor, a progressive variation on the central laissez-faire abstraction of freedom of contract, which had not before been utilized by the Supreme Court to protect employees from the impositions of their employers.

It was left to the leading publicist of race relations in the Progressive period, and the person who provided most of the money for Bailey's appeal, to capture both the promise of the decision and the limit of that promise in the context of the times. Ray Stanard Baker's article "A Pawn in the Struggle for Freedom," in the *American Magazine* (see insert following page 814), led with a full-length photograph of Alonzo Bailey,

---

[179] Wilson v. State, 138 Ga. 489 (1912) (upholding secs. 715 and 716 of the Georgia Penal Code of 1910). In Georgia, a criminal defendant was not allowed to testify but was allowed to make statements, not under oath, and the jury could weigh the statement against the presumption arising from the breach.

[180] 315 U.S. 25 (1942). In this case, Justice Byrnes wrote for a unanimous Court that the Alabama rule barring testimony as to uncommunicated motives was not critical to the holding in *Bailey* and simply served "to accentuate the harshness of an otherwise invalid statute" to convict for fraud on evidence of breach and nothing more. *Ibid.*, at 31.

[181] 1913 Fla. Laws ch. 6528, sec. 3; 1919 Fla. Laws ch. 7917, sec. 2.

[182] 322 U.S. 4 (1944). In *Pollock,* Justice Jackson noted that all the peonage cases had come from the deep South, but added: "This is not to intimate that this section, more than others, was sympathetic with peonage, for this evil has never had general approval anywhere, and its sporadic appearances have been neither sectional nor racial." *Ibid.*, at 11.

shown "just as he came in from his work, in his old soiled overalls, his old greasy hat, his old shoes, the stub of a half-smoked cigarette in his fingers."[183] Like Dred Scott, Bailey had become a "symbol in this new struggle for freedom," but Baker pressed his readers to see Bailey exactly as he was: "Look well at the dull black face and you will see there the unmistakable marks of ignorance, inertia, irresponsibility."[184] Forms of slavery would prevail, Baker warned, so long as "so many negroes are densely ignorant and poverty-stricken, and while so many white men are shortsighted enough to take advantage of this ignorance and poverty." Baker's post-script to *Bailey* injected a note of realistic fatalism about how far the Supreme Court decision would alter the pattern of Southern race relations surrounding agricultural labor. What Baker saw in Alonzo Bailey's "dull black face" revealed also how deeply blacks remained in the mire of stereotypes of black childishness, stupidity, and submissiveness even among the liberal paternalists who were their best white friends in this benighted time.

V.   United States *v.* Reynolds:
The Supreme Court and the "Wheel of Servitude"

The Supreme Court's next encounter with peonage came almost four years after *Bailey*, when the Court again confronted an Alabama law punishing breach of contract, but in the special and rather different context of what was known as the criminal-surety system. In *Following the Color Line*, Baker offered this glimpse of the system in operation:

> One of the things that I couldn't at first understand in some of the courts I visited was the presence of so many white men to stand sponsor for Negroes who had committed various offenses. Often this grows out of the feudal protective instinct which the landlord feels for the tenant or servant of whom he is fond; but often it is merely the desire of the white man to get another Negro worker. In one case in particular, I saw a Negro brought into court charged with stealing cotton.
> "Does anybody know this Negro?" asked the judge.
> Two white men stepped up and both said they did.

---

[183] Baker, "Pawn in the Struggle for Freedom," 608.

[184] Du Bois once complained to Baker: "The great trouble with anyone coming from the outside to study the Negro problem is that they do not know the Negro as a human being, as a feeling, thinking man . . . they continually regard the Negro as in the third person, a sort of outside and unknown personality." W. E. B. Du Bois to R. S. Baker, Apr. 3, 1907, quoted in Baker, *Following the Color Line*, 183, viii (introduction by D. Grantham, Jr.).

The judge fined the Negro $20 and costs, and there was a real contest between the two white men as to who should pay it—and get the Negro. They argued for some minutes, but finally the judge said to the prisoner:

"Who do you want to work for, George?"

The Negro chose his employer, and agreed to work four months to pay off his $20 fine and costs.[185]

Behind the system lay the terror of the chain gang and convict leasing, as Baker pointed out:

If there is no white man to pay him out, or if his crime is too serious to be paid out, he goes to the chain-gang—and in several states he is then hired out to private contractors. The private employer thus gets him sooner or later. Some of the largest farms in the South are operated by chain-gang labour. The demand for more convicts by white employers is exceedingly strong.

This demand exerted powerful pressures on the criminal justice system. The "natural tendency," said Baker, "is to convict as many negroes as possible." Small offenses were punished with sizable fines, and serious crimes were scaled down to misdemeanors so that fines could be assessed and undertaken by employers. One Georgia newspaper reported in 1906 that few misdemeanor convicts reached the chain gang since there were "three farmers to every convict ready to pay the fine."[186]

Alabama was one of two states, along with Georgia, whose statutes expressly sanctioned criminal-surety arrangements.[187] An Alabama statute provided that "the court may allow the defendant to confess judgment, with good and sufficient sureties, for the fine and costs."[188] A companion provision required convicts who contracted with sureties to pay their fines and costs to perform as promised or be convicted and fined again in an amount sufficient to cover the damages suffered by the surety. The employment contracts had to be in writing and approved in open court by the judge before whom the defendant had been sentenced.[189]

---

[185] Baker, *Following the Color Line*, 96–97.

[186] *Ibid.*, 98–99.

[187] Cohen, *Negro Involuntary Servitude*, 53: see also Baker, *Following the Color Line*, 98 et seq.

[188] Ala. Code sec. 7632 (1907) (quoted in *Reynolds*, 235 U.S. at 141).

[189] Ala. Code sec. 6846 (1907) (quoted in *Reynolds*, 235 U.S. at 142).

A. FRAMING THE TEST CASE

The Alabama system was revealed in the story of Ed Rivers, a black man, whose troubles led to the *Reynolds* case. In May 1910, he pleaded guilty to petit larceny in Judge I. B. Slaughter's county court in Monroeville, Alabama, and was fined $15.00 and assessed $43.75 in costs. Rivers had no money so he was sentenced to hard labor for ten days in lieu of the fine and forty-eight days for the costs.[190]

J. A. Reynolds paid Rivers' fine and costs in return for Rivers' agreement to work as a farmhand for nine months and 24 days, at a rate of $6 per month, plus board, lodging, and clothing. Rivers worked for Reynolds for a little more than one month and then quit, despite Reynolds' threats to jail him if he left. Rivers was arrested, brought again before Judge Slaughter, and convicted of failing to perform his surety contract. The fine this time was 1¢, but Judge Slaughter added costs of $87.05, which meant that Rivers faced a chain gang for about 115 days. To avoid this, Rivers entered into another surety contract, with one F. W. Broughton, a neighboring planter, calling for fourteen and a half months labor at $6 per month.[191] Rivers was by now committed to work more than seven times as long as would have been required had he elected to work off his original conviction.

Since 1911, the Justice Department had been committed to challenge the constitutionality of the criminal-surety system, and Rivers' situation seemed an ideal test case to the United States Attorney for the Southern District of Alabama, William H. Armbrecht. The scheme had become an "engine of oppression" against blacks, he wrote to Attorney General Wickersham, and the trivial nature of many of the underlying crimes "gives rise to the thought that the prosecution is [n]ot

---

[190] Section 7634 of the Alabama Code of 1907 provided 10 days imprisonment or hard labor if the unpaid fine was less than $20, 20 days if the fine was $20 to $50, 30 days if the fine was $50 to $100, 50 days for $100 to $150, 70 days for $150 to $200, 90 days for $200 to $300, and 25 additional days for each additional $100 in fines. Section 7635 provided that unpaid costs were to be worked out at the rate of 1 day hard labor for each 75¢. Ala. Code secs. 7634, 7635 (1907) (quoted in *Reynolds,* 235 U.S. at 141–42).

[191] This is as far as the indictment in *Reynolds* revealed Rivers' story, and the end of the story as far as the Supreme Court knew. In fact, Rivers also ran away from Broughton after only a few days of service, was convicted again, and drew a fine of $300.00 and costs of $112.80. At this point, no surety stepped forward and Rivers went to the chain gang to work in a turpentine camp. Rivers was directed by court order to testify before the federal grand jury in Mobile, before which he appeared shackled in chains, and then someone petitioned for habeas in his behalf. At this point, the state released him from the remainder of his sentence. W. Armbrecht to G. Wickersham, June 10, 1911, Justice Department File No. 155322 (hereinafter cited as File 155322).

instigated with any idea of up-holding the majesty of the law, but with the idea of putting these negroes to work."[192] Armbrecht convened a grand jury in Mobile which called Judge Slaughter and Rivers among others in a wide-ranging investigation of the criminal-surety system. In June 1911, the grand jury returned eleven indictments, including charges against Reynolds and Broughton.

The indictments set off a spate of local controversy. The *Mobile Register*, one of Alabama's most influential newspapers, reported:

> A majority of the farmers of Monroe county are anxious that the labor contract be discontinued, as it has a demoralizing effect on labor, some going so far as to state that the negro in some instances is afraid to even leave the place without the permission of the farmer, fearing that he will be arrested before he can get back for violating the contract.

This elicited from Judge Slaughter, who obviously felt that Armbrecht had manipulated the newspaper, a defense of the Alabama statutes and his actions in a letter to the *Register*:

> I am of the opinion, and I do not think it needs any argument on my part, that this is a most humane and salutory statute, for the convict is never placed in shackles as often happens in convict camps, and is treated more as a free citizen than a convict. I do not wish to be understood as criticizing in [*sic*] the convict system of Alabama, but take the best part of it and it is a hard life.[193]

In one of the cases, Slaughter pointed out, a black defendant and his family had begged his surety to save him from the chain gang, and now the surety found himself indicted for acceding to these entreaties. Moreover, the sentencing judge had a duty to ensure that the surety contract

---

[192] W. Armbrecht to G. Wickersham, Oct. 27, 1911, and June 10, 1911, File 155322. Armbrecht, a native of Mobile and a Republican, was appointed by President Roosevelt in 1904 despite the opposition of some blacks who objected to his "lily-white" stance in the Alabama Republican party. Roosevelt himself, of course, supported a "lily-white" Republican party in the South.

[193] Some whites in the South complained that the criminal-surety system encouraged blacks to believe they could escape punishment for crimes.

Walter Clark, president of the Mississippi Cotton Association, told Baker:

> I know planters who expect regularly every Monday to come into court and pay out about so many Negroes. It encourages the Negroes to do things they would not think of doing if they knew they would be regularly punished. I've quit paying fines; my Negroes, if they get into trouble, have got to recognize their own responsibility for it and that what follows.

Baker, *Following the Color Line*, 105.

was "fair and just to both the convicted party and his contractor." The next day, the *Register* editorialized on the controversy, summing up in this remarkable paragraph:

> The Alabama law says this can be done; the United States law says it cannot. With the foregoing facts to base an opinion on, the vast majority of the public must feel a satisfaction that the protecting arm of the federal law is extended in such cases.[194]

Meanwhile Armbrecht was negotiating with the Attorney General of Alabama and lawyers for the indicted defendants to fashion a test case to take to the Supreme Court. He needed their help mainly to avoid a jury. A few years earlier, several defendants involved in criminal-surety arrangements had been tried for peonage in the federal district court in Mobile and acquitted. Armbrecht had good reason to fear that a jury would acquit again, since defendants would be able to claim that they had acted under state laws they believed to be constitutional, and even humane. For their part, Reynolds and Broughton were willing to help make a test case if it could be fashioned so as to avoid the expense and inconvenience of trial, and provided the government would agree that even if they were found guilty of violating the federal peonage law, only a nominal fine would be imposed. Armbrecht agreed. He wanted to test the Alabama surety system, not punish anyone. "The defendants in these cases are no more guilty that [*sic*] probably a thousand others," he wrote Wickersham.[195] Local planters wanted to settle the uncertainty that surrounded surety contracts.[196] All sides,

---

[194] About this editorial Armbrecht wrote to Assistant Attorney General William R. Harr:

The last part of the editorial strikes me with particular force. In order to appreciate this one must recollect that in the south they are very jealous of state rights, and that any interference by the Federal Government with customs established by usage, or any laws passed by the state legislature, whether such customs and laws be right or wrong, usually meets with fierce opposition. The last paragraph . . . is very unusual, especially when it appears in a Democratic newspaper published on the coast of the Gulf of Mexico.

The newspaper stories were attached to a letter from Armbrecht to Harr, June 16, 1911, File 155322.

[195] W. Armbrecht to G. Wickersham, May 11, 1912, File 155322.

[196] On March 24, 1911, Armbrecht wrote Attorney General Wickersham that "certain citizens of Monroe County are willing that the Government should make a test case, provided that if the defendant is convicted a fine only be imposed." Daniel, *Shadow of Slavery*, 191.

There is preserved in the Supreme Court's files a letter to the Court from one W. A. Wadsworth of Orattville, Alabama, who introduced himself thus: "I am a farmer and handle lots of negroes." The law which permitted

moreover, wanted a prompt answer: a test case that would go directly to the United States Supreme Court from the district court in Mobile. Even if a conviction were secured in normal course, it would have to be appealed to the circuit court before going to the Supreme Court on writ of error, a process that could take years.

Prompted by Alabama Congressman George Washington Taylor, the attorney general of Alabama, Robert C. Brickell, also was anxious to resolve the uncertainty that surrounded the criminal-surety system. "[I]t is a matter which vitally affects the enforcement of the criminal laws of Alabama," Brickell wrote to Wickersham, urging that one case be selected to bring the question to the Supreme Court.[197] Armbrecht was pleased to cooperate. With Brickell helping to fashion a test case, Armbrecht wrote Wickersham, the Justice Department would not be charged with oppression.[198] Armbrecht, Brickell, Reynolds' lawyers, and the local state prosecutor met in April 1912 to try to figure out how to get a quick ruling in advance of trial from the federal district court in Alabama involving the construction of a federal statute that could be appealed directly to the Supreme Court under the Criminal Appeals Act of 1907.[199] Interestingly, Brickell wanted the test case to be the one indictment returned by the Mobile grand jury in which a white man named Fields had been held to labor because, as Armbrecht wrote, Brickell "was afraid that political capital might be made of the fact that negroes were being held in this way when, and that in his opinion, the statute was not solely directed to negroes." Armbrecht disagreed, because "after an investigation of nearly a hundred test cases, I found only one white man among them." They finally agreed to use two cases—the case against Reynolds involving the black man, Ed Rivers, and a separate case against Broughton for holding the one white peon Armbrecht had uncovered. They further agreed that if the charges against

---

one person to pay another's fine and then work him, said Wadsworth,

is peonage in its worst form: if a poor man is renting my land and is caught selling liquor or convicted of carrying concealed weapons and fined, say $75.00, his wife and children are to see me at once and demand I pay him out. If I do not pay this fine his wife and children will get another to pay it and move off my place and leave the cotton to rot in the field. . . . We are all guilty in this and can not help ourselves as the law stands.

W. Wadsworth to United States Supreme Court, June 2, 1914, National Archives, Record Group No. 60, Supreme Court File 50–106.

[197] R. Brickell to G. Wickersham, Oct. 17, 1911, File 155322. Taylor's central involvement in bringing the parties together is described in a letter from W. Armbrecht to G. Wickersham, May 11, 1912, File 155322.

[198] W. Armbrecht to G. Wickersham, Oct. 27, 1911, File 155322.

[199] 34 Stat. 1246 ch. 2564 (1907) (current version at 18 U.S.C. sec. 3731 [1976]).

the defendants were upheld, the U.S. Attorney would recommend a fine of $50 and no imprisonment, and that if the judge imposed a harsher sentence, the Attorney General would recommend to the President that the defendants be pardoned.[200]

There was, however, considerable confusion about what litigation strategy to pursue, and this led to delay. Armbrecht and the others in Alabama thought the best approach would be for the defendants to admit the allegations of the indictment but file a plea in bar setting up the Alabama statutes as a defense, with the United States demurring to the plea. If the demurrers were overruled, the United States would appeal to the Supreme Court; if the demurrers were sustained, the judge would direct the jury to find the defendants guilty, and the defendants would appeal. But there were doubts at the Justice Department about whether this procedure would produce a direct appeal. The department countered with another approach entirely—the department would petition for habeas corpus on behalf of selected individuals being held to work under a criminal-surety contract. Armbrecht actually drew up habeas papers in the summer of 1912 and sent them to Washington, but for unknown reasons nothing happened before the Taft Administration left office in March 1913.

Matters then were further delayed as the Wilson Administration took stock. Armbrecht had been replaced, and his successor looked to the new Attorney General, James C. McReynolds, for instructions. McReynolds was dismayed at the delay. In his communications with the Alabama lawyers on the *Reynolds* case, there is an unmistakable tone of urgency, although whether this reflected McReynolds' innate impatience or antipathy to the criminal-surety system is not clear. McReynolds seized the lead in a new round of consultations, again involving Congressman Taylor, Brickell, and the defense lawyers, and now including, amazingly enough, the federal district judge who would hear the *Reynolds* case. Based on advice from Taylor, McReynolds refined the strategy earlier worked out between Armbrecht and Brickell. On November 28, 1913, he issued this gruff instruction to Oliver D. Street, a Special Assistant United States Attorney in Birmingham, to take over the prosecutions:

> Fourteen peonage cases for trial at Mobile December fifteen.[201] Sole object to test constitutionality certain compulsory labor laws particu-

---

[200] W. Armbrecht to G. Wickersham, May 11, 1912, File 155322.

[201] The indictments returned by the federal grand jury in Mobile were divided into three groups. The first were cases like *Reynolds* and *Brough-* *ton,* in which a convict found guilty of a well-established crime confessed judgment with a surety in return for an employment contract. The second class consisted of cases in which conviction had been obtained under the

larly section sixty eight hundred forty six Alabama Code nineteen seven. Plan for test proposed by State Attorney General and parties nearly two years ago. Habeas corpus ordered by this Department one year ago. Nothing done since. Special counsel once employed. Seems unnecessary. Can you not go to Mobile at once and personally handle the situation to bring about desired result? All files and correspondence in district attorney's office there. Answer.[202]

Five days later, McReynolds told Street how to get the case to the Supreme Court. The wire, sent to Street in care of the Alabama attorney general in Montgomery, indicates the care with which defendants' counsel, state officials, federal prosecutors, Alabama Congressmen, and even the federal judge who would hear the case in Alabama fashioned the pleadings to secure an early ruling from the Supreme Court.

Can dispose of present peonage cases by plea in bar in Reynolds case defendant withdrawing plea of not guilty government stipulating truth of facts averred in pleas prepared under test agreement with Alabama Attorney General dated April twenty sixth nineteeen twelve. Judgment to be on plea as criminal appeals act nineteen seven only authorizes appeal from judgment sustaining plea not from order sustaining demurrer. Further proceedings to be in accordance with test agreement. Congressman Taylor today wiring defendants attorneys State Attorney General and Judge Tolman[203] [*sic*] to this effect. To ensure presentation of point will also later institute habeas corpus for a detained workman. Latter however not affecting disposition of peonage cases.[204]

Reynolds and Broughton both withdrew their not guilty pleas, and Reynolds filed a special plea in bar to the indictment while Broughton

---

Alabama contract-fraud statute struck down in *Bailey* and then the convict contracted with a surety. These were convictions decided in the state courts before *Bailey* was handed down. Street wrote that the test case of the first class could establish the illegality of the surety contracts in the second class, although even if *Reynolds* upheld the state criminal surety scheme, there would be an independent basis under *Bailey* for challenging the second class of cases. The third class consisted of simple charges posed to defer trials of the second and third class until a test case of the first class could be taken to the Supreme Court.

O. Street to J. C. McReynolds, Feb. 11, 1914, File 155322. The Attorney General approved, and two test cases from the first class—the cases against Reynolds and Broughton—were arranged. W. Wallace, Jr., to O. Street, Feb. 13, 1914, File 155322.

[202] J. McReynolds to O. Street, Nov. 28, 1913, File 155322.

[203] This was a reference to Judge Harry Toulmin, U.S. District Judge for the Southern District of Alabama, who ruled on the *Reynolds* and *Broughton* cases in the trial court.

[204] J. McReynolds to O. Street, Dec. 3, 1913, File 155322.

demurred to the indictment. Both these pleas had the effect of conceding the facts charged in the indictments but contended that the Alabama criminal-surety statutes did not violate the Thirteenth Amendment or the federal peonage statute. The federal lawyers wanted to be sure one of the cases would come under the Criminal Appeals Act of March 2, 1907,[205] which allowed direct appeals on writ of error to the Supreme Court of district or circuit court decisions that sustained a demurrer or special plea in bar to an indictment based upon either the invalidity of a federal statute or a construction of a federal statute as not reaching facts averred in an indictment.

When the pleas were heard by Judge Harry T. Toulmin[206] on December 15, 1913, he accepted Alabama's position (Brickell appeared for the defendants) that the criminal-surety arrangement was within the Thirteenth Amendment's allowance of involuntary servitude as a punishment for a crime.[207] Criminal-surety contracts did not compel service in payment of a debt, but rather punished for conviction. So the Alamaba Supreme Court had held in numerous cases, Toulmin pointed out, quoting the leading state case:

> The charge against the defendant was not that he refused to pay a debt he had contracted, but that he ran away from the hard labor imposed on him as a punishment. . . . The statute was conceived in the most humane spirit, and offers to convicted offenders the opportunity of selecting their own task master, the kind of service they will render, and of having a voice in the measure of compensation. . . . No one would question the constitutionality of a statute making it indictable for one sentenced to hard labor to escape or flee from service. We regard the present statute as substantially the identical thing tempered to the offender by a humane impulse. . . .[208]

---

[205] 34 Stat. 1246 ch. 2564 (1907) (current version at 18 U.S.C. sec. 3731 [1976]). The reasons for the adoption of the Criminal Appeals Act of 1907 are set out in F. Frankfurter and J. Landis, *The Business of the Supreme Court* (1928), 114–20.

[206] Harry Theophilus Toulmin (1838–1916) studied at the universities of Alabama, Virginia, and Louisiana (now Tulane). After joining the bar in Mobile, he fought as a private in the Confederate Army, was thrice wounded, and rose to the rank of colonel. After the war, he served in the state legislature and as a state judge before President Cleveland appointed him United States District Judge for the Southern District of Alabama in 1886. He served until his death. *Dictionary of American Biography* (1936), XVIII, 602–603.

[207] United States v. Broughton, 213 F. 345 (S.D. Ala.), *reversed sub nom.* United States v. Reynolds, 235 U.S. 133 (1914); United States v. Reynolds, 213 F. 352 (S.D. Ala.), *reversed,* 235 U.S. 133 (1914).

[208] Lee v. State, 75 Ala. 29, 31 (1884).

B.   Criminal Surety Before the Supreme Court

Brickell made much of this "humane impulse" in his brief in the Supreme Court. Criminal-surety arrangements gave one convicted an added option. Longer periods of compulsory service might result, but

> the convict hired out by the county . . . serves in stripes under the watchful eye of an armed guard, often shackled. . . . His companion of the confessed judgment chooses to serve twice or three times as long perhaps, but, such service is usually on the farm where his family is working. His days he spends behind the plow and his nights as he may choose.[209]

If Congress could prohibit the criminal-surety system, it could prohibit convict leasing and could get into wholesale prison reform, a ridiculous arrogation, Brickell thought. How to punish criminals and whether and how to put them to work were state matters, as the Thirteenth Amendment expressly recognized.

Because of the unquestioned acceptance of the notorious convict lease, whereby the state leased out convicts to private interests, Solicitor General John W. Davis' brief for the United States attacking the criminal-surety system had to draw some rather careful distinctions.[210] The liberty of a United States citizen could only be impaired by the judgment of a court for such time as the court determined, based on the state legislature's instructions. The state could not delegate to a private citizen its power to punish, Davis insisted. It might transfer to a private citizen its right in the labor of a convict, but "only when that right is consummate in the State at the time of transfer. . . . [I]t certainly cannot transfer to another the power to compel a greater service than it could itself exact."[211] Under the criminal-surety system, the length and character of the service "are matters of purely private contract . . . and until the convict has in some way broken his agreement the State has washed its hands of the whole transaction." The convict works under threat of arrest if he stops, and "this threat is made good by . . . a new prosecution . . . and a new sentence for an increased amount; this is to be liquidated, perhaps, by a similar contract . . . and so on *ad infinitum*. . . . Once bound to this wheel, there is no escape, and the life of the Father of the Marshal Sea was not more devoid of hope."[212]

---

209 *Brief for Defendants,* 14, United States v. Reynolds, 235 U.S. 133 (1914).

210 *Brief for United States,* 26, United States v. Reynolds, 235 U.S. 133 (1914).

211 *Ibid.,* at 10–11.

212 *Ibid.,* at 11.

Justice Day's opinion for the Court in *Reynolds* was formalistic, repetitive, and even a little defensive, as if he knew the Alabama system was wrong but could not quite put his finger on why. The Court was not prepared to cast doubt on the legality of convict leasing, which was also characterized by forced servitude for private masters, often under barbarous conditions. Moreover, there could be nothing wrong with contracts whereby convicts got the money to pay fines and thereby escape imprisonment. In addition, the state's enforcement of the obligations of such contracts by its criminal law undoubtedly increased the security of such transactions and therefore the opportunities for convicts to make such agreements. Day may also have seen some truth in the state's claim that compared to the chain gang, most surety arrangements were relatively humane. But looked at as a whole, with the distorting effects of racism in the system of law enforcement and with the history of black forced labor, the Alabama criminal-surety system stood as a major support of involuntary servitude. The Court could not know this, however, or at least could not claim that it did. The Court had no knowledge of the criminal justice system in operation; it had only the indictments of Reynolds and Broughton before it. So Day went through a logical exercise. Was the convict working under compulsion to pay his debt to the surety or to satisfy the punishment imposed by the state? The "real substance of the transaction" was that the surety satisfied the state and the convict's service was rendered to reimburse him. Once the deal was struck, the convict was entirely under the surety's control; he could be freed, for example, without state approval. Thus, the debt ran to the surety, not the state. This was the definition of peonage: compulsory service based on debt. Moreover, as Rivers' fate illustrated, the system had a tendency to perpetuate servitude. If the convict refused to work as promised he could be punished anew and might liquidate the new penalty by another, longer obligation. Far from the humane arrangement claimed by the state, "the convict is thus kept chained to an ever-turning wheel of servitude."[213]

The *Reynolds* decision was unanimous,[214] but Justice Holmes issued a brief concurrence to explain why he went along after dissenting in *Bailey*.

> There seems to me nothing in the Thirteenth Amendment or the Revised Statutes that prevents a State from making a breach of contract,

---

[213] United States v. Reynolds, 235 U.S. 133, 146–47 (1914).

[214] McReynolds, who had taken Lurton's place at the beginning of the 1914 Term, did not participate, in view of his involvement as Attorney General.

as well as a reasonable contract for labor as for other matters, a crime and punishing it as such. But impulsive people with little intelligence or foresight may be expected to lay hold of anything that affords a relief from present pain even though it will cause greater trouble by and by. The successive contracts, each for a longer term than the last, are the inevitable, and must be taken to have been the contemplated outcome of the Alabama laws. On this ground I am inclined to agree that the statutes in question disclose the attempt to maintain service that the Revised Statutes forbid.[215]

This grudging little paragraph speaks worlds. Words like imprudent, impulsive, and improvident were the shibboleths of respectable racism in moderate Northern discourse. They were the dignified versions of "shiftless."[216] With the innuendo filled in, Holmes appeared to have meant this: when the state deals with what are presumed to be sensible people, there is nothing wrong with punishing contract breaches, as the *Bailey* dissent argued, including contracts between convicts and sureties. But blacks, being "impulsive people with little intelligence," will turn to surety contracts to avoid even a short period on the chain gang, and then will violate their new obligations when they became onerous, even at the cost of further prosecutions and surety arrangements that dig themselves deeper and deeper into involuntary servitude. Alabama must be taken to have contemplated that its criminal-surety laws would entrap blacks in servitude. This the federal peonage statute forbids.

The irony of Holmes' progression from dissent in *Bailey* to acquiescence in *Reynolds* is that his protective application of federal law rested on a race-conscious approach to the Alabama criminal-surety system in operation, and one that imputed a discriminatory motive to the Alabama legislature at that. But this approach did not lead Holmes to consider whether blacks might be victimized by a criminal process run by whites only, from whose juries blacks were invariably excluded, and which had served to prop up the system of black forced labor since Reconstruction. Blacks were victimized by the criminal-surety laws of Alabama, Holmes was willing to concede, not because the laws were unfair in substance or application, but rather because blacks were stupid and irresponsible.

Holmes was alone in recognizing even obliquely that the victims of Alabama's criminal surety system were predominantly black. Not a word of Day's opinion for the Court referred to race in any manner or context. Thus, *Reynolds* went even beyond *Bailey* in ignoring the racial aspect

---

[215] 235 U.S. at 150 (Holmes, J., concurring).

[216] See generally, R. W. Logan, *The Betrayal of the Negro* (1965), 243–75.

of the case.[217] For this, at least, Alabama Attorney General Brickell must have been thankful.

Reynolds was not received as a decision of much importance, despite its interest as a rare intervention by the Supreme Court in the workings of a state penal system. In contrast to the outpouring of commentary on Bailey, the Reynolds decision produced hardly a ripple in either the popular or academic press. This is odd considering that the criminal-surety system, as Justice Department reports indicated, was a pervasive support for forced labor in Alabama and Georgia. Perhaps it seemed that Reynolds was a foregone conclusion after Bailey, or that the decision did not make much difference, since only two states were affected and convict servitude for private employers remained possible by virtue of the odious convict lease. Probably a more important reason the public and profession took so little note was that Reynolds was decided as governmental concern and public interest about peonage was winding down, after a decade of heightened awareness. The lawyers involved, on the other hand, thought Reynolds was a major case. The Alabama attorney general's concern was evident from the beginning. The case also stuck in John W. Davis' mind as one of the most important that he presented as a Solicitor General, although this may have been partly because it was, along with the Grandfather Clause Cases, one of the first he argued.

After Reynolds, the White Court ruled on two other cases dealing

---

[217] The aftermath of Reynolds sheds light on the arrangements between the federal prosecutors and the defendants to make a test. Counsel for the defendants wrote the Justice Department requesting relief from further prosecution. Their argument, as John W. Davis put it in a letter to the U. S. Attorney in Mobile, was "that they were proceeding in accordance with the statute, which had been declared constitutional by the highest court in Alabama, and that there was no criminal intent on their part." What did the U. S. Attorney think, Davis asked, adding, "[p]erhaps the suggestion is not wholly without merit. . . ." J. Davis to A. Pitts, June 9, 1915, National Archives, Record Group No. 60, File 50–106. The U. S. Attorney replied that he had told the defendants "that the Department of Justice had consented that I let the defendants plead guilty and take a nominal fine without costs and that I thought a fine of $25 would be reasonable enough." Some of the defendants, however, said they could not pay anything and contended that "they all would have been acquitted under the charge of the Court to the jury had they not agreed to let the record be fixed so that an appeal could be taken." The U. S. Attorney added, "I feel deeply for these people. I feel that they have met the Government more than half way in fixing the record in the two cases tried so that a proper interpretation of the statutes could be handed down. . . ." He urged a nominal fine —perhaps $10 for the impecunious— but not so low "that it is beneath the dignity of the Federal Court. . . ." A. Pitts to J. Davis, June 16, 1915, National Archives, Record Group No. 60, File 50–106.

with peonage, actually drawing boundaries around the concept. The first was *Butler* v. *Perry*, decided in 1916. Like a number of states, Florida required ablebodied males from twenty-one to forty-five years of age to work for six ten-hour days on roads and bridges, or in lieu of labor to provide either an ablebodied substitute or $3 a day to the country road and bridge fund. For failing in this duty, one Jake Butler was convicted of a misdemeanor and sentenced to thirty days in jail.[218] Butler claimed that requiring him to work when he had not been convicted of any crime was involuntary servitude. Justice McReynolds disposed of this in a brief, well-researched, and sprightly opinion. Labor on public roads had been from ancient times a duty of citizenship, brought by Roman law to England and then to the colonies. "The system was introduced from England, and, while it has produced no Appian Way, appropriateness to the circumstances existing in rural communities gave it general favor." The Northwest Ordinance of 1787 had prohibited involuntary servitude in language later borrowed by the Thirteenth Amendment, but the Territory and the states later carved out from it required road duty by statute. Most states provided for such duty as late as 1889. The Thirteenth Amendment "was intended to cover those forms of compulsory labor akin to African slavery which in practical operation would tend to produce like undesirable results," not to get in the way of basic obligations of citizenship, such as compulsory service in the military, on juries, on roads, and so forth.[219] It was 1916, and the Court was clearing the way for World War I.

As *Butler* presaged, the claim that the military draft during World War I amounted to involuntary servitude was brushed aside by the Court in the *Selective Draft Law Cases*.[220] At the end of a long, heavily historical, and powerful opinion for the unanimous Court, Chief Justice White was "unable to conceive upon what theory the exaction by government from the citizen of the performance of his supreme and noble duty of contributing to the defense of the rights and honor of the nation . . . can be said to be the imposition of involuntary servitude. . . ."[221]

---

[218] Butler v. Perry, 67 Fla. 405 (1914).

[219] Butler v. Perry, 240 U.S. 328, 331–32 (1916). McReynolds cited Blackstone's *Commentaries* and Vinogradoff's *English Society in the Eleventh Century,* among other authorities reviewed. Butler also claimed that compulsory road work deprived him of property and liberty without due process of law. These claims also fell before the momentum of history. The Fourteenth Amendment was intended "to preserve and protect fundamental rights long recognized under the common law system." 240 U.S. at 333. See generally Note, "Civil Conscription in the United States," *Harv. L. Rev.,* 30:265, 1917.

[220] 245 U.S. 366 (1918).

[221] *Ibid.,* at 390.

VI. Legal Theory and Legal Realism in the Peonage Cases

Does the *Bailey* decision put forward a plausible constitutional theory, if one accepts the premise, as both Hughes and Holmes insisted, that the racial aspect of peonage should be ignored? Or should the decision be understood as a doctrinally disguised response to the continuing legacy of forced labor for blacks in the South? Answers to these questions are elusive, but are nonetheless of first importance in appraising the Supreme Court's work during the Progressive era. If *Bailey* is credible in its professions of race neutrality and its attempt to ground its constitutional doctrine in "the freedom of labor,"[222] it belongs where it is virtually never placed by students of constitutional history, in the camp of decisions, such as *Lochner, Adair,* and *Coppage,* that based rights and legislative inhibitions on the labor contract, and that made freedom of contract theory the backbone of laissez-faire constitutionalism. *Bailey* is an unsettling presence among these warhorses of substantive due process, both conceptually and as a revelation of judicial attitudes. How could a Court suspended in the upper conceptual chambers of freedom of contract theory find in the Thirteenth Amendment a freedom from strict enforcement of contract? To this day, there hovers over the freedom of contract cases the odor of class bias or, at least, benighted indifference to the hard realities of the laborer's bargaining position in an industrial society. Yet *Bailey*'s protection of workers from airtight enforcement of their labor contracts is a constitutional profession on behalf of free labor that is antipathetic to the interest of employers in having an effective legal deterrent to breach of labor contracts on farms and plantations, where constancy of labor may be critical in the planting and harvest seasons. As such, it supports the sincerity, if not the realism, of the protestations of worker interest that mark many of the substantive due process decisions generally thought to be most damaging to the welfare of working people.

On the other hand, if *Bailey* is viewed as a result-oriented response to the exploitation of black workers, it is a constitutional landmark for different reasons. It marks the first decision since *Strauder* v. *West Virginia* in 1880 in which the Supreme Court took the side of black people in an important issue of race relations. Moreover, it marks an early instance of vigorous legal realism on behalf of civil rights, one that sheds light both on the White Court's style of judicial statecraft and on its attitudes toward racial justice.

The question whether *Bailey* rests on a plausible race-neutral principle can be pursued, as Holmes indicated, in two separate but related inquiries. First, does the criminalization of breach of a valid

---

[222] United States v. Bailey, 219 U.S. 219, 245 (1910).

contract to labor compel involuntary servitude? Second, even if the answer to the first question is yes, does the act of taking and not repaying an advance change the matter sufficiently so that punishment would not infringe on the Thirteenth Amendment? Since neither the text nor the legislative history of the Thirteenth Amendment or of the federal peonage statute sheds light on either question, one naturally must look to fundamental principles of contract law and criminal law and the extent to which those traditional principles ought to be read into the Thirteenth Amendment and the federal peonage statute. Whatever aid these areas of legal theory offer on the *Bailey* problem is not necessarily conclusive on the constitutional question. The institutional questions of the power of the states to reorder traditional principles of law respecting labor contracts, the power of Congress to govern in this area, and the appropriate role of the Supreme Court in review under the Thirteenth Amendment and the federal peonage statute must also be taken into account. In short, the *Bailey* decision can be viewed as a prime example of both the promise and the problems of drawing constitutional principles out of the jurisprudence of the common law.

A.   CRIMINAL LAW PERSPECTIVES

The criminal law tradition was at the time of *Bailey*, and remains to this day, staunchly opposed to the notion of criminalizing breach of contract, unless money is received with an aim to swindle. Even recognition that a fraudulent promise can lay the basis for criminal liability has come late and grudgingly to criminal law, because of fear that inferences of fraud may be drawn from mere nonperformance and thereby obscure what the commentary to the Model Penal Code aptly calls the "bright line between theft and breach of contract."[223]

Breaches of contract have been considered violations of private obligations arising from the assent of the parties and not violations of duties owed to the public, and whatever the question-begging content of this formulation, it has served such desirable ends that it has maintained its hold on Anglo-American law theory for centuries.[224] At common law, breach of contract was treated as criminal only when it coincidentally violated duties owed to the public or the state, as where a breach endangered human life or caused serious injury, exposed property to destruction, interrupted vital government services, or violated a contractual relationship thought to require special security (i.e., those involving military personnel or seamen). Additionally, breach of con-

---

[223] Model Penal Code sec. 223.8, commentary at 261 (1980).

[224] See, e.g., J. Stephen, *A General View of the Criminal Law of England* (1863), 4.

tract coincided with the concept of theft where a person received money or property subject to a specific legal obligation to transfer it and failed to make the required disposition.[225]

During the nineteenth century, it gradually became accepted that the crime of theft by deception, or false pretenses as it was commonly called, could encompass the act of receiving money or property in return for a promise to perform a contract that the promisor did not intend, at the time of contracting, to carry out. This was a significant and controversial extension.[226] At common law, the concept of fraud in the crime of theft by deception had been strictly limited to the misrepresentation of external facts. The impulse to punish all manner of swindling led to the more expansive notion that deception could apply to intention, opinion, or any other false representations used to defraud. In 1896, the Supreme Court put the weight of its authority behind this expansion in *Durland* v. *United States*, which held unanimously that the federal mail fraud statute reached a false promise to perform a contract.[227] However, as *Durland* itself illustrates, this expansion of crime of false pretenses was accompanied by insistence on the necessity both of demonstrating fraudulent intent at the time the contract was entered into and of not inferring such intent from the mere fact of nonperformance. Thus, the Alabama Supreme Court's decision in *Ex parte Riley*,[228] which held that a laborer could be punished for the crime of false pretenses if he secured an advance on a promise he intended not to perform, but insisted on clear proof of fraudulent intent independent of the breach, aptly reflected the general approach of criminal law to the problem at the end of the nineteenth century.

Expansion of the concept of deception to cover false intention thus did not submerge the key principle of criminal law theory that fraud should be punished without putting the force of the criminal law behind contractual promises made in good faith. Criminal law theory made a crucial distinction between specious promises and breach of contract

---

[225] See, e.g., J. Stephen, *A Digest of the Criminal Law (Crimes and Punishments)* (4th ed., 1887), 358–65; E. McLain, *A Treatise on the Criminal Law as Now Administered in the United States* (1897), I, 12; J. Prentiss, *New Commentaries on the Criminal Law Upon a New System of Exposition* (1892), II, 379.

[226] For a critique, see G. Fletcher, *Rethinking Criminal Law* (1978), 12, 124; G. Fletcher, "The Metamorphosis of Larceny," *Harv. L. Rev.*, 89:469, 471, 1976.

[227] Durland v. United States, 161 U.S. 306 (1896). In this case, the brief for the defendant asserted: "If there be one principle of criminal law that is absolutely settled by an avalanche of authority it is that fraud . . . must be the misrepresentation of an existing or a past fact, and cannot consist of the mere intention not to carry out a contract in the future." Quoted *ibid.*, at 313. See also Evans v. United States, 153 U.S. 584 (1894).

[228] See discussion *supra*, text accompanying n.105.

due to change of heart or change of circumstances. To maintain the distinction, courts and commentators insisted that mere nonperformance of a contract could only be taken as evidence that there was no intent to perform when the contract was made, in the rare cases where breach almost certainly reflects such a lack of intent. It is consistent with this approach, for example, that most states provide that taking lodging without intent to pay is criminal and that departing without paying is presumptive evidence of fraudulent intent.[229] Some bad-check laws also result in punishing fraudulent promises, with nonperformance treated as presumptive evidence of fraud.[230] But these exceptions do not gainsay the general rule that intent to defraud usually may not be inferred from the mere fact that a promise was not performed.[231]

The imposition of criminal liability on a person who receives money under a contractual obligation to make a specific payment and instead appropriates it also does not run counter to the general principle that contract breach by itself should not be treated as a crime.[232] It has long been the rule that escrows, trustees, lawyers, building contractors holding payments for subcontractors, and other stakeholders commit a crime if they fail to meet the specific obligation for which the money was given and instead treat the money as their own. Such situations are neither credit transactions nor situations where capacity or willingness to perform is understood to be subject to changed circumstances or change of mind.

Thus, the long-accepted position of Anglo-American criminal law is that an individual breaching a contract should not be subject to criminal penalties. There are many reasons of principle and policy behind the tradition. It has been thought inappropriate to employ the moral stigma of the criminal law for contractual nonperformance. As is discussed below, it is economically efficient to permit contract breach where the cost of performance exceeds the value of performance. Contract law is a prime instrument in the efficient allocation of credit in society, and criminal penalties for breach would impair the incentive to choose risks wisely. Moreover, there is obvious futility in using criminal law to punish insolvency.[233] All in all, the jurisprudence of criminal law indicates that to treat breach of a labor contract as a crime would be a stark and dubious deviation from tradition. Alabama's treatment of breach as presumptive evidence of fraud in a setting where

---

[229] Model Penal Code sec. 206.1 (6)(a), comment at 90 (Tent. Draft No. 1 1953).

[230] L. Hall and S. Glueck, *Cases on Criminal Law and Its Enforcement* (2nd ed., 1958), 174.

[231] Model Penal Code sec. 223.3 (1980).

[232] *Ibid.*, sec. 223.8.

[233] See the valuable discussion *ibid.*, sec. 223.8, comment at 258–60.

nonperformance would usually reflect change of heart or circumstances was thus wholly out of keeping with the received jurisprudence of criminal law.

B. PERSPECTIVES FROM CONTRACT THEORY AND PRACTICE

The concept of undue compulsion in the law of contracts is made problematic by the contradiction between freedom and obligation that lies at the heart of the theory of freedom of contract. Freedom is set against itself by the enforcement of promises. At one extreme, John Stuart Mill surely stated a truth good for the Thirteenth Amendment, as well as for classical liberalism, when he posited that "an engagement by which a person should sell himself . . . as a slave, would be null and void."[234] As Mill reasoned, since the justification for enforcing contracts was to enhance the liberty of individuals to control by mutual agreements things that affected them jointly, to enforce contracts undertaking slavery would be theoretically self-defeating. "The principle of freedom cannot require that [one] should be free not to be free."[235] Voluntary slavery is still slavery. Mill was vague about the exact point at which a contract becomes too great an alienation of freedom to be valid. He simply advanced the central idea that there is a point—in time, in degree of dominion, or in the nature of what is promised— beyond which a contractual undertaking freely assumed should not be enforced out of respect for the promisor's autonomy and liberty.[236] As Bruce Ackerman has put it, "[t]here may be a place for the law of bankruptcy, as well as the law of contract, in the ideal liberal state."[237]

Commentators at the other extreme of freedom of contract theory insisted that persons must enjoy a very broad capacity to contract without interference, backed by the assurance of the legal system that they will be held to their promises.[238] The greater the assurance of perform-

---

[234] J. S. Mill, "On Liberty," in *Three Essays* (1912), 125.

[235] *Ibid.,* 126.

[236] *Ibid.,* 125–28. Marx agreed with Mill, for a different reason. When "labour-power" is offered for sale, the seller must be as nearly equal to the buyer as possible. "The continuance of this [equal] relation demands that the owner of the labour-power should sell it only for a definite period, for if he were to sell it rump and stump, once and for all, he would be selling himself, converting himself from a free man into a slave, from an owner of a commodity into a commodity." Equality in the marketplace would be enhanced if labor contracts were only for relatively brief periods, Marx seems to have thought, although why this should be so, as a matter of theory, is by no means clear. K. Marx, *Capital,* S. Moore and E. Aveling, trans. (1906), 1:186.

[237] B. Ackerman, *Social Justice in the Liberal State* (1980), 198.

[238] See, e.g., the statement of Sir George Jessel, M.R.: "[If] there is one thing which more than another public policy requires, it is that men of full

ance, the greater the exchange value of the promise. Freedom of contract theorists insisted in particular on the fullest freedom of contract for laborers. "The property which every man has in his own labour, as it is the original foundation of all other property, so it is the most sacred and inviolable," wrote Adam Smith,[239] and contract is the primary means by which the laborer can get a return. The appeal of this sturdy principle in the Supreme Court during the Progressive era is measured in the line of decisions of which *Lochner, Adair,* and *Coppage* are the signposts.

At the heart of freedom of contract theory, between the extremes of aversion to contracts amounting to slavery and enthusiasm for strict enforcement, lies confusion. "Freedom to dispose of one's own freedom is evidently something of a paradox," Frank Knight wrote in 1947, adding that "[l]iberal doctrine . . . has never had any clear position on this matter."

> It is evident that freedom of contract . . . must be restricted to narrow limits if anything like individual liberty, in a practical common-sense interpretation, is to be maintained (if it is not to run into 'involuntary servitude'). But on the other hand, this inalienability of control over one's own person, meaning especially over its economic powers and capacities—results in placing in an especially weak position anyone who owns productive capacity only as embodied in his own person in the form of labour power.[240]

The problem of the *Bailey* case is central to the paradox Knight puzzled over. As in Mill's writing, the point at which freedom of contract merges into slavery is easiest to conceptualize in terms of a present commitment to a long-in-the-future, open-ended obligation. Threats to the autonomy of parties caught in such contracts are of two sorts: First, an essentially paternalistic concern about whether a promised alienation

---

age and competent understanding shall have the utmost liberty of contracting, and that their contracts entered into freely and voluntarily shall be held sacred and shall be enforced by the Court of Justice." Printing & Numerical Registering Co. v. Sampson, L.R. 19 Eq. 462, 465 (1875), quoted in F. Kessler and G. Gilmore, *Contracts* (2nd ed., 1970).

[239] Smith, *Wealth of Nations,* b. 1, ch. 10, pt. 2, at 151. Smith continued:

The patrimony of a poor man lies in the strength and dexterity of his hands; and to hinder him from employing this strength and dexterity in what manner he thinks proper without injury to his neighbor, is a plain violation of this most sacred property. It is a manifest encroachment upon the just liberty both of the workman, and of those who might be disposed to employ him.

[240] F. Knight, *Freedom and Reform* (1947), 64–65, quoted in Kessler and Gilmore, *Contracts,* 9, n.34.

of freedom should be taken many years later as conveying the promisor's continuing consent may lead to a limitation on internal contractual capacity in the interest of autonomy. Second, an external threat to the promisor's autonomy may be perceived in the undue, and in the sense necessarily nonconsensual, subjection to another's will in an open-ended contract of the "I'll do whatever you want" variety. But Bailey's contract did not pose either of these threats, at least in their gross forms.

Mill and other theorists who have delved into the contradiction between freedom and freedom of contract generally have not gone beyond the broad issue of general contractual validity to the narrower question of the propriety of particular remedies. This was good enough for Holmes as well, as he revealed in his logic of exclusive alternatives: if there is something wrong with Bailey's contract, void it altogether; if the contract is valid, let it be enforced in whatever way the state wants. Holmes was right in regarding Bailey's contract to labor for one year as not remotely the sort of contract Mill or anyone else might have thought generally invalid on the ground of servitude concerns. This was the point of his aside that the Thirteenth Amendment did not bar contracts to labor. But that was not the issue. The question was whether a contract that was not in a general sense a commitment to involuntary servitude might become one if enforced by the particularly compulsive method of the criminal law.

In contrast to the philosophers, the common law tradition has by and large dealt with the tensions between personal autonomy and freedom of contract not at the wholesale level of contractual validity, but in the more discriminating territory of remedial propriety. Certainly traditional contract theory supports Holmes on the general point that as to many contracts, including even contracts to labor in certain ways, undue dominion in Thirteenth Amendment terms has not been thought risked by criminal punishment for nonperformance, at least after a judicial order to perform. Decrees of specific performance come close to surrounding breach of contract with criminal penalties, and courts have not worried that specific performance decrees as a categorical matter compel involuntary servitude.[241] Where specific performance

---

[241] It is true that before a specific performance order is issued, a judge reviews the reasonableness of the demand sought from the breaching party, so that a barrier to oppression is built in and the breaching party has the question of excuse from performance judged before criminal penalties are risked. But under a law making breach a crime, a judge and jury would also look at the reasonableness of the demands imposed in the process of determining whether a breaching party is guilty. Also, in the specific performance situation, it is not breach that gives rise to criminal penalties but rather failure to obey the court's decree. If breach is simply made criminal, once breach occurs criminal liability attaches and presumably could

would be an available remedy, to make breach criminal does not seem much of a step beyond the received tradition. Certainly it is not one that should encounter the Thirteenth Amendment as an obstacle without some clear signal in the constitutional text or the intention of the framers. So we may agree with Holmes that there is no basis in accepted principles of contract law for a flat constitutional rule against criminalizing all contract breaches, however uncommon criminalization may have been.

But if the traditional scope of specific performance is taken as a guide to the particular circumstances in which breach may be criminalized, Hughes' position in *Bailey* rests on considerable authority, because English and American courts have shied away from ordering specific performance of general labor contracts. Specific performance is the exceptional remedy in American and English law, and money damages the normal recourse for contract breach. Specific performance is limited to situations in which damages are inadequate or difficult to measure, such as when the performance breached is somehow without substitute or equivalent.[242] Institutional interest and economic efficiency lie behind traditional limits on specific performance. Money damages will usually involve less judicial supervision, even taking into account the institutional energies spent in determining the appropriate measure of damages and in enforcing payment. More important, where the cost of performance to the reluctant party exceeds the expectation value of the contract to the injured party, to permit breach promotes efficiency so long as damages are paid. For reasons of efficiency, among others, the goal of contract remedies is compensation, not compulsion.[243]

Labor contracts rarely call for services that are without equivalent; substitute performance usually is readily available to employers. Moreover, damages in most instances of breach will be nonexistent or modest, and in any event easy enough to measure. Thus, labor contracts have fit easily into the general preference of contract remedies for damages rather than compulsion to perform. But beyond the pull of these general principles, English and American courts have recognized special features of labor contracts that militate against specific performance. Relations between employer and employee may have deteriorated beyond redemption, and yet personal supervision of open-ended duties by the employer

---

not be cured by belated performance. These differences in timing, however, do not seem to call for a different appraisal under the Thirteenth Amendment of the validity of specific performance as against the validity of treating breach as criminal.

[242] See generally A. Kronman, "Specific Performance," *U. Chi. L. Rev.*, 45:351, 1978.

[243] See E. A. Farnsworth, *An Introduction to the Law of Contracts* (1982), 811–914.

is often the essence of the agreement. Moreover, in many personal service contracts, the services required may be imprecise. Courts shy away from ordering specific performance where obligations are indefinite, as there is an obvious need for precision in decrees backed by the severity of the contempt sanction.[244] Finally, concerns about involuntary servitude have reinforced the courts' aversion.[245] Frederic William Maitland treated servitude concerns as the heart of the matter in his *Lectures on Equity*: "An agreement to serve cannot be specifically enforced, otherwise men might in effect sell themselves into slavery."[246] There is support for the priority Maitland gave to servitude

---

[244] As Lord Selbourne put it in 1873:

There is a considerable class of contracts, such as ordinary agreements for work and labour . . . which are not in the proper sense of the words cases for 'specific performance'; in other words, the nature of the contract is not one which requires the performance of some definite act such as this Court is in the habit of requiring to be performed by way of administering superior justice, rather than leave the parties to their rights and remedies of law. It is obvious that if the notion of specific performance were applied to ordinary contracts for work and labour, or for hiring and service, it would require a series of orders, and a general superintendence, which could not conveniently be undertaken by any Court of Justice; and therefore contracts of that sort have been ordinarily left to their operation at law.

Woverhampton Walsall Ry. v. London North-Western Ry., 16 L.R.-Eq. 433, 439 (1873).

[245] The point was put this way in 1906 by an Iowa judge:

It may . . . be stated to be a universally recognized general rule that the remedy for a violation of contract to perform personal service or labor is at law, and the damages there recoverable constitute the full

measure of relief to which the employer is entitled. . . . Any system or plan by which the court could order or direct the physical coercion of the laborer would be wholly out of harmony with the spirit of our institutions, and his imprisonment would take away his power to make specific performance. Even if such authority existed its exercise would be undesirable. If the relation of employer and employe [*sic*] is to be of value or profit to either it must be marked by some degree of mutual confidence and satisfaction, and when these are gone and their places usurped by dislike and distrust, it is to the advantage of all concerned that their relations be severed. . . . It is the right of the employer to discharge his employe and of the employe to quit his employer's service at any time with or without cause, subject to no other penalty than a judgment for damages for the breach of the contract or hiring.

W. H. Gossard Co. v. Crosby, 132 Iowa 155, 163–64 (1906).

[246] F. W. Maitland, *Equity* (1910), 240. It is somewhat surprising that concerns about involuntary servitude do not have more prominence in the opinions. As one writer explained in 1921, so incontrovertible was the proposition that equity will not decree specific performance of a labor contract that "the very palpability of this

concerns in the absoluteness of the rule against compulsion of labor contracts. All the other grounds for the rule could be vitiated in unusual circumstances. Yet, as Justice Harlan put it sitting on circuit in 1894:

> The rule, we think, is without exception that equity will not compel the actual, affirmative performance by an employe [*sic*] of merely personal services, any more than it will compel an employer to retain in his personal service one who, no matter for what cause, is not acceptable to him for service of that character.[247]

Contracts of the sort involved in *Bailey* exemplify the soundness of history's verdict against compelling the performance of contracts to labor. Agriculture labor contracts differ fundamentally from contracts for the sale of goods, property, or discrete services, where the law of contract remedies sometimes compels performance: relative uncertainty almost always surrounds the laborer's undertaking. He might be asked to do pretty much anything around the farm. The work could be hard or soft, the hours long or short, the employer abusive or considerate. None of this would typically be spelled out in the contract, as it was not in Bailey's contract " 'to work and labor . . . as a farm hand.' "[248] But these unspecified aspects of the laborer's lot could spell the difference between the tolerable and the insufferable.

Criminal enforcement of a one-year contract to do farm labor poses threats to the laborer's autonomy that, though markedly different in degree, are similar to those that troubled Mill about a contract to become a slave. To compel the performance of such an open-ended contractual undertaking by subjecting breaching laborers to harsh criminal penalties would impose a nearly unlimited dominion of employer over laborer, one which the laborer in contracting could not have anticipated and undertaken in any concrete way. Airtight enforcement of such contracts invites oppression and abuse, not in extended time, as in the examples of contracts verging on slavery that caused Mill and Ackerman concern, but in the present, temporarily. The employer's dominion remains *pro tanto* a subversion of the laborer's autonomy. Justice Jackson captured the point with characteristic elegance in *Pollock* v. *Williams*:[249]

> [T]he defense against oppressive hours, pay, working conditions, or treatment is the right to change employers. When the master can com-

---

truism has tended to obscure the principle upon which it is founded." A. Stevens, "Involuntary Servitude by Injunction," *Cornel L.Q.*, 6:235, 250, 1921.

[247] Arthur v. Oakes, 63 F. 310, 318 (7th Cir. 1894).

[248] 219 U.S. 219, 229 (1911) (quoting the contract).

[249] 322 U.S. 4 (1944).

pel and the laborer cannot escape the obligation to go on, there is no power below to redress and no incentive above to relieve a harsh over-lordship or unwholesome conditions of work. Resulting depression of working conditions and living standards affects not only the laborer under the system, but every other with whom his labor comes in competition. Whatever of social value there may be, and of course it is great, in enforcing contracts and collection of debts, Congress has put it beyond debate that no indebtedness warrants a suspension of the right to be free from compulsory service. This congressional policy means that no state can make the quitting of work any component of a crime, or make criminal sanctions available for holding unwilling persons to labor.[250]

Thus Hughes' color-blind rationale for the *Bailey* decision is rooted in more than two centuries of contract law, and is an inviting guide in the philosophically and constitutionally obscure territory where freedom of contract theory and personal autonomy collide. But if Hughes' position in *Bailey* was in harmony with the received practice of contract law, as Holmes probably would have conceded, much of the rationale underlying that practice points the other way. Indeed, it can be argued that all of the factors that normally militate against specific performance of labor contracts, with the exception of servitude concerns, point the other way in the *Bailey* situation. Where an advance has been given and not repaid, employers are measurably damaged; substitute performance, even if readily available, will not cover the loss; and if the breaching laborer has no money out of which to satisfy a judgment, damages are an illusory remedy. Some courts have recognized the breaching party's insolvency to be an instance where money damages are inadequate and specific performance thus required.[251] It would surely not be an unreasonable generalization for the Alabama legislature to regard agricultural laborers as judgment-proof. If the inadequacy of damages is the touchstone of the availability of specific performance, and if the concept is realistic enough to encompass insolvency, it is hard to see why Alabama should not be able to criminalize this particular form of breach. Moreover, the reluctance of courts to supervise complex or undefined tasks is not germane when criminal punishment, rather than specific performance, is the means of compulsion. Problems of vagueness that bedevil the fashioning of an injunction to compel performance of undifferentiated labor contracts are greatly lessened when the question is simply punishment for palpable breach.

In terms of the received tradition of contract law, then, the prob-

---

[250] *Ibid.*, at 18.
[251] See generally H. Horack, "In-

solvency and Specific Performance," *Harv. L. Rev.*, 31:702, 1918.

lem posed in *Bailey* is whether the involuntary servitude objection to specific performance of general labor contracts is sufficiently strong, when none of the other grounds for reluctance to order specific performance are present, to override the inadequacy of damages concern that normally causes courts to move the system of contract remedies from a compensation to a compulsion scheme. The choice is between, on the one hand, protecting the employer against out-of-pocket loss and giving some realistic enforcement to the bargain and, on the other, subjecting the laborer to a compulsion to work that our legal tradition has balked at.

It might even be argued that in theory, Alabama's policy in giving employers a means of heavy compulsion was in the interest of laborers. As Holmes pointed out, echoing one of the dominant themes of freedom of contract theorists, the tighter and more certain the means of contract enforcement the more the laborer can exact for promises, and particularly in the way of advances. Where advances are given and not repaid, judicial invalidation of the risk allocation embodied in Alabama's criminal enforcement of these particular labor contracts almost certainly would be reflected in a readjustment of other terms in the bargain, with the consequence that advances would dry up to the extent that there would be a greater risk of their not being worked off.[252] In theory, then, invalidating the Alabama law cuts off an opportunity for those laborers who want an advance badly enough to trade their right under traditional contract law to break labor contracts with little or no real liability. This is not to claim that the Alabama law had general redistributional effects favoring workers. That question could only be answered by measuring the economic value of the presumptively greater availability of advances under the Alabama statute against the advantages of job mobility secured by the *Bailey* decision. But of course, workers who wanted that mobility could maintain it either by foregoing advances or by using a second advance from a preferred job to repay the first one. Thus, *Bailey* imposes an opportunity cost on laborers; it embodies a paternalistic principle limiting the extent to which laborers can bargain away the freedom, guaranteed them under traditional contract law, to breach contracts without the legal system's intervening to compel them to perform.[253]

---

[252] See generally D. Kennedy, "Form and Substance in Private Law Adjudication, *Harv. L. Rev.*, 89:1685, 1747, 1976.

[253] The charge of paternalism is not fatal to the soundness of the *Bailey* decision. It is paternalism in the end that underlies Mill's position, which even Holmes doubtless would have accepted, that a voluntary contract to become a slave is invalid. See generally the discussion in A. Kronman and R. Posner, *The Economics of Contract Law* (1979), 253–61.

The impact of *Bailey* on employers is hard to assess. Employers who worried about recovering advances in the absence of criminal compulsion to perform would not need to give them, of course, or they could limit their advances to laborers known to be reliable. The cost to employers is not the risk of losing advances, since that risk can be built into the bargain whatever its level of probability, but the loss of an opportunity to secure a very high expectation of performance by the *in terrorem* means of the criminal law. Some of this security can be purchased in the bargain by deferring an attractive payment until the completion of the entire performance. But not all, apparently: employers presumably thought that the Alabama rule served an important interest, since it would otherwise be hard to account for the legislature's tenacity in amending the statute repeatedly to get around the state courts' aversion to criminal liability for breach.

Although the underlying principles of contract theory are somewhat at cross-purposes in relation to the *Bailey* problem, the central lesson is surely strong support for the credibility, if not necessarily the undeniable correctness, of Hughes' elaboration of a positive, race-neutral right. Contract law has consistently denied specific enforcement of general labor contracts. The theory behind this practice has rested to a considerable extent on aversion to the infringement on individual autonomy that would result from legal compulsion to work for another, although, in the jurisprudence of contracts, so many other reasons have supported the principle that the relative weight of the servitude concern is hard to measure. John Stuart Mill and other philosophers of the liberal tradition have lent the weight of their authority to the general notion that there must be limits to the enforcement of promises if freedom of contract is not to slide into slavery. The threats to autonomy that worried them would be present, albeit only temporarily, in compulsion of the sort of contract involved in the *Bailey* case. The criminal law's tradition against punishing breach of contract, together with contract theory's dominant theme of opposing compulsion of labor contracts, is powerful testimony from the common law in favor of Hughes' construction of the Thirteenth Amendment and the federal peonage statute, and corresponding support for the sincerity of Hughes' profession that the racial aspect of peonage was irrelevant to his constitutional rationale. Holmes was clearly bucking the tide of the legal tradition.

C. THE SURPRISING ABSENCE OF APPEALS TO DEFERENCE

In view of the strong support for Hughes' majority position from traditional conceptions of Anglo-American law, the most surprising aspect of Holmes' dissent is the absence of a strong appeal to deference to the legislature in its ordering of rights and liabilities around the employment relation. Arguments based on deference are not really addressed to the analytical weight of such traditional concepts of Anglo-American law as supported Hughes' reading of the Thirteenth Amendment. Nor do they attempt in any direct way to counter the policy arguments supporting the freedom of laborers to break contracts without running into the compulsion of the criminal law. Rather the claim of deference is simply that the legislature must be able to change traditional legal principles, even the most familiar ones, for all the obvious reasons of democratic governance and institutional capacity, and, as Holmes believed, because legal doctrines reflect the struggle for dominance among antagonistic classes, and the legislature is the proper arena for that contest. Deference claims are addressed to attitudes and intuitions about judicial review, not to the analytical processes of interpretation of text and derivation of principles of individual liberty from the traditions of Anglo-American law. It is almost impossible to demonstrate that they are wrong—or right, for that matter—except perhaps in the extreme case where deference would result in swallowing entirely a constitutional guarantee. But certainly deference to the Alabama legislature in the *Bailey* case would not have overridden the core guarantees of the Thirteenth Amendment. Holmes could have been entirely persuaded that the Alabama law was completely out of harmony with traditional principles of contract and criminal law theory and still have insisted on deference as the dispositive element in constitutional interpretation. Had Holmes chosen to respond in this key, he might have rejoined for posterity that the Thirteenth Amendment did not enact Mr. John Stuart Mill's *On Liberty*, if the Alabama legislature preferred to take as its text Mr. Herbert Spencer's *Social Statics*.

Holmes' failure to appeal to deference is all the more surprising since there is no reason to suppose that deference was not an important element in his thinking in 1911. He had not yet had the provocation of the *Grandfather Clause Cases*,[254] *Buchanan* v. *Warley*,[255] the World War I free speech cases,[256] the white primary case,[257] or his most famous property deprivation opinion, *Pennsylvania Coal Co.* v. *Mahon*,[258] to develop a sense of limits on deference in the interest of constitutional guarantees. At the time of *Bailey*, about the only outlet for judicial activism was laissez-faire constitutionalism, to which Holmes had

---

[254] Guinn v. United States, 238 U.S. 347 (1915); Myers v. Anderson, 238 U.S. 368 (1915).

[255] 245 U.S. 60 (1917).

[256] Schenck v. United States, 249 U.S. 47 (1919); Abrams v. United States, 250 U.S. 616 (1919).

[257] Nixon v. Herndon, 273 U.S. 536 (1927).

[258] 260 U.S. 393 (1922).

elected to reply, as his *Lochner*[259] dissent exemplifies, not in the concessionary discourse of principled rejoinder but in disengaged insistence on legislative hegemony. There is no reason to suppose that in 1911 Holmes saw any need for limits on legislative power to regulate employment relations.

That Holmes chose to direct his *Bailey* dissent to the merits of strict contractarianism was thus a sharp departure from his usual approach of disengagement and deference, and the most plausible way of accounting for it is on the ground that Holmes did not really credit his own admonition that "the fact that Alabama [the statute] mainly concerns the blacks does not matter." Holmes seems to have thought that it mattered enough to make the usual arguments for deference to the legislature ring hollow. This would explain why he shouldered the heavy burden of defending the Alabama law's general soundness and consistency with the legal tradition, thereby seeking to negate by implication the realistic inference that the law was simply the latest version of a long series of state efforts to coerce and immobilize black agricultural workers in the South.

The absence of deference in Hughes' opinion is equally striking, especially when one recalls that Hughes was a constant supporter of legislative authority in every other constitutional controversy over freedom of contract that came to the Court during his six-year term as Associate Justice. Like Holmes, Hughes evidently saw little reason to defer to the Alabama legislative judgment in *Bailey*. In sharp contrast to the style of his other opinions dealing with legislation regulating the employment relation, Hughes' opinion in *Bailey* lacks even the kind of rhetorical concessions to legislative authority that were commonplace in the most extravagant assertions of laissez-faire constitutionalism, such as those with which Justice Peckham embroidered his *Lochner* opinion. Most tellingly, by dovetailing the Thirteenth Amendment and the open-ended congressional prohibition of peonage, taking each as an alternative ground for decision, Hughes declined to put the onus of intervention on Congress, and passed up the chance to override claims of deference owed to the Alabama legislature by bowing to the authority of the national legislature. The tone of the *Bailey* opinion is that of an utterly assured Court vindicating a clear command of the Constitution in the face of a brazen legislative effort at subversion. What intuition drove Hughes to discount the usual assumptions of deference to the Alabama legislature on a question that was at least fairly debatable as a matter of general legal theory, had there been no racial connotation to the

---

[259] Lochner v. New York, 198 U.S. 45 (1905). See generally Note, "Governor on the Bench: Charles Evans Hughes as Associate Justice," *Harv. L. Rev.*, 89:961, 969–71, 1976.

problem? Can one imagine a Hughes opinion of such uncompromising activism—and in his fledgling judicial effort in a serious case to boot— had his attitude toward the judicial function in the *Bailey* case not been shaped by the stubborn persistence of forced labor practices for black people in Alabama, a legal and historical context of racial exploitation that rendered inappropriate the usual presumption of constitutionality of legislative action?

This is not to say that Hughes was disingenuous in fashioning a neutral principle of positive right. There is no reason to doubt that Hughes thought a right to breach labor contracts without criminal liability, absent fraud in the making of the contract, was warranted, quite apart from the race-relations concerns that pointed up the need for such a right. But the judicial stance from which Hughes promulgated this neutral principle rested on a realistic appreciation of the continuing legacy of bondage for black people in the South. In their attitudes toward the judicial function in the *Bailey* case, both Hughes and Holmes revealed themselves as realists about the racist character of peonage.

The fact that each took pains to indicate that the Court's approach to peonage should not be conditioned by concerns of race may be attributed to the ennui that gripped Reconstruction principles in the first decade of the twentieth century. Appeals to racial justice had been met with prejudice or indifference in the Supreme Court for more than thirty years. But the exacting judicial scrutiny that Hughes and Holmes gave the Alabama statute, though reasoning to opposite conclusions, carried hints of judicial intervention in the sorry state of race relations in the years to come. The paradox of the *Bailey* decision, and *Reynolds* as well, is that the color-blind doctrine propounded by Hughes evidenced at once that the Court was now willing to attack the racist institution of peonage with a constitutional principle of resilient neutrality and that a race-silent approach was the best tactic to win over a majority of the Justices to the cause of intervention. One can see in the interplay of attitude and doctrine in the *Peonage Cases* the alternating rhythms of principle and prejudice that marked the work of the Supreme Court during the tenure of Chief Justice White.

VII.   The Peonage Decisions in Historical Perspective

After the *Reynolds* decision, executive concern about peonage began to abate, and in the second Wilson Administration, it lapsed into apathy. The Justice Department's enforcement energies had been sustained at a fairly high level since 1906, when Charles W. Russell launched his investigations. The second Roosevelt Administration aroused the most public notice and stirred up a hostile political reaction with its investigations and prosecutions, and Roosevelt deserves substantial credit for making peonage for the first time a major concern of the Justice Department. The Taft Administration maintained the momentum, although as the background of *Reynolds* indicates, it proceeded with more care to enlist the cooperation of state officials with less of an aura of crusading discovery. From 1907 to 1912, the Attorney General's annual reports referred to eighty or so peonage investigations by the Bureau of Investigation each year, although there were never more than a handful of indictments and few convictions. In the first Wilson Administration, investigations and prosecutions actually gained momentum slightly. McReynolds' resuscitation of the stalled *Reynolds* case reflected a general departmental vigor against peonage. The 1913 Attorney General's *Report* showed an average of seven peonage investigations per month by the Bureau of Investigation (producing some twenty-one prosecutions for the year),[260] and the 1914 *Report* indicated an average of nine per month.[261] The number of investigations and indictments was about the same in 1915.[262] After Wilson's reelection in 1916, however, the Justice Department lost interest. In 1916, the number of indictments dropped off to five.[263] The Attorney General's reports for 1917, 1918, and 1919 did not refer to peonage at all. The *Report* for 1920 referred to a number of peonage complaints, but said no prosecutions had been instituted.[264] The 1921 *Report*, however, the first by Harding's Attorney General, Harry M. Daugherty, found peonage to exist "to a shocking extent." It echoed the sentiments of Charles W. Russell fifteen years before:

> Peonage, or the holding of persons in involuntary servitude, still continues in many of the Southern States. The victims are almost always extremely poor, ignorant, and friendless. Many times it appears that county officers conspire with the employers to force these unfortunates into bondage, which is worse than outright slavery. Bureau agents have been instructed to make vigorous efforts to put a stop to this vicious practice and a number of cases have been successfully prosecuted and substantial sentences imposed. Some of the cases reported in the hundreds of reports received have been extremely aggravated and in several instances the poor victims have been murdered when it was discovered by the employer that this bureau was conducting an investigation. In such cases bureau agents have been instructed to work with the State authorities and convictions for murder have resulted

---

[260] *Report of the Attorney General of the United States: 1913* (1913), 46–47.

[261] *Report of the Attorney General of the United States: 1914* (1914), 46.

[262] *Report of the Attorney General*

of the United States: 1915 (1915), 45.

[263] *Report of the Attorney General of the United States: 1916* (1916), 59.

[264] *Report of the Attorney General of the United States: 1920* (1920), 128.

in some instances. The very helplessness of this class of citizens impels the bureau to proceed with all possible vigor and the salutary effect is beginning to appear.[265]

Peonage was a reflection of law, of the corruption of law enforcers, and of lawlessness. The White Court knocked out the main props from the "peculiar system of state laws prevailing in the South, intended evidently to compel services on the part of workingman," but much of the system of laws that Russell described remained. Vagrancy and other open-ended laws that permitted prosecution on discretion, the system of criminal and civil law administered by whites alone, and the informal web of customs that made "the petty officers of the Law—deputy sheriffs, constables, justices of the peace, and the like—an outer cordon of guards to hold the peons in slavery" were left largely untouched by *Bailey* and *Reynolds*. Out of reach entirely were the lawless supports for peonage: the violence and intimidation that infected race relations in the South; the cycle of poverty and debt that bound tenants, sharecroppers, and field hands to the land and to the landlords; and the apathy of powerless, exhausted people.

In the end, more than judicial decisions or law enforcement efforts, it was the wave of black migration northward and to the cities and the increasing demand for factory labor, both intensified by the manpower and material needs of World War I, that broke the wheel of black servitude in the South. The dark years of the Wilson Administration, when Jim Crow laws and black disfranchisement reached their highest levels, saw the beginnings of the Great Migration, which "after emancipation was the great watershed in American Negro history."[266] From 1790, when the first census was taken, to 1910, the focal area of black population had tended steadily to move south and west. The 1920 census for the first time showed the center of black population moving northeast. More than three hundred thousand blacks born in the Southeast, about 5 percent of the total black population of the area, moved away in the decade between 1910 and 1920. Over six hundred thousand left during the 1920s.[267] The constitutionally protected mobility for black workers given expression in the *Peonage Cases* found a physical analogue of far greater social force in the mobility of thousands and thousands of black people away from the aggressive racism of the New South.

---

[265] *Report of the Attorney General of the United States: 1921* (1921), 98, 132.

[266] A. Meier, *Negro Thought in America 1880–1915: Racial Ideologies in the Age of Booker T. Washington* (1963), 170, quoted in Tindall, *Emergence of the New South*.

[267] Tindall, *Emergence of the New South*, 148.

The *Peonage Cases* are a largely forgotten footnote in constitutional law, and not even that in the law of contracts. *Bailey* and *Reynolds* were staples of constitutional law casebooks in the 1920s and 1930s, but by the 1960s, a half century after the decisions, they had become only passing references in the casebooks, if that. The cases have largely dropped from view in the Supreme Court as well. Since 1944, when *Pollock* v. *Williams* was decided, *Reynolds* has not been cited at all. *Bailey* has been cited eleven times in the intervening thirty-seven years, but always on the question of the legitimacy of presumptions in shifting the burden of proof. In the law of contracts, it is fair to say, *Bailey* and *Reynolds* were never noticed as principles controlling the limits of contractual liability. Neither appears in the footnotes of Samuel Williston's exhaustive treatise on contract law, first published in 1924, nor in Arthur Corbin's later work, and the decisions are ignored in the contracts casebooks, old and new. The *Peonage Cases* are not part of the equipment of the modern lawyer, even the specialists in constitutional law or contracts.

Their historical significance to the Progressive era is another matter. *Bailey* and *Reynolds* must be counted as landmarks in the slow process of exorcising the vestiges of slavery from American law. Of all the commitments to the freedman embodied in the Thirteenth, Fourteenth, and Fifteenth amendments that came before the Supreme Court in the Progressive era, only the prohibition against involuntary servitude received unstinting, even imaginative, support.

Why the Court should set itself in firm opposition to peonage, even when dressed up as a punishment for fraud or as a humanitarian alternative to the chain gang, when its response to segregation, disfranchisement, and lily-white criminal law administration was ambivalent if not acquiescent, is a question with no clear answer. Perhaps it was because the Court had, for a time at least, an ally in the executive branch. Peonage was the only aspect of racism in American law and society that the executive branch moved against in this period. Not even lynching drew a comparable response. Peonage was also unlike the other areas of race relations law that came to the Supreme Court in this period in the extent to which white Southerners set themselves against it. Peonage was part of the fabric of Southern race relations, but it was a hidden, shameful part, not one of the proud principles of post-Reconstruction white supremacy, such as segregation or disfranchisement, which were trumpeted through Southern politics. Even the most unrestrained demagogues of racism rarely went so far as to embrace involuntary servitude. The South was disarmed from rising to the defense of peonage; there was some grumbling but no substantial adverse reaction to the Court's intervention. Of the various paths away from racial injustice open to the Supreme Court in the Progressive era, opposition to peonage was the least difficult to traverse.

No doubt the Court's firmness was in part because the principles of the *Peonage Cases* were thought to be needed to protect whites as well as blacks, and were not conceived particularly as commitments to racial justice. It is a sign of the times that the White Court made its most lasting contribution to the constitutional law of race relations in two decisions that, on the surface of their opinions, seemed to have nothing to do with race. In a period when most white people, North and South, assumed the inherent inferiority of blacks, when the segregation and disfranchisement of black people was bedrock in American politics and constitutional doctrine, and when sectional conflict was generally seen as an anachronistic obstacle to commercial community and national progress, the best chance for the constitutional progress of black people lay in the growth of principles of individual liberty that, applied neutrally and without the aim of promoting racial justice, would tend to limit how far the American South could press its vision of apartheid.

CHAPTER X

Black Disfranchisement from the KKK to the Grandfather Clause

T HE MOST DISASTROUS reversal in the condition of blacks between Reconstruction and the turn of the twentieth century concerned the right to vote. The enfranchisement of the large population of mainly illiterate former slaves and the promotion of the labor contract were the twin pillars of the radical program for the freedmen. Both an extraordinary commitment of faith in equality and democracy and an expedient to support the Republican party, black suffrage bore the incubus of its partisan origins. It was certain not only that most Southern whites would view it as a cynical Republican contrivance, but also that many Republicans would put aside their commitment when the sense of party advantage shifted.[1] When change came, it was precipitous. In 1880, a majority of black males in the Southern states voted, and voted Republican in opposition to the white Democratic regimes. Ten years later, the black vote was greatly reduced, though it was still numerous enough to swing close elections. By the turn of the century, it was virtually eradicated, and it would languish in this state until the second half of the twentieth century.[2] The disfranchisement of black people for more than a half century, despite the command of the Fifteenth Amend-

---

[1] C. V. Woodward, *The Burden of Southern History* (1960). An account that suggests white Southerners' attitudes toward black enfranchisement during Reconstruction is P. Lewinson, *Race, Class and Party* (1932), 3–60. The classic account from the white supremacist point of view is W. Dunning, *Essay on the Civil War and Reconstruction* (1965), 353.

[2] For excellent brief discussions, see G. Fredrickson, *White Supremacy* (1981), 184 *et seq.*; Woodward, *Burden of Southern History,* 71 *et seq.*

ment, is one of American history's most formidable challenges to the efficacy and integrity of the concept of constitutional law.

I. *The Constitutional Anomaly of Disfranchisement*

For the white South, the task of eliminating black suffrage posed two serious problems, one external and constitutional, the other internal and political. The constitutional difficulty was how to deprive blacks of the vote without saying so; explicit state laws would force the federal courts to abide by the promise of the Fifteenth Amendment. Buttressing the constitutional barrier were federal statutes regulating elections. These statutes, mostly derived from the Civil Rights Act of 1870, had been enacted precisely to ensure the vote for the freedmen. The political difficulty grew out of the constitutional one; the subterfuges advanced to solve the constitutional problem had the potential to ensnare many whites as well as blacks. Property, literacy, good understanding, or good character tests could normally or by administrative manipulation exclude virtually all black voters, but poor, unschooled whites also had good reason to fear these disfranchising mechanisms. As the end of Reconstruction and the upsurge of agrarian radicalism brought the deep divisions among whites to the surface of Southern politics, black voting, and the mechanisms of its elimination, became a prime focus of contention among factions of Southern whites.

The so-called "Grandfather Clause" was the main contrivance for assuring distrustful poor whites that their rights would not be affected by the program of black disfranchisement that swept through the South around the turn of the century. A loophole was needed through which whites but not blacks could pass to avoid the disfranchising tests, one that would not explicitly contravene the Fifteenth Amendment, that was not quite airtight in its operation, and that permitted at least a lame nonracial rationalization to be conjured up. The cynical pretension of the Grandfather Clause was that property, literacy, or other voter qualifications need not be met by males who had voted before 1867 or had served in the military in the Civil War or in certain earlier wars or who were descended from such persons. Descendants were deemed to possess by inheritance the qualities of civic interest and responsibility of their voting or fighting forebears. Since very few blacks voted before 1867, and none at all in the South, and few had ever served in the military, virtually no blacks would pass through the Grandfather Clause. Most whites, by contrast, were able to meet one of the requirements. The approach was not subtle, but subtlety was not thought to be required.

The Grandfather Clause was thus the distillation of the constitutional and political tensions surrounding black disfranchisement around the turn of the century. More than that, it was the richest example of the ludicrous legal machinations that came out of the Progressive era's unstable mix of reformist rationalism as a mode of racial prejudice, commitment to the reconciliation of North and South and the elimination of "The Negro Question" as a bone of sectional contention, and growing adherence to the ideal of constitutional principle and to the Supreme Court as its anointed guardian. The fate of the Grandfather Clause and the other disfranchising methods that offered themselves for judgment mark critical vantage points for surveying the collision of prejudice and principle in the Supreme Court's race relations decisions during the Progressive era. Thus, when the Grandfather Clause came before the Supreme Court in 1913, it served as well to focus the general questions whether the Supreme Court under Chief Justice Edward Douglass White would reverse or carry forward the repudiation of the Civil War amendments that had taken place during the Chief Justiceships of Morrison Waite and especially Melville Weston Fuller; whether judicial activism in the protection of property and freedom of contract would engender protection for political liberty and civil equality; and whether the Supreme Court could shoulder any burden of constitutional responsibility for the civil and political rights of black people at a time when the political branches were committed to racial separation and political exclusion.

In relation to disfranchisement, these were by no means idle questions in the later part of the Progressive era. Although hindsight has tended to regard the Supreme Court's invalidation of the Grandfather Clause as virtually inevitable, there are many respects in which the Court's action was downright surprising. The Court had previously taken a hands-off attitude toward the political thicket of disfranchisement, in line with the overriding consensus North and South that black voting meant only corruption of elections, incompetence of government, and the engendering of fierce racial antagonisms. Reinforcing these views were prevailing structural conceptions of federalism that placed voting and elections at the core of state sovereignty. Congress had reflected these currents in wiping from the book all the laws left over from Reconstruction that explicitly authorized federal intervention into state officials' handling of voting in state elections, leaving only rather vague and open-ended provisions that almost certainly were not understood to countenance judicial oversight of state regulation of voting qualifications. Since the *Grandfather Clause Cases* came up under these residual statutes, there were serious statutory barriers to judicial intervention that had to be passed before the constitutional issues were ripe for decision. Even these issues, viewed in isolation, were far from certain in outcome. In no case had the Supreme Court ever given the Fifteenth Amendment positive application, and several decisions had strongly hinted that the whole matter of disfranchisement was beyond the judiciary's ken. The Amendment itself was generally regarded in the Progressive era as a misguided and rather embarrassing hangover of Reconstruction radicalism, best ignored or shunted aside by all the federal government, including the courts. Its low estate was captured with deft humor in the pages of the *Harvard Law Review* in an article published in 1910 entitled "Is the Fifteenth Amendment Void?" the opening page of which (see insert following page 814) is a revealing guide to the temper of the times.

A. THE BACKGROUND OF FEDERAL LAW

Whether blacks should be admitted to the political community of white males was a matter of dispute after the Civil War, even among elements of the victorious Republican North. Initial Republican ambivalence about black voting, and perhaps federalism concerns as well, is revealed in the Fourteenth Amendment's suffrage provision, which was intended to induce (not compel) voting rights for blacks in the South (but not in the North) by reducing the congressional representation of states in proportion to the number of adult males barred from the polls. As this effort bore no fruit and as the impracticality of military rule of the South became evident, the radical program for black voting turned to constitutional compulsion.

Even this step was halting, however. Rather than enfranchising all male citizens, the Fifteenth Amendment, adopted in 1870, was cast in negative terms.[3] States were forbidden to deny the vote "on account of race, color, or previous condition of servitude," but that left the states with a wide field for evasion. As Senator Oliver Morton of Indiana pointed out:

> This amendment leaves the whole power in the States just as it exists now, except that colored men shall not be disfranchised for the three reasons of race, color, or previous condition of slavery. They may be disfranchised for want of education or for want of intelligence. . . . [P]roperty or educational tests . . . would cut off the great majority of colored men from voting in those States, and thus this amendment would be practically defeated in all those States where the great body of the colored people live.[4]

Within three decades, Morton's despairing prediction came to pass.

Conscious of its frailty, Congress bolstered the Fifteenth Amend-

---

[3] The Amendment also was cut back to protect only against discrimination denying the right to vote, and not other rights in the electoral process, such as the right relating to candidacy or nomination. See generally J. Pole, *The Pursuit of Equality in American History* (1978), 168.

[4] *Ibid.*, 173.

ment in the year of its adoption with the multiple provisions of the Civil Rights Act of 1870.[5] The fate of these statutes, both in the Supreme Court and in subsequent Congresses, had as critical an impact on the political rights of blacks as any constitutional provision. Several sections of the 1870 Act dealt explicitly with the right to vote in all elections, punishing discriminatory administration of voting qualifications; wrongful refusal to count or give effect to votes; and prevention of anyone from voting by force, bribery, threats, deprivation of employment, ejectment from land or houses, or refusal to renew labor contracts. Violations of these provisions could result in punishment by a fine of up to $500, and imprisonment of not less than one month or more than one year. There were, in addition, several provisions dealing only with congressional elections, punishing illegal voting and violent or corrupt prevention of lawful voting.

There were also two highly important open-ended provisions. Section 6, known as the Ku Klux Klan provision, stated that

> if two or more persons shall band or conspire together, or go in disguise upon the public highway, or upon the premises of another, with intent to violate any provisions of this act, or to injure, oppress, threaten, or intimidate any citizen with intent to prevent or hinder his free exercise and enjoyment of any right or privilege granted or secured to him by the Constitution or laws of the United States,

they should be fined up to $5,000 and imprisoned up to ten years.[6] This was a much more severe penalty than those provided for the franchise offenses. The other catch-all criminal provision, section 17 of the 1870 Act, was carried forward from the 1866 Civil Rights Act,[7] and it punished acting "under color of law" to take away rights secured by the 1866 Act, essentially contract and property rights, rights to sue and give evidence, and rights dealing with personal safety.[8] In 1871, Congress further bolstered the right to vote in congressional elections by detailed statutes requiring federal judges to appoint supervisors of elections to oversee registration and voting and to remain available to review alleged franchise offenses during elections.[9]

Since almost all the provisions of the 1870 and 1871 Acts dealing explicitly with voting would eventually be repealed or cut down by the Supreme Court, the application of the catch-all provisions to franchise

---

[5] 16 Stat. 140 (1870) (repealed by 28 Stat. 36 [1894]).

[6] The reenacted version in the 1870 Civil Rights Act is at 16 Stat. 141, 144 (1871).

[7] 14 Stat. 27 (1866) (Sec. 9 repealed by 71 Stat. 637 [1957]).

[8] 16 Stat. 141, 144 (1871).

[9] Ibid., at 433.

offenses would assume first importance. As enacted, section 17, protecting rights originating in the 1866 Act, surely did not protect voting rights, since the 1866 Act did not deal with the right to vote at all. Whether voting rights were protected by section 6 of the 1870 Act, punishing conspiracies to injure or intimidate persons from exercising or enjoying any right or privilege granted or secured by the Constitution or laws of the United States, was more problematic, although there was much pointing against such coverage. The language of section 6 was surely broad enough to protect the right to vote without discrimination. But since early provisions of the Act explicitly protected voting rights, and provided for lesser penalties, why would Congress punish deprivations of the right to vote more severely in section 6? It could not easily be argued that section 6 was needed to reach *conspiracies* to deprive persons of voting rights, as opposed to individual violations covered by the earlier provisions, because one of the earlier sections reached such conspiracies, but subjected them to the lesser penalties. In the second place, the language of section 6 was clearly directed to violent intimidation by groups such as the Ku Klux Klan. Nonviolent deprivations of the right to vote, as for example by state officials enforcing literacy or other voter qualifications in a discriminatory way, might not be covered, even if violence against would-be voters was. The question whether the statutory successor to section 6 applied to deprivation by state officials of the right to vote would eventually be answered in the affirmative by the Supreme Court in *United States* v. *Mosley*,[10] decided in 1915 along with the *Grandfather Clause Cases*, and the answer given to the statutory question would reveal quite as much about the Court's attitude to black suffrage as the more famous constitutional decisions. The statutory resolution was indeed a predicate of the constitutional discussion.

The Supreme Court first encountered the statutes protecting the right to vote in 1875, when it limited effective federal protection and helped bring down the curtain on Reconstruction. *United States* v. *Reese*[11] invalidated sections of the 1870 Civil Rights Act broadly punishing deprivations of the right to vote in all elections, whether racially motivated or not. These sections went beyond Congress' power, the Court held, because the Fifteenth Amendment "does not confer the right of suffrage upon any one," and only guards against denials of the right to vote on the basis of race. The Court, arguing that the sections were expressly general, declined to limit the statutes by construction to racially motivated franchise offenses, which were within Congress' power to punish under the Fifteenth Amendment.[12]

---

[10] 238 U.S. 383 (1915).
[11] 92 U.S. 214, 217 (1875).
[12] This approach was certainly de-

fensible, but Chief Justice Waite's opinion revealed a general hostility to federal intervention in state elections.

The other 1875 decision that, by implication, cut back federal statutes protecting the right to vote in state elections was *United States v. Cruikshank.*[13] *Cruikshank* involved a celebrated instance of violence in the waning stages of Reconstruction. The legal question presented was whether section 6 of the 1870 Act would support convictions of more than one hundred persons charged with intimidating and killing blacks because of their exercise of various rights, including voting in state elections in Louisiana. The approach of the Court was that except with respect to a narrow class of "attributes of national citizenship," such as the right to petition Congress, and perhaps the right to vote in federal elections, Congress had no power to protect constitutionally secured rights from private violence or interference.[14] This left the right to vote in state elections in the grip of terror, at least so far as federal law was concerned.

Before the 1870 Civil Rights Act, he pointed out, the states controlled all aspects of all elections, and the Act, "a radical change in the practice . . . should be explicit in its terms. Nothing should be left to construction, if it can be avoided." 92 U.S. at 219.

Waite's opinion included language often cited on the problem of when the Court should embark on a narrowing construction of a statute to cure its constitutional overbreadth.

> It would certainly be dangerous if the legislature could set a net large enough to catch all possible offenders, and leave it to the courts to step inside and say who could be rightfully detained, and who should be set at large. This would, to some extent, substitute the judicial for the legislative department of the government. . . .
> To limit this statute in the manner now asked for would be to make a new law, not to enforce an old one. This is no part of our duty.

Ibid., at 221.

[13] 92 U.S. 542 (1875).
[14] Technically, the counts of the indictments relating to lynching blacks who voted were dismissed for failure

to charge that the reason for the crime was the race of the victims, but the Court's reasoning went much further. The Fourteenth Amendment, reasoned the Court, "adds nothing to the rights of one citizen as against another." *Ibid.,* at 554. The implication of this for federal protection of black voters against private violence was clear, because the Fifteenth Amendment's prohibition against racial discrimination in voting was also directed to the states. And so the Court eventually made clear in James v. Bowman, 190 U.S. 127 (1903), when it invalidated a section of the Civil Rights Act of 1870 that prohibited bribing or intimidating anyone attempting to vote "to whom that right is guaranteed by the Fifteenth Amendment." Since the section was not limited to official interference, it was declared beyond Congress' power. The fact that the alleged bribery occurred in a congressional election did not save the statute as applied to federal elections because the statute expressly applied to all elections, reasoned the Court, following the same approach as in United States v. Reese, 92 U.S. 214 (1875); see also United States v. Harris, 106 U.S. 629 (1882).

In limiting Congress, general power to protect the right to vote in state

X: *Black Disfranchisement*

Judicial and legislative withdrawal went hand in hand. First, the codification of federal law in the Revised Statutes of 1873 scattered the civil rights provisions throughout various titles in a way that, as Francis Biddle later said, "effectively concealed the whole scheme for the protection of rights established by the three [Civil War] amendments and five [Civil Rights] acts."[15] Then, in 1878, Congress barred the use of the army to police elections. Republican proposals for federal supervision of federal elections were defeated in 1888 and 1890. The final serious Republican effort of this kind, the Lodge Bill, was defeated in 1891, the year after the Mississippi Constitutional Convention sought to deny blacks the vote.[16] In 1892, the election of Grover Cleveland and a Democratic Congress, on a platform denouncing federal interference in state elections, brought full retreat, and in 1894, Congress repealed all the sections of the 1870 and 1871 Civil Rights Acts providing for federal supervision of elections, or federal remedies for franchise offenses, leaving on the books only naked declarations of the right to vote, unsupported by proper remedies.[17] At this point, Republicans abandoned the cause of black rights, derided as the politics of the bloody shirt, convinced that only a national party, including Southern whites, could compete with the Democrats.

There is no question that Congress in 1894 thought it was pulling the federal courts entirely out of the business of supervising voter registration and polling. The focus of the House committee report, adopted also by the Senate committee, was on getting rid of federal supervisors and marshals at the polls, but the premises were more sweeping. "Let every trace of the reconstruction measures be wiped from the statute books, let the States of this great Union understand that the elections are in their own hands," declaimed the House report. It pledged that

---

elections to preventing only official interference based on race, the Court did not cast doubt on Congress' general power to protect voters in federal elections. In *Ex parte* Yarbrough, 110 U.S. 651 (1884), the Court held, in a celebrated prosecution of Georgia racial violence brought by Emory Speer, then U. S. Attorney and later, as a federal district judge, a controversial foe of peonage and the chain gang, see discussion pp. 849 *et seq., supra,* that Congress had power to protect voters in federal elections from private violence or corruption, whether racially animated or not, and

had done so in a provision of the 1870 Civil Rights Act prohibiting interference with lawful voters in federal elections. See also *Ex parte* Siebold, 100 U.S. 371 (1879).

[15] F. Biddle, "Civil Rights and Federal Law," in *Safeguarding Civil Liberty Today* (1945), 131.

[16] R. Logan, *The Betrayal of the Negro* (1965), 70–78.

[17] 28 Stat. 36 (1894). On the Republicans' abandonment of the political rights of black people, see S. Hirshon, *Farewell to the Bloody Shirt: Northern Republicans and the Southern Negro, 1877–93* (1962).

the repeal would "eliminate the judiciary from the political arena."[18] The constitutional premises of the 1894 repeal were frankly at odds with the Fifteenth Amendment, as the minority reports of both the House and Senate committees made clear in futile protest. Congress' withdrawal from federal protection for voting rights was completed at about the time that the Southern states embarked on a sweeping program to eradicate black suffrage.

B. DISFRANCHISEMENT AND AMERICAN POLITICS

Black voting in the South after the Civil War had always been threatened by terror, fraud, and chicanery, but the decade of the 1890s saw the development of systematic methods of exclusion. During Reconstruction, Southern resistance to black voting was carried by night riders, "bull-dozers," the Ku Klux Klan, and other white-supremacist terrorist groups. Blacks voted in large numbers during Reconstruction, nevertheless. Even the withdrawal of federal troops in 1877 and the final collapse of interracial state governments did not bring an end to black voting. The Redeemers, as the conservative Democrats who controlled politics in the South after Reconstruction were known, for a time acquiesced in black voting and even, to the dismay of the "straight-out" elements of Southern Democracy, permitted fusion movements and token black office-holders. But the conservatives' willingness to permit black political participation was increasingly soured with self-interested political manipulation. Blacks voted in the 1880s amid a growing welter of administrative obstructions. Polling places might be located far from black communities, or moved without notice. Ballots were made confusing and long; intricate separate ballots and ballot boxes would force even sophisticated voters into dependence on election officials. Disfranchising and control devices also appeared in the statutes of many Southern states in the 1870s and 1880s. Poll taxes of a dollar or two, with registration well in advance of elections, coupled with requirements that certificates be preserved and presented at election time, weeded out large numbers of potential voters. Petty larceny was made a suffrage disqualification. Property qualifications and literacy tests were enacted, as well as lengthy residency requirements.[19] In many of the Southern states, these devices succeeded in cutting the black vote by half or even more. Nevertheless, many blacks continued to vote in this period, or at least many black votes were counted, usually to bolster the

---

[18] *Repeal of Federal Election Laws,* H.R. Rep. No. 18, 53rd Cong., 1st Sess. (1893), 7–8; S. Rep. No. 113, 53rd Cong., 2nd Sess. (1893), 2.

[19] See generally Lewinson, *Race, Class and Party,* 66 et seq.; J. Kousser, *The Shaping of Southern Politics* (1974), 40.

strength of the lowland planters against the farmers of the Piedmont, but increasingly blacks voted at the sufferance of the whites in charge.

In the 1880s, the discordant interests of Southern whites, temporarily muted during the struggles of Reconstruction, increasingly come to the surface as the Redeemers' conservative economic policies and relaxed racial paternalism became caught in the storms of agrarian radicalism and class resentment triggered by agricultural depression. One of the struggles that emerged centered on the statutory and administrative obstructions to voting. For one thing, most of these devices, especially the poll tax and literary qualifications, could be turned against poor, illiterate whites as well as blacks. And agrarian radicals came to see that the disfranchising devices permitted the conservatives to enlist black votes when needed. Some Southern radicals even went so far as to challenge the concept of white political supremacy itself and made common cause with black voters.[20]

In the state elections of the 1880s and early 1890s, the conservatives, faced with the alarming prospect of interracial radicalism, bought, intimidated, and fraudulently ran up huge majorities of black voters in lowland counties throughout the deep South in order to beat back the agrarian Populists. At the same time, the conservatives loosed a savage propaganda campaign of race hatred and sectional chauvinism, and even fanned the flames of mob violence, to distract white farmers from their political and economic grievances. In defeat, the Populists capitulated, for the most part, to red-shirt Negrophobia. There is considerable historical dispute about whether disfranchisement originated more in the upland strongholds of agrarian populism or in the lowland areas where blacks were most populous and white planters were ascendant.[21] In any event, as blacks were beset by all shades of the white political spectrum, their right of political participation was the most tempting target; disfranchisement would rededicate Southern Democracy to its central commitment, paper over differences among whites by appeals to white solidarity, and eliminate the menace of black Republicanism.

The forces of white supremacy found support in Progressive reform energies. To Southern Progressives, and many above the Mason-Dixon line as well, disfranchisement and electoral reform were sides of the same coin. Ending black suffrage was conceived as restricting the vote to persons capable of appreciating "the complex problems of modern life," cleansing Southern elections of disgraceful levels of corruption,

---

[20] See Kousser, *Shaping of Southern Politics.*

[21] *Compare* Kousser, *Shaping of Southern Politics,* with Woodward, *Origin of the New South.* See gener-

ally J. Franklin, *From Slavery to Freedom* (1974), 269; L. Harlan, *Separate and Unequal* (1968), 400; C. V. Woodward, *The Strange Career of Jim Crow* (1957), 56 *et seq.*

and eliminating potential allies of poor whites in Populist movements that might resist progressive change.[22] When Ray Stannard Baker wrote that the "good citizens" of Springfield, Ohio, complained that the "venal Negro vote went to the highest bidder," and that "Negroes make themselves conspicuous and obnoxious at primaries and elections, standing around, waiting, and refusing to vote until they receive money in hand," he expressed the Progressives' common excuse for Southern disfranchisement:

> [T]he Negroes of Springfield are disfranchised as absolutely as they are anywhere in the South. . . . [A] purchased voter is a disfranchised voter. The Negroes have no more real voice in the government of Springfield than they have in the government of Savannah or New Orleans. In the South the Negro has been disfranchised by law or by intimidation: in the North by cash. Which is worse?[23]

The Progressives' devotion to imperial adventures abroad further imperiled their moral capacity to object to the exclusion of black people from participation in American democracy. "As America shouldered the White Man's Burden she took up at the same time many Southern attitudes on the subject of race," C. Vann Woodward has well said.[24] And the reverse was just as true. The Big Stick, Dollar Diplomacy, and military interventions were the hallmarks of Northern Progressives' foreign policy, as William E. Leuchtenburg has shown; they "readily accepted the notion that the little brown brother was a ward of the United States, not fit for self-government, because they regarded the southern Negro as a ward when they did not think of him as a corrupt politician attempting to sell his vote to the highest bidder at Republican conventions."[25] Theodore Roosevelt captured the connection between racism at home and imperialism abroad in campaigning against William Jennings Bryan in 1900:

> Mr. Bryan and his associates cannot say enough about the "consent of the governed" doctrine as applying to the Philippines. They dwell

---

[22] Fredrickson, *White Supremacy*, 277; Woodward, *Strange Career of Jim Crow*, 66. See generally A. Stone, "Spectre is Haunting Progressivism," *J. Libertarian Studies*, 3:239, 1979 (reduced public participation in policy making was a general feature of the Progressive movement); R. Hofstadter, *The Age of Reform* (1955), 175 *et seq.*; L. McGraw, "The Progressive Legacy," in L. Gould, ed., *The Progressive Era* (1974), 194.

[23] R. S. Baker, *Following the Color Line* (1964), 202–203.

[24] Woodward, *Strange Career of Jim Crow*, 54.

[25] W. E. Leuchtenburg, "Progressivism and Imperialism: The Progressive Movement and American Foreign Policy, 1898–1916," *Miss. Valley Hist. Rev.*, 39:483, 498, 1952. See also H. Aptheker, *Toward Negro Freedom* (1956), 88.

upon the fact that "no man is good enough to govern another." In North Carolina, and other Southern States, we see before our eyes the process of the disfranchisement of the negro. We see before our eyes the black man governed without his consent by the white man. Be it remembered too, that the men thus disfranchised have always been Mr. Bryan's fellow citizens, most of them born as free as he was born. If our opponents are sincere they must necessarily denounce what has been done in North Carolina with even more bitterness than they have shown in denouncing what has been done in the Philippines. They say that in the Philippines one man is not entitled to govern another, even when the one does so only to protect the other from the rule of a savage oligarchy until he grows able to protect himself. It is a matter of astonishment that such doctrine can be either uttered or listened to without laughter, when it is spoken by and to men who go to their candidate pledging him the votes of their States, because in these States these very men do govern other men without their consent. Until our opponents have removed the beam from their own eye, by applying their "consent of the governed" doctrine at home, let them hold their peace about the Tagal bandits to whom their words give fresh heart to shoot down our soldiers in the Far Eastern archipelago.[26]

Northern Progressives were driven to embrace Southern attitudes toward race, and especially disfranchisement, in countering criticism of American policy in the Philippines and elsewhere. "No Republican leader, not even Governor Roosevelt," exulted Senator Benjamin R. ("Pitchfork Ben") Tillman of South Carolina, "will now dare to wave the bloody shirt and preach a crusade against the South's treatment of the negro. The North has a bloody shirt of its own. Many thousands of them have been made into shrouds for murdered Filipinos, done to death because they were fighting for liberty."[27]

C. THE ERADICATION OF THE BLACK VOTE

Mississippi set the course of the decade when in 1890, the highpoint of the agrarian revolt, the Mississippi Constitutional Convention produced amendments that the historian William A. Dunning termed without overstatement a "bold and undisguised attack on negro suffrage."[28] Under these amendments, a two- or three-dollar annual poll

---

[26] H. Hagedorn, ed., *The Works of Theodore Roosevelt* (1926), 14:384.

[27] Woodward, *Strange Career of Jim Crow,* 55–56. The common paternalistic justification for imperialism, that it brought the splendor of American constitutionalism to "primitive peoples," might have supported a distinction between imperialism abroad and racism at home, but Progressives did not try to press this possibility.

[28] Dunning, *Civil War and Reconstruction,* 379.

tax was required for registration, which took place months ahead of elections; receipts for poll taxes for two years past had to be produced at polling time. Two years' residency in the state and one year in the election district was made a qualification. The list of disfranchising crimes was broadened. To these restrictions, which would indeed exclude many blacks automatically, were added tests open to invidious manipulation. Voters were required to "be able to read and write any section of the Constitution of this State and give a reasonable interpretation thereof to the county registrar," and to demonstrate "a reasonable understanding of the duties and obligations of citizenship."[29] There was little dissembling about the purpose of these devices. As the Mississippi Supreme Court later put it in a revealing opinion, the 1890 convention "swept the circle of expedients to obstruct the exercise of suffrage by the negro race. . . . Restrained by the federal constitution from discriminating against the negro race, the convention discriminated against its characteristics and the offenses to which its weaker members were prone."[30]

The potential of the "Mississippi Plan" to victimize poor whites as well as blacks under its poll tax and elastc literary and civic understanding provisions eventually led to the Grandfather Clause. However, the absence of such a loophole did not defeat the disfranchisement program in Mississippi, where blacks made up about 56 percent of the population, or in South Carolina, where blacks were also in the majority, and which followed the Mississippi Plan in 1895 by adding a requirement of literacy or ownership of $300 worth of property.[31] But when Louisiana, where blacks made up about 43 percent of the population, called a convention in 1898 to take up disfranchising amendments, the objection that the Mississippi Plan could take the vote away from illiterate whites as well as blacks threatened to deadlock the convention. Aiming, in the words of the New Orleans Times-Democrat, "at placing every white voter on the poll list and keeping out nearly every negro, without violating the Federal Constitution,"[32] the Louisiana convention contrived the first Grandfather Clause: males entitled to vote before 1867, their

---

[29] Miss. Const. of 1890, secs. 241–44. See generally Lewinson, Race, Class and Party, 80.

[30] Ratcliff v. Beale, 74 Miss. 247, 266, 20 So. 865, 868 (1896). In explanation of the disfranchising crimes, the Mississippi Supreme Court noted that blacks were "given rather to furtive offenses than to the robust crimes of the whites." Ibid., at 266. Of the poll tax the court said: "Payment of taxes for two years at or before a date fixed many months anterior to an election is another requirement, and one well calculated to disqualify the careless." Ibid., at 266.

[31] Kousser, Shaping of Southern Politics, 91.

[32] J. W. Sumners, "The 'Grandfather Clause,'" Lawyer & Banker & South. Bench & Bar Rev., 7:39, 40, 1914.

sons and grandsons over twenty-one, and foreign-born naturalized males over twenty-one were permitted to register before September 1, 1898, without meeting the literacy or property requirements.[33] The loophole opened by the clause was temporary, although once registered, one stayed eligible. As in Mississippi, there was no hiding the racist purpose. Lieutenant Governor Snyder spoke the sentiments behind the Grandfather Clause when he said at the convention that he was in favor of the proposition that every white man shall vote because he is white, and no black man shall vote, because he is black. We cannot put in law these words, said Snyder, but the result could be attained.[34]

North Carolina followed Louisiana's example in 1900, and the next year Alabama added its version of the Grandfather Clause. "What they want is a scheme pure and simple which will let every white man vote and prevent any Negro from voting," reported the *Birmingham Age-Herald* about the delegates at the Alabama Constitutional Convention of 1901. With an engaging literalism, the delegates fretted even about the efficacy of the Grandfather Clause because "there are in Alabama as in all the States, large numbers of Negroes, who . . . could nevertheless easily establish the identity of white fathers or grandfathers."[35] To meet this difficulty, the drafters of the Alabama version of the clause required that descendants must be "lawful" and converted the provision to an "Old Soldiers" Clause: those who had fought in the Civil War or certain earlier wars and their lawful descendants could register without meeting literacy and property requirements.[36]

Virginia's Grandfather Clause, modeled after Alabama's, was added to the state constitution in 1902, accompanied by assurances to the Virginia Constitutional Convention of 1901–1902 by the author, Carter Glass, later United States Senator, that "discrimination within the letter of the law . . . with a view to the elimination of every Negro voter who can be gotten rid of" was the purpose of the provisions.[37] Georgia put in its Grandfather Clause in 1908, and in the same year, Maryland authorized municipalities to adopt local Grandfather Clauses for local elections.[38]

Not all the Southern states resorted to the full array of franchise restrictions. Florida, Tennessee, Arkansas, and Texas found the poll tax

---

[33] La. Const. of 1898, art. 197, sec. 5.

[34] A. M. Eaton, "The Suffrage Clause in the New Constitution of Louisiana," *Harv. L. Rev.*, 13:279, 281, 1899.

[35] *Birmingham Age-Herald*, June 5, July 12, July 17, 1901 (quoted in Lewinson, *Race, Class and Party*, 84).

[36] For an instructive account of the Grandfather Clause by a supporter of disfranchisement, see Sumners, " 'Grandfather Clause.' "

[37] Quoted in Lewinson, *Race, Class and Party*, 86.

[38] See generally G. Stephenson, *Race Distinctions in American Law* (1910), 305 *et seq.*

sufficient, coupled with confusing multiple ballot box and secret-ballot laws. Moreover, in case direct restrictions failed, another of progressivism's reforms, the political primary, lent itself in the one-party South to excluding blacks from political participation. The "white primary" would prove an effective instrument for racial hegemony, and one stubbornly resistent to constitutional challenge.[39]

The effect of these instruments of racial exclusion was nothing short of spectacular. In Louisiana, for example, more than 130,000 blacks, a majority in twenty-six parishes, voted in 1896 in the last national election before the disfranchising measures. Even discounting fraud, this was significant political participation. In 1900, two years after the new state constitution was drafted, only 5,320 blacks were registered, with no parish having a black majority.[40] By 1904, the number was down to 1,342.[41] In Alabama, after the new constitutional provisions of 1900 went into effect, only 3,000 blacks were registered out of an eligible population of more than 180,000.[42]

The Grandfather Clause did not prevent the disfranchising of many poor or illiterate whites as well. None of the clauses exempted voters from paying poll taxes, and complex ballot procedures remained a snare for the illiterate.[43] But compared with the systematic eradication of black voting in the South, the disfranchisement of poor whites was sporadic and discretionary.

Political exclusion was only the most obvious aspect of a complex movement of racism. Disfranchisement excluded blacks from the jury rolls, since most states selected jury panels from the lists of registered voters, and thus political proscription reinforced the lily-white bias of the administration of justice.[44] Jim Crow laws swept across virtually every aspect of Southern life in this period. Racial lynching, mob violence, terrorism by white vigilante groups, cheered on by the press and Southern demagogues vying with each other in their rhetoric of race chauvinism, created a savage state of racial intimidation around the turn of the century.[45]

---

[39] The progression of white primary cases was: Nixon v. Herndon, 273 U.S. 536 (1927); Nixon v. Condon, 286 U.S. 73 (1932); Grovey v. Townsend, 295 U.S. 45 (1935); Smith v. Allwright, 321 U.S. 649 (1944); Terry v. Adams, 345 U.S. 461 (1953).

[40] Lewinson, *Race, Class and Party,* 81.

[41] Woodward, *Strange Career of Jim Crow,* 68.

[42] Franklin, *From Slavery to Freedom,* 274.

[43] See generally A. Kirwan, *Revolt of the Rednecks* (1964), 64–84; Kousser, *Shaping of Southern Politics,* 72–82.

[44] See generally G. Myrdal, *An American Dilemma* (1944), 524 *et seq.*

[45] See generally Woodward, *Strange Career of Jim Crow;* C. V. Woodward, *Origin of the New South, 1877–1913* (1971), 393.

II. The Supreme Court's Response to "A Fraud Upon the Constitution of the United States"

A. THE COURT'S INITIAL HESITANCY

The Supreme Court's response to black disfranchisement was to confess judicial impotence. The Court handed down three opinions between 1898 and 1904 that were a judicial parallel to Congress' repeal in 1894 of the statutes calling for federal oversight of elections and franchise practices. The result was to disarm the Fifteenth Amendment.

Williams v. *Mississippi*,[46] an 1898 decision that was as fundamental a support for legalized white supremacy as *Plessy* v. *Ferguson*, brought before the Court the disfranchising provisions of the Mississippi Constitution of 1890, though in a roundabout way. Under Mississippi law, officials were to use lists of registered voters "as a guide" in choosing as jurors "qualified persons of good intelligence, sound judgment and fair character."[47] A black man indicted and convicted of murder by all-white grand and petit juries complained that his indictment should have been quashed, that his case should have been removed to federal court, and that his conviction denied his constitutional rights because blacks were routinely excluded from Mississippi juries. The reason for this exclusion, he insisted, was that voter registration under the 1890 Mississippi Constitution was "but a scheme . . . to abridge the suffrage of the colored electors."[48] The literacy and good understanding tests "vest in the administrative officers the full power . . . to ask all sorts of vain, impertinent questions . . . this officer can reject whomsoever he chooses, and register whomsoever he chooses. . . ."[49] All his motions were denied by the Mississippi courts, and the Supreme Court was unanimous in rejecting his claims. There was no "sufficient allegation of an evil and discriminating administration."[50] The Mississippi Constitution and statutes "do not on their face discriminate between the races, and it has not been shown that their actual administration was evil, only that evil was possible under them."[51] But the Court made clear that claims of discriminatory administration would not have a hospitable reception. It noted pointedly that in order to justify removal from a state to a federal court of a case in which equal civil rights were allegedly denied, "such denial must be the result of the constitution or laws of the State, not of the administration of them."[52] The Court stopped short of stating that in direct review of state cases, discriminatory

---

[46] 170 U.S. 213 (1898).

[47] Miss. Code Ann. Sec. 2358 (1892).

[48] 170 U.S. at 214.

[49] *Ibid.*, at 221. Portions of the com-

plaint are quoted in the Supreme Court's opinion, *ibid.*, at 214, 221.

[50] *Ibid.*, at 222.

[51] *Ibid.*, at 225.

[52] *Ibid.*, at 219.

administration against blacks could not ground a constitutional violation, but its drift was unmistakable.[53] The principle of *Yick Wo* v. *Hopkins*[54] would be limited to cases where discriminatory administration was systematic and shown by evidence so conclusive as to amount virtually to a confession by the state authorities. The Court also dismissed the argument that the legislative purpose of the Mississippi amendments should invalidate them. In discussing the poll tax and Mississippi's list of disfranchising crimes, the Court noted that "whatever is sinister in their intention, if anything, can be prevented by both races by the exertion of that duty which voluntarily pays taxes and refrains from crime."[55]

Five years later in the extraordinary decision in *Giles* v. *Harris*,[56] the Supreme Court took the position that remedying discrimination in the registration of voters was simply beyond its capacity, at least when it was as widespread as everyone knew Southern disfranchisement to be. Giles sought equitable relief to require that Alabama registrars register him and "more than five thousand negroes, citizens of the county of Montgomery, Alabama," who had sought to register in 1902.[57] Under the Alabama Constitution of 1901, persons registered before January 1, 1903, remained electors for life unless disqualified by certain crimes, but after that date, voters would have to meet literacy and employment tests, or prove ownership of forty acres of property worth $300. Those entitled to register before January 1, 1903, were those who met residency tests, had paid poll taxes, had served in a war of the United States, including the "war between the States," or were "lawful descendants" of someone who had served, or "who are of good character and who understand the duties and obligations of citizenship under a republican form of government."[58] Few blacks, of course, met the military service or Grandfather Clause tests,[59] and Giles asserted that the good character and under-

---

[53] This hint echoed the position repeatedly taken in debates on the Civil Rights Acts by a minority of Congressmen that the post–Civil War amendments dealt only with state laws that were discriminatory on their face, and that the national government had no power to consider a state's administration or enforcement of laws. See generally E. Schnapper, "Civil Rights Litigation After Monell, *Colum. L. Rev.*, 79:213, 231, 1979. This position describes the realistic effects, though not the doctrinal pretensions, of the jury discrimination cases from Reconstruction through the New Deal period.

[54] 118 U.S. 356 (1886).

[55] 170 U.S. at 222.

[56] 189 U.S. 475 (1903).

[57] *Ibid.*, at 482 (quoting plaintiff's complaint).

[58] Ala. Const. of 1901, art. 8, sec. 180. The other provisions described were secs. 181, 183–88.

[59] Gilbert Stephenson, however, wrote that "a considerable number of Negroes in the Southern States, who were Federal soldiers in the Civil War, have registered under the 'Grandfather Clauses.'" Stephenson, *Race Distinctions in American Law*, 308.

standing test had been intended and administered to "let in all whites and [keep] out a large part, if not all, of the blacks."[60]

In a revealing and candid opinion by Justice Holmes, a majority of the Supreme Court held that the federal courts could not grant relief. Holmes wrote, "[W]e are dealing with a new and extraordinary situation," the allegation that "the whole registration scheme of the Alabama constitution is a fraud upon the Constitution of the United States."[61] But if that were true, "how can we make the court a party to the unlawful scheme by accepting it and adding another voter to its fraudulent lists?"[62] The relief Giles sought was incompatible with the theory of his complaint: if the whole registration machinery was invalid, it was not appropriate to order that machinery to register Giles. It was no answer, Holmes thought, to argue that the fraud would be cured if all qualified blacks were registered, because "there is no probability that any way now is open by which more than a few could be registered."[63] Even if all could be registered, Holmes pointed out, the Alabama Constitution was said to be illegal in its inception, and "it would be a new doctrine in constitutional law that the original invalidity could be cured by an administration which defeated [the Constitution's] intent."[64]

Holmes offered a second, more basic reason for denying affirmative relief. A court of equity should not take jurisdiction unless it could provide relief. "This is alleged to be the conspiracy of a State," and the federal courts have "no constitutional power to control its action by any direct means."[65] If "the great mass of the white population intends to keep the blacks from voting," Holmes argued, putting "a name on a piece of paper will not defeat them."[66] Federal courts could not undertake to supervise the voting in Alabama. The case required an application of the principle that equity would not endeavor to correct a political wrong.[67] "[R]elief from a great political wrong, if done, as alleged by the people of a State and the State itself, must be given by them or by the legislative and political department of the government of the United States."[68] Can any decision better reveal the extraordinary change in the conception of federal judicial power that took place from the beginning to the middle of the twentieth century?

Holmes had left open the possibility of money damages as a remedy

---

60 189 U.S. at 483.
61 *Ibid.*, at 486.
62 *Ibid.*
63 *Ibid.*, at 487.
64 *Ibid.*
65 *Ibid.*, at 487–88.
66 *Ibid.*, at 488.
67 See also Mills v. Green, 67 Fed.

818 (C.C.A.S.C. 1895), *reversed,* 69 Fed. 852 (4th Cir. 1895).
68 189 U.S. at 488. Justices Harlan, Brown, and Brewer dissented, urging that it was well within the judicial power to order that Giles be registered.

for wrongful refusal to register, but when Giles tried this route, along with an action for mandamus, he ran into a bizarre application of the independent-state-ground doctrine. The Alabama courts had given Giles the following shuffle: if the registration provisions of the Alabama Constitution were void, then the registrars were without authority to register anyone, including Giles, and he could not complain of their refusal to do so; on the other hand, if the registration provisions were valid, then the registrars were clothed with a broad quasi-judicial discretion in the exercise of which they were immune from damages. In 1904, in *Giles v. Teasley*, the Supreme Court, in a murky opinion by Justice Day, managed to see in this decision a ground for affirming the state court judgment that was independent of the federal claim not to be deprived of the vote because of race.[69] If the registrars had refused to register Giles under a constitution designed to bar blacks from voting, Day rationalized he had suffered no legal damage "because no refusal to register by a board thus constituted in defiance of the Federal Constitution could have the effect to disqualify a legal voter."[70] And Giles' attempt to mandamus the registrars fell on the theory that if the state constitution were illegal, " 'there would be no board to perform the duty sought.' "[71] "We do not perceive how this decision involved the adjudication of a right claimed under the Federal Constitution against the appellant," Day lamely concluded, adding what was doubtless the dispositive consideration: "The great difficulty of reaching the political action of a State through remedies afforded in the courts, state or Federal, was suggested by this court in *Giles v. Harris*."[72]

The Supreme Court seemed to have closed the circle on voting rights for blacks. With *Cruikshank* having removed private violence, even of massive dimensions, against blacks attempting to vote in state elections from the reach of both judicial and congressional power under the Fourteenth and Fifteenth amendments, with *Reese* and congressional repeal having struck down most of the statutes dealing expressly with official deprivations of the right to vote in state elections, with *Williams* having upheld the "Mississippi Plan" because it did not discriminate on the face of state law, and with *Giles I* and *Giles II* having declared intended systematic disfranchisement beyond the reach of judicial relief, the promise of the Fifteenth Amendment lay in ruin, so far as vindication by the Supreme Court was concerned.

There remained the possibility of criminal prosecution by the executive branch to protect voting rights under the catch-all criminal

---

[69] Giles v. Teasley, 193 U.S. 146 (1904).

[70] *Ibid.*, at 164.

[71] *Ibid.*, at 165 (quoting the lower court decision, 136 Ala. 228, 229–30 (1902).

[72] *Ibid.*, at 166.

civil rights statutes that remained on the books from Reconstruction days. But there was little reason to expect enforcement efforts from Washington. Although the Republicans continued to proclaim a commitment to voting rights for blacks in their party platforms, the promise was plainly empty. Most Republicans accepted lily-white politics as the price of having any hope of gaining a foothold in the South, and excluded blacks from the nascent Republican organizations south of the Mason-Dixon line. Unlike peonage, which the national government prosecuted with some energy in the Progressive era, black disfranchisement was tolerated by the Roosevelt and Taft administration. The Wilson Administration, of course, was not likely to move against it, for it was black disfranchisement, even more than memories of the bloody shirt, that held the Democratic party together in the South. Even if the executive branch had wanted to prosecute state officials who disfranchised blacks, there were serious questions about whether the remaining civil rights statutes would support it. The statutes explicitly protecting voting rights had been repealed in 1894, leaving on the books only general provisions covering deprivation of federally secured rights; these provisions had never been thought to apply to the state officials who deprived blacks of the vote simply by following state disfranchising laws.

B. THE RELUCTANT CHALLENGE TO THE GRANDFATHER CLAUSE

The *Grandfather Clause Cases* of 1915 grew out of the most unlikely circumstances. The disfranchising state governments were almost all one-party political organizations monolithically dedicated to suppressing black political participation. Congress and the executive were acquiescent if not supportive. And the Supreme Court had abandoned the field. The cases arose only as a result of the coalescence of a unique set of circumstances—a state prepared to adopt the most blatant contrivance for barring blacks from the polls; a local Republican party that was not moribund and was desperate for black votes that could swing close state elections; a United States Attorney prepared to press what appeared to be futile criminal cases against election officials in the face of instructions from the Attorney General not to do so; a local federal judge prepared to construe the catch-all federal civil rights statutes to reach deprivations of voting rights; an administration cornered into dubious support of a prosecution taken in the teeth of its explicit instructions; a certification to the Supreme Court of abstract questions of law unencumbered by other questions that might well have disposed of the appeal on nonconstitutional grounds; and, of course, a Supreme Court that was prepared for the first time to recognize some vitality in the Fifteenth Amendment. All these conditions came together in 1910 in Oklahoma, and this strange concatenation of events is the measure of the improbability of the *Grandfather Clause Cases*.

Oklahoma's embrace of the Grandfather Clause was viewed as an embarrassment even by those sympathetic to the disfranchisement movement. For one thing, Oklahoma took what was a temporary expedient in other states and made it a permanent avenue to registration. The creation of a permanent loophole for whites made more blatant what was obvious but could be winked at in other states: that the literacy requirement was intended to bar blacks only. Second, there was vigorous two-party politics in Oklahoma, and blacks made up less than 9 percent of the population, lending credence to the objections of Oklahoma Republicans that, as one put it in a letter to President Taft, the Grandfather Clause was "adopted for the express purpose of disfranchising negro voters, not because they are black, but because they vote the Republican ticket."[73] Even if the Grandfather Clause was viewed not as a partisan measure but as an expression of racism, the small number of black voters made it seem rather gratuitous. "Oklahoma is another state whose negrophobia has been a source of embarrassment to the South," summed up an academic observer in 1914. "It is difficult to find any justification for the policy of disfranchisement in Maryland and Oklahoma. There is not the slightest danger of negro domination. . . . [B]y attempting to disfranchise the negro when it is not necessary, these two states have brought disrepute upon the laudable efforts which are being made to improve the character of the Southern electorate."[74]

Notice of the Oklahoma Grandfather Clause came to the White House in July 1910, a month before the clause was added to the Oklahoma Constitution, in an anxious message to President Taft from J. A. Harris, chairman of the Oklahoma Republican Central Committee:

> The Haskell administration, backed by the democratic organization in this State, are making a determined effort to amend the State constitution so as to deprive ninety per cent. of the African race of the right of suffrage. It is believed that this amendment will be adopted on August 2nd, and will deprive the Republicans of twenty-five thousand votes at the November 1910 election. The effect will be to elect a solid democratic legislature and Congressional delegation in this State. At the last State election, the State was only carried by the democrats by about eleven thousand majority, and under the present conditions in the State, we feel confident of overcoming this majority and electing

---

[73] J. Burford to W. H. Taft, Feb. 10, 1913, Justice and Executive File 150719, National Archives (hereinafter cited as File 150719).

[74] W. R. Smith, "Negro Suffrage in the South," in *Studies in Southern History and Politics* (1964), 231, 251.

a republican governor and State officers in November, if this dastardly effort to rob the colored race of their votes is not consumated.

Harris asked the President to designate special counsel "upon recommendation of the Republican organization in this state" to "prevent this effort to nullify the constitution of the United States."[75]

When Oklahoma was admitted to the Union in 1907, its Constitution had simply enfranchised all resident males over twenty-one. But in January 1910, the Oklahoma legislature submitted the Grandfather Clause amendment for referendum. In their haste to get the clause in place before the 1910 general election, the clause was put to the voters in August, during the primary election. The clause read:

> No person shall be registered as an elector of this State, or be allowed to vote in any election held herein, unless he be able to read and write any section of the Constitution of the State of Oklahoma; but no person who was, on January 1st, 1866, or any time prior thereto, entitled to vote under any form of government, or who at that time resided in some foreign nation, and no lineal descendant of such person, shall be denied the right to register and vote because of his inability to so read and write sections of such Constitution.[76]

In the summer of 1910, these events in Oklahoma met an indifferent response from the administration. Harris' message reached the White House on August 10, 1910, along with a proposed answer (see insert following page 816) from William R. Harr, Acting Attorney General while Wickersham was vacationing, concluding that, under Holmes' opinion in *Giles I,* the federal government could not petition in equity to enjoin the operation of the Grandfather Clause.[77] "I concur in the view of the A.G. that the Executive has no power to intervene or [*sic*] a U.S. Court by equitable proceeding," president Taft wrote across the corner of Harr's letter on August 14.[78] And so nothing was done.

The election in November 1910 bore out Harris' fears.[79] The aim

---

[75] J. Harris to W. H. Taft, July 15, 1910, File 150719.

[76] Okla. Const. of 1910, art. 3, sec. 4a.

[77] This was an extension of Holmes' reasoning in *Giles I,* which was that the federal courts should not cure illegal registration machinery by ordering it to operate in a particular case. An injunction simply suspending the Grandfather Clause need not necessarily have been viewed in this way. But Harr was undoubtedly correct that Holmes' view that systematic disfranchisement was a political question would have led the Court to refuse to enjoin the Grandfather Clause.

[78] W. R. Harr to W. H. Taft, Aug. 10, 1910, File 150719.

[79] J. Harris to G. Wickersham, Aug. 7, 1911, File 150719.

of the Grandfather Clause, he complained to Attorney General Wickersham after the election, was "to deny all colored people the right to vote," and "it was so announced from the stump by practically all of the Democratic candidates for State offices." "Election inspectors had received orders to permit no man to vote who was colored," Harris went on, "and the orders were carried out in practically all portions of the State."[80] There were indeed many complaints from Oklahoma blacks to President Taft and the Justice Department, considerable racial violence, and at least one lynching at the time of the election. United States Attorneys in Oklahoma were hard pressed by local Republican politicians, since the black vote being lost was Republican, and two of them, William R. Gregg of Muskogee and John Embry of Guthrie,[81] wrote the Attorney General suggesting criminal prosecutions of election officials.[82] The statutes under which Gregg and Embry wanted to prosecute were the catch-all civil rights criminal statutes, the Ku Klux Klan provision of the 1870 Act, and the section of the 1866 Act punishing deprivations of rights under color of law. These provisions were codified as sections 19 and 20, respectively, of the Criminal Code of

---

[80] About one week before the election, the Oklahoma Supreme Court upheld the validity of the Grandfather Clause as a "classification based upon a reason":

Any person who was entitled to vote under a form of government on or prior to said date is still presumed to be qualified to exercise such right, and the presumption follows as to his offspring; that is, that the virtue and intelligence of the ancestors will be imputed to his descendants, just as the iniquity of the fathers may be visited upon the children unto the third and fourth generation. But as to those who were not entitled to vote under any form of government on said date, or any prior time, and their descendants, there is no presumption in favor of their qualification, and the burden is upon them to show themselves qualified. This does not apply to any one race, but to every race that falls within this qualification.

Atwater v. Hassett, 27 Okla. 292, 315–16, 111 Pac. 802, 812 (1910). The validity of the clause was again affirmed in Cofield v. Farrell, 38 Okla. 608, 134 Par. 407 (1913).

[81] John Embry (1869–1960) was born in Kentucky and joined the bar there in 1890. In 1891, he moved to the Oklahoma Territory where he practiced law in Chandler, Oklahoma. He served as a probate judge, as mayor of Chandler in 1905–1906, and was elected a member of the territorial legislature, where he sponsored a law establishing segregated schools for black children. He was appointed United States Attorney for the Oklahoma Territory and later for the Western District of Oklahoma. He resigned in 1912, and practiced in Oklahoma City until 1960. *Who Was Who in America* (1960), 4:287.

Gregg does not appear in the standard biographical references.

[82] W. Gregg to G. Wickersham, Nov. 10, 1910; J. Embry to G. Wickersham, Oct. 21, 1910, File 150719.

1909,[83] but still referred to frequently by the section numbers given them in the Revised Statutes of 1874–1878, namely section 5508 and section 5510.[84]

As we have seen, there were difficulties with applying these sections to deprivations of the right to vote,[85] and the Justice Department, again with Taft's approval, took the position that sections 19 and 20 were inapplicable "because they refer to civil rights only." "The only remedy for the situation, aside from Congressional action," Wickersham wrote Embry shortly after the 1910 election, "would seem to be an action at law for damages by an individual affected, in which the [Grandfather] amendment might be declared unconstitutional."[86] The administration, at this point, was unwilling to stir up the South by moving against the Grandfather Clause. Embry, however, under pressure from Oklahoma Republications, went ahead anyway, and procured indictments of two state election officials, J. J. Beal and Frank Guinn. When Harr called him to account for this insubordination, Embry shot back: "If the Department thinks that this law is not applicable to the case, or should not be enforced, I desire that you treat this letter as my resignation and ask the President to accept it at once."[87]

Embry's defiance put the Justice Department in an awkward position. "[T]his flagrant disregard of its instructions can hardly be passed over without notice," Harr wrote to Wickersham:

> [A] United States Attorney who would involve the Department in a political fight of this kind in disregard of its express wishes is a dangerous man to have in office. The political aspect of the matter is not confined to Oklahoma only. If the Government is to institute criminal prosecutions in such cases, its action can not properly be confined to Oklahoma. It must extend to all the Southern States having similar laws, of which there are quite a number.[88]

---

[83] 35 Stat. 1092 (1909) (codified at 18 U.S.C. secs. 241, 242 (1976).

[84] The successive phraseology of these provisions is set out in the appendix to Justice Frankfurter's opinion in United States v. Williams, 341 U.S. 70, 83, 84 (1950).

[85] Gregg and Embry had no doubt that secs. 19 and 20 would punish racially motivated denials of the right to vote that were wrongful under state law, as where a literate black male was turned away. They were unsure of whether criminal prosecutions would lie against officials who merely enforced the Grandfather Clause and refused to register blacks who could not meet the literacy requirement. W. Gregg to G. Wickersham, Nov. 10, 1910; J. Embry to G. Wickersham, Oct. 21, 1910, File 150719.

[86] G Wickersham to J. Embry, Nov. 12, 1910, File 150719.

[87] J. Embry to W. R. Harr, Feb. 4, 1911, File 150719.

[88] W. R. Harr to G. Wickersham, Feb. 11, 1911, File 150719.

But there would be political difficulty in throttling Embry, as well, Harr intimated with some delicacy: "This matter has, however, a broader aspect than that of a mere affront to the Department by the United States Attorney, and so considered, it might not be advisable to treat the insubordination of Mr. Embry too seriously." Embry had "doubtless also been embarrased [sic] and harassed by the political pressure brought to bear upon him to take action," and it "would not seem advisable to take issue openly with the United States Attorney."[89] The statutory question was, Harr conceded, open to doubt. Moreover, even if the statutes were held to apply, Harr thought it "altogether improbable that an Oklahoma jury, which would certainly be composed in part of those favoring the law, would convict State officers of election for enforcing it."[90] Thus, Embry's insubordination would probably be relatively harmless.

What Harr meant by the "political aspect of the matter" is not hard to fathom. The Taft Administration was promoting the cause of sectional reconciliation and seeking to attract white Southerners to the Republican party. For the administration to move against disfranchisement would invite a return to the bloody shirt politics that had closed the ranks of the white South. On the other hand, to force the resignation of a United States Attorney battling against so blatant a disfranchisement mechanism as the Grandfather Clause, which was, after all, only a temporary expedient in every state but Oklahoma, would be an embarrassing revelation of the emptiness of Republican rhetoric, might affect which way Oklahoma would swing in the coming national election, and would demoralize the Republican organization not only in Oklahoma but in other border states where black votes still counted.

Attorney General Wickersham decided that the best tactic was to let Embry pursue his case. "I greatly regret that you should have procured indictments against State election officers," he wrote Embry. "My attention is, however, called to the fact that Judge Campbell[91] . . . has instructed the grand jury in accordance with your own view of the statute, and, under these circumstances I am not prepared to overrule your action in finding the indictments, although I cannot but reiterate my regret that you should have committed the Government . . ."[92] Wickersham did instruct Embry in no uncertain terms to avoid further

---

[89] *Ibid.*

[90] *Ibid.*

[91] Judge Ralph Emerson Campbell of the Eastern District of Oklahoma was born in Pennsylvania in 1867 and took his law degree at the University of Kansas in 1894. He repre-sented the Choctaw, Oklahoma Gulf Railroad before going on the federal bench in November 1907. He was a Republican. *Who Was Who in America* (1960), 1:188.

[92] G. Wickersham to J. Embry, Feb. 17, 1911, File 150719.

prosecutions of the same kind, but even this instruction was ineffectual. Embry had already brought one other prosecution against Oklahoma election officials, and would procure a third indictment a few months later.

Undoubtedly, Wickersham's calculation to let Embry pursue his case rested on the view that an Oklahoma jury would not likely convict state election officials for enforcing the Grandfather Clause.[93] On top of that, Harr had raised serious doubt whether Oklahoma election officials could be said to have acted with the requisite criminal intent even if one or both of the catch-all criminal sections were interpreted to apply to franchise offenses. But, surprisingly, Wickersham and Harr were wrong on both counts. Guinn and Beal, represented by the brother of the Democratic governor, whose fees were paid by the state Democratic party, were convicted on September 29, 1911, in the District Court for the Western District of Oklahoma before Judge John H. Cotteral[94] of violating section 19 of the Criminal Code, the successor to the Ku Klux Klan provision of the 1870 Act, punishing conspiracies to injure, oppress, threaten, or intimidate any citizen in the enjoyment of any right secured by the Constitution or federal laws.[95]

---

[93] In turning down an urgent request from Chairman Harris to appeal rulings by federal district judges in both the Eastern and Western districts of Oklahoma, holding that sec. 20 of the Criminal Code (the catch-all provision that originated in the 1866 Act) did not apply to deprivations of voting rights, Wickersham responded: "[T]hat [Grandfather] clause having been sustained by the Supreme Court of the state, it would undoubtedly be useless to attempt to convict State officers of elections of crime in enforcing it. . . ." J. Harris to G. Wickersham, Aug. 7, 1911; G. Wickersham to J. Harris, Aug. 9, 1911, File 150719.

[94] Judge John Hazelton Cotteral was born in Indiana in 1864, studied at the University of Michigan, and moved his law practice from Garden City, Kansas, to Guthrie, Oklahoma, in 1889. He was chairman of the Oklahoma delegation to the Republican National Convention in 1904, and appointed United States District Judge for the Western District of Oklahoma in 1907. In 1928, he was appointed to the Eighth Circuit Court of Appeals. He died in 1933. *Who Was Who in America* (1960), 1:264.

[95] Judge Cotteral instructed the jury that the Grandfather Clause was invalid, but could be considered

in so far as it was in good faith relied and acted upon by the defendants in ascertaining their intent and motive. . . . [If] the motive actuating the defendants was honest, and they simply erred in the conception of their duty—then the criminal intent requisite to their guilt is wanting, and they cannot be convicted. On the other hand, if they knew or believed those colored persons were entitled to vote, and their purpose was to unfairly and fraudulently deny the right of suffrage to them . . . on account of their race and color, then their purpose was a corrupt one, and they cannot be shielded by their official positions.

The jury evidently was swayed by the widespread evidence that Guinn, Beal,

As the national election approached, the beleaguered administration's attitude toward the Grandfather Clause underwent a metamorphosis.[96] A pivotal question in Taft's struggle for the Republican nomination at the Chicago convention in June 1912 was whether black delegates from the South would bolt to Roosevelt. In the midst of charges and countercharges of bribery and frantic appeals from Roosevelt supporters, the black delegates held firm for Taft, and, among other groups, could have been viewed as the margin of Taft's narrow victory.[97] With Democrats nominating the Southerner Wilson on July 3, and with Roosevelt's commitment to a lily-white strategy for the Progressive party emerging in July and August, the Taft Administration came to see the merit of a visible commitment to black voting rights, especially in a state where black voters might swing the election. Complaints to the White House from Oklahoma blacks denied registration came in over the summer, and by the end of July 1912, the Justice Department telegraphed the United States Attorney in Oklahoma: "You will prosecute complaints similar to those involved in Beall-Quinn [*sic*] case when made by negroes denied registration under grandfather clause."[98] The administration had caught up with John Embry.[99]

and other election officials were determined not to let blacks vote, even if they could satisfy the literacy requirement. The jury charge is quoted in Guinn v. United States, 228 F. 103, 107 (8th Cir. 1915).

[96] This was reminiscent of the administration's concern about Judge William C. Hook's concurrence in the Eighth Circuit's *McCabe* decision, when it considered Hook early in 1912 for the nomination that went to Pitney. See discussion pp. 322–23, *supra*.

[97] Sixty-odd black votes were cast for Taft in the final ballot, in which Taft barely squeaked by with the necessary majority. On the crucial vote giving Elihu Root the chair, the Taft forces carried by fewer than sixty votes. See generally H. Pringle, *The Life and Times of William Howard Taft* (1939), II, 80 *et seq.;* P. Kluger, *Progressive Presidents and Black Americans* (Ph.D. diss., Columbia University, 1974), 216 *et seq.*

[98] J. Fowler to W. Gregg, July 27, 1912, File 150719.

[99] It was not only the political situation that had changed since the summer before. By July 1912, a second federal court had ruled that sec. 19 of the Criminal Code reached deprivations of voting rights. That case, Felix v. United States, 186 F. 685 (5th Cir. 1911), involved violent attacks on would-be voters in Louisiana. Also, another federal court had struck down a Grandfather Clause enacted by the city of Annapolis in a decision that would come to the Supreme Court along with the cases from Oklahoma. Anderson v. Myers, 182 F. 223 (C.C.D. Md. 1910), *affirmed,* 238 U.S. 368 (1915). These decisions gave the Justice Department the stated grounds for its change of heart. But it is not reaching to surmise that the ripening politics of the 1912 Presidential election, particularly Wilson's nomination and Taft's lessened chances in the South, and the emerging challenge of the Progressives made Taft look both to put Oklahoma in the Republican column and to preserve the access of black Republicans to the ballot in other border states that might join the Republican ranks.

X: *Black Disfranchisement*

The approach of the 1912 election in Oklahoma was explosive, as Gregg wrote to Wickersham:

> [T]he state through its election officers is preparing and seems determined to enforce the provisions of the Grandfather Law at the general election to be held in November. Public speeches are being made throughout this district and the question agitated of strictly enforcing the provisions of the state constitution and excluding all colored men who cannot pass the test prescribed therein. Election officers are being selected with a view to accomplishing this result. Public speakers are declaring that it is the duty of the Governor to see that no federal interference is had in the matter of holding the elections in this state even to the extent of calling out the militia.[100]

Governor Lee Cruce indeed threatened to arrest any federal agents who interfered with the elections. On October 23, 1912, Cruce issued a statement that "the grandfather clause is going to be enforced until it is repealed or declared unconstitutional by the Supreme Court." "I am tired of these cheap little partisan Deputy Marshals trying continually to interfere with the administration of the laws in this state," he blustered. "[I]f the local officers in Oklahoma follow my advice, they will put in jail every petty Federal understrapper who tries to interfere with the election officers of Oklahoma in the discharge of their sworn duty."[101] Two days before the election, Cruce sent a letter to Democratic election officials in counties where the black vote was heaviest instructing them not to let any black man vote who could not read and write, and promising to hold them to account for enforcing the Grandfather Clause.[102] On the other hand, rumors were thick in Oklahoma that "the Attorney General had directed that every election official be immediately arrested where a negro is refused the right to vote."[103] A few days before the election, United States Attorney Homer N. Boardman wrote a widely publicized letter to a Democratic official to the effect that state officials would not be permitted to assert a defense of good faith if they enforced the Grandfather Clause. A more flamboyant document, unsigned but attributed to Boardman, and headed "Talk It Over with Your Wife," promised that election officials would go to the penitentiary if they violated federal election laws. The upshot, Gregg predicted, would be "rioting and bloodshed on election day."[104]

---

[100] W. Gregg to G. Wickersham, Oct. 16, 1912, File 150719.

[101] *Dallas Weekly News*, Oct. 25, 1912, p. 1, col. 8.

[102] This was reported to Attorney General Thomas A. Gregory by U. S. Attorney J. Fain in a report on the *Mosley* case, dated Feb. 3, 1916. File 150719.

[103] W. R. Harr to W. Gregg, Oct. 26, 1912, File 150719.

[104] W. Gregg to G. Wickersham, Oct. 16, 1912, File 150719.

Again, the Justice Department looked to the White House for guidance, and on October 29, 1912, a few days before the election, Taft lowered the temperature with these instructions to Harr:

> I think there is no objection to the policy of directing the arrest of election officers for violation of the Federal statutes the day after the election, rather than to precipitate a riot or disturbance of the peace by an attempt to arrest them on election day while they are in other respects discharging their usual lawful functions as officers in the election.[105]

Boardman indeed initiated a major prosecution growing out of the 1912 election, against the chairman and the secretary of the Blaine County Election Board, both Democrats. This case, *United States* v. *Mosley*, became joined to, and in a sense was one of, the *Grandfather Clause Cases* decided by the Supreme Court in 1915. The facts of Mosley would show the extent to which the legal controversy over the Grandfather Clause was enmeshed in the boisterous partisanship of Oklahoma politics.

After Taft's defeat in the 1912 election, the Grandfather Clause controversy continued to occupy the White House, but the focus once again centered on the case against Beal and Guinn. They had appealed to the United States Court of Appeals for the Eighth Circuit, which had certified to the Supreme Court the general question of the validity of the Grandfather Clause. The question now became whether the lame duck administration could present the issue to the Supreme Court before the Democrats took office. "If these cases are not briefed, advanced, argued and submitted before your administration goes out of office, the result will be disastrous," an Oklahoma Republican state senator wrote Taft on February 10, 1913. The Oklahoma Senate and House had passed a formal resolution asking Wilson to pardon Guinn and Beal and to remove the United States Attorney who had prosecuted them,[106] and

---

[105] Taft went on:

I think, however, there is ground for criticism in your suggestion that because the State Supreme Court has held the "grandfather clause" to be within the constitutional power of the State legislature, while the Federal courts have held it to violate the constitution of the United States, in some way or other the election officers could plead the decision of the Supreme Court of the State as an excuse which would relieve them of conviction under the Federal statutes passed for the very purpose of preserving the rights of colored men under the Fifteenth Amendment, against State statutes and, of course, state opinions.

W. H. Taft to W. R. Harr, Oct. 29, 1912, File 150719.

[106] Oklahoma Senate Concurrent Resolution, Nov. 12, 1913.

X: *Black Disfranchisement*

"[i]n the speeches supporting these resolutions the old time states rights doctrine and hostility to the Federal Government were as boldly asserted as in 1861."[107] Early in February, with one month in office remaining, the Taft Administration moved to advance the case, despite the objections of Guinn's and Beal's lawyers. The Supreme Court did advance the case for argument, but it set the date for April 7, a month or so after the new administration would take charge. Whether the April date was dictated by the Court's schedule and docket, or whether the Court did not want a case of such significance presented by a lame duck administration, is uncertain.[108] In any event, as soon as the Wilson Administration came into office, Attorney General McReynolds moved to postpone the argument until the fall of 1913, feeling "that sufficient opportunity has not been given to investigate and prepare for the preparation of the case in such manner as to do full justice to the United States."[109] And so the *Grandfather Clause Cases* were set for argument at the beginning of the October Term 1913.

Doubts that the new administration would carry on the case against the Grandfather Clause were proved wrong, but were far from groundless. It must not have seemed likely that a Democratic administration, headed by a President raised in Virginia, and well stocked with Southerners in key positions, especially at the Justice Department, would move against the disfranchisement of Southern blacks. The men who would have charge of the government's position in the Supreme Court were Attorney General James C. McReynolds of Tennessee and Solicitor General John W. Davis of West Virginia. Not much was known about McReynolds at this time, apart from his antitrust fervor, but he was in fact an obdurate segregationist, and as a Justice, he vigorously opposed federal intervention in state electoral practices.[110] Davis, son of a proslavery father, had been most recently a Democratic Congressman, and was a man of paternalistic conviction of the innate inferiority of blacks. He doubted the wisdom of black suffrage, and his wife would write tongue in cheek to a relative when Davis argued *Guinn* that he felt he "was in danger of winning."[111] Moreover, as the Justice Department was deciding its position in the *Grandfather Clause Cases*, the Wilson

---

[107] J. Burford to W. H. Taft, Feb. 10, 1913, File 150719.

[108] The only recess in this interval was from Mar. 24 to Apr. 7, 1913.

[109] J. Fowler to J. Burford, Apr. 5, 1913, File 150719.

[110] See *infra,* text accompanying notes 214–19.

[111] W. Harbaugh, *Lawyer's Lawyer: The Life of John W. Davis* (1973),

94. Davis was far from a rabid Southern opponent of the Fifteenth Amendment, however. As a Congressman, in connection with debates on the Seventeenth Amendment, involving direct election of Senators, he had broken with his Southern colleagues by refusing to go along with a resolution barring Congress' power to police federal elections. *Ibid.,* 75.

Administration was peremptorily segregating government cafeterias, screening off the desks of black employees, and segregating employees in the Treasury and Post Office departments, thus breaking with the fifty-year tradition of an integrated civil service. And the President himself was declaring that he "honestly thought segregation to be in the interest of the colored people."[112] In August 1913, Booker T. Washington wrote to Oswald Garrison Villard, "I have never seen the colored people so discouraged and bitter as they are at the present time."[113]

And yet, there was considerable ambivalence in Wilson's attitude to the rights of blacks in the early days of his administration. None of the three Presidential candidates in 1912 emerged as singularly sympathetic to blacks, and black leaders and whites active in the early civil rights movement divided their support among Taft, Roosevelt, and Wilson. Moorfield Storey, Oswald Garrison Villard, and W. E. B. Du Bois, among others, thought Wilson was the best prospect for blacks. His campaign promise of "fair dealing" for blacks evoked considerable hope.[114] Wilson indeed was embarrassed by the outcry that greeted his administration's early moves toward segregation, and he may have been receptive to, or at least unlikely to oppose, a gesture in support of black rights.

The *Guinn* case might have seemed suitable for the purpose. Oklahoma's was the only Grandfather Clause that opened a permanent door to registration; all the others were temporary loopholes, and only Georgia's had not already expired. The Mississippi Plan had worked without the need for any Grandfather Clause. To pursue the *Guinn* case might have seemed harmless enough, despite its symbolic importance. There is no evidence that such considerations weighed with Wilson, McReynolds, or Davis, but if they assessed the political implications of supporting invalidation of the Grandfather Clause, it is hard to imagine that these thoughts did not cross their minds.

In the end, however, it was probably simple momentum that enlisted the Wilson Administration. Davis later recalled that when he came into office in mid-August 1913, he "fell heir to cases and issues which were begun long before" and that with this "hangover business . . . you had to pick it up right where it had been dropped. The continuity of the office was absolute. . . . [T]here is a constant flow. You just step into

---

[112] *Ibid.*, 94; see also C. Kellogg, *NAACP* (1967), I, 161 *et seq.*; N. Weiss, "The Negro and the New Freedom: Fighting Wilsonian Segregation," *Pol. Sci. Q.*, 84:61, 1969.

[113] Kellogg, *NAACP*, 164. See generally A. M. Low, "The South in the Saddle," *Harper's Weekly*, 57:20, February 8, 1913.

[114] See generally M. DeW. Howe, *Portrait of an Independent: Moorfield Storey* (1932), 260; Kellogg, *NAACP*, 156.

the river as it goes by."[115] The decisions about what arguments to press in the Supreme Court were his alone, he recalled, and "never, or hardly ever," were interfered with by the Attorney General. With a holding against the Grandfather Clause in the district court, with a jury having found on careful instructions that Beal and Guinn had purposefully deprived blacks of their constitutional rights, with the Court of Appeals having certified pure and simple the question of validity, and with no other state laws at stake, Davis may have thought the department had no choice but to defend the appeal: the Wilson Administration, like its predecessor, may have had its hand forced by events in Oklahoma.

Whatever lay behind the Wilson Administration's decision to press the case, there is no question that when *Guinn* was argued on October 17, 1913, Davis put the constitutional objections to the Grandfather Clause with elegant force. Whatever Davis may have lacked in zeal for the ultimate goal of black suffrage was overcome by his aversion to what he thought a patent evasion of the Constitution, not to mention his fierce determination to excel in a new role. *Guinn* was Davis' second argument. The first, the day before, was the *Pipe Line Cases*.[116]

Davis was opposed by former Senator Joseph W. Bailey of Texas, a doctrinaire states'-righter with whom Davis had crossed swords in Congress on the issue of workmen's compensation for federal employees. "[H]e gets warm physically [as he] leans over his desk entreating the Court as it were, to see the question his way," Davis' wife wrote of Bailey's performance in *Guinn*, adding that her husband, by contrast, was crisp and assured, as if elaborate discussion were an imposition.[117] Bailey tried to deflect the argument away from the Fifteenth Amendment. That Amendment, he claimed, dealt with denials of the vote explicitly on the basis of race, but the Grandfather Clause was neither a denial of the right to vote nor was it based on race. It was the literacy test that abridged voting in Oklahoma, Bailey insisted, and the *Williams* decision had upheld the Mississippi literacy test despite "the frank admission" that it was designed to discriminate against the characteristics of black people. The Grandfather Clause was an extension of voting rights, not an abridgment, and therefore it could not violate the Fifteenth Amendment: "If the State grants me a privilege [to vote, if literate] to which I am entitled under the Constitution of the United States, it does not then abridge or deny my right by granting a greater privilege to my neighbor. . . ." Discrimination in the granting and withholding of

---

[115] J. Davis, *Oral History Transcripts* (Butler Library of Columbia University), 89, 90.

[116] The Pipe Line Cases, 234 U.S. 548 (1914).

[117] Quoted in Harbaugh, *Life of John W. Davis*, 95.

privileges was covered by the Fourteenth Amendment, Bailey argued, but it was settled that that Amendment did not deal with voting.[118]

Davis rested his argument entirely on the Fifteenth Amendment. The Grandfather Clause and the literacy test were together "a suffrage scheme" that discriminated between illiterate whites and illiterate blacks "to the overwhelming and well-nigh universal disadvantage of the latter."[119] Davis' brief was thick with statistics. Of 55,684 blacks in Oklahoma in 1900, only 57 had originally come from the eight Northern states that permitted blacks to vote in 1866. Between 1900 and 1910, Oklahoma's black population had increased by 147.1 percent (compared with an increase of 115.5 percent for whites), the highest increase in any state, and Davis suggested that this produced the racial anxiety that underlay the Grandfather Clause. In any event,

> lengthy analysis is hardly necessary to show the end in view. That is apparent upon the most casual inspection. If the disfranchisement of the illiterate negro were not its purpose, the clause may be declared well nigh devoid of meaning. Nothing more irrational or arbitrary than the tests imposed could be devised if there were no colored race in Oklahoma.[120]

It was true that the Grandfather Clause did not on its face mention race, but "rules of reason" required that it be judged by its operation and effect. Even if some blacks could vote under Oklahoma's suffrage scheme, the Fifteenth Amendment required "that under no condition will any member of any race be excluded for racial reasons."[121]

For many years after, John W. Davis was warmly regarded by the NAACP for the power of his argument in *Guinn*, and much of the goodwill toward Davis stemmed from the high praise of Moorfield Storey, whom Davis cordially encouraged to enter the argument.[122] Storey's brief in *Guinn* was the first of his many submissions to the Supreme Court on behalf of the NAACP, and his presence marked a turning point in the fortunes of black people in the Court.[123] Storey was

---

[118] *Brief for Appellant*, 14–15, Guinn v. United States, 238 U.S. 347 (1915). Bailey concluded that "whatever is sinister in [Oklahoma's] intentions, if any thing, can be easily escaped by both races, if only they will learn to read and write." *Ibid.,* at 28–29.

[119] *Brief for Appellee*, 23, *ibid.*

[120] *Ibid.,* at 24.

[121] *Ibid.*

[122] M. Storey to J. Davis, Oct. 8, 1913, File 150719.

[123] Storey was quite conscious of the value of his prestige in representing the NAACP before the Court. When he was unable personally to deliver his *amicus* brief in *Guinn* he arranged for a prominent white Washington lawyer to file, as this man "would command the respect of the Court." A. Meier and E. Rudwick, "Attorneys in Black and White," in *Along the Color Line: Explorations in the Black Experience* (1976), 135.

one of American law's notable figures, the protégé and biographer of Senator Charles Sumner, president of the American Bar Association, president of the Anti-Imperialist League, and an eloquent, righteous, and tireless embodiment of the abolitionist tradition.[124]

Most of Storey's interventions on behalf of blacks were powerful and assured, but he was tentative about getting involved in his first effort. On September 8, 1913, only a month or so before the *Grandfather Clause Cases* would be argued, he wrote McReynolds that he had been asked by the NAACP to file a brief, but that he

> was not sufficiently familiar with the practice of the court to know whether they are likely to grant this permission. . . . I should regard it as a personal favor if you will let me know what the chances are, and how far you think it desirable for me to undertake to intervene.[125]

Davis replied for the Attorney General that "the Department has no objection whatever," and that the Court would probably allow Storey to intervene. A month later, when Storey sent Davis a copy of his *amicus* brief, he wrote: "The subject is so ably and completely covered in your brief that it would seem an impertinence to attempt to add anything to it except for the unusual importance of the case."[126] And in another letter he added:

> I feel as if it were an impertinence for me to intervene in the case, but the persons who are very much interested in the welfare of colored people desire to be heard, and have asked me to act for them, and they will perhaps be better satisfied if my brief is received.[127]

---

[124] Moorfield Storey (1848–1935) was descended from early colonial stock and was born, took his education, worked, and died in Massachusetts. After graduating from Harvard College in 1866, Storey entered Harvard Law School but left after one year to become secretary to Senator Charles Sumner. He stayed with Sumner until 1869 and was closely involved in the effort to impeach Andrew Johnson. He returned to Boston to practice in 1869 and developed into one of the country's leading commercial lawyers and litigators. He was a leader of the Mugwamp desertion of James G. Blaine for Grover Cleveland in 1884, but his own polit-

ical efforts never met with success. For many years, he was an overseer of Harvard College and in 1896 was President of the ABA. He wrote seven books, over eighty pamphlets and articles, and countless public letters and statements. *Dictionary of American Biography* (1943), XXVIII, 96–97. See generally Howe, *Moorfield Storey;* W. Hixson, *Moorfield Storey and the Abolitionist Tradition* (1972).

[125] M. Storey to J. C. McReynolds, Sept. 8, 1913, File 150719.

[126] M. Storey to J. Davis, Oct. 8, 1913, File 150719.

[127] M. Storey to J. Davis, Oct. 11, 1913, File 150719.

His apologetic tone notwithstanding, Storey's brief was his typical forceful product:

> The purpose and effect of such amendments as this have been openly avowed, and there is not an intelligent man in the United States who is ignorant of them. If it is possible for an ingenious scrivener to accomplish that purpose by careful phrasing, the provisions of the Constitution which establish and protect the rights of some ten million colored citizens of the United States are not worth the paper on which they are written, and all constitutional safeguards are weakened.[128]

In fact, Storey's presence in the case helped Davis considerably. Storey made the Fourteenth Amendment argument against the Grandfather Clause, claiming, in essence, that the clause was a discrimination "implying inferiority in civil society." This effort to apply the Equal Protection Clause to "political" rights and to argue that it embodied a general guarantee against any laws that stigmatized blacks was problematical in 1913, and Davis steered clear of Bailey's challenge to engage on it by telling the Court that he would rest on Storey's brief.[129] *Williams* v. *Mississippi* was not controlling, Storey insisted, because the Grandfather Clause revealed discrimination on its face and not just the possibility of discrimination in administration. Moreover, since *Guinn* came up on certified questions, the remedial problem in *Giles I* and *II* was not before the Court, since the Court was "limited to answering the precise questions of law certified."[130]

---

[128] *Brief for the NAACP,* 4, Guinn v. United States, 238 U.S. 347 (1915). Storey stressed the absurdity of the clause: a black whose ancestors lived in America for many generations could not vote unless he could pass the literacy test, but a "native of Siberia" could vote if naturalized "although he may be unable to read or write, and although he and all his ancestors may have been living in a state of barbarism until within five or six years ago."

[129] Harbaugh, *Life of John W. Davis,* 95. William B. Hixson, Jr., has written that Storey decided not to rely on the Fourteenth Amendment because he feared that the Court might look to the second section of the Amendment and simply call on Congress to reduce the South's representation in Congress. Even if Congress did this, Storey feared the South might be willing to pay this price to disfranchise blacks, and the North might not be inclined to disturb the situation. Hixson, *Storey and the Abolitionist Tradition,* 136–37. But Storey's brief clearly relies on both the Fourteenth and Fifteenth Amendments.

[130] *Brief for the NAACP,* 13, Guinn v. United States, 238 U.S. 347 (1915). A second *amicus* brief attacking the Grandfather Clauses was submitted by Burford and Embry and it cast some light on the administration of the registration provisions. Whites were routinely registered on a simple assertion that an ancestor had the right to vote before 1867, they claimed, whereas some obviously literate blacks were turned away, because their grandfathers could not read! Whites who claimed to be able to read and

X: Black Disfranchisement

About a month after the *Guinn* arguments, the second *Grandfather Clause* case, *Myers* v. *Anderson*, was argued.[131] *Myers* involved a 1908 Maryland statute fixing the qualifications for voters in Annapolis municipal elections.[132] Taxpayers owning at least $500 worth of assessed property, naturalized citizens and their sons, and citizens who were entitled to vote before 1868 in any state or who were descended from such voters were given the vote, so long as they were resident males over twenty-one years of age. Three black men sued the registrars who had refused to register them, seeking damages under section 1979 of the Revised Statutes for acting under color of law to deprive any person of "any rights, privileges, or immunities secured by the Constitution and laws." Federal District Judge Thomas J. Morris[133] held the registrars liable on the ground that the Grandfather Clause was a clear violation of the Fifteenth Amendment. *Giles I* and *II* did not bar recovery, Morris held, because the plaintiffs had not claimed that the entire registration scheme was invalid, but had sought to void only the 1908 provision, leaving in place Maryland's previous, nondiscriminatory registration scheme.[134]

The Maryland officials were represented in the Supreme Court by William L. Marbury, a leader of the Baltimore Bar, who left no stone unturned in a very long, polished brief.[135] "These provisions will be

---

write were also registered routinely, while blacks were subjected to long waits, demands for multiple affidavits about various matters, intricate writing examinations, and were generally given the runaround. *Brief of John H. Burford and John Embry by Permission of the Attorney General,* Guinn v. United States, 238 U.S. 347 (1915).

[131] 238 U.S. 368 (1915).

[132] 1908 Md. Laws 347.

[133] Thomas John Morris, born in 1837 in Baltimore, took his A.B. from Harvard in 1856, was admitted to the bar in 1860, and practiced in Baltimore, privately and for the city government, until 1879, when he was appointed to the district court of Maryland by President Hayes. He was a Republican and a trustee of Johns Hopkins University. He died in 1912. *Who Was Who in America* (1943), 1:868; *Judges of the United States* (1978), 287.

[134] Morris also ruled that it was no defense that the defendants had simply enforced a state law, since the manifest purpose of sec. 1979 was to create liability for enforcement of state laws that were unconstitutional. Nor, he ruled, did the plaintiffs have to show that the registrars had acted with malice or bad faith, since civil, not criminal, liability was at issue. Anderson v. Myers, 182 F. 223 (C.C.D. Md. 1910), *affirmed,* 238 U.S. 368 (1915).

[135] William L. Marbury was born in Maryland in 1858, graduated from Johns Hopkins University and the University of Maryland Law School, and began practicing in Baltimore in 1882. He was a Democrat and was appointed U. S. Attorney for Maryland by President Cleveland in 1894. From 1903 until his death in 1935, he practiced with the firm of Marbury, Gosnell and Williams. *Who Was Who in America* (1960), 1:775.

searched in vain for any reference to race," he said, and to argue that it was racial discrimination to condition the right to vote on whether one's ancestor could vote before 1868 was "a patent fallacy." "It might as well be argued that the property qualification discriminates on account of previous condition of servitude, because if a man had not been held in bondage he would have been able to acquire some property. A slave could not acquire property any more than he could vote."[136] Marbury offered "a simple test" to apply that would uphold the Annapolis suffrage scheme: "each of those clauses admits some negroes and excludes some white men." Beyond this, Marbury made the radical argument that the Fifteenth Amendment reached federal elections only, since determining who should vote in state elections was essential to state sovereignty, and the "power to amend does not include the right or power to destroy the thing to be amended, i.e., the Federal Union."[137] Marbury insisted also that section 1979 protected only "civil rights," not politcal rights, and that in any event the two *Giles* decisions barred liability of individual state officials because "[i]f the plaintiffs had any grievance, it is against the state of Maryland, and their appeal must be to 'the political and legislative department of government.' "[138]

The brief for the three black plaintiffs insisted that the Maryland legislature knew the Grandfather Clause was probably unconstitutional. If a court should strike it down

> well and good—they have satisfied their constituents and done all they could. This putting up of legislation, known to be illegal, or gravely suspected of being illegal, to the courts, and placing upon them the burden and often the odium of striking it down, is only too common in these days.[139]

The brief struck another note of realism in its characterization of Marbury's efforts to use the *Giles* cases to relieve the registrars of liability because the entire scheme was void:

---

[136] *Brief for Plaintiffs in Error,* 49, 51, Myers v. Anderson, 238 U.S. 368 (1915) (emphasis in original removed). "The Fifteenth Amendment does not forbid discrimination on account of some line of demarcation which comes near a race or color line. It is confined to race or color strictly. You cannot, by circumlocution, define a negro; but you are at perfect liberty to draw a line which excludes a great many more negroes than white men." *Ibid.*

[137] *Ibid.,* at 106.

[138] *Ibid.,* at 60.

[139] *Brief for Defendants in Error,* 31, Myers v. Anderson, 238 U.S. 368 (1915). The brief for the three black plaintiffs in the Supreme Court was by Edgar H. Gans, with the assistance of Morris A. Soper and Daniel R. Randall. In the proceedings below, Charles J. Bonaparte, the former Attorney General, had also represented the plaintiffs.

[T]rue, we are violating the Constitution of the United States; true, we suspected this when the law was passed—but we won't let any Court decide it because we have so drawn the law that if our wrongdoing, our violation of the Constitution is alleged, we will show that the registers against whom you bring the action for damages had no official standing. We will effectively nullify the Fifteenth Amendment, because you can not invent a remedy for the wrong.[140]

C. The *Guinn* and *Myers* Decisions

The Supreme Court did not hand down the *Grandfather Clause* decisions for more than a year and a half, until the last day of the next term, an odd delay for a unanimous decision, and one that led Storey to speculate that the Court might be closely divided.[141] There is evidence, though far removed, that this delay was caused by the resistance of Justice Lurton, and Chief Justice White's passion for marshaling the Court. Forty-five years later, William L. Marbury, Jr., of Baltimore, son of the man who had argued in support of the Grandfather Clause, sent Justice Felix Frankfurter this recollection:

There is a story about *Myers* v. *Anderson* and its companion case, *Guinn* v. *United States,* which may interest you. You will note from the report of the cases in 238 U.S. that they were argued in October and November, 1913 but not decided until June, 1915. When they were argued Justice Lurton was still on the court, although in failing health. He was succeeded by McReynolds who had been Attorney General. At that time my father was very close to the Wilson Administration and quite intimate with McReynolds. After the cases were decided, McReynolds told him that when he attended the first meeting of the court he found that the Fifteenth Amendment election cases had been the subject of a terrific controversy. Apparently, Justice Lurton had prepared a dissenting opinion in which he followed my father's argument in the *Myers* case. This so scandalized the Chief Justice that he suggested that Lurton resign. When Lurton refused to do this the majority of the court held up a decision until his death. The case was not decided for nearly a year after McReynolds came to the court and Lurton's dissent never saw the light of day.

All of this father told me many years later and I offer it subject to the uncertainties inherent in the recollection of past events.[142]

---

[140] *Ibid.,* at 32.

[141] After the decision came down, Moorfield Storcy wrote to Joel Spingarn: "I was very much afraid that the court was equally divided, and I am unable even now to understand why the decision should have been delayed so long." M. Storey to J. Spingarn, July 12, 1915, Moorfield Storey Papers, Massachusetts Historical Society.

[142] W. L. Marbury to F. Frankfurter, Sept. 25, 1958 (letter in possession of the author, to be filed in Frankfurter Papers, Library of Congress).

Frankfurter passed the letter on to Professor Alexander Bickel, noting: "What Bill Marbury reports is interesting, but I have heavy doubts about its accuracy."[143]

Surely little in Lurton's outlook should have raised Frankfurter's doubts. Lurton might well have dissented on the ground that the *Giles* decisions should control, or that the Revised Statutes did not reach deprivation of voting rights.[144] But neither of these grounds for dissent should have scandalized White, much less led him to ask Lurton to resign. Thus Marbury's story, if true, would tend to indicate that Lurton was ready to go into wholesale dissent and uphold the constitutionality of the Grandfather Clause under the Fifteenth Amendment. Frankfurter may have doubted that Lurton would go that far, although if anyone on the Court would have, it would have been Lurton.

Marbury's story also raised the question whether Chief Justice White would delay handing down the decision to circumvent Lurton's dissent. White's desire for unanimity was well known. When appointed Chief Justice, it was reported that he said he was "going to stop this dissenting business."[145] Lurton's legal secretary and confidant, Harvey D. Jacob, who lived with Lurton throughout his time on the Court, recalled years later, no doubt echoing Lurton's view, that "Chief Justice White was a great old politician. . . . He'd go walking about visiting judge after judge trying to persuade them to come to his view."[146] But that White would hold up a decision for more than a year in hopes that an ailing dissenting Justice would resign or die seems hard to credit.

The Marbury story is not the only explanation for the delay in decision, nor does it explain the length of the delay. Lurton was not alone, assuming that he did intend to dissent. Justice Lamar initially planned to dissent in *Guinn*, taking the position that the federal statute under which the Oklahoma officials had been convicted did not reach

---

[143] F. Frankfurter to A. Bickel, Sept. 23, 1959. Frankfurter's interest in the *Grandfather Clause Cases* was undoubtedly quickened by his authorship of the Court's opinion in Lane v. Wilson, 307 U.S. 268 (1939), invalidating the registration scheme Oklahoma put in place after the *Guinn* decision on the ground that it perpetuated the discriminatory effects of the Grandfather Clause.

[144] In United States v. Mosley, 238 U.S. 383 (1915), handed down on the same day as *Guinn* and *Myers*, the

Court held that sec. 19 of the Criminal Code, the criminal parallel to sec. 1979, did reach deprivations of voting rights but over an able, lawyerlike dissent by Justice Lamar. It is clear that Lurton agreed with Lamar that sec. 19 did not reach voting rights.

[145] M. Klinkhamer, *Edward Douglas White, Chief Justice of the United States* (1943), 61.

[146] Memorandum by Charles Fairman of conversation with Harvey D. Jacob, June 25, 1936, Lurton Papers, Library of Congress.

franchise offenses. For reasons that are not entirely clear, Lamar ultimately expressed this view by dissenting in the companion case, *United States* v. *Mosley*, rather than in *Guinn*, which has enjoyed, in consequence, an undeserved reputation for unanimity. Lamar was called away from the Court during May and June 1914 on special assignment for the President as a delegate to the so-called ABC Conference to mediate between the United States and Mexico. During Lamar's absence, most of his unwritten majority opinions were reassigned. But there might well have been no one able to take on his dissenting position in *Guinn*, which rested on a complex analysis of legislative history, again assuming that Lurton's dissenting position was based on wholesale constitutional approval of the Grandfather Clause. The *Guinn* decision might have been deferred until Lamar's return so he could write for himself on the statutory problem.

Neither Marbury's claim that White was waiting for Lurton to die nor Lamar's extrajudicial duties in May and June 1914, however, explain why the Court should have waited until the very end of the next term, June 1915, to hand down the decision. Lurton in the meantime had fallen ill on December 3, 1913, about two weeks after *Myers* was argued, and was absent from the Bench for the next four months. When he returned toward the end of the 1913 Term, he was plainly in a weakened state. He died on July 12, 1914, in Atlantic City, New Jersey, where he had gone to rest after the session. The case was not reargued. Nor do new appointments explain the further delay. McReynolds was nominated on August 19, 1914, and was seated by October, but of course he could take no part because of his role in the case as Attorney General.

When *Guinn* and *Myers* came down, almost a year later on June 21, 1915, there was no sign of disunity or doubt. The Court was unanimous, McReynolds taking no part, and the Chief Justice buried the Grandfather Clause under a barrage of certitude. After warming up with a series of such expressions as "beyond doubt," "it is equally beyond the possibility of question," "how can there be room for any serious dispute," White opened all the stops in this wonderful example of his judicial style:

> Indeed, there seems no escape from the conclusion that to hold that there was even possibility for dispute on the subject would be but to declare that the Fifteenth Amendment not only had not the self-executing power which it has been recognized to have from the beginning, but that its provisions were wholly inoperative because susceptible of being rendered inapplicable by mere forms of expression embodying no exercise of judgment and resting upon no discernible reason other than the purpose to disregard the prohibitions of the Amendment by

947

creating a standard of voting which on its face was in substance but a revitalization of conditions which when they prevailed in the past had been destroyed by the self-operative force of the Amendment.[147]

With a modesty that was altogether misplaced, White concluded: "We have difficulty in finding words to more clearly demonstrate the conviction we entertain" that the Grandfather Clause was indeed a denial of the vote based on race; it keyed the right to vote in 1910 to the condition of things before the Fifteenth Amendment for no other conceivable reason than to circumvent its prohibitions.[148]

White took care to limit the scope of the holding. "[N]o right to question the motive of the state" was asserted, nor was the Grandfather Clause condemned "upon the mere ultimate operation of the power," he observed.[149] He protected the *Williams* precedent by insisting that the Oklahoma literacy test was unquestionably valid. Neither motive nor effect condemned the Grandfather Clause, White maintained; rather it was struck down "on its face and inherently considering the substance of things."[150]

There remained the collateral question of whether Oklahoma's literacy test should fall within the Grandfather Clause, not because it in itself was constitutionally deficient, but because without the clause the literacy requirement might not have been imposed. The question was one of state law, White recognized, but in the absence of any state court judgment, he thought the Supreme Court should answer it. Generally an independently legal provision, like the literacy test, would survive the invalidation of an associated provision, but White thought it clear that the overriding intention of the Grandfather Clause was that no one who met its test should have to meet a literacy test in order to vote. This made sense in the political and racial circumstances of Oklahoma. In a state with few blacks and with two-party politics, White must have thought it unlikely that Populist whites would have supported a literacy test without the saving effects of the Grandfather Clause, even though in Mississippi and elsewhere literacy tests were unaccompanied by Grandfather Clauses, and in states other than Oklahoma, the clause was a temporary loophole only. In any event, if White was in doubt about it, he was justified in putting the burden of further political action on those who supported suffrage restriction.

There was not much for White to add in *Myers* v. *Anderson*.[151] The $500 property qualification was clearly constitutional, "as it

---

[147] 238 U.S. at 363–64.
[148] *Ibid.*, at 364.
[149] *Ibid.*, at 359.
[150] *Ibid.*, at 360.
[151] 238 U.S. 368 (1915).

contains no express discrimination repugnant to the fifteenth amendment, and it is not susceptible of being assailed on account of an alleged wrongful motive on the part of the lawmaker or the mere possibilities of its future operation in practice"; yet it had to be thrown out with the Grandfather Clause.[152] Had only the Grandfather Clause been struck out, the absurd result would have been that naturalized citizens and their descendants could have voted freely while native-born citizens could not unless they met the property test.[153]

D. *United States* v. *Mosley:* THE PRESENT IN CONTROL OF THE PAST

Along with *Guinn* and *Myers*, the Supreme Court handed down a third companion case dealing with the right to vote, that, although it turned on statutory construction, was truly constitutional in significance, in manner of reasoning, and in what it revealed about the Court's attitude toward federal protection for the rights of blacks. *United States* v. *Mosley*[154] also came from Oklahoma; it was argued the same day as *Guinn* and held for decision along with it. *Mosley* came up on a truncated record and was not presented to the Court as a race case. But in fact it was, involving the wholesale refusal to count hundreds of black votes in the heated imbroglio over the enforcement of the Grandfather Clause in the 1912 Oklahoma elections.

About a month after the 1912 election, Boardman reported to the Attorney General that the two Democratic members of the three-person Blaine County Election Board, Tom Mosley and Dan Hogan, had, unbeknownst to the Republican member, left out of their official canvass all the votes from eleven precincts where the Grandfather Clause suffrage scheme had not been zealously enforced. The result was to drop some twelve hundred mostly Republican votes, many cast by blacks and Indians, so that the Republican candidate for Congress, who should have won, was narrowly defeated by the Democratic candi-

---

[152] *Ibid.,* at 379.

[153] The conclusion that the property test did not survive was critical to the result in *Myers,* since none of the black plaintiffs could meet the property test, and the refusal to register them would have been proper had the property test remained valid. But since the property test was voided along with the Grandfather Clause, it could not justify the refusal to register. Neither, White held, were the

Giles precedents a defense. The voiding of the Grandfather Clause left the previous Maryland suffrage scheme intact; it did not leave Maryland without any constitutional suffrage scheme. Therefore, the registrars could not escape their duty to register the black plaintiffs. White also rejected offhandedly the contention that sec. 1979 of the Revised Statutes did not cover deprivations of the right to vote.

[154] 238 U.S. 383 (1915).

date, and three county offices went to Democrats rather than Republicans.[155] Boardman proposed to prosecute this election fraud, understandably enough, under section 5515 of the Revised Statutes, which explicitly punished failing to count votes, but "in as much as the Revised Statutes in this office are very incomplete, it has been very hard for us to trace the history of this Statute as to whether it is still in force. . . ."[156] In fact, section 5515 was one of those repealed in 1894, but Assistant General Harr wrote back suggesting that Boardman proceed under section 19 of the Criminal Code.[157] Boardman later concluded that Mosley and Hogan had aimed more at disfranchising Republicans than blacks, because most of the votes not counted were white, and the racial discrimination claim in the case was dropped.[158] But Blaine County had a heavy black vote, and was a hotbed of Grandfather Clause controversy during the 1912 election; and Boardman did not reckon with the possibility that in the precincts omitted from the canvass, black voters, even if a minority, may have held the balance of power. Moreover, the only explanation Mosley and Hogan ever offered for their actions was that blacks had been permitted to register in those precincts without passing the literacy test.

Mosley and Hogan would later contend at their trial in 1916 that they had acted throughout under instructions from the governor and the state Democratic organization. Three days before the elections, Mosley received the following from the head of the State Election Board, B. W. Riley:

> I want to insist that if you have any election officials who are unwilling to enforce the Grandfather Clause they should be removed and others put in, and if you are unable to get those who will enforce it, no election should be held in that precinct. If an election should be held the precinct should not be recognized as the ballots voted would be illegal unless the voters all qualified as required by law.[159]

On election day, Mosley and Hogan claimed that Governor Cruce, state Attorney General Charles West, and Riley told them that the returns from precincts where blacks had been permitted to vote without taking a written literacy test should not be counted. Governor Cruce denied giving any such instructions, but both Boardman and his suc-

---

[155] H. Boardman to G. Wickersham, Dec. 3, 1912, Justice File 164924, National Archives (hereinafter cited as File 164924).

[156] *Ibid.*

[157] W. R. Harr to H. Boardman, Dec. 12, 1912, File 164924.

[158] H. Boardman to G. Wickersham, Mar. 7, 1913, File 164924.

[159] B. Riley to T. Moseley [sic], Nov. 2, 1912, File 164924.

cessor, Wilson's United States Attorney for the Western District of Oklahoma, J. A. Fain, concluded that he had.

None of this was developed in the record that went on appeal to the Supreme Court, because the district court upheld the defendant's demurrer to the indictment, on the ground that section 19 of the Criminal Code did not cover the charges made. The only question for the Supreme Court, therefore, was whether section 19, the statute under which Guinn and Beal also had been convicted, covered a conspiracy by election officials not to count votes. The argument that it did not was based partly on Congress' general repeal of statutes protecting voting rights in 1894 and partly on its origin as section 6, the Ku Klux Klan provision of the Civil Rights Act of 1870. In its original form, section 6 began: "If two or more persons shall band or conspire together or go in disguise upon the public highway, or on the premises of another . . . to injure, oppress, threaten, or intimidate any citizen with intent to prevent or hinder his free exercise and enjoyment of any right or privilege granted or secured by the Constitution or laws," an obvious allusion to the violent activities of the Ku Klux Klan. Moreover, the five previous sections of the Act explicitly protected the right to vote from, among other things, official connivance, and conspiracies, and provided penalties of up to $500 in fines or one year in jail. Section 6, on the other hand, provided for penalties ten times greater. Why would it cover the same conduct earlier prohibited and punish it much more severely? Thus, there were two quite plausible constructions of section 6 that would not have covered the *Mosley* situation: either that the section did not protect the right to vote at all, or that it was concerned with violent intimidation and not with official chicanery.

When section 6 was reworded as section 5508 of the Revised Statutes of 1873, the Ku Klux Klan focus was dropped, as general words were put up front so that it read: "If two or more persons conspire to injure, oppress, threaten, or intimidate any citizen in the free exercise or enjoyment of any right or privilege secured by him by the Constitution," and the clause about going in disguise, alluding to the Klan, was dropped into a secondary place.[160] The other sections of the 1870 Act dealing explicitly with franchise offenses, along with similar provisions from the 1871 Act, were scattered into some seventeen other sections of the Revised Statutes.

As we have seen, almost all of the provisions dealing explicitly with voting were repealed in 1894.[161] Only three sections dealing with the vote were left on the books. Section 2004, broadly affirming the right to vote "without distinction of race," was retained, but the sections

---

[160] 18 Stat. 1073 (1875).   [161] 28 Stat. 36 (1894).

enforcing this right were dropped,[162] and removal to federal court of any action under section 2004 was precluded.[163] Also left on the books was section 5507, prohibiting anyone from preventing or intimidating another from voting by bribery, economic coercion, or violence; but again, the provision setting forth the punishment for violation was dropped. The only other section dealing specifically with the vote that was retained was 2003, which prohibited any federal military presence at state polling places.

The fact that in 1894 Congress left on the books the catch-all provision of section 5508 thus could be taken as an indication that Congress assumed that it did not protect voting rights, at least in ways that would interfere with state officialdom. Moreover, on the particular action charged in *Mosley*, failure by election officials to count votes, Congress had in 1894 repealed section 2008, which penalized anyone who "refuses or omits to receive, count, certify, register, report, or give effect to the vote" of an individual, an exact description of what Mosley was charged with doing. Another repealed provision, section 2009, had punished anyone who "by threats, or any unlawful means, hinders, delays, prevents, or obstructs" any citizen from exercising the right to vote. In sum, the legislative history tended to show that section 19 of the Criminal Code was originally, as section 6 of the 1870 Act, intended to deal with violent intimidation by lawless groups, not with nonviolent official derelictions, and was not in any event intended to protect voting rights from official action. Moreover, it was on this understanding of its scope that Congress left the successor section 5508 on the books in 1894. On the other hand, the words of section 5508 and its successor, section 19 of the Criminal Code, could be read to cover nonviolent official deprivations of voting rights, along with every other kind of deprivation of federal rights, and the original focus on Ku Klux Klan violence had been subordinated.

Holmes' opinion for the Court in *Mosley* insisted that section 6 of the 1870 Act had dealt "with all Federal rights, and protected them in the lump," and that "[a]ny overlapping that there may have been well might have escaped attention, or if noticed, had been approved."[164] As

---

[162] Revised Statutes, secs. 2007–2009 (1875).

[163] 28 Stat. 36, 37 (1894).

[164] Holmes noted at the outset that there was no question of Congress' constitutional power to protect the right to vote in a congressional election. That was clear under *Ex parte Yarbrough*, 110 U.S. 651 (1884). And then Holmes added this, which would be used fifty years later by Justice Douglas in the Georgia "county unit" reapportionment decision, *Gray v. Sanders*, 372 U.S. 368 (1963): "We regard it as equally unquestionable that the right to have one's vote counted is as open to protection by Congress as the right to put a ballot in a box." 238 U.S. at 386.

Congress sought to protect all federal rights from conspiracies, Holmes thought it did not confine the protection to those involving violence, though that class was put in front.

> Just as the 14th Amendment, to use the happy analogy suggested by the Solicitor General [this was a rare compliment to counsel, for Holmes], was adopted with a view to the protection of the colored race but has been found to be equally important in its application to the rights of all, § 6 had a general scope and used general words that have become the most important now that the Ku Klux have passed away.[165]

The general words that had come to the fore in the Revised Statutes subordinated the "going in disguise" clause, and "the present form gives them a congressional interpretation."[166] The 1894 repeal was overlooked entirely as Holmes airily disengaged from the conventional tools of analysis:

> Even if that interpretation would not have been held correct in an indictment under § 6, which we are far from intimating, and if we cannot interpret the past by the present, we cannot allow the past so far to affect the present as to deprive citizens of the United States of the general protection which on its face § 19 most reasonably affords.[167]

Although the plain meaning of section 19 could clearly embrace all conspiratorial deprivation of constitutional rights, peaceful as well as violent, and official as well as private, Holmes' dismissal of the apparent intention of Congress, and of the original wording of the statute, seems clearly actuated by resolve to give section 19 the latitude which the Court thought it "reasonably affords." The Chief Justice, for one, was enthusiastic, and for good reason. "Thank you ever *so* much. It hits the nail right *on the head*," he returned to Holmes.[168] Holmes

---

[165] 238 U.S. at 388.

[166] *Ibid.* This phrase obscured a question of judgment as to how far Congress should have been deemed to have changed the scope of sec. 6 of the 1870 Act by reworking it in the Revised Statutes. The general rule of interpretation was that where the meaning of the Revised Statutes was plain, the courts should not look to the previous legislation for guidance. United States v. Bowen, 100 U.S. 508 (1880). But there were, of course, counterrules of construction. Where the meaning of the Revised Statutes was doubtful, the courts were required to look to the meaning of the statutes that had been revised, and the Revised Statutes were to be given the same meaning they had in the original, unless Congress clearly manifested an intention to change the law. Stewart v. Kahn, 78 U.S. (11 Wall.) 493 (1871); United States v. Le Bris, 121 U.S. 278 (1887). Was it plain that sec. 19 applied to fraudulent refusal by voting officials to count ballots?

[167] 238 U.S. at 388.

[168] Holmes Papers, Harvard Law School Library (emphasis in original).

had taken off White's shoulders the burden of dealing with the statutory question that stood in the way of the *Guinn* decision. As a Southern Democrat who had been in the Senate since 1894, White would have found it very difficult to ignore the evidence of congressional intent. From McKenna came: "Lamar is going to dissent. I promised him to consider his views. I see no answer to this. If he should show me one my assent must [*sic*] without prejudice."[169]

It is quite possible that the offhand, untroubled quality of Holmes' analysis resulted from the fact that the Court heard only one side in *Mosley*. Mosley's lawyer, George H. Gidding, retained by the Democratic State Committee in Oklahoma, did not get his brief in on time, and with the lower court having upheld Mosley's demurrer without opinion, beyond noting that section 19 did not apply, the case against the application of section 19 to Mosley's activities was left entirely to Lamar. He eventually made a careful, persuasive case in dissent, but we know from his letters to the Chief Justice that less than a week before *Mosley* (and the other *Grandfather Clause Cases*) came down, Lamar not only had not written, but had been unable to make White understand, his position on section 19. This is not to say that *Mosley* would have come out differently had the other side been adequately presented. But Holmes, who worked quickly and disliked to revise, might have written a different opinion, and the points Lamar eventually scored in dissent might at least have been addressed, if not actually adhered to.[170]

---

[169] *Ibid.*

[170] Certainly John W. Davis' crisp, forceful brief for the United States gave no hint that anything could be said on the other side. No Fifteenth Amendment question was raised, Davis told the Court, only one of how far Congress had protected the vote in federal elections. The right to vote must entail the right to have the vote counted. *Brief for the United States,* 14, United States v. Mosley, 238 U.S. 383 (1915). "A constitutional guaranty of such significance as this should not be frittered away by a process of hair-splitting definition." It would be a "strained construction" of sec. 19's "sweeping" language to limit it to violent deeds.

The interpretation for which we contend is therefore inevitable. This statute would be but an inefficient instrument to this great end if it forbade interference with the registration of the voter's will by blows, threats, or intimidation, but permitted such obstruction by the safer and surer method of neglecting to return his vote.

Ibid., at 17–18. Davis conceded that when the statute was originally passed in 1870, the chief danger Congress had in mind was violence against blacks trying to vote. But today, "when this particular peril is happily past," the section should not be so restricted. *Ibid.* Then Davis offered the analogy between sec. 19 and the Fourteenth Amendment that Holmes alluded to in his opinion. Davis met the implications of the 1894 repeal head-on. He granted that one of the

X: *Black Disfranchisement*

Justice Lamar's dissent arrayed the evidence against Holmes' interpretation. To read section 19 as Holmes and the Court did was inconsistent with what Congress thought it meant when the statute was adopted, and what Congress thought it meant when it left section 19 on the books in 1894. Moreover, since section 19 reached only conspiracies, the Court's interpretation meant that what was legal if done by one election official was illegal if done by two or more, a dubious construction to strain for. And not only should section 19 be strictly construed because it was penal, but considerations of federal comity should lead the Court to construe federal statutes as making state officials answerable in federal court only when Congress gave clear and explicit directions to that effect. Here, Congress had indeed been explicit: its direction in 1894 was that state officials should not be answerable in federal courts for election offenses. In all its history, the section had never, until the *Grandfather Clause Cases*, been applied against a state election official for depriving someone of the right to vote.[171] It was a lawyerlike dissent in a case that was not decided on lawyerlike considerations.

E. The "Unanimity" of the Grandfather Clause Decisions

One of the striking aspects of the *Grandfather Clause Cases* was that they were unanimous, *Mosley* generally being perceived as a different case. But Lamar's position in *Mosley* would under usual appellate procedures have carried him into dissent in *Guinn* as well. Guinn and Beal, like Mosley, had been convicted under section 19, and Lamar's view of the statute would have required reversal of their convictions, disposing of the need to consider the constitutionality of the Grandfather Clause. Whether Lamar dissented in *Guinn* turned on whether the certification of questions limited to the constitutionality of the Grandfather Clause likewise limited the Supreme Court's scope of review. The Supreme Court's jurisdiction to decide certified questions gave it discretion over whether questions not certified but obviously in the case could be addressed.[172] Thus, the Court in *Guinn* might have brought the

---

repealed sections covered the circumstances of *Mosley* explicitly, but often the same course of conduct was punishable under different statutes, and in any event, sec. 19 punished conspiracies, while the repealed statute had covered individual acts.

[171] *Ex parte* Yarbrough, 110 U.S. 651 (1884), was a prosecution under sec. 5508 for beating a person who had tried to vote, but the defendant was not an election official, and the case involved violent intimidation.

[172] Under sec. 6 of the Judiciary Act of 1891, ch. 517, 26 Stat. 826, 828 (codified as amended in the Judicial Code of 1911, ch. 231, 36 Stat. 1087), the Supreme Court, on receipt of certified questions, "may either give its instruction on the questions . . . or

entire controversy before it, in which case the question of statutory interpretation would have assumed first importance. Lamar at first thought the Court either would or should deal with the statutory question in *Guinn*, because his initial dissenting memorandum was addressed to *Guinn* and to Chief Justice White.

Lamar had trouble getting White to see his position on section 19. "[Y]ou misunderstand me entirely about sec. 19," he wrote to White on June 10, 1915, promising a follow-up written statement of "the views which Justice Lurton and I took on that question and which he repeatedly asked me to write out."[173] White evidently thought Lamar was saying that section 19 had been repealed. "I have never claimed that R.S. 5508 (now Penal Code 19) was repealed," Lamar explained in his second letter, "but have only insisted that its provisions did not apply to the facts set out in the Oklahoma indictments against election officers." Then, after forcefully summarizing the arguments of his *Mosley* dissent, Lamar concluded: "I know how much concern the main question has given you and dislike to trouble you; but even if the question does not have to be answered in the *Guinn* case, it does seem to me that it is necessarily involved in the *Moseley* [*sic*] case."[174]

White's initial drafts of the *Guinn* and *Myers* opinions are not preserved, but Lamar's correspondence indicates that White agreed to some changes that Lamar suggested. In the first place, Lamar objected that the Chief Justice's draft limited the states to making only "reasonable classifications" concerning voter qualifications, and that this was inconsistent with the states' "absolute right to fix qualifications provided they do not infringe the provisions of the 15th Amendment."[175] White conceded on this point: there is no reference in the opinion to "reasonable classifications," and the states' power to qualify the vote on other than racial grounds was treated as beyond question. Second, Lamar was troubled by White's handling of the severability problem. Lamar wanted it made clear that whether the literacy test survived the in-

---

it may require that the whole record and cause may be sent up to it for its consideration, and thereupon shall decide the whole matter in controversy." Although the Supreme Court has had jurisdiction over certified questions from circuit courts since the Act of Apr. 29, 1802, 2 Stat. 156, 159 (1802), the modern form of the jurisdiction took shape with the Judiciary Act of 1891. For a history and discussion of the appellate jurisdiction over certified questions, see J. Moore and A. Vestal, "Present and Potential Role of Certifi-

cation in Federal Appellate Procedure," *Va. L. Rev.*, 35:1, 1949.

[173] J. R. Lamar to E. D. White, June 10, 1915, Lamar Papers, University of Georgia Library.

[174] J. R. Lamar to E. D. White, June 10, 1915, Lamar Papers.

[175] Lamar also objected that "[i]f the courts are to say what is a reasonable classification the result would be that they would constantly be called upon to determine a political question." *Ibid.*

validation of the Grandfather Clause was for the states to decide, even though the Supreme Court needed to decide this local question, since it first arose in federal court. Lamar was worried not about Oklahoma, since, as he wrote to White, "I am quite sure that the Oklahoma voters should not have adopted the literacy test unless at the same time they adopted the Grandfather Clause."[176] But in other states, he thought the literacy or property tests might well survive. White met this point also, and struck out of the final opinion some language of the draft that Lamar feared might make other states feel bound by the Court's holding that the literacy test was not severable from the Grandfather Clause.[177] White's accommodation to Lamar on these two points may have persuaded Lamar to pitch his dissent to *Mosley* and not to *Guinn*.

Whether by confusion or design, Chief Justice White's handling of the statutory problem in *Guinn* was cannily geared to holding a unanimous Court. White focused on the certified questions, and subordinated the statutory question almost to the vanishing point. "The contention concerning the inapplicability of [section 19] . . . or of its repeal by implication, is fully answered by the ruling this day made in [*Mosley*]." Beyond this, there was no discussion to attract Lamar's opposition on the statutory point, and so the fact that *Guinn* was before the Court on certified questions preserved the unanimity of Court and led Lamar to say his piece in *Mosley* instead.

Lamar's dissent in *Mosley* came down on the last day of the 1914 Term, and that was the last day Lamar would sit. He did not feel well at the end of the term, suffered a stroke that summer, and did not resume his seat on the Bench before his death on January 2, 1916. He had other opinions for the Court on that last day of the 1914 Term, but no other dissents, and if, as seems likely, Lamar got out his majority opinions before his lone dissent in *Mosley*, which remained unwritten as late as June 14, the dissent was probably Lamar's last-written utterance as a Justice of the Supreme Court.[178] It was an entirely characteristic, if unknowing, swan song: careful, demonstrating considerable technical

---

[176] J. R. Lamar to E. D. White, June 14, 1915, Lamar Papers.

[177] White's draft had said that the question of severability should be left to the states "if it is possible to do so," and Lamar was afraid that the phrase "indicate[d] that there might be a case in which this court could say that the result was so 'anomalous' that it was 'not possible' for the State court to decide that the provisions were separable." *Ibid*.

[178] Lamar's opinions for the Court on June 21, 1915, were: Chicago, Milwaukee & St. Paul R.R. v. Wisconsin, 238 U.S. 491 (1915); Wells Fargo v. Ford, 238 U.S. 503 (1915); Central Vermont Ry. v. White, 238 U.S. 507 (1915); United States v. Delaware, Lackawanna & Western R.R., 238 U.S. 516 (1915); and Newman v. United States *ex rel.* Frizzell, 238 U.S. 537 (1915).

skill, rooted in the attitudes of Southern landed gentry, and looking to the past, not to the future. The *Mosley* dissent also epitomizes Lamar's genius for friendship on the Court. Despite its forcefulness, there was nothing sharp in it, even in the face of Holmes' rather casual dismissal of the tools of analysis Lamar thought should be brought to bear. And Lamar presented the Chief Justice, whom he cherished, with the prized gift of unanimity in striking down the Grandfather Clause.

Because of the apparent unanimity of the Court, the blatant discrimination inherent in the Grandfather Clause, and the efficacy of other ways of disfranchising blacks, most historians and constitutional scholars have regarded the *Grandfather Clause Cases* as unsurprising—significant to be sure, but foreordained. From the perspective of the Progressive era, however, the *Guinn, Myers,* and *Mosley* decisions were far from inevitable. In the first place, an entirely plausible construction of the federal criminal statute under which the cases were prosecuted was available that would have mooted the Fifteenth Amendment question. Had Justice Lamar's view of section 19 prevailed, not only could *Guinn* have gone the other way, as we have seen, but the Court might well have construed the catch-all civil remedies statute not to reach deprivations of the right to vote by state election officials, producing the opposite result in *Myers* v. *Anderson* as well. Section 1979 of the Revised Statutes used language essentially similar to section 19's, and if the catch-all criminal statute were read not to encompass voting rights, partly to effectuate Congress' intent in the 1894 repeal to withdraw the federal courts from voting rights controversies, it would not have been a strain to construe the catch-all civil statute *in pari materia.*

Buttressing a restrictive reading of the statutes, but potentially a separate threshold as well, was the position Holmes came close to, and may indeed have intended, in *Giles* v. *Harris,* and which underlay *Williams* v. *Mississippi* and *Giles* v. *Teasley* as well: that disfranchisement was essentially a political question, one the federal courts should leave to Congress and the President, or on which they should at least look to the political branches for direction in deciding questions of statutory coverage or of the scope of equitable remedies. From the perspective of *Williams* and *Giles,* the construction of section 19 and section 1979 taken in the *Grandfather Clause Cases* is a distinct surprise. The cases presented the Supreme Court with a choice, and in electing for the first time to use federal law to strike down a state law depriving blacks of the vote, the Court made a notable departure. The departure was not only from what went before, but from what came after. The cases dealing with primaries show that the Supreme Court between the *Grandfather Clause Cases* and *Newberry* v. *United States* in 1921 maintained a commitment to essentially unfettered state control over elections.

The color of the unexpected that historical perspective gives the *Grandfather Clause* decisions is deepened when one takes account of the large contingent element in the Justice Department's role in the cases. The *Guinn* prosecution never would have gotten started had not John Embry disregarded Attorney General Wickersham's explicit instructions, and it may well be the case, though one cannot know, that both the Taft and Wilson administrations pressed on with the challenge to the Grandfather Clause in the federal courts because they felt their hands were forced.

F.   The Aftermath

Notice was widely taken of the significance of a unanimous Supreme Court for the first time striking down a state law disfranchising black people. Moorfield Storey and others in the NAACP exulted. The decision "was a very great victory," "a great step in advance, and indicates that the court has waked up to the situation," Storey wrote Joel E. Spingarn, adding modestly that credit should go to Solicitor General Davis.[179] In another letter, Storey called the decisions "the first step in favor of liberty that the Supreme Court has taken. The fact that it was unanimous and that the Chief Justice gave the opinion adds to its weight."[180] *The Nation* found the decisions "of the utmost Constitutional and political importance. It means as much forward as the Dred Scott case did backward." At the same time, the magazine expressed "full sympathy with the South in the efforts it will now have to make to adjust itself to the new conditions."[181] James C. Hamphill, writing in the *North American Review*, thought it "one of the most important judgments pronounced by the Court in fifty years,"[182] and *The Outlook* hailed it as "[a]mong the most notable decisions of the Supreme Court in recent years."[183] Almost all the approving comments on the decision caught the historical symbolism of White's authorship. *The Independent* thought "[t]his is a great victory for justice, and it is pleasant to note that Chief Justice White, who read the decision, is a citizen of Louisiana and was a Conféderedate [*sic*] soldier."[184] *The Nation* added: "Next to the unanimity of the Court, the most gratifying

---

[179] M. Storey to J. Spingarn, July 12, 1915, Storey Papers.

[180] M. Storey to H. May, July 10, 1915, Storey Papers.

[181] *The Nation,* 100:699, June 24, 1915.

[182] Hamphill, "The South and the Negro Vote," *N. Am. Rev.,* 202:213, 1915.

[183] *The Outlook,* 110:486, 1915.

[184] *The Independent,* 83:3, 4, 1915.

circumstance of its decision is that it was read by Chief Justice White . . . formerly a Confederate soldier."[185]

Paradoxically, the theme of historic importance was offset by a complacent sense that the *Grandfather Clause Cases* would not have much practical impact. Indeed, several newspapers pointed out that the Court itself had pointed the way to continued disfranchisement of blacks. The *Times-Dispatch* of Richmond reassured its readers: "The old-style 'grandfather clauses' have served their purpose—necessary in their day, but no longer vital to the South's protection. It is just as well they are to pass."[186] Another Richmond newspaper, the *News Leader*, said the decision was a "temporary embarrassment," but praised the Court for showing "the line a State may follow in restricting its franchise."[187] The *Times-Picayune* of New Orleans was convinced that the decision "will not increase the number of negroes voting by one." The decision

> is not of the slightest political importance in the South. The question of negro suffrage has been settled—and settled rightly—by the poll-tax and in other ways; and the "grandfather clause" cut little or no part in the settlement; it merely helped to disarm any opposition from the illiterate whites.[188]

The Northern press echoed the conclusion: "It is not clear to us that this Supreme Court decision will have a practical effect," said *The Outlook*,[189] and Hamphill called it "largely academic."[190] The *New York Sun* predicted that "the political hue of the South will remain white," and the *New York Times* assured its readers "the white man will rule his land. The only question left by the Supreme Court's decision is how he will rule it."[191]

There was no such serenity in the states from which the *Grandfather Clause Cases* had come. The *Baltimore Evening Sun* thought the decision would

> unsettle an accepted arrangement that has helped to keep the peace and to prevent the domination of the higher by the lower elements. . . . [T]he misfortune of having waked the sleeping dog in the "grandfather

---

185 *The Nation*, 100:699, June 24, 1915.

186 Quoted in *Literary Digest*, 51:5, 1915.

187 *Ibid.*

188 Quoted *ibid.*, 200. See also the collection of representative comments from Southern newspapers in the *New*

York Times, June 22, 1915, p. 8, col. 2.

189 *The Outlook*, 110:486, 487, 1915.

190 Hamphill, "South and the Negro Vote," 214.

191 *New York Times*, June 23, 1915, p. 10, col. 2.

clause" is that it may revitalize a dead issue and lead to a race and political agitation earnestly to be deprecated.[192]

Harlow's Weekly in Oklahoma City reported that the decision was "the most prominent subject of conversation all over the State," and that Republicans were overjoyed.[193] Governor Cruce immediately set about to find "something just as good as the 'grandfather clause,' " reported the *San Diego Union*, because although less than 10 percent of the state population was black, the two major political parties were "so nearly even in strength that the negro vote might place the Republicans in the ascendency."[194] For a time, Oklahoma Democrats thought to replace the Grandfather Clause with an "Old Soldiers" Clause, under which descendants of men who served in various wars would be permitted to register without satisfying literacy requirements. But this was abandoned as too patent a violation.[195] Instead, a special session of the Oklahoma legislature early in 1916 enacted a new registration law that gave permanent voting privileges to all those registered to vote in the 1914 general election, held of course under the Grandfather Clause suffrage scheme, and gave all others eligible in 1916 only twelve days to get their names on the rolls, unless illness or absence prevented, or be disfranchised for life.[196] Thus was the Grandfather Clause grandfathered in Oklahoma. That the state responded to the *Guinn* decision with such an obvious perpetuation of discrimination suggests how far black disfranchisement was accepted as an appropriate end, the only problem being to find a means that would circumvent the Fifteenth Amendment. Equally revealing is that the federal government did nothing about it. No criminal charges were brought against the officials who administered the scheme, and one is reminded again of the Justice Department's reluctance to bring the Grandfather Clause prosecution in the first place. It was not until 1939 that the Supreme Court, in an opinion by Justice Frankfurter, and with Butler and McReynolds dissenting, struck down the Oklahoma scheme in *Lane* v. *Wilson*,[197] a civil action brought by a black man denied the right to vote. And so after 1915, the Grandfather Clause in Oklahoma continued its sway into the next generation.[198]

---

[192] *Baltimore Evening Sun*, June 22, 1915, p. 6, col. 1.

[193] Quoted in *Literary Digest*, 51: 200, 1915.

[194] *Ibid.*

[195] *Ibid.*

[196] Act of Feb. 26, 1916, ch. 24, secs. 2, 4, 1916 Okla. Sess. Laws 33, 33–35.

[197] 307 U.S. 268 (1939).

[198] Guinn, Beal, Mosley, and the other Oklahoma election officials whom the Justice Department had charged remained caught in the Grandfather Clause controversy for two more years, but eventually escaped. On remand, the Court of Appeals affirmed the convictions of

III. Edward Douglass White: From the KKK to the Grandfather Clause

The favorable notice given his leadership of the unanimous *Grandfather Clause* decisions must have been a tonic for White in the summer of 1915, as it came hard on the heels of a distressing public association of White with the Ku Klux Klan. Along with Woodrow Wilson, White allowed himself to be drawn into controversy over D. W. Griffith's brilliant, innovative, incendiary movie, *Birth of a Nation*. The movie glorified the Klan after the Civil War, and it portrayed the freedman, in the words of the NAACP's publication *The Crisis*, as "an ignorant fool, a vicious rapist, a venal and unscrupulous politician, or a faithful but doddering idiot."[199] When the NAACP embarked on a censorship crusade, Thomas Dixon, the author of the novel *The Clansman*, on which the movie was partly based, engineered a bold scheme. He arranged for the film to be shown to President Wilson and the Cabinet at a private showing at the White House.[200] On the strength of

---

Guinn and Beal, Guinn v. United States, 228 F. 103 (8th Cir. 1915), but Attorney General Gregory recommended that they be pardoned shortly thereafter, and President Wilson granted the pardons on Jan. 17, 1916. 1916 Att'y. Gen. Rep. 356. Four other groups of election officials had been indicted, and their trials had been held for the outcome of the *Guinn* decision. One group was tried and acquitted in February 1916. The U. S. Attorney in charge reported that it was difficult to corroborate the testimony of blacks denied the vote five years before, that evidence of violence was wanting, and that the juries obviously believed the defendants had enforced the Grandfather Clause in good faith. J. Fain to T. Gregory, Feb. 5, 1916, File 164924. Two other sets of indictments were then dismissed by the Justice Department. However, Mosley and Hogan were tried in 1916 and the jury hung, evidently because it believed that the governor and other high state officials had ordered Mosley and Hogan to falsify returns. Despite requests from Oklahoma Governor Robert Lee Wil-

liams and Senator Robert L. Owen that the charges against Mosley and Hogan be dismissed, Attorney General Gregory, on Mar. 25, 1916, ordered that they be retired. There is no record of the results of any retrial. Gregory outlined the department's actions on the various Oklahoma election cases in a letter to Senator Owen. T. Gregory to R. Owen, Apr. 18, 1916, File 164924.

[199] Kellogg, *NAACP,* 143. The film was never shown in Ohio, and it was banned in Pennsylvania as a posthumous libel on Thaddeus Stevens. In many cities, mayors censored the more inflammatory scenes. The greatest furor was in Boston, where Storey, Villard, and the local NAACP chapter tried unsuccessfully to have the film banned altogether. Hixson, *Storey and the Abolitionist Tradition,* 132.

[200] On Feb. 3, 1915, Dixon met for half an hour with the President at the White House—appealing to him as a history scholar and relying on their graduate student days together at Johns Hopkins University—to convince him to see the film. Wilson, still in mourning after the death of his

having shown the film to the President, Dixon managed a meeting with White on February 19, 1915, the day after the White House showing, to try to persuade him, too, to view the film. White was at first reluctant, Dixon later claimed in his unpublished autobiography, but agreed to see the film when told it was about the Klan. Dixon quotes the following interchange, White speaking first:

> "I was a member of the Klan, sir. . . . Through many dark nights, I walked my sentinel's beat through the ugliest streets of New Orleans with a rifle on my shoulder. . . . You've told the true story of that uprising of outraged manhood?"
> "In a way I'm sure you'll approve."
> "I'll be there!" he firmly announced.[201]

Whatever the truth of Dixon's recollections, and he had fish to fry to say the least, the Chief Justice did, as he would later regret, view the film that very evening at its first public showing. At a showing boasting "a large part of the membership of the Senate and House, a sprinkling of the members of the Diplomatic Corps and scores of high officials," including no fewer than thirty-eight Senators, the Chief Justice and Mrs. White were the guests of honor at the film's premiere, sponsored by the National Press Club in the ballroom of the Raleigh Hotel.[202] White's presence at the premiere was not necessarily an endorsement of

---

first wife, said he could not go to a theater but that he would view the film in the White House with Cabinet members and their families. Wilson supposedly told Dixon, however, that news of the private showing was not to be made public. T. Cripps, *Slow Fade to Black: The Negro in American Film, 1900–1942* (1977), 52; A. S. Link, ed., *The Papers of Woodrow Wilson* (1980), 32:142.

Wilson's wishes were not respected, as the press immediately spread word of the Feb. 18 showing. See, e.g., *Wichita Beacon* (Kansas), Feb. 22, 1915, reprinted in Stern, "Griffith: The Birth of a Nation," Part 1, *Film Culture*, 36:75, 1965.

The President apparently was not told what *The Birth of a Nation* was about when he agreed to see it. Later, Dixon was to write to Joseph P. Tumulty: "*Of course I didn't dare allow the President to know the real big purpose back of my film—which was to revolutionize northern sentiments by a presentation of history that would transform every man in my audience into a good Democrat! . . . What I told the President was that I would show him the birth of a new art—the launching of the mightiest engine for moulding public opinion in the history of the world.*" (Emphasis in original.) T. Dixon to J. Tumulty, May 1, 1915, in Link, *Papers of Woodrow Wilson*, 142, n.1.

[201] The excerpt from Dixon's autobiography is quoted in E. Goldman, *Rendezvous with Destiny* (1963), 228–29. See also the account in Cripps, *Negro in American Film*, 52.

[202] *Washington Post,* Feb. 20, 1915, p. 5, col. 5; *Washington Herald,* Feb. 20, 1915, quoted in Stern, "Griffith: Birth of a Nation."

the film's attitudes. Most of the great excitement about the film concerned its technique and scale; it was a window on the future of a major new medium. But White's presence was a coup for the embattled filmmakers.

When Dixon and the film's other promoters traveled the country proclaiming the endorsement of the President and the Chief Justice in cities where the NAACP or church groups tried to bar the showing of the film, Wilson and White reacted in different ways.[203] Although advised by his secretary, Joseph P. Tumulty, publicly to disapprove the film, Wilson hedged: "I would like to do this if there were some way in which I could do it without seeming to be trying to meet the agitation."[204] Wilson did allow Tumulty to say that he had not approved the film, but he did not express outright disapproval until 1918.[205] White, on the other hand, promptly threatened to denounce the film publicly if Dixon and Griffiths continued to claim his support. In a letter to Tumulty, who had received queries about the President's and the Chief Justice's alleged approval, White wrote:

> After talking with you the other day on the subject of the picture show I wrote to the gentleman in New York and had an answer from him. In writing him I told him that I was so situated that if the rumors about my having sanctioned the show were continued that I might be under the obligation of denying them publicly and say, it might be, that I do not approve the show, and therefore if the owners were wise they would stop the rumors. Incidentally in the letter I said: "I have reason to know,—although not authoritatively so—that the name of the President also has been used and that he might perhaps be obliged to take the same course that I have indicated if the rumors are not stopped. I do not speak with any authority, but only by way of rumor."[206]

[203] M. Damrosch to J. Tumulty, Mar. 27, 1915, in Link, *Papers of Woodrow Wilson,* 455; T. Thacher to J. Tumulty, Apr. 17, 1915, in Link, *Papers of Woodrow Wilson,* 33:86. It was originally reported from an unattributed source in MacKaye, "The Birth of a Nation," *Scribner's Magazine,* 102:69, 1937, that after viewing the film, Wilson wiped tears from his eyes and stated: "It is like writing history with lightning. And my only regret is that it is all so terribly true." Link, *Papers of Woodrow Wilson,* 32: 267, n.1. Link tried to ascertain Wilson's true reaction from the last survivor of the White House showing,

Marjorie Brown King, in 1977. Link was told that Wilson appeared preoccupied during the showing, and left after the film without speaking to anyone.

[204] Link, *Papers of Woodrow Wilson,* 33:68. Three years later, during World War I, Wilson finally publicly disapproved the film. A. S. Link, *Wilson: The New Freedom* (1956), 253.

[205] Link, *Wilson: The New Freedom,* 253–54.

[206] E. D. White to J. Tumulty, Apr. 5, 1915, in Link, *Papers of Woodrow Wilson,* 42:486 (footnotes omitted).

It is clear that the producers of the film were informed of White's position. Beneath the surface of these interactions with the President's secretary, one can sense a worried White considerably stirred by having been dragged into public association with Griffith's propaganda.

Dixon's claim that White was a member of the Klan is not corroborated, and is probably an embellishment if not a downright fabrication. White's biographer found no evidence of any Klan affiliation, although she reported rumors that White took part in the street fighting in New Orleans that accompanied the temporary overthrow of the Republican Kellogg regime in September 1874.[207] White was a mainstay of the Redeemer regime of Governor Francis T. Nicholls that took over Louisiana in return for backing Hayes in the disputed Presidential election of 1876. Almost certainly, White would have been prominent in the "White League," the group of Louisiana Democrats that came together in the summer of 1874, dedicated to white supremacy and opposition to the Reconstruction regime of the Kellogg administration. The White League was armed and fought several pitched battles in the streets of New Orleans against the Republican-controlled police and militia in the course of unseating Kellogg for a short time in 1874. Whether White was involved in the fighting seems doubtful, however. He was not among those named by the White League Commanders in a list of persons who led units in the fighting, and given his stature and wartime experience, he almost certainly would have been a leader if he had been involved in the fighting at all.[208] Extensive congressional investigations of the episode did not link him to the fighting,[209] although White personally testified about election fraud and other matters. If White told Dixon about the White League, Dixon might have thought that that was one of the Klan-like organizations that sprang up during Reconstruction, and might have thought that claiming White for the Klan was not too great an embellishment. Not a hint of Klan activity came up on White's nomination as Associate Justice or Chief Justice. And although White was proud indeed of his service for the Confederacy, and marked military and other commemorations with personal ceremonies, no evidence has come down of any similar remembrance of Klan activities. Dixon's account would indicate that

---

[207] Klinkhamer, *Edward Douglas White*, 19.

[208] H.R. Rep. No. 101, 43rd Cong., 2nd Sess. (1875), 213–15; H.R. Rep. No. 261, 43rd Cong., 2nd Sess. (1875), 225–26. See generally P. Howard, *Political Tendencies in Louisiana* (1971), 136–37; E. Lonn, *Reconstruction in Louisiana after 1868* (1917), 181 *et seq.*; E. King, "The Political Situation in Louisiana," in *The Great South* (1972), 89 *et seq.*

[209] H.R. Rep. No. 101, 43rd Cong., 2nd Sess. (1875), 29; *Testimony Taken by the Select Committee on the Recent Election in Louisiana*, House Mis. Doc. No. 34, Pt. 2, 44th Cong., 2nd Sess. (1877), 396.

White was proud of his Klan affiliation, but if so, it is hard to believe that White did not mark his pride in the ceremonial ways with which he liked to remember other events of his past. Dixon's claim that White said he was in the Klan cannot be disproved, and is not altogether implausible, but the weight of evidence points the other way.[210]

White did not act like a Klansman on the Bench, at least not after he took the center seat. True, as Associate Justice he joined the majorities in *Plessy* v. *Ferguson, Williams* v. *Mississippi,* the two *Giles* decisions, and *Berea College* v. *Kentucky.* But as Chief Justice, White's performance in cases involving the rights of black people was a different story. He joined in *Bailey* and *Reynolds,* the two peonage decisions, and in *Buchanan* v. *Warley,* limiting the spread of Jim Crow. He was not with the majority in *McCabe,* but his objections need not necessarily have gone to the merits. Most notably, as the author of the *Grandfather Clause Cases,* White set himself firmly against the position taken by the Senate repeal of the federal election laws in 1894, the very year White left the Senate for the Court, namely, the recognition of state autonomy over elections. Not only in the *Grandfather Clause Cases* but also in the later decisions concerning federal power over primaries, White stood for the supremacy of federal power. It is not the record of a Hughes or a Day, and not close to Harlan, but in race cases during his tenure as Chief Justice, White committed himself to each of the Civil War amendments on behalf of the rights of black people.

When Senator Henry Cabot Lodge, a determined proponent of federal protection for black voting rights, helped to scotch the nomination of Lurton by Theodore Roosevelt in 1906 with his demand for a Republican appointee, he wrote:

> But that which is decisive with me and which I think more important than anything else in such an appointment is that any judge of the Supreme Court for whom we are responsible should be of the nationalist and not of the separatist school, should be a Hamiltonian and not a Jeffersonian. It is a rare thing to find a Democrat who is at heart a Federalist and an old Whig like White and it is not a chance to be taken.[211]

---

[210] If White was a member of one of the secret white supremacy organizations in New Orleans after the war, it would more likely have been the Knights of the White Camellia than the KKK. The Knights was more widespread than the Klan around New Orleans, its activities less violent, and its members more respectable. A. Trelease, *White Terror: The Ku Klux Klan Conspiracy and Southern Reconstruction* (1971), 92 *et seq.*

[211] H. Lodge to T. Roosevelt, Sept. 1, 1906, Box 110, Theodore Roosevelt Papers, Library of Congress.

X: *Black Disfranchisement*

Although Lodge was not writing about race relations, the attitudes he was speaking to had vital bearing on the rights of blacks. Lodge was right about White, and indeed, it was a rare thing to find. A Democrat from the deep South, veteran of the Confederacy, Chief Justice at a time when constitutional principles protecting black people's political and civil rights were in danger of sinking from view, White lent his powerful, nationalist voice to the constructive record of the Supreme Court in race relations cases during the second decade of the twentieth century.

IV. The Retreat to Newberry v. United States: *The Past in Control of the Present*

How markedly the *Grandfather Clause Cases* ran against the drift of constitutional law and statutory construction concerning elections is revealed by comparison not only to the decisions that came before, but also to a series of decisions handed down by the White Court after 1915, culminating in the celebrated *Newberry* decision in 1921. *Newberry* narrowed the statutory scope of section 19, and put election primaries beyond the constitutional reach of federal power altogether. Neither *Newberry* nor the other limiting decisions concerned racial discrimination, but they did smooth the way to one of the most effective techniques of black disfranchisement, the "white primary," which began its dismal sequence in the Supreme Court in 1927.

United States v. *Gradwell*, decided in 1917, was one of four cases decided together involving election fraud.[212] In two of the cases, the indictments charged a conspiracy to defraud the United States under section 37 of the Criminal Code "by corrupting and debauching, by bribery of voters, the general election" of November 1914 in Rhode Island. The other two cases arose from a West Virginia primary to pick the Republican nominee for the United States Senate. One of these also charged a violation of section 37, but for causing unqualified voters to vote in the primary. The same defendants were also charged in a separate indictment with violating section 19, on the theory that by causing unqualified voters to vote, some many times, they had deprived the candidates for the Republican Senate nomination of their "constitutional right" of having only duly qualified Republicans vote, and vote only once.

A unanimous Court affirmed the dismissal of the indictments in all four cases. The conspiracy-to-defraud statute did not apply to elections, Justice Clarke wrote for the Court. Section 37 had originally been passed as part of the revenue laws and these cases were the first attempt

---

[212] 243 U.S. 476 (1917).

to apply it to election fraud. Federal election fraud statutes had existed for a time, but it was "a matter of general as of legal history that Congress, after twenty-four years of experience, returned to its former attitude toward such elections and repealed all these laws," thereby affirming the policy of "entrusting the conduct of elections to state laws, administered by state officers." In view of this policy, and since Congress when it assumed to regulate elections did so in unmistakable terms, it would be "a strained and unreasonable construction" to apply section 37 to elections. As to whether section 19 covered voting fraud in a state primary, it was true that *Mosley* had applied section 19 to certain franchise offenses in a general election, but the section had never been applied to primaries. Clarke had doubts whether Congress' power under Article I, Section 4, to regulate "the times, places, and manner of holding elections for Senators and Representatives" extended to primaries, but even if Congress could regulate primaries generally, the West Virginia primary had peculiar features. It was available only to major parties, and the ballot remained open by petition to other candidates. Any rights which candidates had in such an inconclusive context were derived wholly from state law, Clarke thought, and could not be considered rights under the Constitution or federal law protected by section 19. Congress had never sought to regulate primaries or other nomination procedures, and "it is not for the courts, in the absence of such legislation, to attempt to supply it by stretching old statutes to new uses."[213] Much of this, of course, would have militated against the application of section 19 in the *Grandfather Clause Cases*.

The reprise of Lamar's arguments in his *Mosley* dissent was even clearer in *United States* v. *Bathgate*, where the issue was whether section 19 covered a conspiracy to bribe voters at general elections.[214] Congress' power to reach such conduct was clear, Justice McReynolds wrote for the Court, but its policy had been "to leave the conduct of elections at which its members are chosen to state law alone."[215] The Civil Rights Act of 1870, "[d]eparting from the course long observed,"[216] had of course regulated elections comprehensively, including a specific provision dealing with bribery of voters, but that and kindred sections were repealed in 1894 "[i]n pursuance of a well-understood policy."[217] Of

---

[213] 243 U.S. at 478, 483, 484, 485, 488–89. *The Yale Law Journal* found *Gradwell* "most noteworthy as an exception to the current tendency to extend the scope of the federal laws and leave less and less to the states." *Yale L. J.*, 27:137, 1917. See also *Harv. L. Rev.*, 31:302, 1917; *Va. L. Reg.*, 3:131, 1917.

[214] 246 U.S. 220 (1918). There were also counts charging violations of sec. 37, conspiracy to defraud the United States, but they were dismissed on the authority of United States v. Gradwell, 243 U.S. 476 (1917).

[215] 246 U.S. at 225.

[216] *Ibid.*

[217] *Ibid.*

course, McReynolds said blithely, section 19 meant now what it had when it passed in 1870, and since bribery was specifically denounced by another section, later repealed, section 19 should not be construed to reach bribery of voters, given the general policy "not to interfere with elections within a State except by clear and specific provisions."[218] All of this, of course, had been said by Lamar against the holding in *Mosley*; and that case, it must be remembered, had been presented to the Court as involving not racial discrimination but simple partisan fraud in failing to count votes. The earlier case involved the failure to count the ballots of individual, though unidentified, voters; the present case involved bribery of voters. Grasping at their difference, McReynolds distinguished *Mosley* on the rather strained basis that section 19 was designed to vindicate personal rights "capable of enforcement by a court, and not the political, non-judicable [*sic*] one common to all that the public shall be protected from harmful acts." There were no dissents.[219]

The past most clearly regained control of the present, to recur to Holmes' figure of speech in *Mosley*, and took a claim on the future, too, in the controversial, divisive decision in *Newberry v. United States*, handed down on May 2, 1921, shortly before the death of Chief Justice White. *Newberry* was more than a reversion to judicial attitudes about elections that prevailed before the *Grandfather Clause Cases*; it was a harbinger of constitutional dialectics in the years to come. In its narrow literalism and historical rigidity, in its commitment to qualitative, categorical, conceptual principles of constitutional interpretation, in its candid rejection of functional measures of national interest, and in its overriding of a recent, considered congressional judgment on a matter peculiarly within the ambit of legislative concern, Justice McReynolds' *Newberry* opinion was a window on the troubled course of constitutional adjudication in the decade of the twenties and beyond. The gulf in constitutional philosophy between the majority and the dissenters would promote increasingly bitter divisions within the Court, and between the Court and the political branches, until the debacle of the Court-packing plan in 1937.

Newberry was also the occasion for the final utterance, in dissent, of Chief Justice Edward Douglass White. If any case could be thought to ring down the curtain on the White Court, and on a decade of inconsistent progressivism in constitutional adjudication, *Newberry* was it. It marked an end and a beginning.

Truman H. Newberry, a wealthy businessman from Detroit and former Secretary of the Navy under President Roosevelt, ran against Henry Ford in a close and bitter election for the United States Senate

---

[218] *Ibid.,* at 226.   [219] *Ibid.,* at 226–27.

in Michigan in 1918. That summer, amidst charges of profligate spending, Newberry and Ford won the Republican and Democratic primaries, respectively, and prepared for a campaign that one Michigan newspaper, capturing the temper of the contest, thought would mean "the debauchery of Michigan politics."[220] Reports of Newberry's spending in the primary led Democratic Senator Pomerene of Ohio to call for a Senate investigation, but that action was postponed until after the November election.[221] A federal grand jury, situated, oddly enough, in New York, also investigated the primary, but, according to the *New York Times*, "after considering much evidence the jury was not convinced that there was enough to warrant an indictment."[222]

Ford lost the November election narrowly, but his campaign was not over. He demanded a recount and asked the Senate not to seat Newberry because of alleged violations of the Federal Corrupt Practices Act of 1911, which provided that no candidate for the House or Senate should spend or cause to be spent "in procuring his nomination and election" more than state law permitted, with a ceiling of $5,000 for House candidates and $10,000 for Senate candidates.[223] Michigan

---

[220] *Escanaba Journal*, Aug. 2, 1918, quoted in *Senator from Michigan: Hearing on S. Res. 11 Authorizing Investigation of Alleged Unlawful Practices in the Election of a Senator from Michigan, Before the Senate Committee on Privileges and Elections*, 67th Cong., 1st Sess. (1921), 790. See also S. Ervin, *Henry Ford vs. Truman H. Newberry* (1935), 18–19.

[221] 56 *Cong. Rec.* 10, 386 (1918).

[222] *New York Times*, Oct. 30, 1918, p. 10, col. 7.

[223] Act of Aug. 19, 1911, ch. 33, 37 Stat. 25. The 1911 Act was the first federal restriction on campaign spending. In 1867, Congress prohibited the political assessment of federal employees, and this provision was broadened in the Civil Service Reform Act of 1883, ch. 27, 22 Stat. 403. After 1900, corporate contributions to campaigns came under attack, and the Tillman Act of 1907, ch. 420, 34 Stat. 864, prohibited federally chartered banks or corporations from contributing to candidates for federal election. In 1910, Congress required committees or organizations that at-

tempted to influence the outcome of federal elections in two or more states to disclose, after the election, receipts and expenditures. The 1911 Act, in addition to imposing spending and contribution limits on Senate and House candidates, also imposed disclosure requirements on the candidates themselves, and required disclosure before as well as after elections. These provisions were pulled together in the Federal Corrupt Practices Act of 1925, 43 Stat. 1070 (amended 1947 and 1971), which remained on the books largely unchanged until the Federal Elections Campaign Act of 1971, Pub. L. No. 92–225, 86 Stat. 3 (amended 1974 and 1975). The constitutional problems in regulating political contributions and expenditures are dealt with in Burroughs v. United States, 290 U.S. 534 (1934), and Buckley v. Valeo, 424 U.S. 1 (1976). See generally H. Alexander, *Money in Politics* (1972), 198 *et seq.*; G. Thayer, *Who Shakes the Money Tree? American Campaign Financing Practices from 1789 to the Present* (1973), 52 *et seq.*

limited nomination expenditures to 25 percent of the annual salary of the office sought, and campaign expenditures after nomination to the same amount.[224] Since Senate salaries at the time were $7,500, Newberry was limited by the combination of federal and state law to total election expenditures of $3,750.

Newberry ran afoul of the federal statute because a committee formed to help him raised and spent almost $200,000, most of it before the primary. Newberry did not personally participate in the money raising or spending by this committee, but he knew of its activities, and undoubtedly the prospect that expenditures of such magnitude would be made in his behalf was a factor in his decision to run. Whether and how contributions and expenditures on a candidate's behalf, but not involving the candidate directly, should be regulated is one of the perennial policy problems of campaign finance legislation, and the 1911 Act spoke to the matter opaquely. "No candidate . . . shall give, contribute, expend, use, or promise, or cause to be given, contributed, expended, used, or promised, in procuring his nomination and election, any sum, in the aggregate, in excess" of what state law allowed, was the language of the statute. The Justice Department thought this language covered expenditures by the committee, and in November 1919, Newberry and 134 others involved in his campaign were indicted.[225] Much of the material put before the grand jury had been dug up by a large staff of investigators employed by Henry Ford, who spent a lot of money after the election trying to prove that Newberry had spent too much money before the election.[226]

In the United States District Court for the Western District of Michigan, before Judge Clarence W. Sessions,[227] Newberry and the other defendants pressed two main contentions, one constitutional and one statutory. The constitutional objection was that the indictment should be dismissed because it largely concerned money raised and spent in the primary, and Congress had no power to regulate primaries or other preelection nomination procedures, the Federal Corrupt Practices Act being therefore invalid in that respect. The statutory conten-

---

[224] 1913 Mich. Pub. Act. 109.

[225] Newberry was also charged with having bribed voters, but those counts were dismissed by the trial judge for lack of evidence.

[226] *New York Times,* Nov. 30, 1919, p. 1, col. 1.

[227] Clarence Williams Sessions (1859–1931) attended the University of Michigan and was admitted to the Michigan Bar in 1883. He practiced law in Ionia and Muskegon until 1906, when he became a state circuit judge. In 1911, Taft named him to the federal district court. Sessions was a Republican and championed strict enforcement of Prohibition. The *Newberry* trial in 1919 brought him national publicity. *New York Times,* Apr. 2, 1931, p. 27, col. 3; *Who Was Who in America* (1960), 1:1104.

tion was that money raised and spent by a candidate's supporters, without the candidate's active participation, was not covered by the Act, even if the candidate knew about the activities, banked on them in deciding to run, and encouraged them, indirectly, by a campaign effort. Judge Sessions ruled against Newberry on both points.[228] The jury found Newberry and seventeen other defendants guilty, and Newberry was sentenced to two years' imprisonment in Leavenworth Penitentiary and fined $10,000.

Charles Evans Hughes took Newberry's appeal to the Supreme Court, and it was "[p]ossibly the most controversial case of Hughes's entire career at the bar,"[229] not only because of the political significance of the case, or because the former reform governor took the side of big spending in campaigns, but also because Hughes pressed some constitutional arguments that seem bizarre measured against the central themes of his two careers on the Supreme Court. Hughes artfully combined the claim that the statute had been misconstrued with textual, historical, and libertarian arguments against Congress' power to regulate primaries and election campaigns. The textual question turned on the scope of Congress' power under Article I, Section 4, of the Constitution to regulate the times and manner of holding elections for Senators. This power did not encompass the process of nomination, Hughes urged:

---

[228] In answer to the contention that Congress was powerless to regulate primaries, Judge Sessions said:

[W]hy not? Can it be possible that Congress may protect the political stream from pollution in its lower reaches but is helpless to prevent the dumping of filth and poison into the spring at its source? . . . Theoretically, perhaps, an election without previous nominations is possible, but, practically, it is impossible. . . . In actual practice, the nomination of candidates for public office is as essential to an election as are polling places, ballots, ballot boxes and inspectors. It is no longer open to dispute that Congress may protect and control the latter; by the same reasoning, why not the former? It is common knowledge, and therefore, not to be blindly ignored by courts, that, in a majority of the States of the Union,

under normal conditions, the nomination for the office of United States Senator by the dominant political party is, in fact, the election, and that the subsequent ratification at the polls is little, if any, more than mere formality.

Brief for the United States, 97–98, Newberry v. United States, 256 U.S. 232 (1921). On the issue of statutory construction, Judge Sessions instructed the jury that Newberry violated the statute if he knew that his conduct of the campaign would require more money to be spent than the Act permitted, and that his conduct of the campaign would induce his supporters to raise and spend this excess in his behalf. Judge Sessions' instructions on this point are set out in Justice Pitney's concurrence, 256 U.S. at 292.

[229] M. Pusey, *Charles Evans Hughes* (1952), I, 389.

X: *Black Disfranchisement*

A distinction is at once apparent between the regulation of the manner of holding elections, in order to protect the right of the voter in casting his vote and to secure a fair count of the vote, and the attempt to interfere with or control the activities of the people of the States in the conduct of political campaigns. . . . Upon what ground can it be said that Congress can provide how many meetings shall be held, where meetings shall be held, how many speakers shall be allowed to speak for a candidate, how many circulars may be distributed, how many committees may act in behalf of a candidate, how they shall be organized and what shall be the limit of their honest activity?

To hold that Congress may regulate such modes of popular expression, or may thus impose its will upon the extent of the political activity of the people of the States, is to ignore the fundamental limitation of the power of Congress. No one can read Hamilton's articles in the "Federalist" with respect to this power and believe for a moment that there would have been any chance of ratifying the Constitution had it been proposed to delegate such a power.[230]

Primaries could not be considered part of the election process, Hughes argued, because primaries were unknown to the framers.

[W]hen the Constitution uses a term of definite meaning at the time when the Constitution was adopted, no supposed public policy can justify legislation outside the authority thus limited. . . . Whatever that term meant then, it means now,—no more,—no less. . . . No one would have the hardihood to suggest that within the meaning of the framers of the Constitution the word "elections" had reference to anything else than the taking of the vote for Senators or Representatives.[231]

---

[230] *Brief for Plaintiff in Error,* 48, Newberry v. United States, 256 U.S. 232 (1921).

[231] *Ibid.,* at 56–57. It is interesting, if a bit unfair, to compare this piece of advocacy with one of Hughes' most notable statements as Chief Justice. Writing for the Court in Home Building & Loan Ass'n. v. Blaisdell, 290 U.S. 398 (1934), Chief Justice Hughes wrote:

It is no answer . . . to insist that what the provision of the Constitution meant to the vision of that day it must mean to the vision of our time. If by the statement that what the Constitution meant at the time of its adoption it means to-day, it is intended to say that the great

clauses of the Constitution must be confined to the interpretation which the framers, with the conditions and outlook of their time, would have placed upon them, the statement carries its own refutation. It was to guard against such a narrow conception that Chief Justice Marshall uttered the memorable warning— "We must never forget, that it is a *constitution* we are expounding."

Ibid., at 442–43.

For discussions of the general problem, *compare* R. Berger, *Government By Judiciary* (1977), *with* A. Bickel, "The Original Understanding and the Segregation Decision," *Harv. L. Rev.,* 69:1, 1955.

To this appeal to historical rigidity, Hughes added the dread prospect of the slippery slope:

> If Congress . . . has the power which it has sought to exercise in the statute in question, it has the power to *abolish all primary elections* . . . to establish conventions, to overthrow conventions, to provide any sort of a primary that it may desire to provide. . . .[232]

The government tried to meet these arguments with the simple proposition that the power to regulate the election of its members was a power that Congress had to have as a matter of practical sovereignty. But if a textual anchor was wanted, the government argued, Article I, Section 4, taken with the Necessary and Proper Clause, easily afforded Congress the plenary power to regulate all aspects of the election of its members that national sovereignty required.[233]

Justice McReynolds' opinion for a slim majority consisting of himself, Day, Van Devanter, McKenna, and, surprisingly, Holmes, began by rejecting the notion of inherent sovereign power. Congress had no powers not explicitly granted. The question thus was the reach of Article I, Section 4. To McReynolds, elections meant elections: the final choice. The framers knew nothing of primaries. They were different from elections, being merely ways in which party adherents agreed upon candidates. McReynolds thought history showed that "if the Constitution makers had claimed for this section the latitude we are now asked to sanction, it would not have been ratified."[234] Article I, Section 4, had stirred controversy as a danger to the existence of the states, and Hamilton had assuaged fears about federal control of elections by stressing the narrow scope of Congress' power. "The times, places, and manner of holding elections for Senators and Representatives" thus had a confined meaning when the Constitution was adopted. Even if, as a practical matter, victory in a primary was essential to victory in an election, the primary "is in no real sense part of the manner of holding the election. . . . Birth must precede but it is no part of either funeral or apotheosis."[235] Many things were prerequisites to election: health, education, public discussion, "even the face and figure of the candidate,"[236] but surely authority to regulate the manner of holding elections did not subject these to control. After all, it was settled, so McReynolds thought, that the power to regulate interstate commerce did not carry the power to regulate whatever was essential to commerce. On top of all

---

[232] *Brief for Plaintiff in Error*, 66, Newberry v. United States, 256 U.S. 232 (1921).

[233] *Brief for United States*, 88,

Newberry v. United States, 256 U.S. 232 (1921).

[234] 256 U.S. at 256.

[235] *Ibid.*, at 257.

[236] *Ibid.*

this, McReynolds imposed a conception of state sovereignty so awesomely nonfunctional that he could view a regulation of the method of procuring nomination and election to the United States Senate as an interference "with purely domestic affairs of the State."[237] If this left the states with ultimate power to affect the choice of federal officers, so be it.

Although all the Justices agreed that Newberry's and the others' convictions should be reversed, McReynolds had a majority for his constitutional position only because McKenna, with an important reservation, gave him a fifth vote. McKenna concurred that the Corrupt Practices Act exceeded Congress' powers under the Constitution as of the time the Act was passed in 1911, but he suggested, without elaboration, that the passage of the Seventeenth Amendment in May 1913, which substituted popular for legislative election of Senators, might make a difference should a new statute be passed. McReynolds had dismissed the Seventeenth Amendment because he insisted that a statute must be tested by the powers Congress possessed at the time of its passage. But McReynolds had made clear, without being specific enough to lose McKenna, that the Seventeenth Amendment connoted no expansion of Congress' powers to regulate elections. McReynolds pointed out that as originally proposed by the Senate Judiciary Committee, the Amendment had given the states sole power to regulate Senate elections, taking away what Congress had under Article I, Section 4. This feature of the Amendment was dropped, but even so McReynolds thought it made clear that there was nothing incompatible about popular election of Senators and limited congressional power.

It is remarkable that Holmes helped give McReynolds his majority. *Newberry* stands as a classic McReynolds statement on the scope of national power: committed to hard-edged, categorical boundaries around constitutional words, projecting on the present a very narrow, literal understanding of the past, forthrightly rejecting a functional, relativistic approach to constitutional adjudication, and carving state prerogatives out of a seeming federal domain. It passes belief that Holmes, the author of *Missouri* v. *Holland*,[238] could have thought McReynolds' rationale about the reach of Article I, Section 4, was other than primitive and absurd. That Holmes could join an opinion that was a catalogue of constitutional attitudes he derided testifies to his capacity to swallow an opinion for a result he approved. Holmes must have thought the Corrupt Practices Act was economic and political humbug, and to get rid of it, he was apparently prepared to acquiesce in an opinion limiting federal power. Perhaps First Amendment conceptions lay behind his

---

[237] *Ibid.*, at 258.   [238] 252 U.S. 416 (1920).

vote with McReynolds. The Act put a ceiling on the free marketplace of ideas in political campaigns for egalitarian reasons that Holmes probably thought were foolish and futile. The Act's opaque drafting may also have offended him. But whatever Holmes' reasons, it remains a historical curiosity that he should have sided with McReynolds' extraordinarily restrictive reading of Congress' power.

McReynolds' opinion provoked two long and exceedingly powerful protests, one from Pitney, in which Brandeis and Clarke joined, the other from Chief Justice White writing for himself. Pitney denied that Congress' power to regulate Senatorial primaries depended on any text, but assuming it did, he could not understand why an explicit power to regulate the manner of holding elections should be defined so narrowly. An election was just a process of choice.

> [I]n the essential sense, a sense that fairly comports with the object and purpose of a Constitution such as ours, which deals in broad outline with matters of substance, and is remarkable for succinct and pithy modes of expression, all of the [nominating processes] fall fairly within the definition of "the manner of holding elections.[239]

To put primaries beyond congressional regulation would "leave the general Government destitute of the means to insure its own preservation," and would render the federal government "less than supreme in the exercise of its own appropriate powers; a doctrine supposed to have been laid at rest forever."[240] The Necessary and Proper Clause gave Congress authority to legislate as to all powers vested in the government of the United States. What could be more basic than to maintain a lawmaking body that was representative in its character? The Court must remember that the Corrupt Practices Act amounted to a determination by Congress that

> To safeguard the final elections while leaving the proceedings for proposing candidates unregulated, is to postpone regulation until it is comparatively futile. And Congress might well conclude that, if the nominating procedure were to be left open to fraud, bribery, and corruption, or subject to the more insidious but (in the opinion of Congress) nevertheless harmful influences resulting from an unlimited expenditure of money in paid propaganda and other purchased campaign activities, representative government would be endangered.[241]

All in all, Pitney's *Newberry* concurrence is perhaps his most impressive statement as Justice. Having established that "it is free from

---

[239] 256 U.S. at 280.   [240] *Ibid.*, at 281.   [241] *Ibid.*, at 288.

doubt" that Congress could regulate primaries called to nominate federal candidates, however, Pitney went on to decide that the trial judge had not construed the Corrupt Practices Act properly in instructing the jury. The Act punished excessive contributions and expenditures by candidates, acting directly or by agents. Pitney thought it did not intend to punish candidates who knew others would raise and spend beyond the limit, even if a candidate counted on such expenditures for success and knew that the campaign would, in a general sense, occasion them. The trial judge's instructions, however, blunted the crucial distinction between a candidate's illegal participation in excessive spending and mere active campaigning with knowledge that others would spend beyond the limit. This required reversal.

White's *Newberry* concurrence also ranks as one of his greatest utterances, the more remarkable because it was handed down in failing health less than two weeks before he would enter the hospital for an operation from which he would not recover. It is a measure of White's conviction in the case that he chose to write, given his dislike of individual opinions, since he and Pitney in essence saw eye to eye. It is apparent that White found McReynolds' constitutional analysis repugnant; he indeed offered an antithesis to McReynolds' approach. By establishing a House and a Senate, White reasoned, the Constitution created "reservoirs of vital federal power"[242] concerning their makeup and functions. The states would have had no power to interfere with elections to these bodies without the grant of Article I, Section 4, and all the powers thereby given to the states (except as to the place of choosing Senators) were expressly made subject to a coterminous, overriding congressional power. If there were any doubt about the scope of the Article I, Section 4, power, surely it was removed by the Necessary and Proper Clause. The claim that elections were one thing and primaries another was "a suicidal one."[243] Primaries were in many states more important than the elections (in a footnote White pointed out that in many Southern states, " 'victory in such a primary, on the Democratic side, is practically the equivalent of an election' ").[244] How could one concede a power to regulate elections and deny a power over who is nominated, when that was often controlling?[245]

---

[242] *Ibid.*, at 261 (White, J., concurring in judgment).

[243] *Ibid.*, at 262.

[244] *Ibid.*, at 267, n.1.

[245] *Ibid.*, at 267. To these basic considerations of constitutional structure, White added an interesting reliance on the legislative history of the Seventeenth Amendment, one which arrayed against McReynolds the nationalism of then-Senator George Sutherland of Utah. As first reported by Senator Borah for the Senate Judiciary Committee, the Seventeenth Amendment, after providing for direct election of Senators, had a clause giving the states full authority over the time, place, and manner of electing Sena-

Can any other conclusion be upheld except upon the theory that the phantoms of attenuated and unfounded doubts concerning the meaning of the Constitution, which have long perished, may now be revived for the purpose of depriving Congress of the right to exert a power essential to its existence, and this in the face of the fact that the only basis for the doubts which arose in the beginning (the election of Senators by the state legislatures) has been completely removed by the 17th Amendment?[246]

There are moments in the history of the Supreme Court when the transcendent force of the Constitution seems to dispel the confines of parish and class, and when a Justice evokes a panorama of constitutional development across eras in the nation's history. As the shadows lengthened for Edward Douglass White in the summer of 1921, the *Newberry* case fired his usually circumlocutory and doubting mind with a passionate eloquence and conviction. Can anyone not be moved by the poignancy of the ex-Confederate's nationalist thunder against "the phantoms of attenuated and unfounded doubts concerning the meaning of the Constitution, which have long perished"?

---

tors, thereby taking away Congress' power over such elections. A minority proposal submitted by Senator Sutherland to preserve Congress' power was adopted by the Senate, and the Seventeenth Amendment was ratified in that form. White thought this history, which took place in 1911 when the amendment to extend the Corrupt Practices Act to cover state senatorial primaries was before Congress, put "an end to all doubts as to the power of Congress." *Ibid.*, at 265.

White also countered McReynolds' view of the intent of the framers. The state ratifying conventions were indeed perturbed about congressional power under Article I, Section 4, but the concern was whether Congress might try to regulate the election of state legislatures on the theory that they were to elect Senators. The Federalist and other papers answered this fear by stressing that Congress' only power was over the election of Representatives and Senators, and that election to state legislatures was reserved to the states. But this controversy, White

thought, served only to emphasize the proper distinction between state and federal power. *Ibid.*, at 268.

[246] 256 U.S. at 268–69. White was comparably exercised about the statutory construction issue. He thought the trial judge's instruction plainly told the jury that a candidate was guilty if he or she knew that excess money had been raised and spent in the campaign, even if the candidate had neither raised the money nor directed its expenditure. The statute, on the other hand, was clearly intended to deal with money contributed, raised, or spent by the candidate. The distinction was crucial, White insisted, because on the trial judge's reading, "the greater the public service, and the higher the character, of the candidate, giving rise to a correspondingly complete and self-sacrificing support by the electorate to his candidacy, the more inevitably would criminality and infamous punishment result both to the candidate and to the citizen who contributed." *Ibid.*, at 275.

X: *Black Disfranchisement*

The *Newberry* decision "caused a sensation in the Senate," according to the *New York Times*: "As soon as the result was known little groups of Senators gathered together"[247] to discuss its implications. Senators Borah and Johnson, among others, called for a constitutional amendment to give Congress power to regulate primaries. The amendment boom was short-lived, however, and although bills to start the amending process were introduced in succeeding Congresses, none got out of committee.[248] Eventually, in 1925, the law was amended to conform to the *Newberry* decision by excluding the nomination process from coverage.[249]

Editorial reaction to the decision was mixed. The *New York Times* thought that "even in the face of the great authority of Chief Justice White, the layman who believes that law is common sense finds it hard to resist the reasoning of Justice McReynolds."[250] Both the *Times* and the *New York Tribune* thought the problem likely to solve itself, since the public was disgusted both with free-spending campaigns and with primaries.[251] Academic commentary was uniformly unfavorable. "The argument of the majority is fallacious . . . the decision . . . is deplorable," said the *Columbia Law Review*.[252] The *Michigan Law Review* thought "the majority conclusion is unsound," and it spoke of the "inherent reasonableness of the view of the minority."[253] The *Central Law Journal* thought the decision was "a serious mistake" and that "[n]o line of decisions is more discreditable to the judiciary of this country than those holding that primary election are not 'elections.' "[254] Edwin Corwin noted:

> Altogether, the merits of the question are somewhat divided. In his reading of Article 1, section 4, Justice McReynolds remains unanswered and probably unanswerable. But his assumption that this is the exclusive basis of the power of Congress to enact laws touching the choice of senators and representatives seems untenable. The national government is after all the national government. . . . It would be strange indeed if the government which is vested with the duty of guaranteeing a republican form of government to the states could not adopt the

---

[247] *New York Times*, May 3, 1921, p. 1, col. 4.

[248] See, e.g., S.J. Res. 155, 67th Cong., 2nd Sess., 62 *Cong. Rec.* 1181 (1922); H.R.J. Res. 335, 67th Cong., 2nd Sess., 62 *Cong. Rec.* 7692 (1922); H.R.J. Res. 435, 67th Cong., 4th Sess., 64 *Cong. Rec.* 3098 (1923); H.R.J. Res. 22, 68th Cong., 1st Sess., 65 *Cong. Rec.* 43 (1923).

[249] 43 Stat. 1053, 1070 (1925).

[250] *New York Times*, May 4, 1921, p. 8, col. 2.

[251] *Ibid.; New York Tribune*, May 3, 1921, p. 12, col. 1.

[252] *Colum. L. Rev.*, 22:54, 56–57, 1922.

[253] *Mich. L. Rev.*, 19:860, 862, 864, 1921.

[254] *Central L.J.*, 92:445, 446, 1921.

measures which are necessary to guarantee itself the same kind of government.[255]

Thomas Reed Powell devoted most of his trenchant criticism of the decision to what he regarded as the untenable position of Justice McKenna.[256] Before the Seventeenth Amendment, a distinction might have been drawn between Congress' power to regulate the nomination of popularly elected Representatives and Senators chosen by state legislatures, the latter being both unnecessary and inappropriate. But the Seventeenth Amendment abolished the distinction, and with it the impediment to regulating the nomination of Senators. If the Seventeenth Amendment made a difference, it was in the constitutional character of senatorial nominations, and when the character of a situation governed the scope of a congressional power, the situation should be assessed at the time the statute was applied. The Seventeenth Amendment, in other words, was not a new power to enact regulations, but it might have been viewed as broadening the constitutional basis for existing regulations by eliminating the role of the state legislatures in the election of Senators.

The Supreme Court's unanimous reversal of his conviction was not the end of Senator Newberry's problem with his free-spending campaign, nor of Hughes' involvement with the case. After further investigations, the Senate voted 46 to 41 to seat Newberry on January 12, 1922, but only for the remainder of the Sixty-First Congress. At that time, the Republicans had a majority of twenty-four, but this was soon reduced to thirteen by the November 1922 elections.[257] In the meantime, Hughes, by then Secretary of State, had been drawn back into the case. In August 1922, Hughes received a letter from a Reverend Hugh B. MacCauley that had all the earmarks of a contrivance by the Republican National Committee, asking if Hughes would explain the case because of "[a]llusion to the *Newberry* case made from time to time by Democratic speakers."[258] *Newberry* had indeed become a convenient symbol of vote-buying for the Democrats. Hughes responded vigorously and at length to correct a "most serious injustice." Of Judge Sessions' construction of the Corrupt Practices Act, Hughes said "a more ex-

---

[255] E. Corwin, "Constitutional Law in 1920–1921," *Am. Pol. Sci. Rev.,* 16:22, 25, 1921. T. R. Powell, "The Federal Constitution in 1920–1921," *Mich. L. Rev.,* 20:1, 12, 1921.

[256] E. Corwin, "Major Constitutional Issues in 1920–1921," *American Pol. Sci. Rev.,* 16:22, 25, 1921. T. R. Powell, "The Federal Constitution in 1920–1921," *Michigan L. Rev.,* 20:1, 12, 1921.

[257] Ervin, *Ford vs. Newberry,* 95.

[258] H. MacCauley to C. E. Hughes, Aug. 12, 1922, reprinted in "The Truth About the Newberry Case" (Detroit Free Press Bureau, Aug. 20, 1922), inserted in Ervin, *Ford vs. Newberry.*

traordinary misconstruction of a statute has never come under my observation."

> The plain fact is that Senator Newberry was wrongly and most unjustly convicted and his conviction was set aside. Despite the long period of preparation, the rigid investigation, the careful choosing of their ground, the long drawn out trial, the attempt in every possible way to besmirch, and the zeal, ability and even bitterness of his pursuers, their endeavor to establish a violation of law on the part of Senator Newberry completely failed and accordingly Senator Newberry stood as a senator duly elected by the people of the state of Michigan and entitled to his seat in the senate of the United States.[259]

In his letter, Hughes took umbrage at the Reverend Mr. MacCauley's reference to the fact that Newberry, a Republican, had been vindicated by McReynolds and White, both Democrats. "I deprecate any such allusion, as partisan considerations do not enter into the judicial opinions of the Supreme Court."[260]

The Republican National Committee saw partisan uses in Hughes' letter, however, and a large leaflet boldly titled "The Truth About the Newberry Case, by Charles Evans Hughes, Secretary of State" was soon widely circulated. Hughes now found himself caught in the political tempest swirling around Newberry. *The World* thought the letter "Mr. Hughes's dirtiest day's work." Cartoons were printed showing the Secretary of State stooping to whitewash Newberry. Democrats in the Senate called Hughes' integrity into question.[261]

Shortly after the 1922 election, the *New York Times* reported that a majority of Senators favored unseating Newberry if he did not resign.[262] Three days later, Newberry resigned. "A Democratic Department of Justice . . . through hundreds of agents had hounded and terrified men in all parts of the state into believing that some wrong had been done," he wrote to the governor of Michigan.[263]

The restrictive constitutional doctrine of McReynolds' opinion was longer lived than Newberry's senatorial career. The view that Congress could not regulate primaries persisted until 1941, when, a few months after McReynolds retired, *United States* v. *Classic* in effect overruled *Newberry* by forcibly distinguishing it on the ground that the Seventeenth Amendment had not been considered.[264] In its two decades

---

[259] C. E. Hughes to H. MacCauley, Aug. 16, 1922, *ibid.*

[260] *Ibid.*

[261] *Literary Digest,* 74:16, Sept. 2, 1922. Pusey, *Hughes,* 390.

[262] *New York Times,* Nov. 15, 1922, p. 2, col. 2.

[263] *New York Times,* Nov. 20, 1922, p. 1, col. 5.

[264] United States v. Classic, 313 U.S. 299 (1941).

of life, the *Newberry* doctrine probably had its largest impact not on the question to which it was addressed, but in giving the Court pause as to whether the "white primary" violated the Fourteenth or Fifteenth Amendment. The problem the Court struggled with in these cases was whether state action was present in the exclusion of blacks from primary voting by party organizations having various sorts of official connections. *Newberry* was not exactly on point, but the notion that primaries were beyond the federal regulatory sphere promoted the view that they should not be deemed state action, and *Newberry*'s influence can be gauged by the fact that it was the overruling of *Newberry* by *Classic* that, illogically but ineluctably, led to the Court's decision in 1944 that a party rule without explicit sanction of state law barring blacks from primaries was nevertheless a violation of the Fifteenth Amendment.[265]

V. The White Court and the Paradox of Progress in Race Relations Cases

The basic problem in assessing the White Court's race relations decisions is how much to make of them. The answer is not obvious. It is true that with respect to three of the four most significant legal disabilities pressing down black people—involuntary servitude, disfranchisement, and segregation—the White Court seized the occasion for the first firm rulings limiting the states' powers. With respect to the fourth, the exclusion of blacks from juries, the White Court did nothing. This may be noteworthy in historical terms, but how substantial an achievement for the White Court is another matter. Except for peonage, on which there was a Progressive consensus against the practice above and below the Mason-Dixon line, the White Court did not take the axe to the root of the tree of legalized racism. In striking down the Grandfather Clause as a blatant circumvention of the Fifteenth Amendment, the White Court took pains to protect from any implication of judicial disapproval the literacy, good understanding, citizenship, and other voter qualifications that everyone knew had been used with near-perfect success to deny blacks the vote. And the same Court that prevented Jim Crow laws from spreading to residential segregation, and that insisted that states honor the equality side of the "separate but equal" formula, also left *Plessy* v. *Ferguson* undisturbed and upheld segregation in public transportation in two cases that easily could have gone the other way.

Indeed, it can be argued that the White Court's race relations decisions were reluctant responses to the excesses of racism that found

---

[265] Smith v. Allwright, 321 U.S. 649 (1944).

their way into law in the Progressive era. For example, although the *Grandfather Clause* decisions and *Buchanan* v. *Warley* were critical decisions in the sense that they prevented racial discrimination from becoming an open, accepted legal standard controlling property rights and voting, had the Supreme Court legitimated the racist laws under review, it would virtually have had to put the Fourteenth and Fifteenth Amendments into formal bankruptcy. This would have been a radical step, even for a Court prepared to countenance racism under quite relaxed interpretations of the Fourteenth and Fifteenth Amendments. After all, both *Buchanan* and the *Grandfather Clause Cases* were unanimous (the latter more or less so, depending on how far one takes Lamar's dissent in *Mosley*); one would expect that decisions marking an important shift away from the momentum of racism in American society would not be unanimous.

Doubtless it is true that the excessive, blatant character of the racist laws reviewed by the White Court contributed to its reversal of the thirty-five-year pattern of neglect of black civil rights. But the fact that several of the more notable decisions offered easy, even perhaps appropriate, escapes from decision indicates that the White Court was not forced into its defense of black people's rights. *McCabe* was not ripe for decision, but a bare majority seized the occasion to hand down the first Supreme Court opinion upholding the equality side of the separate but equal formula. The *Grandfather Clause Cases* rested on constructions of federal civil right statutes that need not have been read to cover official machinations denying the right to vote. In *Buchanan* v. *Warley*, there were standing and collusion problems that, although not on careful analysis a barrier to decision, could have drawn to them a Court reluctant to face the merits. Indeed, it was enough to push Holmes to the verge of dissent in view of the confusion surrounding the *jus tertii* concept. The White Court was not faced with the simple choice of upholding or striking down the Grandfather Clause, the Louisville residential segregation ordinance, or the Oklahoma luxury car proviso. These cases presented paths to avoidance at least as accessible as those taken in *Berea College*[266] or in the two *Giles* decisions of the previous decade. It would even have been possible, as Holmes' dissent reflects, for the Court in *Bailey* v. *Alabama*[267] to have viewed the Alabama false pretenses statute as punishing determined fraud rather than mere breach of contract.[268] Alternatively, the Court could have deemed the bar to testimony about uncommunicated motivation to be a denial of due process, leaving the peonage issue unresolved. The holding in *Reynolds*

---

[266] 211 U.S. 45 (1908).
[267] 219 U.S. 219 (1911).

[268] *Ibid.*, at 247 (Holmes, J., dissenting).

might have gone the other way in deference to the broad power of the state to determine how its convicts should be dealt with.

In race cases in the first decade of the twentieth century, the "most important thing" the Supreme Court did, in Brandeis' phrase, was "not doing." In the second decade, with White as Chief Justice, the Supreme Court executed a dramatic shift by its simple willingness to decide. It reached out to put some life into the broken promises of the Civil War amendments.

Important developments in constitutional law can usually be traced, at least with the benefit of hindsight, either to the calculated impact of the appointments process or to the dynamics of constitutional principles that, once loosed, play out their momentum in fairly predictable patterns. Other developments, however, are not susceptible to these typical explanations. Getting at the sources of such developments is a difficult enterprise for the student of constitutional history. The changes wrought in the law of race relations by the White Court are of this last-mentioned, elusive sort, out of kilter with established precedents and with prevailing political and social tendencies as well. Moreover, it is not easy to attribute the White Court's modest but nevertheless pathbreaking rulings in favor of the constitutional claims of black people to the impact of appointments, and certainly not to any calculated use of the appointment power.

Despite Melville Weston Fuller's perfect record of nonsupport for black people's rights, the promotion of Edward Douglass White as the first Chief Justice from the deep South,[269] a man who had fought for the Confederacy and resisted Reconstruction, and who as Associate Justice since 1894 had joined in every majority opinion denying constitutional protection to blacks, including *Plessy* v. *Ferguson* and *Williams* v. *Mississippi*, cannot have raised the hopes of black people. Neither were Taft's other selections promising, on the whole, with the exception of Hughes. Although not much was known about Hughes' disposition toward civil rights, his strong commitment to racial justice on the Bench might have been predicted. In any event, he would have been thought more friendly to blacks than Brewer, the man he replaced, whose stubborn commitment to laissez-faire principles weakened when private choice was overridden in the service of racism. But whatever promise might have been discernible in Hughes' coming was more than offset by Taft's appointment of the fervid secessionist Horace H. Lurton, who was gripped by a romantic paternalism about slavery and who never ruled in favor of the constitutional rights of blacks in little more

---

[269] John Rutledge of South Carolina had a brief, unconfirmed recess appointment as Chief Justice for a few months in 1795.

than four years on the Court. Van Devanter's appointment to fill White's side seat held no predictable significance one way or the other on the future of civil rights, but the replacement of Moody of Massachusetts by Lamar of Georgia, like Lurton a relatively benign but reflexive white supremacist, was clearly a retrograde development. Above all, the death in 1911 of Harlan, the almost constant champion of equal rights in his thirty-four years on the Court, was a blow to the hopes of black people that his replacement by the little-known Pitney did nothing to cushion.

Antipathy to black people's civil rights cannot be said to have been a motivating factor in William Howard Taft's six nominations to the Court between 1909 and 1912, but his appointment of a Confederate Chief Justice, his great personal admiration for his first appointee, Lurton, and his remonstrances that must have lain behind Theodore Roosevelt's assurance to Senator Lodge that Lurton was "right on the Negro question,"[270] reveal a President not much concerned with the claims of racial justice and, in any event, prepared to subordinate them to the national and political advantages of sectional reconciliation, of downplaying an issue that had bitterly divided Republicans and Democrats, and of seeking a foothold in the solid South.

Woodrow Wilson's three appointments to the Court were not at all attuned to questions of race relations, and, despite Wilson's Southern roots and racial attitudes, did not affect the Court's receptivity to claims of racial justice one way or the other. Wilson used his first nomination to replace the unreconstructed Lurton with McReynolds, but although McReynolds would in time deservedly win a reputation as the Court's most obdurate segregationist, during the time White was Chief Justice McReynolds was on the whole not a foe of black aspirations. As Attorney General, he did not prevent the *Grandfather Clause Cases* from going forward, although he probably doubted the applicability of the statute under which the government had pressed the cases. And in by far the most important race case in which he participated as a Justice during White's tenure, *Buchanan* v. *Warley*, McReynolds' support for property rights overcame his commitment to racial separation. Brandeis, of course, would generally prove a supporter of civil rights for black people, although there was little specific in his pre-appointment record to presage this, and Wilson certainly was not concerned about his outlook in race relations cases in naming him. John H. Clarke, Wilson's third appointment, did little to reveal himself on race questions either before or after joining the Court. He went along with

---

[270] T. Roosevelt to H. Lodge, Sept. 4, 1906, in E. Morrison and J. Blum, eds., *Letters of Theodore Roosevelt* (1951), 5:396.

the unanimous decision in *Buchanan* but also joined the majority in the *South Covington* case, upholding a state Jim Crow law as applied to a streetcar line engaged in interstate transit.

In short, neither Taft nor Wilson directed their appointment power to questions of race relations, although Taft's promotion of sectional reconciliation nationally and as a Republican strategy carried negative implications for the achievement of black people's constitutional rights. It is a measure of how immutable race relations seemed in this period, especially in constitutional aspects, that not one of the nine appointments to the Court between 1909 and 1916, whether of a Northern Progressive or a Southern conservative, appears to have been appraised as to its possible effect on race relations by the President, by the Senate, or by the popular press.

Neither did the holdovers from the Fuller Court that served through the White Chief Justiceship—Day, Holmes, and McKenna—carry collectively any particular momentum on race questions one way or the other. To be sure, Day in his nineteen years on the Court emerged, particularly after White became Chief Justice, as, next to Harlan, the Court's firmest supporter of black aspirations, despite his authorship of the curious opinion in the second *Giles* decision. But Holmes in the same period repeatedly lined up against the claims of black people, although he did write the important opinion in *Mosley* that may well have been critical to the holdings in the *Grandfather Clause Cases*. In the decade of the 1920s, when Taft was Chief Justice, Holmes evidenced more sympathy for racial justice. He authored opinions in *Moore* v. *Dempsey*,[271] approving habeas corpus relief for blacks convicted in trials subject to mob domination in the aftermath of the race riot in Phillips County, Arkansas, in 1919, and in *Nixon* v. *Herndon*,[272] striking down a Texas law that barred blacks from voting in Democratic primaries. But during the White Court and before, Holmes was no friend of the constitutional hopes of black people. McKenna, the other holdover from the Fuller Court who served through White's Chief Justiceship, staked out no clear position on race questions. Holmes, Day, and McKenna therefore do not alter the picture one gets from the nine appointments made by Taft and Wilson. The explanation for the White Court's unprecedented recognition of the principles of racial justice in the Thirteenth, Fourteenth, and Fifteenth Amendments is not to be found in the appointments process, nor can it be seen as an expected development based on the subjective views of the individual Justices on race relations.

Although not motivating factors, the atmosphere of settled com-

---

[271] 261 U.S. 86 (1923).   [272] 373 U.S. 536 (1927).

placency and national cohesion about race relations certainly made easier the White Court's ventures into the modest recognition of Reconstruction principles. The false sense of tranquility that pervaded race relations between the success of the disfranchisement movement and World War I meant that recognition of a few baseline civil rights did not seem to threaten set patterns of race relations. On top of this, the impetus to sectional reconciliation that was so strong in this period, and that damaged blacks' hopes of looking to national political processes for protection against racism, appears to have had a positive impact on constitutional perspectives concerning race relations.

The movement toward national cohesion is suggested by White's career. Against the Fuller Court's legacy of neglect for constitutional principles of racial justice—for which White, as Associate Justice, was partly responsible—White's positions in race cases after he became Chief Justice mark considerable progress. The evolution of White's position is probably traceable to the reinforcement given his latent nationalism by his shift to the center seat and by the spirit of national cohesion that gathered momentum in the new century. It may even be that the stimulus of the great War might have been a significant force behind the awakened sense of racial justice in the Court. White was preoccupied with the war. "It is difficult for me to do any work, for I have constantly ringing in my ears the noise of the awful conflict along the Belgian and French border and the appalling thought of the splendid men who are there giving up their lives haunts me day and night," White wrote to George W. Wickersham on November 14, 1914, reflecting the widespread sentiments of official Washington.[273] Of the decisions favoring the rights of black people during White's tenure as Chief Justice, it is worth noting that only *Bailey* v. *Alabama*, the first peonage case, preceded the guns of August. *Buchanan* v. *Warley*, perhaps the most important of all the race decisions in this period, came down after United States' entry into the war. This fact suggests an interesting hypothesis—that the European war's general divisiveness, reflected in race relations by the terrible race riots of 1919, was offset in the Supreme Court by a spirit of national cohesion calling for the recognition of some civil rights.

Paradoxically, some of the White Court's important race relations decisions can be rooted in typical Progressive era concerns and beliefs, despite the fact that in politics and general patterns of social thought the Progressive era was generally retrogressive with respect to racial justice. The Progressive spirit found its clearest expression in the White Court in the peonage cases, where concerns for the freedom of exploited

---

[273] Klinkhamer, *Edward Douglas White*, 64.

workers, horrified fascination with the anachronistic cruelties of peonage in operation, and the subordination of the racial character of the problem all made peonage a prime focus for Progressives' reformist impulses. The generalization that the Progressive era was a time of accelerated racism requires a major exception for the problem of peonage, which was the object of a vigorous reform effort in and out of the courts. The exception, in turn, needs some qualification to the extent that peonage was perceived as a problem afflicting all races.

Less obviously, the Court's response to the disfranchisement of black people, from *Williams* v. *Mississippi* in 1898 to the *Grandfather Clause Cases* in 1915, can also be squared with Progressive impulses. Literacy tests, property qualifications, poll taxes, and disqualification for crimes all fit into reform concerns that voters should be knowledgeable, have a stake in the community, be organized and concerned about civic affairs, and be upright. That these qualifications lent themselves to denying black people the vote did not lessen their intrinsic appeal to Progressive sympathies. The Grandfather Clause, on the other hand, could not easily be squared with Progressive goals about the franchise, although its defenders gamely tried to justify it in these terms. It was not only a patently racist mechanism, but it conferred voting willy-nilly without regard to intelligence or stake in the community. The Grandfather Clause could find no protection in the camouflage of Progressive election reform concerns that helped to shield the other disfranchising mechanisms from serious constitutional scrutiny.

It is hard, on the other hand, to see *Buchanan* v. *Warley* or *McCabe* as even dim reflections of conventional Progressive thinking. As its critics were quick to point out, if *Buchanan* were viewed as affirming property rights, it was a distinctly non-Progressive opinion. *McCabe* is harder to locate in relation to Progressive thinking, but one might well assume that the considerations of practicality and efficiency that Oklahoma adduced in support of its luxury car proviso would have appealed to most Progressives' impatience with the escalation of questions of principle, especially the wholly fictive principle of equality in relation to racial separation. Granted that the term Progressive is not one of sharp definition, it is nonetheless not overly simple to say that the White Court was not in tune with the times in *Buchanan* and *McCabe*.

Conclusion

By some measure, the most attractive explanation of the White Court's advances in the constitutional law of race relations in the second decade of the twentieth century is that these decisions were a by-product of the laissez-faire constitutionalism that took hold in the

Supreme Court in the previous decade. This explanation needs to be handled with care; it lends itself to the exaggerated claim that the race decisions were primarily concerned with protecting property and contract rights and only coincidentally involved race relations.

Both the explanatory power of the linkage to laissez-faire constitutionalism and the necessity for care are illustrated by *Buchanan* v. *Warley*. Contrary to the general impression among historians, *Buchanan* was not a decision that turned on property rights, with segregation merely the happenstancial, invalid restriction on the right to buy, sell, and occupy residential property. Had *Buchanan* involved a comparable nonracial restriction on a use of residential property deemed out of keeping with communal values, the power to regulate almost certainly would have been upheld. On the other hand, the segregation requirement certainly was not by itself a sufficient ground for unconstitutionality either. It was the combination of a racial restriction addressed to personal property rights of substantial importance—not so important as to be immune from regulation in any general sense, but important enough to withstand legislative policies looking to segregation—that produced the result in *Buchanan*. Doubtless the property rights and freedom of contract decisions that were the foundation of laissez-faire constitutionalism conditioned the Supreme Court to invest the property right in *Buchanan* with enough substance to thwart the expansionist logic of segregation. But the right to buy and sell residential property for personal occupancy without racial restriction was not protected to advance the central values of laissez-faire constitutionalism: the right of owners to maximize the economic utility of property and the overall efficiency of a free market economy.[274] Rather, the right in *Buchanan* was conceived of as an attribute of personal autonomy: freedom of choice about where to live within the limits of one's resources and opportunities. The decision should be read as a recognition, in 1917, that black people could claim basic rights of personhood and autonomy as those concepts were then understood.

The *Peonage Cases* also reflect the possibilities of constitutional gains in race relations implicit in the jurisprudence of laissez-faire constitutionalism. The Court's professed race blindness in the *Peonage Cases*, and Hughes' emphasis in *Bailey* on "the freedom of labor upon which alone can enduring prosperity be based," is obviously linked with the concept of freedom of contract. But freedom of contract theory does not speak unambiguously to the baseline question posed, whether breach of labor contracts may be treated as criminal where advances have been

---

[274] *Cf.* T. Jackson and J. Jeffries, "Commercial Speech: Economic Due Process and the First Amendment," *Va. L. Rev.*, 65:1, 25, 1979 (two basic values of economic liberty as perceived by the modern Court).

taken and not repaid. Holmes, who was well versed in the principles of contracts, thought the answer was yes. There is certainly strong support in traditional principles of contract law and criminal law for a constitutional rule that labor contracts may not be enforced with criminal sanctions. But the rather odd neglect, in both Hughes' and Holmes' opinions, of the usual stance of deference to legislative policy choices suggests that implicit concern with the terrible legacy of forced labor for blacks in the South loomed large in the Court's approach, and may well have been the motivating factor in the propounding of a race-neutral, positive right to breach labor contracts without criminal sanctions.

The *Grandfather Clause Cases* have no doctrinal linkage with laissez-faire constitutionalism. But when one explores the conundrum of why the Court chose to intervene in the *Grandfather Clause Cases* when it had an easy statutory escape, and when it had previously adopted a hands-off stance to disfranchisement, one falls back on the activist attitudes toward the judicial function nurtured in the service of property rights and freedom of contract.

The Supreme Court's conception of the judicial function is generally of a piece in any era, although the constitutional landscape changed quite considerably from the beginning to the end of the Progressive era. The unprecedented recognition of constitutional rights for black people under the Thirteenth, Fourteenth, and Fifteenth Amendments that occurred in the later part of the Progressive era was rooted in the institutional revival of the Supreme Court in the early part of the twentieth century, a revival which made its impact felt mainly in the aggressive tenets of laissez-faire constitutionalism, but which produced other, nobler and more lasting, if more tentative, constitutional legacies as well.

Table of Cases

993

Table of Statutes

Index

INDEX

A NOTE ON THE BOOK

This book is set in Linotype Times Roman. Composition by
Maryland Linotype Company, Baltimore, Maryland. Printed
and bound by The Kingsport Press, Kingsport, Tennessee.
Paper is Perkins & Squier Regular Offset manufactured by
P. H. Glatfelter Company, Spring Grove, Pennsylvania.

Woodcut of seal of the Supreme Court by Fritz Kredel.

Typography and binding design by
WARREN CHAPPELL